THE VICTORIA HISTORY
OF THE
COUNTIES OF ENGLAND

EDITED BY C. R. J. CURRIE

THE UNIVERSITY OF LONDON
INSTITUTE OF
HISTORICAL RESEARCH

INSCRIBED TO THE

MEMORY OF HER LATE MAJESTY

QUEEN VICTORIA

WHO GRACIOUSLY GAVE THE TITLE TO

AND ACCEPTED THE DEDICATION

OF THIS HISTORY

THE VICTORIA HISTORY
OF THE
COUNTIES OF ENGLAND

A HISTORY OF
GLOUCESTERSHIRE

VOLUME V

Oxford University Press, Walton Street, Oxford OX2 6DP
Oxford New York
Athens Auckland Bangkok Bombay
Calcutta Cape Town Dar es Salaam Delhi
Florence Hong Kong Istanbul Karachi
Kuala Lumpur Madras Madrid Melbourne
Mexico City Nairobi Paris Singapore
Taipei Tokyo Toronto

and associated companies in
Berlin Ibadan

Oxford is a trade mark of Oxford University Press

Published in the United States
by Oxford University Press Inc., New York

British Library Cataloguing in Publication Data
A catalogue record for this book is available
from the British Library

ISBN 0 19 722787 2

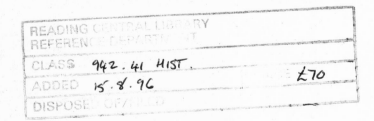
Printed in Great Britain
on acid-free paper by
Butler and Tanner Ltd, Frome

A HISTORY OF THE COUNTY OF GLOUCESTER

EDITED BY N. M. HERBERT

VOLUME V

BLEDISLOE HUNDRED
ST. BRIAVELS HUNDRED
THE FOREST OF DEAN

PUBLISHED FOR

THE INSTITUTE OF HISTORICAL RESEARCH

BY

OXFORD UNIVERSITY PRESS

1996

CONTENTS OF VOLUME FIVE

LIST OF PLATES

For permission to reproduce material in their possession thanks are offered to the Gloucestershire Record Office, the Gloucester Library for items in the Gloucestershire Collection, the Royal Commission on Historical Monuments (England) for items in the National Monuments Record (N.M.R.), Dean Heritage Museum Trust, Monmouth Borough Museums Service, the British Library, Hunting Aerofilms Ltd., Ian Pope, and W. R. Bawden. Plate 34 is reproduced by permission of Keith Allford, Plate 22 by permission of Gerald Smith, and Plates 25 and 44 by permission of Dennis Stephens.

Between pages 184 and 185

LIST OF PLATES

LIST OF MAPS AND OTHER TEXT FIGURES

Figures 1–8, 10, 13–18, 22 were drawn by Philip Moss (Illustration and Design, Hucclecote, Gloucester); the original drafts were prepared by N. M. Herbert and A. R. J. Jurica, based on O.S. Maps 6" (1880s edn.). Figures 11–12 are taken from a redrawing by G. L. Clissold of a map of the western part of the Forest area made in 1608: P.R.O., MR 879 (F 17/1). For permission to reproduce material in their possession thanks are offered to the Gloucestershire Record Office and to the Museum of Fine Arts, Boston (Mass.).

GLOUCESTERSHIRE COUNTY COUNCIL

EDUCATION COMMITTEE, 1994–5

EDITORIAL NOTE

Although numbered Five, this is the eighth volume to be published of the *Victoria History of Gloucestershire* and the seventh since the revival of the Gloucestershire History in 1958. The arrangements by which the Gloucestershire County Council and the University of London collaborate to produce the Gloucestershire History are indicated in the editorial note to *Gloucestershire*, Volume Six. In 1995, however, the Council gave notice that Government limits on local-authority finances would not permit it to continue the partnership in its existing form. When this volume went to press, the Council was negotiating a partnership with Cheltenham and Gloucester College of Higher Education to continue the work of the History. Once again it is the General Editor's pleasure to record the University's gratitude for the Council's continuing generosity during the compilation of this volume.

In 1991 the County Council transferred the supervision of the compilation of the *Victoria History of Gloucestershire* from its Recreation and Leisure Committee to its Education Committee.

The authors and editors of the volume have drawn widely on the help, information, and advice of many people and bodies, too numerous all to be mentioned here but named in the footnotes to the articles with which they helped. All are most cordially thanked. Particular thanks are owed for help and advice to Dr. C. E. Hart, a distinguished historian of the Forest of Dean and its senior verderer, whose papers, deposited in the Gloucestershire Record Office and including many photocopies and transcripts of Public Record Office sources for the history of the Forest, have also much aided the research for this volume, and to Mr. I. J. Standing, curator of Dean Heritage Museum. Among others who have given help with particular aspects of the work, that of Mr. J. E. Everard, deputy surveyor of the Forest of Dean district of Forest Enterprise, Mrs. C. Chamberlain, Mrs. A. Bayliss, Professor J. R. L. Allen, Mr. G. L. Clissold, Mr. B. C. Frith, Mr. O. B. Hepworth, Mr. Ian Pope, and Mr. A. M. R. Watts is warmly acknowledged. Warm thanks are also offered to Professor C. R. Elrington, who after his retirement as General Editor of the Victoria History in 1994 continued to help with the editing of the volume.

For access to records in their possession grateful acknowledgement is made to his Grace the duke of Beaufort for items in the Badminton Muniments, and to Mr. R. J. Berkeley for items in the Berkeley Castle Muniments, and to the National Library of Wales, Hereford Record Office, and Suffolk Record Office. The Clifton diocesan archivist gave permission for access to documents deposited in Bristol Record Office. The staff of Gloucestershire Record Office, under the County and Diocesan Archivist, Mr D. J. H. Smith, continued their indispensable aid and encouragement, and the staff of the Gloucester Library their help with access to the Gloucestershire Collection. The library of the Bristol and Gloucestershire Archaeological Society, of which the senior Local Studies librarian at Gloucester Library, Mr. G. Baker, is honorary librarian, has once again been another valuable resource.

The structure, aims, and progress of the Victoria History as a whole are described in the *General Introduction* (1970) and its *Supplement* (1990).

LIST OF CLASSES OF DOCUMENTS
IN THE PUBLIC RECORD OFFICE

USED IN THIS VOLUME
WITH THEIR CLASS NUMBERS

Office of Land Revenue Records and Enrolments
   LRRO 1   Maps and Plans
   LRRO 5   Deeds and Evidences

Ministry of Agriculture, Fisheries, and Food
   MAF 68   Agricultural Returns: Parish
                   Summaries

Maps and Plans
   MR   Maps, plans, or pictures taken
            from various classes

Probate
   PROB 11   Registered copies of wills proved
              in Prerogative Court of
              Canterbury

Court of Requests
   REQ 1   Miscellaneous Books
   REQ 2   Proceedings

General Register Office
   RG 4   Authenticated Registers, Main Series

RG 9   Census Returns 1861
RG 10   1871
RG 11   1881
RG 12   1891

Special Collections
   SC 2   Court Rolls
   SC 6   Ministers' and Receivers' Accounts
   SC 12   Rentals and Surveys, Portfolios

State Paper Office
           State Papers Domestic
   SP 14   Jas. I
   SP 16   Chas. I
   SP 18   Interregnum

Court of Star Chamber
   STAC 2   Proceedings, Hen. VIII

Court of Wards and Liveries
   WARD 7   Inquisitions post mortem

SELECT LIST OF ACCUMULATIONS
IN THE GLOUCESTERSHIRE RECORD OFFICE

Deposited Collections

D	23	Probyn family of Newland
D	33	Machen family of English Bicknor
D	34	Bell and Hall charities of Newland
D	36	Colchester-Wemyss family of Westbury-on-Severn
D	177	Haines & Sumner of Gloucester (solicitors), including Marling of Clanna and Flaxley charity records
D	326	Guise family of Elmore
D	421	Bathurst family of Lydney
D	543	Yearsley and Wadeson of Mitcheldean (solicitors)
D	608	Twiston-Davies papers deposited by the National Library of Wales
D	637	Vizard & Son of Monmouth (solicitors)
D	1381	Waller& Son of Gloucester (architects)
D	1430	Evans & Ellis of Chepstow (solicitors)
D	1438	Mullings, Ellet, & Co. of Cirencester (solicitors), records of Pyrke family of Littledean
D	1677	Hall and Gage families of Highmeadow
D	1833	Rooke family of Bigsweir
D	2026	Bond family of Redbrook
D	2052	Notes on nonconformity compiled by G. Dutton
D	2172	Rickerby, Mellersh, & Co. of Cheltenham (solicitors)
D	2244	Medieval deeds of the Forest of Dean area
D	2299	Bruton, Knowles, & Co. (estate agents)
D	2428	Land valuation records compiled under the Finance Act of 1910
D	2598	Forest of Dean Methodist circuit
D	2700	Badminton estate records
D	2957	Deeds transferred from the Gloucestershire Collection at Gloucester Library
D	3269	Gloucester municipal charity trustees
D	3270	Governors of Gloucester United schools
D	3469	Charities review papers compiled by L. S. Duirs
D	3921	Documents and papers deposited by Dr. C. E. Hart
D	4431	Deeds collected by Sir Thomas Phillipps
D	4543	Pettit & Westlake of London (solicitors)
D	6993	Forest of Dean verderers' court

Gloucester Diocesan Records (G.D.R.)

T 1	tithe awards
V 5	glebe terriers
vols.	volumes of the diocesan registry
wills	probate copies of wills proved in consistory court

Quarter Sessions Records

Administration

Q/AG	gaols
Q/AL	lunatic asylums
Q/AP	police

Clerk of the Peace

Q/CI	lists and indexes
Q/CL	legal

Finance

Q/FAc	accounts
Q/FR	county rates

Registration

Q/RB	savings banks
Q/REl	elections, land tax
Q/RF	fishing engines
Q/RGf	Forest of Dean encroachments
Q/RI	inclosure awards
Q/RNc	papists' estates
Q/RP	printing presses
Q/RSf	friendly societies
Q/RUm	public works
Q/RZ	miscellaneous

The Court in Session

Q/SG	prisoners
Q/SIb	indictment books
Q/SO	order books
Q/SP	presentments
Q/SR	order rolls
Q/SRh	highway diversions

Other Records

A	Prints
AC	County clerk's department records
CE/M	County council education committee minutes
CE/O	County council education orders
DA	District councils and superseded authorities
DC	County council deeds
EL	Catalogues of records in other archive repositories
G	Boards of guardians

Other Records cont.

G.B.R.	Gloucester Borough Records
GPS	Photographs
HO	Hospitals
K	County council records deposited after 1974
P	Parish records
S	Schools
SB	School boards
SM	School managers

Pamphlets

CH	Charities
ED	Education
FD	Forest of Dean
IN	Industry
NC	Nonconformity
PA	Parish histories
SC	Schools
SL	Sale particulars
SP	Sports

NOTE ON ABBREVIATIONS

Among the abbreviations and short titles used the following may require elucidation:

Abbrev. Plac. (Rec. Com.)	*Placitorum Abbreviatio, Ric. I–Edw. II*, ed. G. Rose and W. Illingworth (Record Commission, 1811)
Acreage Returns, 1905	Board of Agriculture Acreage Returns of 1905, from a MS. copy in possession of the editor, V.C.H. Glos.
Acts of P.C.	*Acts of the Privy Council of England* (H.M.S.O. 1890–1964)
Agric. Returns 1988	Agricultural Returns, Parish Summaries 1988 at Ministry of Agriculture, Fisheries, and Food, Divisional Office, Elmbridge Court, Gloucester
Atkinson, *Map of Dean Forest* (1847)	J. Atkinson, *Plan of Her Majesty's Forest of Dean with High Meadow and Great Doward Woods* (1847)
Atkyns, *Glos.*	R. Atkyns, *Ancient and Present State of Glostershire* (1712)
Award of Dean Forest Mining Com. (1841)	T. Sopwith, *Award of the Dean Forest Mining Commissioners as to the Coal and Iron Mines in Her Majesty's Forest of Dean* (London, 1841)
B. & G. Par. Rec.	*Guide to the Parish Records of the City of Bristol and County of Gloucester*, ed. I. Gray and E. Ralph (B.G.A.S. 1963)
B.G.A.S.	Bristol and Gloucestershire Archaeological Society
B.L.	British Library (used in references to documents transferred from the British Museum)
Badminton Mun.	Records at Badminton House
Berkeley Cast. Mun.	Records at Berkeley Castle
Berkeley MSS.	John Smith, *Berkeley Manuscripts: Lives of the Berkeleys with a Description of the Hundred of Berkeley*, ed. J. Maclean (3 vols. Gloucester, 1883–5)
Bibliotheca Glos.	*Bibliotheca Gloucestrensis: Collections of Scarce and Curious Tracts Illustrative of and Published during the Civil War* (2 vols. Gloucester, priv. print. 1825)
Bigland, *Glos.*	*Historical, Monumental, and Genealogical Collections Relative to the County of Gloucester, Printed from the Original Papers of Ralph Bigland* (3 vols. 1791–1889, issued in parts; vol. iii is unpaginated)
Bk. of Fees	*Book of Fees* (3 vols. H.M.S.O. 1920–31)
Bright, *Nonconf. in Dean*	T. Bright, *Rise of Nonconformity in the Forest of Dean* (Forest of Dean Local History Soc. 1953)
Bryant, *Map of Glos.* (1824)	A. Bryant, *Map of the County of Gloucester in the years 1823 & 1824* (1824)
Cal. Chart. R.	*Calendar of the Charter Rolls preserved in the Public Record Office* (H.M.S.O. 1903–27)
Cal. Close	*Calendar of the Close Rolls preserved in the Public Record Office* (H.M.S.O. 1892–1963)
Cal. Cttee. for Compounding	*Calendar of the Proceedings of the Committee for Compounding with Delinquents, etc.* (H.M.S.O. 1889–92)
Cal. D.L. Pleadings (Rec. Com.)	*Ducatus Lancastriae Calendarium Inquisitiones post mortem, etc. Edw. I–Car. I*, ed. R. J. Harper, J. Caley, and W. Minchin (3 vols. Record Commission, 1823–34)
Cal. Doc. France	*Calendar of Documents preserved in France illustrative of the history of Great Britain and Ireland*, ed. J. H. Round (H.M.S.O. 1899)
Cal. H.O. Papers	*Calendar of Home Office Papers* (H.M.S.O. 1878–99)
Cal. Fine R.	*Calendar of the Fine Rolls preserved in the Public Record Office* (H.M.S.O. 1911–62)
Cal. Inq. Misc.	*Calendar of Inquisitions Miscellaneous (Chancery) preserved in the Public Record Office* (H.M.S.O. 1916–68)
Cal. Inq. p.m.	*Calendar of Inquisitions post mortem preserved in the Public Record Office* (H.M.S.O. 1904–92)
Cal. Inq. p.m. Hen. VII	*Calendar of Inquisitions post mortem, Henry VII* (H.M.S.O. 1898–1955)
Cal. Lib.	*Calendar of the Liberate Rolls preserved in the Public Record Office* (H.M.S.O. 1917–64)

Cal. Mem. R.	*Calendar of the Memoranda Rolls preserved in the Public Record Office* (H.M.S.O. 1969)
Cal. Papal Reg.	*Calendar of Entries in the Papal Registers relating to Great Britain and Ireland* (H.M.S.O. 1893–1961)
Cal. Pat.	*Calendar of the Patent Rolls preserved in the Public Record Office* (H.M.S.O. 1891–1986)
Cal. Proc. in Chanc. Eliz. I (Rec. Com.)	*Calendar of Proceedings in Chancery in the Reign of Queen Elizabeth I, with examples of proceedings from Richard II,* ed. J. Caley and J. Bayley (3 vols. Record Commission, 1827–32)
Cal. S.P. Dom.	*Calendar of State Papers, Domestic Series* (H.M.S.O. 1856–1972)
Cal. Treas. Bks.	*Calendar of Treasury Books* (H.M.S.O. 1904–69)
Cal. Treas. Bks. & Papers	*Calendar of Treasury Books and Papers* (H.M.S.O. 1898–1903)
Cal. Treas. Papers	*Calendar of Treasury Papers* (H.M.S.O. 1868–89)
Camd. Misc. xxii	*Camden Miscellany,* xxii (Camden 4th ser. i), including 'Charters of the Earldom of Hereford, 1095–1201', ed. D. Walker
Cat. Anct. D.	*Descriptive Catalogue of Ancient Deeds in the Public Record Office* (H.M.S.O. 1890–1915)
Cat. of Glos. Colln.	*Catalogue of the Gloucestershire Collection in the Gloucester Public Library,* compiled by R. Austin (Gloucester, 1928)
Close R.	*Close Rolls of the reign of Henry III preserved in the Public Record Office* (H.M.S.O. 1902–75)
Complete Peerage	G. E. C[ockayne] and others, *Complete Peerage...*(2nd edn., 13 vols. 1910–59)
Compton Census, ed. Whiteman	*Compton Census of 1676: a critical edition,* ed. A. Whiteman (British Academy Records of Social and Economic History, new ser. x, London, 1986)
Cur. Reg. R.	*Curia Regis Rolls* (H.M.S.O. 1923–72)
D.N.B.	*Dictionary of National Biography*
Dean Forest Select Cttee. (1874)	*Report from the Select Committee on Dean Forest,* H.C. 272 (1874), vii
Delineations of Glos.	J. and H. S. Storer and J. N. Brewer, *Delineations of Gloucestershire, being views of the Principal Seats of Nobility and Gentry* (London, 1825–7)
Dugdale, *Mon.*	W. Dugdale, *Monasticon Anglicanum,* ed. J. Caley and others (6 vols. 1817–30)
E.H.R.	*English Historical Review*
Eccl. Misc.	*Ecclesiastical Miscellany* (B.G.A.S. Records Section, xi, 1976), including 'Survey of Diocese of Gloucester, 1603', ed. A. C. Percival and W. J. Sheils
Econ. H.R.	*Economic History Review*
Educ. Enq. Abstract	*Education Enquiry Abstract,* H.C. 62 (1835), xli
Educ. of Poor Digest	*Digest of Returns to the Select Committee on Education of the Poor,* H.C. 224 (1819), ix (1)
Ex. e Rot. Fin. (Rec. Com.)	*Excerpta e Rotulis Finium in Turri Londinensi asservatis, Henry III, 1216–72,* ed. C. Roberts (2 vols. Record Commission, 1835–6)
Farr, *Chepstow Ships*	G. E. Farr, *Chepstow Ships* (Chepstow, 1954)
Flaxley Cart.	*Cartulary and Historical Notes of the Cistercian Abbey of Flaxley,* ed. A. W. Crawley–Boevey (Exeter, priv. print. 1887)
Feud. Aids	*Inquisitions and Assessments relating to Feudal Aids preserved in the Public Record Office* (H.M.S.O. 1899–1920)
Finberg, *Early Charters of W. Midlands*	H. P. R. Finberg, *Early Charters of the W. Midlands* (Leicester, 1961)
Finberg, *Glos. Studies*	*Gloucestershire Studies,* ed. H. P. R. Finberg (1957)
Fisher, *Custom and Capitalism*	C. Fisher, *Custom, Work and Market Capitalism: The Forest of Dean Colliers, 1788–1888* (London, 1981)
Fosbrooke, *Glos.*	T. D. Fosbrooke, *Abstracts of Records and Manuscripts Respecting the County of Gloucester, Formed into a History* (2 vols. Gloucester, 1807)
G.B.R.	Gloucester Borough Records (in Glos. R.O.)
G.D.R.	Gloucester Diocesan Records (see above, Glos. R.O. accumulations)
G.R.O.	General Register Office

Gent. Mag.	*Gentleman's Magazine* (1731–1867)
Glos. Ch. Bells	M. Bliss and F. Sharpe, *Church Bells of Gloucestershire* (Gloucester, 1986)
Glos. Ch. Notes	*Gloucestershire Church Notes*, by S. R. Glynne, ed. W. P. W. Phillimore and J. Melland Hall (1902)
Glos. Ch. Plate	*Church Plate of Gloucestershire*, ed. J. T. Evans (B.G.A.S. 1906)
Glos. Colln.	The Gloucestershire Collection, in Gloucester Library, comprising printed works, manuscripts, prints and drawings, etc.
Glos. N. & Q.	*Gloucestershire Notes and Queries* (10 vols. 1881–1914)
Glos. R.O.	Gloucestershire Record Office (see above, Glos. R.O. accumulations)
Glos. Q.S. Archives	*Gloucestershire Quarter Sessions Archives: A Descriptive Catalogue*, compiled by I. E. Gray and A. T. Gaydon (Glos. County Council, 1958)
Glos. Subsidy Roll, 1327	*Gloucestershire Subsidy Roll I Edw. III, 1327* (priv. print. by Sir Thos. Phillipps [? 1856])
Glouc. Cath. Libr.	Gloucester Cathedral Library
Glouc. Corp. Rec.	*Calendar of the Records of the Corporation of Gloucester*, ed. W. H. Stevenson (Gloucester, 1893)
Glouc. Jnl.	*Gloucester Journal* (established 1722)
Greenwood, *Map of Glos.* (1824)	C. & J. Greenwood, *Map of the County of Gloucester in the year 1823* (1824)
H.M.S.O.	Her (His) Majesty's Stationery Office
Harris, 'Wye Valley Ind. Hist.'	P. G. Harris, 'Wye Valley Industrial History' (*c.* 1976, copy in Glos. R.O. libr.)
Hart, *Free Miners*	C. E. Hart, *Free Miners of the Royal Forest of Dean and Hundred of St. Briavels* (Gloucester, 1953)
Hart, *Ind. Hist. of Dean*	C. E. Hart, *Industrial History of Dean* (Newton Abbot, 1971)
Hart, *Royal Forest*	C. E. Hart, *Royal Forest: A History of Dean's Woods as Producers of Timber* (Oxford, 1966)
Hart, *Verderers*	C. E. Hart, *Verderers and Forest Laws of Dean* (Newton Abbot, 1971)
Heref. R.O.	Hereford Record Office
Hist. & Cart. Mon. Glouc. (Rolls Ser.)	*Historia et Cartularium Monasterii Sancti Petri Gloucestriae*, ed. W. H. Hart (Rolls Series, no. 33, 3 vols. 1863–87)
Hist. MSS. Com.	Royal Commission on Historical Manuscripts
Hockaday Abs.	The 'Hockaday Abstracts', being abstracts of ecclesiastical records relating to Gloucestershire, compiled by F. S. Hockaday mainly from diocesan records, in Gloucester Library
Inq. Non. (Rec. Com.)	*Nonarum Inquisitiones in Curia Scaccarii*, ed. G. Vandersee (Record Commission, 1807)
Inq. p.m. Glos.	*Abstracts of Inquisitiones post mortem for Gloucestershire, 1236–1413, 1625–42* (6 vols. issued jointly by the British Record Soc., Index Library vols. xxx, xl, xlviii, and ix, xxi, xlvii, and the B.G.A.S. 1893–1914)
L. & P. Hen. VIII	*Letters and Papers, Foreign and Domestic, of the Reign of Henry VIII* (H.M.S.O. 1864–1932)
Lond. Gaz.	*London Gazette*
Manual of Glos. Lit.	*Bibliographer's Manual of Gloucestershire Literature*, ed. F. A. Hyett and W. Bazeley (3 vols. Gloucester, priv. print. 1895–7)
Mountjoy, *Dean Collier*	T. Mountjoy, *Life, Labours, and Deliverances of a Forest of Dean Collier* (1887)
Mullin, *Forest in Old Photog.*	D. Mullin, *The Forest in Old Photographs from the Dean Heritage Museum Collection* (Gloucester, 1988)
N.L.W.	National Library of Wales
N.M.R.	National Monuments Record, of the Royal Commission on Historical Monuments (England)
Nat. Soc. files	Schools files of the National Society, Church of England Record Centre, South Bermondsey, London
Nat. Soc. *Inquiry, 1846–7*	*Result of the Returns to the General Inquiry made by the National Society* (1849)
Nicholls, *Forest of Dean*	H. G. Nicholls, *The Forest of Dean; an Historical and Descriptive Account* (1858)
Nicholls, *Iron Making*	H. G. Nicholls, *Iron Making in the Olden Times: as instanced in the ancient mines, forges, and furnaces of the Forest of Dean* (1866)

Nicholls, *Personalities of Dean*	H. G. Nicholls, *Personalities of the Forest of Dean* (1863)
P.N. Glos. (E.P.N.S.)	*Place-Names of Gloucestershire* (English Place-Name Soc. vols. xxxviii–xli, 1964–5)
P.R.O.	Public Record Office (see above, P.R.O. classes of documents)
Paar, *G.W.R. in Dean*	H. W. Paar, *Great Western Railway in Dean* (Dawlish, 1965)
Paar, *Severn and Wye Railway*	H. W. Paar, *Severn & Wye Railway* (Dawlish, 1963)
Pat. R.	*Patent Rolls of the Reign of Henry III preserved in the Public Record Office* (H.M.S.O. 1901–3)
Payne, *Glos. Survey*	G. E. Payne, *Gloucestershire: a Survey* (Gloucester [? 1946])
Pearce, 'Water Supply in Dean'	D. A. Pearce, 'History of Water Supply in Forest of Dean' (1983, TS. in Glos. R.O., D 2826)
Phelps, *Forest in Old Photog.* (1983)	H. Phelps, *The Forest in Old Photographs* (Gloucester, 1983)
Phelps, *Forest in Old Photog.* (1984)	H. Phelps, *The Forest in Old Photographs. A Second Selection* (Gloucester, 1984)
Pipe R.	*Pipe Roll*
Plac. de Quo Warr. (Rec. Com.)	*Placita de Quo Warranto...in Curia Receptae Scaccarii Westm. asservata*, ed. W. Illingworth and J. Caley (Record Commission, 1818)
Pleas of the Crown for Glos. ed. Maitland	*Pleas of the Crown for the County of Gloucester, 1221*, ed. F. W. Maitland (1884)
Pooley, *Glos. Crosses*	C. Pooley, *Notes on the Old Crosses of Gloucestershire* (1868)
Poor Law Abstract, 1804	*Abstract of Returns Relative to the Expense and Maintenance of the Poor* (printed by order of the House of Commons, 1804)
Poor Law Abstract, 1818	*Abstract of Returns to Orders of the House of Commons Relative to Assessments for Relief of the Poor*, H.C. 294 (1820), xii
Poor Law Com. 2nd Rep.	*Second Report of the Poor Law Commission*, H.C. 595 (1836), xxxix (1)
Poor Law Returns (1830–1)	*Account of the Money Expended for the Maintenance and Relief of the Poor for the five years ending 25th March 1825, 1826, 1827, 1828, and 1829*, H.C. 83 (1830–1), xi
Poor Law Returns (1835)	*Accounts of the Money Expended 1830, 1831, 1832, 1833, and 1834*, H.C. 444 (1835), xlvii
Proc. C.N.F.C.	*Proceedings of the Cotteswold Naturalists' Field Club*
Public Elem. Schs. 1906	*List of Public Elementary Schools in England and Wales on 1 Jan. 1906* [Cd. 3182], H.C. (1906), lxxxvi
Reg. Bothe	*Registrum Caroli Bothe, Episcopi Herefordensis, 1516–35*, ed. A. T. Bannister (Cant. & York Soc. 1921)
Reg. Bransford	*Calendar of the Register of Wolstan de Bransford, Bishop of Worcester 1333–49*, ed. R. M. Haines (Worcs. Hist. Soc. 1966)
Reg. Cantilupe	*Registrum Thome de Cantilupo, Episcopi Herefordensis, 1275–82*, ed. W. W. Capes (Cant. & York Soc. 1907)
Reg. Gilbert	*Registrum Johannis Gilbert, Episcopi Herefordensis, 1375–89*, ed. J. H. Parry (Cant. & York Soc. 1915)
Reg. Lacy	*Registrum Edmundi Lacy, Episcopi Herefordensis, 1417–20*, ed. A. T. Bannister (Cant. and York Soc. 1918)
Reg. Mascall	*Registrum Roberti Mascall, Episcopi Herefordensis, 1404–16*, ed. J. H. Parry (Cant. & York Soc. 1917)
Reg. Mayew	*Registrum Ricardi Mayew, Episcopi Herefordensis, 1504–16*, ed. A. T. Bannister (Cant. & York Soc. 1921)
Reg. Myllyng	*Registrum Thome Myllyng, Episcopi Herefordensis, 1474–92*, ed. A. T. Bannister (Cant. & York Soc. 1920)
Reg. Orleton	*Registrum Ade de Orleton, Episcopi Herefordensis, 1317–27*, ed. A. T. Bannister (Cant. & York Soc. 1908)
Reg. Spofford	*Registrum Thome Spofford, Episcopi Herefordensis, 1422–48*, ed. A. T. Bannister (Cant. & York Soc. 1919)
Reg. Stanbury	*Registrum Johannis Stanbury, Episcopi Herefordensis, 1453–74*, ed. A. T. Bannister (Cant. & York Soc. 1919)
Reg. Swinfield	*Registrum Ricardi de Swinfield, Episcopi Herefordensis, 1283–1317*, ed. W. W. Capes (Cant. & York Soc. 1909)

Reg. T. de Charlton	*Registrum Thome de Charlton, Episcopi Herefordensis, 1327–44*, ed. W. W. Capes (Cant. & York Soc. 1913)
Reg. Trefnant	*Registrum Johannis Trefnant, Episcopi Herefordensis, 1389–1404*, ed. W. W. Capes (Cant. & York Soc. 1916)
Reg. Trillek	*Registrum Johannis de Trillek, Episcopi Herefordensis, 1344–61*, ed. J. H. Parry (Cant. & York Soc. 1912)
19th Rep. Com. Char.	*19th Report of the Commissioners Appointed to Enquire Concerning Charities* (Lord Brougham's Commission), H.C. 374 (1828), xi (1)
3rd Rep. Com. Woods (1788)	*Third Report of the Commissioners Appointed to Enquire into the Woods, Forests, and Land Revenues of the Crown* (1788, ordered to be printed 1792)
3rd Rep. Com. Woods (1819)	*Third Report of the Commissioners of His Majesty's Woods, Forests, and Land Revenues*, H.C. 474 (1819), xix
4th Rep. Com. Woods (1823)	*Fourth Report...Land Revenues*, H.C. 110 (1823), xi
5th Rep. Com. Woods (1826)	*Fifth Report...Land Revenues*, H.C. 368 (1826), xiv
1st Rep. Dean Forest Com.	*First Report of the Dean Forest Commissioners to the Lords Commisioners of the Treasury*, H.C. 283 (1835), xxxvi
2nd Rep. Dean Forest Com.	*Second Report...Treasury* (bound in one volume with *First Report*)
3rd Rep. Dean Forest Com.	*Third Report...Treasury*, H.C. 515 (1835), xxxvi
4th Rep. Dean Forest Com.	*Fourth Report...Treasury*, H.C. 610 (1835), xxxvi
5th Rep. Dean Forest Com.	*Fifth Report...Treasury* (bound in one volume with *Fourth Report*)
Rep. Dean Forest Cttee. (1958)	*Report of the Forest of Dean Committee 1958* [Cmnd. 686], H.C. (1958–9), xiii
Richardson, *Wells and Springs of Glos.*	L. Richardson, *Wells and Springs of Gloucestershire* (H.M.S.O. 1930)
Roper, *Glos. Effigies*	I. M. Roper, *Monumental Effigies of Gloucestershire and Bristol* (Gloucester, 1931)
Rot. Chart. (Rec. Com.)	*Rotuli Chartarum in Turri Londinensi asservati, 1199–1216*, ed. T. D. Hardy (Record Commission, 1837)
Rot. Hund. (Rec. Com.)	*Rotuli Hundredorum temp. Hen. III & Edw. I in Turri Londinensi et in Curia Receptae Scaccarii Westm. asservati*, ed. W. Illingworth and J. Caley (2 vols. Record Commission, 1812–18)
Rot. Litt. Claus. (Rec. Com.)	*Rotuli Litterarum Clausarum in Turri Londinensi asservati, 1204–27*, ed. T. D. Hardy (2 vols. Record Commission, 1833–44)
Rot. Litt. Pat. (Rec. Com.)	*Rotuli Litterarum Patentium in Turri Londinensi asservati, 1201–16*, ed. T. D. Hardy (Record Commission, 1835)
Rot. Parl.	*Rotuli Parliamentorum* (6 vols. [1783])
Rudder, *Glos.*	S. Rudder, *New History of Gloucestershire* (Cirencester, 1779)
Rudge, *Agric. of Glos.*	T. Rudge, *General View of the Agriculture of the County of Gloucester* (Gloucester, 1807)
Rudge, *Hist. of Glos.*	T. Rudge, *History of the County of Gloucester* (2 vols. Gloucester, 1803)
Select Cttee. on Crown Forests (1854)	*Report from the Select Committee on Crown Forests*, H.C. 377 (1854), x
Select Cttee. on Woods (1849)	*First Report from the Select Committee on the Woods, Forests, and Land Revenues of the Crown*, H.C. 513 (1849), xx
Select Cttee. on Woods (1889)	*Report from the Select Committee on Woods and Forests and Land Revenues of the Crown*, H.C. 284 (1889), xvi
Smith, *Men and Armour*	*Names and Surnames of All the Able and Sufficient Men in Body Fit for His Majesty's Service in the Wars, within the County of Gloucester, Compiled by John Smith, 1608* (1902)
Som. R.O.	Somerset Record Office
Sopwith, *Map of Dean Forest* (1835)	T. Sopwith, *Plan of Coal and Iron Mine Districts in the Forest of Dean* (1835)
Suff. R.O.	Suffolk Record Office

Taylor, *Dom. Glos.*	C. S. Taylor, *Analysis of the Domesday Survey of Gloucestershire* (B.G.A.S. 1887–9, issued in parts)
Taylor, *Map of Glos.* (1777)	I. Taylor, *Map of the County of Gloucester* (1777), republished in *Gloucestershire and Bristol Atlas* (B.G.A.S. 1961)
Tax. Eccl. (Rec. Com.)	*Taxatio Ecclesiastica Angliae et Walliae auctoritate P. Nicholai IV circa A.D. 1291,* ed. S. Ayscough and J. Caley (Record Commission, 1802)
Trans. B.G.A.S.	*Transactions of the Bristol and Gloucestershire Archaeological Society*
Univ. Brit. Dir.	*Universal British Directory of Trade, Commerce, and Manufacture,* ed. P. Barfoot and J. Wilkes (5 vols. 1791–8)
V.C.H.	*Victoria County History*
Valor Eccl. (Rec. Com.)	*Valor Ecclesiasticus temp. Hen. VIII auctoritate regia institutus,* ed. J. Caley and J. Hunter (6 vols. Record Commission, 1810–34)
Verey, *Glos.*	D. C. W. Verey, *Gloucestershire*: vol. i, *The Cotswolds*; vol. ii, *The Vale and the Forest of Dean* (The Buildings of England, ed. N. Pevsner, 1970)
Visit. Glos. 1623	*Visitation of the County of Gloucester, 1623,* ed. J. Maclean and W. C. Heane (Harleian Soc. xxi, 1885)
Visit. Glos. 1682–3	*Visitation of the County of Gloucester, 1682, 1683,* ed. T. FitzRoy Fenwick and W. C. Metcalfe (Exeter, priv. print. 1884)
Williams, *Parl. Hist. of Glos.*	W. R. Williams, *Parliamentary History of the County of Gloucester* (Hereford, priv. print. 1898)

BLEDISLOE HUNDRED

I N 1086 Bledisloe hundred comprised Awre manor and its former members of Bledisloe, Etloe, and Purton (later part of Lydney parish), together with Poulton (later part of Awre parish), Nass (later part of Lydney parish), and two unidentified estates, possibly both within the later Awre parish. It totalled *c.* 19 hides.[1] Most of the later Lydney parish, as a manor of 12½ hides formed between 1066 and 1071 from four separate estates, was part of a separate hundred called Lydney,[2] while Alvington, with 6 hides, was then in Herefordshire as part of Bromsash hundred.[3] By 1221 Lydney and Alvington were part of Bledisloe hundred,[4] having probably been added before the mid 12th century in a reorganization that created the new St. Briavels hundred.[5] Blakeney tithing, in Awre parish, was in St. Briavels hundred until the mid 16th century,[6] but by 1608 it was regarded as part of Bledisloe hundred.[7] Etloe Duchy, a tithing of Awre that became a manor of the duchy of Lancaster in the 14th century,[8] was in the Duchy of Lancaster hundred in the 16th century and the early 17th,[9] but later it was included in Bledisloe.[10] The whole hundred was within the jurisdiction of the Forest of Dean by 1228 and probably from Henry II's reign, but by a new perambulation made in 1300 and confirmed in 1327 Lydney and Alvington parishes and Box manor, in Awre, were excluded.[11]

The hundred was sometimes known as Awre hundred in the early 13th century[12] but otherwise it was called Bledisloe to 1640 when Charles I ordered that the name be changed to Lydney hundred;[13] from that time it was sometimes called the hundred of Lydney alias Bledisloe[14] but more usually the old name alone continued in use.

Henry III gave the hundred to the younger William Marshal, earl of Pembroke, either in 1230, when he gave him Awre manor, or earlier. The king took the hundred in hand again on the earl's death in 1231[15] but in 1233 he granted it in fee to the earl's brother and successor Richard.[16] It then descended with Awre manor until 1668,[17] and later remained part of the Lydney estate of the Winter family and their successors, the Bathursts.[18] Charles Bathurst took the name of the hundred as the title of his barony in 1918 and his viscounty in 1935.[19]

The ancient meeting place of the hundred was evidently in Bledisloe tithing in Awre, probably where the Gloucester–Chepstow road crosses a high ridge northeast of Blakeney village.[20] By 1599 the hundred court met at Lydney,[21] and in the late 17th century and in the 19th it was held at the same time and at the same venue, the Feathers inn, as the Lydney manor court.[22] Court rolls or court papers survive for 1445–6, 1562, 1588, 1595–1600, 1659–60, 1680–3, 1695–1703, 1711, 1716, and 1863–4.[23]

1 *Dom. Bk.* (Rec. Com.), i. 163–4, 167v., 169.
2 Ibid. 164; cf. below, Lydney, manors.
3 *Dom. Bk.* (Rec. Com.), i. 185v.
4 *Pleas of the Crown for Glos.* ed. Maitland, pp. 91–2; P.R.O., JUST 1/274, rot. 10.
5 Below, St. Briavels hundred.
6 P.R.O., JUST 1/274, rot. 11d.; *L. & P. Hen. VIII,* xiv (1), p. 271.　　7 Smith, *Men and Armour,* 57.
8 Below, Awre, manors.
9 *Military Surv. of Glos. 1522* (B.G.A.S. Rec. Ser. vi), 202; Smith, *Men and Armour,* 72.
10 P.R.O., E 179/247/14, rot. 40; *Census,* 1801.
11 Below, Forest of Dean, bounds.

12 *Close R. 1227–31,* 561; P.R.O., C 115/K 2/6683, f. 95v.
13 Glos. R.O., D 421/L 17.　　14 Ibid. M 33, M 77.
15 *Close R. 1227–31,* 561; *Rot. Hund.* (Rec. Com.), i. 176.
16 *Cal. Chart. R. 1226–57,* 174.
17 Below, Awre, manors; *Feud. Aids,* ii. 264; *Cal. Inq. p.m.* xii, p. 194; *Cal. Pat. 1476–85,* 241; Glos. R.O., D 421/L 17, M 84.
18 Below, Lydney, manors; Glos. R.O., D 421/M 33, M 77.
19 Burke, *Peerage* (1963), 258.
20 Below, Awre, intro.
21 Glos. R.O., D 421/M 31.　　22 Ibid. M 32–3, M 77–8.
23 Ibid. M 7, M 13–15, M 29, M 31–33, M 77; D 326/M 16.

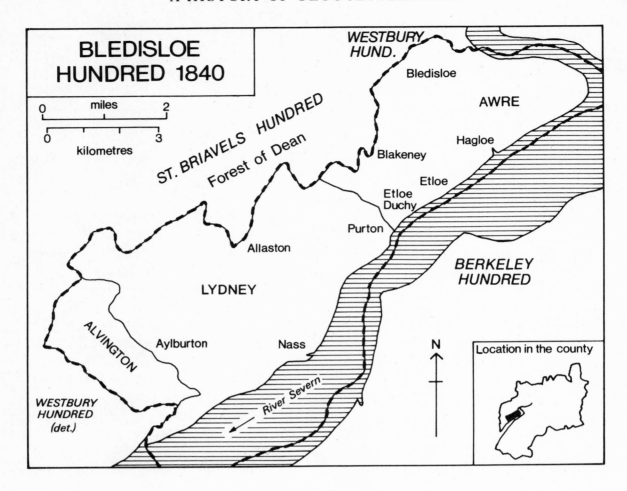

FIG. 1

Llanthony priory claimed that its tenants in the manor of Alvington were exempt from suit to the hundred, and their exemption was confirmed by the lord of the hundred in 1244.[24] Alvington was not represented later in the surviving records of the court until the 1860s. The two large parishes of Awre and Lydney were represented by their various tithings, for which constables were appointed by the court and which paid common fines ranging from 1s. 8d. to 6s.[25]

In each of the years ending at Michaelmas 1317 and 1334 nine ordinary sessions of the hundred court and two leets were held,[26] and roughly the same number of sessions was held in the 1440s, when numerous pleas were heard.[27] The surviving rolls for the late 16th century and the late 17th record only the two leets, held in April and October. In 1659 and early 1660, however, there were sessions of the hundred, hearing mainly pleas of debt, once or twice a month; those sessions, which were held in the name of Sir John Winter's trustees and presided over by leading freeholders of the hundred rather than a steward, may have been only a temporary revival in the particular circumstances of the Interregnum.[28] In the late 16th century the leet enforced the assizes of bread and of ale, appointing breadweighers and aletasters. In 1588 a felon's goods were taken for the lord.[29] In 1640 Sir John

24 P.R.O., C 115/K 2/6683, ff. 95v.–96.
25 Glos. R.O., D 421/M 7, M 13.
26 Berkeley Cast. Mun., General Ser. acct. rolls, Bledisloe hund. acct. 11 Edw. II; Glos. R.O., D 421/

M 16.
27 Glos. R.O., D 421/M 13.
28 Ibid. M 15; cf. below, Lydney, manors.
29 Glos. R.O., D 421/M 7, M 31.

Winter received from Charles I a wide range of franchises in the hundred, some of them probably then only nominal or difficult to enforce; they included goods and chattels of felons, fugitives, and outlaws, treasure trove, wreck, and the right to all royal fish.[30] From the late 16th century there was duplication of leet jurisdiction in the hundred, for a separate view was held for Awre manor, whose lords continued it after 1668, and the Lydney manor court dealt with some matters which strictly belonged to the leet of the hundred.[31]

The three parishes of Bledisloe hundred were bordered on the north-west by the Crown's demesne land of the Forest and on the south-east by the river Severn and gained land from both over the centuries, taking assarts from the royal demesne and reclaiming land from the river. The main ancient route through the hundred, the road between Gloucester and Chepstow, made a rough boundary between the hillsides below the Forest and an area of more gently rolling land and riverside levels. The hillsides, which are formed mainly of the Old Red Sandstone, are broken by a series of narrow, deep valleys by which the Soudley, Blackpool, Newerne, and Cone brooks and a number of other streams drain the central plateau of the Forest, reaching the Severn at muddy inlets, known locally as pills. The slopes were thickly wooded in the Middle Ages and large parts of Lydney remained so later, but in other places the woods gave way to large commons. The lower land was mostly in closes from antiquity but there were some open fields and common meadows on the levels and on the land immediately above them. In Awre only the land around its old village required an Act of parliament to inclose it in 1796, but Alvington's inclosure in 1814 was, for a parish of the Forest area, an unusually major reorganization. Lydney's large commons were inclosed late, in 1864.

Except for Awre village, set in a wide loop of the Severn, the principal settlements, Blakeney, Newerne, Lydney, Aylburton, and Alvington, were based on the main Gloucester–Chepstow road. There were a number of other hamlets but some, such as Box and Nass, were later reduced to one or two farmsteads as holdings were amalgamated. Great medieval magnates, including the Berkeleys, held manors in Awre and Lydney, and Llanthony priory acquired Alvington and Aylburton. There were also many substantial ancient freeholds. In the late 16th century much land was absorbed into an estate built up by the Winters of Lydney, and the Lydney estate remained a substantial one in 1994, its owners, the Bathursts, being survivors of the gentry families who had dominated the Forest area in the 18th and 19th centuries. A smaller estate at Hagloe, in Awre, survived in the ownership of the Crown, but the Clanna estate, formed in the 19th century and based in Alvington, had been dispersed.

The small customary tenancies on the manors gave way in the early modern period to a pattern of medium-sized farms. Cattle were raised on the rich pastures at the riverside, and there were numerous orchards, mainly of the local stire cider apple. From the mid 19th century milk production, aided by railway links, was the principal farming enterprise. Salmon fisheries, worked with putcher weirs, stopping boats, and lave nets, provided an additional source of income for the riverside farmers.

The river Severn, the extensive woodland, and streams for powering mills and forges all contributed to the strong trading and industrial element in the local economy. Iron was worked in movable, bloomery forges in the Middle Ages, and

[30] Ibid. L 17. [31] Below, Awre, loc. govt; Lydney, loc. govt.

Lydney and Alvington were centres of the iron industry in the era of charcoal blast furnaces and water-powered forges in the 17th and 18th centuries. Blakeney was a centre for cornmilling and for tanning, the tanners using oak bark from the Forest. The pills on the river, notably Gatcombe, traded in the products of the Forest area, including timber, iron, coal, cider, and bark. Purton, which was at one of the principal Severn ferries, and Gatcombe were the main outlets for oak timber for naval shipbuilding during the Napoleonic Wars.

Lydney, for many centuries only a minor market town, grew rapidly in significance during the 19th century. After 1812, when a tramroad was built down to a new harbour there, it was one of the main outlets for Forest coal and stone, and its ironworks, adapted to tinplating, became a major employer. Lydney's position was bolstered later by railways, both the main South Wales line, built along the riverside and opened in 1851, and a line linking the Forest to the other side of the Severn by a great bridge at Purton, completed in 1879. Blakeney remained a smaller industrial centre, but the railway built through it to a projected harbour was not a success. Alvington retained some modest industrial activity in the form of paper mills which replaced two of its forges. In the 20th century Lydney town continued to grow: new factories were established there to help offset the decline of industry in the adjoining Forest and housing estates were laid out. In other parts of the hundred agriculture remained a strong element, though subject to the nationwide changes of the late 20th century, including the reduction in the number of farms through amalgamation, the ploughing of old pasture and meadow, and the loss of most of the orchards.

ALVINGTON

THE SMALL parish of Alvington[1] lies on the north-west side of the river Severn, 9.5 km. north-east of Chepstow (Mon.). It was part of Herefordshire in the late 11th century[2] but was joined to Gloucestershire, as part of Bledisloe hundred, before the early 13th century.[3] During the 13th century Alvington was within the jurisdiction of the Forest of Dean but it was among places removed from the Forest by a perambulation made in 1300 and confirmed in 1327.[4]

Alvington parish contained 1,582 a. (640 ha.)[5] until 1935 when 54 a. (22 ha.) of uninhabited farmland adjoining its south end were added from Woolaston.[6] The parish forms a fairly narrow strip of land, rising from level land near the riverside to high land near the edge of the formerly extraparochial Forest. The north end of the later parish was in an area of woodland and waste, where the inhabitants of Alvington and Aylburton, both owned by Llanthony priory, Gloucester, in the late Middle Ages, once intercommoned, and the manorial and parochial boundary there was settled only after litigation in the late 16th century and the early 18th. Afterwards the boundary followed a stone wall along the south side of an ancient assart called Prior's Mesne and then descended a small brook by the west side of Ferneyley wood to its confluence with Woodwards (or Colliers)[7] brook. The north-east boundary then descended Woodwards brook to the riverside level, where there was once a small creek of the Severn called Wose Pill which silted up in the early modern period.[8] The north-west boundary, with Hewelsfield parish, followed the edge of a sharply defined ridge called Bordnage,[9] later Barnage, and the south-west boundary, with Woolaston, descended a brook called Small brook[10] to join Cone brook,[11] which it then followed down to the level. At its south end the parish was divided from the Severn by a narrow strip of land belonging to Woolaston and Aylburton, an unusual arrangement which apparently followed reclamation of that land from the river.[12] The boundary left Cone brook just upstream of an ancient clapper bridge called Mickla bridge and followed drainage ditches to the site of Wose Pill.[13] After the alteration of 1935 the boundary left Cone brook by a drainage ditch further south, near the head of the long inlet called Cone Pill, thus taking in land of Woolaston that had lain north-east of Cone brook.[14]

Except for the part on the alluvial, riverside level, the parish is formed by the Old Red Sandstone.[15] From the level the land rises to Alvington village and a central plateau, lying at 50–60 m. The north-western part of the parish is generally higher, but the land there is broken into by the deep valleys of Cone brook and Woodwards brook; at the north and north-west boundaries the land rises steeply to reach 140 m. near Prior's Mesne and 125 m. at the Barnage ridge. Cone brook has been dammed at several places to make ponds to power forges and mills,[16] and a large fishpond, still maintained in 1994, was made on it in the mid 19th century by the owners of a mansion called Clanna which stood north-east of the brook.[17]

The lower half of the parish, which until inclosure in 1814 contained considerable openfield land, a common meadow, and all the land held by customary tenure,[18] was probably the only part of the parish in cultivation in the early Middle Ages. The upper half, above a line roughly from the confluence of Small and Cone brooks on the south-west boundary across to the north-east boundary east of Park Farm, was for long woodland and commonable waste. About 1145, when Walter of Hereford granted to Llanthony priory all his land at Alvington 'in the moor and the wood',[19] the distinction being made was probably that between the lower and upper parts. The woodland was important to the overall economy of the priory in 1277, when it leased Alvington manor but reserved the wood and the use of Wose Pill for shipping out timber and firewood.[20] In the early 14th century the management of the wood was one of many causes of dissension between on the one hand Llanthony and its tenants in Alvington and Aylburton and on the other Tintern abbey (Mon.) and its tenants in Woolaston and Hewelsfield. The tenants of the manors apparently intercommoned in woodland in the areas later called Woolaston common, Barnage, and Royal Reddings, for by an agreement of 1319 settling relations between the two houses each was to be allowed to coppice parts and after cutting to inclose the coppices against animals for four-year periods in order to allow new growth.[21] In 1300 the north end of the later parish was also part of the extensive wood.[22]

At the dissolution of Llanthony priory in 1539, when the officer who managed the manor for the priory was styled bailiff and woodward, considerable woodland evidently remained.[23] By then, however, some areas in the upper part of the parish may have been cleared, for c. 240 a. of closes there were later claimed as tithe free, a status strictly applicable only to land held in

---

1 This account was written in 1994.
2 Dom. Bk. (Rec. Com.), i. 185v.
3 Pleas of the Crown for Glos. ed. Maitland, p. 91; P.R.O., C 115/K 2/6683, f. 95v.
4 Trans. B.G.A.S. lxvi. 172, 176–93; cf. below, Forest of Dean, bounds.
5 O.S. Area Bk. (1880).   6 Census, 1931 (pt. ii).
7 Below, Lydney, intro.
8 Below, Lydney, intro.; cf. Glos. R.O., D 2099, Alvington ct. bk., ct. 28 Apr. 1774.
9 Glos. R.O., D 1430B/10.
10 Trans. B.G.A.S. lxvi. 178; Glos. R.O., D 2099, Alvington ct. bk., ct. 28 Apr. 1774.
11 So called by the late 13th cent.: V.C.H. Glos. x. 51.

12 Cf. below, Lydney, intro.
13 O.S. Map 6", Glos. XLVII. SW. (1886 edn.).
14 O.S. Map 1/25,000, SO 60; ST 69 (1950–1 edn.).
15 Geol. Surv. Map 1", solid, sheet 35 (1845, revised to 1872).
16 Below, econ. hist.
17 O.S. Map 6", Glos. XLVI. NE. (1884 edn.); Glos. R.O., D 177, lease of Clannaweir Mill 1880.
18 Below, econ. hist.
19 P.R.O., C 115/K 2/6683, f. 91.
20 Ibid. C 115/K 2/6683, ff. 92v.–93v.
21 Ibid. C 115/K 2/6683, ff. 93v.–95v.
22 Trans. B.G.A.S. lxvi. 180.
23 P.R.O., SC 6/Hen. VIII/1224; Glos. R.O., D 1430B/10.

demesne by the priory.[24] About 1586, however, a man aged 50 spoke of lands near Clanna as if they had been inclosed within his memory,[25] and it is possible that the new lords, the Comptons, were responsible for inclosing some parts. Part of the inclosed land, lying north and east of the later Park Farm,[26] formed a deer park, surrounded with palings, in 1606,[27] but that land was leased as farmland by the start of the 19th century. Other tithe-free closes lay north-west and south-east of Clanna, and there was a larger group between the Cone valley and the south-west boundary.[28] About 300 a. at the north end of the parish, though apparently largely cleared of woodland in the early modern period, remained common land until parliamentary inclosure in 1814.[29]

Some of the steeper hillsides remained woodland; there was a total of 117 a. in 1805, all then held in severalty by the lords of the manor. The main woods were Park grove and Yew Tree grove, in the valley of Woodwards brook north-east of the former park, Bargains grove, north-east of Cone brook near the Hewelsfield boundary, and Barnage grove, extending along the same boundary south-west of Cone brook. Barnage grove was in two parts, the lower part called Barnage Common grove having perhaps been subject to common rights more recently than the rest. Much of the woodland, together with Rodmore grove in the adjoining part of St. Briavels, which also belonged to the manor, was oak coppice in 1805,[30] and it had probably long been used to produce wood for sale to local ironmasters for charcoaling. The pattern of woodland was much altered during the 19th century. Most of Barnage grove was felled and turned to farmland after a new farm was established in that area following the inclosure,[31] and Park grove had also been cleared for farmland by 1871.[32] The owners of Clanna planted new land in the Cone valley in the mid 19th century, and Bargains grove and new plantations adjoining and downstream of it became known as Clanna woods. Parts of the former common, in the valley of Woodwards brook north-east of Clanna and in the steep north-east corner of the parish, were also planted.[33] The latter area, known as Meend Plantation, had mixed conifer and hardwood in 1888 when it was sold by a timber merchant to W. B. Marling of Clanna,[34] who planted more conifers there after 1894. In 1919 all the woodland of Alvington belonged to

the Clanna estate, which, including adjoining woods in St. Briavels and Hewelsfield, owned 267 a.[35] Most of the estate's woodland was acquired by the Forestry Commission in 1956.[36]

The Gloucester–Chepstow road, the main thoroughfare through the parish and the only one of importance, was a turnpike between 1757 and 1871.[37] It entered the parish across Woodwards brook by Sandford bridge, which was recorded in 1322[38] and for the repair of which an Alvington man left money in 1490.[39] In the early 1960s the bridge was bypassed by a new stretch of road built to the south-east.[40] The principal side lane from the main road at Alvington village, Clanna Lane, runs northwards to a place called Beanhill green[41] where it forks, one branch leading to the north part of the parish and another towards Hewelsfield, crossing Cone brook by a bridge formerly called Long bridge.[42] The Hewelsfield road once ran close to the south-west bank of the brook and then skirted the lower side of Barnage Common grove; a new, more direct line between Long bridge and Barnage was constructed soon after inclosure in 1814.[43] From the village another lane led southwards to the manor house, Alvington Court, and continued, as Mare Ley Lane,[44] to the riverside at Wose Pill.

About 1145 when the bishop of Hereford confirmed the grant of Alvington manor to Llanthony priory he mentioned the recent devastation of the land and dispersal of the inhabitants,[45] and it is possible that the ordered plan of the village, with a series of long home closes extending north-west and south-east from the main Gloucester–Chepstow road,[46] was created after the grant. At that time the priory built, or rebuilt, a church[47] a short way south-east of the street. Its attempts to establish the village as a market centre in 1265 and later were unsuccessful,[48] and the village remained small and, until the 20th century, confined almost entirely to the roadside.

The earliest house surviving on the street is the principal farmhouse, Duncastle Farm. Its back range is a late-medieval hall house, into which an upper floor was later inserted; a low range adjoining the south-west end was possibly its service wing. About 1800 the old house became the kitchen and service rooms of a long new range built along its street front on the south-east.[49] Two cottages in the village, one heavily restored, are 1½-storeyed buildings of

24 Glos. R.O., D 1430A/31, sale partic. 1805; cf. below, church.
25 Glos. R.O., D 421/L 4, notes of Mr. Neville's case (deposition of John Maddocks).
26 Ibid. plan c. 1710; Q/RI 4 (nos. 121, 123).
27 Ibid. D 33/389.
28 Ibid. D 1430A/31, sale partic. 1805.
29 Ibid. D 421/L 4, plan c. 1710; Q/RI 4.
30 Ibid. D 1430A/31, sale partic. 1805; cf. ibid. Q/RI 4.
31 Below, this section.
32 Glos. R.O., D 177, deeds of Fernleaze Cottage fm.
33 O.S. Maps 6", Glos. XLVI. NE.; XLVII. NW. (1883–4 edn.).
34 Glos. R.O., D 177, deeds of purchase from Jas. Hughes.
35 Ibid. Clanna est. sale papers 1919–20, sale partic. 1919.
36 Inf. from deputy surveyor, Forest Enterprise, Coleford.

37 Chepstow Roads Act, 31 Geo. II, c. 44; Annual Turnpike Acts Continuance Act, 34 & 35 Vic. c. 115.
38 P.R.O., C 115/K 2/6683, f. 101v.
39 Hockaday Abs. ccccxvi.
40 Glos. R.O., DA 28/100/17, mins. 26 Apr. 1960; 26 Sept. 1961.
41 Ibid. D 2099, Alvington ct. bk., cts. 28 Apr. 1774; 9 Oct. 1790; cf. ibid. Q/RI 4.
42 Ibid. Q/RI 4 (no. 83).
43 Ibid. Q/RI 4; O.S. Map 1", sheet 35 (1830 edn.).
44 Glos. R.O., Q/RI 4.
45 P.R.O., C 115/K 2/6683, f. 91.
46 O.S. Map 6", Glos. XLVII. SW. (1886 edn.).
47 Below, church.
48 Below, econ. hist.
49 Glos. R.O., D 1388, plan of Lt.-Gen. Burr's est. 1815.

the 18th century or earlier. The other houses are of predominantly 19th-century appearance, though a short row of cottages, undergoing restoration in 1994, revealed evidence of having been heightened, and several other buildings may have earlier structures as their basis. A number were enlarged and restored in the late 20th century. North of the village street, there was a small farmhouse at Nupend near Clanna Lane by 1601[50] and another further along the lane, near Beanhill green, was recorded in 1770.[51] South of the street, the old manor house at Alvington Court[52] is probably on a site occupied in the Middle Ages, and Courtend, a farmhouse on the lane nearby, dates from the late 18th century.

Additions to the village in the 19th century included a substantial dwelling called Severn Lodge built north-east of the church c. 1820 and a pair of brick villas built on the main road in 1889 by W. B. Marling[53] of Clanna. South of the village on Wyefield Lane, which formerly gave access to an open field of that name, the Lydney rural district council built its isolation hospital in 1896.[54] The hospital closed c. 1950 and part of the buildings was converted into a pair of bungalows.[55] A few other houses and bungalows were added on the lane and near the church later in the 20th century. About 1932 the rural district built six pairs of houses near the bottom of Clanna Lane.[56] Another eight houses were added to the council estate in 1948,[57] and another 26 houses and bungalows in 1968 and 1969.[58]

In the upper part of the parish Clanna, established by the late 16th century,[59] was probably the only early dwelling apart from buildings at forge sites on Cone brook.[60] Before inclosure in 1814 two small cottages were built on encroachments from the common, one near the Hewelsfield boundary north of the later Clanna woods and another, which was enlarged as the farmhouse of Cottage farm after the inclosure, north of Woodwards brook.[61] After the inclosure three new farmsteads were established. Barnage Farm, under the ridge at the north-west, was built shortly before 1828 by William Stevens, who then worked a paper mill at Rodmore in St. Briavels.[62] Glebe Farm, on a high part of the former common at the north end of the parish, and Park Farm, at the south end of the former park, were probably both built before 1830.[63] Later in the 19th century estate buildings were added around Clanna, but the mansion itself was demolished in the early 1950s.[64]

In 1327 41 people were assessed for subsidy at Alvington.[65] In 1551 there were said to be c. 110 communicants in the parish[66] and in 1563 34 households.[67] The population was estimated at 52 families in 1650[68] and c. 200 people in 40 houses c. 1710.[69] There was apparently little change in the 18th century, for 211 people, living in 40 houses, were enumerated in 1801. There was then a fairly steady rise in population, to 340 by 1841 and 408 by 1871. During the next 90 years the population fluctuated between 408 and 342, and between 1961 and 1971 it rose from 407 to 515, presumably accounted for mainly by the enlargement of the council estate. By 1991 the population had fallen again to 459.[70]

The Globe inn, at the junction of the main road and Clanna Lane, had opened by 1805.[71] The village also had a beerhouse in 1856,[72] and by 1891 the Blacksmiths Arms had opened in a building enlarged from a former smithy on the main road.[73] The Globe and the Blacksmiths Arms remained open in 1994. A friendly society met at the Globe in 1805,[74] and in 1815 80 villagers were members of it or other societies.[75] A village hall was built north-west of the churchyard in 1924.[76]

MANOR AND OTHER ESTATES. In 1066 the manor of *ALVINGTON*, then part of the Herefordshire hundred of Bromsash, was held by Brictric.[77] Later claims to it suggest that after the Conquest it was granted to William FitzOsbern (d. 1071), earl of Hereford, whose son Roger de Breteuil forfeited his estates by rebellion in 1075.[78] By 1086 it was held by Thurstan son of Rolf.[79] It was apparently held later by Miles of Gloucester[80] (d. 1143), earl of Hereford, whose son Walter of Hereford granted the manor before 1148 to Llanthony priory, Gloucester. A claim to the overlordship was made then by William son of Reynold, grandson of Roger de Breteuil, and c. 1160 William made a grant of the manor to Walter and received his fealty for it. The claim was continued by William's heir, Reynold de Balon, at the end of the century, but he then quitclaimed his right to Llanthony.[81] The manor was included in a general confirmation of Llanthony's possessions by the Crown in 1199.[82] In 1277 when Bartholomew de Mora gave the adjoining manor of Aylburton to Llanthony the priory gave him Alvington in return, to hold for life at the annual rent of £6,

50 Ibid. D 2957/14.2.
51 Ibid. D 2099, Alvington ct. bk., ct. 28 Apr. 1774.
52 Below, manor.   53 Date and inits. on bldg.
54 Glos. R.O., DA 28/100/1, pp. 39, 47; 100/12, pp. 322–3.
55 Ibid. 100/15, pp. 321–2; 100/16, p. 87.
56 Ibid. 100/11, pp. 160, 167, 220.
57 Ibid. 100/15, pp. 181, 282.
58 Ibid. 100/18, mins. 22 Apr., 22 July 1969.
59 Below, manor.
60 Below, econ. hist. (mills and ironworks).
61 Glos. R.O., Q/RI 4.
62 Ibid. D 177, abs. of title to Clanna Falls est. no. 2.
63 O.S. Map 1", sheet 35 (1830 edn.).
64 Below, manor.
65 *Glos. Subsidy Roll, 1327*, 30.
66 *E.H.R.* xix. 121.
67 Bodl. MS. Rawl. C. 790, f. 29.

68 *Trans. B.G.A.S.* lxxxiii. 86.
69 Atkyns, *Glos.* 218.   70 *Census, 1801–1991.*
71 Glos. R.O., Q/RSf 2; cf. ibid. D 1388, plan of Lt.-Gen. Burr's est. 1815.
72 *Kelly's Dir. Glos.* (1856), 219.
73 *Licensed Houses in Glos. 1891*, 128–9; cf. O.S. Map 1/2,500, Glos. XLVII. 9 (1881, 1903 edns.).
74 Glos. R.O., Q/RSf 2.
75 *Poor Law Abstract, 1818*, 144–5.   76 Date on bldg.
77 *Dom. Bk.* (Rec. Com.), i. 185v.; the identification is confirmed by *Herefs. Domesday* (P.R.S. N.S. xxv), 57.
78 Below, this section; *Complete Peerage*, vi. 447–50.
79 *Dom. Bk.* (Rec. Com.), i. 185v.
80 *Herefs. Domesday*, 79.
81 P.R.O., C 115/K 2/6683, ff. 90v.–91, 96; *Trans. B.G.A.S.* lxxvii. 81–3.
82 *Rot. Chart.* (Rec. Com.), 7.

but in 1285 Bartholomew surrendered his right in return for an annual pension of £45.[83]

Llanthony retained the manor until the Dissolution, after which the demesne farm and site of the manor, at Alvington Court, formed a separate estate, though it was in the same ownership again for parts of the 18th century.[84] The rest of the manor was granted by the Crown in 1547 to Sir William Herbert,[85] who conveyed it in 1550 to Walter Compton.[86] It had passed by 1583 to Walter's son William[87] (d. 1617), whose son and heir Walter[88] conveyed it c. 1622 to William Higford.[89] It was owned by the same or another William Higford in 1640, and later by Thomas Higford (d. 1651) and by Edward Higford (fl. 1658). By 1660 it belonged to Dorothy Higford, a spinster, who died in possession in 1676.[90]

The manor later belonged to John Higford (d. 1706)[91] and it may have passed to his brothers James and the Revd. Henry.[92] By 1716 it was owned by a fourth brother, William Higford (d. 1733) of Dixton, in Alderton, who under his entail was succeeded in turn by his sons James[93] (d. 1742),[94] William (d. 1770),[95] and the Revd. Henry (d. 1795). Henry was succeeded by the heirs of James Higford: John Parsons inherited one moiety and four children of James Davis of Chepstow, namely the Revd. Francis, James, Ann Susanna, and Mary, inherited the other moiety.[96] The share of the younger James Davis (d. 1798) passed to his brother the Revd. Francis (d. c. 1802), who left his shares to Mary.[97] The manor estate, which then included Alvington Court farm but had as its principal residence Clanna in the north part of the parish, comprised almost the whole parish in 1805.[98] In that and the next few years, however, it was dismembered[99] and much of its customary land enfranchised.[1]

In 1806 John Parsons and the two Davis sisters sold the manorial rights with the house called *CLANNA* and a demesne farm of 242 a. to James Proctor Howell. Howell sold that estate in 1820 to William Middleton Noel (d. 1859), who devised it to his nephew Edward Andrew Noel. The Noels bought back some of the lands alienated from the manor at the beginning of the century, and bought land in adjoining parishes,[2] and the estate comprised 654 a. in 1884 when E. A. Noel sold it to

Walter Bentley Marling,[3] brother of Sir William Marling, owner of the adjoining Sedbury Park estate.[4] W. B. Marling further enlarged the Clanna estate by adding farms in Hewelsfield and St. Briavels, and in Alvington, where he bought Glebe farm in 1898.[5] In 1919, when he offered his estate for sale, it comprised 1,966 a. and included eight tenant farms. Some farms were sold separately, while Clanna and the bulk of the estate were bought in 1920 by Richard Pryce-Jenkin of Raglan (Mon.).[6] Pryce-Jenkin died in 1951[7] and his estate was split up during the next few years.[8]

William Compton, who was sometimes described as of Alvington and had servants there in 1608,[9] may have lived at Clanna, where there was a house by 1586.[10] Dorothy Higford was assessed on eight hearths at Alvington in 1672,[11] and John Higford (d. 1706) lived at Clanna.[12] The later Higfords seem to have usually resided on their estate at Dixton.[13] In 1818 Clanna was stone-built and had three sitting-rooms on the ground floor.[14] In 1838 it was a plain but substantial mansion with its principal front facing south-east with views to the Severn and a service range at the rear. The central part of the front was of six bays and two principal storeys with, above the cornice, an attic storey and the plan of the rooms behind it was irregular, suggesting that it survived from an 18th-century house; flanking it were projecting wings, each of two bays and two storeys, probably additions made by W. M. Noel after 1820. In 1885 W. B. Marling made some alterations to the house, mostly internal, and added a billiard room at the north-east end of the main front.[15] He also added many features to the gardens and grounds, among them a home farmhouse with mock timber-framing south-west of the house and, to the north-west, a gardener's cottage in similar style and a walled kitchen garden.[16] In the home woods in the Cone valley the Noels made a fishpond and ornamental waterfall, after which the house was known in the mid 19th century as Clanna Falls.[17] The house was demolished c. 1952, and in 1994, when part of the site was a caravan park, its cellars, some garden walls and ornaments, and the stable block survived. The kitchen garden was then the garden to a new house built at its north-west end in 1989.[18]

---

83 P.R.O., C 115/K 2/6683, ff. 92v.–93v.
84 Below, this section.
85 *Cal. Pat.* 1547–8, 193.   86 Ibid. 1549–51, 203.
87 Glos. R.O., D 421/L 3–4; *Visit. Glos. 1623,* 44.
88 P.R.O., C 142/377, no. 99.
89 Ibid. CP 25/2/299/20 Jas. I Trin. no. 21.
90 Glos. R.O., D 4431, copies of ct. roll; Bigland, Glos. i. 54.
91 Bigland, Glos. i. 54; Glos. R.O., P 12/IN 1/1.
92 Below, this section (Alvington Ct.).
93 For the 18th-century descent, Glos. R.O., D 177/II/1; *Descendants of Higford of Dixton and Alderton* (priv. print. 1839); cf. *V.C.H. Glos.* vi. 192.
94 Bigland, *Glos.* i. 54.   95 G.D.R. wills 1770/71.
96 Glos. R.O., D 2099, Alvington ct. bk.
97 Ibid. D 177, abs. of title to Clanna Falls est. no. 1, recital of deed 1820 (which confuses the manor and Alvington Ct. estates).   98 Ibid. D 1430A/31, sale partic.
99 Ibid. D 177, abs. of title to Clanna Falls est. no. 1; deeds of Yew Tree grove; deeds of Fernleaze Cottage fm.
1 Ibid. Q/RI 4; below, this section.
2 Ibid. D 177, abs. of title to Clanna Falls est. nos. 1–2;

W. M. Noel's purchase in 1820 had been planned, but not completed by his father-in-law Jos. Yates.
3 Ibid. papers of purchase of Clanna Falls est. 1884.
4 Burke, *Peerage* (1963), 1616.
5 Below, Hewelsfield, manor; St. Briavels, manors (Rodmore, Willsbury, Aylesmore); Glos. R.O., D 177, papers of purchase of Glebe fm. 1897–8.
6 Glos. R.O., D 177, Clanna est. sale papers 1919–20.
7 Ibid. P 278/IN 1/31.
8 Inf. from Mr. R. V. Howells, owner of the site of Clanna.
9 Glos. R.O., D 33/384; Smith, *Men and Armour*, 58.
10 Glos. R.O., D 421/L 4, notes of Mr. Neville's case (deposition of John Maddocks).
11 P.R.O., E 179/247/14, rot. 40.
12 *Glos. Ch. Bells*, 110.   13 Cf. *V.C.H. Glos.* vi. 192.
14 Glos. R.O., D 1388/SL 3, no. 9.
15 Ibid. A 12/1; D 2593/2/479; cf. photog. in ibid. D 177, Clanna est. sale papers 1919. sale partic. 1919.
16 Ibid. D 177, Clanna est. sale papers 1919–20, sale partic. 1919; the kitchen garden is dated 1886.
17 O.S. Map 6", XLVII. NW. (1883 edn.).
18 Inf. from Mr. Howells.

The manor house, *ALVINGTON COURT*, and the demesne lands were leased by Llanthony priory in 1537 to Arthur Porter,[19] who received them in fee together with the site of the priory, at Gloucester, in 1540. Arthur (d. 1558 or 1559) was succeeded by his son[20] Sir Thomas Porter (d. 1597), whose son Arthur[21] sold Alvington Court farm in 1599 to Sir Robert Woodruff. Sir Robert (d. 1609) was succeeded by his nephew Robert Woodruff[22] (d. 1638) and Robert by his son Thomas.[23] At the end of the century the estate belonged to Sir George Woodruff who sold it to the lord of the manor John Higford (d. 1706). It then passed in turn to John's brothers,[24] James, the Revd. Henry (d. 1715),[25] and William (d. 1733). William left it to his son William[26] (d. 1770), who gave a life interest to his wife Elizabeth. She married *c.* 1774 James Eaton but separated from him in 1780.[27] On her death or surrender *c.* 1791 the estate reverted to her brother-in-law, the Revd. Henry Higford.[28] In 1805 John Parsons and the two Davis sisters sold Alvington Court farm to William Pride, who sold it in 1808 to Thomas and John Morse. Thomas (d. 1833) left his share to John, who sold the farm in 1837 to Nathaniel Lloyd (d. 1845). Lloyd left it to his brother Thomas, who left it to his nephew John James (d. 1855), a Newnham solicitor.[29] Later owners included Richard Beaumont Thomas (d. 1917), managing director of the Lydney tinplate works. The farm, a compact group of closes in the south-east corner of the parish, covered 206 a. in 1918.[30] In 1994 it was owned and farmed by Mr. and Mrs. G. N. Rogers.

Llanthony priory's manor house at Alvington was recorded from the late 14th century, when between 1377 and 1401 repairs or alterations to a principal chamber, a lesser chamber, and outbuildings were made.[31] Sir Robert Woodruff, who had 10 servants at Alvington in 1608,[32] apparently built a new house at Alvington Court. The surviving farmhouse, a tall stone block of *c.* 1600 with a large lateral stack and some mullioned windows with hoodmoulds, apparently formed the cross wing of a larger house. The main range apparently lay to the east where the wall seems to have been reconstructed early in the 19th century.

A number of farms held by lease for lives under Alvington manor were acquired by James Davis (d. 1780) of Chepstow, heir to a half share of the manor, to which his children eventually succeeded in 1795. In 1805 those leaseholds, including Duncastle farm and comprising 332 a., were held by his widow Martha.[33] Mary and Ann Susanna Davis evidently later bought out the rights that their partner in the manor, John Parsons, owned in those and in other leasehold and copyhold estates and enfranchised them. Following the inclosure of the parish in 1814 Mary, her husband Lt.-General Daniel Burr, and her sister had a substantial estate covering most of the central part of the parish. Daniel died in 1828[34] and Mary, who evidently succeeded to her sister's share, retained the estate until her death in 1836. It passed to her son Daniel Higford Davall Burr[35] (d. 1885), who was succeeded by his son Higford Higford, who had assumed the surname of his distant ancestors in place of Burr. Higford's devisees offered the estate, then 500 a., for sale in 1912. The largest part, Duncastle farm with 314 a., was bought then by Alfred Mullins (d. by 1917), whose executors sold it to W. R. Lysaght of Tidenham. In 1922 Lysaght sold the farm to Leo Chislett,[36] whose son-in-law and daughter, Mr. and Mrs. R. F. Hardacre, owned and farmed it in 1994.

ECONOMIC HISTORY. AGRICULTURE. In 1086 Alvington manor, which had increased four times in value since 1066, had 2 ploughteams and 5 *servi* on its demesne.[37] In 1291 Llanthony priory had 3 ploughlands at Alvington and its adjoining manor of Aylburton,[38] which was presumably, as in the early 16th century, administered with Alvington. A stud of horses which the Crown allowed Llanthony to pasture in the Forest in 1223[39] was probably based at Alvington, for a stud there was reserved to the priory when it leased the manor in 1277. Also reserved in the same lease was a moiety of a new sheephouse, and the priory was running sheep on the manor in 1318 when it complained that Tintern abbey's men had driven off 100 of them.[40] In the early 16th century the basis of the priory's substantial demesne estate was the later Alvington Court farm in the south-east part of the parish but it also included woods, and possibly farmland, in the upper part of the parish and woods and farmland in Aylburton.[41] Alvington Court farm was separated from the manor estate in 1540, but the lords of the manor later had a demesne farm based on Clanna in the upper part of the parish. Clanna farm, including the former park, comprised 242 a. in 1805.[42]

[19] P.R.O., SC 6/Hen. VIII/1224.
[20] Glos. R.O., D 1430B/10; *V.C.H. Glos.* iv. 395.
[21] P.R.O., C 142/253, no. 97.
[22] Ibid. C 142/309, no. 199.
[23] Ibid. C 142/579, no. 57.
[24] G.D.R. wills 1737/131.
[25] Glos. R.O., D 4431, Alvington Ct. deed 1713; P 7/IN 1/2, burials 1715; Hockaday Abs. xcix, 1715. The sources cited in this section confirm that of two Hen. Higfords alive at the period the one who was rector of Alderton was the brother of John, James, and Wm.: cf. *V.C.H. Glos.* vi. 192 and n.
[26] G.D.R. wills 1737/131.   [27] Glos. R.O., D 38A/1.
[28] Ibid. D 2099, Alvington ct. bk., cts. 27 Oct. 1791; 8 Oct. 1792.
[29] Ibid. D 177, deeds of Fernleaze Cottage fm.
[30] Ibid. D 2299/1622.
[31] P.R.O., C 115/K 2/6684, f. 8.
[32] Smith, *Men and Armour*, 58.
[33] Glos. R.O., D 177, abs. of title to Clanna Falls est. no. 1, recital of deed 1820; D 1430A/31.
[34] Ibid. Q/RI 4; for the Burrs, Burke, *Land. Gent.* (1898), i. 727.
[35] Glos. R.O., D 177, deeds of purchase from Jas. Hughes.   [36] Ibid. D 2299/1181.
[37] *Dom. Bk.* (Rec. Com.), i. 185v.
[38] *Tax. Eccl.* (Rec. Com.), 172.
[39] *Rot. Litt. Claus.* (Rec. Com.), i. 559; cf. *Close R.* 1227–31, 533.
[40] P.R.O., C 115/K 2/6683, ff. 92v., 94.
[41] Ibid. SC 6/Hen. VIII/1224; Glos. R.O., D 1430B/10; cf. above, intro.
[42] Above, manor; Glos. R.O., D 1430A/31, sale partic. 1805.

The tenants in 1086 were 12 *villani* with 9 ploughteams.[43] At Alvington and Aylburton in 1291 there were free tenants owing £2 10s. rent and bondmen whose works were valued at £3.[44] In 1540 customary tenants predominated on Alvington manor, paying a total of £23 4s. 7d. in rent while free tenants paid £2 19s. 1d.[45] In 1548 a total of 32 tenants, possibly all the customary tenants, held by copies for terms of years but, that being declared inconsistent with the custom of the manor, they had to exchange them for copies for lives. Most of their estates were then very small, and the largest, comprising four houses and 27 a. and two houses and 22 a. respectively, were presumably the result of amalgamation.[46] In the late 18th century most tenants held either by copy or by lease for lives, but there was little obvious difference between the two types of tenancy, both of which were granted for three lives, paid cash rents and two capons annually, and owed heriots; widows of copyholders had no right of freebench, and entry fines were fixed at the lord's will.[47] The original pattern of tenancies had by then been much obscured by amalgamation and redistribution: in 1805, though the details given of the copyholds and leaseholds still indicated their origin in over 30 estates, they were shared among 22 tenants. The estate held by Martha, widow of James Davis, whose two daughters then owned shares of the manor, included five of the larger leaseholds with a total of c. 150 a. of land. The rest of the Davises' estate, Duncastle farm with c. 180 a. held by lease but with no heriot payable, had possibly originated in lands severed from the manorial demesne. The Davises' estate had the bulk of the open-field land. The other larger estates included 41 a. held by Elizabeth, widow of James Collins (d. 1800), who was the most significant farmer in the village, as she was also tenant at rack rent of the bulk of the Davises' estate. Other tenancies comprised 31 a. and 26 a., while the rest were under 13 a. Two small customary tenements had been taken in hand by the lords and rack rented by 1805,[48] and during the dismemberment of the manor estate in that and succeeding years much of the rest of the customary land, including that of the Davises, was enfranchised.[49] Six other tenancies, to which the Davis sisters acquired all the reversionary right, were enfranchised after 1814 and absorbed in their estate.[50]

By the mid 16th century[51] the open-field arable was apparently confined to three fields. Wye field occupied land south of the village, sloping to the riverside level and the Woolaston boundary, Haw field was on the north-west between the village and the Cone brook valley, and Den field was on the north-east of the village. Earlier,

however, there was evidently an extensive open field on the riverside level, bounded by Aylburton on the north-east and Mare Ley Lane on the south-east. That land was possibly inclosed by Llanthony priory before the Dissolution, and it was held in severalty as part of Alvington Court farm in the early modern period. It was meadowland in 1814 but parts were still called Little and Great Furlong,[52] and the whole area was in ridge and furrow[53] before it was put under the plough in the late 20th century. In the 1780s the rotation in the three open fields was a fallow, followed by clover which was mown in early summer and the aftermath grazed, followed by a spring crop of peas, followed by wheat.[54] Presumably the tenants grew wheat in their closes every fourth year when it was not sown in the fields. Before inclosure in 1814 the three fields contained a total of 108 a.[55]

By the early 17th century there was a common meadow on part of the riverside level between Mare Ley Lane and the south-east boundary of the parish; in 1814 it covered 50 a. Mare Ley, a small piece of land at the parish boundary at the east end of the common meadow, was a common pasture for horses in 1661.[56] In the later Middle Ages the tenants of Alvington and Aylburton intercommoned in a large tract of land, probably then mainly woodland, extending across the north parts of both manors. Alvington common in that area, whose bounds were probably not clearly defined until the early 18th century,[57] comprised 269 a. of the north part of the parish before inclosure in 1814. Land called Clanna green, lying south of the common, between Clanna and the former park, was apparently also commonable waste until the inclosure.[58] Alvington's tenants also had rights of common in the woodland and waste of the royal demesne land of the Forest: it was among parishes recorded as paying herbage money for that right from the early 15th century.[59]

In 1814 the open fields, common meadow, Alvington common, and some small pieces of waste were inclosed under an Act of Parliament of 1810, the expenses being met by a levy on the landowners. The award, which also re-allotted some old inclosures, caused a major reorganization of the principal estates. Of the main owners, J. P. Howell received 21 a. in the common for his manorial rights and 52 a., including another 26 a. in the common, for his Clanna farm; Daniel and Mary Burr and Ann Susanna Davis received 196 a., including 65 a. in the common and 68 a. of the open fields and common meadow; and Thomas and John Morse, for Alvington Court farm, received 48 a., including 33 a. in the common. A new estate, comprising 156 a. and including 120 a. of the common, was created by

43 *Dom. Bk.* (Rec. Com.), i. 185v.
44 *Tax. Eccl.* (Rec. Com.), 172.
45 Glos. R.O., D 1430B/10.   46 P.R.O., SC 2/175/39.
47 Glos. R.O., D 2099, Alvington ct. bk., ct. 28 Apr. 1774.
48 Ibid. D 1430A/31, sale partic. 1805; for the Collinses, mons. in ch.
49 Above, manor.
50 Glos. R.O., Q/RI 4; D 1388, plan of Lt.-Gen. Burr's est. 1815; cf. ibid. D 2299/1181.

51 P.R.O., SC 2/175/39.
52 Glos. R.O., Q/RI 4.
53 Aerial photog. (Royal Air Force, 1946), no. 3103.
54 Glos. R.O., D 2099, Alvington ct. bk., cts. 1783–9.
55 Ibid. Q/RI 4.
56 Ibid.; ibid. D 33/390; D 4431, Alvington ct. roll 1661.
57 Ibid. D 421/L 3–4; cf. below, Lydney, intro.
58 Glos. R.O., Q/RI 4.
59 P.R.O., C 139/84, no. 76; F 14/13; Glos. R.O., D 2026/X 19.

an allotment to the rector of Woolaston in lieu of the tithes. The smaller owners, with common rights or a few strips in the fields, were mainly accommodated with re-allotted old closes, though six cottagers received tiny parcels in the common.[60]

During the 19th and 20th centuries there were nine or ten farms in the parish and a few smallholdings.[61] Adjoining the village the principal farms remained Duncastle farm, comprising the bulk of the Burr family's estate, and Alvington Court. In 1851 the former had 400 a. and employed 12 labourers and the latter had 200 a. and employed 6 labourers; there were then also farms based on Courtend (155 a.) and Severn Lodge (90 a.).[62] In the upper part of the parish the farms were Park farm with the old closes of Clanna farm, Barnage farm, which was added to the Clanna estate in 1859,[63] Cottage farm, which was added to the estate in 1871 and comprised a former part of the common and the land of Park grove,[64] and Glebe farm on the north part of the former common, which passed from the rector to the estate in 1898.[65] In 1919 Park farm had 113 a., Barnage farm 280 a. including 105 a. of the estate's land in Hewelsfield, Glebe farm 95 a., and Cottage farm 52 a.[66] In 1988 nine farms with more than 10 ha. (25 a.) and two smallholdings were returned for the parish; a total of 36 people then worked on the land, but 16 of them were seasonal or casual workers.[67]

In 1866 699 a. of the parish were returned as under crops, mainly wheat, barley, turnips, and clover or grass seeds, compared with 531 a. of permanent grassland. The land returned as under crops fell to 394 a. by 1896 and to 185 a. by 1926. Stock raising, dairying, and sheep farming all increased proportionately, and 442 dairy and beef cattle and 877 sheep were returned in 1926.[68] Land was put back under the plough in the later 20th century, and 139 ha. (343 a.) of arable were returned in 1988, when barley was the principal crop and some land was under maize. Of the largest farms, however, two were then principally concerned with raising cattle and sheep and one with dairying, and there was also a large poultry enterprise.[69] Sixty acres of orchard were returned in 1896[70] but in 1988 only 0.5 ha. (1.2 a.).[71]

MILLS AND IRONWORKS. There was a mill on Alvington manor in 1086,[72] and in the early 13th century and 1318 Llanthony priory had a fulling mill there, somewhere near the village.[73] Iron was worked at Alvington in 1086 when the tenants of the manor owed a render of 20 blooms of iron.[74] Lands called Cinderhill, by Small brook on the south-west boundary, and Cindermead, by Cone brook on the south boundary,[75] recall those activities, but the iron industry may have deserted Alvington by the 13th century when no inhabitants figured in lists of forge-owners of the Forest area. During the 18th century there were three forges on Cone brook in the parish.[76]

A fulling mill held by copy from the manor in 1548 was described as in Alvington wood next to Barnage grove.[77] It was probably at a site on Cone brook by the north-west boundary where Barnage grove formerly adjoined the stream.[78] A forge called Barnage forge later stood there[79] and belonged to the manor estate c. 1695, when it was described as decayed.[80] Between 1701 and 1709 it was among the forges of the Forest area that were worked by the Foley family and its partners.[81] In 1775 it was leased with Rowley forge, with which it was worked until c. 1800.[82] The buildings of Barnage forge survived as part of Thomas Morris's estate in 1814,[83] but were apparently not used later. The dry pond remained in 1994.

Another mill held as copyhold of the manor in 1548 and described as between Rowley and Clanna[84] was possibly on the site of the later Clanna forge, further down Cone brook, west of Clanna.[85] Clanna forge was worked with Rowley forge in 1775 and until c. 1800.[86] In 1824 there was a mill on the site,[87] and it was probably there that the owner of Clanna had a water-powered threshing machine, suitable for conversion to a grist mill, in 1818.[88] In the mid 19th century a leat was constructed to supply the mill from the old Barnage forge pond and from another pond built east of that,[89] and before 1879 F. J. Noble rebuilt the mill to manufacture paper board. Called Clannaweir Mill, it continued in use until 1887 or later.[90]

Rowley Mill, on Cone brook just above its confluence with Small brook,[91] was recorded on the manor estate in 1413[92] and comprised two

---

60   Glos. R.O., Q/RI 4.
61   *Kelly's Dir. Glos.* (1856 and later edns.); P.R.O., MAF 68/1609/6; MAF 68/3295/12.
62   P.R.O., HO 107/2443, where the farmer's name identifies Duncastle: mon. in ch. to Thos. Matthews.
63   Glos. R.O., D 177, abs. of title to Clanna Falls est. no. 2.
64   Ibid. deeds of Fernleaze Cottage fm.
65   Above, manor.
66   Glos. R.O., D 177, Clanna est. sale papers 1919–20.
67   Agric. Returns 1988.
68   P.R.O., MAF 68/26/8; MAF 68/1609/6; MAF 68/3295/12.   69   Agric. Returns 1988.
70   P.R.O., MAF 68/1609/6.   71   Agric. Returns 1988.
72   *Dom. Bk.* (Rec. Com.), i. 185v.
73   P.R.O., C 115/K 2/6683, ff. 92, 95, 102; cf. *Tax. Eccl.* (Rec. Com.), 172. A meadow called Tuck Mill Moor mead in 1814 above Woolaston's Cone Mill was evidently named from that mill: Glos. R.O., Q/RI 4 (nos. 192–3); *V.C.H. Glos.* x. 112.
74   *Dom. Bk.* (Rec. Com.), i. 185v.
75   Glos. R.O., Q/RI 4 (nos. 92, 292–3).

76   Below, this section.
77   P.R.O., SC 6/175/39.
78   Cf. Glos. R.O., Q/RI 4.
79   Hart, *Ind. Hist. of Dean*, 71, 445, assumed the forge was on Small brook near the 19th-century Barnage Fm.
80   Glos. R.O., EL 118, f. 161; cf. ibid. D 177/II/1.
81   *Econ. H.R.* 2nd ser. iv. 324.
82   Below, this section.
83   Glos. R.O., Q/RI 4 (nos. 45–6); cf. below, this section.
84   P.R.O., SC 6/175/39.
85   Glos. R.O., Q/RI 4 (no. 59). Rowley seems to have been originally a general name for land between Cone brook and the SW. boundary: cf. ibid. (nos. 76, 80–1).
86   Below, this section.
87   Bryant, *Map of Glos.* (1824).
88   Glos. R.O., D 1388/SL 3, no. 9.
89   O.S. Map 6", Glos. XLVI. NE. (1884 edn.).
90   Glos. R.O., D 177, lease of Clannaweir Mill 1880; *Trans. B.G.A.S.* xciv. 132.
91   O.S. Map 6", Glos. XLVII. SW. (1886 edn.).
92   P.R.O., C 115/K 2/6682, f. 70.

grist mills under one roof in 1539. The mill descended with Alvington Court from 1540[93] and the forge later at the site belonged to the manor estate in the 18th century and until 1805.[94] In 1646 Robert Kyrle and John Brayne, partners in a number of local ironworks, agreed to build a forge at a place called Atkins Mill or the Burnt Mill in Alvington,[95] and that was presumably at Rowley, for Brayne was later reported to have built a forge at 'Rowland Mill'.[96] By 1703 Rowley forge was worked by the Foleys.[97] In 1775 Rowley, Clanna, and Barnage forges were leased for three lives to David Tanner, and with Tanner's Lydney ironworks they passed in 1790 to the Pidcock family.[98] The stock at Rowley forge was for sale under an execution for debt in 1804,[99] and all three forges had probably ceased working by 1805, though the Pidcocks still held the lease.[1] In 1809 the paper maker Thomas Morris bought the lease,[2] and a paper mill at Rowley was worked by the Morris family until 1841, and later continued under other manufacturers;[3] 7 hands were employed there in 1851.[4] In 1879 F. J. Noble & Co. worked Rowley Mill as a board mill, together with Clannaweir Mill.[5] A leather board maker recorded at Alvington in 1906 and 1914 presumably worked Rowley Mill.[6] In 1927 it was worked by the Gloucester Millboard Co., and apparently closed soon afterwards.[7] A pair of cottages, the ruins of some subsidiary buildings, and the overgrown pond remained in 1994.

The next mill downstream, Cone paper mill, belonged to Woolaston parish.[8] Another mill, also called Cone Mill, stood within Alvington downstream of the Chepstow road and was supplied by a leat from a pond just above the road;[9] it was apparently always worked as a corn mill. It was probably the mill with a tanhouse adjoining or nearby that John Barrow of Badhamsfield, in Newland, owned at his death c. 1645,[10] for members of that family owned Cone Mill in the 18th century. From John Barrow[11] (d. 1775) of Woolaston Grange, it passed to his relatives, members of the Buckle and Harris families, though the tenant in 1814 was Charles Barrow.[12] It continued in use as a corn mill until 1920 or later.[13]

OTHER INDUSTRY AND TRADE. In 1265 Llan-

thony priory was granted a market on Mondays and a fair at the Assumption (15 August), but in 1267 another grant changed the market day to Tuesday and the fair to the feast of St. Laurence (10 August).[14] A third grant, in 1394, confirmed the market day as Tuesday and granted two fairs at Whitsun and the Nativity of the Virgin.[15] The market and fairs presumably never became firmly established and had almost certainly lapsed by 1539.[16] The priory may have hoped that trade in and out of Wose Pill, where it was licensed to levy tolls in 1345,[17] would contribute to the success of the market and fairs.

In 1608 a tucker, four weavers, and a shearman were living at Alvington,[18] the tucker perhaps working the mill at Barnage.[19] That small cloth industry has not been found recorded later. Also living at Alvington in 1608 were two millers and six other tradesmen.[20] Only the usual village tradesmen were recorded during the 17th and 18th centuries, apart from the owner of a sloop in the 1790s.[21] Since Wose Pill had long since silted, his vessel perhaps traded from the nearby Cone Pill in Woolaston. For a small village Alvington was well supplied with craftsmen in the 19th century, with 11 carpenters, 5 smiths, 4 masons, and 3 shoemakers among those enumerated in 1851. There were then also 3 fishermen.[22] In 1870 a small engineering works was run by James Lee, who had patented paper-making machinery[23] and presumably equipped and serviced the local mills. In 1879 there was also a small brewery.[24] There were two smithies on the main road in the 1880s,[25] and the village still had a few tradesmen, together with three or more shopkeepers, in 1939.[26] In 1994 it had a post office and a petrol station.

LOCAL GOVERNMENT. Llanthony priory claimed its manor of Alvington to be free of suit to Bledisloe hundred, and exemption was confirmed by the lord of the hundred in 1244 after his officers had attempted to exact suit.[27] In 1287 the priory held two views each year for Alvington and a small estate called Archer's Hall in Lydney. It also had gallows at Alvington.[28] In the 1530s the priory was apparently holding a single court baron for Alvington and Aylburton and one tithingman served both manors.[29] Court

93 Ibid. SC 6/Hen. VIII/1224; Glos. R.O., D 1430B/10.
94 Glos. R.O., D 177/II/1; ibid. deeds of Fernleaze Cottage fm.; D 421/T 104.   95 Ibid. D 421/E 9.
96 P.R.O., LRRO 5/7A, inq. Sept. 1649.
97 Econ. H.R. 2nd ser. iv. 324.
98 Glos. R.O., D 421/T 104; below, Lydney, econ. hist.
99 Glouc. Jnl. 12 Nov. 1804.
1 Glos. R.O., D 1430A/31, sale partic. 1805.
2 Ibid. D 177, deeds of Fernleaze Cottage fm.; cf. ibid. Q/RI 4.   3 Trans. B.G.A.S. xciv. 131.
4 P.R.O., HO 107/2443; cf. Kelly's Dir. Glos. (1856), 219.
5 Trans. B.G.A.S. xciv. 131–2.
6 Kelly's Dir. Glos. (1906), 22; (1914), 28.
7 Ibid. (1927 and later edns.).   8 V.C.H. Glos. x. 112.
9 O.S. Maps 1", sheet 35 (1830 edn.); 6", Glos. XLVII. SW. (1886 edn.).
10 G.D.R. wills 1645/68.
11 Ibid. 1720/167; Glos. R.O., D 2099, Alvington ct. bk., ct. 17 Nov. 1772.

12 Glos. R.O., Q/RI 4; D 637/II/9/E 2; Bigland, Glos. iii, no. cccv.
13 O.S. Map 1/2,500, Glos. XLVII. 9 (1921 edn.).
14 Cal. Chart. R. 1257–1300, 56, 84.
15 Ibid. 1341–1417, 348–9.
16 Accts. for the man. have no entry for tolls: P.R.O., SC 6/Hen. VIII/1224.
17 Below, Lydney, econ. hist. (other ind. and trade).
18 Smith, Men and Armour, 58.
19 Above (mills and ironworks).
20 Smith, Men and Armour, 58.
21 Farr, Chepstow Ships, 54, 57.
22 P.R.O., HO 107/2443.
23 Kelly's Dir. Glos. (1870), 463.   24 Ibid. (1879), 556.
25 O.S. Map 6", Glos. XLVII. SW. (1886 edn.).
26 Kelly's Dir. Glos. (1939), 27.
27 P.R.O., C 115/K 2/6683, ff. 95v.–96.
28 Plac. de Quo Warr. (Rec. Com.), 244.
29 P.R.O., SC 6/Hen. VIII/1224; Glos. R.O., D 1430B/10.

rolls for Alvington survive for 1548[30] and 1661[31] and a court book for the years 1770–99. Leet jurisdiction was still claimed in the late 18th century.[32] The court probably lapsed at the start of the 19th century with the dismemberment of the manor estate and inclosure.

Alvington had two churchwardens in 1572[33] and later, and their accounts survive from 1829,[34] together with vestry minutes for the years 1831–40.[35] In 1803 the parish expended £87 on poor relief and nine able-bodied and sick poor were on permanent relief and nine people received occasional help.[36] The cost appears to have been fairly well contained during the early 19th century. Between 1813 and 1815 the number on permanent relief was c. 13,[37] and during the late 1820s and early 1830s the relatively modest sum of £159 was the highest annual figure recorded for expenditure.[38] A number of apprenticeships, some to local paper makers, were made in the early 1830s, and in 1832 a family was assisted to emigrate to America. The parish became part of the Chepstow poor-law union in 1836.[39] From 1867 it was part of the Lydney highway board[40] and from 1894 part of Lydney rural district.[41] With the rest of the rural district it was transferred to the new Forest of Dean district in 1974.

CHURCH. Llanthony priory built, or rebuilt, a church at Alvington in the 1140s. Between 1145 and 1148 the bishop of Hereford, Robert of Bethune, consecrated it and gave it the status of a free chapel held directly from himself.[42] Parochial rights over Alvington were claimed, however, by Tintern abbey (Mon.), owner of Woolaston church, and disputes between the two religious houses followed. By an agreement made before 1169 Llanthony renounced all claim to parochial rights in Alvington, except to the tithes of its demesne lands, and Tintern agreed to serve the church on Sundays, three weekdays, and certain feast days. Tintern also surrendered possession of ½ yardland which had formerly belonged to the church. In the early 13th century William, rector of Woolaston, complained that Llanthony had collected tithes from some of the parishioners and had appropriated the ½ yard-land to its own use; Llanthony then surrendered the land to the rector. A later rector claimed Llanthony's demesne tithes but gave up his claim in 1243 in return for a grant of land adjoining the churchyard.[43] In 1318 Tintern abbey, which then had Woolaston church in

hand, was accused by Llanthony of neglecting the cure of souls in Alvington.[44] Alvington church subsequently remained a chapel to Wool-aston.[45]

The rector of Woolaston had no glebe in Alvington in the 18th century,[46] the disputed ½ yardland and the land granted in 1243 having presumably been absorbed long since into Llanthony's demesne estate. Large areas of the parish, including Alvington Court farm and the woods and closes around Clanna, presumably all former parts of the demesne, were tithe free,[47] though an 18th-century rector challenged their status. The rector's tithes in Alvington were valued at £27 7s. 6d. in 1743 and £49 18s. 9d. in 1775. In 1743 he leased them to the separate landholders there, but in 1769 they were held on lease by the curate serving Alvington; in 1775 they were leased among the tenants again.[48] At the inclosure in 1814 the rector's tithes were commuted for 156 a. of land. Most of it was on the former common at the north end of the parish,[49] and in 1898 the rector conveyed Glebe farm there to W. B. Marling in return for an annual payment of £90, which was charged on the farm and on other land of Marling's Clanna estate.[50] The rector still owned 36 a. of glebe in the south part of the parish in 1910.[51]

In 1544 and 1563 a stipendiary curate served Alvington under the rector of Woolaston.[52] In the late 18th century and early 19th the rectors appointed a single curate to serve both Woolaston and Alvington.[53] In 1750 one service was held each Sunday and four communions were held each year.[54] Full services were said to be held in 1825.[55] In 1857 the rector appointed a curate for Alvington, who was to reside there,[56] and in 1872 and until 1914 or later there was a resident curate, styled curate-in-charge.[57] In 1994 Alvington was served by the rector, who then lived in a modern house in Alvington village, the old rectory at Woolaston having been sold.[58]

A small plot of land in Woolaston, comprising ½ a., was given for the repair of Alvington church before 1705.[59] In the 1820s the income, then 10s. a year, was applied to the school at Woolaston, which Alvington children attended.[60]

Alvington church was dedicated to St. Mary in 1523[61] but by the late 18th century it was called *ST. ANDREW,*[62] perhaps by transference from the mother church of Woolaston. It is built of coursed rubble with freestone dressings and comprises chancel with north vestry

30 P.R.O., SC 2/175/39.   31 Glos. R.O., D 4431.
32 Ibid. D 2099.
33 Hockaday Abs. xliv, 1572 visit. f. 8.
34 Glos. R.O., P 12/CW 2/1.   35 Ibid. VE 2/1.
36 *Poor Law Abstract, 1804,*170–1.
37 Ibid. *1818,* 144–5.
38 *Poor Law Returns* (1830–1), p. 66; (1835), p. 64.
39 Glos. R.O., P 12/VE 2/1.
40 Ibid. HB 11/M 2/1.
41 Ibid. DA 28/100/1, p. 8.
42 P.R.O., C 115/K 2/6683, f. 91 (for dating, cf. the mention of Pope Eugenius).
43 Ibid. C 115/K 2/6683, ff 91v.–92v.
44 Ibid. f. 94.
45 Hockaday Abs. ccccxvi.

46 G.D.R., V 5/14T 1; Glos. R.O., P 376/IN 4/4, f. 22.
47 Glos. R.O., D 1430A/31, sale partic. 1805.
48 Ibid. P 376/IN 4/4, ff. 23–4.   49 Ibid. Q/RI 4.
50 Ibid. D 177, purchase of Glebe fm. 1897–8.
51 Ibid. D 2428/1/5.
52 Hockaday Abs. xxx, 1544 stipendiaries, f. 6; Bodl. MS. Rawl. C. 790, f. 29.   53 Hockaday Abs. ccccxvi.
54 G.D.R. vol. 381A, f. 9.
55 Ibid. 383, no. cxxxviii.
56 Hockaday Abs. ccccxvi.
57 P.R.O., ED 7/34/9; *Kelly's Dir. Glos.* (1885 and later edns.).   58 Inf. from the rector.
59 G.D.R., V 5/14T 1.   60 *19th Rep. Com. Char.* 114.
61 Hockaday Abs. ccccxvi.
62 Bigland, *Glos.* i. 53; *Kelly's Dir. Glos.* (1870), 463.

and south chapel, nave with south aisle and south porch, and west tower with north vestry.

A window close to the north-east corner of the chancel and probably also the thick south wall survive from the mid 12th-century church. The three-bayed nave arcade and the unbuttressed tower are both of c. 1300 and may define the extent of an earlier nave. The aisle windows and the south doorway are of the early 14th century, though the windows were renewed in the 19th century. The arches into the south chapel are of the 15th century but the windows in the chapel and those in the nave were renewed in the 19th century in a 14th-century style.

The south chapel was annexed to the manor by c. 1710.[63] About 1780 the church tower was said to be partly of wood,[64] and it perhaps had a timber top stage; the battlemented top with pinnacles may date from alterations made c. 1835 to plans of John Briggs.[65] A thorough restoration of the church in 1857 included the remodelling of the south porch, which formerly had a room above it, the rebuilding of the north wall, and the addition of a small vestry at the north side of the chancel.[66] In 1890, at the cost of W. B. Marling, a new vestry was built at the north-west corner of the church,[67] and c. 1902 the church was reroofed and the south chapel refitted.[68]

A stone slab incised with a cross, used as the altar in the south chapel, is presumably a former coffin slab, and a small coffin slab is set into the south wall of the aisle. Later monuments include a large slab in the chapel with a rhyming inscription to Sir Robert Woodruff (d. 1609) and his wife Mary. The church furnishings mostly date from the restoration of 1857. A new ring of five bells was supplied by Abraham Rudhall in 1704 and 1705, and the tenor and treble were recast by the Loughborough foundry in 1887 and 1905 respectively.[69] A chalice and paten cover were given by Dorothy Higford, lady of the manor, in 1676.[70] A burial ground was consecrated for the new church in the 1140s,[71] and the church presumably retained burial rights from that date. The registers, for christenings, marriages, and burials, survive from 1688.[72] The churchyard has a small but well preserved collection of carved headstones in the local rustic styles of the late 17th century and the 18th.

NONCONFORMITY. A group of Quakers was meeting at Alvington in 1670 and in 1684, when the leading member of the group, Henry Lloyd, died.[73] Only a single Quaker was recorded in the parish in 1735, with one Presbyterian and one Roman Catholic.[74] An unidentified dissenting group registered a house in Alvington in 1806,[75] and in 1817 and 1818 Daniel Edwards, an excise officer living in the village, was leading an Independent meeting.[76]

EDUCATION. In 1818 and until the mid 19th century the poorer children of Alvington attended the National school at Woolaston.[77] About 1850 a parish school was built on the west side of the lane leading to the church by D. H. D. Burr,[78] who transferred it to trustees in 1854.[79] In 1871, when the school was managed by the parish clergy, the churchwardens of Alvington, and E. A. Noel of Clanna, the income came mainly in the form of voluntary contributions, though school pence were also charged.[80] In 1885 the average attendance was 52.[81] In 1910, as Alvington C. of E. school, it had an average attendance of 66 in mixed and infants' departments.[82] By 1932 the average attendance had fallen to 39.[83] The children aged 11 and over went to secondary school at Lydney from 1949, and in 1953 the Alvington school had 22 pupils, taught as one class; about the same number of children from the parish then attended primary school in Woolaston. The Alvington school was closed in 1958.[84]

CHARITIES FOR THE POOR. None known.

AWRE

THE PARISH of Awre[85] lies 16 km. south-west of Gloucester between the river Severn and the Forest of Dean. The large parish contained seven manorial estates, numerous ancient farmsteads, the industrial and trading village of Blakeney which replaced Awre village as the principal centre of population, and the small but commercially significant riverside hamlet of Gatcombe. The whole of Awre parish was included within the jurisdiction of the Forest before 1228 and, apart from the hamlet of Box which was disafforested in the early 14th century, remained within it for as long as it had significance.[86]

63 Atkyns, Glos. 217. 64 Bigland, Glos. i. 53.
65 Glos. R.O., P 12/VE 2/1; cf. below, St. Briavels, church.
66 Glos. R.O., P 12/CW 3/1; cf. painting of ch. before restoration: kept in vestry 1994.
67 Glos. R.O., P 12/CW 3/2; Kelly's Dir. Glos. (1897), 21. 68 Glos. R.O., P 12/CW 3/4.
69 Glos. Ch. Bells, 109–10. 70 Glos. Ch. Plate, 232–3.
71 P.R.O., C 115/K 2/6683, f. 91.
72 Glos. R.O., P 12/IN 1/1–3.
73 Ibid. D 2052. 74 G.D.R. vol. 285B(1), f. 8.
75 Hockaday Abs. ccccxvi.
76 Ibid.; Bright, Nonconf. in Dean, 19.
77 Educ. of Poor Digest, 289; Nat. Soc. Inquiry, 1846–7, Glos. 2.

78 Kelly's Dir. Glos. (1856), 219; O.S. Map 1/2,500, Glos. XLVII. 9 (1881 edn.).
79 Glos. R.O., D 177, deeds of Alvington sch.
80 P.R.O., ED 7/34/9.
81 Kelly's Dir. Glos. (1885), 351.
82 Bd. of Educ., List 21, 1911 (H.M.S.O), 158.
83 Ibid. 1932, 112.
84 Glos. R.O., S 12/2, pp. 32, 45, 67.
85 This account was written in 1989.
86 Trans. B.G.A.S. lxvi. 170–93; below, Forest of Dean, bounds. Box was one of the places which a perambulation of 1300 stated had been afforested by King John, in contradiction to a perambulation of 1228 which included the whole par. in bounds said to have existed from before 1154.

The ancient parish covered 4,520 a. (1,831 ha), or 6,173 a. if all the foreshore and river within its boundaries were included.[87] A wide meander of the river Severn forms a long boundary on the north-east and south-east, the north-west boundary mainly follows watercourses, including Haie brook, and the south-west boundary follows Lanes brook.[88] On the west the boundary with the extraparochial Forest of Dean was an irregular one. From Ayleford in the north it followed the hillside above the valley of Soudley brook, descended close to the main Gloucester–Chepstow road near the bottom of the valley of Blackpool brook at Nibley, crossed the lower slopes of Viney hill, and climbed to take in a rectangular block of land around Hayes wood.[89] The wood was probably a late addition to the parish: it owed a rent to Flaxley manor in 1570,[90] suggesting that it was among late 13th- and early 14th-century assarts whose rents were assigned to Flaxley abbey in 1353.[91] In 1935 the block including Hayes wood, comprising 111 a., was transferred to West Dean civil parish,[92] and in 1953 850 a. of East Dean, including Blakeney Hill woods, Blakeney Hill hamlet, and part of Viney Hill hamlet, were added to Awre parish.[93] The account given here covers the parish as constituted before 1935.

Low-lying land in the east and centre of the parish is formed of the lower lias and red marl, while an extensive level at Awre Point,[94] enclosed by a loop of the Severn, and a smaller area further south, around the sinuous inlet called Brimspill (or Brimspill), are formed of alluvium. The lower land of the parish is bounded by an area of higher ground formed of the Old Red Sandstone:[95] in the north and south are gently rolling hills at around 30–60 m., which culminate in low river cliffs at Box and around Gatcombe, while in the north-west a higher ridge rises to over 106 m. before dropping to the deep valley of Soudley brook near the west boundary. The land is drained principally by Bideford brook, which is formed at Blakeney by the confluence of Soudley[96] (or Forge) brook and Blackpool brook[97] and receives a number of small tributaries before flowing into the Severn at Brimspill. At intervals along the bank small streams reach the river by other muddy inlets, known on the lower Severn as pills.

The scattered nature of settlement, the predominance of ancient closes, and the numerous small groves all suggest that most of the parish emerged from ancient woodland. Hayes wood,

extended at 40 a. in 1570[98] and 56 a. in 1839,[99] was the most substantial piece of woodland surviving in modern times. The smaller groves included Box and Phips groves on the Box farm estate at the north end of the parish, which each covered 8 a. in the 1730s when a local tanner held them on lease, presumably as a source of bark.[1] Only in the east around Awre village was there a fully developed system of open fields and common meadows; that area was inclosed in 1796. Pastoral farming has predominated and orchards were once widespread.[2]

The eastern tip of the parish is formed mainly of land reclaimed from the river Severn. About 350 m. east of Awre village and church the ground falls to a level, which is crossed by a series of reens (drainage ditches) and was once farmed mainly as open fields. Much of the level had presumably been gained from the river before the 12th century when the bank was perhaps on the line of a continuous hedge boundary that was once apparent between a house called Hayward on the southeast and Hamstalls cliff on the north-west.[3] A sea wall, described in 1846 as the main sea wall,[4] once ran along that boundary and remains of it near the north-west end survived until the early 20th century.[5] Land called Hayward, evidently in the area adjoining the house,[6] was reclaimed by the lord of Awre manor c. 1140,[7] and probably at the same period a broad strip of land called the Old Warth (or Wharf) running across Awre Point from near Hayward towards Hamstalls cliff was won from the river.[8] The Old Warth was presumably the land described as 'le Warth ex alia parte Sabrine' belonging to Awre manor c. 1300[9] and the pasture on 'Awre sand' mentioned in 1303.[10] It was in regular use for pasturing cattle by 1319,[11] and later remained common to the tenants of the manor. By the beginning of the 17th century a further strip of land, known as the New Warth (or Wharf), was emerging from the river beyond the Old Warth. It was evidently claimed by the tenants as an extension to the common, but in 1612 they agreed that their lord, Sir Edward Winter, could hold it in severalty,[12] and two years later his tenant Richard White inclosed and drained c. 30 a. by making numerous drainage furrows, two cribs (breakwaters), and a long reen to divide it from the Old Warth.[13]

The reclaimed land remained subject to flooding at very high tides[14] and its banks to wasting by the setting and ebbing of the tide. Cribs to turn or limit the force of the tide were maintained at critical points. At the north-west end

87 *O.S. Area Bk.* (1880).
88 *Trans. B.G.A.S.* lxvi. 180; O.S. Map 1/2,500, Glos. XXXIX. 16 (1880 edn.).
89 O.S. Map 1/2,500, Glos. XXXIX. 12, 15–16 (1880–1 edn.).
90 P.R.O., WARD 7/12/22.
91 *Cal. Chart. R. 1341–1417*, 133.
92 *Census*, 1931 (pt. ii).   93 Ibid. 1961.
94 Taylor, *Map of Glos.* (1777).
95 Geol. Surv. Map 1", solid, sheets 35, 43 (1845 edn., revised to 1872).
96 Glos. R.O., D 3270/19718, Bledisloe man. ct. roll 1671.
97 *Trans. B.G.A.S.* xiv. 361.
98 P.R.O., WARD 7/12/22.   99 G.D.R., T 1/12.
1 G.B.R., J 1/2031; J 4/1, no. 31.

2 Below, econ. hist.
3 O.S. Map 1/2,500, Glos. XL. 5–6 (1880–1 edn.).
4 Glos. R.O., D 3270/19677, pp. 241–2.
5 O.S. Map 1/25,000, SO 70 (1951 edn.).
6 Cf. Glos. R.O., D 3269, deeds of Hayward 1660–1794, deed 1660; G.D.R., T 1/12 (nos. 361, 364).
7 *Cal. Doc. France*, pp. 410–11.
8 Cf. Glos. Colln. RF 30.5; Bodl. MS. Rawl. B. 323, f. 100v.
9 Berkeley Cast. Mun., General Ser. Chart. 3513.
10 *Cal. Inq. p.m.* iv, pp. 117–18.
11 Berkeley Cast. Mun., General Ser. Chart. 2293.
12 Glos. Colln. RF 30.5.
13 G.D.R. vol. 127, depositions 17, 21 May 1616.
14 Bodl. MS. Rawl. B. 323, f. 100v.; G.B.R., B 3/9, f. 428v.; Glos. R.O., D 3270/19677, p. 241.

of the warths there was one called Hamstalls crib in the early 1720s when a second one was built beside it,[15] and by 1732 Amity crib defended the south end of the point.[16] By that time a shift in the main channel of the river had removed part of the New Warth, which was extended at only 15 a. in 1731.[17] Some new ground which appeared in the mid 1740s was soon lost again,[18] but before 1796 a more sustained build-up of land enlarged the New Warth to 49 a.[19] and by the 1840s a new, outer sea wall had been built to defend it.[20] In the late 1840s much work to defend the point, including the rebuilding of the cribs and the addition of new ones, was carried out under the direction of William Clegram of Saul, engineer to the Gloucester and Berkeley canal company.[21] The Old Warth was inclosed and absorbed into the field pattern in 1796[22] but the New Warth remained a notable feature of the landscape in 1989, extending for over a mile along the point. By then a further strip of land, beyond its 19th-century sea wall, had been reclaimed and grassed over, and the long reen built in 1614 on the warth's landward side was dry and partly silted.

South-west of Awre Point, where the main channel of the river generally ran close inshore,[23] the river bank was particularly subject to erosion. The channel may have shifted from the opposite bank shortly before 1234 when land claimed by Awre parish was awarded to Slimbridge.[24] More land was probably lost in the early 17th century, when part of the New Grounds in Slimbridge and warths in other parishes on the opposite bank were being formed,[25] and erosion of the Awre bank removed several dwellings and their home closes around Woodend Lane, south of the village, during the 18th century.[26] If that part of the bank was defended by a sea wall it had vanished between Woodend Marsh, 450 m. north-east of Woodend Lane, and Brimspill by the early 19th century.[27] During 1850 and 1851, to Clegram's plans, a new wall and a series of cribs were built to protect land north-east of Brimspill,[28] but near Woodend Lane erosion continued unchecked[29] and the bank there was still crumbling in the 1980s.

The Severn's fisheries and the river trade were sources of income and employment in the parish.[30] The river's presence was also made evident in the frequent burials of the drowned in Awre churchyard, in many cases victims of shipwreck or other accidents who were carried on to Awre Point by the currents.[31] Vessels often foundered on the dangerous Noose sandbank off the point or in the exposed waters further south.[32] One of the heaviest losses was in 1732 when 17 people drowned in the wreck of a Newnham trow.[33]

The main road through the parish, linking Gloucester and Chepstow (Mon.), probably follows for most of its course a Roman road leading from Newnham to Caerleon (Mon.); the names of Stretfield hill, north of Blakeney, and Oldstreet House, near the south boundary of the parish, presumably derive from that ancient road.[34] The Gloucester–Chepstow road was a turnpike from 1757 until 1871.[35] Improvements carried out under the trust included a new line of road built during 1809 and 1810 to avoid Gurshill in Lydney, beginning near Awre's south-west boundary,[36] and a new, curving descent into Blakeney village from the north-east, built during 1830 and 1831 to replace a steeper and more direct descent called Swan Lane.[37] A road down Viney hill, crossing the Gloucester–Chepstow turnpike at the south end of Nibley green, was by the late 18th century much used for carrying timber from the Forest woods to the riverside at Gatcombe and Purton. That usage led the Crown to pay for its upkeep for some years before 1796 when it was included in the first Forest turnpike Act, some of the funds provided by the Crown under the Act being used on the road.[38] Tollgates were sited at Nibley green and at Etloe House near where the road forked for Gatcombe and Purton.[39] In 1841 the Forest turnpike trustees built a new road down the valley of Blackpool brook to join the Gloucester–Chepstow turnpike at Nibley,[40] where a tollgate was placed on the parish boundary near the bottom of the road.[41] The two roads leading down from the Forest remained turnpikes until 1888.[42] A third route from the Forest, down the west side of the valley of Soudley

[15] G.B.R., B 3/9, ff. 109v., 197; Glos. R.O., D 3270/19672, acct. 1722–8.

[16] Glos. R.O., P 30/IN 1/1, mem. with burials 1732; cf. ibid. D 3270/19743, no. 39.

[17] G.B.R., J 4/1, no. 32.

[18] Glos. R.O., D 3270/19672, accts. 1745–6, 1747–8.

[19] Ibid. 19743, no. 66; Rudge, Hist. of Glos. ii. 119.

[20] Glos. R.O., D 3270/19677, p. 242.

[21] Ibid. pp. 295–301, 315, 346, 386–8, 413, 427–8.

[22] Ibid. Q/RI 13.

[23] Cf. O.S. Map 1/25,000, SO 70 (1951 edn.).

[24] Close R. 1231–4, 429.

[25] Berkeley MSS. iii. 330–1; V.C.H. Glos. x. 139, 163.

[26] Below, this section.

[27] Rudge, Hist. of Glos. ii. 114; Glos. R.O., D 3270/R 106, plan 1828.

[28] Glos. R.O., D 3270/19677, pp. 451, 456, 463, 510–12; cf. O.S. Map 1/2,500, Glos. XL. 9 (1881 edn.).

[29] Glos. R.O., D 3270/19699, pp. 45, 64.

[30] Below, econ. hist.

[31] Glos. R.O., P 30/IN 1/1, burials (particularly 1762–

1809).

[32] e.g. Glouc. Jnl. 7 July 1761; 2 Mar. 1767; 25 Apr. 1768; 31 Jan. 1780; 19 Dec. 1785; 30 May 1814; Bigland, Glos. i. 101.

[33] Glos. R.O., P 30/IN 1/1, mem. with burials 1732.

[34] I. D. Margary, Roman Roads in Britain (1973), 323.

[35] Chepstow Roads Act, 31 Geo. II, c. 44; Annual Turnpike Acts Continuance Act, 34 & 35 Vic. c. 115.

[36] Below, Lydney, intro.

[37] Glos. R.O., D 428/A 4, mins. 4 Sept. 1830; 30 Apr., 4 June 1831.

[38] Dean Forest Roads Act, 36 Geo. III, c. 131.

[39] Atkinson, Map of Dean Forest (1847).

[40] Nicholls, Forest of Dean, 197; Dean Forest Roads Act, 1 & 2 Vic. c. 38 (Local and Personal). The original plan, to have a junction with the main road further NE. and turnpike Millend Lane between Blakeney and Etloe Ho., was not carried out: cf. Glos. R.O., Q/RUm 152; Dean Forest Roads Act, 21 & 22 Vic. c. 86 (Local and Personal).

[41] O.S. Map 1/2,500, Glos. XXXIX. 12 (1881 edn.).

[42] Dean Forest Roads Act, 51 & 52 Vic. c. 193 (Local).

brook to Blakeney,[43] was much improved by the Awre local board of health in 1889[44] at the same time as the Crown built the adjoining part of the road within the Forest.[45]

Awre village was linked to the Gloucester–Chepstow road by the road, usually called the Newnham road, running to the north boundary of the parish and by another road which branched from the Newnham road at Cockshoot, south of Box Farm, and ran past Bledisloe Farm.[46] The latter road, which in its western part was called Chicknalls Lane,[47] survived only as a footpath between Cockshoot and Bledisloe Farm in 1989. An extensive system of footpaths called church ways or burying roads, which the local court leet jury was vigilant in preserving in the 18th and 19th centuries, linked the many scattered farmsteads to Awre church and Blakeney chapel.[48] A footpath making the circuit of the river bank was repaired and improved as part of the Severn Way long-distance path in the 1980s.

Powers for building the main South Wales railway line through Awre were obtained by an Act of 1846 under which the Gloucester and Dean Forest company was to build the line as far as Hagloe and the South Wales company to continue it southwards. In the event the whole line through the parish, opened in 1851, was built by the South Wales company, which amalgamated with the Great Western Railway in 1863.[49] The parish was served by a station at Purton in Lydney, but called Gatcombe station, until 1868 when Awre Junction station was built beside the Awre–Blakeney road at the junction with the new Forest of Dean Central railway. Awre Junction station was closed to passengers and general freight in 1959 and to coal in 1961.[50]

An attempt to build a railway from the Forest into Awre parish was made in 1832. The bill failed in parliament but parts of the line, to be worked by steam locomotives running to Purton by way of a tunnel under Old hill at Nibley, had already been built, and a bridge over the Purton road at the south end of the parish survived in 1989.[51] In 1856 an Act was acquired for the Forest of Dean Central railway, a mineral and goods line to link collieries in the centre of the Forest with the South Wales line and with the Severn at Brimspill, where docks for shipping coal and timber were to be built. The line, running to Awre Junction through Blakeney village, where there was a goods station, was not opened until 1868, by which time the G.W.R. had taken on its operation. It was never a commercial success, running trains only on three days a week at first and even less frequently later, and, although the line was continued to Brimspill, the docks were never made. Traffic ceased to run on

the line west of Blakeney c. 1921 and between Blakeney and Awre Junction in 1949.[52]

Awre parish comprised six tithings, based on ancient manors. Awre tithing included the village and the area enclosed in the loop of the Severn; the large tithing of Bledisloe occupied the area north of a line drawn roughly from Blakeney village to the Severn at Hamstalls Pill, north-west of the house called Hamstalls; Hagloe, apparently coterminous with the ancient manor called Poulton,[53] occupied the centre of the parish and the banks of the Severn between Brimspill and Gatcombe; Etloe tithing extended from the Gloucester–Chepstow road, where it included the south part of Blakeney village, southwards towards Gatcombe; Etloe Duchy, once a manor of the Duchy of Lancaster, occupied the south end of the parish bounded roughly by the Purton turnpike road; and Blakeney tithing comprised the north part of Blakeney village and land lying west of the Gloucester–Chepstow road.

AWRE village, in its isolated situation near the river in the east part of the parish, is a loose collection of small farmsteads. It was once larger, though probably always scattered in plan; a number of houses were lost before the late 18th century, some as a result of the amalgamation of holdings and others by coastal erosion.[54] Most of the houses stand along a low ridge which rises above the eastern level. There is a small concentration near the parish church, around the junction from which the Newnham road leads north-west, the Blakeney road west, Woodend Lane south to the river, and Marsh Road eastwards into the former open fields of the level. The part of the village at the junction, where there was a small green, was known as Churchend in 1493.[55] The Red Hart inn had opened in a building on the south-east by 1796,[56] and in the 19th century the junction was the site of the village pound and a smithy.[57] The inn dates partly from the 17th century, and a house called Bray's Court is 17th-century in origin but was remodelled and enlarged in the early 19th. There are also a few cottages of the late 18th century or early 19th. The medieval manor house called the Lypiatt once stood east of Churchend above the level. On the level the only known dwelling was Hayward, built c. 1680 at the east end of Marsh Road.[58]

South of Churchend a small hamlet called Woodend stood close to the river, around Woodend Lane. Whitescourt on the east side of the lane was recorded as a farmhouse on the manor estate from 1493.[59] It was ruinous in 1857 when it was planned to demolish it[60] and there were only farm buildings at the site in 1989. A cottage of c. 1900 on the opposite side of the lane

[43] Glos. R.O., D 3270/19718, Bledisloe man. ct. roll 1671.
[44] Ibid. DA 1/100/7.
[45] Ibid. DA 40/100/3, pp. 120–1; 4, pp. 2–3, 66–7.
[46] G.D.R., T 1/12.
[47] Glos. R.O., D 3270/19718, ct. 1708.
[48] Ibid. D 3270/19718.
[49] E. T. MacDermot, Hist. G.W.R., revised C. R. Clinker (1972), i. 293–8, 308.
[50] Glos. R.O., D 637/VII/5; Paar, G.W.R. in Dean, 125,

132, 140.
[51] Paar, G.W.R. in Dean, 122.   [52] Ibid. 125–37.
[53] Glos. R.O., D 3270/19743, no. 59.
[54] Below, econ. hist. (agric.).
[55] Glos. R.O., D 421/M 2; D 3269, deeds of land at Awre 1793–1885, deed 1882.   [56] Ibid. D 3270/19743, no. 66.
[57] O.S. Map 1/2,500, Glos. XL. 9 (1881 edn.).
[58] Below, manors.
[59] Glos. R.O., D 421/M 2; cf. G.B.R., J 4/1, no. 28.
[60] Glos. R.O., D 3270/19678, pp. 253, 507.

occupies the site of a small customary tenement called Woodend Close, recorded from the late 17th century,[61] and further north a modern house had by 1989 replaced another ancient tenement called Midways,[62] probably once the home of Richard de Midwey (fl. 1327).[63] Most of the other houses of Woodend were lost as a result of erosion of the river bank. One called Guildings, possibly north-east of the end of Woodend Lane, was under threat in 1691 and another had been lost by 1707. In 1741 the court leet reported that three houses of customary tenants had been washed away and three more were threatened.[64] Just west of the end of the lane stood a freehold farmhouse called Woodend House, which was the home of the Hopkins family until c. 1800 when it was abandoned because of the crumbling of the bank.[65] A house nearby, known as the Garrison by 1721,[66] was taken down c. 1810, though its site was further inland and probably not under threat from erosion.[67] Some of the houses at Woodend were formerly served by Slough Green Lane which led from Woodend Lane round to join the Blakeney road near Hall Farm.[68]

A few small farmhouses, mostly rebuilt in brick or stone in the late 18th century, stand at intervals along the Newnham road north-west of Churchend. They include Upper House Farm, New House Farm, and Fort House, the last probably on the site of the messuage held with a close called Forthay in 1493.[69] Houses once called Howlets and Filkins and a small farmhouse called Brunches, near the north-west end of the village,[70] are all on early sites,[71] the first probably the home of Thomas Howlet in 1493.[72] At a small green, called Vertues green in 1699 and later Awre green,[73] the Newnham road is joined by Northington Lane. Guy Hall, on the west side of the lane, is the remnant of a substantial 16th- or 17th-century house, evidently owned by and named from Guy Hall (d. 1694);[74] his freehold estate, which was divided among several owners after his death,[75] probably included Guy Hall Farm, a gabled 17th-century house of rubble stone on the east side of the lane. Northington Farm, at the north end of the lane,

was rebuilt in stone in the late 18th or early 19th century and extended in the late 19th. Formerly called Cades,[76] it was probably the dwelling of Thomas Cady of Northington in 1462,[77] while Seabrights, the old name of a cottage nearby,[78] recalls Thomas Seabright, a customary tenant in 1493.[79]

On the western fringes of the village, Field House and Hall Farm are substantial and long established farmsteads,[80] and the building of a small group of cottages at a place called Shepherd on the Blakeney road[81] had begun by 1728.[82] The house at Hamstalls, by the river bank north-west of the village, was recorded from 1710[83] and was enlarged c. 1732.[84] In 1796 it was an inn,[85] serving river traffic, and it probably had the sign of the Three Doves in 1824.[86] The inn had closed by 1830.[87] Later in the 19th century Hamstalls was occupied as two dwellings[88] but in the early 20th it became a single residence under the name of the Priory.[89]

BLEDISLOE tithing, like Etloe and Hagloe, probably took its name from an ancient tumulus,[90] which in the case of Bledisloe was presumably the hundred meeting place. It may have been beside the Gloucester–Chepstow road at the highest point of the ridge over which the road runs. A field called Bledisloe field in 1671 lay west of the road at that point[91] and a house called Bledisloe Cottage was built nearby in the mid 19th century. A green called Gallows green, which was inclosed before the mid 17th century and a cottage built on it, lay on the main road in Bledisloe tithing,[92] perhaps further north at the junction with Chicknalls Lane or at Howell's Cross where Howell's Lane[93] branches westwards towards Ayleford. The site of Bledisloe manor was east of the main road, at Bledisloe Farm on Chicknalls Lane.[94]

Settlement in Bledisloe tithing consists of farmsteads scattered widely through the north part of the parish and a few, mostly later, houses on the Gloucester–Chepstow road. A group of closes called Pullminton or Pomerton on the eastern slopes of the valley of Soudley brook[95] apparently includes the site of a deserted medieval hamlet, for three inhabitants of Pullminton were mentioned in 1282[96] and a

---

61 Ibid. 19718, ct. 16 Oct. 1688; 19743, no. 16; 19717, f. 28v.
62 Ibid. D 421/M 5; D 3270/19743, no. 8; 19717, ff. 24v.–25; cf. O.S. Map 1/2,500, Glos. XL. 9 (1881 edn.), where it is named as Meadway Cottage.
63 Glos. Subsidy Roll, 1327, 31.
64 Glos. R.O., D 3270/19718.
65 Ibid. D 3269, deeds of land bought from Ric. White; D 3270/R 97; Rudge, Hist. of Glos. ii. 115. For its site, cf. Glos. R.O., D 3270/R 106.
66 Glos. R.O., D 3270/19718.
67 Ibid. R 97; cf. ibid. R 106.
68 Ibid. D 3269, deeds of land bought from Ric. White, deed 1799; D 3270/R 99, R 106.
69 Ibid. D 421/M 2.
70 O.S. Map 1/2,500, Glos. XL. 5 (1881 edn.).
71 Glos. R.O., D 3270/19718, ct. of surv. 1741.
72 Ibid. D 421/M 2.
73 G.D.R., V 5/30T 3; Glos. R.O., D 3270/19678, p. 200.
74 Glos. R.O., P 30/IN 1/1, burials 1694; D 3269, deeds of Northington 1689–1837.
75 Ibid. D 3270/19718, ct. of surv. 1741.
76 Ibid. 19717, ff. 12v.–13.
77 Ibid. D 421/M 1, ct. of surv. 1595.

78 Ibid. D 3269, deeds of land at Awre 1793–1835, deed 1882.
79 Ibid. D 421/M 2.
80 Below, manors.
81 Cf. O.S. Map 1/2,500, Glos. XL. 9 (1881 edn.).
82 Glos. Colln. RF 30.3.
83 G.B.R., B 3/8, p. 382.
84 Ibid. J 1/2013.
85 Glos. R.O., D 3270/19743, no. 66.
86 The inn of the name marked on Bryant, Map of Glos. (1824), was probably intended for Hamstalls but wrongly placed.
87 Glos. R.O, P 30A/VE 1/1, p. 1.
88 Ibid. D 3270/19677, p. 277.
89 Cf. Kelly's Dir. Glos. (1923), 34.
90 P.N. Glos. (E.P.N.S.), iii. 251–2.
91 Glos. R.O., D 3270/19718, Bledisloe man. ct. roll; G.D.R., T 1/12 (nos. 825, 827).
92 Bledisloe man. ct. roll 1671.
93 Ibid. Awre and Etloe man. ct. 1715.
94 Below, manors.
95 Glos. R.O., D3270/19718, Bledisloe man. ct. roll 1671; G.D.R., T 1/12 (nos. 912–13).
96 P.R.O., E 32/30, rott. 8, 13.

tradition recorded *c.* 1700 tells of a 'town' at the place.[97] There is also evidence of a vanished hamlet at Box in the east part of the tithing, once the site of a manor based on Box Farm on the Awre–Newnham road. If, as suggested below, Box can be identified with an estate recorded in 1086 it already had a population of 17 bordars and their families,[98] and in the 13th century and the early 14th, when it was a separate vill,[99] considerable numbers of people were surnamed of Box or of Box cliff (Boxclive).[1] In 1669 there were some houses or cottages in a field by the road just north of Box Farm called Chapel Hay (later Chapel Hill),[2] possibly the site of a chapel. Maiden Hall, a farmhouse west of Box Farm, was called Little Box Farm in 1694 when it belonged to the James family of Stroat, in Tidenham.[3] The house had been demolished by 1989 when Box Farm, a pair of 19th-century farm cottages, and two modern houses were the only dwellings at Box. Two small farmhouses some way to the south, in Hagloe tithing, also bore the name Box[4] but do not appear to have had any tenurial or other connexion with Box manor.

A house called Cox which stood on the site of Oaklands Farm near the north-west boundary of the parish was recorded from the late 16th century.[5] Hulin's Farm, on the north boundary,[6] was named from the Hulin or Huling family which bought it, with the adjoining Hulin's wood, in 1682. The Hulins sold their farm in 1820 to the Revd. Edward Jones,[7] owner of the adjoining Hayhill estate in Newnham,[8] and by 1839 his estate also included Haiebrook Farm beside the brook on the north-west boundary.[9] In 1989, when the land of the estate was managed from a farmhouse in Newnham,[10] the two farmhouses in Awre stood empty and derelict. Hulin's Farm, originally timber-framed but later mainly walled in rubble or brick, has an early 17th-century range of one storey and attics. A large lateral stack stands close to the north-east corner, joined to the main range by a transeptal roof. A low 19th-century range adjoins on the north side. Haiebrook Farm is a very small L-shaped house of one storey and attics, also of the the early 17th century. At the beginning of the 19th century a two-storeyed block was built in the angle between the two ranges, and it was perhaps at the same time that the old north range was converted to a cider-mill house. Hickman's Court on Chicknalls Lane is another small 17th-century farmhouse, built of rubble stone and with a 19th-century addition. At Hawfield, south of Stretfield hill above Blak-

eney, a small 17th-century farmhouse has been enlarged to a substantial dwelling house: in the 18th century part of the house was heightened and remodelled, early in the 19th century a parallel range with a brick front was added along the south-east side, and in 1922[11] extensive additions in Tudor style were made on the north. New House, built *c.* 1790 on the main road near the junction with Howell's Lane, and Oaklands Park, built near the north boundary *c.* 1818 and later much enlarged, were the principal residences in the north part of the parish in the 19th century.[12] A few houses added on the main road in the early 19th century included two large Regency villas called Kingscroft (later Kingsland) and Underdean.[13] In the late 19th century and the early 20th Underdean was the home of the Jones family, formerly of Nass and Hayhill.[14]

On the west boundary of the parish some houses were built near the Ayleford–Blakeney road, including Hewler's Farm, a three-storeyed farmhouse of the late 17th century, and a few mid 19th-century cottages, loosely connected to the adjoining Forest hamlet of Blakeney Hill. Higher up the road in an area once known as Woodside, lying below the wooded plateau at the edge of the Forest, is a roadside green called Brain's green, perhaps named from George Brain of Woodside who died in 1733.[15] The scatter of cottages called Brain's Green is mainly outside the parish boundary but an earlier, fairly substantial dwelling called Seamsty or Woodside[16] belonged to Awre. It was bought by John Chinn in 1675[17] and later passed to a branch of the A Deane family.[18] Unoccupied from 1788, it fell into disrepair in the early 19th century[19] but was apparently represented later by Woodside House which stood at the north end of the green[20] until demolished in the early or mid 20th century. The settlement on Brain's green was linked to Howell's Lane at the north-west corner of the parish by an ancient lane, disused by 1989, which led from Woodside House into the deep valley of Soudley brook. At Ayleford where it crossed the brook is a stone farmhouse called Rowmedley,[21] built in the 17th century and much altered in the 19th. A house nearby, where Howell's Lane crosses the parish boundary at Haie brook, was a beerhouse called the Two Bridges in the late 19th century and the early 20th.[22]

HAGLOE tithing comprised only scattered farmsteads. Poulton Court, the site of a manor from the early Middle Ages, was later absorbed with almost the whole tithing into the large

[97] Bodl. MS. Rawl. B. 323, f. 101.
[98] *Dom. Bk.* (Rec. Com.), i. 167v.; below, manors.
[99] P.R.O., E 32/28, rot. 3d.; *Bk. of Fees,* i. 306.
[1] *Pleas of the Crown for Glos.* ed. Maitland, p. 93; *Glos. Subsidy Roll, 1327,* 31; P.R.O., E 32/30, rott. 1, 3d.
[2] G.B.R., J 1/1969; J 4/1, no. 31.
[3] Glos. R.O., D 3270/R 29; cf. ibid. R 45.
[4] Below, this section.
[5] Below, manors.
[6] O.S. Map 1/2,500, Glos. XXXIX. 8 (1903 edn.).
[7] Glos. R.O., D 265/T 10.
[8] *V.C.H. Glos.* x. 37.
[9] G.D.R., T 1/12.
[10] Inf. from the owner, Mr. I. M. Kerr, of Newnham.
[11] Inf. from the owner, Mr. P. B. Douglas-Cooper.
[12] Below, manors.

[13] O.S. Map 1", sheet 43 (1831 edn.).
[14] *Kelly's Dir. Glos.* (1879 and later edns.); Burke, *Land. Gent.* (1898), i. 824; Glos. R.O., D 4858/2/4, sale partic. 1966.
[15] Bigland, *Glos.* i. 108.
[16] Taylor, *Map of Glos.* (1777).
[17] Glos. R.O., D 22/T 2.
[18] Ibid. D 265/T 11.
[19] Rudge, *Hist. of Glos.* ii. 118; cf. inscr. to Mary A Deane in chancel of Awre ch.
[20] O.S. Map 6", Glos. XXIX. NE. (1884 edn.); cf. G.D.R., T 1/12, where Stemsey orchard is named on N. side of the ho.
[21] O.S. Map 6", Glos. XXXIX. NE. (1884 edn.); Glos R.O., D 265/T 11.
[22] *Licensed Houses in Glos. 1891,* 144; O.S. Map 1/25,000, SO 60 (1961 edn.).

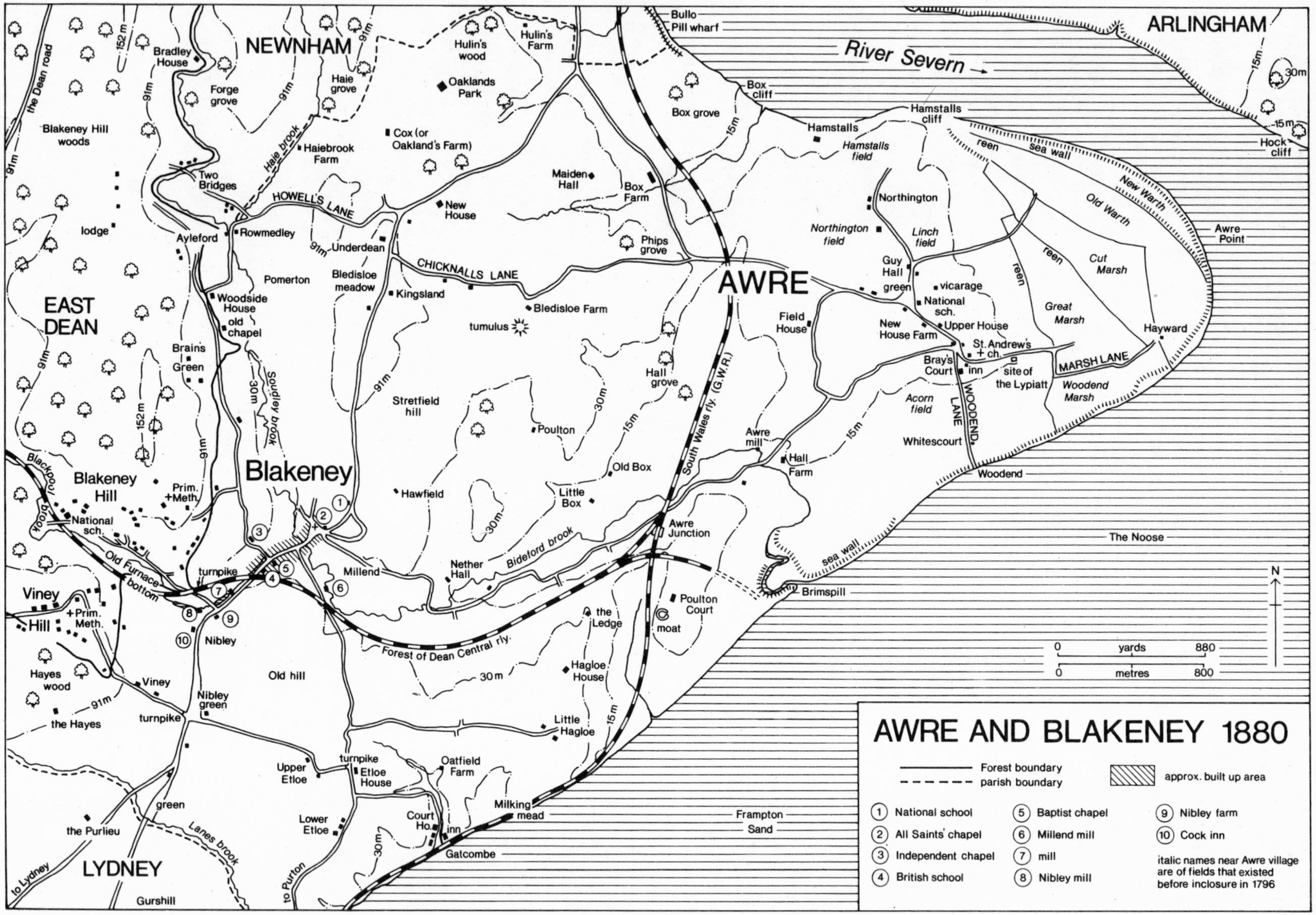

AWRE AND BLAKENEY 1880

ARLINGHAM

River Severn

30m
15m
Hock cliff

NEWNHAM

EAST DEAN

AWRE

Blakeney Hill woods

the Dean road

Bradley House

Forge grove

Haie grove

Two Bridges

Rowmedley

Ayleford

Pomerton

Woodside House
old chapel

Soudley brook

Brains Green

Prim. +Meth.

National sch.

Blackpool brook

Blakeney Hill

Viney Hill

+ Prim. Meth.

Hayes wood

Viney

the Hayes

the Purlieu

LYDNEY

Gurshill

to Lydney

Lanes brook

green

to Purton

turnpike

Lower Etloe

Etloe House

Court Ho.

Upper Etloe

Oatfield Farm

Old hill

Nibley

Nibley green

turnpike

Gatcombe

Cock inn

Milking mead

Little Hagloe

Hagloe House

the Ledge

Poulton Court
moat

Awre Junction

South Wales rly. (G.W.R.)

Forest of Dean Central rly.

Nether Hall

Millend

Hawfield

Stretfield hill

Kingsland

Bledisloe meadow

Underdean

New House

Cox (or Oakland's Farm)

Oaklands Park

Hulin's wood

Hulin's Farm

Maiden Hall

Bledisloe Farm

tumulus

CHICKNALLS LANE

HOWELL'S LANE

Haiebrook Farm

Haie brook

Box Farm

Phips grove

Hall grove

Box grove

Bullo Pill wharf

Box cliff

Hamstalls cliff

Hamstalls

Hamstalls field

Northington

Northington field

Linch field

Guy Hall

green

vicarage

National sch.

New House Farm

Upper House

Field House

St. Andrew's + ch.

site of the Lypiatt inn

Brays Court

Acorn field

Whitescourt

WOODEND LANE

Woodend

Awre mill

Hall Farm

Brimspill

Frampton Sand

Little Box

Old Box

Poulton

Bideford brook

Hagloe

15m

30m

91m

152m

AWRE

Box grove

reen

reen

reen

Sea wall

Old Warth

New Warth

Cut Marsh

Great Marsh

Hayward

MARSH LANE

Woodend Marsh

The Noose

Awre Point

sea wall

15m

N

0		880
yards		
0		800
metres		

Legend

- ① National school
- ② All Saints' chapel
- ③ Independent chapel
- ④ British school
- ⑤ Baptist chapel
- ⑥ Millend mill
- ⑦ mill
- ⑧ Nibley mill
- ⑨ Nibley farm
- ⑩ Cock inn

▨ approx. built up area

——— Forest boundary

– – – parish boundary

italic names near Awre village are of fields that existed before inclosure in 1796

Blakeney

FIG. 2

Hagloe estate, centred on the early 18th-century Hagloe House.[23] The smaller farmsteads of the tithing, few of which survived in the 1980s, were probably established at an early date, most of them deriving from the five customary tenements recorded on Poulton manor in the mid 16th century.[24] At Little Hagloe (formerly Upper Hagloe) in the south part of the tithing two small farmsteads once stood on either side of a lane.[25] That on the south side was recorded from 1525 when the Driver family held it by copy from Poulton manor;[26] the Drivers bought the house and its lands from the manor in 1568 and continued to farm there for the next 200 years.[27] The farmhouse on the north side of the lane was possibly that owned by the Hyman family of Hagloe from 1568 to the 1730s.[28] Later it formed part of the Hagloe estate, which also acquired the farmhouse on the south side in 1900.[29] In the same year the Crown as owner of the estate built a pair of farm cottages[30] at Little Hagloe, and the two farmhouses and their buildings were later abandoned, only some ruins surviving in 1989. A small farmhouse called Merryway, close to the Awre–Blakeney road at the north-east end of Hagloe tithing, was recorded from 1718[31] and demolished c. 1870;[32] another called Old Box, which in 1681 stood north-west of Bideford brook close to the house called Little Box,[33] was also demolished later, leaving only a barn at the site; and at Poulton, north-west of Little Box,[34] only some ruins of a stone farmhouse were to be seen in 1989. Little Box was recorded from the early 18th century[35] and the Ledge (or Lodge), north-east of Hagloe House, from 1656,[36] but both farmhouses were rebuilt in the late 18th century or the early 19th. A few farm cottages stand on the Awre–Blakeney road, including a pair built by the Crown in 1890.[37]

ETLOE was said in 1583 to contain 10 or 12 houses,[38] figures that presumably referred only to scattered dwellings in the south part of the tithing and did not include the part of Blakeney village in Etloe. Several of those scattered dwellings had been demolished by the early 19th century, including ancient customary tenements of the manor of Awre and Etloe called Martins and Barrows on Millend Lane, running south

from Blakeney, and others called Cowleys and Wafields on the cliffs south-west of Gatcombe.[39] Nether Hall, by the Awre–Blakeney road in the north-east of the tithing, was recorded from 1493.[40] Alienated from Awre and Etloe manor in 1656,[41] it later passed to a branch of the A Deanes and to their kinsmen the Bayleys of Bristol.[42] A portion of a late-medieval timber-framed house, including two cut-down base crucks, survives as part of its farm buildings. The east end of the present farmhouse is of a single storey with attics and may be part of the central range and cross wing of a 16th- or 17th-century house, which was partly destroyed in the 18th century when a three-storeyed block was added on the west. The A Deane family also held Etloe House, at the junction of Millend Lane and the Purton turnpike road, and made it the centre of the principal estate of the tithing.[43]

Small groups of dwellings were formed on the Purton turnpike at Upper Etloe west of Etloe House and at Lower Etloe south of the turn to Gatcombe. Lower Etloe, which includes a small 17th-century farmhouse, probably represents some of the former tenant holdings of Etloe Duchy manor. A dwelling by Lanes brook on the south-west boundary, probably at a small green beside the old course of the Gloucester–Chepstow turnpike,[44] was recorded in 1635,[45] and in the same area a building called Chesterley, possibly on a Roman site, was mentioned in 1656.[46]

The riverside hamlet of Gatcombe, from which a busy trade was once carried on,[47] stands by a pill at the end of a long wooded coombe. There was at least one dwelling there by 1495,[48] and in 1583 it was a hamlet of six or seven houses, which size it has remained. In the 1580s its only wealthy resident was said to be a 'Mr. Borough',[49] presumably a successor of Richard Barrow who had a house there in 1547.[50] Barrow's house was possibly on the site of that on the east side of the hamlet, close to the riverside, which became known as Drake's House from a tradition, uncorroborated and recorded only from the late 19th century, that Sir Francis Drake visited Gatcombe.[51] In 1763 the house was probably the inn called the Gatcombe

23 Below, manors.
24 P.R.O., SC 12/2/46, ff. 124–127v.
25 Hockaday Abs. cix, 1794; G.D.R., T 1/12.
26 P.R.O., SC 12/2/46, f. 124.
27 Ibid. CRES 38/654.
28 Ibid. CRES 38/612; G.D.R. wills 1702/235; 1737/32.
29 P.R.O., CRES 38/611, 654.
30 Date and crest on bldg.
31 Glos. R.O., P 30/OV 2/1, rate.
32 Ibid. D 637/VII/5; cf. O.S. Map 1/2,500, Glos. XL. 9 (1881 edn.).
33 19th Rep. Com. Char. 101; cf. G.D.R., T 1/12.
34 P.R.O., CRES 38/628; cf. O.S. Map 1/25,000, SO 60 (1961 edn.).
35 Glos. R.O, P 30/OV 2/1, rates; 19th Rep. Com. Char. 84–5.
36 Glos. R.O., P 30/IN 1/1, burials; P.R.O, CRES 38/616.
37 Date and inits. on bldg.

38 P.R.O., E 134/25 Eliz. I Hil./3.
39 Glos. R.O., D 3270/19718, ct. of surv. 1741; cf. ibid. 19717, ff. 63v.–64, 73v.–74, 79v.–80; G.D.R., T 1/12 (nos. 129–30, 167).
40 Glos. R.O., D 421/M 2.
41 Ibid. D 3270/R 10.
42 G.D.R. wills 1672/103; 1714/9; Bigland, Glos. i. 106–7; Glos. R.O, D 3270/19718, ct. of surv. 1741; Hockaday Abs. cix, 1794.
43 Below, manors.
44 Glos. R.O, D 428/A 1, min. 3 Dec. 1759; O.S. Map 1/2,500, Glos. XXXIX. 16 (1880 edn.).
45 Glos. R.O, P 30/IN 1/1, burials.
46 Ibid. D 3270/R 10.
47 Below, econ. hist. (other ind. and trade).
48 Hockaday Abs. cix.
49 P.R.O., E 134/25 Eliz. I Hil./3.
50 Ibid. SC 12/2/46, f. 123v.
51 J. Bellows, Week's Holiday in Forest of Dean (c. 1880), 10–11.

Boat[52] and by 1792 it was certainly an inn, known then and in the 1830s as both the Sloop and the Ship.[53] It remained open as the Sloop inn in 1879 but closed before 1901.[54] Drake's House was built c. 1600 as two floors with attics which were later raised to make a full third storey.[55] The ground floor may originally have been used for storeage, and the upper floors are reached by a newel stair next to the main doorway. The plan of the upper floors is a large central room with one or two smaller rooms at each end. All the internal walls are of well-finished plank and muntin. In the early 19th century another inn, also having the sign of the Ship, was kept at a house which stands on the west side and slightly higher up the hamlet. That inn was a copyhold under Etloe Duchy manor and was the meeting place of the manor court in 1821, becoming known as the Court House after it closed as an inn, probably in the late 1820s or soon afterwards.[56] The Court House, though largely of the 19th century, incorporates an early 17th-century range, which includes a room with moulded and chamfered beams.

Oatfield Farm, standing above Gatcombe but connected to it by an old hollow way, was apparently the home of Richard Hooper (d. 1639) of Gatcombe;[57] it was owned by the Hooper family in the early 18th century, later passing into the Hagloe estate.[58] The house is a substantial rubble-walled farmhouse of the early 17th century with a lateral stack to the central room, which is flanked by cross passages. To the east there is a two-roomed cross wing and to the west an unheated room which was probably for storeage. There are 19th- and 20th-century additions along the south side and at the north-east corner. Oatfield Farm was sold by the Hagloe estate in 1976 and was extensively restored by its new owner, who also converted a large barn as a conference centre and holiday flats.[59]

BLAKENEY village grew up on the Gloucester–Chepstow road around the junction of the Soudley and Blackpool brooks, which powered a number of mills in and around the settlement. The village was large enough to have a chapel of ease by the mid 16th century and in 1583 it was said to contain 20 or 30 households.[60] About 1775 Blakeney tithing, which included only the north part of the village, was said to be the most populous of the tithings, with 50 families.[61] As a fairly populous village on the main through route and a centre for trade, Blakeney rather than the isolated Awre village became the principal focus of parish life. Blakeney's chapel came

to attract larger congregations than the parish church,[62] the court of the manor of Awre and Etloe was usually held at one of its inns in the 18th century,[63] and by the 1770s the parish vestry usually met in the village. The vestry meetings were held in the church house[64] adjoining the chapel until the house, which also served as an inn called the Bird in Hand, was demolished to make room for the enlargement of the chapel in 1819.[65] The oldest part of the village was presumably the most concentrated group of buildings, in the area called Church Square (actually triangular in shape) in the centre of which the chapel stands. Houses had begun to extend south-westwards along the main road into the part later known as Bridge Street by 1624 when a house by Soudley brook was described as in Blakeney Street.[66] Blackpool brook formed a principal feature of Bridge Street, flowing alongside it for its whole length and crossing at one point from the north-west to the south-east side.[67] The public bridges at Blakeney which the parish repaired in 1688[68] were presumably that known as the town bridge across Blackpool brook and another below, across Soudley brook. In 1790 both were packhorse bridges no more than 5 ft. wide and the parish petitioned the county magistrates to meet part of the cost of rebuilding the lower one to a width of 21 ft. to take vehicles.[69] Blackpool brook was culverted in the north-east part of Bridge Street in the early 20th century.[70]

The oldest surviving house in Blakeney, the former Swan inn, stands east of Church Square at the foot of Swan Lane, which until 1831 was the course of the main road.[71] The building, which dates from the 16th century, has a main block and cross wing and is partly of exposed timber framing; it was restored c. 1985.[72] It was an inn in 1645[73] and until the 1870s when it became a temperance hotel; it apparently closed in the early 20th century.[74] The houses around Church Square were mostly built or rebuilt in the late 18th century and comprise fairly substantial, if plain, dwellings of brick or stone, often rendered. A building opposite the Swan at the entrance to the Awre road had taken over the sign of the Bird in Hand inn from the former church house by 1825[75] and remained an inn until the mid 20th century.[76] The Yew Tree inn west of the chapel had opened by 1817.[77] Bridge Street, which is less closely built up than Church Square, includes a small 17th-century farmhouse on the north-west side and the late 18th-century King's Head inn on the south-east side, but most of the other houses are late

52 *Glouc. Jnl.* 7 Nov. 1763.
53 Ibid. 13 Aug. 1792; Glos. R.O, P 30A/VE 1/1, p. 47; G.D.R., T 1/12; P.R.O., CRES 38/611.
54 O.S. Map 1/2,500, Glos. XXXIX. 16 (1880, 1903 edns.).   55 Below, Plate 22.
56 *Glouc. Jnl.* 17 Dec. 1821; 6 Jan. 1827; inf. (derived from deeds) from Mrs. A. Bayliss, of the Court Ho.
57 Glos. R.O., P 30/IN 1/1, burials; a fireback at the ho. has inits. R and E H and date 1626.
58 Below, manors.
59 Inf. from Mr. E. G. Hoinville, of Oatfield Fm.
60 P.R.O, E 134/25 Eliz. I Hil./3.
61 Rudder, *Glos.* 248.   62 Below, churches.
63 Glos. R.O., D 3270/19718, cts. 1706, 1744, 1758, 1762.
64 Ibid. P 30A/VE 2/1.   65 *19th Rep. Com. Char.* 84.
66 Glos. R.O., D 2845/2.
67 O.S. Map 1/2,500, Glos. XXXIX. 12 (1881 edn.).
68 Glos. R.O., Q/SO 2.
69 Ibid. P 30A/VE 2/1; Q/SR 1790 C.
70 Phelps, *Forest in Old Photog.* (1984), 10.
71 Above, this section.   72 Glos. Colln. RR 49.2.
73 A. W. Crawley-Boevey, *Perverse Widow* (1898), 297.
74 *Kelly's Dir. Glos.* (1870), 469; (1879 and later edns.), s.v. Blakeney.
75 *19th Rep Com. Char.* 85; Glos. R.O., P 30/CH 3/1.
76 O.S. Map 1/2,500, Glos. XXXIX. 12 (1881 edn.); *Kelly's Dir. Glos.* (1939), 48.
77 *Glouc. Jnl.* 21 Apr. 1817.

19th-century buildings in the dark Forest sandstone. The most prominent is Sydenham House, south-west of the King's Head, a substantial L-shaped building. By 1876 it was the home and trading premises of Alfred Butler, a grocer, draper, and miller,[78] who had perhaps built it.

In the late 18th century and the early 19th, probably the period of Blakeney's greatest prosperity, the village was enlarged by the building of stone cottages on Awre Road leading south-east from Church Square, on Lowfield Lane (later renamed Church Way) leading north from the square, and on Millend Lane leading south from Bridge Street to Millend, where there were already a few houses grouped around a corn mill by the 1740s.[79] A small estate of council houses was built in 1949 at Highfield on the west side of the Ayleford road, and others were built in the 1950s on All Saints Road, north of Church Square, and on Awre Road.[80] A few private houses were added in various parts of the village before 1989.

South-west of Blakeney the small roadside hamlet of Nibley had been established by the early 17th century,[81] with a corn mill at the bottom of the Blackpool brook valley one of the earliest buildings.[82] Nibley Farm (in 1989 called Old Nibley Farmhouse) on the south-east side of the road was recorded from 1678[83] but was rebuilt c. 1800. An innkeeper of Nibley who died in 1732[84] may have kept the Cock inn. That inn had certainly opened by 1822 when it was a staging post for a South Wales coach.[85] At the south end of Nibley green, a narrow roadside green extending from Nibley to the junction with the Purton turnpike, a small cottage called Cracked Croft was built before 1741;[86] a larger new house was added to it in the early 19th century and was known as Nibley House in 1989. There was a dwelling at Viney on the road from Nibley green to Viney Hill by 1603,[87] and two small farmhouses, Upper Viney which may date from the 17th century and Lower Viney which is dated 1741, stand there. The Hayes, south of Viney Hill, was the manor house of Blakeney manor.[88]

In 1327 57 people were assessed for the subsidy under Awre 'with its members' and 5 under Blakeney.[89] There were said to be c. 420 communicants in the parish in 1551,[90] 133 households in 1563,[91] and 250 families in 1650.[92] About 1710 the population was estimated at c. 700 in 139 houses,[93] and 952 people in 191

houses were enumerated in 1801. In 1811, out of a total population of 1,035, 346 lived in Blakeney tithing, 332 in Etloe with Etloe Duchy, 194 in Awre, 99 in Bledisloe, and 64 in Hagloe; the figures for Blakeney and Etloe suggest that Blakeney village, straddling the boundary between the two, then had a population of around 550. The population of the parish rose to 1,526 by 1861 and there was then a fairly sharp fall to 1,179 by 1881, followed by a more gradual fall to 1,070 by 1911. It then remained fairly static until 1951 when it was 1,033. Following the addition of the Blakeney Hill area to the parish in 1953, the population was 1,805 in 1961, falling to 1,527 by 1981.[94]

A gas company was formed for Blakeney before 1876 with its works beside the railway at Nibley.[95] It was apparently absorbed by the Lydney gas company in the late 1930s.[96] Blakeney's street-lighting committee mentioned in 1906[97] presumably lit the village streets with gas. Other services for Blakeney were not provided until the mid 20th century. Electricity was laid on to the village by the West Gloucestershire Power Co. in the mid 1930s.[98] Its houses remained dependent on wells for water[99] until the early 1950s when they were supplied under a scheme of the East Dean rural district from a reservoir on Blakeney hill.[1] Some drains had been built by the 1860s[2] but in 1908 some houses discharged sewage into the stream running through the village. Refuse disposal remained the responsibility of the individual householders[3] until 1937 when the rural district extended that service to Awre parish.[4]

Blakeney had a friendly society, meeting at the Swan inn, by 1791,[5] and a lodge of the Oddfellows was founded in the village c. 1824. A brass band formed in the village before 1843[6] was in regular demand for events in the Forest area during the mid 19th century.[7] The village's old National school at the bottom of Lowfield Lane was in use as a public library in 1879.[8] In 1905 the building was vested in trustees for church purposes[9] and it remained in use as a church hall in 1989. A new village hall in Millend Lane was provided before 1927 as a memorial to the dead of the First World War.[10] It had been demolished by 1989 when a community centre, recently built beside a playing field on the north side of the village, housed most social events. In Awre village the school, closed in 1927,[11] was later used as a village hall.

78 Phelps, *Forest in Old Photog.* (1984), 10; *Kelly's Dir. Glos.* (1870), 468; (1879 and later edns.), s.v. Blakeney; *Morris's Dir. Glos.* (1876), 437.
79 Glos. R.O., D 3270/19718, ct. of surv. 1741; ibid. R 161; below, econ. hist.
80 Glos. R.O., DA 24/602/1.
81 P.R.O., REQ 2/163/153.　　82 Below, econ. hist.
83 Glos. R.O., D 3270/19718, ct. 1814; cf. ibid. 19717, ff. 83v.–84.　　84 G.D.R. wills 1732/117.
85 *Glouc. Jnl.* 14 Jan. 1822.
86 Glos. R.O, D 3270/19718, ct. of surv. 1741; cf. ibid. 19717, ff. 85v.–86.
87 P.R.O., REQ 2/163/153.
88 Below, manors.
89 *Glos. Subsidy Roll, 1327,* 31, 44.
90 *E.H.R.* xix. 121.　　91 Bodl. MS. C. 790, f. 27v.
92 *Trans. B.G.A.S.* lxxxiii. 97.
93 Atkyns, *Glos.* 238.　　94 *Census,* 1801–1981.

95 *Morris's Dir. Glos.* (1876), 435; O.S. Map 1/2,500, Glos. XXXIX. 12 (1881 edn.).
96 *Kelly's Dir. Glos.* (1939), 49.
97 Glos. R.O., DA 1/100/9.
98 Ibid. 5, min. 10 Aug. 1934; Payne, *Glos. Survey,* 205.
99 Glos. Colln. RF 30.2; Glos. R.O., DA 1/802, letter 21 Apr. 1927; Payne, *Glos. Survey,* 218.
1 *Citizen,* 28 Sept. 1951; Pearce, 'Water Supply in Dean', 43–4.
2 Glos. R.O., DA 1/100/6, mins. 17 Nov. 1864; 20 Apr. 1865.
3 Ibid. DA 1/802, letter 16 May 1933; Glos. Colln. RF 30.2.
4 Glos. R.O., DA 24/100/12, p. 216.
5 Ibid. Q/RSf 2.　　6 *Glouc. Jnl.* 29 July 1843.
7 Ibid. 30 July 1853; 8, 22 July 1854; 6 Sept. 1862; 2 Aug. 1873.
8 O.S. Map 1/2,500, Glos. XXXIX. 12 (1881 edn.).
9 Glos. R.O., D 3469/5/10.
10 *Kelly's Dir. Glos.* (1927), 51.　　11 Below, educ.

Awre parish was usually without large resident landowners and its leading inhabitants were members of long-established yeoman families, including the A Deanes, Birkins, Trippetts, Hopkinses, Bayleys, Keddicks, Drivers, and a family that took its surname from the place.[12] The Awres, who as late as the 1680s sometimes used the style 'of Awre',[13] were still represented in Awre village in 1989. During the 17th and 18th centuries, presumably because of the close connexion through the river trade, a large number of Bristol men owned land in the parish and many of Awre's inhabitants had relations in that city.[14]

A note inserted in the Awre parish register, probably in the late 17th century, claimed that Thomas Sternhold and John Hopkins, who produced the first English metrical versions of the psalms, published in 1551, both lived in the parish, the former at Hawfield and the latter at Woodend. Although Sternholds and Hopkinses were both well represented in the parish in the 16th century, no contemporary connexion of the two men with the place has been discovered.[15]

MANORS AND OTHER ESTATES. In 1066 Edward the Confessor held the manor of *AWRE*, assessed at 5 hides and contributing half a night's maintenance to the farm of the county, but Alwig the sheriff had separated from the manor three members, Purton in Lydney, Etloe, and Bledisloe, a total of 7 hides, and removed them from the farm.[16] The manor remained in royal hands until the reign of Stephen when it passed to Miles of Gloucester, earl of Hereford,[17] and Robert son of Hugh held it by knight service from Miles (d. 1143) and his son Roger, earl of Hereford. Robert became a monk of Monmouth priory[18] and the manor apparently then reverted to Earl Roger. Awre was among former royal demesne estates between the Severn and the Wye which Henry II confirmed to the earl in 1154 or 1155,[19] and following the earl's rebellion and death in 1155 it was granted to his brother Walter.[20] On Walter's death *c.* 1160 the manor reverted to the Crown,[21] which retained it in hand for the remainder of the century;[22] it was

among the estates in which Henry de Bohun, heir to the earls of Hereford, was required to quitclaim all his rights when created earl in 1200.[23]

In 1204 the Crown granted the manor at farm for life to Walter of Awre the elder (d. *c.* 1221).[24] In 1230 it was granted at fee farm to William Marshal, earl of Pembroke, and his heirs.[25] On William's death in 1231 it passed to his brother Richard[26] and then in turn to his brothers Gilbert,[27] Walter, and Anselm (d. 1245). Anselm's widow Maud, who married Roger de Quincy, earl of Winchester, held the manor in dower until her death in 1252.[28] The manor was then subject to partition among the families of Anselm Marshal's sisters and coheirs.[29] An estate described as half the manor was held in 1276 by William de Valence,[30] who had married Joan, daughter of one of Anselm's sisters, and Joan (d. 1307) probably retained it after William's death in 1296.[31] Before 1316 their son Aymer de Valence, earl of Pembroke, granted that estate to Maurice of Berkeley.[32] Another estate called half the manor was held at his death in 1262 by Richard de Clare, earl of Gloucester, who was son of Isabel, another of Anselm Marshal's sisters.[33] Richard's widow Maud (d. *c.* 1288) held the estate in dower in 1276.[34] In 1280 Richard's son Gilbert de Clare granted it, possibly in reversion on Maud's death, to Roger Mortimer[35] (d. 1282),[36] who had married Maud de Breuse, heir to another of Anselm Marshal's sisters. Maud Mortimer retained the estate[37] until her death in 1301 when she was succeeded by her son Edmund[38] (d. 1304).[39] Edmund's widow Margaret held the estate, then described as a third of the manor, in 1316[40] but had perhaps surrendered it by 1320 when her son Roger Mortimer settled it on the marriage of his daughter Margaret and Thomas of Berkeley.[41]

In 1278 when William de Valence and Gilbert de Clare made an agreement about the advowson of Awre church claims were entered by John de Bohun and William Paynell.[42] The two men, who presumably claimed as other heirs of Anselm Marshal, apparently secured parts of the manor, for *c.* 1300 William Paynell granted lands and the rents and services of tenants at Awre,

[12] For those families, e.g. Glos. R.O., D 421/M 1, ct. of surv. 1595; M 2; D 3270/19743, no. 16; P 30/IN 1/1; Bigland, *Glos.* i. 104–12

[13] Glos. R.O., P 30/IN 1/1, bapt. 1689; marr. 1688.

[14] e.g. ibid. marr. 1610, 1662, 1666, 1687, 1692, 1704, 1729, 1779, 1798; burials 1712, 1714, 1717, 1741, 1745, 1756, 1764; D 265/T 13, deed 1790; D 2845/2; D 2957/30.8; D 3269, deeds of Hayward 1660–1794, deeds 1676, 1686, 1691; D 3270/19718, cts. 1691, 1703, 1705; Bigland, *Glos.* i. 106–9.

[15] I. Gray, 'The Sternhold Mystery', *Trans. B.G.A.S.* lxxxvii. 209–12, where it is suggested, in view of the uncommon surname and a connexion with Glouc., that Sternhold may have been born in the par.

[16] *Dom. Bk.* (Rec. Com.), i. 163.

[17] *Rot. Chart.* (Rec. Com.), 53.

[18] *Cal. Doc. France*, pp. 410–11.

[19] *Rot. Chart.* (Rec. Com.), 53; cf. *Trans. B.G.A.S.* lxxvii. 68–71.   [20] *Pipe R.* 1156–8 (Rec. Com.), 49.

[21] Ibid. 1160 (P.R.S. ii), 28; 1169 (P.R.S. xiii), 114.

[22] Cf. ibid. 1173 (P.R.S. xix), 155; 1195 (P.R.S. N.S. vi), 182.

[23] *Rot. Chart.* (Rec. Com.), 53, 61.

[24] Ibid. 121; *Pipe R.* 1204 (P.R.S. N.S. xviii), 147, and later rolls; cf. *Ex. e Rot. Fin.* (Rec. Com.), i. 70. A grant of the man. to Wm. Longespée, earl of Salisbury, in 1218

apparently implied only the right to receive the annual farm from Wal.: *Rot. Litt. Claus.* (Rec. Com.), i. 365, 367.

[25] *Cal. Pat.* 1225–32, 404.

[26] *Close R.* 1227–31, 561.

[27] *Cur. Reg. R.* xv, p. 248; for the earls of Pembroke, *Complete Peerage*, x. 368–87.

[28] *Close R.* 1242–7, 441; 1251–3, 135; *Ex. e Rot. Fin.* (Rec. Com.), ii. 143.

[29] Cf. *Cal. Pat.* 1364–7, 263–75.

[30] *Rot. Hund.* (Rec. Com.), i. 176.

[31] *Cal. Inq. p.m.* iii, p. 254; *Trans. B.G.A.S.* lxvi. 186.

[32] *Berkeley MSS.* i. 339; cf. *Feud. Aids*, ii. 273.

[33] *Cal. Inq. p.m.* i, pp. 156–7; for the de Clares, *Complete Peerage*, v. 695–702.

[34] *Rot. Hund.* (Rec. Com.), i. 176.

[35] *Abbrev. Plac.* (Rec. Com.), 199.

[36] *Cal. Inq. p.m.* ii, p. 265; for the Mortimers, *Complete Peerage*, ix. 280–4.

[37] *Cal. Close*, 1279–88, 200.

[38] *Cal. Inq. p.m.* iv, pp. 19–20.

[39] Ibid. p. 159.

[40] *Cal. Close*, 1302–7, 175–6; *Cal. Pat.* 1313–17, 491.

[41] *Berkeley MSS.* i. 117.

[42] P.R.O., CP 25/1/75/31, no. 30.

together with the reversion of lands held in dower by Joan, widow of John de Bohun of Midhurst (Suss.), to Thomas of Berkeley, Lord Berkeley (d. 1321). Thomas had a quitclaim from Joan of her rights in 1308.[43] Thomas's son Maurice of Berkeley (d. 1326),[44] who bought Aymer de Valence's share of the manor, granted an estate, apparently comprising tenants' rents in Awre and Etloe, to his own third son John for life,[45] and by 1319 Maurice had apparently transferred his manorial rights and the rest of his estate to his eldest son Thomas. In 1319 the younger Thomas also obtained a lease of his grandfather's land at Awre,[46] and the following year he added the Mortimers' share of the manor to his estate. The lands of the younger Thomas of Berkeley and his brother John were forfeited to the Crown as a result of the family's involvement in the rebellion of 1322.[47] Thomas was restored to his lands in 1327,[48] and the whole manor was united in his possession after the death of his brother in 1332 or 1333.[49]

Thomas, Lord Berkeley, died in 1361 and was succeeded by his son Maurice[50] (d. 1368).[51] The manor was held by Maurice's widow Elizabeth[52] (d. 1389), passing to his son Thomas[53] (d. 1417). It then descended to Thomas's daughter Elizabeth and her husband Richard Beauchamp (d. 1439), earl of Warwick,[54] and in 1445, like the associated Bledisloe hundred, it was presumably held jointly by their three daughters, Margaret, wife of John Talbot, earl of Shrewsbury, Eleanor, wife of Edmund Beaufort, marquess of Dorset, and Elizabeth, wife of George Neville, Lord Latimer.[55] All rights eventually passed to the Latimers, and Elizabeth, who after her husband's death in 1469 married Thomas Wake, held Awre manor at her death in 1480. She was succeeded by her grandson Richard Neville, Lord Latimer, then a minor. From Richard[56] (d. 1530) the manor presumably passed to his son John (d. 1543),[57] whose son John (d. 1577), Lord Latimer, held it in 1555.[58] The last John was succeeded by his daughter Catherine, who married Henry Percy (d. 1585), earl of Northumberland.[59] Catherine and her second husband Francis Fitton sold the manor in 1595 to Sir Edward Winter of Lydney.[60] From Sir Edward (d. 1619) it passed with Lydney to his son Sir John, who in the course of his attempts

to clear his estates of the heavy financial burden imposed on them following the Civil War[61] alienated some of the tenant land in 1656.[62]

In 1668 Sir John Winter, his sons William and Charles, and his mortgagees sold Awre manor to Gloucester corporation, which acquired it in trust as the endowment of Sir Thomas Rich's school in that city. The manor, which by that time was usually called the manor of *AWRE AND ETLOE*, comprised the demesne farms of Lypiatt and Whitescourt, the rents and fines of numerous tenants in Awre, Etloe, Blakeney, and Bledisloe, and valuable fishing rights. Also in 1668 the corporation bought Box farm for the same purpose, and in 1749 Maiden Hall farm and in 1766 Hall farm were added to the trust estate.[63] In 1836 the manor passed from Gloucester corporation to the city's municipal charity trustees and in 1882 it passed to the governors of the Gloucester United Schools.[64] In 1921 the governors were empowered to sell Hall Farm and 364 a. of land,[65] and at the same period they sold Box farm[66] and enfranchised the small amount of copyhold surviving. Of the few remaining manorial assets, the chief rents were redeemed in 1926.[67]

There was possibly no manor house on Awre manor before 1327 when Thomas, Lord Berkeley, built one there, bringing oaks across the river from his estate at Hurst, in Slimbridge.[68] It was presumably the house later called the Lypiatt, which stood on Marsh Lane east of Awre church and was regarded as the manor house in the 17th century.[69] In 1796 the Lypiatt was a stone-built house of 10 rooms.[70] It was demolished in the mid 19th century, before 1879.[71]

The manor of *ETLOE*, severed from Awre manor before the Conquest, was held in 1086 by Roger of Berkeley.[72] That manor appears to have been absorbed once more into Awre manor by the the beginning of the 14th century: Maurice of Berkeley had lands at Etloe c. 1316, presumably acquired with his portion of Awre,[73] and his father Thomas acquired an estate at Etloe, described as within Awre manor, from Thomas Hatholf in 1317.[74] Maurice, Lord Berkeley, bought other lands there in 1366 or 1367.[75] Later Awre manor was thought to include the whole of Etloe tithing, which was occupied mainly by customary tenements held from the manor.[76]

43 Berkeley Cast. Mun., General Ser. Chart. 3513, 1645.
44 For the Berkeleys, *Complete Peerage*, ii. 126–31.
45 *Berkeley MSS.* i. 268.
46 Berkeley Cast. Mun., General Ser. Chart. 2293.
47 *Cal. Fine R. 1319–27*, 96; P.R.O., SC 6/1148/12.
48 *Berkeley MSS.* i. 299, 308.
49 Glos. R.O., D 421/M 4.
50 *Cal. Fine R. 1356–68*, 187–8.
51 *Cal. Inq. p.m.* xii, pp. 194–5.
52 *Cal. Close, 1364–8*, 437.
53 *Cal. Inq. p.m.* xvi, p. 307; *Cal. Close, 1389–92*, 14.
54 *Complete Peerage*, xii (2), 381–2.
55 Glos. R.O., D 421/M 13.
56 *Cal. Pat. 1476–85*, 241; *1485–94*, 125; Glos. R.O., D 421/M 1, ct. 3 Nov. 1595; for the Latimers, *Complete Peerage*, vii. 479–85.
57 It was possibly held in dower, like the Latimers' Purton man., by John's widow, Queen Cath. Parr: below, Lydney, manors.   58 Glos. R.O., D 18/551.
59 *Cal. Proc. in Chanc. Eliz. I* (Rec. Com.), ii. 274.

60 P.R.O., C 142/248, no. 22; C 3/295/10.
61 Ibid. C 142/378, no. 147; cf. below, Lydney, manors.
62 Glos. R.O., D 3270/R 10; cf. ibid. D 4431, deed 2 Apr. 1657.
63 *14th Rep. Com. Char.* H.C. 382, pp. 23–7 (1826), xii.
64 *V.C.H. Glos.* iv. 336–7.
65 Glos. R.O., D 3269, Schemes and orders 1875–1927.
66 M. Burden, *My Brook became a River* (Glouc. 1980), 60.
67 Glos. R.O., D 3270/19743, nos. 38, 87.
68 *Berkeley MSS.* i. 308.
69 Glos. R.O., D 3270/R 2; *14th Rep. Com. Char.* 23; cf. G.B.R., J 4/1, no. 32
70 Glos. R.O., D 3270/19743, no. 66.
71 G.D.R., T 1/12; O.S. Map 1/2,500, Glos. XL. 10 (1880 edn.).
72 *Dom. Bk.* (Rec. Com.), i. 163.
73 *Berkeley MSS.* i. 268; cf. P.R.O., SC 6/1148/12.
74 Berkeley Cast. Mun., General Ser. Chart. 2155.
75 *Berkeley MSS.* i. 371.
76 Glos. R.O., D 3270/19743, no. 39; 19717, ff. 59–92.

A manor later called *ETLOE DUCHY* was perhaps represented by the ploughland at Etloe with which Walter Goscelin was dealing in 1248.[77] The manor belonged to Patrick de Chaworth who died *c.* 1283, leaving as his heir an infant daughter Maud,[78] and in 1305 Maud's husband Henry, earl of Lancaster, owned the manor.[79] Henry (d. 1345) was succeeded by his son Henry, who was created duke of Lancaster in 1351 and died in 1361.[80] At the partition of the duke's estates Etloe was assigned to his daughter Maud[81] and following her death in 1362 probably passed to her sister Blanche, wife of John of Gaunt, and then to their son, the future Henry IV.[82] The Crown held the manor in 1415[83] and retained it[84] until 1609 when it was sold to George Salter and John Williams.[85] It apparently then descended with Minsterworth manor:[86] John Chamberlayne held it at his death in 1628, having devised it to his nephew Thomas Wyndham,[87] Thomas Pury of Taynton owned it in 1669,[88] William Burgess was dealing with it in 1724,[89] and by the 1770s it belonged to Charles Barrow of Highgrove, Minsterworth.[90] At his death in 1789 Barrow was succeeded by his illegitimate daughter Mary Caroline (d. 1837), who married Charles Evans (d. 1819), and their son Edmund Barrow Evans (d. 1868)[91] owned it in 1866.[92] The manor has not been found recorded later.

The manor of *BLEDISLOE*, severed from Awre manor before the Conquest, was held in 1086 by William son of Baderon.[93] It was presumably the estate that Roger of Bledisloe held for ¼ knight's fee from Alan Plucknett in 1285[94] and that John Billing held in 1346.[95] Later it was held by John Greyndour (d. 1416),[96] and it then descended with Abenhall manor in the Baynham and Vaughan families[97] until 1664 when John Vaughan and Frances his wife conveyed it to Thomas Bridgeman and John Horne.[98] It appparently passed to Frances Bridgeman, whose children Thomas Bridgeman and Elizabeth Griffith sold it before 1671 to William Rowles of Cockshoot, in Newnham. Rowles settled it in 1680 on the marriage of his daughter Elizabeth and William Scudamore the younger, of Gloucester, and they sold it in 1682 to John Birkin of Hagloe.[99] It then descended with the

Hagloe estate and was sold to the Crown with that estate in 1853.[1] The manor house and demesne land were possibly retained by John Vaughan when he sold the manor, for he owned an unidentified farm at Bledisloe in 1688.[2] At the beginning of the 18th century Bledisloe farm belonged to the Bellamy family,[3] which retained it until the 1790s.[4] At the beginning of the 19th century the house with *c.* 160 a. of land belonged to Thomas Barber, owner of the nearby Hawfield estate,[5] and in 1839 the farm was owned by Sophia Morse.[6] In the late 1950s the farm was bought by Mr. R. R. Baber, of a family that was prominent as farmers in the parish during the 20th century, and in 1989 he owned and farmed it with Hall farm, near Awre village.[7]

The manor house, at Bledisloe Farm on Chicknalls Lane, was described *c.* 1700 as 'now mean as to building'.[8] It was replaced by a new farmhouse *c.* 1800,[9] a two-storeyed building of brick on a plinth of blocks of industrial slag, with low, stone-built service ranges at the rear. Possibly associated with the site of the manor was a mound which occupied a low ridge to the south of the farmhouse. Excavation in 1964, shortly before the mound was levelled, found evidence of an early timber structure, which the mound replaced in the 12th century, possibly as the motte of a small castle which was left uncompleted; a domestic or farm building was built on the mound later in the Middle Ages.[10]

Soon after the Conquest William FitzOsbern formed a single estate of Nass and Purton, in Lydney, and a third manor called Pontune.[11] Pontune can be identified with the manor of *POULTON* in Awre, which later formed a separate estate, held under the earls of Warwick, overlords of the Lydney manors.[12] It was evidently held in the late 12th century by Roger son of Ralph of Poulton who granted 3 yardlands to Flaxley abbey and also made the abbey another gift for the benefit of the souls of William (d. 1184), earl of Warwick, and his countess;[13] the abbey held the land at Poulton until the Dissolution when it passed with Flaxley manor to the Kingston family.[14] In 1221 Ralph son of Ralph conveyed two ploughlands at Poulton to Ralph of Willington,[15] whose widow Olympia[16] held Poulton manor from the earl of Warwick

77 P.R.O., CP 25/1/74/18, no. 369.
78 *Cal. Inq. p.m.* ii, p. 288.
79 *Cal. Close, 1302–7,* 251.
80 *Complete Peerage,* vii. 401–9; *Cal. Inq. p.m.* xi, p. 105.
81 *Cal. Fine R.* 1356–68, 165.
82 Cf. *Complete Peerage,* vii. 410–18.
83 *Cal. Pat.* 1413–16, 356–7.
84 e.g. P.R.O., CP 25/1/294/76, no. 103; *Cal. D.L. Pleadings* (Rec. Com.), ii. 374.
85 P.R.O., C 54/3768, m. 3.
86 Cf. Rudder, *Glos.* 550.
87 P.R.O., C 142/450, no. 84.
88 Glos. R.O., D 2113/1.
89 P.R.O., CP 25/2/1017/11 Geo. I Mich. no. 31.
90 Rudder, *Glos.* 247.
91 G. E. C. *Baronetage,* v. 235–6, 236 n.; *Glouc. Jnl.* 17 Dec. 1821; and for Chas. Evans's death, Glos. R.O., D 3398, TS. notes on Glouc. bankers: 'Nibletts (later Evans and Jelf)'.
92 Glos. R.O., Q/RF; *Glouc. Jnl.* 6 Jan. 1827.
93 *Dom. Bk.* (Rec. Com.), i. 163.
94 *Feud. Aids,* ii. 240; cf. *Trans. B.G.A.S.* lxvi. 186.
95 *Feud. Aids,* ii. 285.
96 *Cal. Close,* 1413–19, 338.

97 Below, Abenhall, manor; Ruardean, manors; cf. *Cal. Close,* 1447–54, 456; P.R.O., C 139/115, no. 34; C 142/189, no. 82; Glos. R.O., D 36/M 2.
98 P.R.O., CP 25/2/656/16 Chas. II Trin. no. 10.
99 Glos. R.O., D 333/T 3; D 3270/19718, Bledisloe man. ct. roll 1671.
1 P.R.O., CRES 38/611, 613–14; cf. below, this section.
2 Glos. R.O., D 36/T 52.
3 Bodl. MS. Rawl. B. 323, f. 101.
4 Glos. R.O., P 30/OV 2/1, rates; Hockaday Abs. cix, 1794.
5 Rudge, *Hist. of Glos.* ii. 116, 118; *Glouc. Jnl.* 30 Oct. 1815.
6 G.D.R., T 1/12.   7 Inf. from Mr. Baber.
8 Bodl. MS. Rawl. B. 323, f. 101.
9 Cf. Rudge, *Hist. of Glos.* ii. 116.
10 *Trans. B.G.A.S.* lxxxv. 57–69, where the historical background detail is confused and inaccurate.
11 Below, Lydney, manors.
12 *Cal. Inq. p.m.* i, p. 3; ix, p. 196.
13 *Flaxley Cart.* pp. 70, 113.
14 *Valor Eccl.* (Rec. Com.), ii. 486; *L. & P. Hen. VIII,* xviii, p. 124; *Cal. Pat.* 1563–6, pp. 284–5.
15 P.R.O., CP 25/1/73/4, no. 15.
16 Cf. *V.C.H. Glos.* iv. 277.

for 1 knight's fee in 1242;[17] the overlordship of the earls was recorded until 1349.[18] Ralph of Willington, son of Ralph, held Poulton from 1260,[19] and in 1303 it was held by John de Lisle and his wife Joan.[20] John of Willington held it in 1311[21] and was succeeded at his death c. 1338 by his son Ralph.[22] The manor then descended as Westonbirt manor until the attainder of the duke of Somerset in 1552.[23]

In 1555 the Crown sold Poulton manor to William Bridgeman of Mitcheldean and Richard Wilson of Ledbury (Herefs.),[24] but later it may have made a grant of the manor, with Weston-birt, for the benefit of Arthur Basset, who conveyed Poulton to Bridgeman and Wilson and the heirs of Bridgeman in 1567.[25] Bridgeman and Wilson apparently made a partition of the estate under which the former took the manor house, called Poulton Court, the demesne land, and the manorial rights, while the latter took the cus-tomary tenements.[26] Wilson sold at least three, and perhaps all, of the customary tenements to the tenants in 1568,[27] while Bridgeman held Poulton Court and the demesne lands at his death in 1581[28] and his successors to that estate exercised the manorial rights in the 18th and 19th centuries.[29] William Bridgeman was suc-ceeded by his son Thomas, and Thomas (d. 1607) by his son Charles,[30] apparently the Char-les Bridgeman of Littledean who died in 1643.[31] Poulton Court descended to Charles's son Char-les (d. 1647), and the second Charles's son Charles[32] (d. 1680)[33] held it in 1667.[34] John Gainsford held Poulton Court as owner or ten-ant in 1682 and until his death in 1688.[35] At the beginning of the 18th century, when a branch of the Birkin family occupied the house as tenants,[36] Poulton Court was owned by a Mr. Blackwell of Bristol.[37] In 1733 it was owned by Jonathan Blackwell[38] (d. c. 1754) of Northaw (Herts.), who was succeeded by his adopted heir Samuel Killican, who had changed his name to Blackwell.[39] In 1766 Samuel Blackwell, then of Williamstrip, in Coln St. Aldwyns, sold Poulton Court with the Ledge and Merryway farms to James Thomas of Oatfield.[40] It then descended as part of the Hagloe estate to the Crown[41] and remained a farm on that estate in 1989. The

medieval dwelling at Poulton Court was pre-sumably within the circular moat which survives there. The present house has a main range with a tall 17th-century, gabled stone front. At the back a wing with a two-storeyed porch has been much altered but may represent an earlier hall, with service accommodation beyond the hall.

A small estate called the manor of *BLAKE-NEY* was evidently the part of Blakeney tithing later regarded as within St. Briavels hundred:[42] in common with other manors of the hundred it was held from St. Briavels castle for an annual rent and by the service as woodward of a bailiwick in the royal demesne lands of the Forest.[43] The bailiwick of Blakeney was re-corded in the custody of the lord of the manor from 1199,[44] but in 1250 it was forfeited to the Crown.[45] Before 1282 the bailiwick was granted, apparently in fee, to Walter of Aston,[46] but in the 14th century it was granted to other custo-dians for life or during pleasure.[47] In 1486 it was granted in free alms to Llanthony priory, Gloucester.[48] By 1565 the bailiwick had been returned to the lords of Blakeney manor,[49] who remained woodwards until the office lapsed in the mid 19th century.[50]

Blakeney manor was held by Adam of Blak-eney before 1196 when his widow Basile had custody of his lands and heir.[51] She was evi-dently the 'lady of Blakeney' who held Blakeney bailiwick in 1199.[52] In 1201 Thomas of Blakeney owed a fine for having land of which he had been disseised, while Basile owed one for having land in dower.[53] Thomas of Blakeney died in or before 1232 when his son Thomas had seisin of his lands and the bailiwick.[54] The younger Thomas or a successor of the same name died in 1290 or 1291 holding the manor in chief for the annual rent of 19s. paid to St. Briavels castle. His son and heir Thomas was a minor and the manor was occupied until 1295 by William Hathaway, the former constable of St. Briavels.[55] In 1330 Thomas of Blakeney settled his estate on Richard of Haresfield, Richard's wife Eleanor, and their heirs,[56] and Eleanor died holding the estate in 1384 and was succeeded by her grandson John Haresfield[57] who died in 1417 or 1418.[58] Thomas Haresfield held the manor in 1437,[59] and Agnes,

[17] *Cal. Inq. p.m.* i, p. 3.
[18] Ibid. ix, p. 196; P.R.O., C 139/11, no. 28.
[19] *Close R.* 1259–61, 184.   [20] *Feud. Aids*, ii. 251.
[21] *Cal. Chart. R.* 1300–26, 165.
[22] *Cal. Inq. p.m.* viii, p. 110.
[23] *V.C.H. Glos.* xi. 285–6; cf. *Cal. Fine R.* 1391–9, 199–200; *Cal. Close*, 1422–9, 117; P.R.O., SC 12/2/46, ff. 122–31.
[24] *Cal. Pat.* 1554–5, 182.   [25] Ibid. 1556–8, p. 113.
[26] Cf. P.R.O., SC 12/2/46, ff. 122–31.
[27] Ibid. CRES 38/612, 654.   [28] Ibid. C 142/199, no. 84.
[29] Ibid. CRES 38/611, 614, 616. In 1856 and later the Crown was described as owner of the 'manor of Hagloe': *Kelly's Dir. Glos.* (1856), 223; (1879 and later edns.), s.v. Blakeney.
[30] P.R.O., C 142/298, no. 62; G.D.R. wills 1608/139.
[31] Bigland, *Glos.* i. 453.
[32] Glos. R.O., D 4431, deed 1664; G.D.R. wills 1644/14; for death of the second Chas., Glos. R.O., P 30/IN 1/1, burials 1647; cf. Bigland, *Glos.* i. 105.
[33] Glos. R.O., P 30/IN 1/1, burials.
[34] P.R.O., CP 25/2/657/19 Chas. II Trin. no. 23.
[35] *Visit. Glos.* 1682–3, 72; Glos. R.O., P 30/IN 1/1, burials.
[36] Glos. R.O., P 30/IN 1/1, bapt. 1701; G.D.R. wills 1729/86.   [37] Atkyns, *Glos.* 237.
[38] Glos. R.O., P 30/OV 2/1, rate.
[39] P.R.O., PROB 11/812 (P.C.C. 348 Pinfold), ff. 348–50.
[40] Ibid. CRES 38/616.   [41] Below, this section.
[42] *Trans. B.G.A.S.* lxvi. 146, 152–3, 156–8.
[43] Cf. below, St. Briavels hundred.
[44] Below, this section.   [45] P.R.O., C 60/47, m. 13.
[46] Ibid. E 32/30, rot. 35; E 32/31, mm. 11, 17; E 32/32, m. 1.
[47] *Cal. Pat.* 1313–17, 658; 1330–4, 34, 333, 480; 1338–40, 194; 1348–50, 273; 1381–5, 415; 1385–9, 535.
[48] Ibid. 1485–94, 97.
[49] Glos. R.O., D 2026/X 3; P.R.O., WARD 7/12/22.
[50] *3rd Rep. Com. Woods* (1788), 76; Glos. R.O., D 36/Q 2; *5th Rep. Dean Forest Com.* 66, 71.
[51] *Chanc. R.* 1196 (P.R.S. N.S. vii), 108.
[52] *Pipe R.* 1199 (P.R.S. N.S. x), 32.
[53] Ibid. 1201 (P.R.S. N.S. xiv), 44.
[54] *Ex. e Rot. Fin.* (Rec. Com.), i. 223.
[55] *Cal. Inq. p.m.* iii, pp. 2, 195–6.
[56] *Cal. Pat.* 1327–30, 553.
[57] *Cal. Inq. p.m.* xvi, p. 48; *Cal. Fine R.* 1383–91, 88.
[58] Hockaday Abs. ccxxxiii, 1418.
[59] P.R.O., C 139/84, no. 76, where the name of the man is partly illeg. but identifiable by the rent of 19s.

daughter of John Haresfield, inherited it later and married John Barrow. John Barrow, who before 1495 also inherited land in Blakeney and elsewhere in Awre parish from his father Walter,[60] was lord of Blakeney manor in 1508,[61] and the manor evidently passed, with Field Court in Hardwicke, to his son Richard (d. 1563). Richard's son Edmund[62] died in 1570, holding the manor, then called Over Hall, and lands including Hayes wood.[63] Over Hall was presumably the name of the house later called the Hayes adjoining the wood, for in the 18th century the manorial rights of Blakeney were attached to the Hayes.[64]

Edmund Barrow was succeeded in Blakeney manor by his son James (d. 1606), and James by his son Edmund,[65] who was described variously as of the Hayes[66] and of Field Court and died in 1641. Edmund's son John succeeded to the manor[67] and died in 1682 when he was living at Nibley, in Blakeney. In John's lifetime, however, the estate became divided, and was possibly in dispute, between his son George (d. 1696) and Thomas Barrow (d. 1683), a grandson of James Barrow by a second marriage. Thomas was listed as woodward of Blakeney bailiwick in 1673 and 1682 but George was so listed in 1677.[68] George was living at the Hayes in 1672 but in 1681 Thomas, styled of the Hayes, mortgaged Blakeney manor together with the Field Court estate, reserving the Hayes and lands which were stated to have lately been held by George.[69] George was again styled as of the Hayes in 1694, and his son Berea Barrow held the house in 1718. By 1720, however, Thomas Barrow, son of Thomas, held the Hayes, and after his death in 1736 the house and whole estate apparently descended to his daughter Eleanor, wife of the Revd. Thomas Savage[70] (d. 1760). Their son George Savage succeeded and died in 1793,[71] leaving his sisters as coheirs, and in 1794 Sir Thomas Crawley-Boevey of Flaxley, husband of one of them,[72] bought out the interest of the other coheirs in Blakeney manor.[73] In 1820 Blakeney manor and the Hayes were bought by William Ambrose (d. 1843), owner of the Hagloe estate.[74] The manorial rights apparently belonged to J. Mathias in 1879 and to his trustees until 1910 or later.[75] In the earlier 20th century the Hayes was the farmhouse of a small farm owned by the Hayman family.[76] In 1989, when it had been sold by the owner of the farm, the house was derelict and awaiting restoration by its new owners.

The Hayes has a north range of one storey, which has lateral walls of stone rubble but was formerly timber-framed. The gable end is still partly timber-framed and may originally have been internal. At the southern end of the one-storeyed range part of a late-medieval base cruck is buried within a 17th-century chimney stack. The stack is associated with a rebuilding of the early house. That rebuilding was probably in stone, though the internal partitions and the upper floor of the two-storeyed eastern porch are timber-framed. The new block has a cellar, two storeys, and attics, the upper floors being reached by a newel stair in a west projection. In the 19th century a low wing was added to the west side of the single-storeyed range and the roof of the 17th-century block was reconstructed. The house stands at the eastern end of a terraced area which was formerly partly walled and suggests a formal garden of the late 17th century or the early 18th.

Another estate also called the manor of BLAKENEY, probably including part of the village and land in the east end of Blakeney tithing, was recorded in the 14th century. It may have derived from an unnamed estate, comprising ½ hide and a mill, that Walter Arblaster held in Bledisloe hundred in 1086,[77] though an alternative suggestion that Walter's estate lay in the north of Bledisloe tithing adjoining his Ruddle manor, in Newnham, is equally possible.[78] An estate that John, son of Walter of Blakeney, held at Blakeney c. 1300 was probably acquired before 1306 by Thomas, Lord Berkeley.[79] The later Thomas, Lord Berkeley, had a number of tenants at Blakeney in 1333, and his successors to Awre manor were receiving the farm of a manor at Blakeney in 1368 and the farm of its site and demesne in 1457;[80] they still had tenants at Blakeney in the early 17th century.[81] The ancient farmhouse of Nether Hall, which was presumably named in distinction to Over Hall (or the Hayes) and which belonged to Awre manor in 1493,[82] may have been the site of the second Blakeney manor. From the mid 17th century, however, Nether Hall was consistently described and rated as part of Etloe tithing.[83]

A manor called BOX, in the north of the parish, was recorded from the late 12th century, and the circumstances under which in 1300 it

60 Ibid. CRES 38/612, exemplification of depositions 1578; *Cal. Close*, 1485–1500, p. 249.
61 *Cal. Inq. p.m. Hen. VII*, iii, pp. 268–9.
62 P.R.O., CRES 38/612, exemplification of depositions 1578; cf. *V.C.H. Glos.* x. 184.
63 P.R.O., WARD 7/12/22. 64 Rudder, *Glos.* 248.
65 P.R.O., C 142/293, no. 49; the account of the Barrows in the 17th cent. is based on *Genealogist*, N.S. xxx. 76–86.
66 P.R.O., CRES 38/612, deed 1626.
67 Suff. R.O., HA 49/A III(a)/1, deed 1681 (schedule of deeds); cf. P.R.O., LRRO 5/7A, where he held the bailiwick in 1645. 68 Glos. R.O., D 36/Q 2.
69 Suff. R.O., HA 49/A III(a)/1; cf. *V.C.H. Glos.* x. 184, where Thos. is identified incorrectly as a son of Edm. (d. 1641).
70 Glos. R.O., P 30/OV 2/1, rates.
71 *V.C.H. Glos.* x. 184; Rudder, *Glos.* 248; cf. *3rd Rep. Com. Woods* (1788), 76. 72 G. E. C. *Baronetage*, v. 236.
73 Glos. R.O., D 134/T 6.

74 *5th Rep. Dean Forest Com.* 71; cf. G.D.R., T 1/12; below (Hagloe est.).
75 Glos. R.O., DA 1/100/9, min. 15 Sept. 1904; cf. *Kelly's Dir. Glos.* (1870), 468; (1879 and later edns.), s.v. Blakeney. Kelly gives the Crown as owner of Blakeney in 1870 and the Mathiases as lords of Bledisloe later, evidently confusing the two manors.
76 Glos. R.O., D 2428/1/11; *Kelly's Dir. Glos.* (1935), 47.
77 *Dom. Bk.* (Rec. Com.), i. 169.
78 *Trans. B.G.A.S.* cvi. 90–1; Chas. Jones, owner of Ruddle, had land in the north of Bledisloe, apparently including Rowmedley fm., in 1671: Glos. R.O., D 3270/19718, Bledisloe man. ct. roll.
79 Berkeley Cast. Mun., General Ser. Chart. 1245, 1138.
80 Glos. R.O., D 421/M 4; cf. *Cal. Inq. p.m.* xii, p. 194.
81 Glos. R.O., D 421/E 13; D 3270/R 10.
82 Above, intro.
83 Glos. R.O., D 3270/R 10; 19718, ct. of surv. 1741; P 30/OV 2/1.

was excluded from the perambulation of the Forest while the rest of Awre was left in suggest that it had formed a distinct manorial unit from before 1254.[84] It is possible, though no other evidence has been found for the identification, that it was the successor of an unnamed estate of 1 hide and ½ yardland in Bledisloe hundred held by William son of Norman in 1086.[85] About 1190 Box manor formed part of lands at Leighterton and at Box cliff that were held from the heirs of the earls of Hereford for ½ knight's fee.[86] William of Lasborough, who died c. 1261, held a ploughland at Box under the earl of Hereford for ¼ knight's fee. His heir was his daughter Agatha, wife of Henry of Dean,[87] but in 1285 Box was held by Grimbald Pauncefoot and John of the Box.[88] Grimbald, who was constable of St. Briavels and warden of the Forest, died in 1287 and his share was held by his widow Sibyl in 1300, passing to her son Emery Pauncefoot[89] before 1309.[90] By 1346 the two parts were united in the possession of John of the Box,[91] and in 1374 Nicholas Apperley held the estate.[92] No later record of Box has been found until 1577 when Richard Yate conveyed Box manor to Anthony Wye.[93] Anthony or a successor of the same name died in possession of the site of the manor, Box Farm, and the demesne lands in 1629, having settled them on his four daughters.[94] By 1658 Box farm had passed to John Gower of Holdfast (Worcs.),[95] who sold it in 1668 to Gloucester corporation. It remained part of the Sir Thomas Rich trust estate until the early 1920s.[96] It was bought then by F. C. Baber, whose family owned and farmed it until 1989.[97] At Box Farm the high ceilings suggest that the house was reconstructed in the 17th century, but the plan, which included a lateral main stack and stair turret, and the varied thickness of the walls indicate that parts of an earlier building have been incorporated. The interior was refitted in the early 19th century and the porch, which incorporates a staircase, was added late in that century.

In the late 1150s Walter of Hereford granted an estate in Awre to Walter Blund to hold by the serjeanty of service in the donor's chamber. Later, presumably from c. 1160 when Awre manor and Walter of Hereford's other possessions passed to the Crown, the holders of the estate owed service in the royal chamber.[98] By 1174 Walter Blund had been succeeded by his

son Walter.[99] The younger Walter or a successor of the same name held the estate c. 1212.[1] The estate later passed to Walter of Awre who died c. 1278 leaving as his heir an infant son John,[2] whose attainment of full age was verified in 1302.[3] Robert of Awre later succeeded and died before 1326 when his son and heir John came of age.[4] John died in 1344 when his infant heir was Thomas of Awre,[5] who died holding the estate in 1361. The estate, extended as a messuage, 1 ploughland, 6 a. of meadow, and a mill, passed to Thomas's brother John[6] (d. 1382), who left two daughters Joan and Margaret as his heirs.[7] The two married respectively David ap Thomas (also called ap Ivor) and Richard of Awre, who held the estate jointly in 1402.[8]

The reference to a mill among the Awre family's possessions suggests that their estate was later represented by *HALL FARM*, west of Awre village, to which the nearby Hall Mill belonged until 1731.[9] In 1570 and 1606 Hall farm belonged to the Barrows of Blakeney who were thought to hold it by fealty from Lord Stafford (an heir of the Hereford family) as of his manor of Newnham.[10] In 1677 Hall Farm, then known as the Hall or North Hall, and 192 a. belonged to Thomas Blackall of Hackney (Mdx.), who settled the estate on the marriage of his son Thomas. The younger Thomas was presumably the Mr. Blackall of London who owned the estate c. 1700.[11] In 1731 it belonged to Thomas Blackall of Great Haseley (Oxon.).[12] In 1749 it apparently belonged to John Purnell of Dursley, passing c. 1755 to Samuel Blackwell. Blackwell sold it, probably in 1766,[13] to James Thomas of Oatfield Farm, who late in 1766 sold Hall Farm with 140 a. of land to Gloucester corporation.[14] It formed part of the Sir Thomas Rich trust estate until c. 1921. It was bought then by F. Baber,[15] whose family owned and farmed it in 1989. The rear wing of the house has been ascribed to the 17th century[16] but by 1989 recent extensive restoration had obscured any evidence for that. The front range was added or rebuilt in the early 19th century.

Land called the *HAYWARD*, lying at Awre Point east of Awre village, was reclaimed from the river by Robert son of Hugh, owner of Awre manor. He gave it c. 1150 to Monmouth priory[17] but either the grant was never implemented or the land returned later to the manor. In 1204 the Crown granted the Hayward, described as a

[84] *Trans. B.G.A.S.* lxvi. 176–82, 190; cf. below, Forest of Dean, bounds. Allaston, in Lydney, is suggested as the identity of Wm. son of Norman's estate in *Trans. B.G.A.S.* cvi. 90, but it seems more likely that Allaston (if by then cleared and settled) was one of the units formed into Lydney man. between 1066 and 1071: cf. below, Lydney, manors.
[85] *Dom. Bk.* (Rec. Com.), i. 167v.
[86] *Camd. Misc.* xxii. 53.
[87] *Cal. Inq. p.m.* i, p. 139.   [88] *Feud. Aids*, ii. 240.
[89] Ibid. 251; *Trans. B.G.A.S.* lxvi. 186; lxxi. 127–8.
[90] *Cal. Inq. p.m.* v, p. 52.
[91] *Feud. Aids*, ii. 285.   [92] *Cal. Inq. p.m.* xiii, p. 141.
[93] Note in possession of editor, V.C.H. Glos., from P.R.O., CP 25/2/143/1830 (original missing 1989).
[94] *Inq. p.m. Glos.* 1625–42, i. 99–101.
[95] G.B.R., J 1/1967.
[96] *14th Rep. Com. Char.* 23; above, this section.
[97] Inf. from Mr. F. C. Baber.
[98] *Pipe R.* 1161 (P.R.S. iv), 22; *Cal. Inq. p.m.* viii, p. 365.

[99] *Pipe R.* 1174 (P.R.S. xxi), 21.
[1] *Bk. of Fees*, i. 51.
[2] *Cal. Inq. p.m.* ii, p. 163.
[3] Ibid. iv, pp. 76–7.
[4] Ibid. vi, p. 411.
[5] Ibid. viii, p. 365.
[6] Ibid. xi, p. 194.
[7] Ibid. xv, pp. 273–4.
[8] Ibid. xvi, p. 429; *Feud. Aids*, ii. 299.
[9] Below, econ. hist.
[10] P.R.O., WARD 7/12/22; C 142/293, no. 49.
[11] Bodl. MS. Rawl. B. 323, f. 101.
[12] Glos. R.O., D 3270/R 145.
[13] Ibid. R 114; P 30/OV 2/1, rates.
[14] G.B.R., B 3/11, ff. 71, 73; *14th Rep. Com. Char.* 27.
[15] Above, this section.
[16] List of Bldgs. of Archit. or Hist. Interest (Dept. of Environment, 1985).
[17] *Cal. Doc. France*, p. 410.

yardland, with another yardland, a meadow called Honey moor (Hundemore), and 6 a. of land to Walter of Awre the elder,[18] who became farmer of the manor that year. Walter died c. 1221 when custody of his land and heir was granted to Robert de Vernay and Eleanor his wife.[19] The estate, including a messuage, was held by Philip Baderon at his death c. 1278 and descended in direct line to Philip[20] (d. c. 1303), John[21] (d. c. 1332), and Philip[22] (d. 1349). The last Philip was succeeded by his brother Robert Baderon[23] (d. 1361), who left as his heirs two infant daughters Maud and Joan;[24] Robert's widow Joan held a third of the estate in dower until her death in 1396. The younger Joan died in 1397 when her share passed to Maud and her husband John Field.[25] The Barrows, lords of Blakeney manor, owned the estate in 1570 and 1606.[26] The house and some of the land were later detached from the Hayward and Honey moor, which together comprising 50 a. belonged in 1660 to Richard Cox the younger. That small estate, on which a farmhouse was built c. 1680, was owned by the White family between 1769[27] and 1849, later passing to the Gloucester municipal charity trustees.[28] The house at Hayward had been demolished by 1989 when a derelict barn remained at its site.

An estate called *FIELD HOUSE* was held by Richard Trippett (d. 1561), who devised part of the land to his wife Marian, the remainder of the estate evidently passing to his son Thomas.[29] Thomas Trippett of Field House died in 1585, and his eldest son Richard was probably the Richard Trippett of Field House who died in 1627.[30] In 1643 the estate belonged to another Richard Trippett and it passed to his son Richard (d. 1711) and to the younger Richard's son John (d. 1736).[31] John Trippett's heirs were his five daughters, who in 1742 made a partition of the family's estates in Awre and elsewhere in the county: Field House and much of its land were awarded to Elizabeth, wife of William Prestbury, while the farmhouse called Poulton, in Hagloe tithing near the centre of the parish, were awarded with other lands to Perry, wife of the Revd. Whetham Hill of Newnham. William and Elizabeth's Field House estate passed to their son Robert (d. by 1779), whose heirs were his three sisters. The third share of one of them, Perry Allen (later Terrett), passed to her son Thomas Allen, and his son William Allen sold it in 1821 to Robert Prestbury Hooper, son of Elizabeth Hooper, one of the other sisters. In

1831 R. P. Hooper partitioned the estate with Charles Cadogan, son of Robert Prestbury's third sister Joanna Cadogan: Hooper received the house and 92 a. of land for his two thirds and Cadogan received 44 a. for his third. Hooper (d. 1835) was succeeded by his son, also called Robert Prestbury Hooper, who added a small farm at Northington to his estate in 1837. R. P. Hooper died in 1877, and in 1879 his trustees sold the Field House estate to the Gloucester municipal charity trustees.[32] The oldest part of Field House is a long range on the east side which incorporates two cruck trusses and may date from the 16th century. It is linked by a much restored stone range, dated 1859 but of earlier origin, to a gabled, three-storeyed block; the latter, which has walls of exposed close-studded timber framing, may have been the parlour end of the house. There are 19th-century extensions to the north.

A large estate, usually known as the *HAGLOE* estate, originated in lands acquired by the Birkin family, which was recorded in Hagloe from the mid 16th century.[33] John Birkin (d. 1691) of Hagloe was succeeded by his son Richard (d. 1732) and Richard by his son John. John Birkin (d. 1740)[34] devised his lands among his three daughters: Elizabeth's share included Bledisloe manor, bought by the elder John Birkin, Susannah's included lands in Etloe, Hagloe, and Blakeney, and Mary's included Oatfield farm, which her father had inherited from his grandfather Richard Hooper (d. c. 1717). Elizabeth, who on the death of her mother Margaret Birkin in 1749 also received her father's dwelling house, evidently Hagloe House,[35] married Robert Boy and died in 1751. After her death Robert retained her land[36] and lived at Hagloe House until his death in 1800 when he devised his estate to his wife's nephew John Birkin Thomas.[37] Mary died unmarried in 1753 leaving her land to Susannah,[38] who later married James Thomas. Thomas, who took up residence at Oatfield Farm and traded as a merchant from Gatcombe, added Poulton Court to his estate in 1766. At his death in 1780 he was succeeded by his son John Birkin Thomas, who inherited Robert Boy's estate in 1800.[39]

J. B. Thomas died in 1808, leaving to his wife Elizabeth[40] his extensive estate, which comprised a block of farms lying between Gatcombe and Brimspill, including Hagloe House, Poulton Court, Oatfield, the Ledge, Merryway, and a farmhouse at Little Hagloe, together with the

[18] *Rot. Chart.* (Rec. Com.), 125; for the location of Hayward and Honey moor (which adjoined the common meadow of that name), Glos. R.O., D 3269, deeds of Hayward 1660–1794; G.D.R., T 1/12.
[19] *Ex. e Rot. Fin.* (Rec. Com.), i. 70.
[20] *Cal. Inq. p.m.* ii, p. 146.
[21] Ibid. iv, p. 85.
[22] Ibid. vii, p. 303.
[23] Ibid. ix, p. 256.
[24] Ibid. xi, p. 224.
[25] *Cal. Fine R.* 1399–1405, 172–3; *Feud. Aids*, ii. 299.
[26] P.R.O., WARD 7/12/22; C 142/293, no. 49.
[27] Glos. R.O., D 3269, deeds of Hayward 1660–1794.
[28] Ibid. 1829–70; below, this section (New House).
[29] G.D.R. wills 1561/107.
[30] Ibid. 1585/167; Glos. R.O., P 30/IN 1/1, burials 1585, 1627.

[31] Glos. R.O., P 30/IN 1/1, bapt. 1643, 1680; Bigland, *Glos.* i. 106.
[32] Glos. R.O., D 3269, deeds of Field Ho. 1742–1879; cf. below, this section.
[33] P.R.O., CRES 38/612; Glos. R.O., P 30/IN 1/1, burials 1596.
[34] G.D.R. wills 1691/130; 1732/273; Glos. R.O., P 30/IN 1/1, bapt. 1660, 1684; for deaths of members of the fam., Bigland, *Glos.* i. 104–5.
[35] G.D.R. wills 1740/215; for Hooper, ibid. 1717/208.
[36] P.R.O., CRES 38/613.
[37] *Glouc. Jnl.* 29 Dec. 1800; P.R.O., PROB 11/1352 (P.C.C. 8 Abercrombie), ff. 59–60v.
[38] G.D.R. wills 1754/142.
[39] P.R.O., CRES 38/613, 616; cf. below, econ. hist.
[40] Glos. R.O., P 30/IN 1/1, burials 1808; P.R.O., PROB 11/1506 (P.C.C. 855 Loveday), f. 70 and v.

manorial rights of Bledisloe and Poulton and fishing rights in the Severn. In 1810 Elizabeth Thomas married William Ambrose,[41] who also acquired lands in the north of the parish and, with a total of 763 a., was the largest landowner in Awre parish in 1839.[42] Elizabeth died in 1838[43] and William Ambrose, who traded as a timber merchant until declared bankrupt in 1839,[44] died in 1843, leaving the estate at Hagloe heavily mortgaged. One of the mortgagees, Nathaniel Morgan, eventually gained possession and in 1853 sold the Hagloe estate, comprising *c.* 525 a., to the Crown Commissioners of Woods, Forests, and Land Revenues,[45] whose purchase was made partly to facilitate schemes for railway building.[46] The Crown added two farms adjoining the estate on the north, Poulton farm in 1860 and Little Box farm in 1866, and in 1900 added a second farm at Little Hagloe.[47] The Crown remained owner of 702 a. in 1989. By that time most of the farmhouses had been abandoned or sold as private residences and the bulk of the land was farmed from Hagloe House, the chief house of the estate, with a smaller farm based on Poulton Court.[48] Hagloe House was evidently the dwelling house of John Birkin described as new-built in 1737.[49] It was probably built about ten years before that date and has a six-bayed front of red brick with stone dressings. Inside there survives a contemporary staircase of high quality.

An estate based on *ETLOE HOUSE* was built up by the A Deane family, which was recorded at Etloe from the early 16th century.[50] Customary lands of Awre and Etloe manor were held after the death of Matthew A Deane in 1658[51] by his widow Margaret (d. *c.* 1700), passing according to the custom of that manor to his youngest son Robert (d. 1727).[52] Robert was succeeded by his son Matthew[53] who bought a farm at Little Hagloe from the Driver family in 1766[54] and was said to have a large estate in Etloe tithing[55] before his death in 1791. Matthew was succeeded by his son Matthew A Deane of Alderley[56] (d. *c.* 1818) and the younger Matthew by his daughter Margaret.[57] Margaret A Deane (d. 1823) devised her estate to her cousin John Blanch of Bristol,[58] whose family had been customary tenants at Etloe for many years.[59] John Blanch (d. 1833) devised the estate to his nephew

Richard Rosser,[60] and in 1839 Rosser owned 359 a. with Etloe House and farmhouses at Little Hagloe and Upper Etloe; the customary land, which included the site of Etloe House, was then a fairly small part of the total acreage.[61] Rosser (d. 1840) left the estate to his wife Sarah (d. 1847) and then to his son Charles, who died in 1876 having settled it on his four children as tenants in common. The Rossers sold the farm at Little Hagloe to the Crown in 1900[62] and apparently disposed of the rest of their estate then.[63] About 1915 Etloe House and 135 a. belonged to the executors of J. Wheatley.[64] In 1989 that part of the former estate was owned and farmed by a branch of the Baber family. Etloe House, a tall and narrow farmhouse, was built in 1730 at the time of the marriage of Matthew A Deane and his wife Anne.[65]

A house called *COX*, later *OAKLANDS FARM*, at the north end of the parish [66] was the centre of a customary estate of Awre manor in 1573.[67] It was alienated from the manor in 1656 and was probably bought by the tenant Matthew White.[68] Later, possibly by 1690,[69] it passed to Eustace Hardwicke; he was living at the house, then called Hardwicke House, in 1710 and was said to have a good estate in Awre and other parishes.[70] At his death in 1718 he devised the estate to his daughter Patience[71] and in 1720 it was settled on her marriage to Robert Walter of Bristol.[72] By 1741 Cox belonged in right of his wife to John Hardwicke,[73] possibly a second husband of Patience, who died *c.* 1762.[74] John Hardwicke was living at Cox in 1763.[75] It was owned by John Walter in 1770[76] and later by William Marshal (d. by 1794).[77] Cox was sold before 1799 to Thomas Ambrose, from whom the house was leased as a farmhouse at the beginning of the 19th century.[78] In 1839 the house, leased with 73 a., was part of William Ambrose's estates, [79] and *c.* 1850 Oaklands farm was bought by Henry Crawshay and added to his Oaklands Park estate.[80] The farmhouse was rebuilt in the early or mid 19th century.

OAKLANDS PARK, a mansion set in parkland, was built just north-east of Oaklands Farm in the early 19th century. Sir James Jelf, formerly a Gloucester banker and a partner in the nearby Bullo Pill tramroad,[81] apparently built it; he was living there in 1818[82] and in the

41 P.R.O., CRES 38/611; Glos. R.O., P 30/IN 1/1, marr. 1810; cf. ibid. D 608/13/13.
42 G.D.R., T 1/12.   43 Glos. R.O., P 30/IN 1/10.
44 P.R.O., CRES 38/628.
45 Ibid. CRES 38/611.
46 Paar, *G.W.R. in Dean*, 125–6; *31st Rep. Com. Woods*, H.C. 865, pp. 147–9 (1852–3), lvi.
47 P.R.O., CRES 38/628, 644, 654.
48 Inf. from the asset manager (agric. est.), Crown Estate.
49 G.D.R. wills 1740/215.
50 P.R.O., C 1/464/16; Glos. R.O., D 2156/3.
51 G.D.R. wills 1662/123; Glos. R.O., P 30/IN 1/1, burials 1658.
52 Glos. R.O., D 3270/19718, ct. 1700; P 30/IN 1/1, bapt. 1656; Bigland, *Glos.* i. 107.
53 G.D.R. wills 1729/547; Glos. R.O., D 3270/19718, ct. of surv. 1741.
54 P.R.O., CRES 38/654.   55 Bigland, *Glos.* i. 102.
56 P.R.O., PROB 11/1207 (P.C.C. 368 Bevor), ff. 327–328v.; Rudge, *Hist. of Glos.* ii. 117.
57 Glos. R.O., D 3270/R 51.
58 Ibid. R 53.

59 Ibid. D 3270/19743, no. 8; 19718, ct. 1701.
60 P.R.O., CRES 38/654.
61 G.D.R., T 1/12; cf. Glos. R.O., D 3270/19717, ff. 59v.–74.   62 P.R.O., CRES 38/654.
63 Glos. R.O., D 2299/453.   64 Ibid. D 2428/1/11.
65 Date and inits. on bldg.; cf. Glos. R.O., P 30/IN 1/1.
66 O.S. Map 1", sheet 43 (1831 edn.).
67 Glos. R.O., D 421/M 1.   68 Ibid. D 3270/R 10.
69 Ibid. P 30/IN 1/1, bapt. 1690.
70 Ibid. D 2957/101.20; Atkyns, *Glos.* 238.
71 P.R.O., PROB 11/564 (P.C.C. 145 Tenison), ff. 323v.–324v.   72 Glos. R.O., D 2957/30.8.
73 Ibid. D 3270/19718, ct. of surv. 1741.
74 Ibid. 19743, no. 16.   75 G.D.R. wills 1763/144.
76 Glos. R.O., P 30/OV 2/1, rate.
77 Hockaday Abs. cix, 1794.
78 Rudge, *Hist. of Glos.* ii. 116; Glos. R.O., P 30A/VE 2/1, Blakeney ch. seating list 1799.
79 G.D.R., T 1/12.   80 Glos. R.O., SL 313.
81 *V.C.H. Glos.* iv. 140–1; Paar, *G.W.R. in Dean*, 19–20.
82 Glos. R.O., D 3270/19743, no. 16; cf. ibid. Q/SRh 1819 D/1.

1820s, when he ran a marble works at Bullo Pill.[83] In 1830 Oaklands was offered for sale together with 26 a. of wood and a farm of 100 a.[84] but Jelf still owned the house and its park in 1839.[85] About 1850 the house, park, and adjoining land, including Oaklands farm, were bought by the ironmaster Henry Crawshay,[86] who was living at Oaklands Park by 1856.[87] He died in 1879 and his widow Liza Eliza owned Oaklands Park until her death in 1895.[88] In 1899 it was sold to William Gwynne-Evans of Fordham (Essex),[89] whose family owned it until 1976. The house and park were bought then by the Camphill Village Trust, a charity for the care of mentally retarded adults; in 1989 the occupants were employed in craft work and in the large kitchen garden attached to the house.[90] The original house, built by 1818, survives as a low wing at the north end of the present house; it was refitted c. 1830.[91] Some adjacent outbuildings and the lodge on the main road at the parish boundary are contemporary with it. About 1850 Henry Crawshay built a large new house in Renaissance style. It has a main block of two tall storeys with principal fronts to the north-east and south-east and a service block, of the same height but incorporating three storeys, to the west. There were terraced gardens to the south and south-west and a winter garden, unroofed by 1989,[92] and stable block on the west.

In the late 18th century a large estate was built up by John Wade, whose family had been prominent leaseholders under Gloucester corporation since 1710.[93] Wade's estate included land in Bledisloe tithing where, before 1794, he built a residence called *NEW HOUSE* beside the Gloucester–Chepstow road,[94] but most of his land lay in Awre tithing. Between 1767 and 1796 he acquired many of the customary tenements of Awre and Etloe manor,[95] as well as freehold land[96] based on the farmhouse in Awre village later called New House Farm. Additional freehold and customary land, formerly belonging to the Hopkins family, was added to the estate in 1814 and c. 1827.[97] John Wade (d. 1819)[98] was succeeded in his freehold by his grandson John Wade Wait, who also received the customary land by surrender of his younger brother William.[99] In 1839 J. W. Wait owned a total of 527 a. in the parish,[1] and in 1849 he added the small Hayward estate. He died in 1865 and was succeeded by his son John Wade Wait (d. 1868). In 1870 the younger J. W. Wait's trustees sold New

House Farm and most of the freehold adjoining the village to the Gloucester municipal charity trustees, as trustees of the city's almshouses, and most of the customary land to the same body, as lords of the manor and trustees of Sir Thomas Rich's school.[2] The Wait family remained owners of New House and lands in the north of the parish until 1919 or later.[3] New House, a three-storeyed late 18th-century residence,[4] was much reduced in size in the early 20th century when the two upper storeys were removed and replaced by gables. The house was called Severn Lodge in 1989, when its owner had a business there selling garden equipment and a woodworking firm occupied an adjoining part of the grounds.

The Gloucester municipal charity trustees, acting in their capacity as trustees of St. Bartholomew's hospital and the other almshouses of that city, acquired an estate adjoining Awre village by a series of purchases from 1854.[5] The principal acquisitions were made in 1870, when they bought 54 a. from themselves as trustees of Sir Thomas Rich's school and New House Farm, Hayward, and 106 a. from the Wait family,[6] and in 1879, when they bought Field House with 104 a.[7] New House Farm and some land were sold before 1989 when the Gloucester Almshouse and Pension Charities retained Field House and 160 a.[8]

A small farm based on a house in Hagloe called Old Box was bought in 1681 by the trustees of a Newland charity.[9] In 1839 the land, which comprised 41 a., was farmed with the adjoining Little Box farm and the house may by then have been demolished.[10] There was a small barn at the site in 1989 when the charity still owned the land.

Gloucester abbey acquired a meadow in Awre by gift of Adam of Bledisloe in the early 13th century, and in 1336 had a grant of a right of way to it. Known as Monk's mead,[11] the meadow lay near the centre of the parish, south of Hall grove.[12]

The rectory of Awre, belonging to Llanthony priory, Gloucester, from 1351,[13] was leased under the Crown in the late 16th century. It comprised the corn and hay tithes, two tithe barns, one in Awre and one in Poulton, and a few acres of glebe land.[14] In 1607 the Crown sold it to to Thomas James.[15] It descended with the James family's Soilwell estate, in Lydney,[16] until 1657 when it was bought by the Haberdashers'

83 Paar, *G.W.R. in Dean*, 24, 38.
84 *Glouc. Jnl.* 1 May 1830.   85 G.D.R., T 1/12.
86 Glos. R.O., SL 313.
87 *Kelly's Dir. Glos.* (1856), 223.
88 Glos. R.O., SL 313; mon. in Awre churchyard; cf. *Glos. N. & Q.* iv. 285–6.
89 Copy of deed, in possession of Camphill Village Trust.
90 Inf. from Mr. S. Hall, of Camphill Village Trust.
91 Cf. *Glouc. Jnl.* 1 May 1830.
92 Cf. Mullin, *Forest in Old Photog.* 36.
93 G.B.R., B 3/8, p. 383; 9, ff. 140v., 443 and v.; Glos. R.O., D 3270/19672.
94 Rudge, *Hist. of Glos.* ii. 116; cf. Hockaday Abs. cix, 1794.   95 Glos. R.O., D 3270/19743, no. 16.
96 Ibid. no. 1.
97 Ibid. D 3270/R 97, R 106; cf. ibid. 19717, ff. 28v.–29.
98 *Glouc. Jnl.* 17 May 1819.
99 Glos. R.O., D 3270/R 98, R 102–3.

1 G.D.R., T 1/12.   2 Glos. R.O., D 3270/R 106–7.
3 *Kelly's Dir. Glos.* (1879 and later edns.); Glos. R.O., D 2428/1/11.
4 Photocopy of sketch 1840, in possession of Mr. K. C. Uzzell, of Severn Lodge.
5 For purchases not mentioned below, deeds in Glos. R.O., D 3269.
6 Ibid. deeds of land at Awre 1742–1870; D 3270/R 106–7.
7 Ibid. D 3269, deeds of Field Ho. 1742–1879.
8 Inf. from Mr. D. W. Dowding, of Field Ho.
9 *19th Rep Com. Char.* 101.   10 G.D.R., T 1/12.
11 Glouc. Cath. Libr., Reg. Abb. Froucester B, pp. 27–8.
12 Glos. R.O., D 3270/R 132.   13 Below, churches.
14 P.R.O., SC 6/Hen. VIII/1224, rot. 20; E 309/Box 7/23 Eliz. I/2; Hockaday Abs. cix, 1563.
15 P.R.O., C 66/1722, mm. 25–7.
16 Below, Lydney, manors; *Inq. p.m. Glos.* 1625–42, i. 111, 114.

Company and used to endow the livings of Awre and Blakeney.[17]

ECONOMIC HISTORY. AGRICULTURE. In 1086 Awre manor had 1 ploughteam in demesne and a single *servus*,[18] and its demesne remained small in later centuries. The demesne belonging to the earl of Pembroke's part of the manor included 22 a. of arable and 4½ a. of meadow with some pasture in 1296;[19] the Mortimers' part of the manor was described in 1301 as 16½ a. of arable, 5 a. of meadow, and 1½ a. of pasture, with two other pastures,[20] while another survey in 1304 extended it at 21½ a. of arable, 4 a. of meadow, and 2 a. of pasture.[21] In 1329 and in the 1360s the demesne of the reunited manor was an arable enterprise. There were 60 a. of arable, *c*. 40 a. of which were sown each year with wheat, beans, and oats. Two ploughmen, working one team, were retained at an allowance of grain and the harvest was gathered by temporary wage-labour; the works owed by the tenants, apparently comprising only bedrips, were realized as cash. There was no permanent stock other than the plough oxen; any animals received as heriots were transferred to other manors of the Berkeley family across the river. An orchard provided fruit in 1329.[22] By 1457 the demesne land of the manor was leased,[23] and in the 17th and 18th centuries, when it probably included former customary land, it was leased with the manor house called Lypiatt or with the farmhouse called Whitescourt.[24] In 1731 the two farms together comprised 158 a. of land, including a considerable acreage in the open fields.[25]

The tenants on Awre manor in 1086 were 12 *villani* and 8 bordars, working 14 ploughteams between them.[26] Later there was a large tenantry, which was further increased by the addition of land in Etloe in the 14th century. In 1301 there were 26 free tenants and 23 customary tenants on the Mortimers' part of the manor.[27] The total number of holdings may have been reduced in the later Middle Ages: several were in the lord's hands in 1457[28] and in 1493 some holdings included more than one house. In 1493 there were *c*. 25 tenants who held houses or tofts with holdings that ranged in size from a single close to 30 a., besides others who held only parcels of land. The acreages of the holdings were usually multiples of 6, the ancient customary yardland having probably been 24 a. By the late 15th century many of the tenements on the manor were held by 'base tenure',[29] a favourable form of copyhold by inheritance, and there were others held by the more usual form of copyhold for lives.[30] In 1573 the tenants by base tenure asserted that their tenements passed by Borough

English to the youngest son, the youngest daughter, or other next of kin, that they had unrestricted right of alienation, that on succession or purchase the heriot or fine was fixed at the equivalent of a year's rent, and that widows had freebench and guardianship of an heir who was a minor.[31] In 1599 the tenants by base tenure were in dispute over the customs with their new lord Sir Edward Winter and some consulted a lawyer.[32] The dispute was settled by arbitration in 1612: among other matters it was established that tenants could grant leases for up to 12 years without the lord's consent and dispose freely of the timber on their estates.[33]

Later the identities of the customary tenements of Awre and Etloe manor were gradually obscured. They were amalgamated one with another or with lands held by other forms of tenure and most of the houses were abandoned. In 1741 a survey of the manor named 34 ancient customary tenements, held by a total of 22 tenants, in Awre, Etloe, and Bledisloe; 21 (all but one of them in Awre tithing) were base tenures and 13 were copyholds for lives, and each owed a heriot though few by then had houses. There were also various parcels of land held by base tenure but not liable to heriots, evidently lands severed from the ancient tenements.[34] The original pattern was further obscured by later amalgamations and, in Awre tithing, by inclosure in 1796. In the late 18th century a large part of the customary land was included by John Wade in his New House estate,[35] which in 1825 had 118 a. in Awre tithing and 10 a. in Bledisloe tithing and owed heriots in respect of 13 houses, of which no more than four still existed. The other main customary holdings in Awre tithing were then Cades (later Northington farm) with 38 a., which was joined soon afterwards to the New House estate, Brunches with 34 a., and the Awre family's Upper House farm with 32 a. In Etloe tithing many of the holdings passed to the Etloe House estate, which included 59 a. of customary land with the sites of 8 ancient houses in 1825. The other main customary holding in Etloe was then 44 a. based on Nibley Farm.[36] The bulk of the customary land of the New House estate was bought by the lords of the manor in 1870,[37] and most of the other base tenures and copyholds were enfranchised between 1874 and 1886,[38] the process of enfranchisement being completed in the early 1920s.[39]

By the early 17th century Awre and Etloe manor also included leaseholds for years or lives, including the demesne farms and the New Warth.[40] Fourteen of the smaller leaseholds were sold, in most cases to the existing tenants, by Sir John Winter in 1656,[41] swelling the already

[17] G.D.R., V 5/30T 3–4; Rudge, *Hist. of Glos.* ii. 119; cf. below, churches.   [18] *Dom. Bk.* (Rec. Com.), i. 163.
[19] P.R.O., E 149/5, no. 1.
[20] *Inq. p.m. Glos.* 1236–1300, 236.
[21] *Cal. Inq. p.m.* iv, p. 159.
[22] Glos. R.O., D 421/M 4; *Inq. p.m. Glos.* 1359–1413, 50.
[23] Glos. R.O., D 421/M 4.
[24] Ibid. M 5; *14th Rep. Com. Char.* 23.
[25] G.B.R., J 4/1, nos. 28, 32.
[26] *Dom. Bk.* (Rec. Com.), i. 163.

[27] *Inq. p.m. Glos.* 1236–1300, 236.
[28] Glos. R.O., D 421/M 4.   [29] Ibid. M 2.
[30] Ibid.; cf. ibid. M 1, ct. of surv. 1595.
[31] Glos. Colln. RF 30.4.   [32] Glos. R.O., D 421/M 1.
[33] Glos. Colln. RF 30.5.   [34] Glos. R.O., D 3270/19718.
[35] Ibid. 19743, no. 16; cf. above, manors (New House).
[36] Glos. R.O., D 3270/19743, no. 8; cf. ibid. 19717.
[37] Ibid. R 106.   [38] Ibid. 19719; 19743, nos. 6, 12, 14.
[39] Ibid. 19743, no. 87.   [40] Ibid. D 421/M 5.
[41] Ibid. D 3270/R 10.

considerable number of freeholds on the manor. In 1741 there was a number of small leaseholds, usually for 99 years or lives, including some houses built fairly recently on waste land.[42] In the early 1740s the larger farms of the manor estate, comprising the demesne farms of Lypiatt and Whitescourt and Box farm, were held on leases for 15 or 21 years; by the end of the century those farms and Maiden Hall and Hall farms, which had been added to the estate,[43] were rack rented.[44]

In 1086 the former members of Awre manor — Etloe, Bledisloe, and Purton — had 1 team and 2 *servi* in demesne and the tenants were 20 *villani* and 3 bordars with 13 teams.[45] Poulton manor had 40 a. of arable and 5 a. of meadow in demesne in 1329.[46] In 1547 the demesne land of Poulton, held with the manor house on a long lease, covered 230 a., and there were five copyhold tenements on the manor;[47] three or more of the copyholds were enfranchised on 1,000-year leases in 1568.[48] Blakeney manor had six tenants in 1292.[49] Bledisloe manor in 1620 included demesne lands, eight tenants holding on leases for years or lives, and a number of freeholders;[50] the leaseholds were all sold before 1671.[51] The lord of Etloe Duchy enfranchised two customary tenements on his manor in 1669.[52] That manor still included a few copyhold dwellings at Gatcombe in the 1820s.[53]

Only Awre tithing had a fully-developed system of open-field agriculture. The remainder of the parish consisted almost entirely of ancient closes, which in Blakeney and the western part of Bledisloe were probably still being won from the waste of the Forest of Dean in the early Middle Ages. In 1220 Awre was assessed on 11 ploughteams, Poulton on 3½, Etloe (presumably including the Duchy manor) and Box on 2 each, and Bledisloe on 1, and no assessment was given for Blakeney.[54]

In Awre tithing in the early modern period there were six main open fields and a few smaller ones. A compact block of open-field land, occupying the level east of the village, comprised Cut (or Runch) Marsh on the north, Great Marsh in the centre, and Woodend Marsh adjoining the Severn on the south. On slightly higher ground north of the village were Lynch field and Northington field, respectively east and west of Northington Lane, and Hamstalls field, between Northington and the river. A small field called Acorn field lay west of Woodend Lane, another field called Brick Furlong lay north of the church,[55] and another called Woodley Hill lay some way west of the village, on the north side of the Newnham road.[56] The three-course rotation which was evidently followed in the Awre fields in the 14th century[57] continued during later centuries. In the early 18th century the courses were wheat and rye, beans and peas, and a fallow.[58]

The common meadows of the tithing were Rod meadow, adjoining the river west of Hamstalls, Dole (or Dow) meadow, a lot meadow lying east of Lynch field, and Honey Moor, adjoining the river east of Woodend Lane.[59] There was common pasture for sheep in the open fields, where the stint in 1728 was 1 to each acre of land owned, and for cattle in the Old Warth, the strip of reclaimed land extending across Awre Point beyond the open fields. The rights in the Old Warth were enjoyed by all inhabitants of the tithing, including landless cottagers. They were regulated periodically, and rates were levied to meet the cost of prosecuting those pasturing illegally, a hayward's wages, and any other expenses. In 1728 the total stint in the warth was 2 bulls (belonging to Lypiatt farm and the Field House estate), 101 cows, and 23 yearlings and calves.[60] The New Warth, recently formed beyond the Old Warth, was appropriated to the lord of the manor under the agreement between Sir Edward Winter and his tenants in 1612, and most of it was ploughed and cropped in 1614 after his lessee had drained it.[61] Later, usually leased with one of the demesne farms, it was pasture land.[62]

A few small private inclosures were made in Awre tithing, mainly in the fields around Northington.[63] Parliamentary inclosure of the tithing, carried out in 1796 and confirmed by an award the following year, re-allotted c. 300 a. of open field and common meadow, the 64 a. of the Old Warth, where the allotments included plots of ¾ a. for the rights of common attached to each cottage, and many of the old closes, which on some of the farms had been considerably intermixed. A total of 24 owners received allotments in respect of land and rights attached to freehold and customary estates. John Wade was awarded 65 a. for his freehold and customary holdings and added another 21 a. by purchase or exchange, the lords of the manor received 3 a. for right of soil and 37 a. for their rack-rented farmland, William Ryder, owner of a farm at Northington, received 55 a., the owners of Field House received 49 a., and five or six other owners received c. 20 a. or more.[64]

In the remainder of the parish there were only a few small open fields and common meadows and those were mostly inclosed at an early date.

42 Ibid. 19718.
43 Above, manors; G.B.R., J 1/2038A, 2039A, 2040–1.
44 Glos. R.O., D 3270/19672.
45 *Dom. Bk.* (Rec. Com.), i. 163.
46 *Inq. p.m. Glos.* 1302–58, 273.
47 P.R.O., SC 12/2/46, ff. 124–8.
48 Ibid. CRES 38/612, 654.
49 *Cal. Inq. p.m.* iii, p. 2.
50 Glos. R.O., D 36/M 2.
51 Ibid. D 3270/19718.   52 Ibid. D 2113/1.
53 *Glouc. Jnl.* 6 Jan. 1827.
54 *Bk. of Fees*, i. 306–7.
55 Glos. R.O., D 3270/19743, no. 1; G.B.R., J 4/1, nos. 28, 32; G.D.R., T 1/12.

56 Glos. R.O., D 421/M 1, ct. of surv. 1595; D 3270/R 50, R 106.   57 Above, this section.
58 Glos. R.O., D 421/M 1, ct. 26 Apr. 1596; D 3270/19718, cts. 1700, 1747.
59 G.B.R., J 4/1, no. 28; G.D.R., T 1/12.
60 Glos. Colln. RF 30.3.
61 Ibid. RF 30.5; G.D.R. vol. 127, depositions 17, 21 May 1616.
62 Glos. R.O., D 3270/19672; G.B.R., J 4/1, no. 32.
63 Glos. R.O., D 3269, deeds of Northington 1689–1837.
64 Ibid. Q/RI 13 (for which the map does not survive); cf. D 3270/19743, no. 1, which sets out the allotments in a more readily accessible form. For the old closes, G.B.R., J 4/1, nos. 28, 32; B 3/12, f. 67v.

In 1547 one of the tenants on Poulton manor had parcels of arable in Nup field and another had a close of that name, presumably taken from the field. Most of the Poulton tenants then had parcels in a common meadow called Broad mead[65] by Bideford brook, east of Little Box Farm; it was not inclosed until after 1853.[66] Nether Lowfield in Bledisloe, mentioned in 1530,[67] was apparently a small open field in the valley of Soudley brook north of Blakeney. In the same area probably lay the meadow in which Bledisloe tenants owned parcels in 1620.[68] In Etloe c. 1300 a man owned scattered parcels of arable in a field called Brockholebeeches, near the river south-east of the Purton road,[69] but the only later evidence of communal agriculture found was the right of tenants of Awre and Etloe manor in the tithing to pasture animals on Nibley green.[70] From the 1430s or earlier the various tithings all had rights of common in the royal demesne land of the Forest of Dean in return for annual payments called herbage money,[71] but by the mid 19th century only a few parishioners still exercised the rights.[72]

In 1596 Thomas Bridgeman, owner of Poulton Court, was reported to have converted 200 a. of arable to pasture,[73] and the parish presumably shared in the general trend towards pastoral farming evident in the Severnside area in the post-medieval period. There remained, however, a good proportion of arable land, even on the inclosed farms outside Awre tithing. In 1731 Box farm had 74 a. of arable in a total acreage of 170,[74] and in 1792 Poulton Court farm had 61 a. in 212 a. and Oatfield farm had 68 a. in 219 a.[75] In 1801, when the parish was said to contain a total of just under 3,000 a. (a considerable underestimate), 727 a. were returned as under crops. All but a few acres were growing cereals and pulse; there had apparently been little or no attempt to introduce roots into the rotation.[76] Orchards, mostly for cider apples, were widespread. Cider, cider apples, and apples and pears for eating were included in tithing customs in 1699,[77] and all the main farms had cider mills and presses in the 18th century.[78] The Hagloe crab, a cider apple regarded in the late 18th century as second only to the stire in quality, was developed in Hagloe by a Mr. Bellamy c. 1710.[79]

During the 19th century and the early 20th the number of farms in the large parish was c. 35–40, and, with the smallholders and fruit growers, there was a total of 67 agricultural occupiers in 1896 and 1926.[80] In 1851 the largest farms were situated in the east and north of the parish,

where the Waits' New House farm had 330 a. and Hall farm, then including most of the land once held with the old manorial demesne farms, had 300 a. The two farms each employed 10 labourers, while Box farm (260 a.), including the land of Maiden Hall and Hamstalls farms, employed 9. The other large farms were Hickman's Court (196 a.) in Bledisloe, Bledisloe farm (161 a.), and Poulton Court (180 a.). In Hagloe and Etloe tithings in the south of the parish there was a regular pattern of farms, mostly c. 100 a. and employing 2–4 labourers, while the west of the parish had mainly small farms.[81] In 1926 37 farms of over 20 a. were returned, 5 of them having more than 150 a.[82] There had been a considerable reduction in the number of farms by the 1980s, most of the smaller ones having been amalgamated with larger units and their farmhouses sold off or abandoned. In 1988 there were 23 farms of over 10 ha. (25 a.) among a total of 31 holdings returned for the parish. The farms were worked by a total of 104 people, but the smaller ones were worked only on a part-time basis.[83] The largest farms were Hagloe House, from which c. 202 ha. (c. 500 a.), the bulk of the Crown's estate, were farmed, and Hall farm, which was held with Bledisloe farm.

In 1839 Awre parish contained 966 a. of arable as against 2,870 a. of permanent grassland and orchard,[84] and in 1866 1,124 a. of arable were returned, including 401 a. under wheat, 283 a. under other cereals or pulse, and 368 a. under clover, grass leys, roots, or other fodder crops.[85] By the latter date draining had facilitated the ploughing up of some old pasture in the lower parts of the parish. A programme of draining was begun on Box and Hall farms in 1846,[86] and in 1851 three men working as drainers lived in Awre tithing.[87] Animal husbandry included sheep raising, dairying, and cattle raising in 1866 when totals of 1,550 sheep, 202 milk cows, and 727 other cattle were returned.[88] By 1896 the slump in cereals had reduced the total arable acreage to 516. The farms turned increasingly to other enterprises, particularly to dairying. In 1896 375 cows in milk or in calf were returned,[89] and among the farms then concentrating on dairying were Hall and Field House, both in the east part of the parish[90] where much of the former open-field land of Awre tithing had been converted to grassland. In 1926 579 cows in milk or in calf were returned. Other livestock enterprises were then well represented with 472 other cattle, 2,123 sheep, 390 pigs, and 4,866 chickens returned.[91] There was a stud for shire horses at Box farm in 1906,[92] and in the early 1920s E. G.

65 P.R.O., SC 12/2/46, ff. 124–6, 127v.
66 G.D.R., T 1/12; P.R.O., CRES 38/611.
67 Glos. R.O., D 421/M 1, ct. of surv. 1595.
68 Ibid. D 36/M 2.
69 Berkeley Cast. Mun., General Ser. Chart. 1247.
70 Glos. R.O., D 3270/19718, ct. of surv. 1741.
71 P.R.O., C 139/84, no. 76; F 14/13; Glos. R.O., D 2026/X 19.   72 P.R.O., F 3/128, letter 29 Nov. 1860.
73 B.L. Harl. MS. 4131, f. 490.
74 G.B.R., J 4/1, no. 31.   75 P.R.O., CRES 38/611.
76 List & Index Soc. clxxxix, pp. 168, 182.
77 G.D.R., V 5/30T 3.
78 G.D.R. wills 1729/547; 1740/215; Glos. R.O., D 3270/19743, no. 66.

79 Marshall, Rural Econ. of Glos. (1782), ii. 252–3.
80 P.R.O., HO 107/1959; MAF 68/1609/12; MAF 68/3295/16; Kelly's Dir. Glos. (1856 and later edns.).
81 P.R.O., HO 107/1959; for Hall and Box farms, cf. Glos. R.O., D 3270/19678, p. 83; for Poulton Ct., cf. Kelly's Dir. Glos. (1856), 224.   82 P.R.O., MAF 68/3295/16.
83 Agric. Returns 1988.
84 G.D.R., T 1/12.   85 P.R.O., MAF 68/26/8.
86 Glos. R.O., D 3270/19677, pp. 243, 289, 292–3, 352–3, 366, 368, 391.   87 P.R.O., HO 107/1959.
88 Ibid. MAF 68/25/20.   89 Ibid. MAF 68/1609/12.
90 Kelly's Dir. Glos. (1897), 29.
91 P.R.O., MAF 68/3295/16.
92 Kelly's Dir. Glos. (1906), 28.

Courtman, later vicar of Blakeney, kept Wessex saddleback pigs and pedigree poultry at Priory farm (formerly Hamstalls).[93] In 1896 341 a. of orchard were returned in the parish and, though the acreage had fallen by 1926,[94] a number of parishioners specialized in fruit growing and cider making in the early 20th century. A perry pear tree, known as the Blakeney Red, was widely planted, and cider orchards in Bledisloe were acquired before 1927 by Schweppes Ltd.[95]

In the late 1980s dairying remained the principal farming enterprise, with seven specialist dairy farms among the holdings returned in 1988. Several other farms concentrated mainly on cattle and sheep raising, and most also grew wheat and barley. Totals of 2,118 cattle, including 858 cows in milk, 5,329 sheep and lambs, and 373.5 ha. (923 a.) of cereals were returned. Most of the orchards had been grubbed up by 1988, leaving only 14 ha. (35 a.), mainly in the Bledisloe area, where soft fruit was also grown.[96]

MILLS AND IRONWORKS. In the Middle Ages, when the parish was presumably more thickly wooded, ironworking was carried on by some of the small, movable forges then working in the Forest. A movable forge was allowed to operate at Etloe in 1228[97] but was demolished c. 1248 on the orders of the king, who awarded its lessee 10 marks a year in compensation.[98] In 1267, however, he allowed it to be reinstated,[99] and an Etloe man owned a forge in 1282 and another was held by two Blakeney men.[1] The Etloe forge was presumably responsible for the large quantity of cinders that in 1749 was reported to have been dug out of the roadways in the south part of the tithing.[2] A field called Cinders near Northington[3] presumably marked another ancient ironworking site.

By the late 13th century a mill had been built on Blackpool brook above the hamlet of Nibley.[4] It belonged to the Blakeney manor estate[5] and was probably the corn mill that James Barrow rebuilt before 1600.[6] Shortly before 1656 John Barrow built an ironmaking furnace at the site,[7] and before 1692 the Barrows sold the furnace to the ironmaster Paul Foley. Foley (d. 1699) and his son Thomas operated it with partners until 1715. The furnace was not worked later, though the Foley family still owned the site in 1740.[8]

Ruins of the furnace remained at the end of the 18th century.[9] By 1841 a wire mill had been established on the site[10] and it continued to operate until 1856 or later.[11]

Nibley mill, downstream of the furnace site, beside the main road, was presumably the water mill at Nibley with which in 1636 and 1648 members of the Wintle family[12] and in 1701 Richard Chinn were dealing.[13] Edward Chinn owned or occupied Nibley mill in the mid 18th century[14] and William Smith owned it in 1794.[15] In the late 19th century it was worked as a corn mill with a small farm and it apparently went out of use soon after 1906.[16] A 17th-century house, partly timber-framed, and the stone-built mill remained at the site in 1989.

A short way below Nibley mill stood another mill, having a long mill pond extending back alongside the main road as far as the junction with the Blakeney Hill road. It may have been the new-built grist mill at Blakeney offered for sale by James Partridge in 1819 when it was occupied by William Wheeldon.[17] It was in use as a corn mill in the late 19th century.[18] It ceased to work c. 1900[19] and was later converted as a pair of houses. A small, three-storeyed stone building on the east side of Sydenham House in Bridge Street was being worked as a water-powered corn mill by the owner of the house, the shopkeeper Alfred Butler, in 1897 and 1906. The mill, which was presumably supplied by a leat from Blackpool brook, had been converted as a dwelling by 1989.[20]

The lowest of the mills at Blakeney stood at Millend on the south side of the village on a long leat running from near the point where Blackpool and Soudley brooks combine to form Bideford brook.[21] Millend was the site of a mill by 1599[22] and two mills at Blakeney that John Buck held under Awre manor c. 1600 possibly stood there.[23] Those mills were sold by the lord of the manor in 1656, apparently to George Buck, who was then the tenant with his father John.[24] From the mid 18th century mills at Millend were owned with a nearby tannery by the Hayward family, though usually worked by lessees. In 1761 the site included a grist mill, a newly erected bolting mill, and another water wheel which was offered as convenient for a skinner.[25] One part appears to have been used for a while in the cloth industry, for in 1797 William Price held a grist mill and tuck mill

93 Ibid. (1923), 34; (1927), 35.
94 P.R.O., MAF 68/1609/12; MAF 68/3295/16.
95 *Kelly's Dir. Glos.* (1927), 51; (1931), 48; H. Phelps, *Forest of Dean* (1982), 50–1.
96 Agric. Returns 1988.
97 *Close R.* 1227–31, 74; 1237–42, 314, 385.
98 *Cal. Inq. Misc.* i, p. 104.
99 P.R.O., E 32/29, rot. 1.
1 Ibid. E 32/30, rot. 23d.
2 Glos. R.O., D 3270/19718.
3 G.D.R., T 1/12 (no. 499).
4 *Trans. B.G.A.S.* xiv. 361. All but a small part of the site of the mill and the later furnace were outside the par. boundary in the extraparochial Forest: O.S. Map 1/2,500, Glos. XXXIX. 12 (1881 edn.); Glos. R.O., P 30/OV 2/1, rate 1718.
5 *Cal. Inq. p.m.* iii, p. 2; *Cal. Pat.* 1327–30, 553; P.R.O., CP 25/2/299/22 Jas. I East. no. 17.
6 Glos. R.O., D 2026/X 7.   7 Ibid. X 14.
8 Glos. R.O., D 1833/T 13; *Trans. B.G.A.S.* lxxii.

134–6.   9 Hart, *Ind. Hist. of Dean*, 74.
10 Glos. R.O., Q/FR 4/1, f. 65; cf. P.R.O., HO 107/364, s.v. Danby walk.
11 P.R.O., F 16/63 (no. 3681); F 16/70.
12 Ibid. CP 25/2/422/12 Chas. I East. no. 37; CP 25/2/423/24 Chas. I Mich. no. 24.
13 Ibid. CP 25/2/834/13 Wm. III Mich. no. 6.
14 Glos. R.O., P 30/OV 2/1, rates 1738, 1760.
15 Hockaday Abs. cix.
16 *Kelly's Dir. Glos.* (1885 and later edns.), s.v. Blakeney.
17 *Glouc. Jnl.* 19 Apr. 1819.
18 O.S. Map 1/2,500, Glos. XXXIX. 12 (1881 edn.).
19 Hart, *Ind. Hist. of Dean*, 373.
20 Phelps, *Forest in Old Photog.* (1984), 10; *Kelly's Dir. Glos.* (1897), 44; (1906), 44.
21 O.S. Map 1/2,500, Glos. XXXIX. 12 (1881 edn.).
22 Glos. R.O., D 421/M 7.
23 Ibid. E 13; cf. D 2026/X 7.   24 Ibid. D 3270/R 10.
25 *Glouc. Jnl.* 22 Sept. 1761; cf. Glos. R.O., D 3270/19718, cts. 1757, 1760.

under the Haywards. Another part was then occupied by the owners,[26] presumably the bark mill that was worked with their tannery in 1806.[27] The corn mill at Millend was offered for sale by the Haywards in 1813.[28] By 1830 Millend mill belonged to Richard White,[29] and Stephen Adolphus White was working it in 1889.[30] It had gone out of use by 1901,[31] and the small stone mill was occupied as two dwellings in 1989.

A steam-powered corn mill at Blakeney was also held by the White family in the 19th century and may have been near the Millend water mill.[32] Daniel White owned the steam mill in 1830,[33] and in 1856 the miller was Richard White, who was also a maltster and farmer.[34] During the 1870s Stephen Adolphus White, who was then said to have an extensive business as a corn merchant, worked the steam mill.[35]

There was a mill on Awre manor in 1086,[36] possibly the one recorded from 1278 on the estate of the Awre family,[37] an offshoot of the manor. The Awres' mill was apparently that on Bideford brook just west of Hall Farm. Known as Hall Mill by 1639[38] it was in the same ownership as Hall Farm until 1731 when Thomas Blackall sold it to Francis Spring. Spring worked it as a corn mill in the mid 18th century,[39] and his family remained owners until 1834[40] but let the mill from the 1770s.[41] By 1816 it had been converted as a paper mill and was worked by Joseph Lloyd. Thomas Newel was making paper there in 1832 and Benjamin Small of Mitcheldean in 1834, but by 1839 it had been converted back to a corn mill.[42] It remained in use until 1879[43] or later. Some ruins of the mill survived in 1989.

At Gatcombe a works making blacksmiths' anvils was operated by the Foleys and their partners between 1695 and 1705 and was converted as a corn mill c. 1710;[44] no later record of a mill there has been found.

FISHERIES, principally for salmon, provided an additional source of income for the owners and tenants of the manors and farms along the Severn bank. In 1300 John of Box, one of the lords of Box manor, had a fishery at the north end of the parish.[45] That manor probably owned the rights in the stretch of river between the Newnham parish boundary and Hamstalls Pill, which marked the upper limit of the rights held by Awre manor.[46] In 1301 the Mortimers' share

of Awre manor included fisheries at Hamstalls and Woodend,[47] and in the 1320s and 1330s the fisheries were a valuable asset of the manor. In the year 1328–9 a fishery in hand produced 53s. 9¼d., while one at Hamstalls was leased for 13s. 4d., and in 1332–3 the lord received 100s. from his fisheries. The fishermen who worked them under Lord Berkeley also served as manorial bailiffs, and a fish court was held, presumably to deal with poachers.[48] In 1493 the manor fisheries included one called 'Pucherewe', evidently a putcher weir (wickerwork fish traps on a framework of wooden stakes), and a tenant held rights called the gale,[49] the lord's share in cash or kind of the catch of the fishermen.[50] In the 18th century the gale of fishing on Awre manor was usually leased by the lords to a consortium of tenants.[51] The lords of the manor also enjoyed the right to all royal fish,[52] which was exercised in the 1590s and c. 1802 when sturgeon were caught.[53]

In the 18th century and later the main fisheries of Awre tithing were a series of putcher weirs, most of them on the stretch of river between the Hayward and Brimspill. In the same part of the parish the long net, recorded from 1561, was also in regular use.[54] The Baderon family had owned a fishery in 1332 and later,[55] presumably attached to the Hayward estate whose later owners claimed rights.[56] Several weirs belonged to the Hopkinses' Woodend estate in 1747,[57] and in 1851 the right to one in the same area was being disputed by the lords of the manor and a Mr. Cadogan,[58] a member of a family that had been involved in the Awre fisheries since the 1740s or earlier.[59] In 1866 a special commission for fisheries confirmed the right of the lords of the manor to have three ranks of putchers near Brimspill and a single rank nearer to Woodend Lane, and in 1868 the commissioners confirmed a rank belonging to Thomas Cadogan near Woodend Lane and one belonging to the Wait family some way north-east of the lane; together the various weirs contained a total of 977 putchers.[60] The lords of the manor sold their rights to the Cadogans in the 1920s, and members of the family owned and worked the four ranks that were in use in 1989; by that time the traditional wickerwork putchers were being replaced by those made of steel wire. The lave net was also used off Awre in 1989 but the use of the long net there had been given up.[61]

[26] G.D.R. wills 1798/1.   [27] *Glouc. Jnl.* 9 June 1806.
[28] Ibid. 15 Nov. 1813.
[29] Glos. R.O., P 30A/VE 1/1, p. 70; cf. ibid. D 3270/19718, ct. 1829.
[30] *Kelly's Dir. Glos.* (1889), 678.
[31] O.S. Map 1/2,500, Glos. XXXIX. 12 (1903 edn.).
[32] Dan. White lived at Millend in 1830 and S. A. White in 1889: Glos. R.O., P 30A/VE 1/1, pp. 66, 79; *Kelly's Dir. Glos.* (1879), 571.
[33] Glos. R.O., P 30A/VE 1/1, p. 80.
[34] *Kelly's Dir. Glos.* (1856), 224.
[35] Ibid. (1870), 468; (1879), 571.
[36] *Dom. Bk.* (Rec. Com.), i. 163.
[37] *Cal. Inq. p.m.* ii, p. 163; xv, pp. 273–4.
[38] Glos. R.O., P 30/IN 1/1, burials.
[39] Ibid. D 2957/30.5; D 3270/R 114, R 145.
[40] Ibid. D 3270/R 155.
[41] Ibid. P 30/OV 3/4.
[42] *Trans. B.G.A.S.* xciv. 132; Glos. R.O., D 3270/R 148–58.

[43] *Kelly's Dir. Glos.* (1879), 561.
[44] *Trans. B.G.A.S.* lxxii. 140.   [45] Ibid. lxvi. 181.
[46] Cf. *Glouc. Jnl.* 8 Feb. 1808.
[47] *Inq. p.m. Glos. 1236–1300*, 236.
[48] Glos. R.O., D 421/M 4.   [49] Ibid. M 2.
[50] Cf. *Berkeley MSS.* iii. 321.
[51] G.B.R., B 3/9, ff. 411, 437v.; 10, f. 83; Glos. R.O., D 3270/19672, accts. 1764–5, 1781–2, 1799–1800.
[52] Glos. R.O., D 3270/19718, ct. of surv. 1741.
[53] Ibid. D 421/M 1; D 3270/19672, acct. 1802–3.
[54] G.D.R. wills 1561/107; *Glouc. Jnl.* 26 Nov. 1764; 30 May 1803.   [55] *Cal. Inq. p.m.* vii, p. 303; xi, p. 224.
[56] Glos. R.O., D 3269, deeds of Hayward 1660–1794.
[57] Ibid. deeds of land bought from Ric. White.
[58] Ibid. D 3270/19677, pp. 524–7.
[59] G.B.R., B 3/10, f. 83; *Glouc. Jnl.* 30 May 1803.
[60] Glos. R.O., Q/RF.
[61] Inf. from Mr. C. Cadogan, of Awre; cf. Phelps, *Forest in Old Photog.* (1984), 65–8.

In 1547 the gale of fishing between Brimspill and Gatcombe Pill belonged to Poulton manor,[62] and rights in that stretch of river descended with the manor to the Hagloe estate.[63] In 1770 and 1779 James Thomas, lord of Poulton, leased to groups of fishermen the right to use the long net, lave net, stop net, or any other kind of net, reserving the right to royal fish, which he claimed for the manor, and to putcher weirs, which were apparently attached to individual farms. Changes in the river could evidently much affect the size of the catch, and the lease of 1770 provided for the rent to be raised from £5 to £12 if a shift of the channel caused a pool to form below Brimspill.[64] In 1737 a house at Gatcombe belonging to the Oatfield Farm estate, probably the later Sloop inn, had a fishery attached, and ranks of putchers were leased with Poulton Court in 1792.[65] About 1913 the tenant of Poulton Court had c. 600 putchers in the river adjoining the farm.[66] The farmer still operated a rank there in 1989, while at Gatcombe two ranks were worked by the owners of the Court House, who had bought rights from the Hagloe estate c. 1979.[67]

A fishery belonging to Etloe Duchy manor in 1283[68] presumably comprised rights below Gatcombe. The right to use two stop nets (large nets operated from boats held on cables broadside to the tide) was confirmed to the owner of the Duchy manor in 1866; one net was used off Purton and the other between Purton and Gatcombe.[69] From 1878 the rights belonging to Etloe Duchy, together with rights of the Bathurst family to use stop nets in Wellhouse Bay below Purton, in Lydney, were leased by Charles Morse, owner of the Court House at Gatcombe. His descendants, who later bought the rights, worked the fishery from Gatcombe for the next 100 years, and in the 1920s owned 10 stopping boats. The boats, which were built and repaired in outbuildings at the Court House, usually took up their station in Wellhouse Bay, where a building called the fish house provided accommodation for the fishermen during the season. Most of the salmon caught were sent by rail to London. Three boats were kept at Gatcombe by Mrs. Ann Bayliss (née Morse) in 1989 but they had not been used for about three years due to difficulties in getting them repaired and renewing the nets.[70] In 1922 over 70 men from Blakeney and the surrounding area fished with lave nets off Gatcombe, selling their catch to the Morses,[71] and a few men still used lave nets there in 1989.

OTHER INDUSTRY AND TRADE. A salt pan, producing 30 packloads of salt, was recorded among the assets of Awre manor in 1086.[72] The pan, and a salt house mentioned c. 1600,[73] were evidently near the river bank at Woodend, where they were later recalled by the name Salthouse orchard.[74]

Trade on the river Severn employed the men of Awre parish from at least 1282 when two inhabitants were accused of using their boats to carry wood stolen from the Forest to Bristol and elsewhere.[75] In 1354 the profits of Awre rectory included offerings given by merchants voyaging overseas.[76] Goods were landed or loaded at various places on the river bank, including Brimspill and Hamstalls.[77] Eight of 11 sailors listed in the parish in 1608 lived in Awre tithing,[78] suggesting that considerable trade was then carried on from that part of the parish. Possibly there was then a regular landing at Woodend, which erosion of the bank later made difficult to use. Vessels brought limestone to Woodend in the 1820s when there was a limekiln near the end of Woodend Lane,[79] and later in the century and in the early 20th Bristol and Chepstow stone for roadmaking was landed there.[80]

Most of the trade was concentrated on the small hamlet of Gatcombe, where there was a sheltered anchorage for larger vessels, as well as a pill into which smaller boats could be drawn. Much trade entering the Severn came no higher than Gatcombe, the larger vessels preferring not to encounter the dangerous sandbanks further upstream, and for several centuries Gatcombe was one of Gloucester's chief outlets for maritime trade.[81] The hamlet had the status of a creek of the port of Bristol in 1479 when a Gatcombe vessel was trading in fish from Ireland,[82] and custom dues taken at Gatcombe creek were granted to a royal servant in 1485.[83] Gatcombe figured largely in litigation between the cities of Gloucester and Bristol which followed the creation of a new port based on Gloucester in 1580. Differing views were advanced as to its value as a haven, some maintaining that at spring tides ships of up to 80 tons could lie there and others that it could safely be used only by ships of up to 40 tons, but its importance to Gloucester was made clear. Trade with Ireland in fish and other commodities was carried on, as well as some trade with the Continent. In the early 1580s a customs officer, based at Newnham by the officials of the new port, attended regularly at Gatcombe to search vessels.[84]

A reference to a mariner of Gatcombe who died in 1669[85] is one of the few records found of the hamlet's role in the river trade in the 17th century. At the beginning of the 18th century iron from Blakeney furnace was shipped there

62 P.R.O., SC 12/2/46, ff. 126v., 131.
63 Glos. R.O., D 608/13/13.
64 P.R.O., CRES 38/614.   65 Ibid. CRES 38/613–14.
66 A. O. Cooke, *Forest of Dean* (1913), 199–200.
67 Inf. from Mrs. A. Bayliss, of the Court Ho.
68 *Cal. Inq. p.m.* ii, p. 288.   69 Glos. R.O., Q/RF.
70 Inf. from Mrs. Bayliss; cf. B. Waters, *Severn Tide* (1955), 124–6; Phelps, *Forest in Old Photog.* (1984), 69–71.
71 Notebook, in possession of Mrs. Bayliss.
72 *Dom. Bk.* (Rec. Com.), i. 163.
73 Glos. R.O., D 421/E 13.   74 Ibid. D 3270/R 106.
75 P.R.O., E 32/30, rott. 2, 4.
76 Ibid. C 115/K 1/6681, f. 207.

77 Glos. Colln., list of landing places in port of Glouc. c. 1790; Glos. R.O., D 1559, diary transcript, entries for 18 June, 2 July 1783.   78 Smith, *Men and Armour*, 55–7.
79 Bryant, *Map of Glos.* (1824).
80 Glos. R.O., DA 1/100/6, mins. 15 Oct. 1863; 20 Dec. 1866; 7, min. 16 May 1889; 9, min. 16 Jan. 1908.
81 Cf. *V.C.H. Glos.* iv. 43, 126, 128.
82 P.R.O., E 122/19/14, f. 25.
83 *Cal. Pat.* 1485–94, 58; cf. ibid. 271.
84 P.R.O., E 134/25 Eliz. I Hil./3; East./14; G.B.R., B 2/1, ff. 90v., 91v., 94v.
85 G.D.R. wills 1669/158; cf. Glos. R.O., P 30/IN 1/1, burials 1669.

for Bristol and for the Midlands.[86] Goods for Gloucester merchants and tradesmen continued to pass through Gatcombe throughout the 18th century with trade in copper and maltsters' coal from the South Wales ports becoming particularly important.[87] At the end of the century a Birmingham copper company used Gatcombe as a transit point, establishing a warehouse there.[88] One or two Gatcombe vessels were involved in the regular trade carried on between the Severn and Ireland, chiefly in oak bark and cider. In the 1760s and 1770s James Thomas of Oatfield Farm traded with South Wales and Ireland, his boats including the *Susanna* and the *John Birkin* named after his wife and son;[89] J. B. Thomas was dealing in bark, probably for the Irish trade, in 1789.[90] In the early and mid 18th century several generations of the Cupitt family were mariners and merchants at Gatcombe,[91] and in the late 18th and early 19th the Barretts, including Richard Barrett, owner of two sloops which were lost in a gale in 1775, were among mariners there.[92] About 1790 five sloops and a brig were based at the hamlet.[93]

In the late 18th century and the early 19th Gatcombe was a centre of the timber trade. During the Napoleonic Wars it was one of the main shipping points for the oak timber sent from the Forest to the naval dockyards.[94] A navy purveyor living at Blakeney in 1801[95] and a timber haulier of Etloe mentioned in 1809 were among those employed in that trade.[96] At a place called Milking mead, a narrow coombe in the cliffs just upstream from Gatcombe, a timber yard belonged to the Oatfield Farm estate in the early 1790s when there was a wharf and warehouse adjoining;[97] in 1843 a small dwelling there was described as formerly a barkhouse[98] and had presumably been used by the Thomases in the Irish trade. William Ambrose, owner of Oatfield and the Hagloe estate from 1810, traded as a timber merchant[99] and had the yard in hand in the 1830s. Another, larger yard, called Gatcombe timber yard, occupied a field on the west side of the hamlet;[1] a gully in the cliffs enabled the timber to be lowered to the water's edge, where a small stone-built, high-water quay was constructed sometime during the early or mid 19th century.[2] In the early 19th century Gatcombe timber yard was occupied by a Chepstow

timber company, which was succeeded as tenant by William Ambrose; in 1831 he sublet it to the Commissioners of the Navy.[3] There was another yard at the south end of the parish where timber was collected for shipping from Purton.[4] At Milking mead a ruined limekiln survived next to the former timber yard in 1989, recalling another trade once carried on.[5]

Twelve mariners and three watermen, together with a number of mariners' wives, whose husbands were evidently away at sea, were enumerated in the parish in 1851. Most lived in Etloe and Hagloe tithings[6] and were associated with the trade at Gatcombe, which was enjoying its final period of activity. The South Wales railway line, then under construction along the foreshore, obstructed access to the timber yards and cut off the mouth of the pill with a low viaduct. A few mariners and pilots still lived in Awre parish in the later 19th century and the early 20th,[7] some probably employed in vessels using the nearby Lydney and Bullo Pill harbours.

Shipbuilding was established in the parish by 1608 when shipwrights were living in Blakeney and Hagloe and a ship carpenter in Etloe;[8] a shipwright of Blakeney was mentioned in 1662.[9] All were perhaps employed at Gatcombe, where several vessels were built in the mid 17th century.[10] In 1787 J. B. Thomas and a partner owned a shipbuilding yard, probably at Milking mead, and launched a brig of over 300 tons.[11] In 1804 when Thomas offered the yard for letting he claimed that vesels of over 600 tons had been built there.[12] Snows of 198 and 129 tons built in 1803 and 1834 respectively were probably more typical of the vessels built at Gatcombe. The latter boat was built by James and Thomas Shaw,[13] who in 1839 occupied a building below Gatcombe timber yard, close to the site of the quay mentioned above.[14] Members of the Shaw family were still boatbuilders in the parish in the 1850s,[15] though the railway line presumably prevented the building of all but very small craft at Gatcombe. In 1851 there was also a boatyard at Hamstalls, where a shipwright Charles Cooper was employing 18 workers;[16] it apparently closed soon afterwards.

Apart from that connected with the river, the trade and industry of Awre parish was concentrated on Blakeney village, where the streams provided water for mills (described above) and

86 *Trans. B.G.A.S.* lxxii. 135.
87 *Glouc. Jnl.* 2 Apr. 1775; 26 June 1775; cf. P.R.O., E 190/1267/14; 1268/10; 1269/5.
88 *Glouc. Jnl.* 12 Oct. 1801; 18 May 1818.
89 P.R.O., E 190/1263/1, 9, 11; 1265/7; 1269/7, 9; *Glouc. Jnl.* 7 Nov. 1763; 26 June 1775; for the Thomases, cf. above, manors (Hagloe).   90 Glos. R.O., D 421/E 34.
91 P.R.O., E 190/1263/1, 9, 11; G.D.R. wills 1723/76; 1761/52; 1771/54.
92 *Glouc. Jnl.* 6 Feb., 7 Aug. 1775; tombstone to Jas. Barrett (d. 1844) in Glouc. city cemetery (moved from St. Luke's ch., Glouc.).
93 Glos. Colln., list of landing places in port of Glouc. c. 1790.
94 *Glouc. Jnl.* 1 Aug. 1785; 29 May 1797; 25 Aug. 1806; Dean Forest Roads Act, 36 Geo. III, c. 131.
95 Farr, *Chepstow Ships*, 65.
96 *Glouc. Jnl.* 18 Sept. 1809.
97 P.R.O., CRES 38/611, est. terrier 1792; CRES 38/616, deed 1795; cf. G.D.R., T 1/12.

98 Glos. R.O., D 608/13/13.
99 Ibid. D 637/I/71; Farr, *Chepstow Ships*, 130.
1 G.D.R., T 1/12; Glos. R.O., P 30A/VE 1/1, pp. 41, 91.
2 Cf. O.S. Map 1/2,500, Glos. XXXIX. 16 (1880 edn.); it survived in 1989 on the river side of the railway embankment.   3 Glos. R.O., D 4371/1.
4 G.D.R., T 1/12; cf. below, Lydney, econ. hist. (other ind. and trade).
5 Cf. O.S. Map 1/2,500, Glos. XXXIX. 16 (1880 edn.).
6 P.R.O., HO 107/1959.
7 *Kelly's Dir. Glos.* (1856 and later edns.).
8 Smith, *Men and Armour*, 56–7.
9 Glos. R.O., D 22/T 1.
10 Ibid. D 2026/X 14, s.v. ports upon Severn.
11 *Glouc. Jnl.* 24 Dec. 1787; cf. Bigland, *Glos.* i. 102.
12 *Glouc. Jnl.* 28 May 1804.
13 Farr, *Chepstow Ships*, 76, 141.
14 G.D.R., T 1/12.
15 P.R.O, HO 107/1959; *Kelly's Dir. Glos.* (1856), 224.
16 P.R.O., HO 107/1959.

tanneries and the main Gloucester–Chepstow road stimulated commerce. By the beginning of the 18th century — on what authority is not known — fairs were held at Blakeney on May Day and All Saints[17] (altered in 1752 to 12 May and 12 November). In the mid 18th century,[18] and until they lapsed in the early 20th, they dealt principally in livestock.[19]

Blakeney's role as a centre for crafts and trade had apparently begun by the 1270s and early 1280s when there was a smith, a weaver, and a baker in Blakeney tithing and a baker and butchers in Etloe tithing,[20] in which the south part of the village lay. In 1608 32 tradesmen were listed in Blakeney and Etloe tithings, compared to only 9 in the other parts of the parish. Apart from the usual village craftsmen, the tradesmen in Blakeney and Etloe included 2 grindstone hewers, possibly working in quarries on Blakeney hill in the adjoining extraparochial Forest, 5 nailers, 4 weavers, a mercer, and a tanner.[21] Nailmaking may have had a continuous existence at Blakeney until the mid 19th century, though only sporadic references have been found.[22] Weavers were recorded there until the early 18th century[23] and, as mentioned above, later in that century there was probably a fulling mill at Millend.[24] In 1649, at a time when much wood was being taken illegally from the royal demesne woodlands of the Forest, 5 timber dealers and 2 cardboard makers were recorded at Blakeney.[25]

Tanning, an industry associated with the Forest bark trade, was again recorded at Blakeney in 1655, 1682, and 1711.[26] A tanhouse in Etloe tithing, apparently at Millend, belonged to the Barrows of Blakeney manor in 1721. In the 1750s it was occupied by William Swayne, one of a family which owned a tannery at Underhill, in Newnham.[27] By 1763 Thomas Hayward occupied it,[28] and he or another Thomas Hayward died, a prosperous man, in 1797, leaving the business to his son John.[29] John offered the tannery for letting in 1806.[30] Tanning continued at Blakeney until 1865 or later.[31]

The numbers of tradesmen and shopkeepers increased in the early 19th century as Blakeney began to serve the growing Forest settlements on the hillsides above, as well as benefiting from the increase in traffic on the turnpike road. Blakeney acquired some of the features of a small town, though its trades and crafts were generally of a humble character. In 1851 142 tradesmen,

craftsmen, and shopkeepers were enumerated in Blakeney and Etloe tithings, with over 40 different trades represented.[32] A brewery was opened before 1870 and was worked until c. 1915.[33] There was a branch bank by 1897.[34] The village derived little benefit from the mineral railway built through it to the Forest and opened in 1868,[35] but the growth of motor transport in the early 20th century helped to maintain trade and supported a garage by 1927.[36] In 1931 20 shopkeepers and 15 other tradesmen or small businessmen were listed in the village,[37] but in the mid 20th century its role declined, partly as a result of the growth of Lydney as a business and shopping centre. In 1989 business activity in Blakeney was limited to 8 shops, 2 public houses, a restaurant, a garage, and a building firm.

The parts of the parish outside Blakeney village had few rural tradesmen. In the late 19th century and the early 20th Awre village had one or two shopkeepers and a blacksmith, and the rural part of Etloe had one or two craftsmen.[38]

LOCAL GOVERNMENT. In 1276 the lords of Awre manor claimed the right to return of writs, pleas of *vee de naam*, the assize of bread and ale, and gallows.[39] The gallows belonging to the lords, who also held Bledisloe hundred, were presumably at Gallows green in Bledisloe tithing beside the Gloucester–Chepstow road.[40] In 1741 the lords of Awre and Etloe manor also claimed estrays, felons' and fugitives' goods, and wrecks;[41] a wreck was adjudged to belong to the lords in 1727[42] and the dangerous waters off Awre Point made it a franchise that they could often exercise.

View of frankpledge was also claimed, and court rolls for the leet and court baron survive for 1588 and for the years 1594–1600;[43] there are also rolls and full sets of court papers for the years 1688–1881. In the late 17th century joint courts leet and baron were held twice a year but from c. 1700 only one a year was held, with separate courts baron when required for the surrenders and admissions of the customary tenants. The October leet continued until 1881 but the court baron was held only every other year from 1800 until 1864, after which tenures were dealt with at the offices of the Gloucester solicitors who were stewards of the manor.[44] In

17 Atkyns, *Glos.* 238.
18 *Glouc. Jnl.* 31 Oct. 1763; 26 Mar., 2 Apr. 1764.
19 *Kelly's Dir. Glos.* (1879 and later edns.).
20 *Rot. Hund.* (Rec. Com.), i. 182; P.R.O, E 32/29, rott. 4d., 6; E 32/30, rott. 3, 23d.
21 Smith, *Men and Armour*, 55–7; the totals of tradesmen given here exclude the sailors.
22 Glos. R.O., P 30/IN 1/1, burials 1742; P.R.O., HO 107/1959.
23 Glos. R.O., P 30/IN 1/1, burials 1648, 1702; D 3270/R 10.
24 Above (mills and ironworks). Selwyn James of Awre was described as a clothier in 1749 but possibly his business was based in Dursley, from which he had recently moved: Glos. R.O., D 3270/R 39–45.
25 P.R.O., LRRO 5/7A, presentments 1649; depositions 1649, nos. 30–1.
26 Glos. R.O., D 2957/30.40; P 30/IN 1/1, burials 1682, 1711.

27 Ibid. P 30/OV 2/1, rates 1721, 1755–7; cf. ibid. D 2957/215.60–1.   28 Glos. R.O., P 30/OV 2/1, rate.
29 G.D.R. wills 1798/1.
30 *Glouc. Jnl.* 9 June 1806.
31 Glos. R.O., P 30A/VE 1/1, p. 79; *Slater's Dir. Glos.* (1858–9), 204; *Glouc. Jnl.* 2 Dec. 1865.
32 P.R.O., HO 107/1959.
33 *Kelly's Dir. Glos.* (1870), 469; (1879 and later edns.), s.v. Blakeney.
34 Ibid. (1897), 44.   35 Above, intro.
36 *Kelly's Dir. Glos.* (1927), 51.   37 Ibid. (1931), 48.
38 Ibid. (1856–70), s.v. Awre; (1879 and later edns.), s.vv. Awre, Blakeney; for the Awre smithy, Glos. R.O., D 3270/R 106.
39 *Rot. Hund.* (Rec. Com.), i. 176.
40 Glos. R.O., D 3270/19718, Bledisloe man. ct. roll.
41 Ibid. Awre and Etloe ct. of surv. 1741.
42 Ibid. ct. 24 Oct. 1727.   43 Ibid. D 421/M 1, M 7.
44 Ibid. D 3270/19718–19.

the 1670s one of the biannual courts met at Awre and the other at Blakeney but in the 18th century the court usually met at Blakeney.[45] In 1808, however, an inn at Awre, presumably the Red Hart, was described as the accustomed meeting place[46] and the Red Hart was the usual venue later.

In the court two homages made presentments, one for Awre and one for Etloe with the part of Bledisloe that belonged to the manor, but there was one leet jury for the whole manor. The numbers and descriptions of the manorial officers elected in the court varied but in the early 18th century they were usually two constables for Awre and a tithingman each for Awre, Etloe, and Bledisloe. The upkeep of the reens and sea walls of Awre tithing occupied much of the court's time.[47] Such matters were also the responsibility of the Commissioners of Sewers for the Upper Level of the Severn in whose jurisdiction Awre was included. In the early 18th century the commissioners' court employed a surveyor at Awre and made orders for repairs,[48] but in 1712, after distress was taken from some tenants to enforce payment of a rate, local dissatisfaction with the commissioners led the Awre and Etloe court leet to inaugurate its own system for the upkeep of the walls and appoint its own surveyors.[49]

Rolls of the court baron for Bledisloe manor survive for 1620, 1671, 1704, 1743, 1801, 1813, and 1819.[50] There is a roll of 1819 for Poulton manor court, which then claimed leet jurisdiction and elected a constable for Hagloe tithing.[51] A court baron for Etloe Duchy manor was held at the Ship inn (later the Court House) at Gatcombe in 1821.[52]

Early records of parish government surviving are churchwardens' accounts for 1670–1722,[53] overseers' accounts for 1717–75,[54] and vestry minutes from 1770.[55] The parish had two churchwardens, one chosen by the vicar and the other by the vestry, and in the 18th century the one chosen by the vestry had particular responsibility for Blakeney chapel and was sometimes called the chapelwarden.[56] The six tithings each repaired their own roads, appointing separate surveyors,[57] and there were three overseers of the poor, one for Awre, one for Hagloe and Bledisloe, and one for Blakeney and the two Etloe tithings.[58]

In 1683 the church house in Awre village was used as a poorhouse and a pauper was housed in a cottage there owned by the parish. The church house at Blakeney had also been used for the poor but by 1683 the Barrow family, owners of the manor, had appropriated it to their own

use.[59] Measures for poor relief taken by the parish authorities in the later 18th century included employing women at spinning flax,[60] apprenticing pauper children, and paying a subscription to the Gloucester infirmary. A plan made in 1791 to build a workhouse to hold 50 paupers was evidently not implemented. In 1821 measures were taken for more efficient management of the poor, a building was adapted as a workhouse in 1822, and the poor were put out to farm in 1823. The measures reflected a sharp rise in the number of paupers. About 20 adults and some children were receiving regular weekly relief in the 1770s; between the late 1780s and 1810 c. 40 paupers were usually on relief and by the early 1820s the numbers had risen to over 70.[61]

In 1835 the parish was included in the Westbury-on-Severn poor-law union.[62] In 1863 a local board of health was formed for the parish, holding its meetings at Blakeney.[63] The board, which employed one officer as its surveyor and inspector of nuisances, initially a joint appointment with the Westbury and Newnham boards, and another as rate collector, was almost entirely concerned with the upkeep of the roads, even after its assumption of the powers of an urban sanitary authority. It was replaced by an urban district council under the Act of 1894.[64] The urban district, which also did little for the provision or improvement of public services, was abolished in 1935.[65] Apart from the area added to West Dean parish, Awre parish then became part of the East Dean rural district,[66] with which it was included in the Forest of Dean district in 1974.

CHURCHES. Awre had a church, with 1 yardland attached to it, in 1086.[67] Robert son of Hugh, who held Awre manor in the 1140s, granted the church to Monmouth priory, and c. 1150 the gift was confirmed by his overlord Roger, earl of Hereford, and by the diocesan, the bishop of Hereford, who licensed the priory to appropriate the church on the death of the then rector.[68] The grant to Monmouth was possibly nullified on Earl Roger's rebellion or perhaps was never implemented; no later evidence of any connexion with the priory has been found, and in 1226 the church remained a rectory in the gift of the Crown, owner of the manor.[69] In 1278 the earls of Gloucester and Pembroke, owners of portions of the manor, agreed to make alternate presentations. There were then other claimants to the advowson,[70] which was evidently in dispute in the early 14th

45 Ibid. 19672; 19718, cts. 1706, 1744, 1758, 1762.
46 *Glouc. Jnl.* 13 June 1808.
47 Glos. R.O., D 3270/19718.
48 Ibid. D 272/2/2; G.B.R., J 1/1991.
49 Glos. R.O., D 3270/19718.
50 Ibid. D 36/M 2; D 3270/19743, no. 60; P.R.O., CRES 38/612–14.   51 Glos. R.O., D 3270/19743, no. 59.
52 *Glouc. Jnl.* 17 Dec. 1821.
53 *B. & G. Par. Rec.* 55.
54 Glos. R.O., P 30/OV 2/1.
55 Ibid. P 30A/VE 2/1.
56 G.D.R. vol. 285B(3), pp. 1–2; cf. Glos. R.O., P 30A/VE 2/1, mins. 1805 sqq.

57 Glos. R.O., P 30A/VE 2/1, min. 1788.
58 Ibid. P 30/OV 2/1, acct. 1754–5.
59 G.D.R., V 5/30T 2.   60 Glos. R.O., P 30/OV 2/1.
61 Ibid. P 30A/VE 2/1.
62 *Poor Law Com. 2nd Rep.* p. 524.
63 *Kelly's Dir. Glos.* (1889), 665.
64 Glos. R.O., DA 1/100/6–8.
65 Ibid. 1–5, 9; cf. Glos. Colln. RF 30.2.
66 *Census,* 1931 (pt. ii).
67 *Dom. Bk.* (Rec. Com.), i. 163.
68 *Cal. Doc. France,* pp. 410–11.
69 *Cal. Pat.* 1225–32, 60; *Bk. of Fees,* i. 376.
70 P.R.O., CP 25/1/75/31, no. 30; cf. above, manors.

century: the bishop collated to the rectory in 1302 and the rector appointed then had a presentation from the Crown in 1307.[71] Thomas of Berkeley, lord of the manor, presented in 1349,[72] and in 1351 he gave Awre church to Llanthony priory, Gloucester, in exchange for the manor of Coaley, the priory having licence to appropriate the church. A vicarage was ordained in 1354[73] and the living remained a vicarage. An ancient chapel at Blakeney had the status of a perpetual curacy after receiving an endowment in the mid 17th century and became the centre of a separate ecclesiastical district in 1853.[74] In 1952 the livings of Awre and Blakeney were united,[75] and in 1982 they were made a united benefice with Newnham vicarage.[76]

The advowson of Awre vicarage passed with Llanthony priory's rectory estate to the James family and to the Haberdashers' Company.[77] In 1545, however, it was exercised by William Francombe under a grant from Llanthony for one turn,[78] and in 1568 Robert Alfield of Gloucester presented under a grant from Edward Barnard of Flaxley, whose right possibly also derived from a grant by Llanthony.[79] In 1982 the Haberdashers' Company and the bishop of Gloucester were assigned alternate presentations to the united benefice.[80]

Under the ordination of the vicarage in 1354 Llanthony priory retained all the great tithes, a barn and threshing floor, and some mortuaries, while the vicar was awarded the glebe house, glebe lands, small tithes, and other profits.[81] In 1418 a disagreement between the vicar and the priory over the division of the mortuaries was resolved,[82] and in 1479 the vicar and priory secured a confirmation of the original endowment.[83] The mode of tithing the putcher weirs on the river bank was in dispute in 1625: the vicar claimed a tithe of the total catch from each, but the fishermen claimed that by custom he worked the weir on his own account one day in every ten, taking whatever was trapped then.[84] In 1699 the vicar's tithes were mostly taken in kind, with cash payments fixed only for milk, cider, garden produce, and wood.[85] In 1769 the vicar refused to accept the validity of those moduses and established his right to take the tithes in kind.[86] In 1839, when a third portion of them was on lease to the curate of Blakeney, the small tithes were commuted for a total corn rent charge of £450 7s. 2d.[87] In the 17th century the vicar's glebe comprised a few parcels in the common meadows and open fields and some small closes,[88] and following inclosure in 1796 it amounted to 8 a.[89] The vicarage house, east of Northington Lane, was rebuilt as a substantial three-storeyed dwelling in the early 19th century. The vicars of the united benefice lived at Blakeney after 1952 and at Newnham after 1982.[90]

In 1657 the Haberdashers' Company, under a bequest made to it by a Mr. Hammond for purchasing impropriate rectories and augmenting livings, bought the lay rectory of Awre and used the great tithes to augment the vicarage and endow Blakeney chapel. Under the terms of Hammond's bequest the incumbent of any living so augmented was required to hold no other benefice, to be absent from his cure no more than 40 days in a year, and to preach at least once a Sunday.[91] After 1657 the parish was divided into two roughly equal parts for the collection of the great tithes, those from one division being assigned to the vicar and those from the other to the curate of Blakeney. That arrangement, under which vicar and curate shared the cost of maintaining the chancel of the parish church, continued[92] until c. 1780. The Haberdashers then granted a lease of all the tithes to the vicar who was to pay £50 a year to the curate of Blakeney,[93] and before 1839 another arrangement was made by which the vicar held two thirds of the great tithes and the curate one third, while the vicar leased to the curate one third of his small tithes. The great tithes were commuted in 1839 for a total corn rent charge of £400.[94]

In 1291 Awre church was valued at £40.[95] The vicarage was worth £10 4s. 7d. in 1535[96] and £48 in 1650.[97] About 1710 and in 1750 it was worth £100, about half the value being derived from the portion of the great tithes,[98] and in 1856 it was worth £572.[99]

Among early incumbents of Awre, Walter Blund and Henry of Awre, who succeeded Walter in 1226, were from local landowning families.[1] Thomas of Berkeley's steward William of Syde[2] was rector from 1349 until the grant to Llanthony in 1351.[3] John Winston, vicar in the early 1520s, was several times proceeded against by the diocesan authorities for immorality.[4] In 1548 the vicar Anthony Aldwyn had failed to read the homilies or preach quarterly sermons.[5] His curate Philip Huling[6] succeeded to the vicarage in 1553, was deprived in 1554, and was reinstated several years before his death c. 1568.[7]

71 *Reg. Swinfield*, 381; *Cal. Pat.* 1307–13, 12. The advowson was claimed by Marg., widow of Edm. Mortimer, in 1305: *Cal. Close*, 1302–7, 276.
72 *Reg. Trillek*, 375.
73 P.R.O., C 115/K 1/6681, ff. 205–7.
74 Below, this section.
75 *Lond. Gaz.* 22 July 1952, p. 3945.
76 *Glouc. Dioc. Year Bk.* (1981), 30.
77 *Reg. Trillek*, 386; *Reg. Mayew*, 277; Hockaday Abs. cix; cf. above, manors.
78 Hockaday Abs. cix, 1532, 1545.
79 Ibid. 1566, 1568.
80 *Glouc. Dioc. Dir.* (1987), 52.
81 P.R.O., C 115/K 1/6681, f. 207.
82 Ibid. C 115/K 2/6682, f. 106v.
83 *Reg. Myllyng*, 50–2.
84 G.D.R. vol. 148, depositions 22 Feb. 1625.
85 Ibid. V 5/30T 3.   86 *Glouc. Jnl.* 25 Dec. 1769.
87 G.D.R., T 1/12.   88 Ibid. V 5/30T 1, 3.
89 Glos. R.O., D 3270/19743, no. 1.
90 *Glouc. Dioc. Year Bk.* (1952–3), 8; (1981), 79; (1983), 79.
91 Glos. R.O., P 30/IN 1/1, mem. after burials 1704.
92 G.D.R., V 5/30T 3; Glos. R.O., P 30/IN 1/1, mem. after bapt. 1727, 1748; OV 2/1, rates.
93 Bigland, *Glos.* i. 102; cf. Rudge, *Hist. of Glos.* ii. 119.
94 G.D.R., T 1/12.   95 *Tax. Eccl.* (Rec. Com.), 161.
96 *Valor Eccl.* (Rec. Com.), ii. 501.
97 *Trans. B.G.A.S.* lxxxiii. 97.
98 Atkyns, *Glos.* 236; G.D.R. vol. 381A, f. 1.
99 G.D.R. vol. 384, f. 12.
1 *Cal. Pat.* 1225–32, 60; cf. above, manors.
2 *Berkeley MSS.* i. 341.
3 *Reg. Trillek*, 375; P.R.O., C 115/K 1/6681, f. 206.
4 Hockaday Abs. cix.   5 Ibid.
6 *E.H.R.* xix. 121.
7 Hockaday Abs. cix; cf. G.D.R. wills 1561/107.

Huling's successsor John Williams, who failed in many of his duties and by 1576 had let the benefice to farm,[8] later lost possession of the vicarage and was claiming it at the institution of John Street in 1581. Henry James, a relation of the patron, was instituted in 1636[9] and died in 1643 after being imprisoned by parliamentary troops.[10] Jonathan Bird held the living in 1650 and died in 1653.[11] William Marshall was admitted to the living in 1657 and subscribed in 1662, remaining vicar until his death in 1667.[12] The living was later held by two vicars of high church views,[13] James Whiting who served from 1671 to *c.* 1677 when he was drowned at Purton passage, and Charles Chapman who served from 1677 to 1707.[14] Jackman Morse, vicar 1721–65, held the living with Huntley rectory from 1727,[15] in spite of the terms under which the benefice had been augmented. He did, however, remain resident at Awre, as did Charles Sandiford,[16] vicar 1780–1826, who was also curate of Blakeney from 1786, vicar of Tirley from 1788, and archdeacon of Wells from 1815. His successor at Awre, Joseph Malpas,[17] remained vicar for the next 50 years.[18]

In the 18th century and the earlier 19th many parishioners worshipped at both the parish church and Blakeney chapel; in the 1790s most of the owners of farmhouses had pews at both places.[19] In 1750 full Sunday services were held at the parish church with an afternoon service at Blakeney,[20] and in 1825 one service was held at each on Sunday, morning and afternoon alternately. At the latter date Blakeney was said to attract congregations of 400–500, compared to 50–60 at Awre.[21] On the Sunday of the ecclesiastical census in 1851 Blakeney's congregations of 211 in the morning and 231 in the afternoon were more than twice those at Awre.[22] From the 1760s some inhabitants of the adjoining Forest hamlets were married and baptized in the parish, presumably at Blakeney chapel, and were buried at the parish church. It was probably from 1820, when a grant from the Crown aided rebuilding, that some free sittings in Blakeney chapel were appropriated to Forest inhabitants, but in 1835 they were said never to have made use of them.[23]

In the early 18th century there was said to have once been a chapel at Poulton Court.[24] No other record has been found and the supposition may have been suggested by the fact that the rectory was sometimes called the rectory of Awre and Poulton, the vicarage often being similarly designated.[25] That usage, at least for the rectory, may derive only from the existence of rectory tithe barns at both places.[26] There was a chantry dedicated to the Virgin Mary in Awre church by 1339;[27] its lands were sold by the Crown in 1563.[28]

The parish church of *ST. ANDREW*, which bore that dedication by the mid 12th century,[29] is built of coursed rubble and ashlar and comprises chancel, nave with north aisle and south porch, and west tower. The church was rebuilt in the mid 13th century as a large building with a long chancel and a nave and north aisle of six bays. The aisle is a little earlier in style than the chancel.[30] The porch was added in the 14th century and the upper part of the tower was reconstructed in the 15th. Several of the windows were added in the 15th century, though they were much restored in the 19th. The church was restored in 1875 under F. S. Waller at a cost of £2,500, all but £300 of which was provided by Henry Crawshay of Oaklands Park. The work included repewing and refitting and the removal of plaster ceilings from the nave and aisle, where the roofs were reconstructed.[31]

The octagonal font is probably of the early 15th century,[32] and there is a 15th-century oak rood screen, its lower part renewed. A niche which survives over the south door once contained a statue of the Virgin Mary, which attracted offerings in the 1350s.[33] A massive, roughly hewn dugout chest stands under the tower. A ring of six bells was cast for the church by Abraham Rudhall in 1712; the treble was recast by Thomas Rudhall in 1775 and the second and tenor by John Rudhall in 1821.[34] The plate includes a chalice and paten cover of 1576 and a tankard flagon of 1749 which was given to the church in 1827.[35] Much of the floor of the church is still paved with the tombstones of the numerous yeoman families of the parish, and the churchyard has a large and varied collection of carved headstones of the 18th century and the early 19th. The registers survive from 1538.[36]

At Blakeney the chapel of *ALL SAINTS*, so called by 1750 but *c.* 1710 said to be dedicated to SS. Philip and James,[37] was recorded from 1551 when it was a chapel of ease to the parish church.[38] After 1657, when the Haberdashers' Company endowed it with half the great tithes of the parish,[39] it came to be regarded as a

[8] G.D.R. vol. 40, f. 259.
[9] Hockaday Abs. cix; *Visit. Glos. 1682–3*, 98.
[10] Glos. R.O., P 30/IN 1/1, list of vicars.
[11] *Trans. B.G.A.S.* lxxxiii. 97; Glos. R.O., P 30/IN 1/1, burials 1653.
[12] Hockaday Abs. cix; Glos. R.O., P 30/IN 1/1, burials 1667.
[13] *D.N.B.* s.v. Billingsley, Nic.; cf. below, this section.
[14] Hockaday Abs. cix; Glos. R.O., P 30/IN 1/1, list of vicars; ibid. burials 1707.
[15] Hockaday Abs. cix; ccxlviii.
[16] Glos. R.O., P 30/IN 1/1–2; P 30A/VE 2/1.
[17] Hockaday Abs. cix; cxxvii; *Fasti Ecclesiae Anglicanae* (1854), i. 162.
[18] *Morris's Dir. Glos.* (1876), 435; *Kelly's Dir. Glos.* (1885), 357.
[19] Hockaday Abs. cix, 1794; Glos. R.O., P 30A/VE 2/1, min. 1 Sept. 1799.
[20] G.D.R. vol. 381A, f. 1.
[21] Ibid. 383, no. cv.
[22] P.R.O., HO 129/334/1/1/1–2.
[23] Glos. R.O., P 30/IN 1/1; *3rd Rep. Dean Forest Com.* 6, 32.
[24] Bodl. MS. Rawl. B. 323, f. 101.
[25] *Inq. p.m. Glos.* 1625–42, i. 111; Hockaday Abs. cix.
[26] P.R.O., SC 6/Hen. VIII/1224, rot. 20.
[27] *Reg. Bransford*, 183.
[28] *Cal. Pat.* 1560–3, 573.
[29] *Cal. Doc. France*, p. 410; cf. *Cal. Close*, 1302–7, 276.
[30] No architectural evidence remains for work carried out on the chancel on two occasions in the late 14th cent.: P.R.O., C 115/K 2/6684, f. 8v.
[31] *Kelly's Dir. Glos.* (1885), 357; *Morris's Dir. Glos.* (1876), 435.
[32] *Trans. B.G.A.S.* xliv. 188.
[33] P.R.O., C 115/K 1/6681, f. 207.
[34] G.D.R., V 5/30T 4; *Glos. Ch. Bells*, 128.
[35] *Glos. Ch. Plate*, 12.
[36] Glos. R.O., P 30/IN 1/1.
[37] G.D.R. vol. 381A, f. 1; Bodl. MS. Top. Glouc. c. 3, f. 191v.
[38] *E.H.R.* xix. 121.
[39] Some of the details of the chapel's hist. are given above with the account of the par. ch.

perpetual curacy, and curates, often called chaplains, were nominated by the Haberdashers.[40] It was not, however, assigned a particular area to serve and was used by inhabitants of the whole parish. The chapel was being used for marriages by the 1680s and for baptisms by 1708 but did not keep separate registers until 1813;[41] a burial ground was provided in 1892.[42] The living was worth £60 a year in 1750, most of the income being supplied by the portion of the great tithes.[43] In 1856 it was worth £250.[44] In 1853 the chapel was assigned a separate ecclesiastical district, comprising the southern half of the parish,[45] and the living, later styled a vicarage, continued in the gift of the Haberdashers.[46] There was no glebe house until 1951. Moira House, north-east of the chapel, was then acquired,[47] and it served as the residence of the vicars of the united benefice of Awre and Blakeney from 1952 to 1982.

The curate of Blakeney from 1667 was Nicholas Billingsley,[48] who had been deprived of the living of Weobley (Herefs.) in 1662. His continuing lack of conformity attracted the hostility of two successive vicars of Awre and of the diocesan bishop, Robert Frampton, and he was suspended before 1690. He later declined the offer of Bishop Edward Fowler to reinstate him and ministered to nonconformists at Blakeney and elsewhere in the county.[49] From 1693 to 1727 the curate was Richard Mantle[50] who was also rector of English Bicknor from 1710,[51] and from 1744 Roynon Jones, of the family which owned the Nass estate, in Lydney, was curate.[52]

In the early 18th century Blakeney chapel was a small single-cell building with a gallery.[53] It was enlarged in 1748 when the nave was lengthened and a new aisle and chancel were added; the cost was met by subscription.[54] In 1799 the gallery was rebuilt and a new one added.[55] In 1820 the chapel was rebuilt to the designs of Samuel Hewlett as a plain single-cell building with a small west tower, a low south porch, and large galleries. The new building was planned to seat 700 and about a third of the cost was met by the Crown[56] because it was intended to serve inhabitants of the adjoining part of the Forest. Some internal refitting was carried out in 1880,[57] and in 1906–7 the chapel was restored and a small eastern apse added to the designs of Prothero and Phillott of Cheltenham.[58] The

bowl of the font is a 15th-century water stoup, discovered near Gatcombe during building of the South Wales railway.[59] The single bell was cast by Abraham Rudhall in 1719.[60] The plate includes a chalice of 1669, given to the chapel in 1766.[61]

NONCONFORMITY. Nonconformity at Blakeney apparently originated with Nicholas Billingsley who was suspended as curate of the Anglican chapel shortly before 1690.[62] A group led by him registered a house for dissenting worship in the village in 1691 and other houses there were registered the same year.[63] In 1697 Billingsley performed the marriage of his son Richard, described as a meeting teacher, in the meeting house.[64] The meeting at Blakeney, styled Presbyterian, had 100 members c. 1715, and its minister David Thomas[65] registered his house there for worship in 1727.[66] In 1735 the meeting was supported by funds from London; the congregation was then described as very small[67] and it numbered only 12 in 1750.[68] In 1773 the meeting was described as Presbyterian or Congregationalist[69] and it was presumably represented later by the Congregationalist or Independent cause at Blakeney.

A group associated with William Bishop, minister of the Independent meeting at Gloucester, registered a house at Blakeney in 1795. A prominent member was Richard Stiff,[70] who had come to the village in 1783 and was active in preaching to nonconformists there and in the adjoining part of the extraparochial Forest until his death in 1816.[71] In 1823 a small chapel called Blakeney Tabernacle was built by the Revd. Isaac Bridgman just inside the parish boundary at Brain's Green beside the road to Ayleford. Bridgman was a former curate at Holy Trinity church, Harrow Hill, in the Forest, who had found difficulty in confining his views to established church doctrine.[72] Anglican liturgy was at first used for the services, but in 1825 the congregation joined the Independents. Bridgman, who remained minister until c. 1828,[73] also registered a house in Etloe in 1827.[74] In 1849 the congregation left the Brain's Green chapel for a new one, also called the Tabernacle, built in Blakeney village on the Ayleford road.[75] In 1851 the new chapel, then styled Independent but later Con-

---

40 Glos. R.O., P 30/IN 1/1, mem. after bapt. 1721; Hockaday Abs. cxxvii; G.D.R. vol. 384, f. 24.
41 Glos. R.O., P 30/IN 1/1; P 50/IN 1/1.
42 Ibid. P 50/IN 1/7.
43 G.D.R. vol. 381A, f. 1; cf. Atkyns, Glos. 238.
44 G.D.R. vol. 384, f. 24.
45 Lond. Gaz. 26 Aug. 1853, p. 2360.
46 Kelly's Dir. Glos. (1870), 468; (1885), 369.
47 Glos. R.O., P 50/IN 3/9.
48 Hockaday Abs. cix.
49 D.N.B.; G.D.R. vols. 227; 233; 251, f. 44v.; Life of Rob. Frampton, ed. T. Simpson Evans (1876), 175–7, where he is named as Benjamin.
50 Hockaday Abs. cix; Glos. R.O., P 30/IN 1/1, mem. after bapt. 1721.   51 Hockaday Abs. cxxii.
52 Glos. R.O., P 30/IN 1/1, mem. after bapt. 1743.
53 Atkyns, Glos. 238.   54 Bigland, Glos. i. 102.
55 Glos. R.O., P 30A/VE 2/1.
56 Ibid. mins. 15 July 1819; 3 Jan. 1820; cf. ibid. P 50/CW 3/1; P.R.O., HO 129/334/1/1/2.

57 Glos. R.O., P 50/CW 3/1.   58 Ibid. CW 3/4–7.
59 Trans. B.G.A.S. xlix. 144–5, 162–3.
60 Glos. Ch. Bells, 151.
61 Glos. Ch. Plate, 24–5.   62 Above, churches.
63 Glos. R.O., Q/SO 3 (list at end).
64 Ibid. P 30/IN 1/1.   65 Ibid. D 2052, s.v.1717.
66 Hockaday Abs. cix.
67 G.D.R. vol. 285B(1), f. 4.   68 Ibid. 381A, f. 1.
69 Trans. Cong. Hist. Soc. v. 217.
70 Hockaday Abs. cix, 1793; cxxvii, 1795; cf. V.C.H. Glos. iv. 324.
71 J. Stratford, Good and Great Men of Glos. (1867), 411; Glouc. Jnl. 9 Dec. 1816.
72 Stratford, Good and Great Men, 411–12; Glouc. Jnl. 25 Aug. 1823.
73 Bright, Nonconf. in Dean, 18.
74 Hockaday Abs. cix.
75 Glos. R.O., NC 14; below, Plate 16. The Brain's Green chap. was later converted to a dwelling, which it remained in 1989.

gregational, had average congregations of 265 in the morning and 205 in the evening.[76] In 1972, when it became part of the new United Reformed Church, the church at Blakeney had 20 members and two lay preachers under a settled minister who also served chapels in nearby parishes.[77] The chapel closed in 1988.[78]

From 1818 a group of Baptists met at Blakeney under the leadership of John Watkins of Lydney. The group was attached to the Baptist church at Coleford until 1821 when it became a separate church. In 1833, when the membership was c. 37,[79] a chapel was built on the south side of the main street.[80] In 1851 it had average congregations of 250 in the morning and 170 in the evening.[81] The chapel was restored in 1874.[82] In 1989 the Baptist church had c. 25 members under a minister. Shared services were then held with the congregation of Blakeney's Anglican church on two Sunday afternoons each month.[83]

A small group of Wesleyan Methodists met in a room at Blakeney from 1817, and c. 1832, when there were c. 9 members, it was served by travelling preachers or by the ministers of local chapels.[84] No later record of Wesleyans at Blakeney has been found.

EDUCATION. Two schoolmasters were teaching at Blakeney in 1572 but one had failed to obtain a licence from the diocesan authorities and the other was declared contumacious and suspended by them.[85] Another schoolmaster was teaching in the parish in 1605[86] and two were recorded in 1623, one at Blakeney.[87] Nicholas Billingsley, curate of Blakeney, was teaching a school in 1682,[88] and the same year another man was licensed to teach a private school in the parish.[89] Some of the masters recorded at Blakeney evidently held their school in the church house which in 1683 was said to have been used for that purpose from time immemorial.[90] William Brown, described as a baker and schoolmaster, died in 1750.[91] In 1818 the only school for the poor recorded in the parish was a Sunday school attended by 120 children.[92]

By 1833 there were two National schools in the parish, said to have been started in 1830; they were supported by subscriptions and pence and taught a total of 133 children. One was evidently at Blakeney[93] and the other in Awre village. Awre National school was provided with a new building in 1855, built on part of the green at the junction of the main village street and Northington Lane; the site was given by the lords of the manor, the Gloucester charity trustees,[94] who in 1856 agreed to give £10 a year towards running the school.[95] In 1874 the income was mainly from voluntary contributions, a shortfall being made up by the vicar.[96] The school had an average attendance in 1885 of only 36,[97] and in 1910, as Awre C. of E. school, of only 34. The average attendance was down to 24 by 1922 and the school closed in 1927.[98]

Blakeney National school was evidently one of the schools said to have opened in 1830, though it was later said to have been built in 1827 and enlarged in 1831,[99] in which year the building, north of Blakeney chapel at the entrance to Lowfield Lane, was secured by a trust deed.[1] It was again recorded in 1856,[2] and in 1872 it was teaching c. 90 children and was supported mainly by voluntary contributions and pence.[3] In 1873 the old building was replaced by a new school, built beside the main Gloucester road above the village on a piece of rectory glebe land leased by the Haberdashers' Company to the vicar of Blakeney. In 1885 it had an average attendance of 80,[4] and in 1910, as Blakeney C. of E. school, it had accommodation for 176 and an average attendance of 98 in mixed and infants' departments. The average attendance fell to 51 by 1922 and to 32 by 1932, and the school was closed in 1935.[5] The building was a private house in 1989.

By 1852 there was also a British school at Blakeney[6] but it was apparently re-established and placed under a new management committee in 1865. In 1865 it had an attendance of 60 and was supported mainly by pence, the children paying 2d., 3d., or 4d. a week depending on the number of subjects they studied.[7] The school, on the south side of Bridge Street near the west end of the village, was rebuilt in 1873. In 1885 the average attendance was 70[8] and in 1904 it had an average attendance of 129 in mixed and infants' departments.[9] The school was renamed Blakeney Council school in 1905 when it was transferred to the county council, and the building was enlarged during 1907 and 1908 to accommodate the children from Blakeney Woodside C. of E. school, at Blakeney Hill.[10] The average attendance was 197 in 1910[11] and rose to 250 by 1922. The school was enlarged to accommodate 380 before 1932 but in 1938 the average attendance was 232.[12] In 1989, as Blakeney County Primary school, it had 101 children on its roll.[13]

76 P.R.O., HO 129/334/1/1/4.
77 Cong. Year Bk. (1972), 94.
78 Inf. from Mrs. R. Peaty, sec., Blakeney Bapt. ch.
79 Bright, Nonconf. in Dean, 26–8.
80 Glouc. Jnl. 22 June 1833.
81 P.R.O., HO 129/334/1/1/3.   82 Inscr. on chap.
83 Inf. from Mrs. Peaty.   84 Bright, Nonconf. in Dean, 33.
85 Hockaday Abs. xliv, 1572 visit. ff. 3–4.
86 G.D.R. vol. 97, f. 222v.   87 Ibid. vol. 152.
88 Ibid. vol. 243, p. 221.
89 Hockaday Abs. cix.   90 G.D.R., V 5/30T 2.
91 Glos. R.O., P 30/OV 2/1, note after acct. 1749–50.
92 Educ. of Poor Digest, 290.
93 Educ. Enq. Abstract, 302; cf. below, this section.
94 P.R.O., ED 7/34/21; Glos. R.O., D 3270/19678, p. 200.   95 Glos. R.O., D 3270/19678, p. 441.
96 P.R.O., ED 7/34/21.

97 Kelly's Dir. Glos. (1885), 357.
98 Bd. of Educ., List 21, 1911 (H.M.S.O.), 158; 1922, 102; 1932, 112.   99 P.R.O., ED 7/34/23.
1 Glos. R.O., D 3469/5/10.
2 Kelly's Dir. Glos. (1856), 223.
3 P.R.O., ED 7/34/23.
4 Glos. R.O., P 50/SC 2; Kelly's Dir. Glos. (1885), 369.
5 Bd. of Educ., List 21, 1911 (H.M.S.O.), 158; 1922, 102; 1932, 112; 1936, 118.
6 Glouc. Jnl. 31 Jan. 1852; Kelly's Dir. Glos. (1856), 223.
7 P.R.O., ED 7/34/22.
8 Kelly's Dir. Glos. (1885), 369.
9 Public Elem. Schs. 1906, 181.
10 Glos. R.O., CE/M 2/3, p. 224; 5, p. 95; 6, p. 23.
11 Bd. of Educ., List 21, 1911 (H.M.S.O.), 158.
12 Ibid. 1922, 102; 1932, 112; 1938, 125.
13 Educ. Services Dir. 1989–90 (co. educ. dept.), 4.

CHARITIES FOR THE POOR. Richard Hart of Gurshill, Lydney, by will dated 1665 gave £15 to the poor of Awre parish.[14] The principal with other funds was used in 1707 to buy back the church house at Blakeney, which had been taken from the parish. Later the rent of the house, which was £4 14s. 6d. c. 1780, was distributed to the poor.[15] After the house was demolished in 1819 £5 was paid out of the church rates instead. About 1825 it was intended to replace the £15 principal[16] but the charity had been lost by 1865.[17]

James Stokes by will dated 1745 gave three bushels of wheat, to be delivered at Blakeney chapel by the tenant of Little Box farm and distributed among the poor of Blakeney and Etloe tithings.[18] In 1913 the Crown as owner of the farm gave £30 stock to replace the bequest.[19] Thomas Terret by will of 1771 gave £10, the interest to be distributed to the poor of the same two tithings,[20] and Matthew A Deane of Etloe House by will dated 1791 gave £20, the proceeds to be distributed in bread at Blakeney chapel among the poor of Blakeney, Etloe, and Etloe Duchy tithings.[21] The sums given by Terret and A Deane were lent out together on security[22] and had been lost by 1865.[23]

In 1825 the vicar Charles Sandiford bought the Bird in Hand inn, at Blakeney, for £280 and settled it on trustees; they were to use the rent, initially £18 a year, to maintain the church clock, pay the clerk £3 a year for winding it, and buy flannel and blankets for the poor. The inn was sold c. 1863 and the proceeds, apparently c. £400, were invested in stock.[24] John Blanch of Etloe House by will dated 1824 left £100, the proceeds to be distributed among the poor.[25] A Scheme of 1918 amalgamated the eleemosynary part of the Sandiford charity with the Blanch charity, authorizing a distribution in flannel and blankets or sums of up to £2 10s. to meet particular cases of need.[26]

Harriet Barber by will proved 1883 left £1,000 for the poor. Frederick Barber by will proved 1887 gave £50, the income to be distributed in bread.[27] Mrs. E. B. Wait in 1902 left £150, the income to be distributed in sheets, flannel, and serge petticoats to the poor of Awre, excluding inhabitants of Blakeney ecclesiastical parish;[28] the charity was apparently implemented but lapsed some time after 1919.[29] Mary Teesdale by will proved 1924 left a sum for the poor of Blakeney,[30] and Edward Bennett by will proved 1946 left a bequest, represented in 1948 by £700 stock, the income to be used to pay 10s. each to 30 aged inhabitants of Blakeney ecclesiastical parish.[31]

A Scheme of 1972 formed the Stokes, Teesdale, and Bennett charities into the Blakeney United Charities for the relief of old people of Blakeney ecclesiastical parish in cash or kind. A Scheme of 1974 amalgamated the eleemosynary Sandiford charity and the Blanch, Frederick Barber, and Harriet Barber charities and applied the income to the relief of cases of need in the whole of the ancient parish.[32]

LYDNEY

THE LARGE parish of Lydney[33] lay 21 km. southwest of Gloucester on the west bank of the river Severn. It contained the small town of Lydney with an adjoining village called Newerne, the village of Aylburton, and scattered farmsteads in the tithings of Purton, Nass, and Allaston. Aylburton developed separate institutions of parish government and assumed the status of a civil parish in the late 19th century, while remaining a chapelry of Lydney.

Although Lydney had a market from 1268 and some inhabitants later held by burgage tenure, the town remained small and insignificant for much of its history. The parish was dominated by its landowners, particularly after the late 16th century when most of the land was formed into a large estate by the Winters, who were succeeded in possession by the Bathursts in 1723. The estate was unusually rich in non-agricultural resources, including fisheries, mineral deposits, and extensive woodland, and its owners also profited from the establishment of ironworks at the start of the 17th century and the reclamation of saltmarsh in the early 18th. In the early 19th century the building of a tramroad and harbour to serve the coal trade of the Forest of Dean began to transform Lydney's economy, which later benefited from the growth of the ironworks into a tinplate factory and from railway building. In the mid 20th century the town's success in attracting new industry made it one of the main centres of employment for the Forest region, and by 1990 it had been much enlarged by suburbs.

The ancient parish covered 7,077 a. (2,864 ha.), with Aylburton later forming a separate parish of 1,883 a. (762 ha.).[34] In 1935 29 a. (12 ha.), near New Mills in the angle formed by the Newerne stream and a tributary brook, were added to Lydney from West Dean.[35] The whole parish lay within the jurisdiction of the Forest of Dean by 1228, but it was disafforested in the

14 G.D.R. wills 1666/107.   15 Bigland, Glos. i. 102.
16 19th Rep. Com. Char. 84.
17 Glos. N. & Q. vii. 23.
18 19th Rep. Com. Char. 84–5.
19 Glos. R.O., D 3469/5/10.
20 19th Rep. Com. Char. 85.
21 P.R.O., PROB 11/1207 (P.C.C. 368 Bevor), f. 328v.
22 19th Rep. Com. Char. 85.
23 Glos. N. & Q. vii. 23.
24 Glos. R. O., P 30/CH 3/1; D 177, Char. Com. authori-

zation for sale 1863; 19th Rep. Com. Char. 85.
25 Glos. R.O., D 3270/R 55.
26 Ibid. D 3469/5/10.   27 Ibid.
28 Ibid. P 30/CH 4/1; cf. Kelly's Dir. Glos. (1906), 44.
29 Glos. R.O., P 50/CH 1.
30 Ibid. D 3469/5/10, Scheme 1972.
31 Ibid. Scheme 1948.   32 Ibid. Schemes.
33 This account was written in 1990.   34 Census, 1931.
35 Ibid. (pt. ii); cf. O.S. Map 6", Glos. XLVII. NW. (1883 edn.).

early 14th century.[36] As a result, a number of its woods were termed purlieus in the 16th century,[37] a name retained by one large wood, the later Purlieu common in Purton. Former parts of the royal demesne woodland adjoining the parish, the Snead (later called Maple Hill) and Kidnalls, covering *c.* 280 a. on the east side of the valley of the Newerne stream, are included in this account. The two woods were granted on lease by the Crown in 1626,[38] and the reversion was included in a grant of the bulk of the royal Forest land to Sir John Winter in 1640.[39] He retained it when he surrendered his other rights under the grant in 1662,[40] and the Snead and Kidnalls descended as part of his Lydney estate and were regarded as outside the Forest bounds. They remained extraparochial until 1842 when they were included in the new township of West Dean.[41]

The long north boundary, between the ancient Lydney parish and what were formerly parts of Newland and the extraparochial Forest, follows an irregular course across the hillsides. At its west end above Alvington parish it includes the former Prior's Mesne estate, which was assarted from the royal demesne of the Forest in 1306 by Llanthony priory.[42] The priory owned both Aylburton and Alvington manors, which left the boundary between them a matter of dispute after the Dissolution. Prior's Mesne was claimed by the lords of both manors in the 1580s[43] and was later secured by the lord of Aylburton. About 1710 the owners of the two manors were disputing common land lying south of Prior's Mesne (at the later Glebe farm) and it was claimed on the part of the owner of Aylburton that the boundary at that point was Woodwards brook running west and south of the disputed land;[44] in that dispute the owner of Alvington evidently established his claim, for the land was later part of Alvington common, with the parish boundary north and east of it, joining the brook at the south side of Ferneyley wood.[45] A feature described as the Forest ditch or the great old ditch defined the boundary between Prior's Mesne and the land in Alvington common *c.* 1710. It was no longer discernible in 1990 but on part of the boundary, south of the house called Aylburton Lodge, there was a drystone wall of massive dimensions, apparently part of a longer wall built following the dispute.[46]

The south-west boundary descends Woodwards brook into the riverside meadows but close to the river makes a sharp south-westerly turn along a drainage dyke to the inlet called Cone Pill, including the whole river frontage of Alvington and part of that of Woolaston.[47] That illogical boundary, evidently in part the result of

land being gained from the river,[48] was presumably not established until after 1277 when Llanthony priory became owner of Aylburton as well as Alvington; it was perhaps still not settled in 1318 when the priory and Tintern abbey (Mon.), owner of Woolaston, were disputing part of the Stirts, the tract of land on the river side of the boundary.[49] By 1602 the Stirts was accepted as being part of Aylburton but, having formed part of Llanthony's demesne, it was claimed not to be tithable to Lydney church.[50] The north-east boundary of Lydney parish descends a brook, called Lanes brook by 1300,[51] to reach the Severn at Purton Pill, and the river forms the long south-east boundary.

The boundary between the civil parish (formerly chapelry or tithing) of Aylburton and the rest of the ancient parish descends Park brook beside Lydney woods and park and crosses the level to the Severn by an irregular course, which was partly determined after alterations in the river bank.[52] A straight stretch on the north-east of land called Aylburton mead is marked by a double ditch and a bank, possibly the 'Meredich' (boundary ditch) mentioned as a bound of land in the mead in 1229.[53]

The north-east part of the parish is rolling countryside, lying at 30–80 m. south-east of the main Gloucester–Chepstow road, where a hill called Gurshill by the 13th century[54] is the main feature, and rising to *c.* 140 m. at Needs Top on the north boundary. On the Severn the land ends in river cliffs, which are at their steepest between the wood called Warren grove and the headland called Nass Point, upstream of the entrance to Lydney harbour.[55] The headland, from which the tithing of Nass was named,[56] was a more pronounced feature of the riverside before new land formed in a large bay to the south-west of it.[57] In the south-west part of the parish the main road forms a rough division between a wide riverside level and steep well wooded slopes which reach over 200 m. at Prior's Mesne. The level is formed of alluvium, the east and central areas of the Old Red Sandstone, and the higher ground to the north-west of Drybrook Sandstone with the coal measures above; in Aylburton tithing there is also an intervening band of carboniferous limestone.[58]

Most of the broad tract of level ground in the south part of the parish has been reclaimed from the Severn over the centuries. The inner edge of the level is most clearly defined below Aylburton village, where a branch of Park brook follows it to a place called Stockwell green, 325 m. south-east of the main Chepstow road and *c.* 1.4 km. from the present river bank, and a lane

[36] *Trans. B.G.A.S.* lxvi. 172–9, 187–93.
[37] Glos. R.O., D 421/M 23–4, where some woods are listed as 'groves' and others as 'purlieus', but the distinction being made is not clear.
[38] Ibid. D 421/19/8; cf. ibid. D 2026/X 3.
[39] Ibid. D 421/E 5.   [40] Ibid. D 421/19/19.
[41] Ibid. D 421/E 16, E 23; Forest of Dean Poor Relief Act, 5 & 6 Vic. c. 48.
[42] Below, manors.   [43] Glos. R.O., D 421/L 3–4.
[44] Ibid. L 4.   [45] Cf. ibid. Q/RI 14.
[46] Ibid. D 2099, Alvington ct. bk., ct. 1774.
[47] Woolaston formerly included meadowland on the NE. side of Cone brook, transferred to Alvington in 1935: O.S.

Map 6", Glos. XLVII. SW. (1886 edn.); *V.C.H. Glos.* x. 102–3.   [48] Cf. below.
[49] P.R.O., C 115/K 2/6683, f. 94; C 115/L 1/6689, f. 179v.
[50] G.D.R. vol. 89, depositions 9 Mar., 13, 28 Apr. 1602.
[51] *Trans. B.G.A.S.* lxvi. 180; O.S. Map 6", Glos. XLVII. NE. (1891 edn.).   [52] Cf. below, this section.
[53] P.R.O., C 115/K 2/6683, ff. 79 and v., 86v.
[54] P.R.O., CP 25/1/74/24, no. 548; C 138/40, no. 52.
[55] Glos. R.O., Q/RUm 37/1.
[56] *P.N. Glos.* (E.P.N.S.), iii. 259.
[57] Below, this section.
[58] Geol. Surv. Map 1", solid, sheet 35 (1845 edn., revised to 1872).

follows it from Stockwell green into Alvington parish. To the north-east, the excavation of a Roman villa, *c.* 200 m. south-east of the Chepstow road, revealed that the site had been a small headland on an early river bank.[59] A tradition was recorded in the 1770s that the river once ran close to the south side of Lydney churchyard,[60] which is *c.* 1.6 km. from the present bank.

The physical evidence suggests that most of the level, extending to a line some way south-east of the mid 19th-century South Wales railway, was won from the river within the Romano–British period.[61] At the time of the first documentary record, in the early 13th century, the part belonging to Aylburton tithing was known by the general designation of Aylburton's marsh and was farmed as open field and common meadow.[62] Land was recorded, among other places, at 'the hill' in the marsh, evidently a low rise where the railway runs through a cutting, and in the Stirts, the part of Aylburton tithing that extends in front of Alvington and Woolaston to Cone Pill.[63] Woodwards brook then entered the river at the north-east end of the Stirts by an inlet called Wose Pill,[64] which later silted but remained visible in field boundaries. Of the remains of the sea walls (actually earthen banks) traversing the level, one crossing the Stirts from Cone Pill to Wose Pill probably marks the line of an early-medieval river bank. From Wose Pill a long sea wall ran north-eastwards to the site of the early 19th-century Lydney harbour,[65] part following a stretch of the boundary between Lydney and Aylburton tithings which runs roughly parallel to the river. It is suggested that the sea wall was built to contain an early-medieval inundation of the level.[66] A field on the landward side of a surviving stretch of the wall, in which ridge and furrow was visible in 1990, was known as Shortlands by 1322[67] and may have been named after its strips were truncated by the inundation.

The addition of land to the level was apparently in progress once more by the early 14th century. A 30-acre pasture called the New Stirts was recorded in 1312[68] and was probably in the outer part of the Stirts which in distinction to the inner part appears not to have been cultivated in strips.[69] In 1322 there was land, designated 'at Foremarsh', adjoining Wose Pill,[70] probably on its north-east side in front of Shortlands. By the mid 16th century a narrow strip of land called Aylburton Warth[71] had begun to form in front of the Stirts and there was land, known as the Marsh,[72] on the river side of the old sea wall between Wose Pill and the site of the later harbour. In the early 19th century Aylburton Warth, including the silted pill, covered *c.* 80 a., and the Marsh, most of which was in Lydney tithing with a smaller, south-western part in Aylburton, covered *c.* 195 a. A later major addition was land called the New Grounds in front of the Marsh.[73] Silting against the bank there had begun by 1664[74] and *c.* 300 a. had emerged from the river by 1682 when Charles Winter, owner of the Lydney estate, and William Jones, owner of Nass manor, both laid claim to it.[75] Before the dispute could be resolved the river's channel shifted, washing away the new land, but in 1730 it began to form again in much the same place and the dispute was renewed by the successors of Winter and Jones.[76] By arbitration in 1734 the bulk of the New Grounds, said to be 240 a., was awarded to the Lydney estate and the north-eastern end, later said to be *c.* 40 a., to Nass manor.[77]

Part of the New Grounds had apparently been washed away again by the beginning of the 19th century when it covered only *c.* 207 a.[78] Land there was certainly lost in the mid 19th century, when a new sea wall and breakwaters were built to defend the bank,[79] and again in the mid 20th, when the bank was reinforced by piling stones.[80] Further down river, however, there was a build up of land against Aylburton Warth in the first half of the 20th century, roughly doubling the part of Aylburton lying in front of Alvington.[81]

A number of streams crossed the parish to drain into the Severn at the level. The original pattern has been much altered by the changing river bank, the needs of the Lydney ironworks, and by the building of the new harbour. At the start of the 19th century the Newerne stream[82] (sometimes called Cannop brook or the Lyd), flowing down the centre of the parish through Newerne village, formed the head of an inlet called Lydney Pill at a point just north of the later South Wales railway line;[83] Plummer's

59 Glos. R.O., D 3921/III/20.
60 Rudder, *Glos.* 524.
61 Inf. from Professor J. R. L. Allen, of Reading University. For the area, below, Fig. 3.
62 P.R.O., C 115/K 2/6683, ff. 78 and v., 80v., 81 and v., 99v.; cf. below, econ. hist. (agric.).
63 P.R.O., C 115/K 2/6683, f. 80 and v.; for the Stirts, cf. G.D.R., T 1/117.
64 P.R.O., C 115/K 2/6683, ff. 79v.–80, 101v.; C 115/K 2/6684, f. 140.
65 For the wall, only parts of which survived in 1990, Glos. R.O., D 421/T 30, mortgage 5 Jan. 1653/4; P 209A/IN 3/1, f. 16; aerial photog. (Royal Air Force, 1946), no. 3093.
66 Inf. from Prof. Allen.
67 P.R.O., C 115/K 2/6683, f. 101v.; cf. G.D.R., T 1/117.
68 P.R.O., C 115/L 1/6689, f. 176 and v.
69 Aerial photogs. (R. A. F., 1946), nos. 3093, 3103.
70 P.R.O., C 115/K 2/6683, f. 101v.
71 Glos. R.O., D 421/M 10.   72 Ibid. E 12, M 23.
73 For the outer lands of the level, Glos. R.O., P 209A/IN 3/1; D 421/T 102; O.S. Map 1", sheet 35 (1830 edn.); G.D.R., T 1/117, where, however, some of the original boundaries and acreages had been altered as the result of the

building of the harbour. It should be noted that from the 1880s the O.S. maps apply the name 'New Grounds' to both the Marsh and New Grounds, the name 'Lydney Marsh' to land further north formerly called Great Cowleaze, and the name 'Aylburton Warth' to both the Stirts and Aylburton Warth: O.S. Maps 6", Glos. XLVII. SW. (1886 edn.); 1/25,000, SO 60 (1961 edn.).
74 *Trans. B.G.A.S.* lxvi. 242.
75 Glos. R.O., D 421/L 2; cf. ibid. L 8, plan 1682.
76 Ibid. L 7–8.
77 Ibid. L 17, T 68.
78 Ibid. T 102, lease 1806; P 209A/IN 3/1.
79 G.D.R., T 1/117; O.S. Map 6", Glos. XLVII. SW., SE. (1886, 1889 edns.).
80 Glos. R.O., DA 28/100/14, pp. 428, 476–7, 545; 18, min. 26 Jan. 1965.
81 Cf. O.S. Maps 6", Glos. XLVII. SW. (1886 edn.); 1/25,000, ST 69 (1951 edn.).
82 *Trans. B.G.A.S.* lxvi. 180; Glos. R.O., D 421/M 32.
83 Cf. Glos, R.O., D 421/E 30, plan 1809, where the old warehouse (marked 'storehouse') indicates the place to which the pill was once navigable; cf. below, econ. hist. (other ind. and trade).

brook (formerly called Woodfield[84] or Nass brook[85]), crossing the north-eastern part of the parish, reached that pill further south at a place called Cross Pill; and Park brook (formerly Pailwell brook),[86] flowing down to Aylburton, had a branch running from that village across the fields to the ironworks called Lower Forge, north-west of the head of the pill. Lower Forge was also supplied by a stream which rose on Red hill, north-east of Lydney park, and served an iron furnace near the point where it crossed the Chepstow road, and, by the late 17th century, by a long leat which branched from the Newerne stream north of the Chepstow road.[87] At some time between 1778 and 1790 the lessee of the Lydney ironworks built a narrow canal[88] from Upper Forge at the north boundary of the parish down to Lower Forge. The canal, usually known as the Cut, runs close to the Newerne stream in the upper part of its course but in its lower course, which presumably adapted the existing leat, it takes a more direct line some way west of the stream, crossing the Chepstow road between Lydney and Newerne; from Lower Forge there was also a short branch of the canal down to the head of Lydney Pill.[89] About 1814 another lessee of the ironworks built a new feeder stream to Lower Forge, replacing the existing branch of Park brook;[90] it left the brook north-east of Aylburton village and ran through the lower part of Lydney park to join the Red hill stream south of the Chepstow road.[91]

Following the formation of the New Grounds in the entrance to Lydney Pill in the 1730s, the pill reached the Severn by a long channel, winding along the north-west side of the new land to emerge downstream of it at the point where the boundary between Lydney and Aylburton was fixed, and by a lesser channel called the Eastern Way, taking a more direct course down the north-east side of the new land.[92] The building of Lydney harbour between 1810 and 1813[93] obscured the upper part of the pill and took most the water that had drained into it. By 1990 the Eastern Way had silted up, while the main channel, which by the early 20th century entered the river some way above its old mouth, was reduced in size and distinguished from the many drainage ditches crossing the level only by its sinuous course.[94]

Woodwards brook, on the south-west boundary of the ancient parish, has also been called at various times Sandfords, Colliers, and Ferneyley brook.[95] Wose Pill, where it entered the river, also received a western branch of Park brook, flowing from Aylburton village and sometimes called Stockwell brook. After the silting of the pill the combined brook took a circuitous course along the north-west side of Aylburton Warth to Cone Pill.[96] By the mid 20th century, however, it had been diverted into a large new drainage dyke built down through the Stirts and the warth.[97]

The slopes of the north-western half of the parish were once covered by a continuous belt of woodland, which was probably not significantly depleted until the early modern period. In the eastern part of the parish the pattern of ancient, inclosed farms, including one named Hurst,[98] was presumably formed from woodland in Anglo-Saxon or early medieval times. In 1086 Lydney manor included a wood measuring 1 league by ½ league.[99] A large wood, comprising that later called Old Park wood with adjoining woodland between Park brook and the Newerne stream, belonged to the earl of Warwick's Lydney manor in the 13th century.[1] The parish being then within the jurisdiction of the Forest, the wood was several times forfeited to the Crown for contravention of the forest laws against waste. Similar penalties were incurred in respect of woods belonging to the lords of Aylburton manor,[2] probably including the later Aylburton common and the wood to the north called Old Bargains.

In the late 16th century all the several woodland on the north-western slopes of the parish passed to the Winters' Lydney estate, which had 1,679 a. (including the extraparochial Snead and Kidnalls) in 1678.[3] In 1839 there were c. 1,400 a. of woodland in the parish, all of it belonging to the Lydney estate except for some small groves on the cliffs in Purton and Nass and a wood on the Prior's Mesne estate in Aylburton.[4] From the early 17th century much of the produce of the woodland of the Lydney estate was consumed by its ironworks,[5] and in the late 18th century timber and bark were supplied to local merchants, tanners, and shipbuilders.[6] The main tract of woodland, lying east of Park brook, included the great wood called Old Park, which had presumably been imparked by one of the

[84]   Glos. R.O., D 637/II/8/T 1, marr. settlement 1739; D 428/A 2, mins. 7 June, 6 Sept. 1806.
[85]   Ibid. D 421/M 79.
[86]   P.R.O., C 115/K 2/6683, f. 89; Glos. R.O., D 421/L 3.
[87]   Taylor, *Map of Glos.* (1777); below, econ. hist. For Park brook, cf. Glos. R.O., D 421/T 45, where a lease of Millend mill in 1759 limited the miller to using the water when it was not needed by the ironworks downstream. For the leat, ibid. E 16, where the forge stream or 'cut' was mentioned in distinction to the Newerne stream as a boundary of Elm farm, N. of Newerne, in 1678.
[88]   Glos. R.O., D 421/E 34, T 69. As the canal existed by 1790, it was presumably built by David Tanner, whose lease of 1778 gave powers for it, rather than by his successors the Pidcocks as suggested by Hart, *Ind. Hist. of Dean*, 91, 93; cf. below, econ. hist. (mills and ironworks).
[89]   Glos. R.O., Q/RUm 37/1; D 4880/2. Between Upper and Middle forges its course was later replaced by the large forge ponds.
[90]   Ibid. D 4880/1; cf. ibid. D 421/E 46.

[91]   O.S. Map 6", Glos. XLVII. NW. (1883 edn.); Glos. R.O., D 4880/2.   [92]   Glos. R.O., D 421/L 11; Q/RUm 37/1.
[93]   Below, this section.
[94]   Greenwood, *Map of Glos.* (1824); O.S. Maps 6", Glos. XLVII. SW., SE. (1886, 1888 edns.); 1/25,000, SO 60 (1950 edn.).
[95]   *Trans. B.G.A.S.* lxvi. 180; P.R.O., C 115/K 2/6683, f. 101v.; Glos. R.O., D 421/L 4; M 32, undated presentment; O.S. Map 6", Glos. XLVII. SW. (1886 edn.).
[96]   Glos. R.O., D 421/M 32, ct. 1688; O.S. Map 6", Glos. XLVII. SW. (1886 edn.).
[97]   Aerial photog. (R.A.F., 1946), no. 3093.
[98]   *P.N. Glos.* (E.P.N.S.), iii. 259.
[99]   *Dom. Bk.* (Rec. Com.), i. 164.
[1]   *Trans. B.G.A.S.* lxvi. 180.
[2]   P.R.O., E 32/28, rot. 8; E 32/29, rot. 8d.; E 32/30, rot. 23; cf. *Close R.* 1251–3, 320; *Cal. Close*, 1279–88, 325.
[3]   Glos. R.O., D 421/E 16.   [4]   G.D.R., T 1/117.
[5]   Below, econ. hist.
[6]   Glos. R.O., D 421/E 34, E 52, E 56; L 18, letters 19, 30 Mar., 24 June 1772.

earls of Warwick after Lydney was excluded from the Forest. South of Old Park wood the lords of the manor created a second park, called the new park or the deer park, before the mid 17th century.[7] Later it was planted and landscaped as an amenity of a large manor house built at its south end in the late 17th century.[8] Kidnalls and some other outlying woods were sold to the Forestry Commission before 1947.[9] In 1990 the Lydney estate retained 485.5 ha. (1,200 a.) of broadleaved woodland and conifer plantation, which was managed primarily as a commercial timber enterprise, though game was preserved in some parts.[10]

Other woodland, which was subject to common rights, was gradually cleared of trees to become open pasture. Allaston Meend, comprising a compact area south of the house called Soilwell and a long roadside strip extending down Primrose hill on the road to Newerne,[11] was denuded of trees in the early 17th century by the Winters to make charcoal for their iron furnace. The last trees, a grove adjoining Soilwell, were felled by Charles Winter in 1677 during a dispute with the owners of Soilwell over rights in the common.[12] Aylburton wood,[13] later called Aylburton common, which covered c. 220 a. in the central part of Aylburton tithing, contained only a few trees by 1722. The Purlieu, at the north-east end of the parish, was still well wooded in 1722, as were two smaller commons, the Tufts, on the north boundary by the Newerne stream, and Needs Top,[14] on the north boundary west of the Purlieu. The commons, which covered a total of 542 a. in 1839, were inclosed in 1864.[15] Little of the former common land was ever put under the plough, and in 1990 some parts, including the bracken-covered south-west slopes of Aylburton common, remained rough grazing.

On Camp hill, a spur of land overlooking Park brook at the south end of Old Park wood, an Iron Age hillfort was used as the site of an extensive complex of Roman buildings. Some walls still stood to a height of several feet in the early 18th century. Later that century there was some digging and removal of artefacts on the site, and the owner Charles Bathurst excavated there after 1804.[16] Detailed excavation during 1928 and 1929 revealed that in the early Romano-British period the occupants of the site had engaged in iron mining and that in the 4th century A.D. a temple with a pilgrims' guesthouse, baths, and other associated structures were built. The finds, including votive objects,[17]

were housed in a private museum built on to Lydney Park house in 1937,[18] and the footings of the buildings excavated were left open to view. Two classical statues, once thought to be Roman but evidently made c. 1700 as garden ornaments, formerly stood at the eastern approach to the temple site[19] but were moved in the mid 20th century to the gateway of a new garden laid out in a valley below. Little Camp hill, a smaller hill south of Camp hill, is crowned by the earthworks of a Norman castle.[20]

An ancient road known as the Dean road, thought to be Roman, can be traced from Highfield hill, on the main Gloucester–Chepstow road north-east of Newerne, through Allaston tithing, and into the Forest; considerable remains of kerbstones and paving survive on a disused stretch east of Soilwell.[21] The Gloucester–Chepstow road, which runs south-westwards through the parish and provided the main street of its three villages, is thought to be on a Roman route, but only parts of the road follow the ancient course. Until 1810 it crossed Lanes brook from Awre parish on a different course, following a lane up Gurshill,[22] beyond which an ancient lane continued to Nass by way of Warren grove and Cliff Farm.[23] The old alignment up Gurshill suggests that the original importance of that part of the road was as a route to a river crossing near Nass Point.[24] The route to Lydney perhaps once branched from the Nass road north of Warren farmhouse and followed a footpath that leads past Hurst Farm. By the 18th century, however, it turned sharply westwards at Gurshill to join the course of the present road at Woodfield bridge on Plummer's brook, and that was the route adopted as the Gloucester–Chepstow turnpike road in 1757. In 1809–10 the turnpike trust avoided Gurshill by building a new line of road from Awre parish across the Purlieu to Woodfield bridge.[25] South-west of Lydney town the Chepstow road once followed a straight course to Aylburton village, giving its name to the small hamlet of Overstreet, on the site of which the first Lydney Park house was built c. 1690.[26] In 1736 the road was diverted to the south-east,[27] rejoining its former course just south of the house, and in 1818 a further alteration moved it from north to south of the buildings of Park Farm.[28] South-west of Aylburton village the Chepstow road left the parish at Sandford bridge[29] until the early 1960s when the bridge was bypassed by a road improvement.[30]

7 Ibid. T 20, T 30; G.D.R., T 1/117.
8 Below, manors.
9 *Forest of Dean* (National Forest Park Guide, 1947), plan at end.
10 Inf. from Mr. O. B. Hepworth, agent to the Lydney Park est.
11 For the commons, O.S. Map 1", sheet 35 (1830 edn.); G.D.R., T 1/117.
12 Glos. R.O., D 421/L 6.   13 Ibid. E 12, M 9.
14 Ibid. E 32.   15 Ibid. P 209A/SD 1/1.
16 W. H. Bathurst, *Roman Remains at Lydney Park, Glos.* ed. C. W. King (1879), 1–4; Rudder, *Glos.* 525; *Archaeologia*, v. 207–8.
17 R. E. M. and T. V. Wheeler, *Excavation of Prehistoric, Roman, and Post-Roman Site in Lydney Park, Glos.* (Rep. of Research Cttee. of Soc. of Antiquaries, ix, 1932).
18 C. E. Hart, *Lord Bledisloe of Lydney* (1957), 20.
19 Wheeler, *Lydney Park*, 137.   20 Below, manors.
21 A. W. Trotter, *Dean Road* (Glouc. 1936), 5–11; in 1990

much less remained visible than in the 1930s.
22 Taylor, *Map of Glos.* (1777); Glos. R.O., D 428/A 2, min. 6 Sept. 1806; A 3, mins. 5 Dec. 1807; 17 Dec. 1808.
23 G.D.R., T 1/117; Glos. R.O., D 637/II/8/T 1, marr. settlem. 1739.
24 Cf. I. D. Margary, *Roman Roads in Britain* (1973), 323–4, where the possible significance of that route is noted but the new line of turnpike made in 1809–10 is assumed to be part of a Roman alignment.
25 Chepstow Roads Act, 31 Geo. II, c. 44; Glos. R.O., D 428/A 3, mins. 17 Dec. 1808; 2, 23 Sept. 1809; 3 Mar., 20 Oct., 1 Dec. 1810.   26 Below, this section.
27 Glos. R. O., P 209/IN 1/1, mem. at end.
28 Ibid. Q/SRh 1818 D/1.
29 P.R.O., C 115/K 2/6683, f. 101v.; O.S. Map 6", Glos. XLVII. SW. (1886 edn.).
30 Glos. R.O., DA 28/100/17, mins. 26 Apr. 1960; 26 Sept. 1961.

A lane which climbs steeply up the east side of Gurshill from Purton hamlet to join the old Gloucester–Chepstow road was a turnpike under the Forest of Dean trust from 1796 to 1888;[31] there was a tollbooth just east of the junction. On the Gloucester–Chepstow road, which remained a turnpike until 1871, a turnpike gate was put up in 1759 at the north-east end of Lydney town at the junction with the Bream road,[32] which was the principal route up to the Forest until 1902 when Lydney rural district built Forest Road as part of a new main road up the Newerne valley.[33] In the east part of the parish much of the old road system has gone out of use, partly as a result of the building of railways across it in the mid 19th century. The road between Gurshill and Nass, mentioned above, was joined at Warren grove by a road linking Purton hamlet to Nass by way of Wellhouse,[34] and another road, providing a route between Purton hamlet and Lydney town, branched off at Warren grove to join Nass Lane at Crump Farm.[35]

A passage across the Severn from Purton hamlet to the place of the same name in Berkeley parish was evidently in use by 1282 when Hamelin the ferryman (le passur) was among owners of boats at Lydney's Purton.[36] The rights in the passage evidently belonged to the lord of Purton manor in 1325.[37] In 1574 a three-quarter share in the passage was sold by Thomas Morgan to Sir William Winter.[38] The Winters acquired the other quarter share and leased the passage together with the house called Purton Manor to the Donning family before 1607,[39] and the passage then descended with the Purton Manor estate.[40] In 1600 the keeper of the passage was presented at quarter sessions for excessive charges.[41] In 1726 Martin Inman, whose family continued as lessees for the next 150 years,[42] operated Purton passage with a number of boats and kept the passage house inn. In 1740 the removal of a large rock from the river bed on the Berkeley side caused the river to shift its channel with the result that only a single crossing could be made each day. Much custom had been lost by 1750, when the river returned to its old channel, and the passage was damaged by a further shift the following year.[43] It appears to have been in full use again by the end of the century.[44] In the late 18th century and the early 19th people often forded the river at Purton but some, misjudging the times of the tide, were drowned.[45] Purton passage was closed in 1879 when the Severn railway bridge, which included a footway, was opened just downstream of it. The railway company compensated the owner and took the ferryman into its employ.[46]

Plans for a tramroad to link the mines of the west part of the Forest with the Severn at Lydney and the Wye at Lydbrook were under discussion from 1799, and an Act of 1809 authorized the building of the Lydney and Lydbrook Railway which, at its south end, was to follow the Newerne valley down to Lower Forge. A further Act of 1810, which renamed the project the Severn & Wye Railway and Canal, gave powers for a tramroad to a place just south of the head of Lydney Pill and for a harbour, in the form of a short canal, extending from the end of the tramroad to the Severn between Nass Point and the branch of the pill called the Eastern Way. The undertaking was completed in 1813, and in 1821 a new outer harbour and lock were added at the river end and the tramroad was extended the full length of the harbour. Locomotives were run on the tramroad from 1864. Parts of it were abandoned in 1868 when a railway line was laid beside it, but stretches remained in use for some years to serve the Lydney tinplate works.[47]

The South Wales railway, which became part of the G.W.R. system in 1863, was built across the south-east side of the parish in 1851.[48] A station was built near the head of Lydney harbour and another, called Gatcombe station, at Purton.[49] In 1868 the Severn & Wye Co. laid a broad gauge railway beside its tramroad north of the G.W.R. line; it was opened in 1869 and converted to standard gauge in 1872. A station was built at what became known as Lydney Junction, at the terminus of the line just north of the G.W.R. line, and another was built at Lydney town. In 1872 an Act authorized the building of the Severn Bridge railway, which was to run from Lydney Junction, cross the Severn by a bridge from Purton to Sharpness, and join the Midland Railway's Bristol–Gloucester line at Berkeley Road. The massive Severn railway bridge, designed by G. W. Keeling and G. W. Owen, was begun in 1875 and completed in 1879. It was formed of a series of bowstring girders on tubular piers and had a pair of wide central spans and 19 lesser spans. Severn Bridge station was built at the approach to the bridge on the Lydney side and the station at Lydney Junction was replaced by another at the start of the new line. At the opening of the railway in 1879 it was amalgamated with the Severn & Wye and in 1894 the combined railway passed into the joint control

[31] Dean Forest Roads Acts, 36 Geo. III, c. 131; 51 & 52 Vic. c. 193 (Local).

[32] G.D.R., T 1/117; Glos. R.O., D 428/A 1, mins. 9 Aug., 5 Nov. 1759; Annual Turnpike Acts Continuance Act, 34 & 35 Vic. c. 115.

[33] Glos. R.O., DA 28/100/1, pp. 97–8, 247; *80th Rep. Com. Woods*, H.C. 247, p. 3 (1902), xxi; *81st Rep. Com. Woods*, H.C. 232, p. 3 (1903), xviii.

[34] Glos. R.O., D 421/M 83.

[35] Ibid. M 79; and for all three roads, G.D.R., T 1/117.

[36] P.R.O., E 32/30, rot. 24.

[37] Berkeley Cast. Mun., General Ser. Chart. 1571, 2445.

[38] Glos. R.O., D 421/T 14. [39] Ibid. E 13, f. 31v.; M 83.

[40] Ibid. D 637/II/8/T 2; below, manors.

[41] B.L. Harl. MS. 4131, f. 554.

[42] Glos. R.O., D 189/VII/1; P 209A/IN 3/1, f. 23; *Glouc. Jnl.* 17 Apr. 1750; Bigland, *Glos.* ii. 161; R. M. Huxley, *Rise and Fall of Severn Bridge Railway* (Glouc. 1984), 65.

[43] Glos. R.O., D 189/VII/1.

[44] *Glouc. Jnl.* 10 Feb. 1783; 1 Jan. 1798.

[45] Ibid. 14 Feb. 1791; W. Wickenden, *Poems and Tales* (1851), pp. li–liv. [46] Huxley, *Severn Bridge Railway*, 25, 65.

[47] Paar, *Severn and Wye Railway*, 14–24, 72, 123, 147; for the harbour, cf. Glos. R.O., Q/RUm 37/1.

[48] E. T. MacDermot, *Hist. G.W.R.* revised C. R. Clinker (1972), i. 298, 308.

[49] O.S. Map 1", sheet 35 (1830 edn.: revision with railways added, 1878).

of the G.W.R. and M.R. Passenger services north of Lydney town were withdrawn in 1929.[50] In 1960 two oil tankers collided in the Severn at night and were carried against the railway bridge, bringing down two spans. The bridge was not reopened and was demolished between 1967 and 1970. The former Severn & Wye line between Lydney town and Severn Bridge station was closed in 1964,[51] but the line north of the town was used to carry stone ballast until 1976, being officially closed in 1980. In 1983 the part of the line north of the town was bought by the Dean Forest Railway Co., a steam preservation society which had occupied premises at an old colliery at Norchard since 1978. In 1990 the society ran steam trains on parts of the track and had plans to reopen the line between Lydney town and Parkend.[52] By then the station on the main South Wales line, the only one surviving in the parish, had been reduced to an unmanned halt.

The reasons for the development of the two separate but closely adjoining villages of LYDNEY and NEWERNE are obscure. Lydney was presumably in existence by the 9th century when an estate of the name was recorded, and Newerne, meaning 'the new house',[53] was probably founded before 1066. The two villages apparently became part of a single estate soon after 1086 when William FitzOsbern united various manors in the area. A later division, before 1285, into two manors called Lydney Warwick and Lydney Shrewsbury[54] was not, as might have been expected, based on the two separate settlements, for in 1558 both manors had tenants in both places.[55] Nor can the continuing distinction between the two settlements be readily related to an attempt made in the 13th century to establish a borough and market town. A market was granted in 1268[56] and there were 25 burgages on Lydney Shrewsbury manor in 1322.[57] The market's site was later, and probably from the 13th century, at Lydney's medieval town cross, and perhaps the bulk of the burgages were in Lydney, but the later disposition of Lydney Shrewsbury's tenants[58] suggests that some of the burgages mentioned in 1322 were in Newerne.

The attempt to establish a borough and market town was ultimately unsuccessful and the twin settlements remained small and physically distinct until the mid 19th century. Lydney, which in 1818 contained only c. 37 houses and was styled a village, was formed by Church Road, which branched from the main Gloucester–Chepstow road south-eastwards to the parish church, and by the the main road from the junction with Church Road north-eastwards as far as the junction with the road from Bream. Newerne village, which had c. 27 houses in 1818, began c. 200 yd. beyond the Bream road at the foot of a short hill, where the Severn & Wye tramroad and the later railway crossed the main road, and extended beyond the Newerne stream as far as the junction with Nass Lane.[59] The Newerne stream, which was bridged by a county bridge,[60] formerly flowed along the south-east side of Newerne's street to the Nass Lane junction,[61] but in 1924 it was diverted into a new channel running south-east from the bridge.[62]

In Lydney town the main concentration of houses was probably always on the Gloucester–Chepstow road, which became known as High Street, but Church Road was also fairly well built up in late medieval and early modern times, so that the town cross and small market place at the junction of the two streets were more obviously the hub of the town than was the case in the early 19th century. Some buildings used for trade once stood around the church: a shop next to the churchyard was mentioned in 1416[63] and another, opposite the churchyard, in 1527.[64] A building called the Shambles stood nearby in 1558.[65] Dairy Farm, on the west side of the road near the church, presumably occupies the site of the dairy house mentioned c. 1600,[66] but it was rebuilt in the early 19th century and was derelict in 1990. At least two other farmhouses, one called the Chantry, stood on Church Road north-west of Dairy Farm in the late 17th century,[67] and there were some old cottages further up the road, nearer to the market place.[68] The town cross at the market place dates from the 14th century and has a pedestal with ogee-headed niches raised high on a stepped base; its missing shaft and head were renewed in 1878 in memory of the Revd. W. H. Bathurst.[69] A small market house adjoined the cross until the 1870s.[70] A church house, recorded from c. 1600,[71] was on the east side of the market place and the pound was on the west.[72] The houses along Lydney's High Street and Newerne's single main street (later called Newerne Street) were apparently small and of little architectural distinction.[73] Those in High Street included by 1656 the Feathers,[74] the town's chief inn, often known simply as the Lydney inn. Its full sign was given in 1681 as the Hand of Feathers and in the late 18th century as the Plume of Feathers[75] and was derived from the crest of the Winter family,[76] owners of the Lydney estate. A

50 Paar, *Severn and Wye Railway*, 73–5, 81, 94, 102–10, 114–17. For the Severn bridge, below, Plate 29.
51 Huxley, *Severn Bridge Railway*, 120–1, 127–48.
52 Inf. from Mr. D. Ponter, Dean Forest Railway Co.
53 *P.N. Glos.* (E.P.N.S.), iii. 259.
54 Below, manors.   55 Glos, R.O., D 421/M 23.
56 *Cal. Chart. R.* 1257–1300, 114.
57 P.R.O., E 142/26.
58 Cf. Glos. R.O., D 421/M 23.
59 O.S. Map 1", sheet 35 (1830 edn.); G.D.R., T 1/117; Glos. R.O., P 209A/IN 3/1.
60 Glos. R.O., Q/CI 2, p. 18.
61 O.S. Map 6", Glos. XLVII. NW. (1883 edn.).
62 Date on bridge.   63 Glos. R.O., D 421/M 19.

64 Ibid. M 20.   65 Ibid. M 23; cf. ibid. M 26.
66 Ibid. E 13, f. 7v.   67 Ibid. T 16.
68 G.D.R., T 1/117; O.S. Map 6", Glos. XLVII. NW. (1883 edn.).
69 Inscr. on cross; cf. Pooley, *Glos. Crosses*, plate at pp. 64–5.
70 Below, econ. hist. (market and fairs).
71 Glos. R.O., D 421/E 13, f. 5v.
72 O.S. Map 6", Glos. XLVII. NW. (1883 edn.).
73 Cf. *Univ. Brit. Dir.* iii (1794), 566.
74 Glos. R.O., D 421/T 30.
75 Ibid. M 32, T 101; D 3270/R 23; *Glouc. Jnl.* 8 Apr. 1771.
76 Burke, *General Armory* (1884), 1124.

short way south-west of the Feathers a 16th-century house called the Old Manor House survived until 1975.[77] The houses on the north-west side of High Street included the King's Head inn, which closed before 1766,[78] and two which remained farmhouses into the early 19th century, Malthouse Farm, near the market place, and Elm Farm, recorded from 1678 by the junction with the Bream road.[79] Newerne included at least one inn, the Swan, by 1777.[80]

Lydney and Newerne were refashioned as a result of the industrialization of the parish in the 19th century. In 1990 nothing survived which, on external evidence, dated from before the late 18th century and most of the houses were no older than the mid 19th. Newerne could still be regarded as a separate village in 1851[81] but the gap between it and Lydney was filled later, with a new police station and magistrates' court of 1876[82] one of the first buildings to go up on what became known as Hill Street. In the long main street that resulted from the amalgamation of the two settlements the houses were generally small and of poor quality, many having shops on the ground floor. Among the few larger houses are the early 19th-century Althorpe House by Bream Road, which was the home of the coal proprietor David Davies (d. 1868),[83] and Severn House, built beside the railway, apparently c. 1829, as the headquarters of the Severn & Wye Railway Co.[84] The Feathers hotel was rebuilt in the early 19th century and extended in the early 20th. In Newerne Street the Swan, on the south-east side, was joined by a number of public houses, including the Bridge inn, built at Newerne bridge in 1844,[85] and the Royal Albert, opened before 1851 opposite the end of Nass Lane.[86]

Expansion of the town away from the main street in the late 19th century took the form of small dwellings for industrial workers, usually built in pairs of the local dark Forest stone. It began in the 1850s when houses were built on Albert Street, the road leading from Newerne towards Primrose Hill,[87] and Queen Street, leading off Albert Street, was laid out and built up.[88] At the same period or soon afterwards cottages were built some way out of Newerne on Tutnalls Lane (later Tutnalls Street), which runs southwards along a low ridge overlooking the Newerne stream.[89] In the 1880s a number of short streets of similar small dwellings were formed on the south-east side of the main street of Lydney and Newerne,[90] and in the 1890s and the early years of the next decade houses were built on Stanford Road, leading off Bream Road on the other side of the main street.[91] The focus of the expanding town remained the old market place and cross: in 1888–9 a town hall, designed in Jacobean style by W. H. Seth Smith, was built there in the angle of the Chepstow road and Church Road, and in 1896 the Lydney Institute, in a similar style, was built on the Chepstow road adjoining.[92]

During the 20th century Lydney was much enlarged, principally by the progressive formation, mainly with council estates, of the suburb of Tutnalls on the ridge bounded by Tutnalls Street and Nass Lane. Before the First World War speculative development in and around the town included 49 houses in two long terraces called Mount Pleasant built shortly before 1909 at what was then a fairly isolated site in the south part of Tutnalls.[93] A few small houses were also added to those on Tutnalls Street at the same period.[94] On the north side of the town Grove Road, leading from Stanford Road up to a new cottage hospital, was laid out in 1908–9 and its lower part built up with semidetached houses,[95] and at the same time a small group of houses was built on Spring Meadow Road,[96] a street formed between the new Forest Road of 1902 and the road up to Primrose Hill. In 1919 Lydney rural district council bought land on the east side of Tutnalls Street and by 1924 had completed 50 council houses, mainly in short terraces, centred on Severn Road.[97] During the next three years a private developer built another 40 small semidetached houses on an adjoining part of the site under a scheme subsidised by the council.[98] Between 1926 and 1928 the council built 55 semidetached houses on Spring Meadow Road[99] and the same private developer undertook another subsidised scheme on the adjoining part of Forest Road.[1] Between 1930 and 1933 the council built 86 houses, of a small semidetached type found best suited to local needs, in two estates adjoining Regent Street and Oxford Street on the south-east side of the town.[2] In 1935, partly to rehouse occupants of

[77] Below, manors.   [78] Glos. R.O., D 421/T 71.
[79] Ibid. E 16; P 209A/IN 3/1, ff. 9, 14; G.D.R., T 1/117 (nos. 152, 463).
[80] *Glouc. Jnl.* 6 Oct. 1777; cf. Glos. R.O., P 209A/IN 3/1, f. 30.
[81] Ibid. D 637/I/73.   [82] Date on bldg.
[83] G.D.R., T 1/117; *Kelly's Dir. Glos.* (1856), 322; inscr. in churchyard.
[84] Paar, *Severn and Wye Railway*, 21; Glos. R.O., D 421/L 21.
[85] Date on bldg.; O.S. Map 6", Glos. XLVII. NW. (1883 edn.).
[86] P.R.O., HO 107/2443; Phelps, *Forest in Old Photog.* (1983), 23.
[87] Fifteen building plots on the SW. side of the street were for sale in 1848 and were presumably the sites of the 15 houses that were being built in 1851: Glos. R.O., D 637/I/73; P.R.O., HO 107/2443; cf. G.D.R., T 1/117 (no. 583).
[88] O.S. Map 6", Glos. XLVII. NW. (1883 edn.); one is dated 1855.
[89] O.S. Map 1/2,500, Glos. XLVII. 7 (1880 edn.).
[90] One in Regent St. is dated 1889, and one in Victoria Rd. 1887.

[91] One is dated 1896; cf. Glos R.O., D 2516/11/2, min. 1 Feb. 1898.
[92] *Kelly's Dir. Glos.* (1889), 835; C. E. Hart and C. Watts, *Recreation Centre and Town Hall, Lydney* (1968), 19, 21. The Institute was demolished in 1994 (after completion of this par. hist.).
[93] Glos. R.O., D 2428/1/7.
[94] One is dated 1910.
[95] Glos. R.O., DA 28/100/2, pp. 182, 205; 3, pp. 53, 91, 96, memorials 1909, 1910 (loose at back of vol.).
[96] Ibid. 2, p. 246; 3, p. 111; D 2516/11/2, min. 14 July 1909.
[97] Ibid. DA 28/100/5, pp. 29, 70, 146, 176, 189; 6, pp. 68, 143, 191.
[98] Ibid. 6, pp. 117, 128, 168, 199–200; 7, pp. 117, 154; 8, pp. 70, 102. For the housing estates of the 1920s and 1930s, cf. O.S. Map 1/25,000, SO 60 (1961 edn.).
[99] Glos. R.O., DA 28/100/7, pp. 191–2; 8, pp. 21, 180; 9, pp. 2–3, 35, 81, 106, 120.
[1] Ibid. 9, p. 151; 10, pp. 156, 176; cf. ibid. 13, p. 638.
[2] Ibid. 10, pp. 237, 247, 286, 329, 345–6, 359; 11, pp. 62, 119, 122, 250, 252, 315.

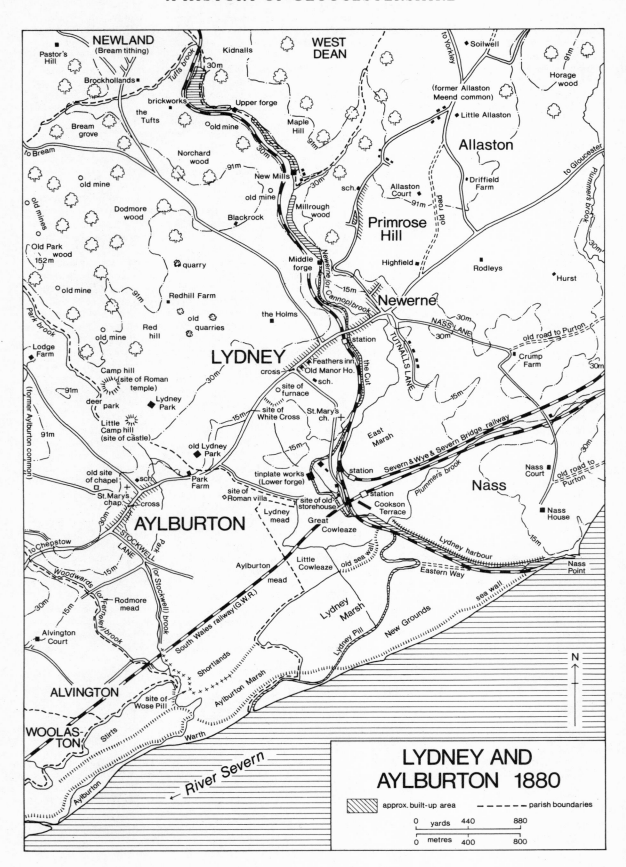

FIG. 3

houses in Albert Street demolished under a clearance scheme,[3] the council began another estate at Tutnalls adjoining Nass Lane.[4] There was private building during the 1920s and 1930s on Highfield Road (the Gloucester road northeast of the town),[5] on the upper part of the road to Primrose Hill, which was called Chapel Road until 1932 when it was renamed Springfield Road,[6] and on the upper part of Grove Road, where some large detached villas were put up.[7] The largest private scheme of the years between the wars comprised over 40 semidetached houses built in 1938 at Templeway, north-west of and parallel to Lydney High Street.[8]

After the Second World War, against a background of the national housing shortage and the needs of the new factories that were established in Lydney, the rural district council continued to develop its Tutnalls estates. Until its schemes could be completed a hutted camp in the grounds of Nass House, occupied by the American army during the war, was used until the mid 1950s as temporary housing.[9] The council enlarged the Nass Lane estate in the late 1940s,[10] and in 1950 began a large new estate based on Harrison Way, where 120 houses had been built by 1957.[11] In 1956 it began building small semidetached bungalows for old people at Klondyke Avenue on the north side of Tutnalls, and that estate eventually included c. 100 such dwellings.[12] In the late 1960s and the early 1970s the council built some blocks of low-rise flats at Tutnalls and in the town, on the west side of Bream Road.[13] By 1972 there were 666 council-owned dwellings in Lydney.[14] Private building began again in 1957 with the first houses of the Highfield estate, in the angle of Nass Lane and Highfield Road;[15] in 1964 the Lakeside estate of over 100 houses, on the south edge of Tutnalls,[16] and the Templeway West estate, on land of the Holms farm adjoining Templeway, were begun;[17] and in 1966 the Lynwood Park estate on the east side of Springfield Road was begun.[18] All those estates were enlarged at intervals during the next 25 years, the Lynwood Park estate merging with another estate higher up the hill to engulf the 19th-century hamlet of Primrose Hill.

On the main street of the town there was piecemeal redevelopment during the later 20th century. The Lydney end of the town remained relatively little affected in 1990, while the Newerne end had become the principal shopping area, aided in particular by a new bus station opened at Hams Road at the north end of Tutnalls Street in 1960[19] and by the building of a large supermarket with adjoining public car park on the north-west side of the main street in the 1970s.[20]

North of Lydney town there were a few outlying dwellings, the earliest of them probably the Holms, west of the Bream road. In 1558 it was the centre of a freehold estate belonging to the Hyett family,[21] which sold it to the Winters in 1600,[22] and the farmhouse was rebuilt in the 19th century. There was a farmhouse at Blackrock on the Bream road further north by 1600.[23] Three ironworks on the Newerne stream above Newerne had groups of cottages for the workers by 1844.[24] Most of the cottages were dilapidated in 1889 and were probably demolished soon afterwards when the works were abandoned, leaving a small group at New Mills, the middle site, in 1990. Of the works themselves there were then only some ruins at Upper Forge, but the beds of the great ponds, which filled the valley bottom for over a mile,[25] and the stone-built dams remained.

South of Lydney town the harbour, the railways, and the growth of the tinplate works at Lower Forge caused sporadic building at the far end of Church Road in the 19th century. Two short rows of cottages, one of them on the site of an old warehouse, were built early in the century near the old head of Lydney Pill, just north of the later South Wales railway line.[26] South of the railway, beside the head of the harbour, the Severn & Wye Railway Co. built Cookson Terrace, named after its chairman Joseph Cookson, in 1859.[27] It is formed of nine gabled dwellings, of which the central one is larger than the others and housed the Railway hotel until c. 1970.[28] Before 1880 the part of Church Road between the church and the bridge over the Cut was diverted to the west and renamed Station Road,[29] and three terraces of cottages were built on its new straight course in 1898–9.[30] From the early 1940s land adjoining Station Road and on the north-east side of the harbour was extensively developed for industry.[31]

South-west of Lydney town, by the boundary of Aylburton tithing, a small hamlet called Overstreet formed on the main Chepstow road.[32] In the early 17th century it contained several houses,[33] but most were replaced or became outbuildings to the large manor house called Lydney Park that was built there c. 1690.[34]

3 Ibid. 11, pp. 379–80; 12, pp. 70–1, 315.
4 Ibid. 12, pp. 129–30, 156, 223, 252, 394; 13, pp. 293, 354, 398.
5 Ibid. 6, p. 91; 7, pp. 168, 182; 9, p. 124; 13, pp. 67, 287.
6 Ibid. 11, p. 223.
7 Ibid. 6, pp. 155–6; 7, p. 52; 10, p. 291; 11, p. 253; 12, p. 467; 13, p. 67.
8 Ibid. 13, pp. 67, 184, 205, 222, 237, 287, 317.
9 Ibid. 15, pp. 163–4, 180, 295; 17, min. 25 Sept. 1956; cf. O.S. Map 1/25,000, SO 60 (1961 edn.).
10 Glos. R.O., DA 28/100/14, p. 728; 15, pp. 65, 217, 227, 247, 372.
11 Ibid. 16, pp. 59, 69, 98, 305, 451; 17, min. 22 Jan. 1957. For housing estates of the 1950s and 1960s, cf. O.S. Map 6″, SO 60 SW. (1971 edn.).
12 Glos. R.O., DA 28/100/16, pp. 544, 572; 17, mins. 26 June, 27 Nov., 18 Dec. 1956; 17 Dec. 1957; 18, mins. 11 Aug. 1964; 10 Aug. 1965; 9 Aug. 1966; 28 Mar. 1967.
13 Ibid. 18, min. 26 Sept. 1967; 19, mins. 25 Nov. 1969; 23 Mar. 1971.   14 Lydney Par. Official Guide (1972), 21.
15 Glos. R.O., DA 28/100/17, mins. 25 June, 26 Nov. 1957;

26 May, 27 Oct. 1959; 22 Mar., 23 Aug. 1960; 22 Oct. 1963.
16 Ibid. 18, min. 11 Aug. 1964; 19, min. 23 Dec. 1969.
17 Ibid. 18, mins. 11 Aug. 1964; 22 Feb. 1966.
18 Ibid. mins. 25 Oct. 1966; 24 Jan. 1967.
19 Ibid. 17, mins. 26 May, 22 Dec. 1959; 26 Jan. 1960.
20 Cf. Lydney Par. Official Guide (1972), 8.
21 Glos. R.O., D 421/M 23.   22 Ibid. D 421/13.
23 Ibid. D 421/E 13, f. 6.   24 Ibid. E 46.
25 Ibid. D 4880/2; cf. below, econ. hist. (mills and ironworks).   26 Cf. Glos. R.O., D 421/E 30.
27 Ibid. P 209/CW 2/4, min. 29 Nov. 1860; date on rainwater heads; cf. Paar, Severn and Wye Railway, 71.
28 O.S. Map 1/2,500, Glos. XLVII. 10 (1880 edn.); Glos. R.O., DA 28/100/18, min. 28 Nov. 1967; 19, mins. 25 May 1971; 25 Jan. 1972.
29 G.D.R., T 1/117; O.S. Map 6″, Glos. XLVII. NW. (1883 edn.).   30 Dates on bldgs.
31 Below, econ. hist. (other ind. and trade).
32 Bodl. MS. Top. Glouc. c. 3, f. 191v.
33 Glos. R.O., D 421/E 13, f. 9v.; T 13; Inq. p.m. Glos. 1625–42, i. 111.   34 Below, manors.

Overstreet Farm mentioned in 1660 and again in 1715[35] was probably on the site west of the manor house that was later occupied by stables and a keeper's house. In the early 19th century a substantial farmhouse called Park Farm was built south-west of the manor house for the home farm of the Lydney estate.[36] Lydney Park was demolished and replaced by a new house built on the hillside to the north-west in the late 19th century but the estate was still farmed and administered from buildings at the old site in 1990.

The tithing of NASS (usually spelt Naas in the late 20th century), south-east of Lydney, was settled by 1066.[37] Nass Court, site of the ancient manor house, and Nass House, built in the mid 17th century, stand close to the river at the end of Nass Lane and were once part of a larger hamlet. In 1651 there were three small farmhouses on the same part of the lane, but in the following year William Jones, owner of Nass House, bought them[38] and he probably demolished them soon afterwards.[39] In 1651 there was also a dwelling at Plummer's Farm, where Nass Lane crosses Plummer's brook, and another at Crump Farm, where the lane joined the old road from Purton hamlet; both farmhouses were tenanted by members of the Crump family,[40] which probably bought the freehold of Crump Farm later in the 17th century.[41] Cliff Farm, which stands above the river on the old Purton–Nass road, probably occupies the site of a farmhouse which William Jones also added to his estate in 1652.[42] All three of the outlying farmhouses in Nass tithing were rebuilt during the 18th century or the 19th.

PURTON tithing, at the north-east end of the parish, was also inhabited by 1066,[43] and later comprised scattered farmsteads and a small hamlet on a cliff above the mouth of Lanes brook. The inhabitants of the hamlet gained their livelihood in part from the river trade, fisheries, and the passage across the Severn. A chantry chapel founded there in 1360[44] was probably intended to serve travellers using the crossing, who were later accommodated by a passage house inn. The inn, mentioned from 1726,[45] had the sign of the Ship in the early 19th century[46] and became the Severn Bridge hotel after the opening of the nearby railway bridge;[47] it remained open as the Old Severn Bridge hotel in 1990. In 1651 the hamlet included a manor house and a number of small farmhouses.[48] In 1990 it comprised only the manor house, the substantial early 18th-century hotel building, and two smaller houses.

The farmsteads of Purton tithing were mostly built on hilltop sites. Two were the centres of medieval freehold estates: Wellhouse, overlooking the river south of Purton hamlet, was demolished in the 18th century,[49] and Warren, above the Plummer's brook valley, was unoccupied from c. 1930[50] and survived as a roofless ruin in 1990. Warren was rebuilt in the earlier 17th century as a stone farmhouse on a symmetrical plan. The main range, which is raised above a rock-cut cellar, has a central two-storeyed porch on the westside and a staircase projection on the east. The round-headed wooden doorway with carved decoration in the spandrels was one of the few features still intact in 1990. A house near the road junction at the summit of Gurshill, and Nursehill and the Wards, further south, were all recorded from the early 17th century. In 1607 Nursehill was on lease to a branch of the Donning family of Purton,[51] which bought the freehold later in the century.[52] The farmhouse is a long range of the earlier 17th century, described as new-built in 1651,[53] but it was much altered in the 19th and 20th centuries. Stone gate-piers were built opposite the west entrance in the later 17th century. A house beside Lanes brook where the Gloucester–Chepstow road entered the parish was mentioned at the beginning of the 17th century,[54] and another called Purlieu House in 1739[55] was perhaps at the site of Purlieu Farm, where the farmhouse was replaced by a bungalow in the later 20th century. On the Purlieu common four cottages were built by squatters before 1680[56] but at the inclosure in 1864 only two survived, on an encroachment adjoining the parish boundary.[57] That no significant settlement was established was presumably due to the vigilance of the commoners, who in 1807 were reported to be active in suppressing encroachments and illegal dwellings.[58] On the former Needs Top common, just within the parish, near the Forest settlement of Oldcroft, a few cottages were built soon after the inclosure.[59]

ALLASTON tithing lay between Plummer's brook and the Newerne stream. Its principal farmsteads, called Soilwell, Allaston Court, Rodley Manor, and Hurst, were established in the Middle Ages as the centres of small manors.[60] Driffield Farm (formerly Lower Allaston Farm)[61] on Driffield Road, leading up the hill from the main Gloucester road, is an L-shaped 17th-century farmhouse which was altered in the 19th century. A farmhouse stood at the Hulks by the Yorkley road near the north end of the

35 Glos. R.O., D 421/T 13.   36 G.D.R., T 1/117.
37 *Dom. Bk.* (Rec. Com.), i. 164.
38 Glos. R.O., D 421/M 79, T 11; cf. below, manors.
39 Cf. Glos. R.O., D 421/L 2, where his grandson Wm. said in 1683 that most of the former tenant land of the est. was in hand.
40 Ibid. M 79, where that held by John Crump, with the Nass–Lydney road SW. and a brook E., was evidently at Plummer's Farm and that held by Thos. Crump, adjoining the Nass–Lydney and Nass–Purton roads, at Crump Farm.
41 Bigland, *Glos.* ii. 162.
42 Glos. R.O., D 421/M 79 (the ho. held by John Winter adjoining the Purton–Nass road), T 11; cf. G.D.R., T 1/117.
43 *Dom. Bk.* (Rec. Com.), i. 164.

44 Below, manors.   45 Glos. R.O., D 189/VII/1.
46 Ibid. P 209A/IN 3/1, f. 23.
47 *Kelly's Dir. Glos.* (1889), 836.
48 Glos. R.O., D 421/M 83.
49 Below, manors (Soilwell; Wellhouse).
50 Glos. R.O., DA 28/100/10, pp. 215–16, 253.
51 Ibid. D 421/E 13, f. 31 and v.; M 83; T 14.
52 Ibid. D 637/II/8/L 3.   53 Ibid. D 421/M 83.
54 Ibid. M 83; E 13, f. 32.
55 Ibid. D 637/II/8/L 3, T 1.
56 Ibid. D 421/M 29, M 32.
57 Ibid. P 209A/SD 1/1.   58 Ibid. D 421/L 19.
59 Cf. O.S. Map 6″, Glos. XXXIX. SE. (1884 edn.).
60 Below, manors.   61 G.D.R., T 1/117.

tithing in 1668[62] but the site comprised only farm buildings in the early 19th century.[63] A pair of farm cottages was later built there and was being restored as a single house in 1990. About 1820 a large villa called Highfield was built beside the Gloucester road north-east of Newerne, perhaps for the ironmaster John James (d. 1857), who was living there by 1839.[64]

By 1680 five cottages had been built on Allaston Meend common and, in spite of the manor court's repeated orders that they be demolished, were still there 25 years later.[65] Those cottages, though none of that date survived in 1990, evidently began the formation of the hamlet of Primrose Hill, on the narrow strip of Allaston Meend that extended down the road to Newerne. In the early 19th century there were two loose groups of cottages, one around the junction with the lane to Allaston Court (later Court Road) and the other at a place called Lower Meend near the south end of the common. Following inclosure,[66] the building of cottages for industrial workers between the two older groups in the late 1860s and the 1870s enlarged Primrose Hill into a long roadside settlement. The new cottages, mostly of the dark Forest sandstone, were set square on to the road unlike the pre-inclosure dwellings.[67] A school was built for the hamlet in 1876 and a mission church in 1903,[68] and the Severn View public house near Lower Meend had opened by 1880.[69] Before the First World War and during the 1920s and 1930s there was much infilling with new houses and bungalows,[70] and from the 1950s bungalows were built along the road above Primrose Hill, linking the hamlet to a small group of late 19th-century cottages near the junction with Driffield Road. In the late 1960s and early 1970s a large private housing estate, mainly of bungalows, was built on the east side of Primrose Hill on land of Allaston Court farm,[71] and it was extended in the late 1980s.

AYLBURTON village, in the south-west part of the ancient parish, was a populous settlement from the early Middle Ages and had a chapel of ease by 1219.[72] The village evolved as a single long street on the Gloucester–Chepstow road, but its chapel was built high above the village on a spur of land, where there may have been a prehistoric fortification.[73] At the junction of the village street and the lane that led up to the chapel (called Chapel Hill) stands a stepped 14th-century cross, similar to that at Lydney. At the start of the 17th century there were houses at the head of Stockwell Lane, which led from the south-west end of the village to the fields on the riverside level and the site of Wose Pill, and others at Millend

(later Milling) at the north-east end of the village.[74] Between those two points the street was evidently built up with small farmhouses, for 17 houses with small farms attached belonged to the Winter's Aylburton manor in 1718.[75] Only a few of the early farmhouses survived in 1990 and those had been much altered in the modern period. The oldest (no. 32, Aylburton High Street) was possibly the messuage of one of two freehold estates absorbed by Aylburton manor in the late 16th century.[76] Its entrance probably preserves the line of the screens passage of a small medieval hall, from which there survives an embattled dais beam, with cut-back shields and heads, and a smoke-blackened central cruck truss and windbrace. North of the hall the service end was reconstructed in the 17th century, perhaps when an upper floor and chimney stack were inserted in the hall, and the adjoining dwelling on the south appears to preserve the form of a 17th-century cross wing. A small L-shaped 17th-century building, housing the Cross inn in 1990, stands at the foot of Chapel Hill, and Old Court House, on the south-east side of the village street, is another small farmhouse of similar type, much altered and restored. Cross Farm, south-west of the junction with Chapel Hill, incorporates part of an early house but was remodelled in the late 19th century; a small factory for processing bacon was built adjoining it in 1922.[77] A short row of cottages near the bottom of the lane leading up towards Coleford is probably 17th-century in origin.

The consolidation of the farmland into two or three large farms and the growth in the number of tradesmen and tinplate workers in Aylburton led to much alteration in the character and appearance of the village during the 19th century. In the mid 19th century a continuous row of cottages, mostly faced in roughcast, was built along the south-east side of the street from opposite the Coleford road to near Park brook, and between 1890 and 1910 stone-built estate cottages, usually in pairs, were built for the Lydney estate in various parts of the village.[78] The medieval chapel was taken down in 1856 and re-erected on a site more convenient for the villagers near the bottom of the Coleford road, which was named Church Road. A school was built on the opposite side of Church Road in 1870.[79] Between 1936 and 1938 Lydney rural district built four pairs of council houses on Stockwell Lane,[80] and in 1950–1 it built a small estate called Milling Crescent east of Church Road,[81] adding some old people's bungalows there in the late 1950s and early 1960s.[82] Later

[62]   Glos. R.O., D 3270/R 21; cf. G.B.R., J 4/1, no. 26.
[63]   G.D.R., T 1/117.
[64]   Ibid.; Glos. R.O., P 209/MI 1, p. 75. In 1990 it was called Rocklands and a smaller ho. nearby, formerly Highfield Villa, was called Highfield: cf. O.S. Map 6", Glos. XLVII. NE. (1891 edn.).
[65]   Glos. R.O., D 421/M 29, M 31–4.
[66]   O.S. Map 1", sheet 35 (1830 edn.); Glos. R.O., P 209A/SD 1/1.
[67]   O.S. Map 6", Glos. XLVII. NW. (1883 edn.); one is dated 1877.   [68]   Below, churches; educ.
[69]   O.S. Map 6", Glos. XLVII. NW. (1883 edn.).
[70]   Glos. R.O., DA 28/100/3, p. 67; 7, pp. 121, 143, 154; 10, pp. 21, 291; 11, pp. 61, 318, 328, 425; 12, pp. 286, 409, 423; 13, pp. 169, 205, 238.

[71]   Ibid. 19, mins. 27 Jan. 1970; 28 Nov. 1972.
[72]   B.L. Harl. MS. 6203, pp. 71–2.
[73]   G.D.R., T 1/117; the field on the NE. slope of the spur was called Bury field.
[74]   Glos. R.O., D 421/E 13, ff. 3v.–5.
[75]   Ibid. T 30.   [76]   Below, manors.
[77]   Glos. R.O., DA 28/100/6; cf. Country Life, 23 Aug. 1924, 283.
[78]   A pair at the NE. end of the village is dated 1896 and others, in Church Road, are dated 1908 and 1910.
[79]   Below, churches; educ.
[80]   Glos. R.O., DA 28/100/12, pp. 206, 295, 411; 13, pp. 108, 132, 286.
[81]   Ibid. 15, pp. 418, 489; 16, p. 122.
[82]   Ibid. 17, mins. 25 Sept. 1956; 15 Aug. 1961.

in the 20th century a few small private houses were added to the village street, and some larger, detached dwellings were built on Chapel Hill near and above the old site of the chapel.

The few ancient outlying dwellings of Aylburton tithing included Lodge Farm, established before 1717 by the owners of the Lydney estate on the west side of the park woodlands,[83] and Prior's Mesne Lodge (later Prior's Lodge) high on the north boundary. The south part of the Prior's Mesne estate, a former coney warren, was sold in the 1830s[84] and later formed the grounds of three houses. A small farmhouse called the Warren, which stood close to the St. Briavels boundary by the early 18th century,[85] was perhaps the home of the warrener employed on the estate in 1703;[86] it was enlarged to form a substantial house c. 1890.[87] Another farmhouse, built a short way north-east of the Warren by the early 19th century, was enlarged and remodelled in Tudor style in the middle of the century and given terraced gardens, becoming known as Prior's Mesne House.[88] In the 1890s its owner Surgeon-General Henry Cook created a 'wild garden' of exotic plants in part of its grounds.[89] Part of the former warren lying east of the Alvington road was sold in 1832 by James Croome of Berkeley to his brother Daniel, an attorney, who built himself a house there before 1843, later enlarging it. In 1858 a new owner William Knight built Devonshire Villa (later Aylburton Lodge) beside Croome's house, which was demolished a few years later to make way for a coachhouse and stables.[90] South of the Prior's Mesne estate, Rockwood, a Regency villa with verandah and ground-floor bow windows, was built beside the Aylburton–Coleford road c. 1815.

Aylburton common, occupying much of the lower slopes of the tithing, was apparently not settled at all before the beginning of the 19th century. Before 1818 six or seven small cottages were built on encroachments at Upper Common where lanes form a triangle on a plateau.[91] A few more houses were added in the same area after inclosure in 1864, and in the later 20th century most of the older cottages were restored and extended and new houses built among them. Other houses were built after inclosure near the lower edge of the common in the valley of Woodwards brook, where the Traveller's Rest beerhouse had opened by 1880.[92] About 1907 Sandford Terrace,[93] a row of brick houses, was built further down the valley, overlooking the Chepstow road, and other houses were built in the same area later in the century.

In 1327 94 inhabitants of the parish were assessed for subsidy, 42 of them in Aylburton.[94] In 1563 there were said to be 155 households in the parish, 50 of them in Aylburton.[95] In 1603 there were said to be 509 communicants,[96] and in 1608 171 able-bodied men were mustered, distributed as 60 in Aylburton tithing, 52 in Lydney tithing, 24 in Allaston tithing, 19 in Purton tithing, and 16 in Nass tithing.[97] In 1650 a total of only 104 families was recorded, which, if accurate, suggests a loss of population, perhaps accentuated by local dislocation during the Civil War.[98] About 1710 the population was estimated at c. 700 in 153 houses,[99] and there had apparently been little change by c. 1775, when there were said to be 661 inhabitants, made up of 246 in Lydney, 231 in Aylburton, 105 in Allaston, 44 in Purton, and 35 in Nass.[1] By 1801 the total population had risen to 1,032, with 783 in Lydney, Allaston, Purton, and Nass, and 249 in Aylburton. In the earlier 19th century, as the parish began to benefit from its docks and tinplate works, the population increased by some 2½ times. Lydney and the three north-eastern tithings had 1,989 inhabitants by 1851, and the population of that area continued to grow steadily, reaching 3,559 by 1901, 4,811 by 1951, and, following the growth of housing estates, 7,246 by 1981. Aylburton tithing (later the civil parish) also maintained a steady rise in population during the 19th century and early 20th: it rose to 588 by 1851, 731 by 1901, and 921 by 1921. There was then a decline to 718 by 1981.[2]

Although the parish had a number of lesser gentry families in the early modern period, including the Jameses of Soilwell and the Joneses of Nass, the influence of the owners of the large Lydney estate was paramount. It continued after the industrialization of the town, with the Bathursts providing many of the new amenities, but industrialists also played a role in the community, among them R. B. Thomas (d. 1917), managing director of the Lydney tinplate works,[3] and G. B. Keeling (d. 1894), secretary and later managing director of the Severn & Wye Railway Co.[4]

Some inns of the town are mentioned above. There was a total of 14 public houses in 1891.[5] A friendly society with 70 members was meeting in Lydney by 1804.[6] A mechanics' institute was founded in 1843[7] and in 1897 there was a mutual improvement society.[8] By 1879 assembly rooms had opened at Newerne,[9] and from 1889 the new town hall was the principal public meeting place. The town hall was built by a non-profit making limited company, which vested it in trustees in 1957, and in 1968 it was transferred to the parish council.[10] The Lydney Institute, opened in 1897

83 Ibid. Q/RNc 1, p. 92.   84 Below, manors.
85 Glos. R.O., D 421/L 4.   86 Ibid. D 608/9/10.
87 Ibid. D 2299/2921.   88 Ibid. 5438.
89 *A Glos. Wild Garden* (1903); cf. *Cat. of Glos. Colln.* p. 713.
90 Deeds of Aylburton Lodge, in possession of Mr. A. M. R. Watts, of Prior's Lodge; for Dan. Croome, *Hunt's Dir. Glos.* (1849), 120.
91 Cf. Glos. R.O., P 209A/IN 3/1, ff. 51–2; Bryant, *Map of Glos.* (1824).
92 O.S. Map 1/2,500, Glos. XLVII. 5 (1881 edn.).
93 Glos. R.O., DA 28/100/2, p. 136.
94 *Glos. Subsidy Roll, 1327,* 30–1.
95 Bodl. MS. Rawl. C. 790, f. 27v.   96 *Eccl. Misc.* 99.

97 Smith, *Men and Armour,* 53–5.
98 *Trans. B.G.A.S.* lxxxiii. 97; cf. below, this section.
99 Atkyns, *Glos.* 541.
1 Rudder, *Glos.* 528–30.   2 Census, 1801–1981.
3 D. Wainwright, *Men of Steel* (1986), 20, 50–2, 58–9.
4 *Kelly's Dir. Glos.* (1870), 594; (1885), 520; Paar, *Severn and Wye Railway,* 27–8.
5 *Licensed Houses in Glos.* (1891), 128–31.
6 *Poor Law Abstract, 1804,* pp. 170–1.
7 *Kelly's Dir. Glos.* (1870), 593.
8 Ibid. (1897), 233.
9 O.S. Map 1/2,500, Glos. XLVII. 6 (1880 edn.).
10 Hart and Watts, *Recreation Centre,* 19, 25–6.

principally to house the school of science and art, also included a library, reading room, and billiards room,[11] and it came to be used as a social club by the workers at the tinplate factory.[12] The Regent Hall, in Bath Place at Newerne, was built in 1930 by the Lydney branch of the Labour party but was also used by other organizations, including a W.E.A. branch, whose members started a public library in a disused shop in Newerne Street in the mid 1930s.[13] A branch of the county library had opened by 1957 and moved to new premises in Hill Street in 1963.[14] There was a Lydney band in 1859,[15] and a new drum and fife band was formed in 1890 and a brass band in 1892.[16] A cinema called the Lydney Picture House was opened in 1913 and closed in 1964.[17] A newspaper, the *Lydney Herald*, was published for a few months in 1863, and another, the *Lydney Journal*, appeared between 1865 and 1867. The *Lydney Observer*, a weekly, was begun in 1875,[18] and continued publication in 1990 as part of the Forest of Dean Newspapers group.

In 1789 Thomas Bathurst organized horse races on Lydney mead south of the town. Apparently a new venture that year,[19] the meeting does not seem to have become a regular event. From the late 19th century Lydney developed a strong sporting tradition. A rugby club was formed in 1887 and *c.* 1920 moved to a ground south of Newerne. The team became one of the most successful in the region, many players reaching the county side.[20] A football club for Lydney and Aylburton was formed *c.* 1887 and was succeeded by a new Lydney club *c.* 1911; a hockey club was formed *c.* 1905;[21] and a cricket club played on a pitch in Lydney park in the early 20th century.[22] A golf club, with links near the Holms, was formed in 1909,[23] and in the mid 20th century a golf course was laid out south of Tutnalls.[24] In 1920 an open-air swimming bath was built near the Chepstow road south-west of the town and given to the inhabitants of Lydney and Aylburton by Charles Bathurst, later Viscount Bledisloe.[25] After the Second World War most sporting activities were concentrated on a new recreation ground laid out south of Newerne, between the Newerne stream and the Cut, where Viscount Bledisloe and the local industrialist John Watts gave land in 1946. They inaugurated the Lydney Recreation Trust, and during the next eight years marshy land was drained, by diverting part of the stream and digging a lake, and cricket and football pitches and tennis courts were formed. A new cricket square laid later was used for occasional county

games after 1963. In 1968 the trustees conveyed the whole recreation ground, which other gifts had enlarged to 51 a., to the Lydney parish council.[26] In 1990 the council also administered Bathurst Park, a public park north-east of Church Road, which Charles Bathurst and his son (later Viscount Bledisloe) gave to the town in 1892 to mark the latter's coming of age.[27] A yacht club was established *c.* 1962 with its premises at a former boatbuilding yard at the entrance to Lydney harbour.[28]

In Aylburton an inn called the Hare and Hounds had opened by 1796 when two friendly societies for inhabitants of the village met there.[29] The inn, which stood near the north-east end of Aylburton, was demolished in the mid 20th century,[30] but two other public houses, the George and the Cross, both open by the 1870s,[31] served the village in 1990. A field adjoining the village was used as a recreation ground from 1898, and from *c.* 1933 a local committee managed it as a playing field. A village hall was built on the south-east side of the village street in 1920–1 as a memorial to the dead of the First World War.[32]

Mains water was supplied to Lydney town in 1902 when Lydney rural district built a pumping station at Ferneyley springs near the west boundary of Aylburton and a reservoir above Lodge Farm near its east boundary.[33] In the early 1950s boreholes at Rodmore, in St. Briavels parish, and old mine workings at the Tufts were tapped for additional supplies, and a new reservoir was built at Chapel Hill, in Aylburton, in 1956. From 1969 the supply was supplemented from the Buckshaft scheme of the North West Gloucestershire water board, in which the rural district was a partner, and from 1976 most of the town and parish received river Wye water from the Mitcheldean works of the Severn-Trent water board.[34] Aylburton had a supply from 1912 when a subscription was raised to lay pipes from a spring above the village, and some houses continued to use that source after 1950 when the rural district's mains were extended to the village.[35] The Lydney Gas Light and Coke Co. was established by local businessmen in 1860, reviving a company first formed in 1856. It built its works beside the Cut south of Newerne and began to supply Lydney and Newerne in 1861, when 44 street lamps were lit at the expense of the parish vestry and 200 private users were connected. Extensions to the mains matched the growth of the town in the late 19th century and early 20th, and in 1915 there were 149 public lamps, then the responsibility of the

[11] Glos. R.O., D 5627/3/1.
[12] *Tinplaters of Lydney and Lydbrook*, ed. B. Rendell and K. Childs (n.d.), 65: copy in Glos. R.O., PA 209/11.
[13] Ibid. 63–4; Glos. R.O., DA 28/100/10, pp. 280, 325–6.
[14] Glos. R.O., DA 28/100/17, min. 17 Dec. 1957; Glos. Colln. R 195.24.
[15] *Glouc. Jnl.* 23 July 1859.   [16] Hart, *Lord Bledisloe*, 29.
[17] C. E. Hart, *Watts of Lydney 1851–1965* (Coleford, 1965), 27.   [18] B.L. newspaper cat.
[19] *Glouc. Jnl.* 5 Oct. 1789; Glos. R.O., D 214/F 1, no. 87.
[20] *Lydney and District Official Guide* (c. 1960), 31; Hart and Watts, *Recreation Centre*, 7.   [21] Hart, *Lord Bledisloe*, 25.
[22] Ibid. 23; *Lydney and District Official Guide* (c. 1960), 31.

[23] *Glouc. Jnl.* 25 Sept. 1909.
[24] O.S. Map 6", SO 60 SW. (1971 edn.).
[25] *Kelly's Dir. Glos.* (1923), 246.
[26] Hart and Watts, *Recreation Centre*, 3–15.
[27] Plaque at park gates.   [28] *Glos. Life*, Mar. 1974, 47.
[29] Glos. R.O., Q/RSf 2.
[30] G.D.R., T 1/117; W.I. hist. of Aylburton (1957, TS. in Glos. Colln.), 52.   [31] *Kelly's Dir. Glos.* (1879), 699.
[32] W.I. hist. of Aylburton, 37–41.
[33] Glos. R.O., D 177, water supply papers 1898–1902; Payne, *Glos. Survey*, 221.
[34] Pearce, 'Water Supply in Dean', 92–4, 102–3.
[35] W.I. hist. of Aylburton, 31; Pearce, 'Water Supply in Dean', 92.

parish council.[36] In 1946 the company took over the Coleford gas company and began a considerable extension to its area of supply, continued after nationalization in 1948.[37] The Lydney gasworks were closed in 1957.[38] Electricity was laid on to the town *c.* 1925 by the West Gloucestershire Power Co., which had built its power station at Norchard colliery in the parish.[39] A sewerage system was built by the rural district council *c.* 1900[40] with the main outfall running under the fields to the Severn beyond the New Grounds.[41] A treatment plant was built and new sewers laid in the 1970s. A volunteer fire brigade for the town had been formed by 1912.[42] In 1932 the rural district established a new brigade and built a fire station at the entrance to Oxford Street, which remained in use after the brigade was absorbed by the county fire service in 1948.[43]

A cottage hospital to serve Lydney and Aylburton was opened in a house in Aylburton village in 1882 by Mary, wife of Charles Bathurst; it was maintained by subscriptions, collections, and the patients' contributions. In 1908 it moved to a new building at the top of Grove Road, north of Lydney town. The hospital was enlarged between 1935 and 1937 by the addition of a maternity wing and out-patient department, given by Viscount Bledisloe as a memorial to his first wife, and a new physiotherapy centre was completed in 1963 as a memorial to Viscount Bledisloe. The hospital passed to the local hospital management board in 1948[44] and, as the Lydney and District hospital, it remained open under the Gloucester district health authority in 1990. The authority also ran a health centre on the north of Newerne Street. In 1955 a cemetery, managed by Lydney parish council, was opened on the west side of Church Road.[45]

During the Civil War there were some minor actions and considerable destruction and plundering at Lydney. Sir John Winter fortified his manor house, White Cross, as a royalist stronghold, and the fighting, mainly during 1644 and early 1645, included skirmishes at Soilwell and Nass where the parliamentary forces of Gloucester had placed garrisons in an attempt to contain Winter.[46]

The composer Herbert Howells (1892–1983) was born and educated at Lydney,[47] and the Chaucerian scholar Professor Nevill Coghill (1899–1980) lived at Aylburton in his later

years.[48] F. S. Hockaday (d. 1924), a colliery proprietor who lived at Highbury House[49] on the north side of the town, devoted many years to studying and indexing the archives of Gloucester diocese.[50]

MANORS AND OTHER ESTATES.

Burgred, king of Mercia 852–74, granted an estate at Lydney to Ethelred. Ethelred evidently gave it to Glastonbury abbey (Som.),[51] but in 972 an estate of 6 'mansae' in Lydney belonged to Pershore abbey (Worcs.).[52] Soon after the Norman Conquest four estates in Lydney were granted by their lords to William FitzOsbern, earl of Hereford, who formed them into a single manor: they were the 6 hides of Pershore abbey, 3 hides of the bishop of Hereford, and a total of 3½ hides held by two thegns.[53] An estate of 2½ hides at 'Niware' which was formerly part of Herefordshire but which the sheriff of Gloucestershire added to his county 'in the time of Earl William' can probably be identified as Newerne[54] and may have been one of the thegns' estates. It seems most likely that FitzOsbern's new manor comprised the later Lydney, Allaston, and Aylburton tithings. Nass, Purton, and Poulton (in Awre) were also amalgamated by FitzOsbern, for whom the Lydney area evidently had a strategic and logistical significance in the years immediately following the Conquest, presumably as a crossing-point of the Severn; he also built a small castle on the opposite bank, in Berkeley.[55]

FitzOsbern's estates passed to the Crown on the rebellion of his son Roger in 1075, and the later pattern of tenures and overlordships indicates that all of Lydney parish, with the probable exception of Aylburton, was included in a royal grant to the earls of Warwick. William (d. 1184), earl of Warwick, is the first found recorded in connexion with the Lydney estates[56] but the earls may have been in possession for many years before that.[57]

Later the part of the parish based on the twin settlements of Lydney and Newerne was included in two manors, one held in demesne by the earls of Warwick and the other held from them by the Talbot family. The earls' manor, which became known as *LYDNEY WAR-WICK*,[58] was recorded from 1205, when during the minority of Henry, son of Earl Waleran, it was granted to Thomas Basset,[59] Henry's future father-in-law. It descended with the earldom of Warwick until the late 15th century.[60] In

36 Glos. R.O., D 2516/11/1–2.
37 *Lydney and District Official Guide* (*c.* 1960), 29.
38 J. Powell, *Look at Lydney* (1975), 22.
39 Glos. Colln. JR 13.9.
40 Glos. R.O., DA 28/100/1, pp. 97–8, 111, 117, 135.
41 Payne, *Glos. Survey*, 236.
42 Glos. R.O., DA 28/100/3, p. 149.
43 Ibid. 11, pp. 129, 152, 213, 227, 241; 15, p. 296.
44 R. A. J. Bell, *Hist. of Lydney and District Hosp.* (1964): copy in Glos. R.O., PA 209/2.
45 Glos. R.O., DA 28/100/16, p. 438.
46 Below, manors; *Bibliotheca Glos.* i, pp. lxxxvii, ci–cii, cvi; ii. 95, 129, 133, 143, 147.
47 *Musical Times*, 1 Feb. 1920, 88; *Who's Who* (1983), 1109; (1984), 49.   48 *Who Was Who, 1971–80*, 158–9.

49 *Glouc. Jnl.* 22 Nov. 1924.   50 *Trans. B.G.A.S.* xlvi. 379–83.
51 Finberg, *Glos. Studies*, 1–4.
52 Finberg, *Early Charters of W. Midlands*, p. 59.
53 *Dom. Bk.* (Rec. Com.), i. 164.
54 Ibid. 181; cf. *Trans. B.G.A.S.* cv. 121–2, where an alternative suggestion that it was at a place in the Cannop brook valley, in the centre of the uncultivated royal demesne woodland of the Forest, seems unlikely.
55 *Dom. Bk.* (Rec. Com.), i. 163, 164.
56 *Cur. Reg. R.* i. 280; above, Awre, manors (Poulton).
57 *Rot. Chart.* (Rec. Com.), 53, implies that Lydney was alienated by the Crown before the end of Hen. I's reign.
58 P.R.O., C 142/378, no. 147; Glos. R.O., D 142/T 29.
59 *Pipe R.* 1205 (P.R.S. N.S. xix), 100, 102.
60 For the earls, *Complete Peerage*, xii (2), 363–94.

1317 it was granted to Hugh Despenser the elder during the minority of Thomas de Beauchamp;[61] in 1397 on the forfeiture of a later Earl Thomas de Beauchamp it was granted to John de Montague, earl of Salisbury;[62] and Margaret, widow of the younger Thomas, held it in dower from 1401 to 1406.[63] In 1478 and 1486 it was in the hands of the Crown during the minority of Edward, heir of the attainted and executed George, duke of Clarence and earl of Warwick, [264] but in 1487 it was in possession of Anne, widow of Richard Neville, earl of Warwick. She granted it that year to the Crown.[65] The Crown retained Lydney Warwick manor[66] until 1547 when it granted it to Thomas Seymour, Lord Seymour,[67] who was attainted and executed in 1549. In 1550 the manor was granted to John Dudley, earl of Warwick,[68] who sold it in 1551 to Sir William Herbert,[69] created that year earl of Pembroke. Pembroke sold it in 1560 to William Winter,[70] with whose other Lydney estates it then descended.

A manor later called *LYDNEY SHREWS-BURY*[71] was held by Richard Talbot from the earl of Warwick in 1285;[72] the overlordship of the earls of Warwick was recorded until the mid 16th century.[73] Richard Talbot died in 1306 and Sarah Talbot, apparently his widow, held the manor in 1316.[74] It passed to Richard's son Gilbert, later Lord Talbot, whose estates were forfeited temporarily after his capture at Boroughbridge in 1322. From Gilbert (d. 1346)[75] the manor descended in direct line to successive Lords Talbot, Richard[76] (d. 1356), Gilbert (d. 1387),[77] and Richard. Richard granted it in 1392 to Joan, daughter of Thomas of Woodstock, duke of Gloucester, on her betrothal to his son Gilbert. On Joan's death in 1400 it reverted to Richard's widow Ankaret,[78] who married Thomas Neville (d. 1407)[79] and died in 1413.[80] Ankaret was succeeded by her son Gilbert, Lord Talbot[81] (d. 1418). His daughter Ankaret died in infancy in 1421 and the manor passed to her uncle John Talbot, later earl of Shrewsbury.[82] It then descended with the earldom of Shrewsbury,[83] Catherine, widow of John Talbot (d. 1473), holding it in dower.[84] In 1552 Francis Talbot, earl of Shrewsbury, conveyed Lydney Shrewsbury to the earl of Pembroke,[85] who sold it, probably with Lydney

Warwick in 1560 and certainly by 1562,[86] to William Winter.

William Winter's father John Winter (d. 1546), a sea captain of Bristol and Deptford (Kent), owned a house at Lydney,[87] and William was described as late of Lydney in 1554 when he was pardoned for joining Wyatt's rebellion.[88] William, who was knighted in 1573 and was one of the commanders against the Armada in 1588,[89] added numerous estates in the parish to the two Lydney manors and was succeeded at his death in 1589 by his son Edward.[90] Edward, who also followed a naval career and was knighted in 1595,[91] was warden of the Forest and constable of St. Briavels 1601–8.[92] He died in 1619 and was succeeded by his son John,[93] who was knighted in 1624 and became secretary to Queen Henrietta Maria in 1638. In 1640, for a large sum of money, he had a grant in fee of the bulk of the royal demesne land of the Forest.[94] In the Civil War Sir John led the royalist forces in the Forest area, engaging in numerous skirmishes with the parliamentary garrison of Gloucester until driven from Lydney in 1645.[95] His estate was discharged from sequestration in 1647,[96] but in 1649 he was among 12 leading royalists condemned to perpetual banishment and confiscation, and, failing to leave England, he was imprisoned in the Tower.[97] In 1651 or 1652 he bought the estate back from the commissioners for delinquents' lands, but to meet the resulting debts many farms in Purton, Nass, and the adjoining parish of Awre were sold to the tenants, and Sir John and his son and heir William also negotiated a long series of mortgages. In 1668, when a further large sale of lands in Awre and Allaston was made,[98] Sir John still had some rights in the estate[99] but he had evidently released them to William by 1674 when William made a will leaving an annuity to his father.[1] William Winter (d. by 1677) was succeeded by his brother (Sir) Charles[2] (d. 1698), who left the estate to his widow Frances.[3] Before 1714 she married Thomas Nevill but, continuing to style herself Dame Frances Winter, retained sole control of the estate. The estate was still subject to the earlier mortgages, part of the burden being cleared by the sale of lands in Aylburton in 1718. Dame Frances died in 1720,[4] and in 1723 her heirs and

[61] *Cal. Pat.* 1317–21, 123–4; *Inq. p.m. Glos.* 1302–58, 168.
[62] *Cal. Pat.* 1396–9, 213–14.
[63] *Inq. p.m. Glos.* 1359–1413, 246.
[64] *Cal. Pat.* 1476–85, 124; 1485–94, 94.
[65] *Cal. Close*, 1485–1500, p. 90.
[66] P.R.O., DL 29/638/10366; Glos. R.O., D 421/M 20; *L. & P. Hen. VIII*, xvi, p. 643.   [67] *Cal. Pat.* 1547–8, 26.
[68] Ibid. 1549–51, 71.   [69] Ibid. 357.
[70] Ibid. 1560–3, 205; Glos. R.O. D 421/T 30, abs. of title.
[71] P.R.O., C 142/378, no. 147; Glos. R.O., D 421/T 29.
[72] *Feud. Aids*, ii. 240.
[73] *Inq. p.m. Glos.* 1359–1413, 245–6; P.R.O., SC 2/175/74.
[74] *Feud. Aids*, ii. 273. For the Talbots, *Complete Peerage*, xii (1), 609–20.
[75] P.R.O., E 142/26; *Cal. Inq. p.m.* viii, p. 519.
[76] *Cal. Close*, 1346–9, 385.
[77] *Cal. Inq. p.m.* xvi, p. 467.
[78] *Inq. p.m. Glos.* 1359–1413, 225; *Cal. Close*, 1399–1402, 261.   [79] *Inq. p.m. Glos.* 1359–1413, 245–6.
[80] P.R.O., C 138/5, no. 52.
[81] Glos. R.O., D 421/M 19.

[82] P.R.O., C 139/154, no. 29.
[83] *Complete Peerage*, xi. 698–712.
[84] *Cal. Pat.* 1467–77, 397, 541.
[85] Ibid. 1550–3, 428.
[86] Glos. R.O., D 421/M 21; cf. ibid. T 30, abs. of title.
[87] Hockaday Abs. cclxv; *D.N.B.* s.v. Winter, Sir Wm.
[88] *Cal. Pat.* 1554–5, 201–2.   [89] *D.N.B.*
[90] P.R.O., C 142/227, no. 204.
[91] *D.N.B.* s.v. Winter, Sir Wm.; Glos. R.O., D421/E 1.
[92] Glos. R.O., D 421/E 3; Hart, *Royal Forest*, 86.
[93] P.R.O., C 142/378, no. 147.
[94] *D.N.B.*; Glos. R.O., D 421/E 5; D 421/19/15.
[95] *Bibliotheca Glos.* ii. 39, 63–4, 66, 72, 95, 124, 133, 137, 143.   [96] Glos. R.O., D 421/19/18.
[97] *D.N.B.*; cf. Glos. R.O., D 421/M 79, M 83.
[98] Glos. R.O., D 421/T 14, T 30; below, this section (Allaston); above, Awre, manors.
[99] Glos. R.O., D 421/T 22.
[1] Ibid. F 2. Sir John was still alive in 1676 and possibly in 1683: ibid. E 3; *Visit. Glos. 1682–3*, 206.
[2] Glos. R.O., D 421/F 2, L 6.
[3] Ibid. T 28.   [4] Ibid. T 29–30.

trustees sold the Lydney estate to Benjamin Bathurst, a son of Sir Benjamin Bathurst of Cirencester.[5]

Benjamin Bathurst (d. 1767), who was successively M.P. for Cirencester, Gloucester, and Monmouth,[6] apparently made his Lydney estate over to his son Thomas before 1759.[7] Thomas (d. 1791)[8] was succeeded by his brother Poole Bathurst (d. 1792), who devised it to his widow Anne with reversion to his nephew Charles Bragge.[9] Bragge, who succeeded on Anne's death in 1804[10] and assumed the name Bathurst, was Chancellor of the Duchy of Lancaster 1812–23 and died in 1831. The estate, which in 1818 comprised 3,435 a. of farmland, woodland, and parkland in the parish,[11] passed successively to his sons Charles (d. 1863) and the Revd. William Hiley Bathurst[12] (d. 1877), to William's son Charles (d. 1907), and to Charles's son Charles. The youngest Charles Bathurst, who was governor-general of New Zealand 1930–5, was created Baron Bledisloe in 1918 and Viscount Bledisloe in 1935.[13] He died in 1958 and the estate and viscounty passed to his son Benjamin (d. 1979)[14] and then to Benjamin's son Christopher. Some farms and woodland in the north-east part of the parish were sold in the 20th century but other land in Aylburton and in the adjoining parish of Alvington was acquired, and the estate comprised over 1,214 ha. (3,000 a.) in 1990.[15]

An early lord of Lydney presumably occupied the small castle which stood on Little Camp hill in Lydney park, overlooking the Park brook valley. Built some time in the 12th century and probably demolished soon after the end of that century, it comprised a rectangular keep, a walled inner court, and an outer bailey defended by a ditch and bank.[16] A manor house was recorded on Lydney Warwick manor in 1315[17] but there was no house in 1369.[18] The Talbots had a capital messuage on their manor in 1322,[19] and in 1558 the site of Lydney Shrewsbury manor was called Abbot's Court.[20] The reason for that name is obscure, as there appears to have been no monastic owner in that part of the parish after Pershore abbey in the 11th century. A house in the main street of Lydney, a short way north-east of the market place, was known as the Old Manor House in 1880[21] and was probably the original dwelling of the Winter family. John Winter's house was evidently a substantial one in 1538 when he complained that it had been attacked by a mob led by members of the

Baynham family,[22] and his son William's mansion was described as next to the cross in 1558.[23] The Old Manor House, a gabled building apparently dating from the 16th century but with later additions, was demolished in 1975.[24]

Sir William Winter, probably soon after he bought the two Lydney manors, built a large new house called White Cross[25] just beyond the south-west end of the town, on the south-east side of the Chepstow road. White Cross was fortified by Sir John Winter during the Civil War and in May 1644, under his wife Mary, it withstood an attack by the parliamentary forces of Edward Massey. When he was forced to leave Lydney in April 1645 Sir John burned the house down.[26] Part of it apparently remained standing in 1673, by which time an ironmaking furnace had been built on the north-east part of the grounds. William Winter was then living at a house called the Court,[27] perhaps the one later called the Old Manor House. The site of White Cross was later marked only by earth banks, presumably raised as part of its Civil War defences.

A new manor house, known as Lydney Park, was built by Sir Charles Winter at Overstreet at the south end of the deer park, close to Aylburton village. He apparently completed it in 1692.[28] It was a tall, plain house on an **L** plan, having three storeys and attics and a front of seven bays to the south-east. Improvements that Benjamin Bathurst was making in the late 1720s[29] may have included the seven-bay orangery that later adjoined the north-east corner. In the early 1770s the entrance front was to the south-west, where there was a walled garden[30] and a stable block. About 1830, as part of alterations designed by Thomas Greenshields, the orangery was remodelled and a floor of service rooms added above it.[31] Landscaping of the adjoining parts of the park in the late 1720s included the planting of clumps of elms,[32] and in 1736 the main Chepstow road, which ran next to the house, was diverted to the south-east and the park extended to the new line.[33] By the early 1770s the park had a number of ornamental features, and a terrace and Gothick summer house had been built on Red hill on the north-east side of it.[34]

In 1877 a new Lydney Park house was built further north and higher up the hillside than the old one, which was demolished, except for part of the stable block, in 1883. The new house, a Tudor-style mansion in rusticated stonework with a castellated tower at one corner, was designed by C. H. Howell.[35] From 1940 to 1948 it was occupied by a school and Viscount Ble-

5 Ibid. T 22, T 28; Rudder, *Glos.* 528.
6 Williams, *Parl. Hist. of Glos.* 209. For the Bathursts, Burke, *Peerage* (1963), 257–8.
7 Glos. R.O., D 421/T 45; Rudder, *Glos.* 523.
8 Glos. R.O., P 209/IN 1/2.
9 Fosbrooke, *Glos.* ii. 193; Glos. R.O., D 421/L 16.
10 Glos. R.O., P 209/IN 1/2.
11 Ibid. P 209A/IN 3/1.   12 Ibid. D 421/E 31.
13 Hart, *Lord Bledisloe.*   14 Inscr. in ch.
15 Inf. from Mr. O. B. Hepworth, agent to the est.
16 *Antiq. Jnl.* xi. 240–61.
17 *Inq. p.m. Glos.* 1302–58, 158.   18 Ibid. 1359–1413, 54.
19 P.R.O., E 142/26.   20 Glos. R.O., D 421/M 23.
21 O.S. Map 6", Glos. XLVII. NW. (1883 edn.).
22 P.R.O., STAC 2/23/218.
23 Glos. R.O., D 421/M 23. The grounds of the Old Manor Ho. may then have extended to the market place and

cross with no other houses intervening.
24 List of Bldgs. of Archit. or Hist. Interest (Min. of Housing, 1952); Glos. R.O., GPS 209/3–5; *Wyntours of the White Cross* (White Cross sch. 1986), 20–1.
25 Glos. R.O., D 421/E 3, depositions 1617; cf. Atkyns, *Glos.* 539.
26 *Bibliotheca Glos.* i, pp. lxxxvii, cvi; ii. 39, 95, 147.
27 Glos. R.O., D 421/T 22; for the furnace, below, econ. hist. (mills and ironworks).
28 Bodl. MS. Top. Glouc. c. 3, f. 191v.; *Glos. N. & Q.* ii. 497.
29 Glos. R.O., D 421/E 53, accts. 1728–9.
30 Rudder, *Glos.* plate at pp. 524–5 (below, Plate 12) .
31 Glos. R.O., D 421/E 39; cf. Hart, *Lord Bledisloe*, 49.
32 Glos. R.O., D 421/E 53, L 16.
33 Ibid. P 209/IN 1/1, mem. at end.
34 Ibid. D 421/E 45; Rudder, *Glos.* plate at pp. 524–5.
35 Hart, *Lord Bledisloe*, 49; Glos. Colln. prints 182.10.

disloe lived at Redhill House, built in the late 19th century on the north-east side of the park. From 1950 Lydney Park was occupied by his son and eventual successor, who created an ornamental garden in a wooded valley north-west of the house.[36]

In 1066 Earl Harold held the manor of *NASS*, assessed on 5 hides, and soon after the Conquest William FitzOsbern joined it to the manors of Purton and Poulton (in Awre) to make a single estate.[37] Following the rebellion of FitzOsbern's son Roger, Nass, Purton, and Poulton were in the king's hands in 1086 and they later resumed their separate identities, apparently after inclusion in a royal grant to the earls of Warwick.[38] Nass manor is recorded again in 1300 when Walter of Nass was its lord,[39] and in 1322 Walter held a house and 50 a., presumably comprising only the demesne land, from the Talbots' manor;[40] the manor continued to be held from Lydney Shrewsbury manor.[41] Thomas Rigg and Catherine his wife held Nass manor in 1400,[42] and in 1419 their daughter Joan held it with her husband Robert Greyndour.[43] Nass manor then descended with Clearwell, in Newland, until 1611 when it was among estates of the Baynham family[44] that passed to the Vaughans. Between 1658[45] and 1668 John Vaughan of Ruardean sold the manor with the house and farm called Nass Court, to William Jones, owner of the Nass House estate, who had been lessee of the farm since 1650 or earlier.[46]

The Jones family was established at Nass by 1577, when William Jones owned a small freehold,[47] and it later bought from the Winters a larger estate. The Winters' estate at Nass included land that Joan Greyndour gave to endow a chantry at Newland in 1446 and William Winter bought in 1559,[48] and possibly also land that Joan and her second husband alienated in 1481.[49] In 1607 Sir Edward Winter owned several small farms, one of which was on lease to Charles Jones;[50] in 1651 three were on lease to Charles's son William, who bought the freehold of the estate the following year.[51]

William Jones's combined estates at Nass passed at his death in 1667 or 1668[52] to his son Charles (d. 1689). About 1679 Charles settled Nass on the marriage of his son William,[53] whose widow Anne held it in 1685.[54] It passed to Roynon Jones (d. 1732),[55] whose widow Anne

settled Nass House and a large part of the estate on the marriage of her son William in 1735; she retained Nass Court and other lands, which were confirmed to her for life in 1763.[56] William Jones died in 1775[57] and the Nass estate then passed in direct line of descent to Roynon (d. 1817),[58] the Revd. Edward[59] (d. 1847), Edward Owen Jones[60] (d. 1872), and William Charles Nigel Jones (d. 1915).[61] In 1916 the estate, comprising Nass House, Nass Court, Cliff Farm, and c. 440 a., was offered for sale by its mortgagees. John Biddle, tenant of one of the farms,[62] bought the estate c. 1920, and his family owned and farmed it in 1990.[63]

Early owners of Nass manor may have built a small castle there. In 1558 Nass cliff was known alternatively as 'Nass Castle',[64] and in 1737 the Joneses claimed that a castle had anciently stood on their manor.[65] Its most likely site appears to be at Nass Point, at the south end of the cliff, guarding the entrance to Lydney Pill. A hall and farm buildings were recorded on the manor in 1443,[66] probably at the site of Nass Court, on the west side of Nass Lane. The small farmhouse at Nass Court contains one early 17th-century window and may date from a rebuilding of that date but it has been much altered at a later period. On the lane to the east stands a buttressed barn of eight bays which formerly had a base-cruck roof and probably dates from the 16th century. Nass House, on the lane further south, is a large late 17th-century mansion. It was probably built by William Jones in the 1660s after he had enlarged his estate but it may be on the site of an earlier dwelling of the Jones family. The house, which is largely built of rubble but incorporates some blocks of ashlar, has a north front of seven bays and a south front of six bays with a centre that is recessed to a staircase tower. The elevations are gabled but the tower is capped by a flat roof with a cupola. A service wing was added on the west, probably in the early 18th century, when several of the rooms in the house were panelled. A walled forecourt abuts the house on the south side, and on the north there was a long avenue of lime trees,[67] felled in the mid 20th century. The house, which has undergone little alteration since it was built, was apparently little used by the Joneses after c. 1770 when they built a new house at Hayhill on their Ruddle manor, in Newnham.[68]

36 Hart, *Lord Bledisloe*, 17; Lydney Park guide (c. 1985).
37 *Dom. Bk.* (Rec. Com.), i. 164.
38 Above, this section.
39 *Trans. B.G.A.S.* lxvi. 186; cf. P.R.O., C 115/K 2/6683, f. 89 and v.   40 P.R.O., E 142/26.
41 Ibid. C 140/84, no. 39; Glos. R.O., D 421/M 19, ct. 21 Apr. 23 Hen. VI; D 421/E 13, f 21.
42 P.R.O., CP 25/1/290/59, no. 11.
43 *Cal. Inq. p.m. Hen. VII*, i, p. 47; *Trans. B.G.A.S.* vi. 183.
44 Below, Newland, manors; *Cal. Inq. p.m. Hen. VII*, i, p. 47; P.R.O., C 142/33, no. 69; C 142/189, no. 82; N.L.W., Dunraven MSS. 260.
45 Below, Ruardean, manors (Hathaways); *Cal. S.P. Dom. 1580–1625*, 545; P.R.O., CP 25/2/555/1658 Mich. no. 57.
46 Glos. R.O., D 421/L 2; *Cal. Cttee. for Compounding*, iii. 2362.   47 Glos. R.O., D 421/M 84.
48 N.L.W., Dunraven MSS. 325; *Cal. Pat. 1558–60*, 359.
49 P.R.O., CP 25/1/79/94, nos. 51–3.
50 Glos. R.O., D 421/E 13, ff. 12v., 32v.
51 Ibid. M 79, T 11.

52 P.R.O., PROB 11/328 (P.C.C. 133 Hone), ff. 161v.– 162v.
53 Glos. R.O., D 421/L 2; P.R.O., PROB 11/397 (P.C.C. 158 Ent), ff. 155–157v.   54 Glos. R.O., D 421/L 7.
55 Ibid. L 9, L 11; Bigland, *Glos.* ii. 160.
56 Glos. R.O., D 177/III/10.   57 Ibid. P 209/IN 1/2.
58 Ibid. IN 1/11, which also records the burial of his eldest son Roynon in 1814: cf. *Glouc. Jnl.* 10 Jan. 1814. For the Joneses, Burke, *Land. Gent.* (1898), i. 824.
59 G.D.R., T 1/117; Glos. R.O., D 1272, deeds of Nass man. 1818–43.   60 Glos. R.O., P 209A/SD 1/1.
61 Ibid. D 6993/1, ct. 9 May 1916; *Kelly's Dir. Glos.* (1914), 248.   62 Glos. Colln. RX 195.1.
63 Inf. from Mr. E. Biddle.
64 Glos. R.O., D 421/M 23.   65 Ibid. L 8.
66 P.R.O., C 139/115, no. 34.
67 Glos. Colln. RX 195.1; for the ho. (where access was not possible in 1990), below, Plate 11.
68 *V.C.H. Glos.* x. 38; cf. Glos. R.O., D 1272, deeds of Nass man. 1818–43; P 209A/SD 1/1; *Kelly's Dir. Glos.* (1910), 242.

Before 1066 the manor of *PURTON* was severed from Awre manor, to which it had been attached as a contributor to the royal farm, and, as mentioned above, it was later included in FitzOsbern's amalgamation of manors.[69] By the early 13th century Purton had been acquired by Maurice de Gant (d. *c.* 1230) who granted it at farm to his tenants.[70] In 1242 Maurice's widow Margaret Somery held Purton with Over (in Almondsbury) from the earl of Warwick as ¼ knight's fee.[71] It later passed to Maurice's nephew and heir Robert de Gurney (d. *c.* 1269), whose son Anselm[72] granted the manor shortly before 1285 to his son William.[73] By 1303 Purton was held by John ap Adam,[74] who had married Elizabeth de Gurney, daughter of William's brother John. John ap Adam died *c.* 1311, and in 1325 his son Thomas granted the whole or the bulk of his Purton estate to John of Walton for life.[75] In 1328, however, Thomas granted the manor to William of Cheltenham, who then or later had a grant from John of Walton of his interest.[76] It is probable that in those transactions William of Cheltenham was acting for his patron Thomas of Berkeley, Lord Berkeley, and that later he had the manor in his own right by gift of Lord Berkeley.[77] In 1360 William gave 12 houses and 12 yardlands at Purton, evidently the bulk of the estate, as the endowment of a chantry chapel,[78] and in 1366 he granted the remainder of his estate to Maurice, Lord Berkeley, reserving a life interest, which however he surrendered to Maurice the following year.[79]

The chantry estate and the Berkeleys' estate both continued to be known as Purton manor. The former was sold by the Crown in 1549 after the dissolution of the chantries to Sir John Thynne and Thomas Throckmorton,[80] and before 1560 it was acquired by William Winter.[81] The other estate descended with Tucknall manor in Lydney and with Awre manor,[82] and in 1546 it was held in dower by Queen Catherine Parr, formerly the wife of John Neville, Lord Latimer.[83] Later it seems to have become regarded as part of Tucknall manor, a survey of which in 1577 included free rents in Purton and the fishing rights adjoining the tithing,[84] and it evidently passed to the Winters with Tucknall in 1595. Much of the land at Purton was sold to

the tenants in the 1650s[85] but the Winters and their successors the Bathursts retained the manorial rights and some farmland.[86]

Purton Manor, the chief house of the chantry estate, and the demesne lands belonging to it were sold by the Winters in 1657 to William Donning,[87] whose family had leased them from before 1607.[88] In 1673 William (d. 1680) settled most of his estate on the marriage of his son Thomas,[89] who held it at his death in 1714.[90] In 1740 and 1752 the estate belonged to Sir John Hynd Cotton, Bt., and others.[91] By 1791 the owner was Edward Eliot, Lord Eliot (d. 1804),[92] and the estate, comprising Purton Manor farm, which had absorbed the adjoining Wellhouse farm, and Hill farm, based on a house at Gurshill, passed to his son John Craggs Eliot,[93] who was created earl of St. Germans in 1815. The earl (d. 1823) was succeeded in his estates and title by his brother William, who sold Hill farm in 1830 to Charles Mathias of Lamphey Court (Pemb.), the promoter of a scheme to build a railway line from the Forest to Purton Pill.[94] Purton Manor and the rest of the estate were acquired before 1839 by James Croome of Breadstone, in Berkeley.[95] Croome (d. 1865) was succeeded by his eldest son John James Croome but his younger son Thomas Breadstone Croome[96] owned the estate by 1870.[97] James Croome and his successors enlarged their estate to include most of the farms of the east part of the parish, and at his death in 1909 T. B. Croome owned Purton Manor, Warren, Hill, Hurst, Rodley Manor, and Crump farms, a total of *c.* 900 a. The estate passed to James Croome-Jackman (d. 1925), and was apparently sold and split up before the Second World War.[98] Purton Manor farm was bought in the late 1940s by Mr. D. J. Aldridge and he and his family owned and farmed it together with adjoining farms in 1990.[99]

Purton Manor, which stands on a cliff overlooking the Severn, was the home of the priests who served the adjoining chantry chapel until the mid 16th century.[1] The low west range of the present house was probably built in the 16th century as the central room of a house which was otherwise demolished in the early 17th century when the three-storeyed east block was built.

69 *Dom. Bk.* (Rec. Com.), i. 163, 164.
70 *Cal. Inq. p.m.* i, p. 226; for Maur. and his heirs, *Berkeley MSS.* i. 50–54.
71 *Cal. Inq. p.m.* i, p. 3, where she appears as Marg. 'de Gomery'.   72 Ibid. p. 226; cf. P.R.O., E 32/30, rot. 24.
73 *Feud. Aids*, ii. 240.
74 Ibid. 251; cf. *Cal. Inq. p.m.* v, p. 402, where 'Cenere' is evidently a mistake for Over.
75 Berkeley Cast. Mun., General Ser. Chart. 2445.
76 Ibid. 2650, 1571.
77 *Berkeley MSS.* i. 342.
78 *Cal. Pat.* 1358–61, 477.
79 Berkeley Cast. Mun., General Ser. Chart. 3576, 3578–9, 3594.
80 *Cal. Pat.* 1548–9, 329–30.
81 Glos. R.O., D 421/M 82.
82 *Berkeley MSS.* i. 378; *Cal. Inq. p.m.* (Rec. Com.), iv. 31, 192; cf. below, this section (Tucknall); above, Awre, manors.
83 P.R.O., C 142/74, no. 78; *Complete Peerage*, vii. 483–4.
84 Glos. R.O., D 421/M 84.
85 Ibid. T 14.
86 Rudder, *Glos.* 528; G.D.R., T 1/117; Glos. R.O., P

209A/SD 1/1; D 421/T 16.
87 Glos. R.O., D 673/II/8/T 2, marr. settlem. 1673.
88 Ibid. D 421/E 13, ff. 11v.–12, 31v.
89 Ibid. D 673/II/8/T 2; G.D.R. wills 1680/211.
90 Atkyns, *Glos.* 541; Glos. R.O., P 209/IN 1/1, burials 1713/14.
91 Glos. R.O., D 189/VII/1.
92 Ibid. P 209/MI 1, pp. 107–8; cf. ibid. D 421/E 42, draft agreement 1792; for Eliot and his successors, Burke, *Peerage* (1963), 2143.
93 Glos. R.O., P 209A/IN 3/1, ff. 20, 25; cf. below, this section (Wellhouse).
94 Glos. R.O., EL 425; Paar, *G.W.R. in Dean*, 122. Hill fm. was then called Gurshill fm.: cf. G.D.R., T 1/117.
95 G.D.R., T 1/117; cf. below, this section (Soilwell).
96 Deeds of Prior's Lodge, in possession of Mr. A. M. R. Watts, succession duty acct. 1866; *Cal. Grants of Probate* (1866).
97 *Kelly's Dir. Glos.* (1870), 593.
98 Glos. R.O., D 2428/1/7; D 2299/3469; *Kelly's Dir. Glos.* (1914 and later edns.).
99 Inf. from Mr. Aldridge.
1 Hockaday Abs. cclxv, 1549; Glos. R.O., D 421/M 83.

That block has a near symmetrical plan with one room on either side of a central stair; the older range became the kitchen and other service accommodation was provided in a two-storeyed lean- to in the angle between the two ranges. The north-eastern ground- floor room has a moulded plaster ceiling and an overmantel bearing the date 1618 and the initials of members of the Donning family, then the tenants.[2] West of the house is a 17th-century stable block with three gables and decorated circular windows.

Lands at Lydney that the brothers Ralph and Niel de Mundeville held under the overlordship of Waleran (d. 1204), earl of Warwick, apparently comprised or included an estate that was later called the manor of *TUCKNALL*. They were succeeded by Richard de Mundeville,[3] who held ½ knight's fee from the earl of Warwick in 1242.[4] The estate passed to Philip de Mundeville[5] who apparently granted it to John of Nass and Walter (or William) Warren; in 1285 they held ⅙ knight's fee from Philip.[6] In 1303 Walter Warren held ⅒ fee at Tucknall[7] and his estate, which was later held from Lydney Warwick manor, passed to another Walter Warren by 1346,[8] and to Thomas, son of Henry Warren, who in 1350 sold it to Thomas of Berkeley, Lord Berkeley.[9] It then descended with Awre manor,[10] passing to Sir Edward Winter in 1595.[11] Tucknall manor has not been found named among the Winters' estates after 1619,[12] and in 1677 it was described as having been absorbed in Lydney Shrewsbury manor.[13] In 1577 it comprised a widely scattered group of lands in the eastern tithings of the parish, most of them held freely from it by chief rents. The name of the manor was taken from a place south-east of Newerne, surviving in a corrupt form as Tutnalls: Tucknalls green[14] and other lands called Tucknalls were mentioned in that area in the late 17th century.[15]

Before 1538 Walter Yate of Arlingham bought from William Bashe, vicar of Arlingham, a reversionary right to lands in Lydney parish after the life interest of James Cooke,[16] and at his death in 1546 Walter held the manor of *ALLASTON* from the Latimers' Purton manor.[17] He apparently left it, together with his Wellhouse estate at Purton, to a younger son John Yate,[18] who in 1557 conveyed the house called Allaston Court and lands, then said to be held from Lydney Warwick manor, to Thomas Browne.[19] In or shortly before 1568 Allaston manor was acquired by William Winter.[20] The Winters sold much of the land, including Allaston Court farm, in 1668 to Gloucester corporation as trustee of Sir Thomas Rich's school in that city,[21] and the corporation also acquired Driffield farm from Dame Frances Winter in 1712 in a belated adjustment to meet the value of the lands agreed at the sale of 1668.[22] The Gloucester United Schools Governors, successors to the corporation's trust,[23] sold their 292- acre Allaston estate in 1907.[24] Most of it, including Allaston Court and Driffield farms, was bought then or shortly afterwards by Charles Bathurst and added once more to the Lydney estate.[25] A farm called Little Allaston and the manorial rights had continued as part of that estate after 1668.[26] The Lydney estate sold most of its Allaston lands in the mid 20th century. Allaston Court farm was acquired by the tenants, the Liddington family, which retained the house and a small acreage in 1990, most of the land having been sold for building.[27] Allaston Court was rebuilt in the late 17th century as a gabled stone farmhouse of two storeys and attics,[28] and in the early 19th century it was doubled in size by an extension to the southwest.

An estate at the north end of Allaston tithing known as *SOILWELL*, and sometimes as Sully, was said in the late 17th century to have been an assart from the waste of the Forest,[29] and the fact that it was held directly from the Crown without the intervening lordship of the earls of Warwick or their successors also indicates such an origin.[30] It was evidently the land called the park of Sully that John of Sully held in 1284 when he was given deer from the Forest to stock it.[31] No later record of the estate has been found before c. 1600 when it was among estates in the parish that had been acquired by Thomas James, merchant and alderman of Bristol.[32] The small Warren estate in Purton, named from the family that owned it from 1322 or earlier,[33] came to Thomas before 1581[34] from his mother Margaret, daughter of William Warren of St. Briavels,[35] and Thomas also bought the Rodleys estate in Allaston.[36] Thomas James (d. 1619)[37]

[2] T and M D, probably for Thos. and Marg.: cf. G.D.R. wills 1639/140; Glos. R.O., D 421/M 83.
[3] P.R.O., C 115/K 2/6683, f. 76 and v.
[4] *Cal. Inq. p.m.* i, p. 3.
[5] P.R.O., C 115/L 1/6689, f. 172 and v.
[6] *Feud. Aids*, ii. 240.
[7] Ibid. 251   [8] Ibid. 285.
[9] Berkeley Cast. Mun., General Ser. Chart. 3352.
[10] *Cal. Pat.* 1485–94, 125; Glos. R.O., D 421/M 84; above, Awre, manors.
[11] P.R.O., C 142/248, no. 22; C 3/295/10.
[12] Ibid. C 142/378, no. 147.
[13] Glos. R.O., D 421/L 6.
[14] Ibid. M 29, ct. 1668, which mentioned the lane (probably the later Tutnalls Lane) leading from Tuttels (probably at the later Tuthill Ho.) to Tucknalls green: cf. O.S. Map 6", Glos. XLVII. NE. (1891 edn.).
[15] Glos. R.O., D 421/E 16.
[16] P.R.O., C 1/932, nos. 16–17.
[17] Ibid. C 142/74, no. 78.
[18] G.D.R. wills 1546/221; *Visit. Glos. 1682–3*, 209–10.
[19] Glos. R.O., D 421/M 23; P.R.O., CP 25/2/71/589, no. 16.

[20] Glos. R.O., D 421/6.
[21] Ibid. D 3270/R 21; *14th Rep. Com. Char.* H.C. 382, p. 25(1826), xii.
[22] Glos. R.O., D 3270/R 23, R 26.
[23] Cf above, Awre, manors.
[24] Glos. Colln. (H) G 5.1 (9); M. Burden, *My Brook became a River* (Glouc. 1980), 36.
[25] Glos. R.O., D 2428/1/7.
[26] Ibid. D 421/L 6; P 209A/SD 1/1; G.D.R., T 1/117.
[27] Inf. from Mr. G. D. L. Liddington.
[28] Cf. G.B.R., J 4/1, no. 27.
[29] Glos. R.O., D 421/L 6.
[30] *Inq. p.m. Glos.* 1625–42, i. 113.
[31] *Cal. Close*, 1279–88, 253. Land E. of Soilwell ho. was later known as the Park: G.D.R., T 1/117.
[32] Glos. R.O., D 421/L 6; cf. *V.C.H. Glos.* x. 65; Smith, *Men and Armour*, 53.
[33] P.R.O., E 142/26; C 138/40, no. 52; *Cal. Inq. p.m.* xi, p. 467; Glos. R.O., D 421/M 23.
[34] Glos. R.O., D 421/M 27; cf. *Inq. p.m. Glos.* 1625–42, i. 111, 113.   [35] Below, St. Briavels, manors (Stowe).
[36] Below, this section.   [37] *V.C.H. Glos.* x. 65.

was succeeded by his son Edward[38] (d. 1628), Edward by his infant son Thomas,[39] who came of age c. 1647[40] and died in 1671,[41] and Thomas by his son Thomas, a minor in the guardianship of his mother Elizabeth until c. 1680.[42] The last Thomas (d. 1702), who lived at Warren, devised his estates, apart from Rodleys, to his son Edward,[43] but Soilwell and Warren passed, probably before 1707,[44] to Thomas's brother William (d. 1727). William was succeeded by his son William,[45] who was clerk of the peace for Gloucestershire from 1723 until his death in 1742.[46] The younger William left his estates to be sold,[47] but his daughter Frances James was described as of Soilwell at her death in 1766.[48] The James family sold the estate to Richard Williams, who apparently sold to John Townley, the owner in 1791.[49] Peregrine Townley owned it in 1802. His estate was offered for sale in 1838, when Warren was bought by James Croome and added to the Purton Manor estate.[50] Soilwell belonged in 1839 to Blanche Taylor.[51] In 1864 John Trotter Thomas of Coleford owned the house and 124 a.[52] He sold the estate in 1870 to Arnold Thomas, whose widow put it up for sale in 1920.[53] Lord Bledisloe bought it soon afterwards and the farmland remained part of the Lydney estate in 1990,[54] Soilwell house having passed into separate ownership.

There was apparently a house at Soilwell by the late Middle Ages. It was rebuilt in 1661[55] as a tall house of stone with two storeys and attics, the ground floor raised on cellars; it has a three-room plan with three chimney stacks on the rear wall. The entrance is by a porch at one end of the central hall and a stair turret rises from a doorway at the other end. The principal rooms were fitted with panelling in the mid 18th century when a small addition was made at the back. The walled front garden with cross paths may be contemporary with the house.

Before 1204 the brothers Ralph and Niel de Mundeville, apparently owners of Tucknall manor,[56] gave 1½ yardland at a place called Archer's Hall in Lydney to Alan, chamberlain of Waleran, earl of Warwick. Alan granted the land to Kenilworth priory (Warws.) but later granted it to Llanthony priory, Gloucester, which had a quitclaim from Kenilworth[57] and had two tenants at Archer's Hall in 1287.[58] Llanthony apparently alienated the estate before the Dissolution.[59] It was presumably the small manor in the south part of Allaston tithing that was held from Tucknall in the 16th century[60] and was known as ARCHER'S HALL, ALLASTON, or RODLEYS. William Kingscote (d. 1524) of Kingscote owned houses and lands there, and his son William[61] had the manor at his death in 1540. William, son of the younger William, succeeded[62] and his son Christopher Kingscote conveyed the manor in 1590 to Thomas James.[63] Rodleys manor then descended with Soilwell[64] until 1689 when Thomas James (d. 1702) conveyed it to his brother Richard, who died without issue in 1694.[65] Rodleys then reverted to Thomas, who settled it on his wife Joan, and in 1711 Joan joined in a settlement of the manor on their son Edward and his heirs.[66] By 1752 the manor house was occupied by Thomas James,[67] who died in 1761.[68] Edward Jones owned Rodleys manor c. 1775 and in 1791,[69] George Jones owned the house and 95 a. in 1839,[70] and the representatives of Elizabeth Anne Jones owned that estate in 1864.[71] It later formed part of the Croome family's estate.[72] The house, known as Archer's Hall or Rodleys in 1564[73] and as Rodley Manor in the 20th century, was rebuilt in the early 19th century. By 1990, when part of the farmland had been built on, the house was derelict.

In 1285 small unidentified estates were held from the earl of Warwick by Richard de Alington, who had 1/10 knight's fee, Thomas Pavy, who had 1/6 knight's fee, and Hugh de Chavelinworth, who had 1/6 knight's fee.[74] Richard's estate was perhaps the 1/10 knight's fee in 'Yerdeshulle' that was held by members of the Wyle (or Byle) family in the early 14th century and by Richard Barrett in 1402.[75] The place name has been identified as Gurshill[76] and possibly the estate was later represented by one of the farms in that area.

38 Glos. R.O., D 421/L 6; cf. Visit. Glos. 1682–3, 98.
39 Inq. p.m. Glos. 1625–42, i. 110–14; Hockaday Abs. cclxvii, 1628.
40 Hockaday Abs. cclxvii, 1650.
41 For Thos. and his successors, Visit. Glos. 1682–3, 98 (where the forenames of Thos. and his son Thos. appear incorrectly as Jas.); Bigland, Glos. i. 238–9; Glos. R.O., P 278/IN 1/1, burials.
42 Glos. R.O., D 421/L 6; Hockaday Abs. cclxvii, 1682.
43 G.D.R. wills 1702/31.
44 Glos. R.O., D 421/M 34, ct. 1707; D 637/II/8/T 3 (bounds of Wellhouse est. given in deed 1716).
45 G.D.R. wills 1727/107; Glos. R.O., D 326/L 16.
46 Glos. Q.S. Archives, pp. xi, 87; Glos. R.O., D 678/fam. settlems. 57D/123–30, 273.
47 Glos. R.O., D 326/L 16.
48 Glos. R.O., P 278/IN 1/3; cf. Bigland, Glos. i. 239.
49 Rudder, Glos. 530, where Townsend is presumably a mistake for Townley; Glos. R.O., P 209/MI 1, p. 111.
50 Glos. R.O., D 637/I/71; D 608/13, no. 12.
51 G.D.R., T 1/117.
52 Glos. R.O., P 209A/SD 1/1.
53 Ibid. D 2299/1862.
54 Inf. from Mr. Hepworth.
55 An inscr., which had been removed or covered up by 1990, read 'Edificat Sully A.D. 1437, Redificat Soilwell Manor 1661': List of Bldgs. of Archit. or Hist. Interest (Dept. of Environment, 1988).
56 Above, this section.
57 P.R.O., C 115/K 2/6683, f. 76 and v.; C 115/L 1/6689, f. 172 and v.
58 Plac. de Quo Warr. (Rec. Com.), 244.
59 Cf. P.R.O., SC 6/Hen. VIII/1224.
60 Ibid. C 142/62, no. 105; Glos. R.O., D 421/E 13, f. 23.
61 P.R.O., C 142/42, no. 115; for the Kingscotes, Visit. Glos. 1623, 99–100.
62 P.R.O., C 142/62, no. 105.
63 Trans. B.G.A.S. xvii. 132.
64 Above, this section; Inq. p.m. Glos. 1625–42, i. 110–14; Glos. R.O., D 421/L 6.
65 Glos. R.O., D 6/F 9; for Ric., ibid. P 278/IN 1/1, burials 1694; Bigland, Glos. i. 238.
66 G.D.R. wills 1702/31; Glos. R.O., D 6/F 9.
67 Berkeley Cast. Mun., General Ser. T, box 25, letters 3 July 1752; 13 Apr. 1755.   68 Bigland, Glos. ii. 160.
69 Rudder, Glos. 530; Glos. R.O., P 209/MI 1, p. 104.
70 G.D.R., T 1/117.
71 Glos. R.O., P 209A/SD 1/1.
72 Above, this section (Purton).
73 G.D.R. wills 1565/82; cf. Glos. R.O., D 421/L 6.
74 Feud. Aids, ii. 240.   75 Ibid. 251, 285, 298.
76 P.N. Glos. (E.P.N.S.), iii. 258.

A small manor called *HURST* in Allaston was held by Thomas Rigg and Catherine his wife in 1400[77] and passed with Nass manor to the Greyndours.[78] It was probably the estate, including 2 messuages and 120 a., that John and Joan Barre conveyed to Thomas Morgan in 1466,[79] for Thomas a Morgan, alderman of Gloucester, owned Hurst at his death in 1534.[80] Men called Thomas Morgan of Hurst, probably fathers and sons in succession, died in 1568,[81] c. 1613,[82] 1664, and 1704, and Richard Morgan of Hurst died in 1717.[83] Hurst was later owned by Probert Morgan (d. 1759),[84] whose widow held it c. 1775,[85] and the Morgan family still owned the estate in 1791.[86] In 1839 the house and 233 a. belonged to Henry Morgan Clifford.[87] In 1864 and 1926 Hurst was part of the Croome family's estate.[88] In 1942 it was bought by a branch of the Biddle family, and in 1990 the farm, covering 240 a., was owned and worked by Mr. D. R. Biddle.[89] The house, which stands on a low hill in the south part of Allaston tithing, has a north range of two storeys and attics with a four-bayed, cruck-framed roof. About 1800 the west end of that range was refronted and a new wing was built against its south side.

A small estate in Purton tithing, held from the Latimers' Purton manor, was called the manor of *WELLHOUSE* in 1546 but has not been found described as a manor later. It was owned by Walter Yate (d. 1546), who devised it to a younger son John,[90] and it passed with Allaston manor to William Winter before 1568. In 1542 Walter Yate had leased the house and lands for 60 years to Laurence Gough,[91] whose family retained the lease until its expiry.[92] In 1623 Sir John Winter leased Wellhouse with 106 a. to George Donning, who was succeeded by his son Thomas.[93] Thomas bought the freehold from the Winters in 1659[94] and died in 1675 or 1676.[95] The estate later passed to William Donning of Nursehill (d. 1715) and at a partition of his estates among his daughters was divided between Mary, wife of the Revd. Thomas Mantle, and Isabel, later the wife of Samuel Dudbridge of Woodchester.[96] By 1745 Wellhouse had been acquired by the owners of the adjoining Purton Manor estate, with which it then descended. Most of the house had fallen down by 1745 and its site, south-west of Purton hamlet overlooking the part of the river called Wellhouse Bay, was

marked later only by a barn,[97] of which ruins remained in 1990.

Aylburton was not named in Domesday Book but in 1300 was thought to be ancient demesne of the Crown[98] and so it was presumably among the Lydney estates amalgamated by FitzOsbern. It was apparently not among the land later granted to the earls of Warwick,[99] for it was held directly from the Crown in 1285.[1] The earliest record found of the manor of *AYLBURTON* was in 1167 when it was held by Hugh de Lacy[2] (d. 1186), whose son Walter succeeded to it in 1189.[3] In the early 13th century Walter granted the manor, excepting a moiety of the tenant land which was in the possession of William son of Warin, to Philip de Coleville[4] (fl. 1229, 1244).[5] Philip was succeeded before 1258 by William de Coleville,[6] who shortly before 1272 granted the manor to Bartholomew de Mora.[7] Another estate in Aylburton, perhaps comprising the lands reserved in Walter de Lacy's grant, was held by Vivian de Roshale in 1258, passing by 1270 to Fulk de Lacy,[8] who granted it to Bartholomew de Mora.[9] In 1277 Bartholomew granted Aylburton manor to Llanthony priory, Gloucester,[10] which retained it until the Dissolution.

In 1559 the Crown sold Aylburton manor to William Winter,[11] and two smaller freehold estates at Aylburton were added to the Winters' Lydney estate in 1599. In 1367 Thomas Gainer was dealing with an estate comprising a plough-land and other lands,[12] and his estate was presumably one of the two freeholds for which Thomas Buck and Edward Cottington did homage to the prior of Llanthony in 1515.[13] Thomas's estate passed to Matthew Buck (d. 1540), whose son and heir Thomas[14] was presumably the Thomas Buck who bought the other estate from John Cottington of Leigh upon Mendip (Som.) in 1573. In 1599 James Buck sold the two estates, each with a chief house, to Sir Edward Winter.[15] In 1718 Dame Frances Winter sold the bulk of the tenant land belonging to the Lydney estate in Aylburton to John Lawes,[16] but much of it was evidently bought back later by the Bathursts, who were the only large landowners in the tithing in 1818.[17] A court and other buildings were mentioned on the manor in 1277,[18] but by the early 16th century Llanthony priory maintained a manor house

77 P.R.O., CP 25/1/290/59, no. 11.
78 Ibid. C 139/115, no. 34.
79 Ibid. CP 25/1/79/93, no. 12.
80 Ibid. C 142/57, no. 50. 81 G.D.R. wills 1568/128.
82 Ibid. 1612/252. 83 Bigland, *Glos.* ii. 158–9.
84 Ibid. 159; cf. *Glouc. Jnl.* 24 July 1759.
85 Rudder, *Glos.* 530.
86 Glos. R.O., P 209/MI 1, p. 105.
87 G.D.R., T 1/117.
88 Glos. R.O., P 209A/SD 1/1; D 2299/3469; above, this section. 89 Inf. from Mr. D. R. Biddle.
90 P.R.O., C 142/74, no. 78; G.D.R. wills 1546/221.
91 Glos. R.O., D 421/6.
92 Hockaday Abs. cclxvi, 1571; Glos. R.O., D 421/E 13, f. 10v. 93 Glos. R.O., D 421/M 83.
94 Ibid. T 14. 95 G.D.R. wills 1675/162.
96 Glos. R.O., D 637/II/8/T 3; for Wm.'s death, ibid. P 209/IN 1/1.
97 Ibid. D 189/VII/1, letters 29 July, 4 Aug. 1745; G.D.R., T 1/117.

98 *Trans. B.G.A.S.* lxvi. 190.
99 Above, this section. 1 *Feud. Aids*, ii. 240.
2 *Pipe R.* 1167 (P.R.S. xi), 144.
3 Ibid. 1186 (P.R.S. xxxvi), 122; 1188 (P.R.S. xxxviii), 112.; W. E. Wightman, *Lacy Fam. in Eng. and Normandy* (1966), 201–2. 4 P.R.O., C 115/K 2/6683, f. 77.
5 Ibid. C 115/K 2/6683, ff. 86v.–87.
6 Ibid. E 32/28, rot. 2d.; E 32/29, rot. 8d.
7 Ibid. C 115/K 2/6683, ff. 77v., 86.
8 Ibid. E 32/28, rot. 2d.; E 32/29, rot. 8d.
9 Ibid. C 115/K 2/6683, f. 77v.; *Feud. Aids*, ii. 240.
10 P.R.O., C 115/K 2/6683, f. 77v.
11 *Cal. Pat.* 1558–60, 359; the sale was to Winter and to Edw. Baeshe, who released his right to Winter: Glos. R.O., D 421/T 32. 12 P.R.O., CP 25/1/78/74, no. 475.
13 Ibid. C 115/L 2/6691, f. 80.
14 Ibid. C 142/69, no. 75.
15 Glos. R.O., D 421/T 31. 16 Ibid. T 30.
17 Ibid. P 209A/IN 3/1, ff. 37–43.
18 P.R.O., C 115/K 2/6683, f. 88v.

only on its adjoining manor of Alvington, with which Aylburton was administered.[19]

An estate, comprising land in the north of Aylburton tithing, in Bream tithing of Newland, and in St. Briavels, was based on a house at the parish boundary that was called at various times PRIOR'S MESNE LODGE, BREAM LODGE, and PRIOR'S LODGE. It originated in 212 a. of the waste of the Forest that the Crown allowed Llanthony priory to assart in 1306.[20] The priory's tenants of Aylburton and Alvington manors were allowed to common in the assarted land, usually known as Prior's Mesne, and after the Dissolution the lords of the two manors disputed the right of soil. A large house built there by William Compton of Alvington in or shortly before 1581 was demolished by a mob, supposedly instigated by Sir William Winter, lord of Aylburton. In 1584, however, the Crown claimed ownership of Prior's Mesne and sold it to two speculators, whose right was acquired soon afterwards by Winter. Successfully resisting the continuing claim that it was part of Alvington manor, the Winters later held it in severalty.[21] Prior's Mesne Lodge had been built by 1656 when the Winters sold it with the north part of Prior's Mesne and lands in the adjoining parishes to John Parry of London,[22] who sold his estate in 1662 to William Powlett. The southern part of Prior's Mesne, comprising a large coney warren, was sold by the Winters to James Barrow of Bream, who sold it before 1681 to William Powlett, his brother-in-law.[23] Powlett (d. 1703), a serjeant at law,[24] left the estate to James Barrow's son John, who died childless c. 1713, with successive remainders to James (d. by 1718), his wife Barbara, their daughter Mary Lawrence, and Mary's younger children.[25] The subsequent descent in the Lawrence family is complicated, but later occupants of the estate, though not necessarily owners of all rights in it, were Mary's son Powlett Lawrence (d. by 1756), his brother Barrow Lawrence (d. 1770), and Barrow's daughter Ann, wife of Thomas Baron. On Baron's bankruptcy in 1775 assignees took possession of the estate and mortgaged it for the benefit of his creditors, and in 1794 the mortgagee John Paul foreclosed.[26]

In 1802 John Paul sold the Prior's Mesne estate to John Wade of Awre and John Matthews of Newnham. In 1803 Wade released his right to Matthews (d. 1808), whose trustees sold the estate, which then comprised 410 a. in Aylburton and the adjoining parishes and was reputed to be a manor, to Josias Verelst in 1812. Verelst

(d. 1819) left it to his wife Margaret[27] who offered it for sale in 1820.[28] It was bought then or later by Robert Purnell of Dursley, who sold 208 a., the former coney warren lying west of the Aylburton–Coleford road, to James Croome in 1832. Croome sold the warren piecemeal before 1839[29] and it later formed the pleasure grounds for a number of houses,[30] but in 1845 he bought from Purnell the remainder of the estate, including Prior's Mesne Lodge and land on the east side of the road. Croome died in 1865 and his son J. J. Croome sold Prior's Mesne Lodge in 1870 to James Hughes, a timber merchant. It changed hands fairly frequently later, and in 1961 was bought by a Lydney businessman Mr. A. M. R. Watts,[31] the owner in 1990.

Prior's Lodge (as it was usually called in the 20th century) incorporates at its west end a small L-shaped house of the earlier 17th century. In the 1690s Wiliam Powlett[32] added to the east end a taller block, which included a well staircase with corkscrew balusters. In the late 18th century the house was remodelled externally and given pediments above the east and west elevations. Refitting continued in the early 19th century and towards the end of that century service rooms were built into a shallow central recess in the north elevation. Just below the house on Park brook there was a small lake called Prior's (or Chelfridge) pool in 1608,[33] possibly a fishpond dating from Llanthony priory's ownership. Josias Verelst apparently enlarged it in the early 19th century.[34] He also built the entrance lodge on the road west of the house.[35]

In 1219 when Lire abbey (Eure) granted its church of Lydney to the dean and chapter of Hereford it reserved to itself 1 yardland in Nass and ½ yardland in Lydney.[36] The ½ yardland was held from the abbey by Walter Wyther at his death in 1270[37] and was evidently the house and 12 a. held by his son-in-law William Boter (d. c. 1285).[38] Lire's property in the parish has not been traced later.

The Lydney rectory estate belonging to the dean and chapter of Hereford from 1219[39] comprised the corn tithes of the parish and of the chapelry of St. Briavels. It was granted on long leases during the 18th and 19th centuries.[40] The rectory was valued at £100 in 1603[41] and at £160 c. 1710,[42] and the tithes of Lydney and Aylburton were commuted for a corn rent charge of £420 in 1839.[43] The dean and chapter had a house or farm building at Lydney in 1270 when they were accused of harbouring poachers who supplied them with venison from the Forest.[44]

19 Ibid. SC 6/Hen. VIII/1224.
20 Ibid. C 115/K 2/6683, f. 89.
21 Glos. R.O., D 421/L 3–4.
22 Ibid. T 30.
23 Ibid. D 608/9/10; D 421/L 4.
24 Ibid. P 209/IN 1/1.
25 Ibid. D 608/9/10; for John Barrow, G.D.R. wills 1713/357.
26 Glos. R.O., D 608/9/10.　27 Ibid.
28 Ibid. D 421/E 57.
29 Deeds of Aylburton Lodge, in possession of Mr. A. M. R. Watts; G.D.R., T 1/117.
30 Above, intro.
31 Deeds of Prior's Lodge, in possession of Mr. Watts.

32 Letter from Powlett to Barbara Barrow 9 Jan. 1694 (photocopy in possession of Mr. Watts); Glos. R.O., D 608/9/10, recital of Powlett's will 1703.
33 P.R.O., MR 879 (F 17/1).
34 Deeds of Prior's Lodge, deposition 24 Feb. 1906.
35 Glos. R.O., D 608/9/10, recital of deed 1812.
36 B.L. Harl. MS. 6203, p. 71.
37 Cal. Inq. p.m. i, pp. 235–6.
38 Ibid. ii, p. 335, though the land is there said to be held of the earl of Warwick.　39 Below, churches.
40 Glos. R.O., D 326/L 16; P 209/MI 1, p. 100; G.D.R., V 5/195T 1; T 1/117.
41 Eccl. Misc. 99.　42 Atkyns, Glos. 540.
43 G.D.R., T 1/117.　44 P.R.O., E 32/29, rot. 5.

A small meadow adjoining the vicarage house was owned by the chapter until 1805, when it granted it to the vicar,[45] and may have been the site of the rectory buildings.

ECONOMIC HISTORY. AGRICULTURE. In 1086 the new manor formed from four estates at Lydney by William FitzOsbern had 3 teams in demesne.[46] In 1315 100 a. of underwood and heath subject to the commoning rights of tenants was the only demesne land mentioned on Lydney Warwick manor,[47] but in 1527 there was demesne land, meadow, and pasture leased among tenants.[48] The manor later called Lydney Shrewsbury had 44 a. of arable and 10 a. of meadow in hand in 1322 and other demesne land was held by a tenant.[49] By 1426 the demesne of Lydney Shrewsbury was all on lease.[50] The ancient demesne lands of the two manors were apparently represented later by the group of closes on the Lydney estate lying south-west of the town on either side of the Chepstow road.[51] Nass manor in 1066 had 1 team in demesne, while Purton and Poulton (in Awre) had 2 teams and 2 *servi* between them.[52] In 1444 Nass manor had 100 a. of arable, 6 a. of meadow, and 20 a. of wood in demesne.[53]

In 1066 of the four estates at Lydney later amalgamated by FitzOsbern, the largest, that of Pershore abbey, had as tenants 6 *villani* with 4 teams, but in 1086 a possibly incomplete statement of the tenants ascribed only 8 bordars to the united manor.[54] In 1315 Lydney Warwick manor included 24 free tenants,[55] and in 1558 its tenant land was mainly in small parcels held freely, though there were also 5 customary tenants and 2 tenants at will.[56] In 1322 the later Lydney Shrewsbury manor had 22 free tenants, mostly holding small parcels of land, a number of bondmen, some of whom occupied holdings of 18 a. in return for cash rents, mowing work, and 8 days' reaping, and 25 tenants of burgages, owing 12d. rent each, suit of court, heriots, and reliefs.[57] Burgage tenure, presumably introduced in the 13th century in connexion with the establishment of a market,[58] has not been found recorded after 1443,[59] but some of the burgages were evidently represented later by the tenements in Lydney and Newerne held freely from Lydney Shrewsbury in 1558. That manor then had other freeholders who held land with no houses, 9 copyholders, and 4 tenants by indenture.[60] In 1066 the tenants of Nass manor were 10 *villani* and 2 bordars with 9 teams between them, and those of Purton and Poulton 15 *villani* and 2 bordars, also with 9 teams.[61] The 12 houses and 12 yardlands recorded on Purton manor in

1360 were probably held by customary tenants;[62] later evidence suggests that the yardland on the manor comprised 24 a.[63] A brief extent of Nass manor in 1444 mentioned only rents of free tenants.[64]

The fragmentation of the north-east part of the parish into numerous small manors perhaps hastened the decline of the traditional customary tenures. Apart from those mentioned above on the two Lydney manors in 1558, there were 6 or more customary tenants on Purton manor in 1579,[65] 2 on Tucknall in 1577,[66] and at least one on Allaston in 1568.[67] Customary tenures comprised only a small proportion of holdings by c. 1600 when a rental, possibly incomplete, of the Winters' five manors and other estates in the north- east part of the parish listed over 67 tenancies by indenture for years or lives, 22 tenancies at will, and 17 copyholds, besides numerous small freeholds.[68] Some of the manors that remained independent of the Winters' Lydney estate, that is Soilwell, Hurst, Rodleys, and the reduced Nass manor, probably comprised only single demesne farms.

By the 17th century, and probably for many centuries previously, there was a pattern of scattered, small or medium-sized, enclosed farms in the north-east part of the parish. In 1651 there was a total of 26 tenant farms on Purton manor and the Winters' part of Nass manor: 8 of them had between 7 and 18 a., 16 had between 23 and 57 a., and there were two larger farms — Purton Manor with 78 a. and Wellhouse with 106 a.[69] Most of those farms became freeholds following sales by the Winters in the 1650s and 1660s and some were consolidated in larger units, including those at Nass which were taken in hand after being sold to the Jones family.[70] Copyhold tenure is not found recorded after 1651 and probably ended in the north-east part of the parish in the late 17th century. By the late 18th century the farms which remained part of the Lydney estate were usually held by leases for 7, 14, or 21 years.[71]

Aylburton tithing remained a more compact unit and retained a more traditional system of tenures. In 1539, when the demesne land was on lease with that of the neighbouring Alvington manor, Llanthony priory was receiving rents from free and customary tenants,[72] and c. 1600 Aylburton manor had 17 freeholds, 22 tenements held on leases for years or lives, 17 copyholds, and various parcels of land held at will.[73] In 1718, when the Winters sold much of the tenant land, the manor included 16 leasehold farms, ranging in size from 7 to 64 a.[74] and almost all based on small farmhouses on the village street. The consolidation of the land into two or

45 G.D.R., V 5/195T 3.
46 *Dom. Bk.* (Rec. Com.), i. 164.
47 *Inq. p.m. Glos.* 1302–58, 158.
48 P.R.O., SC 12/8/4.   49 Ibid. E 142/26.
50 Glos. R.O., D 421/M 19.
51 Ibid. D 3270/R 1; cf. G.D.R., T 1/117.
52 *Dom. Bk.* (Rec. Com.), i. 164.
53 P.R.O., C 139/115, no. 34.
54 *Dom. Bk.* (Rec. Com.), i. 164.
55 *Inq. p.m. Glos.* 1302–58, 158.
56 Glos. R.O., D 421/M 23.
57 P.R.O., E 142/26.   58 Above, intro.

59 Glos. R.O., D 421/M 19.   60 Ibid. M 23.
61 *Dom. Bk.* (Rec. Com.), i. 164.
62 *Cal. Pat.* 1358–61, 477.
63 In 1651 six holdings on the man. were 23–25 a.: Glos. R.O., D 421/M 83.   64 P.R.O., C 139/115, no. 34.
65 Glos. R.O., D 421/M 82.   66 Ibid. M 84.
67 Ibid. D 421/6.   68 Ibid. D 421/E 13.
69 Ibid. M 79, M 83.   70 Ibid. T 11, L 2.
71 Ibid. T 44, T 49, T 59, T 74, T 102.
72 P.R.O., SC 6/Hen. VIII/1224.
73 Glos. R.O., D 421/E 13, ff. 3v.–5.
74 Ibid. T 30.

three large farms by the early 19th century[75] perhaps followed the buying back of much of the land for the Lydney estate.

In the 16th and 17th centuries only vestiges survived of open fields, which outside Aylburton tithing had probably never been extensive. In 1558 tenants on Lydney Shrewsbury manor had parcels of arable in Church field,[76] lying west of the upper part of Church Road, and in 1651 tenants of Purton manor had arable in a field called Moor field.[77] A small open field called Broad Holes (perhaps originally Broad Doles) survived at Tutnalls in 1839[78] and was apparently inclosed before 1864. A principal part of the medieval open fields of the two Lydney manors was apparently in land later called Great and Little Cowleaze, comprising c. 60 a.[79] within the old sea wall west of the head of Lydney harbour, for it was covered by ridge and furrow in the mid 20th century.[80] In 1793, and probably for many years previously, the two Cowleazes were under grass and held in severalty by the Lydney estate.[81]

Land called Foremarsh, where tenants of the Lydney manors had common meadow in 1558, was presumably in the north-east part of the tract of land later called the Marsh, extending across Lydney and Aylburton tithings on the outside of the old sea wall. Tenants then also had meadow in Eastmarsh, lying beside the Newerne stream south-west of Tutnalls, and in South mead,[82] which was probably the common meadow later called Lydney mead, south of Lower forge. The Marsh and Eastmarsh were later held in severalty by the owners of the Lydney estate but Lydney mead, which contained 37 a. in 1818,[83] remained uninclosed until 1864.

In the Middle Ages the open fields of Aylburton tithing were mainly on the inner part of its level, then usually known as Aylburton's marsh. Until extensive new ploughing in the later 20th century the land there was largely in ridge and furrow, the main exceptions being at Aylburton mead, on the east, adjoining Lydney tithing, and at the smaller Rodmore mead, on the west, adjoining Woodwards brook by the lane leading from Stockwell green to Alvington Court;[84] there was meadow land in both areas in the 13th century.[85] Most of the arable of Aylburton tenants mentioned during the 13th century and the early 14th was in the level, some of it specified as on the hill in the marsh, a low rise west of Aylburton mead, in Shortlands, south of the hill and just within the old sea wall, and at Rodmore, presumably adjoining Rodmore mead.[86] There was also some arable on the higher ground between the edge of the level and the Chepstow road: land was mentioned in Kingarstone, on the

north-east side of Stockwell Lane, and in 'la Buttine',[87] probably the open field later called Bittam or Bitterns by Woodwards brook near the Alvington boundary. In the early 13th century some tenants had arable in the Stirts[88] in the part of Aylburton that lay south-east of Alvington. Land called the New Stirts, which was probably in the outer part of the Stirts and recently reclaimed, was used as a common pasture at the beginning of the 14th century. In 1312 and 1331 tenants released common rights there to Llanthony priory, which had a grant of other land in the Stirts in 1317,[89] and by the early 16th century the priory held the Stirts in severalty as part of its demesne farm based in Alvington.[90]

In the later 16th century tenants of Aylburton manor had open-field arable in Shortlands, Bitterns, Aylburton field, and the Wurthen, the last two being perhaps parts of the level, and they had common meadow in Aylburton mead, Rodmore mead, and in Aylburton's part of the Marsh, beyond the old sea wall. Aylburton Warth, which had formed at the riverside beyond the Stirts, was a common pasture for cows in 1565[91] and later. Most of Aylburton's open-field land was enclosed by private agreement and converted to grassland. In 1818 the uninclosed land remaining in the tithing was 7 a. in Bitterns field, 69 a. of meadow (most of it held by farms on the Lydney estate) in Aylburton mead, 6 a. in Rodmore mead, and Aylburton Warth, which was then stinted for a total of c. 65 cows.[92]

The tenants had extensive common of pasture on the hills, principally on the Purlieu and Allaston Meend in the north and on Aylburton common.[93] In Aylburton common the tenants of Alvington manor, formerly in the same ownership, intercommoned with those of Aylburton in the late 16th century.[94] Common rights in some other areas of the woodland and waste were restricted by the manorial lords after the Middle Ages. In 1577 tenants of Tucknall manor claimed that Sir William Winter had inclosed Dodmore wood, north of Lydney Park woods, and other grounds which had been common to them.[95] Later the Winters extinguished rights which the men of Aylburton and Alvington claimed in Prior's Mesne in the 1580s, turning c. 200 a. there into a coney warren. That large warren became farmland in the mid 18th century[96] and parts were later planted.[97] Although the parish was excluded from the Forest in the early 14th century, all its tithings continued to claim common rights in the royal demesne land in return for an annual payment of herbage money.[98]

The emergence of the saltmarsh called the

75 Ibid. P 209A/IN 3/1, ff. 37–43.
76 Ibid. D 421/M 23. For the sites of fields, meadows, and pastures mentioned in the next paras., G.D.R., T 1/117; and for the level, cf. above, intro.
77 Glos. R.O., D 421/M 83.   78 G.D.R., T 1/117.
79 Cf. Glos. R.O., P 209A/IN 3/1, f. 16.
80 Aerial photog. (Royal Air Force, 1946), no. 3093.
81 Glos. R.O., D 421/T 68.
82 Ibid. M 23.   83 Ibid. P 209A/IN 3/1.
84 Aerial photog. (R.A.F., 1946), nos. 3093, 3103.
85 P.R.O., C 115/K 2/6683, f. 79 and v.

86 Ibid. ff. 78–81v., 99v., 101v.
87 Ibid. ff. 85v., 101v.   88 Ibid. f. 80 and v.
89 Ibid. C 115/L 1/6689, ff. 176–177v.
90 G.D.R. vol. 89, depositions 9 Mar. 1601/2.
91 Glos. R.O., D 421/M 10, E 12.   92 Ibid. P 209A/IN 3/1.
93 Above, intro.   94 Glos. R.O., D 421/L 3.
95 Ibid. M 84.   96 Ibid. L 3–4; D 608/9/10.
97 Deeds of Aylburton Lodge, in possession of Mr. Watts, deed 1832.
98 P.R.O., C 139/84, no. 76; Berkeley Cast. Mun., General Ser. no. 16.

New Grounds from the river in the 1730s added a valuable asset to the Lydney estate, whose owners secured title to most of the land[99] and later leased the remainder from the Nass estate. The New Grounds won a wide reputation as pasture for horses and cattle, which were sent from neighbouring parts of Gloucestershire, Monmouthshire, and Herefordshire. In the period 1779–84 the 'tack' fees brought in £300–£360 a year.[1] In the 1790s and the early 19th century the New Grounds, Lydney's part of the Marsh, and other meadows and pastures between the Marsh and the Chepstow road, a total of 469 a., were leased out by the Bathursts at an annual rent that varied betwen £545 and £650. The lessees, who included from 1793 to 1796 a Slimbridge farmer and a Frocester farmer, took outsiders' animals at tack fees, while the owners reserved to themselves pasture for 120 sheep.[2]

Inclosure by Act of parliament in 1864 covered the commons of the Purlieu, Allaston Meend, Aylburton common, Needs Top, the Tufts, and Stockwell green, with Bitterns open field, Lydney mead, Aylburton mead, Rodmore mead, and Aylburton Warth (then called the Cow Pastures). The Revd. W. H. Bathurst was awarded 278 a. in respect of his Lydney estate and 31 a. for the rights of soil, and he retained the right to work minerals on all the lands, subject to the payment of compensation to other owners. James Croome was awarded 45 a. for his Purton Manor, Prior's Mesne, and other estates, allotments of 5 a.–22 a. were made in respect of nine other estates, and the great majority of allottees received only a few perches of land in respect of common rights attached to houses and cottages.[3]

By 1818, when there had been much amalgamation among the many small holdings that had existed in the 17th century, the parish contained c. 30 farms of over 20 a.[4] On the Lydney estate the largest farms were the home farm (339 a.) based on the new farmhouse later called Park Farm near the manor house, Cross farm (178 a.) based on a house in Aylburton village street,[5] Dairy farm (179 a.) with its farmhouse on Church Road, and Malthouse farm (203 a.) with its farmhouse in Lydney High Street and other buildings at the Holms. A considerable acreage was kept in hand together with Redhill farmhouse and the park. The New Grounds and other large pastures remained on a separate lease in 1818 but later were added to Dairy farm, which in 1851 had 600 a. and employed 20 farm labourers.[6] The other main farms in the parish in 1818 were Nass Court (216 a.) and Cliff farm (119 a.) on the Nass estate, two farms on the Purton Manor estate (143 a. and 119 a. respectively), Nursehill and two adjoining farms held

together (a total of 206 a.), Hurst farm (195 a.), Crump farm (170 a.), Soilwell (166 a.), and Driffield farm (137 a.). Another 14 farms on the Lydney estate or belonging to smaller owners had between 20 a. and 100 a. Pastoral farming predominated on the larger and low-lying farms in 1818 when there was very little arable on the home farm, on Dairy farm, which was so called in 1778,[7] or on Nass Court farm, described in 1803 as a dairy and grazing farm well known for its cheese.[8] Most of the other farms had over a third of their acreage under the plough and some, on the higher land in Allaston and Purton, had over half. In 1818 most farms apparently followed a three-course rotation of a traditional type, with wheat in one year, barley, oats, beans, and peas in the second, and a fallow, with some clover, in the third. Only two farms had introduced turnips, which amounted to only 8 a. in 1818, and only one was using grassland leys.

In 1839 of the tithable land of the parish, excluding the woods and commons, 1,355 a. were arable and 2,931 a. meadow and pasture.[9] There was little change during the mid 19th century, the inclosure of 1864 presumably coming too late to result in widespread conversion of the former common land to arable. In 1866 1,234 a. were returned as under crops, mainly cereals and peas and beans but including 183 a. of roots.[10] The acreage under crops fell to 816 a. by 1896 and to 478 a. by 1926,[11] the decline being matched by an increase in the amount of dairying and grazing. In 1866 255 milk cows and 573 other cattle were returned, in 1896 the comparable figures were 284 and 948, and in 1926 545 and 851. The number of sheep returned rose from 2,684 in 1866 to 4,584 in 1896, falling to 3,139 by 1926. Orchards were fairly widespread, with 145 a. being returned in 1896.[12]

The number and size of the farms remained little altered in 1926 when there was a total of 61 agricultural occupiers in the parish, 2 having over 300 a., 11 having 100 a.–300 a., 15 having 20 a.–100 a., and the rest having under 20 a. A total of 95 full-time farm labourers and 22 casual workers was then employed.[13] In 1904 Charles Bathurst, later Lord Bledisloe, who was an advocate of co-operative principles in agriculture,[14] founded the Lydney and District Farmers' Co-operative Society, which built its stores near the top of Church Road. A provender mill was built at the site in the 1920s and the society became a large supplier of animal feed, seed corn, and fertilizer.[15] About 1923 Lord Bledisloe reorganized part of his estate in line with his ideas, introducing a profit-sharing scheme for the employees, small factories for processing bacon and cheese, and direct marketing by means of farm shops and delivery vans.[16] The scheme, which operated under the style

[99] Above, intro.   [1] Glos. R.O., D 421/E 34–5.
[2] Ibid. T 68, T 102; *Glouc. Jnl.* 27 Apr. 1801; 1 May 1809.   [3] Glos. R.O., P 209A/SD 1/1.
[4] Inf. for 1818 in this para. is from ibid. IN 3/1, which excludes the Prior's Mesne est., where there were another one or two farms.
[5] Cf. ibid. D 421/E 26.
[6] Cf. G.D.R., T 1/117; P.R.O., HO 107/2443.
[7] Glos. R.O., D 421/T 49.   [8] *Glouc. Jnl.* 8 Aug. 1803.

[9] G.D.R., T 1/117.   [10] P.R.O., MAF 68/26/8.
[11] Ibid. MAF 68/1609/6; 3295/12.
[12] Ibid. MAF 68/25/9; 1609/6; 3295/12.
[13] Ibid. MAF 68/3295/12.
[14] Glos. Colln. (H) H 8.4; VA 3.28.
[15] *Lydney and District Official Guide* (c. 1960), 35; *Lydney Par. Official Guide* (1972), 7; cf. Glos. R.O., D 2428/1/7.
[16] *Country Life*, 23 Aug. 1924, 282–5; cf. Glos. R.O., DA 28/100/6, pp. 59, 123.

Bledisloe Farms Ltd., apparently came to an end before 1931.[17]

In the later 20th century Lydney's suburban expansion, together with industrial and recreational development, took much farmland, and amalgamations reduced the number of working farms. In 1988 32 agricultural holdings were returned in Lydney and Aylburton, 19 of them farms of over 10 ha. (25 a.); 68 people worked the farms, which also gave some seasonal casual employment, but most of the smaller holdings were worked only on a part-time basis. Dairying was the main enterprise carried on by the larger farms but sheep raising, beef cattle, and cereals (including a considerable acreage of maize) were all represented; 2,607 cattle (about a third of them dairy cows), 3,282 sheep and lambs, and 432 ha. (1,067 a.) of crops were returned.[18] In 1990 on the Lydney estate, which was then concentrated in the south-western part of the ancient parish, 485.5 ha. (1,200 a.) were in hand and farmed from Park Farm, and 303.5 ha. (750 a.) were let, the principal tenant farms being the Holms farm and Prospect farm, the latter based on a farmhouse at Chapel Hill in Aylburton. In the north-eastern part of the parish 182 ha. (450 a.) were farmed by the Aldridge family's Purton Manor Farms, and there were other substantial family-run farms at Hurst, Nass Court, and Nursehill.[19]

MILLS AND IRONWORKS. There were apparently two or three mills on the Newerne stream at Lydney in the Middle Ages, probably at sites which were later occupied by ironworking forges. In 1086 a mill was recorded on the Lydney manor created by William FitzOsbern,[20] and the earl of Warwick built a new mill on his manor before 1282.[21] In 1443 a mill called Newerne mill belonged to Nass manor,[22] and in 1558 two corn mills belonged to Lydney Warwick manor.[23] About 1600 the Lydney estate included a mill called Over Mill near Millrough wood.[24]

A mill recorded on Aylburton manor in 1244 was sold by the lord of the manor in 1272.[25] Llanthony priory had a fulling mill at Aylburton in 1535.[26] That was presumably the one later called Wood Mill, on Woodwards brook c. 600 m. upstream of the Chepstow road,[27] and known as Tucker's Mill in 1632. Then a copyhold of the manor,[28] it had possibly been worked

as a fulling mill until a few years previously, as a tucker was recorded at Aylburton in 1608.[29] Wood Mill remained part of the Lydney estate and was in use as a grist mill[30] until the late 19th century or the early 20th.[31] There was another mill on Aylburton manor c. 1600,[32] probably at Millend (later Milling) on Park brook at the north-east end of the village. In 1717 there was an anvil works at Millend,[33] but the works had been replaced by a grist mill by 1759 when Thomas Bathurst granted it on lease.[34] No later record of a mill at Millend has been found.

About 1267 William Wyther built a mill at Purton.[35] The only mill found recorded later in the north-east part of the parish was Woodfield Mill standing on Plummer's (formerly Woodfield) brook below the Gloucester road. Woodfield Mill was a new-built grist mill in 1651 when William Donning held it from Purton manor as part of Nursehill farm,[36] and it was owned with Nursehill by the Donnings in 1739.[37] The mill had been demolished by the mid 19th century.[38]

The large quantities of cinders that were dug from the slopes of Allaston in the early 18th century[39] and field names such as Cinder hill and Cinder mead that occur in several other places[40] are evidence of ironworking in the parish in the Middle Ages. Henry, earl of Warwick, had confirmation of his right to work a forge at Lydney in 1221,[41] and later in the 13th century two or three Lydney men worked movable forges within the Forest of Dean, probably in Lydney itself.[42] Another forge was recorded at Lydney in 1437.[43]

Shortly before 1600 Sir Edward Winter built an iron furnace and a forge on the Newerne stream, which he dammed to create large ponds.[44] Other forges and an iron slitting mill were built later,[45] and Sir Edward and his son Sir John ran the ironworks on an extensive scale, charcoaling wood from their estate, parts of which they denuded of trees,[46] and from demesne woodlands of the Forest leased from the Crown.[47] During the Civil War, until they were burnt by the parliamentary troops of Edward Massey in 1644, the ironworks were an important asset of local royalists.[48] After Sir John's flight in 1645 the House of Commons granted the works to Massey,[49] who was rebuilding one of the forges later that year. Massey leased them in 1647 to John Gifford, who destroyed much timber in the Lydney woods. Gifford remained

17 Kelly's Dir Glos. (1923 and later edns.).
18 Agric. Returns 1988.
19 Inf from Mr. O. B. Hepworth, agent to the Lydney est., and local farmers.
20 Dom. Bk. (Rec. Com.), i. 164.
21 P.R.O., E 32/31, m. 4.   22 Ibid. C 139/115, no. 34.
23 Glos. R.O., D 421/M 23.   24 Ibid. E 13, f. 6v.
25 P.R.O., C 115/K 2/6683, ff. 86, 87.
26 Valor Eccl. (Rec. Com.), ii. 425.
27 O.S. Map 6", Glos. XLVII. SW. (1886 edn.).
28 Glos. R.O., D 421/M 9.
29 Smith, Men and Armour, 54.
30 Glos. R.O., D 421/T 46, T 102.
31 Kelly's Dir. Glos. (1856 and later edns.); O.S. Map 6", Glos. XLVII. SW. (1886 edn.).
32 Glos. R.O., D 421/E 13, ff. 4-5.
33 Ibid. Q/RNc 1, p. 99.   34 Ibid. D 421/T 45.
35 P.R.O., E 32/31, m. 4; Cal. Inq. p.m. i, pp. 235-6; ii, p. 335.

36 Glos. R.O., D 421/M 83.
37 Ibid. D 637/II/8/T 1, T 3.
38 Cf. G.D.R., T 1/117.
39 G.B.R., J 1/1994; Glos. R.O., D 3270/19672, accts. 1717-18, 1722-3.
40 G.D.R., T 1/117 (nos. 307-8, 346, 897-8).
41 Rot. Litt. Claus. (Rec. Com.), i. 452; ii. 123.
42 P.R.O., E 146/1/25; E 32/29, rot. 2; E 32/30, rot. 23d.
43 Berkeley Cast. Mun., General Ser. acct. roll 426.
44 Bibliotheca Glos. ii. 95; the furnace was at or near the later New Mills: ibid. D 421/E 16.
45 For a detailed account of the Lydney ironworks, Hart, Ind. Hist. of Dean, 44-5, 82-93, 177-91.
46 Glos. R.O., D 421/E 1, L 6; D 2026/X 20, petition against Wm. Winter.
47 Hart, Royal Forest, 87-8, 101-2, 125; Glos. R.O., D 421/E 4.
48 Bibliotheca Glos. ii. 95.
49 Ibid. i, p. clxxxviii.

in possession in 1650 after Massey defected to the royalists and forfeited his estate.[50] From 1653 the ironworks were worked by John Wade, the parliamentary administrator of the Forest.[51] After the recovery of his estate Sir John Winter resumed ironworking, using a new furnace, at the south-west end of Lydney town on part of the grounds of White Cross house,[52] and forges on the Newerne stream called Pill forge (later Lower forge), near the head of Lydney Pill,[53] New forge (later Middle forge), c. 600 m. above Newerne village,[54] and Slitting Mill forge (later Upper forge), adapted from the former slitting mill on the parish boundary south-west of Kidnalls.[55] The Winters worked the furnace and forges until c. 1720,[56] Slitting Mill forge being replaced by a corn mill before 1717.[57] In 1714 an agreement was made to supply 80 tons of iron a year to a Bristol ironmonger.[58]

In 1723 the Lydney ironworks were leased to John Ruston of Claines (Worcs.). He and later lessees had the right to buy from the estate an annual allowance of wood and any cinders or ore found on it and were also given the use of Lydney Pill and a warehouse there.[59] Ruston surrendered most of the premises in 1731 and the owner Benjamin Bathurst employed the works on his own account for a few years.[60] By 1740 the ironworks were occupied by Rowland Pytt of Gloucester, who was apparently then in partnership with a Mr. Raikes,[61] and Pytt's son Rowland succeeded him as lessee,[62] probably by 1748. The younger Rowland died before 1768, when his two executors, themselves ironmasters, renewed the lease. From 1775 the lessee was David Tanner of Tintern (Mon.),[63] who took a comprehensive new 99-year lease in 1778.[64] In 1789 Tanner sold the lease to his mortgagees who sold it the following year to four members of the Pidcock family, described as Staffordshire glassmasters. The Pidcocks produced iron at Lydney until 1813 when they sold the lease back to the Bathursts. The works then comprised the furnace at White Cross, which was probably abandoned soon afterwards, Upper forge, which had been rebuilt on the slitting mill site, Middle forge, Lower forge, which had an iron rolling mill attached, and the narrow canal[65] built in the late 18th century from Upper forge down to Lower forge and Lydney Pill.[66]

In 1814 the Lydney forges were leased to John James, who in the early 1820s built a new forge called New Mills roughly half way between Upper forge and Middle forge. By 1844 James was using Lower forge as a tinplating works.[67]

His family surrendered the lease in 1847 and a new one was granted to members of the Allaway family, ironmasters and tinplate manufacturers.[68] In 1864 W. Allaway & Sons were producing c. 1,000 boxes of tinplate each week as well as some sheet iron, and they were employing c. 400 workers,[69] most of them from Lydney parish where the works remained the principal source of employment until the mid 20th century.[70] From 1876 the works were leased to Richard Thomas, who already occupied tinplate works at Lydbrook.[71] In 1889, after the firm had spent £6,000 on improvements and new machinery at Lower forge, it took a new lease which empowered it to remove the machinery from the three upper sites and drain their ponds,[72] and the upper sites were abandoned soon afterwards as manufacture was concentrated at Lower forge. Richard Thomas & Co., in which Richard was succeeded as managing director by his son Richard Beaumont Thomas in 1888, became one of the principal tinplate manufacturers in the country, acquiring other mills in South Wales. In 1941 the Lydney works closed but they reopened in 1946 under the name of Richard Thomas & Baldwin. With the nationalization of steel in 1951 the works became part of the Steel Co. of Wales and continued under that style until they closed in 1957.[73]

FISHERIES. A fishery in the Severn recorded in 1086 belonged either to Purton manor or to Poulton manor (in Awre),[74] and there were fisheries on Purton manor in 1269.[75] William Warren, owner of Warren farm and other lands in Purton and Nass, had several 'stages' (*stationes*) for fishing, probably putcher weirs, in the river in 1419.[76] In 1577 the earl of Northumberland, lord of Tucknall and one of the Purton manors, claimed the rights in the stretch of river from Purton Pill on the parish boundary downstream to Nass manor, and his tenants then held stages at Purton Pill, Wellhouse Rock, and elsewhere.[77] In 1651 the tenant of the Wards farm under Purton manor had five stages at Wellhouse Rock and the tenant of Nursehill had one further downstream.[78] Later the Winters and Bathursts in respect of their various manors claimed the fishing rights in the whole stretch of river adjoining the parish, though the Joneses claimed the rights adjoining their Nass manor; the Joneses' claim was upheld in 1738 but fishery leases granted by the Bathursts began to acknowledge their rights only c. 1790.[79] The right to sturgeon and other royal fish within Bledisloe hundred

[50] P.R.O., LRRO 5/7A, depositions 1645, no. 31; depositions 1649, no. 2; *Cal. Cttee. for Compounding*, ii. 2142-3.
[51] Hart, *Ind. Hist. of Dean*, 18-19.
[52] Glos. R.O., D 421/T 28, mtge. 8 Apr. 1704; T 30, abs. of title (mtge. 27 May 1673); cf. G.D.R., T 1/117 (nos. 225, 227).
[53] Glos. R.O., D 421/T 30, abs. of title (mtges. 10 June 1652, 27 May 1673); for the sites of the forges, ibid. D 4880/2.
[54] Ibid. D 421/T 18, mtge. 1663; T 20, tithe agreement 1698.
[55] Ibid. T 16, lease 1661; T 28, mtge. 8 Apr. 1704.
[56] Ibid. T 28.   [57] Ibid. T 69; Q/RNc 1, p. 102.
[58] Ibid. D 421/L 14.   [59] Ibid. T 18.
[60] Ibid. L 15.   [61] Ibid. E 45.
[62] *Glouc. Jnl.* 10 Apr. 1775; for the Pytts, cf. *V.C.H. Glos.* iv. 127; Glos. R.O., D 3117/349.

[63] Glos. R.O., D 421/E 45, L 20.   [64] Ibid. T 69.
[65] Ibid. T 104, E 47.   [66] Above, intro.
[67] Glos. R.O., D 421/E 46.   [68] Ibid. T 105.
[69] Nicholls, *Iron Making*, 59.
[70] Below, this section (other ind. and trade); Glos. R.O., DA 28/100/17, min. 30 July 1957.
[71] Glos. R.O., D 4880/1; *Tinplaters of Lydney and Lydbrook*, 25; cf. below, Forest of Dean, industry (ironworks).   [72] Glos. R.O., D 4880/2.
[73] *Tinplaters of Lydney and Lydbrook*, 26-7, 44-5.
[74] *Dom. Bk.* (Rec. Com.), i. 164.
[75] *Cal. Inq. p.m.* i, p. 226.
[76] P.R.O., C 138/40, no. 52.
[77] Glos. R.O., D 421/M 84; cf. above, manors.
[78] Glos. R.O., D 421/M 83; cf. ibid. T 14, deed 1659.
[79] Ibid. L 2, E 41-2; cf. ibid. D 326/F 24.

was granted by the Crown to Sir John Winter in 1640, and his successors reserved those fish in their leases in the 18th century.[80]

In 1866 the Bathursts' fisheries included six stop nets used in Wellhouse Bay and two used just below the New Grounds near the entrance to Lydney Pill, besides a weir with 650 putchers at Aylburton Warth. Nass manor then had 300 putchers and 1 putt at Fairtide Rock below Nass cliff, the Purton Manor estate had 2 putts near Wellhouse Rock, and the owner of the Wards had 40 putchers in Wellhouse Bay.[81] From the late 19th century the Bathursts' Wellhouse Bay fishery was leased by the Morse family of Gatcombe which operated stopping boats until c. 1986.[82] The putcher weir at Fairtide Rock, reached by means of a ladder down the cliff face, was worked from 1916 or earlier by the Biddle family, tenants of Cliff farm and later owners of the Nass estate.[83] In 1990 the Biddles' putcher weir and that at Aylburton Warth, worked by a tenant under the Lydney estate, remained in use, and lave nets were employed on the sandbanks off Aylburton,[84] where they had been recorded in frequent use in the 1760s.[85]

OTHER INDUSTRY AND TRADE. Although Lydney had a market from 1268, the town was of little importance as a commercial centre before the 19th century. There was, however, a varied pattern of employment in the parish, provided by the ironworks, fisheries,[86] river trade, woodlands, and mineral deposits.

From the early Middle Ages Lydney Pill and Purton Pill were minor centres of the Severn trade. Three owners of boats at Purton and one at Lydney were presented at the forest eyre of 1270 for trading regularly to Bristol in wood and venison stolen from the Forest,[87] and in 1282 seven boats based at Purton Pill and six based at Lydney Pill were reported to trade in stolen timber.[88] Wose Pill, in Aylburton at the mouth of Woodwards brook,[89] was used by Llanthony priory, owner of Aylburton and Alvington, to ship out wood and bring in other supplies,[90] and it was used for general trade in 1345 when the priory was empowered to take tolls there.[91] In 1282 iron ore was shipped there.[92] In 1343 a Lydney vessel was arrested for an act of piracy committed near Falmouth (Cornw.),[93] and in 1347 Lydney was mentioned among places on

the Severn where customs were collected.[94] Lydney Pill,[95] Purton Pill,[96] and Wose Pill, then called Aylburton Pill,[97] were all in use for trade in the late 16th century, though in 1608 two boatmen were the only parishioners listed as obtaining a living directly from the river trade.[98]

During the 17th and 18th centuries Lydney Pill was used to ship out the iron, coal,[99] bark, and timber produced on the Lydney estate.[1] During the Commonwealth period the government used it as the main shipping place for Forest timber for the navy.[2] Occasionally a Lydney vessel was employed in the trade to Ireland from the Severn,[3] and trade with Bristol continued on a regular basis. A trow and three small sloops that were based at the pill c. 1790 were used in the Bristol trade.[4] It was said that vessels of 150 tons could reach the head of the pill in the early 18th century but the formation of the New Grounds made access difficult and at the start of the 19th century the pill was used only at the highest spring tides.[5] The owners of the Lydney estate maintained a warehouse at the head of the pill from the late 16th century until the opening of the new harbour in 1813, and a second warehouse, built nearby before 1723, was used by the lessees of the ironworks.[6] Purton Pill was used for shipping out coal from the Forest mines[7] until the opening of Lydney harbour. In the late 18th century and the early 19th it was also an outlet for navy timber,[8] which was collected in a yard on the north side of the pill in Awre parish.[9] About 1790 two vessels were based permanently at Purton, a brig which carried the navy timber to Plymouth and a sloop used in the Bristol trade.[10]

Ships were being built in the parish in 1608 when its inhabitants included two shipwrights and a ship carpenter.[11] In 1656 Lydney Pill was chosen as the site for building a frigate for the navy under the direction of master shipwright Daniel Furzer. The vessel was launched in 1657 and was followed by a second frigate in 1660, but silting of the foreshore around the pill later led Furzer to transfer his operations downstream to Cone Pill.[12] A ship carpenter was living at Nass in 1733.[13]

Exploitation of the mineral deposits of the parish had begun by Roman times when iron ore was dug in Old Park wood,[14] which is riddled with workings of later centuries.[15] In 1282 the

80 Ibid. D 421/E 41, L 17.   81 Ibid. Q/RF.
82 Above, Awre, econ. hist. (fisheries).
83 Glos. Colln. RX 195.1; B. Waters, *Severn Tide* (1955), 168–9.   84 Inf. from Mr. Hepworth, Mr. E. Biddle.
85 Glos. R.O., D 421/L 17.
86 Above, this section.
87 P.R.O., E 32/29, rott. 5d., 8.
88 Ibid. E 32/30, rot. 24; cf. ibid. E 32/31, m. 16, where the place called Newe(n) was presumably Lydney Pill, where the Newerne stream entered the river.
89 Above, intro.
90 P.R.O., C 115/K 2/6683, f. 92v.; C 115/K 2/6684, f. 127v.
91 Ibid. C 115/K 2/6684, f. 140.
92 Ibid. E 32/31, m. 16.
93 *Cal. Pat.* 1343–5, 68.   94 Ibid. 1345–8, 277.
95 Glos. R.O., D 421/E 3, depositions 1617 (Ric. Witt).
96 P.R.O., E 134/25 Eliz. I Hil./3; E 134/25 Eliz. I East./14.
97 Ibid. E 134/25 Eliz. I East./14; E 178/132.
98 Smith, *Men and Armour*, 53–4.

99 Glos. R.O., D 421/T 18, T 69.
1 Ibid. E 52, agreement 1750; E 56, agreements 1793, 1795.
2 Hart, *Royal Forest*, 287; *Cal. S.P. Dom.* 1655, 518, 533; 1656–7, 428, 529, 570; 1658–9, 552.
3 P.R.O., E 190/1249/13–14; E 190/1259/11.
4 Glos. Colln., list of landing places in port of Glouc. c. 1790.
5 Glos. R.O., D 421/E 49, notes of meeting 7 Mar. 1809.
6 Ibid. M 31, T 18, T 69. The owners' wareho. was presumably that recorded in 1809 at Nat. Grid SO 633018 (ibid. M 30) and later replaced by cottages, while Stationroad Cottages, to the N., may incorporate the lessees' wareho.
7 Hart, *Free Miners*, 132; Glos. Colln., list of landing places; Glos. R.O., D 421/E 49, letter 6 Mar. 1808.
8 *Glouc. Jnl.* 8 Sept. 1794; 16 Mar. 1818.
9 G.D.R., T 1/12.   10 Glos. Colln., list of landing places.
11 Smith, *Men and Armour*, 54–5.
12 *Trans. B.G.A.S.* lxvi. 238–45.
13 Glos. R.O., D 421/L 8.
14 *Trans. B.G.A.S.* lxxviii. 86–91.
15 O.S. Map 6", Glos. XLVII. NW. (1883 edn.).

earl of Warwick claimed the iron ore and coal found in his Lydney woods, and ore was mentioned as an asset of his estate in 1318.[16] A coal mine in Norchard wood was worked for the Winters in the early 17th century,[17] and in 1765 a collier agreed with Thomas Bathurst for sinking pits in the Tufts.[18] In Kidnalls wood, on the east side of the Newerne stream, coal was presumably being worked in 1660 when a gin house was mentioned there.[19] The anomalous status of Kidnalls following its exclusion from the Forest led to the Bathursts having to defend their right to the coal there against incursions by free miners in the late 18th century.[20] An abortive lease of the Lydney ironworks drawn up in 1733 assumed that Benjamin Bathurst could supply to the lessees 1,000 tons of coal a year from his pits, and the right to raise coal on the estate was included in the lease of the ironworks granted in 1778.[21] The Pidcocks, lessees from 1790, made use of that right, bringing the coal down to Lydney Pill by means of the ironworks canal. In 1810 their colliery comprised two pits and a level. They retained the right to dig coal when they gave up the ironworks in 1813.[22] Stone was quarried throughout the upland area of the parish. Hearth stones, some of them used in local iron furnaces, were dug in the upper part of Aylburton tithing in the late 17th century,[23] and the Lydney estate had a stone and tile quarry at Pailwell, near the head of Park brook, in 1723.[24] In 1778 the lessee of the ironworks was given the right to work quarries at Pailwell, Aylburton common, Kidnalls, and the Snead, and on Red hill, where he had the use of a limekiln.[25]

In 1608 25 tradesmen and craftsmen were listed under Lydney (probably meaning the tithing, which also included most of Newerne village), 14 under Aylburton, and 19 under the three northern tithings. The Lydney tradesmen and craftsmen included three tanners, a mercer, and a nailer, Aylburton had a nailer, a parchment maker, and the tucker mentioned above, and in Purton tithing there were a clothier and two weavers.[26] Tanning may have remained a local industry for many years, though the only later reference found was in 1678, when there was a tanhouse at Newerne.[27] Weaving continued in the parish until the late 17th century.[28]

A directory of c. 1790 described Lydney as a mean, inconsiderable town and listed only a small group of tradesmen, together with a surgeon and one shopkeeper. Its market had lapsed by then, and the town apparently gained little benefit from its position on a main turnpike route: there was no regular coach service and only one good inn.[29] Lydney's economic significance dates from the building of the tramroad and harbour at the beginning of the 19th century, and its growth was stimulated by the development of the tinplate works[30] and by the opening of the South Wales railway in 1851 and the Severn Bridge railway in 1879.[31]

The Severn & Wye tramroad and the new harbour were completed in 1813,[32] and in 1816 Lydney was given the status of a creek of the port of Gloucester and customs officers were stationed there.[33] The wharves at the head of the harbour and the right to wharfage, guaranteed at £500 a year by the Severn and Wye Co., were allotted to the landowner Charles Bathurst; his successor sold the wharves to the company in 1853.[34] Coal was the main cargo handled. The wharves were leased to the mining companies of the part of the Forest coalfield served by the tramroad, nine having premises at Lydney in 1859.[35] In 1856 700 tons of coal were being shipped daily, most of it being carried in small coasting vessels to the ports of the Bristol Channel,[36] and in 1879 nine coal merchants or coal shippers were based at the harbour.[37] Other products of the Forest sent out through Lydney included pig iron, bark, timber, and paving stones. Tinplate, brought from the works at Lower forge by a short private tramroad, was shipped at the head of the harbour. Among incoming goods was salt, for which a warehouse was built in conjunction with the Droitwich Salt Co. in 1825.[38] In 1821 the Lydney Trading Society was established to run a freight and passenger service along the tramroad from Lydbrook and a weekly vessel to Bristol.[39] Two companies were running vessels to Bristol by the 1850s.[40] Boatbuilding was started at the harbour by David Davies in 1834,[41] and a second yard had opened by 1856.[42] A ropemaker was in business there in 1859.[43] The tramroad and harbour stimulated the mining of coal and ore in the upland parts of the parish. In 1839 the Pidcocks' successors, still mining there under the right granted in 1778, planned to instal steam engines,[44] and later there were coal workings at Norchard,[45] Kidnalls, and the Tufts.[46]

By 1851 Lydney had grown into a busy centre: apart from the large body of men employed at the tinplate factory and ironworks, the inhabitants of Lydney town and Newerne included c.

[16]   P.R.O., E 32/31, m. 17; *Inq. p.m. Glos.* 1302–58, 168.
[17]   Glos. R.O., D 421/E 3.
[18]   Ibid. E 23.   [19]   Ibid. T 30.
[20]   Ibid. E 23, E 44; *4th Rep. Dean Forest Com.* 31–2; cf. above, intro.   [21]   Glos. R.O., D 421/T 69.
[22]   Ibid. L 19, T 104; E 49, bond 1809; *Glouc. Jnl.* 24 Sept. 1792; 21 May 1810.   [23]   Glos. R.O., D 421/E 9, L 4.
[24]   Ibid. T 18.   [25]   Ibid. T 69.
[26]   Smith, *Men and Armour*, 53–5.
[27]   Glos. R.O., D 421/E 16.
[28]   Hockaday Abs. cclxvii, 1663, 1674.
[29]   *Univ. Brit. Dir.* iii (1794), 566.
[30]   Above, this section (mills and ironworks).
[31]   Above, intro.   [32]   Ibid.
[33]   Glos. R.O., D 421/E 50.
[34]   Paar, *Severn and Wye Railway*, 21, 71.
[35]   Glos. R.O., D 421/E 50; *Slater's Dir. Glos.* (1858–9),

204.
[36]   Paar, *Severn and Wye Railway*, 30, 145.
[37]   *Kelly's Dir. Glos.* (1879), 699.
[38]   Paar, *Severn and Wye Railway*, 148–9; Paar, *G.W.R. in Dean*, 149–50.
[39]   Paar, *Severn and Wye Railway*, 59, 61; *Glouc. Jnl.* 19 Mar. 1821.
[40]   *Slater's Dir. Glos.* (1858–9), 205; *Kelly's Dir. Glos.* (1856), 322.
[41]   Paar, *Severn and Wye Railway*, 148.
[42]   *Kelly's Dir. Glos.* (1856), 322–3.
[43]   *Slater's Dir. Glos.* (1858–9), 204.
[44]   Glos. R.O., D 421/L 19.
[45]   G. J. Field, *Look Back at Norchard* (Cinderford, 1978), 29.
[46]   Glos. R.O., D 637/I/72; P 209A/SD 1/1; *Diary of a Cotswold Parson*, ed. D. Verey (Dursley, 1978), 176.

150 tradesmen, craftsmen, and shopkeepers, following 38 different trades.[47] The professions were represented by a solicitor, a doctor, and a vetinerary surgeon, and the wealthier class of inhabitants was augmented by coal proprietors, mining engineers, civil engineers, and others connected with local industry.[48] A bank, a branch of the Gloucestershire Banking Co., was opened in the town in 1840.[49] Aylburton village also had a high proportion of tradesmen, craftsmen, and shopkeepers by the mid 19th century, c. 60 (excluding tinplate and iron workers) being enumerated in 1851, together with two solicitors and a doctor.[50]

In the later 19th century and the early 20th the local economy was dominated by the tinplate works, the railways, and the docks, which together employed large numbers in Lydney, Newerne, and Aylburton, as well as most of the inhabitants of the new cottages built at Primrose Hill and Tutnalls. In 1881 277 inhabitants of the ancient parish worked at the tinplate works and forges, 122 (including clerical staff) on the railways, and 53 at the docks and in associated trades such as boatbuilding. There were also 30 men (including management staff) employed in mining and quarrying, most of the miners living at Primrose Hill and the adjoining parts of Allaston.[51] An iron foundry, established in the town in 1859, later specialized in making points, crossings, and other equipment for the railways,[52] and the building and maintenance of rolling stock, including the private wagons of the mining companies, became a significant local industry; three firms of wagon builders had opened workshops near Lydney Junction by 1897,[53] and one firm continued to repair stock at a factory in Church Road until 1962.[54] By 1905 the Amalgamated Society of Railway Servants had opened a branch at Lydney, and the Dock, Wharf, Riverside, and General Workers union also had a branch there by 1917.[55] At Lydney harbour the coal trade remained dominant, with nine coal tips and three cranes in use in 1897, when the harbour handled a total of 265,000 tons of goods. Steamers ran passenger services to Bristol, and boatbuilding continued until 1937.[56]

The coal and iron mines on the Lydney estate in the upper part of the parish were taken over by the Park Iron Mines and Collieries Co. Ltd. in 1891.[57] In the 20th century the principal colliery was at Norchard, which from 1911 was run by Park Colliery Co., a new company formed by Charles Bathurst. It amalgamated with Princess Royal colliery, in the Forest, in 1930 and was later worked from a level dug at

Pillowell until it closed in 1965.[58] From 1923 it fuelled the power station of the West Gloucestershire Power Co., which was built on an adjoining site beside Forest Road and became the main source of electricity supply in the county; the power station closed in 1967 and was later demolished.[59] Two small coal mines, called the Hulks and Sulla, near the Yorkley road[60] were also worked during the first part of the century.[61] Other industry in the upper part of the parish in the late 19th century and early 20th included a brickworks at the Tufts beside the railway,[62] a brick and tile works beside the Yorkley road near Soilwell,[63] and a chemical works on the parish boundary north of the Tufts,[64] which was in production from 1887 to 1948 making tar, naphtha, and acetate.[65]

From the 1920s trade at Lydney harbour declined with the closure of collieries in the Forest. Its coal trade came to an end c. 1960 when the coal tips and the railway serving them were closed.[66] The last significant activity was the carriage of imported timber from Avonmouth for the Pine End plywood works on the north side of the harbour. The works ceased to obtain its supplies by water in 1977,[67] and powers to close the harbour and fill in its entrance were obtained in 1978. The closure was not enforced, however, and in 1980 the British Transport Dock Board and British Rail sold the harbour and adjoining land to the river authority, Severn- Trent Water, which in 1990 was attempting to promote tourist and leisure use.[68]

In the mid 20th century Lydney was successful in attracting new industry, enabling it to surmount the loss of its harbour trade and, potentially a more serious blow, the closure of its tinplate works in 1957. The opening of factories in the area around the harbour made Lydney one of the main centres of employment for inhabitants of the Forest following the decline of coal mining and other traditional industries. A large site on the north-east side of the harbour was used during the Second World War as a salvage depot for military vehicles, and from 1945 under the auspices of the Royal Forest of Dean Development Association it was laid out as an industrial estate,[69] originally served by railway sidings.[70] Among the main firms attracted to the estate, where c. 1,000 people were being employed by 1960, were the J. Allen (later the London) Rubber Co., which took over a local enterprise making rubber gloves, and Duramin Engineering, which built bodywork for commercial vehicles.[71] Particularly active in the

47 Those employed in labouring tasks, including navvies building the S. Wales railway, and some other minor occupations are excluded from the total.
48 P.R.O., HO 107/2443.
49 Dean Forest Mercury, 28 July 1950.
50 P.R.O., HO 107/2443.   51 Ibid. RG 11/5221.
52 Morris's Dir. Glos. (1876), adverts. p. 189.
53 Kelly's Dir. Glos. (1897), 233.
54 Glos. R.O., DA 28/100/14, p. 626; Powell, Lydney, 22.
55 Glos. R.O., DA 28/100/1, p. 441; 4, p. 170.
56 Paar, Severn and Wye Railway, 148–9; Kelly's Dir. Glos. (1897), 232; for the harbour, below, Plates 9,23.
57 Glos. R.O., D 421/T 91.
58 Field, Norchard, 41–59.
59 Ibid. 66–73; Glos. Colln. JR 13.9; Payne, Glos. Survey, 205.

60 O.S. Map 1/25,000, SO 60 (1950 edn.).
61 Glos. Colln. (H) G 5.1 (9); Glos. R.O.,D 2299/1862.
62 O.S. Map 6", Glos. XLVII. NW. (1883 edn.).
63 Kelly's Dir. Glos. (1914), 249; O.S. Map 1/25,000, SO 60 (1950 edn.).
64 O.S. Map 1/2,500, Glos. XXXIX. 14 (1922 edn.).
65 Hart, Ind. Hist. of Dean, 348–51.
66 Paar, Severn and Wye Railway, 149.
67 Glos. Life, Nov. 1968, 22; inf. from Lydney Products Ltd.
68 Glos. Colln. RR 195.7 (1).
69 Dean Forest Mercury, 29 June 1945; cf. Glos. R.O., DA 28/100/13, pp. 479, 548; 14, pp. 474, 718.
70 O.S. Map 1/25,000, SO 60 (1961 edn.).
71 Lydney and District Official Guide (c. 1960), 33–4; Glos. R.O., DA 28/100/17, mins. of ind. cttee. 9 June 1960.

establishment of the estate and in other schemes to bring industry and employment to Lydney was the Watts family, shopkeepers in the town from the mid 19th century but later branching out in other ventures. John Watts ran bus services in the Forest and South Wales from the early 1920s and was the principal promoter of the amalgamation of a number of operators into the Red and White bus company in 1937. His brother Arthur Watts was active in the vehicle and tyre trade and in engineering. The Watts Tyre and Rubber Co., mainly concerned with remoulding and retreading, was based at the industrial estate after the Second World War, later moving to larger premises at the old tinplate works. Another of the family's firms, making solid fuel boilers and oil burners, traded on the estate until 1960 when it was sold to Allied Ironfounders Ltd.,[72] which moved to a site south of the tinplate works in 1964 but closed its factory in 1968.[73] Adjoining the industrial estate, close to the harbour entrance, the Pine End works was established in 1940 as a 'shadow' factory to make plywood for aeroplanes and gliders. After the war two large timber firms took over the factory and continued to make plywood from West African hardwoods,[74] employing over 600 workers in 1968.[75] Other firms which settled in Lydney included Albany Engineering, makers of pumps and hydraulic equipment, which opened a factory in Church Road in 1945,[76] the British Piston Ring Co. (later Brico Metals), which built a large foundry south of Tutnalls in 1962,[77] and J. R. Crompton, which opened a paper mill north of the former tinplate works in 1965.[78] By 1968 Lydney was a prosperous industrial centre, with c. 5,000 people employed in its factories.[79]

The industrial recession of the late 1970s and the early 1980s much reduced employment, and two large firms, the London Rubber Co. and Duramin, closed their factories.[80] Only a few hundred people were employed on the industrial estate by 1982. The estate was bought then by Beachley Property Ltd., which divided it into small units, and by 1990 over 1,000 people worked there in a total of c. 70 small manufacturing and service enterprises.[81] In the late 1980s, when Lydney's industry began to benefit from the improved access to the M4 motorway provided by a new bridge over the Wye at Chepstow, another industrial estate was begun south-west of the former tinplate works. In 1990 the great majority of inhabitants of the Lydney housing estates, besides others from a wider area, worked in local factories. Among the main

employers, the Watts group of companies, under its holding company Watts of Lydney Ltd., employed c. 470 at Lydney making industrial tyres, selling tyres and other vehicle components, distributing vehicles, and making urethane products; Brico Metals, which became Lydmet Ltd. after a reorganization in its controlling group in 1981, employed c. 450 making camshaft castings and valve seats; the Pine End works, which after a management buy-out in 1988 traded as Lydney Products Ltd., employed c. 200 producing plywood for the building trade, boatbuilders, and vehicle manufacturers; and the paper mill employed 162, mainly making long-fibred tissues for use in teabags and other household products.[82]

MARKET AND FAIRS. In 1268 the earl of Warwick was granted the right to hold a market on his Lydney manor on Mondays.[83] In the Middle Ages, as later, the market probably centred around the medieval town cross at the junction of High Street and Church Road, but a building called the Shambles which stood near Lydney church in 1558[84] may also have been used on market days. By the early 18th century, on what authority is not known, two fairs were held on 23 April and 28 October. By 1725 both the market, for which the day had been changed to Wednesday, and the fairs had lapsed and measures were taken to revive them. Toll-free trading at the fairs was offered and the lord of the manor promised free access to Lydney Pill for traders coming by boat. The following year a new market house was built,[85] presumably the one that adjoined the north-west side of the town cross[86] until demolished in the 1870s.[87] In the 1760s the two fairs (held on 4 May and 8 November after the calendar change) were principally cattle fairs,[88] and an advertisement to encourage cattle dealers to attend was published in 1776.[89]

The market had lapsed once more by the early 1790s and may not have been held again[90] until the 1880s, when there was a fortnightly cattle market at the Feathers inn.[91] In 1933 a dealer or auctioneer of Ross-on-Wye (Herefs.) planned to start monthly livestock sales at the 'old cattle market', a field adjoining Church Road just south-east of the market place, and a produce market behind the Cross Keys inn on the opposite side of the road.[92] The stock market apparently continued until the Second World War. The two annual fairs had been joined by a third, held on 25 June for wool and livestock, by 1870, and they continued until the Second World War[93] on a site at Newerne on the south-east side of the main street.[94]

72 Hart, *Watts of Lydney*; inf. from Mr. A. M. R. Watts.
73 Glos. R.O., DA 28/100/18, mins. 22 Sept., 22 Dec. 1964; 26 Mar., 28 May 1968.
74 Ibid. 13, pp. 548, 564–5, 628; 14, pp. 36, 237; inf. from Lydney Products Ltd. The factory was established by the Aeronautical and Panel Plywood Co. but traded in the war and for many years afterwards as Factories Direction Ltd.
75 *Glos. Life*, Nov. 1968, 22–3.
76 Glos. R.O., DA 28/100/14, pp. 626. 677.
77 Inf. from Lydmet Ltd.
78 Inf. from J. R. Crompton Ltd.
79 *Glos. Life*, Nov. 1968, 22. 80 Inf. from Mr. Watts.
81 Inf. from Beachley Property Ltd.
82 Inf. from Watts of Lydney Group Ltd.; Lydmet Ltd.;

Lydney Products Ltd.; J. R. Crompton Ltd.
83 *Cal. Chart. R.* 1257–1300, 114.
84 Glos. R.O., D 421/M 23; cf. ibid. M 26.
85 *Glouc. Jnl.* 4 Oct. 1725; 5 Apr. 1726.
86 G.D.R., T 1/117.
87 Glos. R.O., P 209/CW 2/4, min. 10 Apr. 1871; O.S. Map 6", Glos. XLVII. NW. (1883 edn.).
88 *Glouc. Jnl.* 24 Oct. 1763; 23 Apr. 1764.
89 Ibid. 22 Apr. 1776.
90 *Univ. Brit. Dir.* iii (1794), 566; *Hunt's Dir. Glos.* (1849), 117.
91 *Kelly's Dir. Glos.* (1885), 519.
92 Glos. R.O., DA 28/100/11, pp. 197, 310–11, 352.
93 *Kelly's Dir. Glos.* (1870 and later edns.).
94 Cf. *Dean Forest Mercury*, 3 Feb. 1950.

LOCAL GOVERNMENT. Court rolls for Lydney Shrewsbury manor survive for several years in the period 1416–45,[95] for Lydney Warwick manor for the years 1524, 1527–8,[96] and 1548 or 1549,[97] and for both manors for the years 1555, 1562, and 1574.[98] By 1607, for which year a draft roll survives, a single court was being held for both manors.[99] A court roll for Allaston manor survives for 1568 when the court met at Wellhouse, in Purton, and also exercised jurisdiction over the Wellhouse estate,[1] and a roll for Purton manor survives for 1579.[2] By 1677, and probably for many years earlier, the Winters were holding a single court baron for all the manors included in their Lydney estate,[3] and rolls for that joint court survive for several years in the period 1681–1707[4] and for the years 1863–4.[5] Leet jurisdiction was exercised by the court of Bledisloe hundred, which belonged to the Winters from 1595.[6] By the late 17th century the hundred court was being held on the same day as the court baron and at the same venue, the Feathers inn, and there was some duplication in the matters presented in the two courts.[7] The two courts continued to be held on the same day at the Feathers in the 19th century.[8] The hundred court appointed constables for the tithings of Lydney, Aylburton, and Purton, and one for Allaston and Nass.[9]

Of the manors which remained outside the Lydney estate, a court met for Rodleys manor until 1654 or later.[10] At Nass the manor court had lapsed by 1683 because almost all the holdings on the manor had passed into the lord's hands.[11]

The surviving records of parish government for Lydney include the accounts of the two churchwardens from 1763 and vestry minutes from the early 19th century. A poorhouse mentioned in 1772[12] was perhaps the building called the church house adjoining the market place. In 1803 20 people in Lydney parish, excluding Aylburton, received permanent relief from the parish and 39 people occasional relief, and c. 40 were receiving permanent relief each year at the end of the Napoleonic Wars.[13] There was the usual steady rise in the annual cost of relief during the early 19th century,[14] but the fact that the large and populous parish did not find it necessary to build a workhouse indicates that poor relief was not a great burden. From 1854 a considerable body of ratepayers opposed the payment of church rates, and as a result the rates were levied only for the upkeep of the church fabric, a voluntary subscription being opened for other churchwardens' expenses.[15]

Aylburton tithing and chapelry had its separate parish officers and relieved its own poor. It had two churchwardens in the 16th century[16] but by the late 18th century and until 1914 there was a single officer, styled chapelwarden; his accounts survive from 1769,[17] and there are vestry minutes from 1854.[18] In 1784 the Aylburton ratepayers resisted an attempt by the Lydney vestry to levy a church rate on them for repairs to the parish church.[19] By the later 19th century Aylburton had come to be regarded as a parish in its own right and it had its own parish council under the Act of 1894.[20]

In 1836 Lydney and Aylburton were included in the Chepstow poor- law union.[21] In 1867 a Lydney highway board was established covering all the Gloucestershire parishes in the union except St. Briavels,[22] and in 1894 the Gloucestershire parishes of the union were formed into the Lydney rural district. The business of the rural district council was dominated by the affairs of the growing town of Lydney, particularly its housing schemes, and until 1945 the council appointed a Lydney parochial committee, comprising the Lydney councillors and members of the parish council, to deal with the detail of matters exclusive to Lydney parish. The council was usually chaired by a Lydney councillor[23] and from 1898 it met at Lydney's town hall, moving in 1956 to a council chamber in new offices built the previous year in the same part of the town.[24] In 1974 the Lydney rural district became part of the new Forest of Dean district. The council offices continued in use as the treasurer's department of the new council. Lydney parish council exercised considerable responsibilities in the later 20th century, including management of a cemetery, a park, and the large recreation trust property.[25]

CHURCHES. The church at Lydney, recorded in the mid 12th century,[26] was evidently an early foundation built to serve a wide area on the south side of the Forest of Dean. The churches at Hewelsfield and St. Briavels were chapels to it until the mid 19th century, and Aylburton[27] has remained annexed as a chapelry. In the mid 16th century, but at no other period, the church at Lancaut was also said to be a chapel to Lydney.[28]

Lydney church passed to Lire abbey (Eure), in Normandy, presumably by gift of the abbey's founder William FitzOsbern (d. 1071). By the early 13th century the abbey had appropriated the church, and a vicarage, comprising a third of the profits, had been ordained. In 1219 Lire granted the church to the dean and chapter of Hereford, reserving a sufficient portion to the vicar and glebe land to itself.[29] In 1271 the dean and chapter bought out a right that William de

95 Glos. R.O., D 421/M 19.   96 Ibid. M 20.
97 P.R.O., SC 2/175/74.   98 Glos. R.O., D 421/M 21.
99 Ibid. M 22.   1 Ibid. D 421/6.
2 Ibid. M 82.   3 Ibid. L 6.
4 Ibid. M 32, M 34.   5 Ibid. M 77.
6 Above, Bledisloe hundred.   7 Glos. R.O., D 421/M 32–3.
8 Ibid. M 77.   9 Ibid. M 33, M 77.
10 Ibid. L 6.   11 Ibid. L 2.
12 Ibid. P 209/CW 2/4.
13 *Poor Law Abstract, 1804,* 170–1; *1818,* 144–5.
14 Ibid.; *Poor Law Returns* (1830–1), 66; (1835), 64.
15 Glos. R.O., P 209/CW 2/4.

16 Hockaday Abs. cclxvi, 1563; xlvii, 1576 visit. f. 129.
17 Glos. R.O., P 209/CW 2/1–2; P 384/VE 2/1.
18 Ibid. P 209/VE 2/1.
19 Ibid. CW 2/1.   20 Ibid. VE 2/1.
21 *Kelly's Dir. Glos.* (1870), 593; cf. Glos. R.O., P 278/VE 2/1.
22 Glos. R.O., D 1219/3.   23 Ibid. DA 28/100/1–19.
24 Ibid. 1, p. 101; 16, pp. 432, 573.   25 Above, intro.
26 Dugdale, *Mon.* vi (2), 1092, 1094.
27 B.L. Harl. MS. 6203, p. 72; Hockaday Abs. cclxvi, 1552; G.D.R. vol. 382, f. 18.
28 *Valor Eccl.* (Rec. Com.), ii. 501; cf. *V.C.H. Glos.* x. 77.
29 B.L. Harl. MS. 6203, pp. 70–3.

Beauchamp, earl of Warwick, claimed in the advowson of the church.[30] In 1274 when the vicar's portion was found inadequate a new portion, to be at least a third of the profits, was ordered to be assigned.[31] The living, which has remained a vicarage, was in the gift of the dean and chapter of Hereford[32] until 1929 when by an exchange of advowsons it passed to the Lord Chancellor on behalf of the Crown.[33] By grant of the patrons the advowson was exercised in 1552 by John Crocker and Gilbert Wheeler, in 1554 by Thomas Church, in 1570 by William Winter, and in 1595 by Sir Edward Winter.[34]

In 1291 the church and its chapels were valued at £53 6s. 8d. and the vicar's portion at £13 6s. 8d.,[35] and in 1535 the vicarage was valued at £23 18s. 8d.[36] In 1650 the vicarage was worth £60,[37] in 1750 £260,[38] and in 1856 £799.[39] In Lydney parish the impropriators owned the corn tithes and the vicar all the other tithes,[40] and there was a similar division in the St. Briavels chapelry, except in some small areas that were tithable to others;[41] in Hewelsfield the vicar took all the tithes.[42] A total of 406 a. in Lydney parish, mostly Prior's Mesne and the Stirts, formerly of Llanthony priory, was tithe free in 1839.[43] In the late 17th century and the 18th the owners of the Lydney estate usually took a lease of the vicar's tithes arising in their demesne lands and woods.[44] In 1839 the vicar's tithes in Lydney and Aylburton were commuted for a corn rent charge of £680.[45] There was apparently no vicarage glebe until 1805 when the impropriators gave the vicar a meadow of c. 1 a. adjoining the vicarage house.[46] The house, on the north side of the churchyard, was burnt down in the Civil War. It was rebuilt by the vicar Edward Jones before 1680[47] and was enlarged in the 1720s.[48] It was rebuilt in Tudor style in 1840–1.[49]

In 1281 Reynold, vicar of Lydney, was given leave of absence for three years to go on crusade[50] and in 1285 he was given two years' leave for study.[51] The cure was served by a canon of Hereford in 1289 while the vicar Gilbert of Chevening studied at Oxford.[52] Lydney was a centre of Lollardism in the late 15th century.[53] In 1470 two Lydney men were required to abjure heresies which included denial of transubstantiation and purgatory, opposition to pilgrimages and images, and the assertion that the clergy forbade the use of the scriptures in English 'solely from envy'. Two years later at

least 11 other parishioners were found to have voiced similar opinions; one owned an English translation of St. Matthew's gospel and several had met in a private house where a preacher, Thomas Packer of Walford (Herefs.), addressed them.[54] About 1497 two parishioners, Ellen Griffith and a man called Spenser, were burnt at Lydney as heretics.[55]

Thomas Turner, vicar from 1570 to his death in 1595,[56] was reported in 1576 to have popish tendencies: he omitted many of the offices, administered communion in a pre-Reformation chalice, perambulated in a surplice, and read the gospels at Aylburton village cross. He was also accused of immorality and censured for excessive familiarity with his parishioners.[57] In 1593 Turner was among clergy characterized as 'slender scholars and of life suspected'.[58] His successor Anthony Sterry was also rector of Abenhall.[59] Morgan Godwin, instituted in 1641, had deserted his cure by 1645 to join the royalist forces.[60] Hopewell Fox, of a prominent puritan family of clergy,[61] was vicar in 1650 and held the cure until his death in 1662.[62] Between the late 17th century and the early 19th, when several incumbents were prebendaries of Hereford cathedral or had other livings in Herefordshire, the parish was often in the care of stipendiary curates.[63]

In 1360 William of Cheltenham founded a chantry chapel, dedicated to St. Leonard, in Purton hamlet and endowed it with the bulk of his Purton manor.[64] The chantry was probably also intended to serve as a chapel of ease, for at the time of its dissolution in 1549 it was said to have been founded to provide services for the inhabitants of the hamlet in winter.[65] Probably it was also used by travellers crossing the river at Purton passage. William granted the advowson of the chantry to Maurice, Lord Berkeley, in 1365[66] and it descended with the Berkeleys' Purton manor.[67] The chantry and its lands were acquired by the Winters before 1560,[68] and the chapel, which stood among the outbuildings of Purton Manor, had been converted as a barn by 1651.[69]

Two chantries in Lydney church, one dedicated to St. Mary and the other to the Holy Cross, existed by 1328.[70] The Holy Cross chantry possibly lapsed soon afterwards, as a chantry founded in the church in 1375 by John Chardborough and Julia his wife, Walter of Aust, and John Gainer and endowed with a substantial

30 *Charters and Rec. of Heref. Cath.* ed. W. W. Capes (Heref. 1908), 125.
31 Ibid. 133. 32 Hockaday Abs. cclxvi.
33 *Lond. Gaz.* 17 Dec. 1929, pp. 8191–2.
34 Hockaday Abs. cclxvi.
35 *Tax. Eccl.* (Rec. Com.), 161.
36 *Valor Eccl.* (Rec. Com.), ii. 501.
37 *Trans. B.G.A.S.* lxxxiii. 97.
38 G.D.R. vol. 381A, f. 4. 39 Ibid. 384, f. 134.
40 Ibid. V 5/195T 1; T 1/117.
41 Ibid. T 1/153. 42 Ibid. T 1/100.
43 Ibid. T 1/117; for the Stirts, cf. ibid. vol. 89, depositions 9 Mar. 1602.
44 Glos. R.O., D 421/T 20, E 28.
45 G.D.R., T 1/117. 46 Ibid. V 5/195T 3.
47 Ibid. 1.
48 Glos. R.O., P 209/IN 1/1, mem. at end.
49 Ibid. MI 1, p. 72. 50 *Reg. Cantilupe*, 290.
51 *Reg. Swinfield*, 545. 52 Ibid. 212, 526.

53 Cf. J. A. F. Thompson, *Later Lollards, 1414–1520* (1965), 40–2, 47.
54 *Reg. Stanbury*, 118–26. 55 *Reg. Mayew*, 109–10.
56 Hockaday Abs. cclxvi.
57 G.D.R. vol. 40, ff. 225, 257.
58 Hockaday Abs. lii, state of clergy 1593, f. 13.
59 Ibid. cclxvi; *Eccl. Misc.* 99.
60 Hockaday Abs. cclxvii.
61 *Glos. N. & Q.* ii. 412–15.
62 *Trans. B.G.A.S.* lxxxiii. 97; Bigland, *Glos.* ii. 160.
63 Hockaday Abs. cclxvii–xx; G.D.R. vol. 382, f. 18; Rudder, *Glos.* 530; *Trans. B.G.A.S.* xcvi. 6; Glos. R.O., P 209/IN 1/1–2. 64 *Cal. Pat.* 1358–61, 477.
65 Hockaday Abs. cclxv, 1549.
66 Berkeley Cast. Mun., General Ser. Chart. 3573.
67 *Reg. Spofford*, 351; *Reg. Myllyng*, 37–8; *Reg. Mayew*, 274; *Reg. Bothe*, 340, 346; cf. above, manors.
68 Above, manors. 69 Glos. R.O., D 421/M 83.
70 *Reg. T. de Charlton*, 95, 99.

estate[71] later had the same dedication.[72] From 1432 or earlier the advowson of Chardborough's Holy Cross chantry was exercised by the Berkeleys and Latimers, owners of Tucknall and one of the Purton manors.[73] The lands of St. Mary's and Holy Cross chantries were granted in 1559 to William Winter and Edward Baeshe;[74] Winter became sole owner of the lands and they presumably formed the farm later based on the house called the Chantry in Church Road.[75]

At Primrose Hill a corrugated iron mission church, dedicated to Holy Trinity, was put up in 1903 and replaced by a new brick church in 1933.[76]

The parish church of *ST. MARY*, which bore that dedication by the early 13th century,[77] is built of rubble with ashlar dressings and has a chancel with north chapel and south vestry, an aisled and clerestoried nave with north porch and south vestry, and a west tower with spire.

No part of the fabric of the present church appears to survive from before the 13th century when the chancel, aisled nave, and west tower were built, forming a church of notable size and quality. The upper stage of the tower and the spire were added in the early 14th century and the north chapel was possibly added in the late 14th century to house the chantry founded in 1375.[78] In the 15th century the nave was raised and given a clerestory, which includes an east window, and some new windows were inserted in the aisles. The north chapel was rebuilt by Sir William Winter before 1589[79] and became the private chapel of his family and later of the Bathursts;[80] it housed the organ from 1860 to 1938 and was rededicated as a chapel in 1940.[81] The church was severely damaged by fire during fighting in the Civil War and remained roofless in the late 1660s when plans for restoration were in hand.[82] The nave and aisles retain the wagon roofs installed then. A small vestry was added on the south side of the chancel in 1841. Between 1849 and 1853 a general restoration and refitting of the church was carried out under Fulljames and Waller.[83] The top of the spire, which had been rebuilt in 1784,[84] was again rebuilt in 1896 when much additional expense was incurred because scaffolding blew down and damaged other parts of the church.[85] The south porch was extended c. 1937 to form a choir vestry.[86]

The church has an octagonal stone font of the 15th century.[87] A coffin slab with the effigy of a priest, probably of the early 14th century, was formerly in the churchyard[88] but in 1990 was

kept under the tower. A wooden chancel screen was inserted in 1906.[89] The east window of the Bathursts' chapel has stained glass depicting the Franz Joseph glacier, in New Zealand, given in 1941 by Viscount Bledisloe.[90] The communion plate was stolen in 1833 and a new chalice and paten were given by Charles Bathurst; a new flagon was acquired by subscription in 1847.[91] A chalice and paten, which were found walled up in the old Lydney Park house when it was demolished in the late 19th century, were given to the church by Viscount Bledisloe (d. 1958).[92] A ring of six bells was supplied in 1700 by Abraham Rudhall, who recast one of them in 1703; others were recast in 1797 (by John Rudhall), in 1841, and in 1971. The ring was augmented to eight by the addition of two bells by John Taylor of Loughborough (Leics.) in 1900, and to ten by two more bells from the Loughborough foundry in 1974.[93] The parish registers, which survive from 1678, include entries for some inhabitants from Yorkley and other nearby parts of the Forest and Newland parish.[94] The churchyard was extended to the south following the diversion of Church Road in the mid 19th century.[95] The older part contains a large number of carved headstones dating from the late 17th century to the early 19th.

The chapel of ease of *ST. MARY* at Aylburton, known by that dedication by 1750 but dedicated to St. John in 1471,[96] was established before 1219.[97] Aylburton had a chaplain in 1436[98] and in the mid 16th century a stipendiary curate had particular responsibility for the chapel.[99] No later evidence has been found for such an arrangement until c. 1903 when the assistant curate of the parish was based at Aylburton at the request of the villagers and of Charles Bathurst, who contributed to his stipend during the next few years.[1] Later in the 20th century the assistant curate lived in the village in a house rented from the Lydney estate, but that arrangement ended c. 1985.[2] In 1750 and 1825 the chapel was used only for an afternoon service on Sundays, the villagers attending the parish church in the morning.[3]

Aylburton chapel stood at Chapel Hill, above the village on the lane leading up to Aylburton common.[4] In 1855–6 the chapel was dismantled and rebuilt, with the same materials and in almost exactly the same form, at a lower and more convenient site, on the lane which became known as Church Road. The cost was borne by

71 *Cal. Pat.* 1374–7, 108.
72 *Trans. B.G.A.S.* viii. 289.
73 *Reg. Spofford*, 358, 360, where Ric. Beauchamp, earl of Warw., held it, evidently by right of one of the manors of his wife Eliz. Berkeley rather than by right of Lydney Warwick manor; *Reg. Stanbury*, 184; *Reg. Mayew*, 282.
74 *Cal. Pat.* 1558–60, 359.
75 Glos. R.O., D 421/T 16, lease 1683.
76 *Kelly's Dir. Glos.* (1910), 242; (1935), 248; Glos. R.O., D 3921/II/5.
77 B.L. Harl. MS. 6203, p. 72; G.D.R. wills 1543/35.
78 Bigland, *Glos.* ii. 155; above, this section.
79 Hockaday Abs. cclxvi, 1589.
80 Atkyns, *Glos.* 540.
81 R. A. J. Bell, *Parish Church of St. Mary, Lydney* (1983), [10, 38].
82 G.D.R. vol. 219.
83 Glos. R.O., P 209/CW 2/4; MI 1, p. 73.

84 Ibid. CW 2/4.   85 *Glos. N. & Q.* vii. 54–5, 115.
86 Bell, *Ch. of St. Mary*, [38].
87 *Trans. B.G.A.S.* xliv. 195.
88 Roper, *Glos. Effigies*, 444.
89 Bell, *Ch. of St. Mary*, [22].   90 Ibid. [13].
91 Glos. R.O., P 209/CW 2/4; *Glos. Ch. Plate*, 140.
92 *Trans. B.G.A.S.* li. 75; Bell, *Ch. of St. Mary*, [35].
93 *Glos. Ch. Bells*, 422–3; cf. Bell, *Ch. of St. Mary*, [35].
94 Glos. R.O., P 209/IN 1/1–2.   95 Cf. above, intro.
96 G.D.R. vol. 381A, f. 4; Hockaday Abs. cclxv, 1471.
97 B.L. Harl. MS. Rawl. 6203, pp. 71–2.
98 *Reg. Spofford*, 210.
99 Bodl. MS. Rawl. C. 790, f. 27v.; Hockaday Abs. xxx, 1544 stipendiaries, f. 6; cclxvi, 1562.
1 Glos. R.O., P 384/VE 2/1, min. 13 Dec. 1907.
2 Inf. from the vicar of Lydney, the Revd. D. Evans.
3 G.D.R. vol. 381A, f. 4; 383, no. cxviii.
4 G.D.R., T 1/117.

Charles Bathurst.[5] The chapel, which is of rubble with ashlar dressings, comprises chancel, nave with south aisle and porch, and west tower. The fabric dates mainly from a rebuilding in the early 14th century, but some of the windows were renewed at the removal to the new site. The fittings include a 15th-century stone pulpit and a plain, cylindrical stone font which cannot be definitely dated but is possibly Norman.[6] The plate includes a chalice given in 1710,[7] and there is a single bell, cast in 1733 by William Evans of Chepstow.[8] The chapel kept separate registers from 1856, when the new site included a burial ground.[9]

In the early 1860s a lay preacher Frederick Bryan held meetings at Aylburton common in the open in summer and in a cottage in winter. A small mission room was built at Bryan's instigation in 1867, and it was enlarged in 1869. Apart from the period c. 1892–1901, services continued under lay readers, and the room was still used for two services a month in 1990.[10]

ROMAN CATHOLICISM

ROMAN CATHOLICISM. The Winter family were recusants at least from the time of Sir John,[11] who inherited the Lydney estate in 1619. Its presence encouraged the survival of a group of Catholics at Lydney: 20 were recorded there in 1676[12] and 35 c. 1720.[13]

From the 1940s Roman Catholics heard mass in various centres in Lydney, and in 1977 a small church was built at the north-east end of Newerne and opened as a chapel of ease to Cinderford. In 1990 it had an average congregation of 75, drawn from Lydney, Aylburton, and other villages.[14]

PROTESTANT NONCONFORMITY

PROTESTANT NONCONFORMITY. There was a group of Quakers at Aylburton by 1660 when all those at a meeting there were arrested and the 15 men among them imprisoned.[15] At the same period some of the group were persecuted, and on occasion physically assaulted, by the vicar of Lydney, Hopewell Fox.[16] In 1676 and 1677 the Gloucestershire quarterly meeting assisted the Aylburton Quakers to purchase a site and build a meeting house in Coleford, where presumably there was less danger of persecution. By 1679 they were meeting in the new meeting house together with Quakers already established at Coleford,[17] to which some

or all of the Aylburton members may have moved.

In 1796 Independents under William Bishop, minister at Gloucester, registered a house in Lydney for worship.[18] Another house, at Newerne, was registered in 1804 and one at Aylburton in 1807, but the Independent cause did not become firmly established in the parish.[19]

Baptists, attached to the church at Coleford, were meeting in the house of John Trotter at Lydney by 1819, and in 1836, when the group had 30 members, a chapel was built on land bought by Trotter on the north-west side of the main street.[20] In 1851 the chapel had average morning congregations of 140 and average evening congregations of 180.[21] Enlargement and renovation of the chapel, including the addition of a schoolroom, were completed in 1877.[22] In 1990 the Baptist church had 25 adult members under a settled minister.[23]

Wesleyan Methodist ministers of the Cardiff circuit preached at Lydney from 1803 but abandoned their mission a few years later. The cause was later revived under ministers of the Monmouth circuit[24] and houses were registered for worship in 1816 and 1819.[25] In 1850 the Wesleyans built a chapel in the later Swan Road at Newerne. It had average congregations of 100 in 1851.[26] The chapel was closed in 1956 and Methodist worship in Lydney was centred on Springfield Methodist church.[27] At Aylburton Wesleyans held open-air meetings at the village cross in 1910. Later a temporary building was used until 1915 when a chapel was built on the south-east side of the village street. A hall was built adjoining the chapel in 1966.[28] In 1990 Aylburton Methodist church had 17 members and was served as part of the Forest of Dean circuit.[29]

Primitive Methodists converted two cottages at Newerne into a chapel in 1850, and in 1851 congregations at afternoon and evening services averaged 100.[30] In 1869 a new chapel called Ebenezer was built on the road to Primrose Hill (later Springfield Road)[31] and the old chapel was sold in 1871.[32] After the Methodist Union of 1932 the Springfield Road chapel became the Springfield Methodist church, and in 1990, as part of the Forest circuit, it had 73 members.[33] A group of Primitive Methodists, never numbering more than 10 members,[34] met in a house at New Mills from 1856 to 1868,[35] and there was a small meeting near Soilwell in 1859.[36]

A Congregational church, using a corrugated

5 Glos. R.O., P 209/MI 1, pp. 73–4; cf. ch. guide (1985).
6 Cf. *Trans. B.G.A.S.* xlix. 132, 152.
7 *Glos. Ch. Plate*, 141.   8 *Glos. Ch. Bells*, 129.
9 *Glos. Par. Rec.* 55; G.D.R. vol. 384, f. 31v.
10 Ch. guide (1985); inf. from the vicar.
11 *Cal. S.P. Dom.* 1637–8, 74; 1639, 427; Glos. R.O., Q/SO 4, p. 515.   12 *Compton Census*, ed. Whiteman, 544.
13 Glos. R.O., Q/SO 4, p. 515.
14 Inf. from the Revd. J. Halpin, par. priest of Cinderford.
15 Glos. R.O., D 2052, Aylburton.   16 Ibid. Lydney.
17 Ibid. D 1340/A 1/M 1, mins. 30 Mar. 1676; 28 June, 27 Sept. 1677; 28 Mar. 1678; 27 Mar., 26 June 1679.
18 Hockaday Abs. cclxix; cf. *V.C.H. Glos.* iv. 324.
19 Hockaday Abs. cclxx; Bright, *Nonconf. in Dean*, 18–19.
20 Bright, *Nonconf. in Dean*, 28–9; *Earlier Hist. of Baptist Ch., Lydney*, 3: copy in Glos. R.O., NC 36.
21 P.R.O., HO 129/576/3/3/7.

22 *Earlier Hist. of Baptist Ch.* 6.
23 *Baptist Union Dir.* (1990–1), 76.
24 Bright, *Nonconf. in Dean*, 33.
25 Hockaday Abs. cclxx.
26 P.R.O., HO 129/576/3/3/8; cf. O.S. Map 6″, Glos. XLVII. NW. (1883 edn.).   27 Glos. R.O., D 2598/1/26.
28 G. E. Lawrence, *Kindling the Flame* (1974), 37–9: copy in Glos. R.O., D 2598/23/1.
29 Inf. from the Revd. R. M. Styles, of Lydney.
30 Glos R.O., D 2598/4/6, min. 16 Dec. 1850; P.R.O., HO 129/576/3/3/9.
31 *Glouc. Jnl.* 23 Oct. 1869; O.S. Map 6″, Glos. XLVII. NW. (1883 edn.).   32 Glos. R.O., D 421/T 62.
33 Inf. from the Revd. R. M. Styles.
34 Glos. R.O., D 2598/4/9.
35 Ibid. 4/6, mins. 10 Dec. 1856; 9 Mar. 1868.
36 Ibid. min. 12 Dec. 1859.

iron building in Tutnalls Street, was formed in 1906.[37] A new brick chapel was built in 1928.[38] In 1990, as a United Reformed church, it had 10 adult members and was served with other churches of the Forest area.[39]

Among other meetings were those of the Salvation Army recorded from 1884 to c. 1895,[40] the Latter Day Saints recorded from 1902 to the early 1920s,[41] and the Jehovah's Witnesses recorded in the 1960s.[42] The Elim Pentecostal church at Gloucester had members in Lydney by 1957;[43] from c. 1959 the church used the former Methodist chapel in Swan Road,[44] which it continued to occupy in 1990.

EDUCATION. Dame schools and other small private schools were teaching 142 children in the parish in 1833. Lydney had a church Sunday school by 1818[45] and one was being held in part of Aylburton chapel in 1847. A National school, probably supported by Charles Bathurst,[46] was opened before 1839 in a building at the site of the old furnace at the south-west end of Lydney town.[47] Bathurst was wholly supporting the school in 1856 when c. 200 children were said to attend.[48] About 1865, when it was for girls and infants, it had an average attendance of 126 and an income from voluntary contributions and school pence, the Revd. W. H. Bathurst making up a deficiency.[49]

In 1866 the Revd. W. H. Bathurst gave a site on the north-east side of Church Road and a new church school was built, funded by subscription and a government grant.[50] In 1885 it had accommodation for 300 and an average attendance of 228, organized in boys', girls', and infants' departments.[51] The school was enlarged in 1892 and 1899, bringing the accommodation up to 530.[52] In 1910, called Lydney C. of E. school, it had an average attendance of 263.[53] From 1919 the older children attended the new senior council school in the town,[54] and in 1922 Lydney C. of E. school, organized as junior mixed and infants, had an average attendance of 112, falling to 41 by 1938.[55] It accepted controlled status in 1950.[56] In 1973 it moved into the former secondary school buildings in Bream Road,[57] and it had 127 children on its roll in 1990.[58]

Primrose Hill C. of E. school opened in 1876 in a new building[59] on the west side of the road at Primrose Hill. In 1885 it had accommodation for 100 children and an average attendance of 80, in mixed and infants' departments.[60] It was enlarged in 1886, increasing the accommodation to 160.[61] Average attendance was 129 in 1910, falling to 50 by 1932, when the school was organized as junior mixed and infants.[62] It accepted controlled status in 1950.[63] It moved to a new building on the housing estate east of Primrose Hill, opened in 1976,[64] and had 174 children of primary school age on the roll in 1990.[65]

Lydney Council school opened in 1906[66] in a new building near the entrance of Nass Lane and in 1909 a second building was opened on an adjoining site for its infants' department.[67] In 1910 the school had accommodation for 328 and an average attendance of 257. After the opening of a senior school at Lydney in 1919 it had junior mixed and infants' departments and the name was changed to Lydney Junior Council school. In 1938 it had an average attendance of 271.[68] Later it was organized as separate junior and infants' schools, which merged once again in 1976, and in 1977 it moved into the former girls' secondary school building further along Nass Lane. In 1978 the school was renamed Severnbanks Primary school.[69] It had 313 children on its roll in 1990.[70]

Aylburton C. of E. school opened in 1870 in a schoolroom built opposite Aylburton chapel, mainly at the cost of the Revd. W. H. Bathurst; he also made up a deficiency in its running costs, which otherwise were supplied from school pence.[71] In 1885 it was a mixed school with accommodation for 160 and an average attendance of 96.[72] By 1910 there was a separate infants' department and the average attendance was 118.[73] After 1919 the older children of Aylburton attended the senior school at Lydney,[74] and Aylburton C. of E. school had an average attendance of 62 in 1938.[75] It accepted controlled status in 1949.[76] In 1990 it had 52 primary school children on its roll.[77]

In 1915 plans for a senior school at Lydney resulted in a new building being put up in Bream Road, but it was used as a hospital for the remainder of the First World War.[78] In 1919 the

37 *Cong. Year Bk.* (1972), 94; *Kelly's Dir. Glos.* (1927), 258.
38 Date on bldg.
39 *United Reformed Ch. Year Bk.* (1989–90), 62.
40 G.R.O. Worship Reg. no. 27877.
41 *Kelly's Dir. Glos.* (1902 and later edns.).
42 G.R.O. Worship Reg. no. 67801.
43 Glos. R.O., D 2598/1/26, letter 8 Apr. 1957.
44 G.R.O. Worship Reg. no. 67149.
45 *Educ. of Poor Digest*, 303; *Educ. Enq. Abstract*, 319.
46 Nat. Soc. *Inquiry, 1846–7*, Glos. 12–13.
47 G.D.R., T 1/117.
48 *Kelly's Dir. Glos.* (1856), 322.
49 P.R.O., ED 7/35/204.
50 *Kelly's Dir. Glos.* (1870), 593.
51 Ibid. (1885), 520.   52 Ibid. (1902), 235.
53 *Bd. of Educ., List 21, 1911* (H.M.S.O.), 164.
54 P.R.O., ED 7/35/204B.
55 *Bd. of Educ., List 21, 1922* (H.M.S.O.), 105; *1932*, 116; *1938*, 41.
56 *Lydney and District Official Guide* (c. 1960), 26.
57 Glos. R.O., SM 209/5/M 2, pp. 81, 87.
58 *Educ. Services Dir. 1990–1* (co. educ. dept.), 22.

59 P.R.O., ED 7/35/205.
60 *Kelly's Dir. Glos.* (1885), 520.
61 Ibid. (1902), 235.
62 *Bd. of Educ., List 21, 1911* (H.M.S.O.), 164; *1922*, 105; *1932*, 116.
63 *Lydney and District Official Guide* (c. 1960), 26.
64 Glos. R.O., SM 209/5/M 2, p. 121.
65 *Educ. Services Dir. 1990–1*, 27.
66 P.R.O., ED 7/35/204A.
67 Glos. R.O., S 209/3/1, p. 1.
68 *Bd. of Educ., List 21, 1911* (H.M.S.O.), 164; *1922*, 105; *1938*, 128; P.R.O., ED 7/35/204B.
69 Glos. R.O., SM 209/3/M 3.
70 *Educ. Services Dir. 1990–1*, 32.
71 P.R.O., ED 7/34/24; *Kelly's Dir. Glos.* (1870), 593.
72 *Kelly's Dir. Glos.* (1885), 520.
73 *Bd. of Educ., List 21, 1911* (H.M.S.O.), 158.
74 P.R.O., ED 7/35/204B; W.I. hist. of Aylburton, 25.
75 *Bd. of Educ., List 21, 1938* (H.M.S.O.), 125.
76 W.I. hist. of Aylburton, 27.
77 *Educ. Services Dir. 1990–1*, 6.
78 *Kelly's Dir. Glos.* (1927), 259; Glos. R.O., CE/M 2/12, pp. 130, 181; 14, pp. 212–13.

building was opened as Lydney Senior Council school and took the older children from the local elementary schools.[79] In 1922 it had mixed accommodation for 240 and an average attendance of 146. In 1938 the average attendance was 126.[80] Under the Act of 1944 the school became the Lydney Secondary Modern school[81] and in 1961 it was divided into separate boys' and girls' secondary schools, the latter in new buildings in Nass Lane.[82] The schools were closed in 1973 when the boys' school had an attendance of c. 370 and the girls' school c. 350.[83]

In 1902 a committee was formed to promote secondary education in the Lydney area, and in 1903 it opened a secondary school for boys and girls, supported by fees, in the Lydney Institute building. By 1905 the school had over 100 pupils. The Board of Education granted recognition only on condition that better accommodation was provided, and extensions to the Institute building were completed in 1907, half the cost being provided by the county council and half raised locally.[84] In 1908 a Board of Education Scheme created a governing body, including six representatives of the county council, to administer the school together with the Lydney Institute and School of Art. The secondary school was to take children aged from 8 to 19; no limit was set on the catchment area but children from Lydney, Aylburton, and Alvington were to have preference if space became limited.[85] The buildings were extended in the 1930s, and in 1936 the school had 500 pupils, including some who came from places on the other side of the Severn by railway. In 1932 the name was changed from Lydney Secondary school to Lydney Grammar school,[86] and it remained an assisted grammar school under the Act of 1944.[87] Attendance was over 500 when the school closed in 1973.[88]

In 1973 secondary education in the area was reorganized: Lydney Grammar, Lydney Boys' and Girls' Secondary schools, and a secondary modern school at Bream were closed and their pupils transferred to two new comprehensive schools, Whitecross, at Lydney in the enlarged buildings of the grammar school, and Wyedean, at Sedbury, in Tidenham;[89] Wyedean for a few years used the former girls' secondary school in Nass Lane as one of its buildings.[90] In 1988 Whitecross comprehensive school had 919 children aged from 11 to 18 on the roll.[91] From 1989 it took children up to 16 years, those of sixth-form age going to the Royal Forest of Dean College at Five Acres,[92]

and there were 789 children on the roll at Whitecross in 1990.[93]

The Lydney Institute, providing science and art classes, was opened in 1889 in the new town hall at the market place.[94] Later known as the Lydney Institute and School of Art and Science, it was by 1894 a recognized centre for training elementary school teachers for the district.[95] A new building for the Institute was opened adjoining the town hall in 1897 and a new science wing was added[96] in 1902. Under the Scheme of 1908, mentioned above, the Institute was to provide instruction in art, science, commercial subjects, and domestic science for day and evening students.[97] Art tuition appears to have predominated later.[98] In the early 1960s, known as the Lydney School of Art and Evening Technical Institute, it prepared students for art examinations and ran evening classes in commercial and domestic subjects.[99] In 1966 it was amalgamated with the technical college at Cinderford to form the West Gloucestershire College of Further Education; the art department of the new college remained at Lydney for a few years.[1]

CHARITIES FOR THE POOR. In 1683 there was an almshouse with four rooms near Lydney town cross.[2] It was apparently still in use c. 1775[3] and was perhaps replaced by the row of six tenements on the south-west side of Church Road which was occupied as almshouses in 1839. The almshouses in Church Road were owned by the Bathursts,[4] who apparently supported them until the foundation of the War Memorial Trust almshouses in the 1920s.[5]

Thomas Donning by will dated 1655 gave 20s. a year to the poor of Purton tithing,[6] and his brother William Donning by will dated 1680 charged the bequest on a house and plot of land.[7] Thomas Morgan of Hurst by will dated 1660 gave, together with a bequest for three sermons, 20s. a year to the poor of the parish. Richard Hart of Gurshill by will dated 1665 gave £15 to be laid out on land and the proceeds distributed to the poor. The principal had not been laid out in 1683.[8] The three charities had probably lapsed by c. 1780 when a bequest of £5 by Eleanor Lewis, whose will was the subject of litigation, was said to be the only charity given for Lydney,[9] and they and the Lewis charity were certainly defunct by the 1820s.[10]

The Revd. Richard Gwatkin (d. 1789) left £100, the interest to be distributed among eight

[79] P.R.O., ED 7/35/204B.
[80] Bd. of Educ., List 21, 1922 (H.M.S.O.), 105; 1938, 128.
[81] Lydney and District Official Guide (c. 1960), 27.
[82] Glos. R.O., SM 209/1/M 4; cf. Lydney Par. Official Guide (1972), 8, and street plan.
[83] Glos. R.O., D 5627/3/4; below, this section.
[84] Glos. R.O., D 5627/3/1.   [85] Ibid. 3/3.
[86] Lydney Grammar Sch. 1903–73, 11, 19, 71: copy in Glos. R.O., SC 32.
[87] Lydney and District Official Guide (c. 1960), 26.
[88] Glos. R.O., D 5627/3/4.
[89] Lydney Grammar Sch. 4; Glos. R.O., D 5627/3/4.
[90] Glos. R.O., S 209/2/4, entry 21 July 1976.
[91] Educ. Services Dir. 1988–9, 41.
[92] Notice issued by co. educ. dept. 11 Nov. 1988.

[93] Educ. Services Dir. 1990–1, 44.
[94] Glos. R.O., D 5627/3/1.
[95] Kelly's Dir. Glos. (1894), 227.
[96] Glos. R.O., D 5627/3/1.   [97] Ibid. 3/3.
[98] Kelly's Dir. Glos. (1935), 248.
[99] Lydney and District Official Guide (c. 1960), 27.
[1] Glos. R.O., SM 209/2/M 5, mins. 1 July 1966; 27 Oct. 1967; rep. of grammar sch. headmaster, Spring 1970.
[2] G.D.R., V 5/195T 2.
[3] Rudder, Glos. 530.   [4] G.D.R., T 1/117.
[5] O.S. Map 1/2,500, Glos. XLVII. 6 (1922 edn.); Kelly's Dir. Glos. (1910 and later edns.); below, this section.
[6] G.D.R., V 5/195T 2.   [7] Ibid. wills 1680/211.
[8] Ibid. V 5/195T 2; wills 1666/107.
[9] Bigland, Glos. ii. 158.   [10] 19th Rep. Com. Char. 85.

poor people of the parish, half in cash and half in soap and candles. The principal was received in 1789 and used on church repairs and £5 interest for it was paid out of the parish rates.[11] In 1854, when some parishioners opposed the levying of church rates, a subscription was opened to replace the principal and pay the interest until the full sum could be raised. The £100 had been raised by 1865 when it was laid out on stock. From the 1850s until 1889 £3 was usually received for the charity and distributed as directed, most of the recipients being the occupants of the almshouses in Church Road. Later the income fell to under £3[12] and only 50s. was being received in 1971 when a Scheme applied it to the poor in cash or kind.[13] By 1990 the Gwatkin charity had been amalgamated with the War Memorial Trust.[14]

In 1839 trustees for the poor of Aylburton held a row of four almshouses on the north-west side of the village street near the cross.[15] Later in the 19th century, when the almshouses were re-garded as church property, the occupants were chosen by the Aylburton vestry.[16] The alms-houses remained in use until c. 1940[17] and were sold in 1944 and later demolished. The proceeds, c. £250, were invested in stock, and a Scheme of 1945 applied the income to poor people of Aylburton civil parish who were members of the Church of England.[18] An income of £6 was being distributed in 1990.[19]

Christopher Willoughby of Bishopstone (Wilts.) by deed of 1680 gave a rent charge of £16 a year to the churchwardens of Aylburton: £4 each was to be given to two poor women of Aylburton, £4 10s. distributed among four other poor people, and the remainder used on pay-ments for a sermon, for the vicar or curate for keeping a record of the charity distribution, and for the clerk and churchwardens. The charity was distributed as directed from 1681 and con-tinued to be so in 1990.[20]

The War Memorial Trust was founded by Lord Bledisloe in 1927. He built a group of four almshouses on Church Road just north of the church, to be occupied by dependants of Lydney men killed in the First World War, men disabled in the war, or, failing either, poor inhabitants of the parish; the occupants were to pay a rent sufficient to cover maintenance of the buildings but the trustees were empowered to remit the rent where appropriate. The almshouses were modernized c. 1973 to make two houses and four flats. Lord Bledisloe also founded the Bledisloe-New Zealand War Memorial Trust in 1944 when he gave £2,500, the income to aid men of Lydney and Aylburton to emigrate to New Zealand, of which he had been governor-general. The recipients were to be men who had served in one of the two world wars or their lineal descendants. A Scheme of 1957 opened the charity to inhabitants of Lydney rural district when there were no suitable recipients from Lydney or Aylburton.[21]

[11] Glos. R.O., P 209/CH 2.
[12] Ibid.; ibid. CW 2/4.
[13] Ibid. D 3469/5/100.
[14] Inf. from the vicar.   [15] G.D.R., T 1/117.
[16] Glos. R.O., P 209/CW 2/1, mins. 20 Sept. 1855; 16 Oct. 1856; 2, mins. 18 Apr. 1895, and *passim*.
[17] Ibid. DA 28/100/12, p. 366.
[18] Ibid. D 3469/5/100.
[19] Inf. from the vicar.
[20] Glos. R.O., P 209/CH 1; *19th Rep. Com. Char.* 86; inf. from the vicar.
[21] Glos. R.O., D 3469/5/100.

ST BRIAVELS HUNDRED

ST. BRIAVELS hundred was created between 1086 and 1220, probably before 1154 to provide an administrative structure for the area then within the Forest of Dean.[1] The history of the hundred and of the Forest administration remained closely entwined.

In 1086 the area of the later hundred was divided between two counties and three hundreds. Lydney hundred, in Gloucestershire, included Hewelsfield and Wyegate, both added to the Forest since 1066 and apparently depopulated, and St. Briavels (then named Lydney);[2] Westbury hundred, in Gloucestershire, included English Bicknor and a manor called Dean;[3] and Bromsash hundred, in Herefordshire, named from a tree at a road junction in Weston under Penyard,[4] included Staunton, 'Brocote', and Whippington (all depopulated and added to the Forest waste before 1066), Ruardean, and Lea.[5] The woodland and waste of the royal Forest, which evidently covered much of the area, was not directly described in the Domesday survey.

St. Briavels hundred was recorded in 1220 when, in a listing by hundreds, its vills were grouped as the separate responsibility of the constable of St. Briavels, John of Monmouth.[6] In 1248, under the heading 'Forest of Dean', they were described as a separate hundred,[7] and in 1270 the hundred was named as St. Briavels.[8] As a royal hundred with unusually full jurisdiction, it was sometimes called the liberty of St. Briavels in the late 13th century. Among its vills were Mitcheldean, Littledean, and Abenhall (all apparently offshoots of the Domesday manor called Dean), Hewelsfield and Staunton, which had re-emerged as manorial units, and St. Briavels, English Bicknor, Ruardean, and part of Lea.[9] All those older manors had probably been much enlarged by assarting from the Forest waste, a process which had created two new manors and parishes. Newland (formerly called Welinton) had a church by 1216 and its parish, later in widely scattered parts, was defined in 1305 by a grant of the tithes from all recent assarts from the Forest.[10] Flaxley was created by Roger, earl of Hereford, c. 1150 as the endowment of his foundation, Flaxley abbey.[11]

In Westbury-on-Severn parish Northwood tithing, which originated as a manor called Walmore formed by assarting in the 12th century,[12] was part of the hundred until 1608 or later; it was listed with Westbury hundred from 1672, though detached parts of the Forest demesne in the same area called Walmore common and Northwood green remained in St. Briavels. Blakeney, in Awre parish, was also in the hundred to the 16th century but was regarded wholly or partly as within Bledisloe hundred by 1608.[13] Blythes Court manor, in Newnham parish, may have originated as part of St. Briavels hundred, though not found recorded as such: like manors of the hundred it owed service as a woodward of a Forest bailiwick and a

[1] Below, Forest of Dean, bounds.
[2] *Dom. Bk.* (Rec. Com.), i. 166v.–167.
[3] Ibid. 167v.
[4] Cf. P.R.O., E 32/31, m. 13.
[5] *Dom. Bk.* (Rec. Com.), i. 181–182v., 185v.
[6] *Bk. of Fees*, i. 308; the Crown pleas for the vills were presented as a separate group in 1221: *Pleas of the Crown for Glos.* ed. Maitland, pp. 47–9.
[7] P.R.O., JUST 1/274, rot. 11d.
[8] Ibid. E 32/29, rot. 1.
[9] Ibid. JUST 1/278, rott. 55–6; *Cal. Inq. Misc.* i, p. 414.
[10] Below, Newland, intro.; churches.
[11] Below, Flaxley, intro.; manor.
[12] *V.C.H. Glos.* x. 80, 91.
[13] For constituents of the hundred, *Military Surv. of Glos. 1522* (B.G.A.S. Rec. Ser. vi), 72–85, where the Glos. part of Lea is identified wrongly as Lea Bailey; *L. & P. Hen. VIII*, xiv (1), p. 271; Smith, *Men and Armour*, 31–46; P.R.O., E 179/247/14, rott. 37–9; *Census*, 1831. For Northwood and Blakeney, cf. *Trans. B.G.A.S.* lxvi. 154, 156–8

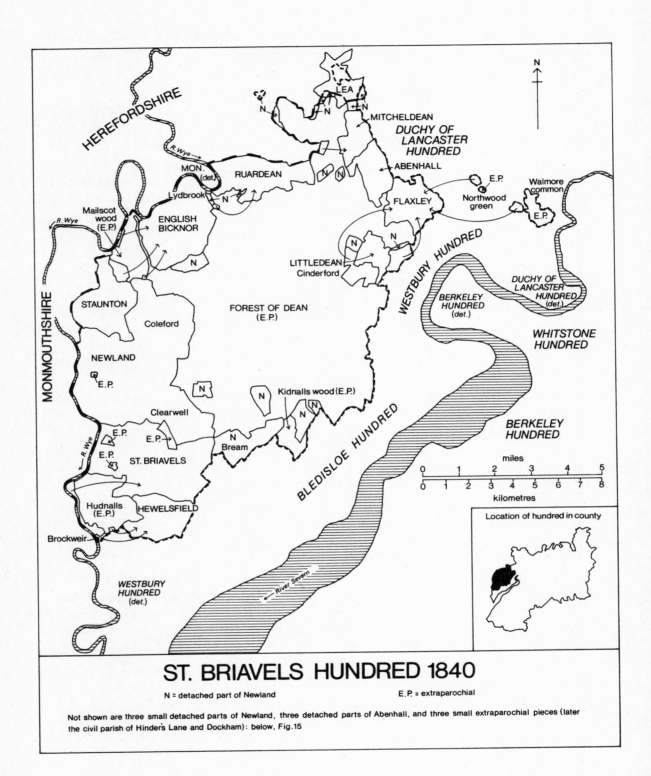

ST. BRIAVELS HUNDRED 1840

N = detached part of Newland   E.P. = extraparochial

Not shown are three small detached parts of Newland, three detached parts of Abenhall, and three small extraparochial pieces (later the civil parish of Hinder's Lane and Dockham): below, Fig.15

FIG. 4

chief rent to St. Briavels castle.[14]   A part of Lea parish remained in Herefordshire in Greytree hundred: in 1831 it was said to contain 380 a. while the Gloucestershire part of the parish, which was in three divisions, one of them including the church and some of the village, contained 150 a.[15] In 1844 the Gloucestershire part was transferred to Herefordshire,[16] and the whole parish is reserved for one of the Herefordshire volumes of this History. In the same area, Herefordshire gained in the 1880s some detached parts of Lea Bailey, a tithing of Newland, and in 1965 much of Lea Bailey Inclosures, formerly in the extraparochial Forest.[17]

The hundred or liberty was centred on St. Briavels castle and manor. In the early Middle Ages that estate supported the royal officer known as the constable of St. Briavels, who administered the Forest and acted as escheator and rent collector for the manors of the hundred. Ten of the manors of the hundred (if Blythes Court is included) supported woodwards of Forest bailiwicks[18] and paid rents to the constable and to his successors as holders of the castle estate.[19] The exceptions were Flaxley, which was given to Flaxley abbey in free alms,[20] and Hewelsfield. Hewelsfield's lack of a bailiwick, and the fact that it was the only place in the hundred removed from the Forest in the early 14th century among vills claimed to have been afforested after 1154, suggest that it was a late addition to the hundred. It also paid no rent, but that was presumably the result of its grant to Tintern abbey (Mon.) in free alms in the late 13th century.[21] Apart from Hewelsfield, the parishes of the hundred remained in the Forest jurisdiction, which was exercised over manorial lands until 1668.[22]

The St. Briavels hundred court was kept at the castle by the constable, usually acting through a deputy. It met every three weeks in theory but in the early 15th century the actual number of sessions each year was 13 or 14, and that was the usual number in the late 16th century, when customary adjournments for holidays explained the discrepancy. The court day was Monday, briefly changed to Tuesday in the Interregnum. Ordinary sessions, usually termed the court of pleas or three weeks' court, were combined with the court leet for the hundred on three Mondays, near Michaelmas, St. Hilary, and Hockday. The court also acted as a court baron for the royal manors of St. Briavels and Newland,[23] and in the early 15th century parcels of waste in those manors, some the sites of mills, were granted to new tenants in the court.[24] By the 18th century almost its only function as a court baron was receiving the suit of free tenants of the manors. When St. Briavels castle and the two manors were leased away from the constableship[25] the constable continued to hold the courts, though in the late 16th century, but possibly not later, the lessee received the profits.[26] For many years during the 17th century and the early 18th the constableship and the lease were held by the same man, making it uncertain whether the right of holding the courts belonged with the constableship or with the lease. In 1755 when constableship and lease passed into separate tenure again Thomas James, who was both deputy constable and steward of the castle estate,

[14]   Below, this chapter.   [15]   *Census*, 1831; G.D.R., T 1/112.
[16]   Counties (Detached Parts) Act, 7 & 8 Vic. c. 61; *Census*, 1851
[17]   Below, Newland intro. (Table I); Mitcheldean, intro.
[18]   Below, Forest of Dean, forest admin. (early hist.).
[19]   Glos. R.O., D 2026/X 19; Berkeley Cast. Mun., General Ser. 16; cf. P.R.O., C 139/84, no. 76 (which describes a third of the estate, given in dower, and is not a complete rental).   [20]   *Flaxley Cart.* pp. 16–17.
[21]   *Cal. Chart. R.* 1300–26, 89; cf. below, Hewelsfield, manor.
[22]   Below, Forest of Dean, bounds.

[23]   P.R.O., E 134/25 & 26 Eliz. I Mich./17; Berkeley Cast. Mun., General Ser. acct. roll 426; Glos. R.O., D 2026/L 8, M 1, M 3; for the change of day, *Acts & Ords. of Interr.* ed. Firth & Rait, ii. 1115.
[24]   Glos. R.O., D 33/103, 120, 124; P.R.O., SC 6/850/20; SC 6/858/14.
[25]   For the constableship and lease, below, St. Briavels, manors; Forest of Dean, wardens.
[26]   P.R.O., E 112/15, no. 9; E 134/25 & 26 Eliz. I Mich./17; REQ 2/4/306.

began to hold the courts leet in right of the lessee, while continuing the court of pleas in right of the constable. The division was emphasized in 1764 when the constable appointed a separate deputy to hold the court of pleas, while the steward continued the leet.[27] From that time, though constable and lessee were the same again in the years 1766–1810 and both courts continued on the same day at the castle, the courts were regarded as entirely distinct.[28] Court rolls survive for some sessions in the years 1633–5 and 1641,[29] and there are court books for the years 1719–1839, which from 1755 record only the court of pleas.[30] Some court papers for the separate leet survive for the 19th century and the early 20th.[31]

The deputy constable, appointed by the constable of St. Briavels, presided over the courts, but by the late 16th century two or more of the chief freeholders of St. Briavels manor sat with him; the failure of such freeholders to attend caused the abandonment of some sessions in the 1570s. The deputy constable's practice of appointing his own deputy, who in his turn deputized someone else to preside, also called in question the legality of some sessions at that period, and further problems were caused when the clerk, appointed by the deputy constable to record proceedings, sent an unqualified person in his place.[32] During the 18th century, when the constable of St. Briavels appointed a number of local gentry as his deputies, one with legal training, usually a member of the James family of Lydney and Coleford, presided.[33] Under the duke of Beaufort, constable 1812–35, two Newnham solicitors were appointed as deputy constables to hold the court of pleas, one also having the style of recorder. Jurymen, in theory drawn from the whole hundred, were by the early 19th century in the court of pleas almost always from St. Briavels parish itself. That court appointed a bailiff as its executive officer,[34] and c. 1743 a Mitcheldean man was appointed as a second bailiff,[35] presumably to carry out processes in the more distant parishes on the north-east side of the Forest.

The court of pleas remained an active court for minor civil cases. In the early 17th century some pleas of trespass concerned small parcels of land and were settled after two or more suitors were appointed to 'view' the land and report to the court.[36] By the early 15th century small estates were conveyed in the court by fine, in the same mode as in the Court of Common Pleas;[37] fines were still levied in 1782[38] but the practice was said in 1832 to be long discontinued.[39] By the early 18th century actions for debt predominated[40] and they were almost the whole business in the early 19th century. In the 1830s c. 200 pleas were heard each year for debts of up to £20, though most were for under £5. Examples were cited in 1832 of a man who recovered a debt of £2 at a cost of £11 14s. and of another who was imprisoned for six months for a debt of £6, and the court was then said to be of little benefit except to the group of local attorneys who were admitted to plead there. A complex system of fees had developed, most taken by the deputy constables for their salary while others went to the attorneys and to the bailiff.[41]

The castle, which earlier had been a prison for those indicted by the Forest

[27] Badminton Mun. FmH 2/1/1; FmS/G 2/4/5; Glos. Colln. 15931.

[28] *1st Rep. Dean Forest Com.* 13; St. Briavels Court Act, 5 & 6 Vic. c. 83; in both sources 'hundred court' evidently means the separate leet.

[29] Glos. R.O., D 2026/M 3.   [30] Glos. Colln. 15930–4.

[31] P.R.O., CRES 5/151; F 3/587; F 14/14, 16.

[32] Ibid. E 112/15, no. 9; E 134/25 & 26 Eliz. I Mich./17; Glos. R.O., D 2026/X 4.

[33] Glos. Colln. 15930–1; Badminton Mun. FmS/G 2/3/3, ff. 5–6; FmS/G 2/4/4; cf. below, Coleford, econ. hist.

(other ind. and trade); Lydney, manors (Soilwell; Rodleys).

[34] *1st Rep. Dean Forest Com.* 3, 12–14.

[35] Glos. Colln. 15930, ct. 28 Feb. 1742/3.

[36] Glos. R.O., D 2026/M 3.

[37] Ibid. D 33/104, 306, 310.

[38] Glos. Colln. 15933.

[39] *1st Rep. Dean Forest Com.* 3, 19.

[40] Glos. Colln. 15930.

[41] *1st Rep. Dean Forest Com.* 3–22; *Returns relating to Hundred Courts,* H.C. 338-III, pp. 28–30 (1839), xliii; *Court of Requests,* H.C. 619, pp. 42–3 (1840), xli.

courts, was used by the late 17th century to confine undischarged debtors.[42] A room in one of its gatehouse towers was used in the early 19th century, and rooms above were occupied by the gaoler and his family.[43] In the early 1830s the gaoler allowed the prisoners, who usually numbered less than six, the run of the castle and sometimes trusted them to wander outside it. They were supported entirely by charity until *c.* 1825 when an allowance of 3*s.* 6*d.* a week each was made from the St. Briavels parish poor rates. The gaoler received some fees, and he was allowed to keep an alehouse in the castle until *c.* 1820 when it was closed and he was given a salary of £25 instead.[44]

In 1842 an Act abolished the court of pleas and its prison and established instead a court of requests for recovering debts of up to £15 in the hundred. It was to hold sessions at Coleford for the parishes of the west part of the hundred and at Littledean for those of the east.[45] In 1847 the court of requests was replaced by a county court for the district.[46]

An important part of the business of the hundred leet in the 16th century and the early 17th was its attempts to regulate commoning in the royal demesne land of the Forest.[47] The leet also administered the assizes of bread and of ale in 1627, appointing two men for each parish or tithing to enforce them. A constable then attended from each parish to make presentments,[48] but by the early 18th century the court found it difficult to ensure their attendance and very little leet business was done at the three annual sessions with that designation.[49] The separate leet, held for the lessee of the St. Briavels castle estate from 1755, met twice a year in the early 19th century.[50] It lapsed for some years in the mid 19th century and was revived *c.* 1862[51] after the estate had been taken in hand by the Crown. In the early 20th century, when the deputy surveyor of the Forest, as chief local agent of the Crown Commissioners of Woods, acted as steward, it was held no more than once a year; a session in 1921 was perhaps the last. In its later years, though styled the court leet and court baron for the manor and hundred of St. Briavels and the manor of Newland, it apparently dealt only with matters within St. Briavels parish.[52] Several of the local manor courts of the hundred also exercised leet juridisction within their manors in the late medieval and early modern periods.[53]

Over 20,000 a. in the centre of St. Briavels hundred, which remained royal demesne land of the Forest of Dean, was only sporadically settled before the mid 18th century and was extraparochial until the mid 19th. Its history is summarized below, at the head of the account of the Forest,[54] and what follows here relates principally to the parochial lands of the hundred.

The ancient parishes of St. Briavels hundred lie around the edge of a plateau of high land, most of which is occupied by the formerly extraparochial Forest. The parishes on the west side, including Newland and St. Briavels, are mainly on the high land, with steep slopes to the river Wye; English Bicknor and Ruardean, on the north side, are mainly on the slopes from the plateau edge to the river; and a group of smaller parishes, including Mitcheldean, occupy a system of valleys at the plateau's north-east edge. The Old Red Sandstone forms much of the valleys

[42] Hart, *Royal Forest*, 299; *Trans. B.G.A.S.* iii. 334–5.
[43] P.R.O., F 3/587, surv. 1835.
[44] *1st Rep. Dean Forest Com.* 4, 16–18.
[45] St. Briavels Court Act, 5 & 6 Vic. c. 83.
[46] Small Debts Act, 9 & 10 Vic. c. 95; P.R.O., F 3/587, letter 19 June 1888.
[47] P.R.O., E 134/34 Eliz. I Hil./23; E 134/36 Eliz. I Hil./21; Glos. R.O., D 2026/L 8.

[48] Glos. R.O., D 2026/L 8.
[49] Glos. Colln. 15930–1.
[50] P.R.O., F 3/587, surv. 1835; F 14/14.
[51] Ibid. F 3/727.
[52] Ibid. CRES 5/151; F 14/16.
[53] Below, Abenhall, Littledean, Mitcheldean, Ruardean (loc. govt. sections).
[54] Below, Forest of Dean, intro.

and the hills rising from the Wye, carboniferous limestone, containing iron ore deposits, outcrops around the plateau's edge and forms high cliffs above the river in and near English Bicknor, and the sandstones and shales of the coal measures form the central plateau. Lodgegrove brook, Greathough (or Lyd) brook, the upper Red brook, and the lower Red brook (later Valley brook) are among the streams draining from the high land to the Wye, and Westbury and Longhope brooks are among those draining the north-eastern valleys. Woodland, which with the mineral deposits and the availability of water power determined the mainly industrial role of the hundred, was cleared from much of the parochial land during the early Middle Ages, leaving some substantial stretches on hillsides too steep for cultivation in Flaxley and some of the Wye Valley parishes. Woodland regained some land from agriculture after 1817 with the planting of c. 1,000 a. of the Highmeadow estate in Staunton, Coleford, and English Bicknor. With the late clearance and settlement of much of the land, there was hardly any customary tenure and only a few small open fields; no parish required an Act of parliament for inclosure. The small freehold, often carried on with a trade or craft, was the typical holding in much of the hundred, and even in parishes where substantial estates were formed after the Middle Ages farms remained modest in size, mainly concerned with animal husbandry. Commoning rights in the royal demesne land of the Forest were a cherished asset of the many smallholders, whose vigorous defence of them was inherited in the modern period by those parishioners who settled as squatters on the demesne itself.

The local Cistercian abbeys of Flaxley and Tintern (Mon.) were among manorial owners; otherwise most manors were held in the Middle Ages by small lay lords, with the Greyndours and their successors the Baynhams prominent at the end of the period. Several small castles were established, but only that of St. Briavels, because of its role as an administrative centre, was long maintained. The area retained a strong body of resident gentry in later centuries, most of them serving in the Forest administration as officers by tenure or appointment. The Throckmortons and later the Wyndhams succeeded to the Baynhams' western estates based on Clearwell, in Newland, and another substantial estate was established on the west side of the Forest by the Halls, who built a large mansion at the site of the deserted village of Highmeadow and were succeeded by the Viscounts Gage. Smaller, but locally influential, landowners included the Machens of Eastbach, in English Bicknor, the Catchmays and Rookes of Bigsweir, in St. Briavels, and the Bonds of Redbrook, in Newland. In the north-eastern parishes the chief landowners were the Vaughans, successors to other Baynham estates, the Colchesters, who built a mansion at the Wilderness near Mitcheldean in the 1670s, the Pyrkes of Littledean, and the Boeveys (later Crawley–Boeveys), who lived at Flaxley in a mansion formed from the buildings of the medieval abbey.

For many centuries river transport was probably more important than roads for distributing the products of local industry, which were shipped at creeks on the Severn in adjoining hundreds, the larger river ports of Chepstow and Monmouth, and small landing places on the Forest bank of the Wye; Brockweir, at the lowest point of the hundred on the Wye, was a small community of watermen engaged mainly in the Bristol trade. The principal road routes crossing the hundred were from Gloucester to Monmouth and Wales: one ran through Mitcheldean and the northern part of the Forest and another through Littledean and the central Forest, both converging originally on Coleford. The northern route was largely refashioned in the turnpike age, when, among other improvements, a new Wye Valley road of the 1820s with a bridge at Bigsweir helped to improve accessibility to the western edge of the area. Mitcheldean, where the northern route to Monmouth was crossed by an ancient route from the Severn at Newnham to Ross-on-Wye (Herefs.) and Hereford, was the principal market town in the late medieval and early modern periods; it was supported also by a succession of industries, including clothmaking and pinmaking. Coleford, part of Newland parish until 1894, became the principal centre on the west side of the hundred, securing a market and fairs in 1661. Littledean was a minor market centre in early modern period. Newland did some trade in the 16th century, but it later settled into a more residential role and, with its gentry houses, almshouses, and grammar school grouped around a large church and churchyard, was the most picturesque (in a conventional sense) village in the hundred.

The hundred's mineral wealth and woodland gave most of its villages a strong industrial element: places such as Ruardean, Littledean, and Clearwell had miners, ironworkers, quarrymen, charcoal burners, and makers of barrel staves and hoops, trenchers, shovels, and cardboard. For the miners the boundaries of St. Briavels hundred defined the limit of their customary rights, so that the hundred, unlike most in Gloucestershire, retained a popular significance in modern times. In the Middle Ages numerous itinerant bloomery forges and some larger fixed works were supported by the woodland of the manors and royal demesne. In the 13th century some of the iron produced went to make crossbow bolts at St. Briavels under the direction of the constable, and a specialist trade carried on in later centuries was nailmaking at Littledean. In most parishes the inefficient medieval forges left large mounds of iron slag, or cinders, which were later dug out and rendered down in the water-powered blast furnaces that were established from c. 1600. Bishopswood at the boundary of Ruardean and Walford (Herefs.), Flaxley, Gunn's Mills in Abenhall, and Redbrook in Newland were among sites of the iron industry in the era of water power. At some of those and some other mill sites corn milling, cloth fulling, and paper making were carried on at various times in the 17th and 18th centuries, and Redbrook was the site of copper works. Tanneries, using Forest oak bark, operated in several parishes.

In the 19th century the main centre of activity in the hundred shifted to the royal demesne land of the Forest, where by 1851 there was a larger population than in the old parishes.[55] The development of deep coal mining and other industry in the central Forest, however, affected most of the parishes, where the agricultural and traditional elements were further submerged by large contingents of miners. The villages of Ruardean, Littledean, and Bream, in Newland, were enlarged and mainly rebuilt and came to share the character of the newer hamlets adjoining them within the Forest demesne. Some small coal and iron mines were worked in Ruardean, Coleford, and other parishes until the early 20th century. Lime burning was a significant trade in St. Briavels and Mitcheldean, among other parishes, and in Mitcheldean cement was made and the red sandstone was quarried. Among tramroads built early in the 19th century to serve the Forest mines and quarries one led to Monmouth through Coleford and Redbrook, which remained an industrial hamlet dominated by a large tinplate works. Another tramroad led to the river bank at Lydbrook, an industrial village, mainly on the extraparochial

55 *V.C.H. Glos.* ii. 177.

land, between English Bicknor and Ruardean, and to coal wharves established in Ruardean to supply Herefordshire. Steam railways, including the Wye Valley line which operated from 1876 to 1964, and the short lived Coleford to Monmouth line of 1883–1916, were of little significance in the parishes. Coleford prospered, however, as the main business and retail centre on the west side of the coalfield and was also the principal local base for the nonconformist churches. Mitcheldean, partly because of the development of the new Forest town of Cinderford in that area, had a more limited role, with a brewery the main employer in the town itself. Among the smaller settlements, Staunton after the planting of much of the adjoining farmland became a community of forestry workers. Hudnalls, a tract of extraparochial common land near the Wye added to St. Briavels and Hewelsfield in 1842, was colonized by smallholders and craftsmen, who were largely replaced from the end of the century by a wealthier, residential population.

A wire and cable works established in 1912 at Stowfield, in English Bicknor, became a major employer in the mid 20th century, when the loss of employment by the closure of the Forest deep mines was compensated partly by new factories at Mitcheldean and Coleford. More traditional industry was still represented in the late years of the century by large quarries for roadstone near Coleford and Newland. Most of the villages became residential and dormitory communities for Gloucester and other places outside the Forest area. New housing estates and bungalows were added to most of them and the plain stone cottages of the miners, quarrymen, and forestry workers were restored and enlarged.

ABENHALL

THE ANCIENT parish of Abenhall, formerly also called Abinghall,[1] which lay 16 km. west of Gloucester, was flanked on the south-west by the extraparochial Forest of Dean and included part of the market town of Mitcheldean.[2] Almost rectangular in shape, the parish covered only 770 a.[3] (311.6 ha.) and was divided from Mitcheldean parish to the north-west mostly by the old course of the Gloucester–Monmouth road, following in 1620 the bed of a stream which ran only in the winter months;[4] the road was lined in places with houses belonging to Mitcheldean town.[5] On the north-east, at Whitemoor, Abenhall was apparently bounded before the 17th century by a great ditch.[6] The parish included a small peninsula of land containing the southern part of a high tract of land called the Wilderness west of the Monmouth road and three small detached pieces to the south-east within a peninsula of the Forest reaching to Shapridge.[7]

The links between Abenhall and Mitcheldean, which at one time were both within the jurisdiction of the Forest,[8] were presumably partly tenurial in origin.[9] Abenhall, although regarded as a member of Mitcheldean in 1316[10] and assessed for the subsidy with it in 1327,[11] formed a separate manor to which a bailiwick in the Forest was attached by 1301.[12] In the mid 14th century the parish included land described as a new assart.[13] One of the detached pieces contained part of Gunn's Mills built on the royal demesne of the Forest in the early 15th century[14] and included in Abenhall by 1620.[15] The parish boundaries with the Forest in that area were a matter of dispute in the mid 18th century.[16] The detached pieces, containing 7 a., were transferred to East Dean civil parish in 1885 and were in that part of East Dean acquired by Littledean in 1953.[17] The main part of Abenhall was united with Mitcheldean parish in 1935.[18] The following account relates to the ancient parish of Abenhall apart from the northern end, including the land at the Wilderness, the history of which, dominated by settlement and economic activity connected with Mitcheldean town, is given under Mitcheldean parish. The account also includes the part of Gunn's Mills within the Forest.

Abenhall lies on the Old Red Sandstone. The land rises from deep valleys to over 200 m. in the east, the lowest parts being at just under 100

m. in the south-east and north-east. The southern half of the parish is drained by tributaries of Westbury brook, flowing in valleys with bottoms of alluvial soil,[19] and the northern corner is crossed by the wooded valley of Longhope brook. Most of the land has long been agricultural and in the later Middle Ages there were several open fields in the parish. The greater part of the surviving woodland, estimated at 122 a. for the whole parish in 1838, was on the eastern side and included Abenhall grove, which adjoined extensive woods in Longhope and Flaxley.[20] Wilk wood, on the south side of the valley of Longhope brook, was mentioned in 1458.[21] Its ownership was divided between the manor and the Pyrke family by 1624 when Jasper Lugg, who ran a tannery in Mitcheldean, took a lease of the manor's part.[22] The Pyrke family's part, later included in its Dean Hall estate, was exploited by timber merchants from Newnham and Chaxhill in the 1860s.[23]

It has been supposed that the Littledean–Mitcheldean road running east of Gunn's Mills and northwards through Abenhall was part of a Roman road linking Lydney and the Severn crossing at Newnham with the settlement at Ariconium near Weston under Penyard (Herefs.).[24] The later importance of the road, described in 1227 as a great highway,[25] is confirmed by the levying of toll on wagons passing through Abenhall between Newnham and Hereford and elsewhere in the later 15th century[26] and by the claim of the lord of the manor, in 1642, to a customary payment from every wain or cart passing to or from Lea (Herefs., formerly Glos. and Herefs.) with wares.[27] The road originally ran past Abenhall church, east of which it was joined by a route from Shapridge.[28] The latter route, described as a horse way in 1227,[29] was evidently used as a road from Flaxley in 1675. By the early 17th century the road from Littledean took a more direct course, bypassing the church to the west,[30] and in 1988 the original course, which it joined at Folly Farm, survived north of the church only as a bridle path. In 1769 the section of the road through Abenhall was turnpiked as part of a route linking Mitcheldean with the Gloucester–Newnham road at Elton, in Westbury-on-Severn. The section of the Gloucester–Monmouth road leading up the valley of Longhope brook and turning

---

[1] G.D.R., T 1/1; O.S. Map 6", Glos. XXXI. NE. (1884 edn.); *Kelly's Dir. Glos.* (1939), 21. This account was written in 1988.   [2] Below, Fig. 6.

[3] *O.S. Area Bk.* Abinghall (1880); Little Dean (1878).

[4] Glos. R.O., D 36/M 2, f. 2v.

[5] Ibid. D 2123, p. 63; G.D.R., T 1/1, 123.

[6] Glos. R.O., D 36/M 10.

[7] G.D.R., T 1/1; O.S. Maps 6", Glos. XXIII. SE. (1883 edn.); XXXI. NE. (1884 edn.).

[8] *Trans. B.G.A.S.* lxvi. 166–207.

[9] Taylor, *Dom. Glos.* 25, 404.

[10] *Feud. Aids,* ii. 275.

[11] *Glos. Subsidy Roll, 1327,* 44.

[12] Below, manor. Apart from the ancient tenurial link, the lords of Abenhall held part of Mitcheldean manor by the mid 13th cent. and until the late 17th.

[13] P.R.O., C 135/83, no. 13.

[14] Ibid. SC 6/850/20; G.D.R., T 1/1.

[15] Glos. R.O., D 36/M 2, f. 2v.

[16] Ibid. D 23/L 2; D 36/E 50; *Cal. Treas. Bks. & Papers,* 1742–5, 276, 483–4.

[17] *O.S. Area Bk.* Little Dean (1878); *Census,* 1891, 1961.

[18] *Census,* 1931 (pt.ii).

[19] Geol. Surv. Map 1/50,000, solid and drift, sheet 234 (1972 edn.).

[20] G.D.R., T 1/1.   [21] Glos. R.O., D 36/E 1, f. 22.

[22] Ibid. D 4431, agreement 2 June 14 Chas. II; D 637/II/3/T 1; below, Mitcheldean, econ. hist. (other ind. and trade).

[23] Glos. R.O., D 1438, est. papers; cf. ibid. Littledean and Notgrove deeds 1766–1851, deed 6 Nov. 1773.

[24] A. W. Trotter, *Dean Road* (1936), 40–4; I. D. Margary, *Roman Roads in Britain,* ii (1957), p. 64; *V.C.H. Glos.* x. 35.   [25] *Flaxley Cart.* pp. 108–9.

[26] Glos. R.O., D 36/M 1.   [27] Ibid. M 10.

[28] Cf. Trotter, *Dean Road,* 40–4; Margary, *Roman Roads,* ii, p. 64.   [29] *Flaxley Cart.* pp. 108–9.

[30] Glos. R.O., D 23/T 39; cf. ibid. D 4431, deed 1 Apr. 13 Jas. I.

south-westwards at Barton Corner to follow the Mitcheldean boundary was turnpiked in 1747.[31] Both turnpikes were discontinued in 1880.[32]

Settlement in Abenhall, which contained only 22 houses c. 1710[33] and 38 houses in 1801,[34] was scattered except where it belonged to Mitcheldean town. In the centre of the parish, above the valley of Westbury brook's main tributary, was a small group of buildings including the church and the medieval manor house. In the late 19th century, when that house was demolished and a school was built, the only dwellings there were a new rectory house and Church Farm.[35] The farmhouse, south of the church, dates from a rebuilding in 1858 by the lord of the manor, Edmund Probyn,[36] and the outbuildings, apparently remodelled at the same date, incorporate earlier ranges. A cottage was built next to the school in the early 20th century.[37] North-west of the church on the Mitcheldean road a farmstead known as the Folly, which had belonged to the Bridgeman family of Prinknash, was sold to Thomas Pyrke of Littledean in 1740. At that time the farmhouse, which had fallen into decay, was used as a barn. A new farmhouse, built soon afterwards by the Pyrkes,[38] was refronted and refenestrated in the 20th century. Further south a house known as Fernyfield dates from the 1860s.[39] There were a few dwellings near the Forest boundary in the later 17th century.[40] On the western side of the parish several buildings on the east side of Jubilee Road, at Plump Hill, belonged to Abenhall in the mid 19th century. They included Green Farm,[41] a small 19th-century house. Home Farm, a brick house, was built c. 1900 on the site of a barn called Barefields in the mid 18th century.[42] Further south there was a dwelling at Ladygrove House by 1624,[43] and of three dwellings in 1840 at the Spout (later Spout Lane)[44] only one remained in 1988. At Shapridge, south-east of Abenhall, there was a small farmhouse next to the Forest boundary in the later 17th century.[45] Perhaps that known in 1715 as Old Abenhall,[46] it was rebuilt shortly before 1865, probably by Edmund Probyn.[47]

In the later Middle Ages there was a small settlement beside the Gloucester–Mitcheldean road in the valley of Longhope brook.[48] Known as Barton, presumably from a barton on the manor estate, the part of the hamlet north of the road included a mill by 1280 and a chapel by 1444.[49] By the 16th century, when the settlement contained the church house of Abenhall, one tenement had disappeared and another had fallen into ruin,[50] and by 1785 only a mill near the Longhope boundary remained.[51]

The muster roll of 1542 lists 30 names for Abenhall[52] and an estimate of 50 communicants was made for the parish in 1551.[53] There were said to be 24 households in 1563,[54] 89 communicants in 1603,[55] and 60 families in 1650.[56] Population figures for the whole parish included part of Mitcheldean town, which accounted for many of Abenhall's residents. The population, estimated c. 1710 at 88,[57] grew in the 18th century and was reckoned c. 1775 to be more than 158.[58] The increase continued in the early 19th century, the population standing at 185 in 1801 and 239 in 1841, and after a slight decline in the 1840s reached a peak of 307 in 1871; about half of the parishioners lived in the town in 1851. The population, like that of Mitcheldean, fell in the late 19th century and the early 20th, but between 1921 and the time of the union with Mitcheldean in 1935 it recovered from 189 to 230.[59]

In 1821 an innkeeper lived in Abenhall.[60] The Rising Sun, a beerhouse standing apart on the Littledean road in the south of Abenhall in 1831,[61] was burned down in 1865.[62] The houses in Jubilee Road used standpipes erected by the rural district council in 1897 in an extension of a small scheme for supplying water to Horsepool bottom in the adjoining part of the Forest. The standpipes were removed in 1925 when the scheme was superseded by the main supply.[63]

MANOR. Abenhall was presumably among those lands called Dean which William son of Norman held in 1086 and which Edward the Confessor had exempted from the payment of geld in return for the guarding of the Forest.[64] In the 13th century a woodward held land and the bailiwick of Abenhall in the Forest from the Crown in fee by a cash rent.[65] The land became part of *ABENHALL* manor, which in 1301 was held from the Crown by the serjeanty of keeping the bailiwick and by a cash rent of 20s. paid at Newnham to the constable of St. Briavels castle.[66] The office of woodward of the bailiwick descended with the manor until the late 18th century.[67] In the late 14th century and the 15th, however, the manor was thought to be held from St. Briavels castle by knight service.[68]

31 Glouc. & Heref. Roads Acts, 9 Geo. III, c. 50; 20 Geo. II, c. 31.
32 Annual Turnpike Acts Continuance Act, 43 & 44 Vic. c. 12.
33 Atkyns, *Glos.* 199.   34 *Census*, 1801.
35 G.D.R., T 1/1.   36 Date and inits. 'E. P.' on ho.
37 Cf. O.S. Map 6", Glos. XXXI. NE. (1903 edn.); Glos. R.O., D 2299/1098.
38 Glos. R.O., D 1438, Littledean and Notgrove deeds 1766–1851, deed 6 Nov. 1773; D 18/288.
39 Ibid. D 2299/1247.   40 P.R.O., F 17/7.
41 G.D.R., T 1/1; O.S. Map 6", Glos. XXXI. NE. (1884 edn.).
42 Glos. R.O., D 2172/1/43.
43 P.R.O., E 134/22 Jas. I Mich./35.
44 G.D.R., T 1/1.
45 P.R.O., F 17/7; cf. *2nd Rep. Dean Forest Com.* 34.
46 Glos. R.O., Q/RNc 1, p. 66.
47 Ibid. D 637/VII/1.   48 Ibid. D 36/E 1, ff. 40v.–41v.
49 Ibid. D 1448/T 26; D 4431, deed St. Mary Magdalen 22 Hen. VI.   50 Ibid. D 36/E 1, ff. 39v.–41v.

51 Ibid. D 2123, pp. 91, 93.
52 *L. & P. Hen. VIII*, xvii, p. 499.
53 *E.H.R.* xix. 120.   54 Bodl. MS. Rawl. C. 790, f. 28v.
55 *Eccl. Misc.* 99.   56 *Trans. B.G.A.S.* lxxxiii. 97.
57 Atkyns, *Glos.* 199.   58 Rudder, *Glos.* 210.
59 *Census*, 1801–1931; P.R.O., HO 107/1959.
60 Glos. R.O., P 1/IN 1/7.   61 Ibid. Q/RUm 128.
62 *Glouc. Jnl.* 14 Oct. 1865.
63 Glos. R.O., DA 24/100/1, p. 256; 2, p. 29; 6, pp. 152–3, 159; 9, pp. 255, 281; Pearce, 'Water Supply in Dean', 32–4.
64 *Dom. Bk.* (Rec. Com.), i. 167v.; below, Mitcheldean, manor; cf. Taylor, *Dom. Glos.* 25, 204.
65 Below, this section.   66 *Cal. Inq. p.m.* iv, p. 13.
67 P.R.O., C 139/115, no. 34; Glos. R.O., D 2026/X 3; D 36/Q 2; *3rd Rep. Com. Woods* (1788), 76.
68 *Cal. Inq. p.m.* xiv, pp. 140–1; P.R.O., C 139/115, no. 34; C 140/34, no. 53; *Cal. Close, 1447–54*, 455–6; *Cal. Fine R. 1461–71*, 295–6.

The first men known to have held the manor were surnamed of Abenhall.[69] William, a woodward in 1216 and 1237,[70] was presumably the lord of Abenhall, and his son Ralph (fl. 1255)[71] had evidently acquired a moiety of Mitcheldean manor by the 1240s, when he was paying 30s. rent to the Crown.[72] The same or another Ralph, keeper of the bailiwick in the 1260s,[73] was succeeded in Abenhall manor at his death c. 1301 by his son John.[74] In 1317 John's brother and heir Ralph granted the manor, described as a messuage and two ploughlands, to another brother Reynold.[75] Reynold (d. c. 1341) was succeeded by his son Ralph,[76] and Ralph died c. 1347 leaving an infant daughter Margaret as his heir.[77] Margaret and her husband Lawrence Greyndour obtained seisin of Ralph's lands in 1358[78] and her second husband Robert of Huntley retained them after her death in 1357. Her son and heir John Greyndour[79] later held Abenhall manor and part of Mitcheldean manor and at his death in 1415 or 1416 was succeeded by his son Robert.[80] At Robert's death in 1443 a third of Abenhall manor passed in dower to his wife Joan, who later married John Barre, and two thirds to his daughter Elizabeth, wife of Reynold West, Lord La Warre. After Elizabeth's death in 1452 her second husband John Tiptoft, earl of Worcester,[81] retained her part until his death in 1470 when it reverted to her heir William Walwyn. From William (d. 1471) it passed to his daughter Alice, wife of Thomas Baynham,[82] to whom the rest of the manor reverted at Joan Barre's death in 1484.[83] Thomas died in 1500[84] and from Alice the manor, together with part of Mitcheldean, descended until 1696 usually with an estate in Ruardean.[85] In 1527 Sir Christopher Baynham settled Abenhall manor on the marriage of his son George and Cecily Gage,[86] and in 1565 their son Richard (d. 1580) held the woodwardship of Abenhall.[87] In 1611 the estates passed to the Vaughans, a leading Roman Catholic family, from whom they were confiscated several times.[88] In 1696 Abenhall manor was sold, to pay the debts of John Vaughan (d. 1694) and his dead brother

Thomas, to Richard Vaughan of Courtfield in Welsh Bicknor (Mon., later Herefs.). Richard (d. 1697) left the manor to John Vaughan, the son of his second marriage, who sold it in 1724 to Stephen Cooke of Leigh.[89] Stephen settled the manor on his son Thomas, who sold it in 1740 to John Howell.[90] From John (d. 1778) it passed to his grandson Edmund Probyn of Newland.[91] By 1799 Edmund had given the manor to his son John, rector of Abenhall and archdeacon of Llandaff (Glam.),[92] who was succeeded at his death in 1843 by his son John.[93] By the mid 1850s John had settled 403 a. in Abenhall on his son Edmund and in 1872 Edmund sold that land to Henrietta Davies and Charles Barton,[94] the latter of whom had acquired Folly farm (90 a.) from Duncombe Pyrke in 1870.[95] Henrietta, one of the owners of the nearby Wilderness estate,[96] died in 1877 leaving Charles, her niece's husband, the land she had purchased.[97] Charles's estate had passed to his daughter Katherine Barton by 1906 and was broken up after her death in 1912,[98] when it covered 530 a. Church and Folly farms were purchased by their tenants, c. 175 a. by Frederick Hart, and c. 125 a. by the Gloucestershire county council's smallholdings committee.[99]

The manor house was recorded from 1301[1] and the site may have included the hall mentioned in 1444 and 1471.[2] In 1481 Thomas and Alice Baynham were licensed to have an oratory in the house.[3] The manor house was occupied by a tenant by 1625,[4] and Thomas Dowle, a later farmer of the demesne, was assessed on two hearths in 1672.[5] The house stood east of the church[6] and was demolished with its outbuildings in the mid 19th century.[7]

ECONOMIC HISTORY. Two ploughteams were recorded at Abenhall in 1220[8] and two ploughlands in 1317.[9] The manor included 60 a. of arable in 1301 and 140 a. of arable in demesne and 6 a. of wood in 1317.[10] In 1341 it included 80 a. of arable in open fields and 4 a. of coppice woodland but no meadow land or pasture in

[69] The descent of the man. is detailed in J. Maclean, 'Hist. of Manors of Dene Magna and Abenhall', *Trans. B.G.A.S.* vi. 140–60.
[70] *Rot. Litt. Claus.* (Rec. Com.), i. 334–5, 442–3, 533; *Cur. Reg. R.* xvi. 12.
[71] P.R.O., CP 25/1/74/20, no. 450.
[72] Ibid. E 146/1/25; cf. ibid. E 32/32, m. 2; below, Mitcheldean, manor.
[73] P.R.O., E 32/29, rott. 1d., 5d.
[74] *Cal. Inq. p.m.* iv, p. 13.
[75] Ibid. vi, pp. 1–2; *Cal. Pat.* 1313–17, 639.
[76] *Cal. Inq. p.m.* vi, p. 97; viii, pp. 225–6.
[77] Ibid. ix, pp. 4–5.   [78] *Cal. Close*, 1354–60, 477.
[79] *Cal. Inq. p.m.* xiv, pp. 140–1.
[80] *Cal. Close*, 1413–19, 338; *Cal. Fine R.* 1413–22, 144.
[81] P.R.O., C 139/115, no. 34; C 139/149, no. 23.
[82] Ibid. C 140/34, no. 53; C 140/37, no. 26; *Cal. Close*, 1447–54, 455–6; *Cal. Fine R.* 1461–71, 295–6.
[83] *Cal. Inq. p.m. Hen. VII*, i, pp. 3, 47.
[84] *Trans. B.G.A.S.* vi. 149.
[85] Below, Ruardean, manors (Hathaways); cf. P.R.O., C 142/33, no. 69; C 142/340, no. 192.
[86] P.R.O., C 142/113, no. 49.
[87] Glos. R.O., D 2026/X 3; cf. P.R.O., C 142/189, no. 82.
[88] P.R.O., C 142/340, no. 192; cf. *Trans. B.G.A.S.* vi. 152–6.
[89] Glos. R.O., Q/RNc 4/1; J. H. Matthews, *Vaughans of Courtfield* (1911), 24–5; Marshall Bridges, said to be lord of the manor in Atkyns, *Glos.* 199, had been Ric. Vaughan's trustee.
[90] *Trans. B.G.A.S.* vi. 157–8.
[91] Bigland, *Glos.* i. 1; ii. 260.
[92] Glos. R.O., D 23/E 4, E 9; Fosbrooke, *Glos.* ii. 165; for the Probyns, *Trans. B.G.A.S.* vi. 195–6; Burke, *Land. Gent.* (1898), ii. 1218.
[93] Glos. R.O., D 637/IV/4.
[94] Ibid. D 2714, Shelley fam. deeds, deed 28 Sept. 1867.
[95] Ibid. D 1438, Littledean and Notgrove deeds 1766–1851, endorsement on deed 18 Feb. 1851.
[96] Below, Mitcheldean, manor.
[97] Glos. R.O., D 2362, deeds 1784–1899, will of H. Davies.
[98] *Kelly's Dir. Glos.* (1906), 17; *Glouc. Jnl.* 18 May 1912.
[99] Glos. R.O., D 2299/1098; *Mins. of Glos. County Council*, xxv. 341.
[1] P.R.O., C 133/100, no. 6; C 135/85, no. 13.
[2] Ibid. C 139/115, no. 34; C 140/34, no. 53.
[3] *Reg. Myllyng*, 206.
[4] N.L.W., Courtfield MSS. 240, which shows that in 1625 Joan Vaughan held a moiety of the ho.
[5] P.R.O., E 179/247/14, rot. 39; Glos. R.O., Q/RNc 4/1.
[6] Bigland, *Glos.* i. 1.
[7] Cf. G.D.R., T 1/1; Glos. R.O., D 637/VII/1.
[8] *Bk. of Fees*, i. 308.   [9] *Cal. Pat.* 1313–17, 639.
[10] P.R.O., C 133/100, no. 6; C 134/53, no. 4.

severalty and in 1347 it had, in addition to 60 a. of arable, 60 a. of new assarts, 2 a. of meadow, and 4 a. of wood.[11] In 1444 the manor had 100 a. of arable, 4 a. of meadow, and 20 a. of woodland.[12] In the later 15th century the demesne was possibly held in hand by Thomas Baynham, who by 1464 farmed that part, but not the woodland, belonging to Joan Barre in dower.[13] In 1620 two tenants held moieties of the demesne[14] and in 1685 most of the demesne was farmed by Thomas Dowle.[15]

The freeholders recorded on the manor numbered 35 in 1301, 10 in 1317, and 24 in 1341 and 1347. The customary tenants were described in 1301 as 24 cottars owing autumn bedrips, perhaps commuted. In 1317, however, there were 6 cottars holding a yardland between them and performing labour services in August and September, and in 1347 eight tenants worked for two days in the harvest.[16] Tenure by lease was recorded from 1562,[17] and in 1620 on Joan Vaughan's estate in Abenhall and Mitcheldean, where some tenants had accumulated holdings, there were 18 leaseholders, mostly with tenures for 3 lives or 80 or 99 years with heriots and additional rents of hens or capons payable. Five of the holdings were on lease for 21 years. While the largest holdings were presumably the moieties of the demesne, most were probably less than 15 a. and several were c. 2 a. Many of the tenants lived in Mitcheldean town as did most of the c. 28 freeholders, who owed cash rents to the estate.[18] Rentals of the Vaughan family's estate in 1634 and 1685 both listed a total of c. 29 tenants.[19]

In the mid 14th century the open arable in Abenhall lay in more than one field, including that known in 1327 as Old Abenhall field.[20] At least one open field remained in the early 15th century, when a grant of two dole lands in it was made,[21] but most, if not all, farmland had been inclosed by the mid 16th century, when arable land in the northern part of the parish included pieces known as pit furlong and pit dole.[22] The parish contained several sheepcots in the 17th century.[23] Meadow land was confined mostly to the valley of Longhope brook, where Long meadow (12 a.) lay athwart the stream and partly in Mitcheldean.[24] Although Abenhall was said in the later 18th century to include a considerable area of common land overgrown with ferns and bushes,[25] no commonable land was identified in the parish in 1838.[26] In the late 13th century Ralph of Abenhall claimed common

rights for himself and his men throughout the Forest of Dean[27] and in the 1740s John Howell asserted similar rights for the manor of Abenhall within the bailiwick of Abenhall.[28] In 1762 the parish paid 3s. 4d. herbage money for common rights in the extraparochial land of the Forest,[29] and five landholders exercised those rights in 1860.[30]

A rental of 1780 listed eight tenants on Abenhall manor,[31] which in 1799 included farms of 85 a., 80 a., 54 a., and 26 a. The largest, held by the Scudamore family[32] for most of the 18th and 19th centuries, was Church farm.[33] Folly farm on the Pyrke family's estate comprised 83 a. in 1773.[34] Of eight farmers living in the parish in 1831 five employed labour, the number of resident farmhands being 25.[35] In 1840 the principal holdings were Church farm with 156 a., Shapridge farm with 105 a., Folly farm with 87 a., and 91 a. farmed from Gunn's Mills. On the west side of the parish were several smaller holdings, including those centred on Green Farm (30 a.) and Barefields (12 a.).[36] The pattern of landholding remained much the same in the early 20th century[37] and the west side of the parish, where Katherine Barton created two new tenancies c. 1911,[38] was confirmed as an area of smallholdings in 1913, when most of the land there was acquired by the county council's smallholdings committee. At that time 13 people had holdings of 18 a. or less[39] and Church, Shapridge, and Folly farms, all with over 100 a., were the largest farms in the parish.[40] The number of recorded agricultural occupiers, most of them tenant farmers, rose from 12 in 1896 to 22 in 1926, when 7 had under 50 a., another 4 under 20 a., and another 9 under 5 a.[41]

In the late 18th century more land in the parish was devoted to arable than to pasture.[42] In 1801 the main crops were wheat and barley[43] and in 1838 the parish was reckoned to contain 306 a. of arable and 239 a. of meadow and pasture.[44] In 1866, although c. 65 a. in the southern part of Abenhall grove had been cleared for arable,[45] the proportions of arable and grassland were much the same, with wheat, turnips, and grass leys being the main crops in the rotation and 162 a. being permanent grassland.[46] Sheep farming was of importance, 711 sheep being recorded that year, and only a few cattle and pigs were then kept.[47] In the later 19th century and the early 20th much land under the plough was turned permanently to grass and in 1926, when permanent grassland covered some 424 a., the amount of

11 Ibid. C 135/65, no. 6; C 135/83, no. 13.
12 Ibid. C 139/115, no. 34.
13 Glos. R.O., D 36/M 1.   14 Ibid. M 2, f. 3.
15 Cf. ibid. M 4; Q/RNc 4/1.
16 P.R.O., C 133/100, no. 6; C 134/53, no. 4; C 135/65, no. 6; C 135/83, no. 13.
17 G.D.R. wills 1562/29.
18 Glos. R.O., D 36/M 2, ff. 3–6.
19 Ibid. f. 25 and v.; M 4.   20 Ibid. E 1, f. 18v.
21 Ibid. D 4431, deed Thurs. after St. David 7 Hen. IV.
22 Ibid. D 36/E 1, ff. 31–45.
23 Ibid. M 2, f. 9; D 4431, deed 23 Oct. 15 Chas. II.
24 Ibid. D 2123, pp. 79, 83.
25 Rudder, Glos. 209; Rudge, Hist. of Glos. ii. 86.
26 G.D.R., T 1/1.   27 P.R.O., E 32/32, m. 2.
28 Glos. R.O., D 23/L 2.   29 Ibid. P 1/OV 2/2.
30 P.R.O., F 3/128, letter 29 Nov. 1860.

31 Glos. R.O., D 23/E 4.   32 Ibid. E 9.
33 Ibid. D 637/VII/1; Kelly's Dir. Glos. (1870), 460; (1889), 655.
34 Glos. R.O., D 1438, Littledean and Notgrove deeds 1766–1851.   35 Census, 1831.
36 G.D.R., T 1/1; cf. O.S. Map 6", Glos. XXXI. NE. (1884 edn.).   37 Glos. R.O., D 2299/1098.
38 Ibid. DA 24/100/6, p. 138.
39 Mins. of Glos. County Council, xxv. 341, 357.
40 Glos. R.O., D 2428/1/1.
41 P.R.O., MAF 68/1609/15; MAF 68/3295/16.
42 Bigland, Glos. i. 1; Rudge, Hist. of Glos. ii. 86.
43 List & Index Soc. clxxxix, pp. 168, 181.
44 G.D.R., T 1/1.
45 Ibid.; Glos. R.O., D 637/VII/1.
46 P.R.O., MAF 68/26/8.
47 Ibid. MAF 68/25/20.

cereals and root crops grown was minimal. The flocks and beef herds were enlarged in the early 20th century, 1,330 sheep and 146 cattle, including dairy cows, being returned in 1926 compared with 549 and 87 respectively in 1896.[48] Orchards, recorded in Abenhall from the early 15th century,[49] were scattered throughout most parts of the parish in 1840[50] and covered over 32 a. in 1926.[51]

Abenhall manor had a water mill in the early 14th century.[52] Two dilapidated water mills recorded there in the 1340s[53] were presumably on Longhope brook, where two mills later stood. Barton mill, recorded in 1280,[54] was a corn mill in the 17th century.[55] It was sold to Nathaniel Pyrke in 1693[56] and, after several more changes of ownership, to Maynard Colchester in 1747.[57] He closed it soon afterwards.[58] The other mill, perhaps that which the lady of the manor had in hand in the early 16th century,[59] stood downstream at the boundary with Longhope.[60] It belonged to William Bridgeman (d. 1581), whose son Thomas[61] sold it, then a grist mill called Wyatt's Mill, in 1597 to John Ayleway.[62] The site passed with Ayleway's estate, which became part of the Colchester family's possessions in 1641,[63] and the mill had disappeared by 1623.[64] A corn mill built in its place by Robert Kirke, a Mitcheldean mercer, in the early 1630s[65] was worked until the mid 18th century with Barton mill.[66] Known later as Abenhall mill, it operated until the late 19th century.[67] Some 19th-century buildings survived in 1988.

Gunn's Mills, on a short tributary of Westbury brook, stood west of the Littledean–Mitcheldean road below Shapridge. At its greatest extent, in the mid 19th century, it formed a complex of buildings and ponds spread over four adjacent sites.[68] The principal buildings and the earliest ranges were at the lowest site,[69] which was that part of the Crown demesne on which John Cone of Mitcheldean built a water mill in or shortly before 1435.[70] In 1540 John Counteys and his wife Margaret, the daughter and heiress of another John Cone, quitclaimed a corn mill there to Richard Brayne.[71] The clothier William Gunn, the Braynes' tenant by 1596,[72] was operating two fulling mills there in 1601[73] and

enlarged the mill pond in 1610. A furnace for casting iron was built there after 1625 and was owned by Sir John Winter in 1634.[74] John Brayne seized it in 1644[75] and Winter had regained possession by 1653.[76] The furnace was apparently not in use in 1680[77] and was rebuilt in 1682 and 1683,[78] perhaps by Messrs. Hall and Scudamore who were later said to be partners in a new forge at Gunn's Mills.[79] The site, which after the Restoration was apparently held for a time by the constable of St. Briavels castle on behalf of the Crown, passed to William Brayne (d. 1693), who left it to his daughters Margaret Maddox, later wife of Joseph Halsey, and Rebecca.[80] They sold Gunn's Mills in 1702 to the ironmaster Thomas Foley of Stoke Edith (Herefs.)[81] and the Foleys produced iron there intermittently until at least 1736.[82] By 1741 the ironworks had been converted as a paper mill, worked by Joseph Lloyd[83] (d. 1761).[84] His business, including a corn mill a short distance upstream,[85] was continued by his wife Hannah and his son Joseph.[86] The latter, who purchased Gunn's Mills in 1780,[87] increased paper production by converting the corn mill as part of the paper manufactory and by erecting new buildings on a third site, further upstream within the Forest. Although his son Joseph took over the business in 1805[88] he retained an interest in it until 1816.[89] After the younger Joseph's death in 1842 Gunn's Mills was occupied by tenants under the Lloyd family.[90] It was idle between 1848 and 1851 when paper making was resumed by John Birt. He provided several new buildings and installed new machinery, including steam engines, and, having bankrupted himself,[91] was succeeded as lessee in 1855 by Aaron Goold. At Goold's death in 1862 his three sons took over the business, which ceased in 1879 following the diversion of water from the stream to the new Cinderford waterworks.[92] The machinery had been removed by 1890 when a farmer bought Gunn's Mills.[93]

In the 20th century many of the buildings were demolished or fell into ruin and the ponds were drained or filled in. At the lowest site the surviving ruins in 1988 included the furnace,

48   Ibid. MAF 68/1609/15; MAF 68/3295/16.
49   Glos. R.O., D 4431, deed Mich. 12 Hen. IV; D 36/E 1, f. 21v.; D 23/T 39; Q/RNc 1, pp. 61–6.
50   G.D.R., T 1/1; cf. Glos. R.O., PA 1/1.
51   P.R.O., MAF 68/3295/16.
52   Ibid. C 133/100, no. 6; C 134/53, no. 4.
53   Ibid. C 135/65, no. 6; C 135/83, no. 13.
54   Glos. R.O., D 1448/T 26; D 4431, grant of Hen. of Dean to Hugh Godwin; ibid. D 36/E 1, ff. 40, 92v.
55   Ibid. D 36/M 2, f. 3v.; P.R.O., E 134/22 Jas. I Hil./3.
56   Glos. R.O., D 4431, deed 25 Sept. 5 Wm. and Mary.
57   Ibid. D 36/T 1.
58   Ibid. T 59, deed 16 June 1758.   59   Ibid. E 1, f. 29v.
60   Cf. ibid. D 2123, pp. 91–3; G.D.R., T 1/1.
61   P.R.O., C 142/199, no. 84.
62   Glos. R.O., D 36/E 1, f. 88; N.L.W., Courtfield MSS. 785, presentments 25 Oct. 1598.
63   Below, Mitcheldean, manor; cf. P.R.O., C 142/305, no. 135.
64   Cf. Glos. R.O., D 36/E 3, ff. 67v., 68v.; Inq. p.m. Glos. 1625–42, i. 60–4.
65   Glos. R.O., D 36/E 2, f. 41; M 78, ff. 13v.–14.
66   Ibid. D 4431, deed 10 Jan. 12 Chas. I; cf. ibid. D 36/E 10, ff. 27v.–28; E 12, f. 112v.; M 78, f. 62 and v.; T 1.
67   Cf. O.S. Map 6", Glos. XXIII. SE. (1883, 1903 edns.).
68   Glos. R.O., Q/RGf 1/7; O.S. Map 6", Glos. XXXI. NE. (1884 edn.).
69   G.D.R., T 1/1.   70   P.R.O., SC 6/850/20.
71   Ibid. CP 25/2/14/82, no. 8; cf. Glos. R.O., D 36/M 2, f. 2v.
72   P.R.O., CP 25/2/146/1906, no. 1; Glos. R.O., D 2172/1/75.
73   P.R.O., CP 25/2/147/1923, no. 4.
74   Glos. R.O., D 421/E 4.
75   P.R.O., LRRO 5/7A, depositions 1645, nos. 7, 13.
76   Glos. R.O., D 36/M 11.   77   Hart, Free Miners, 103.
78   Glos. Soc. Ind. Arch. Jnl. (1974), 17–18.
79   Bodl. MS. Top. Glouc. c. 3, f. 137.
80   G.D.R. wills 1693/144; cf. Hart, Verderers, 107.
81   Glos. R.O., D 2172/1/75; D 2957/1.1.
82   Atkyns, Glos. 199; Hart, Ind. Hist. of Dean, 63–4, 70.
83   Glos. R.O., P 145/IN 1/3; D 36/E 50; cf. Glouc. Jnl. 19 July 1743.
84   Bigland, Glos. i. 5.
85   Glos. R.O., D 2172/1/43; 1/75; D 2528, p. 22, plan G.
86   Glouc. Jnl. 22 Dec. 1761.   87   Glos. R.O., D 2172/1/75.
88   Ibid.; cf. ibid. Q/RGf 1/7.
89   Lond. Gaz. 2 Nov. 1816, p. 2074.
90   Glos. R.O., D 2172/1/75; Trans. B.G.A.S. vi. 304–5; lxxi. 157–8.
91   Glos. Soc. Ind. Arch. Jnl. (1974), 35; Glouc. Jnl. 5 May 1855.
92   Glos. R.O., D 2172/1/75; EN, A. N. Goold.
93   W. H. Townley, 'Ind. Sites in Vale of Castiard', 8: copy in ibid. IN 41; Kelly's Dir. Glos. (1894), 133.

rebuilt in 1682 and 1683 apparently to an earlier plan with a square hearth, and, on top of it, a rubble and timber-framed building provided for the paper mill in the mid 18th century.[94] On the west of the site the former mill house incorporates a brick range of the early 19th century[95] from which the third storey was removed in 1921, when it was a farmhouse.[96] By the late 1980s, when a building contractor operated from the site, lawns covered the area, formerly a pool, south of the house. At the next two sites upstream, the higher of which contained the corn mill operating in the mid 18th century[97] and washing mills in the mid 19th,[98] the buildings had disappeared. Those remaining at the highest site, within the Forest, were among those built by Joseph Lloyd in the late 18th century or early 19th and included a former paper mill and a range converted as a dwelling in the 1970s.[99]

The urban growth at the Mitcheldean end of Abenhall and the proximity of the Forest of Dean led to a diversification of employment in the parish, evident in 1608 when 48 men, including apprentices, followed a variety of trades compared with 13 engaged in agriculture.[1] In 1831 there were 28 families in the parish supported by agriculture and 17 by trade.[2] The trade and industry located at the northern end of the parish, including quarrying, were integral to the town's economy and are treated in Mitcheldean's history.[3] Among the inhabitants of the rural part of Abenhall in 1851 were a shoemaker, a sawyer, a shopkeeper, a miner, and an engine driver.[4]

LOCAL GOVERNMENT. By the mid 1460s a court usually met twice a year in Abenhall to combine view of frankpledge and a court baron for Abenhall manor and part of Mitcheldean manor. It dealt with cases of assault, bloodshed, and illicit gaming and enforced the assize of ale[5] and in 1482 it heard pleas of debt and trespass.[6] A court book survives for 1620–1, a court roll for 1642, and records of presentments and other court papers for 1581–1607, 1622–40, 1653, 1687, and 1691. In those years the court, sometimes sitting as a court of survey, also dealt with tenurial and other estate matters, including management of woodland, and with affrays, the assize of bread, and the maintenance of highways and watercourses. In 1603 it ordered the repair of the Abenhall parish stocks. Much of its business related to Mitcheldean town and it appointed two clerks for the town's market as well as two constables, two aletasters, and two bread weighers. The last two offices had been combined by 1620 and their holders later acted also as fish and flesh tasters. By 1624 a leather sealer was also appointed. The offices of clerks of the market had evidently lapsed by the late 1620s.[7]

Two churchwardens were recorded in Abenhall from the mid 16th century.[8] In 1825 the vestry ordered them to replace the parish stocks, which were near the churchyard. The money needed for church maintenance was allotted out of the poor rate in 1824,[9] but a separate church rate was levied after the reform of the poor law in 1834. In the mid 19th century there was only one churchwarden, usually the head of the Scudamore family of Church farm who also served as surveyor of the highways.[10] Poor relief was administered in the late 18th century and the early 19th by one overseer, although in the 1820s two overseers were appointed. The usual forms of relief were applied and c. 5 people received regular payments in the early 1760s and c. 10 in the mid 1790s;[11] 19 people were given regular help in 1803.[12] From 1786 the parish subscribed to the Gloucester infirmary[13] and for two years from 1825 the vestry retained a surgeon. From 1823 the poor were farmed by the governor of the Littledean workhouse, to which most of them were admitted.[14] The annual cost of relief, having risen from £65 in 1776 to £140 in 1803 and £278 in 1815,[15] had fallen by 1825 to £166; and it remained at that level, apart from 1832 and 1833[16] when the parish helped a woman and her children to emigrate to America and apprenticed a boy to a Mitcheldean nailer.[17] Abenhall was included in Westbury-on-Severn poor-law union in 1835,[18] in East Dean and United Parishes rural district in 1895,[19] and, as part of Mitcheldean civil parish, in the Forest of Dean district in 1974.

CHURCH. The church at Abenhall was recorded from 1291. At that time the rector of Westbury-on-Severn had a portion of 2s. in it,[20] indicating that it probably originated as a chapel of Westbury church; the portion was still paid in 1535.[21] The benefice was a rectory, the first known incumbent being instituted in 1318,[22] and it was united with Mitcheldean rectory in 1946.[23] In 1912 the adjoining part of the Forest, namely Shapridge and parts of the Edge Hills area and

94 Hart, *Ind. Hist. of Dean*, 70–1; *Glos. Soc. Ind. Arch. Jnl.* (1974), 17–18.
95 Glos. R.O., D 3921/II/16.
96 Townley, 'Ind. Sites in Castiard', 9.
97 Glos. R.O., D 2528, p. 22, plan G. 98 G.D.R., T 1/1.
99 *Glos. Soc. Ind. Arch. Jnl.* (1974), 37–8; cf. P.R.O., MR 415 (F 16/47); Glos. R.O., Q/RGf 1/7.
1 Smith, *Men and Armour*, 35–6. 2 *Census*, 1831.
3 Below, Mitcheldean, econ. hist. (other ind. and trade).
4 P.R.O., HO 107/1959. 5 Glos. R.O., D 36/M 1.
6 N.L.W., Courtfield MSS. 787.
7 Glos. R.O., D 36/M 2, M 5–14; N.L.W., Courtfield MSS. 342–3, 785, 790.
8 Hockaday Abs. xxix, 1543 subsidy, f. 9; xliv, 1572 visit. f. 5; xcv, 1703.
9 Glos. R.O., P 1/VE 2/1; *Morris's Dir. Glos.* (1867), 427.
10 Glos. R.O., P 1/CW 2/1; ibid. VE 2/1; for the Scud-amores, above, econ. hist.
11 Glos. R.O., P 1/OV 2/1–2; ibid. VE 2/1, which includes overseers' accts. for the years 1821–3, 1824–7, and 1833–4. 12 *Poor Law Abstract, 1804*, 172–3.
13 Glos. R.O., HO 19/8/1.
14 Ibid. P 1/VE 2/1; P 110/VE 2/1.
15 *Poor Law Abstract, 1804*, 172–3; *1818*, 146–7.
16 *Poor Law Returns* (1830–1), p. 66; (1835), p. 65.
17 Glos. R.O., P 1/VE 2/1.
18 *Poor Law Com. 2nd Rep.* p. 524.
19 Glos. R.O., DA 24/100/1.
20 *Tax. Eccl.* (Rec. Com.), 161.
21 *Valor Eccl.* (Rec. Com.), ii. 501; cf. *V.C.H. Glos.* x. 98–9.
22 *Reg. Orleton*, 385; cf. Hockaday Abs. xcv.
23 *Glouc. Dioc. Year Bk.* (1950–1), 34–5; cf. *Lond. Gaz.* 4 Jan. 1929, pp. 137–8.

Plump Hill, had been transferred from Holy Trinity parish to Abenhall for ecclesiastical purposes.[24]

The advowson belonged to the lord of the manor in 1317[25] and descended with the manor until the mid 19th century.[26] The Crown filled vacancies in 1349 and 1351 when it had custody of the manor,[27] and in 1472 John Barre, whose wife was entitled to every third turn by reason of dower, made a presentation.[28] The Crown was said to be patron in 1563.[29] In 1623, at the first vacancy under the Roman Catholic Vaughan family, a presentation by Joan Vaughan's trustees was quashed and a nominee of Oxford University was instituted.[30] Later vacancies under the Vaughans were each filled by a patron for the turn.[31] After 1846, when John Probyn (d. 1863) settled the advowson, subject to his life interest, in trust for sale, the patronage changed hands several times.[32] The bishop of Worcester acquired it by an exchange in 1893 and it passed to the Lord Chancellor, acting for the Crown, as part of an exchange in 1908.[33] The Lord Chancellor, who after the union of benefices was entitled to exercise the patronage alternately with the Diocesan Board of Patronage, relinquished his right to the board c. 1970.[34]

The rector owned all the tithes of the parish. By the late 1670s moduses had long been accepted for milch cows, calves, and garden produce; workhorses and oxen were exempted from payments by parishioners for the grazing of livestock.[35] The tithes were commuted from 1839 for a corn rent charge of £140.[36] In the early 16th century the rector rented a house and land from the lady of the manor for 2s. 3d.;[37] the house, on a close given for a chantry in the church, was rebuilt by the rector after 1529 and was sold in 1549.[38] In the later 16th century the glebe comprised c. 17 a. and a cottage, and in the late 1670s it contained c. 31 a. and no buildings.[39] It covered c. 27 a. in 1840[40] and was sold c. 1919.[41] James Davies, rector from 1837, built a large rectory house, for the completion of which Queen Anne's Bounty granted £200 in 1846.[42] The house, standing west of the church

on land formerly part of the manor,[43] was sold c. 1949.[44] The rectory was valued at £4 in 1291,[45] £4 5s. 5d. clear in 1535,[46] £50 in 1750,[47] and £142 in 1856.[48]

Because of the living's poverty many of Abenhall's rectors, as in 1291, were pluralists.[49] In 1334 the rector, John Honsom, was imprisoned at St. Briavels for poaching in the Forest of Dean.[50] William Budge, rector from 1529, was said in 1548 to have been non-resident for three years. He was deprived in 1554 for being married[51] but served the parish again in 1563 when the rectory was vacant and he had the living of Mitcheldean.[52] Several rectors enjoyed long incumbencies, notably Anthony Sterry, who was presented in 1568[53] and became a graduate after 1584, when he was living in Oxford.[54] Later he was also vicar of Lydney, where he resided,[55] and employed a curate at Abenhall. Curates were also employed by Sterry's successor at Abenhall, Edward Potter,[56] rector from 1623 and vicar of Longhope from 1626. Described as a preaching minister in 1650, Potter had been deprived of the rectory by 1655 and had recovered it by 1662, only to be deprived again by 1669.[57] Richard Hall, rector of Mitcheldean, also held Abenhall from 1685 until his death in 1723.[58] John Probyn, presented in 1785 by his father from whom he later acquired the manor, became archdeacon of Llandaff (Glam.)[59] but lived in Newland, where he became vicar for a short time, and later in Longhope, where he was a landowner.[60] Abenhall was often served for him by curates, including from 1813 his son Edmund, to whom he gave the rectory in 1827. Both Edmund (d. 1837)[61] and his successor James Davies, who took up residence in the parish, employed curates.[62] Davies, a friend of prominent Tractarians, remained rector until 1873.[63]

Obits in the church were founded by John Woodward and by Lady (Alice) Dennis. The latter's foundation was supported from the close on which the rector had his house[64] and presumably commemorated her first husband Thomas Baynham (d. 1500),[65] to whose anniversary the

24 *Kelly's Dir. Glos.* (1919), 21; Glos. R.O., P 1/IN 3/2.
25 *Cal. Inq. p.m.* vi, pp. 1–2.
26 Hockaday Abs. xcv; *Trans. B.G.A.S.* vi. 140–60, 171–9.   27 *Cal. Pat.* 1348–50, 273, 362; 1350–4, 61.
28 Hockaday Abs. xcv.
29 Bodl. MS. Rawl. C. 790, f. 28v.
30 *Trans. B.G.A.S.* vi. 154, 177; P.R.O., E 134/22 Jas. I Hil./3; IND 17004, p. 59.
31 Hockaday Abs. xcv.
32 *Trans. B.G.A.S.* vi. 160; Glos. R.O., P 206/IN 1/10; *Kelly's Dir. Glos.* (1885), 348.
33 *Lond. Gaz.* 21 July 1893, pp. 4127–8; 3 Mar. 1908, pp. 1480–1.
34 Ibid. 4 Jan. 1929, pp. 137–8; *Glouc. Dioc. Year Bk.* (1950–1), 34–5; (1969), 26–7; (1971), 26–7.
35 G.D.R., V 5/1T 2–3.   36 Ibid. T 1/1.
37 Glos. R.O., D 36/E 1, ff. 29–30; cf. *Valor Eccl.* (Rec. Com.), ii. 501.
38 Hockaday Abs. xcv; *Cal. Pat.* 1549–51, 99, 103.
39 G.D.R., V 5/1T 1–3.   41 Glos. R.O., D 2299/1760.
40 Ibid. T 1/1.
42 Hockaday Abs. xcv; G.D.R., F 4/1; Hodgson, *Queen Anne's Bounty* (suppl. 1864), pp. xiv, lxv.
43 Cf. G.D.R., T 1/1 (no. 88); O.S. Map 6", Glos. XXXI. NE. (1884 edn.).
44 Glos. R.O., D 2299/9818.
45 *Tax. Eccl.* (Rec. Com.), 161.

46 *Valor Eccl.* (Rec. Com.), ii. 501.
47 G.D.R. vol. 381A, f. 1.   48 Ibid. 384, f. 1.
49 e.g. *Tax. Eccl.* (Rec. Com.), 161; G.D.R. vol. 285B(3), pp. 1–2.
50 *Cal. Close*, 1333–7, 240.
51 Hockaday Abs. xcv.
52 Bodl. MS. Rawl. C. 790, ff. 27, 28v.
53 Hockaday Abs. xcv.
54 Ibid. xlix, state of clergy 1584, f. 45; lii, state of clergy 1593, f. 4.
55 Bigland, *Glos.* ii. 158; G.D.R. wills 1627/11.
56 Glos. R.O., P 1/IN 1/1; G.D.R., D 1/1, 181.
57 Hockaday Abs. xcv; *Walker Revised*, ed. A. G. Matthews, 176; *Trans. B.G.A.S.* lxxxiii. 97.
58 Hockaday Abs. xcv; Bigland, *Glos.* i. 446; Glos. R.O., P 220/IN 1/1.
59 Hockaday Abs. xcv; above, manor.
60 Glos. R.O., D 23/E 9; D 23A/17; Hockaday Abs. ccxcvii.
61 Hockaday Abs. xcv; Glos. R.O., P 1/IN 1/7; *Trans. B.G.A.S.* vi. 196.
62 Hockaday Abs. xcv; Glos. R.O., P 1/IN 1/7–8; P.R.O., HO 107/1959.
63 O. W. Jones, *Isaac Williams and his Circle* (1971), 12, 19, 74–5, 121–36.
64 Hockaday Abs. xcv.
65 Above, manor.

rector paid 2s. in 1535.[66] The endowments of both obits were sold to William Sawle and William Bridges in 1549.[67] Land held for church purposes in the early 16th century was appropriated by Joseph Vaughan before 1577.[68]

The church of *ST. MICHAEL*, so called by c. 1710[69] although it bore a dedication to St. James in 1444[70] and to St. Augustine in 1452 and 1580,[71] is built of sandstone rubble and has a chancel with north organ chamber, a nave with south aisle and porch, and a south-west tower.[72] The nave and chancel, which have no division between them, are of the later 13th century and the aisle and tower were added in the early 14th century, the chancel windows being renewed at that time. In the 15th century a new west window was put into the tower and the upper part of the tower was remodelled or rebuilt. On the tower, above a blocked west doorway, a carving of a shield bearing picks and spades, tools of miners,[73] was replaced by a copy in 1982.[74] The nave roof, which is unframed, may be 15th-century. The south doorway and its rear arch are round-headed and, although similar to plain 12th-century work, are probably of 1749, when the aisle was rebuilt with its roof to a lower pitch.[75] The porch, which also has a round-headed doorway, was presumably added at that time. The aisle windows, of which that on the south side was round-headed in the late 18th century,[76] were given 14th-century style tracery, apparently after 1857[77] and before the church was restored to designs by A. W. Maberly in 1874. At the restoration, financed by a fund inaugurated by J. W. Gregg, who was both rector and patron, the ceiling and a west gallery were removed from the nave and a vestry was built.[78] The organ chamber was created c. 1885 by extending the vestry westwards.[79]

The font, which dates from the 15th century, is of local workmanship and the octagonal bowl is richly carved, six faces displaying family coats of arms and two the implements of miners and smiths.[80] The glass includes 14th-century fragments, perhaps portraying St. Catherine, in the chancel north window.[81] The chancel contains memorials to members of the Pyrke family, notably brasses to Richard (d. 1609), his wife, and two sons, and an ornate monument erected by Mary (née Colchester) to her husband Nathaniel (d. 1715).[82] There are three bells, the treble cast in the 14th century, the second by John Pennington in 1655, and the tenor probably by Roger and Richard Purdue in 1682.[83] Among

the plate are a paten given by Mary Pyrke in 1732 and a chalice acquired in 1734.[84] The surviving registers, which begin in 1596, include many entries for Mitcheldean during the incumbency of Richard Hall (1685–1723) and distinguish all entries for the extraparochial Forest of Dean from 1813.[85]

NONCONFORMITY. There were said to be no recusants in Abenhall in 1603[86] but absenteeism from church was commonly reported by the early 17th century. Dissent grew after the Restoration; at least 6 men stayed away from church in 1676 and a Quaker lived in the parish in 1685.[87] In 1695 a house was registered for worship by Presbyterians,[88] presumably the Independent group which in 1715 had the same minister as the Mitcheldean Independent church. Other parishioners belonged to the Mitcheldean church at that time.[89] The Independents also had a meeting in Abenhall in the early 19th century[90] when they used a house on the Gloucester road at the end of Mitcheldean town.[91]

EDUCATION. In 1833 a Sunday school supported by voluntary contributions and teaching 20 children was begun in Abenhall[92] and in 1846 the parish had two dame schools with 20 and 6 day and 29 and 7 Sunday pupils respectively.[93] A school built west of the church near the Littledean–Mitcheldean road in 1850 housed a day school, which in 1875, as Abenhall C. of E. school, had a daily attendance of 30 and was supported by voluntary contributions and pence. It was then owned and controlled by Henrietta Davies[94] and later it was supported by the Barton family. The school, which had an average attendance of 50 in 1885 and 23 in 1902,[95] became in 1903 one of the first to be closed by the county education committee, the children being transferred to schools at Mitcheldean and Plump Hill.[96] The building continued in use as a Sunday school and was apparently given to the parish by the representatives of Katherine Barton in 1913. It served as a parish room for many years[97] but was unused in 1988.

In 1930 the county education committee opened a senior school for Mitcheldean and adjoining parishes in new buildings in the north of Abenhall.[98] The school, the average attendance at which was 181 by 1938,[99] became a secondary modern school under the 1944 Educ-

66 *Valor Eccl.* (Rec. Com.), ii. 501.
67 *Cal. Pat.* 1549–51, 99, 103.
68 Glos. R.O., D 36/E 1, ff. 28v., 42; G.D.R. vol. 40, f. 248v.
69 Atkyns, *Glos.* 199.   70 P.R.O., C 139/115, no. 34.
71 Ibid. C 139/149, no. 23; C 142/189, no. 82.
72 Evidence on a later 17th-cent. map (P.R.O., F 17/7) of a spire is unsupported.
73 Nicholls, *Iron Making*, 26.
74 *Glos. and Avon Life*, July 1982, 50.
75 Rudder, *Glos.* 210; Glos. R.O., D 4335/31.
76 Bigland, *Glos.* i. 1.   77 Cf. *Glos. Ch. Notes*, 103–4.
78 Glos. R.O., D 4335/31; *Glouc. Jnl.* 15 Aug. 1874; *Kelly's Dir. Glos.* (1879), 552; (1902), 17.
79 Glos. R.O., P 1/VE 2/1.
80 *Trans. B.G.A.S.* xl. 39, 43–5, 51, and plate I; detail from font reproduced below, Fig. 19.
81 *Trans. B.G.A.S.* vi. 277.

82 Bigland, *Glos.* i. 3.   83 *Glos. Ch. Bells*, 103.
84 *Glos. Ch. Plate*, 1.
85 *B. & G. Par. Rec.* 43; Glos. R.O., P 1/IN 1/1–11.
86 *Eccl. Misc.* 99.
87 Glos. R.O., D 2052; cf. Hockaday Abs. xcv, 1572.
88 Glos. R.O., Q/SO 3.   89 Bright, *Nonconf. in Dean*, 14.
90 *Glouc. Jnl.* 23 Oct. 1809; G.D.R. vol. 383, no. civ.
91 Below, Mitcheldean, nonconf.
92 *Educ. Enq. Abstract*, 300.
93 Nat. Soc. *Inquiry, 1846–7*, Glos. 2–3.
94 P.R.O., ED 7/37, Abenhall C. of E. sch.
95 *Kelly's Dir. Glos.* (1885), 348; (1902), 17.
96 Glos. R.O., CE/M 2/1, p. 73; 2, pp. 44–5.
97 Ibid. P 1/VE 2/1; ibid. CW 2/1; cf. ibid. D 2299/1098; D 2428/1/1.   98 Ibid. SM 1/1/M 1, pp. 1–8.
99 *Bd. of Educ., List 21, 1932* (H.M.S.O.), 112; *1938*, 128.

ation Act and at a reorganization of Forest of Dean secondary education in 1985 was made a comprehensive school called Dene Magna school. New buildings had been added to the site in 1961 and 1980, and in 1988 there were 568 pupils on the roll, drawn from a wide area including Westbury-on-Severn and Ruardean.[1]

CHARITIES FOR THE POOR. None known.

ENGLISH BICKNOR

THE RURAL parish of English Bicknor lies 8 km. ENE. of Monmouth on the boundary with Herefordshire and Monmouthshire.[2] It is bounded on the north by the river Wye and like Welsh Bicknor, the parish on the opposite side of the river,[3] took its name from a bank.[4] Two short sections of Offa's Dyke, once the boundary between the lands of the English and the Welsh, were built in the north-east of English Bicknor near the river.[5]

Part of English Bicknor, probably adjoining the later village, was settled by 1066[6] and the cultivated area was later increased by assarting from the Forest of Dean woodland and waste.[7] The parish, which was within the Forest's jurisdiction by the early 13th century and so remained as long as that jurisdiction had significance,[8] covered c. 2,377 a. in the early 19th century and included several detached parts divided from the main block by the large tract of extraparochial land called Mailscot.[9] Mailscot, which was alienated from the royal demesne of the Forest in 1625[10] and came to be regarded as outside the Forest,[11] is included in this account.

The main part of English Bicknor was compact and regular in shape with its north boundary following the course of the Wye from Lydbrook in the north-east downstream to Coldwell, where the river turns north describing a large loop to pass the promontory called Symonds Yat rock. Elsewhere the parish adjoined the extraparochial royal demesne of the Forest save in the north-east at Lower Lydbrook, where it touched Ruardean and a detached part of Newland, and on a section of the south boundary, where it touched the detached part of Newland called Hoarthorns farm.[12] English Bicknor's boundaries included a tributary stream of the Wye at Lower Lydbrook and several sections of the Coleford–Goodrich (Herefs.) road on the west at Hillersland and Redinhorne. A landmark on the south boundary at Short Standing was the Gospel Oak, which was replaced by another oak before 1725.[13] An area of the Forest demesne at Hangerberry, to the east, was claimed for the parish in a long suit begun in 1743 by Viscount Gage, lord of English Bicknor manor.[14]

To the west the wedge of extraparochial land called Mailscot or Mailscot wood extended northwards from Coalpit hill to Symonds Yat rock and was bounded on the west by the river Wye and on the south-east by a track known in 1625 as the green way or the hunter's path. In 1625 it was reckoned to cover c. 430 a.,[15] but its true area was c. 832 a.[16] On the south-west side of Mailscot an area of 141 a., which included Braceland, formed a detached part of English Bicknor[17] bounded on the south and west by the ancient course of Whippington brook, known in 1282 as 'Wybaltunes' brook.[18] The brook disappeared underground below Coalpit hill before the 18th century, and in 1993 the dry ditch on its course was visible in places down to Oldstone (formerly Obson's) well, on the west side of Mailscot, where the brook surfaced a short distance above the Wye.[19] The other parts of English Bicknor adjoining Mailscot were a narrow strip of meadow land on the river bank opposite Whitchurch (Herefs.) and a small piece of land at Broomhill Tump in the south-east corner.[20]

The west part of Mailscot, adjoining Whippington brook, had apparently included an estate called 'Wiboldingtune' which had, however, reverted to the Forest waste by 1066. The bishops of Hereford, to whom ownership of the estate and its fishery was ascribed in 1086,[21] had a weir in the river Wye there in the late 13th century, and a clearing of 90 a. between the Bicknor–Staunton highway and the river was known as Bishop's slade in 1282.[22] An assart of 40 a. near Whippington brook in 1317 was presumably the parochial land at Braceland, which belonged to Staunton manor in 1579. The parochial land further west, perhaps the grove of Henry the carter in 1317, was in 1579 a copse of c. 80 a. belonging to Richard Baynham of Clearwell.[23] The piece of English Bicknor at Broomhill Tump was probably one of the two assarts held with English Bicknor manor in 1301.[24]

In 1842 Mailscot was added to English Bicknor

[1] Inf. from head teacher; *Educ. Services Dir. 1988–9* (co. educ. dept.), 37.
[2] This account was written in 1993.
[3] Herefs., formerly Mon.: *Census*, 1831, 1881.
[4] *P.N. Glos.* (E.P.N.S.), iii. 211; iv. 158.
[5] C. Fox, *Offa's Dyke* (1955), 184–5.
[6] *Dom. Bk.* (Rec. Com.), i. 167v.
[7] Cf. *Inq. p.m. Glos.* 1236–1300, 231.
[8] *Trans. B.G.A.S.* lxvi. 166–202; below, Forest of Dean, bounds.
[9] G.D.R., T 1/25. [10] Glos. R.O., D 23/E 29.
[11] Ibid. D 1677/GG 1320; Hart, *Royal Forest*, 294.
[12] G.D.R., T 1/25, 128, 151.
[13] P.R.O., F 14/2A, rot. 1 and d.

[14] Glos. R.O., D 23/E 35; D 1677/GG 1180–1331; Hart, *Royal Forest*, 197.
[15] Glos. R.O., D 23/E 29; P.R.O., E 178/5307.
[16] Figure obtained by comparing area of Eng. Bicknor parish before and after 1842. [17] G.D.R., T 1/25.
[18] *Trans. B.G.A.S.* xiv. 364.
[19] P.R.O., F 14/2A, rot. 1; F 14/6; MR 691 (LRRO 1/240); O.S. Map 6", Glos. XXX. SE. (1884 edn.).
[20] G.D.R., T 1/25.
[21] *Dom. Bk.* (Rec. Com.), i. 182; *Trans. B.G.A.S.* cv. 123.
[22] *Tax. Eccl.* (Rec. Com.), 168; *Trans. B.G.A.S.* xiv. 364–5.
[23] *Cal. Pat.* 1317–21, 14–15; *Trans. B.G.A.S.* vii. 238–9; P.R.O., MR 879 (F 17/1).
[24] *Inq. p.m. Glos.* 1236–1300, 231.

to give the parish an area of 3,209 a. The transfer included land by the Wye, south-west of Symonds Yat rock,[25] but it excluded a long strip of land containing closes on the east side of the road at Hillersland and Redinhorne. That land, sandwiched between Bicknor and Mailscot and extending to Symonds Yat rock, had remained part of the royal demesne in 1625[26] and was included in West Dean township in 1842.[27] In 1935 it was transferred to English Bicknor and at the same time the north-east corner of the parish was transferred to the new civil parish of Lydbrook.[28] In 1965 16 a. on the side of the Wye valley south-west of Symonds Yat rock were transferred to Goodrich, leaving English Bicknor with 2,958 a. (1,197 ha.).[29] The account printed here deals with the parish as constituted between 1842 and 1935 save for the area in the north-east forming part of Lydbrook village, which is treated below with the Forest of Dean.

Much of English Bicknor is above the 120-m. contour and the land is generally hilly, rising to 224 m. in the east above Hangerberry and the Lydbrook valley. Most of the parish lies on the sandstone beds of the Forest of Dean coalfield, but in the north and west the land is formed by carboniferous limestone and in the north-east the underlying Old Red Sandstone is revealed.[30] To the north and west the ground falls steeply to the Wye and in places the limestone forms cliffs above the river. The highest are on the north side where Coldwell rocks and Symonds Yat rock rise almost perpendicularly for c. 90 m. Symonds Yat rock was the site of an ancient fort controlling several crossings of the Wye and defended on three sides by the steep drop to the river and on the south by a series of five banks and ditches running across the promontory.[31] The name Symonds Yat, first recorded in 1256,[32] was used for the gorge west of the rock. The cliffs have long provided nesting-places for birds of prey and in 1648, in a lease of land at Redinhorne, George Wyrall, the landowner, reserved hawks' eyries.[33] Coldwell is also known as Crowsmarsh[34] and one of the prominent limestone outcrops to the east was known as Raven cliff by 1685.[35] The number of kites, hawks, and ravens in the area declined in the early 19th century[36] but peregrine falcons nested in Coldwell rocks in 1993. Limestone has been quarried extensively in the parish and coal has

been mined on the west side and in Mailscot. Several streams disappear underground through swallow holes recorded in the later 18th century[37] and in places the flow of water was reduced by schemes to prevent flooding in the coalfield in the early 20th century.[38] In 1993 the principal stream flowed northwards in a valley between English Bicknor village and Eastbach, to the south-east, and joined the Wye at Stowfield, in the north-east of the parish. A stream flowing into the Wye at Coldwell was called Hollow brook in 1256.[39]

Some land in the south was not cleared for cultivation until after 1282[40] and the Crown regarded closes in the Eastbach, Joyford, Short Standing, and Hillersland areas as ancient assarts in the early 17th century.[41] In the 17th century common arable fields survived in several places but most land was farmed in closes. There was some rich meadow land on the banks of the river Wye.[42] Most of the surviving woodland, which in 1840 covered 362 a. of the ancient parish,[43] clothed the slope of the Wye valley. The belt of woodland on the north side of the parish included three small commons or wastes, Chepstow grove, Common grove, and an area at Coldwell rocks, where the rights of English Bicknor manor tenants to pasture animals and take brushwood were recorded in 1639.[44] In the mid 19th century Chepstow grove or wood, where parishioners continued to take firewood, was regarded as parish property[45] and from 1938 it was managed under the name of the Poor's Land charity.[46] Court wood, known in 1282 as Martin's Cockshoot,[47] and other land near the Wye were landscaped in the later 18th century to create scenic walks overlooking the river between Bicknor Court and Symonds Yat rock.[48] On the east side of the parish Hangerberry wood, planted after 1608,[49] covered 25 a. in 1792[50] and was enlarged in the mid 19th century.[51] At Braceland, where an inclosure of oak and beech was created in the early 1620s,[52] 70 a. of farmland were planted as part of the Highmeadow woods after being acquired by the Crown in 1817.[53] That land had been cleared by the mid 1960s when it was used as a holiday camping site.[54] The decision of the owners of Mailscot wood in the later 1620s to fell timber for charcoaling and mining operations and to inclose the land provoked riots in 1631[55] and left

25 Dean Forest Poor-Relief Act, 5 & 6 Vic. c. 48; O.S. Area Bk. (1881).
26 P.R.O., E 178/5307.
27 Glos. R.O., Q/RGf 1/4; P.R.O., F 16/64.
28 Census, 1931 (pt. ii).   29 Ibid. 1971.
30 Geol. Surv. Map 1/50,000, solid and drift, sheet 233 (1974 edn.); Geol. of Forest of Dean Coal and Iron-Ore Field (H.M.S.O. 1942), 18, 20, 31, 38.
31 Trans. B.G.A.S. iv. 302; cxii. 59–61.
32 Cal. Pat. 1247–58, 524.
33 Glos. R.O., D 33/420 (abs. of deed in ibid. D 33/218).
34 P.R.O., F 17/117(2), pp. 8–14, 17–18; MR 691; G.D.R., T 1/25; H. A. Machen, 'Hist. Eng. Bicknor' (1954), TS. in Glos. R.O., PA 138/1), 4.
35 Glos. R.O., D 33/248.
36 Nicholls, Forest of Dean, 204.
37 Taylor, Map of Glos. (1777).
38 Richardson, Wells and Springs of Glos. 29, 92; Machen, 'Hist. Eng. Bicknor', 17–18.
39 Cal. Pat. 1247–58, 524; Trans. B.G.A.S. xi. 271; the name Holywell brook was recorded in the mid 18th cent.:

Glos. R.O., D 23/E 35, surv. of river Wye.
40 Cf. Trans. B.G.A.S. xiv. 364–5.
41 Glos. R.O., D 33/188C, 188G, 273; P.R.O., C 66/2168, no. 3.
42 Below, econ. hist.   43 G.D.R., T 1/25.
44 Trans. B.G.A.S. xi. 270–1.
45 Glos. R.O., P 138/VE 2/1, min. 28 Oct. 1858; cf. 19th Rep. Com. Char. 87; G.D.R., T 1/25.
46 Glos. R.O., D 3469/5/59; below, char.
47 Trans. B.G.A.S. xiv. 364–5; P.R.O., MR 879.
48 Bigland, Glos. i. 185; Brayley and Britton, Beauties of Eng. and Wales, v. 716; cf. Glos. R.O., D 637/II/6/F 3.
49 P.R.O., MR 879.
50 Ibid. F 17/117(2), p. 1.
51 G.D.R., T 1/25; O.S. Map 6", Glos. XXXI. NW. (1883 edn.).   52 Glos. R.O., D 1677/GG 673.
53 P.R.O., F 17/117(1), p. 1; G.D.R., T 1/25.
54 Hart, Royal Forest, 246.
55 Hist. MSS. Com. 23, 12th Rep. I, Cowper, i, pp. 429–30; Acts of P.C. 1630–1, pp. 284–5; Cal. S.P. Dom. 1631–3, 4.

only 100 trees standing there.[56] The wood, later replanted, became part of the Highmeadow estate in 1676[57] and the woodland west of Braceland was added to it. In 1792 the wood covered 728 a. and waste land was confined to 19 a. on the side of the Wye gorge at New Weir and 15 a. on Coalpit hill.[58] Mailscot accounted for most of the 1,033 a. of woodland in the enlarged parish in 1905.[59]

The road pattern in English Bicknor has altered much since the Middle Ages when several routes ran south-west across the parish and through Mailscot wood.[60] The Bicknor–Staunton highway crossing Coalpit hill in 1282 was the main road between Lydbrook and Monmouth. From Lydbrook it followed Probert's Lane and it entered English Bicknor village from the east along Godwin's Lane. West of the village it followed a route below Bicknor Court to reach Mailscot midway between Hillersland and Redinhorne, but by the 17th century traffic for Monmouth followed the Coleford road from the village before turning west along Red House Lane to join the road to Mailscot.[61] The Coleford road, known in 1402 as New Street,[62] ran south from the village and turned south-west at Dryslade Farm to follow an ancient route past a medieval chapel and over Wormall (formerly Horemore) hill.[63] It had become the main road to Monmouth and the route through Mailscot had been abandoned by the later 18th century.[64] The Joyford road, branching south from the Coleford road at Dryslade Farm, is called Bicknor Street.

East of the village a road branching from the Lydbrook road in the valley below Upper Tump Farm and running south to the Forest was perhaps that known in 1282 as Eastbach way. At Eastbach it was crossed by a road which ran west to a junction with the Coleford road near the entrance to Red House Lane.[65] The section of that road south of the village was closed in 1851 when Edward Machen, owner of the Eastbach estate, improved the road between Eastbach and the village. Soon afterwards several roads in the north-east were abandoned in favour of new roads built by the rector, John Burdon, to provide work for unemployed farm labourers. The road from Stowfield to Lower Lydbrook on a course near the river Wye was completed in 1853, and the road from the village to Stowfield by way of Millway grove was finished in 1855 at

the same time as a road linking Eastbach with Stowfield and Lower Lydbrook.[66] The Goodrich road at Hillersland and Redinhorne was maintained to the county boundary below Symonds Yat rock by the Dean Forest turnpike trustees from 1827 until 1888.[67] It formed part of an old route between Coleford and Ross-on-Wye (Herefs.) but in the 19th century traffic for Ross used the road through Hangerberry and Lydbrook[68] or, by 1880, the road through Bicknor village and Lower Lydbrook.[69] In Mailscot, where the burden of highway maintenance fell on St. Briavels hundred in the 18th century,[70] a path running north-west to the river at the Slaughter was described in 1792 as a coach road.[71] In 1867 a new bridge carried a road from Braceland to Staunton over Whippington brook below Coalpit hill.[72] In the 17th century wayside crosses apparently marked several road junctions in the parish.[73] Campion's cross was east of the village on Godwin's Lane[74] and the high cross, recorded in 1595, presumably stood west of the village where the road to Coleford turned south.[75]

The Ross–Monmouth railway opened in 1873 crossed the Wye into Bicknor at Stowfield and followed the river before entering a tunnel under Symonds Yat rock to resume a course along the river bank below Mailscot wood.[76] The Severn & Wye railway, completed the following year, ran through Lower Lydbrook to join the Ross–Monmouth line at Stowfield.[77] Stations were built at the junction (Lydbrook Junction) and at Symonds Yat south-west of the tunnel.[78] The Severn & Wye line, on which passenger services ceased in 1929, closed in 1956 and the line between Lydbrook Junction and Monmouth in 1959. The line to Ross was used by goods traffic for a few more years[79] and the bridge over the Wye at Stowfield survived as a footbridge in 1993. Upstream near Lower Lydbrook the church of Welsh Bicknor, which some Lydbrook people attended in 1851,[80] was reached by a ferry across the river in the later 19th century and the early 20th.[81]

Settlement in English Bicknor was scattered throughout the parish and included sites abandoned after the Middle Ages.[82] The older surviving houses are of stone. The village grew up around a Norman castle on a spur in the centre of the parish.[83] The medieval parish church stands in the castle's outer bailey. To the

[56] Hart, *Royal Forest*, 107.
[57] Glos. R.O., D 23/E 29; below, manor.
[58] P.R.O., F 17/117(2), pp. 1, 8–9; MR 691.
[59] Acreage Returns, 1905.
[60] *Glevensis*, xxii. 58–60.
[61] *Trans. B.G.A.S.* xiv. 364–5; P.R.O., MR 879.
[62] Glos. R.O., D 33/63.
[63] P.R.O., MR 879; MR 691; for the chapel, below, church.
[64] Taylor, *Map of Glos.* (1777); Glos. R.O., D 1677/GG 1545, no. 16.
[65] *Trans. B.G.A.S.* xiv. 365; P.R.O., MR 879.
[66] Glos. R.O., P 138/VE 2/1; Q/SRh 1852 C/1; 1853 D; 1855 A/3; 1870 D/2; Machen, 'Hist. Eng. Bicknor', 16; for Edw. Machen, below, manor.
[67] Dean Forest Roads Act, 7 & 8 Geo. IV, c. 12 (Local and Personal); Dean Forest Turnpike Trust Abolition Act, 51 & 52 Vic. c. 193 (Local).
[68] *Trans. B.G.A.S.* iv. 303.

[69] O.S. Maps 6", Glos. XXX. NE., SE. (1883–4 edn.); XXXI. NW. (1883 edn.).
[70] Glos. R.O., Q/SO 4, p. 194.
[71] P.R.O., MR 691.   [72] Ibid. F 14/6.
[73] *Trans. B.G.A.S.* xi. 271, 273; Glos. R.O., D 1677/GG 722.
[74] Glos. R.O., D 1677/GG 477; P.R.O., MR 691.
[75] Glos. R.O., D 33/170; a lower cross was recorded in 1623: ibid. P 138/IN 1/1.
[76] Paar, *G.W.R. in Dean*, 113; O.S. Maps 6", Glos. XXX. NE., SE. (1883–4 edn.).
[77] Paar, *Severn and Wye Railway*, 79.
[78] *Morris's Dir. Glos.* (1876), 493.
[79] Paar, *Severn and Wye Railway*, 87, 94, 116.
[80] P.R.O., HO 129/577/2/1/1.
[81] O.S. Map 6", Glos. XXXI. NW. (1883 and later edns.).
[82] P.R.O., MR 879.
[83] Below, manor.

north-east in the barbican is the former rectory house and to the south-west school buildings dating from the 1830s also encroach on the castle site. In the mid 19th century, when two bridges provided access to the churchyard, part of a ditch was filled in to enlarge the rector's garden and in 1880 part of the castle motte was excavated during work to make a garden for the schoolmaster.[84] South-east of the church a small cluster of buildings in the late 18th century[85] included an inn[86] and the parish or church house, recorded from 1548.[87] Nearby was the pound, recorded in 1725.[88] To the south-west Bicknor House, formerly known as the Great House, dates from the late 18th century when it became the residence of William Ambery (d. 1791).[89] Enlarged in the early 19th century, it was occupied until the mid 1880s by members of the Machen and Davies families.[90] To the west, where the Coleford road turns south, was a farmhouse built probably after 1608[91] and known as Cross House in 1792.[92] A house to the south was rebuilt in 1756.[93] Later buildings in the village included an almshouse, erected in 1858 in place of the inn by the churchyard.[94] In the late 20th century a few houses and bungalows were built at the entrance to the Eastbach road and on the Coleford road.

Further south on the Coleford road building had begun by 1402,[95] and in 1608 there were scattered farmhouses and cottages there and on the Joyford road. On the Coleford road the main range of Whitehouse Farm, John Jordan's residence in 1608,[96] was probably built in the 16th century when its south end was an open hall of three bays. North of the hall was a bay which was defined by stone cross walls and beyond that a room which has been much altered. In the 17th century a lateral stack and an upper floor were put into the hall, the side walls being raised to give the new floor more height. In 1667 a parlour wing was added behind the hall[97] and about that time, if not before, the bay north of the hall was made into a pantry. One of the trusses in the hall was moved northwards when a new stair was put in but the stair, dating from the late 17th century and of high quality, does not appear to be in the position for which it was made. The house, which was part of a freehold estate owned by Henry Davies of Chepstow in

1766, was a farmhouse on the Eastbach estate from 1864[98] until 1962 and it was extensively restored after it became a private house in 1987. A barn, in different ownership from 1987,[99] has been converted as a house and two holiday cottages. Dryslade Farm, further south on the site of a house recorded in 1565,[1] was part of an estate inherited in 1754 by William Lane (d. 1789)[2] and was rebuilt in the 19th century. Nearer the village Cowmeadow Farm was built c. 1820 next to older farm buildings.[3] Bicknor Cottage, to the south, was built in the later 18th century on the site of an inn[4] and became the Machen family's principal residence in 1895.[5] To the south-west an estate of 16 council houses was created south of the entrance to Red House Lane between 1949 and 1952, and in 1993 later houses and bungalows in that area filled the west side of the Coleford road as far as a village hall built in 1934. Eight council houses further south on the road also date from 1934.[6]

A medieval chapel and house by the Coleford road on the hillside south-east of Dryslade Farm had been demolished by the late 18th century.[7] South of Dryslade Farm early dwellings on Bicknor Street included a small farmhouse at the place called Shallis hill.[8] Several more cottages were built on roadside encroachments in the 18th century.[9] Some fell into ruin in the mid 20th century and at least two, including one dated 1745, were pulled down.[10] At Joyford, on the boundary between the former extraparochial land of the Forest and land belonging to English Bicknor and Newland, there were a few cottages and a water mill within Bicknor in 1608.[11] On the Coleford road near the Forest boundary at Short Standing there was a farmhouse called Sterts c. 1356.[12] To the south a house also within Bicknor was occupied in the mid 1830s by the minister of the Berry Hill church[13] and became the Sterts farmhouse in the 20th century.[14]

In the east settlement began at Eastbach before 1221[15] and included several farmhouses and cottages in the Middle Ages.[16] The dwellings, of which at least three were abandoned before 1639,[17] were strung out on the eastern side of the valley. East of Bicknor village, perhaps in the area known in the later 16th century as Nether (or Lower) Eastbach,[18] there were two farmhouses east of the old road from the village

84 *Trans. B.G.A.S.* iv. 303–5; liii. 7–8.
85 P.R.O., MR 691.   86 Ibid. F 17/117(2), p. 29.
87 Ibid. p. 22; Hockaday Abs. cxxii, 1548; G.D.R., V 5/128T 2.
88 P.R.O., F 14/2A, rot. 2d.; F 17/117(2), p. 1.
89 Glos. R.O., D 33/421, deposition 28 Aug. 1840.
90 *Kelly's Dir. Glos.* (1856–89 edns.); *Trans. B.G.A.S.* lxiv. 104.
91 P.R.O., MR 879.
92 Ibid. F 17/117(2), pp. 3–4; MR 691.
93 Date on bldg.; cf. P.R.O., MR 879.
94 Inscr. on bldg.; below, char.
95 Glos. R.O., D 33/63.
96 P.R.O., MR 879.
97 Date with the inits. probably of another John Jordan on wing; cf. G.D.R. wills 1660–1/7.
98 Glos. R.O., D 637/II/6/E 1–2.
99 Inf. from the owner of Whitehouse, Canon B. G. Carne.
1 G.D.R. wills 1565/16.
2 Glos. R.O., D 2957/128.21; cf. ibid. D 2957, abs. of title 110; for Lane, below, Mitcheldean, educ.; *V.C.H. Glos.*

iv. 133.
3 Glos. R.O., D 23/E 38, E 42.
4 Ibid. D 33/421.
5 *Trans. B.G.A.S.* lxiv. 107.
6 Machen, 'Hist. Eng. Bicknor', 9–11.
7 Below, church; *Glos. Subsidy Roll, 1327*, 44; Glos. R.O., D 33/358.
8 Glos. R.O., D 33/420 (abs. of deed in ibid. D 33/223); cf. ibid. D 637/II/6/E 1, plan 1766.
9 P.R.O., F 14/1, ct. 21 June 1774; F 17/117(2), pp. 9–14; MR 691.
10 O.S. Maps 1/2,500, Glos. XXX. 12 (1922 edn.); SO 5713, 5813–14 (1960 edn.); Machen, 'Hist. Eng. Bicknor', 10.
11 P.R.O., MR 879; below, econ. hist.
12 Glos. R.O., D 33/420 (abs. of deed in ibid. D 33/42).
13 P.R.O., F 17/17.
14 Machen, 'Hist. Eng. Bicknor', 13.
15 *Eyre Rolls, 1221–2* (Selden Soc. lix), p. 73.
16 Cf. *Glevensis*, xxii. 60; *Trans. B.G.A.S.* civ. 234.
17 *Trans. B.G.A.S.* xi. 272, 275–6.
18 Glos. R.O., D 33/270, 282; D 1677/GG 437A, 440.

to Lydbrook in the late 18th century.[19] Lower Tump Farm, the older of the two,[20] had belonged to William Bennett (d. 1761)[21] and, to the south, Upper Tump Farm, formerly known as Lewis House, to the Revd. John Benson (d. 1713).[22] In 1910 both farms were in the same ownership[23] and in the late 20th century Upper Tump Farm and its outbuildings, having become dilapidated,[24] were restored. To the south-east, perhaps in the area called Over Eastbach in the later 16th century,[25] the principal building in 1993 was Eastbach Court.[26] At Carterspiece, to the south, a small farmhouse near the Forest boundary in 1608[27] was rebuilt in the late 18th century or the early 19th. By 1758 there were also a few cottages higher up to the northeast on the boundary[28] and in 1993 the hamlet included a new house.

At Stowfield in the north-east settlement began before 1282[29] and there were two or three cottages in 1639.[30] Stowfield Farm, the only house there in the late 18th century, was one of the main farms on the Highmeadow estate[31] and, having been sold by the Crown in 1825,[32] became a freehold estate owned in the late 19th century and the early 20th by the Aldrich-Blake family.[33] A pair of estate cottages was built to the east on the Lydbrook road at Tumps hill in 1872.[34] In the early 20th century H. W. Smith began industrial development at the railway junction near the river bank to the north-west.[35] Stowfield House, which he built on Tumps hill before 1920 in grounds including a lodge on the Lydbrook road,[36] became a boys' home at the end of the Second World War and was a geriatric hospital from 1956[37] to 1993. Enlargement of the house has incorporated an outbuilding in it.[38] In the mid 20th century a small housing estate was created on the hillside north of Stowfield House and a few houses were built further east on the Lydbrook road. Southeast of Stowfield House H. W. Smith built a pair of cottages,[39] and in 1993 a charitable trust opened a residential home for disabled people in new buildings just above the house.[40]

West of English Bicknor village the principal house in the mid 16th century was Bicknor Court.[41] In the early 17th century there was a ruined farmhouse nearby.[42] A later farmhouse standing south-west of the Court was rebuilt in 1862.[43] In the late 18th century there was an old house lower down to the north-east.[44] To the north at Common grove, where encroachments on common land began before 1774,[45] there was a single cottage in 1792.[46] By the 1840s six or seven dwellings had been built there,[47] some of them on Rosemary Topping, the hill to the west.[48] Several fell into ruin and were demolished in the early 20th century[49] and three or four remained in 1993.

In the north-west a number of scattered cottages to the east of Redinhorne, including a timber-framed dwelling of c. 1610 and several older buildings, have disappeared.[50] In 1993 a barn was a camping centre for young people. Cottages were built on extraparochial land adjoining the Coleford–Goodrich road both at Redinhorne and, to the south, at Hillersland.[51] Hillersland Farm, within English Bicknor, was built in the 17th century. To the south-east at Blackthorns Farm, which belonged to the Wyrall family in 1608[52] and became part of the Eastbach estate in 1735,[53] a bungalow was built southwest of the farmhouse in the later 20th century.[54] Within Mailscot cabiners resident in 1628 were expelled.[55] A woodman's lodge was built northwest of Hillersland before 1748.[56]

At Symonds Yat, in the gorge west of the rock, most early houses were on the west side of the river, in Whitchurch parish, where ironworks were built in the 17th century.[57] The settlement, which included houses on the east side of the river on former extraparochial land and on land belonging to Goodrich,[58] was also called New Weir[59] after a weir constructed there in the 1660s. On the extraparochial land, where two cottages were pulled down, probably in the 1630s, on the orders of Crown officials,[60] a lock keeper's house was built near the weir when work to improve the Wye navigation began in the mid 1690s.[61] In the late 18th century a ferry crossed the river below the weir to the ironworks.[62] By 1792 five cottages had been built on encroachments on the eastern side of the gorge[63] and in 1851 there were 12 cottages there belong-

19   P.R.O., F 17/117(2), pp. 23–4; MR 691.
20   Ibid. MR 879.
21   Glos. R.O., D 900; G.D.R. wills 1761/180; Bigland, *Glos.* i. 189.
22   P.R.O., F 14/2A, rot. 2; *Alumni Oxon. 1500–1714*, i. 109; cf. P.R.O., F 14/1; F 17/117(2), pp. 23–4; MR 691.
23   Glos. R.O., D 2428/1/23/3, p. 15.
24   Machen, 'Hist. Eng. Bicknor', 13; O.S. Map 1/2,500, SO 5815 (1960 edn.).   25   Glos. R.O., D 33/270.
26   Below, manor.   27   P.R.O., MR 879.
28   Ibid. F 17/96; F 17/117(2), pp. 20–1; MR 691.
29   Ibid. E 32/30, rot. 19.
30   *Trans. B.G.A.S.* xi. 273, 276.
31   P.R.O., F 17/117(2), pp. 1–2; MR 691.
32   *5th Rep. Com. Woods* (1826), 110.
33   Glos. R.O., Q/RUm 361/2; D 2428/1/23/3, pp. 7–8; Burke, *Land. Gent.* (1937), 179–80.
34   Date, with inits. of F. J. Aldrich-Blake, on bldg.
35   Below, econ. hist.; O.S. Maps 6", Glos. XXX. NE. (1905, 1924 edns.); 1/2,500, SO 5817 (1976 edn.).
36   Glos. R.O., D 2299/2467; O.S. Map 6", Glos. XXXI. NW. (1924 edn.).
37   W.I. hist. of Lydbrook (c. 1959, TS. in Glos. Colln.), 20, 33.
38   Cf. O.S. Map 6", Glos. XXXI. NW. (1924 edn.).
39   Glos. R.O., D 2299/2467.

40   Inf. from secretary, Orchard Trust, Stowfield.
41   Below, manor; P.R.O., MR 879.
42   *Trans. B.G.A.S.* xi. 271.
43   P.R.O., MR 691; F 3/878.
44   Ibid. F 17/117(2), p. 7; MR 691.   45   F 14/1.
46   Ibid. F 17/117(2), p. 11; MR 691.
47   Ibid. HO 107/364; HO 107/2444.
48   G.D.R., T 1/25; O.S. Map 6", Glos. XXX. NE. (1883 edn.).
49   O.S. Map 6", Glos. XXX. NE. (1905, 1924 edns.); Machen, 'Hist. Eng. Bicknor', 15.
50   Glos. R.O., D 33/186; P.R.O., MR 879.
51   Below, Forest of Dean, settlement.
52   Cf. P.R.O., MR 879.   53   Glos. R.O., D 33/189.
54   Ibid. 259; below, manor.
55   Below, Forest of Dean, settlement (intro.).
56   Glos. R.O., D 1677/GG 1238.
57   T. D. Fosbroke, *Wye Tour* (1826), 46; *Kelly's Dir. Herefs.* (1870), 392; below, econ. hist.
58   G.D.R., T 1/25.
59   O.S. Map 6", Glos. XXX. NE. (1883 edn.).
60   Glos. R.O., D 272/1/14.
61   Ibid. D 2079/III/149; S. D. Coates and D. G. Tucker, *Water Mills of Middle Wye Valley* (Monmouth District Mus. Service, 1983), 55.
62   Fosbroke, *Wye Tour*, 47.
63   P.R.O., F 17/117(2), pp. 8–9; MR 691.

ing to English Bicknor.[64] Among buildings erected near the river in the later 19th century, when Symonds Yat had become a popular tourist resort,[65] was the main range of the Rocklea (later Royal) hotel. Another house was adapted as a temperance hotel by 1900[66] and was the Forest View hotel in 1993. Near the rock's summit, a popular viewpoint over the Wye, a refreshment kiosk and picnic site were built in 1956 and additional car parks were provided later.[67] North of the rock, there were three cottages on the Goodrich road in 1792,[68] and a school, a nonconformist chapel, and several more cottages were built in the 19th century.[69]

South-east of Symonds Yat rock there was a cottage on waste land by the river below Coldwell rocks in the early 17th century.[70] Several more cottages were built there in the 18th century[71] and there were perhaps as many as a dozen dwellings, including some in Goodrich, along the river bank in the early 19th century. Several fell into ruin before 1866[72] and some were apparently demolished a few years later to make way for the Ross–Monmouth railway.[73] The last cottage there in Bicknor was abandoned in the early 20th century.[74]

At Braceland a small farmhouse recorded in 1721[75] was a woodman's cottage on the Highmeadow estate in 1792.[76] In 1814 it was rebuilt[77] as a hunting lodge but by the mid 1820s, under the Crown Commissioners of Woods, it housed an assistant to the deputy surveyor of the Forest of Dean.[78] The house, which became a private residence in the 1860s,[79] was a lodging house in the mid 1930s[80] and was converted as an adventure centre for young people by the county education committee in the mid 1960s.[81] To the south in 1851 the hamlet of Coalpit Hill, then regarded as an extraparochial place, contained five dwellings.[82] In 1993 there were two cottages there and a pair of brick cottages, built by the Crown in 1905,[83] to the north-east.

Six tenants were recorded in English Bicknor in 1086[84] and 20 people were assessed there in 1327 for the subsidy.[85] The muster roll of 1539 gives 33 names for the parish,[86] and the number of communicants was estimated at 177 in 1551[87] and 206 in 1603.[88] The figure of 25 households given for the parish in 1563 was clearly an

underestimate.[89] There were said to be 100 families in Bicknor in 1650[90] and the population was estimated c. 1710 at 300 in 60 houses[91] and c. 1775 at 500.[92] The number of inhabitants, 465 in 1801, rose to 598 in 1831 and then fell slightly. The decline was offset partly by the parish's enlargement in 1842, and the population in 1851 was 584. In the later 19th century and the early 20th the population fluctuated, rising to 665 in 1881, dropping to 544 in 1901, and rising again to 671 in 1921. A decline after 1921 was caused mainly by the transfer of more than a third of the inhabitants to the new civil parish of Lydbrook in 1935, and a recovery in population to 523 in 1951 was not sustained. In 1991 Bicknor parish had 416 inhabitants.[93]

Among the alehouses in the parish in the 1660s was one outside the village in the north part of the Coleford road. Known in 1698 as the White Hart, it closed before 1791.[94] In the village the Bear inn, perhaps the victualler's house recorded in 1774,[95] stood next to the churchyard and was the venue for a friendly society in 1787.[96] The principal meeting place in the parish in the early 19th century,[97] it closed c. 1857.[98] A village hall built some way along the Coleford road in 1934[99] was the premises of an association football club in 1993. At Symonds Yat there was an unlicensed alehouse by the river in the 1630s.[1] The Rocklea hotel, the only licensed house there within English Bicknor in the later 19th century,[2] was renamed the Royal hotel in 1901 or 1902.[3]

Before the First World War the history of English Bicknor was dominated by the Bicknor Court, Eastbach, and Highmeadow estates. Charles Machen, the principal landowner from 1893,[4] provided a water supply from a reservoir near Blackthorns Farm to a standpipe in the village.[5]

MANOR AND OTHER ESTATES. An estate of ½ hide in English Bicknor was held by Morganwy in 1066 and by William son of Norman in 1086.[6] Henry I granted land there that had belonged to Wulfric of Dean to Miles of Gloucester c. 1131.[7] Ralph Avenel, who held land in English Bicknor from the Crown in

64 Ibid. HO 107/2444.　　65 Below, econ. hist.
66 O.S. Map 6", Glos. XXX. NE. (1883 and later edns.).
67 Dean Forest & Wye Valley (H.M.S.O. 1974), 88.
68 P.R.O., F 17/117(2), pp. 9–10; MR 691.
69 Below, nonconf.; educ.
70 P.R.O., MR 879; Trans. B.G.A.S. xi. 270.
71 P.R.O., F 14/2A, rot. 2d.; F 17/117(2), pp. 9–14; MR 691.
72 G.D.R., T 1/25; Glos. R.O., Q/RUm 359.
73 O.S. Map 6", Glos. XXX. NE. (1883 edn.).
74 Machen, 'Hist. Eng. Bicknor', 15.
75 Glos. R.O., D 23/T 4.
76 P.R.O., F 17/117(2), p. 6; MR 691.
77 Glos. R.O., D 1677/GG 1545, no. 113; GG 1549.
78 C. Heath, Excursion down the Wye (1826), s.v. Braceland; P.R.O., HO 107/364.
79 Kelly's Dir. Glos. (1863), 266; (1870), 527, 544.
80 Ibid. (1935), 114.
81 Dean Forest & Wye Valley, 20; inf. from warden, the Wilderness, Mitcheldean.
82 P.R.O., HO 107/2444.
83 Inscr. on bldg.
84 Dom. Bk. (Rec. Com.), i. 167v.
85 Glos. Subsidy Roll, 1327, 43–4.
86 L. & P. Hen. VIII, xiv (1), p. 271.
87 E.H.R. xix. 120.　　88 Eccl. Misc. 99.
89 Bodl. MS. Rawl. C. 790, f. 28.
90 Trans. B.G.A.S. lxxxiii. 97.
91 Atkyns, Glos. 279.
92 Rudder, Glos. 289.　　93 Census, 1801–1991.
94 Glos. R.O., Q/SIb 1, ff. 16, 164v.; D 33/421.
95 P.R.O., F 14/1.
96 Glos. R.O., Q/RSf 2; P.R.O., F 17/117(2), p. 29; MR 691.
97 Glouc. Jnl. 10 Oct. 1803; Glos. R.O., P 138/VE 2/1, min. 23 Mar. 1828.
98 Glos. R.O., P 138/IN 1/9, burial 3 Feb. 1856; D 3469/5/59.
99 Machen, 'Hist. Eng. Bicknor', 9.
1 Glos. R.O., D 272/1/14; Hart, Free Miners, 101.
2 O.S. Map 6", Glos. XXX. NE. (1883, 1905 edns.); Licensed Houses in Glos. 1903, 56–7.
3 80th Rep. Com. Woods, H.C. 247, pp. 3–4 (1902), xxi.
4 Below, manor.
5 Glos. R.O., D 33/427; Richardson, Wells and Springs of Glos. 92.
6 Dom. Bk. (Rec. Com.), i. 167v.
7 Reg. Regum Anglo-Norm. ii, no. 1723.

1190,[8] also had custody of a bailiwick in the demesne woodland of the Forest of Dean.[9] He was succeeded c. 1217[10] by his son William Avenel, who obtained seisin of the land, castle, and bailiwick of English Bicknor in 1223.[11] William died c. 1236 holding 2 ploughlands there.[12] In 1282 his successor held the bailiwick[13] and in 1301 the manor of *BICKNOR*, later *ENGLISH BICKNOR*, was held by custody of the bailiwick and by a cash rent paid at Newnham to the bailiffs of St. Briavels.[14] The manor continued to be held for the rent, paid to the holders of St. Briavels castle, and by the office of woodward of Bicknor bailiwick until the 19th century.[15]

William Avenel's daughter and heir Douce became the ward of Robert de Mucegros in 1236 and evidently took the name Cecily and married Robert's son John[16] (d. 1275). Bicknor manor, part of Cecily's inheritance,[17] may have been held in the later 1270s by her son Robert de Mucegros (d. 1280)[18] and at her death c. 1301 it passed to Robert's daughter Hawise, wife of John de Ferrers[19] (d. c. 1312) of Chartley (Staffs.). Hawise and her third husband John de Bures,[20] who was lord of Bicknor in 1316,[21] settled part of the manor in 1330 on their daughter and son-in-law Catherine and Giles Beauchamp (d. 1361)[22] but John held the whole manor after Hawise's death and at his own in 1350, and Hawise's grandson and heir John de Ferrers[23] held it from 1351.[24] John de Ferrers died in 1367 and his wife Elizabeth, who married Reynold of Cobham, held the manor until her death in 1375. It passed to her son Robert de Ferrers,[25] who was granted livery of his inheritance in 1381.[26] Robert was succeeded in 1413 by his son Edmund,[27] who assigned the manor in dower to his mother Margaret in 1413,[28] and Edmund in 1435 by his son William,[29] upon whose marriage the manor was settled in 1442.[30] William died in 1450 and his wife Elizabeth in 1471,[31] and the manor descended through Walter Devereux, Lord Ferrers (d. 1485) and husband of William's daughter Anne (d. 1469), to Walter's son John Devereux, Lord Ferrers, who was granted livery in 1486.[32] From John (d.

1501) the manor passed with the barony of Ferrers to his son Walter. The latter, created Viscount Hereford in 1550, died in 1558 and his grandson and heir Walter Devereux, who became Lord Bourchier in 1571 and earl of Essex in 1572, died in 1576 leaving his son Robert as his heir.[33] English Bicknor manor evidently shared the same descent as the Devereux family titles and after Robert Devereux's execution in 1601 for treason it has held by his wife Frances. She married Richard de Burgh, earl of Clanricarde and, from 1628, of St. Albans,[34] who in 1608 was described as lord of English Bicknor in her right.[35] At Frances's death in 1632 the manor passed to her son Robert Devereux, earl of Essex.[36]

In 1633 the earl of Essex sold the manor to Benedict Hall of Highmeadow,[37] who had already acquired land in the parish.[38] From Benedict the manor, which included land at Whitecliff and elsewhere in Newland parish,[39] descended as part of the Highmeadow estate.[40] In 1726 Viscount Gage, the owner of Highmeadow, sold several farms in Bicknor to John Hopkins.[41] Following its purchase of the Highmeadow estate in 1817 the Crown[42] sold much of its farmland in Bicknor,[43] and in 1840 it retained c. 220 a., mostly woodland, in the ancient parish.[44] The Crown also retained the manorial rights which, together with the woodland, were managed for it in 1993 by the Forestry Commission.[45]

The castle, part of Ralph Avenel's estate in the early 13th century,[46] was a Norman fortification in the centre of the parish. It comprised a motte on the south side of a ditched enclosure with an outer bailey to the north and east and a later barbican to the north, both defended by ditches.[47] The capital messuage recorded in the early 14th century[48] was presumably on part of the site, and in 1627 a building known as castle hall stood near the church,[49] which is in the outer bailey. The hall had been demolished by the late 18th century and a small house south-east of the church, perhaps the remains of the ancient manor house,[50] was pulled down soon afterwards.[51] In 1880 excavation of the castle motte destroyed a small stone chamber.[52]

8   *Pipe R.* 1190 (P.R.S. N.S. i), 57.
9   Ibid. 1199 (P.R.S. N.S. x), 32.
10   *Pat. R.* 1216–25, 127.
11   *Ex. e Rot. Fin.* (Rec. Com.), i. 109.
12   *Cal. Inq. p.m.* i, p. 1.
13   *Trans. B.G.A.S.* xiv. 364.
14   *Cal. Inq. p.m.* iv, p. 9; P.R.O., C 138/2, no. 26.
15   *Cal. Inq. p.m.* xii, p. 117; P.R.O., C 139/75, no. 33; E 315/429, f. 126; F 14/13; Glos. R.O., D 1677/GG 784; D 2026/X 19; D 36/Q 2; *3rd Rep. Com. Woods* (1788), 76.
16   *Trans. B.G.A.S.* iv. 311–17.
17   *Cal. Close,* 1272–9, 172.
18   *Rot. Hund.* (Rec. Com.), i. 176; *V.C.H. Glos.* viii. 190.
19   *Cal. Inq. p.m.* iv, p. 9.
20   *Complete Peerage,* v. 305–8.
21   *Feud. Aids,* ii. 275.
22   P.R.O., CP 25/1/77/57, no. 45; *V.C.H. Glos.* viii. 190.
23   *Cal. Inq. p.m.* ix, p. 402; *Complete Peerage,* v. 313.
24   *Cal. Fine R.* 1347–56, 292.
25   *Cal. Inq. p.m.* xii, pp. 116–17; xiv, p. 102.
26   *Complete Peerage,* v. 315–16.
27   P.R.O., C 138/2, no. 26.
28   *Cal. Close,* 1413–19, 101.
29   P.R.O., C 139/75, no. 33.   30   *Cal. Pat.* 1441–6, 52.
31   *Complete Peerage,* v. 320–1; cf. *Cal. Pat.* 1452–61, 232.

32   *Complete Peerage,* v. 321–5.
33   *Cal. Inq. p.m. Hen. VII,* ii, p. 284; *Complete Peerage,* vi. 478–9; v. 140–1.
34   *Complete Peerage,* iii. 230–1; v. 141–2; Glos. R.O., D 1677/GG 606, 750.
35   Smith, *Men and Armour,* 41.
36   *Complete Peerage,* v. 142; Glos. R.O., D 1677/GG 772.
37   Glos. R.O., D 1677/GG 784, 820.
38   Ibid. GG 666, 758, 783.
39   *Trans. B.G.A.S.* xi. 277.
40   Below, Staunton, manor.
41   Glos. R.O., D 23/T 29; D 3304.
42   Ibid. D 33/425.
43   *4th Rep. Com. Woods* (1823), 96; *5th Rep. Com. Woods* (1826), 108, 110.
44   G.D.R., T 1/25.
45   P.R.O., F 3/727–8; *Kelly's Dir. Glos.* (1939), 166; inf. from asset manager (agric. est.), Crown Estate.
46   *Pat. R.* 1216–25, 127.
47   *Trans. B.G.A.S.* iv. 303–5; liii. 7–8.
48   *Inq. p.m. Glos.* 1236–1300, 230; 1302–58, 341–2.
49   P.R.O., MR 879; Glos. R.O., D 1677/GG 726, 772.
50   P.R.O., F 17/117(2), p. 3; MR 691; Bigland, *Glos.* i. 185.
51   Cf. G.D.R., T 1/25.
52   *Trans. B.G.A.S.* iv. 304; liii. 8.

The church of Hereford had an estate of 3 hides called Whippington, probably on the west side of Mailscot. It formed part of the Herefordshire hundred of Bromsash, but was waste by 1066 and remained so in 1086 when it was said to belong rightly to the bishop of Hereford.[53]

An estate based on *BICKNOR COURT*, known in 1639 as Brooces,[54] may have included land acquired in the 1330s and 1340s by William Breuse. William's son John also acquired land in English Bicknor and his estate there passed to Simon Basset. In 1358 Simon, an M.P., conveyed that estate to John of Pulesdon,[55] presumably a descendant of Nicholas of Pulesdon whose land in the parish was forfeit to the Crown in 1322.[56] In 1392 John's son and heir Alexander sold the estate to John Greyndour of Newland and his wife Isabel[57] and in 1402 they granted it to John Lascelles of Chepstow (d. by 1405) and his wife Margaret. In 1411 Margaret quitclaimed her rights in the estate to Richard Staunton and his wife Florence,[58] and in 1443 Richard Staunton, lord of Staunton, conveyed it to trustees for William Walwyn of Bickerton (Herefs.). In 1454 William conveyed it to John Ashurst, who acquired more land in Bicknor, some of it from William.[59] John Ashurst, who had been appointed constable of St. Briavels in 1449,[60] died c. 1487,[61] and the Bicknor Court estate, which he was later said to have held in the right of his wife Joan, passed to his son Thomas. Thomas (fl. 1508) was succeeded by his brother Philip, who in 1530 sold the estate to John Copinger, but in 1532 a life interest in it was awarded to William Wyrall, who claimed to have bought it from Thomas, his brother-in-law.[62] Copinger took possession following Wyrall's death in 1534 but was expelled by Wyrall's grandson, William Wyrall,[63] to whom Copinger quitclaimed the estate later in 1534. The younger William Wyrall retained the estate in 1549 and his son William settled it in 1574 on the marriage of his son George (d. 1610) to Bridget Winter (d. 1635).[64] Their grandson George Wyrall, who bought land in the parish in 1627,[65] inherited the estate in 1635 and after his death in 1648 it evidently descended in the direct male line to William (d. c. 1661), Jephthah (d. 1702), and George (d. 1726).[66] George left the estate to his mother Martha.[67] She sold some land[68] and after her death in 1739 Bicknor Court apparently passed to her daughters Martha (d. 1750) widow of John Machen, Sarah (d. 1766) wife of Robert Ryder, and Barbara (d. 1745) wife of Richard Davies as joint owners and then to Barbara's son George Davies.[69] George, who changed his surname to Wyrall,[70] owned over 336 a. in the parish in 1792.[71] In 1808 he was succeeded by his daughter Mary Wyrall (d. 1826), under whose will the estate passed to Edward Machen (formerly Davies) and a life interest in Bicknor Court to her companion Mary Ann Davies.[72] In 1832 Edward Machen inherited the Eastbach estate, with which Bicknor Court descended until 1903 when Charles Machen sold the house and c. 266 a. to John Gunter of Huntsham, in Goodrich (Herefs.).[73] Gunter died in 1904[74] and his trustees retained Bicknor Court and its lands. From the 1920s the estate had a succession of owners[75] before Edward Gwilliam bought it in 1968. In 1977 Bicknor Court was sold with 33 a. to V. A. Fisher and in 1986 it was bought by Mr. A. J. Johnston.[76]

The late-medieval Bicknor Court, from which John Copinger's agent was evicted by William Wyrall in 1534[77] and which a tenant occupied in 1541,[78] probably included the two lower floors at the west end of the present north front of the stone house. In 1574, when Wyrall's son William retained the hall of the house for his own use, there were rooms to the south, possibly in a wing, and a detached gatehouse,[79] and in 1608 the house apparently had a U-shaped plan open to the east and there was a garden to the south and a walled rabbit warren to the north.[80] The hall was presumably the present kitchen, on the north side next to the medieval part of the house. Its large stone fireplace, decorated with lozenges, dates from the mid 17th century and in the north-east room contemporary panelling, decorated similarly on its frieze, may be in situ or may have come from the hall. The stair hall and the room to the south are of the later 17th century. The house, for which Jephthah Wyrall's uncle George Wyrall was assessed on three hearths in 1672,[81] was occupied by tenants in the late 17th century.[82] In the late 18th century an east front of five bays and three storeys was built and a new staircase was installed as part of a general refitting for George Wyrall, who later used the house as an occasional

53 *Dom. Bk.* (Rec. Com.), i. 182; *Trans. B.G.A.S.* cv. 123.
54 *Trans. B.G.A.S.* xi. 271.
55 Glos. R.O., D 33/23–5, 30, 64, 420 (abs. of deeds in ibid. D 33/31, 33, 35–6, 40, 45).
56 *Cal. Fine R.* 1319–27, 97, 175; cf. P.R.O., E 142/31, rot. 5.
57 Glos. R.O., D 33/420 (abs. of deed in ibid. D 33/59).
58 Ibid. D 33/64–5, 72.
59 Ibid. 106, 110–11, 112B–113, 118–19.
60 Below, Forest of Dean, wardens.
61 Hockaday Abs. cxxii.
62 P.R.O., REQ 1/5, ff. 170–173v.; REQ 2/3/97; J. Maclean, 'Remarks on Manor and Advowson of Eng. Bicknor', *Trans. B.G.A.S.* i. 89–91; *Trans. B.G.A.S.* lxiii. 199–200.
63 P.R.O., STAC 2/9, no. 183; Hockaday Abs. cclxv; for Wyrall fam. pedigrees, Rudder, *Glos.* 288–9; *Trans. B.G.A.S.* i. 68–9.
64 Glos. R.O., D 33/139, 143, 153.
65 Ibid. D 1677/GG 714A.
66 Ibid. D 33/241, 244, 420 (abs. of deeds in ibid. D 33/204, 206–8, 223); G.D.R. wills 1702/60; Bigland, *Glos.* i. 189.
67 G.D.R. wills 1729/494.
68 Glos. R.O., D 33/259–60.
69 G.D.R. wills 1738/26; Bigland, *Glos.* i. 188.
70 Rudge, *Hist. of Glos.* ii. 389.
71 P.R.O., F 17/117(2), pp. 17–19.
72 Mon. in church; Glos. Colln RR 128.1, in which T. T. Matthews claimed the est. in 1884 by inheritance; *Trans. B.G.A.S.* i. 91–3, which gives an incorrect date for Geo. Wyrall's death.
73 Below, this section; Glos. R.O., D 33/427.
74 Glos. R.O., P 138/IN 1/9.
75 *Kelly's Dir. Glos.* (1910 and later edns.); Machen, 'Hist. Eng. Bicknor', 7, 11.
76 Inf. from Mr. Johnston. 77 P.R.O., STAC 2/9, no. 183.
78 Glos. R.O., D 33/358.
79 Ibid. 153.
80 P.R.O., MR 879.
81 Ibid. E 179/247/14, rot. 39d.; *Trans. B.G.A.S.* i, pedigree at pp. 68–9.
82 Glos. R.O., D 33/248, 250, 256.

residence.[83] After Mary Ann Davies's death in 1858 the house was occupied by tenants, including from 1876 Sir John Maclean, a retired civil servant and antiquary,[84] and between 1883 and 1895 it was the residence of its owners, the Machens.[85]

Land at *EASTBACH* was held under English Bicknor manor by Alexander Baynham (d. 1524)[86] and descended with an estate in Mitcheldean to Joseph Baynham.[87] Joseph, the owner in 1608,[88] died in 1613 and his son and heir Alexander[89] had sold all or part of the Eastbach land to Edward Machen of Gloucester by 1616. In 1633 Edward settled his Eastbach estate on his son Richard (d. 1673) and in 1675 it was settled on Richard's widow Mary.[90] From Mary (d. 1678)[91] it passed to her son Edward Machen of Abenhall (d. 1708), who left it to his daughter Elizabeth, wife of Thomas Tomkins (d. 1711).[92] Elizabeth (d. 1712) was succeeded by her brother Richard Machen (d. 1735), from whom the estate, including lands he had purchased from John Hopkins and others, passed to his brother Edward.[93] Edward, who had bought Blackthorns farm in English Bicknor in 1730,[94] was succeeded at his death in 1740 by his nephew Edward Tomkins.[95] The nephew took the additional surname of Machen and died in 1778 leaving the estate in turn to his wife Hannah (d. 1789) and James Davies.[96] James, who took the surname Machen under the terms of Edward's will but sometimes used that of Davies,[97] owned over 453 a. in the parish in 1792.[98] He became deputy surveyor of the Forest of Dean in 1806.[99] At his death in 1832 the Eastbach estate passed to his son Edward Machen[1] (formerly Davies), who was deputy surveyor from 1808 until 1854.[2] Edward, who had purchased 350 a. in the parish from the Crown and had inherited the Bicknor Court estate in the 1820s,[3] died in 1862[4] and was succeeded by his son Edward, rector of Staunton. Edward (d. 1893) left the estate in turn to his wife Sophia (d. 1893) and son Charles[5] (d. 1917), who sold Bicknor Court and its land[6] and was succeded in turn by his wife Lucy (d. 1932) and son Henry. The estate, which was further reduced by sales after 1917,[7] passed from Henry (d. 1958)[8] to his son and daughter, James Machen and Joan Agutter, and they sold the remaining part.[9] Eastbach Court and most of the land were purchased by the tenant Ernest Knight and in 1964 were bought by the Symonds family, which having built a new house higher up to the south-east, sold Eastbach Court and *c.* 12 ha. (*c.* 30 a.) to David Rowe-Beddoe in 1989 and retained *c.* 101 ha. (*c.* 250 a.) in 1993.[10]

The house called Eastbach Court in 1639[11] was presumably on the site of the messuage owned by Alexander Baynham in 1524[12] and of the present stable block, in the south end of which are moulded beams of the later 16th century. The house, occupied by Sir Robert Woodruff in 1608[13] and by Edward Machen's brother-in-law George Wyrall in 1633,[14] was assessed on six hearths in 1672.[15] The date 1723 on the stable weathervane may refer to work undertaken a few years before the building of the present house.[16] The house, built of ashlar, has main fronts of five bays, that to the west having a rusticated ground floor with prominent keystones and a pedimented doorcase, and the interior retains its original staircase and panelled rooms.[17] A service wing to the north was added in the early 19th century, and following James Machen's death in 1832 his wife Lucy kept the house with *c.* 100 a. until her death in 1855.[18] The Machen family lived at Eastbach Court until 1883.[19] There are 18th- and 19th-century barns to the south.

Mailscot wood, adjoining the parish on the west, was part of the royal demesne of the Forest until 1625 when it was granted to Sir Edward Villiers for £20 a year. He died in 1626 and Mailscot was held for a time by his wife Barbara. His son and heir William became Viscount Grandison while a minor in 1630 and died in 1643 leaving an only child Barbara. She married Roger Palmer, created earl of Castlemaine in 1661, and, having become mistress to Charles II, was created duchess of Cleveland in 1670. In 1676 she sold Mailscot to Henry Benedict Hall,[20] with whose Highmeadow etate it descended.

[83] Bigland, *Glos.* i. 185; Brayley and Britton, *Beauties of Eng. and Wales*, v. 716; cf. P.R.O., F 17/117(2), p. 18.
[84] Glos. R.O., D 2299/748; P 138/IN 1/9; *Kelly's Dir. Glos.* (1856–85 edns.); for Maclean, *Trans. B.G.A.S.* xix. 168–9; I. Gray, *Antiquaries of Glos. and Bristol* (B.G.A.S. 1981), 110.   [85] *Trans. B.G.A.S.* lxiv. 106.
[86] P.R.O., C 142/42, no. 112.
[87] Ibid. C 142/149, no. 129; C 142/164, no. 62; below, Mitcheldean, manor.
[88] P.R.O., MR 879.
[89] Ibid. C 142/335, no. 32.
[90] Glos. R.O., D 33/276; D 1677/GG 656; for the Machens, H. A. Machen, 'Machen Fam.' *Trans. B.G.A.S.* lxiv. 96–112.   [91] Bigland, *Glos.* i. 188.
[92] G.D.R. wills 1709/59; *Trans. B.G.A.S.* lxiv. 101.
[93] P.R.O., PROB 11/675 (P.C.C. 13 Derby), ff. 106–108v.   [94] Glos. R.O., D 33/259.
[95] G.D.R. wills 1740/216.
[96] Ibid. 1780/53.   [97] Glos. R.O., D 1833/T 6.
[98] P.R.O., F 17/117(2), pp. 15–17.
[99] Ibid. LR 4/20/5.
[1] Glos. R.O., P 138/IN 1/9; D 637/II/6/E 2.
[2] Ibid. LR 4/20/5.
[3] *4th Rep. Com. Woods* (1823), 96; *5th Rep. Com. Woods* (1826), 108; above, this section.
[4] Nicholls, *Personalities of Dean*, 90.

[5] Glos. R.O., D 33/437.   [6] Above, this section.
[7] *Trans. B.G.A.S.* lxiv. 108; Glos. R.O., D 33/427.
[8] Mon. in church.
[9] Burke, *Land. Gent.* (1937), 1469; inf. from Canon Carne.
[10] Inf. from Mr. John Symonds and Mr. and Mrs. Rowe-Beddoe.   [11] *Trans. B.G.A.S.* xi. 271.
[12] P.R.O., C 142/42, no. 112.   [13] Ibid. MR 879.
[14] Glos. R.O., D 1677/GG 778; *Trans. B.G.A.S.* lxiv, pedigree at pp. 96–7.
[15] P.R.O., E 179/247/13, rot. 24.
[16] *Trans. B.G.A.S.* lxiv. 102–3, which mentions an account book detailing building work in the 1760s after a fire; cf. Bigland, *Glos.* i. 185.
[17] A staircase of identical design at Frampton Court has been attributed to the Bristol architect John Strahan: *V.C.H. Glos.* x. 145–6; H. Colvin, *Biog. Dict. of Brit. Architects* (1978), 787–8; similar staircases of *c.* 1730 are at Hagloe House (above, Awre, manors), Newland House (below, Newland, manors), and the Victoria hotel, Newnham (*V.C.H. Glos.* x. 33).
[18] G.D.R., T 1/25; Glos. R.O., D 1833/T 6; P 138/IN 1/9.   [19] *Trans. B.G.A.S.* lxiv. 105–6.
[20] Glos. R.O., D 23/E 29; *Complete Peerage*, iii. 280–2; vi. 75; C. E. Hart, *Commoners Of Dean Forest* (1951), 25. Payment of the £20 rent lapsed long before 1681: *Cal. Treas. Bks.* 1681–2, 165, 342.

The wood covered 728 a. in 1792[21] and it remained part of the Crown's Highmeadow woods, managed by the Forestry Commission, in 1993.

ECONOMIC HISTORY. In 1086 William son of Norman's Bicknor estate had half a ploughteam with six bordars in demesne and since 1066 its value had doubled to 10s.[22] In 1220, by which time much more land was probably being cultivated, there were nine ploughteams in Bicknor.[23] At least one ploughland lay barren in 1383.[24] The manorial demesne, which comprised two ploughlands in 1236, included 120 a. of arable and 8 a. of meadow in 1301[25] and 60 a. of arable and 3 a. of meadow in 1351.[26] The meadow land was on the southern bank of the river Wye and its fertility was enhanced by occasional flooding.[27]

In the Middle Ages there were several open fields near the village, notably to the south-west where Horemore field adjoined Mailscot wood in the 13th century.[28] Ockwall field, north of Horemore field,[29] and Crows field were recorded in the early 15th century[30] and Windmill field, north of the village, in 1608.[31] Pye meadow, south of the village, was under arable crops in 1568[32] and was described as a common field in 1608.[33] In the 1560s there was an open field at Eastbach called Turn field.[34] Inclosure of the fields was evidently piecemeal[35] and parts of Horemore, Ockwall, and Windmill fields survived in the early 17th century together with a small open field by the Joyford road in the south.[36] In the 1630s the parishioners had pasture rights in three small commons within English Bicknor[37] and ran cattle on the extraparochial land of the Forest.[38] Earlier, sheep had also been pastured on the Forest waste.[39] In 1725 tenants in the parish claimed common rights for cattle and pigs in the Forest for a yearly payment of 2s.[40] Later the parish paid 1s. herbage money for common rights there,[41] and three landholders exercised them in 1860.[42] In 1631 new enclosures in Mailscot were destroyed by mobs of local people anxious to preserve their common rights[43] but the Dean reafforestation Act of 1668 confirmed that Mailscot, granted away by the Crown in 1625, had ceased to be subject to such rights.[44] Apples, turnips, beans, and peas were grown in the parish in the early 17th century.[45] In 1636 two farmers on the Bicknor Court estate in the Hillersland area were required to plant specific numbers of fruit trees, mostly crabs.[46] Plums were also cultivated before 1685,[47] and in the early 19th century English Bicknor was said to have excellent orchards of cider apples and other fruit.[48] Under a share-cropping agreement of 1655 a tenant of the Bicknor Court estate undertook to plant hops in a field near Redinhorne.[49] Hop cultivation continued in 1685,[50] and in 1792 a field adjoining orchards next to Millway grove, north-east of the village, was known as the Hop Yard.[51]

The manor included £23 7s. 7¼d. in rents from 124 free tenants in 1301[52] and 20s. in rents from 16 free tenants in 1351.[53] In the early 17th century the majority of parishioners followed non-agricultural trades and of 80 listed in 1608 only 9 were described as yeomen and 10 as husbandmen.[54] In 1639 the manor received rents from 31 freeholders in the parish and, by custom, a single heriot on the death of each freeholder with one or more dwellings.[55] In the mid 17th century tenants on the Bicknor Court estate had leases for life or lives and paid rents of hens or capons besides cash rents.[56] Many chief rents owed to the lord of the manor were redeemed in the late 1860s.[57]

In 1792 there were three farms of more than 240 a. in the parish, three farms of c. 140–200 a., nine farms of c. 50–100 a., and one farm of 23 a. Of the farms on the Highmeadow estate Stowfield (261 a.) and Cross House (199 a.) were held by leases renewed in 1793 for 16 years and Carterspiece (58 a.) was held at will. The farmland at Braceland was attached to Broomhill farm, to the south-east in Coleford tithing of Newland. The largest farm in English Bicknor was the home farm of the Eastbach estate covering 285 a.[58] Most of the 41 agricultural occupiers recorded in the parish in 1896 were tenant farmers,[59] and in the early 20th century the Eastbach estate included a farm of 345 a., three farms with 123–157 a., three farms with 55–99 a., three farms with 10–39 a., and several smaller holdings.[60] Also in the parish at that time

21 Below, Staunton, manor; P.R.O., F 17/117(2), pp. 1–14; Glos. R.O., D 33/425.
22 *Dom. Bk.* (Rec. Com.), i. 167v.
23 *Bk. of Fees*, i. 308.
24 *Cal. Inq. p.m.* xv, pp. 290–1.
25 *Inq. p.m. Glos.* 1236–1300, I, 231.
26 Ibid. 1302–58, 342.
27 *Cal. Inq. p.m.* xii, p. 117.
28 Glos. R.O., D 33/6.
29 P.R.O., MR 879.
30 Glos. R.O., D 33/63, 91, 93, 355.
31 P.R.O., MR 879.
32 Glos. R.O., D 33/151.
33 P.R.O., MR 879.
34 Glos. R.O., D 1677/GG 440, 446.
35 Ibid. D 33/88.
36 P.R.O., MR 879.
37 *Trans. B.G.A.S.* xi. 270–1.
38 Ibid. i. 77–8.
39 G.D.R. vol. 122, depositions 4, 15 Apr. 1616.
40 P.R.O., F 14/2A, rot. 2d.
41 Nicholls, *Forest of Dean*, 124; *5th Rep. Dean Forest Com.* 67.
42 P.R.O., F 3/128, letter 29 Nov. 1860.
43 Hist. MSS. Com. 23, *12th Rep. I, Cowper*, i, pp. 429–30; *Acts of P.C.* 1630–1, pp. 284–5; *Cal. S.P. Dom. 1631–3*, 4.
44 Hart, *Royal Forest*, 294.
45 G.D.R. vol. 122, depositions 15 Apr. 1616.
46 Glos. R.O., D 33/420 (abs. of deeds in ibid. D 33/207–8).
47 Ibid. D 33/248.
48 Bigland, *Glos.* i. 185; Brayley and Britton, *Beauties of Eng. and Wales*, v. 716.
49 Glos. R.O., D 33/420 (abs. of deed in ibid. D 33/224).
50 Ibid. D 33/248.
51 Ibid. D 177, Pencoyd and Eng. Bicknor draft deed 1792; Q/SRh 1855 A/3.
52 *Inq. p.m. Glos.* 1236–1300, 231.
53 Ibid. 1302–58, 342.
54 Smith, *Men and Armour*, 41–3.
55 *Trans. B.G.A.S.* xi. 270–7.
56 Glos. R.O., D 33/420 (abs. of deeds in ibid. D 33/215, 217–19, 223, 234, 244).
57 P.R.O., F 14/6.
58 Ibid. F 17/117(2), pp. 1–8, 15–32, 42–3; MR 691.
59 Ibid. MAF 68/1609/6.
60 Glos. R.O., D 33/423.

were three farms with over 200 a. and one with 140 a.[61] Of 20 agricultural holdings recorded in 1926 a majority were worked by tenants and one had over 300 a., three over 150 a., four over 100 a., and nine under 50 a. Together the farms provided regular employment for 36 labourers.[62] Most of the farmers owned their land in 1988, when of 16 agricultural holdings returned for the parish seven had 20 ha. (c. 50 a.) or less, five had 50 ha. (c. 123 a.) or more, and another two had 100 ha. (c. 247 a.) or more. Most of the smaller farms were worked on a part-time basis.[63]

If it was true that the parish had a very small area under arable crops c. 1775,[64] much land came under the plough in the late 18th century.[65] In 1784 the farm at Bicknor Court was devoted equally to tillage and pasture and a farm at Short Standing was predominantly arable.[66] In 1792 the parish contained over 1,200 a. of arable, 325 a. of meadow, and 330 a. of pasture.[67] Wheat and barley were the main arable crops in 1801 when 631 a. were said to be growing corn, legumes, or roots.[68] In the late 1830s the acreages of arable, meadow, and pasture were much the same as they had been in 1792,[69] but by 1866, when 733 a. were permanently under grass and large flocks of sheep were kept, the area under crop rotation, growing mainly wheat, barley, turnips, and grass seeds, had contracted to 1,158 a. In addition to the sheep, which numbered 1,441, small herds of beef and dairy cattle and pigs were kept.[70] More land was turned to permanent grass in the later 19th century and the early 20th century, 1,286 a. being returned as permanent grassland and 473 a. as crops in rotation in 1926. During that period the dairy herds were enlarged, 103 dairy cattle being returned in 1926[71] compared with 40 in 1866,[72] and in the early 20th century the flocks, which had decreased in size by 1896, were enlarged considerably, 2,157 sheep being returned in 1926. Orchards covered at least 75 a. in 1896 and 43 a. in 1926. Commercial poultry farming, which had been introduced by 1926,[73] continued in the late 1980s, when most land in the parish remained under grass and the principal farms were devoted to sheep, dairy, and beef farming.[74]

In 1200 Ralph Avenel had a grant of a Monday market at English Bicknor[75] but no later record of it has been found.

Many inhabitants have lived by working the natural resources of the parish and the adjoining Forest. Ironmaking began in or near English Bicknor long before 1217[76] when Ralph Avenel had two itinerant forges in English Bicknor or the adjoining Crown woodland.[77] As many as four such forges worked simultaneously in that area later in the 13th century.[78] The early ironworks left behind substantial heaps of cinders in the parish,[79] one tip being at a field known in 1565 as Cinderhill close.[80] Removal of cinders for resmelting evidently began before 1621 when Benedict Hall reserved those on his land at Braceland for his own use,[81] and by agreement in 1692 cinders were to be dug on the Bicknor Court estate and sent to Parkend and ironworks at Bishopswood and Blakeney.[82] Deposits of cinders had still not been exhausted by 1800.[83] Charcoal burning was recorded in 1184[84] and took place over many centuries in Mailscot wood, where there were at least nine charcoal pits in 1279[85] and where much timber was felled for charcoaling and mining operations in the late 1620s.[86] A charcoal burner was active in the woods on Rosemary Topping just before the First World War.[87] Trades supported by local woodland were represented in the early 17th century by carpenters, turners, a cooper, and makers of cardboard, platters, saddletrees, and trenchers.[88] In 1656 a timberman lived at Carterspiece[89] and in 1744 two men living near Hangerberry were woodcutters.[90]

Lime was made in Bicknor for local use in building and farming by the early 17th century[91] and field names of the late 18th century indicate that limekilns had operated in many places.[92] The limestone crags above the Wye have been extensively quarried: at Symonds Yat a miner had a kiln in the late 17th century[93] and quarries operated in the late 18th century.[94] A kiln below Coldwell rocks continued in use in the mid 19th century[95] as did kilns at Stowfield and Common grove.[96] Kilns were also built north-east of the village on the east side of Millway grove.[97] Lime was burnt at Common grove in the late 1930s.[98] Among quarries worked after the First World War was one at Eastbach.[99] Sand and gravel were dug at Redinhorne before 1577[1] and in the early 20th century,[2] and land near Joyford was called the Clay Pits in 1608.[3] Stoneworking in Mailscot

[61] Ibid. D 2428/1/23/3, pp. 5, 7, 12–13, 15.
[62] P.R.O., MAF 68/3295/6.
[63] Agric. Returns 1988.   [64] Rudder, Glos. 288.
[65] Cf. Bigland, Glos. i. 185.
[66] Glouc. Jnl. 13 Dec. 1784.
[67] P.R.O., F 17/117(2), pp. 1–8, 15–29.
[68] List & Index Soc. clxxxix, p. 171.
[69] G.D.R., T 1/25.
[70] P.R.O., MAF 68/25/9; MAF 68/26/8.
[71] Ibid. MAF 68/1609/6; MAF 68/3295/6.
[72] Ibid. MAF 68/25/9.
[73] Ibid. MAF 68/1609/6; MAF 68/3295/6.
[74] Agric. Returns 1988.
[75] Rot. Chart. (Rec. Com.), 79.
[76] Cf. New Regard of Forest of Dean, iii. 50–3.
[77] Rot. Litt. Claus. (Rec. Com.), i. 334–5.
[78] P.R.O., E 146/1/25; E 32/29, rot. 2; E 32/30, rot. 23d.; E 32/31, m. 16.
[79] Rudge, Hist. of Glos. ii. 88, 385.
[80] G.D.R. wills 1565/16.
[81] Glos. R.O., D 1677/GG 673.

[82] Ibid. D 33/251.
[83] Rudge, Hist. of Glos. ii. 88, 385.
[84] Pipe R. 1184 (P.R.S. xxxiv), 148.
[85] Hart, Royal Forest, 45.   [86] Ibid. 101, 107.
[87] A. O. Cooke, Forest of Dean (1913), 142–51.
[88] Smith, Men and Armour, 42–3; P.R.O., E 137/13/4; E 178/3837, depositions 1614; Glos. R.O., D 33/198.
[89] Glos. R.O., D 33/420 (abs. of deed in ibid. D 33/227).
[90] Ibid. D 1677/GG 1253.
[91] Ibid. D 33/189.
[92] P.R.O., F 17/117(2), pp. 1–8, 22–7; MR 691.
[93] Glos. R.O., D 23/E 35, surv. of river Wye; D 272/1/14, ct. 21 June 1688.
[94] Fosbroke, Wye Tour, 44.
[95] Glos. R.O., D 23/E 38; P.R.O., HO 107/364.
[96] Glos. R.O., D 637/II/6/E 4; G.D.R., T 1/25.
[97] Personal observation.
[98] Machen, 'Hist. Eng. Bicknor', 19.
[99] Glos. R.O., D 33/424.   [1] Ibid. D 1677/GG 483.
[2] Machen, 'Hist. Eng. Bicknor', 21.
[3] P.R.O., MR 879.

included a millstone quarry in the west, near the river Wye.[4]

One miner was recorded in English Bicknor in 1608[5] and coal was dug near Blackthorns Farm a few years later for use in making lime.[6] The inclosure of Mailscot by the Villiers family was made partly in order to mine coal there, and in the riots of 1631 colliers were attacked and pits filled in.[7] Those pits may have been on Coalpit hill, which was known by that name in 1792.[8] In the 18th and 19th centuries coal was mined in the western part of the parish, including on Wormall hill where Farmer's Folly colliery worked intermittently.[9] In the mid 1830s mining resumed on Coalpit hill,[10] and in 1851 12 of the 15 miners resident in English Bicknor lived at Joyford.[11] In Mailscot wood Highmeadow colliery, west of Hillersland, had a tramway and rope-worked incline down to the river Wye and the Ross–Monmouth railway in 1878; it closed before 1900.[12] Small-scale mining continued intermittently at Short Standing and Hillersland until after the Second World War and Farmer's Folly colliery was in production in 1955. The re-opened Highmeadow colliery was among several mines worked in the early 1940s.[13]

The earliest mills known to have belonged to English Bicknor, a corn mill and a fulling mill on the manor in 1301,[14] were presumably at Lydbrook, which became an industrial centre with mills and, from the late 16th century, ironworks.[15] In 1608 William Parlour operated a corn mill in the south at Joyford.[16] Its water supply was improved in 1675[17] and the mill was sold to John Morgan in 1677 and to Richard Hawkins of Coleford in 1685.[18] In the mid 19th century it was worked by William Copner[19] (d. 1876).[20] It ceased operating in the mid 1890s[21] and the building and adjoining mill house survived in 1993. Field names recorded in 1608 may indicate the sites of a water mill north-east of the village towards Stowfield and a windmill north of the village.[22] In the early 18th century the Bicknor Court estate included a corn mill[23] and in 1792 there was a cider mill by the Wye at Coldwell rocks.[24]

In the later 16th century the usual rural trades and crafts were found in Bicknor[25] and in 1608 parishioners included three tailors, two shoemakers, a butcher, a hatter, a saddler, and a smith. Some trades recorded in 1608, notably those of an ironworker, a tanner, a dyer, and three weavers,[26] were presumably associated with industries at Lydbrook.[27] Among parishioners were a glover in 1629,[28] a feltmaker in 1648,[29] and a nailer in 1706.[30] In 1664 a Ruardean basket maker obtained a lease to cultivate osier beds in the river at Stowfield[31] and in 1841 one person living below Coldwell rocks and two people living at Coalpit Hill practised the same craft.[32] Gloucestershire inhabitants at Symonds Yat (or New Weir) earning a living from trade on the Wye included two watermen and a barge master in 1851[33] and a boatman in 1905,[34] and a few barges and trows were built there, perhaps on the west side of the river, between 1808 and 1856.[35] Tourists visited Symonds Yat by river from the late 18th century[36] and following the opening of a railway station there in the mid 1870s hotels and refreshment rooms were built on both sides of the river[37] to cater for the influx of visitors.[38] In 1993 a summer tourist industry and adventure activities, including canoeing, continued to thrive there.

H. W. Smith & Co., formed by 1910 to make electric wire and cable,[39] moved from works at Trafalgar colliery in the Forest to a factory, begun in 1912, by the railway junction at Stowfield. Known as the Lydbrook cable works, the factory was enlarged considerably during the First World War when it employed 650 people and mainly produced cable for field telephones.[40] Acquired by the Edison Swan Electric Co. in the mid 1920s, the works later employed up to 1,200 from an area including Cinderford and Ross-on-Wye (Herefs.) to make power cables[41] and closed in 1965 with the loss of 840 jobs. The factory was taken over the following year by Reed Corrugated Cases Ltd.,[42] a manufacturer of boxes and other packaging materials, known from 1991 as SCA Packaging Ltd., and it em-

4 *New Regard of Forest of Dean*, iv. 57–8.
5 Smith, *Men and Armour*, 43.
6 Glos. R.O., D 33/189.
7 Hist. MSS. Com. 23, *12th Rep. I, Cowper*, i, pp. 429–30; Hart, *Commoners of Dean*, 26.
8 P.R.O., F 17/117(2), pp. 4, 8–9; MR 691.
9 G.D.R. wills 1728/111; Taylor, *Map of Glos.* (1777); *Glouc. Jnl.* 14 Jan. 1793; *Award of Dean Forest Mining Com.* (1841), 56–7, 142–5, 165–6; Sopwith, *Map of Dean Forest* (1835); Glos. R.O., Q/RUm 173/1, plan A 1; D 637/II/6/E 7.
10 *Award of Dean Forest Mining Com.* (1841), 65.
11 P.R.O., HO 107/2444.
12 O.S. Map 6", Glos. XXX. SE. (1884, 1903 edns.); Paar, *G.W.R. in Dean*, 151.
13 O.S. Map 6", Glos. XXX. SE. (1903, 1924 edns.); *Geol. of Forest of Dean Coal and Iron-Ore Field* (H.M.S.O. 1942), 38; Glos. R.O., D 33/424.
14 *Inq. p.m. Glos. 1236–1300*, 230–1.
15 Below, Forest of Dean, industry (ironworks; mills).
16 Smith, *Men and Armour*, 43; P.R.O., C 66/2168, no. 3.
17 Glos. R.O., D 1677/GG 979.
18 Ibid. D 3269, Joyford Mill deeds 1638–1707.
19 P.R.O., HO 107/364.
20 Glos. R.O., P 138/IN 1/9.
21 *Kelly's Dir. Glos.* (1894), 150; (1897), 153; O.S. Map 6", Glos. XXX. SE. (1903 edn.).

22 P.R.O., MR 879.
23 Ibid. CP 25/2/1015/3 Geo. I East. no. 21.
24 Ibid. F 17/117(2), p. 11; MR 691.
25 Glos. R.O., D 33/160, 170; D 1677/GG 440, 534.
26 Smith, *Men and Armour*, 42–3.
27 Below, Forest of Dean, industry (ironworks; mills; other ind. and trade).
28 Glos. R.O., D 891.   29 Ibid. D 33/282.
30 Ibid. D 2957/128.5.   31 Ibid. D 1677/GG 937.
32 P.R.O., HO 107/364, s.vv. Eng. Bicknor, Worcester walk.
33 Ibid. HO 107/2444.   34 Glos. R.O., D 33/424.
35 Farr, *Chepstow Ships*, 84, 159, 179.
36 Fosbroke, *Wye Tour*, 37–48.
37 *Morris's Dir. Glos.* (1876), 493; *Kelly's Dir. Herefs.* (1885), 1245; *Kelly's Dir. Glos.* (1902), 157; (1910), 162.
38 P.R.O., F 3/824.
39 *Kelly's Dir. Glos.* (1910), 241.
40 *Dean Forest Mercury*, 14 Nov. 1919; according to K. S. Woods, *Development of Country Towns in SW. Midlands during the 1960s* (Oxf., 1968), 56, the factory was built in 1908.
41 Woods, *Country Towns in SW. Midlands*, 57; Glos. R.O., D 3921/III/7.
42 *Citizen* (Glouc.), 23 Sept. 1964; H. Phelps, *Forest of Dean* (1982), 24.

ployed 450 people in 1985 and 270 in 1993.[43] Temco Ltd., established by H. W. Smith in the early 1920s to make fine stainless steel wire, had a factory near the cable works[44] and employed 107 people in 1985 when the firm moved to Cinderford.[45]

The Wye fishery belonging to English Bicknor manor in the late 13th century[46] presumably extended, as it did in 1639, from Lydbrook down to Coldwell.[47] It included a weir,[48] which was decayed in the late 16th century[49] and was presumably just below Stowfield adjoining the field known in 1608 as Weir field.[50] Fishing rights between Lydbrook and Stowfield, which apparently did not belong to the manor in 1725,[51] were acquired, under a grant of 1874, from the Crown by the owner of Stowfield farm.[52] The bishops of Hereford, who had a fishery in the Wye at Whippington in 1086,[53] retained a weir, called Bishop's weir, adjoining Mailscot in the late 13th century.[54] The priory of Llanthony Prima, owner of a fishery downstream, at Hadnock (later Mon.),[55] kept a boat at Bishop's weir in 1282. Upstream William de Valence had a weir at Symonds Yat in 1282. That weir, described as being under Doward[56] in Whitchurch (Herefs.), may have been the ancient weir on the remains of which New weir was constructed south-west of Symonds Yat rock in the 1660s. In the mid 1680s New weir was raised to provide power for ironworks on the Herefordshire side and a sluice or lock on the Gloucestershire side was filled in. That work obstructed barges and reduced salmon stocks in the river,[57] and under an Act of 1696 to improve the Wye navigation the weir's owner, the earl of Kent, opened a new lock on the Gloucestershire side. Further grants of fishing rights in the river by the earl, lord of Goodrich manor, were to be void[58] but in the early 18th century his successor, the duke of Kent, disputed the fishery adjoining Mailscot with Benedict Hall,[59] who in 1696 had granted a lease of fishing rights between New weir and Dixton together with a cottage near the weir.[60] In 1730 the duke and Viscount Gage, Hall's successor, agreed to hold the fishery and the narrow strip of the river bank downstream of the weir below Mailscot jointly and the duke undertook to maintain the weir and the lock.[61] In the late 18th century, when fishermen continued to use small round boats known as truckles on the

river below the weir,[62] two fish houses stood on the bank below Mailscot.[63] After the ironworks closed c. 1814 the weir fell into decay and by 1826 it had been removed and the lock had been filled in.[64] In 1851 a fisherman lived nearby and another lived at Coldwell.[65]

LOCAL GOVERNMENT. Gallows in St. Briavels hundred possessed by Robert de Mucegros c. 1276[66] were presumably at English Bicknor, where his mother Cecily had gallows and a tumbrel and claimed view of frankpledge and waif in 1287.[67] Later lords of the manor also claimed the twice-yearly view of frankpledge.[68] For the manor court, which met twice in 1639 as a court of survey,[69] court rolls for 1725 and 1804 and court books for the periods 1769–1801 and 1866–77 have survived. The court, convened intermittently by the mid 18th century, dealt with tenurial matters and encroachments on the lord's waste and met in 1725 at the White Hart.[70] In the early 19th century it met at the Bear once a year[71] and in the later 19th century it met intermittently at Braceland, later at Blackthorns Farm, and its main business became perambulating the manor boundaries. The court apparently last convened in 1912.[72]

The parish had two churchwardens in 1543 and later.[73] Poor relief was administered by overseers, mentioned in 1661,[74] and in the early 18th century it was financed in whole or in part from parish property comprising a few plots of land, 2 a. of coppice, and a rent charge of 2s., while the church house was used as a poorhouse.[75] In the 1820s the income from the property was distributed among widows on parish relief.[76] The cost of relief, £78 in 1776, rose sharply from the late 18th century, as many people living in the new hamlets of the extraparochial Forest of Dean claimed settlement in the parish, and at £342 in 1803, when 70 people were being helped, 30 of them regularly, was one of the highest in parishes bordering the Forest.[77] In 1813, when £871 was spent, 60 and 28 people received regular and occasional help respectively and another 7 were accommodated in a new parish workhouse,[78] built next to the church house with loans provided by William Ambery and Mary Wyrall.[79] From 1821 relief was administered under the direction of a select vestry and from 1822 or 1823

43 *Citizen*, 6 Nov. 1985; inf. from sales support manager, SCA Packaging Ltd.
44 Hart, *Ind. Hist. of Dean*, 208–9; Glos. R.O., D 3921/III/7.   45 *Citizen*, 3 Oct. 1985.
46 *Inq. p.m. Glos.* 1236–1300, 230–1.
47 *Trans. B.G.A.S.* xi. 271.
48 *Cal. Inq. p.m.* xii, p. 217; *Public Works in Med. Law*, i (Selden Soc. xxxii), 157, 166.
49 Glos. R.O., D 1677/GG 528.
50 P.R.O., MR 879.   51 Ibid. F 14/2A, rot. 2d.
52 Ibid. F 14/6.
53 *Dom. Bk.* (Rec. Com.), i. 182.
54 *Tax. Eccl.* (Rec. Com.), 168.   55 Ibid. 170.
56 P.R.O., E 32/31, m. 16.
57 Glos. R.O., D 272/1/14.
58 Wye & Lugg Navigation Act, 7 & 8 Wm. III, c. 14; Coates and Tucker, *Water Mills of Middle Wye Valley*, 55.
59 Glos. R.O., D 1677/GG 1282.
60 Ibid. D 23/E 32; P.R.O., F 14/2A, rot. 2d.
61 Glos. R.O., D 2079/III/149; cf. ibid. D 1677/GG 1125, 1320.

62 Fosbroke, *Wye Tour*, 47–8.
63 Glos. R.O., D 1677/GG 1319; P.R.O., MR 691.
64 Heath, *Excursion down the Wye*, s.v. New Weir; for site of lock, Glos. R.O., Q/RUm 14.
65 P.R.O., HO 107/2444.
66 *Rot. Hund.* (Rec. Com.), i. 176.
67 *Plac. de Quo Warr.* (Rec. Com.), 246; above, manor.
68 Glos. R.O., D 1677/GG 1230; P.R.O., F 14/2A, rot. 2d.
69 *Trans. B.G.A.S.* xi. 269–79.
70 P.R.O., F 14/1–2B, 6.
71 *Glouc. Jnl.* 10 Oct. 1803; 15 Oct. 1804; 14 Dec. 1807; 1 May 1809.   72 P.R.O., F 3/727–8.
73 Hockaday Abs. xxix, 1543 subsidy, f. 9; G.D.R., V 5/128T 1–3.   74 Glos. R.O., D 33/419/8.
75 G.D.R., V 5/128T 2; Bigland, *Glos.* i. 185.
76 *19th Rep. Com. Char.* 87.
77 *Poor Law Abstract, 1804*, 172–3; *3rd Rep. Dean Forest Com.* 6, 29.
78 *Poor Law Abstract, 1818*, 146–7.
79 *19th Rep. Com. Char.* 86–7.

the poor, both in and out of the workhouse, were farmed by a succession of contractors usually for less than £240 a year. A surgeon was employed to attend the poor in 1830.[80] The total cost of relief fell dramatically after 1813,[81] and had been reduced to £230 a year by the early 1830s,[82] when many of those helped lived in the Forest.[83] The parish was included in the new Monmouth poor-law union in 1836[84] and became part of West Dean rural district under the 1894 Local Government Act[85] and part of Forest of Dean district in 1974.

CHURCH. English Bicknor church, which stands in the outer bailey of a Norman castle,[86] dates from the 12th century.[87] It was recorded from 1221 when, during the minority of the lord of Bicknor, the Crown presented to it,[88] and it remained a rectory. The advowson descended with the manor until the mid 17th century.[89] In 1972 the benefice was united with Christ Church, Berry Hill, and land at Hillersland and Mailscot, including Symonds Yat rock, was added to the ecclesiastical parish.[90] The north-eastern corner of English Bicknor had been included in 1852 in the district of a new church at Lydbrook.[91]

In 1288 the bishop made a grant of the rectory *in commendam* with the consent of the lady of the manor.[92] In the later Middle Ages the Crown occasionally presented to the living by reason of a minority.[93] After 1506 the patronage was granted away for each turn but the lord of the manor filled a vacancy in 1538 after his grantees had renounced their right. At the next vacancy in 1558, when the lord was a minor, the right of the patron for the turn superseded the claim of the Crown.[94] The lords of the manor continued to grant away the patronage until at least 1638[95] and had relinquished the advowson by the late 1660s when it belonged to Thomas Godwin, the rector. In 1669 it was acquired from the dying Godwin by William Hughes, vicar of Newland, to ensure his succession to the living. Hughes, whose title was dubious, conveyed the advowson to Francis Harris and Thomas Lister in 1679 and they conveyed it to Samuel Harris, their

appointee as Hughes's successor, in 1680.[96] Harris, whose title to the advowson was secured in 1687 by grant from Thomas Marshall, Godwin's grandson,[97] sold it to Richard Mantle in 1698.[98] William Hodges presented at the next three vacancies, his first nominee, in 1710, being Richard Mantle and his last, in 1731, John Beale, who had acquired the advowson from Thomas Mantle. Beale died in 1744 and his trustees, after presenting a successor, sold the advowson to Somerset Jones (d. 1768). Claimants under the latter's will exercised the patronage together in 1777, after which the advowson was sold to John Davies.[99] He conveyed it in 1780 to the visitors of John Michel's foundation in Queen's College, Oxford.[1] In the 1870s F. J. Aldrich-Blake (d. 1904), a local landowner and rector of Welsh Bicknor, acquired the advowson[2] and in 1906 Mary Machen owned it. By 1939 the Society for the Maintenance of the Faith had a share in the patronage[3] and after the union of benefices in 1972 was entitled to fill the second of every four vacancies.[4]

The rectory was valued at £16 13s. 4d. in 1292.[5] In 1414 a pension of £8 from its revenues was awarded to a former rector.[6] The glebe comprised 8 a. in 1678.[7] All the tithes belonged to the rector[8] and in 1642 they were farmed for £90, a sum the farmer had difficulty raising, particularly after he was compelled by imprisonment to help pay for a parliamentary garrison at Newnham.[9] The tithes were also farmed in the late 17th century.[10] In 1842 they were commuted for a rent charge of £392[11] and by the mid 1870s the Crown had added 16 a. to the glebe in place of its share of the charge.[12] The rectory was valued at £11 10s. 9½d. in 1535,[13] £70 in 1650,[14] £120 in 1750,[15] and £300 in 1856.[16]

The rectory house stood north-east of the church[17] where the rector had his garden in 1330.[18] The rector was assessed for five hearths in 1672[19] and his outbuildings included a barn of eight bays in 1704.[20] The house was rebuilt in the 1730s[21] and enlarged in the late 19th century, when additional stables and kennels were also provided.[22] It was sold after the union of benefices in 1972.[23]

80 Glos. R.O., P 138/VE 2/1.
81 *Poor Law Abstract, 1818*, 146–7.
82 *Poor Law Returns* (1830–1), p. 66; (1835), p. 65.
83 *3rd Rep. Dean Forest Com.* 29, which says that c. £330 was spent on relief in 1833.
84 *Poor Law Com. 2nd Rep.* p. 535.
85 Glos. R.O., DA 25/100/1, pp. 1–10.
86 *Trans. B.G.A.S.* iv. 303–4; liii. 7.
87 Below, this section.
88 *Pat. R. 1216–25*, 285; above, manor.
89 *Reg. Orleton*, 319, 321; *Cal. Inq. p.m.* xii, p. 117; *Trans. B.G.A.S.* xi. 271; Hockaday Abs. cxxii.
90 Glos. R.O., P 227/IN 3/5.
91 *Lond. Gaz.* 20 Apr. 1852, pp. 1118–19.
92 *Reg. Swinfield*, 527 and n.
93 *Cal. Pat. 1374–7*, 173, 189, 288; 1377–81, 443; *Reg. Mayew*, 274 and n.   94 Hockaday Abs. cxxii.
95 Glos. R.O., D 1677/GG 833; cf. *Trans. B.G.A.S.* i. 84–5, where the advowson is said to have belonged to Sir John Bridgeman in 1630.
96 *Trans. B.G.A.S.* i. 80; P.R.O., E 134/2 Jas. II Mich./18.
97 Glos. R.O., D 3833/5.   98 *Trans. B.G.A.S.* i. 81.
99 Hockaday Abs. cxxii; Glos. R.O., D 3833/5.

1 *Trans. B.G.A.S.* i. 81.
2 *Kelly's Dir. Glos.* (1870), 544; (1879), 643; *Clergy List* (1868); for the Aldrich-Blake fam. estate, above, intro.
3 *Kelly's Dir. Glos.* (1906 and later edns.); for Mary Machen, *Trans. B.G.A.S.* lxiv. 106.
4 Glos. R.O., P 227/IN 3/5.
5 *Tax. Eccl.* (Rec. Com.), 161.
6 *Reg. Mascall*, 82–4.   7 G.D.R., V 5/128T 1.
8 Ibid. 2–3.   9 P.R.O., C 3/458/15.
10 Ibid. E 134/2 Jas. II Trin./5; Glos. R.O., N.R.A. rep. on deeds held by Holmes, Campbell, & Co., of Littlehampton, Suss.
11 G.D.R., T 1/25.
12 *Trans. B.G.A.S.* i. 82 n.
13 *Valor Eccl.* (Rec. Com.), ii. 501.
14 *Trans. B.G.A.S.* lxxxiii. 97.
15 G.D.R. vol. 381A, f. 2.   16 Ibid. 384, f. 20.
17 O.S. Map 6", Glos. XXX. NE. (1883 edn.).
18 Glos. R.O., D 33/23; cf. G.D.R., V 5/128T 1.
19 P.R.O., E 179/247/14, rot. 39d.
20 G.D.R., V 5/128T 2.
21 Ibid. vol. 285B(3), pp. 1–2.
22 Machen, 'Hist. Eng. Bicknor', 8.
23 Glos. R.O., P 227/IN 3/5.

The rector in 1324 was a Frenchman.[24] The rectors in 1357 and 1410 were dispensed to be absent for three years.[25] Chaplains living in the parish in 1352 and 1369[26] may have been among curates serving the church in the later 14th century,[27] and between 1376 and 1403 the benefice changed hands eight times by exchange.[28] John May, instituted in 1414, was rector for over 40 years. Between the mid 16th century and the early 19th century the rectors were often pluralists and many employed curates at Bicknor.[29] Walter May, who became treasurer of Hereford cathedral, was rector 1538–58[30] and in 1551 his curate, a former monk, was found to be particularly ignorant.[31] Henry Taylor, rector 1559–92, had a living in Herefordshire and may have taken up residence after 1563. He was considered neither a scholar nor a preacher.[32] Morgan Godwin, instituted in 1639, was succeeded in 1641 by his brother Thomas, chancellor of Hereford diocese, and Thomas (d. 1644)[33] by his son Thomas, who remained rector until his death in 1669.[34] His successors William Hughes (d. 1679) and Samuel Harris (d. 1710) were also vicars of Newland.[35] Duncombe Pyrke Davies, rector 1780–1815, lived at Monmouth, where he was vicar from 1798.[36] Edward Feild, rector from 1833 and, in 1840, the first school inspector appointed by the National Society, left Bicknor in 1844 to become bishop of Newfoundland.[37] John Burdon, rector from 1844, was also for a time rector of Welsh Bicknor.[38] George Hustler, his successor at English Bicknor in 1877, bankrupted himself by keeping hounds[39] and died in 1905 while following the hunt.[40] For much of his incumbency C. F. Doddrell, rector 1905–34, also held the living of Welsh Bicknor.[41]

A chapel built probably before 1282[42] stood west of the Coleford road near an ancient road junction.[43] It bore a dedication to St. Laurence in 1402[44] and was apparently in use in 1558.[45] Its ruins were removed in the mid 18th century.[46]

The parish church, which bore a dedication to ST. MARY THE VIRGIN by 1514,[47] has a chancel with north and south chapels (the north chapel used as a vestry), an aisled and clerestoried nave with south porch, and a west tower. It is mostly of sandstone rubble with ashlar dressings but the chancel is of squared blocks of pink gritstone. The original plan probably had a central tower located at the west end of the present chancel and flanked by transepts. To the north the arch that became the first bay of the north arcade is richly decorated in the Herefordshire style of the 12th century. The chancel walls and the nave arcades are late 12th-century and the west tower was built in the 13th century. The tower, presumably a replacement for the central tower, apparently contained one or more bells in the late 14th century[48] and was given a new upper stage in the 15th century. The nave was given a clerestory and a new roof in the early 16th century. The aisles and porch were apparently rebuilt as part of repairs and other improvements carried out in 1839[49] and the chancel's east wall was probably rebuilt during restoration work in 1908 when memorial glass to the Revd. John Burdon was put in its window.[50] In 1936 the sanctuary was restored at the expense of Burdon's son Rowland.[51]

The Norman font is plain and tub-shaped.[52] The church floor incorporates several coffin lids of the 14th century and there are three recumbent effigies in the north aisle. Two of the effigies date from the early 14th century and are said to be of Cecily de Mucegros (d. c. 1301) and of a female relative. The other effigy, of a priest, dates from the mid 14th century[53] and was in the north chapel in 1868.[54] The chapel was the mortuary chapel of the Wyrall family in the 17th and 18th centuries.[55] In the south chapel memorials to members of the Machen and Davies families include a wall monument with a portrait of Edward Tomkins Machen (d. 1778). The chapel also has a screen of c. 1500. In the north aisle panels displaying the Lord's Prayer, the Ten Commandments, and the Creed were the gift in 1794 of the rector, the landowner James Davies, and William Ambery.[56] The ring of five bells was recast by Abraham Rudhall in 1709.[57] The church plate includes a chalice and paten given by George Wyrall in 1707 and a paten of 1723 given by the Revd. George Hustler. Lucy Machen and Edward Feild were donors of plate in the mid 19th century.[58] The churchyard monuments include a collection of tombchests mostly of the 18th century. The parish registers survive from 1561 with some gaps.[59]

24 *Cal. Close, 1323–7*, 211.
25 *Reg. Trillek*, 397; *Reg. Mascall*, 189.
26 *Cal. Pat. 1350–4*, 305; Glos. R.O., D 2244/61.
27 *E.H.R.* xliv. 448.
28 Hockaday Abs. cxxii; *Reg. Gilbert*, 125; *Reg. Trefnant*, 191.
29 Hockaday Abs. cxxii.
30 Ibid. cxxii, ccxcvi; *Trans. B.G.A.S.* xcii. 102.
31 *Trans. B.G.A.S.* xlix. 82; *E.H.R.* xix. 120.
32 Hockaday Abs. xlvii, 1576 visit. f. 23; xlix, state of clergy 1584, f. 43; lii, state of clergy 1593, f. 13; cxxii.
33 Ibid. cxxii; *D.N.B.* s.v. Godwin, Francis; P.R.O., C 3/458/15.
34 Glos. R.O., P 138/IN 1/1–2; Hockaday Abs. cxxii; Bigland, *Glos.* i. 187.
35 Hockaday Abs. cxxii, ccxcvi.
36 Ibid. cxxii; G.D.R. vol. 382, f. 17.
37 Hockaday Abs. cxxii; W. H. Tucker, *Memoir of E. Feild, Bishop of Newfoundland* (1877), 17, 20; *D.N.B.*
38 *Clergy List* (1865, 1868 edns.).
39 Machen, 'Hist. Eng. Bicknor', 8; G.D.R., D 16/3/4.
40 *Glos. Countryside*, Oct. 1933, 136–7.
41 Photog. in vestry.
42 P.R.O., E 32/30, rot. 19; *Glos. Subsidy Roll, 1327*, 44.
43 For site, P.R.O., MR 879; Taylor, *Map of Glos.* (1777), marks the chapel E. of Bicknor Street.
44 Glos. R.O., D 33/63.
45 Hockaday Abs. ccxcvi.
46 G.D.R., V 5/128T 2; Bigland, *Glos.* i. 185.
47 Hockaday Abs. cxxii.
48 *E.H.R.* xliv. 448.
49 Glos. R.O., D 33/442; *Glos. Ch. Notes*, 144.
50 Glos. R.O., P 138/VE 2/1; *Kelly's Dir. Glos.* (1910), 161.
51 *Kelly's Dir. Glos.* (1939), 165.
52 *Trans. B.G.A.S.* xlix. 133, 153.
53 Roper, *Glos. Effigies*, 434–8.
54 *Glos. Ch. Notes*, 145.
55 Atkyns, *Glos.* 279; Bigland, *Glos.* i. 187–8.
56 Inscr. on panels; for Davies, above, manor.
57 Bodl. MS. Rawl. B. 323, f. 102; *Glos. Ch. Bells*, 296.
58 *Glos. Ch. Plate*, 81.
59 *B. & G. Par. Rec.* 65.

NONCONFORMITY. In 1616 a member of the Wyrall family was not attending the parish church[60] and George Wyrall (d. 1726) and his successors at Bicknor Court[61] in the 18th century were Roman Catholics.[62] In the early 19th century several protestant nonconformist meetings were established at Lydbrook[63] and in 1827 the pastor of the Baptists there registered a house in Bicknor for worship. At Symonds Yat (or New Weir), where a house was registered in 1818,[64] the Coleford Baptists held services in the early 1850s[65] and built a small chapel on the Goodrich road, at the county boundary, in 1881.[66] That meeting had 7 members in 1993.[67]

EDUCATION. An elderly schoolmaster of English Bicknor died in 1809[68] and the parish had a church Sunday school funded by subscription in 1819.[69] In the 1820s many children attended a day school at Berry Hill[70] and in 1833 a private day school in the parish taught c. 12 children.[71] In 1834 the rector Edward Feild started a day school[72] in a new building south-west of the church. It was supported by members of the Machen and Davies families, and in 1836 a separate schoolroom was built to the south for the girls' department and an infant department was started.[73] The school became a National school financed by subscription, including an annual grant provided by the Commissioners of Woods acting for the Crown, and pence. In 1847 it taught 91 children in boys' and girls' departments.[74] It was enlarged in 1873[75] and the average attendance was 59 in junior mixed and infant departments in 1904.[76] Attendance rarely exceeded that figure after the First World War,[77] and in 1992 as English Bicknor C. of E. school it had 43 children on its roll.[78] The schoolroom built in 1836, which became the teacher's house,[79] had been demolished by 1992 and classrooms erected in its place.

At Symonds Yat an infant school, dated 1838, on the Coleford–Goodrich road[80] may have been the day school in Bicknor supported by subscriptions and pence and teaching 52 infants in 1847.[81] It was open in 1866[82] and had closed by 1896, having been under the same management as the parish's National school. The building was a house in 1905.[83]

CHARITIES FOR THE POOR. Richard Terrett by will proved 1748 left a rent charge of 5s. to buy bread for 10 parishioners on Christmas Day.[84] Distribution of the charity lapsed in the mid 19th century.[85] In the early 1820s William Ambery and Mary Wyrall used £10 10s. annual interest from loans for building the parish workhouse in gifts to the poor, £10 being distributed in wheat at noisy gatherings. William (d. 1823) bequeathed the interest on his loan to provide £5 for the poor on Christmas Eve and Mary (d. 1826) bequeathed her loan as a gift.[86] By a Scheme of 1865 Ambery's charity was endowed with the former workhouse and church house, and, under the name of the charity of George Wyrall, land and a 2s. rent charge long used by the parish for the benefit of the poor were placed in the same trust. The endowments combined provided an annual income of £9 2s. From 1938 the two charities were administered with the Poor's Land charity.[87] The buildings had been sold by the early 1990s when the three charities had a combined annual income of c. £1,770 for cash payments to the poor and needy.[88]

In 1858 an almshouse was built on the site of the former Bear inn beside the churchyard, given for a parish almshouse by Edward Feild, the former rector. The almshouse, for the maintenance of which Edward Machen gave £100 stock in memory of his mother Lucy, was run by the incumbents of English Bicknor and Staunton and members of the Machen family.[89] At first it housed six elderly widows[90] and later residents received the surplus income from a £100 bequest of William Allaway, by will proved 1894, for repairing his family vault at English Bicknor. Allaway's charity was administered by the almshouse trustees from 1935 and was assigned to the almspeople shortly before 1971,[91] when its income was £2 and that of the almshouse was £90.[92] The almshouse, where alterations had reduced accommodation to five places, had only one occupant in 1973.[93] It was sold under a Scheme

60 Glos. R.O., D 2052.
61 Ibid. Q/SO 4; above, manor.
62 Misc. vii (Cath. Rec. Soc. ix), 135; Nicholls, Personalities of Dean, 128–9; cf. G.D.R. vol. 285B(1), f. 4.
63 Below, Forest of Dean, prot. nonconf.
64 Hockaday Abs. cxxii.
65 P.R.O., HO 129/577/1/1/31.
66 Story of Coleford Bapt. Ch. (1971) (copy in Glos. R.O., NC 42), 13; O.S. Map 6", Glos. XXX. NE. (1905 edn.).
67 Inf. from minister, Coleford Bapt. church.
68 Glos. R.O., D 5102/2.
69 Educ. of Poor Digest, 299.   70 G.D.R. vol. 383, no. cxii.
71 Educ. Enq. Abstract, 303.
72 Tucker, Memoir of E. Feild, 12, 17.
73 Glos. R.O., D 33/442; G.D.R., T 1/25; cf. P.R.O., F 3/26.
74 Nat. Soc. Inquiry, 1846–7, Glos. 4–5; Nicholls, Forest of Dean, 175.   75 Kelly's Dir. Glos. (1885), 454.
76 Public Elem. Schs. 1906, 184.
77 Bd. of Educ., List 21, 1922 (H.M.S.O.), 104; 1932, 115; 1938, 127.
78 Schools and Establishments Dir. 1992–3 (co. educ.

dept.), 16.
79 Trans. B.G.A.S. iv. 303–4; Kelly's Dir. Glos. (1885), 454; Glos. R.O., D 2428/1/23/3 and annotated copy of O.S. Map 1/2,500, Glos. XXX. 8 (1902 edn.).
80 Inscr. on bldg.
81 Nat. Soc. Inquiry, 1846–7, Glos. 4–5.
82 Glos. R.O., Q/RUm 359.
83 P.R.O., F 3/411; Glos. R.O., D 33/424.
84 G.D.R. wills 1748/75.
85 19th Rep. Com. Char. 87; Glos. R.O., CH 21, W. Dean rural district, p. 8.
86 19th Rep. Com. Char. 86–7; Glos. R.O., P 138/IN 1/9; ibid. VE 2/1, mins. 24 Dec. 1827; 24 Dec. 1828.
87 Glos. R.O., D 3469/5/59; above, local govt.; intro.
88 Inf. from Mrs. B. G. Britton, of Hillersland, clerk to trustees of char.
89 Date and inscr. on bldg.; Glos. R.O., D 3469/5/59.
90 Glos. Colln. R 128.1; Tucker, Memoir of E. Feild, 16; cf. Glos. R.O., P 138/IN 1/9.
91 Glos. R.O., D 3469/5/59.
92 Ibid. CH 21, W. Dean rural district, p. 7.
93 Ibid. CH 22, pp. 99–100.

of 1982 and the proceeds of the sale were used to create a fund, known as Lucy Machen's charity, which in 1993 provided help, mainly in cash payments, to poorer inhabitants of English Bicknor, Hillersland, and Staunton.[94] The former almshouse was converted as flats.

COLEFORD

THE PARISH and former market town of Coleford, 7 km. ESE. of Monmouth, was originally part of Newland parish.[95] Coleford formed a tithing occupying the north-east corner of the main block of the parish which, being created by assarting from the woodland and waste of the Forest of Dean, had many detached parts.[96] The town, whose name appears in the form Coverd or Cover in the late 17th century,[97] grew up in the centre of the tithing at a ford through which charcoal and iron ore were probably carried before 1282.[98] It had its own chapel by the late 15th century and it had emerged as the principal settlement on the west side of the Forest of Dean by the early 17th century.[99] The town's prosperity was enhanced by a grant of a market in 1661 and by the growth of the Forest's mining, ironmaking, and quarrying industries from the late 18th century. Coleford's population rose throughout the 19th century, and in 1894 the tithing was made a separate civil parish.[1] Detached pieces of Newland at Hoarthorns Farm, Lower Lydbrook, Reddings near Lydbrook, and Pope's Hill near Littledean, long regarded as parts of the tithing,[2] had been transferred to other parishes in 1883 and 1884.[3] In the mid 20th century Coleford ceased to have a market but after the Second World War new factories were built there to help to replace the Forest's traditional industries. The town, which continued to grow as a residential area, remained a shopping centre of local importance in 1994.

Coleford comprises 2,060 a. (c. 833.5 ha.) and is irregular in shape. It makes a substantial indent into the former extraparochial area of the Forest of Dean to the east and its boundary mostly follows ancient roads and tracks, including on the south-west routes from Highmeadow to Whitecliff and from Whitecliff to Millend and on the south routes over Mill hill and along Pingry Lane to the road from Chepstow (Mon.) to Coleford. The north-western boundary includes the course of Whippington brook.[4] This account of Coleford deals with the whole of the civil parish, apart from the Lane End district on the eastern boundary, which is treated below

with the Forest of Dean, and land at Highmeadow on the west, which is treated below with Staunton. It includes that part of Whitecliff hamlet, on the south-west, which remained in Newland after 1894, and the detached part of Newland at Hoarthorns Farm, 210 a. (c. 85 ha.) north-east of Berry Hill,[5] which included part of Joyford hamlet and was transferred to West Dean township or civil parish in 1883.[6]

Coleford is in a basin surrounded by low hills, which rise to 225 m. in the north at Berry Hill, 220 m. in the east at Broadwell Lane End, and 215 m. in the south-west at Breckness Court. Apart from the north-west corner, where the land falls towards the valley of Whippington brook, drainage is to the upper part of Valley brook, which rises near Broadwell Lane End and flows in a valley bisecting Coleford from north-east to south-west. In 1282 Valley brook was called Thurstan's brook,[7] and later different parts in Coleford had different names, including Gout brook in 1769 for the section in the town[8] and Whitecliff brook for the section below it.[9] There was a royal fishpond on the brook on the west side of Pool green in the north-east in 1282.[10] It and a millpond recorded upstream of it in 1608[11] were filled in after 1777.[12] The town grew up where two other streams joined Thurstan's brook, Coller (in 1769 called Coalway) brook rising near Edenwall, to the south-east, and Sluts brook near Crossways, to the north-west.[13] The problem of flooding was exacerbated in the early 18th century by water from mines above the town,[14] but the development of Speedwell colliery within the Forest in the later 19th century reduced the amount of water in Thurstan's brook to a trickle.[15] Coller and Sluts brooks were diverted and culverted as part of a flood prevention scheme carried out between 1979 and 1983.[16]

The carboniferous limestone on which Coleford lies contains deposits of iron ore and on the high ground of the north and east it is overlaid by the sandstone and shales of the Forest of Dean coalfield. Several productive coal seams, including the Coleford High Delf, outcrop in

94 Inf. from Mrs. S. J. Milford, of Eng. Bicknor, clerk to trustees of char.
95 G.D.R., T 1/128; the following account was written in 1994.
96 Below, Newland, intro.
97 Ogilby, *Britannia* (1675), plate 15; Glos. R.O., D 1340/A 1/M 1; cf. Atkyns, *Glos.* 574; Rudder, *Glos.* 568.
98 Cf. *Trans. B.G.A.S.* xiv. 364; *P.N. Glos.* (E.P.N.S.), iv. 113.
99 P.R.O., MR 879 (F 17/1).
1 *Census, 1801–1901; Manual of Glos. Lit.* ii. 166.
2 Glos. R.O., P 227/OV 1/1; T. Bright, 'Hist. Coleford Bd. of Health' (1956, TS. in ibid. PA 93/1), 7.
3 Below, Newland, intro. (Table I).
4 O.S. Maps 6", Glos. XXX. SE.; XXXVIII. NE. (1903 edn.).

5 *O.S. Area Bk.* Newland (1881).
6 Below, Newland, intro. (Table I).
7 *Trans. B.G.A.S.* xiv. 364.
8 Glos. R.O., P 310/MI 1, pp. 3–4.
9 Bright, 'Hist. Coleford Bd. of Health', 7.
10 *Trans. B.G.A.S.* xiv. 364.   11 P.R.O., MR 879.
12 Taylor, *Map of Glos.* (1777).
13 Glos. R.O., P 310/MI 1, pp. 3–4, where Coller brook was also called Thurstan's brook.
14 Bodl. MS. Top. Glouc. c. 3, f. 139.
15 P.R.O., F 3/865; M. Mushet, *Something about Coleford and the Old Chapel* (1877), 20: copy in Glos. Colln. 10957 (21).
16 C. E. Hart, *Coleford: The Hist. of a W. Glos. Forest Town* (1983), p. xxvi. Hart's book is a comprehensive and detailed hist. of Coleford.

Coleford.[17] Iron ore, stone, and coal have been dug, and in several places, notably the area in the west called Scowles, the ground is riddled with abandoned mines and quarries. In some places the ground is covered by cinders, the slag produced by early ironworks. In the 20th century large-scale quarrying near Scowles and at Whitecliff produced two vast pits, which were both disused in 1994.

The process of assarting by which Newland parish was created was in progress in the later Coleford tithing by 1225, when Hugh of Kinnersley cleared land in the south-west corner on the estate later called Breckness Court.[18] Much land remained part of the Forest woodland and waste in 1282 when Thurstan's brook and the road to Broadwell marked the southern boundary of the Forest's Bicknor bailiwick.[19] Several landowners were required in the early 17th century to compound for their land as assarts made from the royal demesne.[20] Once cleared the land was usually cultivated in closes but an area at Scowles became a common.[21] In the late 18th century there were small scattered pieces of woodland in Coleford tithing including several in the north-west corner by Whippington brook,[22] where the Crown Commissioners of Woods planted over 200 a. of farmland between 1824 and 1827 to provide timber for naval use.[23] That woodland, forming part of the Highmeadow woods, was managed by the Forestry Commission from 1924,[24] and an area on the east side, at Berry Hill, was cleared to form the Christchurch holiday campsite, opened in 1939.[25] In the later 20th century the area of farmland was reduced further by the growth of housing and industrial estates outside the town centre, and golf courses were created at Edenwall and Five Acres, in the south-east and north-east respectively.

Several ancient routes in Coleford tithing fell into disuse after the town became the focal point of roads in the area.[26] The green way recorded in 1282[27] was possibly part of a track running above the valley of Thurstan's brook and to the south-east of Scowles (in 1434 Greenway Scowles).[28] The track apparently became a way between Coleford and Newland church but, although a field on its route was known in 1792 as Church Path,[29] it was replaced long before 1608 by a road in the valley.[30]

Coleford town and Whitecliff hamlet, to the south-west, grew up on the valley road, which ran out of the Forest at Mile End to follow Thurstan's brook from Pool green, north-east of the town. The ford from which the town was named was presumably the crossing of Coller brook, where a bridge was built before 1608.[31] The road, of which the section between Mile End and Pool green was known in 1317 as the Derkesty[32] (later Dark Stile),[33] was an important route from Mitcheldean[34] and in the later 17th century traffic between Gloucester and South Wales used the section leading to the town.[35] At the south-west end of Whitecliff the road forked for Highmeadow and Millend and both routes have been used by travellers between Coleford and Newland village.[36] The Highmeadow road was the main route to Newland in the 16th century[37] and was used by travellers between Coleford and Monmouth in the early 18th century.[38] On the turnpiking of the road beyond Highmeadow in 1755[39] it became the main coach road between Coleford and South Wales.[40] A road running from the Forest at Broadwell to a junction with the road from Mitcheldean at Pool green was known in 1317 as the pool way,[41] after the fishpond by the green.[42] That road, which originally continued west of the green and north of the town along Stank Lane, recorded in 1479,[43] became the road from Littledean and Newnham to Coleford[44] and in the later 18th century it was also used by travellers from Gloucester.[45]

An ancient route known in 1345 as the coal way ran north-westwards from the Forest boundary at Coalway Lane End and down Lord's hill to join the main road through Coleford east of Coller brook.[46] Known later as Coller Lane,[47] it was used by travellers from Blakeney and Purton passage on the river Severn in the later 17th century.[48] The road entering the south side of Coleford town was known as the ore way in 1306.[49] It was later the main route from Chepstow[50] and in the mid 18th century it was used by travellers between Bristol and Hereford,[51] who continued northwards from the town through Berry Hill where the road divided, within the Forest, for English Bicknor and Goodrich (Herefs.).[52] South of the town at High Nash, known in 1306 as Windbridge Ash,[53] the Chepstow road was joined by an old road from Whitecliff called Rock Lane and an old road from Milkwall, on the Forest boundary,[54] known

17 Geol. Surv. Map 1/50,000, solid and drift, sheet 233 (1974 edn.).
18 Rot. Litt. Claus. (Rec. Com.), ii. 52; below, manors.
19 Trans. B.G.A.S. xiv. 364.
20 P.R.O., C 66/2168, no. 3.
21 Glos. R.O., D 23/T 24; Berkeley Cast. Mun., General Ser. T, box 25, Scowles papers 1790s.
22 P.R.O., F 17/117(2), pp. 33, 42; MR 691 (LRRO 1/240).
23 Ibid. F 17/117(1), pp. 6–8, 11; Glos. R.O., P 227/OV 1/1; below, Forest of Dean, forest admin. (replanting and reorganization).
24 Lond. Gaz. 25 Mar. 1924, pp. 2510–13.
25 Dean Forest & Wye Valley (H.M.S.O. 1974), 14.
26 Hart, Coleford, 5–9.   27 Trans. B.G.A.S. xiv. 364.
28 Glos. R.O., D 1677/GG 205.
29 P.R.O., MR 691; the field may have been that called Church Way in 1635: Inq. p.m. Glos. 1625–42, i. 220–1.
30 P.R.O., MR 879.   31 Ibid.
32 Glos. R.O., D 33/12.
33 Ibid. D 1677/GG 1545, no. 16.

34 Ibid. D 33/70; N.L.W., Dunraven MSS. 324.
35 Ogilby, Britannia (1675), p. 30, plate 15.
36 Below, Newland, intro.
37 Glos. R.O., D 1677/GG 436, 465.
38 Ibid. Q/SP 1/5, no. 21.   39 Below, Staunton, intro.
40 Glos. R.O., D 1677/GG 1545, no. 16.
41 Ibid. D 33/12.   42 Above, this section.
43 Glos. R.O., D 1677/GG 281.
44 Ibid. D 33/70; Q/SO 1, f. 71; N.L.W., Dunraven MSS. 324.
45 3rd Rep. Com. Woods (1788), 83.
46 Glos. R.O., D 2244/28; D 2957/86.9.
47 Ibid. D 608/4/4; Hart, Coleford, 8.
48 Glos. R.O., Q/SO 1, ff. 71, 182v.
49 Ibid. D 1677/GG 24; D 2957/86.12A.
50 P.R.O., MR 879; MR 691.
51 Glouc. Jnl. 22 Nov. 1762.
52 Taylor, Map of Glos. (1777).
53 Glos. R.O., D 1677/GG 24.
54 O.S. Map 6", Glos. XXXVIII. NE. (1884 edn.).

in 1501 as Tufthorn Lane.[55] The road from Milkwall perhaps passed the place known as Put Oak's green in 1413.[56] Further south Pingry Lane, joining the Chepstow road at Perrygrove and known in 1608 as Breckness Court Lane,[57] provided a route from Clearwell village. The Staunton road branching from the Berry Hill road north of the town was part of the main road between Gloucester and South Wales in 1675[58] but most traffic for Wales apparently took the road through Whitecliff in the 18th century.[59] In 1794, however, the road between Crossways, on the Staunton road, and Highmeadow, part of a route running across the north of Coleford from Five Acres, on the Forest boundary, was described as a public road to Monmouthshire.[60]

In 1796 the roads converging on Coleford town from Mile End, Broadwell, and Coalway and the road to Highmeadow by way of Whitecliff were turnpiked as part of a new Forest of Dean trust.[61] Edmund Probyn, a local landowner, was levying tolls at Scowles for the maintenance of the road to Highmeadow by way of Crossways in the later 1790s[62] but that road was administered by the Forest trust by 1824.[63] The Staunton road beyond Crossways came under the trust in 1831 when, on improvements to the road in Staunton village, it became the main Coleford–Monmouth road.[64] The road north out of Coleford town to Berry Hill, where tolls were collected in the later 1790s at its junction with the road from Five Acres to Highmeadow,[65] also came under the Forest trust in 1831[66] but the Chepstow road south out of the town remained outside it.[67] In 1840 the trust had tollhouses at the junctions at Pool green, Crossways, Berry Hill, and the bottom of Whitecliff.[68] In 1841 a new turnpike was built, branching from the Mitcheldean road at Edge End, within the Forest, and running north of the town to the Staunton road at the Long stone, within Staunton, and it became the main Gloucester–Monmouth route.[69] The roads of the Forest trust were disturnpiked in 1888.[70] In 1991 a bypass road was opened south-east of the town running from the Coalway road below Lord's hill to the Chepstow road north of Perrygrove.[71] A junction between the Chepstow road and the bypass was formed east of High Nash and part of the old road south of High Nash was closed.

A tramroad opened in 1812 to link mines in the Forest with Redbrook and Monmouth en-

tered Coleford north of Broadwell and, after crossing the Mitcheldean road north-east of Pool green, ran along the side of the valley of Thurstan's brook through the town and Whitecliff. The descent at Pool green was by means of an incline apparently controlled by ropes.[72] The tramroad was little used after Monmouth acquired a rail link to the South Wales coalfield in the mid 19th century and its track had been removed by 1880.[73] The first railway to reach Coleford, a branch line from Parkend opened by the Severn & Wye Railway Co. in 1875, ran through Milkwall to a goods and passenger station on the south-east side of the town.[74] A railway from Monmouth, using parts of the old tramroad route, was completed in 1883. It included a short tunnel at Whitecliff and it crossed the Newland road to run to a goods and passenger station next to that of the Severn & Wye Co. A junction was made between the two railways in 1884 after the Monmouth line had been taken over by the G.W.R. From 1916, when the Monmouth line closed west of Whitecliff, stone from the main Whitecliff quarry was carried by rail through Parkend[75] and in 1951 the junction at Coleford was improved. The Severn & Wye line, on which passenger services had ceased in 1929,[76] was abandoned in 1967 and the track between Whitecliff and Parkend had been removed by 1971.[77] Some railway buildings at Coleford, including a goods shed, were incorporated in a railway museum opened in 1988.[78] Also surviving in 1994 were the bridges which had carried the Monmouth railway across the Highmeadow road just beyond Whitecliff and the Newland road just outside the town and, on the Highmeadow road north-west of the railway bridge, the ruins of the bridge that had carried the Monmouth tramroad.

By the mid 14th century hamlets called Coleford and Whitecliff had grown up along the road in the valley of Thurstan's brook. Coleford, which had eight or more houses in 1349[79] and was described as a street in 1364,[80] had a chapel by 1489.[81] The chapel stood on a rise at the south-western corner of a large open area west of Coller brook, and that area, triangular in shape with the main north–south route through Coleford at its western end,[82] became the site of a market in the mid 17th century.[83] A cross, perhaps that recorded in 1499,[84] stood north-east of the chapel in 1608.[85] In the early 17th century

55 Glos. R.O., D 2957/86.12A.
56 Ibid. D 2957/214.13.   57 P.R.O., MR 879.
58 Ogilby, *Britannia* (1675), p. 30, plate 15.
59 Above, this section.
60 Berkeley Cast. Mun., General Ser. T, box 25, Scowles papers 1790s; Taylor, *Map of Glos.* (1777).
61 Dean Forest Roads Act, 36 Geo. III, c. 131.
62 Glos. R.O., D 1677/GG 1545, no. 16.
63 Ibid. Q/RUm 107; Bryant, *Map of Glos.* (1824).
64 Dean Forest Roads Act, 1 & 2 Wm. IV, c. 42 (Local and Personal); below, Staunton, intro.
65 Glos. R.O., D 1677/GG 1545, no. 16.
66 Dean Forest Roads Act, 1 & 2 Wm. IV, c. 42 (Local and Personal).
67 Bryant, *Map of Glos.* (1824), marks it as a turnpike.
68 G.D.R., T 1/128; for the Whitecliff tollhouse, below, Plate 27.
69 Nicholls, *Forest of Dean*, 197.
70 Dean Forest Turnpike Trust Abolition Act, 51 & 52

Vic. c. 193.
71 Inf. from co. surveyor's dept.
72 Paar, *G.W.R. in Dean*, 86–9, 96–7.
73 Ibid. 111–14; O.S. Map 6", Glos. XXXVIII. NE. (1884 edn.).
74 Paar, *Severn and Wye Railway*, 98–100; O.S. Map 6", Glos. XXXVIII. NE. (1884 edn.).
75 Paar, *G.W.R. in Dean*, 96–7, 113–18.
76 Paar, *Severn and Wye Railway*, 98–100, 116.
77 R. Anstis, *Story of Parkend* (1982), 68; Hart, *Coleford*, 334.
78 Mullin, *Forest in Old Photog.* 121; *Dean Forest Mercury*, 1 Apr. 1988.
79 N.L.W., Dunraven MSS. 339.
80 Glos. R.O., D 2244/56.
81 Ibid. D 2957/86.8; below, churches.
82 P.R.O., MR 879.
83 Below, econ. hist. (markets and fairs).
84 N.L.W., Dunraven MSS. 271.
85 P.R.O., MR 879.

Coleford retained an essentially linear plan with several houses facing the later market place and many more in Newland Street, the road to Whitecliff, and, east of the Coller brook, in Gloucester Road, the road to Mitcheldean. The houses on the north-west side of Gloucester Road were in plots running down to Thurstan's brook. By the early 17th century much of High Street, the Chepstow road, had been built up and there were a few houses north of Thurstan's brook on the Berry Hill road, later St. John Street but in 1858 called Birmingham Street. There were also a few houses in an area known later as the Spout on the north-east side of a back lane, later Bank Street but in 1858 called Victoria Street, linking the road down Lord's hill with the Berry Hill and Staunton roads. North of the town a few houses stood on Sparrow hill, on the Berry Hill road, and a more continuous line extended along the north-west side of the Mitcheldean road to Poolway,[86] where a small outlying hamlet had been established by the late 15th century.[87]

Following the grant of a market in 1661[88] much building took place within the town and c. 1710 it was reckoned to have 160 houses.[89] The market place was reduced by encroachments, notably a new market house built in 1679 on the site of the cross mentioned above.[90] In the late 1730s and early 1740s Viscount Gage tried by asserting manorial rights to prevent an enlargement of the chapel and other building in the town centre,[91] but encroachments continued and in several places streams were culverted and houses built over them. At the end of the century the fronts of houses and shops on the south-east side of the market place projected beyond that of the Plume of Feathers, which occupied part of the site of an inn opened before 1654. By 1800 also infilling had completed the building up of St. John Street.[92] In the late 18th century and the early 19th the town also expanded along its other streets and most of its older houses were rebuilt. Some new building was stimulated by the opening of the new tramroad in 1812,[93] and William Williams, a collier, built several houses on the north-west side of Gloucester Road before 1830.[94]

Among the older surviving buildings in the market place the Old White Hart, at the entrance to St. John Street, dates from the 17th century. The two adjoining cottages were rebuilt in the early 18th century for another inn[95] and a row of three houses at the entrance to High Street was built in the same period. Poolway House, at

Poolway, has three bays dating probably from the late 16th century with a heavily timbered roof and, on the ground floor, a relocated plank and muntin wall. The house was enlarged westwards in the 17th century and extensively refitted in the 18th century. Many of the town's new fronts of the years 1795–1830 were to a uniform design with fluted keystones. The town's principal inn, the Angel on the north side of the market place, was refronted or rebuilt during that period. Of the town's few larger houses Bank House, on the north-east side of Bank Street, is pedimented and was probably built for James Coster before 1786. It was acquired by the Crown in 1861 as an office for the deputy gaveller of the Forest and it also housed a branch of the Gloucestershire Banking Co. from 1862;[96] it was the Forestry Commission's administrative headquarters for its Forest of Dean district in 1994. The town's larger houses of the period 1795–1830 include one on the south side of Newland Street, acquired by the industrialist James Teague (d. 1818)[97] and occupied as flats in 1994. Rock House, further down the valley and overlooking the street, was built north of the tramroad probably in the mid 1820s. In 1867 it was the home of W. H. Fryer,[98] who probably built the adjoining gothic folly later known as Rock Castle.[99] Lawnstone House, at the top of High Street, was in 1840 the residence of the solicitor William Roberts[1] and from 1927 the offices of West Dean rural district council,[2] which enlarged the building in the early 1950s.[3] Higher up at Cinder Hill, on the road to High Nash, Forest (formerly Tump) House was acquired by the metallurgist David Mushet in 1810 and became a hotel in the mid 20th century.[4] East of the town there were a few cottages on the Coalway road at Lord's Hill by 1777[5] and a school and a parsonage house were built there in the late 1830s.[6] Further along the road a large building was erected in 1875 for Bell's Grammar school.[7]

Among changes in the town centre in the later 19th century, the market house (or town hall) was rebuilt on a larger scale in 1866[8] and the chapel, which had been rebuilt in 1820, was pulled down in 1882, its tower being retained for a clock tower.[9] The most ornate building of the period was the Baptist chapel of 1858 in Newland Street,[10] and James Ward, the principal assistant of the deputy surveyor of the Forest of Dean,[11] added a new front to the house on Sparrow hill known by the late 1870s as Sunny Bank.[12] Most of the town's growth in the later

86 Ibid.; Glos. R.O., P 93/SC 1/1.
87 Glos. R.O., D 2957/86.8; N.L.W., Dunraven MSS. 324.
88 Glos. R.O., D 1677/GG 1439.
89 Atkyns, Glos. 574.
90 Bodl. MS. Top. Glouc. c. 3, f. 139; below, econ. hist. (markets and fairs).
91 Glos. R.O., D 678/fam. settlements 57D/150–1, 279; D 1677/GG 1282.
92 P.R.O., MR 691; for the Plume of Feathers, Glos. R.O., D 608/4/1; Cal. S.P. Dom. 1654, 156.
93 Above, this section.
94 Glos. R.O., D 608/4/9.
95 Ibid. D 2926/6; G.D.R. wills 1721/62.
96 Hart, Coleford, 11, 372–3.
97 R. Anstis, Ind. Teagues and Forest of Dean (1990), 19, 74.

98 Morris's Dir. Glos. (1867), 668.
99 Glos. R.O., D 637/I/52; inf. from Mr. I. J. Standing, of Rock Ho.   1 G.D.R., T 1/128.
2 Hart, Coleford, 376, 378.
3 Dean Forest Mercury, 26 Aug. 1955.
4 Hart, Coleford, 372; for Mushet, below, econ. hist. (mills and ironworks); Forest of Dean, industry (ironworks).
5 Taylor, Map of Glos. (1777).
6 P.R.O., ED 7/34/86; G.D.R., F 4/1.
7 Date on bldg.; below, educ.
8 Glos. R.O., DC/H 35; Glos. Chron. 16 Feb. 1867.
9 Below, churches.
10 Glos. R.O., D 2722/31; below, Plate 15.
11 Kelly's Dir. Glos. (1870), 527; P.R.O., RG 11/5223, s.v. Newland (Coleford).
12 G.D.R., T 1/128; O.S. Map 6", Glos. XXXVIII. NE. (1884 edn.).

19th century was on the north-west side where the British Land Society laid out several new roads in 1858. Building on the estate, which had been enlarged by 1866,[13] included an entrance lodge of 1868 for a cemetery at the end of Victoria Road[14] and the parish church of St. John, consecrated in 1880, on a site in Boxbush Road overlooking the town centre.[15] Of the new houses on the town's outskirts,[16] the most prominent was the Coombs, built high up on the Berry Hill road in the late 1850s, in château style with a central tower, for Isaiah Trotter. It was a health cure centre in 1945 when the writers Laurence Housman and Vera Brittain were among visitors,[17] and later it was a home for the elderly, additional accommodation being provided c. 1980.[18]

The town's expansion after the First World War began on the south side where Coleford urban district council completed 20 pairs of new houses at High Nash in 1923. Between 1926 and 1928 the council built 30 houses in Albert and Victoria Roads, on the north-west side.[19] Most building in the mid 20th century was on the north side where the Sunny Bank council estate, originally comprising 50 houses built in 1940 and 1941 between the Berry Hill and Staunton roads, was enlarged after the Second World War. In the same period the road up Sparrow hill was closed and the Berry Hill road was diverted to leave the Staunton road further out.[20] From the 1950s there was considerable private building on the north-east side of the town[21] and by 1994 housing estates covered the land between the Coombs and Poolway. The area between Poolway and Lord's Hill, on the east side, was filled by piecemeal council and private development, beginning in 1960 with the Eastbourne council estate at Poolway.[22] In the late 20th century houses were also built on the south side of the town where the new bypass had attracted several small estates by 1994.

In the older part of the town new buildings in the early 20th century included two banks in the market place in the early 1920s[23] and a labour exchange on the Coalway road at the bottom of Lord's hill in 1937.[24] In the 1960s and 1970s several buildings were demolished to make way for new developments, which included a police station and magistrates' court, opened in 1964, on the south-east side of Gloucester Road.[25] Traffic congestion in the market place was eased by the demolition of the town hall in 1968 and

the introduction of a gyratory system around the clock tower.[26] The top end of High Street was widened in 1970, the buildings on the east side being replaced by a row of new shops,[27] and in the later 1980s former railway land to the east was redeveloped to include a car park, a supermarket, and a small shopping centre. West of High Street new district council offices were completed behind Lawnstone House in 1990,[28] and at Cinder Hill a doctor's surgery was built on a circular plan in 1993.

Whitecliff, a long straggling hamlet on the Newland road south-west of Coleford town, took its name from a rock face on the south-east side of the valley near the junction of Rock Lane.[29] It was called Whitecliff Street in 1275.[30] In 1349 it had 22 or more houses[31] and in the early 17th century it included several dwellings on the Highmeadow road beyond the junction of the road to Millend.[32] In the late 18th century cottages and small farmhouses were strung out along the Newland road[33] and by the mid 19th there was a cluster of cottages at the entrance to Rock Lane.[34] Whitecliff House, at the north-east end of the hamlet, was built in the early 19th century to the popular local design with fluted keystones. To the south-west Whitecliff Farm, part of an estate owned by the Revd. John Shipton in 1840,[35] was demolished c. 1935.[36] Near the south-west end of Whitecliff a mid 18th-century farmhouse, said to have been on the site of a house occupied by the Wyrall family until the later 15th century,[37] had fallen into ruin by the late 19th century and its site became a tip for spoil from a quarry in the mid 20th century.[38]

Several farmsteads were established on the high open land of the tithing, some of them before 1608, and several roads leading from the town were gradually built up, mainly with small cottages during the 18th and 19th centuries. In 1714 fifteen people were presented for building cottages on the Staunton road,[39] and by 1792 buildings were scattered along it almost to Crossways.[40] In the early 19th century several cottages were built in the Crossways area on the side of the road to Berry Hill, to the north-east,[41] and in 1908 a house called Rushmere was built on the Staunton road beyond Crossways.[42] Owen Farm, which stands south of Crossways and was bought by Ralph Owen (d. 1731),[43] is probably 17th-century in origin, but it has been extensively remodelled. It bears the crest of Edward Bell's charity, which bought it in 1823.[44] Scowles

13 Glos. R.O., P 93/SC 1/1; Q/SRh 1868 B/1.
14 Date on rainwater heads; for cemetery, below, this section.   15 Below, churches.
16 e.g. Glos. R.O., D 177, Eastbourne Ho. deeds.
17 Hart, *Coleford*, 371; for Trotter, below, econ. hist.; Forest of Dean, industry (other ind. and trade).
18 O.S. Map 1/2,500, SO 5711 (1974, 1992 edns.).
19 T. Bright, 'Hist. Coleford Urban District Council' (1957, TS. in Glos. R.O., PA 93/2), 15–17.
20 Glos. R.O., DA 25/600/2; O.S. Map 1/2,500, SO 5711 (1960 edn.).
21 Cf. O.S. Maps 1/2,500, SO 5710–11 (1960 edn.).
22 Glos. R.O., DA 25/600/2; Hart, *Coleford*, 443.
23 Glos. R.O., DA 5/100/5, pp. 317, 416.
24 Date on bldg.; cf. Hart, *Coleford*, 427.
25 *Dean Forest Mercury*, 6 Nov. 1964.
26 Hart, *Coleford*, 447.
27 O.S. Map 1/2,500, SO 5710 (1960, 1973 edns.); Hart, *Coleford*, 455.

28 *Citizen* (Glouc.), 2 Oct. 1990.
29 Glos. R.O., D 23/T 23.   30 Ibid. D 2244/11.
31 N.L.W., Dunraven MSS. 339.
32 P.R.O., MR 879.
33 Ibid. MR 691; F 17/117(2), pp. 37, 49–51.
34 Ibid. HO 107/2444, s.v. Newland (Coleford); G.D.R., T 1/128.   35 G.D.R., T 1/128.
36 Hart, *Coleford*, 363–4.
37 Rudge, *Hist. of Glos.* ii. 89; for the Wyralls at Whitecliff: Glos. R.O., D 33/62, 69, 73–4, 96, 98, 100, 121.
38 Mushet, *Something about Coleford*, 26–7; Hart, *Coleford*, 362–3.
39 Glos. R.O., D 1677/GG 1368.
40 P.R.O., MR 691.
41 Glos. R.O., D 1677/GG 1545, no. 118A; G.D.R., T 1/128.
42 Hart, *Coleford*, 391.
43 Glos. R.O., D 5377/3/1; Bigland, *Glos.* ii. 264.
44 Glos. R.O., D 34/9/69.

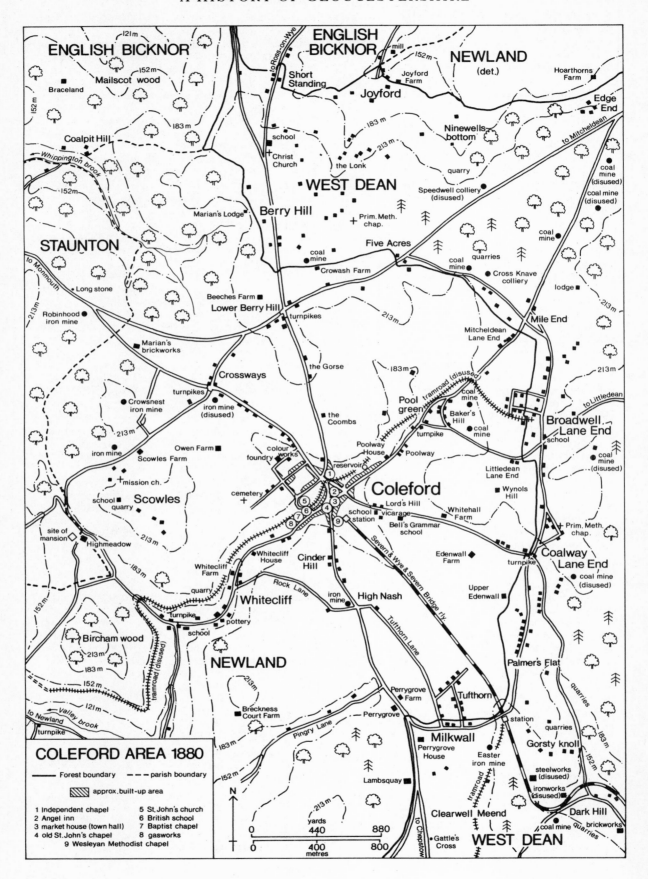

ENGLISH BICKNOR

Mailscot wood

Braceland

Coalpit Hill

Whippington brook

152 m

STAUNTON

to Monmouth

Long stone

Robinhood
iron mine

Marian's
brickworks

Crowsnest
iron mine

iron mine
(disused)

iron mine

Owen Farm

Scowles Farm

mission ch.

school

Scowles

quarry

site of
mansion

Highmeadow

Bircham wood

to Newland
turnpike

Valley brook

ENGLISH
BICKNOR

mill

to Ross-on-Wye

Short
Standing

school

Christ
Church

WEST DEAN

Berry Hill

Marian's Lodge

Beeches Farm

Lower Berry Hill

turnpikes

Crossways

turnpikes

Joyford
Farm

Joyford

the Lonk

Prim. Meth.
chap.

Five Acres

coal
mine

Crowash Farm

the Gorse

the
Coombs

colour
works

foundry

cemetery

NEWLAND
(det.)

Hoarthorns
Farm

Edge
End

to Mitcheldean

Ninewells
bottom

quarry

Speedwell colliery
(disused)

coal
mine

coal
mine
(disused)

coal
mine
(disused)

coal
mine

quarries

Cross Knave
colliery

lodge

Mile End

Mitcheldean
Lane End

tramroad (disused)

Pool
green

Baker's
Hill

turnpike

coal
mine

coal
mine

Broadwell
Lane End

school

coal
mine
(disused)

to Littledean

Littledean
Lane End

Poolway
House

Poolway

reservoir

Coleford

Lord's Hill

Wynols
Hill

Whitehall
Farm

Prim. Meth.
chap.

Coalway
Lane End

coal mine
(disused)

school
station

Bell's Grammar
school

vicarage

Edenwall
Farm

turnpike

Whitecliff
House

Whitecliff
Farm

quarry

Turnpike

pottery

Whitecliff

school

Cinder
Hill

Rock Lane

iron
mine

High Nash

Severn & Wye & Severn Bridge rly

Upper
Edenwall

Tufthorn Lane

Palmer's Flat

quarries

NEWLAND

Breckness
Court Farm

Pingry Lane

Perrygrove
Farm

Perrygrove

Tufthorn

station

Milkwall

Perrygrove
House

Gorsty knoll

quarries

steelworks
(disused)

Lambsquay

Easter
iron mine

tramroad

ironworks
(disused)

Clearwell Meend

Gattle's
Cross

WEST DEAN

Dark Hill

brickworks

coal mine

quarries

N

COLEFORD AREA 1880

— Forest boundary
--- parish boundary

▨ approx. built-up area

1 Independent chapel   5 St. John's church
2 Angel inn   6 British school
3 market house (town hall) 7 Baptist chapel
4 old St. John's chapel   8 gasworks
     9 Wesleyan Methodist chapel

yards
0   440   880
0   400   800
        metres

FIG. 5

Farm, a plain stone farmhouse on the Cross-ways–Highmeadow road, was built shortly after 1674 on the site of a ruined sheephouse, acquired that year by the Probyn family of Newland,[45] and has been remodelled. Squatters built cottages on Scowles common from the start of the 19th century,[46] creating a hamlet with 36 households in 1851. The small community of miners and quarrymen[47] had its own church and school from the mid 19th century.[48]

North of Coleford there was a house on the Berry Hill road at the Gorse in the later 18th century.[49] Further north scattered building began close to the Forest boundary at Berry Hill before 1566.[50] In the late 18th century there was a cluster of houses, including several farmhouses, at the crossroads formed by the Berry Hill road and the road between Five Acres and Highmeadow[51] (later the main Gloucester–Monmouth road), and in 1851 there were 17 houses at Berry Hill belonging to Coleford tithing.[52] At the crossroads, sometimes called Lower Berry Hill to distinguish it from more extensive settlement on the extraparochial land of the Forest,[53] a farmhouse south of the Gloucester road was demolished in 1964 as part of a road improvement scheme.[54] To the west there was at least one dwelling in 1585 at the place called Knaven Green, and Beeches Farm, north-west of the crossroads, is on the site of a farmstead established by the late 16th century.[55] Marian's Farm, a small farmhouse further north, was recorded in the mid 18th century.[56] It was retained for use as a woodman's lodge by the Crown Commissioners of Woods when they planted the farmland there in the mid 1820s.[57] To the north-east, a farmhouse called Broomhill Farm was built next to Mailscot wood c. 1700,[58] but was abandoned on the creation of the new plantations; its ruins had been removed by 1840.[59] On the east side of Berry Hill the farmstead recorded at Crowash Farm, on the Forest boundary, from 1676[60] was demolished in the later 20th century when more houses were built to the north. A farmhouse and barn standing next to the Forest at Five Acres were possibly built in the 17th century. In the mid 18th century there was also a cottage there[61] and in the 19th and 20th centuries several houses were built nearby, on the south side of the Monmouth road. Merryweathers (formerly Lit-tle Five Acres) Farm is on the site of a building recorded in 1608.[62]

Among the scattered farmsteads on the east side of Coleford the house at Folly Farm, on the Mitcheldean road beyond Poolway, was used as a barn by 1787.[63] Broadwell Farm, on the Forest boundary at the place once known as King's Broadwell, was recorded in 1789.[64] Whitehall, a small farmhouse on the Coalway road, was built in the late 18th century. At Wynols Hill, where a house was recorded in 1499,[65] a three-storeyed house built in the mid 17th century belonged to the Skynn family of Clearwell in 1699.[66] During the Second World War it was part of a prisoner of war camp[67] and soon afterwards it was demolished.[68] The main range of Edenwall Farm, standing in a valley below the Coalway road on the site of a house recorded in 1608,[69] incorporates a farmhouse and a barn. To the south-east a small 18th-century farmhouse or cottage on the Forest boundary, sometimes called Upper Edenwall,[70] was rebuilt after 1881.[71] There was at least one dwelling at Milkwall, on the Forest boundary south-east of Coleford, in 1628.[72] Of the farmsteads established near the boundary west of Milkwall possibly after 1608,[73] Perrygrove Farm, east of the Chepstow road, was known as Cover House and belonged to the Skynn family in 1727.[74] Much lower down Pingry Lane a medieval house called Breckness Court had been abandoned by the early 18th century when it was replaced by a farmhouse on a site above the valley.[75]

In the later 19th century several housing estates were developed to the east of Coleford by the British Land Society. The first, at Baker's Hill north-east of Poolway,[76] contained five houses in 1856.[77] The other estates, on the Forest boundary and including one at Tufthorn next to Milkwall, are recorded, together with 20th-century housing in the Lane End district, under the history of the Forest.[78] In the 20th century there was also much building north-west of Milkwall on Tufthorn Avenue (formerly Lane), where 46 council houses were built between 1929 and 1933[79] and where the remaining land was filled with houses and industrial buildings after the Second World War.[80] In the 1960s several houses were built on the north side of the Coalway road as part of ribbon development extending from Coalway Lane End.[81]

45 Ibid. D 23/T 24; D 637/II/1/T 1; P 227/IN 1/2, burial 27 Dec. 1685.
46 P.R.O., MR 691; G.D.R., T 1/128.
47 P.R.O., HO 107/2444, s.v. Newland (Coleford).
48 Below, churches; educ.
49 Taylor, *Map of Glos.* (1777).
50 Glos. R.O., P 227/IN 1/1.   51 P.R.O., MR 691.
52 Ibid. HO 107/2444, s.v. Newland (Coleford).
53 O.S. Map 6", Glos. XXX. SE. (1884 edn.).
54 Hart, *Coleford*, 386.
55 Glos. R.O., P 227/IN 1/1; P.R.O., MR 879; MR 691.
56 P.R.O., F 17/96; F 17/117(2), p. 43; MR 691.
57 Ibid. F 17/117(1), pp. 7, 11; *2nd Rep. Dean Forest Com.* 29; G.D.R., T 1/128.
58 Glos. R.O., D 1677/GG 1044; P.R.O., F 17/117(2), p. 42; MR 691.
59 *2nd Rep. Dean Forest Com.* 29; G.D.R., T 1/128.
60 Glos. R.O., D 4493/1–15; G.D.R., T 1/128.
61 P.R.O., F 17/96.
62 Ibid. MR 879; O.S. Map 6", Glos. XXX. SE. (1884 edn.).
63 Hockaday Abs. clxxvi, Christ Church 1816.

64 G.D.R. wills 1794/54.
65 N.L.W., Dunraven MSS. 271.
66 Glos. R.O., D 2957, abs. of title 148; P 227/IN 1/2, baptism 4 Feb. 1673.
67 Hart, *Coleford*, 371–2; below, Forest of Dean, settlement.   68 O.S. Map 1/2,500, SO 5810 (1960 edn.).
69 P.R.O., MR 879.
70 O.S. Map 6", Glos. XXXVIII. NE. (1884 edn.).
71 P.R.O., RG 11/5223, s.v. Newland (Coleford).
72 Glos. R.O., P 227/IN 1/1–2; D 891, Coleford deeds 1655–1817.   73 Cf. P.R.O., MR 879.
74 N.L.W., Mynde Park MSS. 441, 908.
75 Below, manors.
76 Bristol R.O. 35721, Coleford papers 1855–96.
77 Glos. R.O., D 661.
78 Below, Forest of Dean, settlement.
79 Bright, 'Hist. Coleford U.D.C.' 17.
80 Glos. R.O., DA 25/600/2; O.S. Maps 1/2,500, SO 5709 (1960, 1972 edns.); SO 5809 (1960, 1978 edns.); below, econ. hist. (other ind. and trade).
81 O.S. Map 1/2,500, SO 5810 (1960, 1973 edns.).

Hoarthorns Farm, an isolated farmstead in the detached part of Newland north-east of Berry Hill, was held under English Bicknor manor in 1565[82] and was part of the Eastbach estate by 1616.[83] The farmhouse was rebuilt in the early 19th century and was sold with some land in the mid 20th century.[84] To the west the small hamlet of Joyford in 1608 included cottages on both sides of the boundary between the detached part of Newland and English Bicknor.[85] Joyford Farm, a small house possibly of the 17th century, belonged to Newland[86] and was sold with part of the Highmeadow estate to John Hopkins in 1726.[87]

In 1672 seventy households were assessed for hearth tax in Coleford tithing[88] and c. 1710 the town contained 160 houses.[89] Between 1811 and 1831 the tithing's population rose from 1,551 to 2,193, the increase reflecting the growth in the coal industry. In the mid 19th century it increased more slowly and in 1871 it was 2,718. In 1901 Coleford civil parish had a population of 2,541, rising to 2,781 in 1921 and, after a small decrease in the 1920s, to 2,945 in 1951. Population growth accelerated in the 1950s and there were 5,075 inhabitants in 1991.[90]

A gas company formed in 1840 built its works in Newland Street[91] and supplied shops and houses in the town. Gas street lighting, delayed at first by lack of agreement among the townspeople,[92] was by 23 lamps in 1871.[93] The company, which also supplied Whitecliff,[94] was taken over by the Lydney gas company in 1946 and gas manufacture ceased at Coleford c. 1950, after nationalization.[95] Electricity was brought to the town by the West Gloucestershire Power Co. c. 1924.[96] In 1868 a volunteer brigade was formed to operate a fire engine brought to the town from Gloucester by an insurance company.[97] A brigade formed in 1931 became part of the county fire service in 1948. It was based on a station next to the rural district council's offices in High Street before 1964, when a new fire station opened on the east side of Cinder Hill.[98]

In 1821 Coleford had a dispensary supported by subscriptions and employing an apothecary or surgeon. It apparently closed through lack of funds, some people preferring to support the Monmouth dispensary.[99] There was a lack of burial space within the town and on the closure of Newland churchyard to burials of Coleford residents in 1867[1] a burial board laid out a cemetery on the west side of the town. The cemetery, which included chapels for Anglicans and nonconformists linked by a corridor surmounted by a bellcot, opened in 1868 and was managed jointly by Coleford and Newland parish councils after 1894. It was enlarged in 1947 and the chapels were demolished in 1976.[2]

Coleford lacked basic sanitary services in the mid 19th century when the town's streams were used as sewers and water was taken from wells and from troughs alongside Thurstan's brook at the Spout. From 1873 a local board of health maintained a water cart, which had been acquired by subscription, and from 1877 it piped water from a small reservoir on the north-east side of the town to standpipes in or near the market place. That system, which in 1892 also served two houses, was extended to Whitecliff in 1899. Despite small schemes near Scowles and Berry Hill the higher parts of Coleford were without piped water until 1932 when water was supplied from a reservoir in Staunton in a joint scheme of the urban district council and West Dean rural district council. Pollution of the town's streams increased as the flow of water dwindled in the later 19th century and the unculverted sections of Thurstan's brook downstream in Whitecliff remained a nuisance in the mid 20th century. Between 1931 and 1935 the urban district council built sewers to replace surface gutters.[3] In the late 1940s and the early 1950s the West Dean council provided a sewerage system for the town with treatment works by Valley brook below Newland village.[4]

Coleford town probably had several victualling houses in 1600.[5] The number of public houses increased as the town grew in importance and in 1830 there were seven or eight inns, most of them in the market place, and a larger number of beerhouses.[6] On the north side of the market place the inn known as the Angel in 1725 had opened by the 1650s. For many years it housed an excise office[7] and in the mid 18th century it was the town's principal coaching inn and it was used for public meetings and assemblies.[8] A beam across the gap between it and the market house and bearing its name was taken down c. 1862.[9] Another inn open in 1654[10] was an important meeting place in the later 17th century;[11] part of its site, on the south-east side of the market place, became a separate house in 1738

82 Glos. R.O., P 227/IN 1/1; D 1677/GG 445.
83 Ibid. D 1677/GG 635, 656; D 33/276; for the Eastbach est., above, Eng. Bicknor, manor.
84 Glos. R.O., D 33/423; Glos. Colln. RR 86.10 (1), p. 17.
85 P.R.O., MR 879; for Joyford, above, Eng. Bicknor, intro.; below, Forest of Dean, settlement.
86 O.S. Map 6", Glos. XXX. SE. (1884 edn.); 2nd Rep. Dean Forest Com. 29.
87 Glos. R.O., D 23/T 29.
88 P.R.O., E 179/247/14, rot. 38.
89 Atkyns, Glos. 574.
90 Census, 1811–1991.
91 Glos. Colln. RF 86.7; date on bldg.
92 Hunt's Dir. Glos. (1849), 97.
93 Bright, 'Hist. Coleford Bd. of Health', 26.
94 Payne, Glos. Survey, 256.
95 Lydney and District Official Guide (n.d.), 29; Hart, Coleford, 274.
96 Bright, 'Hist. Coleford U.D.C.' 19.
97 Glouc. Jnl. 15 Feb. 1868; Kelly's Dir. Glos. (1870), 526.
98 Dean Forest Mercury, 23 Oct. 1964; O.S. Map 1/2,500, SO 5710 (1960, 1973 edns.).
99 Glos. R.O., D 2926/24; Glouc. Jnl. 26 Mar. 1821.
1 Glos. R.O., D 637/I/84.
2 Hart, Coleford, 302, 462; Bright, 'Hist. Coleford U.D.C.' 1–2.
3 Bright, 'Hist Coleford Bd. of Health', passim; Bright, 'Hist. Coleford U.D.C.' passim; Glos. R.O., D 3921/II/12; Hart, Coleford, 473.
4 Glos. R.O., DA 25/100/27, p. 2017; 29, p. 2394; deeds of Tanhouse Fm., Newland, in possession of Mr. P. W. Chamberlain.
5 B.L. Harl. MS. 4131, f. 553.
6 Pigot's Dir. Glos. (1830), 367; cf. ibid. (1842), 102.
7 Glos. R.O., D 1677/GG 1282, 1368, 1558.
8 Glouc. Jnl. 14 Aug. 1750; 7 Mar. 1758; 3 June 1760; 14 Oct. 1782.
9 Glos. R.O., D 637/I/37; Hart, Coleford, 382, shows the beam in a photog. of c. 1860.
10 Cal. S.P. Dom. 1654, 156.
11 P.R.O., E 134/2 Jas. II Trin./5.

and the inn, then known as the Plume of Feathers, was called the Flower de Luce in 1752. The name had reverted to the Plume of Feathers, more commonly the Feathers, by 1784.[12] The north-west side of the market place had the Coach and Horses inn in 1719,[13] and the White Hart, which stood next to it in 1730,[14] was called the Old White Hart in 1787. The King's Head, opened at the east end by the entrance to Gloucester Road before 1785,[15] was a stopping-place for a Gloucester and Monmouth coach in 1830[16] and was the terminus of a Gloucester coach in 1849.[17] The sites of the Red Lion, mentioned in 1732,[18] and the Three Parrots, mentioned in 1755,[19] are not known. The Jovial Collier or Colliers, recorded from 1766,[20] and the Bear, opened by 1798[21] and renamed by 1826 the Royal Oak and later the Lamb,[22] were in Gloucester Road.[23] The Red Lion mentioned in 1802[24] was just outside the town at Cinder Hill.[25] In the 1840s and 1850s there were at least a dozen other public houses in the market place and the streets leading from it.[26] The Jenny Lind, recorded in 1856,[27] was at the Spout and was known as the Queen's Head in 1881. In 1881 there was also a coffee house in St. John Street.[28] The Angel, the Feathers, the Old White Hart, and the King's Head survived in 1994.

In Whitecliff the sign of the Folly, recorded in 1757,[29] belonged in 1851 to a beerhouse at the entrance to Rock Lane.[30] In the lower part of Whitecliff the Nag's Head, opened by 1790,[31] was known in the 1830s as the Traveller's Rest[32] and was the hamlet's only public house in 1910.[33] It closed after 1935.[34] In 1861 there was an inn at Crossways and several other public houses in the north part of Coleford tithing. The Cross Keys, at the Lower Berry Hill crossroads,[35] was presumably that called the New Inn in 1856.[36] An inn there in 1994 was called Pike House.

A friendly society was meeting at the Jovial Collier in 1766. From 1777 many similar societies meeting at inns in and near the town had their rules enrolled[37] and in 1807 Coleford had 11 benefit societies with an average membership of 100. The largest, meeting at the Angel, had 223 members.[38] A savings bank was established in the town in 1838[39] and an equitable and industrial society, presumably a co-operative venture, had been formed by 1889.[40] There was a circulating library in the town in the late 1840s[41] and a mechanics' institute founded in 1855 opened a reading room and library there. The institute, reorganized in 1859, closed in the early 1860s[42] and the town had a privately owned reading room in 1863.[43] In the 1930s a library was run from a stationer's shop.[44] A branch of the county library at Cinder Hill in 1959[45] was later housed in a former chapel in High Street and in 1964 moved to new premises in Bank Street.[46] The market house of 1679 also served as a town hall and remained an important meeting place until its demolition in 1968.[47] Among groups using it in the late 1860s was a masonic lodge.[48] A community centre built in Bank Street in 1967 was enlarged in 1979.[49] Other meeting places in 1994 included the wooden Maycrete Hall, built at Cinder Hill c. 1930 as a centre for the unemployed.[50] A drill hall built in High Street in 1906 was converted a few years later as a cinema,[51] which remained open, under the name of the Studio, in 1994. The town had a brass band in 1864.[52]

In 1831 a printing press was set up in Coleford[53] and from the early 1860s several weekly newspapers for the Forest area were printed in the town. The most successful was the *Dean Forest Guardian*, started in 1874 as a Conservative publication.[54] It was printed at Cinderford from 1922, when it came under the same ownership as papers in Cinderford and Lydney,[55] and publication ceased in 1991, when the three papers were amalgamated under the title of the *Forester*.[56]

Sports clubs in Coleford included the Forest of Dean cricket club founded before 1842.[57] Coleford's first rugby football club was formed in 1877 and association football and hockey clubs were also formed before the First World War. For many years the August fête of a branch of the Ancient Order of Foresters was a major athletics event.[58] In 1919, to honour the award

[12] Glos. R.O., D 608/4/2; Q/RSf 2; Hockaday Abs. clxv, 1752.
[13] G.D.R. wills 1721/62.   [14] Glos. R.O., D 2926/6.
[15] Ibid. Q/RSf 2.
[16] *Pigot's Dir. Glos.* (1830), 367.
[17] *Hunt's Dir. Glos.* (1849), 104.
[18] Glos. R.O., D 608/4/1.
[19] Ibid. D 891, Coleford deeds 1655–1817.
[20] Ibid. Q/RSf 2; P 227/OV 1/1; *Slater's Dir. Glos.* (1852–3), 120.   [21] Glos. R.O., Q/RSf 2.
[22] Ibid. P 227/OV 1/1; Q/REl 1A, St. Briavels; deeds at Dean Heritage museum, Soudley.
[23] *Morris's Dir. Glos.* (1867), 667.
[24] Glos. R.O., Q/RSf 2.
[25] Ibid. P 227/OV 1/1; Q/REl 1A, St. Briavels; G.D.R., T 1/128.
[26] *Pigot's Dir. Glos.* (1842), 102; Hart, *Coleford*, 253–8; P.R.O., RG 9/3980, s.v. Newland (Coleford).
[27] *Kelly's Dir. Glos.* (1856), 272.
[28] P.R.O., RG 9/3980, s.v. Newland (Coleford); RG 11/5223, s.v. Newland (Coleford).
[29] Glos. R.O., D 637/II/1/T 1.
[30] P.R.O., HO 107/2444, s.v. Newland (Coleford).
[31] Glos. R.O., Q/RSf 2.
[32] *Pigot's Dir. Glos.* (1830), 367; *Robson's Dir. Glos.* (1839), 75; cf. *Morris's Dir. Glos.* (1876), 542; P.R.O., RG 10/5298, s.v. Newland (Coleford).

[33] Glos. R.O., D 2428/1/23/1, p. 60.
[34] *Kelly's Dir. Glos.* (1935), 134.
[35] P.R.O., RG 9/3980, s.v. Newland (Coleford).
[36] *Kelly's Dir. Glos.* (1856), 271.
[37] Glos. R.O., Q/RSf 2.
[38] *Glouc. Jnl.* 17 Aug. 1807.
[39] Glos. R.O., Q/RB 4; *Pigot's Dir. Glos.* (1842), 101–2.
[40] *Kelly's Dir. Glos.* (1889), 747.
[41] *Hunt's Dir. Glos.* (1849), 100.
[42] Glos. R.O., PA 227/7; Hart, *Coleford*, 291–2.
[43] *Kelly's Dir. Glos.* (1863), 253.
[44] Ibid. (1927), 144; (1939), 135.
[45] O.S. Map 1/2,500, SO 5710 (1960 edn.).
[46] *Dean Forest Mercury*, 4 Sept., 4 Dec. 1964.
[47] Bodl. MS. Top. Glouc. c. 3, f. 139; below, econ. hist. (markets and fairs).
[48] *Morris's Dir. Glos.* (1867), 670.
[49] Hart, *Coleford*, 449.
[50] Ibid. 461.   [51] Ibid. 403–4.
[52] *Glouc. Jnl.* 27 Aug. 1864.
[53] Glos. R.O., Q/RP 1.
[54] Hart, *Coleford*, 292–3; *Manual of Glos. Lit.* ii. 166; B.L. index of newspapers at Colindale, s.vv. Cinderford, Coleford.
[55] Hart, *Coleford*, 401.   [56] *Forester*, 1 Oct. 1991.
[57] *Glouc. Jnl.* 21 May 1842.
[58] Hart, *Coleford*, 322, 416.

of the Victoria Cross to Angus Buchanan, a local man, land on the west side of the town was purchased by public subscription for a recreation ground.[59] It included a playing field, a bowling green, and tennis courts; the courts were abandoned before 1980.[60] Another playing field was laid out some way north-west of the recreation ground in the late 1930s.[61] A golf club founded in 1907[62] had links between High Nash and Whitecliff;[63] they were ploughed up during the Second World War.[64] In the early 1970s the former Bell's Grammar school at Lord's Hill was converted as a country club and, in 1973, the adjoining farmland at Edenwall was laid out as a golf course.[65] In 1994 another golf club had a new course in the north-east of Coleford, extending from the Mitcheldean road to Five Acres.

In 1643 royalist troops marching on Gloucester from South Wales dislodged a parliamentary garrison stationed at Coleford to intercept them.[66] Natives of Coleford have included the writer Mary Howitt (1799–1888)[67] and the metallurgist Robert Mushet (1811–91), who by experiment in a barn on the town's outskirts discovered a refinement of the Bessemer process.[68]

MANORS AND OTHER ESTATES. As land in Coleford was cleared for settlement in the Middle Ages a number of estates were formed. Some, notably Breckness Court, owed chief rents to the royal manor of Newland, part of the St. Briavels castle estate.[69] In 1275 at least one house, in Whitecliff, was held from William Ely the younger for a cash rent, suit of court, and heriots,[70] and in 1349 John Joce of Newland received chief rents from houses and lands in Coleford and Whitecliff. John's successors, owners of the Clearwell estate,[71] continued to take rents in Coleford and Whitecliff in 1462.[72]

The *BRECKNESS COURT* (formerly *BRECKNOCKS COURT*) estate in the south-west corner of Coleford tithing[73] originated as an assart which Hugh of Kinnersley created under grant from the Crown before 1225.[74] The estate, which was styled a manor from the early 17th century,[75] was restored to Hugh in 1233 after seizure for the Crown.[76] It passed to John of Kinnersley, who held 151 a. from the Crown for 44s. 5d. rent and was succeeded c. 1255 by his son Hugh, a minor.[77] In 1277 Hugh of Kinnersley sold the estate to Richard de Carew, bishop of St. Davids,[78] who died in 1280[79] having settled the reversion of a messuage, 3 ploughlands, and rents worth 73s. 4d. in Newland on Erneburga, wife of Thomas of Brecon.[80] In 1319 Erneburga and her then husband John ap Howel granted that estate to John's son Howel and in 1343 Howel settled it on himself and Maud la Kele and entailed it on her children Robert and Catherine.[81] Richard Aubrey was the lord of Breckness Court in 1366.[82] The estate's descent has not been traced during the next two centuries. In 1585 Walter Jones lived on it,[83] and in 1608 it belonged to Thomas Jones and Hugh Jones,[84] who in 1623 were described respectively as of Llanwarne and Little Dewchurch (both Herefs.).[85] In 1635 Thomas's son Edward had an interest in the estate[86] and in 1707 William Jones and others, among them Penelope the widow of Edward Jones (d. 1685), conveyed a moiety of it, known as Breckness Court farm and including the site of the main house, to John Symons of Clearwell.[87] The other moiety was owned in 1692 by Thomas Jones[88] of Little Dewchurch and sold in 1710 by his widow Rachel and daughter Lettice, the wives of Benjamin Mason and Richard Oswald respectively, to William Davies. It comprised land on the south-east side of Pingry Lane, in Clearwell tithing,[89] and its descent has not been traced. From John Symons (d. 1721) Breckness Court farm descended with the Symons family's lands elsewhere in Newland parish until the break-up of that estate in the late 19th century[90] and was acquired before 1894 by E. R. Payne.[91] The Payne family had 54 a. at Breckness Court in 1910[92] and owned land there in the 1940s.[93]

In 1225 the Crown gave Hugh of Kinnersley five oaks to build a house on his estate.[94] Known in 1334 as Kinnersley Court and in 1358 as Brecknocks Court,[95] it stood on a moated site north of Pingry Lane[96] and was probably occupied as a farmhouse in the early 17th century.[97] The site, in 1840 part of a field called Moat meadow,[98] had been abandoned by c. 1711 when

59 Plaque on entrance gates.   60 Hart, *Coleford*, 421.
61 Inscr. on entrance gates.
62 *Glouc. Jnl.* 25 Sept. 1909.
63 O.S. Map 6", Glos. XXXVIII. NE. (1924 edn.).
64 Hart, *Coleford*, 421.
65 Ibid. 379, 431; *Glos. and Avon Life*, Oct. 1976, 42–5.
66 *Bibliotheca Glos.* ii, p. xxxiv.
67 *D.N.B.*   68 Ibid.; Hart, *Coleford*, 237.
69 Below, Newland, manors; *Inq. p.m. Glos.* 1625–42, i. 220–1; Glos. R.O., D 2026/X 19; Berkeley Cast. Mun., General Ser. 16; for Breckness Ct., below, this section.
70 Glos. R.O., D 2244/11.
71 N.L.W., Dunraven MSS. 339; below, Newland, manors.
72 Glos. R.O., D 1677/GG 1225.
73 N.L.W., Mynde Park MSS. 286, 908; G.D.R., T 1/128; O.S. Map 6", Glos. XXXVIII. NE. (1884 edn.).
74 *Rot. Litt. Claus.* (Rec. Com.), ii. 52.
75 *Inq. p.m. Glos.* 1625–42, i. 221.
76 *Close R.* 1231–4, 232.
77 *Cal. Inq. p.m.* i, p. 324; cf. Glos. R.O., D 2026/X 19.
78 *Cal. Pat.* 1272–81, 199; *Cal. Chart. R.* 1257–1300, 204.
79 *Handbook of Brit. Chronology* (1961), 279.
80 P.R.O., CP 25/1/75/31, no. 34.
81 *Cal. Pat.* 1317–21, 384; 1343–5, 109; cf. Glos. R.O.,

D 1677/GG 50.
82 Glos. R.O., D 33/420 (abs. of deed in ibid. D 33/49).
83 Ibid. P 227/IN 1/1.   84 P.R.O., MR 879.
85 Glos. R.O., D 2026/X 19.
86 *Inq. p.m. Glos.* 1625–42, i. 220–1; for the Jones fam. of Llanwarne, J. Duncumb, *Hist. and Antiquities of Herefs.* (edn. by J. H. Matthews, 1913), ii. 94–5.
87 P.R.O., CP 25/2/926/6 Anne Trin. no. 34; F 3/128; N.L.W., Mynde Park MSS. 1296–7.
88 P.R.O., CP 25/2/898/4 Wm. and Mary Trin. no. 13.
89 Glos. R.O., D 5377/3/1; D 5730/1/1; G.D.R., T 1/128.
90 Berkeley Cast. Mun., General Ser. 16; Bigland, *Glos.* ii. 257; below, Newland, manors.
91 Glos. R.O., D 2299/191.
92 Ibid. D 2428/1/23/1, p. 58.
93 'Assart or Ancient Settlement? Preliminary Rep. on Breckness Court' (Forest of Dean Local Hist. Soc. 1985), 10–11: copy in ibid. FD 36; cf. ibid. DA 5/510/3, p. 42.
94 *Rot. Litt. Claus.* (Rec. Com.), ii. 52.
95 Glos. R.O., D 1677/GG 50, 87.
96 'Assart or Ancient Settlement?' 12–18; N.L.W., Dunraven MSS. 325, deed 1446.
97 Glos. R.O., P 227/IN 1/1, baptism 7 Sept. 1628.
98 G.D.R., T 1/128 (no. 1042).

John Symons converted a barn on higher ground some way to the north as a farmhouse.[99] That house was abandoned long before 1985[1] but it was standing as part of a range of farm buildings in 1994.

Land in Coleford belonging to Staunton manor presumably once formed part of the Staunton bailiwick of the Forest.[2] In 1345 Philip, son of John of Staunton (d. 1339), made a grant of lands in Coleford,[3] and in 1413 the lord of Staunton owned land at Edenwall.[4] In 1478 the lord of Staunton's possessions in Coleford were said to include 100 a. and to be held from Flaxley abbey but in 1526 they were held from the St. Briavels castle estate.[5] In 1579 Staunton manor included land and chief rents in many parts of Coleford, including Tufthorn, Lord's Hill, and Edenwall.[6] Other chief rents from houses and land at Whitecliff and elsewhere were acquired from Charles Thornbury by William Hall of Highmeadow in 1589,[7] and passed with the rights of Staunton manor from 1620. In the 18th century claims of the Gage family, owners of the Highmeadow estate and lords of Staunton,[8] over Coleford, particularly over the town's market place, caused conflict with local people and with the earls of Berkeley, lessees of the royal manor of Newland.[9] The Crown, which owned Staunton manor from 1817,[10] sold several small strips of land in the market place in 1866.[11]

Flaxley abbey, which made a grant of land in the north-west quarter of Coleford in 1430,[12] received rents in Newland, Coleford, and Staunton valued at £17 3s. 6d. in 1535.[13]

ECONOMIC HISTORY. AGRICULTURE. Much of Coleford was held by free tenants owing chief rents to the royal manor of Newland,[14] the rents being determined when the land was cleared or in the early 17th century when the owners made compositions with the Crown.[15] In the 14th and 15th centuries many houses and small holdings owed chief rents to the Joce family and their successors to the Clearwell estate.[16]

In the later Middle Ages a large part of Coleford was meadow land, including in 1478 land at Pool green.[17] Arable land, which on the Breckness Court estate in the south-west corner of the tithing evidently comprised 3 ploughlands in 1278,[18] included a small open field on the hillside at High Nash in 1344.[19] In the later 15th century there were several other small open fields on the hills in the south part of Coleford, the field called Ducknells being high above Whitecliff. Holdings in the fields were described in terms of 'day-works', the number of days needed presumably for ploughing.[20] Along with freeholders elsewhere in the parishes bordering the Forest of Dean, Coleford's landholders enjoyed common rights on the royal demesne land of the Forest.[21] On the west side of the tithing Scowles common,[22] covering 23 a. in 1792, was used by local people in the later 18th century for grazing sheep during the months the Forest was closed to livestock. Ownership of the common, claimed at that time for Newland manor by the lessee of the St. Briavels castle estate, was confirmed to the lord of Staunton manor in 1798.[23] There was a new sheephouse at Wynols Hill in 1654.[24] An older sheephouse north-east of Scowles was in ruins in 1674.[25] Hops were grown in the tithing before 1618,[26] and in the early 18th century several orchards near the town grew cider apples of the variety called stire.[27] There were also orchards on Hoarthorns farm, north-east of Berry Hill, in 1796.[28]

In the late 18th century much land in Coleford was worked by tenant farmers. By 1792 most of the farmland at the north-west end of the tithing had been incorporated in two farms on the Highmeadow estate, both held by leases renewed in 1793 for 16 years. Broomhill farm had 142 a., including 56 a. to the north-west at Braceland in English Bicknor, and Marian's farm 140 a., including 16 a. in Staunton and 21 a., formerly a separate farm, at Knaven Green. On the same estate a farm of 19 a. at Whitecliff had been added to Cherry Orchard farm (in Newland and Staunton), and a tenant at will farmed 26 a. at Lower Berry Hill. There were half a dozen other farms, all with under 50 a., in the north-west quarter of Coleford in 1792. They included Scowles farm, which was part of the Probyn family's estate, Owen farm, and Whitecliff farm.[29] In the south part of the tithing in 1814 Breckness Court and Perrygrove farms, on the Symons family's estate, contained 65 a. and 64 a. respectively;[30] Breckness Court had been tenanted before 1712.[31]

The area of farmland in Coleford was reduced in the mid 1820s when new timber plantations were created in the north and Broomhill and Marian's farms were lost.[32] In 1840 Coleford

99 N.L.W., Mynde Park MSS. 1296–7; G.D.R., T 1/128.
1 'Assart or Ancient Settlement?' 19.
2 Trans. B.G.A.S. xiv. 363–4.
3 Glos. R.O., D 2244/28; below, Staunton, manor.
4 Glos. R.O., D 2957/214.13.
5 Trans. B.G.A.S. vii. 234–6.   6 Ibid. 238–43.
7 Glos. R.O., D 1677/GG 527.
8 Below, Staunton, manor.
9 Glos. R.O., D 678/fam. settlements 57D/279; D 1677/GG 1212, 1282, 1543; Berkeley Cast. Mun., General Ser. T, box 25.
10 Below, Staunton, manor.   11 P.R.O., F 14/10.
12 Glos. R.O., D 1677/GG 195.
13 Valor. Eccl. (Rec. Com.), ii. 486.
14 Above, manors; Inq. p.m. Glos. 1625–42, i. 220–1; Glos. R.O., D 2026/X 19; Berkeley Cast. Mun., General Ser. 16.
15 P.R.O., C 66/2168, no. 3; cf. below, Forest of Dean, forest admin. (exploitation 1603–68).
16 Above, manors.
17 Glos. R.O., D 1677/GG 1224–5.
18 P.R.O., CP 25/1/75/31, no. 34; above, manors.
19 Glos. R.O., D 2244/26.
20 Ibid. 151; N.L.W., Dunraven MSS. 271; for Ducknells, P.R.O., MR 879.
21 Below, Newland, econ. hist.
22 Glos. R.O., D 23/T 24.
23 Berkeley Cast. Mun., General Ser. T, box 25; P.R.O., F 17/117(2), p. 45; MR 691.
24 Glos. R.O., D 2957, abs. of title 148.
25 Ibid. D 23/T 24; P.R.O., MR 879.
26 P.R.O., C 66/2168, no. 3.
27 Bodl. MS. Top. Glouc. c. 3, f. 139v.
28 Glos. R.O., photocopy 815.
29 P.R.O., F 17/117(2), pp. 4, 36–7, 42–4, 49–51, 53; MR 691.
30 N.L.W., Mynde Park MS. 908.
31 Ibid. 1296–7.
32 P.R.O., F 17/117(1); G.D.R., T 1/128.

contained 17 farms of over 20 a. The largest were Edenwall (123 a.), Whitecliff (106 a.), Pingry (92 a.), and Five Acres (83 a.). At that time the detached part of Newland north-east of Berry Hill contained Hoarthorns farm (176 a.), which was part of the Eastbach estate in English Bicknor, and a small farm at Joyford.[33] In 1896 a total of 69 agricultural holdings was returned for Coleford parish, most of them worked by tenants.[34] The number of farms declined in the 20th century. Thirty-nine, all under 100 a. and most under 50 a., were returned in 1926, when farming provided regular work for 32 people.[35] From the late 1950s the area of cultivation contracted as land was taken for industrial, residential, and recreational use,[36] and in 1988, when most farmland was owner-occupied, 19 holdings were returned for the parish. One farm had more than 100 ha. (247 a.), but most of the others had less than 20 ha. (49 a.) and were worked on a part-time basis.[37]

In the mid 19th century a greater area of Coleford was devoted to arable than to grassland.[38] The main crops were wheat, barley, grass seeds, and turnips, and in 1866 the arable land, 1,068 a., included 120 a. lying fallow. At that time 794 a. were permanent grassland and beef and dairy cattle and pigs were kept as well as much larger numbers of sheep.[39] In the later 19th century the numbers of beef and dairy cattle grew, and the move from arable to livestock farming continued in the early 20th century, when the sheep flocks were enlarged. In 1926, when 1,102 a. were returned as permanent grassland and only 117 a. as arable, the number of sheep was 2,305 compared with 1,152 in 1866 and the numbers of beef and dairy cattle 165 and 121 compared with 92 and 50 in 1866. There was at least one commercial poultry farm in Coleford in 1926.[40] During the Second World War the size of the dairy herds increased[41] but in 1988, when most of Coleford's farmland remained under grass, the principal farms were devoted to sheep and beef farming.[42]

MILLS AND IRONWORKS. In 1594 Charles Thornbury quitclaimed to Thomas Baynham a mill[43] on Thurstan's brook at Pool green. It was held in 1608 by William Thornbury[44] and was possibly the corn mill owned in 1667 by Thomas Foley of Great Witley (Worcs.).[45] Another building at Pool green in 1608, downstream of William Thornbury's mill and on or below the dam of the king's fishpond,[46] was evidently the corn mill bought by Benedict Hall of Highmeadow in 1637.[47] Nothing is known of the mills above the town after the mid 17th century.

The site of the highest mill on the brook below the town was occupied in 1840 by a building called the old mill.[48] Downstream a grist mill operating in Whitecliff in 1694[49] may have been the mill near the centre of the hamlet in 1792 at the site of the later ironworks.[50] During the Napoleonic Wars a mill next to the ironworks made black paint from yellow ochre.[51] It was worked by Isaiah Birt, one of the ironworks' owners, who in 1806 obtained a patent for the manufacture of black paint, and it remained in use until 1813 or later.[52] In 1618 William Worgan owned a mill at Whitecliff cross,[53] at the south-west end of the hamlet, where Elizabeth Worgan held a grist mill under a grant from William Probyn of Highmeadow in 1657.[54] That was probably the Whitecliff mill belonging to the Highmeadow estate in 1675 and 1707.[55] A steam mill at Whitecliff, apparently started c. 1820,[56] was in use in the mid 1850s.[57] None of the mills below the town was in use in 1880.[58] The location of a water mill on the Breckness Court estate, demolished before 1673, is unknown.[59]

Ironworking in Coleford in the Middle Ages or earlier produced large quantities of waste material or cinders.[60] Some formed prominent mounds, of which several were in the north-west part of the tithing towards Staunton.[61] The earlier ironworks were evidently moveable forges operating on the royal demesne woodland of the Forest of Dean.[62] An oresmithy, or furnace, was operating at Whitecliff in 1361,[63] and the hamlet had a number of furnaces and forges in the 15th and 16th centuries.[64] In the later Middle Ages iron was also worked in Coleford town,[65] where there was a furnace next to the chapel in 1539.[66]

In 1797 James Teague, a local mine owner, formed a partnership with Midland industrialists including Samuel Botham of Uttoxeter (Staffs.) to build a coke-fired furnace at Whitecliff. After flooding halted construction work Teague's company was re-formed with Thomas Halford, a London stockbroker, as a member and the furnace, near the centre of the hamlet, was blown in probably in 1801 or 1802. A second furnace was built beside it before 1808.[67] The ironworks supplied tinplate works but their output was limited by the quality of coke used. In 1809 Halford, who had taken over the ironworks,

33 G.D.R., T 1/128. 34 P.R.O., MAF 68/1609/6.
35 Ibid. MAF 68/3295/6.
36 Above, intro.; below (other ind. and trade).
37 Agric. Returns 1988. 38 G.D.R., T 1/128.
39 P.R.O., MAF 68/26/8.
40 Ibid. MAF 68/25/9; MAF 68/1609/6; MAF 68/3295/6.
41 Payne, Glos. Survey, 95.
42 Agric. Returns 1988.
43 P.R.O., CP 25/2/145/1897, no. 2.
44 Ibid. MR 879; Nicholls, Forest of Dean, 258.
45 Glos. R.O., D 1833/T 13. 46 P.R.O., MR 879.
47 Glos. R.O., D 1677/GG 826.
48 G.D.R., T 1/128.
49 Glos. R.O., D 2926/10.
50 P.R.O., F 17/117(2), p. 50; MR 691.
51 Hart, Ind. Hist. of Dean, 245–6; New Regard of Forest of Dean, iii. 85.
52 I. J. Standing, 'Whitecliff Ironworks', Glos. Soc. Ind.

Arch. Jnl. (1981), 37; (1986), 9; cf. Glos. R.O., D 637/V/4, where the mill was said in 1810 to have belonged to Jas. Powell.
53 P.R.O., C 66/2168, no. 3.
54 Glos. R.O., D 1677/GG 933.
55 Ibid. GG 981, 1084–5.
56 Ibid. D 637/I/45. 57 Hart, Coleford, 265.
58 O.S. Map 1/2,500, Glos. XXXVIII. 4 (1882 edn.).
59 N.L.W., Dunraven MSS. 270.
60 New Regard of Forest of Dean, i. 37–8; iii. 85.
61 Glos. R.O., D 23/T 23; D 33/230, 358.
62 Below, Forest of Dean, industry (ironworks).
63 Glos. R.O., D 1677/GG 92A.
64 Ibid. GG 495; D 2244/121.
65 Ibid. D 2244/135; D 2957/86.11.
66 Ibid. D 1677/GG 389.
67 Standing, 'Whitecliff Ironworks', Glos. Soc. Ind. Arch. Jnl. (1980), 18–23; for Teague, Anstis, Ind. Teagues, 45–52.

enlisted the help of David Mushet, a noted metallurgist, to increase productivity but the works remained unprofitable and Mushet withdrew from the venture after a few months. The furnaces were abandoned several years later, perhaps by 1812, and Halford was declared bankrupt in 1816. Some of the fittings were sent to Cinderford in 1827,[68] and the surviving ruins were maintained for their archaeological and industrial interest in the late 20th century.[69]

OTHER INDUSTRY AND TRADE. The exploitation of Coleford's mineral resources began long before 1397 when its first known miner was recorded.[70] Ancient surface iron mines known locally as scowles gave the name to the limestone outcrop in the west of the tithing. Generations of Newland parishioners also quarried stone at Scowles, which in the mid 18th century was riddled with abandoned workings.[71] Coal was presumably dug on the higher ground in the east part of Coleford by the late 16th century, when a miner acquired a lease of land bordering the royal Forest at Broadwell.[72] Six miners were listed in Coleford in 1608.[73]

By the late 17th century iron-ore mining had been abandoned in favour of the digging up of cinders left by early ironworks. The owners of the Highmeadow estate exploited cinder deposits by the Staunton road and in the 1720s supplied cinders to the Redbrook furnace. Cinders were also quarried at Cinder Hill and, in the 1760s, in the town and at Whitecliff.[74] The building of the Whitecliff ironworks stimulated ore prospecting in the early 19th century, notably by David Mushet who in 1809 developed Boxbush mine near the town centre.[75] In 1835 ore was mined north of Scowles, between Whitecliff and High Nash, and at Perrygrove. In the early 1870s Scowles pit, by the Crossways–Highmeadow road, sent ore to the Parkend ironworks,[76] and Crowsnest pit, to the north, supplied ironworks in South Wales.[77] Crowsnest mine later yielded a quantity of yellow ochre.[78] In 1873 two pits were opened at Crossways but they and several new iron-ore mines at High Nash were abandoned not long afterwards. Two drift mines at Whitecliff extracted small amounts of ore in the later 1890s.[79]

Coal mining continued in the north and east parts of Coleford from the 17th century.[80] In the east a mine, known in 1735 as Gentlemen Colliers,[81] included a working pit at Littledean Lane End near Broadwell in 1835. At that time there were also working coal mines in the Poolway and Berry Hill areas, some of the pits north of Poolway belonging to Cross Knave colliery. Although coal mining declined in Coleford after 1850, when new pits were opened within the Forest,[82] there were several pits and levels on the east side of the tithing in the later 19th century[83] and mining continued at Poolway until the 1960s.[84] The principal colliery owner there employed 45 men in the early 1940s.[85] Coal was also mined north of the town in the 1940s and the opencast method was used to extract coal at the Gorse and at Edenwall in the 1960s.[86]

A marl pit recorded in 1354[87] may have been in Coleford tithing. Limestone was quarried at the south-west end of Whitecliff before the 17th century.[88] One of the two grindstone hewers listed in Coleford in 1608[89] worked at Bixhead, in the Forest, in 1621.[90] In the 18th century residents of Whitecliff and Berry Hill worked as stone cutters.[91] Limekilns operated at Whitecliff,[92] and Scowles, where a kiln was built before 1734, supplied much lime to Monmouthshire. In the later 18th century Viscount Gage, who claimed manorial rights at Scowles, opposed the building of new kilns there, but a kiln erected in 1793 under a grant from the St. Briavels castle estate was rebuilt after it had been pulled down on Gage's orders.[93] In the late 18th century lime was also burnt on Hoarthorns farm, north-east of Berry Hill.[94] The opening of the Monmouth tramroad in 1812[95] stimulated quarrying at Whitecliff and there were three new limekilns at the south-west end of the hamlet in 1836.[96] The quarries on the west side of the Forest offered additional jobs to Coleford men[97] and in 1851 G. E. Payne, a Coleford stone merchant, had nine employees.[98] At Whitecliff, where lime burning continued intermittently,[99] a quarry on the north side of the valley was worked for roadstone in 1870[1] and was enlarged after the construction of the Monmouth railway. It later sent stone by rail through Coleford and Parkend[2] and by the mid 1960s it formed a massive crater reaching into the hillside as far as Scowles.[3] Several quarries were worked at Scowles in

68 *Glos. Soc. Ind. Arch. Jnl.* (1980), 24–6; (1981), 34–6; (1986), 3–9; Anstis, *Ind. Teagues*, 60, 67.
69 *Glos. Soc. Ind. Arch. Jnl.* (1986), 11, 19; *Glos. and Avon Life*, June 1980, 50–1.
70 N.L.W., Dunraven MSS. 324.
71 Berkeley Cast. Mun., General Ser. T, box 25, Scowles papers 1790s; Hart, *Free Miners*, 30.
72 Glos. R.O., D 33/169.
73 Smith, *Men and Armour*, 36–7.
74 Glos. R.O., D 1677/GG 1368; P 310/MI 1, p. 16; Berkeley Cast. Mun., General Ser. T, box 25, Scowles papers 1790s. 75 Hart, *Coleford*, 235.
76 Ibid. 234, 295; *Award of Dean Forest Mining Com.* (1841), 191–2.
77 Paar, *G.W.R. in Dean*, 111.
78 Hart, *Ind. Hist. of Dean*, 246.
79 Glos. R.O., D 34/9/71B; Hart, *Coleford*, 290.
80 Ogilby, *Britannia* (1675), plate 15.
81 Nicholls, *Forest of Dean*, 235.
82 I. J. Standing, 'Mining of Coal in Coleford district before 1850', *Glos. Soc. Ind. Arch. Jnl.* (1980), 40–1; Hart, *Coleford*, 241.
83 O.S. Map 6", Glos. XXXVIII. NE. (1884 edn.); Hart,

Coleford, 294; *Kelly's Dir. Glos.* (1885), 434.
84 *Glos. Countryside*, Apr.–June 1954, 162; Hart, *Coleford*, 445. 85 Glos. R.O., AP/R 1/SE 2A/F 2.
86 Hart, *Coleford*, 379, 445.
87 Glos. R.O., D 2244/47. 88 P.R.O., MR 879.
89 Smith, *Men and Armour*, 36–7.
90 Glos. R.O., D 2026/L 5.
91 Ibid. D 543, Whitecliff deeds 1747–1828; D 637/II/4/T 3; D 2656; Bigland, *Glos.* ii. 264–5.
92 P.R.O., F 17/117(2), pp. 49–50; MR 691.
93 Berkeley Cast. Mun., General Ser. T, box 25; Glos. R.O., D 1677/GG 1545, no. 40.
94 Glos. R.O., photocopy 815. 95 Above, intro.
96 Glos. R.O., D 637/VII/31.
97 *Glouc. Jnl.* 28 Mar. 1808; 18 Nov. 1816; below, Forest of Dean, industry (quarrying).
98 P.R.O., HO 107/2444, s.v. Newland (Coleford); G.D.R. wills 1854/116.
99 Glos. R.O., D 2299/191; *Kelly's Dir. Glos.* (1889), 747.
1 Hart, *Coleford*, 297.
2 Paar, *G.W.R. in Dean*, 117–18; I. Pope and P. Kerau, *Severn & Wye Railway*, iii. 559–60, 566.
3 O.S. Maps 1/2,500, SO 5609–10 (1972–3 edn.).

1870.[4] A quarry opened to the north-west, between the Crossways–Highmeadow road and the parish boundary, in the late 19th century[5] was exploited for roadstone[6] and in the later 20th century it ate deeply into the hillside.[7] Both it and the Whitecliff quarry were idle in 1994.

Iron was worked in Coleford and Whitecliff in the later Middle Ages,[8] and among the metal trades established before 1333 was nailmaking.[9] A sharesmith lived in Coleford in 1387[10] and one of the more prosperous residents in 1534 was an iron merchant.[11] In 1608 metal trades in the tithing were represented by 4 smiths and 2 nailers and other trades by 4 carpenters, 1 cooper, 3 shoemakers, 2 tailors, 2 butchers, 3 tanners, 2 glovers, and 2 weavers.[12] While some of those tradesmen presumably lived at Whitecliff, where there was a tannery in the 17th century,[13] and some possibly in the detached part of the tithing at Lydbrook, the retailing trades centred on Coleford town where residents included a chandler in 1640[14] and a mercer in 1658.[15]

Following the grant of a market in 1661[16] the town's economy depended both on market trade and on retail business, and in the early 18th century its community of small shopkeepers and innkeepers relied on the custom of miners from the surrounding countryside.[17] Shopkeepers in 1751 included an ironmonger,[18] and the three shops on the Highmeadow estate in 1756 were presumably in the town.[19] A brewery was recorded in Coleford in 1686[20] and there were several small malting businesses in the town in the 18th century.[21] A silkweaver lived there before 1727.[22] From the later 17th century Coleford also provided opportunities for professional men. Surgeons were recorded from 1702[23] and an apothecary lived in the town in 1751.[24] At least one attorney practised at Coleford in 1700[25] and among resident attorneys in 1745 was Thomas James.[26] James, later of Rodleys, in Lydney,[27] was agent of the St. Briavels castle estate and his practice remained in his family[28] until William Roberts acquired it in 1829.[29]

Although Coleford was on an important route between Gloucester and South Wales[30] road traffic was of minor importance for the town's economy in the mid 18th century.[31] Improvements to roads in the Forest in the late 18th century increased traffic through Coleford[32] but from 1841 the town was bypassed by the Gloucester–Monmouth road.[33] In the late 1840s there was a thrice-weekly coach service between Coleford and Gloucester[34] and in the mid 1850s a daily service to the railway at Lydney was started.[35]

With the expansion of mining and quarrying in the Forest from the later 18th century[36] Coleford grew in importance as a market and business centre for the area. In 1830 its shopkeepers included 5 grocers and drapers, 2 linen drapers, a grocer, an ironmonger and butcher, a druggist, and a bookseller.[37] In 1856 there were shops selling confectionery and music.[38] The grocery and drapery business run by Thomas Trotter in 1830[39] was the town's largest retailing concern in 1881[40] but was later replaced as the main clothes store by a similar business started by E. A. Trotter in 1866.[41] The number of professional people also grew, 2 attorneys and 3 surgeons being recorded in 1830[42] and 3 solicitors and 4 surgeons in 1856.[43] Richard White, a draper and general shopkeeper, was also in business as an auctioneer and land agent by 1805[44] and John Briggs, an auctioneer and surveyor established in the town by 1838, also practised as an architect. Coleford had a branch of a Herefordshire bank in 1839[45] and the Gloucestershire Banking Co. opened a branch in the town in 1862.[46] In the mid 19th century some of the more prosperous mine owners and industrialists of the Forest area lived in Coleford and several mining and civil engineers took up residence,[47] notably John Atkinson on his appointment as deputy gaveller for the Forest in 1838.[48]

The town also had a number of small industries. A silk-throwing factory sited in Newland Street, presumably the silk mill opened c. 1790,[49] employed 80 or more people before it closed c. 1826.[50] In the early 19th century tanning, a traditional industry in the Forest area, was carried on at two places, one of which, at the Spout,

4 Hart, *Coleford*, 296.
5 O.S. Map 6", Glos. XXXVIII. NE. (1884 and later edns.).   6 Hart, *Ind. Hist. of Dean*, 309.
7 Cf. O.S. Maps 1/2,500, SO 5510–11 (1976 edn.).
8 Above (mills and ironworks).
9 Glos. R.O., D 33/26; D 2244/23.
10 Ibid. D 2957/86.1.   11 Hockaday Abs. ccxcv.
12 Smith, *Men and Armour*, 36–7.
13 Glos. R.O., D 1677/GG 741, 952.
14 Ibid. D 2926/3.   15 Ibid. D 33/231.
16 Below (markets and fairs).
17 Bodl. MS. Top. Glouc. c. 3, f. 139; for inns, above, intro.
18 Glos. R.O., D 608/4/1.
19 Ibid. D 1677/GG 1358.
20 P.R.O., CP 25/2/778/2 Jas. II Trin. no. 25.
21 G.D.R. wills 1742/78; Glos. R.O., D 608/4/7.
22 *Cal. Reg. Glouc. Freemen 1641–1838* (B.G.A.S. Rec. Ser. iv), 90.
23 Hockaday Abs. clxv, 1743; ccxcvii, 1702, 1719.
24 Glos. R.O., D 637/II/1/T 1.
25 Ibid. D 2026/L 9.
26 Ibid. D 1677/GG 1228; D 678/fam. settlements 57D/268; G.D.R. wills 1762/188.
27 Above, Lydney, manors.
28 Berkeley Cast. Mun., General Ser. T, box 25; *Glouc.*

Jnl. 9 June 1806.
29 P.R.O., F 14/13; F 3/128.   30 Above, intro.
31 *Glouc. Jnl.* 28 Aug. 1750; 7 Mar. 1758.
32 Ibid. 13 Sept. 1784; 29 Aug. 1796; 3 Jan. 1814; below, Forest of Dean, settlement.
33 Above, intro.
34 *Hunt's Dir. Glos.* (1849), 104.
35 *Slater's Dir. Glos.* (1852–3), 121; (1858–9), 180.
36 Below, Forest of Dean, industry.
37 *Pigot's Dir. Glos.* (1830), 367.
38 *Kelly's Dir. Glos.* (1856), 271–2.
39 *Pigot's Dir. Glos.* (1830), 367.
40 P.R.O., HO 107/2444, s.v. Newland (Coleford); RG 11/5223, s.v. Newland (Coleford).
41 Hart, *Coleford*, 224; *Forester*, 28 Feb. 1992.
42 *Pigot's Dir. Glos.* (1830), 367.
43 *Kelly's Dir. Glos.* (1856), 271–2.
44 *Glouc. Jnl.* 18 Apr. 1808; Glos. R.O., D 23/E 7; D 608/4/7.
45 *Robson's Dir. Glos.* (1839), 74–5; G.D.R., F 4/1.
46 Hart, *Coleford*, 372–3.
47 *Pigot's Dir. Glos.* (1842), 102; *Morris's Dir. Glos.* (1876), 541–5.
48 Hart, *Free Miners*, 62.   49 Bigland, *Glos.* ii. 257.
50 Hart, *Ind. Hist. of Dean*, 401–2; Glos. R.O., P 227/OV 1/1.

was converted as a brewery just before 1833.[51] The brewery closed in the late 19th century.[52] Isaiah Trotter, a maltster in 1842,[53] became the town's leading corn merchant.[54] Of Coleford's traditional metal crafts nailmaking survived in the late 1850s.[55] A coachbuilder had moved from Berry Hill to the town by 1861[56] and one of the town's blacksmiths specialized in making agricultural implements in 1870.[57] In 1876 there was a foundry in Albert Road.[58] It and a nearby paint factory or colour works, established by 1870,[59] closed before 1900.[60]

A pottery recorded at Whitecliff in 1720[61] was possibly that making casting pots for the nearby ironworks in 1803.[62] The pottery, which employed 16 men and boys in 1851,[63] continued in production in the early 1880s[64] but was disused in 1898.[65] In the 1920s a mortar mill operated at a builders' yard in the part of Whitecliff adjoining the town.[66] A brickyard on the Staunton road beyond Crossways was occupied in 1821 by James Machen, owner of the Eastbach estate, and in the following year by James Hall.[67] Hall revived brickmaking there in the later 1840s.[68] The yard, which became known as Marian's brickworks,[69] ceased production c. 1940, and the kilns and some buildings were demolished in the early 1950s to make way for a saw mill and fence factory.[70]

After the Second World War the Royal Forest of Dean Development Association encouraged the establishment of businesses in Coleford to counter the loss of jobs in the mining and quarrying industries. The Bristol firm of H. W. Carter & Co. Ltd., makers of Ribena blackcurrant juice and other fruit drinks, occupied a new factory west of High Nash from 1947. The factory was acquired by Beecham Foods Ltd. in 1955 and became a major employer.[71] From 1990 it was owned by SmithKline Beecham, which had c. 450 full-time employees there in 1994.[72] A firm making women's and children's clothes, which moved to Coleford in 1950,[73] closed its factory after a few years.[74] By the late 1950s factories were being built on an industrial estate in Tufthorn Avenue, south-east of the town.[75] The main one was built in 1961 for a company using waste material from the Pine End works in Lydney to make table tops and moulded

products for cars and domestic appliances.[76] In the 1970s the factory manufactured room partition and ceiling components and by the mid 1980s its workforce had risen to over 300. It employed fewer people by 1989, when it switched to making concrete slabs from stone quarried at Tidenham.[77] Henry Sykes Ltd., a London pump manufacturer, established a depot on the Tufthorn estate in 1963 and built a components factory there in 1965.[78] The factory, which in 1983 became the main centre of pump production for the Sykes group of companies,[79] employed 130 people in 1986 and, as part of the SPP Group, was enlarged in 1987.[80] In the later 1980s, following the loss of many jobs in the Forest area, more factories were built in Tufthorn Avenue and, beginning in 1986, the Mushet industrial estate was laid out to the north-east, where the bypass opened in 1991.[81] Businesses there in 1994 included a producer of extrusion and capstan machines, one of several small engineering firms established in Coleford in the early 1960s.[82]

Although Coleford market was in decline in the later 19th century and lapsed in the mid 20th century, the town remained an important centre for services such as banking to the surrounding countryside. Some old-established retail businesses were replaced by branches of chain stores, and following the building of new shops on the south-east side of the town in the late 1980s several shops in the town centre, notably in 1992 Trotter's store, closed.[83]

MARKETS AND FAIRS. The medieval cross at the centre of Coleford[84] may have been the focal point for informal market trade in the 16th century. In 1642 the commander of a parliamentary garrison in Coleford started a market in the town because the nearest chartered market, in Monmouth, was under royalist control. The Coleford market was held on Wednesdays and Fridays until opposition from Monmouth forced its closure.[85] A market house, evidently at the site of the cross, was burned down in 1643 when royalist forces seized the town.[86]

In 1661 seven men including leading tradesmen in the town had a grant of a Friday market and fairs on 9 June and 24 November.[87] They

[51] Glos. R.O., P 227/OV 1/1; D 637/I/41; G.D.R., T 1/128.
[52] O.S. Map 1/2,500, Glos. XXXVIII. 4 (1882, 1902 edns.).
[53] Pigot's Dir. Glos. (1842), 102.
[54] Hunt's Dir. Glos. (1849), 101; Kelly's Dir. Glos. (1856 and later edns.); below (markets and fairs).
[55] Slater's Dir. Glos. (1858–9), 180.
[56] P.R.O., HO 107/2444, s.v. W. Dean; RG 9/3980, s.v. Newland (Coleford).
[57] Morris's Dir. Glos. (1867), 669; Kelly's Dir. Glos. (1870), 527.
[58] Morris's Dir. Glos. (1876), 543.
[59] Kelly's Dir. Glos. (1870), 527.
[60] O.S. Map 1/2,500, Glos. XXXVIII. 4 (1882, 1902 edns.).
[61] Glos. R.O., D 637/II/1/T 1; cf. G.D.R. wills 1720/180.
[62] Rudge, Hist. of Glos. ii. 104.
[63] P.R.O., HO 107/2444, s.v. Newland (Coleford).
[64] Ibid. RG 11/5223, s.v. Newland (Coleford); O.S. Map 6", Glos. XXXVIII. NE. (1884 edn.).
[65] Glos. R.O., DA 5/510/1, p. 55.
[66] Ibid. 3, p. 36; Kelly's Dir. Glos. (1927), 143.
[67] Glos. R.O., P 227/OV 1/1; Bryant, Map of Glos. (1824); for the Eastbach est., above, Eng. Bicknor, manor.
[68] 26th Rep. Com. Woods, H.C. 611, p. 87 (1849), xxvii;

[69] O.S. Map 6", Glos. XXX. SE. (1884 edn.).
[70] Glos. R.O., AP/R 1/SE 2A/F 35–6; Hart, Coleford, 229.
[71] Hart, Ind. Hist. of Dean, 423, 429; Glos. R.O., D 3921/V/21.
[72] Inf. from secretary to site director, SmithKline Consumer Healthcare, Royal Forest Factory, Coleford.
[73] Hart, Ind. Hist. of Dean, 423.
[74] W.I. hist. of Coleford (1959, TS. in Glos. Colln.), 13.
[75] O.S. Map 1/2,500, SO 5709 (1960 edn.).
[76] Glos. R.O., D 3921/V/21.
[77] Dean Forest Mercury, 16 Oct. 1987; 13 Sept. 1991.
[78] Glos. R.O., D 3921/V/21.
[79] Dean Forest Mercury, 19 Aug. 1983.
[80] Ibid. 13 Mar. 1987; Citizen, 3 Nov. 1987.
[81] Citizen, 22 Mar., 3 June 1986.
[82] Glos. R.O., D 3921/V/21.
[83] Forester, 28 Feb. 1992; 22 Jan. 1993.
[84] N.L.W., Dunraven MSS. 271; P.R.O., MR 879.
[85] Glos. Colln. LF 1.1, f. 27 and v.
[86] Bibliotheca Glos. ii, pp. xxxiv, cxlix.
[87] Glos. R.O., D 1677/GG 1439; cf. ibid. D 33/231–2; Cal. S.P. Dom. 1654, 156.

Glos. R.O., D 637/II/5/B 3.

held the market and the fairs in the town centre, where a new market house was built on the site of the cross in 1679 with a grant of £40 from the Crown and contributions from Sir Baynham Throckmorton of Clearwell, Henry Benedict Hall of Highmeadow, and several other landowners.[88] In the early 18th century the shares of the original owners of the market rights were acquired by William Davies of Clearwell, later of Bream.[89] Viscount Gage, who claimed the market place and house as part of Staunton manor, asserted that his predecessor Henry Benedict Hall had granted use of them only for the lives of the recipients of the 1661 charter, and in 1743 William Harper, to whom Davies had sold his rights, conveyed the market place and house to Lord Gage and the market rights to Gage's son William Hall Gage. The market rights descended with Staunton manor and the Highmeadow estate until 1822 when the Crown sold them to George Morgan, the lessee. At his death in 1840 Morgan, landlord of the Old White Hart inn, left them to his nephew Thomas Morgan,[90] and in the early 1860s the tolls were leased by the landlord of the Old White Hart.[91] In 1866 the market rights were bought by Isaiah Trotter, who formed a limited company to administer the market and rebuild the market house.[92]

The market and fairs became a mainstay of the town's economy in the late 17th century.[93] In 1756 the market house and tolls were farmed for £7 a year.[94] At that time the two principal markets were held in early May and early October. The June fair, held on 20 June following the calendar change of 1752, had come to specialize in the sale of wool[95] and in 1782, to counter an attempt by Monmouth to monopolize the local trade in Welsh wool, a second wool fair was held on 16 July.[96] The November fair, which was principally a cheese fair,[97] moved to 5 December,[98] continued to deal also in livestock,[99] but it did little trade by 1830.[1] The Friday livestock market, which in 1811 included a toll-free sheep market in late August,[2] became restricted to the last Friday of each month.[3] The market and fair tolls were worth over £70 a year in the 1840s. At that time the June fair, the tolls of which were leased for £12 in 1844,[4] was also the town's principal pleasure fair and was held over two days.[5] In 1884, in an attempt to revive its business, the market was moved to the third Tuesday in each month. Pig sales, the main business at that time, were later halted until an

area was paved for them in 1899. In the early 20th century there was an annual stock market in early December.[6] The monthly livestock market, held on the fourth Tuesday in the mid 1920s,[7] gradually declined, partly because of traffic problems in the town centre, and together with the other markets and fairs it lapsed in the 1940s.[8] An autumn sheep sale started near Coleford in the 1920s was held within the Forest at Clearwell Meend for a time and was conducted by the Coleford branch of the farmers' union at Coalway Lane End in the early 1980s.[9]

Part of the market house destroyed in 1643[10] may have been incorporated in the new one built in 1679, which was raised on arches and reached by a wide staircase.[11] Both market place and house, known as the Cross, were improved by Viscount Gage in 1744[12] and the market house was enlarged and remodelled in a Tudor style in 1866–7. The new building had a hall and a reading room on the ground floor and a long assembly room on the upper floor.[13] From 1948 it was the headquarters of a community association, which improved it in 1951 and 1952 for use as a community centre. It was demolished in 1968 to ease traffic movement in the town centre.[14]

LOCAL GOVERNMENT. Coleford was subject, as a tithing, to the parish government of Newland, which is discussed below. The Newland parish workhouse opened in the mid 1780s was in Coleford town, at the corner of St. John and Bank Streets.[15] In 1836 the tithing was included in the Monmouth poor-law union as part of Newland.[16]

In the early 18th century two constables policed the town and its market[17] but later only one constable was appointed for the whole tithing.[18] In 1786 an association for the prosecution of felons was formed to combat crime in the town. The association, which also covered Newland and several adjoining parishes, apparently lapsed in the early 1790s and was revived in 1814.[19] Magistrates were holding sessions at the Angel inn by 1841[20] and the county constabulary had a station in the town in 1849.[21] In the early 1860s a large house at the bottom of Lord's hill was converted as a police station and petty sessional court.[22] In 1840 there was an old pound next to the former Newland workhouse in the town and a pound at Whitecliff.[23] A town crier was recorded in 1863.[24]

88 Bodl. MS. Top. Glouc. c. 3, f. 139; Glos. R.O., DC/H 35.
89 Glos. R.O., D 1677/GG 984, 1082, 1108, 1363.
90 Ibid. DC/H 35; G.D.R. wills 1840/213.
91 Glos. R.O., D 637/I/37.   92 Ibid. DC/H 35.
93 Bodl. MS. Top. Glouc. c. 3, f. 139.
94 Glos. R.O., D 1677/GG 1358.
95 Glouc. Jnl. 8 May 1753.
96 Ibid. 28 May 1781; 10 June 1782.
97 Rudder, Glos. 568.
98 Univ. Brit. Dir. ii (1793), 573.
99 Glouc. Jnl. 31 Oct. 1763; 11 Dec. 1815.
1 Pigot's Dir. Glos. (1830), 366–7.
2 Glouc. Jnl. 19 Aug. 1811.
3 Glos. Chron. 16 Feb. 1867.
4 Glos. R.O., DC/H 35.
5 Pigot's Dir. Glos. (1842), 101; Glouc. Jnl. 25 June 1853.
6 P.R.O., F 3/130; F 14/9.
7 Rep. on Midland Markets (H.M.S.O. 1927), 115.
8 Hart, Coleford, 435.

9 Citizen, 2 Oct. 1981; H. Phelps, Forest of Dean (1982), 104–5.
10 Bibliotheca Glos. ii, p. cxlix.
11 Bodl. MS. Top. Glouc. c. 3, f. 139; H. Phelps, Forest to Severn (1994), 44; below, Plate 3.
12 Glos. R.O., D 1677/GG 1216, 1282.
13 Ibid. DC/H 35; Glos. Chron. 16 Feb. 1867.
14 Coleford Social Guide (1955), 7; Hart, Coleford, 447.
15 Below, Newland, local govt.; G.D.R., T 1/128.
16 Poor Law Com. 2nd Rep. p. 535; cf. Kelly's Dir. Glos. (1856), 271.
17 Bodl. MS. Top. Glouc. c. 3, f. 139.
18 Below, Newland, local govt.
19 Trans. B.G.A.S. c. 228–9; Glos. R.O., D 891, Newland assoc. order bk. and papers 1787–92.
20 Glos. R.O., D 891, petty sessions' draft min. bk. 1841–2.   21 Hunt's Dir. Glos. (1849), 104.
22 Glos. R.O., Q/AP 22/3; Q/CI 4.
23 G.D.R., T 1/128.
24 Kelly's Dir. Glos. (1863), 253.

In the 19th century some services were provided for Coleford by voluntary effort[25] and in 1871 a local board of health was formed.[26] The board, which was also responsible for detached parts of the tithing until their transfer to other parishes in 1883 and 1884,[27] was dissolved in 1894 when Coleford became a parish and urban district.[28] The parish retained the status of urban district until 1935 when it became part of West Dean rural district.[29] In 1974 it was included in the new Forest of Dean district.

CHURCHES. A chapel recorded in the centre of Coleford in 1489[30] was presumably built by local people for their own use. Damaged during the Civil War, it fell into ruin and c. 1690 some townspeople rebuilt it with voluntary contributions and employed a minister to read services and preach. In 1705 the Crown granted £300 as an endowment to support the minister, William Harrison, and those of his successors appointed by the bishop.[31] The grant provided an income of £15 for Harrison, who was also rector of Staunton,[32] but in the mid 1730s the principal was lent out at the annual interest of £13 10s.[33] At that time the chapel was served by Thomas Hill, rector of Staunton,[34] whom Viscount Gage may have appointed to assert his claim to rights in the chapel.[35] In 1764 the vicar of Newland was licensed to hold the chapel, and at the next vacancy, in 1795, the bishop made his first appointment.[36] The £300 endowment was used after 1750 to buy a farm in Herefordshire, which yielded an income of £18 c. 1775.[37] The living, styled a perpetual curacy in 1764,[38] received grants from Queen Anne's Bounty in and after 1772[39] and Scowles farm had been added to the endowment by 1835.[40] A glebe house was built at Lord's Hill in 1838.[41] In 1856 the living was worth only £105.[42]

The vicars of Newland continued to minister to parts of the tithing outside the town until 1872,[43] when the bulk of the tithing was created a district for the Coleford chapel.[44] The impropriator and the vicar of Newland assigned their tithe rent charges from the district to the living in 1873,[45] and the two farms remained part of the endowment until sold in 1893 and 1921 respectively.[46] The benefice was styled a vicarage in 1876.[47] In 1880 a new church was opened[48] and in 1890 the ecclesiastical parish was enlarged to take in adjoining parts of the Forest of Dean in the Lane End district.[49] Mission churches for that area were built at Broadwell and Milkwall.[50] In 1922 the benefice was united with Staunton, which was also in the bishop's patronage. The vicarage house at Lord's Hill was retained for the united benefice[51] and in 1970 was replaced by a house opposite the church.[52]

Coleford chapel, in which a monthly Friday lecture was given c. 1708,[53] was used only for Sunday afternoon services in 1750.[54] Thomas Thomas, perpetual curate from 1795, was master of Bell's Grammar school in Newland village.[55] From 1803 the afternoon service at Coleford was taken for him by P. M. Procter, vicar of Newland, who began a mission to the Forest's miners at Berry Hill the following year.[56] Henry Poole, who served Coleford chapel as curate from 1818, succeeded Thomas in 1819 and himself employed curates at Coleford from 1822, when he opened a church at Parkend for missionary work in the Forest.[57] Poole resigned Coleford in 1834 and the next three incumbents remained only a few years. J. L. Sisson, perpetual curate from 1843, was forced by differences with the congregation to appoint a curate in his place in 1851.[58] He resumed his duties in 1854 and retained the living until 1866.[59] Of his successors only E. H. Brice, vicar 1902–27, had a longer incumbency.[60]

In 1850 a new schoolroom in Scowles hamlet was licensed for a mission served from Newland church.[61] Within a few years the building was used only for that purpose[62] and from 1872 it was a chapel of ease to Coleford.[63] The chapel was used for prayers and sermons only[64] and in the late 19th century it was closed during the summer.[65] A small building with a west bellcot and one bell,[66] it closed before 1968[67] and was converted as a house.

Coleford's medieval chapel, in the town centre, bore a dedication to ST. JOHN THE BAPTIST in 1534,[68] but its successor on the same site was known as St. John the Evangelist in the mid 1870s.[69] The old chapel was a small single-cell building with a west bellcot and porch in 1608.[70] For its repair from the ruin into which

[25] Above, intro.   [26] Glos. R.O., DA 5/100/1.
[27] Bright, 'Hist. Coleford Bd. of Health', 12; below, Newland, intro. (Table I).
[28] Glos. R.O., DA 5/100/2; *Manual of Glos. Lit.* ii. 166.
[29] *Census*, 1931 (pt. ii).   [30] Glos. R.O., D 2957/86.8.
[31] *Cal. Treas. Bks.* 1685–9, 675; 1704–5, 167, 477; Hockaday Abs. ccxcvii, 1705.
[32] Atkyns, *Glos.* 575, 688.   [33] G.D.R. vol. 285B(2).
[34] Ibid. 285B(3), pp. 3–4, 7–8.
[35] In Glos. R.O., D 1677/GG 1216, Hill is described as Gage's 'creature' at Staunton.
[36] Hockaday Abs. clxv; *Glouc. Jnl.* 9 Feb. 1795.
[37] G.D.R. vol. 381A, f. 6; Rudder, *Glos.* 568.
[38] Hockaday Abs. clxv.
[39] Hodgson, *Queen Anne's Bounty* (1845), p. cclxxxiv.
[40] Glos. R.O., D 34/9/69.   [41] G.D.R., F 4/1.
[42] Ibid. vol. 384, f. 68.   [43] Glos. R.O., D 637/I/84.
[44] *Lond. Gaz.* 14 May 1872, pp. 2290–1.
[45] Glos. R.O., P 93/IN 3/1.   [46] Ibid. 2.
[47] *Morris's Dir. Glos.* (1876), 540.
[48] Below, this section.
[49] *Lond. Gaz.* 8 July 1890, pp. 3775–7.

[50] Below, Forest of Dean, churches.
[51] *Lond. Gaz.* 25 Apr. 1922, pp. 3223–4.
[52] Glos. R.O., P 93/IN 3/8.
[53] Bodl. MS. Top. Glouc. c. 3, f. 139.
[54] G.D.R. vol. 381A, f. 6.   [55] *Glouc. Jnl.* 9 Feb. 1795.
[56] Glos. R.O., D 2297; P. M. Procter, *Origin of Established Ch. and Nat. Day Sch. in Forest of Dean* (1819), *passim*; below, Forest of Dean, churches (Christ Church).
[57] Hockaday Abs. clxv; below, Forest of Dean, churches (St. Paul).   [58] Hockaday Abs. clxv; G.D.R., V 6/32.
[59] Glos. R.O., P 93/IN 1/6.
[60] *Kelly's Dir. Glos.* (1870 and later edns.).
[61] Hockaday Abs. clxv.   [62] Below, educ.
[63] *Kelly's Dir. Glos.* (1889), 746.
[64] Mushet, *Something about Coleford*, 6.
[65] Glos. R.O., P 93/IN 4/3/6–7.
[66] Hart, *Coleford*, 296, 302; for site, O.S. Map 6", Glos. XXXVIII. NE. (1884 edn.).
[67] *Dean Forest Mercury*, 13 Dec. 1968.
[68] Hockaday Abs. ccxcv.
[69] *Morris's Dir. Glos.* (1876), 540.
[70] P.R.O., MR 879.

it had fallen after damage during the Civil War,[71] money was being collected by 1686, when the Crown gave timber from the Forest for that purpose,[72] and it was rebuilt on its existing plan a few years later.[73] Private pews were installed before 1721[74] and to increase the seating it was decided in 1737 to add an aisle.[75] Supported by Lord Berkeley, the congregation obtained £150 for the project from the Crown in 1740[76] but Viscount Gage, who claimed to own the site as part of the waste of Staunton manor, stopped building work and threatened to erect limekilns on either side of the chapel.[77] The aisle, on the south side, was apparently completed after 1750.[78] In the late 18th century the chapel also had a west gallery.[79]

In 1820 the chapel was rebuilt on a larger scale under the direction, and partly at the expense, of the perpetual curate, Henry Poole.[80] The new building, towards which the Crown contributed £250,[81] was, like Poole's later church at Parkend, on an octagonal plan with chancel and west tower.[82] It also had north and south galleries and a west organ gallery, and in the 1870s desks and a high pulpit obscured the congregation's view of the chancel.[83] Known as the New Chapel, it soon proved too small for the growing congregation and the cramped site in the market place gave no scope for enlargement.[84] In 1880 it was replaced by a larger church in Boxbush Road and in 1882 it was demolished, the stone being used to build a school next to the new church.[85] The tower, which contained a bell cast by Abraham Rudhall in 1718[86] and a clock bought by public subscription in 1863,[87] was retained as a clock tower and in 1945 the adjoining ground was laid out as a public garden.[88]

The new church in Boxbush Road was begun in 1878 and consecrated in 1880. It was then called St. John the Baptist,[89] but in 1994 was *ST. JOHN THE EVANGELIST*. Built of red sandstone rubble with white sandstone dressings, it was designed by F. S. Waller & Son in a late 13th-century style. The apsidal chancel and the tall nave with an open timber roof with crown posts and arch braces had been finished by the time of the church's consecration[90] and the south transept was completed in 1886.[91] A north porch and east vestries were added in 1890[92] and a north transept was built in 1907.[93] Some fittings were brought from the chapel in

the town centre, including the organ, which was replaced by a new instrument in 1906.[94] A carved oak reredos to a design by Sir Charles Nicholson was erected in 1920 as a war memorial.[95] The single church bell was probably cast in or just before 1880.[96] The registers, which record births from 1768 (baptisms from 1782) and marriages from 1872, include a few burials in the years 1784–6.[97]

ROMAN CATHOLICISM. From 1855 the Roman Catholic missionary to Monmouth also worked in the Coleford area, where many members of his congregation lived. Although he started a Sunday school in 1860 and a Catholic day school opened in the town in 1862, the mission to Coleford lacked a chapel and it lapsed before 1882, presumably on the priest's departure from Monmouth.[98] On the establishment of a new mission from Monmouth in 1930 mass was said in a house in Newland Street. Later in 1930 a resident priest was put in charge of the mission and in 1933 a church dedicated to St. Margaret Mary was built at High Nash.[99] Later a presbytery and a hall were built next to the church[1] and in 1994, when its parish extended from Symonds Yat in the north to Beachley in the south, the average congregation numbered 60.[2]

PROTESTANT NONCONFORMITY. Nonconformity took root in Coleford in the mid 17th century, when the town's medieval chapel was in decay,[3] and ten people were presented in 1667 for not attending Newland parish church.[4] The nine protestant dissenters recorded in Newland parish in 1676 were perhaps all Coleford people.[5] The town's nonconformist meetings prospered in the 19th century and their strength was reflected in controversy over the payment of church rates in the mid 1830s.[6]

In 1660 three or more Coleford men were among those arrested at a Quaker meeting in Aylburton and imprisoned.[7] Quakers evidently met in Coleford before 1676, when the Gloucestershire quarterly meeting helped the Aylburton Quakers to purchase land and build a meeting house there,[8] and several Quakers were persecuted for attending meetings in the town in 1677.[9] The new meeting house was by the main

71 Hockaday Abs. ccxcv, 1705; *Trans. B.G.A.S.* lxxxiii. 98.
72 *Cal. Treas. Bks.* 1685–9, 675.
73 Ibid. 1704–5, 167; Bodl. MS. Top. Glouc. c. 3, f. 139.
74 Hockaday Abs. ccxcvii.
75 Glos. R.O., D 678/fam. settlements 57D/282.
76 *Cal. Treas. Bks. & Papers*, 1739–41, 291.
77 Ibid. 215; Glos. R.O., D 678/fam. settlements 57D/151, 153, 279; D 1677/GG 1282.
78 G.D.R. vol. 381A, f. 6; below, Plate 3.
79 Bigland, *Glos.* ii. 257.
80 Nicholls, *Personalities of Dean*, 156–7; Glos. R.O., D 2926/24.   81 *3rd Rep. Dean Forest Com.* 6.
82 G.D.R., T 1/128; below, Forest of Dean, churches (St. Paul).
83 *Glouc. Jnl.* 22 May 1880.
84 Mushet, *Something about Coleford*, 39–40; P.R.O., F 3/29.
85 Glos. R.O., P 93/CW 3/1/1; P.R.O., F 3/25.
86 Mushet, *Something about Coleford*, 9.
87 P.R.O., F 3/29.
88 Glos. R.O., P 93/CW 3/1/10.

89 *Glouc. Jnl.* 22 May 1880.
90 Glos. R.O., P 93/SP 1/1; *Kelly's Dir. Glos.* (1885), 432.
91 P.R.O., F 3/29; Glos. R.O., P 93/IN 4/3/5, par. mag. Mar. 1886.
92 Glos. R.O., P 93/IN 4/3/6, par. mag. Nov. 1890.
93 Ibid. 8, par. mag. Dec. 1907.   94 P.R.O., F 3/29.
95 *Kelly's Dir. Glos.* (1923), 136.
96 *Glos. Ch. Bells*, 238.
97 Glos. R.O., P 93/IN 1/1–13.
98 Bristol R.O. 35721, Coleford papers 1855–96.
99 Glos. R.O., D 5467/6/1; Hart, *Coleford*, 459.
1 O.S. Map 1/2,500, SO 5710 (1960 edn.).
2 Inf. from parish priest.   3 Above, churches.
4 Glos. R.O., Q/SIb 1, f. 153.
5 *Compton Census*, ed. Whiteman, 544.
6 Below, Newland, local govt.
7 J. Besse, *Abstract of Sufferings of Quakers*, ii (1738), 169–70.
8 Glos. R.O., D 2052.
9 *Cry of Oppression and Cruelty inflicted upon Quakers in Glos.* [1677], 5–6.

road in Whitecliff, and Coleford and Aylburton people met together in it in 1679. The meeting had virtually lapsed by 1718 and the meeting house and its burial ground were sold in 1720 or 1721.[10] A revival in the Quaker interest at Coleford following a meeting in the market house in 1753 was short lived.[11] A Quaker meeting established in the early 1920s lapsed later, but it revived in the 1970s and used the vestry of Coleford Baptist chapel in the 1980s.[12]

In the later 17th century John Skinner, minister of a Baptist church at Ryeford, in Weston under Penyard (Herefs.), preached to a congregation in Coleford.[13] The meeting may have used a house registered for worship in 1689[14] and may have been the independent meeting described as 'something considerable' in the early 1690s.[15] After Skinner's death in 1694[16] the Coleford Baptists had their own minister for a few years[17] and their church, presumably that holding a weekly service in 1705,[18] had 50 members in 1715.[19] The church, which sent missions to the extraparochial area of the Forest,[20] was sustained in the mid 18th century mainly by William Birt (d. 1765), a householder in Coleford and pastor of a church in King's Stanley. In 1770 his widow obtained the help of a preacher from Pontypool (Mon.).[21] The church may have gained more members in 1786, when a house in the town was registered,[22] but its meeting place was almost in ruins in 1793.[23]

In 1799 thirteen Baptists, including members of the Trotter family, re-formed the church at Coleford with William Bradley as its minister and built a small chapel, registered in 1800, in Newland Street. The new church grew rapidly, notably during John Fry's pastorate 1814–39,[24] and in 1824 it had 112 members and a large Sunday school.[25] In 1818 some Baptists registered Wynols Hill house, where John Trotter lived, for worship.[26] The Newland Street chapel, which had its own burial ground, was enlarged twice, the second time in 1828. In 1858, on the opening of a larger chapel further along the street, it was retained as a schoolroom.[27] The new chapel, designed in a debased Romanesque style by C. G. Searle,[28] had 308 members in 1868[29] and continued to support the estab-

lishment of daughter churches in the Forest.[30] The chapel, which had galleries on three sides, was remodelled internally in 1971 with a meeting room on a new upper floor and schoolrooms below.[31] It had 80 members and its own minister in 1994.[32] The former chapel or schoolroom, to the north-east, housed a day school between 1863 and 1880[33] and was enlarged in 1887.[34] It was converted as three dwellings c. 1980.[35]

George Whitefield preached in the market house in 1739 and John Wesley visited the town in 1756 and in 1763, when his followers had a meeting there.[36] A Methodist society visited by ministers of the Countess of Huntingdon's Connexion used the market house in 1788.[37] In 1789 it opened a new chapel in Newland Street and in 1791 it registered two houses in Newland parish for worship.[38] The chapel, known as the Countess of Huntingdon's chapel,[39] closed in 1819.[40] In 1824 a g Methodist missionary to the Forest of Dean registered two houses in Coleford[41] and by 1840 Wesleyans were meeting in the Countess of Huntingdon's chapel.[42] In 1851, following a split in the congregation, the chapel was in the hands of Wesleyan Reformers and attendance was down by a third.[43] The Wesleyan loyalists apparently held services at the Angel inn[44] and later in 1851, under the leadership of John Adams (d. 1899), a local glazier,[45] they built a chapel called Ebenezer at the top of High Street. That chapel, at which a new schoolroom was built in 1871,[46] closed c. 1947.[47] The Wesleyan Reformers' church in Coleford is not recorded after 1851.

Houses in Whitecliff and Coleford were registered as places of worship for unidentified groups in 1826 and 1834 respectively.[48] In 1842 Thomas Loder, an Independent minister in Monmouth, built a chapel in Bank Street.[49] It had its own minister from 1843[50] and under Robert Stevens, minister 1858–96,[51] it was a centre of missionary work in the Forest.[52] In 1872 a manse was built at Poolway. The chapel was fitted with side galleries in the mid 1850s and was repewed in 1871.[53] It had two rear schoolrooms and was styled Congregational in 1876.[54] The meeting had 110 members in 1900[55] and employed E. R. Vaughan as minister for

10 Glos. R.O., D 2052; D 891, Coleford deeds 1655–1817, deed 1771.
11 Ibid. Q/SO 8, f. 72v.; D 1340/A 1/M 10, pp. 164, 166, 179.
12 Hart, Coleford, 457; W.I. hist. of Coleford, 19.
13 Glos. R.O., D 2722/31.
14 Ibid. Q/SO 3.
15 A. Gordon, Freedom after Ejection (1917), 46; cf. ibid. 145, 240.
16 Calamy Revised, ed. A. G. Matthews, 444.
17 Glos. R.O., D 2722/31.
18 Hockaday Abs. ccxcvii.
19 Trans. Bapt. Hist. Soc. ii. 99.
20 Below, Forest of Dean, prot. nonconf. (Baptists).
21 Hart, Coleford, 180.
22 Hockaday Abs. ccxcvii.
23 Glos. R.O., D 2722/31.
24 Ibid.; Hockaday Abs. clxv.
25 Bright, Nonconf. in Dean, 26.
26 Hockaday Abs. ccxcvii.
27 Glos. R.O., D 2722/31; G.D.R., T 1/128; O.S. Map 1/2,500, Glos. XXXVIII. 4 (1882 edn.).
28 Glos. R.O., D 2722/9; below, Plate 15.
29 Glos. R.O., D 2052.
30 Ibid. D 2297; below, Forest of Dean, prot. nonconf. (Baptists).

31 Glouc. Jnl. 20 Feb. 1971.   32 Inf. from minister.
33 Below, educ.   34 Date on bldg.
35 Hart, Coleford, 453.   36 Glos. R.O., D 2052.
37 Ibid. D 1050.   38 Hockaday Abs. ccxcvii.
39 Glos. R.O., D 1050, mem. 13 Apr. 1792.
40 Ibid. D 2297.
41 Hockaday Abs. clxv; below, Forest of Dean, prot. nonconf. (Wesleyan Methodists).
42 G.D.R., T 1/128.
43 P.R.O., HO 129/577/1/4/14.
44 Ibid. HO 129/577/1/4/15; Hart, Coleford, 192.
45 P.R.O., HO 107/2444, s.v. Newland (Coleford); Hart, Coleford, 306–11.
46 Glos. R.O., D 2598/8/1; O.S. Map 1/2,500, Glos. XXXVIII. 4 (1882 edn.).
47 Glos. R.O., D 2598/1/26.
48 Hockaday Abs. ccxcvii, clxv.
49 Morris's Dir. Glos. (1876), 541.
50 Glos. R.O., D 5533/1/1.
51 Ibid. D 5533/4/4.
52 Below, Forest of Dean, prot. nonconf. (Congregationalists and Independents).
53 Glos. R.O., D 5533/1/1; Hart, Coleford, 311.
54 Morris's Dir. Glos. (1876), 541.
55 Glos. R.O., D 2052.

over 30 years from 1924.[56] The chapel shared a minister with other Congregational churches in the Forest area by the late 1960s[57] and, having joined the United Reformed Church, it had 10 members in 1984.[58] After its closure c. 1990 the chapel was divided into flats.

A mission hall built in Bank Street in the late 19th century[59] was used by Plymouth Brethren. It closed after 1959 and was demolished in the late 1960s.[60] Members of a pentecostalist sect, the Assemblies of God, who moved from Bristol in the late 1940s as employees of H. W. Carter & Co., started a church in Coleford and in the late 1950s held services in Maycrete Hall. The church, which had a resident minister from 1956, built a meeting place, called Mount of Olives, on the Eastbourne housing estate at Poolway in 1960.[61] A branch of the Church of the Latter Day Saints worshipped in the former Methodist chapel in High Street between 1966 and 1969[62] and had built a church on a housing estate at Wynols Hill by 1976.[63] The High Street chapel was demolished in a road widening scheme in 1970.[64]

EDUCATION. In the early 18th century Coleford had a school supported by subscriptions from, among others, Maynard Colchester (d. 1715), a founder of the S.P.C.K.[65] A schoolmaster was living in Coleford in the 1790s and he was one of several there in 1815.[66] In 1819 there were c. 100 school places in three day schools and a Sunday school, all supported by subscriptions.[67] In 1825 a church school was built at the south-west end of Whitecliff for the whole of Newland parish. Known later as Newland National school,[68] it opened in 1826 and was supported by subscriptions and pence. In 1833 it taught 74 boys and 65 girls on weekdays and much smaller numbers on Sundays, when other Sunday schools were open in the town,[69] and in 1846 up to 92 boys and 58 girls, taught in separate departments, attended on weekdays.[70] The school's income included the proceeds of an annual sermon in 1855[71] and a grant from the Crown later. The school had an average attendance of 46 in 1877[72] and it closed in 1887 after attendance had fallen to 24.[73] Under a Scheme

of 1889 the proceeds from the sale of the building were used for prizes for schoolchildren in Newland ancient parish and for religious instruction.[74]

Another National school recorded in Coleford in 1830[75] was presumably the infant school run by Anglicans in the former Countess of Huntingdon's chapel in Newland Street at that time.[76] A National school possibly started in 1835 as a Sunday school[77] occupied a new building at Lord's Hill from 1838.[78] Supported by subscriptions and pence, it received an annual grant from the Crown from 1841[79] and taught 65 boys and 78 girls separately in 1846.[80] The average attendance had dropped to 15 by 1867, but following the appointment of a trained master that year it began to grow[81] and from 1869 the school had junior mixed and infant departments under separate management.[82] The school was enlarged in 1877 when, as St. John's C. of E. school, it had an average attendance of 136. In 1882, following an influx of children previously taught at a British school,[83] the junior department was reorganized with the boys in a new building next to St. John's church in Boxbush Road.[84] The infant school moved to a new building next to the church in 1896[85] and the three departments of St. John's school had a combined average attendance of 306 in 1904.[86] The boys' school was enlarged in 1910.[87] In 1930, when the older boys and girls were transferred to a new secondary school in Bowens Hill Road,[88] the school at Lord's Hill was closed and the younger children were taught together in the buildings by the church.[89] The average attendance at St. John's school was 151 in 1932 and 196 in 1938.[90] Between 1966 and 1974 the school moved in stages to the site of the school in Bowens Hill Road, which had been vacated,[91] and in 1994 it had 234 children on its roll.[92] The buildings in Boxbush Road were converted for use as a day hospital and a clinic.[93] The former school building at Lord's Hill was used as a parish room and church hall in 1959[94] and was converted for use as a holiday and youth centre by the diocese in 1979.[95]

The Coleford Baptists had a Sunday school with 260 pupils in 1824.[96] Baptists also started another Sunday school in Newland parish in

56 Hart, *Coleford*, 455.
57 *Congregational Year Bk.* (1972), 94.
58 *United Reformed Ch. Year Bk.* (1984–5), 62.
59 O.S. Map 1/2,500, Glos. XXXVIII. 4 (1882, 1902 edns.).
60 Hart, *Coleford*, 457–9; O.S. Map 1/2,500, SO 5710 (1960 edn.).
61 Hart, *Coleford*, 461; inf. from Miss V. Armstrong, of Coleford; for H. W. Carter & Co., above, econ. hist. (other ind. and trade).
62 Glos. R.O., co. highways dept. deeds, file 105.
63 Below, Forest of Dean, prot. nonconf. (other churches).
64 G. E. Lawrence, *Kindling the Flame* (1974), 30: copy in Glos. R.O., D 2598/23/1; W.I. hist. of Coleford, 19.
65 A. Platts and G. H. Hainton, *Educ. in Glos.: A Short Hist.* (1954), 24–6, 29–30.
66 Glos. R.O., D 149/R 38.
67 *Educ. of Poor Digest*, 304.
68 P.R.O., ED 7/37, Newland Nat. sch.; for site, O.S. Map 6", Glos. XXXVIII. NE. (1884 edn.).
69 *Educ. Enq. Abstract*, 322.
70 Nat. Soc. *Inquiry, 1846–7*, Glos. 12–13.
71 P.R.O., ED 7/37, Newland Nat. sch.

72 Ibid. F 3/25.
73 Glos. R.O., P 93/IN 4/3/5, par. mag. June 1887.
74 Ibid. D 3469/5/112.
75 *Pigot's Dir. Glos.* (1830), 367.
76 Glos. R.O., D 2297.
77 *Pigot's Dir. Glos.* (1842), 101; Hart, *Coleford*, 341–2.
78 P.R.O., ED 7/34/86.
79 Ibid. F 3/25.
80 Nat. Soc. *Inquiry, 1846–7*, Glos. 12–13.
81 P.R.O., F 3/25.
82 Ibid. ED 7/34/86; Glos. R.O., S 93/8/1–2.
83 P.R.O., F 3/25.
84 Glos. R.O., S 93/8/1, 4; P 93/IN 4/3/4, par. mag. Dec. 1882.
85 Ibid. S 93/8/2; P 93/SC 2/1.
86 *Public Elem. Schs. 1906*, 183.
87 Glos. R.O., S 93/8/16.   88 Ibid. S 93/1/2.
89 Ibid. S 93/8/3; Hart, *Coleford*, 429.
90 *Bd. of Educ., List 21, 1932* (H.M.S.O.), 114; *1938*, 126.
91 Hart, *Coleford*, 429.
92 *Schools and Establishments Dir. 1994–5* (co. educ. dept.), 33.   93 Hart, *Coleford*, 440, 476.
94 W.I. hist. of Coleford, 14.
95 Hart, *Coleford*, 429; inf. from vicar of Coleford.
96 Bright, *Nonconf. in Dean*, 26.

1828[97] and ran a free school, presumably at their Newland Street chapel, in 1830.[98] In 1851 the former Countess of Huntingdon's chapel in Newland Street, then occupied by Wesleyan Reformers, was temporarily a British school.[99] In 1863 a new British school opened in the former Baptist chapel in Newland Street. Teaching boys and girls, it was financed by subscriptions and pence.[1] It also received a grant from the Crown and it had 185 children on its roll when it closed in 1880.[2]

Coleford had several small day and boarding schools in the mid 19th century,[3] including in 1858 a boarding school run by a former minister of the town's Independent chapel.[4] In 1862 a Roman Catholic convert took lodgings in the town and started a day school in Gloucester Road. The school soon had 40 pupils, most of them protestants. Some children moved to the British school opened the following year.[5] In 1867 the Catholic school taught 30 children and the Independents had a school with 170 pupils.[6] Neither school is recorded later. In the late 19th century there were several private girls' schools in Coleford.[7]

A schoolroom built at Scowles in 1849 by C. W. Grove, curate of Newland, was paid for by voluntary contributions[8] and from 1850 was also used for church services.[9] In 1858 J. F. Brickdale (later Fortescue-Brickdale) of Newland built a new school there on the suggestion of his daughter Mary and at his death in 1867 he left her the building and an annuity of £50 for its maintenance.[10] In 1877 it was a mixed school teaching juniors and infants and it had an average attendance of 72.[11] In 1879 Mary Brickdale, who ran it as a church school largely at her own expense, increased the accommodation and built a house for its teachers, who were to be a married couple. On the closure of Coleford British school in 1880 attendance rose and from 1883 the junior and infant departments were run separately. Not long before her death in 1895 Mary Brickdale appointed managers for the school, and in 1897 the Revd. H. A. G. Graham gave £1,000 stock as an endowment and the two departments were merged to form the Brickdale Memorial school. It was managed with other church schools in Coleford from 1903.[12] The average attendance was 69 in 1904[13] and 48 in 1938.[14] The school

closed in 1969[15] and the buildings, which had remained in the ownership of the Fortescue-Brickdale family until 1922,[16] were converted for domestic use.

Coleford Senior Council school was opened by the county council in 1930 to take children aged nine years and over from St. John's school. Occupying a new building in Bowens Hill Road, it also took children from other local elementary schools[17] and had an average attendance of 161 in 1932 and 87 in 1938.[18] It became a secondary modern school under the 1944 Education Act and closed in 1966. The children were transferred to Berry Hill Secondary school at Five Acres.[19]

In 1876 Bell's Grammar school, part of an early 17th-century charitable foundation, moved from Newland to a new building at Lord's Hill in Coleford.[20] At Lord's Hill the number of pupils rose to over 30 before dropping sharply to 5 in the late 1890s. In the early 20th century the school grew rapidly. Girls were admitted from 1905 and the number of pupils passed 150 in 1932.[21] The school, which was run by the separate Educational Charity of Edward Bell and Others from 1908,[22] was enlarged in the 1920s.[23] It became a secondary grammar school under the 1944 Act[24] and had 300 pupils in 1959.[25] In 1968 the pupils were transferred to the new Royal Forest of Dean Grammar school at Five Acres,[26] and the Lord's Hill buildings were sold in 1971 and converted as a hotel and country club.[27] Under a Scheme of 1973 the charity was renamed Bell's Foundation and it provided special benefits for the secondary schools at Five Acres and financial help for their pupils, preference being given to those resident in Newland ancient parish.[28]

An art school was established in 1872 and had premises in Newland Street. It apparently closed soon after 1876.[29] In the 1890s evening classes on mining, science, and art started in Coleford with support from the county council. The science and art classes, organized from the Lydney Institute, continued until 1905 or later.[30]

CHARITIES FOR THE POOR. Coleford, as part of Newland, benefited from its almshouse charities, and in the 1820s the Newland eleem-

[97] *Educ. Enq. Abstract*, 322.
[98] *Pigot's Dir. Glos.* (1830), 367.
[99] P.R.O., HO 129/577/1/4/14.
[1] Ibid. ED 7/37, Coleford Brit. sch.
[2] Ibid. F 3/25; Glos. R.O., P 93/IN 4/3/4, par. mag. Aug. 1880.
[3] *Pigot's Dir. Glos.* (1842), 102; *Hunt's Dir. Glos.* (1849), 103; P.R.O., HO 107/2444, s.v. Newland (Coleford); *Slater's Dir. Glos.* (1852–3), 119.
[4] *Slater's Dir. Glos.* (1858–9), 179; Glos. R.O., D 5533/1/1.
[5] Bristol R.O. 35721, Coleford papers 1855–96; Glos. R.O., D 637/I/49.
[6] *Glos. Chron.* 16 Feb. 1867.
[7] *Morris's Dir. Glos.* (1876), 543; *Kelly's Dir. Glos.* (1889), 747; (1894), 127.
[8] P.R.O., HO 129/577/1/3/9; ED 7/34/87.
[9] Hockaday Abs. clxv.
[10] Glos. R.O., D 1317; P 227/IN 1/27.
[11] P.R.O., ED 7/34/87.
[12] Glos. R.O., P 93/SC 4/1–2; ibid. IN 4/3/6, par. mag. Sept. 1895.
[13] *Public Elem. Schs.* 1906, 183.

[14] *Bd. of Educ., List 21, 1938*, 126.
[15] *Dean Forest Mercury*, 13 Dec. 1968.
[16] Glos. R.O., D 3469/5/112.
[17] Ibid. CE/M 2/19, p. 366; 20, pp. 211–12; S 93/1/2; Hart, *Coleford*, 429.
[18] *Bd. of Educ., List 21, 1932*, 114; *1938*, 126.
[19] Glos. R.O., S 93/1/2–4; below, Forest of Dean, educ. (secondary schools).
[20] Glos. R.O., D 34/2/5; T. Bright, 'Hist. Bell's Grammar Sch.' (1968, TS. in ibid. SC 6/4), 4; below, Newland, educ.; char.
[21] W.I. hist. of Coleford, 16–17; Bright, 'Hist. Bell's Grammar Sch.' 4–6.
[22] Glos. R.O., D 3469/5/112.
[23] Bright, 'Hist. Bell's Grammar Sch.' 5.
[24] Cf. Glos. R.O., CE/M 2/29, ff. 26, 122.
[25] W.I. hist. of Coleford, 17.
[26] Bright, 'Hist. Bell's Grammar Sch.' 6; below, Forest of Dean, educ. (secondary schools).
[27] Hart, *Coleford*, 431.   [28] Glos. R.O., D 3469/5/112.
[29] *Morris's Dir. Glos.* (1876), 541, 546.
[30] Glos. R.O., SB 15/4, pp. 7–8; D 4480/4; Platts and Hainton, *Educ. in Glos.* 101.

osynary charity endowed with land in Awre, bought with funds from Henry Hall's charity, was distributed in Coleford and Bream tithings.[31] A Newland charity endowed by a member of the Morton family in the late 16th century with a rent charge of 6s. 8d. from a house in Coleford was evidently used later for Coleford's poor and had lapsed by the early 19th century.[32]

Coleford was among the many places for which John Harvey Ollney by will proved 1836 established a Christmas coal and blanket charity. It apparently received £200 and the charity, which had an income of over £6, was confined to Anglicans in the mid 19th century.[33] The distribution of blankets ceased in the 1890s and 24 people received coal in 1910.[34] Thomas James by will proved 1859 left £200 for a Christmas charity to be distributed with the Ollney charity. The James charity, with an income of c. £6, provided cash payments, most of 5s., to c. 25 Anglicans. In 1894 William James increased the principal to £700 stock, and from 1896 the charity was distributed among inhabitants of the enlarged ecclesiastical parish of Coleford. In 1910 cash payments were made to 74 people.[35] Later 46 people received cash payments from the Ollney and James charities, which had a combined income of £23, and in the 1960s the number of recipients was reduced.[36] Joseph Dennis by will proved 1879 left the reversion of £600 stock to the poor of Coleford parish for a Christmas charity. Called the Dennis Parker charity,[37] it had an income of £13 c. 1970, when it was applied with the part of Henry Hall's charity mentioned above.[38]

By his trust deed of 1892 Isaiah Trotter conveyed a row of ten single-storeyed almshouses that he had built at the Gorse in 1889 to the minister and deacons of Coleford Baptist church as free housing for 5 men and 5 women who had lived within 2 miles of the church and were preferably members of it. The almshouses were first occupied a few years later, and in 1899 Trotter endowed the charity with £8,000 stock.[39] From 1962 the occupants paid a small rent,[40] and in 1991 the charity's catchment area was extended to include most of the Forest region.[41]

FLAXLEY

FLAXLEY lies 14.5 km. WSW. of Gloucester on the north-eastern edge of the Forest of Dean. It was formerly the site of a Cistercian abbey[42] and the ancient parish, which covered 1,749 a. (707.8 ha.),[43] was formed from land given to the monks, much of it in the mid 12th century by the abbey's founder, Roger, earl of Hereford.[44] The following account of Flaxley deals with the ancient parish except for settlement north of the Littledean–Coleford road, which is treated below with Cinderford in the history of the Forest of Dean.

The parish, which was once within the Forest's jurisdiction,[45] lay in five portions. The main part was an irregular area of 1,044 a. flanked by the extraparochial Crown demesne of the Forest on the south and west.[46] It contained the abbey, which Earl Roger founded in the valley of Westbury brook in a clearing surrounded by chestnut trees, namely in 'a certain place in the valley of Castiard called Flaxley'.[47] It also contained the woods around the abbey, which Henry III granted to the monks for firewood in 1227.[48] The grant included Castiard and Timbridge wood on the north side.[49] Banks and ditches were constructed to mark the limits of the monks' lands[50] but those around Timbridge wood, presumably in the area north of Gaulet where Blaisdon parish later had a detached piece, had been destroyed by 1229, allegedly by Richard of Blaisdon.[51] The boundaries of the main part of Flaxley, most of which were specified in the grant of 1227, were marked roughly by dells, watercourses, and ancient tracks; on the northeast it was divided from Blaisdon by Longhope (or Blaisdon) brook and on the west it was bounded for a distance by the Littledean–Mitcheldean road and on the south-east by a route linking Blackmore's Hale, a settlement on the boundary of the Forest below Pope's Hill,[52] and Blaisdon.

The principal detached portion of Flaxley covered 395 a., sandwiched between Littledean on the north-east and the extraparochial Forest on the south and west. It was very irregular in shape, lying in two areas joined together by a neck of land at St. White's on the Littledean–Coleford road,[53] and it evidently contained land which had belonged to Walfric and his son Geoffrey and which Earl Roger included in his endowment of Flaxley abbey. Among that land was 'Wastadene', which by 1158 was a grange of

31 Below, Newland, char.; 19th Rep. Com. Char. 100–1.
32 Bigland, Glos. ii. 260; G.D.R., V 5/214T 3.
33 Glos. R.O., P 93/CH 1/1; cf. V.C.H. Glos. vii. 86, 121.
34 Glos. R.O., P 93/CH 1/2.   35 Ibid. P 93/CH 1/1–4.
36 Glos. R.O. CH 21, W. Dean rural district, p. 5.
37 Ibid. D 3469/5/112.
38 Ibid. CH 21, W. Dean rural district, p. 6.
39 Ibid. D 2722/11; Kelly's Dir. Glos. (1889), 746; (1894), 125.
40 Glos. R.O., D 2722/25.
41 Inf. from minister, Coleford Bapt. church.
42 This account was written in 1988. A hist. of Flaxley abbey is given in V.C.H. Glos. ii. 93–6.
43 O.S. Area Bk. Flaxley (1880); Little Dean (1878); Westbury upon Severn (1880).
44 Flaxley Cart. p. 16; after the Dissolution land in

Dymock, which had belonged to the monks, was said to be in Flaxley par.: G.D.R. wills 1544/79; P.R.O., C 3/196/23; cf. Rudder, Glos. 410.
45 Trans. B.G.A.S. lxvi. 166–207.
46 O.S. Area Bk. Flaxley (1880); cf. O.S. Maps 6", Glos. XXXI. NE. (1884 edn.); XXXII. NW. (1891 edn.).
47 Flaxley Cart. p. 16; cf. P.N. Glos. (E.P.N.S.), iii. 232; Dean Forest & Wye Valley (H.M.S.O. 1956), 66.
48 Rot. Litt. Claus. (Rec. Com.), ii. 125, 171.
49 Flaxley Cart. pp. 108–9.
50 Cf. Trans. B.G.A.S. xiv. 360, 367.
51 Cur. Reg. R. xiii. 359; xiv. 10, 82–3, 315–16; cf. V.C.H. Glos. x. 6–7.   52 Cf. V.C.H. Glos. x. 84.
53 O.S. Area Bk. Little Dean (1878); cf. O.S. Map 6", Glos. XXXI. SE. (1883 edn.).

the abbey,[54] later known as the grange of Ardland or St. White's.[55] The portion's southern
area, containing the principal buildings of the
grange,[56] was bounded in several places by ancient tracks, including one leading eastwards
from St. White's towards Littledean, and it
extended eastwards almost as far as the Littledean–Newnham road. On the south it ran up
against a part of the Forest that was granted to
the abbey in 1258 and became known as Abbots
wood.[57] The northern area, bounded on the east
by the lane known later as Littledean Hill Road[58]
and containing in 1591 land called Mousell and,
to the north, the Meend[59] (later Packers or
Flaxley Meend),[60] became part of the town of
Cinderford. In 1883 the portion was transferred
to East Dean township or civil parish and in
1953, when East Dean was dismembered, the
areas north and south of the Coleford road were
included in the new civil parishes of Cinderford
and Ruspidge respectively.[61] Another detached
portion of Flaxley covered 207 a. east of Littledean in a compact area bounded on the north
by the Littledean–Gloucester road and on the
south by a track, sunken for part of its course,
known as Lumbars Lane. Above it on a bank
marking the western boundary is Littledean
Camp,[62] which has been identified with 'the old
castle of Dean' standing above land given to the
Cistercians by Earl Roger.[63] The portion, which
contained at the north-eastern corner near Camp
Farm a tiny detached part of Westbury-on-
Severn,[64] was transferred to Littledean in 1883.[65]
Two smaller portions lay east of the main part
of the parish. They comprised 45 a. between
Blaisdon and Westbury at Wintle's Farm, north
of Northwood green, and 58 a. within Westbury
to the west of Walmore common,[66] and they were
absorbed respectively by Blaisdon in 1883 and
Westbury in 1882. The main part of Flaxley,
which by the addition of the detached part of
Blaisdon north of Gaulet in 1883 contained
1,066 a.,[67] was united with Blaisdon in 1935.[68]

The main part of Flaxley is crossed from west
to east by the Westbury brook valley, called the
valley of Castiard in the 12th century,[69] and is
made up mostly of hills rising to 150 m. in the
north-west and to 175 m. in the south-west on
Welshbury. The lower ground, in the south-
east, is formed by the Keuper Marl and the

higher ground by the Old Red Sandstone; alluvial soil covers the principal valley bottoms.[70]
Fortifications on Welshbury, so called by 1227,[71]
are thought to have formed an extensive Iron
Age fort.[72] The land has remained heavily
wooded and the cleared areas, which include the
eastern part towards Boseley, the northern corner at Gaulet, and narrow belts of land along the
floor of the central valley and below Welshbury,
were by the later 18th century used principally
for meadow and pasture. North-east of Flaxley
Abbey, the house formed after the Dissolution
from the abbey buildings, a small park was laid
out and stocked with deer by the mid 18th
century.[73] The woodland, which measured 521
a. in 1905,[74] was administered by the Forestry
Commission from 1952.[75]

The portions of the parish near Littledean lie
on more steeply sloping land, climbing to 237
m. at St. White's and 180 m. at Littledean
Camp. In 1265, during the barons' war, a beacon
was lit at Ardland (St. White's) as a signal to the
king's party captive in Gloucester.[76] The ground
is formed by sandstone and in the west, at St.
White's, by limestone, a thin band of which,
running NE.–SW., contains an outcrop of iron
ore.[77] Although mining and quarrying have
taken place at St. White's the land has been
devoted mostly to pasture. A grove or coppice
containing 10 a. next to the Forest west of St.
White's was recorded in 1591[78] and some woodland has survived south-east of St. White's and
east of Littledean. In the late 19th century there
was a rifle range south-east of Littledean Camp[79]
and in the mid 20th century the Cinderford golf
club had its course at St. White's.[80]

The principal road through the main part of
Flaxley leads up the central valley towards
Mitcheldean. Its original course evidently
crossed Westbury brook to ascend a bridle path,
mentioned in 1227, running along the parish
boundary east of Shapridge towards Abenhall
church.[81] It was later diverted[82] to join the
Littledean–Mitcheldean road on the parish
boundary near Gunn's Mills and was turnpiked
in 1769 as part of a route from Elton, on the
Gloucester–Newnham road, to Mitcheldean.[83]
By 1824 a tollgate had been placed at the junction with the Blaisdon road,[84] which itself was a
turnpike between 1833 and 1866.[85] The Elton–

54 Flaxley Cart. pp. 16, 18.
55 Glos. R.O., D 2172/1/54.   56 Below, manor.
57 Flaxley Cart. pp. 109–10; O.S. Map 6", Glos. XXXI.
SE. (1883 edn.).
58 Cf. surv. of Sir Thos. Crawley-Boevey's estates 1797
(nos. 4, 8): copy in Glos. R.O., MF 285; Greenwood, Map
of Glos. (1824).
59 Glos. R.O., D 2172/1/71.
60 Surv. of Crawley-Boevey est. 1797 (no. 8); Glos. R.O.,
P 145/OV 2/1; Atkinson, Map of Dean Forest (1847); Kelly's
Dir. Glos. (1879), 647.
61 O.S. Area Bk. Flaxley (1880); Census, 1891, 1961.
62 O.S. Area Bk. Little Dean (1878); cf. O.S. Maps 6",
Glos. XXXI. SE. (1883 edn.); XXXII. SW. (1883 edn.).
63 Flaxley Cart. p. 16; Trans. B.G.A.S. lxxvii. 57–8.
64 O.S. Map 1/2,500, Glos. XXXII. 9 (1881 edn.).
65 O.S. Area Bk. Flaxley (1880); Census, 1891.
66 O.S. Area Bk. Westbury upon Severn (1880); cf. O.S.
Maps 6", Glos. XXXII. NE., NW. (1884–91 edn.).
67 O.S. Area Bk. Flaxley (1880); Census, 1891; cf. O.S.
Map 6", Glos. XXXII. NW. (1891 edn.).
68 Census, 1931 (pt. ii).   69 Flaxley Cart. p. 16.
70 Geol. Surv. Map 1/50,000, solid and drift, sheet 234

(1972 edn.).
71 Flaxley Cart. p. 108; in Taylor, Map of Glos. (1777),
it is called Edgbury Hill.
72 C. E. Hart, Arch. in Dean (1967), 16–17.
73 Glouc. Jnl. 3 Mar. 1761; Bigland, Glos. i. 583; Delineations of Glos. 127–8.   74 Acreage Returns, 1905.
75 Inf. from deputy surveyor, Forest Enterprise, Coleford; Dean Forest & Wye Valley, pp. iii–iv, 30–1.
76 Trans. B.G.A.S. lxv. 116; V.C.H. Glos. iv. 20.
77 Geol. Surv. Map 1/50,000, solid and drift, sheet 234
(1972 edn.); sheet 233 (1974 edn.); Atkinson, Map of Dean
Forest (1847).
78 Glos. R.O., D 2172/1/71.
79 O.S. Map 6", Glos. XXXI. SE. (1883, 1903 edns.).
80 Glos. R.O., SM 109/2/M 2, p. 148; Dean Forest &
Wye Valley, 6.   81 Flaxley Cart. p. 108.
82 Cf. Glos. R.O., D 23/T 39; D 4431, deed 1 Apr. 13 Jas. I.
83 Glouc. & Heref. Roads Act, 9 Geo. III, c. 50; Taylor,
Map of Glos. (1777).
84 Greenwood, Map of Glos. (1824).
85 Huntley Roads Acts, 3 Wm. IV, c. 75 (Local and
Personal); 29 & 30 Vic. c. 100 (Local and Personal); Glos.
R.O., Q/RUm 128.

Mitcheldean turnpike was discontinued in 1880.[86] The Blaisdon road was a continuation of a way from Blackmore's Hale. That way, recorded in a Forest perambulation of 1282[87] and known as Dirty Lane in 1833,[88] was rebuilt where it marked the Flaxley boundary south-west of the Mitcheldean–Elton road between 1925 and 1927.[89]

Several important routes crossed the part of Flaxley south of Littledean and were recorded in 1591.[90] One, descending southwards from Littledean towards Abbots wood and Soudley, was supposed to have been part of a Roman road linking Ariconium with Lydney.[91] It was crossed by two tracks, which ran westwards from the Littledean–Newnham road and have been largely abandoned.[92] The northern one formed a junction with the old route from Littledean to St. White's at a spring known by 1679 as Pennywell,[93] but owing to its steepness traffic between Newnham and St. White's took a longer route through Littledean and Callamore in the later 18th century.[94] In the late 1820s the more direct route between Littledean and St. White's was replaced by a new road to Nailbridge running north-westwards across Flaxley Meend from a point between Pennywell and St. White's.[95] The new road crossed a track known as Mousell Lane.[96]

Flaxley abbey, known also as the abbey of Dean,[97] stood by Westbury brook, the course of which has been varied to serve not only the abbey precinct and the later manor house, called Flaxley Abbey, and its grounds but also a number of ironworks.[98] The only abbey buildings to survive, notably part of the claustral ranges, have been incorporated in the manor house.[99] The grange recorded next to the abbey in 1227[1] may have occupied the site to the north-west where several farm buildings later stood.[2]

A chapel standing before the abbey gate in 1253[3] was probably on a different site to the later parish church, which was some way south-west of Flaxley Abbey on the Mitcheldean–Elton road.[4] In 1695 there was a church house next to Flaxley Abbey.[5] The village of Flaxley has remained very small with a few cottages, one having a timber frame, scattered along the road

east of the church and along the southern end of the Blaisdon road, in which was a pound in the late 19th century and the early 20th.[6] In 1856 the church was replaced by a new building to the west. Other buildings added to the village in the 19th century included a school and a vicarage house. There are also several cottages strung out at intervals along Westbury brook, on which there was a succession of forges in the 17th and 18th centuries.[7]

The rest of Flaxley, which was even more sparsely populated, contained a number of ancient farmsteads. In the main part, at the head of a remote valley in the north, was Gaulet, where a family called a Fowle lived in the 1540s.[8] The house, a long range of one storey and attics with an east cross wing of two storeys, has a lobby entrance plan and early 17th-century mullioned and transomed windows.[9] Monk Hill Farm at the eastern boundary is probably of the later 16th century.[10] It has a central range of three bays with thin raised crucks and two lower cross wings, the eastern wing, originally timber-framed, having stone walls. A farmstead had been established at the place known in 1565 as Tibbs Cross,[11] on the edge of the Forest below Welshbury, by the later 18th century.[12]

The earliest settlement in the portions of Flaxley near Littledean was evidently at the abbey's grange of Ardland or St. White's.[13] The grange occupied the site of St. White's Farm, west of a track leading southwards from the Coleford road to Abbots wood,[14] and included a chapel or hermitage, which was dedicated to St. White (*Candida*).[15] After the Dissolution a new house called the Grange, standing south-west of Littledean, became the principal residence in that part of Flaxley.[16] By 1661 settlement had also taken place further south in the area known as Sutton,[17] where two 18th-century farmhouses belonging to Flaxley have survived.[18] In 1988 one, Baynham Farm, was unoccupied, having been replaced by a bungalow nearby, and the other, Wellington's Farm, on the Soudley road, was a centre for pony trekking. By the road opposite the latter in 1872 was a pound for Abbots wood.[19] A farmstead to the east, at Maidenham, was abandoned in the mid 20th century and its house and outbuildings had been

86 Annual Turnpike Acts Continuance Act, 43 & 44 Vic. c. 12.   87 Trans. B.G.A.S. xiv. 360.
88 2nd Rep. Dean Forest Com. 34.
89 Glos. R.O., DA 24/100/9, pp. 212–14, 268, 272, 370; 10, pp. 418–20, 476–8.
90 Ibid. D 2172/1/71; cf. ibid. D 36/E 12, ff. 43v.–44; D 4543/2/1/3.
91 A. W. Trotter, Dean Road (1936), 34–6; I. D. Margary, Roman Roads in Britain, ii (1957), p. 64.
92 Cf. O.S. Map 6", Glos. XXXI. SE. (1883 edn.).
93 Glos. R.O., D 2123, p. 159; D 36/E 12, ff. 43v.–44; M 55.
94 Newnham Ferry to St. White's Road Act, 23 Geo. III, c. 104; Bryant, Map of Glos. (1824).
95 Nicholls, Forest of Dean, 197; cf. Greenwood, Map of Glos. (1824); O.S. Map 1", sheet 43 (1831 edn.). The route of the new road varied considerably from that specified in Dean Forest Roads Act, 7 & 8 Geo. IV, c. 12 (Local and Personal); Glos. R.O., Q/RUm 107.
96 Surv. of Crawley-Boevey est. 1797 (no. 8); P.R.O., HO 107/1959.
97 Flaxley Cart. pp. 1, 17; V.C.H. Glos. ii. 93.
98 W. H. Townley, 'Ind. Sites in Vale of Castiard', 14–16: copy in Glos. R.O., IN 41; Glos. Soc. Ind. Arch. Jnl. (1974), 18–19.   99 Below, manor.

1 Flaxley Cart. p. 108; Cal. Chart. R. 1226–57, 11.
2 Atkyns, Glos. plate at pp. 436–7, reproduced below, Plate 6.   3 B.L. Harl. Ch. 43 A.39.
4 Atkyns, Glos. plate at pp. 436–7; below, church.
5 N.L.W., Mynde Park MS. 1685.
6 O.S. Map 6", Glos. XXXII. NW. (1891, 1924 edns.).
7 Below, econ. hist.
8 Trans. B.G.A.S. lii. 289–90; Hockaday Abs. cxxvi, Blaisdon, 1544.
9 Access was not possible in 1988.
10 The site may have been that called Monk Toft in 1612: Glos. R.O., P 145/IN 1/1, list of churchwardens.
11 Ibid. D 2026/X 3.
12 Cf. P.R.O., MR 415 (F 16/47).
13 Glos. R.O., D 2172/1/54.
14 O.S. Map 6", Glos. XXXI. SE. (1883 edn.); below, manor.   15 Reg. Bothe, 355, 359; below, church.
16 O.S. Map 6", Glos. XXXI. SE. (1883 edn.); below, manor.
17 P.R.O., E 134/13 Chas. II East./24; G.D.R. wills 1742/148; cf. Greenwood, Map of Glos. (1824).
18 Cf. surv. of Crawley-Boevey est. 1797 (nos. 5, 13); O.S. Map 6", Glos. XXXI. SE. (1883 edn.).
19 Glos. R.O., Q/RI 52.

demolished by 1988.[20] The Grove, standing in a deep valley, was the principal farmstead in the part of Flaxley east of Littledean; its house, dating from the 17th or 18th century, has been much enlarged. In the later 20th century farming was centred on a new bungalow and farm buildings above the valley to the north and the Grove was a camping centre. Camp Farm on the Littledean–Gloucester road[21] incorporates part of a house of the late 16th century or early 17th with crucks. A barn on the west end has been converted as a house. At the Moors, in the south-western corner of that part of Flaxley, a farmhouse was built shortly before 1691 on a small freehold estate belonging to William Pritchard in the right of his wife Mary Bridgeman.[22] The farmhouse was rebuilt as a private residence in 1988. A dwelling had been established at Wintle's Farm, north of Northwood green, by 1699 when it was part of Walmore manor in Westbury-on-Severn;[23] possibly it was there by 1559 when a Northwood man was described as a Flaxley parishioner.[24]

The muster roll of 1539 listed 7 men for Flaxley and those of 1542 and 1546 gave 12 and 17 names respectively.[25] In 1563 there were said to be 20 households in the parish[26] and in 1603 the number of communicants was put at 100.[27] In 1650 there were said to be 30 families.[28] The population, estimated c. 1710 at 200 and c. 1775 at 196,[29] evidently fell considerably in the late 18th century, but in the early 19th century it increased steadily, rising from 135 in 1801 to 272 in 1861.[30] The rise was mostly caused by building in the part of the parish at Cinderford,[31] which quadrupled Flaxley's population in the 1860s. The boundary changes of the early 1880s left Flaxley with a rural population which declined from 127 in 1881 to 82 in 1901. It remained about the same when the parish was united with Blaisdon in 1935.[32]

In the mid 1280s a lay brother sold ale for the abbot of Flaxley.[33] A victualler may have lived in Flaxley in 1670[34] and another parishioner's licence to sell ale was withdrawn in 1677.[35] A house called the Greyhound, which in 1693 had land in Flaxley and Westbury[36] and later was rated as part of Flaxley,[37] presumably stood at the east end of the village on the parish boundary. Flaxley had an old parish library in 1825.[38]

In the earlier Middle Ages several monarchs stayed at Flaxley abbey, probably while hunting in the Forest of Dean. John paid several visits in the early 13th century[39] and Henry III was there in 1229 and 1256.[40] In 1353 Edward III compensated the abbey for expenses incurred during his frequent visits.[41] In 1234 several followers of the rebel Richard Marshal, earl of Pembroke, took refuge in the abbey.[42] After the Dissolution Flaxley remained for four centuries essentially the possession of the owners of Flaxley Abbey. They included, from 1692, Catharina Boevey (d. 1727),[43] whose charitable work extended far beyond the parish and who was commemorated by a monument in Westminster abbey; she was reputedly the 'perverse widow' portrayed in the *Spectator* as being wooed by Sir Roger de Coverley.[44] After her death Flaxley Abbey passed to the Crawley-Boeveys, who dominated parish life until the mid 20th century.

MANOR AND OTHER ESTATES. According to tradition Roger, earl of Hereford, founded Flaxley abbey to mark the spot in the valley of Castiard where his father Miles of Gloucester had been killed hunting in 1143.[45] In 1158 Henry II made a new grant to the monks of Roger's gifts and added other lands, including an assart under Castiard called Vincents Land.[46] Among the abbey's other benefactors were William de Mynors, lord of Westbury manor in the late 12th century, and William of Dean, lord of Mitcheldean and at one time Roger's tenant, who both gave land at or near Castiard, and William of Dean's son Geoffrey.[47] In 1227 Henry III granted the monks woodland around the abbey in place of a general right to take fuel throughout the Forest of Dean.[48] By such grants the abbey built up an estate which included Flaxley and land in neighbouring parishes.[49]

In 1537 Flaxley abbey and its possessions, including the manor of *FLAXLEY*, were granted to Sir William Kingston[50] (d. 1540), and in 1543 and 1544 they were confirmed to his son Sir Anthony[51] (d. 1556). The latter's son Edmund, who apparently was illegitimate,[52] conveyed Flaxley manor in 1565 to his brother-in-law Edward Barnard.[53] Edward, who was acting as a trustee for Edmund, devised the estate at his death in 1570 to Edmund's son Anthony. From Anthony (d. 1591) it passed to his son William[54] (d. 1614), who was succeeded by his uncle Edmund Kingston[55] (d. 1623).

20 Cf. surv. of Crawley-Boevey est. 1797 (no. 9); Glos. R.O., D 2299/685.
21 P.R.O., MR 415.
22 Glos. R.O., D 2957/101.11, 17, 27–30.
23 Ibid. Q/RNc 1, p. 88.   24 G.D.R. wills 1559/208.
25 *L. & P. Hen. VIII*, xiv (1), p. 271; xvii, p. 499; xxi (2), p. 206.
26 Bodl. MS. Rawl. C. 790, f. 28v.
27 *Eccl. Misc.* 99.   28 *Trans. B.G.A.S.* lxxxiii. 97.
29 Atkyns, *Glos.* 437; Rudder, *Glos,* 450.
30 *Census*, 1801–61.
31 Below, Forest of Dean, settlement.
32 *Census*, 1861–1931.
33 P.R.O., JUST 1/278, rot. 56.
34 Glos. R.O., P 145/IN 1/2.
35 Ibid. Q/SO 1, f. 141v.
36 Ibid Q/RNc 1, pp. 86–7; cf. ibid. D 4543/2/1/1.
37 Ibid. P 145/OV 2/1.   38 G.D.R. vol. 383, no. cxiii.
39 *Cur. Reg. R.* v. 79; itin. of John in *Rot. Litt. Pat.* (Rec. Com.).

40 *Close R.* 1227–31, 187; 1254–6, 341, 432–3.
41 *Cal. Chart. R.* 1341–1417, 133.
42 *V.C.H. Glos.* ii. 94–5.   43 Below, manor.
44 A. W. Crawley-Boevey, *Perverse Widow* (1898), *passim*; Bigland, *Glos.* i. 584.
45 *Flaxley Cart.* pp. 1–4; *V.C.H. Glos.* ii. 93.
46 *Flaxley Cart.* pp. 16, 18–19.
47 Ibid. pp. 134–5, 138–9; *V.C.H. Glos.* x. 85; *Trans. B.G.A.S.* vi. 125–6, 199.
48 *Flaxley Cart.* pp. 108–9.
49 Ibid. *passim*: some of the lands granted have not been identified; cf. *V.C.H. Glos.* x. 7, 40, 91.
50 *L. & P. Hen. VIII*, xii (1), p. 353; for the Kingstons, *Trans. B.G.A.S.* vi. 285–7, 292–5.
51 *L. & P. Hen. VIII*, xvii (1), p. 124; xix (1), p. 379.
52 P.R.O., C 142/107, no. 50.
53 *Cal. Pat.* 1563–6, pp. 284–5.
54 P.R.O., C 142/231, no. 94; G.D.R. wills 1570/27; cf. Smith, *Men and Armour*, 41; *V.C.H. Glos.* xi. 50.
55 P.R.O., C 142/347, no. 90.

Edmund's Flaxley estate passed to his son William,[56] who sold it in 1648 to the merchants William and James Boeve (later Boevey), members of London's Dutch community. In 1654 James conveyed his interest to William, his half brother, and the latter assigned a moiety of the estate to his half sister Joanna, widow of Abraham Clarke. Joanna, who bought the other moiety after William's death in 1661,[57] died in 1664 leaving Flaxley to her son Abraham Clarke (d. 1683) and he left the estate to his cousin William, son of James Boevey.[58] William Boevey died in 1692 and under his will the estate passed in turn to his wife Catharina (d. 1727) and a kinsman Thomas Crawley, who assumed the name Crawley-Boevey.[59] Thomas died in 1742[60] and his son and heir Thomas Crawley-Boevey[61] enlarged the estate in the 1760s by purchasing land in Westbury-on-Severn adjoining the main part of Flaxley.[62] Thomas (d. 1769) was succeeded by his son Thomas Crawley-Boevey,[63] heir in 1789 to a baronetcy, and from Sir Thomas (d. 1818) the estate descended with the baronetcy from father to son, through Thomas (d. 1847), Martin (d. 1862), Thomas (d. 1912), and Francis (d. 1928), to Launcelot.[64] Land in Flaxley Meend was sold off in 1839 and later[65] and the break up of the rest of the estate, under way by 1910, was completed by Sir Launcelot,[66] who sold over 500 a. of woodland at Flaxley to the Forestry Commissioners in 1952[67] and Flaxley Abbey and just under 200 a. to F. B. Watkins in 1960.[68] Mr. Watkins, a local industrialist,[69] remained the house's owner in 1988.

The abbey, dedicated to St. Mary, was under construction by 1158[70] and appears to have had a cruciform church with a south cloister, which was c. 30.5 m. (100 ft.) from east to west.[71] Henry III gave timber for the church and abbey buildings in 1229 and 1231.[72] The abbey, particularly its refectory, was in disrepair in 1515,[73] and in 1536, on the eve of its dissolution, the church was said to have been destroyed by fire and its bells sold to help pay for a rebuilding.[74] The buildings were presumably demolished soon after 1536, apart from the western claustral range which became a manor house known as Flaxley Abbey. The northern end of that range was destroyed by fire in 1777.[75] The surviving part includes a late 12th-century vaulted undercroft of five bays with a tall narrow archway, probably over a staircase, on its east side and a cross wing at its south end. On the ground floor the wing is divided lengthways into two compartments, the wider one, on the north, being tunnel-vaulted and the other being open. In the late 12th century the wing was clearly a reredorter and the upper room in the west range was presumably the dormitory for the lay folk. In the later 14th century the upper room in the wing was reconstructed as a hall or great chamber with an open roof of high quality; it probably formed part of the abbot's lodging or the guest suite. A lower range to the east of the wing, occupied after the 1960s by a room called the Bow Room, incorporates part of the walls of the southern claustral range.[76] A short length of the south wall of the nave of the abbey church, including the lower part of its 12th-century east doorway into the cloister, survives in a late 17th-century brick orangery; the east wall of the orangery must be on the site of the west wall of the transept. The site of the chapter house, which is reported to have had an apsidal east end, was excavated in 1788 and seven coffin lids, presumably from abbots' tombs, were found.[77]

The western range was presumably retained after the abbey's dissolution because it provided domestic accommodation of some quality. Among its occupants were Edward Barnard (d. 1570)[78] and Abraham Clarke, who was assessed on 8 hearths in 1672.[79] No evidence survives for new building or conversion work before the late 17th century when William Boevey carried out extensive alterations,[80] which included a brick extension on the east side of the main range. Part of that extension is occupied by an oak staircase, which is next to the site of its late 12th-century predecessor and was aligned with the main, west entrance to the house. It leads to a corridor, along the east side of the upper floor, which served a series of newly fitted principal rooms.[81] The orangery to the north-east was also part of the improvements initiated by William Boevey.[82] Following the fire of 1777 the house was altered to designs by Anthony Keck.[83] The northern half of the main range, which had been destroyed, was replaced by a cross wing matching that on the south end. The main addition was to the south-east where a new block, built against the south side of the cross wing and the lower range to the east, provided an entrance hall

56   Ibid. CP 25/2/420/3 Chas I. Trin. no. 15; 5 Chas. I Mich. no. 29.
57   Glos. R.O., D 4543/2/2/1, ff. 1, 18v.; Crawley-Boevey, *Perverse Widow*, 15–19.
58   Crawley-Boevey, *Perverse Widow*, 60–2.
59   Ibid. 63, 75, 106, 123; Glos. R.O., D 5895/1; P 145/IN 1/3.
60   Glos. R.O., P 145/IN 1/4.
61   Crawley-Boevey, *Perverse Widow*, 314–15; for several generations daughters and younger sons of the Crawley-Boeveys were called Crawley only: ibid. 318–20 nn.
62   Glos. R.O., D 4543/2/1/1; D 4543/4/1.
63   Crawley-Boevey, *Perverse Widow*, 315–18; Glos. R.O., Q/REl 1A, St. Briavels 1776.
64   Burke, *Peerage* (1963), 267–70; Glos. R.O., P 145/OV 2/1; *Kelly's Dir. Glos.* (1856 and later edns.).
65   Glos. R.O., D 4543/2/2/3; G. E. Lawrence, *Kindling the Flame* (1974), 17: copy in ibid. D 2598/23/1.
66   Ibid. D 2299/685, 3325, 4482; D 4543/5/3–7; *V.C.H. Glos.* x. 92.
67   Inf. from deputy surveyor, Forest Enterprise, Coleford; Hart, *Royal Forest*, 240.
68   Glos. R.O., SL 568; *Country Life*, 12 Apr. 1973, 980.
69   Below, Forest of Dean, industry (other ind. and trade).
70   *Flaxley Cart.* pp. 1, 17–19; *V.C.H. Glos.* ii. 94.
71   For discussions of the abbey buildings, *Trans. B.G.A.S.* vi. 280–3; xliii. 57–60.
72   *Close R.* 1227–31, 188, 495.
73   *Reg. Mayew*, 286.
74   *V.C.H. Glos.* ii. 95.
75   *Glouc. Jnl.* 14 Apr. 1777.
76   Inf. from Mr. F. B. Watkins.
77   Bigland, *Glos.* i. 583; cf. *Flaxley Cart.* plate V; in 1988 the three surviving lids were in the orangery.
78   G.D.R. wills 1570/27.
79   P.R.O., E 179/247/13, rot. 24d.
80   Bodl. MS. Top. Glouc. c. 3, f. 193.
81   For a view of the W. front in the late 17th cent., B. Watkins, *Story of Flaxley Abbey* (1985), p. x.
82   Atkyns, *Glos.* plate at pp. 436–7, reproduced below, Plate 6; dated rainwater heads of 1751 and 1765, respectively on the W. and E. sides of the main range of the ho., seem unrelated to any major structural work.
83   *Delineations of Glos.* 127.

flanked by principal rooms, all being decorated in Adam style. The ground-floor bay on the east front of the lower range was presumably added at the same time. By the mid 1820s the west window of the great chamber had been redesigned with Gothic tracery,[84] perhaps for Sir Thomas Crawley-Boevey (d. 1847) who later added Gothic buttresses and battlements on the west front and a south porch and battlements on the south-east block.[85] The undercroft and the great chamber were restored in 1913.[86] After 1960 extensive repairs and alterations were carried out under Oliver Messel. The Bow Room was formed from several small rooms and was linked to the orangery by an arcaded passage.[87]

Gardens laid out around the house by William Boevey and completed after his death in 1692 by his wife Catharina[88] included to the east a large formal parterre incorporating canals on the south and east sides. On the west side of the house were three enclosed forecourts, the northernmost containing a small formal garden with corner pavilions on the north side, and to the north-west was a group of outbuildings including a house and barn.[89] By the late 18th century, possibly as part of the alterations following the 1777 fire, the formal gardens and forecourts had been removed, lawns laid around the house, and a new kitchen garden created beyond the outbuildings.[90] The last were replaced by new farm buildings in the 18th and 19th centuries, and an outbuilding was erected further east in the early 19th century with a Gothic front intended as an eye-catcher from the main house. The formal gardens were restored after 1960 to a modified plan which included canals and ponds on the east side of the house.[91]

After the Dissolution the grange of Ardland or St. White's became part of a leasehold estate centred on a house called *THE GRANGE* and comprising most of the portion of Flaxley between Littledean and the Forest of Dean.[92] William Parker held a lease of the grange, originally granted by Flaxley abbey, in 1544 when Sir Anthony Kingston granted a lease in reversion to Hugh Huntley. The latter lease passed to Richard Copley, who sold it in 1576 to Henry Ockall.[93] A lease of the Grange and land was granted by the abbey in 1536 to Henry Brayne of London. Henry, a resident of Bristol at his death in 1558, devised it to his son Robert (d. 1570), whose widow Goodith granted it to his

servant Thomas Hawkins.[94] Thomas died *c.* 1606 leaving the lease in turn to his wife Margaret and son James[95] but his title was contested by Robert Brayne's uncle Richard Brayne (d. 1572) of Littledean and by Richard's grandson Thomas Brayne.[96] Thomas Brayne, who in 1591 obtained from Anthony Kingston a lease for 370 years of the house, then said to be in Littledean, and land, including St. White's farm, died in 1604. His executor sold that lease to pay his debts in 1611 and James Hawkins, a lawyer, purchased it the following year.[97] James, who continued to face claims from the Braynes, died in 1637 leaving the Grange, subject to the life interest of his wife Jocamina, to his son James (d. 1678).[98] Another son John (d. 1674) acquired St. White's farm, which he left to his wife Sarah[99] (d. 1689). His son James (d. 1722) devised it with the Grange, which he had inherited from his uncle, to his kinswoman Mary Young (d. 1742). She left the estate to her nephew George Skipp[1] (d. 1783), who in 1781 agreed to sell it to his son George to free it from debt.[2] The son built up an estate of *c.* 300 a. in Littledean and Flaxley.[3] Among his purchases was Court farm in Littledean, which contained land, notably *c.* 40 a. at Mousell, included in the Grange estate under the long lease of 1591; from 1772 the Mousell land was claimed by its owners as freehold,[4] a claim which the Crawley-Boeveys denied.[5]

George Skipp died in 1804 and doubts about the authenticity of his will led to a division of the Grange and St. White's farm between his wife Frances, his children George, Catherine, and Penelope, and his grandsons Peter and John Shaw as tenants in common. A moiety of the estate, representing the interests of Frances (d. 1823) and George (d. 1837), who left his lands to his wife Hannah, was vested in 1845 in George's son Francis, and Francis's share of the Grange and of 41 a. was sold in 1861 to the ironmaster Henry Crawshay[6] (d. 1879)[7] and in 1883 to Francis Montagu Lloyd.[8] The other moiety of the estate, which Penelope Skipp, wife of Joseph Lloyd (d. 1842) of Abenhall, secured by acquiring the interests of the Shaws and of her sister Catherine, wife of Thomas Bate, was shared at her death in 1864 between her sons and was eventually acquired in full by F. M. Lloyd, her grandson. He died in 1922 leaving the Grange in turn to his wife Edith (d. 1939)

[84] Cf. Atkyns, *Glos.* plate at pp. 436–7; *Delineations of Glos.* plate facing p. 119.
[85] Crawley-Boevey, *Perverse Widow*, 317 n.
[86] *Trans. B.G.A.S.* xliii. 58–9.
[87] *Country Life*, 29 Mar., 5, 12 Apr. 1973, 842–5, 908–11, 980–4, which has a full description and many photogs.
[88] Bodl. MS. Top. Glouc. c. 3, f. 193; Crawley-Boevey, *Perverse Widow*, 75.
[89] Atkyns, *Glos.* plate at pp. 436–7.
[90] Surv. of Sir Thos. Crawley-Boevey's estates 1797 (no. 1): copy in Glos. R.O., MF 285; cf. Bigland, *Glos.* i. 583; *Delineations of Glos.* 127–8, plate facing p. 119.
[91] *Country Life*, 12 Apr. 1973, 983–4.
[92] Cf. surv. of Crawley-Boevey est. 1797 (nos. 4, 11).
[93] Glos. R.O., D 2172/1/54.
[94] P.R.O., C 3/274/35; PROB 11/49 (P.C.C. 12 Stonard), ff. 93v–95; PROB 11/53 (P.C.C. 12 Holney), f. 90v.; *Trans. B.G.A.S.* vi. 296–7.
[95] G.D.R. wills 1607/143.
[96] Glos. R.O., D 2172/1/72; cf. *Trans B.G.A.S.* vi. 296–9.

[97] Glos. R.O., D 4431, deed 7 Sept. 23 Chas. II; D 2172/1/71; P.R.O., PROB 11/104 (P.C.C. 53 Harte), ff. 38v.–40v.; cf. *Trans. B.G.A.S.* vi. 287.
[98] Glos. R.O., D 2172/1/54; 1/72; D 4431, deed 7 Sept. 23 Chas II; G.D.R., V 1/147.
[99] Bigland, *Glos.* i. 453; G.D.R. wills 1678/68.
[1] Glos. R.O., P 110/IN 1/2–3; G.D.R. wills 1694/285; 1723/256; 1742/160.
[2] Glos. R.O., D 2172/1/76.
[3] Surv. of Crawley-Boevey est. 1797 (nos. 4, 7–8, 10–11, 21); cf. Glos. R.O., D 2957/101.11, 29–31.
[4] Glos. R.O., D 543, Mitcheldean brewery, Smith v. Wintle legal papers 1907; cf. ibid. D 2957/101.8–10, 32; Glos. Colln. RF 101.2.
[5] Glos. R.O., D 4543/2/1/2; D 4543/4/1; surv. of Crawley-Boevey est. 1797 (nos. 4, 8).
[6] Glos. R.O., D 2172/1/55; D 1438, misc. papers (Skipp fam. pedigree); D 2568, deed 1846.
[7] *Glos. N. & Q.* iv. 285–6.
[8] Glos. R.O., D 2172/1/55; D 2299/608.

and his son Leslie Skipp Lloyd.[9] The latter owned it until 1960 when the estate reverted to Sir Launcelot Crawley-Boevey, who sold it.[10]

The Grange, which stood a short distance south-west of Littledean near the Soudley road,[11] had been built by 1536.[12] In 1591 it was Thomas Hawkins's residence[13] and in 1606 it included a new room used by his son James as a study.[14] The house, which was rebuilt c. 1672,[15] was of local sandstone with limestone dressings and comprised a three-storeyed block with string courses and gables on the east and north sides and a lower south wing.[16] In the early 19th century it was let as a private residence, the occupants including May-nard Colchester in 1820,[17] John Wright Guise in 1825,[18] and the ironmaster Stephen Allaway in 1841 and 1852.[19] Later it fell into ruin[20] and by the turn of the century it had been abandoned and some fittings removed by F. M. Lloyd to a house, renamed by him the Grange, in nearby Newnham parish.[21] The shell was pulled down in 1962[22] and the fabric used in the restoration of the gardens at Flaxley Abbey.[23]

In 1904 St. White's farm, which comprised 101 a., came into the possession of Thomas Harrison Burdess by his purchase of the moieties held by F. M. Lloyd and Eleanor Phillips. Eleanor's moiety derived from Elizabeth Bradley and in 1865 had been vested in, as trustee for sale under Elizabeth's will, her husband Thomas Adams Phillips (d. c. 1892),[24] the owner by 1870 of Mousell farm (44 a.).[25] T. H. Burdess died in 1915 and after his wife Hannah surrendered St. White's farm in 1954 Sir Launcelot Crawley-Boevey sold the freehold to the tenant farmer, Jesse Virgo.[26] The farmhouse, on the site of the medieval grange,[27] dated from a rebuilding in the 19th century. In the mid 20th century it was occupied by the Cinderford golf club[28] and in the later 1980s it contained several dwellings.

Part of Flaxley passed with the abbey's manor of Walmore in Westbury-on-Severn, which Sir Anthony Kingston alienated in 1544.[29] Thomas Crawley-Boevey (d. 1742) purchased some of the land[30] but the manor retained Camp Farm and 62 a. in Flaxley until at least 1840.[31]

ECONOMIC HISTORY. The name of the parish suggests that flax was grown in a clearing in the Westbury brook valley before the place was given to the Cistercians for an abbey in the mid 12th century.[32] In 1227 the monks had a grange next to the abbey and a field to the south. Most of the surrounding land remained wood-land[33] and from that time the abbot resisted claims by the lords of the neighbouring manor of Longhope to pasture rights in it.[34] Land in the east towards Boseley, in the north at Gaulet, and in the south-west below Welshbury were cleared for cultivation in closes,[35] those clear-ances evidently being for the monks as there is no record of the land being subject to tithes. The monks had established a grange or farm at 'Wastadene' near St. White's by 1158 and the clearance of the land east of Littledean, begun before it was given to them, had not been completed by 1158 when 100 a. were said to have been assarted.[36] The land north of the Little-dean–Coleford road known as Mousell and the Meend was evidently among early clearances.[37] In 1282 the abbey estates supported at least 11 ploughteams.[38] In 1291 the estate next to the abbey included 3 ploughlands and £1 6s. 8d. rent of assize, and in Dean, presumably on its land near Littledean, the monks had 3 ploughlands, yielding 10 loads of hay, and 5s. rent of assize.[39] At that time the monks were also sheep farm-ers,[40] the abbey having been active in the wool trade by the early 13th century.[41] Its flocks, which were reduced in size by murrain in the late 1270s,[42] included 140 ewes and 100 wethers in 1291. It also had 35 cows that year.[43] From the time of its foundation the abbey had the right to pasture its livestock, including cattle and pigs, in the Forest of Dean.[44] Later Flaxley landhold-ers enjoyed common rights in the extraparochial land of the Forest,[45] and in 1860 three people exercised those rights.[46] In Abbots wood, that part of the Forest acquired by the monks in 1258,[47] the owners of St. White's and Mousell farms retained pasture rights for their horses, cattle, and sheep until 1872.[48]

The farmland and woodland next to the abbey were apparently in the hands of one or more

9 Ibid. D 2172/1/55; D 4543/2/1/3; Trans. B.G.A.S. vi. 304–5.
10 Glos. R.O., D 2172/1/71; Watkins, Flaxley Abbey, 279.
11 Trans. B.G.A.S. xlix. 264; O.S. Map 6", Glos. XXXI. SE. (1883 edn.).
12 P.R.O., C 3/274/35; cf. Glos. R.O., D 2172/1/72.
13 Glos. R.O., D 2172/1/71.
14 G.D.R. wills 1607/143.
15 P.R.O., E 179/247/13, rot. 24d.
16 Trans. B.G.A.S. xlix. 264–7; Glos. R.O., D 4304/7, 10; S. M. Crawley-Boevey, Dene Forest Sketches (n.d.), plate facing p. 200.
17 Glos. R.O., P 145/OV 2/1.
18 Ibid. P 110/IN 1/5.
19 P.R.O., HO 107/365; Glos. R.O., D 421/T 105.
20 Trans. B.G.A.S. vi. 285; cf. Country Life, 5 Dec. 1914, 765.
21 Trans. B.G.A.S. xlix. 264–6; Glos. R.O., D 4304/5; Kelly's Dir. Glos. (1894), 248; (1897), 253; cf. V.C.H. Glos. x. 34.
22 Dean Forest Mercury, 20 Apr. 1962.
23 Watkins, Flaxley Abbey, 279.
24 Glos. R.O., D 4543/2/1/3.
25 Ibid. Q/RI 52; cf. ibid. D 2172/1/55.
26 Ibid. D 4543/2/1/3; D 4543/5/6.
27 Ibid. D 2172/1/54–5; 1/71; D 4543/4/1; P.R.O., C

3/274/41; Taylor, Map of Glos. (1777).
28 Dean Forest & Wye Valley, 6.
29 Glos. R.O., Q/RNc 1, pp. 84–9; L. & P. Hen. VIII, xix (1), p. 507; cf. V.C.H. Glos. x. 91, which states incorrectly that Sir Ant. alienated the man. in 1540.
30 Glos. R.O., Q/RNc 4/5; D 4543/2/1/1.
31 Surv. of Crawley-Boevey est. 1797 (nos. 1, 10, 21); Glos. R.O., Q/RUm 169/2.
32 P.N. Glos. (E.P.N.S.), iii. 232; Flaxley Cart. p. 16.
33 Flaxley Cart. pp. 108–9.
34 Inq. p.m. Glos. 1236–1300, 109.
35 Cf. surv. of Sir Thos. Crawley-Boevey's estates 1797 (nos. 1–3, 6): copy in Glos. R.O., MF 285.
36 Flaxley Cart. pp. 16, 18.
37 Cf. Glos. R.O., D 2172/1/71.
38 Trans. B.G.A.S. xxxiii. 270.
39 Tax. Eccl. (Rec. Com.), 171.   40 V.C.H. Glos. ii. 94.
41 Cur. Reg. R. xiii. 527.
42 Cal. Pat. 1281–92, 2.
43 Tax. Eccl. (Rec. Com.), 174.
44 Flaxley Cart. pp. 16, 18.
45 5th Rep. Dean Forest Com. 65 and n.
46 P.R.O., F 3/128, letter 29 Nov. 1860.
47 Flaxley Cart. pp. 109–10; cf. P.R.O., E 134/13 Chas. II East./24.
48 Glos. R.O., Q/RI 52.

lessees in 1535,[49] by which time the grange of Ardland or St. White's was also leased from the abbey.[50] In 1797, when Sir Thomas Crawley-Boevey had 788 a., mostly woodland and the grounds of Flaxley Abbey, in hand, the largest farms in the parish were Monk Hill farm (138 a.) and Gaulet farm (96 a.) in the main part and Grove farm (122 a.) and St. White's farm (103 a.) near Littledean. Among the smaller farms were three or four at Maidenham and Sutton, one of which had been formed by the amalgamation of two holdings, and two north of the Littledean–Coleford road.[51] By the late 1840s the ironmasters Henry Crawshay and Stephen Allaway had acquired the tenancies respectively of the farms at Sutton and farmland at the Grange, and 100 a. in that area were farmed from Maidenham.[52] Several smaller farms survived in the early 20th century and the size of the principal farms remained virtually unchanged.[53] In the main part of the parish there were seven agricultural occupiers, six of them in 1896 being tenant farmers, and in 1926 three had over 100 a. and two under 20 a.[54] The home farm of Flaxley Abbey, which in 1960 with 119 a. was occupied by a tenant,[55] was among the five or six larger farms in the ancient parish in 1988.

Arable farming was of minor importance in Flaxley in the later 18th century when the land, apart from the woods, was devoted mostly to pasture.[56] Some land north of the Littledean–Coleford road remained marginal and covered with furze in the mid 19th century.[57] In 1801 only 187 a. were returned in the whole parish as under crops, wheat accounting for half of the area and barley, oats, beans, potatoes, and peas for the rest.[58] The presence of a butcher at Tibbs Cross in 1841 and 1851 indicates the importance of livestock to the local economy.[59] Arable cultivation had increased by 1866 when 287 a. were returned as arable and 359 a. as permanent grassland and the main crops in the rotation were wheat, oats, barley, turnips, and grass leys.[60] Sheep farming had continued and near Littledean a large flock was kept on Maidenham farm in the mid 19th century.[61] Herds of beef and dairy cattle had been established in the parish by 1866, when 143 cattle were returned together with 389 sheep and 64 pigs.[62] At the end of the century agriculture in the main part of the parish was dominated by the flocks and herds. Arable farming was of little significance and in 1905 the areas of permanent grassland and arable were measured at 525 a. and 16 a. respectively. In the early 20th century the flocks were increased, 685 sheep being returned in 1926 compared with 215 in 1896, and smaller numbers of cattle and pigs were kept.[63] Near Littledean Maidenham farm was used together with the adjoining part of the Forest in the 1920s as a sheep walk.[64] In 1988 the farmland in Flaxley and near Littledean remained devoted primarily to sheep rearing and dairying and some beef cattle were kept.

Fruit was grown at St. White's before 1591[65] and there were six orchards on the Flaxley Abbey estate in 1692.[66] Other parts of the parish also contained orchards in the late 18th century[67] and at least 47 a. in the main part were covered with fruit trees in 1896.[68] In 1960 the area around Flaxley Abbey retained many orchards and included a market garden.[69] Among fruit grown was the Blaisdon Red variety of plum, developed in the neighbouring parish. Several orchards had been grubbed by the early 1980s.[70] In 1695 a garden within the grounds of Flaxley Abbey was, according to its name, devoted to the cultivation of hops.[71]

Roger, earl of Hereford, granted Flaxley abbey an iron forge at Ardland in the mid 12th century, and under Henry II's charter of 1158 the abbey was entitled to operate an itinerant forge as freely as the forges belonging to the Crown demesne.[72] The forge, which was set up in places in the Forest of Dean,[73] has not been found recorded after 1258 when the monks were given Abbots wood in the royal demesne woodland of the Forest to provide fuel for it.[74] It may have been located for a time east of St. White's at Pennywell, where a substantial hill or tump was formed on the boundary with Littledean by the tipping of cinders from early ironworks.[75] The abbot's household may have included a miller in 1221[76] and the grange next to the abbey had both a water mill and a fulling mill in 1291.[77]

In the 17th and 18th centuries some six sites on Westbury brook in Flaxley were associated with mills or ironworks.[78] Flaxley mill, on the highest just within the parish, may have existed by 1633[79] and have been worked by one of the millers resident in the parish in the 1660s.[80] In the late 18th century it was a grist mill attached

[49] *Valor Eccl.* (Rec. Com.), ii. 486.
[50] Glos. R.O., D 2172/1/54; P.R.O., C 3/274/35; cf. *Valor Eccl.* (Rec. Com.), ii. 486.
[51] Surv. of Crawley-Boevey est. 1797 (entry before no. 1, nos. 1–13, 21).
[52] Glos. R.O., D 4543/2/1/2; D 4543/4/1; P.R.O., HO 107/1959.
[53] Glos. R.O., D 2299/398, 685, 928, 4482.
[54] P.R.O., MAF 68/1609/12; MAF 68/3295/16.
[55] Glos. R.O., SL 568.
[56] Rudder, *Glos.* 449; Bigland, *Glos.* i. 582.
[57] Glos. R.O., D 2172/1/55; G. A. Allan, *Church Work in Forest of Dean* (copy in Glos. Colln. L 9.6), 20.
[58] *List & Index Soc.* clxxxix, p. 172.
[59] P.R.O., HO 107/365; HO 107/1959.
[60] Ibid. MAF 68/26/9.
[61] H. Phelps, *Forest of Dean* (1982), 74.
[62] P.R.O., MAF 68/25/20.
[63] Ibid. MAF 68/1609/12; MAF 68/3295/16; Acreage Returns, 1905.
[64] Glos. R.O., D 2299/7188.

[65] Ibid. D 2172/1/71.
[66] Ibid. D 5895/1.
[67] Surv. of Crawley-Boevey est. 1797 (nos. 1, 3, 5–6, 10, 12).
[68] P.R.O., MAF 68/1609/12.
[69] Glos. R.O., SL 568.
[70] Phelps, *Forest of Dean*, 146; cf. *V.C.H. Glos.* x. 9.
[71] N.L.W., Mynde Park MS. 1685.
[72] *Flaxley Cart.* pp. 16, 18.
[73] P.R.O., E 146/1/25.
[74] *Flaxley Cart.* pp. 109–10.
[75] Glos. R.O., D 2123, p. 159; below, Littledean, econ. hist. (other ind. and trade).
[76] *Pleas of the Crown for Glos.* ed. Maitland, pp. 47–8.
[77] *Tax. Eccl.* (Rec. Com.), 171; cf. Townley, 'Ind. Sites in Castiard', 15.
[78] Townley, 'Ind. Sites in Castiard', 10–17; *Glos. Soc. Ind. Arch. Jnl.* (1974), 10–19.
[79] *Glos. Soc. Ind. Arch. Jnl.* (1974), 18; O.S. Map 6", Glos. XXXI. NE. (1884 edn.).
[80] Glos. R.O., P 145/IN 1/2.

to a small farm[81] and it was worked as such until after 1912.[82] The buildings remained the centre of a farm[83] but a stone range adjoining the farmhouse, which had housed the mill, had fallen into decay by the early 1970s.[84] In 1974 the buildings were restored for Omega Electric Ltd., which in 1984 employed 9 people making computer systems for industrial and commercial use.[85] The former farmhouse, dating from the 17th century, has a box-framed upper storey. An outbuilding to the west had been converted as a house by 1988.

In 1635 two forges were recorded at Flaxley[86] and by 1674 a furnace and two forges belonging to the Flaxley Abbey estate[87] were held by Paul Foley of Stoke Edith (Herefs.).[88] The furnace, downstream of Flaxley Abbey,[89] was worked for Foley by John Hellier in 1680.[90] Catharina Boevey may have taken the works in hand[91] but the Shropshire ironmaster Richard Knight, a partner of the Foleys, operated the furnace in 1695, when he sent pig iron to Bewdley (Worcs.), and in 1710.[92] At that time the Flaxley Abbey ironworks included three forges, one of which may have been next to the furnace.[93] A forge downstream of the Blaisdon road, at the boundary with Westbury, was in use in 1693[94] and belonged to Walmore manor, in Westbury, until 1731 when Thomas Crawley-Boevey purchased it.[95] The Crawley-Boeveys retained the furnace in hand in the early 1740s and possibly in the later 1760s,[96] and several forges operated upstream of Flaxley Abbey until at least the early 1780s.[97] By the end of the century the ironworks, described as very large and extensive,[98] were run by John Soule[99] and the furnace was fed mainly with Lancashire ore shipped to Newnham. The forges downstream hammered the iron into bars, ploughshares, and other items. The furnace, which because of a shortage of charcoal was not in continuous use,[1] was apparently abandoned in 1818.[2] It was pulled down and ponds associated with it were drained.[3] The forges, notably that below the Blaisdon road, possibly remained in use for several years.[4] In 1827 one former forgeman was a wireworker[5] and in 1851 a blacksmith occupied a forge above the Blaisdon road.[6]

A corn mill erected by Thomas Brayne of Littledean[7] was evidently the new mill included in the lease of the Grange estate acquired by Thomas in 1591. The mill, on a stream at a place called Sandbach green near Littledean,[8] was probably owned by Abraham Astill in 1703 and was purchased by Thomas Crawley-Boevey in 1727. It evidently ceased to work long before 1847 when its site could not be identified.[9]

In 1608 a group of clothworkers including four coverlet weavers and three broadweavers lived in Flaxley. A carpenter, a tanner, a glover, a tailor, a sailor, and a fishmonger were also among parishioners in 1608,[10] as were evidently three pinmakers, two cordwainers, a butcher, a baker, and a narrow weaver in the 1660s and a blacksmith in the 1700s.[11] The village had a smithy in 1769[12] and a blacksmith still worked at the same site in 1988.[13] In the mid 19th century the village also had a sawyer and a carpenter.[14]

Iron ore was mined at St. White's c. 1270 but the abbot of Flaxley, acting as landowner, removed the miners and filled in the workings. Despite the abbey's opposition mining was resumed some years later by Grimbald Pauncefoot, the warden of the Forest of Dean, and, although it yielded little ore, continued in 1287.[15] In the 17th century several Flaxley men worked as miners and colliers.[16] Most of the 21 families in the parish not supported by agriculture in 1831[17] probably lived in the St. White's, Mousell Lane, and Dockham Road areas of Cinderford, where Flaxley parishioners in 1851 included several ore and coal miners and a few tradesmen.[18] The establishment of new ironworks in Cinderford in the late 1820s was followed by the opening of large mines nearby,[19] and Buckshraft (later Buckshaft) iron mine, of which William Crawshay was an owner, extended under land belonging to Flaxley by the early 1840s.[20] Those mines were closed in 1899.[21] A site east of St. White's Farm was mined for a short period after the First World War. There had been a limekiln at the same site in the mid 19th century.[22]

The main part of Flaxley may have contained a limekiln and a brickyard on separate sites

81 Surv. of Crawley-Boevey est. 1797 (entry before no. 1).
82 Glos. R.O., D 4543/2/1/2; D 4543/4/1; D 2299/928.
83 Kelly's Dir. Glos. (1914 and later edns.).
84 Hart, Ind. Hist. of Dean, 374.
85 Citizen (Glouc.), 13 Mar. 1984.
86 P.R.O., SP 16/282, f. 253.
87 Cf. G.D.R. wills 1645/42; P.R.O., E 179/247/13, rot. 24d.
88 Hart, Ind. Hist. of Dean, 24, 43.
89 Atkyns, Glos. plate at pp. 436–7, reproduced below, Plate 6.
90 Glos. R.O., D 36/E 30.
91 Watkins, Flaxley Abbey, 304–7; cf. Glos. R.O., D 36/E 31; M 72.
92 Hart, Ind. Hist. of Dean, 63, 81; H. R. Schubert, Hist. Brit. Iron and Steel Ind. (1957), 375.
93 Atkyns, Glos. 436, plate at pp. 436–7.
94 Glos. R.O., D 2557/T 1.
95 Ibid. Q/RNc 1, pp. 84–6; 4/5.
96 Ibid. D 36/E 12, ff. 128v.–129; below, Mitcheldean, econ. hist. (other ind. and trade).
97 Taylor, Map of Glos. (1777); P.R.O., F 17/4.
98 Univ. Brit. Dir. ii (1792), 775.
99 Glouc. Jnl. 19 Dec. 1796; 17 Aug. 1807.
1   Rudge, Hist. of Glos. ii. 96–7; surv. of Crawley-Boevey est. 1797 (no. 1).
2   Watkins, Flaxley Abbey, 308.
3   Nicholls, Iron Making, 55.
4   Cf. Bryant, Map of Glos. (1824); Glos. R.O., P 145/OV 2/1.
5   Glos. R.O., P 145/IN 1/7.
6   P.R.O., HO 107/1959.
7   Glos. R.O., D 2026/X 7.
8   Ibid. D 2172/1/71; P.R.O., PROB 11/104 (P.C.C. 53 Harte, will of Thos. Brayne), f. 39.
9   Glos. R.O., D 4543/2/1/1; 2/2/1, ff. 18v.–19, 58.
10 Smith, Men and Armour, 41.
11 Glos. R.O., P 145/IN 1/2–3.
12 Ibid. D 4543/2/1/1–2; D 4543/4/1.
13 Cf. Kelly's Dir. Glos. (1856 and later edns.); Phelps, Forest of Dean, 148.
14 P.R.O., HO 107/1959.
15 Inq. p.m. Glos. 1236–1300, 144–5.
16 Smith, Men and Armour, 41; Glos. R.O., P 145/IN 1/2; P.R.O., E 134/1651 Hil./10; E 134/13 Chas. II East./24.
17 Census, 1831.   18 P.R.O., HO 107/1959.
19 Nicholls, Iron Making, 56–62.
20 Award of Dean Forest Mining Com. (1841), 179–80, 189–90; Glos. R.O., Q/RUm 173/2, plans F, G; D 2172/1/55.
21 Hart, Ind. Hist. of Dean, 233.
22 Glos. R.O., D 4543/2/1/2; D 4543/4/1; O.S. Map 6", Glos. XXXI. SE. (1883 and later edns.); Trans. B.G.A.S. xlix. 268.

before 1690.[23] A resident of Gaulet was trading in bark in 1767,[24] and among the small industries dependent on the area's extensive woodland was charcoal burning.[25] The charcoal was presumably sent to the Flaxley ironworks in the 17th and 18th centuries and its production by the traditional method, using pits and earth kilns, survived around Flaxley well into the 20th century.[26]

LOCAL GOVERNMENT. By his charter of 1198 Richard I granted Flaxley abbey extensive franchises in its lands, including pleas of infangthief and exemption from hundred and shire courts.[27] Court rolls for Flaxley manor in 1681 and 1751 and presentments made to the court in 1734 and 1739 survived in 1963 but their whereabouts was not known in 1988.[28]

Flaxley had two churchwardens in 1576[29] and 1703.[30] In the late 16th century and the early 17th the principal farmers possibly filled the office in annual rotation. There were also two surveyors of the highways in 1597[31] and two overseers of the poor in 1658.[32] By 1727 there was only one churchwarden and one overseer[33] and by 1788 those offices were held together. The overseer's accounts, which survive from 1788, incorporate his account as churchwarden until 1804 when the offices were held separately again. Later there were two overseers. The usual forms of poor relief were applied during that period, and in 1793 or 1794 the poor were inoculated at the parish's expense. In the late 1780s upwards of 7 or 8 people were receiving regular weekly pay;[34] regular help was given in 1803 to 18 people, including 6 who were disabled and 10 who did not live in the parish, and in 1813 to 12 people. The cost of relief, which rose considerably in the late 18th century, was £139 in 1803 and £205 in 1813.[35] From 1823 the poor were farmed by the governor of the Littledean workhouse, to which they were sent,[36] and the parish thereby kept down the cost of relief to £141 in 1825 and to c. £108 a year in the early 1830s.[37] Most relief went to persons living in the extraparochial Forest of Dean.[38] Flaxley was included in the Westbury-on-Severn poor-law union in 1835[39] and in East Dean and United

Parishes rural district in 1895.[40] The united parish of Blaisdon and Flaxley became part of the Forest of Dean district in 1974.

CHURCH. Flaxley abbey, which presumably provided a place of worship for laity from its beginning, sought a licence in 1253 to hold services in a new chapel before the abbey gate.[41] In the late 16th century Flaxley had a chapel served by a curate.[42] The chapel was in the gift of the owners of Flaxley Abbey, who paid the curate a stipend,[43] and the living, although described in 1650 as a vicarage,[44] was more correctly styled a donative in the 18th century.[45] By 1839 it was called a perpetual curacy and by 1870 more usually a vicarage.[46] In 1923 the benefice was united with Blaisdon[47] and in 1976 Westbury-on-Severn was added to the united benefice.[48] For ecclesiastical purposes Flaxley in 1880 lost land at Cinderford to the new district of Woodside (later the parish of St. Stephen, Cinderford)[49] and in 1909 gained Pope's Hill in the Forest and land in Dirty Lane from Holy Trinity parish and Westbury-on-Severn.[50] Flaxley's boundaries were revised again when the benefice was enlarged in the late 1970s.[51]

After the union with Blaisdon the Crawley-Boeveys enjoyed the right of presentation alternately with Mary MacIver and her trustees.[52] Sir Launcelot Crawley-Boevey (d. 1968) retained his interest after selling Flaxley Abbey and from the late 1970s his son Sir Thomas Crawley-Boevey, Bt., was entitled to fill every fourth vacancy in the enlarged benefice.[53]

Tithes were never taken in Flaxley, the abbey, as a Cistercian house, having been exempt from their payment from land which it had brought into cultivation.[54] Nevertheless the lay owners of Flaxley Abbey were said to hold an impropriation,[55] valued at 100 marks in 1603[56] and at £40 c. 1710,[57] and the Grange estate acquired by Thomas Brayne in 1591 was charged with paying 13s. 4d. a year to the impropriator or the tenants of his rectory estate.[58] As a Cistercian foundation the abbey had also been exempt from episcopal visitations,[59] and later owners of Flaxley Abbey claimed peculiar jurisdiction in Flaxley parish.[60] Visitations were held from the

[23] Glos. R.O., D 5895/1; cf. surv. of Crawley-Boevey est. 1797 (no. 3).
[24] Glos. R.O., D 36/E 7/1.
[25] Cf. N.L.W., Mynde Park MS. 1686.
[26] B. Waters, *Forest of Dean* (1951), 136–40; cf. Glos. R.O., D 3921/II/34; Phelps, *Forest in Old Photog.* (1983), 42–3; below, Plate 24.
[27] *Flaxley Cart.* pp. 29, 111–12.
[28] Glos. R.O., N.R.A. rep. on Flaxley Abbey Mun.
[29] Hockaday Abs. xlvii, 1576 visit. f. 134.
[30] Ibid. cxcvii.
[31] Glos. R.O., P 145/IN 1/1.
[32] Ibid. 2.   [33] *19th Rep. Com. Char.* 92.
[34] Glos. R.O., P 145/OV 2/1.
[35] *Poor Law Abstract, 1804*, 172–3; *1818*, 146–7.
[36] Glos. R.O., P 110/VE 2/1; P 145/OV 2/1.
[37] *Poor Law Returns* (1830–1), p. 66; (1835), p. 65.
[38] *3rd Rep. Dean Forest Com.* 28.
[39] *Poor Law Com. 2nd Rep.* p. 524.
[40] Glos. R.O., DA 24/100/1.
[41] B.L. Harl. Ch. 43 A.39.
[42] Bodl. MS. Rawl. C. 790, f. 28v.; Hockaday Abs. xliv, 1572 visit. f. 9.
[43] Bodl. MS. Top. Glouc. c. 3, f. 193; Atkyns, *Glos.* 436;

Rudder, *Glos.* 450; P.R.O., HO 129/334/1/8/21.
[44] *Trans. B.G.A.S.* lxxxiii. 97.
[45] Bodl. MS. Top. Glouc. c. 3, f. 193; P.R.O., C 78/1423, no. 5; G.D.R. vol. 382, f. 21; Bigland, *Glos.* i. 583.
[46] Hockaday Ab. cxcvii; *Kelly's Dir. Glos.* (1856 and later edns.).
[47] *Lond. Gaz.* 26 May 1922, pp. 4041–2; *Kelly's Dir. Glos.* (1927), 50, 178.
[48] Glos. R.O., P 227/IN 3/5; cf. *Glouc. Dioc. Year Bk.* (1977), 22–3; (1978), 21.
[49] *Lond. Gaz.* 13 Aug. 1880, pp. 4451–3; *B. & G. Par. Rec.* 98.   [50] Glos. R.O., P 354/VE 3/4.
[51] Ibid. P 227/IN 3/5.
[52] *Kelly's Dir. Glos.* (1927), 178; (1939), 171; *V.C.H. Glos.* x. 8–10.
[53] *Glouc. Dioc. Year Bk.* (1966–7), 26; *Dioc. of Glouc. Dir.* (1987), 49; *Who Was Who, 1961–70*, 254.
[54] *V.C.H. Glos.* x. 94; cf. Glos. R.O., D 2299/398.
[55] Bodl. MS. Rawl. C. 790, f. 28v.; Rudder, *Glos.* 450.
[56] *Eccl. Misc.* 99.   [57] Atkyns, *Glos.* 436.
[58] Glos. R.O., D 2172/1/71.
[59] *V.C.H. Glos.* ii. 94.
[60] Bodl. MS. Rawl. C. 790, f. 5; cf. P.R.O., HO 129/334/1/8/21.

late 16th century,[61] but in 1828 the curate denied the diocesan registry's authority to demand submission of a glebe terrier.[62]

In 1603 the curate's stipend was £5[63] and in 1650 the living's value £10.[64] Later the curate had a stipend of £8, to which Catharina Boevey added £4 a year. In 1727 a Chancery order directed that £1,200 she had left to provide for the reading of prayers, the catechizing of children, and the visiting of the sick be used to augment the curate's living,[65] and in 1737 Bradley farm, covering 108 a. in Longhope, Mitcheldean, and Newland, was bought with the bequest. The land was placed under the same trustees as Catharina Boevey's apprenticing and book charities but later, apparently by 1760,[66] the curate managed it.[67] In 1835 the curate's income, comprising rent from the farm and the £8 stipend, was £98.[68] The living was valued at £108 in 1856 and £143 in 1870.[69] Bradley farm was sold in 1880.[70] In the absence of a glebe house the curate lived in Mitcheldean in the 1660s.[71] In 1777 he lived in Elton, in Westbury-on-Severn,[72] presumably in accommodation provided by the trustees of the apprenticing and book charities, who by 1817 had built Broughtons on their estate there as a residence for the Flaxley curate.[73] William Crawley stayed at Broughtons after resigning the living in 1846 and his successors, who did not obtain use of the house until 1863,[74] lived in the village.[75] In 1886 a vicarage house was built south of the church[76] by Sir Martin Crawley-Boevey's widow Elizabeth (d. 1892), who also added £1,000 to the endowment of the living.[77] That house remained in use for the united benefice in 1988.

Edward a Fowle, the first known curate, had been appointed by 1563 and was possibly one of the family living at Gaulet.[78] In 1576 he was found to be unlicensed[79] and was censured for wearing a cope at Easter and for not preaching quarterly sermons.[80] The rector of Blaisdon served the chapel in 1584[81] and may have been assisted later by John Harvey, a layman who was accused in 1591 of administering the chalice at Easter.[82] In 1622 the curate was reported for not reading canonical services and prayers.[83] Most

curates served for a few years only before the late 17th century when longer ministries became the rule.[84] Thomas Tyrer (d. 1743), curate from 1719, was also rector of Hope Mansell (Herefs.).[85] His successor Charles Crawley,[86] brother of Thomas Crawley-Boevey (d. 1769), served the chapel for nearly 40 years. After his death in 1780[87] the living was given to John Longdon (d. 1808), a distant relative by marriage and incumbent of Barnwood and Winstone,[88] under whom the Flaxley chapel was served by a succession of curates.[89] Between 1810 and 1846 the living was held in turn by Charles and William Crawley, sons of Sir Thomas Crawley-Boevey (d. 1818).[90] Thomas Wetherell, who was perpetual curate 1852–73, employed stipendiary curates from 1862.[91] One appointed c. 1864 without the bishop's knowledge was banned from participating in services.[92] Richard Crawley-Boevey, vicar 1883–90 by the gift of his brother,[93] took up residence in the vicarage provided by his mother.[94]

At St. White's a chapel or hermitage was surrendered to Flaxley abbey by an anchorite, who was said to have been given the site by Henry II.[95] Anchoresses lived there in 1225 and 1241[96] and an anchorite was collecting alms to repair the building and the road leading to it in 1519, when it bore a dedication to St. White. The chapel was last recorded in 1530 when it was said to be dedicated to SS. White and Radegund.[97]

The chapel before the abbey gate[98] was probably not that used by the parishioners after the Dissolution. That building, which lacked a pulpit in 1576,[99] stood some way south-west of Flaxley Abbey by the road from Elton to Mitcheldean and was a small, low single-cell building with a wooden west bell turret.[1] The chapel, which was said c. 1708 to be dedicated to St. Laurence,[2] was rebuilt on a slightly larger scale in 1727 at the expense of Mary Pope, the executrix of Catharina Boevey who had intended to replace it. The new chapel was a plain building with a west tower and spire.[3] In 1851, when it was uncertain if it was dedicated like the medieval abbey to St. Mary the Virgin, it had

61 Hockaday Abs. xliv, 1572 visit. f. 9; lxxiii, 1703 Heref. archd. visit. f. 2.
62 G.D.R., V 5/133T 2.   63 Eccl. Misc. 99.
64 Trans. B.G.A.S. lxxxiii. 97.
65 P.R.O., C 78/1423, no. 5; Atkyns, Glos. 436.
66 Glos. R.O., D 2362, deeds 1718–1892; 19th Rep. Com. Char. 91–2.
67 Cf. Glos. R.O., Q/REl 1A, Duchy of Lanc., Longhope, upper division.
68 3rd Rep. Dean Forest Com. 33.
69 Kelly's Dir. Glos. (1856), 287; (1870), 547.
70 Glos. R.O., D 2362, deeds 1718–1892.
71 Ibid. P 220/CH 2; cf. ibid. P 145/IN 1/2, burials 1671.
72 Taylor, Map of Glos. (1777).
73 Glos. R.O., D 177, Flaxley Char., min. bk. 1834–1937, min. 12 Mar. 1834; acct. bk. 1811–22; cf. V.C.H. Glos. x. 84.
74 Hockaday Abs. cxcvii; Glos. R.O., D 177, Flaxley Char., min. bk. 1834–1937.
75 Glos. R.O., D 4543/2/1/2; D 4543/4/1, P.R.O., HO 107/1959.   76 Glos. R.O., D 1381/5R.
77 Mon. in church; Burke, Peerage (1963), 269.
78 Bodl. MS. Rawl. C. 790, f. 28v.; cf. above, intro.
79 Hockaday Abs. xlvii, 1576 visit. f. 134.
80 G.D.R. vol. 40, f. 227.
81 Hockaday Abs. xlix, state of clergy 1584, f. 46.

82 Trans. B.G.A.S. xci. 179.
83 Glos. R.O., D 2052.   84 Hockaday Abs. cxcvii.
85 Glos. R.O., P 145/IN 1/3–4.
86 Bigland, Glos. i. 583.
87 Crawley-Boevey, Perverse Widow, 302, 314; Glos. R.O., P 145/IN 1/4.
88 Crawley-Boevey, Perverse Widow, 258 n., 302; Glos. N. & Q. v. 232.
89 G.D.R., V 1/101; Glos. R.O., P 145/IN 1/4.
90 Crawley-Boevey, Perverse Widow, 319–20; Hockaday Abs. cxcvii.
91 G.D.R. vols. 384, f. 95; 385, p. 100.
92 Glos. R.O., P 110/IN 4/2; P 145/IN 1/7.
93 Burke, Peerage (1963), 269; Crockford (1894), 310.
94 Kelly's Dir. Glos. (1889), 774; above, this section.
95 Flaxley Cart. pp. 78, 143; cf. Rot. Litt. Claus. (Rec. Com.), i. 430.
96 Rot. Litt. Claus. (Rec. Com.), ii. 44, 51; Close R. 1237–42, 273.
97 Reg. Bothe, 355–6, 358–9.
98 B.L. Harl. Ch. 43 A.39.   99 G.D.R. vol. 40, f. 227.
1 Atkyns, Glos. 436, plate at pp. 436–7, reproduced below, Plate 6.
2 Bodl. MS. Top. Glouc. c. 3, f. 193.
3 Hockaday Abs. cxcvii; Bigland, Glos. i. 583–4; Nicholls, Forest of Dean, 188.

130 seats, all appropriated for the tenants and household of Sir Martin Crawley-Boevey.[4] The chapel was replaced in 1856 by a new church a few yards to the west and was pulled down.[5]

The church, which was dedicated to *ST. MARY THE VIRGIN*, is built of red gritstone with grey sandstone dressings and has a chancel with north organ chamber and a nave with north aisle, north-west tower and spire, and wooden south porch. It was designed by George Gilbert Scott in an early 14th-century style[6] and was paid for by William Gibbs, brother-in-law of Sir Martin Crawley-Boevey. The organ was enlarged in 1888 as a memorial to Gibbs's widow Matilda (d. 1887).[7] The church contains some fittings from the earlier chapels, notably monuments to Abraham Clarke (d. 1683), William Boevey (d. 1692), and Catharina Boevey (d. 1727),[8] and a bell cast by Abraham Rudhall in 1727.[9] The oldest surviving pieces of plate, a chalice with paten cover and a credence paten, date from 1777.[10] The east window of the organ chamber contains medieval glass portraying the arms and badge of Llanthony priory.[11] The registers begin in 1562 and contain entries for inhabitants of the adjoining parts of the extra-parochial Forest of Dean from the late 1690s.[12]

NONCONFORMITY.

Five nonconformists were recorded in Flaxley in 1676.[13] They presumably included Edward Cox, a Quaker, perhaps of Gaulet, who died in 1710.[14] Five Presbyterians were recorded in the parish in 1735.[15] No record has been found of any dissenting meeting place in the parish,[16] apart from those established at Cinderford in the mid 19th century[17] which included the Strict Baptist chapel listed under Flaxley in 1876.[18]

EDUCATION.

In the early 18th century Catharina Boevey supported a charity school in Flaxley teaching 30 children and on Sundays dined 6 of the pupils in turn and heard them say their catechism.[19] In 1819 the parish had a school teaching 20 children and was served by a Sunday school at Littledean.[20] Flaxley had its own Sunday school in 1825,[21] and in 1833 the day and the Sunday school, both supported by a lady, presumably one of the Crawley-Boeveys, taught 20 and 43 children respectively.[22] In 1840 Sir

Thomas Crawley-Boevey built a school at the end of the village by the Blaisdon road,[23] and in 1846 it housed boys' and girls' schools newly united to the National Society. They were financed by subscriptions and pence and taught 71 day pupils and 83 Sunday pupils.[24] In 1871 the day school, managed by the vicar for Sir Thomas Crawley-Boevey, had an average attendance of 46 children and the building was also used for a winter evening school.[25] The day school had an average attendance of 59 in 1894,[26] including children from Pope's Hill. It closed in 1901.[27] The Sunday school continued for some years to use the building,[28] which later served as a village hall.

CHARITIES FOR THE POOR.

By will dated 1626 George Coulstance, a Gloucester pewterer, gave a rent charge of 20s. for the poor of his native Flaxley.[29] The charity, which was apparently distributed in the late 18th century,[30] had lapsed by the later 1820s.[31]

Sums of £60 and £100 left respectively by Abraham Clarke (d. 1683) for the poor and William Boevey (d. 1692) for apprenticeships[32] passed to the latter's wife Catharina. She placed children as apprentices[33] and by will proved 1727 added £240 to the capital to provide apprenticeships for children chosen by the lord of the manor. Following a suit over Catharina's bequests the money, together with £200 she had left for the distribution of religious books among the inhabitants of Flaxley and adjoining parishes, was laid out in 1734 on land in Elton. The land was vested in trustees, who applied two thirds of the income to apprenticeships and a third to books.[34] The book charity was distributed by the curate of Flaxley chiefly among his parishioners. Apprenticeship premiums, determined by the Crawley-Boeveys, were increased in 1847 to encourage masters to take children. Full distribution of the income ceased in 1872 and regular payments in 1908. They both resumed in 1928, by which time the income, derived from investments, was £145.[35] The charities, in which Blaisdon shared after 1935,[36] were placed under separate trusts by Schemes of 1961. In 1970 the apprenticeship charity's income of c. £146 was used partly for educational expenses of students. The book charity's income was c. £75.[37]

4 P.R.O., HO 129/334/1/8/21.
5 Nicholls, *Forest of Dean*, 191; G.D.R., V 6/41.
6 *Glouc. Jnl.* 20 Sept. 1856, which implies, incorrectly, that Sir Martin Crawley-Boevey paid for the new bldg.
7 *Kelly's Dir. Glos.* (1894), 157; Burke, *Peerage* (1963), 269.
8 Cf. Atkyns, *Glos.* 436–7; Bigland, *Glos.* i. 583–5.
9 *Glos. Ch. Bells*, 303.
10 *Glos. Ch. Plate*, 85.
11 *Trans. B.G.A.S.* xlvii. 314, plate XVI.
12 *B. & G. Par. Rec.* 140; Glos. R.O., P 145/IN 1/1–8.
13 *Compton Census*, ed. Whiteman, 544.
14 Glos. R.O., D 2052.   15 G.D.R. vol. 285B(1), f. 5.
16 Cf. ibid. 383, no. cxiii.
17 Glos. R.O., Q/RZ 1; below, Forest of Dean, prot. nonconf.
18 *Morris's Dir. Glos.* (1876), 495–6.
19 Crawley-Boevey, *Perverse Widow*, 114–15, 139.
20 *Educ. of Poor Digest*, 299.
21 G.D.R. vol. 383, no. cxiii.
22 *Educ. Enq. Abstract*, 315.

23 Date and inits. 'T. C. B.' on bldg., which was in Westbury par.: O.S. Map 6", Glos. XXXII. NW. (1891 edn.).
24 Nat. Soc. *Inquiry, 1846–7*, Glos. 8–9; Nat. Soc. files, Flaxley Meend.
25 P.R.O., ED 7/37, Flaxley Nat. Mixed sch.
26 *Kelly's Dir. Glos.* (1894), 157.
27 Glos. R.O., SB 15/5, p. 90.
28 O.S. Map 6", Glos. XXXII. NW. (1903, 1924 edns.).
29 Glos. R.O., P 154/14/CH 7.
30 Bigland, *Glos.* i. 583.
31 Cf. *19th Rep. Com. Char.* 91–2.
32 Atkyns, *Glos.* 436–7; Crawley-Boevey, *Perverse Widow*, 62, 75.
33 Crawley-Boevey, *Perverse Widow*, 139.
34 Ibid. 126–8; *19th Rep. Com. Char.* 91–2; Glos. R.O., D 134/T 19.
35 Glos. R.O., D 177, Flaxley Char., min. bk. 1834–1937; acct. bks. 1811–22, 1813–1937.
36 Ibid. letters 1937–40; cf. *V.C.H. Glos.* x. 11.
37 Glos. R.O., CH 21, E. Dean rural district, p. 8.

Anne Wetherell, widow of a former vicar of Flaxley,[38] founded a charity by will proved 1888. In 1970 the income of £2 was distributed in firewood to old age pensioners or was allowed to accumulate for use in emergencies.[39]

HEWELSFIELD AND BROCKWEIR

HEWELSFIELD and Brockweir, called until 1994 Hewelsfield,[40] is a small parish by the river Wye 8 km. NNE. of Chepstow (Mon.). In 1842 an adjoining tract of extraparochial land, which became known as Hewelsfield common, was added to Hewelsfield for civil parish purposes,[41] and the parish was further enlarged in 1935 by the addition of an arm of Woolaston parish, comprising 219 a. and extending down the south side of the valley of Brockweir brook to the Wye at the village of Brockweir.[42] This account covers the parish as constituted between 1842 and 1935 and includes Hewelsfield village, scattered settlement on Hewelsfield common that was created by squatters from c. 1800 and was later inhabited by more prosperous residents, and most of the former trading village of Brockweir; a few buildings in the south part of Brockweir that lay within Woolaston, including Townsend (or Brockweir) Farm and a Moravian church, are covered in the history of Woolaston in another volume.[43]

There was a settlement, then called Hiwoldestone, at Hewelsfield in late Anglo-Saxon times. William I placed it within the Forest of Dean and it was probably depopulated and its fields returned to the waste, but it evidently had an inhabited settlement and manor again by the mid 12th century, when a church was recorded.[44] During the 12th century the names Hiwoldestone and Hewelsfield were both used.[45] The reconstituted manor was probably at first outside the jurisdiction of the Forest of Dean, but was within it during the 13th century, and was excluded again under a perambulation of 1300, which found it to be among the manors afforested since the beginning of Henry II's reign.[46]

Until 1842 Hewelsfield parish was in three parts and had a total of 1,102 a. The main, and by far the largest, part comprised farmland on high ground, having Hewelsfield village as its centre and Aylesmore brook as most of its north boundary. Below and to the west, a detached part of only a few acres lay on the north side of Brockweir brook, which flows down from the main part of the parish to the Wye, and on the bank of the Wye another detached part of Hewelsfield parish included the part of Brockweir village lying north of Brockweir brook.[47] The extraparochial land later called Hewelsfield common was bounded on the south by the two small parts of the parish and by Brockweir brook, on the east by the main part of the parish, on the north by fields of St. Briavels parish, and on the west, on the later parish boundary, by another brook flowing down to join the Wye at Brockweir. The south-east part of Hewelsfield common, on steep slopes below the ridge called Hart hill, was manorial land in the 13th century, occupied by a wood of the lords of Hewelsfield called Harthill wood. With the rest of Hewelsfield it was removed from the Forest by the perambulation of 1300: the revised bounds of the Forest were then traced from the Wye up Brockweir brook to a 'mere (or boundary) brook', which was evidently a small brook that joined Brockweir brook east of a ridge called Mill hill, and, leaving Harthill wood on the right hand side and the Forest on the left, to Aylesmore brook.[48] The north and west parts of Hewelsfield common were in the detached tract of the royal demesne land of the Forest known as Hudnalls, and were surveyed as part of it in 1608. The small tributary of Brockweir brook east of Mill hill then marked the boundary between Hudnalls and Harthill wood; it was called Black brook in 1608, while the name Mere (or Meer) brook was used then and later for the more westerly brook, on the later parish boundary.[49]

Harthill wood, the south-east part of Hewelsfield common, was usually called Harthill common during the 17th and 18th centuries, when it was common to the men of Hewelsfield;[50] it is not known whether the lords of the manor continued to claim manorial rights there.[51] The inhabitants also commoned in the west and north parts of Hewelsfield common, which were called Brockweir common by the late 18th century though included under the general designation of Hudnalls.[52] The name Mere brook, as recorded in 1608, suggests that the later parish boundary was already used then to define the areas of the extraparochial land of Hudnalls in which the men of Hewelsfield and St. Briavels respectively exercised their rights, and in the late 18th century and the early 19th the brook was regarded, and sometimes perambulated, as an unofficial parish boundary.[53] In the early 19th century the name Brockweir

38 Burke, *Land. Gent.* (1898), ii. 1577; Glos. R.O., P 145/IN 1/17, entries 18 Apr. 1873, 15 Mar. 1888.
39 Glos. R.O., CH 21, E. Dean rural district, p. 8.
40 Notice by Forest of Dean district council, 14 June 1994, posted at Brockweir. This account was written in 1994.
41 Dean Forest Poor-Relief Act, 5 & 6 Vic. c. 48; Glos. R.O., P 175/CW 2/1, min. 23 Mar. 1843.
42 *Census*, 1931 (pt. ii).
43 *V.C.H. Glos.* x. 102–18.
44 *Dom. Bk.* (Rec. Com.), i, 167; below, manor; church.
45 *Cal. Doc. France*, pp. 411, 413; Dugdale, *Mon.* vi (2), 1094.
46 *Trans. B.G.A.S.* lxvi. 176–82, 193; below, Forest of

Dean, bounds.
47 G.D.R., T 1/100; for old boundaries, below, Fig. 10.
48 P.R.O., E 32/29, rot. 5; *Trans. B.G.A.S.* lxvi. 178, 180.
49 P.R.O., MR 879 (F 17/1); cf. below, St. Briavels, intro.
50 Suff. R.O., HA 49/A III(d)/1; Bodl. MS. Rawl. B. 323, f. 110v.; Rudder, *Glos.* 498.
51 A roughly drawn plan of c. 1680 suggests that the marquess of Worc., then lord, may have been doing so: P.R.O., F 17/7.
52 Glos. R.O., P 209/MI 1, pp. 18–19; G.D.R., T 1/100.
53 Glos. R.O., P 209/MI 1, p. 19; *3rd Rep. Dean Forest Com.* 26.

common came to be applied generally to all the extraparochial land east of Mere brook, including Harthill common,[54] but Hewelsfield common was the usual name by 1880.[55] Its addition to the three parts of the ancient parish in 1842 created a single unit of 1,592 a.[56]

The upper part of the enlarged parish is situated on a spur of land at c. 200 m., the land falling away steeply on most sides, towards the Wye below Hart hill and Cows hill on the west, towards Woolaston and the Severn on the south, and into the valleys of Cone brook and its tributary, Aylesmore brook, below Clay hill on the west and north. The higher land is on carboniferous limestone, while the land sloping to the Wye is on the Old Red Sandstone.[57] Brockweir brook, so called by 1300, forming the valley running from west of Hewelsfield village down to the Wye at Brockweir,[58] was usually called Harthill brook in the early modern period,[59] and in 1726 at Brockweir it was referred to as Grange brook, probably recalling a medieval grange of Tintern abbey (Mon.).[60] Mere brook, mentioned above, flowing through Hudnalls to Brockweir, was still called by that name in 1826,[61] but in 1748 it was called Smith's brook.[62]

A wood of the lord of the manor John of Monmouth mentioned in 1246 was presumably Harthill wood, in the south-east part of the extraparochial land.[63] In 1270, when Harthill wood was within the Forest, it was temporarily forfeited to the Crown on account of a misdemeanour by the woodward employed by the owner, Tintern abbey.[64] By the early 17th century, when the name Harthill common was used,[65] the wood had probably been much depleted by unrestricted grazing. In the early 19th century encroachments on the whole of the extraparochial area[66] produced a pattern of small closes, contrasting with the more regular pattern of larger fields in the ancient parish. Offa's Dyke descends the hillside near the south-western end of the former extraparochial area and crosses Brockweir brook at the upper detached part of the ancient parish, where the dyke was enlarged in the mid 13th century to form a mill dam.[67]

Ancient routes running up from the river Severn at Alvington and Woolaston met at Hewelsfield village and continued by way of Aylesmore, on the north boundary of the parish, to St. Briavels village.[68] The Chepstow to St. Briavels road, passing the village a short way to the west, was, however, the most important route through the parish in the modern period;

it was repaired by the parish under indictment in 1812.[69] Later the road from the village to meet it at the crossroads called Tumpkinhales was improved and widened, and the old St. Briavels road by way of Aylesmore was closed in 1837. The latter was then described as a deep hollow lane, much of it impassable to carriages,[70] in which form most of it survived in 1994. An ancient road along the bank of the Wye, leading from a ferry opposite Tintern abbey through Brockweir village towards Redbrook and Monmouth bridge, had a pitched surface in parts c. 1800 and was once of considerable local importance,[71] but it survived only as a path in the 20th century. In the early 17th century the only road across Hewelsfield common was apparently one linking St. Briavels and Brockweir, descending by what was later called Prince's hill.[72] In the early 19th century encroachment on the common created a network of minor lanes,[73] which survived in 1994 though many of them only as unmade tracks. Of various lanes crossing the common from east to west, two were used as routes between Hewelsfield village and Brockweir in the mid 19th century. In 1876 the parish decided to maintain one which took a more northerly and higher course (called Hewelsfield Common road in 1994) rather than a lower one, probably that later called Bailey Lane,[74] and the Lydney highway district agreed to bear the cost of repairing the higher route in 1882.[75] All the roads leading up the hills from Brockweir village remained difficult to negotiate in the 19th century and goods were usually carried by donkeys. The building of a bridge across the Wye at Brockweir later encouraged improvement of the roads. A bus service between Chepstow and Coleford ran through the village from 1928, and the following year a halt was opened on the Wye Valley railway on the Monmouthshire side of the bridge.[76]

A ferry over the Wye at Brockweir was in operation by the early 1830s and was possibly then a recent innovation, for bringing workers over to a shipbuilding yard from the Monmouthshire bank. In the late 19th century, when a small rowing boat was sculled across, passengers were charged 1d., providing the ferry's owner Edwin Dibden with an income of c. £120 a year. When the bridge was opened he sued its promoters unsuccessfully for loss of business.[77] The bridge, of flat girders on steel piers and stone abutments, was begun in 1905 and opened the following year.[78] The scheme was promoted from 1894 by prosperous residents who had

54   Glos. R.O., P 175/CW 2/1, note of pop. figures after acct. 1821–2; Census, 1841.
55   O.S. Map 6", Glos. XLVI. NE. (1884 edn.).
56   O.S. Area Bk. (1881).
57   Geol. Surv. Map 1", solid, sheet 35 (1845 edn., revised to 1872).
58   Trans. B.G.A.S. lxvi. 178, 180.
59   P.R.O., MR 879; Taylor, Map of Glos. (1777).
60   Glos. R.O., D 608/6; cf. below, econ. hist.
61   Glos. R.O., D 1430A/29; cf. Taylor, Map of Glos. (1777).
62   Glos. R.O., Q/RNc 4/14.
63   Close R. 1242–7, 434.
64   P.R.O., E 32/29, rot. 5; E 32/30, rot. 4.
65   Suff. R.O., HA 49/A III(d)/1.
66   Below, this section.
67   C. Fox, Offa's Dyke (1955), 191; below, econ. hist.

68   Cf. below, St. Briavels, intro.
69   Glos. R.O., Q/SR 1813.
70   Ibid. Q/SRh 1837 C/4.
71   C. Heath, Hist. and Descriptive Accounts of Tintern Abbey (Monmouth, 1801), [11–12]; Glos. R.O., D 1430B/13, ct. proc. 19 Jan. 1907; cf. below, St. Briavels, intro.
72   P.R.O., MR 879.
73   O.S. Map 1", sheet 35 (1830 edn.); cf. ibid. 6", Glos. XLVI. NE. (1884 edn.).
74   Glos. R.O., P 175/OV 2/1, mins. 22 Apr. 1875; 25 Mar. 1876; cf. O.S. Maps 6", Glos. XLVI. NE. (1884 edn.); SE. (1891 edn.).
75   Glos. R.O., P 175/CW 2/1; Q/SRh 1882 East.
76   W.I. hist. of Brockweir (1959, TS. in Glos. Colln.), 16.
77   Glos. R.O., D 1430B/13.
78   Ibid. ct. proc. 18 Jan. 1907.

settled in the area, and it was built as the private enterprise of three of them, who raised subscriptions and secured grants from Lydney rural district and from Gloucestershire and Monmouthshire county councils; the local authorities eventually supplied three quarters of c. £4,800 needed and subscribers the remainder.[79]

Hewelsfield village, on high ground at the junction of various lanes leading up from the Severn and Wye, was presumably the site of 'Hiwoldes stone', from which the place was named in the 11th century. The church, built by the mid 12th century,[80] stands in a circular churchyard, possibly indicating a re-used pagan site.[81] In modern times, and probably in the 16th century,[82] the village around it was very small, comprising only the house called Hewelsfield Court, standing on the east side of the old road to St. Briavels, and a few small houses and cottages on the lanes that converge on the churchyard. Surviving documentary evidence does not show whether the village was larger in the Middle Ages, but it is possible that Hewelsfield Court farm which dominated it by the early modern period was created from a number of smaller freeholds, each with its own farmhouse.[83] One house that has vanished, called Haresley House, stood west of Hewelsfield Court in 1733.[84] A two-storeyed house on the east side of the churchyard, later the Parrot inn, was apparently built in 1706.[85] The few buildings were supplemented by a schoolroom and a small nonconformist chapel during the 19th century.[86]

Of the few outlying farmsteads in the upper part of the ancient parish, Harthill Court, at the top of Hart hill north-west of the village, was established by the late Middle Ages.[87] In 1633 a small farmhouse called Bayly stood at the head of the Brockweir brook valley near the boundary with Hewelsfield common;[88] it was demolished before 1840.[89] By 1629 there was a dwelling or dwellings, part of the Rodmore estate (in St. Briavels), at Royle Reddings above the Cone brook valley at the east side of the parish.[90] In the south part of the parish only a barn and yard stood at the site of Poolfield Farm in 1818,[91] and a farmhouse was built before 1840 when it was called Hill Farm.[92] Cowshill Farm in the southwest part of the main part of the parish was apparently also established as a farmstead at the same period; the lands there were farmed from a house in the village in 1781.[93]

Brockweir, on the bank of the Wye where the Brockweir and Mere brooks fall into the river, had some houses by the late 13th century,[94] and provided a substantial part of the parish's population by the mid 16th century.[95] River trade was its main support until the late 19th century.[96] The houses are of stone with rendering and are clustered tightly on narrow lanes. The oldest building, the Malthouse, on the south side of the road leading to the waterside, presumably formed part of the buildings of a grange that Tintern abbey owned at Brockweir in the early 16th century.[97] The south part is a 15th-century range, the ground floor entered through its west wall and the first floor having near central doorways on the north and south. The north staircase also served a 16th-century north-west range and may have been within a porch, entered by the four-centred doorway that has been reset further north. The north-east angle, between the two ranges, was infilled in the 19th century, when the roofs of the older ranges were reconstructed. Part of the building was used as a malthouse in the earlier 19th century, when it belonged to a prominent local family called Jane,[98] and from 1968 a pottery was carried on there.[99] On the opposite side of the road a two-storeyed building, housing a shop in 1994, retains two 15th-century cusped windows and a stone newel stair in its rear wall. A house by Brockweir bridge, known as the Manor House, is a substantial building of c. 1600, the front to the river retaining a large gable and several original windows. It appears to have had a three-roomed plan, each room having a chimney stack. Service and staircase projections to the rear were later incorporated in a 19th-century extension, and the north end of the house was much altered in the 20th century. Glenwye, by the riverside to the south, is a 17th-century house, originally on a three-roomed plan, the central room heated by a fireplace in the side wall. The other houses of Brockweir were mostly built or rebuilt during the 18th century. In the smaller detached part of the ancient parish, in the valley above, a decayed house formerly belonging to James Cutt was recorded in 1759;[1] it had gone by 1840 when the land was called Cutt's orchard.[2]

In the extraparochial land, later called Hewelsfield common, encroachment by squatters had begun by 1794[3] and several cottages had been built by 1812.[4] By 1830 cottages were scattered widely on a network of narrow lanes,[5] and by 1841, shortly before it was added to Hewelsfield parish, the area contained 53 dwellings.[6] In the late 19th century, encouraged partly by the opening of the Wye Valley railway on the Monmouthshire side of the river in 1876,[7] private

---

[79] Ibid. AC/C 3/1/1–2. The action by Dibden, who was declared bankrupt as a result, and another by his mother over access to her cottage, increased the promoters' total liability to c. £6,500.
[80] Above, this section.
[81] Cf. *V.C.H. Ches.* i. 239–41.
[82] Cf. below, this section (population).
[83] Below, manor; econ. hist.
[84] Glos. R.O., D 637/III/7; cf. G.D.R., T 1/100.
[85] Date, with inits. 'J. P.', on bldg.; below, this section.
[86] Cf. O.S. Map 6", Glos. XLVI. NE. (1884 edn.).
[87] Below, manor.
[88] Suff. R.O., HA 49/A III(d)/1; cf. ibid. A III(b)/28.
[89] G.D.R., T 1/100.
[90] *Inq. p.m. Glos.* 1625–42, i. 110–14.

[91] Glos. R.O., P 175/IN 3/1, f. 6; cf. ibid. D 1833/E 1.
[92] G.D.R., T 1/100.
[93] Glos. R.O., D 4018/T 18; cf. ibid. P 175/IN 3/1, f. 8; G.D.R., T 1/100.
[94] P.R.O., E 32/30, rot. 6d; for the village, below, Plate 10.
[95] Below, this section.   [96] Below, econ. hist.
[97] *Valor Eccl.* (Rec. Com.), iv. 370.
[98] Glos. R.O., D 1430A/1–2.
[99] Inf. from the owner, Mr. F. B. Naylor.
[1] Glos. R.O., D 1430A/1.   [2] G.D.R., T 1/100.
[3] Glos. R.O., P 209/MI 1, p. 19.
[4] Ibid. D 892/T 70; P 175/IN 1/2, entries for Brockweir common, Hudnalls, and Harthill.
[5] O.S. Map 1", sheet 35 (1830 edn.).
[6] *Census*, 1841.   [7] Paar, *G.W.R. in Dean*, 113.

residents and retired people settled in the area and enlarged the cottages or built new houses. By 1880 house names such as Wye View, Belmont, Bellevue House, and Woodbine Cottage reflected the changing character of the common. In 1907 it was found that on the Gloucestershire bank of the river within a 2¼ mile radius of Brockweir (which included also St. Briavels common and adjoining areas in St. Briavels) 48 houses had been enlarged or new built in the previous 12 years; some of the houses were let to holidaymakers during the summer months.[8] One substantial house, Harthill Grange, set in landscaped grounds and with a stable block, was built on the north part of Hewelsfield common shortly before 1877.[9] It was demolished in the mid 20th century.[10] New building, mainly bungalows but including four council houses in 1931 on a lane called Belmont Road, continued in the area during the 1920s and 1930s,[11] and began again in the early 1960s.[12] Hewelsfield common remained a popular residential area in 1994 with detached houses scattered over the hillsides. Most were then modern in character, and the very few early 19th-century cottages that had survived were incorporated in larger dwellings.

In 1551 there were reported to be c. 80 communicants in the parish[13] and in 1563 20 households.[14] At that period the small population was roughly divided between the two villages: in 1539 14 men were mustered under Hewelsfield and 10 under Brockweir[15] and the corresponding figures in 1546 were 11 and 9.[16] Later the balance swung fairly heavily towards Brockweir. The population was estimated at 40 families in 1650,[17] c. 200 people in 40 houses c. 1710,[18] and 253 people in 54 houses c. 1775.[19] In 1801 298 people in 62 houses were enumerated,[20] and by 1821, in the ancient parish and in the growing number of dwellings on Hewelsfield common, there were 434 people.[21] In 1841 the parish had a population of 319 and the common 212. In the next 60 years there were comparatively sharp alterations in the level of population in the enlarged parish, probably due mainly to the changing nature of the households on Hewelsfield common: between 1851 and 1861 the numbers fell from 497 to 417 and between 1891 and 1901 from 409 to 353, with a rise again to 442 by 1921. There was a gradual fall in the mid 20th century, but between 1981 and 1991 there was a recovery from 383 to 414.[22]

A church house, evidently in Hewelsfield village, had been demolished by 1683 but a house

at Brockweir then had that designation[23] and remained in possession of the parish until c. 1896.[24] The Parrot inn, at a house by Hewelsfield churchyard, where a friendly society met in 1805,[25] remained open until the first decade of the 20th century.[26] At Tumpkinhales on the Chepstow road, west of the village, there was an inn called the Carpenter's Arms by 1834, and in 1840 there was also a beerhouse there;[27] the inn closed after 1959.[28] At Brockweir an inn called the George, on the south side of the road to the river bank, was recorded from 1793 and had changed its name to the New Inn by 1840.[29] In 1840 the village had three other public houses, called, in connexion with its trade, the Ship, the Severn Trow, and the Bristol. There was then also a beerhouse called the Spout north of the village in a row of cottages that was later formed into a single dwelling called Spout House.[30] The Bristol was called the Sloop in 1844 when a friendly society met there.[31] By 1891 the New Inn and another called the Royal Arms were the only public houses in the village;[32] the latter closed after 1959,[33] leaving only the New Inn, which by 1994 had changed its name to the Brockweir inn.

Brockweir, approached as much by water as by road, was an isolated community with an independent character. The minister appointed to its new Moravian church in 1832[34] described the life of its watermen as being centred on beerhouses, skittle alleys, and cockfighting and said that it had the reputation of a 'city of refuge' for lawless elements.[35] Nonconformist chapels, a school, the decline of its trade, and an influx of outsiders to the area had all helped to temper its character by 1906 when the opening of the bridge over the Wye ended its comparative isolation. In the late 19th century the Moravians built a hall, which was used by the villagers in general, near their church in the part of the village within Woolaston, and by 1900 a small reading room had been opened.[36] In 1935 a new village hall and reading room, called the Mackenzie Hall after Professor John Mackenzie who gave it, was opened by the roadside some way above the village to serve Brockweir and the Hewelsfield common area.[37]

MANOR AND OTHER ESTATES. In Edward the Confessor's reign an estate of 3 hides at Hewelsfield was held by Wulfheah (Ulfeg).[38] After the Conquest it was perhaps held briefly

8 Glos. R.O., D 1430B/13, ct. proc. 24 Jan. 1907; cf. O.S. Map 6", Glos. XLVI. NE. (1884 edn.).
9 Glos. R.O., D 637/VII/16.
10 W.I. hist. of Brockweir, 27.
11 Glos. R.O., DA 28/100/6, pp. 45, 81, 133; 9, p. 35; 11, p. 193; 13, p. 321; for the council houses, ibid. 10, p. 385; 11, pp. 25, 46.
12 Ibid. 17, mins. 15, 21 Aug. 1961; 13 Aug., 22 Oct. 1963.   13 E.H.R. xix. 121.
14 Bodl. MS. Rawl. C. 790, f. 27v.
15 L. & P. Hen. VIII, xiv (1), p. 271.
16 Ibid. xxi (2), p. 206.
17 Trans. B.G.A.S. lxxxiii. 98.
18 Atkyns, Glos. 479.   19 Rudder, Glos. 499.
20 Census, 1801.
21 Ibid. 1821; cf. Glos. R.O., P 175/CW 2/1, note after acct. 1821–2.
22 Census, 1841–1991.

23 G.D.R., V 5/161T 4.
24 Glos. R.O., P 175/CH 1/1, mins. 12 Dec. 1895; 17 Dec. 1896; cf. ibid. OV 2/1, mins. 23 Jan. 1851; 24 Mar. 1853.
25 Ibid. Q/RSf 2; cf. G.D.R., T 1/100.
26 Kelly's Dir. Glos. (1906 and later edns.).
27 G.D.R., T 1/100; Glos. R.O., P 175/VE 2/1, min. 17 Aug. 1834.
28 W.I. hist. of Brockweir, 4.
29 Glos. R.O., D 1430A/1–2; cf. G.D.R., T 1/100.
30 G.D.R., T 1/100.
31 Glos. R.O., Q/RZ 1; cf. ibid. P 175/VE 1/1.
32 Licensed Houses in Glos. 1891, 128.
33 W.I. hist. of Brockweir, 4.   34 Cf. V.C.H. Glos. x. 118.
35 Glos. R.O., P 278/MI 13.
36 O.S. Map 1/2,500, Glos. XLVI. 10 (1902 edn.); V.C.H. Glos. x. 118.
37 W.I. hist. of Brockweir, 13, 25, 29; inscr. on bldg.
38 Dom. Bk. (Rec. Com.), i. 167.

by William FitzOsbern, earl of Hereford, whose foundation Lire abbey (Eure), in Normandy, later owned Hewelsfield church as a chapelry of Lydney.[39] The Hewelsfield estate later passed to the lord of Monmouth, William son of Baderon, but before 1086 by William I's command it was placed in the Forest of Dean and probably depopulated.[40] Later a new manor called *HEWELSFIELD* was formed and returned to the ownership of the lords of Monmouth. In 1246 it was held by John of Monmouth, great-grandson of William son of Baderon, who was succeeded at his death in 1248 by his son John (d. *c.* 1256).[41] The younger John granted it, with his honor of Monmouth, to Prince Edward,[42] who in 1266 granted it in free alms to Tintern abbey (Mon.).[43] In 1279 or 1280 Edward as king took the manor into his hands, but in the latter year he restored it to the abbey at a fee farm of 61*s.* 5*d.*, from which the monks were discharged in 1330.[44] A rent of 51*s.* and other services owed from Hewelsfield were acquired by Amice de Lacy before 1269[45] and sold by her son Fulk to the monks before 1280.[46] Hewelsfield manor was retained by Tintern until the Dissolution, when the abbey also had a grange at Brockweir, which probably comprised buildings in that village and land adjoining in Woolaston parish. Manor and grange were granted with the other abbey estates in 1537 to Henry Somerset, earl of Worcester.[47] The manorial rights of Hewelsfield passed to his descendants, earls of Worcester and dukes of Beaufort.[48]

A large estate based on the house called *HEWELSFIELD COURT* was sometimes called a manor but presumably originated as a free tenancy or tenancies held under the manor. It was owned, probably by 1542,[49] by William Warren (d. 1573), who was also an important landowner in St. Briavels. It passed to George Gough, who married William's daughter Mary,[50] and Mary apparently held it as a widow in 1608.[51] Their son William Gough apparently succeeded to their Hewelsfield estate, and it later passed to William's son Richard. Richard Gough left it to his daughters Alice, wife of Sir Nicholas Throckmorton, and Eleanor, wife of Sir William Catchmay of Bigsweir, in St. Briavels.[52]

Sir Nicholas Throckmorton died in 1664 and Alice in 1669,[53] and their share of the estate, probably including Hewelsfield Court, was sold

by their heirs before 1689 to Robert Symonds.[54] Robert's son Thomas succeeded him before 1719 and died in 1760, having settled it on his wife Penelope, and their son Thomas Symonds Powell succeeded. Thomas died in 1793 and in that year his heir completed his agreed sale of the estate to William Turner of Upton Bishop (Herefs.).[55]

Eleanor Catchmay, the other daughter of Richard Gough, died in 1662.[56] A part of her share was presumably the estate owned by William Catchmay (d. 1691)[57] of Hewelsfield. William settled his estate on his wife Barbara[58] (d. 1712), and it passed to their son William[59] (d. 1714),[60] who settled it on his wife Elizabeth. Elizabeth later married a Mr. Perkins and died before 1733 when, under an agreement between her heirs, her Hewelsfield land was assigned to her daughter Elizabeth, the wife of John Jane. The estate, which included Haresley House, standing opposite Hewelsfield Court, passed to John's son Edmund Jane (d. by 1776) of Chepstow, whose son Thomas succeeded and was probably the same Thomas who sold it to William Turner, owner of the other share of the estate, in 1797.[61] Poolfield farm at Hewelsfield, which the Rooke family of Bigsweir owned *c.* 1780[62] and until 1818[63] or later, may have been another part of Eleanor Catchmay's share of the estate, descending in the main line of her heirs.[64]

William Turner died in 1805 and was succeeded by his son Samuel (d. 1833), whose devisees completed a sale of the estate he had agreed with W. H. Peel of Aylesmore, in St. Briavels; it then comprised Hewelsfield Court and *c.* 420 a.[65] With other lands in Hewelsfield bought by Peel,[66] it descended with Aylesmore until 1892. Hewelsfield Court and 366 a. of land were then sold to W. B. Marling[67] and formed part of the Clanna estate, based in Alvington, until the mid 20th century.[68] Other lands in the parish, including Cowshill and Poolfield farms, were bought in the same period by Marling's brother Sir William Marling, Bt., and Sir William's son Col. Perceval Marling[69] and formed part of their Sedbury Park estate, based in Tidenham, until *c.* 1921.[70] Hewelsfield Court farm was bought in the 1950s by its tenants, the Simmons family, which owned and farmed it in 1994.[71]

The Goughs lived at Hewelsfield,[72] evidently

39 Below, church; above, Lydney, churches.
40 *Dom. Bk.* (Rec. Com.), i. 167, where the manor is entered only as a former possession of Wm. son of Baderon with no current tenantry or value.
41 *Close R.* 1242–7, 434; Sanders, *Eng. Baronies*, 64–5.
42 *Rot. Hund.* (Rec. Com.), i. 176; P.R.O., E 32/30, rot. 21d.
43 *Cal. Chart. R.* 1300–26, 89.
44 *Cal. Pat.* 1272–81, 404; *Cal. Close*, 1330–3, 4–5.
45 P.R.O., JUST 1/275, rot. 47.
46 *Cal. Chart. R.* 1300–26, 89; *Cal. Close*, 1279–88, 17.
47 *L. & . P. Hen. VIII*, xii (1), pp. 350–1; P.R.O., SC 6/Hen. VIII/2498; for Brockweir, cf. above, intro.; below, econ. hist.
48 P.R.O., C 142/340, no. 192; Atkyns, *Glos.* 479; Bigland, *Glos.* ii. 85.
49 *L. & . P. Hen. VIII*, xvii, p. 499.
50 P.R.O., C 142/177, no. 91; cf. below, St. Briavels, manors (Stowe).
51 Smith, *Men and Armour*, 43.
52 *Visit. Glos. 1682–3*, 74–5; Bigland, *Glos.* ii. 85.
53 Glos. R.O., P 175/IN 1/1.
54 Ibid.; Atkyns, *Glos.* 479.

55 Glos. R.O., D 637/III/7; cf. ibid. I/65, agreement 1793.
56 Bigland, *Glos.* ii. 86.   57 Ibid. 88.
58 G.D.R. wills 1691/34.
59 Ibid. 1712/115; Glos. R.O., P 175/IN 1/1.
60 G.D.R. wills 1714/151.
61 Glos. R.O., D 637/III/7.
62 Ibid. D 1833/E 1.
63 Ibid. P 175/IN 3/1, f. 6.
64 Cf. St. Briavels, manors (Bigsweir).
65 Glos. R.O., D 637/I/65; cf. ibid. P 175/IN 3/1, ff. 2–3.
66 G.D.R., T 1/100; Glos. R.O., D 262/T 29.
67 Below, St. Briavels, manors; Glos. R.O., D 177, Hewelsfield Ct. and Highgrove papers 1892.
68 *Kelly's Dir. Glos.* (1914), 226; (1939), 232; Glos. R.O., D 177, Clanna est. sale papers 1919–20.
69 *Kelly's Dir. Glos.* (1885 and later edns.); Glos. R.O., D 2428/1/40; cf. Burke, *Peerage* (1963), 1616.
70 Glos. Colln. RV 306.1; *V.C.H. Glos.* x. 63.
71 Inf. from Mr. J. W. Simmons, of Hewelsfield Court.
72 P.R.O., C 142/177, no. 91; *Visit. Glos. 1682–3*, 74.

at Hewelsfield Court, and one of the Throckmorton family was assessed on 7 hearths at Hewelsfield in 1672.[73] In the early 18th century Robert Symonds lived at Hewelsfield Court,[74] which later was usually tenanted. About 1830 it was rebuilt as a tall, square, stone farmhouse, but a substantial part of the older house, adjoining the new block on the west, was retained and used as a farm building. The old range dates from the 16th century and includes a garderobe turret and a large first-floor room, heated from a lateral stack. In 1994 it and some of the other farm buildings were being remodelled to form dwellings.

An estate called *HARTHILL* was styled a manor from the mid 16th century and in 1612 was held by fealty from the lord of Hewelsfield, the earl of Worcester.[75] It may have been held by William Wyther who was a landowner in Hewelsfield in 1300,[76] and John Wyther of Harthill was mentioned in 1346.[77] John Greyndour held Harthill, comprising a house and ploughland, at his death in 1415 or 1416, and was succeeded by his son Robert.[78] It descended with the Clearwell estate, in Newland,[79] until 1640 when Sir Baynham Throckmorton sold it to John Gonning of Bristol and his son John.[80] It then descended with the Great House estate, in St. Briavels, returning to the same ownership as Clearwell in the early 18th century.[81] The Harthill estate, comprising Harthill Court and 136 a. in 1840,[82] passed with Clearwell until 1870[83] or later, but by 1881 it belonged to Francis Lamb,[84] who lived at a large new house called Harthill Grange built on the north part of Hewelsfield common.[85] Edward Lamb owned the estate in 1910 and 1939.[86] By 1994 Harthill Court and the farmland were in separate ownerships. The south end of a long service wing at Harthill Court probably survives from a rebuilding of the farmhouse in the late 18th century, while its north end was added in the early 19th century. About 1860 a taller block, containing the principal rooms, was added at the south end of the house. An outbuilding, much altered, incorporates a 17th-century window head.

Monmouth priory owned a small estate in Hewelsfield, presumably given to it by one of the lords of Monmouth before the mid 13th century. In the 1440s the estate comprised a few small free tenements and some parcels of land that had apparently escheated to the priory.[87] That estate was retained by the priory until the Dissolution.[88]

ECONOMIC HISTORY.

Little evidence for the early agricultural history of Hewelsfield has been found, but the original pattern of tenure, as in other manors created on the Forest fringes, was probably one of small freeholds. The medieval manor apparently had little agricultural land in demesne, though it did include some woodland.[89] An extent of 1276 mentioned only a pasture capable of supporting 20 cattle and 100 sheep. The value of the manor was then mainly in the form of rents of free tenants, who also owed four barbed arrows each, while bedrips and some other customary services were valued at under 10s. The whole value was only £6 3s. 5½d.[90] The survey of Tintern abbey's lands at the Dissolution mentioned only free rents at Hewelsfield and a grange at Brockweir,[91] the land of which was probably in the adjoining part of Woolaston parish, represented later by Townsend (or Brockweir) farm.[92] The principal freehold estate at Hewelsfield in the post-medieval period, based on Hewelsfield Court, was perhaps an amalgam of smaller freeholds.[93]

A field called Wigdons, beside the Woolaston road near the south boundary of the parish, where small parcels of arable were mentioned in 1733, was apparently then an open field.[94] Two small areas of steep hillside, one below Clay hill near the east side of the parish and one below Cows hill at the west boundary, were recorded as common land from c. 1700;[95] in 1840 both were called Hewelsfield cliff.[96] A larger common enjoyed by the inhabitants in the 17th and 18th centuries was Harthill common in the extraparochial lands of the parish, and, probably from the Middle Ages, the inhabitants commoned in adjoining parts of the Forest demesne land called Hudnalls.[97] Both Hewelsfield and Brockweir were among the villages and hamlets that claimed common and estovers in the Forest demesne in the early 17th century.[98]

In 1818 the Hewelsfield Court estate formed a single tenancy of 421 a.,[99] and it remained much the largest farm in the parish during the 19th and 20th centuries. The farmer employed between 20 and 30 labourers in 1851,[1] and by 1877, when the farm comprised 463 a., extensive ranges of farm buildings adjoined the house.[2] The other main farms in 1818 were Harthill Court with 127 a., Poolfield farm with 80 a., and Cowshill, Royle Reddings, and another farm which each had c. 60 a.; there were then four other farms with over 20 a.[3] From the beginning

73 P.R.O., E 179/247/14, rot. 39.
74 Atkyns, *Glos.* 479; Glos. R.O., D 637/III/7, recital of deed 1793.
75 Hockaday Abs. ccxcv, 1548; P.R.O., C 142/340, no. 192.
76 *Trans. B.G.A.S.* lxvi. 179.
77 *Cal. Pat.* 1345–8, 174.
78 *Cal. Close*, 1413–19, 338.
79 Below, Newland, manors; Hockaday Abs. ccxcv, 1548; P.R.O., C 142/377, no. 92.
80 Suff. R.O., HA 49/A III(d)/1–2.
81 Ibid. A III(a)/2; N.L.W., Dunraven MSS. 334; below, St. Briavels, manors.   82 G.D.R., T 1/100.
83 *Kelly's Dir. Glos.* (1870), 580.
84 G.D.R., T 1/100.
85 *Kelly's Dir. Glos.* (1885), 504; cf. O.S. Map 6", Glos. XLVI. NE. (1884 edn.).
86 Glos. R.O., D 2428/1/40; *Kelly's Dir. Glos.* (1939), 232.
87 P.R.O., SC 2/175/61.

88 Ibid. SC 6/Hen. VIII/7319, where the land is identified only as 'in the Forest of Dean'.
89 Above, intro.
90 P.R.O., C 145/34, no. 16.
91 *Valor Eccl.* (Rec. Com.), iv. 370.
92 Cf. *V.C.H. Glos.* x. 110; Glos. R.O., Q/RI 144; D 262/E 27.
93 Above, manor.
94 Glos. R.O., D 637/III/7; cf. G.D.R., T 1/100.
95 Bodl. MS. Rawl. B. 323, f. 110v.; cf. Glos. R.O., D 247/30B.
96 G.D.R., T 1/100; cf. O.S. Maps 6", Glos. XLVI. NE., SE. (1884 edn.).   97 Above, intro.
98 P.R.O., E 112/82, no. 300.
99 Glos. R.O., P 175/IN 3/1, ff. 2–3.
1 P.R.O., HO 107/2443.
2 Glos. R.O., D 262/T 29.
3 Ibid. P 175/IN 3/1.

of the 19th century smallholdings were established by the encroachment of Hewelsfield common,[4] and nine farmers were listed in that area in 1879[5] and seven in 1894.[6] In 1896 a total of 38 agricultural occupiers was returned in the enlarged parish of Hewelsfield.[7] In 1920 the principal farms were Hewelsfield Court (364 a.), then part of the Clanna estate, and Poolfield (232 a., including land in Woolaston) and Cowshill (108 a.), both part of the Sedbury Park estate; the Clanna estate also included Royle Reddings farmhouse and 105 a., then farmed as part of Barnage farm in Alvington.[8] In 1988, when all were owner-occupied, the farms were Hewelsfield Court, two others with over 50 ha. (124 a.), three of 20–40 ha., and ten smallholdings worked part-time. A total of 28 people then worked the farms.[9]

In 1801 321 a. of arable were returned in the parish, mainly growing wheat and barley.[10] In 1818 the larger farms were predominantly arable, Hewelsfield Court having 245 a. out of 421 a., Harthill 75 a. of 127 a., and Poolfield 60 a. of 80 a. They grew barley, wheat, and oats, with turnips, clover, cinquefoil, leys, and fallow as the other elements in the rotation.[11] In 1866 756 a. of arable were returned compared to 422 a. of permanent grass;[12] the livestock comprised c. 100 cattle and c. 390 sheep.[13] By 1896 the amount of cropped land returned had fallen to 302 a., and there had been a considerable increase in the livestock, which included 75 dairy cows.[14] By 1926 there had been a further increase in livestock farming, with 349 cattle, including 131 cows in milk, and 813 sheep returned; 186 a. were then used as rough grazing.[15] In 1988 the principal farms were engaged in dairying and stock raising, 568 cattle and 1,559 sheep being returned; 48 ha. (119 a.) of crops were returned, almost all barley.[16]

A water mill built by the abbot of Tintern at Hewelsfield shortly before 1270 straddled the boundary between Tidenham chase and the Forest and was presented at two eyres as a resort of poachers and as an impediment to the passage of deer from the chase to the Forest.[17] The mill was evidently at a site on Brockweir brook, partly in the small detached part of Hewelsfield and partly in Woolaston parish; the spur of land above called Mill hill was presumably named from it. Still surviving there in 1994 was the dry millpond and a large, stone-capped mill dam,

which incorporated a stretch of Offa's Dyke. No record has been found of the mill in use in the post-medieval period. Further down the brook at Brockweir village there was a corn mill by 1758, owned by a branch of the Jane family.[18] It remained in use until the early 20th century,[19] and the stone mill building survived in 1994.

Among many inhabitants of Brockweir village employed in the trade of the river Wye was John Gethin, who left two boats to his sons in 1571.[20] One of his sons was probably the John Gethin who was killed on his boat in the Kingsroad, in the Bristol Channel, during an affray with Bristol merchants in 1587.[21] In 1608 13 sailors, five of them surnamed Gethin, were mustered from Hewelsfield parish.[22] During the 18th and the early 19th centuries Brockweir was a transhipment port, where goods brought down in barges from Herefordshire were put in larger craft, usually trows of 60–80 tons, for carriage to Bristol.[23] It also sent wood and iron from the Forest area to Bristol,[24] and presumably, as in the late 19th century, the returning boats carried groceries and household necessities.[25] Surviving title deeds of the 18th and early 19th centuries suggest that almost all the inhabitants of the village were then employed on the river.[26] In 1851 2 mariners and 16 watermen lived in Hewelsfield parish, and 2 mariners, 3 sailors, and 8 watermen in the adjoining parts of St. Briavels.[27] The Bristol trade continued throughout the 19th century, with the Bowens and Dibdens the families principally involved.[28] Trade declined with the opening of the Wye Valley railway in 1876, and continued on a limited scale into the early 20th century.[29]

A ship carpenter lived at Brockweir in 1748[30] and small river craft were perhaps then built at the village. About 1826 the building of seagoing vessels, including brigs and schooners, was begun there by John Easton of Hereford. His yard closed in or soon after 1836 but another yard, in a close on the upstream side of the village,[31] had been started by Hezekiah Swift of Monmouth (d. 1835). Swift's business was continued by his son Thomas, who built brigs, schooners, and barques, some of the last over 300 tons, besides sloops and trows, until c. 1848.[32] The building of small craft continued at Brockweir until the end of the century.[33]

In 1608 a joiner, a butcher, and a weaver were living in Hewelsfield parish.[34] Thirteen trades-

4   Cf. above, intro.
5   Kelly's Dir. Glos. (1879), 684.
6   Ibid. (1894), 209.
7   P.R.O., MAF 68/1609/6.
8   Glos. R.O., D 177, Clanna est. sale papers 1919–20.
9   Agric. Returns 1988.
10 List & Index Soc. clxxxix, p. 173.
11 Glos. R.O., P 175/IN 3/1.
12 P.R.O., MAF 68/26/8.
13 Ibid. MAF 68/25/9.
14 Ibid. MAF 68/1609/6.
15 Ibid. MAF 68/3295/12.   16 Agric. Returns 1988.
17 P.R.O., E 32/29, rot. 7d.; E 32/30, rot. 21d.; E 32/31, m. 5.
18 Glos. R.O., D 637/III/6; cf. G.D.R., T 1/100.
19 O.S. Map 1/2,500, Glos. XLVI. 10 (1902 edn.); Glos. R.O., D 2428/1/40.
20 Hockaday Abs. ccxliii.
21 Adams's Chronicle of Bristol, ed. F. F. Fox (Bristol, 1910), 121.
22 Smith, Men and Armour, 43.

23 Rudder, Glos. 307; Heath, Tintern Abbey, [11]; Glos. R.O., D 1430B/13, ct. proc. 19 Jan. 1907; cf. Glouc. Jnl. 20 June 1814.
24 Bigland, Glos. ii. 85.
25 W.I. hist. of Brockweir, 3.
26 e.g. Glos. R.O., D 608/6; D 637/I/67; D 1775; D 2957/161.1–4.
27 P.R.O., HO 107/2443.
28 Kelly's Dir. Glos. (1856 and later edns.); Harris, 'Wye Valley Ind. Hist.' Brockweir, 4, 8.
29 W.I. hist. of Brockweir, 4; W. J. Creswick, Where I was Bred (Coleford, c. 1970), 24.
30 Glos. R.O., Q/RNc 4/14.
31 Farr, Chepstow Ships, 21–2, 123, 127, 135, 139; G.D.R., T 1/100; cf. Glos. R.O., D 1430B/13, ct. proc. 19 Jan. 1907.
32 Farr, Chepstow Ships, 21–2, 137–70, 182–4; Harris, 'Wye Valley Ind. Hist.' Brockweir, 6–8.
33 Kelly's Dir. Glos (1879), 684; (1897), 212.
34 Smith, Men and Armour, 43.

men and craftsmen, excluding those employed in the river trade, were enumerated in the parish in 1851, mainly living at Brockweir or on Hewelsfield common.[35] In 1879 Brockweir had 3 shopkeepers, a butcher, and a carpenter, while 2 masons lived on the common and a butcher at Tumpkinhales.[36] There was a smithy in Hewelsfield village during the later 19th century.[37] Brockweir had a number of shopkeepers until the mid 20th century.[38] In 1994 there was a pottery at the house called the Malthouse and one other small shop.

The weir that gave Brockweir its name was mentioned c. 1150 when Monmouth priory held it by gift of Baderon, lord of Monmouth.[39] Members of the de Clare family had a fishery at Brockweir, attached to property on the Monmouthshire bank, in the early 14th century,[40] and Tintern abbey held the weir in 1331.[41] Tintern's rights presumably passed to the earl of Worcester at the Dissolution, and in 1866 the extensive Wye fisheries of the duke of Beaufort included a crib opposite Brockweir on the Monmouthshire bank and the right to use a stop net there.[42] The remains of the ancient weir were visible in 1994 as rocky shallows under Brockweir bridge.

LOCAL GOVERNMENT. No court rolls for Hewelsfield manor are known to survive, but rolls of 1444 and 1449 survive for a court held for Monmouth priory's small estate.[43] Leet jurisdiction over Hewelsfield was exercised by the St. Briavels hundred court.[44]

The surviving records of parish government include churchwardens' accounts from 1795 and vestry minutes from 1832.[45] The parish had two churchwardens in the early modern period,[46] but there was only one in the late 18th century[47] and until c. 1857, from which time two were elected.[48] In 1803 £59 was expended on poor relief and eight people received regular relief.[49] The annual cost reached £149 in 1814, with 12 people on permanent relief,[50] but in the 1820s and 1830s it was usually kept below £100.[51] In 1833 the poor were farmed for £80. A salaried assistant overseer had by then been appointed and the church house at Brockweir was used as a poorhouse.[52] Hewelsfield parish was included in the Chepstow union in 1836.[53] It was included in the Lydney highway district in 1867,[54] and in 1894 it became part of Lydney rural district.[55]

It was transferred with the rest of the rural district in 1974 to the Forest of Dean district, in which the parish, under its new style of Hewelsfield and Brockweir, remained in 1994.

CHURCH. The church at Hewelsfield had been founded by the mid 12th century.[56] Its ownership, with that of St. Briavels church, was then disputed between Monmouth priory, a foundation of the lords of Monmouth, who may have recovered the manor by then, and Lire abbey (Eure), which claimed the church as a chapel to its church of Lydney. About 1166 the dispute was decided in favour of Lire,[57] and the church remained a chapel to Lydney.[58] In or shortly before 1855 a separate living, variously described as a perpetual curacy or rectory, was created, to which the dean and chapter of Hereford, patrons of Lydney, presented.[59] In 1963 the living was united with that of St. Briavels, which was in the same patronage.[60]

All the tithes of Hewelsfield belonged to the vicar of Lydney, who was awarded a corn rent charge of £131 1s. for them in 1840.[61] The whole rent charge was presumably applied to the new benefice, which was said to be worth £130 a year in 1856.[62] In 1894 the net income of the incumbent was £78.[63] In 1635 there was a small glebe house south-west of the churchyard for the use of the curate serving the chapelry,[64] and in 1706 it was a two-roomed cottage with a thatched roof.[65] The vicar of Lydney repaired it in the 1820s.[66] It was sold after the union of the benefices in 1963, the incumbent living at St. Briavels.[67]

The vicar of Lydney appointed curates to serve Hewelsfield from the early 16th century,[68] and from the mid 17th century the same man usually also served St. Briavels.[69] In 1650, when there was said to be a rector for the parish with an income of £30, temporary provision had perhaps been made by the Commonwealth government.[70] At the beginning of the 18th century one service was being held each Sunday,[71] and in 1750 and 1825 it was either in the morning or afternoon, alternately with St. Briavels.[72]

The church of *ST. MARY MAGDALENE*, so called by 1508,[73] is built of coursed rubble and ashlar and comprises chancel, central tower with north transept, and nave with north aisle, south porch, and a small vestry or cell adjoining the west side of the porch.

35 P.R.O., HO 107/2443.
36 *Kelly's Dir. Glos.* (1879), 684, 731.
37 O.S. Map. 6", Glos. XLVI. NE. (1884 edn.).
38 *Kelly's Dir. Glos.* (1939), 232.
39 *Cal. Doc. France*, p. 413.
40 *Cal. Inq. p.m.* iv, p. 227; v, p. 335.
41 *Cal. Close*, 1330–3, 370–1.
42 Glos. R.O., Q/RF.   43 P.R.O., SC 2/175/61.
44 Glos. R.O., D 2026/L 8; Glos. Colln. 15930, ct. 1 May 1721.
45 Glos. R.O., P 175/CW 2/1; VE 2/1; OV 2/1.
46 Hockaday Abs. ccxliii, 1563; G.D.R., V 5/161T 1.
47 Glos. R.O., P 175/CW 2/1.   48 Ibid. OV 2/1.
49 *Poor Law Abstract, 1804*, 172–3.
50 Ibid. *1818*, 146–7.
51 *Poor Law Returns* (1830–1), pp. 66–7; (1835), p. 65.
52 Glos. R.O., P 175/VE 2/1.
53 Ibid. OV 2/1.   54 Ibid. HB 11.
55 Ibid. DA 28/100/1, p. 212.
56 *Cal. Doc. France*, pp. 411, 413.
57 Dugdale, *Mon.* vi (2), p. 1094; cf. below, St. Briavels,

church.
58 B.L. Harl. MS. 6203, pp. 72–3; *Eccl. Misc.* 102; G.D.R. vol. 383, no. cxx.
59 Hockaday Abs, ccxliii, 1850, 1855; *Kelly's Dir. Glos.* (1856), 311.
60 Glos. R.O., P 175/IN 3/3.
61 G.D.R., V 5/161T 2; T 1/100.
62 *Kelly's Dir. Glos.* (1856), 311.
63 *Crockford* (1894), 1669.
64 G.D.R., V 5/161T 1.   65 Ibid. 5.
66 Ibid. 7; cf. Glos. R.O., P 175/IN 3/1, f. 1.
67 Glos. R.O., P 175/IN 3/3.
68 Hockaday Abs. xxx, 1544 stipendiaries, f. 7; xlvii, 1584 state of clergy, f. 45.
69 G.D.R. vol. 285B(3), pp. 4–5, 7–8; vol. 321; Hockaday Abs. cccxxviii, 1681, 1804, 1824.
70 *Trans. B.G.A.S.* lxxxiii. 98.
71 G.D.R., V 5/161T 6.
72 Ibid. vol. 381A, f. 4; 383, no. cxx.
73 Hockaday Abs. ccxliii, 1509.

The nave and aisle are of the 12th century, though externally much restored. The chancel, tower, porch, and cell are of the 13th century. The north transept is 14th-century in origin, but it is thought to have been extended in the 16th century, possibly to house a burial chapel of the Gough family, which was mentioned in the late 18th century.[74] The church's west window was inserted in the late 13th century, and there are 14th-century windows on both sides of the chancel. The church was restored under the direction of William Butterfield in the mid 1860s, when new windows were put into the south side of the nave, the roofs were renewed, and the church refitted.[75] In the 1970s the roofs were repaired and the whole church retiled, and in the early 1980s the interior was restored and redecorated.[76]

The font, with an octagonal bowl on a circular pedestal, dates from the early 13th century.[77] There is a ring of six bells: (i) by John Taylor of Loughborough 1866, added to the ring in 1979; (ii) by William Evans 1733; (iii) by John Pennington 1634; (iv) recast by Mears of London 1864; (v) by William Evans 1746; (vi) a late 15th-century bell from a Gloucester foundry.[78] The plate includes a chalice and paten cover of 1695, and a paten given by the curate Edgar Lloyd in 1849.[79] The registers survive from 1664.[80]

NONCONFORMITY. The history of the Moravian church opened in 1832 in the south part of Brockweir village is given under Woolaston in another volume.[81] Houses at Brockweir and in the adjoining area that were registered for worship from 1812 were probably used by Wesleyan Methodists,[82] who c. 1818 opened a chapel in the south part of the extraparochial land that was later added to St. Briavels parish.[83] Before 1846 the Wesleyans opened a chapel called Salem in the north part of Brockweir village.[84] It closed before 1914 and was later demolished. During the early 20th century several groups, including Quakers, Pentecostalists, and Christian Scientists, held meetings in private houses in Brockweir and the surrounding area.[85]

From c. 1816 Daniel Edwards, a lay preacher, led an Independent meeting in Hewelsfield,[86] and in 1822 the group built a small chapel called Zion on the west side of Hewelsfield village. In 1851 it had an average congregation at its evening service of 45.[87] In 1908 it was an out-station of the Congregational chapel in St. Briavels village.[88] It had closed by 1994.

EDUCATION. In 1851 a small National school was built west of the parish church. It was taught by a mistress and supported by voluntary contributions, pence, and the rent of one of the church houses;[89] from 1864 part of the income of the Church and Poor charity was applied to it.[90] The school had an average attendance of only 25 in 1875,[91] and it was closed before 1885 when the children from the upper part of the parish attended the National school in St. Briavels village.[92] The building at Hewelsfield remained in use as a Sunday school[93] until sold by the parish in the early 1970s.[94]

At Brockweir an infant school run by the Moravians in the part of the village within Woolaston parish was apparently reconstituted as a British school in 1873.[95] In 1875, however, it was replaced by a school held in the same building by a school board[96] formed the previous year for Hewelsfield and St. Briavels. In 1885 the board school had accommodation for 60 children and an average attendance of 34 children from Brockweir and the south part of St. Briavels parish.[97] In 1896 the board built a new school on the south part of Hewelsfield common by the road leading up from Brockweir.[98] In 1904, called Brockweir Council school, it had an average attendance of 97 and was organized as mixed and infants' departments.[99] The average attendance was 85 in 1938.[1] The number on the roll had fallen to 18 by 1992[2] and the school was closed the following year.[3]

CHARITIES FOR THE POOR. Lands belonging to the parish in 1683, including the church house at Brockweir and the site of the old church house at Hewelsfield village, were thought to have been given by a number of donors for the repair of the church; they were valued at £6 16s. 6d. a year in 1683,[4] and in 1864 they comprised 11 a.[5] Elizabeth Williams by will dated 1724 gave rent charges of 20s. a year for eight poor widows, 10s. for the repair of the church, and 5s. for a sermon on Good Friday; by the 1820s the land charged was divided among several owners, causing problems in ob-

74 Bigland, *Glos.* ii. 85; ch. guide (1987).
75 P. Thompson, *William Butterfield* (1971), 446.
76 Ch. guide (1987).
77 *Trans. B.G.A.S.* xxxviii. 194, 211.
78 *Glos. Ch. Bells*, 376–7.
79 *Glos. Ch. Plate*, 120–1; cf. Glos. R.O., P 175/OV 2/1, min. 18 Apr. 1849.
80 Glos. R.O., P 175/IN 1/1–2.
81 *V.C.H. Glos.* x. 118.
82 Hockaday Abs. cccxxviii, 1812; ccxliii, 1813, 1821, 1825.
83 Below, St. Briavels, nonconf.
84 Hockaday Abs. ccxliii, 1846; cf. O.S. Map 1/2,500, Glos. XLVI. 10 (1881 edn.).
85 W.I. hist. of Brockweir, 18.
86 Bright, *Nonconf. in Dean*, 19.
87 P.R.O., HO 129/576/3/5/13; Hockaday Abs. ccxliii, 1822.
88 Glos. Colln. J 11.48 (16); cf. O.S. Map 1/2,500, Glos. XLVI. 12 (1902 edn.).

89 P.R.O., ED 7/37.
90 Glos. R.O., D 3469/5/112.
91 P.R.O., ED 7/37.
92 *Kelly's Dir. Glos.* (1885), 504; Glos. R.O., P 175/CH 1/1, min. 3 Mar. 1887.
93 O.S. Map 1/2,500, Glos. XLVI. 12 (1902 edn.).
94 Glos. R.O., P 175/SC 1.
95 *V.C.H. Glos.* x. 118; P.R.O., ED 7/34/168.
96 P.R.O., ED 7/34/168; Glos. R.O., D 1430B/13, sale partic. 1907.
97 *Kelly's Dir. Glos.* (1885), 504, 557.
98 Ibid. (1897), 212.
99 *Public Elem. Schs. 1906*, 185.
1 *Bd. of Educ., List 21, 1911* (H.M.S.O.), 127.
2 *Schools and Establishments Dir. 1992–3* (co. educ. dept.), 9.
3 Co. educ. cttee. mins. 1 Mar. 1993.
4 G.D.R., V 5/161T 4.
5 Glos. R.O., D 3469/5/112.

taining the payments.[6] A bequest of John Matthews (d. 1639) for the poor and for a sermon was lost after 1683.[7]

A Scheme of 1864 amalgamated the parish lands charity and the Williams charity to create the Hewelsfield Church and Poor charity; the annual income, then £17 a year, was to be divided, apart from the 5s. for the sermon, between the church fabric, the parish school, and the poor;[8] all but a small part of the land was sold in the mid 1890s and the proceeds invested in stock. In 1882 the poor's part was distributed in doles of 5s. to women and 2s. 6d. to men, and in the early 1940s it was distributed in 9s. doles.[9] The part assigned to the church fabric and the payment for the sermon were made a separate ecclesiastical charity, though under the same trustees, in 1899. The part for the school was formed into a separate educational endowment a few years later,[10] and during the early 20th century was applied to the upkeep of the old school building, which was then in use as a Sunday school.[11]

LITTLEDEAN

LITTLEDEAN, which once had a market and was a centre of ironworking and metal trades, lies 17 km. WSW. of Gloucester.[12] As defined in 1878 the ancient parish, one of the smallest in rural Gloucestershire, contained 495 a. and was very irregular in shape.[13] It was bounded by the once extraparochial Forest of Dean on the north and by detached parts of Flaxley and Newland elsewhere, and on the south, beyond Dean hill, a peninsula of Littledean to the west of Newnham touched the Forest at Blaize Bailey. On Dean hill the parish included a small area which as late as 1863 had been a detached part of the Forest.[14] Littledean's boundaries followed a straight ridgeway on Littledean hill to the west and ancient tracks in places elsewhere. The eastern boundary with part of Flaxley took in Littledean Camp, a small earthwork probably of the late 11th century or early 12th, which has been identified as 'the old castle of Dean' recorded in the mid 12th century.[15] The earthwork was acquired in 1987 by the Dean Heritage museum.[16] The name Littledean, used in its Latin form Dean Parva in 1221,[17] distinguished it from nearby Mitcheldean (Dean Magna),[18] with which it presumably had a tenurial connexion in 1086.[19] Littledean, which remained a member of Mitcheldean in 1316,[20] had a church by the later 12th century.[21]

In 1883 Littledean absorbed the parts of Flaxley and Newland, together with a small detached piece of Westbury-on-Severn, to the east.[22] In 1953, on the dismemberment of East Dean civil parish, it took in part of the Forest to the north, including Pope's Hill, Shapridge, and Edge Hills, to more than double its area to 1,568 a. (634.5 ha.).[23] The following account covers the parish as it existed before 1883 and the former extraparochial land on Dean hill.

The parish lies at the heads of valleys which drain to the north, north-east, and south. It takes in the surrounding hillsides rising to over 240 m. on Littledean hill and, less steeply, to over 185 m. in the east and south-east. Only in the north-east does the land fall below the 120-m. contour. Littledean was included within the ancient boundaries of the Forest of Dean[24] but woodland was cleared early and only 7 a. survived in 1839.[25] The Old Red Sandstone forms the land save in the west where it is overlaid by strata of carboniferous limestone and sandstone containing deposits of haematite ore. The limestone and the ore, which outcrops in a thin band running NE.–SW. just below the ridge,[26] have been quarried and mined and the ore was used by many rudimentary ironworks in the Middle Ages. Throughout the parish, particularly at Callamore on the west side and on Dean hill, were areas of waste ground, parts of which were used for dumping slag or cinders from those ironworks. Agriculture was predominantly pastoral and was carried on in small closes. In the 1580s Thomas Brayne created a deer park west of Littledean village[27] but it has not been found recorded in use after the early 17th century.[28]

Littledean stood at the centre of a network of tracks. They included roads said to have been used by the Romans linking Gloucester with the Forest of Dean, and Newnham and Lydney with Ariconium, near Weston under Penyard (Herefs.).[29] The route from Newnham, used in 1255 by travellers to Monmouth[30] and in the later 15th century by travellers to Hereford,[31] entered the parish on Dean hill and curved north, descending through the village and past the church towards Mitcheldean. The section running along the west side of Chestnuts hill was

[6] 19th Rep. Com. Char. 93.
[7] G.D.R., V 5/161T 4.
[8] Glos. R.O., D 3469/5/112.   [9] Ibid. P 175/CH 1/1.
[10] Ibid. D 3469/5/112.   [11] Ibid. P 175/CH 1/1.
[12] This history was written in 1989.
[13] O.S. Area Bk. (1878); cf. O.S. Maps 6", Glos. XXXI. SE., NE. (1883–4 edn.). According to 3rd Rep. Dean Forest Com. 5, the area in 1831 was 780 a.
[14] G.D.R., T 1/114; P.R.O., HO 107/1959; Kelly's Dir. Glos. (1863), 303; in 1785 the extraparochial area was said to belong to Newnham: Glos. R.O., D 2123, p. 159.
[15] Flaxley Cart. p. 16; Trans. B.G.A.S. lxxvii. 48–60.
[16] Dean Forest Mercury, 13 Mar. 1987.
[17] Pleas of the Crown for Glos. ed. Maitland, 77.
[18] P.N. Glos. (E.P.N.S.), iii. 225, 236.

[19] Below, manors.
[20] Feud. Aids, ii. 275.   [21] Below, church.
[22] Census, 1891; O.S. Area Bk. (1878); O.S. Map 6", Glos. XXXI. SE. (1883 edn.).
[23] Census, 1961.   [24] Trans. B.G.A.S. lviii. 109.
[25] G.D.R., T 1/114.
[26] Geol. Surv. Map 1/50,000, solid and drift, sheet 234 (1972 edn.); sheet 233 (1974 edn.); Atkinson, Map of Dean Forest (1847).   [27] Glos. R.O., D 2026/X 7.
[28] Ibid. D 2957/101.22.
[29] O.S. Map 6", Glos. XXXI. SE. (1883 edn.); I. D. Margary, Roman Roads in Britain, ii (1957), p. 64; cf. V.C.H. Glos. x. 35; Trans. B.G.A.S. lxxvii. 48.
[30] Cal. Pat. 1247–58, 435.
[31] Glos. R.O., D 36/M 1.

described *c.* 1282 as a high road (*summum iter*)[32] and survived as a green way in the mid 18th century, when it was no longer the main route between Littledean and Mitcheldean.[33] A route to the Forest ran north-west from the village centre along Broad Street before forking for Callamore and St. White's. The route to St. White's formed a junction at Pennywell with a track running west from the Newnham road at Dean Hall[34] but in the later 18th century traffic from Newnham to St. White's and Coleford took the longer and slightly less steep route through the village and Callamore where the road to the Forest divided.[35] The road running north-west through Callamore is called the Ruffitt and that running south-west from Callamore Reddings Lane, a name recorded in 1674.[36] The route from Lydney, by way of Soudley, originally crossed Broad Street[37] to follow an ancient way turning east to the church and a market place. That way was stopped in the mid 17th century[38] and, further west, George Lane, branching northwards from Broad Street, was the principal road between Littledean and Mitcheldean by the mid 18th century.[39]

The Littledean–Gloucester road, branching east from the old Mitcheldean road, follows the valley down to Elton and apparently once took a more northerly course, known in 1565 as Washbrook Lane, along the south side of Chestnuts hill.[40] From 1769 to 1880 it was a turnpike beginning in the centre of the village.[41] The village's other streets and the road through Callamore to St. White's were turnpiked in 1783 as part of the main route between Newnham and the Forest of Dean.[42] A tollgate was erected on Dean hill[43] and in 1819 the road was diverted from the east side to the west side of Dean Hall at the expense of the house's owner, Joseph Pyrke.[44] In the late 1820s, when the trust administering that route lapsed,[45] the more direct route between Littledean and St. White's was replaced by a new road running higher up the hillside from the bottom of the Ruffitt. The new road, built by the Forest turnpike trust, turned northwestwards for Nailbridge at the point, east of St. White's, where it rejoined the old route,[46] and in the 1870s there was a tollgate just below the junction.[47] The Forest turnpike trustees had responsibility for George Lane from 1796[48] until their powers were abolished in 1888.[49]

Littledean village grew up on the old Newnham–Mitcheldean road. The church, dating from the later 12th century, stands at the northeast end and just beyond it was a large pond, which was filled in *c.* 1850.[50] The village was possibly represented in 1282 by a dozen cottages, seven of them relatively new, on 2½ a. of land held under Henry of Dean[51] and in 1542 it may have contained the building called the church house.[52] The junction of Broad Street, some way south of the church, took the name the Cross from a high cross erected there by 1458.[53] It served as a market cross by 1573,[54] having a low wooden penthouse built against it to shelter traders,[55] and was removed in 1821 to improve the road junction.[56] The top of the shaft, which had carvings of small figures in niches below a finial, was placed in the grounds of the Grange, just outside the village, before being moved in the 1890s to a garden in Newnham.[57] By 1976 part of the shaft was in the garden of Littledean House hotel.[58] The village extends along the three roads leading from the Cross. Many of the houses were rebuilt in the local sandstone in the 18th and 19th centuries but several earlier ones survive. The house east of the Cross has an early 18th-century street front with a pediment. To the north in Church Street is a house with a timber frame and a jettied upper floor, which may date from the 15th century, and to the south in Silver Street, so called in 1715,[59] is a 17th-century cottage. The south side of Broad Street contains a 17th-century gabled house and, further west at the corner of the Soudley road, the former White Lion inn[60] dates from the 17th century and was altered in the early 19th. Court Farm, much further along the street, was the site of a medieval house.[61] Frogmore, near the church, is an early 18th-century painted brick house of five bays. In the 1980s it was the home of members of the Colchester-Wemyss family,[62] which had once owned Littledean manor and a large estate nearby. At the Cross, on the south side of Broad Street, is a house built in 1764 by William Howell, a coal miner.[63] Further along

32   *Trans. B.G.A.S.* xiv. 360.
33   Taylor, *Map of Glos.* (1777); Glos. R.O., D 36/E 12, ff. 56v.–57: the farmstead known as the Greenway evidently took its name from the road.
34   Glos. R.O., D 2123, p. 159; D 36/E 12, ff. 43v.–44, 68v.–69; cf. O.S. Map 6", Glos. XXXI. SE. (1883 edn.).
35   Cf. Newnham Ferry to St. White's Road Act, 23 Geo. III, c. 104; Bryant, *Map of Glos.* (1824).
36   Glos. R.O., DA 24/100/2, pp. 233–4; D 36/T 16.
37   A. W. Trotter, *Dean Road* (1936), 34–9.
38   Glos. R.O., D 36/M 55; cf. G.D.R., T 1/114 (nos. 125, 166).
39   Taylor, *Map. of Glos.* (1777); Glos. R.O., D 2123, p. 159.
40   Glos. R.O., D 2026/X 3.
41   Glouc. & Heref. Roads Act, 9 Geo. III, c. 50; Annual Turnpike Acts Continuance Act, 43 & 44 Vic. c. 12.
42   Newnham Ferry to St. White's Road Act, 23 Geo. III, c. 104; Bryant, *Map of Glos.* (1824).
43   Glos. R.O., D 2123, p. 159.
44   Ibid. Q/SRh 1819 C/2.
45   Newnham Ferry to St. White's Road Act, 45 Geo. III, c. 109 (Local and Personal).
46   Nicholls, *Forest of Dean*, 197; cf. Greenwood, *Map of Glos.* (1824); O.S. Map 1", sheet 43 (1831 edn.). The route varied considerably from that specified in Dean Forest Roads Act, 7 & 8 Geo. IV, c. 12 (Local and Personal); Glos. R.O.,

Q/RUm 107.
47   O.S. Map 6", Glos. XXXI. SE. (1883 edn.).
48   Dean Forest Roads Act, 36 Geo. III, c. 131.
49   Dean Forest Turnpike Trust Abolition Act, 51 & 52 Vic. c. 193.
50   Cf. G.D.R., T 1/114; O.S. Map 6", Glos. XXXI. SE. (1883 edn.).
51   P.R.O., E 32/30, rot. 18.
52   Glos. R.O., D 2172/1/51.
53   Ibid. D 36/E 1, ff. 21–2, 27v.–28; cf. Hockaday Abs. cclx, 1493.   54   G.D.R. wills 1574/40.
55   Bodl. MS. Top. Glouc. c. 3, f. 193; Bigland, *Glos.* i. 451; Glos. R.O., D 4304/5, which includes an illustration.
56   *Gent. Mag.* xcii (1), 19.
57   *Trans. B.G.A.S.* vi. 267; Glos. R.O., D 4304/5: in the 1860s it was placed temporarily in the rectory garden.
58   Glos. R.O., PA 110/5, which mistakenly suggests that the fragment came from a cross at Nightingale's Cross, at the north-west end of the village.
59   Glos. R.O., D 36/E 11, ff. 38v.–39.
60   Surv. of Sir Thos. Crawley-Boevey's estates 1797 (no. 7): copy in Glos. R.O., MF 285.
61   Below, manors.   62   Local inf.
63   G.D.R. wills 1765/148; date on bldg. with inits. of Wm. and his wife Margaret.

the north side of the street, on the site of a house which had belonged to Ketford Brayne (d. 1705),[64] is a house bearing the date 1812 and the initials of Richard Smith and his wife Ann.[65] Among other buildings put up in the 19th century were a rectory house, a chapel, and a manse in Broad Street and a school in Church Street. After the Second World War the village's appearance was altered by the removal of some old cottages and by the building of council houses and private dwellings in small estates off the principal streets.[66]

The north-west end of the village centred on Nightingale's Cross, so called by 1591,[67] where the road forked for Callamore and St. White's; a great elm standing there was a prominent landmark in the 18th century.[68] That part of the village presumably included the dwelling said in 1436 to be in Nightingale Street.[69] The architectural history of Brayne Court (formerly the Red House), standing at the entrance to the Ruffitt, has been obscured by an extensive restoration of the 1920s when additions were made to the building and early fittings were introduced.[70] A 16th-century block, now the stair-hall, may have been a parlour and solar to a hall to the east. The hall was remodelled in the early 17th century when it probably had a screens passage across the east end and service rooms, largely demolished by the late 18th century, beyond that.[71] A cross wing at the west end of the house probably dates from the early 17th century and provided additional parlour accommodation. Known as the Upper House, it was the residence in 1694 of Anne Brayne and in 1716 of her son John.[72] There was some refitting c. 1700 and again in the early 19th century. Soon afterwards, presumably in 1855 when the house was converted as three cottages, a carved overmantel with the arms of the Brayne family was removed.[73] To the south-east Littledean House hotel, which opened as a boarding house in 1906,[74] occupies a number of former houses and outbuildings. The main block, originally a two-storeyed house, was extended westwards and heightened by a storey in the early 19th century. That work was possibly undertaken by Joseph Bennett, a maltster and grocer,[75] who resided there in 1838[76] and is said to have moved the overmantel from Brayne Court to the house.[77] To the west a two-storeyed range of the 19th century once contained service rooms and stables and coach houses. To the east a low early 19th-century wing joins the main block to a cottage, which has been much altered but retains a small 16th-century window in a gable, and beyond that is a short link to a small two-storeyed house bearing the date 1737. The east end of the hotel has been converted from a three-storeyed commercial building which fronts a former malthouse, in which there is a kiln. Among the houses at the bottom of the Ruffitt is one dated 1824.

North-east of the village on the Gloucester road a house of correction,[78] opened in 1791, was one of several built in the county according to ideas promoted by Sir George Onesiphorus Paul, Bt. Designed by William Blackburn (d. 1790) and completed under the supervision of his brother-in-law William Hobson,[79] it incorporated a two-storeyed building with a central block, containing an office, committee room, chapel, infirmaries, and accommodation for keeper and turnkey, and east and west wings, containing the cells; open arcades on the ground floor of the wings had been filled in by 1812. Around the building were four courtyards and the whole was surrounded by a perimeter wall with a gatehouse on the south side. In 1844 the ground-floor cells were enlarged and a third storey was added to the central block, one room of which became a schoolroom. From 1854 the building was used as a police station and remand prison and in 1874 the east wing was remodelled as a petty sessional court. During the Second World War the cells were used as a store by the county record office and Gloucester cathedral. The police station was closed in 1972 and the building, which continued to house archives until 1979, was purchased by an insurance company in 1985 for a record and computer centre.[80]

Outside the village the parish contains scattered dwellings including Dean Hall, by the Newnham road, which for over two centuries belonged to the Pyrke family and was the principal residence in Littledean. In the 17th and 18th centuries several small settlements were formed by squatter development on waste ground just outside the Forest, notably at Callamore in the west but also on Dean hill in the south-east and at Waterend Lane (formerly Waterlane End) on the old Mitcheldean road in the north. At least 15 of the people ejected from the extraparochial Forest in the mid 17th century put up cottages or cabins in Littledean,[81] evidently in those places, but most of the dwellings were built or rebuilt in the 18th and 19th centuries. Building at Callamore, including the site of the farmstead at Colloegrove, began before 1618.[82] In 1679 there were 22 squatters living there,[83] the highest cottages presumably being at Littledean Hill where later buildings marked the eastern limit of the town of Cinderford in 1989.[84] On Dean hill, at the place sometimes known as Pleasant Stile, there were

[64] Glos. R.O., D 36/E 11, ff. 39v.–40; D 2123, pp. 156, 159; *Visit. Glos. 1623*, 209 and n.
[65] Glos. R.O., D 36/E 14–15; G.D.R. wills 1817/164.
[66] Glos. R.O., DA 24/602/1; P 110/SC 1/1; *Dean Forest Mercury*, 7 May 1971.
[67] Glos. R.O., D 2172/1/71.
[68] Ibid. D 36/E 11, ff. 39v.–40; D 2123, p. 159.
[69] P.R.O., SC 6/868/15, rot. 3.
[70] Glos. R.O., PA 110/1.
[71] Cf. ibid. D 2123, p. 159; G.D.R., T 1/114.
[72] Glos. R.O., D 543, Mitcheldean brewery, legal papers Smith *v.* Wintle 1907.
[73] Ibid. D 4304/20.
[74] Ibid. PA 110/2; *Kelly's Dir. Glos.* (1910 and later edns.).

[75] *Slater's Dir. Glos.* (1852–3), 148.
[76] Dean Forest Roads Act, 1 & 2 Vic. c. 38 (Local and Personal), s. 2.
[77] Glos. R.O., PA 110/1; D 4304/20.
[78] Para. based on J. R. S. Whiting, *House of Correction* (1979), 18–23, 34–5, 41–4, 113–16, and plates at pp. 64–5.
[79] Glos. R.O., Q/AG 7, pp. 113–14, 124.
[80] *Dean Forest Mercury*, 3 Jan. 1986.
[81] Glos. R.O., D 36/M 63, M 67–8.
[82] Ibid. D 4431, deed 22 Sept. 16 Jas. I.
[83] Ibid. D 36/M 55.
[84] Ibid. D 2123, p. 159; O.S. Map 6", Glos. XXXI. SE. (1883 edn.); for Cinderford, below, Forest of Dean, settlement.

three squatter cottages in 1679.[85] The larger surviving buildings include Temple Farm, an early 18th-century farmhouse known in 1797 as Solomon's Temple.[86] The late 18th-century Hill House was probably the house being built in 1793 for the merchant Joseph Boughton (d. 1801).[87] Dean Cottage was built in the mid 1850s by Duncombe Pyrke for his sisters Charlotte and Emily.[88] At Waterend Lane five squatter cottages belonged to Littledean in 1679.[89] Further north a homestead built by Richard Taylor (d. 1712) became known as the Greenway.[90]

Twelve inhabitants of Littledean were assessed for the subsidy in 1327.[91] In 1548 there were said to be 240 communicants in the parish[92] but the figure was probably nearer 200.[93] In 1563 the number of households was 62[94] and in 1603 the number of communicants was given as 140.[95] In 1650 the parish was said to contain 132 families.[96] The parish's population, estimated c. 1710 at 320 in 70 houses,[97] grew quickly in the later 18th century and early 19th, being estimated c. 1775 at 423[98] and enumerated as 541 in 1801 and 754 in 1811. After falling to 617 in 1831 it rose to 947 in 1851, after which it declined to 769 in 1901. The boundary changes of 1883 added little to the population, which fluctuated between 782 and 906 in the early 20th century, but the parish's enlargement in 1953 brought a substantial increase and in 1961 the population was 1,378. In 1981 it had fallen to 1,293.[99]

Five keepers of victualling houses were recorded in the parish in 1596[1] and 14 alehouse-keepers or ale vendors in 1667.[2] In the later 18th century the number of inns and alehouses was much smaller, those that had closed including the Red Lion, recorded in 1670, in Broad Street.[3] The White Lion at the corner of Broad Street and the Soudley road was recorded from 1797.[4] The Cross Keys south-west of the Cross had opened by 1739[5] and the Bell in Church Street by 1779.[6] The Golden Heart at the corner of Broad Street and George Lane, open in 1785,[7] had been renamed the George by 1819.[8] The King's Head north-west of the Cross was recorded from 1796.[9] In 1870 there were six inns and beerhouses in the parish, including the Swan in the Ruffitt,[10] and in 1889 one beerhouse at Littledean Hill was within Littledean.[11] There were five public houses in Littledean in 1903[12] and the George and the King's Head remained open, with Littledean House hotel, in 1989. Littledean had two friendly societies in 1803[13] and societies met in the Bell and Cross Keys inns in 1813. Other societies' rules were enrolled in 1823 and 1842.[14] The village had a brass band in 1843, and a band organized by temperance supporters played at a horticultural show in the village school in 1865.[15] Later a room at a chapel in the village was used for meetings and in 1950 a stable at the rectory house was converted as a church hall. Both places were partly superseded by a village hall built by the district council before 1981. The church hall was closed in 1984[16] and was converted as a house.

In April 1643 Sir William Waller led a force from Chepstow (Mon.) against Prince Maurice, who had lodged in Littledean. The royalists withdrew from the village, enabling Waller to pass through their line, but they engaged the rearguard covering his march to Gloucester.[17] In May 1644 cavalry sent by Edward Massey, commander of the Gloucester garrison, surprised and defeated a royalist garrison at Littledean and later massacred a group of soldiers who had broken the terms for their surrender.[18]

MANORS AND OTHER ESTATES. Littledean with Mitcheldean and Abenhall was presumably part of the estate called Dean held by William son of Norman in 1086[19] and apparently had a castle soon afterwards.[20] Woodland there belonging to the Crown was cleared for cultivation by William of Dean (d. c. 1259), the lord of part of Mitcheldean, who paid a rent of 2s. to St. Briavels castle for it. William's son and heir Henry of Dean made further clearances at Littledean[21] and at his death c. 1292 was seised there of assarted land, for which he owed the same rent of 2s., and 2 yardlands held from the Crown for a cash rent of 6d.[22] Henry's lands descended with his Mitcheldean estate to his grandson William of Dean, who at his death c. 1319 had in Littledean a messuage, 51 a., and rents worth £3 17s. 5d. from 18 freehold estates.[23] His lands, placed in the guardianship of his wife Isabel in

85 Glos. R.O., D 36/M 55.
86 Surv. of Crawley-Boevey est. 1797 (no. 21).
87 Glouc. Jnl. 17 June 1793; 23 Mar. 1801.
88 Glos. R.O., D 4304/17; cf. Slater's Dir. Glos. (1852–3), 148; (1858–9), 215; Burke, Land. Gent. (1846), ii. 1089; Glos. R.O., D 1388/SL 5, no. 53.
89 Glos. R.O., D 36/M 55.
90 G.D.R. wills 1711/40; Glos. R.O., D 36/E 12, ff. 56v.–57.
91 Glos. Subsidy Roll, 1327, 44.
92 P.R.O., E 301/23, no. 36.
93 Cf. E.H.R. xix. 121.
94 Bodl. MS. Rawl. C. 790, f. 28v.
95 Eccl. Misc. 99.
96 Trans. B.G.A.S. lxxxiii. 98.
97 Atkyns, Glos. 382.
98 Rudder, Glos. 402.   99 Census, 1801–1981.
1 B.L. Harl. MS. 4131, ff. 484, 500.
2 Glos. R.O., Q/SIb 1, ff. 145v., 148, 149v., 151 and v., 154.
3 Ibid. D 4431, deed 20 Dec. 22 Chas. II; D 36/E 12, ff. 43v.–44, 65v.–66.
4 Surv. of Crawley-Boevey est. 1797 (no. 7).
5 Glos. R.O., D 543, Littledean deeds 1664–1875.

6 Ibid. Bell inn deeds 1734–1860.
7 Ibid. D 2123, pp. 157, 159.
8 Ibid. P 110/VE 2/1; D 2568.
9 Ibid. Q/REl 1A, St. Briavels.
10 Kelly's Dir. Glos. (1870), 590–1; Glos. R.O., DA 24/100/5, p. 237.
11 Kelly's Dir. Glos. (1889), 753.
12 Licensed Houses in Glos. 1903, 136–7.
13 Poor Law Abstract, 1804, 172–3.
14 Glos. R.O., Q/RSf 2; RZ 1.
15 Glouc. Jnl. 15 July 1843; 5 Aug. 1865.
16 Glos. R.O., P 110/IN 3/5; ibid. CW 2/5.
17 Bibliotheca Glos. i. 32, 196–7; ii, pp. xxxviii–xxxix; Vindication of Ric. Atkyns (1669), 20–1.
18 Bibliotheca Glos. i. 93, 327–8; the tradition that the massacre was at Dean Hall is recorded in ibid. ii, pp. lxxxvi–lxxxvii.
19 Dom. Bk. (Rec. Com.), i. 167v.; below, Mitcheldean, manor; cf. Taylor, Dom. Glos. 25, 204.
20 Above, intro.
21 P.R.O., E 32/30, rot. 18; Inq. p.m. Glos. 1236–1300, 24.
22 Inq. p.m. Glos. 1236–1300, 159–60.
23 Ibid. 1302–58, 172–3, 204–6; below, Mitcheldean, manor.

1320, were eventually divided between his infant daughters Joan and Isabel.[24] The Littledean possessions later became known as the manor of *LITTLEDEAN*.[25] Custody of a bailiwick in the royal demesne woodland of the Forest was probably held with the Littledean lands before 1282 when the bailiwick was in the king's hands.[26] It was restored some time after 1319[27] to the lords of the part of the manor acquired by Isabel of Dean,[28] and in 1565 the Littledean bailiwick, also known as Badcocks Bailey, was held by Richard Baynham (d. 1580) evidently by virtue of his reversionary right to that part of the manor.[29] The estate later passed to the Vaughans and they were recorded as woodwards of the bailiwick until the late 17th century.[30]

William of Dean's elder daughter Joan received his Mitcheldean possessions and in 1436 her descendant Robert Baynham[31] had rents totalling £3 2s. 7d. in Littledean.[32] Robert died later in 1436 and his Littledean and Mitcheldean estates descended to William Baynham (d. 1568) and were retained by William's widow Anne in jointure in 1573. By 1608 William's son Joseph[33] held a quarter of Littledean manor[34] and at his death in 1613 was succeeded by his son Alexander.[35] The Littledean estate apparently passed with Mitcheldean in 1694 to Maynard Colchester.[36]

Isabel, William of Dean's other daughter, married Ralph of Abenhall[37] (d. c. 1347), whose daughter and heir Margaret, wife in turn of Lawrence Greyndour and Robert of Huntley, had rents in Littledean at her death in 1375.[38] By 1354 Isabel was married to John Basset,[39] who died in 1362 leaving infant daughters, Margaret and Alice (d. 1367).[40] Margaret married Walter Brown and in 1383 they conveyed a quarter of Littledean manor to John Greyndour,[41] the son and heir of Margaret of Huntley.[42] John died in 1415 or 1416 and his part of the manor descended with his estate in Abenhall and Mitcheldean, which passed at the death of Thomas Baynham in 1611 to the Vaughan family.[43] By 1634 the Vaughans' share of the manor was described as two thirds[44] and

in 1659 John Vaughan sold it to Henry Heane, whose family already owned land in Littledean.[45] Henry, who was vicar of Olveston, died in 1661 and his share of the manor passed first to his wife Elizabeth and secondly, in 1676, to his son Henry, rector of Great Witcombe.[46] In 1679 John Parker of Hasfield, the mortgagee, took possession of the estate, which included fishing rights in the river Severn near Broadoak.[47] He died in 1692 leaving it to his daughters Mary, Eleanor, Margaret, and Elizabeth, who sold it in 1700 to Maynard Colchester of Westbury-on-Severn.[48] Maynard, who had apparently inherited another portion of the manor,[49] was regarded as sole lord of Littledean[50] and the manorial rights passed with his Wilderness estate near Mitcheldean and belonged in the early 20th century to M. W. Colchester-Wemyss.[51] A house in which the Misses Parker held courts from 1693 became known locally as the manor house.[52] It stood near the church on the west side of Church Street.[53]

Flaxley abbey had acquired lands in Littledean by 1269.[54] Known sometimes as the manor of *LITTLEDEAN*[55] they were granted with the abbey's other estates to Sir William Kingston in 1537.[56] Some of the Littledean land descended, under a long lease granted by Anthony Kingston in 1591 and acquired by James Hawkins in 1612, with the Grange estate in Flaxley.[57] Anthony Kingston's son William[58] was among the lords of Littledean in 1608.[59] The Kingstons' successors at Flaxley owned land in Littledean[60] and included the Crawley-Boeveys, who had sold some cottages by the mid 1730s.[61] Sir Thomas Crawley-Boevey, Bt., retained 5 a. in the parish in 1839.[62]

The Brayne family, which owned a substantial estate in Littledean in the 17th century, was descended from Richard Brayne to whom John Greyndour in 1388 granted the reversion of a house and 36 a. held for life by Margery Hayward.[63] The house, known in the early 17th century as *HAYWARDS* or *THE COURT HOUSE*,[64] became the chief house of an estate which passed from Richard Brayne (d. 1572) in

[24] *Cal. Close*, 1318–23, 173–4.
[25] *Cal. Pat.* 1381–5; P.R.O., C 139/149, no. 23; C 142/189, no. 82.
[26] *Trans. B.G.A.S.* xiv. 367–8.
[27] *Inq. p.m. Glos.* 1302–58, 169–71.
[28] Below, this section.
[29] Glos. R.O., D 2026/X 3; P.R.O., C 142/189, no. 82.
[30] Below, this section; Hart, *Royal Forest*, 275; Glos. R.O., D 36/Q 2.   [31] Below, Mitcheldean, manor.
[32] P.R.O., SC 6/858/15, rot. 3 and d.
[33] Ibid. C 139/79, no. 15; C 142/42, no. 112; C 142/149, no. 129; C 142/164, no. 62.
[34] Smith, *Men and Armour*, 33; Glos. R.O., D 33/271.
[35] P.R.O., C 142/335, no. 32.
[36] Below, Mitcheldean, manor.
[37] *Trans. B.G.A.S.* vi. 130.
[38] *Cal. Inq. p.m.* ix, pp. 4–5; x, p. 360; xiv, pp. 140–1.
[39] *Cal. Chart. R.* 1341–1417, 141.
[40] *Cal. Inq. p.m.* xi, p. 224; xv, p. 193.
[41] *Cal. Pat.* 1381–5, 59, 267, 295.
[42] *Cal. Inq. p.m.* xiv, pp. 140–1.
[43] Above, Abenhall, manor; below, Mitcheldean, manor; P.R.O., C 139/149, no. 23; C 142/113, no. 49; C 142/340, no. 192; E 134/22 Jas. I Hil./3; Glos. R.O., D 36/E 29, M 49.
[44] P.R.O., CP 25/2/527/9 Chas. I Hil. no. 7.
[45] Glos. R.O., D 36/T 16.
[46] Ibid.; W. C. Heane, *Gen. Notes relating to Heane Fam.*

(1887), 9, 11–12.
[47] Glos. R.O., D 36/E 32, M 54–6.
[48] Ibid. T 16; *V.C.H. Glos.* viii. 284.
[49] Above, this section.
[50] Atkyns, *Glos.* 381.
[51] Below, Mitcheldean, manor; Rudder, *Glos.* 402; *Kelly's Dir. Glos.* (1856–1927 edns.).
[52] Glos. R.O., D 36/M 64–8; E 9, ff. 34v.–35.
[53] Ibid. E 11, ff. 31v.–32; T 16; D 2957/101.5.
[54] P.R.O., JUST 1/275, rot. 35d.; C 139/84, no. 76; cf. *Valor Eccl.* (Rec. Com.), ii. 486.
[55] P.R.O., JUST 1/275, rot. 35d.; CP 25/2/420/5 Chas. I Mich. no. 29.
[56] *L. & P. Hen. VIII*, xii (1), p. 353; cf. ibid. xviii (1), p. 124.
[57] Glos. R.O., D 2172/1/71; above, Flaxley, manor.
[58] P.R.O., C 142/231, no. 94.
[59] Smith, *Men and Armour*, 33.
[60] Surv. of Sir Thos. Crawley-Boevey's estates 1797 (nos. 7, 9, 21): copy in Glos. R.O., MF 285; Glos. R.O., D 4431, deed 22 Feb. 18 Chas. II; above, Flaxley, manor.
[61] Glos. R.O., D 543, Littledean deeds 1733–91; Bell inn deeds 1734–1860.
[62] G.D.R., T 1/114.
[63] *Cal. Pat.* 1381–5, 295; in 1437 Littledean landholders included John Brayne: P.R.O., C 139/84, no. 76.
[64] P.R.O., C 142/385, no. 18; it was also known as the Court Place: Glos. R.O., D 2172/1/72.

turn to his wife Jane and his grandson Thomas Brayne.[65] From Thomas (d. 1604) it passed in jointure to his wife Catherine,[66] who married John Winford[67] and retained the estate in 1638. By 1641 it had reverted under Thomas's will to Ketford Brayne,[68] who, though a royalist, escaped sequestration.[69] Ketford died in 1682[70] and John Brayne, who fell heavily into debt, sold the house and some land in 1710 to Eustace Hardwicke. In 1715, as part of a settlement of Chancery suits between them, Eustace conveyed the house and land back to John and in 1716 John sold the estate, which included land in adjoining parts of Flaxley and Newland, to his attorney and principal creditor, Walter Roberts of Ross-on-Wye (Herefs.). Walter (d. by 1734) was succeeded by his son James. In 1770 James sold the estate to the attorneys Robert Pyrke and Selwyn James of Newnham and in 1775 they conveyed it to trustees for sale to pay their joint debts. After his partner's death in 1780 Selwyn James took legal action to force a sale and c. 1785 the estate was sold to George Skipp.[71] George, who also acquired the adjoining Grange estate, died in 1804 and the Court House and its lands evidently passed in turn to his wife Frances (d. 1823) and son George.[72] George (d. 1837) left the estate to his wife Hannah and in 1845 she conveyed the house and c. 155 a. to her son Francis Skipp.[73] In 1861 the house and most of the land were sold to the ironmaster Henry Crawshay (d. 1879) and in 1884 they were bought by the Mitcheldean brewer Thomas Wintle. He died in 1888 and his trustees sold the house and 60 a. in 1906 to William Smith, the tenant farmer.[74] In 1984 the house and some land were bought by Mr. Frank Thorpe.[75] The Court House, which had become a farmhouse by the early 18th century[76] and was later known as Court Farm, was on the south side of Broad Street near the north-western end of the village.[77] It was occupied by a farm bailiff by the early 1850s[78] and was rebuilt as a bailiff's house in the 1860s or 1870s.[79]

A house outside the village by the Newnham road, known by 1628 as Littledean Hall and later as *DEAN HALL*,[80] became the centre of an estate built up by the Pyrke family. The house belonged until 1611 to the Cockshoot estate in Newnham, which Richard Brayne settled in 1552 on his son John,[81] later described as of Newent. In 1599 John, together with his son Richard, sold the estate to his nephew Thomas Brayne (d. 1604) and in 1606 Richard, who under Thomas's will had a reversionary right, acquired it outright from Thomas's widow Catherine.[82] Richard sold the house in Littledean in 1611 to Richard Brayne of Bristol, a grocer, who sold it in 1612 to Charles Bridgeman of Poulton Court in Awre.[83] Charles, who bought land around the house, made it his residence[84] and at his death in 1643 left the small estate to his wife Catherine[85] (fl. 1657). His grandson Charles Bridgeman sold it first in 1657 to John Wade,[86] the chief administrator of the Forest of Dean,[87] and having bought it back from Wade in 1662,[88] secondly in 1664 to Thomas Pyrke of Abenhall,[89] a landowner at Mitcheldean.[90] Thomas took up residence in the house and enlarged the estate,[91] which at his death in 1702 passed to his wife Anne in jointure. She released it in 1703 to his son and heir Nathaniel in return for an annuity.[92] Nathaniel, who in 1710 added the Cockshoot to the estate,[93] died in 1715 leaving his son Thomas as his heir.[94] From Thomas (d. 1752) the estate passed in turn to his wife Dorothy (d. 1762) and his great-nephew Joseph Watts.[95] Joseph, who changed his surname to Pyrke, took possession in 1764[96] and died in 1803 leaving the estate of 185 a. in Littledean and Newnham to his son Joseph Pyrke[97] (d. 1851). From the latter it passed to his son Duncombe (d. 1893), whose son Duncombe[98] broke it up by sales. In 1897 H. J. Austin, a Lancaster architect, bought the house and c. 30 a. and in 1898 he sold the same to John Penberthy.[99] Penberthy, who bought other land in and around Littledean,[1] died in 1927 and,

65 P.R.O., C 142/164, no. 61; PROB 11/54 (P.C.C. 20 Daper), ff. 148v.–150; for the Braynes, *Trans. B.G.A.S.* vi. 296–9.

66 P.R.O., PROB 11/104 (P.C.C. 53 Harte), ff. 38v.–40v.

67 Glos. R.O., D 4431, deed 20 Aug. 13 Jas. I.

68 Ibid. D 1681/T 13; cf. P.R.O., PROB 11/104 (P.C.C. 53 Harte), ff. 38v.–40v.; C 142/288, no. 112; C 142/385, no. 18.

69 *Cal. Cttee. for Compounding*, i. 87.

70 G.D.R., V 1/147.

71 Glos. R.O., D 543, Mitcheldean brewery, legal papers 1907; D 2957/101.8–10, 12, 19–21, 32.

72 Above, Flaxley, manor; cf. Glos. R.O., P 110/VE 2/1, poor rate 1820; D 36/E 13, ff. 47v.–48; G.D.R., T 1/114 suggests that Geo., the son, shared the Court Ho. estate as well as the Grange with others.

73 Glos. R.O., D 2568, deed 31 Dec. 1846; D 1438, misc. papers, Skipp fam. pedigree; D 543, Mitcheldean brewery, legal papers 1907.

74 Ibid. D 543, Court Farm sale partics. 1860; Mitcheldean brewery, legal papers 1907; deed (copy) 2 Feb. 1884; D 2299/608; *Glos. N. & Q.* iv. 285–6.

75 Inf. from Mr. F. Thorpe.

76 Glos. R.O., D 543, Mitcheldean brewery, legal papers 1907.

77 Ibid. D 2957/101.20; O.S. Map 6", Glos. XXXI. SE. (1883 edn.).

78 P.R.O., HO 107/1959; *Kelly's Dir. Glos.* (1856), 320.

79 Cf. Glos. R.O., D 2299/608.

80 Ibid. D 4431, deeds 20 July 4 Chas. I; 6 Dec. 4 Jas.

II; Atkyns, *Glos.* 381.

81 Glos. R.O., D 4431, deed 28 Mar. 6 Edw. VI.

82 Ibid. deed 6 May 4 Jas. I; P.R.O., PROB 11/104 (P.C.C. 53 Harte), ff. 38v.–40v.; for the Braynes, *Trans. B.G.A.S.* vi. 296–9.

83 Glos. R.O., D 4431, deeds 10 May 9 Jas. I; 28 Jan. 10 Jas. I; 20 Aug. 13 Jas. I.

84 Ibid. deeds 2 Apr. 16 Jas. I; 20 Apr. 17 Jas. I; 20 Sept. 18 Jas. I; D 2957/101.23.

85 G.D.R. wills 1644/14; Bigland, *Glos.* i. 453.

86 Glos. R.O., D 4431, deed 15 Apr. 1657.

87 Hart, *Royal Forest*, 140, 150.

88 Glos. R.O., D 4431, deed 1 May 14 Chas. II.

89 Cf. ibid. deed 8 Sept. 16 Chas. II; P.R.O., CP 25/2/656/16 & 17 Chas. II Hil. no. 23.

90 Below, Mitcheldean, intro.

91 Glos. R.O., D 4431, deeds 21 Feb. 18 Chas. II; 18 Mar. 24 Chas. II; 20 Oct. 27 Chas. II; 26 May 31 Chas. II.

92 Ibid. deeds 28 and 29 Apr. 2 Anne; Bigland, *Glos.* i. 452.

93 Glos. R.O., D 4431, deed 11 Aug. 9 Anne.

94 Bigland, *Glos.* i. 3; G.D.R. wills 1715/319.

95 Bigland, *Glos.* i. 452–3; G.D.R. wills 1752/38; Fosbrooke, *Glos.* ii. 162.

96 Glos. R.O., D 1438, Littledean and Notgrove deeds 1766–1851.

97 Ibid. Pyrke fam. wills 1702–1852; G.D.R., T 1/114, 129.

98 Glos. R.O., D 1438, Pyrke fam. wills 1760–1858; Burke, *Land. Gent.* (1898), ii. 1227.

99 Glos. R.O., D 1438, Littledean sale papers.

1 Ibid. D 2299/3829.

following the death of his wife Eleanor in 1938, his daughter Eleanor, wife of E. W. Jacques,[2] sold the house to M. G. Corbet-Singleton (d. 1964). Corbet-Singleton's widow Enid left it in 1975 to Mr. David Macer-Wright, whose son, Mr. D. M. Macer-Wright, was the owner in 1989.[3]

The north–south range of Dean Hall is probably of the 16th century and has a conventional three-roomed plan. In the early 17th century a new parlour wing, apparently re-using older foundations, was added to the north end. A service wing to the west of the south end of the main range may also be of the 17th century but it was remodelled in the 18th and 19th centuries. Minor additions were made to the north wing in the early 19th century and it was refronted to incorporate the attics and given a central entrance porch in 1852.[4] At the same time gates were built to the south on the Newnham road at the end of a drive which followed the old line of the road on the east side of the house.[5] From the late 1850s the house, while it belonged to the Pyrke family, was occupied by tenants, including from 1877 the barrister F. E. Guise (d. 1893).[6]

In 1688 Lincoln College, Oxford, acquired a rent charge of £14 in Littledean to support scholarships established under the will of Thomas Marshall.[7] The college apparently received a rent of £12 in the late 18th century.[8]

In the later Middle Ages the tithes of Littledean belonged to St. Bartholomew's hospital, Gloucester,[9] which by the later 16th century usually leased them to the curate of Littledean. The rent charge for which they were commuted in 1840 was used to augment the incumbent's living in 1867.[10] Tithe-free land in the parish presumably represented the estate of Flaxley abbey, which as a Cistercian house was exempt from paying tithes from land which it had brought into cultivation.[11]

ECONOMIC HISTORY.
AGRICULTURE. In the 1230s corn was grown on assarted land in Littledean held by William of Dean.[12] In 1282, as a result of encroachments on Crown land by William and his son Henry, Henry held 26 a. of cultivated land, a pasture close containing 15 a.,

and 2 a. of woodland in Littledean, and seven tenants under him, including 5 cottagers, shared 2½ a. there.[13] In addition to the assarts Henry of Dean's estate in Littledean in 1292 included 2 yardlands described as thicket or undergrowth,[14] and in 1319 that of William of Dean, most of whose 102 a. of assarted land was evidently there, included a yardland (48 a.) of arable, 3 a. of meadow, and rents from 18 freeholders.[15] In 1436 Robert Baynham, holding a part of the manor, received rents ranging between 4d. and 2s. 2d. for 65 holdings from 43 tenants, most if not all freeholders, and rents ranging from 6d. to 8s. for seven holdings outside the manor in Littledean and Newnham.[16] On another part of the manor 13 freeholders and 3 leaseholders paid chief rents to Baynham Vaughan in 1632[17] and at least 23 freeholders paid rents to John Parker in 1686.[18] In 1785 Maynard Colchester received chief rents from 20 small freehold estates, two or three of them outside the manor at Blackmore's Hale and Elton in Westbury-on-Severn.[19] By ancient custom some freeholders owed heriots and, from 1653 at the latest, a fine on selling any land.[20] Such customary payments were claimed in Littledean as late as 1906.[21] In 1535 Flaxley abbey had rents and farms worth £10 17s. 2d. clear from its lands in Littledean and, presumably, adjoining parts of Flaxley and Newnham.[22] In or soon after 1618 owners of former assarts, many of which were contiguous to the Forest, secured their titles by paying compositions to the Crown.[23]

William of Dean's estate, as extended in 1319, had 2 neifs, both owing rents and three days' work in the harvest, in Littledean.[24] In 1686 John Parker received rents from at least 14 leaseholders, 3 of whom owed an additional payment of a hen.[25] A few tenancies were at will.[26] In the early 18th century many cottage holdings created by squatter development were held under the Colchesters on leases for three lives or 99 years.[27] In 1785 Maynard Colchester had 6 tenants holding ½ a.–9¼ a. at rack rent, 33 cottage tenants, and a tenant holding 3½ a. in Littledean.[28]

By the 16th century most land in the parish was in closes of pasture or meadow[29] and several orchards had been planted.[30] Among the livestock kept sheep were most numerous, one flock

[2] *Glouc. Jnl.* 28 Jan. 1927; mons. in churchyard.
[3] Inf. from Mr. D. M. Macer-Wright.
[4] Date on porch; photog. in Glos. R.O., D 4031/2, reproduced below, Plate 14; cf. view of ho. on map of Littledean par. 1836, in possession of Mr. D. M. Macer-Wright.
[5] Date and inits. of Duncombe Pyrke on gates; cf. Glos. R.O., Q/SRh 1819 C/2.
[6] Glos. R.O., D 1438, Littledean estate papers; *Kelly's Dir. Glos.* (1856–97 edns.); Burke; *Peerage* (1963), 1087.
[7] P.R.O., CP 25/2/778/3 & 4 Jas. II Hil. no. 13; *V.C.H. Oxon.* iii. 165 and n.
[8] Bigland, *Glos.* i. 451 n.
[9] *Cal. Papal Reg.* vi. 395–6; *V.C.H. Glos.* x. 47.
[10] Below, church.
[11] G.D.R., T 1/114; cf. *V.C.H. Glos.* ii. 94.
[12] P.R.O., E 146/1/25.
[13] Ibid. E 32/30, rot. 18.
[14] *Inq. p.m. Glos.* 1236–1300, 159–60; *Cal. Inq. p.m.* iii, p. 37, where the translation of the word *riffletum* as 'osier bed' is an unlikely reading.
[15] *Inq. p.m. Glos.* 1302–58, 172–3.
[16] P.R.O., SC 6/858/15, rot. 15 and d.; C 139/79, no. 15.
[17] Glos. R.O., D 36/M 49.
[18] Ibid. M 50.
[19] Ibid. D 2123, pp. 156–9; cf. ibid. D 36/E 9, E 11–13.
[20] Ibid. D 4431, ct. roll 17 Oct. 1653.
[21] Ibid. D 543, Court Farm sale partics. 1860; D 2299/608.
[22] *Valor Eccl.* (Rec. Com.), ii. 486; cf. above, Flaxley, econ. hist.; *V.C.H. Glos.* x. 40.
[23] Glos. R.O., D 4431, deed 22 Sept. 16 Jas. I; cf. P.R.O., C 66/2168, no. 3; Hart, *Royal Forest*, 100.
[24] *Inq. p.m. Glos.* 1302–58, 172.
[25] Glos. R.O., D 36/M 50.
[26] Ibid. M 65–6.
[27] Ibid. E 85.
[28] Ibid. D 2123, pp. 150–5, 159; cf. ibid. D 36/E 9, E 11–13.
[29] Hockaday Abs. cclx, 1493; Glos. R.O., D 2172/1/52; 1/56; D 2957/101.1; D 4431, deeds 6 Nov. 22 Eliz. I; 8 Feb. 27 Eliz. I; P.R.O., E 309/Box 1/5 Eliz. I/16, no. 1.
[30] Glos. R.O., D 4431, deeds 28 Mar. 6 Edw. VI; 8 Feb. 27 Eliz. I; 15 Mar. 43 Eliz. I; P.R.O., C 142/164, no. 61.

using a sheepcot erected near Collafield by 1638,[31] but many people also had pigs[32] and some cattle.[33] Tenants of land in Littledean enjoyed common rights in the extraparochial land of the Forest of Dean, including Abbots wood, in the mid 17th century.[34] Those rights, for which the parish paid 3s. 4d. herbage money in the late 18th century,[35] were exercised by six people in 1860.[36] Five Littledean holdings continued to enjoy common rights for horses, cattle, and sheep in Abbots wood until 1872.[37] Throughout the parish, and particularly on the west side, were areas of waste ground. Some of that land was evidently used for grazing and an area on Dean hill was described as a common in 1618.[38] Inclosure of the waste, which had begun by the mid 17th century and continued into the 20th, was mostly for cottages and gardens.[39] Some land taken in from the waste on the north-east side of the parish adjoining Chestnuts hill had been planted with orchards or potatoes by 1754.[40] In 1801 only 46 a. in the parish were said to be under arable crops, mostly wheat and barley.[41] In 1866, when the area returned as arable was 70 a., half of which grew turnips and other forage crops, permanent grassland accounted for at least 260 a.[42] The numbers of sheep and pigs returned were 290 and 179 respectively and very few cattle were recorded.[43] At the end of the century and in the early 20th even less land was under arable cultivation and most was given over to grassland and sheep farming. Some beef and dairy cattle were kept.[44] A market gardener lived in Littledean in 1885[45] and orchards covered at least 66 a. in the enlarged parish in 1896.[46] Cider production on one farm expanded in the early 20th century into a business supplying cider and perry wholesale to inns in a wide area, an enterprise that failed after 1950.[47] Littledean had a small area of commercial plum orchards in the later 1980s when most of the land remained under grass and one of the larger farms was devoted to dairying and another to sheep raising.[48]

There have been many smallholdings and few large farms in Littledean. Parishioners usually combined husbandry with a trade[49] and in 1831 only 9 of 158 families depended chiefly on agriculture for a livelihood. Many more families evidently derived some support from farming[50]

and in 1851 the inhabitants included 2 full-time farmers, 2 farm bailiffs, and a haulier, an innkeeper, and a teacher with small farms, and 44 agricultural labourers.[51] In the late 1830s Court farm, part of which was in Flaxley, had 120 a.,[52] Dean Hall farm 55 a., and most other holdings under 20 a.[53] In 1863 the inhabitants, apart from the two principal farmers, were labourers, craftsmen and small shopkeepers.[54] Court farm, the tenancy of which had passed to the ironmaster Stephen Allaway by the early 1850s,[55] had been reduced to 60 a. by 1883.[56] For the enlarged parish 31 separate holdings, most worked by tenants, were returned in 1896.[57] Some amalgamation had taken place by 1926[58] when 16 separate holdings were returned, of which 7 were under 20 a. and another 6 under 50 a.[59] In the later 1980s Littledean had two farms with 100 ha. (c. 247 a.) or more and at least eight holdings of 20 ha. (c. 50 a.) or less worked by part-time farmers.[60]

MILLS. In the early 1280s there was an old mill north-east of Littledean below Chestnuts hill[61] and in 1382 two men surnamed 'atte mill' were granted land in Littledean.[62] A mill, apparently that belonging to John Player in 1515,[63] stood below Chestnuts hill on the stream north of the Gloucester road and was owned by the Pomfrey family in the mid 16th century. Richard Pomfrey, a weaver, sold it in 1577 to Thomas Pinfold, a Stroud mercer,[64] and in 1597, when Pinfold sold it to Rowland Heane, it was a grist mill.[65] Ownership of the mill, which was occupied in 1619 by John Swift[66] and was operated from 1674 by Ephraim Sansom of Blackmore's Hale, descended to Thomas Heane of Tockington, who in 1679 sold it to Thomas Pyrke.[67] The mill was in use in 1785[68] but the principal building had been removed by 1836.[69] Another building, dating from the early 19th century and standing downstream on the parish boundary,[70] was derelict in 1989.

OTHER INDUSTRY AND TRADE. Littledean was the home of ironworking and metal trades by the mid 13th century, when four itinerant forges fuelled by timber or charcoal were operating there.[71] Henry of Dean felled a grove before 1282 to provide charcoal[72] and among the forges at

31 Glos. R.O., D 2957/101.25.
32 Ibid. D 36/M 57–61.
33 Ibid. D 4431, deed 15 Mar. 43 Eliz. I.
34 P.R.O., E 134/13 Chas. II East./24.
35 Glos. R.O., P 110/OV 2/1; ibid. CW 2/1; 5th Rep. Dean Forest Com. 65 and nn., 67.
36 P.R.O., F 3/128, letter 29 Nov. 1860.
37 Glos. R.O., Q/RI 52.
38 Ibid. D 4431, deed 2 Apr. 16 Jas. I.
39 Ibid. D 36/M 51–68, M 74; DA 24/100/3, pp. 98–9; 12, pp. 21–2.   40 Ibid. D 36/M 68.
41 List & Index Soc. clxxxix, p. 174.
42 P.R.O., MAF 68/26/9.   43 Ibid. MAF 68/25/20.
44 Ibid. MAF 68/1609/12; MAF 68/3295/16; Acreage Returns, 1905.   45 Kelly's Dir. Glos. (1885), 440.
46 P.R.O., MAF 68/1609/12.
47 H. Phelps, Forest of Dean (1982), 132–4.
48 Agric. Returns 1988.
49 Cf. Kelly's Dir. Glos. (1856), 320; (1863), 303–4.
50 Census, 1831; cf. ibid. 1811.
51 P.R.O., HO 107/1959.
52 Glos. R.O., D 2172/1/55.

53 G.D.R., T 1/114.   54 P.R.O., ED 7/34/194.
55 Glos. R.O., P 110/CW 2/3; Kelly's Dir. Glos. (1856), 320.
56 Glos. R.O., D 2299/608.
57 P.R.O., MAF 68/1609/12.
58 Cf. G.D.R., T 1/114; Glos. R.O., D 2299/3829.
59 P.R.O., MAF 68/3295/16.
60 Agric. Returns 1988.
61 Trans. B.G.A.S. xiv. 360.
62 P.R.O., CP 25/1/78/79, no. 48.
63 Hockaday Abs. cclx.   64 Glos. R.O., D 2957/101.1.
65 Ibid. D 4431, deed 6 Aug. 39 Eliz. I.
66 Ibid. D 36/T 16; it was called Swift's Mill on a late 17th-century map: P.R.O., F 17/7.
67 Glos. R.O., D 4431, deeds 20 Dec. 22 Chas. II; 3 Nov. 26 Chas. II; 26 May 31 Chas. II.
68 Ibid. D 2123, p. 159; cf. ibid. D 36/E 11, ff. 38v.–39; E 12, ff. 55v.–56.
69 Map of Littledean par. 1836.
70 O.S. Map 6", Glos. XXXI. SE. (1883 edn.).
71 P.R.O., E 146/1/25; cf. ibid. E 32/29, rot. 2; E 32/31, m. 15.
72 Hart, Royal Forest, 261.

work in Littledean at that time was one belonging to a sharesmith.[73] Nailmaking had been established by 1327, when a nailer was one of the wealthier inhabitants,[74] and became the most important trade in Littledean. Seventeen nailers listed in 1608 included men of some wealth, notably members of the Robinson family[75] whose descendants were in the trade until the 19th century.[76] Among the craftsmen of the parish in 1608 were also two pinners.[77]

The early forges and furnaces, one of which was owned by Richard Brayne (d. 1504), smelted ore mined locally.[78] The scale of the industry is indicated by the deposits of cinders or slag found by roads throughout the parish in the later 17th century.[79] In the west at Callamore and Pennywell and in the south-east they formed prominent tumps.[80] Littledean was one of the principal ironworking centres in the Forest area in the early 1560s, when three local smithholders or ironmasters, including members of the Hawkins family, bought most of the coppice wood in the Crown demesne woodlands for making charcoal.[81] Metal trades, principally nailmaking, remained a major source of employment long after 1672, when five or more forges were operating in the parish.[82] By the later 17th century the cinder tips were being removed for resmelting[83] and in 1680 John Parker agreed to sell cinders on the waste ground of his manorial estate to the Flaxley furnace; they were being taken there from Pennywell in 1710.[84] The Colchesters removed cinders from Callamore in the mid 18th century[85] but the digging of cinders had apparently ended by the 1780s.[86]

Miners were recorded in Littledean from the mid 13th century[87] and eleven miners and a collier were listed in the parish in 1608.[88] The number of coal miners probably increased in the 17th century,[89] when squatters migrated from the Forest to Littledean,[90] and 12 coal miners were exempted in 1718 from paying parish rates on their cottages evidently because of poverty.[91] The mining community was centred on Callamore, where at least eight coal miners lived in 1728.[92] Coal has been mined on that side of the

parish[93] but most colliers presumably worked in adjoining parts of the Forest. A marlpit was dug in Littledean before 1280[94] and deposits of iron ore and ochre to the west and south-west of Littledean had been exploited by the 17th century.[95] In 1608 a parishioner was employed carrying red ochre (raddle).[96] In the late 17th century limestone was quarried and burnt at Callamore,[97] at the top end of which a limekiln, perhaps that standing near Colloegrove in 1668,[98] continued to operate in the early 18th century.[99]

Littledean's importance as an industrial and local trading centre is indicated by the large number of craftsmen and tradesmen listed in the parish in 1608; of the 107 men named only 6 were described as husbandmen.[1] Nearby woodland supported several industries and crafts, including the making of hoops in the 1550s,[2] shovels and trenchers in the 1600s,[3] and saddletrees in the 1640s.[4] It also supplied bark for tanning, which had been introduced to Littledean by 1597.[5] The principal tannery, worked by Rowland Heane (d. 1610) and his son David (d. 1619),[6] was near the church[7] and possibly remained in use in the mid 1740s.[8] Two glovers were listed in 1608.[9] In the 1790s the merchant Joseph Boughton, a member of a Broadoak family, lived in Littledean and was active in the timber trade.[10] Although cloth was stolen at Littledean in 1377[11] and a few weavers lived in the parish in the late 16th century[12] and several clothiers in the later 17th century,[13] the textile trades were not strong. Three weavers were listed in 1608, when the inhabitants included two chapmen, a tinker, and a bone lacemaker and the more usual country crafts and trades were represented by a smith, four carpenters, two joiners, three butchers, and a tiler.[14] In 1766 there was a thatcher.[15] Few members of the professional classes have pursued careers in Littledean. Exceptions were an architect and a surgeon, both of the Steel family, in the early 18th century.[16]

In the later 18th century many poor inhabitants continued to depend on nailmaking and mining for a livelihood.[17] Although several nailmakers such as Philip Robinson (d. 1809), who

73 P.R.O., E 32/30, rot. 23d.
74 *Glos. Subsidy Roll, 1327*, 44; cf. P.R.O., SC 6/858/13, rot. 3 and d.
75 Smith, *Men and Armour*, 34–5.
76 Glos. R.O., D 543, Littledean deed 24 Feb. 9 Wm. III; D 36/E 12, ff. 61v.–62; *Glouc. Jnl.* 7 Aug. 1809.
77 Smith, *Men and Armour*, 34.
78 Hockaday Abs. cclx, 1504.
79 Glos. R.O., D 36/M 52–68.
80 Ibid. E 13, ff. 6v.–8; M 74; D 2123, pp. 152, 155, 159; G.D.R., T 1/114.
81 Glos. R.O., D 2026/X 3; P.R.O., PROB 11/54 (P.C.C. 20 Daper, will of Ric. Brayne), ff. 148v.–150.
82 P.R.O., E 179/247/14, rot. 37d.
83 Glos. R.O., D 36/M 52–68, M 74.
84 Ibid. E 30–1, M 72.   85 Ibid. E 13, ff. 7v.–8.
86 Cf. Rudder, *Glos.* 401; Bigland, *Glos.* i. 451.
87 P.R.O., JUST 1/275, rot. 35d.; cf. Glos. R.O., D 2172/1/61; D 2957/101.1.   88 Smith, *Men and Armour*, 34.
89 Cf. Glos. R.O., Q/SIb 1, ff. 3v.–4.
90 Ibid. D 36/M 55, M 63, M 67; Hart, *Free Miners*, 207, 247.
91 Glos. R.O., Q/SO 4, p. 190.
92 Ibid. D 36/E 85.
93 O.S. Map 1/2,500, Glos. XXXI. 12 (1886 edn.).
94 P.R.O., E 32/30, rot. 21.
95 Bodl. MS. Rawl. B. 323, f. 106v.; for mining of ochre,

below, Forest of Dean, industry.
96 Smith, *Men and Armour*, 34.
97 Glos. R.O., D 36/M 65–6.   98 Ibid. D 1681/T 15.
99 Ibid. D 36/E 9, ff. 35v.–36; E 11, ff. 32v.–33.
1 Smith, *Men and Armour*, 33–5.
2 P.R.O., REQ 2/251/44.
3 Smith, *Men and Armour*, 34; cf. Hart, *Royal Forest*, 86 and n.
4 P.R.O., LRRO 5/7A, cert. of timber felled, May 1647.
5 Glos. R.O., D 4431, deed 6 Aug. 39 Eliz. I.
6 G.D.R. wills 1611/126; 1619/22; Bigland, *Glos.* i. 453; Smith, *Men and Armour*, 33–4.
7 Glos. R.O., D 36/M 59; D 4431, deeds 20 Sept. 14 Jas. I; 18 Mar. 24 Chas. II.
8 Ibid. D 36/R 1; E 12, ff. 56v.–57, 129v.–130; Q/RNc 4/13.
9 Smith, *Men and Armour*, 34.
10 *Univ. Brit. Dir.* ii (1792), 776; *Glouc. Jnl.* 15 Apr., 17 June 1793; 23 Mar. 1801; cf. *Trans. B.G.A.S.* xcvii. 98–9.
11 P.R.O., JUST 1/293, rot. 1.
12 Ibid. REQ 2/251/44; Glos. R.O., D 2957/101.1.
13 P.R.O., E 134/13 Chas. II East./24; Glos. R.O., D 1681/T 15; cf. Bigland, *Glos.* i. 454.
14 Smith, *Men and Armour*, 33–5.
15 Glos. R.O., D 543, Littledean deed 11 Mar. 1766.
16 Ibid. P 110/CW 3/1; Bigland, *Glos.* i. 454.
17 Rudder, *Glos.* 401.

took over his uncle's business in 1776[18] and acquired some coalworks, prospered, the trade was mostly in the hands of poor labourers working individually.[19] In 1851 it gave employment to 28 parishioners[20] but in the later 19th century it was gradually abandoned and by the First World War had virtually ceased.[21] The mining population of the west part of the parish grew as new and deeper mines were opened, particularly from the late 1820s, around Cinderford.[22] In 1851 it comprised 49 coal miners and 15 iron miners[23] and in 1872 or 1873 the Forest branch of the Amalgamated Association of Miners formed a lodge in Littledean.[24] Among the new pits in the Forest the St. Annals, Perseverance, and Buckshraft iron mines, which extended under Littledean, were closed in 1899.[25] From the 18th century quarrying and limeburning in Littledean were probably on a small scale.[26] In the late 19th century two quarries were reopened, one of them, in the Ruffitt above Callamore, by M. W. Colchester-Wemyss. The other, near St. White's, was worked after the First World War.[27]

In the mid 19th century other inhabitants followed trades usually found in large villages and some, including in 1851 a coal agent, a tinplate worker, a patten-ring maker, a stock taker at an iron foundry, and a number of coke workers and railway labourers, presumably worked in the industrial area centred on Cinderford. There was also a number of small shopkeepers in Littledean,[28] where in 1912 the Cinderford co-operative society opened a shop.[29] A small malting industry, established by the mid 18th century,[30] was represented in the early 1850s by three maltsters, of whom one, Joseph Bennett, also traded as a grocer, draper, ironmonger, druggist, and nailmaker. At that time other residents included two curriers and an auctioneer[31] and several ran lodging houses.[32] After the First World War the number of craftsmen and tradesmen in the parish fell,[33] and by the 1950s most of the working population travelled to factories at Cinderford and Gloucester or were employed in the Forest's remaining coal mines.[34] In 1989 the village retained several shops, and above Callamore and by the Gloucester road were coal merchants' yards.

MARKET AND FAIRS. Littledean was evidently a mart of some importance in 1276, when a monk of Leonard Stanley priory was dealing there in a wide range of merchandise.[35] In the late Middle Ages a market may have been held near the church[36] but in 1573 and later it centred on the market cross.[37] Leather was presumably traded in 1659, when Henry Heane's court appointed a searcher and sealer of leather.[38] Grain, butter, and cheese were the principal commodities bought and sold in a Saturday market at the end of the 17th century. Dealing practices, such as forestalling, engrossing, and badging of corn, drove away business and an attempt to revive the market in 1757[39] was unsuccessful.[40] Fairs held in Littledean on Whit Monday and 15 November (26 November after the calendar change of 1752) dealt in livestock, metalware, and clothing in 1724 and were mainly for the sale of pedlary in the mid 1760s.[41] In 1794 a wool fair was organized for 18 July.[42] In the mid 19th century the November fair dealt in cattle, sheep, and pigs. Together with the Whitsun fair, which had apparently been revived by 1885, it had been discontinued by the mid 1920s,[43] when a Monmouth firm of auctioneers conducted two sheep sales, in August and September, handling over 3,000 animals, including a few cattle, each year.[44] One annual sheep sale was held in 1989.[45]

LOCAL GOVERNMENT. William of Dean (d. c. 1319) held a court for Littledean.[46] The court held for the part of the manor which passed to the Vaughan family in 1611 exercised view of frankpledge and occasionally met as a court of survey.[47] Among its surviving records are papers for 1623,[48] for several years in the period 1659–1701, and for 1754[49] and a court roll for 1653.[50] The court, which apart from tenurial matters dealt with disturbances of the peace and unlicensed alehouses and enforced the assize of bread and of ale, was mostly concerned with the maintenance and cleanliness of streets, streams, and wells and the regulation of encroachments and quarrying, including digging for cinders, on waste land. The lord also claimed waifs, strays, felons' goods, and deodands.[51] The court, which in 1659 appointed an aletaster, a bread weigher, and a searcher and sealer of leather,[52] requested the lord in 1700 to repair the manor's common pound and fined two former constables in 1701

18 *Glouc. Jnl.* 4 Mar. 1776; Glos. R.O., P 110/IN 1/4.
19 *Univ. Brit. Dir.* ii (1792), 775–6; Bigland, *Glos.* i. 451.
20 P.R.O., HO 107/1959.
21 Cf. *Kelly's Dir. Glos.* (1856–1914 edns.).
22 Nicholls, *Iron Making*, 56–62; cf. *Slater's Dir. Glos.* (1852–3), 148; O.S. Maps 6", Glos. XXXI. SE., NE. (1883–4 edn.).
23 P.R.O., HO 107/1959.
24 Fisher, *Custom and Capitalism*, 75, 186.
25 *Award of Dean Forest Mining Com.* (1841), 178–80, 182, 186–7, 189–90, 198–9; Glos. R.O., Q/RUm 173/2, plans D, G; Hart, *Ind. Hist. of Dean*, 233.
26 Glos. R.O., P 110/VE 2/1, min. 2 Aug. 1826; P.R.O., HO 107/1959; *Kelly's Dir. Glos.* (1856), 320.
27 O.S. Map 6", Glos. XXXI. SE. (1883 and later edns.); Glos. R.O., D 2299/608; DA 24/100/1, p. 111; P 110/VE 2/2, p. 16.
28 P.R.O., HO 107/1959; ED 7/34/194.
29 *Glouc. Jnl.* 3 Aug. 1912.
30 Cf. Glos. R.O., D 2568, deeds 24 and 25 Mar. 1813; D 36/E 12, ff. 65v.–66.
31 *Slater's Dir. Glos.* (1852–3), 148.

32 P.R.O., HO 107/1959.
33 *Kelly's Dir. Glos.* (1914–39 edns.).
34 Glos. R.O., PA 110/2.
35 *Rot. Hund.* (Rec. Com.), i. 182.
36 Glos. R.O., D 36/M 55; cf. above, intro. (roads).
37 G.D.R. wills 1574/40; above, intro.
38 Glos. R.O., D 36/M 52.
39 *Glouc. Jnl.* 11 Jan. 1757; cf. Atkyns, *Glos.* 381.
40 Rudder, *Glos.* 401; *Univ. Brit. Dir.* ii (1792), 775.
41 *Glouc. Jnl.* 11 May 1724; 31 Oct. 1763; 28 May 1764; cf. Glos. R.O., D 5692/1; Bigland, *Glos.* i. 451.
42 *Glouc. Jnl.* 7 June 1794.
43 *Kelly's Dir. Glos.* (1856 and later edns.).
44 *Rep. on Midland Markets* (H.M.S.O. 1927), 115, 160.
45 Inf. from Mrs. J. R. Felton, of Littledean House hotel.
46 *Inq. p.m. Glos.* 1302–58, 172–3.
47 P.R.O., E 134/22 Jas. I Hil./3; Glos. R.O., D 36/E 29.
48 N.L.W., Courtfield MSS. 790.
49 Glos. R.O., D 36/M 52–68.
50 Ibid. D 4431, ct. roll 17 Oct. 1653.
51 Ibid. D 36/M 55.
52 Ibid. M 52.

for not having set watch and ward during the summer of that year.[53] It continued to deal with encroachments on the waste at least until 1834.[54]

Two churchwardens were recorded in 1445[55] and from 1543.[56] By 1716 they also administered poor relief[57] but in 1805 the offices of churchwarden and overseer of the poor were separated, the churchwardens being responsible for the administration of several charities. Most of the money needed for the church was taken from the poor rate until 1834, after which church rates were levied regularly. During the period 1799–1810, if not for longer, each overseer accounted half the year.[58] Poor relief took the usual forms, including apprenticeships for children.[59] In 1818 the vestry ordered the badging of all paupers receiving parish pay and instructed lodging house keepers not to admit tramps. The parish subscribed to the Gloucester infirmary and by 1813 it retained a surgeon or doctor to attend the poor. From 1816 one or two salaried overseers were employed.[60] In the early 19th century the parish maintained its poor in a number of houses, including some built for that purpose and some belonging to a charity.[61] In 1822 it opened a workhouse in the former Red Lion inn[62] and appointed a governor to farm the poor in it for £240, the inmates' earnings, and bastardy payments. From 1823 the workhouse was also used by the parishes of Abenhall and Flaxley, and from 1824 it was run as a pin factory. In 1826 Littledean parish had 13 bedsteads in the workhouse.[63]

Six people received regular help in 1709.[64] The cost of poor relief, which was £64 in 1776 and c. £75 in 1785, had risen to £240 by 1803 when 21 people were given regular and 22 occasional aid. By 1813 the number receiving occasional help had doubled and the cost of relief had risen to £345. After that the annual cost fell[65] and in the late 1820s and the early 1830s it sometimes was less than £200 and only twice was more than £300.[66] Many of the paupers assisted by the parish in the early 1830s lived within the extraparochial area of the Forest of Dean.[67] In 1835 Littledean was included in Westbury-on-Severn poor-law union[68] and from 1895 it was in the East Dean and United Parishes (later the East Dean) rural district.[69] In 1974 Littledean became part of the new Forest of Dean district.

CHURCH. Architectural evidence shows that Littledean had its own church or chapel by the later 12th century. In 1405 Littledean was a chapelry of Newnham[70] but by 1413 the inhabitants had appointed a chaplain and were paying him tithes and other offerings which St. Bartholomew's hospital, Gloucester, claimed as appropriator of Newnham church.[71] In the mid 15th century, before 1460, the hospital conceded control of the chapel and the choice of priest to the inhabitants and, for a rent of 53s. 4d., granted them the tithes and other profits in Littledean. The patronage, which under a confirmation of that concession in 1477 was conditional on the rent's payment,[72] was exercised by a group of inhabitants in 1514.[73] By 1573 it had reverted, together with the tithes, to the hospital's governors, Gloucester city corporation,[74] and in 1836 both advowson and tithes passed with the hospital governorship to the Gloucester municipal charity trustees.[75]

A chaplain described in 1508 as rector of Littledean served the church and was presumably receiving the tithes.[76] From the later 16th century Littledean was served by curates nominated by Gloucester corporation or by the farmer of the tithes. In practice the curate often farmed the tithes[77] but in 1603, when they were valued at £20, he had a stipend of £6.[78] From 1684 the corporation combined the curacy with that of Newnham[79] and the curate held the tithes of both parishes at farm.[80] Littledean came to be regarded as a perpetual curacy.[81] The Littledean tithes were taken in kind in 1680[82] and were commuted in 1840 for a rent charge of £115.[83] In 1847, when the livings of Littledean and Newnham were separated under a Chancery decree of 1844, the hospital's governors took the rent charge in hand and paid the perpetual curate a stipend of £70.[84] The living, which also benefited from two sermon charities, was valued at £90 in 1856.[85]

In 1866 the governors of St. Bartholomew's hospital sold the advowson and rent charge to William Lockett, the perpetual curate.[86] The

53 Ibid. M 67–8.
54 Ibid. M 51.
55 Hockaday Abs. cclx.
56 Ibid. xxix, 1543 subsidy, f. 6; xlvii, 1576 visit. f. 133; cclx, 1703, 1732, 1766, 1800.
57 Glos. R.O., P 110/OV 4/1.
58 Ibid. OV 2/1; ibid. CW 2/1.
59 Ibid. OV 4/1.
60 Ibid. OV 2/1; ibid. VE 2/1.
61 Poor Law Abstract, 1804, 172–3; 19th Rep. Com. Char. 91; Glos. R.O., P 110/VE 2/1.
62 Cf. Glos. R.O., D 1438, workhouse trust deed 1822; D 36/E 13, ff. 33v.–34.
63 Ibid. P 110/VE 2/1; P 1/VE 2/1; P 145/OV 2/1.
64 Ibid. D 36/R 1.
65 Poor Law Abstract, 1804, 172–3; 1818, 146–7.
66 Poor Law Returns (1830–1), p. 66; (1835), p. 65.
67 3rd Rep. Dean Forest Com. 6, 25, 28.
68 Poor Law Com. 2nd Rep. p. 524.
69 Glos. R.O., DA 24/100/1; Census, 1931 (pt. ii).
70 Reg. Mascall, 18; cf. Reg. Lacy, 80; E.H.R. xliv. 451.
71 Cal. Papal Reg. vi. 395–6; cf. V.C.H. Glos. x. 47.
72 Glouc. Corp. Rec. pp. 410–11; V.C.H. Glos. ii. 121.
73 Hockaday Abs. cclx.

74 G.B.R., B 3/1, ff. 39v., 61; J 3/16, ff. 10v.–12, 169–170v.; V.C.H. Glos. iv. 352.
75 Glos. R.O., D 3269, char. trustees' min. bk. 1844–56, ff. 148–50, pp. 428–30; D 3270/19678, pp. 503–4; V.C.H. Glos. iv. 351. In 1659 two thirds of the advowson were sold with part of Littledean man. to Hen. Heane but there is no other evidence that lords of the man. ever had any right to the patronage: Glos. R.O., D 36/T 16.
76 Hockaday Abs. cclx.
77 G.B.R., B 3/1, ff. 39 and v., 61, 88; J 3/16, ff. 10v.–12, 169–170v., 280v.–282v., 300v.–302; Glos. R.O., D 3296, hospitals' lease bk. 1630–1703 (1), ff. 81v.–83v., 134; (2), ff. 218–21, 256–7.   78 Eccl. Misc. 99.
79 G.B.R., B 3/3, p. 865; G.D.R., V 1/147, 167.
80 G.B.R., B 3/3, p. 865; 8, pp. 85, 601; 9, ff. 210 and v., 433 and v.; J 1/2032, 2083; Glos. R.O., D 3269, St. Barth. hosp., lease bk. 1760–87, ff. 94v.–96.
81 Hockaday Abs. cclx; G.D.R., T 1/114.
82 G.D.R., V 5/101T 1.   83 Ibid. T 1/114.
84 Glos. R.O., D 3269, char. trustees' min. bk. 1844–56, ff. 148–50, pp. 419–40; char. trustees' acct. bk. 1851–6, ff. 9, 29, 57.
85 G.D.R. vol. 384, f. 78; below, this section.
86 Glos. R.O., D 3270/19679, pp. 478–9, 487.

following year the living was endowed by Lockett and the Ecclesiastical Commissioners with the rent charge and a further £80 a year and was declared a rectory.[87] Lockett conveyed the advowson later in 1867 to the trustees of the Church Patronage Society.[88] In 1984 the benefice was united with that of Woodside, also known as Cinderford St. Stephen, which was in the same gift.[89] Littledean was enlarged for ecclesiastical purposes in 1909, when the adjoining part of the Forest at Chestnuts hill was transferred to it, and in the late 1970s, when land to the south was added from Flaxley.[90]

In 1594 a house in Littledean was known as the parish priest's house[91] but in 1680 and later the curacy lacked a residence.[92] A grant of £400 from Queen Anne's Bounty[93] was used in 1822 to buy a house in Broad Street.[94] That building, part of which had once been a malthouse,[95] was pulled down and replaced by a new house in the later 1860s, and a field behind it was acquired as glebe in 1878.[96] After the union of benefices in 1984 the house was sold and the incumbent lived at Cinderford.[97]

Under the will of George Morse of Henbury, dated 1668, the curate of Littledean was to receive 10s. a year for a sermon but the bequest was evidently never paid.[98] Two other sermon charities, founded under the wills of Eustace Hardwicke (d. 1718) and Dorothy Pyrke (d. 1762), yielded £1 11s. for the incumbent.[99] The value of the Pyrke sermon charity, which in 1906 was consolidated with a clothing charity,[1] remained unchanged at £1.05 in the late 1980s when the incumbent received £5 for Hardwicke's sermon.[2]

In the early 16th century several chaplains or chantry priests served in the church. One accused of incontinency absconded with a woman in 1508 and another accused in 1522 of fathering two children remained in office in 1525.[3] George Pomfrey, curate in 1551,[4] was a former canon of Llanthony priory and chantry priest in the church. From 1563 he also held Rodmarton rectory[5] and in 1572 was non-resident.[6] In 1612 the curate was presented for not preaching monthly sermons and for conducting irregular marriages of minors.[7] Following the death in

1636 of an aged and enfeebled curate and petitions from many parishioners his assistant Walter Ridler became curate.[8] Soon afterwards Bishop Goodman suspended him for preaching that Roman Catholics were damned[9] but Ridler, although denounced as 'an inconformable minister' by opponents of his puritan patrons,[10] retained the cure until 1651. His successor Thomas Ashfield,[11] a preaching minister who had served the church for a stipend of £22 in 1650,[12] subscribed to the Act of Uniformity in 1662. In the early 1670s Henry Heane, rector of Great Witcombe and heir to part of Littledean manor, had the cure.[13] Of the men who served the cures of both Littledean and Newnham John White, admitted in 1714, was also rector of Mitcheldean from 1723[14] and his successor John Winfield, admitted in 1727, accepted Churcham vicarage in 1733 and was dismissed in 1739 because of non-residence.[15] James Parsons, perpetual curate from 1800,[16] had by 1822 appointed separate curates for Littledean and Newnham. He later resided in Littledean and served the parish in person until 1845. Under H. M. Willis, his successor at Littledean in 1847,[17] the replacement in 1849 of Joseph Bennett, a long serving churchwarden who had refused to let charity money be used for a new village school, led some members of the congregation to withhold church rates until Willis resigned in 1857. The next incumbent, J. J. Hedges (d. 1864), faced opposition from Bennett over the restoration of the church.[18]

A chantry dedicated to the Holy Trinity was established in Littledean church in 1412 or 1413. Its founder, Philip Hook (d. 1406), endowed it with Stantway manor in Westbury-on-Severn.[19] At its dissolution the chaplain had an income of £6 3s. 2d. and the endowments included his house and rents in Westbury and Littledean. They were granted in 1550 to John Butler and Hugh Partridge.[20] In 1468 there was a chantry of St. Mary in the church. In 1548 its chaplain, who said a morrow mass, had an income from land in Littledean and Westbury of £2 18s. 2d., which the parishioners had often used for repairing the church, highways, and a conduit bringing water to the village.[21] The Littledean

---

87 *Lond. Gaz.* 16 July 1867, p. 3977; 20 Aug. 1867, p. 4613; G.D.R. vol. 385, p. 82.
88 G.D.R., D 5/1/31; *Kelly's Dir. Glos.* (1870), 590.
89 *Glouc. Dioc. Year Bk.* (1986), 34–5; Glos. R.O., P 110/MI 1/1; cf. G.D.R., D 5/1/31.
90 Glos. R.O., P 110/MI 1/1; P 227/IN 3/5; P 354/VE 3/4.
91 P.R.O., E 134/36 & 37 Eliz. I Mich./33; cf. G.B.R., J 3/16, ff. 10v.–12.
92 G.D.R., V 5/101T 1; ibid. vols. 285B(3), pp. 3–4; 381A, f. 6.
93 Hodgson, *Queen Anne's Bounty* (1845), p. cclxxxv.
94 Glos. R.O., P 110/IN 3/5.
95 Ibid. D 3269, char. trustees' min. bk. 1844–56, ff. 155–6.
96 Ibid. P 110/IN 3/3, 5.
97 Ibid. MI 1/1; *Glouc. Dioc. Year Bk.* (1986), 34–7, 75.
98 Glos. R.O., D 333/F 15; G.D.R., V 5/101T 2.
99 Bigland, *Glos.* i. 451; G.D.R. wills 1762/16; *19th Rep. Com. Char.* 90–1; cf. Glos. R.O., P 110/CW 2/1, 3; ibid. OV 2/1.
1 Glos. R.O., D 3469/5/93; CH 21, E. Dean rural district, p. 11.
2 Inf. (1992) from Mrs B. Sleeman, of Pleasant Stile, clerk to Littledean par. char. trustees.
3 Hockaday Abs. cclx.

4 *E.H.R.* xix. 121.
5 Hockaday Abs. cclx, cccxxv; *Trans. B.G.A.S.* xlix. 67, 92, 105.   6 Hockaday Abs. xliv, 1572 visit. f. 5.
7 Ibid. lii, state of clergy 1593, f. 6; G.D.R. vol. 116.
8 Bigland, *Glos.* i. 453; *Cal. S.P. Dom.* 1637–8, 286–7; G.B.R., B 3/2, p. 70.
9 G. Soden, *Godfrey Goodman, Bishop of Glouc. 1583–1656* (1953), 244, 254–5.
10 *Cal. S.P. Dom.* 1637–8, 187, 285–6; cf. *V.C.H. Glos.* iv. 90.   11 G.B.R., B 3/2, pp. 374, 617, 626–7.
12 *Trans. B.G.A.S.* lxxxiii. 98.
13 Hockaday Abs. cclx, ccccxiii; above, manors.
14 G.B.R., B 3/8, p. 557; Hockaday Abs. cclxxx.
15 G.B.R., B 3/9, ff. 210, 433; K 1/29; Hockaday Abs. clii.
16 Cf. *V.C.H. Glos.* x. 47.
17 Hockaday Abs. cclx, ccxcviii; Glos. R.O., D 3269, char. trustees' min. bk. 1844–56, ff. 148–50, pp. 432–40.
18 Glos. R.O., P 110/IN 4/2; ibid. CW 2/1, 3; D 3270/19678, pp. 488, 503–4.
19 *Cal. Pat.* 1408–13, 418; 1436–41, 177; P.R.O., PROB 11/2A (P.C.C. 12 Marche), f. 88v.; C 145/307, no.3.
20 Hockaday Abs. cclx; *Cal. Pat.* 1549–51, 280; cf. *Cal. Pat.* 1580–2, p. 144.
21 Hockaday Abs. cclx; P.R.O., LR 2/191, f. 56 and v., which says that the land belonged to Holy Trinity chantry.

land, which the Crown leased in 1563 to Robert and Goodith Brayne,[22] was said in 1594 to include houses once occupied by the chantry priest and a bellman.[23] Thomas Brayne of Mitcheldean by will proved 1531 left land for an obit in Littledean church.[24]

The church, which had been dedicated to *ST. ETHELBERT* by 1406,[25] is built of coursed rubble and has a chancel with north chapel, a clerestoried nave with north aisle and south porch (the porch used as a vestry), and a west tower with the stump of a spire. The responds of the chancel arch and the south wall of the nave date from the later 12th century. In the 14th century the chancel, including the arch, was rebuilt and the aisle was added. The chapel had been built by 1413 to accommodate the Holy Trinity chantry[26] and was by 1504 the mortuary chapel of the Braynes.[27] The clerestory and the tower and spire were also added and some windows were enlarged in the 15th century.[28] The chapel retains its original roof and the chancel, nave, and aisle have 17th-century ceilings. An early 16th-century south doorway in the chancel has been blocked. Much tracery had been mutilated or removed by 1849, when the church was described as in bad order, dirty, and ill kept. Earlier the porch had been closed, the pulpit placed against the south wall of the nave, east and west galleries erected, and a corner of the chapel adapted as a vestry.[29] Piecemeal restoration began in 1863 and the galleries had been taken down by 1869.[30] Damage to the building by a storm in 1893 necessitated the removal of the spire in 1894 and further restoration work, notably on the tower.[31]

Windows in the chapel and aisle contain fragments of medieval glass.[32] The church has a cloth formed by two medieval chasubles sewn together and used in the late 18th century to cover the reading desk.[33] A 17th-century communion table stands in the chapel. The font has an octagonal bowl probably of medieval date.[34] George Pomfrey, the curate, by will proved 1575 left 3s. 4d. towards casting church bells.[35] In 1752 a peal of six bells was cast by William Evans of Chepstow (Mon.) and in 1894 one bell, which had been broken, was recast.[36] The church plate dates from the 19th century.[37] The organ, dated 1790,

was bought in the mid 20th century.[38] There are 18th-century wall monuments to members of the Pyrke family and among the floor tablets is one to Ketford Brayne (d. 1705).[39] The churchyard contains a number of 18th-century tombchests and carved headstones. The surviving registers date from 1684.[40]

NONCONFORMITY. Several parishioners refused to attend the parish church in the late 16th century and the early 17th[41] and some Roman Catholics were alleged to have obtained the curate's suspension in 1637.[42] William Brayne disturbed the incumbent during prayers in 1616[43] and John Brayne's house was licensed in 1672 as a place of worship for a Presbyterian group.[44] Independents registered a house in the village in 1724[45] but no dissenters were reported in the parish in 1750.[46] Independents meeting at Littledean Hill from the late 1790s under the preacher Richard Stiff moved to a house in Broad Street, which they registered in 1805 and converted as a chapel. In 1813 an adjoining house was incorporated in the chapel, which was taken down to make room for a new building in 1820 when the congregation worshipped, temporarily, in premises called the Club Room.[47] The new chapel, built chiefly through the efforts of the Gloucester minister William Bishop, was opened in 1821.[48] It sent missions to the Forest of Dean, notably to Pope's Hill and Drybrook,[49] and had David Prain as resident minister in the later 1820s.[50] It was enlarged in 1847 and had attendances averaging over 200 in 1851.[51] A manse was built in Broad Street *c.* 1870.[52] The chapel, to which a schoolroom was added in 1885,[53] was described as Congregational from the later 19th century[54] and had 60 members in 1900.[55] It later shared a minister with other churches and in 1972 joined the United Reformed Church. Services were well attended in 1989.[56]

Two houses registered on the same day in 1815 by John Wright, a Newent minister, were said to be in Littledean but one may have been at Cinderford.[57] A house in Silver Street was registered in 1823.[58] The congregation for which Isaac Denison, a Wesleyan Methodist minister

22 P.R.O., E 309/Box 1/5 Eliz. I/16, no. 1.
23 Ibid. E 134/36 & 37 Eliz. I Mich./33.
24 Hockaday Abs. cclxxx.
25 P.R.O., PROB 11/2A (P.C.C. 12 Marche, will of Phil. Hook), f. 88v.
26 Ibid. DL 7/1, no. 26; in 1572 the chapel was apparently known as Whorls aisle: P.R.O., PROB 11/54 (P.C.C. 20 Daper, will of Ric. Brayne), ff. 148v.–150.
27 Hockaday Abs. cclx.
28 Cf. *Trans. B.G.A.S.* vi. 278–9.
29 *Glos. Ch. Notes*, 63–4; undated plan in church.
30 Glos. R.O., P 110/CW 2/2; ibid. IN 4/2; D 4304/20.
31 Ibid. P 110/CW 3/3–4; ibid. VE 2/2, pp. 31–44; D 1381/YU; for views of ch. with spire, ibid. P 110/MI 1/1; D 4031/2.
32 Cf. Bigland, *Glos.* i. 451; *Trans. B.G.A.S.* xlvii. 308.
33 *Trans. B.G.A.S.* xi. 257–8; Bigland, *Glos.* i. 451.
34 The bowl is ascribed to the 18th cent. in *Trans. B.G.A.S.* xlix. 130; Verey, *Glos.* ii. 288.
35 G.D.R. wills 1574/40.
36 *Glos. Ch. Bells*, 416–17; Glos. R.O., P 110/VE 2/2; ibid. CW 3/3.
37 *Glos. Ch. Plate*, 137; cf. Glos. R.O., P 110/VE 2/1, mins. 24 Aug. 1825; 14 Aug. 1828.

38 Inf. from Mr. R. Jones, former churchwarden; cf. *Trans. B.G.A.S.* xciii. 173.
39 Cf. *Visit. Glos. 1623*, 209 and n.
40 *B. & G. Par. Rec.* 183; Glos. R.O., P 110/IN 1/2–13.
41 Glos. R.O., D 2052.
42 Soden, *Godfrey Goodman*, 244, 254–5.
43 Glos. R.O., Q/SIb 1, f. 152v.; D 2052.
44 *Cal. S.P. Dom.* 1672, 402.
45 Hockaday Abs. cclx.   46 G.D.R. vol. 381A, f. 6.
47 Glos. R.O., D 2297; Hockaday Abs. cclx; cf. below, Forest of Dean, prot. nonconf.
48 *Glouc. Jnl.* 24 July 1820; 5 Feb. 1821; J. Stratford, *Good and Great Men of Glos.* (1867), 417.
49 Below, Forest of Dean, prot. nonconf.
50 P.R.O., RG 4/766; Glos. R.O., D 2297.
51 P.R.O., HO 129/334/1/7/20.
52 *Glouc. Jnl.* 20 Apr. 1872.
53 Date on schoolroom.
54 *Kelly's Dir. Glos.* (1879), 630; (1885), 439–40.
55 Glos. R.O., D 2052.
56 *United Reformed Ch. Year Bk.* (1986–7), 62; inf. from church sec., Mr. E. Radley.
57 Hockaday Abs. cclx.
58 G.D.R. vol. 344, f. 113v.

living in Littledean, registered a house in 1824 presumably attended the Wesleyan chapel opened at Littledean Hill later that year.[59] Bible Christians sent a mission to Callamore in or before 1837.[60] In 1842 a Baptist preacher from Dursley visited Littledean once a month and in 1846 a member of Cinderford Baptist church registered a house in the parish.[61]

EDUCATION. William Ipsley (fl. 1548), the priest of St. Mary's chantry in Littledean, kept a school.[62] Dorothy Pyrke by will proved 1762 left £200 for a sermon and a school at Littledean. A woman was to have a salary of £4 4s. for teaching 10 poor children to read and the school 10s.-worth of books a year.[63] There is no evidence when the school started but it was in existence in 1815.[64] In the mid 1820s Joseph Pyrke, who had the principal sum in hand, made the payments specified in the bequest and his wife Elizabeth frequently visited the school,[65] which in 1845 was held in the cottage of the teacher, an elderly, ill-qualified woman.[66] The Independents, who had started a Sunday school by 1814,[67] supported a school teaching 86 children in 1819.[68] It may have been the day school recorded in 1825[69] and the British school faced in 1845 with closure because of dwindling attendances. During that period Littledean had half a dozen fee-paying schools.[70] A Sunday school founded to serve Littledean and the surrounding area was financed by voluntary contributions and taught c. 80 children in 1819, when the master and mistress together were paid £11.[71] It may have been the Sunday school attended by the pupils of Dorothy Pyrke's charity school in the mid 1820s[72] and supported by subscriptions and conducted in the church in the mid 1840s.[73]

In 1848 a National school opened opposite the church in a new building on land provided by Joseph Pyrke. Funds for its construction were not readily forthcoming and for some years the building remained uncompleted. The school, with which Dorothy Pyrke's charity school merged, was managed by the incumbent[74] and had a single department and an average attendance in 1863 of 60.[75] A wing was added for an

infants' school in 1871[76] and the building was enlarged further in 1896 and 1912.[77] Some overcrowding had resulted from the entry in 1901 of children from Pope's Hill and Flaxley.[78] The school, in which the mixed and infants' departments were amalgamated in 1916,[79] had average attendances of 199 in 1910 and 148 in 1938.[80] Problems in raising funds to maintain the school led the managers to apply for controlled status in 1947.[81] More classrooms were provided in the 1960s[82] and, as Littledean C. of E. Voluntary Controlled Primary school, it had 97 children on its roll in 1989.[83] Dorothy Pyrke's bequest had been invested by 1887, when its income for educational purposes was assigned as prizes for local schoolchildren. The educational charity was administered separately from 1906 and, under a Scheme of 1930,[84] it paid the the primary school c. £30 a year in the late 1980s.[85]

Zachariah Jolly, once master at Edward Protheroe's school in Cinderford,[86] ran a private school in Littledean by 1863. It continued until at least 1879.[87]

CHARITIES FOR THE POOR. The charity of Thomas Bartlem, who by will proved 1714 left the rent of a house for the poor, became due after the death of his widow in 1715[88] and was distributed in bread worth £1 5s.[89] It lapsed when the parish sold the house but was revived and was paid out of the poor rate by 1799, the money raised by the sale having been used to build poorhouses.[90] The charity was met out of the rents of parish property from 1837. From 1846 the value of the bread distributed was £1 10s.[91] Following the sale of the property c. 1850 the charity was funded from the poor rate but by the mid 1860s it had been discontinued.[92]

Eustace Hardwicke by will proved 1718 gave two fields and an orchard for maintaining his tomb, paying for a sermon, and providing £1-worth of twopenny loaves for the poor hearing the sermon.[93] The surplus income from the land was applied, as the donor had intended, in green coats for the elderly.[94] From 1819 the charity's income was £18,[95] double that in the later 18th century,[96] and from 1827 £1 10s. was laid out on

59 Hockaday Abs. cclx; G. E. Lawrence, *Kindling the Flame* (1974), 14: copy in Glos. R.O., D 2598/23/1; cf. G.D.R. vol. 383, no. cx; below, Forest of Dean, prot. nonconf.
60 Glos. R.O., D 2598/5/8.
61 *Hist. Baptist Ch. Cinderford* (1910) (photocopy in Glos. R.O., NC 40), 2–3; Hockaday Abs. cclx.
62 P.R.O., E 134/36 & 37 Eliz. I Mich./33; Hockaday Abs. cclx.
63 G.D.R. wills 1762/16.
64 *Poor Law Abstract, 1818*, 146–7.
65 *19th Rep. Com. Char.* 90–1; Burke, *Land. Gent.* (1846), ii. 1089.
66 Nat. Soc. files, Dean, Little; cf. Nat. Soc. *Inquiry, 1846–7*, Glos. 8–9.
67 *Glouc. Jnl.* 11 July 1814.
68 *Educ. of Poor Digest*, 297.
69 G.D.R. vol. 383, no. cx.
70 Nat. Soc. files, Dean, Little; *Educ. Enq. Abstract*, 313.
71 *Educ. of Poor Digest*, 297, 299.
72 *19th Rep. Com. Char.* 91.
73 Nat. Soc. *Inquiry, 1846–7*, Glos. 8–9.
74 Nat. Soc. files, Dean, Little; Glos. R.O., P 110/IN 4/2.
75 P.R.O., ED 7/34/194.
76 Glos. R.O., D 2186/83; the wing is dated with the inits.

'T. F.' and 'W. S.', presumably those of the churchwardens.
77 *Kelly's Dir. Glos.* (1914), 145.
78 Glos. R.O., SB 15/5, p. 90; CE/M 2/1, p. 148.
79 Ibid. CE/M 2/13, p. 151.
80 *Bd. of Educ., List 21, 1911* (H.M.S.O.), 163; *1938*, 128.
81 Nat. Soc. files, Dean, Little; Glos. R.O., CE/M 2/30, f. 82.
82 Glos. R.O., P 110/SC 1/1.
83 *Educ. Services Dir. 1989–90* (co. educ. dept.), 19.
84 Glos. R.O., D 3469/5/93.
85 Inf. (1992) from Mrs. B. Sleeman.
86 Nicholls, *Forest of Dean*, 171.
87 *Kelly's Dir. Glos.* (1863), 303; (1879), 630.
88 G.D.R. wills 1714/136; Glos. R.O., P 110/IN1/3.
89 Bigland, *Glos.* i. 451.
90 *19th Rep. Com. Char.* 90; Glos. R.O., P 110/OV 2/1.
91 Glos. R.O., P 110/CW 2/1, 3.
92 Ibid. IN 4/2; CH 21, E. Dean rural district, p. 11.
93 P.R.O., PROB 11/564 (P.C.C. 145 Tenison), ff. 323v.–324v.; the tomb, in the churchyard, was under a pyramid which Hardwicke had erected and which had disappeared probably by 1929: Atkyns, *Glos.* 382; Glos. R.O., D 3469/5/93.
94 Glos. R.O., P 110/OV 2/1.
95 Ibid. VE 2/1; ibid. CW 2/1.
96 Bigland, *Glos.* i. 451.

bread. Up to *c.* 70 people, nearly all women, received clothing.[97] The orchard was used as allotments in the 1920s and 1930s.[98] The bequest of Dorothy Pyrke (d. 1762) for a sermon and school provided also for a second clothing charity for the elderly.[99] It was distributed by Joseph Pyrke in the mid 1820s.[1] Another bread charity was founded by Ann Matthews (d. 1800),[2] who by will gave rents from property in Littledean for three doles, each worth 30*s.*[3] In 1870 the income of the Hardwicke and Matthews charities was assigned, subject in respect of Hardwicke's to the repair of the founder's tomb and the sermon payment, to a wider range of needs, including assistance to schools teaching Littledean children. Dorothy Pyrke's trust, as regulated in 1887, continued, subject to her sermon and educational charities, to provide clothing, and when it was reorganized in 1906 the sermon and clothing charities were consolidated

as the Charity of Dorothy Pyrke for Sermon and Poor. By a Scheme of 1929 that charity was brought under the same trust as the Hardwicke and Matthews charities and the trust's income was used to pay for the two sermons and to provide help for the poor and for local schools.[4] In the late 1980s the income was *c.* £300, of which up to £150 was given to the village primary school.[5]

In 1961 £160 from the assets of a local horticultural society, then being wound up, was assigned to provide payments at Christmas to residents aged over 70. In 1969 a bequest of £150 by Mrs. E. G. M. Evans was added to the fund,[6] which had ceased to function by the late 1980s.[7]

Jane Walter by deed of 1760 gave £40 to provide bibles equally for the poor of Littledean and Mitcheldean. The charity lapsed after a few years as a result of the loss of the principal sum.[8]

MITCHELDEAN

THE PARISH and former market town of Mitcheldean lies 16.5 km. west of Gloucester.[9] Mitcheldean, once part of the Forest of Dean,[10] was usually called Dean until the mid 13th century.[11] Afterwards it was generally known as Micheldean or Great Dean, in the Latin form Dean Magna, to distinguish it from nearby Littledean.[12] The form Mitcheldean was in use by the mid 17th century[13] and the parish was occasionally called Michael Dean, from the dedication of its church, by that time.[14] Littledean and presumably Abenhall had tenurial links with Mitcheldean[15] and were regarded as members of it in 1316.[16] The town of Mitcheldean, which lay partly in Abenhall, was a centre for industries based on the products of the adjacent Forest. It supported a cloth industry by the later 13th century and had a market from 1328. The town prospered in the 17th century but was in decline as an industrial centre and market by the end of the 18th and became primarily a shopping centre of local importance. After the Second World War the presence of a factory owned by Rank Xerox Ltd. was a major influence on Mitcheldean, which expanded as a residential area.

The ancient parish of Mitcheldean covered only 627 a. and was irregular in shape with a detached part to the west at Blackwell meadows. The main part, containing 579 a.,[17] lay above 125 m. at the head of the valley of Longhope brook,

which is drained to the south-east, and rose to *c.* 200 m. on the side of Breakheart hill to the east. To the west, above the town, was the extraparochial Forest of Dean, into which the parish made a substantial indent, rising steeply up Stenders hill and reaching 275 m. at the Wilderness in the south-eastern corner. The parish boundaries, which were those of the manor of Mitcheldean as described in 1619,[18] were marked mostly by hedges and lanes. The south-eastern boundary with Abenhall included a section of the Gloucester–Monmouth road, following the bed of a stream which ran only in the winter months,[19] and it crossed the upland area of the Wilderness. Blackwell meadows, separated from the rest of the parish by part of the Forest known as Mitcheldean Meend, was a compact area of 48 a. on the boundary with Herefordshire[20] and paid tithes to Mitcheldean by 1583.[21] It was transferred to East Dean civil parish under the Divided Parishes Act of 1882. Mitcheldean civil parish, which as a result of other changes in the 1880s was bounded on part of the north by Herefordshire, was enlarged considerably in 1935, when Abenhall and part of Longhope to the north-east were added to it, and again in 1953, when it gained a substantial part of East Dean to the west including Blackwell meadows. The area added in 1953 also contained Lea Bailey Inclosures, most of which, in a peninsula of the county extending north-westwards,

[97] Glos. R.O., P 110/CW 2/1, 3; *19th Rep. Com. Char.* 90.
[98] Glos. R.O., P 110/CH 1/1; O.S. Map 6", Glos. XXXI. SE. (1924 edn.).
[99] G.D.R. wills 1762/16.
[1] *19th Rep. Com. Char.* 90–1.
[2] Glos. R.O., P 110/IN 1/4.
[3] *19th Rep. Com. Char.* 91; cf. Glos. R.O., P 110/OV 2/1; ibid. CW 2/1, 3.
[4] Glos. R.O., D 3469/5/93.
[5] Inf. (1992) from Mrs. B. Sleeman.
[6] Glos. R.O., P 110/CH 1/1.
[7] Inf. from Mrs. Sleeman.
[8] Bigland, *Glos.* i. 451; *19th Rep. Com. Char.* 90.
[9] This history was written in 1988.
[10] *Trans. B.G.A.S.* lxvi. 166–207.

[11] *Dom. Bk.* (Rec. Com.), i. 167v.; *Bk. of Fees*, i. 308; *Pat. R.* 1216–25, 395.
[12] *P.N. Glos.* (E.P.N.S.), iii. 234; cf. ibid. 225.
[13] Glos. R.O., D 36/T 29; D 543, deeds 1694–1876.
[14] Ibid. D 3833/10; Greenwood, *Map of Glos.* (1824); cf. Bodl. MS. Rawl. B. 323, f. 106.
[15] Above, Littledean, intro.; manors; Abenhall, intro.; manor.   [16] *Feud. Aids*, ii. 275.
[17] *O.S. Area Bk.* Mitcheldean (1880); Ruardean (1878).
[18] *Trans. B.G.A.S.* vi. 207.
[19] Glos. R.O., D 36/M 2, f. 2v.
[20] *O.S. Area Bk.* Ruardean (1878); P.R.O., MR 415 (F 16/47).
[21] Glos. R.O., D 4431, deed 6 Feb. 25 Eliz. I; cf. ibid. D 36/M 78, f. 4v.; *Trans. B.G.A.S.* vi. 207.

was transferred to three Herefordshire parishes in 1965 to leave Mitcheldean with 1,064 ha. (2,629 a.).[22] The following account deals with the main part of the ancient parish and the northern end of Abenhall, including part of the Wilderness, where settlement and economic activity were an integral part of the history of Mitcheldean town. Blackwell meadows is treated as part of the Forest.

Mitcheldean lies on the Old Red Sandstone save in the south-west where the high ground on Stenders hill and at the Wilderness is formed by carboniferous limestone. In the latter an outcrop of iron ore runs north–south in a thin band.[23] Longhope brook, which rises north of the town, was known in 1436 as Casbrook (later Carisbrook).[24] Drainage was also provided by a tributary stream rising west of, and flowing down through, the town, where it was known by 1625 as the churchyard brook.[25] Mitcheldean once had considerable waste land but by the 16th century most of the land had been inclosed and was used mainly for meadow or pasture. The principal woods surviving in the late 1830s were Scully grove (14 a.) on Stenders hill, Lady grove (17 a.) occupying a strip of land on the hillside east of the Wilderness, and Land grove (27 a.) lying east of Mitcheldean above Longhope brook and belonging to the Colchester family's Wilderness estate.[26] A park mentioned in 1347[27] was presumably located east of the town where parkland, belonging to part of Mitcheldean manor held with Abenhall manor, was used for farming by the mid 15th century.[28] Part of the Wilderness was included in a paddock or small park formed by 1740 for the Colchesters' mansion there.[29] Quarries at the Wilderness and in the valley of Longhope brook were exploited on a large scale in the 19th century and the early 20th. Abandoned limestone workings on Stenders hill were purchased in 1974 by the Gloucestershire Trust for Nature Conservation and have been designated a site of special scientific interest.[30]

A road from Littledean by way of Abenhall, said to have been part of a Roman route linking Lydney and the Severn crossing at Newnham with Ariconium, near Weston under Penyard (Herefs.),[31] was formerly the principal thoroughfare through Mitcheldean. North of the town it forked for Newent and Ross-on-Wye (Herefs.),[32] the Ross road by way of Lea (Herefs., formerly Glos. and Herefs.) forming the way towards Hereford mentioned in 1320.[33] The Newnham–Hereford route, on which traffic was subject to toll in Mitcheldean before the 17th century,[34] remained of some importance in the early 19th century.[35] In the south of the town, on the boundary between Mitcheldean and Abenhall, it was crossed by the Gloucester–Monmouth road, the area around the crossroads being known as the Merrin (formerly Mere End).[36] On the Gloucester side the road, which turns south-eastwards at Barton Corner east of the town,[37] had been used by the Romans.[38] On the Monmouth side it originally left the town by Silver Street, which ran southwards from the Merrin[39] and in the 16th century was used by traffic for Littledean,[40] but its steep ascent to the Forest over Plump hill was difficult to negotiate and in the mid 18th century traffic usually followed an alternative route turning northwards at the Merrin and westwards in the town centre to climb Stenders hill to the Forest. The Stenders road, which also carried much of Mitcheldean's market trade,[41] had been the way to Ruardean in 1411.[42]

In 1747 the Gloucester road, beginning at the Merrin, was turnpiked. In 1769 the powers of its trustees were extended to cover the principal roads through the town and parish, thereby including Mitcheldean in a network of turnpiked roads reaching also to Ross, Hereford, and Newnham.[43] Those roads remained turnpiked until 1880[44] and tollgates were placed at the Merrin, at the northern end of the town, and on Stenders hill.[45] The road up Stenders hill remained an important route to the Forest after 1841 when the Forest of Dean turnpike trust built a new road leading south-westwards from the Merrin and over Plump hill towards Monmouth. The new road, which incorporated a straightened section of Silver Street,[46] was a turnpike until 1888.[47] After the completion of the railway line from Gloucester to Hereford by the Great Western Railway in 1855 Mitcheldean was served from a station on the Ross road 1½ mile (3 km.) north of the town in Lea.[48] The line was closed in 1964.[49]

22 *Census*, 1891; 1931 (pt. ii); 1961–71.
23 Geol. Surv. Map 1/50,000, solid and drift, sheet 233 (1974 edn.); sheet 234 (1972 edn.); Atkinson, *Map of Dean Forest* (1847).
24 P.R.O., SC 6/858/15, rot. 5; Glos. R.O., D 36/E 1, f. 87v.; M 78, f. 35.
25 Glos. R.O., D 36/M 75, rot. 3d.
26 G.D.R., T 1/1, 123.
27 Glos. R.O., D 4431, deed c. Annunc. B.V.M. 21 Edw. III.
28 Ibid. D 36/E 1, ff. 20 and v., 27–9, 35v.–36; cf. G.D.R., T 1/123 (nos. 157, 159).
29 Glos. R.O., D 36/E 12, f. 72v.; D 2123, pp. 65, 69.
30 Glos. Colln. R 203.12.
31 A. W. Trotter, *Dean Road* (1936), 40–4; I. D. Margary, *Roman Roads in Britain*, ii (1957), p. 64; *V.C.H. Glos.* x. 35.
32 Cf. Glos. R.O., D 4431, deed Nativity 16 Hen. VI.
33 Ibid. deed Mon. after St. Luke 14 Edw. II.
34 Below, econ. hist. (other ind. and trade); cf. above, Abenhall, intro.
35 *Paterson's Roads* (1829), 609.
36 Glos. R.O., D 4431, deeds St. Mat. 33 Edw. III; Thurs. before SS. Phil. and Jas. 17 Ric. II.
37 Ogilby, *Britannia* (1675), p. 30, plate 15.

38 Margary, *Roman Roads*, ii, pp. 59–60.
39 Glos. R.O., D 2123, pp. 63, 69; cf. Ogilby, *Britannia*, p. 30, plate 15.
40 Glos. R.O., D 36/E 1, f. 33v.; D 2957/1.2.
41 Ibid. D 36/M 78, f. 19v.; Badminton Mun. FmS/G 2/4/4.
42 Glos. R.O., D 2957/303.2.
43 Glouc. & Heref. Roads Acts, 20 Geo. II, c. 31; 9 Geo. III, c. 50.
44 Annual Turnpike Acts Continuance Act, 43 & 44 Vic. c. 12; cf. Huntley Roads Act, 29 & 30 Vic. c. 100 (Local and Personal).
45 Glos. R.O., D 2123, pp. 63, 93; Bryant, *Map of Glos.* (1824); O.S. Map 6", Glos. XXIII. SE. (1883 edn.).
46 Nicholls, *Forest of Dean*, 197; Nicholls, *Iron Making*, 6; cf. G.D.R., T 1/1, 123; O.S. Map 1/2,500, Glos. XXIII. 16 (1881 edn.). The route of the new road varied from that specified in Dean Forest Roads Act, 1 & 2 Vic. c. 38 (Local and Personal); Glos. R.O., Q/RUm 152.
47 Dean Forest Turnpike Trust Abolition Act, 51 & 52 Vic. c. 193.
48 E. T. MacDermot, *Hist. G.W.R.* revised C. R. Clinker (1972), i. 207, 454–5.
49 *V.C.H. Glos.* x. 6.

The town of Mitcheldean was created by building alongside the road from Littledean to Newent and Ross and, to a lesser extent, along the road to Stenders and the plan that it had assumed by the late 14th century remained basically the same until the mid 20th. The road junction in the town centre is known as the Cross and the main road running northwards is called High Street. South of the Cross the Littledean road leads over a rise known as Hawker hill and down Merrin Street to the Merrin, from where the town developed southwards along Silver Street. The Stenders road running westwards from the Cross was known by 1469 as the Millend (later Millend Street) from a mill standing on the churchyard brook to the north,[50] but the section west of the entrance to New Street has been renamed Stenders Road. New Street, which leads southwards and turns westwards to run parallel with the road, had taken that name by 1396[51] and was described later as leading towards the Wilderness.[52] Other less important streets included Brook Street, so called by 1384,[53] which ran north-eastwards from High Street by the churchyard brook.[54]

The early development of the town occurred around the Cross. A cross erected there by 1430 was known as the high cross by 1471.[55] It incorporated a covered area for market traders in the mid 17th century[56] and displayed a clock in the mid 18th.[57] To the north-west, on the south side of the churchyard brook, stood the church and, further west, a medieval manor house. The churchyard was hemmed in tightly on the east by buildings facing High Street and on the west by a lane (later Church Lane) leading northwards towards Lea Bailey.[58] South-east of the churchyard was an area known in the mid 18th century as the Scallions.[59] Expansion of the town northwards along High Street was under way by 1320[60] and a site for the market had been established beyond the churchyard brook by 1431.[61] The lines of the market place have been obscured but they evidently defined a small area on the east side of the street and contained a cross or market house, known in 1537 as the chipping cross,[62] which was rebuilt in the mid 1760s.[63] The buildings in High Street also included a row of four dwellings known in 1488 as the High Rents,[64] which belonged to a chantry and were used in 1549 as poorhouses.[65] By the

16th century some houses had been built on the road between the market place and the fork of the Newent and Ross roads, that area being known in 1503 as Garons End (later Townsend).[66] Shrewsbury barn, on the Ross road, had been pulled down by 1696.[67] In the early 17th century New Street contained 8 dwellings said to have been erected on waste land cleared from the Forest.[68]

The Merrin, at the southern end of the town, had been settled by the mid 14th century[69] and a cross erected at the crossroads there by 1411.[70] By that time building had begun in Merrin Street and Silver Street,[71] the latter so called in 1825.[72] Thomas Pyrke, a member of a prominent landed family established at Mitcheldean by the late 14th century,[73] resided at the Merrin in 1663.[74] The oldest surviving building there, Abenhall House on the east side of the Littledean road, was enlarged in the 18th century. By the later 18th century several terraced cottages had been built in the southern part of Silver Street, but along the Gloucester road the town's development had been limited to two houses on the south side.[75]

From the mid 16th century many buildings in the town were rebuilt[76] and more houses and shops were provided by infilling. Among the few early buildings to escape later redevelopment is a row of three timber-framed houses of the 16th century on the south side of Millend Street. It includes, in the centre, the former Jovial Colliers inn and, to the east, a cottage once occupied as two dwellings.[77] An outbuilding of 5 bays north-east of the churchyard and a timber-framed house on the east side of Merrin Street possibly also date from the 16th century. The town, inhibited from spreading along streets leading off High Street by mounds of slag or cinders from old ironworks,[78] developed in its basic plan into a long and very narrow, crooked street of low buildings.[79] A house had been erected at the Bull Ring, the area east of High Street and south of Brook Street, by 1635.[80] The south part of the market place, on the corner of High Street, was filled before 1635 by a building which later became the White Horse inn,[81] but the north part remained largely open in 1705.[82] East of the Cross a tall gabled house, possibly that called the New House in 1609,[83] was known as the Dunstone later in the century.[84] By 1740 it had

[50] Glos. R.O., D 4431, deed 14 July 9 Edw. IV; D 36/M 78, ff. 5v.–22; P 220/VE 2/2, f. 214.
[51] Ibid. D 4431, deed Easter Sun. 19 Ric. II.
[52] Ibid. D 36/E 1, f. 4.
[53] Trans. B.G.A.S. lxii. 110.   [54] Glos. R.O., Q/SRh 1964.
[55] Ibid. D 4431, deeds Fri. before Nativity 9 Hen. VI; Sun. after Nativity B.V.M. 11 Edw. IV.
[56] Ibid. D 36/M 78, f. 34v.; P 220/CH 2.
[57] Ibid. P 220/VE 2/2, ff. 93–8.
[58] Ibid. D 2123, p. 63; Q/SRh 1860 C/1.
[59] Ibid. D 36/E 86; cf. ibid. E 12, f. 82v.
[60] Ibid. D 4431, deed Mon. after St. Luke 14 Edw. II.
[61] Ibid. deed St. And. 10 Hen. VI.
[62] Ibid. D 36/E 1, f. 89v.; M 10.
[63] Rudder, Glos. 401; below, econ. hist. (markets and fairs).
[64] Glos. R.O., D 36/E 1, ff. 4, 23v.; M 78, f. 8.
[65] Hockaday Abs. cclxxx.
[66] Glos. R.O., D 36/E 1, ff. 18, 31 and v., 88.
[67] Ibid. f. 31; M 78, ff. 13v., 72.
[68] Ibid. E 3, f. 49v.
[69] Ibid. D 4431, deed St. Mat. 33 Edw. III.
[70] Ibid. deed Mich. 12 Hen. IV; D 36/M 10; Trans. B.G.A.S. vi. 207.
[71] Glos. R.O., D 4431, deeds Fri. before Nativity 9 Hen. VI; 1 Aug. 24 Hen. VI.   [72] Ibid. P 1/VE 2/1.
[73] Ibid. D 4431, deeds Thurs. after Nativity St. John the Baptist 9 Ric. [? II]; Thurs. before SS. Phil. and Jas. 17 Ric. II; eve of Trin. 1 Hen. VI; cf. Inq. p.m Glos. 1625–42, i. 165–7, 180–2, 192–6; Bigland, Glos. i. 1, 445, 451.
[74] Glos. R.O., D 4431, deed 23 Oct. 15 Chas. II.
[75] Ibid. D 2123, p. 63.
[76] Cf. ibid. D 36/E 12, ff. 74v., 138v., 150v., 151v., 158v., 159v.; M 78, f. 23v.; T 26.
[77] G.D.R., T 1/123 (nos. 17–20); Phelps, Forest in Old Photog. (1983), 116.
[78] Below, econ. hist. (other ind. and trade).
[79] Bodl. MS. Rawl. B. 323, f. 106; Rudder, Glos. 400; Gent. Mag. xcii (1), 17.
[80] Glos. R.O., D 36/E 6, rot. 8d.; D 149/T 1155.
[81] Ibid. D 36/E 6, rot. 10; M 78, ff. 6v., 51v.
[82] Ibid. T 25.
[83] Inq. p.m. Glos. 1625–42, i. 192–3.
[84] Bigland, Glos. i. 449.

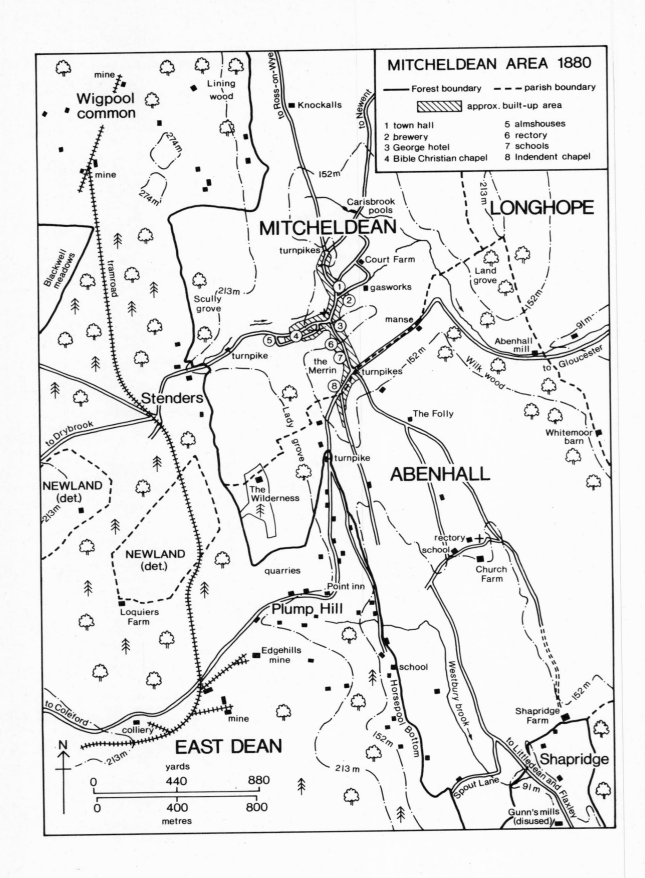

FIG. 6

176

become the George inn.[85] The top part of the building, including the gables, was removed in 1947.[86] A row of six dwellings at the Cross, on the west side of the Littledean road, was known in 1610 as Messengers Rents.[87] In the later 18th century the town fell into economic decline and decay.[88] The high cross was pulled down in the mid 1770s[89] and many buildings were in ruins c. 1790.[90] In the early 19th century there was much rebuilding and by 1822 most of the derelict buildings had been replaced or removed.[91] Several of the town's more substantial houses date from that period, including two in New Street, on one of which a stone bearing the date 1683 and the initials R. and M.D. has been reset, and one at the Merrin. Tusculum, a large house in grounds north of Stenders Road, may have been older;[92] it was demolished c. 1970. Between 1828 and the late 1850s several buildings in front of the church in High Street were pulled down, one or two at a time, to enlarge the churchyard,[93] which in 1860 was also extended on the west following a diversion of Church Lane.[94] The rectory house west of Hawker Hill, on the Littledean road, was rebuilt in 1849[95] and a school was built in its grounds, lower down towards the Merrin, in 1850.[96] New buildings in the later 19th century included a brewery in Brook Street in 1868,[97] and the opening of cement works on Stenders hill may have encouraged the building of several brick houses in Stenders Road at the turn of the century.[98] Most of the houses at the Abenhall end of the town date from the 19th century. Abenhall Lodge (formerly Woodville), the most substantial, stands south-east of the Merrin and was built in the later 1860s, probably for the solicitor J. J. G. Borlase.[99] A house on the Gloucester road was built in the early 1850s as a manse.[1] Council house building began in 1938 with six dwellings at Townsend.[2]

The town, which had changed little in extent from the late 14th century, expanded considerably after the Second World War. The growth was stimulated by the factory of British Acoustic Films (later Rank Xerox), which was established in the Brook Street brewery.[3] Many council houses were built particularly on the east side of the town near the factory, beginning in 1949

with the Eastern Avenue estate at the Bull Ring,[4] and private housing was provided later in estates on the west side of the town and west of the Ross road. The factory was itself considerably enlarged, notably in the early 1970s when farmland to the north-east was levelled for the construction of workshops, and it came to dominate the town's appearance as well as its economic and social life.[5] To prevent traffic congestion in the town the main road was widened in places from the early 1960s, particularly in High Street where many shops and houses were demolished, the Ross road was diverted before 1971 to leave the Newent road further out,[6] and an entrance to the factory was made from the Gloucester road at Barton Corner in the early 1970s.[7] In 1964 part of Brook Street and a lane to Court Farm, which the factory was to cover, were closed.[8] In the redevelopment of the town a row of shops, a library (1984), and a surgery (1983) were built on the east side of High Street[9] and several houses were provided by small infill schemes. Other new buildings included an old people's home east of Townsend, opened by the county council in 1971, and a row of council maisonettes for the elderly on the east side of Hawker Hill.[10]

Settlement outside the town was limited to a few farmsteads and scattered cottages.[11] Court Farm, immediately north-east of the town on the site of the chief house of the Ayleway family's estate in the early 17th century, was pulled down c. 1970 to make way for an extension of the Rank Xerox factory.[12] Knockalls, on the Ross road, was the farmhouse of a small freehold estate belonging in 1693 evidently to Sir William Forester[13] and in 1773 to Edward Hearne.[14] It was rebuilt in the early 19th century and became part of the Wilderness estate in 1907.[15] At the Wilderness a mansion formerly belonging to the Colchester family dates from the late 17th century.[16]

Thirty-eight inhabitants of the estate called Dean were recorded in 1086[17] and twenty-five inhabitants of Mitcheldean and Abenhall were assessed for tax in 1327.[18] The muster roll of 1542 gives 52 and 30 names for Mitcheldean and Abenhall respectively.[19] In 1548 there were said to be 268 communicants in Mitcheldean parish[20]

[85] Glos. R.O., D 36/E 12, f. 157v.
[86] Phelps, *Forest in Old Photog.* (1983), 123.
[87] Glos. R.O., D 36/E 1, f. 15v.; E 6, rot. 8; M 84.
[88] Rudder, *Glos.* 401.
[89] Glos. R.O., P 220/VE 2/2, ff. 119–20.
[90] *Univ. Brit. Dir.* ii (1792), 775; cf. Rudge, *Hist. of Glos.* ii. 90.
[91] *Gent. Mag.* xcii (1), 17–18; cf. Phelps, *Forest in Old Photog.* (1983), 24, 113; Mullin, *Forest in Old Photog.* 49–50.
[92] Cf. Glos. R.O., D 2123, p. 63; G.D.R., T 1/123. A proposal in 1868 to convert the house as a private asylum was evidently not carried out: Glos. R.O., Q/AL 38/8 (1–2).
[93] Glos. R.O., P 220/VE 2/4–6; cf. ibid. VE 2/2, f. 215; ibid. CW 3/2–4; G.D.R., T 1/123; O.S. Map 1/2,500, Glos. XXIII. 16 (1881 edn.).
[94] Glos. Colln. 18490 (3), pp. 22–3; Glos. R.O., Q/SRh 1860 C/1.
[95] G.D.R., F 4/1.
[96] Glos. R.O., P 220/CH 5/4.
[97] Ibid. D 543, Mitcheldean brewery papers.
[98] Cf. O.S. Map 6", Glos. XXIII. SE. (1883 and later edns.).
[99] *Kelly's Dir. Glos.* (1870), 459–60, 598.
[1] *Glouc. Jnl.* 18 Jan. 1851; O.S. Map 6", Glos. XXIII.

SE. (1883 edn.).
[2] Glos. R.O., DA 24/100/12, pp. 302, 336.
[3] Below, econ. hist. (other ind. and trade).
[4] Glos. R.O., DA 24/602/1; 'Memories of Mitcheldean' (Bristol Univ. dept. of extra-mural studies, 1965), 5: copy in Glos. Colln. RR 203.4.
[5] *Glos. and Avon Life*, Nov. 1977, 42–5; *The Times*, 15 Sept. 1966; *Dean Forest Mercury*, 9 June 1972.
[6] Glos. R.O., GPS 220/1–6, 13–20, 22–4, 29.
[7] *Dean Forest Mercury*, 9 June 1972.
[8] Glos. R.O., Q/SRh 1964.
[9] *Dean Forest Mercury*, 10 Feb. 1984; *Lydney Observer*, 2 Dec. 1983.
[10] *Glos. and Avon Life*, Nov. 1977, 45.
[11] Cf. Glos. R.O., D 36/E 12, ff. 83v., 94v., 155v.
[12] Below, manor.
[13] Glos. R.O., P 220/VE 2/1, pp. 135, 149.
[14] Ibid. P 220/CH 5/1.
[15] Ibid. D 543, sale partics. 1918.
[16] Below, manor.
[17] *Dom. Bk.* (Rec. Com.), i. 167v.
[18] *Glos. Subsidy Roll, 1327*, 44.
[19] *L. & P. Hen. VIII*, xvii, p. 499.
[20] P.R.O., E 301/23, no. 39; cf. *E.H.R.* xix. 120.

and in 1563 92 households.[21] The number of communicants in 1603 was 366[22] and of families in 1650 more than 250.[23] The parish's population, which included most of the townspeople, was estimated c. 1710 at 600 in 120 houses and c. 1775, when the place was in economic decline, was put at 590.[24] It had fallen to 563 by 1801 and to 535 by 1811, after which it rose gradually, apart from a slight decline in the 1840s, to reach 742 by 1871, when Abenhall's population, which included the rest of the townspeople, was also at a peak. A gradual drop in Mitcheldean's population, only partly accounted for by the loss of Blackwell meadows, then followed and by 1931 it had sunk to 511. The enlargement of the parish in 1935 increased its population considerably and industrial development and new housing from the 1940s brought a substantial rise in the numbers living in the town; in 1951 the parish as constituted before 1935 had 762 inhabitants. The boundary changes of 1953 and 1965 also greatly altered the parish's population, which in 1971 was 2,211. In 1981 there were 2,741 residents, of whom all but 62 were in private households.[25]

In the early 17th century Mitcheldean had a common water supply[26] piped from a spring in Scully grove to several cisterns in the town, one of them at the high cross.[27] There were also several public watering places north of the town, including Carisbrook pools by the Newent road.[28] The cisterns were closed c. 1815 and pumps were placed over them.[29] The piped system, maintained by the vestry out of parish rates, had been extended by 1844 to provide six pumps.[30] It also supplied some houses and was taken over by a limited company formed in 1868, which constructed a small reservoir near the source.[31] The supply was later polluted by cement works next to the reservoir[32] and before 1900 a borehole was sunk at the works and a new reservoir built higher up within the Forest. The company, which came under the control of Francis Wintle, the owner of a brewery in the town, also supplied a few houses in the Abenhall part of the town.[33] There public wells at the Merrin and Silver Street, the former recorded in 1590,[34] were sealed in 1929 following the provision in Abenhall of a mains supply from the Cinderford waterworks. The rural district council extended that supply throughout the town after the Second World War and took over the water company's concern in 1955.[35] The churchyard brook was long used as a sewer[36] and in 1867 the vestry culverted the section through the town below the churchyard.[37] From the 1890s the sanitary authority built several drains in the town and in 1936 and 1937 it constructed a sewerage system with a treatment plant by Longhope brook.[38] In the later 1860s the vestry lit the town with gas supplied by the Mitcheldean Gas Light and Coke Co., which had been formed in 1865 and which built its works east of the town in Brook Street.[39] The works, which passed into private hands before 1897, supplied gas to shops and houses in the parish and to the Wilderness.[40] At nationalization in 1948 they ceased to manufacture gas but were used for storage until c. 1970 when the site was incorporated in the Rank Xerox factory.[41] Electricity was brought to the town c. 1930 by the West Gloucestershire Power Co.[42]

Although only two innholders and one victualler were recorded in the parish in 1608,[43] Mitcheldean had many inns and alehouses and at least 14 people were brewing and selling ale in 1625.[44] The comparatively high number of inns in the 17th and 18th centuries reflected the town's status as a market and industrial centre as well as its position on roads to Newnham, Hereford, Gloucester, and South Wales. Most inns were near the Cross and the market place. South of the Cross the Swan or Black Swan, on the east side of Hawker Hill, and the George, on the west side, had opened by 1581 and 1620 respectively.[45] Both had closed by 1740 when the Dunstone, east of the Cross, was trading as an inn under the sign of the George.[46] It became the town's principal coaching inn[47] and in the mid 19th century, before the advent of the railway, remained a stopping place for coaches to Gloucester and Coleford.[48] In the late 17th century and the early 18th at least three inns, one called the Shears in 1695, faced High Street from the churchyard.[49] Among the inns of or near the market place were the Garons, recorded in 1616,[50] and the Talbot, opened on the east side by 1619 and closed by 1696. To the south

21 Bodl. MS. Rawl. C. 790, f. 27.
22 Eccl. Misc. 98.   23 Trans. B.G.A.S. lxxxiii. 98.
24 Atkyns, Glos. 381; Rudder, Glos. 401.
25 Census, 1801–1981.
26 Glos. R.O., D 36/M 75, rott. 2d., 15d.; M 76.
27 Gent. Mag. xcii (1), 17; Trans. B.G.A.S. lviii. 281–3 and plate II, a photog. of the cistern excavated at the Cross in 1936.
28 Glos. R.O., D 36/M 75, rot. 3d.; M 78, f. 35; O.S. Map 6", Glos. XXIII. SE. (1883 edn.); cf. P.R.O., SC 6/858/15, rot. 5; G.D.R., T 1/123 (nos. 202, 215–16, 249–51).
29 Gent. Mag. xcii (1), 17; Glos. R.O., P 220/VE 2/3.
30 Glos. R.O., P 220/VE 2/5–6.
31 Ibid. D 543, Mitcheldean waterworks papers; D 36/T 47.   32 Ibid. D 2759/15.
33 Pearce, 'Water Supply in Dean', 82–3; Richardson, Wells and Springs of Glos. 45, 121; O.S. Map 6", Glos. XXIII. SE. (1903 edn.).
34 N.L.W., Courtfield MSS. 785.
35 Glos. R.O., DA 24/100/10, passim; 14, passim; Pearce, 'Water Supply in Dean', 35, 84.
36 Cf. N.L.W., Courtfield MSS. 785, presentments 15 Oct. 1588; Glos. R.O., D 36/M 78, ff. 34–5.
37 Glos. R.O., P 220/VE 2/6.

38 Ibid. DA 40/100/4, pp. 45, 104–5, 116, 120, 136; DA 24/100/5, p. 126; 12, pp. 98, 187–8; Payne, Glos. Survey, 235.
39 Glos. R.O., P 220/VE 2/6; D 543, Mitcheldean gasworks papers; O.S. Map 1/2,500, Glos. XXIII. 16 (1881 edn.).
40 Kelly's Dir. Glos. (1894 and later edns.); Payne, Glos. Survey, 259.
41 'Memories of Mitcheldean', 4–5; cf. Glos. R.O., GPS 220/1.
42 Payne, Glos. Survey, 205; Glos. R.O., IN 10; Kelly's Dir. Glos. (1931), 258.
43 Smith, Men and Armour, 31–3.
44 Glos. R.O., D 36/M 75, rot. 2.
45 Ibid. E 1, f. 37; E 12, f. 104v.; T 25; P.R.O., C 142/383, no. 114.
46 Glos. R.O., D 36/E 12, ff. 104v., 130v.–131v., 157v.
47 Univ. Brit. Dir. ii (1792), 775; Nicholls, Forest of Dean, 196.
48 Robson's Dir. Glos. (1839), 89; Slater's Dir. Glos. (1852–3), 144.
49 Glos. R.O., D 36/E 12, ff. 80v., 152v.; T 55–6; D 149/T 1155; P 220/CH 2; cf. ibid. P 220/VE 2/2; D 2123, pp. 61, 63.
50 Ibid. D 36/E 2, f. 4v.; E 6, rot. 9d.

the building on the corner of High Street was used as part of the Talbot in 1642[51] and had taken the sign of the White Horse by 1674 to become an important meeting place and, in the late 18th century, a contender for the town's coaching trade.[52] The Swan or White Swan opened north of the market house c. 1712.[53] Further south, on the west side of High Street, the Lion or Red Lion opened by 1621.[54] A house at the junction of the Ross and Newent roads had the name of the Bell before 1581[55] and an inn with that name in 1740 was in New Street.[56] The Seven Stars, opened by 1756, was on the west side of Hawker Hill.[57] At the Merrin cross-roads an inn, which had probably opened by 1651, was called the Cross Keys in 1703.[58] The positions of some of the town's 18th-century inns, including the King's Arms, a coaching inn advertised in 1764 but closed by 1779, are not known.[59] The George, Red Lion, Seven Stars, and White Horse remained open in 1839 when Millend Street had the Jovial Colliers and High Street also the Rose and Crown.[60] The Lamb inn, facing the Monmouth road at the Merrin, opened shortly before an Abenhall friendly society held its first feast day there in 1856[61] and the Greyhound opened in High Street c. 1865.[62] The Seven Stars and Rose and Crown had closed by 1910[63] and only the George, Lamb, and White Horse survived by the mid 1960s and remained open in 1988. The former Red Lion was a youth hostel from 1936 until its demolition in the mid 1980s.[64]

A friendly society was meeting at the White Horse inn in 1809.[65] Another society met at the George from 1838 and one for women at the town's charity schools from 1844.[66] The market house was converted as a town hall in 1861.[67] An institute opened by 1885 housed a reading room. It closed c. 1900[68] but its work was revived for a few years by a club for young men formed in 1904.[69] Mitcheldean had its own brass band by 1843.[70] It lapsed during the First World War.[71] Cricket and rugby football clubs were formed before 1894.[72] Local activities in the late 19th century included an annual ploughing match from 1864.[73] After the First World War the centre of social activities was St. Michael's Hall, a former chapel in Stenders Road, which was demolished c. 1970.[74] In 1935 Francis Wintle gave the parish council a recreation ground on the west side of Townsend[75] and in 1975 a community centre was built there.[76] A branch of the county library was housed in a new building in High Street from 1984.[77] In the 1960s and 1970s accommodation was provided at the Rank Xerox factory for social and sporting activities.[78] An earlier benefactor was the industrialist Timothy Bennett (d. 1861), who on Christmas Day distributed beef to poor parishioners at his house in the town.[79]

In April 1643 part of the royalist army led by Prince Maurice was quartered at Mitcheldean,[80] and in July 1645 the Scots army commanded by Alexander Leslie, earl of Leven, camped there before laying siege to Hereford.[81]

MANOR AND OTHER ESTATES. Mitcheldean was presumably in those lands called Dean totalling 2 hides and 2½ yardlands, exempted by Edward the Confessor from the payment of geld in return for the guarding of the Forest of Dean and held in 1066 by the thegns Godric, Elric, and Ernui and in 1086 by William son of Norman.[82] William's estate seems to have passed to his son Hugh (fl. 1130) and later to Miles of Gloucester (d. 1143) and his son Roger, earl of Hereford, from whom William of Dean held an estate and an office in the Forest for 20s. rent.[83] That estate became known as the manor of DEAN or MITCHELDEAN[84] and the office was probably the woodwardship of the later bailiwick of Mitcheldean. William was described as the king's forester and his son Geoffrey of Dean[85] held the bailiwick in 1199.[86] Geoffrey's son William, recorded in the early 13th century as a tenant of the Crown by serjeanty,[87] was presumably the William of Dean (d. c. 1259) who held a moiety of the manor, comprising 2 ploughlands and 6 marks rent in Mitcheldean, from the Crown for a cash rent of 10s.[88] Custody of the bailiwick had been forfeited to the Crown in 1250.[89] William's estate passed to his descendants, who paid

[51] Ibid. E 1, f.4v.; E 2, f. 40v.; M 78, ff. 6v., 15v., 64v.
[52] Ibid. P 220/VE 2/1; *Glouc. Jnl.* 6 Oct. 1761; 9 Oct. 1775.
[53] Glos. R.O., D 36/E 11, f. 52v.; E 13, ff. 17v.–18; D 2123, pp. 61, 63.
[54] Ibid. D 36/E 1, f. 2; E 3, f. 72v.; M 78, f. 52; D 3833/10.
[55] Ibid. D 36/E 1, f. 31.
[56] Ibid. E 12, f. 153v.
[57] Ibid. P 220/VE 2/2; D 2123, pp. 59, 63.
[58] Ibid. D 4431, deed 23 July 1651; D 36/T 31; cf. ibid. D 149/T 1155.
[59] Cf. ibid. D 36/E 12, ff. 74v., 139v., 157v.; T 25; T 59; P 220/VE 2/2; for the King's Arms, *Glouc. Jnl.* 3 Dec. 1764; 7 June 1773; 13 Dec. 1779.
[60] G.D.R., T 1/123.
[61] Glos. R.O., D 543, Lamb inn deeds 1853–80; *Glouc. Jnl.* 2 Aug. 1856.
[62] Glos. R.O., D 543, Mitcheldean brewery papers, draft conveyance 25 Mar. 1878; *Kelly's Dir. Glos.* (1870), 598.
[63] Glos. R.O., D 2428/1/1.
[64] 'Memories of Mitcheldean', 8; H. Phelps, *Forest of Dean* (1982), 144.
[65] Glos. R.O., Q/RSf 2.
[66] Ibid. Q/RZ 1; *Glouc. Jnl.* 29 July 1848.
[67] *Morris's Dir. Glos.* (1876), 527; Glos. R.O., PA 220/2.
[68] *Kelly's Dir. Glos.* (1885–1902 edns.).

[69] Glos. Colln. 18490 (2): par. mag. nos. 11–30.
[70] *Glouc. Jnl.* 10 June, 22 July 1843.
[71] 'Memories of Mitcheldean', 7.
[72] *Kelly's Dir. Glos.* (1894), 234.
[73] *Glos. Chron.* 20 Oct. 1864; *Glouc. Jnl.* 28 Oct. 1865; Glos. R.O., D 543, notice 14 Sept. 1875.
[74] 'Memories of Mitcheldean', 7; below, nonconf.
[75] *Dean Forest Mercury*, 5 July 1935.
[76] Ibid. 12 Dec. 1975.   [77] Ibid. 10 Feb. 1984.
[78] Glos. R.O., PA 220/3; *Glos. and Avon Life*, Nov. 1977, 45.
[79] *Glouc. Jnl.* 29 Dec. 1849; 3 Jan. 1857; 20 Apr. 1861.
[80] *Bibliotheca Glos.* i. 196.
[81] Hist. MSS. Com. 29, *13th Rep. I, Portland*, i, pp. 249, 362.
[82] *Dom. Bk.* (Rec. Com.), i. 167v.; cf. Taylor, *Dom. Glos.* 25–6.
[83] *Trans. B.G.A.S.* vi. 124–6, 199; *Pipe R.* 1130 (H.M.S.O. facsimile), 77.
[84] *Cal. Inq. p.m.* vi, p. 97; *Cal. Chart. R.* 1327–41, 84; a detailed account of the man. is given in J. Maclean, 'Hist. of Manors of Dene Magna and Abenhall', *Trans. B.G.A.S.* vi. 123–209.   [85] *Flaxley Cart.* pp. 138–9.
[86] *Pipe R.* 1199 (P.R.S. N.S. x), 32.
[87] *Bk. of Fees*, i. 343.   [88] *Cal. Inq. p.m.* i, p. 119.
[89] Below, Forest of Dean, forest admin. (officers and courts).

the rent to the St. Briavels castle estate.[90] The bailiwick, from which a separate bailiwick of Littledean was created before 1282, remained in the custody of others until 1319 or later,[91] but by 1384 it was held with part of Mitcheldean manor by Joan of Dean.[92] It apparently remained with the lords of that part until the late 18th century.[93]

William of Dean's moiety of Mitcheldean manor passed at his death c. 1259 to his son Henry of Dean,[94] sometimes also surnamed of Lasborough.[95] From Henry (d. c. 1292) it descended in turn to his son William of Dean (d. c. 1310) and to William's son William of Dean (d. c. 1319). The latter's heirs were his infant daughters Joan and Isabel[96] and in 1320 their mother Isabel was granted his lands for their use.[97] By 1328 the moiety of Mitcheldean manor was in the hands of William's elder daughter Joan and her husband John Esger.[98] By 1334 Joan had married Ralph Baynham (ap Eynon), who was dead in 1366,[99] and later she granted a rent of £10 from the manor to her son Thomas Baynham, who was probably dead in 1376 when the rent was confirmed to his wife Joan. Joan of Dean was alive in 1384 when her heir was said to be her daughter Margaret, wife of William of the hall, constable of Grosmont (Mon.),[1] but by 1395 her share of the manor had passed to John Baynham, a minor and the son and heir of Thomas Baynham.[2] John (fl. 1411)[3] had been succeeded by 1418 by Robert Baynham (d. 1436), whose share of the manor was described as two thirds and by then evidently included the right to fill two of every three vacancies in Mitcheldean rectory. Robert's son and heir Thomas, a minor,[4] by 1471 also held the other part of the manor, together with Abenhall, in the right of his second wife Alice Walwyn. At his death in 1500 his own part passed to Sir Alexander Baynham, his son by his first marriage,[5] and from Sir Alexander (d. 1524) the estate, by then usually known as the manor of Mitcheldean, descended, apparently in turn, to his sons John (d. 1528) and William[6] (d. 1568). William's son and heir Robert died in 1572 leaving his brother Joseph as his heir but William's widow Anne retained the manor in jointure in 1573.[7] Joseph was apparently seised of the manor in 1574, when he granted it to

Thomas Horn,[8] and 1594,[9] but in 1608 it was held by Sir Robert Woodruff in the right of his wife Mary, the widow of Robert Baynham.[10] Mary, who survived Sir Robert Woodruff (d. 1609), died in 1610[11] and the manor reverted to Joseph Baynham. Joseph (d. 1613) was succeeded by his son Alexander,[12] who sold his Mitcheldean estate in 1619 to Nicholas Roberts[13] of London and later of Stanton Harcourt (Oxon.).[14]

Nicholas, who in 1630 purchased an estate in Mitcheldean and Abenhall including much of the Wilderness,[15] died in 1637. His estate descended with land he had acquired in Westbury-on-Severn, being purchased with it in 1641 by Richard Colchester,[16] and from the late 17th century was centred on a house built at *THE WILDERNESS* by Duncombe Colchester. Duncombe, who was knighted in 1674 and died in 1694, settled the new house and its land in 1689 on the marriage of his son and heir Maynard and Jane Clarke (d. 1741). Maynard (d. 1715)[17] left Mitcheldean manor in turn to his brother Henry (d. 1719) and Henry's son Maynard,[18] who added the remainder of the manor to the Wilderness estate in 1740.[19] After the death of a later Maynard Colchester in 1860 the Colchester estates passed to his sisters Dorothea, Henrietta Davies, and Arabella and his great-nephew Maynard Willoughby Wemyss as tenants in common. Henrietta, to whom Arabella and Dorothea conveyed their interests in return for annuities, died in 1877 leaving her share of the estates to Maynard and her niece Dorothea Barton. Maynard, who assumed the surname Wemyss-Colchester, changed in 1882 to Colchester-Wemyss, enlarged the Wilderness estate in the period 1878–82 and bought out Dorothea Barton's interest in it in 1899.[20] The house had been sold with 41 a. in 1887 to Helen Lucas.[21] M. W. Colchester-Wemyss disposed of most of the remaining land c. 1919,[22] and in 1930, when he was succeeded as lord of the manor by his son Sir Maynard Francis Colchester-Wemyss, the principal landowner in Mitcheldean was Francis Wintle,[23] the former owner of a brewery in the town.[24]

The ancient manor house, standing west of the church,[25] presumably represented the house recorded on William of Dean's estate in 1319[26] and

90 *Cal. Inq. p.m.* iii, p. 37; vi, pp. 96–7; vii, pp. 17–18.
91 Below, Forest of Dean, forest admin. (officers and courts); *Cal. Inq. p.m.* vi, p. 97.
92 *Cal. Pat.* 1381–5, 404.
93 Glos. R.O., D 2026/X 3; D 36/Q 2; Hart, *Royal Forest*, 275; *3rd Rep. Com. Woods* (1788), 76.
94 *Cal. Inq. p.m.* i, p. 119.
95 *Cal. Close*, 1279–88, 225, 250.
96 *Cal. Inq. p.m.* iii, p. 37; vi, pp. 96–7; vii, pp. 17–18.
97 *Cal. Close*, 1318–23, 173–4.
98 P.R.O., C 53/115, m. 17; in 1327 Wm. Esger was among the principal residents of Mitcheldean: *Glos. Subsidy Roll, 1327*, 44.
99 *Trans. B.G.A.S.* vi. 130, 167.
1 *Cal. Pat.* 1374–7, 372; 1381–5, 404.
2 *Trans. B.G.A.S.* vi. 168.
3 Glos. R.O., D 2957/203.2.
4 *Trans. B.G.A.S.* vi. 131, 168; P.R.O., C 139/79, no. 15; below, church.
5 *Trans. B.G.A.S.* vi. 131–2; above, Abenhall, manor; cf. P.R.O., C 1/425/58.
6 P.R.O., C 142/42, no. 112; C 142/48, no. 102.
7 Ibid. C 142/149, no. 129; C 142/164, no. 62.

8 Glos. R.O., D 36/E 1, f. 18; cf. *Cal. Pat.* 1572–5, p. 340; P.R.O., CP 25/2/142/1816, no. 16.
9 P.R.O., E 134/36 Eliz. I Hil./21.
10 Ibid. C 142/305, no. 135; Smith, *Men and Armour*, 31.
11 Bigland, *Glos.* i. 54.
12 Glos. R.O., D 36/E 1, ff. 14v.–16v.; P.R.O., C 142/335, no. 32.
13 Glos. R.O., D 36/E 3, f. 61v.
14 Ibid. T 24.   15 Below, this section.
16 *Inq. p.m. Glos.* 1625–42, ii. 42–6, 159–62; Glos. R.O., D 36/E 3, ff. 140–1; cf. *V.C.H. Glos.* x. 87.
17 Glos R.O., D 36/T 55; for the Colchesters, *Trans. B.G.A.S.* vi. 189–93.
18 Glos. R.O., D 36/T 56; P 354/IN 1/2.
19 Ibid. D 36/T 25.
20 Ibid. D 2362, deeds 1784–1899; mortgages 1871–1921; for the Colchester estates in 1877: ibid. D 177/VI/4.
21 Ibid. D 2362, mortgages 1871–1921, deed 27 Feb. 1878.
22 Ibid. D 543, sale partics. 21 Dec. 1918; 14 Aug. 1920.
23 *Kelly's Dir. Glos.* (1923 and later edns.); *V.C.H. Glos.* x. 87.
24 Below, econ. hist. (other ind. and trade).
25 Cf. Glos. R.O., D 36/E 2, ff. 23–24v.; M 78, f. 17 and v.
26 P.R.O., C 134/61, no. 27.

the Baynhams' residence in the early 15th century.[27] The manor house, occupied by a tenant by 1437, became known as the Court Hall or House[28] and was in disrepair in 1642. It had been pulled down by 1696 when the Colchesters held courts elsewhere on their estate.[29]

The Wilderness, also called Hill House, was begun by Duncombe Colchester before 1672[30] on a site commanding extensive views over the Forest of Dean and Vale of Gloucester.[31] It probably had an L-shaped plan and parts of its walls survive in the south-eastern corner of the existing house. In the 1690s it was occupied by Duncombe's son-in-law Nathaniel Pyrke[32] and in 1715, when it had 25 rooms, it was the home of Jane Colchester (d. 1741).[33] After her death it was the Colchesters' principal residence[34] and by 1785 the south front had been extended westwards.[35] In 1824 the house was rebuilt and remodelled by Elizabeth Colchester, who added the service wing on the north-west and a room to the north of the new main staircase.[36] Shortly afterwards a billiard room was built to the north of that room and by the late 1870s a south-facing conservatory was added at the north-eastern corner of the billiard room.[37] From 1884 the Wilderness was used as a sanatorium for women from Barnwood House Hospital, the trustees of which bought the house and its grounds from F. L. Lucas in 1896.[38] After the sanatorium was closed in 1919 the East Dean and District Joint Hospital Board purchased the house for use as an isolation hospital.[39] Later, until 1965, it was a geriatric hospital and in 1968 the county education committee bought it for use as a residential centre for field studies,[40] which it remained in 1988. To the south-west an 18th-century range of two storeys had become a coach house and stables by 1840.[41] In 1785 the house's grounds included an enclosed forecourt to the south, beyond which were avenues or walks to the south and south-west, and a terrace to the east.[42] The forecourt had been removed and a second terrace created by 1840.[43]

By the 1240s a moiety of Mitcheldean manor was held from the Crown by Ralph of Abenhall

for 10s. rent.[44] It evidently descended with his Abenhall manor[45] to Alice Walwyn, whose husband Thomas Baynham[46] (d. 1500) owned the other moiety.[47] Alice, who later married Sir Walter Dennis, died in 1518 and the Abenhall estate, which her son Sir Christopher Baynham inherited, retained a moiety of Mitcheldean,[48] described as a third of the manor in 1611 when the estate passed to the Vaughan family.[49] In 1696 the Vaughans' part of Mitcheldean was purchased by Nathaniel Rudge, a mercer in the town, and in 1714 his mortgagee Augustine Rock, a Bristol stuffmaker, sold it to William Hughes, a Mitcheldean attorney.[50] William died intestate in 1723[51] and Maynard Colchester purchased his share of the manor from his widow Anne and son William in 1740,[52] thereby uniting the two parts of the manor in the Wilderness estate.[53]

An estate mostly comprising leasehold land in Mitcheldean and Abenhall belonged to William Bridgeman, who was given part of it, including a house in Mitcheldean, by his father John (d. 1548).[54] William, who in 1549 purchased some land belonging to a chantry in Mitcheldean church,[55] died in 1581 and his son and heir Thomas[56] sold bits of the estate piecemeal to John Ayleway. John's purchases included much of the Wilderness,[57] which was held from the Crown as of St. Briavels castle in free socage.[58] John (d. 1607) was succeeded by his son John,[59] who came of age in 1619.[60] He died in 1626 and his brother and heir William[61] sold the estate in 1630 to Nicholas Roberts,[62] owner of part of Mitcheldean manor with which it descended.[63] John Ayleway's house, which after his death in 1626 was occupied, sometimes only in part, by a tenant, came to be regarded as the manor house by the end of the century when Maynard Colchester held courts in it.[64] The house, which was at Court Farm, immediately north-east of the town, was later used as a farmhouse and was rebuilt in the early 19th century. It was demolished c. 1970 to make way for an extension of the Rank Xerox factory.[65]

Flaxley abbey, the abbot of which was described

27 Glos. R.O., D 2957/203.2; *Cal. Close*, 1422-9, 459, 471.
28 P.R.O., SC 6/858/15, rot. 5; Glos. R.O., D 36/E 2, ff. 23-24v.; M 19, f. 1v. A tenement called 'the castle' was recorded on the estate in the early 15th cent.: Glos. R.O., D 36/E 1, f. 6; cf. *Cal. Pat.* 1374-7, 220.
29 Glos. R.O., D36/M 78, ff. 17 and v., 36, 47, 63-4.
30 P.R.O., E 179/247/24, rot. 39; cf. Ogilby, *Britannia* (1675), p. 30, plate 15. The ho. was in Abenhall and part of its grounds, including some outbuildings, in Mitcheldean: O.S. Map 6", Glos. XXXI. NE. (1884 edn.).
31 Bodl. MS. Top. Glouc. c. 3, f. 139v.; Atkyns, *Glos.* 199.
32 Glos. R.O., D 36/M 78, f. 61; Bigland, *Glos.* i. 3.
33 Glos. Colln. RF 328.1.
34 Glos. R.O., D 36/E 16, T 59; Bigland, *Glos.* i. 1; P.R.O., HO 107/1959; cf. *V.C.H. Glos.* x. 88.
35 Glos. R.O., D 2123, p. 69.
36 Nicholls, *Forest of Dean*, 251; Nicholls, *Personalities of Dean*, 63; cf. G.D.R., T 1/1.
37 O.S. Map 1/2,500, Glos. XXXI. 4 (1881 edn.).
38 Glos. R.O., D 3725, Barnwood Ho. Trust, rep. 1884, 1896; *Kelly's Dir. Glos.* (1894), 234.
39 Glos. R.O., D 3725, Barnwood Ho. Trust, rep. 1919, 1920.
40 Ibid. D 3921/V/24; *Glos. and Avon Life*, Sept. 1975, 40-1.
41 G.D.R., T 1/1.
42 Glos. R.O., D 2123, pp. 65, 69.

43 G.D.R., T 1/1.
44 P.R.O., E 146/1/25.
45 Above, Abenhall, manor; *Cal. Inq. p.m.* vi, pp. 1-2, 97; *Cal. Close*, 1413-19, 338; P.R.O., C 139/115, no. 34.
46 P.R.O., C 140/34, no. 53.
47 *Trans. B.G.A.S.* vi. 131-2; above, this section.
48 P.R.O., C 142/33, no. 69.
49 Ibid. C 142/340, no. 192; cf. Glos. R.O., D 23/T 1.
50 Glos. R.O., D 36/T 25; P 220/IN 1/1.
51 Bigland, *Glos.* i. 446; G.D.R. wills 1722/39.
52 Glos. R.O., D 36/T 25.   53 Above, this section.
54 Hockaday Abs. cclxxx; for the Bridgemans, *Visit. Glos. 1623*, 26-8.
55 Glos. R.O., D 36/E 1, f. 91v.; cf. ibid. f. 33.
56 P.R.O., C 142/199, no. 84.
57 Glos. R.O., D 36/E 1, ff. 87v.-93.
58 *Inq. p.m. Glos.* 1625-42, ii. 42-6.
59 P.R.O., C 142/305, no. 135.
60 Glos. R.O., D 36/E 3, f. 65v.
61 *Inq. p.m. Glos.* 1625-42, i. 60-4.
62 Glos. R.O., D 36/E 1, f. 95.
63 Cf. *Inq. p.m. Glos.* 1625-42, ii. 42-6.
64 Ibid. i. 60-1; ii. 43; Glos. R.O., D 36/M 78, ff. 13v., 47, 63; M 79; Colchester's tenant in the early 18th cent. acted for him as woodward of the bailiwick: Glos. R.O., D 36/E 10, ff. 33v.-34, 77v.-78.
65 Phelps, *Forest in Old Photog.* (1983), 24; *Dean Forest Mercury*, 9 June 1972.

in 1316 as one of the lords of Mitcheldean with Abenhall and Littledean,[66] acquired land in Mitcheldean,[67] where a few pieces were held from Flaxley manor in the late 16th century and the early 17th.[68] Little Malvern priory (Worcs.) had 6s. 2d. in rents of assize from Deerhurst and Mitcheldean in 1535.[69]

ECONOMIC HISTORY. AGRICULTURE. In 1086 William son of Norman, whose estate in Dean had increased in value from 33s. in 1066 to 44s., had 3 ploughteams in demesne there and his tenants, of whom three owed a total rent of 8s., were 38 bordars sharing 7½ teams.[70] The estate is presumed to have included land in Mitcheldean, Abenhall, and Littledean,[71] and in 1220 three ploughteams were recorded in Dean and two in Abenhall.[72] William of Dean's estate as surveyed in 1259 had 2 ploughlands in Mitcheldean and Henry of Dean's estate in 1292 had a ploughland there.[73] In 1319 the estate of Henry's grandson William included 80 a. of arable and 3 a. of meadow in Mitcheldean and 102 a. of assarted land, of which much was at Littledean and 4 a. at Bradley to the north-east of Mitcheldean.[74] In 1282 fourteen men had parcels of land, all under 3 a., described as old assarts,[75] and in 1322 a holding included 66½ a. of pasture which had been recently assarted.[76] The shape of the parish, which, together with Abenhall, included a large indent into the extra-parochial Forest of Dean on high land west of the town, suggests that land there was taken from the Forest for cultivation at a relatively late date. Assarting and inclosure of the Wilderness was under way in 1333,[77] and in 1436 Robert Baynham's estate had, in addition to 40 a. of arable, 10 a. of meadow, and 16 a. of pasture, 100 a. of newly broken land and 200 a. of waste.[78] Lady grove was described as part of the new assarts in 1436[79] and land west of the town was included in a survey of assarted lands in the early 17th century. In 1619, before he sold his estate to Nicholas Roberts, Alexander Baynham paid the Crown a composition for a large number of assarts including Scully grove.[80]

In 1319 William of Dean had 18 neifs, each owing works for 3 days in the autumn, in Mitcheldean. There were also 30 freeholders paying him rents worth £4 4s. in total.[81] Some freeholders were presumably tradesmen or craftsmen in the small town, and many of the 134 parishioners listed in 1608 probably combined husbandry with a trade.[82] Many of the tenants and freeholders recorded in 1620 on Joan Vaughan's estate in Abenhall and Mitcheldean lived in the town.[83] In 1623 Nicholas Roberts's estate had c. 37 tenants holding by leases, most of which were for 3 lives or 99 years with heriots and additional rents of capons payable. It also included rents from 37 freeholders for 88 tenements,[84] for each of which he claimed a heriot until agreeing in 1626 that by ancient custom a single heriot was owed on the death of each freeholder.[85] In 1635 the estate, which by then had land in Abenhall, contained few purely agricultural holdings, most, including the freeholds, being buildings in the town with or without a few acres of land attached to them. Some parcels of land were held at will,[86] as in 1642 were a few buildings which had presumably encroached on the town's market place and streets. Leaseholds for 21 years, common while Alexander Baynham had owned the estate between 1613 and 1619, or for 7 years had become the most usual form of tenure by 1696.[87] As for heriots from freeholds, Maynard Colchester in 1723 denied claims, based on the practice of the other part of the manor, that they were owed only for holdings with a dwelling.[88]

No evidence has been found for open fields in Mitcheldean, the field of Bradley mentioned in the later 13th century probably lying to the north-east in Longhope.[89] In the late 16th century most of the cultivated land was in small closes and was used as pasture and meadow.[90] Sheep farming was important by the 14th century, when several shepherds were employed,[91] and flax was among the crops grown in the parish in 1340.[92] In the early 16th century Sir Alexander Baynham's demesne included an arable field, ten meadow or pasture closes, and an orchard, which he may have had in hand, and a few pieces, notably land occupied as twelve gardens, which had been leased to tenants.[93] There were many small orchards in and around the town in 1635.[94] Although the parish retained some waste land, presumably on road sides, in 1839, no evidence has been found for land in it subject to common rights.[95] About 1280 Henry of Dean, as woodward of a bailiwick, claimed common rights for himself and his men throughout the Forest of Dean,[96] and Richard Colchester

66 *Feud. Aids*, ii. 275.
67 Hockaday Abs. cclxxx; P.R.O., C 142/56, no. 22.
68 *Inq. p.m. Glos.* 1625–42, i. 63; ii. 45; P.R.O., C 142/413, no. 95.
69 *Valor Eccl.* (Rec. Com.), iii. 244; P.R.O., SC 6/Hen. VIII/4039, rot. 19.
70 *Dom. Bk.* (Rec. Com.), i. 167v.
71 Taylor, *Dom. Glos.* 25.
72 *Bk. of Fees*, i. 308.
73 *Cal. Inq. p.m.* i, p. 119; iii, p. 37.
74 P.R.O., C 134/61, no. 27.
75 Ibid. E 32/30, rot. 19.
76 Ibid. SC 6/1147/12, m. 4.
77 Ibid. C 143/226, no. 13.
78 Ibid. C 139/79, no. 15.
79 Glos. R.O., D 36/E 1, f. 98.
80 Ibid. E 3, ff. 49 and v., 61v.; cf. Hart, *Royal Forest*, 100.
81 P.R.O., C 134/61, no. 27.
82 Smith, *Men and Armour*, 31–3; cf. G.D.R. wills

1605/211.
83 Glos. R.O., D 36/M 2, ff. 3–6; above, Abenhall, econ. hist.
84 Glos. R.O., D 36/M 19, ff. 1–2v.
85 Ibid. M 75, rot. 8d.
86 Ibid. E 6, rott. 6d.–19.
87 Ibid. M 78, ff. 9v.–23v., 58–68; E 6, rott. 12–17d.
88 Ibid. M78/f. 72v.; E 48.
89 Ibid. D 4431, grant of Hen. of Dean to Hugh Godwin.
90 Ibid. D 36/T 24; P.R.O., C 142/199, no. 84; C 142/305, no. 135; cf. Glos. R.O., D 36/E 3, ff. 49 and v., 72–9, 200–214v.; M 78, ff. 5–23v.
91 Glos. R.O., D 1448/T 27; D 4431, deeds Thurs. after Nativity B.V.M. 2 Ric. II; Thurs. after Nativity St. John the Baptist 9 Ric. II.
92 *Inq. Non.* (Rec. Com.), 416.
93 *Trans. B.G.A.S.* vi. 206.
94 Glos. R.O., D 36/E 6, rott. 6d.–19.
95 Cf. G.D.R., T 1/123.
96 P.R.O., E 32/32, m. 4.

claimed similar rights in 1642.[97] In the mid 1680s the parish paid 7s. herbage money for common rights in the extraparochial land of the Forest,[98] and in 1860 four people exercised those rights.[99]

In 1785 the Wilderness estate included farms of 105 a. and 72 a. and eight small holdings of between 4 a. and 30 a. at Mitcheldean.[1] In 1831, when about a fifth of the families in the parish depended on agriculture, there were 16 farmers or smallholders, of whom 7 employed labour, and 16 agricultural labourers.[2] In 1839 two farms in the parish had over 100 a., the larger one being Court farm, and a farm at Knockalls had 42 a.[3] There was also a number of smallholdings in the parish in the late 19th century and the early 20th bringing the total of agricultural occupiers to c. 15. In 1926 eight of them had under 20 a.[4] and two rented land by the Ross road from the county council.[5] Court farm, which in 1918 had covered 170 a. in Mitcheldean and the adjoining part of Longhope, remained the largest farm until after the Second World War.[6] In 1988 the enlarged parish, including Abenhall, returned 21 holdings, of which 2 had 40–50 ha. (c. 100–125 a.) and 16, presumably those worked part-time, had 20 ha. (c. 49 a.) or less.[7]

In the late 18th century two thirds of the cultivated land in the parish were devoted to pasture.[8] Of the 105 a. under crops in 1801 barley and wheat accounted for 95 a. and pota-toes, oats, and peas for the remainder.[9] In the early 19th century more land was used for arable cultivation, Knockalls grove (11 a.) at the north end of the parish being grubbed up for that purpose in the late 1820s or 1830s,[10] and in 1839 it was estimated that the parish contained 220 a. of arable and 340 a. of meadow and pasture.[11] The trend had evidently been reversed by 1866, when much of the land was devoted to sheep farming, and later in the century, as cereal production fell, more land was turned to perma-nent grass and herds of beef and dairy cattle were established. The acreage of corn returned in 1896 was down to 49 a. compared with 108 a. in 1866 while permanent grassland rose during that period to 427 a. from 262 a. Orchards accounted for at least 22 a. in 1896. The introduction of cattle was partly at the expense of the flocks, 506 sheep and 112 cattle being returned in 1896 compared with 635 and 15 in 1866. The number of pigs returned rose from 42 in 1866 to 67 in

1896.[12] By 1878 two fields (c. 7 a.) south of the Gloucester road, belonging to the town's charity school, had been divided into 36 allotment gar-dens and a field at Townsend had also been given over to allotments.[13] In the early 20th century the flocks were increased considerably, with 1,068 sheep being returned in 1926.[14] The farms, which were mixed, continued to depend on sheep farming and dairying and many retained cider orchards in the mid 20th century.[15] In the 1960s and 1970s the area of agricultural land was greatly reduced by the creation of new housing estates and the vast extension of the Rank Xerox factory. In the later 1980s nearly all the farmland of the enlarged parish, including Abenhall, was under grass. The principal farms were devoted mainly to dairying but they also raised sheep and beef cattle. Pigs were also reared and one holding was a poultry farm.[16]

MILLS. A miller lived in Mitcheldean in 1282[17] and two water mills were recorded there in 1319.[18] A mill driven by the churchyard brook and standing on the west side of the town was in use in 1371, when Richard atte Mill was among Mitcheldean's inhabitants, and it had a steeply inclined race or shoot.[19] It was held from the part of the manor inherited by Robert Baynham (d. 1436)[20] and the freehold belonged, possibly by 1573, to Thomas Bridgeman and was conveyed in 1598 to Anthony Callow.[21] The mill was worked by William Bennett in 1629[22] and possibly remained in use in 1642, but by 1696 it had been pulled down.[23] Wind-mill hill, recorded in 1689 north-west of the town,[24] was possibly the site of an earlier wind-mill.

OTHER INDUSTRY AND TRADE. Mitcheldean was a centre of ironworks by the early 13th century, when itinerant forges or smithies be-longing to William of Dean and William of Abenhall were worked in Mitcheldean or the nearby demesne woodland of the Forest.[25] Eight such forges operated in the Mitcheldean area in the mid 13th century[26] and the number increased later in the century. In 1270 at least one nailer was at work there.[27] Indirect evidence suggests that the small town had a substantial body of tradesmen before the 14th century.[28] Residents included one or more tailors in 1270[29] and a shoemaker in 1280,[30] and among the wealthier

97 Glos. R.O., D 36/M 78, f. 24v.
98 Ibid. P 220/VE 2/1.
99 P.R.O., F 3/128, letter 29 Nov. 1860.
1 Glos. R.O., D 2123, pp. 71–83.
2 Census, 1831.   3 G.D.R., T 1/123.
4 P.R.O., MAF 68/1609/15; MAF 68/3295/16.
5 Mins. of Glos. County Council, xxxiv. 31; Glos. R.O., K 871/2/2/191.
6 Glos. R.O., D 543, sale partics. 21 Dec. 1918; Kelly's Dir. Glos. (1914–39 edns.).
7 Agric. Returns 1988.   8 Bigland, Glos. i. 443.
9 List & Index Soc. clxxxix, p. 175.
10 Cf. Greenwood, Map of Glos. (1824); G.D.R., T 1/123 (no. 233).
11 G.D.R., T 1/123.
12 P.R.O., MAF 68/25/20; MAF 68/26/9; MAF 68/1609/15.
13 Glos. R.O., P 220/CH 5/2, 4, 7; O.S. Map 1/2,500, Glos. XXIII. 16 (1881 edn.).
14 P.R.O., MAF 68/3295/16.
15 'Memories of Mitcheldean', 19.

16 Agric. Returns 1988.
17 P.R.O., E 32/30, rot. 19.
18 Ibid. C 134/61, no. 27.
19 Glos. R.O., D 4431, deed Mon. after All Saints 45 Edw. III; cf. ibid. deed 14 July 9 Edw. IV; D 36/E 1, f. 17v.
20 P.R.O., SC 6/858/15, rot. 5; Glos. R.O., D 36/E 1, f. 15.
21 P.R.O., CP 25/2/142/1813, no. 9; CP 25/2/146/1915, no. 21; Glos. R.O., D 36/E 6, rot. 7.
22 Glos. R.O., D 36/M 75, rot. 18.
23 Ibid. M 78, ff. 6, 50.
24 Ibid. T 55.
25 Rot. Litt. Claus. (Rec. Com.), i. 334–5, 442–3.
26 P.R.O., E 146/1/25; cf. Glos. R.O., D 4431, grant of Hen. of Dean to Hugh Godwin.
27 P.R.O., E 32/29, rot. 2; E 32/30, rot. 23d.; E 32/31, m. 16.
28 Cf. above (agric.).
29 P.R.O., E 32/29, rott. 4d., 6.
30 Glos. R.O., D 1448/T 26.

inhabitants in 1327 were two carpenters, two nailers, and a weaver.[31] Also recorded were the son of a mason and a tiler in 1347[32] and a baker in 1367.[33] In addition to nailmaking, metal trades were represented by a locksmith and a spurrier working in the town in the 1370s and the mid 1380s respectively.[34] There may have been wiremaking at the Merrin, where land was called Wirehouse Close in 1576.[35] Place-name evidence from the mid 16th century also indicates that charcoal was made just outside the town.[36]

Ironworking continued in the later Middle Ages, when furnaces, known as oresmithies,[37] were supplied with ore mined presumably at the Wilderness or in the adjoining royal demesne.[38] Slag from the works was tipped in many parts of the town to form cinder hills, the most notable being in Brook Street.[39] The masters running the industry were known as smith-holders and several were also engaged in mining and husbandry in the early 16th century.[40] One parishioner, by will proved 1570, required the user of his anvil and bellows to distribute 12d. a year to the poor on Good Friday.[41] In the early 16th century eight smithies, presumably including several forges, were working on Sir Alexander Baynham's estate[42] but in the 1540s, when several smithies were used for other purposes, the town's iron industry was in decline[43] and at the end of the century it was not of primary importance.[44] Many, if not all, of the miners living in Mitcheldean at that time[45] presumably mined iron ore at the Wilderness.[46] Limestone was being quarried there by 1634, when a man was granted liberty to burn lime.[47]

The cloth industry had been established in Mitcheldean by the later 13th century when a weaver witnessed local deeds.[48] Many townsmen in the later 14th century and the early 15th had surnames derived from the trades of weaver, fuller, and shearman,[49] and weavers were recorded in 1436,[50] in 1532,[51] and in 1586.[52] Mitcheldean's earliest known clothier was Robert Stanton (fl. 1585).[53] In the later 16th century wool was evidently the staple of Mitcheldean's trade,[54] and in 1608 among the townspeople, many of whom were listed under Abenhall, were 4 clothiers, 24 weavers, and 5 tuckers. In addition to the cloth industry the town thrived in 1608 as a centre of crafts and of retail and service trades. Clothing trades were represented by 3 mercers, 5 tailors, 3 glovers, and 10 shoemakers, metal trades by 5 smiths, 4 cutlers, 2 nailers, and a brazier, leather trades by 3 tanners, 2 curriers, and probably a saddler, and building trades by a thatcher, a tiler, a plasterer, a mason, and a sawyer. As well as the other usual tradesmen such as butchers, bakers, and carpenters, there were 3 sieve makers, 2 innkeepers, a victualler, a cook, a miner, a lime burner, a basket maker, a dish carrier, a tooth drawer, and a sailor. The prosperity of the town and its social composition are indicated by the 38 people named as servants and the 10, including the barrister Edward Trotman and the clothier William Gunn, styled gentlemen.[55]

The continuing importance of metal trades and the diversity of clothing trades in the early 17th century is underlined by the presence of a locksmith and a hosier in the town.[56] Cloth manufacture also remained important and before 1617 the clothier John Hathway installed looms in a brewhouse in New Street.[57] Clothiers ranking among the town's leading inhabitants included Edward Morse, who in 1622 purchased two turns in the patronage of the rectory and in 1625 was among prominent men taking a lease of profits from the market and fair.[58] Dyers lived in the town in the 1620s.[59] Weavers still worked in Mitcheldean then but the manufacture of coarse cloth had given way to pinmaking as the town's chief industry by the end of the 17th century[60] and had disappeared by the end of the 18th.[61] Flax dressing and feltmaking were other trades in the town in the mid 18th century.[62]

Pinmaking, which had been established in Mitcheldean by 1628,[63] provided much employment in the early 18th century[64] when, together with the market and fairs, it was the mainstay of the town's trade.[65] The craft, which was in the hands of small masters, died out in the 18th century with a lack of investment. One pinmaker moved to Bristol but the decline chiefly benefited Gloucester where the industry was flourishing.[66] The disappearance of pinmaking left leather manufacture as Mitcheldean's principal indus-

31 *Glos. Subsidy Roll, 1327,* 44.
32 Glos. R.O., D 4431, deed Sun. after St. Augustine 21 Edw. III.   33 Ibid. D 36/E 1, f. 4.
34 Ibid. D 4431, deeds Mon. after Mich. 45 Edw. III; Mon. after St. Edw. the Confessor 49 Edw. III; *Trans. B.G.A.S.* lxii. 138.
35 Glos. R.O., D 4431, deed 12 Sept. 18 Eliz. I.
36 Ibid. D 36/E 1, f. 14; D 127/562.
37 Ibid. D 36/E 1, ff. 7, 17v.; D 4431, deeds St. Benedict 44 Edw. III; Mon. after Mich. 45 Edw. III.
38 Cf. Bodl. MS. Top. Glouc. c. 3, f. 193; Nicholls, *Forest of Dean,* 214.
39 Glos. R.O., D 36/E 1, ff. 89v., 91; E 2, f. 13; M 78, f. 19; D 2123, pp. 79, 83; cf. *Trans. B.G.A.S.* ii. 225, 234; Glos. Colln. 18490 (3), p. 27.
40 Glos. R.O., D 36/E 1, f. 89v.; *L. & P. Hen. VIII,* i (1), p. 215; cf. Rudge, *Hist. of Glos.* ii. 12.
41 G.D.R. wills 1570/74.
42 *Trans. B.G.A.S.* vi. 200–6.
43 Glos. R.O., D 36/E 1, ff. 22v., 89v.
44 Ibid. f. 91; cf. Smith, *Men and Armour,* 31–3, 35–6.
45 Cf. Glos. R.O., D 4431, deeds Mich. 23 Hen. VII; 20 May 2 & 3 Phil. and Mary; 23 Oct. 18 Eliz. I.
46 Cf. Bodl. MS. Top. Glouc. c. 3, f. 193.
47 Glos. R.O., D 36/F 4/1.

48 Ibid. D 4431, grant of Hen. of Dean to Hugh Godwin.
49 e.g. ibid. deeds Mon. after Mich. 45 Edw. III; Tues. before St. Geo. 40 Edw. III; Sun. after All Saints 14 Hen. IV.
50 Ibid. deed Fri. before Trin. 14 Hen. VI.
51 Hockaday Abs. cclxxx.
52 Glos. R.O., D 4431, bond 17 Apr. 28 Eliz. I.
53 Ibid. deed 26 Dec. 28 Eliz. I.
54 Cf. *Univ. Brit. Dir.* ii (1792), 775.
55 Smith, *Men and Armour,* 31–3, 35–6: those named included the son and the servant of two mercers not themselves listed.
56 Glos. R.O., D 36/E 2, ff. 19v., 24v.; P.R.O., E 134/22 Jas. I Hil./3.
57 Glos. R.O., D 36/T 26.
58 Ibid. E 3, f. 159v.; E 2, f. 34 and v.
59 Ibid. E 2, f. 33; D 4431, deed 7 Sept. 18 Jas. I.
60 Ibid. P 1/IN 1/2; P 220/IN 1/1; ibid. OV 4/1; Atkyns, *Glos.* 381.
61 Bigland, *Glos.* i. 443; *Univ. Brit. Dir.* ii (1792), 775.
62 Glos. R.O., D 36/E 12, ff. 105v.–106; D 2957/203.3, 6; P 220/CW 3/2–3.
63 Ibid. D 36/E 2, f. 37v.   64 Ibid. P 220/IN 1/1.
65 Bodl. MS. Top. Glouc. c. 3, f. 139v.
66 Rudder, *Glos.* 401; Glos. R.O., P 220/OV 4/1, indenture 1762; cf. *V.C.H. Glos.* iv. 130–1.

1. The Buck stone, at Staunton, *c.* 1895

2. Old iron-ore workings known as the Devil's Chapel, at the Scowles, near Bream

3. Coleford town centre in 1797 showing the west end of the market house and the chapel, rebuilt in the late 17th century and enlarged by a south aisle *c.* 1755

4. Mitcheldean church from the south-east, *c.* 1780

5. Highmeadow House from the north-east, *c.* 1700; Newland church is shown in background

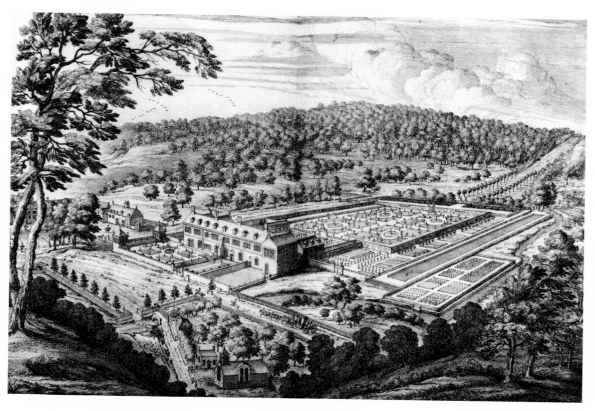

6. Flaxley Abbey from the south-west, *c.* 1710, with the parish church and (*at right*) the furnace and a forge of Flaxley ironworks

7. Newland village from the north; Newland House and the Old School House stand west of the churchyard and Birchamp House on the hillside east of the village

8. St. Briavels from the west in 1947, before the enlargement of the village

9. Lydney harbour, *c.* 1900, looking from its head towards the river

10. Brockweir before the bridge was built over the Wye in 1906

12. Lydney Park, *c.* 1770

14. Dean Hall, Littledean: the north front remodelled in 1852

11. Nass House: the south front

13. Clearwell Court from the north-west, with the stable range in foreground

16. Blakeney Congregational (formerly Independent) chapel

17. Zion chapel (Bible Christian), Upper Soudley, in the early 20th century

15. Coleford Baptist chapel

18. Ruardean church and village, looking north-west over Wye Valley

19. Blakeney Hill in the early 20th century

20. Flour Mill colliery in the Oakwood valley, near Bream

21. Cannop colliery in the 1930s, with coal wagons on a siding of the Severn Bridge & Severn & Wye railway

23. Schooner at coal tip in Lydney harbour

22. The former Sloop inn (Drake's House) at Gatcombe, with in foreground boats used for stop net fishing

26. Brass at Newland church with crest of iron miner with pick, candle, held in teeth, and hod

24. Charcoal burner with hearth and equipment, c. 1930

25. Members of the Gwilliam family, free miners, at coal level near Christ Church, c. 1955

27. Tollhouse and gate at Whitecliff, near Coleford, 1888, at abolition of Forest turnpike trust

28. Block of stone being hauled on tramroad at Bixslade

29. The Severn railway bridge at Purton, completed in 1879; Severn Bridge
station is in the foreground

30. Lower Lydbrook from the south, with the railway viaduct completed in 1874

31. Cinderford ironworks, *c.* 1890

32. Workers at quarry of the South Wales Portland Cement Co., in Mitcheldean, *c.* 1913

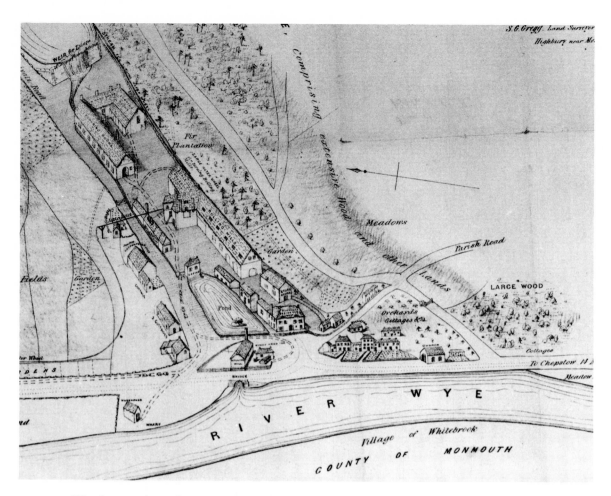

33. Tinplate works at Lower Redbrook in 1848; buildings shown near the river include the Anglican and Wesleyan chapels, both converted barkhouses

34. Tinplate workers at Lydbrook in the early 20th century, with tinplates and tongs and other tools

35. Newland church, *c.* 1860, shortly before its restoration; the Old School House is in background

36. St. Paul's church, Parkend

37. The chapel-schoolroom (later Christ Church) at Berry Hill, opened in 1813

38. Pillowell school with Yorkley village beyond, *c.* 1910

39. The Speech House from the north-west, *c.* 1895, after enlargement; the straight joint in north wall marks the end of the late 17th-century building

40. St. Briavels castle in 1775

41. The verderers' court room at the Speech House, *c.* 1850

42. Forest officers at the Speech House, *c.* 1865, including (*seated*) verderers D. Pyrke, E. Probyn,
E. O. Jones, and C. Bathurst, (*standing behind, holding hat*) deputy surveyor Sir J. Campbell,
and (*standing against wall*) the three keepers

44. Free miner with coal truck, near Christ Church, *c.* 1955

43. The Dean road nearing its crossing of Blackpool brook, *c.* 1920 (before a new road was laid alongside this section)

try.[67] Tanning, introduced to the town by the early 1540s,[68] was carried on at several sites.[69] In the mid 1620s, when tanners, glovers, and dyers were polluting the churchyard brook, Jasper Lugg had a tannery north of Stenders Road.[70] It was operated until 1777, when its lessee was bankrupt, and had fallen into ruin by 1786.[71] The only other tannery of any size, in Brook Street, may have been operating by the mid 1540s.[72] By the late 17th century its use was intermittent and c. 1744 it was converted as potash works.[73] Glove making, using deerskins from the Forest, continued in the town until at least the mid 1780s[74] and among leather workers living in the town c. 1790 were a fellmonger, a currier, and a saddler.[75] A small leather factory survived the turn of the century.[76] The town continued to support a wide variety of other trades. Notable among the craftsmen was George Voyce (d. 1722), the first of a dynasty of clockmakers.[77] Other occupations recorded included stiller in 1699, barber in 1700, and millwright in 1715.[78] The professions were fairly well represented in Mitcheldean during its period of importance as a market and industrial centre. The earliest known of several surgeons was licensed in 1683[79] and attorneys were resident by 1703.[80]

The decline of much of Mitcheldean's traditional industry in the 18th century was evident in the state of many of its buildings in the mid 1770s[81] and some wealthier families had abandoned the town by the early 19th century. The poor turned for a livelihood to collecting cinders left by ancient ironworks.[82] Landowners were selling cinders, rich in iron, to furnaces for resmelting by the early 18th century[83] and Maynard Colchester supplied furnaces at Flaxley and Newent from his Wilderness estate, notably from a large tip in Mitcheldean town, in the early 1740s.[84] Although an agreement of 1747 between Colchester and two Bristol ironmasters for the construction of a furnace near the town came to nothing,[85] the cinders were consumed rapidly and accessible deposits had been exhausted by the end of the century.[86] Another activity associated with the needs of furnaces outside Mitcheldean was charcoal burning: under an agreement of 1767 for the purchase of timber

Thomas Crawley-Boevey, owner of the Flaxley ironworks, was entitled to work charcoal pits in woods on the Wilderness estate.[87] The Colchesters' exploitation of their woodland in the 18th century also included sales of bark and by an agreement of 1785 timber went to ironworks at Ayleford in Newnham.[88] A timber merchant lived in Mitcheldean in 1817.[89]

Road traffic was an important element in the town's economy long before the early 17th century when a customary payment called wheelage was claimed on both parts of the manor from every cart or wain passing with merchandise to or from Lea or one of the two nearby navigable rivers.[90] In the later 18th century the town contained several inns and lodging houses[91] but in the mid 1770s, despite the turnpiking of the principal roads, the townspeople derived little profit from traffic.[92] Some wagons serving Monmouth and Brecon passed through, including in 1750 a passenger and goods service operated by a London carrier, but most traffic between Gloucester and South Wales evidently preferred a more northerly route skirting the Forest of Dean by way of Ross.[93] Improvements to the Forest roads, particularly those made after 1796, boosted traffic through Mitcheldean and the town's inns benefited accordingly.[94]

With the decline of its industry and market trade Mitcheldean settled into a more limited economic role principally as a minor service and retailing centre. Small retailers gaining a living c. 1790 included 3 shopkeepers, 3 mercers, 2 bakers, a butcher, a carpenter, a saddler, a tailor, a hatter, and a breeches maker,[95] and among the shopkeepers and small tradesmen recorded in 1842 were several grocers, drapers, tailors, and a chemist.[96] In the early 19th century metal trades, which included nailmaking and tinplate working, provided little employment.[97] Among the nailers was John Griffiths (d. 1861),[98] whose family continued in business at the Merrin until c. 1912.[99] The town's corn trade clearly remained more important than the presence of a single mealman c. 1790 suggests,[1] for a few corn dealers were resident in the mid 19th century and were also engaged in other businesses such as milling and malting.[2] The town and its neighbourhood also continued to offer scope for professional

67 Bigland, *Glos.* i. 443.
68 Glos. R.O., D 36/E 2, f. 13.
69 Ibid. M 2, f. 3; M 10; D 1230/4.
70 Ibid. D 36/M 75, rott. 3d., 5d., 13d.; E 2, f. 45.
71 Ibid. M 78, ff. 14, 50v., 63v.; E 12, ff. 96v.–97; E 49.
72 Ibid. E 2, f. 13.
73 Ibid. M 78, f. 48v.; T 31; D 2957/203.4, 8; D 5851/3/1.
74 Ibid. D 36/E 12, f. 102v.; E 13, ff. 16v.–17; *Gent. Mag.* xcii (1), 18.
75 *Univ. Brit. Dir.* ii (1792), 775.
76 Brayley and Britton, *Beauties of Eng. and Wales,* v. 708.
77 G. Dowler, *Glos. Clock and Watch Makers* (1984), 102–6; for fuller details of Voyce fam., Glos. R.O., P 220/IN 1/1; ibid. VE 2/1–2; *Univ. Brit. Dir.* ii (1792), 775.
78 Glos. R.O., P 220/IN 1/1; ibid. CW 3/2.
79 Hockaday Abs. cclxxx.
80 Glos. R.O., P 220/IN 1/1.
81 Rudder, *Glos.* 401; cf. *Univ. Brit. Dir.* ii (1792), 775.
82 Rudge, *Hist. of Glos.* ii. 90; *Gent. Mag.* xcii (1), 17–18.
83 Atkyns, *Glos.* 381.
84 Glos. R.O., D 36/E 12, ff. 128v.–129; cf. *Trans. B.G.A.S.* lxxii. 134–5.
85 Glos. R.O., D 36/E 16.

86 Rudge, *Hist. of Glos.* ii. 12–18, 90.
87 Glos. R.O., D 36/E 7/2; above, Flaxley, econ. hist.
88 Glos. R.O., D 36/A 7; E 7/1, 3; E 12, ff. 129v.–130.
89 Ibid. F 22.
90 Ibid. E 2, f. 34 and v.; M 10.
91 Ibid. P 220/VE 2/2, f. 155; ibid. 3, min. 23 Apr. 1799.
92 Rudder, *Glos.* 401.
93 *Univ. Brit. Dir.* ii (1792), 775–6; *Glouc. Jnl.* 28 Aug. 1750; 13 Sept. 1784.
94 Nicholls, *Forest of Dean,* 194–6; Dean Forest Roads Act, 36 Geo. III, c. 131; *Glouc. Jnl.* 29 Aug. 1796; Rudge, *Hist. of Glos.* ii. 90.
95 *Univ. Brit. Dir.* ii (1792), 775.
96 *Pigot's Dir. Glos.* (1842), 120–1.
97 *Gent. Mag.* xcii (1), 18; Glos. R.O., P 1/IN 1/7; P 220 IN 1/3.
98 Glos. R.O., P 1/IN 1/11; *Pigot's Dir. Glos.* (1842), 121.
99 G.D.R., T 1/1; *Slater's Dir. Glos.* (1852–3), 144; *Kelly's Dir. Glos.* (1856–1914 edns.), s.vv. Abenhall, Mitcheldean.
1 *Univ. Brit. Dir.* ii (1792), 775.
2 *Pigot's Dir. Glos.* (1842), 121; *Kelly's Dir. Glos.* (1856), 326; P.R.O., HO 107/1959.

men, represented *c.* 1790 by 2 attorneys and a surgeon[3] and in 1842 by 3 attorneys and 4 surgeons. In the 1920s and 1930s there was also an auctioneer in the town.[4] An architect, Alfred Smith, was resident in the early 1880s.[5]

In the later 19th century the town's industrial life was revived by the opening of a brewery and by exploitation of limestone and sandstone on the Wilderness estate. Brewing developed from the malting industry, which had been established by 1715[6] and was represented by 3 maltsters *c.* 1790.[7] In the mid 19th century the principal maltsters were the corn merchants Timothy Bennett, who was also a colliery owner, and Thomas Wintle.[8] Wintle built a brewery in Brook Street in 1868 and, as his operations there expanded, put up new buildings, notably a malthouse in 1870. The business was run from 1890 by his son Francis and from 1923, when it owned 72 licensed houses in the surrounding area, by a limited company.[9] The maltings were damaged by fire in 1925.[10] Brewing ended in 1930 when the company, which with 50 employees was the only large-scale business in the town, was taken over by the Cheltenham Original Brewery Co., but malting continued until the mid 1940s.[11]

Quarrying and mining continued near Mitcheldean from the 17th century and several townsmen found employment as stone cutters and masons or as coal miners in the Forest.[12] Lime kilns were operating on the Wilderness estate in 1791[13] and a mason was granted a lease of a quarry at the Wilderness in 1818.[14] Iron ore continued to be mined there and the nearby Westbury Brook mine ran beneath the old workings in the mid 19th century.[15] Small sandstone quarries were being worked near the town by the late 18th century.[16] Those north of the Gloucester road, which yielded red sandstone, were exploited on a large scale from 1882 and became known as the Wilderness quarries.[17] Those quarries, at which brickworks were established in 1885,[18] were purchased in 1900 by Forest of Dean Stone Firms Ltd.[19] Soon after the First World War the works were closed with the loss of 150 jobs[20] and since then the quarries have been worked only occasionally.[21] Limestone quarrying at the Wilderness expanded after 1885 when cement works were built on

Stenders hill.[22] Quarries were opened on both sides of the road[23] but the enterprise, which gave employment to up to 200 men, ended when the works closed just after the First World War.[24] A saw mill was opened behind Mitcheldean churchyard in the early 1890s and continued in use well into the 20th century.[25] Other new enterprises with a shorter life included a shoe factory established by the mid 1890s[26] and a coach building business recorded in 1906.[27]

In 1941 British Acoustic Films Ltd. brought 54 employees from London to the former brewery in Brook Street and during the war it made anti-aircraft devices and firefighting equipment there and increased its workforce to 250. After the war the factory, the development of which owed much to Frederick Wickstead, made cinematic equipment and as part of the Rank Organization from 1948 it was run by Rank Precision Industries Ltd. From 1964 it concentrated on the production of xerographic machines, introduced in 1960 because of foreign competition in the cinematic trade, and in 1965 it became the main manufacturing plant for Rank Xerox Ltd., an exporter of copying and duplicating machinery. The factory continued to grow until the later 1970s when it covered 27 ha. (*c.* 67 a.) and the workforce numbered 4,800. Most employees, including former miners, came from the Forest and *c.* 700 employees lived in the town.[28] In the early 1980s Rank Xerox closed parts of the factory and reduced its workforce to *c.* 1,200. To create jobs the company launched schemes which in 1984 converted the former brewery buildings as workshops for small businesses and in 1986 opened a trading and industrial estate on the eastern side of the factory site. In 1986 the workshops housed 48 businesses employing 250 people and the estate 4 businesses, including an insurance company with 350 employees and the research and development department of a security systems firm with 90 employees.[29] After the Second World War few other businesses in Mitcheldean employed more than a handful of people.[30] One, a joinery started before the war, had moved by 1980 to the former cement works on Stenders hill.[31] In 1988 the site also accommodated an engineering firm, which was started in 1975 and employed 33 people, mostly women, in 1980 to

3 *Univ. Brit. Dir.* ii (1792), 775.
4 *Pigot's Dir. Glos.* (1842), 120; *Kelly's Dir. Glos.* (1856 and later edns.).
5 Glos. R.O., P 220/IN 1/4.
6 Ibid. CW 3/2.
7 *Univ. Brit. Dir.* ii (1792), 775.
8 *Pigot's Dir. Glos.* (1842), 121; *Kelly's Dir. Glos.* (1856), 326; P.R.O., HO 107/1959.
9 Glos. R.O., D 543, Mitcheldean brewery papers; *Ind. Glos. 1904*, 56–7: copy in ibid. IN 11.
10 *Glouc. Jnl.* 4 Apr. 1925.
11 Ibid. 15 Mar. 1930; 'Memories of Mitcheldean', 18.
12 Glos. R.O., D 36/E 86,T 34; P 1/IN 1/7–8; P 220/IN 1/3–4; ibid. OV 4/1; P.R.O., HO 107/1959; *Univ. Brit. Dir.* ii (1792), 775.
13 Glos. R.O., P 220/VE 2/2, f. 74.
14 Ibid. D 36/E 86.
15 Nicholls, *Iron Making*, 62–3; *Award of Dean Forest Mining Com.* (1841), 199–200; Glos. R.O., Q/RUm 173/2, plans B, D; for Westbury Brook mine, below, Forest of Dean, industry (mining from 1770s).
16 Bigland, *Glos.* i. 1; cf. G.D.R., T 1/1 (no. 30).

17 *Ind. Glos. 1904*, 56; *Kelly's Dir. Glos.* (1889), 840; Glos. R.O., D 3921/II/31.
18 *Kelly's Dir. Glos.* (1885), 525; cf. O.S. Map 6", Glos. XXIII. SE. (1883 and later edns.).
19 Hart, *Ind. Hist. of Dean*, 306.
20 *Glouc. Jnl.* 26 July 1919.
21 'Memories of Mitcheldean', 17.
22 Glos. R.O., D 2362, Wilderness cement works deeds; P 220/VE 2/6, min. 4 Nov. 1887.
23 O.S. Map 6", Glos. XXIII. SE. (1883 and later edns.).
24 Hart, *Ind. Hist. of Dean*, 313–14; *Glouc. Jnl.* 26 July 1919.
25 *Kelly's Dir. Glos.* (1889–1919 edns.); O.S. Map 6", Glos. XXIII. SE. (1903 edn.).
26 Glos. R.O., DA 24/100/1, p. 40.
27 *Kelly's Dir. Glos.* (1906), 244.
28 *Glos. and Avon Life*, Nov. 1977, 42–3; Hart, *Ind. Hist. of Dean*, 422–3, 425, 431, plate facing p. 405; *The Times*, 15 Sept. 1966; *Citizen* (Glouc.), 21 Apr. 1972.
29 *Citizen*, 15 July 1983; 20 June 1984; 12 July 1986; *Dean Forest Mercury*, 20 Feb. 1987.
30 *Glos. and Avon Life*, Nov. 1977, 43.
31 *Kelly's Dir. Glos.* (1939), 264; Glos. Colln. R 203.9.

make electronic equipment.[32] By 1964 a road haulage firm had established a depot at the Merrin and had acquired the quarries north of the Gloucester road,[33] where several small industrial units had been built by 1987. A motor bus service, started by Frederick Cottrell in 1921, continued in his family in 1988.[34]

MARKETS AND FAIRS. In 1328 Reynold of Abenhall and Joan Esger, together with her husband John, had a grant of a market on Mondays and a three-day fair at Michaelmas on the manor of Mitcheldean.[35] Stalls or shops were recorded in Mitcheldean from 1366[36] but although a Monmouth man was selling shoes there in 1447 there is no evidence that the town was a trading centre of any great importance. It attracted traders from neighbouring parishes on the north-east side of the Forest of Dean, including in 1447 several butchers.[37] Fish was apparently sold in the town in 1477.[38] By 1431 the market was held at the north end of High Street,[39] on the east side of which the cross or market house known as the chipping cross was built before 1537.[40] Ownership of the building was divided between the two parts of the manor, the western end belonging to that part held for most of the 17th century by the Vaughan family.[41]

The market presumably once dealt in wool, which was evidently a staple of the town's trade for some time.[42] In the late 16th century and the early 17th corn, butter, cheese, meat, and leather were bought and sold in the Monday market, which had spilled over into the town's main street and was attended by dealers from Newnham, Berkeley, Gloucester, and Monmouth. The courts of the lords of both parts of the manor attempted, through the market officers, to regulate the quality and weight of goods and check forestalling.[43] By 1675 fairs had been established on Easter Monday and 9 July in addition to Michaelmas.[44] The July fair lapsed before 1696[45] and a fair held on the Monday after All Saints' Day lapsed after 1722.[46] In the 17th century the tolls of the corn market and the fairs were shared by the two lords, the corn tolls being taken by the lord on whose side of the market house the corn was pitched.[47] Nicholas Roberts's tolls, farmed for £5 10s. in 1623,[48] were granted in 1625, together with the customary payment

of wheelage and the right to appoint the bellman or toll collector, to nine leading townsmen at a rent of £2,[49] and the Colchesters' tolls were farmed for £6 in 1678 and £11 in 1714.[50] In the late 17th century the Vaughans' tolls were farmed by the same tenant and toll from corn pitched on the side of the market place, in a penthouse next to the former Talbot inn and under a gallery next to the White Horse, was held at will from the Colchesters by another person.[51] By the mid 17th century butter and cheese were traded at the high cross, known by 1659 also as the butter cross.[52] The cross, where shelter was presumably provided as at the Littledean cross by a penthouse around the shaft,[53] was leased from the churchwardens. The butter and cheese market was probably restricted to the two fair days long before 1750,[54] when the cross was leased for life to Benjamin Bonnor, a Gloucester brazier.[55] The fairs, of which the Michaelmas fair was held on 10 October following the calendar change of 1752, specialized in cattle, sheep, and horses in the mid 18th century.[56]

In 1740, when he became the sole lord of the manor, Maynard Colchester (d. 1756) had the tolls of the corn market and the fairs, valued at £9 10s., in hand. Profits from the tolls, which were derived mostly from the market, fell and from 1750 they were farmed for £7 a year. They were taken in hand again a few years later[57] and the corn market, some of the business of which was conducted in the White Horse and other inns,[58] was revived for a time by Maynard's son, Maynard Colchester, who in the mid 1760s rebuilt the market house and obtained new measures.[59] The decline of business continued later in the century and the tolls were farmed again from the early 1770s, the rent being reduced to £3 by 1783.[60] The corn market was dealt a hard blow in 1795 by bread riots in the Forest, which deterred farmers from sending grain, and the business of the meat market had declined considerably by that time.[61] The butter and cheese market evidently continued for several years after the high cross was pulled down in the mid 1770s.[62] In the early 19th century the fairs dealt in livestock and cheese[63] and in 1814 an additional fair was held on 8 July for dealings also in wool.[64] By the early 1840s the business of the Monday market and the fairs was merely

[32] *Citizen*, 15 Oct. 1980.
[33] Glos. R.O., D 3921/V/21, p. 80; Hart, *Ind. Hist. of Dean*, 431.
[34] 'Memories of Mitcheldean', 10; *Glos. and Avon Life*, Nov. 1977, 45.
[35] P.R.O., C 53/115, m. 17.
[36] Glos. R.O., D 4431, deed Tues. before St. Geo. 40 Edw. III.
[37] Hockaday Abs. cclxxx.
[38] Glos. R.O., D 36/M 1, rot. 3.
[39] Ibid. D 4431, deed St. And. 10 Hen. VI.
[40] Ibid. D 36/E 1, f. 89v.
[41] Ibid. M 10; M 78, f. 71v.
[42] *Univ. Brit. Dir.* ii (1792), 775.
[43] N.L.W., Courtfield MSS. 342–3, 785; Glos. R.O., D 36/M 75, M 77–8; cf. below, local govt.; above, Abenhall, local govt.
[44] Ogilby, *Britannia* (1675), p. 30.
[45] Glos. R.O., D 36/M 78, f. 70.
[46] *Glouc. Jnl.* 23 Apr. 1722.
[47] Glos. R.O., D 36/E 5, p. 177; M 10; M 78, ff. 64v.–65,

70; M 79, rot. 12; M 80; T 25, deed 2 Oct. 1705.
[48] Ibid. M 19, f. 2v.
[49] Ibid. E 2, f. 34 and v.
[50] Ibid. E 8, ff. 109, 127, 136, 138; 10, ff. 79v.–80; 11, ff. 79v.–80, 83v.–84, 117v.–118.
[51] Ibid. E 5, p. 177; M 13; M 78, ff. 64v.–65, 70.
[52] Ibid. P 220/CH 2; ibid. VE 2/2, f. 214.
[53] Ibid. D 36/M 78, f. 34v.; above, Littledean, econ. hist. (market and fairs).
[54] Glos. R.O., P 220/VE 2/1–2.
[55] Ibid. CW 3/2.
[56] *Glouc. Jnl.* 26 Sept. 1763; 2 Apr. 1764.
[57] Glos. R.O., D 36/E 12, ff. 123v.–124.
[58] Glos. Colln. 18490 (2): par. mag. no. 11.
[59] Rudder, *Glos.* 400–1; *Glouc. Jnl.* 20 July 1767; Bigland, *Glos.* i. 443.
[60] Glos. R.O., D 36/E 12, ff. 123v.–124.
[61] Nicholls, *Forest of Dean*, 83–5.
[62] Glos. R.O., P 220/VE 2/2, ff. 119–28.
[63] Rudge, *Agric. of Glos.* 339.
[64] *Glouc. Jnl.* 4 July 1814.

nominal.[65] The market was discontinued in 1861 and the fairs had lapsed by 1870.[66]

In the mid 17th century the chipping cross was a market house with an open ground floor and an upper storey supported on pillars.[67] The stone building which replaced it in the mid 1760s had an open arcaded ground floor and an upper room,[68] which was converted in 1861 by some inhabitants for use as a town hall.[69] The building remained part of the Wilderness estate until after the First World War,[70] and from the 1920s, when it was acquired by the owners of the town's brewery and the ground floor was filled in, it was used for storage.[71] In 1964 the Rank Organization gave it to the parish council[72] and in 1988 it remained the town hall.

LOCAL GOVERNMENT. Profits of court for Mitcheldean manor were recorded in 1319.[73] The courts held for both parts of the manor following its division[74] had similar powers in the early 17th century and presumably long before that. One was the Abenhall manor court, which exercised jurisdiction over part of Mitcheldean by the 1460s.[75] For the other court, held for the part of Mitcheldean acquired by the Colchester family in 1641, court papers for 1625–9, 1631, and 1695–6, a court roll for 1642, and a book with records of courts for 1642 and 1696 survive.[76] During that period the court usually met twice a year to combine view of frankpledge with a court baron and occasionally was convened as a court of survey. Like the Abenhall court it dealt with tenurial and other estate matters, heard pleas of affray and bloodshed, and enforced the assize of bread and of ale. In 1696 Maynard Colchester claimed a gun as a deodand after a suicide.[77] The government of the town and the regulation of the market provided the bulk of the business of both courts, which were particularly concerned with ensuring that streets were kept in repair and clean and that watercourses and cisterns were not polluted. Like the Abenhall court Nicholas Roberts's court, which in 1627 dealt with a butcher trading without having completed his apprenticeship, appointed two constables, two aletasters who also acted as bread scrutineers, two leather sealers, and two clerks of the market in the mid 1620s.[78] The duties of the bellman and crier, whose appointment belonged to Roberts and his successors, included collecting the market and fair tolls[79] and in the late 18th century possibly checking the weights and measures used.[80] The office of crier survived the market and fairs.[81] In 1691 the Abenhall court heard claims that its lord, John Vaughan, was not providing a standard bushel for use in the market[82] and in 1696 Nathaniel Rudge, to whom the Vaughans' powers in Mitcheldean had passed, was presented in his own court for not keeping his part of the market house and a pound in repair.[83] The pound was presumably that near the Merrin which had been put to other use by the end of the 18th century.[84] Another pound, probably that recorded in 1611,[85] was at the corner of Millend Street and Church Lane and by 1727 was maintained by a tenant of the Colchesters in return for the profits from it and the occupancy of a nearby house.[86] That pound was moved to the entrance of New Street in the early 19th century.[87]

Mitcheldean had two churchwardens in 1458[88] and later.[89] The money needed by them for church maintenance came in part from cottages given to the parish.[90] The parish vestry had general supervision of poor relief as its main responsibility by the late 18th century and became more active in town government in the mid 19th. Administration of relief was in the hands of two overseers, who by the mid 18th century accounted in turn for 6 months.[91] There were two surveyors of the highways for the parish and by 1722 the two constables were chosen yearly by the vestry.[92] The parish maintained stocks and a pillory until at least the mid 18th century.[93]

Poor relief took the usual forms and in the later 17th century there were usually c. 13 people receiving regular assistance.[94] In 1683 the remaining part of a former schoolhouse was used as a poorhouse and some income for relief came from two cottages, one of them a former almshouse, given to the parish; a cottage between Stenders Road and New Street, later said to have been given for the use of the poor, provided income solely for repairing the church and was pulled down in 1689.[95] In 1696 and until 1715 a house in Millend Street served as a poorhouse.[96] Fewer people were helped in the mid 18th century, when the former almshouse was used

65 Pigot's Dir. Glos. (1842), 120.
66 Cf. Morris's Dir. Glos. (1876), 527; Kelly's Dir. Glos. (1863), 309; (1870), 597–8.
67 Glos. R.O., D 36/M 10; M 78, f. 71v.
68 Cf. ibid. GPS 220/7, 26.
69 Morris's Dir. Glos. (1876), 527.
70 Glos. R.O., D 543, sale partics. 21 Dec. 1918.
71 Ibid. PA 220/2; GPS 220/8; 'Memories of Mitcheldean', 20.
72 Citizen, 18 Aug. 1964.   73 P.R.O., C 134/61, no. 27.
74 Cf. ibid. C 139/79, no. 15; C 139/115, no. 34.
75 For the Abenhall ct. and its rec., above, Abenhall, local govt.
76 Glos. R.O., D 36/M 75–80.   77 Ibid. M 78, f. 72.
78 Ibid. M 75; N.L.W., Courtfield MSS. 342–3, 785, 790.
79 Glos. R.O., D 36/E 2, f. 34 and v.; M 79, rot. 12.
80 Bigland, Glos. i. 443.
81 Kelly's Dir. Glos. (1879), 703; 'Memories of Mitcheldean', 7; cf. above, econ. hist.
82 Glos. R.O., D 36/M 14.
83 Ibid. M 15–16, which suggest that Rudge continued the practice of combining view of frankpledge with a ct.

baron.   84 Ibid. E 15.
85 Ibid. D 33/271; cf. ibid. D 36/M 78, ff. 5v., 20.
86 Ibid. D 36/E 12, ff. 122v.–123; D 2123, pp. 60, 63.
87 Ibid. D 36/T 36; G.D.R., T 1/123; O.S. Map 1/2,500, Glos. XXIII. 16 (1881 edn.).
88 Glos. R.O., D 36/E 1, f. 4.
89 Hockaday Abs. xxix, 1543 subsidy, f. 6; xliv, 1572 visit. f. 4. The churchwardens' accts. for the periods 1655–6, 1673–1701, and 1749–1859 are included in Glos. R.O., P 220/VE 2/1–2.
90 G.D.R., V 5/203T 3; below, church.
91 Vestry mins. for 1759–1907 are in Glos. R.O., P 220/VE 2/2–6; overseers' accts. for 1665–6, 1673–1701, and 1749–1846 are included, together with the workhouse guardian's accts. from 1790, in ibid. VE 2/1–2; ibid. OV 2/1–3.
92 Ibid. VE 2/2.   93 Ibid. VE 2/1–2; OV 2/4.
94 Ibid. VE 2/1; for a hist. of poor relief between 1660 and 1834, ibid. MI 4.
95 G.D.R., V 5/203T 3–4; Glos. R.O., P 220/VE 2/1; cf. Glos. R.O., P 220/VE 2/2, f. 214; ibid. CW 3/2, lease 18 Aug. 1718.
96 Glos. R.O., D 36/M 78, f. 67; E 10, ff. 52v.–53.

as a poorhouse, but from the mid 1770s, when the town's industry was in decline, many more parishioners needed regular assistance and by the mid 1780s their number averaged c. 25. Action to enforce the badging of paupers was taken in 1787 and 1815 and there were several moves, as in 1750, 1799, and 1814, to prevent lodging house keepers from accommodating paupers without settlement in the parish.[97] In 1790 a parish workhouse was opened with 15 inmates in a rented house. It had a guardian, a post regularly combined with that of assistant overseer and enjoying a salary in 1806,[98] and a salaried governess had been installed by 1799.[99] The inmates, who were put to work heading pins for Gloucester manufacturers or spinning hemp, usually numbered 9 in the early 19th century, while parishioners on permanent out-relief usually numbered over 20. From c. 1810 the workhouse was run primarily as a poorhouse.[1] The parish subscribed to the Gloucester infirmary from 1777[2] and a surgeon was retained from 1821. In 1821 the vestry also appointed a salaried overseer but from 1823 the poor were farmed by a succession of contractors chosen by annual tenders and having the use of the workhouse and the parish's poorhouses.[3] Most apprenticeships made by parish officers from the mid 18th century were financed by the funds of a charity.[4] The annual cost of poor relief stood at £95 in 1776 and rose to well over £400 in 1813.[5] It had fallen considerably by 1823, when the poor were taken at farm for £200,[6] and was kept down to c. £240 in the late 1820s and to c. £195 in the early 1830s.[7]

Mitcheldean became part of the new Westbury-on-Severn poor-law union in 1835.[8] Proposals by the vestry for the formation of a local board of health were turned down in 1866 because of Mitcheldean's small population.[9] The poor-law union as the sanitary authority for the parish from 1872 was succeeded in 1895 by East Dean and United Parishes rural district[10] and in 1935 by East Dean rural district.[11] In 1974 Mitcheldean became part of the new Forest of Dean district.

CHURCH. Mitcheldean church presumably originated as a chapel of Westbury-on-Severn church but had evidently become a parish church by 1223 when claims to the patronage were advanced by William of Dean on the one hand and by the patrons and rector of Westbury on the other.[12] In 1291 the rector of Westbury had a portion in Mitcheldean church,[13] which by then was a rectory in the patronage of the lords of the manor, the first known presentation being that made in 1280 by Henry of Dean.[14] The benefice was united with Abenhall rectory in 1946.[15]

The advowson of Mitcheldean rectory was divided at an early date between the two parts of the manor, the right to present at every third vacancy belonging by 1417, and presumably from the division, to that part of the manor acquired by the lords of Abenhall.[16] The other, greater share of the advowson belonged to that part of the manor acquired by the Baynhams, who in the late 14th or early 15th century may have usurped a turn belonging to the Greyndours. Two vacancies arising in 1395 were filled by Thomas of Woodstock, duke of Gloucester, as guardian of John Baynham,[17] and the Crown made a presentation in 1438, presumably by reason of the minority of Thomas Baynham.[18] In 1550 John Pengry presented to the rectory under a grant. At the next vacancy, filled in 1552 by William Baynham, the advowson was claimed by Sir Christopher Baynham, formerly lord of Abenhall, and the following vacancy was filled in 1555 by the bishop.[19] William Baynham's share of the advowson passed with his estate to Joseph Baynham,[20] by whose grant Thomas Horn of Rodley presented in 1574. Patrons for a single turn filled the three vacancies arising in the 17th century,[21] the first two under a grant of 1622 by Nicholas Roberts[22] and the third, in 1679, in place of the Roman Catholic John Vaughan.[23] From 1740, when the two parts of the manor were re-united, the advowson descended wholly with the Colchester estates, passing in 1930 to Sir M. F. Colchester-Wemyss.[24] By 1934 it had been transferred to the Diocesan Board of Patronage,[25] which after the union of benefices had an alternate right of presentation with the Lord Chancellor and from c. 1970 enjoyed sole right of patronage.[26]

The rector took the tithes of the whole parish including Blackwell meadows.[27] In 1681 crops and animals were tithable in kind, apart from garden produce for which a composition was paid.[28] The tithes, parts of which were farmed out in 1550[29] and in 1811,[30] were commuted in

97 Ibid. P 220/VE 2/2–3.
98 Ibid. OV 2/1–2; ibid. VE 2/2, ff. 203–8.
99 Ibid. VE 2/3.
1 Ibid. OV 2/1–2; *Poor Law Abstract, 1804*, 172–3; *1818*, 146–7; cf. *Univ. Brit. Dir.* iii (1794), 195; *Glouc. New Guide* (1802), 152, 161.
2 Glos. R.O., P 220/VE 2/2, f. 184.
3 Ibid. VE 2/3–5.
4 Ibid. OV 4/1–3; cf. ibid. P 220/CH 3/2; ibid. VE 2/2, ff. 219–25, 235–7; below, charities.
5 *Poor Law Abstract, 1804*, 172–3; *1818*, 146–7.
6 Glos. R.O., P 220/VE 2/4.
7 *Poor Law Returns (1830–1)*, p. 67; (1835), p. 65.
8 *Poor Law Com. 2nd Rep.* p. 524.
9 Glos. R.O., P 220/VE 2/6.
10 Ibid. DA 40/100/1–4; DA 24/100/1.
11 *Census*, 1931 (pt. ii).
12 *Pat. R. 1216–25*, 395; *V.C.H. Glos.* x. 85, 98.
13 *Tax. Eccl.* (Rec. Com.), 161.
14 *Reg. Cantilupe*, 250–1.

15 *Glouc. Dioc. Year Bk.* (1950–1), 34–5; cf. *Lond. Gaz.* 4 Jan. 1929, pp. 137–8.
16 *Cal. Close, 1413–19*, 338; cf. Glos. R.O., D 36/M 78, ff. 25v., 70v.
17 *Trans. B.G.A.S.* vi. 168; above, Abenhall, manor.
18 *Cal. Pat. 1436–41*, 221, 223; *Cal. Fine R. 1430–7*, 305.
19 Hockaday Abs. cclxxx; above, Abenhall, manor.
20 Cf. P.R.O., C 142/149, no. 129; C 142/164, no. 62.
21 G.D.R., D 1/192; Hockaday Abs. cclxxx.
22 Glos. R.O., D 36/E 3, f. 159v.; cf. ibid. f. 62.
23 Ibid. M 78, f. 70v.; above, Abenhall, manor; church.
24 Hockaday Abs. cclxxx; *Kelly's Dir. Glos.* (1856–1931 edns.); cf. *V.C.H. Glos.* x. 87.
25 G.D.R., D 1/192.
26 *Lond. Gaz.* 4 Jan. 1929, pp. 137–8; *Glouc. Dioc. Year Bk.* (1950–1), 34–5; (1969), 26–7; (1971), 2–7.
27 *Trans. B.G.A.S.* vi. 207.
28 G.D.R., V 5/203T 1.
29 Hockaday Abs. cclxxx.
30 G.D.R., B 4/3/849.

1840 for a corn rent charge of £176 13s.[31] The rector's glebe, recorded from the later 13th century,[32] included 10 a. in two closes outside the town in 1619.[33] It was estimated as 8 a. in 1681[34] and was reduced to 5 a. in the mid 19th century.[35] The church was worth £6 13s. 4d. and the rector of Westbury's portion 2s. in 1291.[36] The benefice, in which the rector resigning in 1418 was awarded a pension of £10,[37] was valued at £10 5s. 10d. in 1535,[38] £10 15s. 0¾d. in 1603,[39] £40 in 1642 and 1650,[40] and £50 in 1750.[41] It was allotted £200 by Queen Anne's Bounty in 1796[42] and was valued at £141 in 1856.[43]

In 1436 a tenement called the priest's chambers was held under the Baynhams by a tenant.[44] The rectory house recorded from 1597 stood west of Hawker Hill.[45] It was said to be decayed in 1605[46] and it contained 10 rooms in 1681 when a barn was among the outbuildings.[47] The house, to which a schoolroom was added in 1812,[48] had fallen into decay by 1849 when it was rebuilt to designs of Francis Niblett.[49] It remained in use for the united benefice in 1988.[50]

A trust established in 1790 under the will of William Lane paid the rector of Mitcheldean or his curate two guineas for sermons on Good Friday and the Sunday after Trinity and three guineas for catechizing poor children and superintending a charity school. From 1913, when the trust was reorganized, the salary for catechizing was paid by Lane's School Foundation to the rector or a teacher. The value of the sermon charity was increased in the 1970s.[51]

The rector in 1346 was licensed to be absent for a year[52] and a later rector in 1442 was given leave to be non-resident for three years.[53] Geoffrey Hereford, bishop of Kildare and suffragan of Hereford, held the rectory from 1465 until his death in or before 1469.[54] Thomas More, rector from 1485, enjoyed a long incumbency,[55] during which a Lollard sympathizer, who had addressed a meeting in Mitcheldean, did penance at the church in 1511.[56] Thomas Baynham, More's successor in 1524, was accused of fathering a child but retained the living. There were at least four rectors in the course of

the 1550s, one being deprived under Mary for being married.[57] William Budge, who lost Abenhall under the same circumstances, was rector in 1559.[58] In 1576 and 1584 a curate served the church for a non-resident rector.[59] By that time puritanism had a committed supporter in Mitcheldean in Anthony Bridgeman, possibly a member of a local landowning family,[60] who in 1589 proposed abolition of collegiate and cathedral churches and of ecclesiastical pluralism.[61]

Hugh Griffith (d. 1623), rector from 1592,[62] employed a curate in 1593[63] and was presented in 1605 for not preaching monthly sermons and not catechizing on Sundays.[64] Other long incumbencies were those of Richard Stringer (1623–75), Richard Hall (1679–1723) who from 1685 also served Abenhall, and Richard Roberts (1727–70) who, after being dispensed in 1737 to hold the living of Kentchurch (Herefs.), usually employed curates.[65] Roberts's successor resigned in 1773 rather than take up residence, as the parish vestry had insisted,[66] and the next rector, after moving to another parish by 1786, engaged curates at Mitcheldean.[67] Edward Jones, rector 1802–1847, was also non-resident and employed curates.[68] The first was his brother Henry Prowse Jones, whose absence in 1807 led the vestry to complain about the irregularity of services.[69] Jones's later curates took an active part in parish life, notably Henry Berkin (1809–14), who undertook a mission to the adjoining part of the extraparochial Forest of Dean, and George Cox, whose curacy lasted from 1830 to 1847 when Edward Machen became rector.[70] Machen rebuilt the rectory house and set about restoring the church and enlarging the churchyard.[71] His successor Charles Edward Dighton, rector 1857–78, lived near Bristol between 1869 and 1871.[72] Between 1890 and 1910 seven men were instituted to the rectory.[73]

Several chantries were founded in Mitcheldean church, some probably by 1420 when three stipendiary priests were recorded there; one, a former rector, also had the £10 pension mentioned above.[74] Chantries dedicated to St. George and the Holy Trinity had been united

31 Ibid. T 1/123.
32 Glos. R.O., D 4431, grant of Hen. of Dean to Hugh Godwin; D 36/E 1, f. 89v.
33 Ibid. D 36/E 1, f. A.
34 G.D.R., V 5/203T 1.
35 Ibid. T 1/123; P.R.O., IR 29/13/135; Kelly's Dir. Glos. (1856), 326.
36 Tax. Eccl. (Rec. Com.), 161.
37 Trans. B.G.A.S. vi. 168.
38 Valor Eccl. (Rec. Com.), ii. 500.
39 Eccl. Misc. 98.
40 Glos. R.O., D 36/M 78, f. 25v.; Trans. B.G.A.S. lxxxiii. 98.   41 G.D.R. vol. 381A, f. 3.
42 Hodgson, Queen Anne's Bounty (1845), p. cclxxxv.
43 G.D.R. vol. 384, f. 78.
44 P.R.O., SC 6/858/15, rot. 5.
45 Glos. R.O., D 4431, deed 22 Feb. 39 Eliz. I.
46 G.D.R. vol. 97, f. 230.   47 Ibid. V 5/203T 1.
48 P. M. Procter, Origin of Established Ch. and Nat. Day Sch. in Forest of Dean (1819), 23 n.
49 G.D.R., F 4/1; the porch is dated 1850: Glos. Colln. 18490 (3), p. 18.
50 Cf. Lond. Gaz. 4 Jan. 1929, pp. 137–8.
51 Glos. R.O. P 220/CH 5/4; for the trust, below, educ.
52 Reg. Trillek, 395.   53 Reg. Spofford, 371.
54 Reg. Stanbury, 186, 193; Handbook of Brit. Chronology (1961), 339, in which Geof. is said to have died before 1464.
55 Hockaday Abs. cclxxx.

56 Reg. Mayew, 109–11; cf. J. A. F. Thomson, Later Lollards, 1414–1520 (1965), 48 and n.
57 Hockaday Abs. cclxxx.
58 G.D.R. vol. 15, p. 240; above, Abenhall, church.
59 Hockaday Abs. xlvii, 1576 visit. f. 132; xliv, state of clergy 1584, f. 45.
60 Smith, Men and Armour, 31–2; G.D.R. wills 1638/13.
61 Cal. S.P. Dom. 1581–90, 578; Rec. of Early Eng. Drama. Cumb., Westmld., and Glos. ed. A. Douglas and P. Greenfield (Toronto, 1986), 267–8, 333–5.
62 Hockaday Abs. cclxxx; G.D.R., D 1/192.
63 Hockaday Abs. lii, state of clergy 1593, ff. 4, 6.
64 G.D.R. vol. 97, f. 230.
65 Hockaday Abs. cclxxx; Bigland, Glos. i. 446; Glos. R.O., P 220/IN 1/1.
66 Hockaday Abs. cclxxx; Glos. R.O., P 220/VE 2/2.
67 Hockaday Abs. cclxxx; Glos. R.O., P 220/IN 1/2; G.D.R. vol. 382, f. 19.
68 Hockaday Abs. cclxxx, cxxxv; V.C.H. Glos. x. 37.
69 Glos. R.O., P 220/VE 2/3.
70 Ibid. IN 1/2–3; cf. ibid. P 220/CH 5/3–4; ibid. VE 2/2–5; for Berkin, also Nicholls, Personalities of Dean, 132–7; Nicholls, Forest of Dean, 157–61.
71 Glos. Colln. R 203.4; 18490 (3), pp. 18–19, 22–3.
72 Hockaday Abs. cclxxx; Glos. R.O., P 220/CH 5/4; Glouc. Jnl. 11 Mar. 1916.
73 G.D.R., D 1/192; Kelly's Dir. Glos. (1914), 258.
74 Reg. Lacy, 87; Trans. B.G.A.S. vi. 168.

by 1514 and their endowments supported a chaplain, who celebrated two obits for the founders.[75] At their dissolution the chaplain had an annual income of £5 12s. 1½d.[76] The endowments, made up mostly of tenements in the town and land in Mitcheldean and Abenhall, were granted by the Crown in 1549 to Sir John Thynne and Thomas Throckmorton,[77] who sold at least part of them to William Bridgeman.[78] Three other obits, one of them founded by the rector Thomas More (d. by 1524), were celebrated in the church in the mid 1540s. The church's lady chapel had its own priest in 1532 but the wishes of Thomas Baynham (d. 1532), who left an estate in Market Lavington (Wilts.) for the foundation of a chantry at Mitcheldean, were evidently not followed.[79]

Several cottages in the town were given to the parish[80] and in the later 17th century four of them, including a former almshouse, provided income for repairing the church.[81] Half of the income from one cottage belonged, under a grant probably of 1490, to Longhope parish[82] and between 1828, when the building was demolished and its site incorporated in the churchyard, and 1865 Mitcheldean paid Longhope a rent of 25s.[83] A cottage in Millend Street, said to have been given in the 16th century by a member of the Bridgeman family,[84] was probably used as a school in the early 1770s.[85] It was occupied as two dwellings by 1828[86] and was retained by the parish in 1910.[87] A church house, formerly used for a school, was recorded in the churchyard in the mid 18th century and was pulled down c. 1787.[88] Charities for the repair of the church and the benefit of the five senior choir members were founded under the will of Alexander Smith Porter (d. 1849) of Worcester, but the parish did not receive a principal sum of £107 1s. 9d. until 1863 following litigation. The income, two thirds of which went towards church repairs,[89] provided £2 9s. 4d. for distribution to choir members in 1905.[90]

The church, which bore a dedication of *ST. MICHAEL* by 1420,[91] is built of sandstone rubble and ashlar. It has a chancel with north and south chapels and north-east vestry and a clerestoried nave, two north aisles, a south aisle with crypt, and a south-west tower with spire and south porch. The low north-west buttress

of the nave probably dates from the 13th century and the nave and chancel, which had no division between them, probably date from that time or earlier. The south chapel and aisle, tower, and porch were added in the early 14th century and the north chapel and aisle may have been of a similar date. The top stage of the tower and spire were possibly added in the early 15th century. The outer north aisle, which was built in the mid 15th century[92] during alterations later associated with Thomas Baynham (d. 1500),[93] extends eastwards to the limit of the chapels and is wider than the inner aisle with which it shares a roof. In the later 15th century the nave arcades were rebuilt, the clerestory and a new roof were added, a large west window was put into the nave, and the south aisle windows were given new tracery. In reconstructing the arcades, which have four-centred arches, much of the 14th-century moulded stonework was re-used. Only the arch between the chancel and south chapel survives in its 14th-century form. The rood staircase, against the south wall, continues down into the 14th-century crypt and is probably of the late 15th century. Wooden panelling placed between the chancel and nave above the rood loft has been retained and bears late 15th-century paintings, uncovered c. 1830, which depict the Last Judgment and the Passion.[94]

The spire may have fallen, damaging the south aisle, in or before 1731 when a brief was sought for the repair of the church.[95] The work, for which collections were made in 1733, was considerable[96] and included a new roof for the aisle.[97] The spire was rebuilt, possibly in the early 1740s, by Nathaniel Wilkinson of Worcester.[98] In 1837 a vestry was completed on the site of an earlier room,[99] which may have been pulled down by 1773 when meetings were held in what was then called the lower chancel, perhaps the north chapel.[1] A west gallery for the singers was installed in the church in 1765 and a gallery for the pupils of the town's charity schools was erected in the south aisle in 1790.[2] The latter was maintained by the schools and was entered by an external stair up to a window until 1837 when it was enlarged.[3] At a partial restoration of the church in 1853 the eastern bay of the chancel

75 Glos. R.O., D 4431, deed 25 Jan. 5 Hen. VIII; *Valor Eccl.* (Rec. Com.), ii. 500.
76 Hockaday Abs. cclxxx.
77 *Cal. Pat.* 1548–9, 331; cf. P.R.O., E 315/67 (2), ff. 298–299v.
78 Glos. R.O., D 36/E 1, f. 91v.
79 Hockaday Abs. cclxxx; cf. *V.C.H. Wilts.* x. 90–1.
80 Cf. Glos. R.O., D 36/E 1, ff. 4, 23.
81 Ibid. P 220/VE 2/1; G.D.R., V 5/203T 3–4.
82 Cf. Glos. R.O., D 4431, deed 24 Dec. 6 Hen. [VII or VIII], by which John Hart granted the cottage to two Mitcheldean and two Longhope men; *18th Rep. Com. Char.* H.C. 62, pp. 326–7 (1828), xx(i) which records the tradition that the cottage was granted to Longhope by Walter Gifford or Pekks during Henry VII's reign.
83 Glos. R.O., P 220/VE 2/2, 4, 6; P 206/CH 2.
84 Ibid. P 220/CH 2.
85 Ibid. VE 2/2, f. 214 and vestry min. 8 Oct. 1771.
86 Ibid. VE 2/4.   87 Ibid. D 2428/1/1.
88 Ibid. P 220/VE 2/2, ff. 130, 214; cf. G.D.R., V 5/203T 3–4.
89 Glos. R.O., P 220/CH 8.
90 Ibid. P 220/CH 5/4.
91 Hockaday Abs. cclxxx; *Cal. Pat.* 1436–41, 221, 223;

the form St. Michael the Archangel was used in 1524: Glos. R.O., D 4431, deed Annunc. B.V.M. 15 Hen. VIII; from the late 19th cent. the dedication was frequently extended to St. Michael and All Angels: *Trans. B.G.A.S.* vi. 269; xxxiv. 200; *Glouc. Dioc. Year Bk.* (1963–4), 24; *Dioc. of Glouc. Dir.* (1987), 48.
92 J. H. Middleton, 'Ch. of St. Michael and All Angels, Mitcheldean', *Trans. B.G.A.S.* vi. 269–77, maintains that there had been an earlier outer N. aisle.
93 Bigland, *Glos.* i. 444; above, manor.
94 *Gent. Mag.* ci (2), 409–11; *Trans. B.G.A.S.* vi. 273–7; lxxxvi. 203.
95 Glos. R.O., Q/SO 5, f. 150.
96 *Glos. N. & Q.* i. 346–7; ii. 402; iii. 334; iv. 14; cf. Bigland, *Glos.* i. 444.
97 *Glouc. Jnl.* 11 Sept. 1909.
98 Hockaday Abs. cclxxx; Colvin, *Biog. Dict. Brit. Architects* (1978), 897; for the ch., below, Plate 4.
99 Glos. R.O., P 220/VE 2/5.
1 Ibid. P 220/CH 3/2; ibid. VE 2/2–5.
2 Ibid. P 220/VE 2/2, f. 108; *Gent. Mag.* xcii (1), 114; Glos. Colln. 18490 (3), p. 19.
3 Glos. R.O., P 220/CH 5/2–4.

was rebuilt and enlarged, the tracery of some windows was renewed, and, the galleries having been removed, the church was almost completely repewed. The work, to designs by Henry Woodyer,[4] was financed by the rector Edward Machen and by subscription.[5] The crypt, which had been used as a charnel house,[6] was cleared out in 1886.[7] In the early 1890s the rector E. H. Firth paid for further restoration work, notably on the north aisles, and commissioned a wooden screen and arch placed between the chancel and nave in 1893. The church organ stood in the north chapel by that time.[8] Later the east end of the outer aisle was fitted as a vestry and in 1988 the north-east vestry was used as a store.

The Norman font, decorated with figures of the apostles standing in the niches of an arcade, had been mutilated by the late 18th century and the lower part had been turned upside down and a new bowl formed in it. The upper part was replaced in 1882 when the font was restored.[9] A wooden, octagonal pulpit dating from the 15th century stands in the church but is not used,[10] a new one having been provided in 1922 as a memorial to the dead of the First World War.[11] Among the features of the work associated with Thomas Baynham (d. 1500) are the ceilings of the north aisles, which have carvings of angels holding shields, and glass which was set in the outer aisle's east window until the restoration of 1853; after the restoration fragments of that glass, depicting angels with musical instruments, were reset haphazardly in three windows on the north side.[12] Glass in several other windows was replaced in the later 19th century and the early 20th by stained glass, much of it as memorials, and the glass of the chancel's east window dates from c. 1970.[13] Brasses believed to portray Margaret Hody and Alice Walwyn (d. 1518), the wives of Thomas Baynham (d. 1500), survive. They were removed from a monument in the outer north aisle during the restoration of 1853, when a floor tablet to the Revd. Richard Stringer (d. 1675) was moved from the chancel to the south chapel.[14] Several wall monuments of the 18th century survive. A large reredos sculpted with full-size figures by W. G. Storr-Barber was installed in 1913.[15]

In the early 18th century the church had five bells,[16] some probably belonging to a peal recast c. 1680.[17] Three new bells were added by sub-scription in 1760 when the peal was recast at the Gloucester foundry of the Rudhall family. The tenor was recast at the same foundry in 1783 and again in 1819, another by G. Mears & Co. in 1864 at the expense of Henrietta Davies, and a third by John Taylor & Co. in 1924. A sanctus bell was recast by Thomas Rudhall in 1773.[18] The church had a clock by the 1650s and a new one was acquired by subscription in the early 1760s when a new set of chimes was obtained from Bristol.[19] The plate includes a chalice and paten cover of the later 16th century.[20] The registers survive from 1680 and contain many entries for Abenhall.[21]

NONCONFORMITY. Although there were said to be no recusants in Mitcheldean in 1603[22] several parishioners were regularly absent from services by that time. In 1623 a man was reported to have interrupted the rector during prayers and in 1639 a marriage was said to have taken place in an alehouse.[23] By 1676, although only four nonconformists were recorded,[24] Dissent was widespread and in 1682 thirteen people were reported for staying away from the parish church. Two were, or had been in 1669, described as Anabaptists,[25] and most may have been members of an Independent church founded, according to tradition, in 1662. That church had a resident minister in 1715, when its membership, including Abenhall residents, was put at 120.[26] In 1728 the minister's house was registered for worship by members of Gloucester's Independent church[27] and in 1735 the meeting, described as Presbyterian, had 20 members, drawn apparently from four families.[28] In the same year a man was convicted for pulling down the pulpit and several pews and for damaging graves in the chapel yard,[29] which was on the west side of Silver Street.[30] During the ministry of Benjamin Cadman (c. 1760–1800) the chapel, which had members from Abenhall and Longhope, supported a successful mission to Ruardean.[31] Under Cadman's successor John Horlick, minister of both the Mitcheldean and Ruardean churches for c. 50 years, there was a large increase in the congregation,[32] which in 1851 numbered well over 150.[33] The chapel was rebuilt in 1822 and provided with a schoolroom in 1842, and Samuel Addington of London paid for extensive alter-

4 *Glouc. Jnl.* 23, 30 July 1853; 11 Sept. 1909.
5 Glos. Colln. 18490 (3), pp. 18–19; Glos. R.O., P 220/VE 2/6.
6 Cf. Glos. R.O., P 220/VE 2/2, f. 141; *Trans. B.G.A.S.* vi. 277, 353–6.
7 Glos. Colln. 18490 (3), p. 21; R 203.8.
8 Ibid. 18490 (3), pp. 9–15; Glos. R.O., D 2593, Mitcheldean church papers.
9 *Trans. B.G.A.S.* xxxiv. 200 and n., 205; *Glouc. Jnl.* 11 Sept. 1909.
10 *Gent. Mag.* ci (2), 409–11; Glos. Colln. 18490 (3), pp. 4–5; Verey, *Glos.* ii. 300.
11 'Memories of Mitcheldean', 13.
12 *Trans. B.G.A.S.* vi. 273; liii. 2; *Glouc. Jnl.* 11 Sept. 1909; cf. Bigland, *Glos.* i. 444.
13 Cf. Glos. Colln. 18490 (3), pp. 24, 29–31; Verey, *Glos.* ii. 300.
14 *Trans. B.G.A.S.* vi. 130–1, 263; liii. 2; cf. Bigland, *Glos.* i. 444, 446 and n.
15 Inscr. in church.

16 Bodl. MS. Rawl. B. 323, f. 106.
17 G.D.R., V 5/203T 3.
18 Glos. R.O., P 220/VE 2/1–2; *Glos. Ch. Bells*, 63, 437–9.
19 Glos. R.O., P 220/VE 2/1–2.
20 *Glos. Ch. Plate*, 146–7.
21 Glos. R.O., P 220/IN 1/1–4.
22 *Eccl. Misc.* 98.   23 Glos. R.O., D 2052.
24 *Compton Census*, ed. Whiteman, 544.
25 Glos. R.O., D 2052.
26 Bright, *Nonconf. in Dean*, 14.
27 Hockaday Abs. cclxxx; cf. *V.C.H. Glos.* iv. 324.
28 G.D.R. vol. 285B(1), f. 4; (3), pp. 3–4.
29 Glos. R.O., Q/SG 1, 1735–40.
30 Ibid. D 36/E 12, f. 79v.; G.D.R., T 1/123 (no. 2); P.R.O., IR 29/13/135.
31 J. Stratford, *Good and Great Men of Glos.* (1867), 409; Glos. R.O., P 220/CH 5/1; Hockaday Abs. cccxxvi, 1775.
32 Stratford, *Good and Great Men*, 412–13; Bright, *Nonconf. in Dean*, 1–2.
33 P.R.O., HO 129/334/1/10/26.

ations in 1850.[34] The meeting received a few gifts to maintain the minister, including in 1769 land in Abenhall from Edward Heane,[35] on which a manse was built in the early 1850s.[36] In 1900 the chapel, which was called Congregational from the later 19th century, had 40 members and 84 children attended its Sunday school in 1900.[37] It had ceased to have a resident minister by the mid 1960s, when the average attendance was 12.[38] In 1977, several years after the church had joined the United Reformed Church, the chapel was taken over by the Mitcheldean Christian Fellowship, an independent evangelical church which continued to worship there in 1988.[39]

Dissenting groups registered houses in Mitcheldean in 1797 and 1824.[40] An Independent meeting in Abenhall, recorded in 1809 and 1841, used a house on the Gloucester road at the end of the town.[41] In 1814 a few Wesleyan Methodists, who had been holding services for several years, opened a small chapel behind High Street near the Bull Ring.[42] The meeting remained small and the chapel, which was visited by ministers of the Ledbury circuit[43] and in 1851 drew a congregation of 25,[44] had been closed by 1855.[45] In 1856 it was purchased by a group of Bible Christians,[46] who moved in 1861 to a new and larger chapel on the south side of Stenders Road.[47] That chapel, which had 35 members in 1885,[48] came under the United Methodist Church formed in 1907.[49] It was closed in 1913 and a gift to support a resident minister was assigned to a minister at Drybrook.[50] In 1918 the building was purchased by Anglicans for use as a parish hall[51] and c. 1970 it was demolished to make an entrance to a housing estate.

Roman Catholic priests from Cinderford celebrated mass in Mitcheldean for a number of years after the Second World War. The services were discontinued before 1965.[52]

EDUCATION. Mitcheldean had a schoolhouse before 1545 when the building belonged to a chantry.[53] A schoolhouse in the churchyard, believed to have been given to the parish by a member of the Bridgeman family,[54] was in use in the early 17th century,[55] perhaps by the unlicensed teachers mentioned in 1602 and 1637.[56] In 1683 the building, part of which had fallen down, was a poorhouse.[57] By 1771 and

until 1776 a school was kept in another of the parish's houses, probably that in Millend Street.[58] Charity schools for boys and girls supported by voluntary subscriptions were established in the town in 1784. They also provided evening classes and were soon teaching 50 children on weekdays and Sundays.[59]

In 1790 the boys' school was reorganized to benefit from William Lane's trust. Lane (d. 1789), a Gloucester lawyer[60] and native of Mitcheldean, left £1,000 in trust to support, among other things, a charity school teaching not less than 20 children on Sundays as well as other days and to pay its teacher a salary of £15. The trustees, the lord of the manor John Colchester and the feoffees of Jonathan Parker's charity, invested the principal in stock in 1790 and the school, managed by the trustees and the parish priest, taught c. 30 boys, for whom uniforms were purchased in 1795. Lane's trust fund, the school's sole source of finance, was augmented by purchases of stock, made in 1808 with bequests totalling £300 left by Lane's widow Amy (d. 1807) and made later with surplus income.[61] Lane's school shared premises with the girls' school, which continued to depend on voluntary contributions, chiefly £15 15s. a year from John Colchester, and had c. 25 pupils in 1795. The schools' anniversaries were celebrated together by a music festival in the church and a dinner. At the festival, held irregularly after 1805, a collection was taken for the girls' school, surplus income of which was invested in stock from 1795.[62] The management of the girls' school was gradually assimilated with that of Lane's foundation, particularly in 1830 when part of its funds was used to buy c. 7 a. in Abenhall.[63] The schools, which had moved by 1835 to a house on the west side of High Street,[64] taught 40 boys and 40 girls in 1847.[65] From 1850 they were accommodated in a new building, designed by Fulljames and Waller, on the west side of Hawker Hill in the grounds of the rectory house.[66] In 1855 the master assisted the rector in teaching evening classes, and an infants' school was established in 1871 when the building was enlarged.[67] From 1857 the schools, which continued to enjoy the support of the Colchester family, admitted children from adjoining Forest hamlets on the payment of pence and received an annual grant of £5 5s. from the Crown's

34 Glos. R.O., D 2297; *Glouc. Jnl.* 7 Oct. 1822; 18 Jan. 1851.
35 Glos. Colln. RF 203.2; Glos. R.O., P 220/CH 5/1, 7.
36 Above, intro.
37 *Kelly's Dir. Glos.* (1856 and later edns.); Glos. R.O., D 2052.
38 'Memories of Mitcheldean', 14.
39 Local inf.; cf. Glos. R.O., free church surv.
40 Hockaday Abs. cclxxx.
41 *Glouc. Jnl.* 23 Oct. 1809; Glos. R.O., P 220/CH 5/2.
42 Glos. R.O., D 2297; DC/H 129; cf. G.D.R., T 1/123 (no. 166).
43 G. E. Lawrence, *Kindling the Flame* (1974), 13: copy in Glos. R.O., D 2598/23/1; cf. ibid. D 2598/2/17.
44 P.R.O., HO 129/334/1/10/27.
45 G. E. Lawrence, *Bible Christians in Forest of Dean*, ed. H. R. Jarrett (1985), 29.
46 Glos. R.O., DC/H 129.
47 Ibid. D 2598/11/1; O.S. Map 1/2,500, Glos. XXIII. 16 (1881 edn.).
48 Glos. R.O., D 2598/5/2.
49 Lawrence, *Kindling the Flame*, 48.

50 Glos. R.O., D 2598/11/1.
51 Ibid. P 220/VE 2/7–8.
52 Ibid. D 5467/6/1; 'Memories of Mitcheldean', 14.
53 *Trans. B.G.A.S.* vi. 206; Glos. R.O., D 36/E 1, f. 22v.
54 G.D.R., V 5/203T 3–4; Glos. R.O., P 220/CH 2.
55 Glos. R.O., D 36/E 6, rot. 12d.; M 78, f. 9v.
56 G.D.R. vol. 91, f. 36v.; 195, p. 160.
57 Ibid. V 5/203T 3–4.
58 Glos. R.O., P 220/VE 2/2, f. 214 and vestry min. 8 Oct. 1771.
59 *Glouc. Jnl.* 29 Aug. 1785; Bigland, *Glos.* i. 445.
60 *V.C.H. Glos.* iv. 133.
61 Glos. R.O., P 220/CH 5/4; *19th Rep. Com. Char.* 95–6; mon. in church.
62 Glos. R.O., P 220/CH 5/2–4; char. board in church porch; cf. *Bristol Jnl.* 13 Aug. 1791.
63 Glos. R.O., P 220/CH 5/1–3, 7.
64 Ibid. VE 2/5, min. 24 July 1835; G.D.R., T 1/123 (no. 70).
65 Nat. Soc. *Inquiry, 1846–7,* Glos. 12–13.
66 Glos. R.O., P 220/CH 5/4.
67 P.R.O., ED 7/35/221; Glos. R.O., P 220/CH 5/4.

Commissioners of Woods. The payment of pence for the children of parishioners, introduced in 1856 but discontinued in 1857, was resumed in 1874, the payment being refunded for those who attended regularly. In the 1880s there were other moves to limit the number of free pupils and reduce the deficit in expenditure.[68] In 1889 the average attendance was 113[69] and in 1893 the building was enlarged again with help from the National Society to which the schools affiliated.[70] The boys' and girls' schools merged about that time[71] and Mitcheldean Endowed school had an average attendance of 162 in mixed and infants' departments in 1904.[72] The endowments were administered from 1913 by a body called Lane's School Foundation.[73] The average attendance at the school fell from 150 in 1922 to 73 in 1938.[74] With the growth of the town a temporary schoolroom was added in 1958[75] and additional buildings were provided to the east from the late 1960s. In 1988 there were 219 children on the school's roll.[76]

In 1810 the Revd. Henry Berkin started a Sunday school and in 1812 he built a room next to the rectory house for it.[77] The school, intended for children from the adjoining Forest hamlets, was supported financially by, among others, the National Society and the duke of Beaufort, warden of the Forest, and it taught several hundred children, but it did not survive Berkin's departure from the parish in 1814.[78] The Independents ran a Sunday school at their chapel from c. 1812[79] and it taught 64 boys and 56 girls in 1833.[80]

In 1819 there were two dame schools in the parish[81] and in 1833 two infants' schools, begun that year, taught 4 boys and 13 girls at their parents' expense.[82] There was a school at the northern end of the town in 1840[83] and a preparatory school, one of two day schools other than the charity schools recorded in 1842, remained open until at least 1879.[84] A boarding school, begun in 1830, taught 30 boys and 10 girls in 1833[85] and there was a boarding school in the early 1850s,[86] a day school run by a music seller in 1876,[87] and a private school for girls at the end of the century.[88]

CHARITIES FOR THE POOR. The Mitcheldean almshouse mentioned in 1572[89] was presumably that north of the churchyard brook behind the church in 1616.[90] By 1660 it was administered by the churchwardens and occupied by a tenant,[91] the rent being used by 1683 to repair the church and relieve the poor.[92] The building, which in the mid 18th century was a poorhouse,[93] was pulled down c. 1853.[94] In 1857 Henrietta Davies built a pair of almshouses south of Stenders Road. The occupants paid a nominal rent and received a small weekly allowance. In 1868 Mrs. Davies, who managed the almshouses until her death, endowed the charity with £1,200 and it was renamed the Wilderness Charity.[95] In the 1960s and 1970s part of the endowment used for improvements to the building was replaced out of the income from the balance and the almspeople made small weekly contributions towards their maintenance.[96] The almshouses remained in use in 1988.[97]

Robert Stanton by will dated 1588 left a rent charge of 6s. 8d. for the poor.[98] The rent was witheld before 1655 and, although it was paid in the 1680s and 1690s,[99] its distribution among the poor had ceased by the early 18th century.[1] Richard Walwyn of Newent by will dated 1701 gave £20 to the poor, the interest to be distributed yearly, and Jonathan Parker of London by will dated 1719 left £200 to provide clothing and apprenticeships for children. Both sums were used in 1722 to buy land in Ruardean and the income was applied to Parker's charity except for 20s. a year paid for Walwyn's charity.[2] The bequest of William Morse of Stone in Berkeley, who by will dated 1726 gave £100 for the town's poor, was also laid out on land in Ruardean, which was later administered with Parker's charity.[3] Walter Little by will proved 1733 left £20 for the poor[4] but the parish, which had received half of the bequest by 1735,[5] evidently obtained only £15. That sum was lent out, the interest of 15s. a year being shared among the poor, and from 1778, when the principal was appropriated for the use of the church, 15s. a year was paid from the church rate.[6] A sum of £14, arising from a gift by Andrew Crew and producing 14s. a year for the poor, was similarly lent out and, in 1789, appropriated.[7]

68 Glos. R.O., P 220/CH 5/2, 4.
69 Kelly's Dir. Glos. (1889), 841.
70 Nat. Soc. files, Mitcheldean Endowed.
71 Cf. Kelly's Dir. Glos. (1894), 234.
72 Public Elem. Schs. 1906, 187.
73 Glos. R.O., P 220/CH 5/4.
74 Bd. of Educ., List 21, 1922 (H.M.S.O.), 106; 1932, 116; 1938, 129.
75 'Memories of Mitcheldean', 15.
76 Educ. Services Dir. 1988-9 (co. educ. dept.), 19.
77 Nat. Soc. files, Dean East Holy Trin.; Procter, Origin of Ch. in Dean, 23 n.
78 Nicholls, Forest of Dean, 157-8; Nicholls, Personalities of Dean, 133-7.
79 Glos. R.O., D 2297.
80 Educ. Enq. Abstract, 321.
81 Educ. of Poor Digest, 304.
82 Educ. Enq. Abstract, 321.
83 G.D.R., T 1/123 (no. 81).
84 Pigot's Dir. Glos. (1842), 120; Kelly's Dir. Glos. (1856), 326; (1879), 703.
85 Educ. Enq. Abstract, 321.
86 Slater's Dir. Glos. (1852-3), 144.
87 Morris's Dir. Glos. (1876), 528.

88 Kelly's Dir. Glos. (1894), 235; (1897), 238; (1902), 240.
89 Hockaday Abs. cccxxxviii.
90 Glos. R.O., D 36/E 2, f. 17v.; M 78, f. 9v.
91 Ibid. P 220/VE 2/1; lease 20 Sept. 1684 in ibid. OV 4/1.
92 G.D.R., V 5/203T 3.
93 Glos. R.O., P 220/VE 2/2, f. 214.
94 Ibid. CW 3/2; ibid. VE 2/6.
95 Ibid. D 36/T 46; Morris's Dir. Glos. (1865-6), 686.
96 Glos. R.O., D 3469/5/107; CH 22, p. 103.
97 Inf. (1995) from Mrs. Phyllis Christopher, clerk to the Wilderness Charity.
98 Glos. R.O., P 220/CH 1.   99 Ibid. VE 2/1.
1 Bodl. MS. Top. Glouc. c. 3, f. 139v.
2 Glos. R.O., P 220/CH 3/1; char. board in church porch.
3 Glos. R.O., P 220/CH 3/1; in 19th Rep. Com. Char. 94 and later references the donor is incorrectly called Wm. Nourse.
4 G.D.R. wills 1733/153.
5 Ibid. B 4/2/L 51.
6 Glos. R.O., P 220/VE 2/2, ff. 119, 216.
7 Ibid. ff. 132, 216-18; Crew was born in Alderley in 1650: ibid. P 6/IN 1/1; char. board in church porch incorrectly gives his birth place as Alderton.

The Walwyn, Morse, Little, and Crew charities were distributed together at Christmas by 1749. The amount dispensed varied according to the income of the Morse charity, which was £4 in 1749 and £7 from 1800, and the Little charity was not paid between 1761 and 1768.[8] The Stanton charity was distributed with the others from 1829, when payment of the rent charge resumed, but it and the Little and Crew charities were discontinued in 1847.[9] The Walwyn and Morse charities usually took the form of doles of 2s. 6d. in the later 19th century.[10] The Parker charity, which had an income of £10 in 1749, was applied as intended under the trust of 1722. From the mid 18th century frequent apprenticeships were made, mostly for boys, over a wide area and in 1785 the feoffees decided to end placing children with parishioners, a practice which had led to abuse of the charity.[11] In 1790 the feoffees were in open conflict with the rector, who, sharing with them in the management of the school to be funded by William Lane's trust, claimed the sole right to nominate children for apprenticeships.[12]

Mitcheldean benefited from John Harvey Oll-ney's Christmas coal and blanket charity for various Gloucestershire parishes, receiving £200 principal in 1839 and distributing the income in blankets.[13] Harriett Blunt by will proved 1859 gave £100 for coal in winter.[14] Under a Scheme of 1910 a trust established in 1908 to manage the Walwyn, Parker, and Morse charities under the title of the United Charities also administered the Ollney and Blunt charities,[15] which after the Second World War were distributed in cash.[16] In 1937 the Parker charity was assigned to young people aged under 21 taking up and following trades. At a reorganization in 1971 the other charities were amalgamated to form the Mitcheldean Welfare Trust, which had an income of £75 for the needy. The Parker charity, which then had an income of £122, was managed by the same trustees[17] and in 1988 it made small grants to young people in apprenticeships or further education.[18]

Jane Walter by deed of 1760 gave £40 to provide bibles equally for the poor of Mitcheldean and Littledean at Christmas. The charity lapsed after a few years when the principal sum was lost.[19]

NEWLAND

NEWLAND,[20] a village situated on the east side of the river Wye 5.5 km. south-east of Monmouth, was the centre of a large parish with complex boundaries and settlements of differing character. Coleford, a market town from the late 17th century, became the principal centre of population, while Newland, a picturesque village grouped around a large church and churchyard, remained small and mainly residential. In the villages of Clearwell and Bream and in Whitecliff hamlet, adjoining Coleford, a large proportion of the inhabitants worked in mining, quarrying, and other Forest trades, but Clearwell was also the centre of one of the principal estates of the Forest area, and the parish contained other substantial freehold farms. Upper and Lower Redbrook hamlets, which grew up on the banks of the Wye, were purely industrial settlements, with mills, ironworks, and copper works.

Newland parish was created in the early Middle Ages by asserting from the Forest of Dean woodland and waste, and its formation was well under way by the start of the 13th century, when its church was built. It was called Welinton in 1220[21] and was described as the 'new land of Welinton' in 1232 and 1247,[22] but later it was called simply Newland (*Nova Terra*). In 1305 the appropriator of the church, the bishop of Llandaff, was granted the tithes from all recent and future assarts from the Forest waste[23] and, though the fullest interpretation of the grant was prevented by the claims of other churches of the Forest area,[24] widely scattered parcels of land thus became part of Newland parish. Besides its main block, formed of the tithings of Coleford, Newland, and Clearwell, the parish had 22 detached parts,[25] and in 1881 its total area was 8,797 a. (3,560 ha.).[26]

Coleford tithing became a separate civil parish in 1894,[27] and the detached parts were added to other parishes between 1883 and 1935 (see Table I). Ten of them, lying at or near the north-east fringes of the Forest, had formed the hamlet or tithing called Lea Bailey, which was distinct from but in some places adjoined both the Forest woodland of the same name and the parish of Lea (Glos. and Herefs.). Inhabitants of Lea Bailey tithing were sometimes married in Newland church,[28] but the tithing was only

8 Glos. R.O., P 220/VE 2/2, ff. 216–18, 226–32; ibid. P 220/CH 3/2; ibid. CH 6.
9 Ibid. VE 2/2, ff. 259–60, 323–35; *19th Rep. Com. Char.* 94.
10 Glos. R.O., P 220/CH 3/2; ibid. CH 7.
11 Ibid. P 220/VE 2/2, ff. 219–25, 235–7; ibid. CH 3/1–2; ibid. OV 4/1–3.
12 Ibid. P 220/CH 4; above, educ.; cf. Glos. R.O., P 220/CH 3/2, min. 26 Mar. 1790.
13 Ibid. P 220/CH 7.
14 Ibid. reg. wills 1859, ff. 334v.–337v.
15 Ibid. D 3469/5/107.
16 Ibid. P 220/CH 5/4.
17 Ibid. D 3469/5/107; CH 21, E. Dean rural district, p. 13.
18 Inf. from Mrs. Christopher.
19 Bigland, *Glos.* i. 445; *19th Rep. Com. Char.* 90.
20 This account was written in 1992.

21 *Bk. of Fees*, i. 308; *Rot. Litt. Claus.* (Rec. Com.), i. 393, 413, 469. The references to the building of the parish church at 'Welinton' were presumably unknown to Atkyns (*Glos.* 574), whose statement that it was the original name of Clearwell village has been followed by other writers. The name was possibly taken from a farmstead at Newland village: cf. below, this section.
22 *Pat. R.* 1225–32, 477; *Cal. Pat.* 1232–47, 510.
23 *Cal. Pat.* 1301–7, 319.
24 Ibid. 547; *Cal. Close*, 1307–13, 85; *Rot. Parl.* i. 200, 317; *Reg. Orleton*, 319–20.
25 For the ancient parish, G.D.R., T 1/128; below, this section (Table I).
26 *Census*, 1881.
27 Ibid. 1901.
28 Glos. R.O., P 227/IN 1/1, marr. 1623; 2, marr. 1719, 1730, 1733.

No.	Location or usual name	On map	Date of transfer	Transferred to	
1*	N. of Lower Lea Bailey Incl.	XXIII. SE	1883	Lea	a
2*	W. of Lower Lea Bailey Incl.	,,	,,	Weston under Penyard	a
3*	,,	,,	,,	,,	a
4*	part of Howley grove (N. of Mitcheldean)	,,	,,	Lea	a
5*	W. of Lea Bailey	XXIII. SW	1884	Hope Mansell	b
6	Morse grounds (at Drybrook)	XXXI. NE	1883	East Dean	c
7	Loquiers farm (SW. of Mitcheldean)	,,	,,	,,	c
8	at Reddings (nr. Lydbrook)	XXXI. NW	1884	Ruardean	b
9	at Lower Lydbrook	,,	,,	,,	b
10*	adjoining Cinderford town on NE.	XXXI. SE	,,	East Dean	d
11	near Pope's Hill	,,	1883	Littledean	e
12	at Ellwood	XXXVIII. SE XXXIX. SW	,,	West Dean	c
13	Whitemead park	XXXIX. SW	,,	,,	c
14	Yorkley Court	XXXIX. SE, SW	1935	,,	f
15	Badhamsfield (nr. Yorkley)	,,	,,	,,	f
16	Oakwood Mill (N. of Bream)	XXXIX. SW	1883	,,	c
17	Hoarthorns farm (NE. of Berry Hill)	XXX. SE XXXI. SW	1883	,,	e
18	Bream	XXXIX. SW XLVII. NW	1935	,,	f
19*	at Lea Line	XXIII. SE	1883	Lea	g
20*	Woodgreen (nr. Blaisdon)	XXXII. NW	1890	Blaisdon	e
21*	Knacker's Hole (nr. Hope Mansell)	tithe map	1884	Walford	e
22*	in Lea village	tithe map	1883	Lea	c

Notes. The maps referred to in nos. 1–20 are sheets of O. S. Map 6", Glos. (1883–4 edn.). All detached parts are shown (but not so clearly located) on the Newland tithe map, G.D.R., T 1/128. The O.S. numbered the parts in separate sequences for those in Lea Bailey tithing and those not, as well as in a single sequence covering all; the comprehensive sequence is used here, and two parts which lay in areas where the O.S. survey was completed in 1887 after the transfers had been made are numbered here 21–22. The parts marked * formed Lea Bailey.

Sources for the transfers are:

a   O.S. Maps 1/2,500, Glos. XXIII. 7, 11 (1881 edn. overprinted with boundary changes 1886); *O.S. Area Bk.* Newland (1881), added page.

b   L.G.B.O. Confirmation Act, 46 & 47 Vic. c. 80 (Local).

c   Divided Parishes and Poor Law Amendment Act, 45 & 46 Vic. c. 58.

d   L.G.B.O. Confirmation Act, 46 & 47 Vic. c. 137 (Local).

e   *Census,* 1891.

f   *Census,* 1931; ibid. (pt. ii).

g   *O.S. Area Bk.* Newland (1881), added page.

intermittently administered by the Newland parish officers and was possibly never rated to the parish. From the late 17th century it relieved its own poor,[29] and it was regarded as a separate parish by 1882.[30] Land called the Glydden, later part of David's grove, near Lower Redbrook on the slopes above Valley brook, was a detached part of the extraparochial Forest within Newland until absorbed by the parish in the mid 19th century.[31] The Glydden was recorded as common land in 1410[32] and covered 23 a. in 1787.[33] After the loss of the various parts and the addition from West Dean in 1935 of the west part of Clearwell Meend, 57 a. of land between Clearwell village and the Chepstow–Coleford road, Newland civil parish was left as a compact area of 4,771 a. based on Newland and Clearwell villages.[34]

Coleford tithing, with the detached part numbered 17, is given a separate parish history in this volume, the detached parts numbered 1–11, 16, 19, and 21–2 are treated in the history of the extraparochial Forest of Dean, and no. 20 is included as part of the history of Blaisdon in another volume.[35] This parish history includes Newland and Clearwell tithings, together with the larger detached parts lying close by at Bream, Yorkley, Whitemead, and Ellwood (nos. 12–15, 18); however, some aspects of those detached parts in the modern period, when they were affected by the development of the largely extraparochial hamlets of Bream's Eaves, Whitecroft, Pillowell, Yorkley, and Ellwood, are covered in the history of the extraparochial Forest. The history of the deserted hamlet and vanished mansion called Highmeadow, on the boundaries of Staunton parish, Newland tithing, and Coleford tithing, is included wholly under Staunton.

Part at least of the later parish of Newland was settled and cultivated in the Anglo-Saxon period when there was a manor called Wyegate, probably based on Wyegate Green above the valley of Mork brook. Before 1086, however, Wyegate was taken out of cultivation and included in the royal demesne land of the Forest.[36] Assarting presumably proceeded steadily during the 12th and early 13th centuries, and in 1220 the manor of Newland was extended at 10 ploughteams.[37] Payers of newly assessed rents for assarts who were listed in 1219 included two men surnamed of Welinton and others[38] with surnames that suggest a connexion with the later parish.[39] About 1245 it was reported that different parts of Newland had been 'assessed', presumably for rents for new assarts, under the three constables

of St. Briavels who served between 1207 and 1230.[40] By the mid 13th century much of the area around the new parish church at Newland village had evidently been taken into cultivation, besides a narrow strip of land on the banks of the Wye, comprising the manor of Wyeseal.[41]

In 1282 most of Clearwell tithing, the south part of the parish, still lay within the royal demesne land of the Forest. The eastern bounds of the Forest bailiwick of Bearse were then Horwell hill (later Bream's Meend), Oakwood brook, and Spoon green at the south end of the land later called Clearwell Meend. From Spoon green its bounds traversed the later parish to a cross at Thurstan's brook, evidently somewhere near Millend, for Thurstan's brook was then the name of the upper part of Valley brook. Whether the boundary reached that point by the road that became the main village street of Clearwell or ran further south through the area called Platwell is not clear. From Thurstan's brook the boundary of the bailiwick then turned south along the edge of the cultivated land of Newland to Stowe on the boundary with St. Briavels, and — including the land later called Bearse common, which long remained part of the royal demesne — ran south-east to Rodmore, later part of St. Briavels parish.[42]

Most of the land between the site of Clearwell village and the St. Briavels boundary was taken into cultivation in the earlier 14th century when the Crown appointed commissioners to value and dispose of unwanted parts of its demesne waste.[43] Four acres in the Platwell area that were granted out of the Forest waste in 1306[44] were probably part of a much larger block then disposed of: the assarting of other large parts of Bearse bailiwick, later included in Lydney and St. Briavels, is recorded the same year.[45] In 1317 John of Wyesham was licensed to assart land called Noxon, covering 280 a. between the later Lydney–Coleford road and Oakwood brook.[46] In 1323 William Joce, ancestor of the owners of the Clearwell estate, was allowed to assart 80 a. at 'Drakenhord', evidently the land later called Dragon's Ford south-west of the road junction called Trow green, and 20 a. at 'Muchelcleye', presumably in the area later called Clays northeast of Trow green.[47] In 1338 a successor, John Joce, was licensed to assart another 116 a. in 'St. Briavels, Newland, Drakenhord, Overesene, Holiwalle',[48] and later in 1338 and in 1342 Joce made grants of land at Drakenhord and 'Overnese', which was in the same area as Drakenhord.[49] The wide tract called Broadfields,

[29] Ibid. D 2026/R 6.
[30] *Census*, 1891.
[31] Crown Land Revenue Act, 54 Geo. III, c. 70, s. 10; P.R.O., MR 415 (F 16/47); G.D.R., T 1/128.
[32] Glos. R.O., D 2957/214.12.
[33] P.R.O., MR 415.
[34] *Census*, 1931 (pt. ii); cf. O.S. Map 1/25,000, SO 50 (1951 edn.).
[35] *V.C.H. Glos.* x. 6.   [36] Below, manors.
[37] *Bk. of Fees*, i. 308.
[38] *Pipe R.* 1219 (P.R.S. N.S. xlii), 13.
[39] Lands of Ellen and John Ball may have been those later called Balls by Valley brook below Newland village, of Wal. of Ketifort those later called Ketford's lands, and of Adam Bateric the later Batridge field below Highmeadow: P.R.O., MR 879 (F 17/1); below, manors (Lower Redbrook

Fm.).
[40] P.R.O., E 146/1/25; and for dating, below, Forest of Dean, wardens
[41] Below, manors.
[42] P.R.O., E 32/31, m. 12. For the identification of Horwell hill, Spoon green, and Thurstan's brook, P.R.O., MR 879; and for Bearse common, below, St. Briavels, intro.
[43] Cf. *Cal. Fine R.* 1307–19, 164, 183; for that area, below, Fig. 8.   [44] Glos. R.O., D 1677/GG 12.
[45] Prior's Mesne: above, Lydney, manors; Gainer's Mesne: below, St Briavels, intro.
[46] Below, manors.
[47] P.R.O., C 143/157, no. 9; cf. ibid. MR 879; G.D.R., T 1/128.
[48] *Cal. Fine R.* 1337–47, 67; P.R.O., C 143/239, no. 20.
[49] N.L.W., Dunraven MSS. 325–6.

bounded by the Lydney–Coleford road, the Chepstow–Coleford road, and the boundary with St. Briavels, later belonged to the Clearwell estate[50] and was probably all taken by the Joces in the earlier 14th century. The Reddings (or Ridings), lying on the St. Briavels boundary east of Stowe hamlet,[51] were probably part of 200 a. which in 1361 Grace Dieu abbey (Mon.) claimed had been assarted since 1226 adjoining its grange at Stowe, and the abbey itself was licensed to assart land west of Stowe, near Wyegate Green, in 1338.[52] In James I's reign when owners of assarts made anciently from the demesne land of the Forest were required to compound for them, the bulk of Clearwell and Newland tithings was included.[53]

Of the detached parts of Newland lying east of Clearwell tithing, Whitemead, evidently inclosed by the Crown itself, was recorded in 1283.[54] Land at Bream had been cleared and settled by the mid 14th century, and there was farmland at Ellwood by the same period.[55] In 1282 the meadow of Yorkley was mentioned,[56] and in 1310 land in the Yorkley area was held by John ap Adam,[57] whose name is presumably preserved in that of Badhamsfield farm. An assart of 36 a. at Yorkley was mentioned in 1338.[58]

In its completed form the part of the parish comprising Newland and Clearwell tithings formed a roughly rhomboidal block of land, bounded on its west side by the river Wye and on the north by part of the Newland village to Monmouth road and the upper Red brook. On the north-east the boundary with the tithing and later parish of Coleford followed ancient routes running from Highmeadow to Whitecliff, Whitecliff to Millend, over Mill hill (north of Clearwell village), and, by Pingry Lane, to the Chepstow–Coleford road near Milkwall. The east boundary, with the extraparochial Forest, skirted the edge of Clearwell Meend, on the south side of which a boundary marker called Cradocks stone stood in 1282 and 1608,[59] and followed Oakwood brook. The south boundary, with St. Briavels parish, followed an ancient track running westwards from the Lydney–Coleford road at Bream Cross, skirted the detached part of the Forest waste called Bearse common, and reached the Wye by way of Stowe and Wyegate Green. The largest detached portion of the parish, including Bream village, covered 748 a.[60] lying south-east of the main part of the parish and divided from it by a strip of extraparochial Forest c. 120 yds. wide near Bream Cross. Its boundary with the ancient parish of Lydney was formed in part by Pailwell

(later Park) brook on the south-west and Tufts brook, a tributary of Cannop brook, on the south-east, while to the north it had a long irregular boundary with the extraparochial Forest. The two detached portions further east at Yorkley were also sandwiched between Lydney parish and the Forest and were divided from each other by a strip of roadside waste along the Lydney to Yorkley village road. The western portion, comprising the Yorkley Court estate, covered 281 a. and the eastern one, comprising Badhamsfield farm, 77 a.[61] Collectively the three portions at Bream and Yorkley formed the tithing of Bream. The island of Newland within the Forest at Ellwood, which was regarded as part of Clearwell tithing,[62] covered 134 a.[63] The portion called Whitemead park, further into the Forest near Parkend village, covered 229 a. in 1776.[64]

On the west side of the parish the land rises steeply from the Wye, and much of Newland and Clearwell tithings is at 170–200 m. In the south is gently rolling, open land, while in the north the land is more rugged, with the main feature the sinuous valley of the lower Red brook[65] (later called Valley brook), which performs a jack-knife turn between Newland village and the Wye. On the north boundary a stream that was also called Red brook in the late Middle Ages descends to Upper Redbrook hamlet in a steep-sided valley formerly called Ashridge Slade. A high wooded ridge, called Ashridge in 1608[66] but later Astridge, divides the valleys of the two Red brooks and is matched on the north-east by the heights of Bircham (called Birchover in the Middle Ages)[67] and Highmeadow. The land of the home part of the parish is formed mainly of the Old Red Sandstone, while carboniferous limestone forms the eastern fringes and the detached parts,[68] where iron, stone, and coal were dug in numerous small workings.[69] At Noxon Park wood, in the south-east of Clearwell tithing, the ground has been gashed and pitted by iron-ore mining, and in a wood south of Bream village called the Scowles (the local name for old workings[70]) a similar area of broken ground was popularly known as the Devil's Chapel.[71] Offa's Dyke traverses the west side of the parish[72] above the Wye, where two farmhouses on its course are called Coxbury and Highbury. In Highbury wood, where it follows the top of the ridge and is lined by ancient yew trees, the dyke is a pronounced feature of the landscape.

The hillsides above the Wye and much of the sides of the Red brook valleys have remained thickly wooded. There were c. 500 a. of wood-

50 P.R.O., MR 879.
51 Cf. ibid.
52 Cal. Pat. 1361–4, 11; Cal. Fine R. 1337–47, 65; cf. below, St. Briavels, manors (Stowe).
53 Glos. R.O., D 34/1/1; D 2026/E 21; D 1677/GG 657.
54 Cal. Close, 1279–88, 219.
55 N.L.W., Dunraven MSS. 339, rental of John Joce; ibid. 325, deeds 1357, 1384; Glos. R.O., D 2244/44.
56 P.R.O., E 32/31, m. 11.
57 B.L. Harl. MS. Ch. 111, c. 32.
58 Cal. Inq. p.m. viii, p. 108.
59 P.R.O., E 32/31, m. 12; MR 879.
60 O.S. Area Bk. Newland detached no. 18 (1880).
61 Census, 1931 (pt. ii).
62 Glos. R.O., P 227/OV 1/1.

63 G.D.R., T 1/128.
64 P.R.O., F 17/161.
65 Glos. R.O., D 2244/42.
66 Ibid. D 33/103; D 2026/T 11; P.R.O., MR 879.
67 Glos. R.O., D 2244/46; N.L.W., Dunraven MSS. 339, rental 1430 (s.v. Millend).
68 Geol. Surv. Map 1", solid, sheets 35, 45 (1845 edn., revised to 1872).
69 O.S. Maps 6", Glos. XLVII. NW.; XXXIX. SW. (1883 edn.).
70 Hart, Ind. Hist. of Dean, 242.
71 Bryant, Map of Glos. (1824); Nicholls, Iron Making, 213; above, Plate 2.
72 C. Fox, Offa's Dyke (1955), 186–8.

land in those areas in 1840, then belonging to the Bigsweir estate, based in St. Briavels, or to the Newland Valley estate.[73] At Noxon the owners of the Clearwell estate maintained a large deer park in the 16th and early 17th centuries[74] and later had 120 a. of woodland there. Noxon Park wood was acquired in 1907 by the Crown Commissioners of Woods,[75] who from 1817 had owned Bircham wood, covering c. 40 a. on the hill east of Newland village, as part of the Highmeadow estate.[76] In the detached lands, the Crown's Whitemead park was used as farmland by the early 18th century, but in 1808 the Commissioners planted 204 a. with timber, and they bought and planted 110 a. of the parish at Ellwood c. 1818.[77] From 1924[78] the Crown woodlands were managed by the Forestry Commission's Dean surveyorship, partly as conifer plantations, and before 1958 the Commission added Forge and Astridge woods, on the north side of Valley brook, to their holdings in the parish.[79] The woodland above the Wye remained in private ownership in 1992, though Highbury wood was then managed by the Nature Conservancy as a reserve.

In the early 17th century the owners of the Clearwell estate had a walled coney warren on the high ground west of Clearwell Court and land south of the house was a small park.[80] Later a larger area, including the warren, was inclosed in a walled deer park.[81] Some small open fields once lay north-west of Newland village but most of the parish after its clearance from the Forest was farmed in large closes.[82] The Newland oak, one of the largest trees recorded in England, stood in a field north of Newland village.[83] In 1906 its circumference at 5 ft. from the ground was 43 ft. 6 in. The tree collapsed in a storm in 1955, and remnants of the stump remained in 1992, together with a sapling taken from it and planted alongside.[84]

The spine of the road system that developed to link the villages and hamlets of the parish was provided by the route running from Bream Cross at the south-eastern corner of the main part of the parish, where roads from Lydney and Aylburton met, through Clearwell and Newland villages to the Wye at Upper Redbrook hamlet, where it joined a route to Monmouth. Roads converging on the central route at Newland village included Highmeadow way, recorded in 1369,[85] descending steeply from Highmeadow hamlet on the north-east and in the 16th century

also providing the main route between Coleford and the village,[86] a lane from the Wye at Lower Redbrook hamlet following the valley of Valley brook, a lane called French way in 1422 (later French Lane) which provided a more direct way from Lower Redbrook hamlet by climbing over Astridge and meeting the Valley brook road at the south-west corner of Newland village,[87] and the principal route from St. Briavels, called Inwood Lane (later Rookery Lane), running from Stowe across the high plateau via Inwood Farm.[88] South-east of Newland village the main spinal route was joined at a place called Scatterford by a road from Coleford and Whitecliff. At the north-west end of Clearwell village a crossroads, mentioned c. 1300[89] and usually called Wainlete or Wainland,[90] was formed on it by Margery Lane, which branched from Inwood Lane at the Margery pool north of Stowe, and by Pingry Lane, which ran north-east from Wainlete to Coleford.[91] On the west side of the parish an ancient route between St. Briavels and Monmouth, later called Coxbury and Wyegate Lane, ran from Wyegate Green across the high ground on the edge of the Wye Valley and descended to the river at Lower Redbrook hamlet. There it joined a riverside road, recorded in 1445, leading from Brockweir to Monmouth.[92] In 1801 about a mile of that riverside road south of Lower Redbrook was formed by a causeway of pitched stones.[93]

South of Clearwell village Shop House, whose name is a corruption of Sheep House,[94] and a place called Troll mead in 1282, later Trow green,[95] are crossroads on the main spinal route. At Shop House it was crossed by a route from the Wye at Bigsweir, which left the parish at Spoon green at the south end of Clearwell Meend, and at Trow green it was crossed by a road from Chepstow and St. Briavels to Coleford, which converged with the Bigsweir road before it reached Spoon green. In 1608 parts of both those routes were named as Cockshoot Lane but later the name was used only for the Bigsweir road between Stowe and Shop House. The Chepstow–Coleford road was called Clay Lane north-east of Trow green in 1608[96] and Spoon green was later known as Clay Lane End. At Bream Cross on the parish boundary the main spinal route was joined by a road from St. Briavels that was called the portway in 1310.[97]

In 1282, before the area was assarted, a number of clearings were recorded in the south part of

73 G.D.R., T 1/128.
74 Below, manors.
75 P.R.O., CRES 38/669, deed and sale partics. 1907; ibid. 672, deed 1880.
76 Glos. R.O., D 23/E 42; G.D.R., T 1/128; cf. below, Staunton, manor.
77 Below, manors (Whitemead Pk.); *3rd Rep. Com. Woods* (1819), 19; G.D.R., T 1/128.
78 *Lond. Gaz.* 25 Mar. 1924, pp. 2510–13.
79 Hart, *Royal Forest*, 232, 235, 240; *Rep. Dean Forest Cttee.* (1958), map at end.
80 N.L.W., Dunraven MSS. 260, deed 1637; cf. P.R.O., MR 879.
81 Atkyns, *Glos.* plate at pp. 574–5; G.D.R., T 1/128; cf. *Glouc. Jnl.* 8 Sept. 1788.
82 Below, econ. hist. (agric.).
83 O.S. Map 6", Glos. XXXVIII. NE. (1884 edn.).
84 Hart, *Royal Forest*, 243 n.
85 Glos. R.O., D 1677/GG 97, 220; D 2957/214.54;

P.R.O., MR 879.
86 Glos. R.O., D 1677/GG 436, 465.
87 Ibid. D 33/82–3; O.S. Map 6", Glos. XXXVIII. NE. (1884 edn.).
88 P.R.O., MR 879; O.S. Map 6", Glos. XXXVIII. NE. (1884 edn.).
89 Glos. R.O., D 33/4.
90 Ibid.; ibid. D 1677/GG 177; cf. *P.N. Glos.* (E.P.N.S.), iii. 239.
91 O.S. Maps 6", Glos. XXXVIII. NE., SE. (1884 edn.).
92 Below, St. Briavels, intro.; O.S. Map 6", Glos. XXXVIII. SE. (1884 edn.); Glos. R.O., D 33/96.
93 C. Heath, *Historical and Descriptive Accounts of Tintern Abbey* (Monmouth, 1801), [5, 12].
94 Below, this section.
95 P.R.O., E 32/31, m. 12; MR 879.
96 Ibid. MR 879; for Cockshoot Lane, N.L.W., Dunraven MSS. 327, deeds 1716, 1787.
97 Below, St. Briavels, intro.

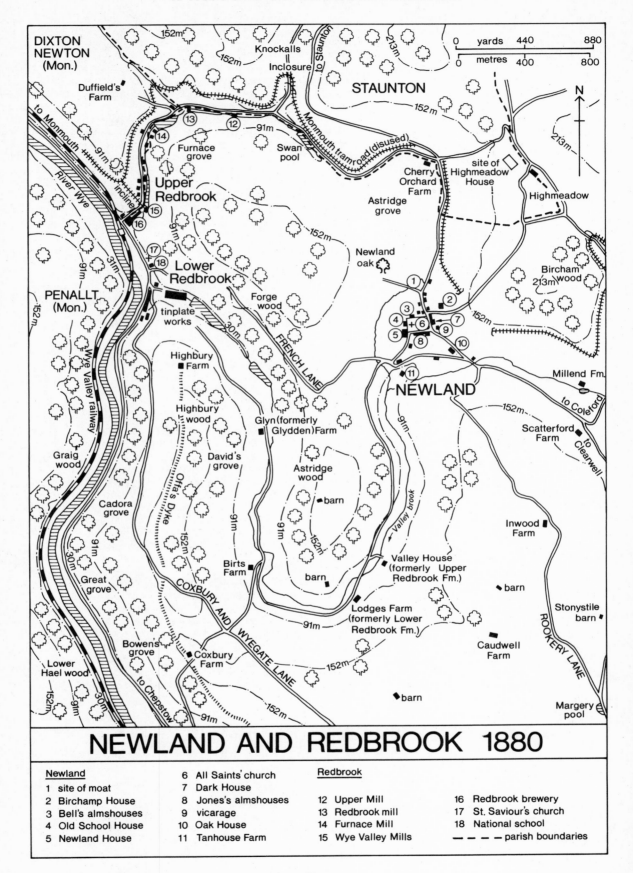

NEWLAND AND REDBROOK 1880

Newland			Redbrook	
1 site of moat	6	All Saints' church		
2 Birchamp House	7	Dark House		
3 Bell's almshouses	8	Jones's almshouses	12 Upper Mill	16 Redbrook brewery
4 Old School House	9	vicarage	13 Redbrook mill	17 St. Saviour's church
5 Newland House	10	Oak House	14 Furnace Mill	18 National school
	11	Tanhouse Farm	15 Wye Valley Mills	– – – – parish boundaries

Fig. 7

the parish. Such clearings in forest land were often made alongside paths for the security of travellers,[98] and some presumably corresponded to the later road system, but they are not easy to locate from the landmarks given. One called the 'Longreode' and described as running between Willsbury and Troll mead was possibly alongside the track which runs north from Willsbury green in St. Briavels, crosses the portway at a house called Roads House, and continues northwards to Trow green as a footpath. Another called 'Smetherede' ran from the Longreode to Oakwood brook and may have been on the portway or on the line of a footpath further north; the name suggests that it was a route used by the ironworkers of St. Briavels to carry their ore from the iron mines of the Noxon area. 'Sponnerede', which ran from a place called 'Bersesenese' to Spoon green in 1282,[99] may have corresponded to the part of the St. Briavels to Coleford road between Bearse common and Spoon green.

Many crossroads and junctions on the old roads seem to have been marked by wayside crosses in the Middle Ages. They included village crosses at Newland and Clearwell,[1] and, recorded in 1608, Crockets cross on French Lane west of Newland village, and Hodgeway cross, on Highmeadow way near the Staunton boundary.[2] There were perhaps once others at Wyegate Green,[3] and at the place called Blindway cross in 1685, where Coxbury and Wyegate Lane met a lane leading from farmsteads on Valley brook to Wyeseal on the Wye.[4]

The road on the northern boundary of the parish from Highmeadow down through Upper Redbrook hamlet was turnpiked in 1755,[5] and during the late 18th century and the early 19th it was part of the main Coleford to Monmouth route.[6] The road joining it at Cherry Orchard Farm, running from Coleford through Whitecliff, Millend, and Newland village, was turnpiked under the Forest of Dean trust established in 1796. The Forest trust also covered the road from Clearwell village towards Coleford, following the Forest boundary to Milkwall.[7] In 1827 the same trust was extended to include the Lydney to Newland village road between Bream Cross and Scatterford and also the Chepstow–Coleford road by way of Bearse common, Trow green, and Clay Lane End.[8] Under an Act of 1824 a new Wye Valley road from Chepstow to Monmouth was built, incorporating much of the old riverside route within the parish, and at the same time a branch from near the new Bigsweir bridge to the Forest, by way of Cockshoot Lane, Shop House, and Clay Lane End, was turnpiked.[9] In 1840 there were tollhouses at Trow

green, Clay Lane End, Scatterford (later moved north-westwards to the junction with Rookery Lane), and above Upper Redbrook hamlet.[10] The upper Red brook valley road was disturnpiked in 1878,[11] the Wye Valley and Bigsweir roads in 1879,[12] and the roads of the Forest trust in 1888.[13] The ancient main routes on the steeper ground lost their importance in the turnpike era and most of them, including Highmeadow way, Coxbury and Wyegate Lane, and parts of Rookery Lane, remained narrow, unmade bridle paths in 1992. In the late 19th and early 20th centuries a ferry operated on the Wye at Lower Redbrook hamlet.[14]

The Monmouth tramroad, opened in 1812 to link the Forest mines and Monmouth, crossed the parish east of Newland village, where its course included a short tunnel below Bircham wood. In the upper Red brook valley it ran in Staunton and Dixton Newton (Mon.), over the boundary, but a branch, by means of an incline crossing the road and stream at Upper Redbrook hamlet, served wharfs on the Wye at Lower Redbrook. Only a modest traffic ran to Redbrook and the tramroad as a whole was little used after the mid 19th century when Monmouth was provided with a rail link to the South Wales coalfield.[15] In 1883 the Coleford railway to Monmouth was opened, using the old tramroad route, except for some short deviations, and serving Newland by a small station within Staunton parish near Cherry Orchard Farm. The railway was closed in 1916. The Wye Valley railway between Chepstow and Monmouth opened in 1876 and included a station at Upper Redbrook, where the line crossed from the Monmouthshire to the Gloucestershire bank of the Wye. The line was closed to passenger traffic in 1959 and to freight in 1964.[16] Remains from the railways and tramroad in 1992 included the cast iron bridge of the Wye Valley line across the river and the stone bridge of the tramroad incline across the road in Upper Redbrook.

Early settlement in the area took the form of scattered hamlets, often themselves of a dispersed nature but usually based on single streets running along the valleys. In Newland and Clearwell tithings a widespread pattern of settlement evident by the mid 14th century became less marked as a result of changes in the early modern period. The hamlets of Highmeadow and Ashridge, on the boundary with Staunton,[17] and the old settlement of Redbrook, on Valley brook between Newland village and the Wye, lost most of their houses, leaving only one or two large farmsteads. At Newland village, however, dispersed groups of dwellings were given a focus

98 Cf. *Close R.* 1234–7, 1, 248; *Cal. Pat.* 1247–58, 435; in Latin termed *trenchea* and in O.E. *reod*: cf. *P.N. Glos.* (E.P.N.S.), iv. 166.

99 P.R.O., E 32/31, m. 12.   1 Below, this section.

2 P.R.O., MR 879.

3 Glos. R.O., D 33/191.   4 Ibid. D 2026/T 40.

5 Monmouth Roads Act, 28 Geo. II, c. 31.

6 Glos. R.O., D 1677/1545, no. 16; Bryant, *Map of Glos.* (1824); cf. below, Staunton, intro.

7 Dean Forest Roads Act, 36 Geo. III, c. 131.

8 Ibid. 7 & 8 Geo. IV, c. 12 (Local and Personal).

9 Abbey Tintern and Bigsweir Roads Act, 5 Geo. IV,

c. 29 (Local and Personal); cf. Glos. R.O., Q/RUm 90.

10 G.D.R., T 1/128; O.S. Map 6", Glos. XXXVIII. NE. (1884 edn.).

11 Annual Turnpike Acts Continuance Act, 1878, 41 & 42 Vic. c. 62.

12 Ibid. 1874, 37 & 38 Vic. c. 95.

13 Dean Forest Turnpike Trust Abolition Act, 51 & 52 Vic. c. 193.

14 O.S. Map 1/2,500, Glos. XXXVIII. 2 (1885, 1922 edns.).

15 Paar, *G.W.R. in Dean*, 85–9, 96–102, 111–12.

16 Ibid. 113, 117–18, 120–1.

17 Below, Staunton, intro.

by new building around the church and churchyard, and at Clearwell a group of hamlets coalesced to form a substantial village.

At NEWLAND village the parish church was built shortly before 1216[18] on a low, flat-topped hill, sheltered by higher hills except to the south where the valley of Valley brook descends to the Wye. The top of the hill was presumably then unoccupied, giving scope for laying out the large rectangular churchyard, but the later disposition of the village suggests that there were already houses on the lower ground round about. They probably included a dwelling or dwellings near the source of the stream called Black brook on the Monmouth road north of the hill, and it was perhaps there that the name Welinton, used in the early 13th century for the area that the church was built to serve,[19] may have originated; the name is thought to mean a farmstead by a willow copse,[20] and there is an ancient moated site on Black brook on the west side of the Monmouth road. Other groups of houses that may be of early origin stood further down Black brook below and west of the hill and in the valley on the south side of the hill. The church and churchyard had attracted building around them by the mid 14th century. The church became the most significant point of reference in the large, dispersed parish: in the late Middle Ages and until the 17th century the village was known as Churchend,[21] and late-medieval property deeds when identifying roads converging on the place from other hamlets usually gave 'the church of All Saints' as the destination.[22] From the 17th century, however, the name Churchend was replaced by the name of the parish. The village was a minor market centre in the 15th and 16th centuries.[23] Later, as Coleford became established as the principal trading centre of the area, Newland village became residential in character, having a number of substantial gentry houses, two sets of almshouses, a grammar school, and in the mid 18th century a successful private school.[24] In the late 18th century the picturesque setting, the fine church in its well kept churchyard, and the several elegant houses gave it the reputation of one of the most attractive villages in the county.[25]

The church has remained the dominant feature of Newland village and the large churchyard its focus.[26] The main thoroughfare, on the Lydney–Monmouth road, runs along the east side of the churchyard, and a village cross stood at the junction with the lane to Highmeadow in 1511 and 1608.[27] North of the churchyard two houses mentioned in 1404 as at Blackbrook Street[28] were presumably near the moated site by the Monmouth road. A house within the moat became

the residence of the priest of Greyndour's chantry in Newland church in 1446, and it was demolished in the 18th century.[29] By the mid 14th century there were several houses on a lane running along the south side of the churchyard,[30] and that lane was probably the site of butchers' shambles in the 16th century;[31] from 1617 most of its south side was occupied by a row of almshouses built for the charity of William Jones.[32] The hillside south of the churchyard, formerly called Wolf hill, and the valley below had several houses in the 15th century. The lane there, leading from the Clearwell road towards Redbrook, was called Nether Churchend Street in 1472, but it appears also to have been called Warlows way at that period. Before it divides into French Lane and the valley lane at the south-west corner of the village, it is joined by a lane, known as Payns Lane in 1425[33] and later Savage Hill,[34] descending steeply from the churchyard. In the early modern period the valley south of the village was the site of tanneries,[35] and in 1695 the road there was known as Barkhouse Lane from that trade,[36] but in the 20th century it was called Laundry Road. West of the hill three or four houses stood by Black brook, above its crossing by French Lane, in the early 17th century.[37] Their later disappearance was presumably the result of the incorporation of that area in the grounds and garden prospect of Newland House, built on the hill above.

The earliest surviving house in Newland village appears to be the Old School House, on the west side of the churchyard, formerly housing a grammar school founded by Edward Bell. Its earlier, north–south, range is apparently the building that was under construction for the school in 1576.[38] The southern end of that range was demolished in the early 20th century,[39] and the remaining portion is of a single storey with attic, having a large internal stack near the north end with a cross passage beyond it. There is some evidence that the range originally extended further north and was curtailed at the building of the east–west range, which is of two storeys and attics and is dated 1639. The plan of the later range, presumably designed specifically for the purposes of the school, provides heated rooms at each end, that to the east being larger, and two small, unheated rooms in the centre. All are joined by a passage, which is alongside the cross passage of the north–south range. Spout Farm, on the main street near the north end of the village, was recorded from 1669.[40] It is a small L-shaped rubblestone farmhouse of the mid 17th century, with an addition of c. 1800 at its south end.

18 Below, churches.   19 Above, this section.
20 *P.N. Glos.* (E.P.N.S.), iii. 237.
21 e.g. Glos. R.O., D 2244/31; D 34/9/15; D 1677/GG 1225; Smith, *Men and Armour*, 40.
22 e.g. Glos. R.O., D 2244/13, 42; N.L.W., Dunraven MSS. 324, deed 1426; 325, deed 1423.
23 Below, econ. hist. (other ind. and trade).
24 *Glouc. Jnl.* 6 Oct. 1761; 19 Oct. 1772.
25 Rudder, *Glos.* 567, 569; Brayley and Britton, *Beauties of Eng. and Wales*, v. 718.
26 For the village, above, Plate 7.
27 Glos. R.O., D 2957/214.54; P.R.O., MR 879.
28 Glos. R.O., D 2957/214.8.
29 Below, manors (Newland House).

30 Glos. R.O., D 2244/31, 78.
31 Ibid. D 1677/GG 348; D 2957/214.67.
32 Below, char.
33 Glos. R.O., D 2957/214.24, 31, 38, 76A; D 2244/105, 153; D 2026/T 66.
34 O.S. Map 1/2,500, Glos. XXXVIII. 7 (1921 edn.).
35 Below, econ. hist. (other ind. and trade).
36 Glos. R.O., D 2026/E 18.
37 P.R.O., MR 879; cf. Glos. R.O., D 33/338 (where the lane leading to Crokers cross is evidently French Lane).
38 Below, educ.
39 Inf. from Mrs. C. Chamberlain, of Newland; cf. Bigland, *Glos.* ii, plate facing p. 257; above, Plate 35.
40 Glos. R.O., D 637/II/1/T 1.

Newland House, a substantial house at the south-west corner of the churchyard, was the home of the Probyns, who were the principal gentry family at Newland in the 18th century[41] and evidently did much to establish it as a popular residential village. A house in the main street east of the churchyard was rebuilt c. 1694 by William Probyn, whose family held it on long leases from Bell's charity. Before 1816 it became the Ostrich inn,[42] the sign derived from the Probyn crest.[43] The Dower House (formerly Dark House), in the same group of buildings, was apparently the house that Sir Edmund Probyn left to his sister Frances in 1742, with reversion to his nephew William Hopkins.[44] Later it belonged to Edmund Probyn (d. 1819) who left it to two daughters while they remained unmarried.[45] The main part of the house is of the early 18th century and of five bays with a hipped roof. About 1820 a room with a canted bay was added at the south-west and later in the 19th century two wings were added at the rear. Parts of an early 18th-century staircase survive, but the interior of the original house has been largely refitted.

On the hillside south-east of the village a house called Woofields, later Oak House, was leased in 1695 by George Bond of Redbrook to a carpenter who was to 'finish' the house; the carpenter sold the lease in 1700, and in 1712 the house was described as recently erected.[46] It was apparently owned or occupied by members of the Probyn family in the later 18th century[47] and in 1840 belonged to Edmund Probyn's daughter Susan Dighton, whose family lived there until the early 20th century.[48] In 1968 it became a home for mentally retarded people.[49] The central part of the north wing of Oak House has exceptionally thick walls retained from an earlier building, possibly a barn which stood at the site in 1665.[50] The new house of c. 1700 had a main block facing south-east and a recessed kitchen wing to the north-west. The entrance hall has fittings of high quality, and a square garden room has a venetian window and an elaborately coved ceiling. The room at the north-east end of the main front was redecorated in the early 19th century, and later that century a large first-floor drawing room was formed above the kitchen wing. During restoration after 1968 the service areas of the house were much altered and a new block was added at the rear.

Tanhouse Farm, on Valley brook at the south-west of the village, also dates from c. 1700, and is a four-square house with a front of five bays with timber mullion and transom windows. A small forecourt with pineapple and acorn finials surmounting its wall completes the symmetry of the design. The interior has been partly rearranged but retains a contemporary oak staircase. A branch of the Probyn family owned and worked a tannery there in the 18th century.[51] The Lecturage, at the east end of William Jones's almshouses and formerly the residence of the lecturer supported by that charity,[52] and South Lodge, on Savage Hill, are other fairly substantial early 18th-century houses. Birchamp House, in the north-east part of the village by the lane to Highmeadow, was built shortly before 1808, when it was called Newland Cottage.[53] Before 1820 it was improved and enlarged to form a substantial classical-style residence.[54]

CLEARWELL was probably settled rather later than Newland but eventually became a larger village. It developed on land which in the late 13th century was at the northern edge of the Forest waste of Bearse bailiwick,[55] and it formed around three roads which run down shallow valleys to a central junction. In the later Middle Ages the groups of houses on the three roads were apparently regarded as separate hamlets: those on the road running north-west towards Newland were distinguished as Clearwell (or Clearwell Street) and Wainlete, which as mentioned above was the old name of the crossroads at the road's north-west end, those on the road running east to Clearwell Meend and the extra-parochial Forest as Peak, and those on the road running south towards Lydney as Platwell (or Platwell Street).[56] At the central junction a substantial cross on a high, stepped plinth was erected in the 14th century; it was restored and its missing finial replaced in the mid 19th century.[57] It was called the high cross in 1624 and the upper cross in 1705,[58] suggesting that a second village cross once stood at the Wainlete crossroads, which place was later known as Lower Cross.[59] The source of water which gave its name to the north-west street and ultimately to the whole village is a clear and copious spring emerging at the foot of the hillside a short way west of the cross and flowing along the north-east side of Clearwell Street as one of the main feeders of Valley brook. A pool at the spring was surrendered by a tenant to the lady of Clearwell in 1484,[60] and it was presumably the owners of the estate who enclosed the spring in a small stone wellhouse in the 19th century.

Clearwell Street and Platwell had dwellings by c. 1300,[61] and in 1349 there were 8 or more

41 Below, manors.
42 Glos. R.O., D 34/9/30, 62, 69.
43 Fairbairn's Crests, i. 392.
44 Glos. R.O., D 637/II/1/T 1; cf. Taylor, Map of Glos. (1777), which marks 'Hopkin Esq.' there.
45 P.R.O., PROB 11/1616 (P.C.C. 233 Ellenbro'), f. 288; cf. G.D.R., T 1/128; Glos. Countryside, July 1932, 50.
46 Glos. R.O., D 2026/E 18, T 60; Newland Valley est. deeds, in possession of Mr. and Mrs. P. W. Chamberlain, of Tanhouse Fm., Newland: Upper Redbrook fm. 1712–93, marr. settlm. 1712. The crest of the Bonds of Redbrook, on the fireplace in the entrance hall, confirms the identification: Burke, General Armory (1884), 98.
47 Taylor, Map of Glos. (1777).
48 Trans. B.G.A.S. vi. 195–7; G.D.R., T 1/128; Glos. R.O., D 2428/1/23/2.
49 Inf. from Mr. S. Horn, of Oak House.

50 Glos. R.O., D 2026/T 49.
51 Below, econ hist. (other ind. and trade).
52 G.D.R., T 1/128.
53 Glouc. Jnl. 21 Mar. 1808; Glos. R.O., Q/RUm 30.
54 Glouc. Jnl. 10 July 1820; Glos. R.O., D 637/VII/22.
55 Above, this section.
56 Glos. R.O., D 1677/GG 1225; D 2244/18, 33; N.L.W., Dunraven MSS. 324, deeds 1360, 1416, 1484; 325, deeds 1419, 1484; Hist. MSS. Com. 55, Var. Colln. IV, Glemham Hall, pp. 177, 180.
57 Pooley, Glos. Crosses, 61–4; cf. N.L.W., Dunraven MSS. 324, deed 1416.
58 N.L.W., Dunraven MSS. 329, deeds 1705, 1708; Suff. R.O, HA 49/A III(d)/1.
59 P.R.O., HO 107/2444.
60 N.L.W., Dunraven MSS. 324.
61 Glos. R.O., D 33/3–4.

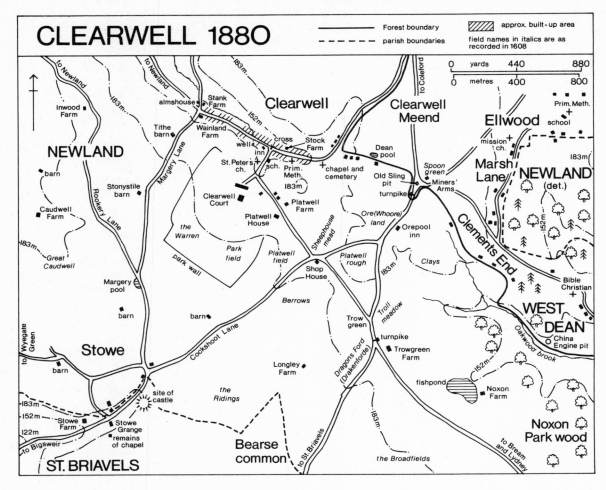

FIG. 8

houses at Clearwell and 15 or more at Platwell and 'Platwell gate'.[62] In 1462 14 houses were mentioned at Clearwell and Wainlete, 13 at Platwell, and 16 at Peak.[63] In 1608 the north-west street and the east street, for which the name Peak remained in use until the 18th century,[64] were closely built up, with the main concentrations of houses around the central road junction and Wainlete. Platwell, more detached from the other settlements, was then a fairly compact hamlet. Later, a number of houses on the west side of the street at Platwell[65] were removed to make way for the kitchen gardens of the adjoining manor house called Clearwell Court, and by the early 19th century Platwell was a small, dispersed group of farmhouses and other dwellings.[66]

Most of the houses that formed Clearwell village in 1608 were replaced by plain stone cottages in the late 18th century and the 19th, but several older farmhouses survive. At Stank Farm, north of Lower Cross, a small 17th-century house with a prominent central porch was extended to the north in the 19th century. The

former Stock Farm[67] (in 1992 comprising Tudor Cottage and Tudor Farmhouse Hotel) in the east street is an L-shaped 17th-century house with an 18th-century wing added on the east. The Wyndham Arms, west of the central road junction, is a substantial 17th-century house, partly timber-framed, and there is an early 18th-century house north of the cross. On the east side of the street at Platwell a house called Baynhams incorporates a small 17th-century dwelling with a central gable and a west chimney stack, flanked by a staircase; it has walls of rubble but may have originally been timber-framed. The house was much altered in character in the early 20th century when Adeline Vereker (d. 1930), wife of the owner of Clearwell Court, enlarged it to the north and east and introduced many 17th- and 18th-century fittings, salvaged from other buildings.[68] Platwell Farm, further south, was owned with a freehold estate by the Skynn family during the 17th and earlier 18th centuries.[69] A substantial new farmhouse was built in the mid 19th century; its predecessor stood further south[70] where a farm building

62 N.L.W., Dunraven MSS. 339.
63 Glos. R.O., D 1677/GG 1225.
64 Cf. N.L.W., Dunraven MSS. 329, deed 1705; 323, deed 1772.
65 P.R.O., MR 879.   66 G.D.R., T 1/128.
67 Ibid.; O.S. Map 1/2,500, Glos. XXXVIII. 12 (1881

edn.).
68 Inf. from the owner, Mrs. J. A. Couldridge; memorial to Mrs. Vereker, in garden.
69 Inq. p.m. Glos. 1625–42, i. 231–2; N.L.W., Mynde Park MSS. 441, 613, 985, 1056.
70 G.D.R., T 1/128.

incorporates 17th-century windows. Platwell House, on the west side of the road, was owned from the late 17th century to the mid 19th by the Hoskins family, landowners in Newland and St. Briavels.[71] A low service wing on the northwest has heavy floor joists of 16th-century character. The principal range, to which it adjoins, is in part timber-framed and may survive from an L-shaped house which was rebuilt in stone and enlarged in the 17th century. In the mid or late 18th century a staircase was built in the entrant angle and the west front remodelled with a central doorway and an ogee-headed first-floor window. The interior retains fittings of c. 1700 and of the late 18th century.

In 1830 a chapel of ease was built for Clearwell village at the east end, on the road leading to the Forest. It was replaced in 1866 by a new church built by the countess of Dunraven, owner of the Clearwell estate, near the entrance to Clearwell Court in part of Platwell Street; that part of the street became known as Church Street. The countess had built a village school on the street in 1859,[72] and a few estate cottages were added in the same part of the village later in the century. Although containing the residence of the owners of a large landed estate, Clearwell in the 19th and early 20th centuries was inhabited mainly by small freeholders, often engaged in village crafts or mining and quarrying.[73] In 1907 only 9 cottages in the village belonged to the estate, together with three farmhouses, the Wyndham Arms, and a substantial house built opposite the grounds of Clearwell Court in the mid 19th century as the residence of the estate bailiff.[74] West Dean rural district built five pairs of council houses on the Newland road beyond Lower Cross in the 1930s[75] and a terrace of houses just south-east of Lower Cross, replacing the farmhouse of Wainland Farm, in 1957.[76] In the mid and late 20th century the north-west street was further altered by new private houses, some of them replacing older buildings. Clearwell was a fairly populous residential village in 1992, when it included two hotels, at the former manor house and the Wyndham Arms, two other public houses, and a post office and shop.

REDBROOK, as a settlement name, has been used loosely over the centuries to cover the whole area traversed by the two brooks that descend to the river Wye. Its main use was originally for a scattered settlement in the valley of Valley brook between Newland village and the river. That settlement was referred to as Redbrook Street in 1352[77] and as Over Redbrook in 1596,[78] and its two principal farmsteads were called Upper and Lower Redbrook Farms until the early 19th century.[79] A hamlet that formed beside the Wye at the foot of Valley brook was usually identified as Wye's Green before the 18th century,[80] and a group of mills near the foot of the northern valley, though sometimes said to be 'at Redbrook', was more usually identified as 'in Ashridge Slade' in the 15th and 16th centuries.[81] The names Lower and Upper Redbrook for the two riverside hamlets became established only in the later 18th century.[82]

The settlement called Redbrook Street in 1352 probably comprised several groups of dwellings at intervals along Valley brook. In 1608 there were houses at the sites of Upper and Lower Redbrook Farms on the left bank of the stream c. 1.5 km. below Newland village and three or four dwellings on the opposite bank close by. Downstream, where the valley road was joined by the lane from Blindway cross near the site of the later Birts Farm, stood another small group, and another group of about four houses stood further downstream, above the site of the later Glyn Farm.[83] Most of the smaller houses were demolished when large parts of the valley were absorbed into a single estate based on Upper Redbrook Farm, but two new farmhouses were built in the lower part of the valley. Birts Farm was evidently the house and farm buildings that were under construction on land called Birts bought by George Bond of Upper Redbrook Farm in 1642,[84] and Glyn (formerly Glydden or Clidden) Farm was built before 1800.[85] In 1992 the small stone house at Birts Farm, no longer a farmhouse, had recently been heavily restored, while Glyn Farm was used as a pony trekking centre. Highbury Farm, high above the stream at the lower end of the valley, was recorded from 1696,[86] and the low, stone farmhouse may date from the 17th century. About 1800,[87] however, a castellated Gothick facade was attached to its northern end, and it was known as Highbury Cottage in the early 19th century when successive owners were men from London, Wolverhampton, and Norfolk, presumably attracted there by the vogue for Wye Valley scenery at that period.[88]

The riverside hamlets called Upper and Lower Redbrook were industrial in origin, having a number of mills by the end of the Middle Ages and a variety of industries later.[89] Their character, as it survived in 1992, was mainly set by building in the dark Forest sandstone during the 19th century, when the Monmouth tramroad of 1812, the Wye Valley turnpike road of 1824, and the Wye Valley railway of 1876 aided industrial growth. Upper Redbrook is a straggling settlement in the deep valley of the upper Red brook, originally based on a series of mills. The buildings stand beside the brook and the Newland–Monmouth road, some within Newland and some within Dixton Newton parish

71 Ibid. wills 1685/253; ibid. T 1/128; Bigland, Glos. i. 241; cf. below, St. Briavels, manors (Stowe).
72 Below, churches; educ.   73 P.R.O., HO 107/2444.
74 Glos. Colln. (H) G 5.1 (8).
75 Glos. R.O., DA 25/600/1, 3.
76 Ibid. 2; cf. O.S. Map 1/2,500, Glos. XXXVIII. 8 (1881 edn.).
77 Glos. R.O., D 2244/40.   78 Ibid. D 33/171.
79 Below, manors; Newland Valley est. deeds, misc. bdle., plan in affidavit 1823.
80 Glos. R.O., D 33/171; D 1677/GG 402; D 2026/T 52, T 64.

81 Ibid. D 33/103; D 2026/T 11.
82 Taylor, Map of Glos. (1777); Glos. R.O., D 2166, deeds 1748, 1762.
83 P.R.O., MR 879.
84 Glos. R.O., D 2026/T 41.
85 Ibid. D 637/VII/22.
86 Newland Valley est. deeds, Highbury fm. 1696–1824.
87 Cf. Glos. R.O., D 637/VII/22, where the house (then called Wright's Fm.) is described as unfinished.
88 Newland Valley est. deeds, Highbury fm. 1696–1824.
89 Below, econ. hist.

(Mon.). By about 1830 a long terrace of 18 workmen's tenements had been built near the foot of the valley.[90] Later in the century more cottages and some larger houses, built for millers and other industrialists, were added in the valley, and the terrace was replaced or remodelled c. 1900 as eight dwellings. Lower Redbrook formed a more compact settlement at the foot of Valley brook. Six cottages had been built by 1712 on the land called Wye's Green below a copper works which had been established there.[91] In 1827 the large tinplate works, which had replaced the copper works, owned 18 workmen's cottages,[92] most of them on the turnpike road, facing the river. A larger house of c. 1700, once occupied by the manager of the works,[93] was demolished in the late 20th century.[94] A chapel of ease and a school were built in 1872[95] on the main road north of Lower Redbrook, and a group of council houses built north of them between 1930 and 1934[96] linked the two Redbrook hamlets. In 1939 the Highbury estate of 24 council houses was built on the hillside south of Valley brook at Lower Redbrook.[97]

South of the Redbrook hamlets, on the narrow strip of meadowland that borders the Wye below its wooded hillsides, the only early dwelling recorded was the house called Wyeseal, established by the mid 13th century near the boundary with St. Briavels.[98]

The smaller settlements in Newland and Clearwell tithings included Stowe on the south boundary where the old road between Newland village and St. Briavels, the road from Bigsweir to the Forest, and other lanes converged. The hamlet was sometimes called Stowe Green from a substantial green that lay south of the Bigsweir road, partly in St. Briavels parish.[99] It was encroached on and quarried away during the 19th and 20th centuries.[1] There was at least one dwelling at Stowe by c. 1300[2] and there were several in the 15th century.[3] In 1608, apart from Stowe Grange and Stowe Farm, which are in St. Briavels parish, there were seven houses dispersed on the various lanes. One small farmhouse, straddling the boundary where a lane from Wyegate joined the Bigsweir–Forest road,[4] was known as the 'two parish house' in 1653.[5] The older houses within Newland were all removed before the mid 19th century except for two, and those, known later as Stowe Hall and Stowegreen Farm,[6] were rebuilt. A few new cottages added for limeburners and farm labourers gave the hamlet a population of 8 households in 1851.[7]

Wyegate Green, on the south boundary high above the Mork valley, was apparently the site of an Anglo-Saxon settlement that was added to the Forest waste in the late 11th century.[8] In 1608 three houses stood on the west side of the narrow green which lay on the ancient lane from St. Briavels to Lower Redbrook hamlet.[9] In 1851 there were a few farm labourers' cottages at Wyegate Green,[10] and two survived, recently restored, in 1992.

At Millend, between Newland and Clearwell villages, a small, dispersed hamlet, containing five or more houses in 1462,[11] formed around mills on the upper part of Valley brook. A small former farmhouse on the east side of the road leading to Whitecliff dates in part from the 17th century and there are two substantial late 19th-century houses on the road. In 1478 a house was recorded at or near the site of Scatterford Farm, at the junction of that road and the Lydney–Monmouth road. Originally the centre of a small freehold farm,[12] in the 1720s Scatterford became part of an estate that was acquired in Newland by the Symons family.[13] The house has an irregular, double-pile plan with a broad central corridor. Its plan developed from additions made to an earlier house in the 17th century, but its character in 1992 owed much to a recent restoration. The western corner of the building is of medieval origin and has a later inserted ceiling, divided into six compartments by moulded beams, and a large fireplace with a formerly external doorway beside it. It formed the south-west end of a range which was probably shortened in the 17th century, when the house was enlarged by an addition to the south-east and given a new entrance range facing north-east. The use of quarter-round, chamfered ceiling beams throughout suggests that the enlargement took place over a relatively short period. The new entrance range had a two-storeyed central porch but with an asymmetrical arrangement of windows and chimneys, perhaps because it was partly re-using an earlier building. Many alterations, including the removal of the porch, were made during the 18th and 19th centuries, and an extensive restoration, with some additions, was carried out after 1986.[14]

In 1608 a few dwellings, later demolished or rebuilt, stood on a lane that climbed over the south end of Clearwell Meend at the parish boundary, some of them just above Clearwell village and others at the east end of the lane, near Spoon green.[15] Some labourers' cottages and a farmhouse were built in the early 19th century on that lane near a pond called Dean pool.[16] Lambsquay, on the parish boundary near the

90   Glos. R.O., D 2166, plan of Upper Redbrook c. 1830.
91   Newland Valley est. deeds, Upper Redbrook fm. 1712–93, marr. settlm. 1712; Glos. R.O., D 2026/T 64.
92   Glos. R.O., D 639/13.
93   Ibid. 14, a sketch of works and hamlet 1848, detail reproduced above, Plate 33.
94   Cf. Harris, 'Wye Valley Ind. Hist.' Lower Redbrook, 2.
95   Below, churches; educ.
96   Glos. R.O., DA 25/600/3.
97   Ibid. 2.   98   Below, manors.
99   P.R.O., MR 879.
1   Ibid. F 3/128; cf. O.S. Map 6", Glos. XXXVIII. SE. (1884 edn.).
2   Glos. R.O., D 2244/2.
3   Ibid. D 1677/GG 1225.

4   P.R.O., MR 879.
5   N.L.W., Dunraven MSS. 260, deed 1653; cf. D 1833/T 3.
6   G.D.R., T 1/128.   7   P.R.O., HO 107/2444.
8   Below, manors.   9   P.R.O., MR 879.
10   Ibid. HO 107/2444.
11   Glos. R.O., D 1677/GG 1225.
12   Ibid. 1224; N.L.W., Dunraven MSS. 271, deed 1538; 325, deed 1598; Mynde Park MS. 415; P.R.O., MR 879.
13   N.L.W., Mynde Park MSS. 301, 1254; G.D.R., T 1/128.
14   Inf. from and plans in possession of the owner, Mr. J. B. Benson.
15   P.R.O., MR 879.
16   Cf. ibid. HO 107/2444.

north end of Clearwell Meend, had some dwellings by 1465.[17] About 1800 a substantial house was built there beside the Chepstow–Coleford road.[18] In the late 19th century it was occupied by Edwin Payne (d. 1897), a stone merchant,[19] and in 1992 it was a hotel.

The farmsteads of the high, open land in the south of the main part of Newland parish were established as, or else became, tenant farms to the main estates and were built or rebuilt of stone in the plain vernacular style of the 18th and early 19th centuries. The area is also dotted with large stone barns. Farmhouses were recorded from the 16th century at Inwood[20] on Rookery Lane, at Caudwell[21] above the Valley brook valley, and at Coxbury[22] high above the Wye Valley where the track between Valley brook and Wyeseal crossed Offa's Dyke. A small farmhouse at Shop House at a road junction south of Clearwell village took its name from a sheephouse belonging to the Clearwell estate.[23] Of the principal farmhouses of the Clearwell estate in the south-east part of the parish, Trowgreen and Longley (formerly Longney) may not have been established until the 18th century,[24] but Noxon dates in part from the 17th century.[25] The name of Stonystile barn, on Margery Lane, west of Clearwell, was recorded as that of a field in 1505,[26] and may derive from the stone-slab stile in a wall there. A new farmhouse and barn were built at Stonystile c. 1721[27] but in 1992 a 20th-century house adjoined older farm buildings. Tithe barn, on the same lane nearer Clearwell village, belonged to the Newland rectory estate.[28] In the mid and late 20th century some of the big, isolated barns had new houses built beside them or were themselves converted as dwellings.

BREAM village, in the largest of the detached portions of Newland parish, had five or more dwellings by 1462.[29] A chapel of ease was built there before 1505,[30] probably as much because of the distance from the parish church as because of the number of inhabitants. In 1608 the village remained small, with houses spaced loosely along the Lydney–Newland road in a low valley and with some others in the entrance to a road that branched northwards to Parkend in the extraparochial Forest.[31] In an undated record of the late 17th century it was said that only c. 24 families then lived in Bream tithing,[32] a description which may also have included the two detached portions at Yorkley. The earliest surviving house at Bream village, standing near the entrance to the Parkend road, is dated 1637 with

initials which are probably for George Gough, a Bristol man who was buying land in the area in the 1620s.[33] It is an early 17th-century house on an L plan, with a contemporary porch at the south-east of the main, east–west, range. That range probably once extended further east where a 19th-century building now stands. The house, which was the New Inn during the 19th and early 20th centuries, was restored in the 1980s.[34] Bream Court Farm, near the west end of the main street, is a small rubble-built farmhouse of the late 17th century.

The other houses at Bream are mainly cottages built in the mid and later 19th century when the village became part of a larger settlement, which included the area called Bream's Eaves on extra-parochial land to the north, and took on the character of the other mining hamlets of the Forest fringes. Its chapel was rebuilt as the centre of a new ecclesiastical parish and the whole settlement was served by a school and by nonconformist chapels over the Forest boundary.[35] Until the beginning of the 20th century the junction of the old village street and the Parkend road remained a focal point of village life but by the middle of the century, when two public houses there closed and some shops were demolished, the centre of gravity had shifted to High Street on the part of the Parkend road within the formerly extraparochial land.[36] A small estate of private houses was built in the old village, east of the road junction, in the 1980s.

The principal early farmhouse of the Bream area was at Pastor's Hill east of the old village,[37] and a farmhouse was recorded from 1578 at Brockhollands, further south near the Lydney boundary.[38] From the late 18th century cottages were built in the north-east of the parochial land of Bream, later forming part of the Forest hamlets of Whitecroft and Pillowell.[39]

The detached parts of Newland at Yorkley, divided by the road running north from Lydney to Yorkley village, probably had dwellings by the early 14th century. Seven cottages mentioned on Lord Berkeley's manor of Yorkley in 1346 may, however, have been in Lydney parish, from which the manor received rents.[40] In the early modern period the parts of Newland at Yorkley appear to have contained only two farmhouses, Yorkley Court[41] in the west part and Badhamsfield in the east part. Badhamsfield, as mentioned above, probably derives its name from medieval ownership by the ap Adam family and the farmhouse was recorded by that name

[17] N.L.W., Dunraven MSS. 271.
[18] *Glouc. Jnl.* 12 Feb. 1816; Glos. R.O., D 5377/3/1, deed 1824.
[19] Mon. in Clearwell cemetery; Paar, *Severn and Wye Rly.* 48.
[20] Glos. R.O., D 2957/214.83; D 2026/T 39, deed 1670.
[21] N.L.W., Dunraven MSS. 326, deed 1569.
[22] Glos. R.O., P 227/IN 1/1, bapt. 1562, 1566; D 2026/T 40.
[23] P.R.O., MR 879, where Sheephouse meadow adjoins it; cf. N.L.W., Dunraven MSS. 260, deed 1637.
[24] Cf. Glos. R.O., D 214/T 78, abs. of title (deeds 1671, 1685); N.L.W., Dunraven MSS. 339, rental 1757.
[25] Below, manors.
[26] Glos. R.O., D 1677/GG 306.
[27] N.L.W., Mynde Park MS. 302.
[28] Below, manors.

[29] Glos. R.O., D 1677/GG 1225.
[30] Below, churches.   [31] P.R.O., MR 879.
[32] Glos. R.O., D 2026/X 8.
[33] N.L.W., Dunraven MSS. 327, deed 1624; cf. Glos. R.O., P 227/IN 1/1, marr. 1635.
[34] Below, this section; W. A. Camm, *Bream through the Ages* (1979), 43.
[35] Below, churches; Forest of Dean, settlement.
[36] Cf. Camm, *Bream through the Ages*, 9, 20, 43–4.
[37] Below, manors.
[38] Glos. R.O., P 227/IN 1/1.
[39] P.R.O., HO 107/2444; below, Forest of Dean, settlement.
[40] Below, manors; Berkeley Cast. Mun., General Ser. acct. roll 326.
[41] Below, manors.

in 1626,[42] but the surviving house is no earlier than the late 18th century and was heavily restored in the mid 20th. By 1775 c. 10 cottages had been built on parish land at the north-west boundary of Yorkley Court farm[43] as part of the developing village of Yorkley. In the mid 19th century land within the parish was colonized by a larger group of cottages called Yorkley Wood.[44]

In Whitemead park, an island of the parish within the extraparochial Forest, a farmhouse had been built by 1651, when there were also eight small cottages there.[45] The cottages, some of them occupied by people working an iron furnace at Parkend, were presented as illegal encroachments in 1656 and were probably demolished soon afterwards. In the early 18th century the park contained only a farmhouse at its north boundary[46] and a second farmhouse was built in the east part shortly before 1751 when the park became two farms, divided by Cannop brook.[47] Early in the 19th century, when most of the park was included in a new timber plantation, the eastern farmhouse was demolished and the northern one adapted as the residence of the Forest's deputy surveyor.[48]

The island of Newland at Ellwood contained a number of houses by 1608.[49] A farmhouse on the north boundary, later called Ellwood Farm, belonged to the Symons family's estate in the 18th century,[50] and another farmhouse belonged then to the Newland House estate.[51] From c. 1819, when the Crown planted most of the farmland of the parochial land at Ellwood, a farmhouse at the south-east corner, adjoining the Forest hamlet of Little Drybrook, became a woodman's lodge[52] called Ellwood Lodge. From the 1860s, however, it was leased as a private house[53] and the Forestry Commission sold it in 1968.[54] The older part of Ellwood Lodge is a small late 17th-century house with a two-roomed plan and a large gable-end stack. It was extended in the late 18th century by the addition of a short wing in front of its west end and in the early 19th century by a block beyond the eastern gable. In the mid 19th century the west end was remodelled: the floor levels were raised and the roof of the old house was reconstructed. In the north part of the parochial land at Ellwood a number of cottages were built near Ellwood Farm in the mid 19th century to form, with other cottages beyond the boundary, the hamlet of Ellwood.[55]

In 1327 18 people, a small proportion of what was probably already a substantial population, were assessed for the subsidy in Newland parish.[56] In 1349 78 houses were listed at Clearwell, Coleford, and Whitecliff alone and the list was probably not comprehensive for those areas.[57] The parish was said to have c. 700 communicants in 1551,[58] 250 households in 1563,[59] 850 communicants in 1603,[60] and 300 families in 1650.[61] About 1710 the population was estimated at c. 2,200 living in 480 houses, 160 of the houses said to be in Coleford tithing,[62] and c. 1775 the population was estimated at c. 2,997.[63] In 1811 in the three tithings covered in this parish history — Newland, Clearwell (including the detached part at Ellwood), and Bream (including the detached parts at Yorkley) — there was a total of 1,524 people; Coleford tithing then had 1,551 and Lea Bailey tithing 72.[64] In Newland, Clearwell, and Bream tithings the population was 1,745 by 1831 and 2,316 in 1861, most of the increase occurring in Bream tithing with the growth of the mining hamlets of the area. In 1901 the population of Newland civil parish was 1,877, rising to 2,061 by 1931. In 1951, after the loss of the parts at Bream and Yorkley, the population of the civil parish was 1,148, declining to 877 by 1971 and rising again to 924 by 1991.[65]

In 1600 Newland parish contained eight or more victualling houses, presumably scattered through its constituent villages, including Coleford.[66] The Ram inn where the parish vestry met in 1754 and 1765 was presumably in Newland village.[67] The Ostrich, open by 1816,[68] was the only public house there in modern times. A former smithy at the north end of the village became the village meeting room c. 1920,[69] given by the Roscoe family of Birch-amp House as a memorial to the war dead.[70]

In Clearwell village an inn or lodging house (*hospitium*) that was granted on lease in 1518 with the consent of the parishioners of Newland may have been used as a church house.[71] The village had the Carpenters Arms inn by 1787, the Butchers Arms by 1802,[72] and the Wyndham Arms, named from the family at Clearwell Court, by 1821.[73] In 1906 its public houses were the Wyndham Arms, the Butchers Arms, the Lamb, and at least one beerhouse,[74] and in 1992 the Wyndham Arms at the central road junction, by then enlarged as a substantial hotel, and the

42   P.R.O., CRES 38/612, deed 1626; cf. G.D.R. wills 1645/68.
43   Glos. R.O., D 2528.
44   Below, Forest of Dean, settlement.
45   P.R.O., E 317/Glos./20.
46   Glos. R.O., D 2026/X 14.
47   Berkeley Cast. Mun., General Ser. 16; ibid. General Ser. T, box 25, lease 1750; P.R.O., F 17/161.
48   Below, manors; cf. G.D.R., T 1/128.
49   P.R.O., MR 879.
50   N.L.W., Mynde Park MSS. 303, 1951; G.D.R., T 1/128.
51   Glos. R.O., D 637/II/1/T 1, deeds 1757, 1794.
52   *3rd Rep. Com. Woods* (1819), 19; G.D.R., T 1/128.
53   P.R.O., F 3/45–6.
54   Inf. from the owners, Mr. and Mrs. J. F. Evans.
55   P.R.O., HO 107/2444; below, Forest of Dean, settlement.

56   *Glos. Subsidy Roll, 1327*, 6.
57   N.L.W., Dunraven MSS. 339.
58   *E.H.R.* xix. 120.
59   Bodl. MS. Rawl. C. 790, f. 28.   60   *Eccl. Misc.* 99.
61   *Trans. B.G.A.S.* lxxxiii. 98.
62   Atkyns, *Glos.* 575.   63   Rudder, *Glos.* 570.
64   *Census*, 1811; and for the constituent parts of the tithings, Glos. R.O., P 227/OV 1/1.
65   *Census*, 1831–1991.
66   B.L. Harl. MS. 4131, f. 553.
67   Glos. R.O., P 227/VE 2/2.
68   Above, this section.
69   O.S. Map 1/2,500, Glos. XXXVIII. 3 (1902, 1922 edns.).
70   Plaque in room; cf. *Kelly's Dir. Glos.* (1923), 266.
71   Glos. R.O., D 2957/214.54.
72   Ibid. Q/RSf 2.   73   Ibid. P 227/OV 1/1.
74   *Kelly's Dir. Glos* (1906), 125; Glos. R.O., D 2299/392.

Butchers Arms in the east street and the Lamb in the west street remained open. A friendly society had been formed in Clearwell village by 1787.[75] A cottage hospital was opened by the countess of Dunraven in 1869.[76] A recreation ground was laid out at the west end of the village before 1934, and during the late 1930s Col. Charles Vereker of Clearwell Court organized unemployed men in building an open-air swimming pool.[77]

At Orepool on the Chepstow–Coleford road near the east boundary of the parish an inn had opened by 1851 and remained open as the Orepool inn in 1992. The hamlet of Stowe had a beerhouse in 1851,[78] probably the Travellers Rest, which was so called by 1891[79] and was still open in 1992.

Upper Redbrook hamlet had three public houses by 1856: the Bush was at the bottom of the hamlet near the river, just within Dixton Newton, and the Queen's Head and the Founders Arms were further up the hill.[80] Only the Bush remained open in 1992. At Lower Redbrook the King's Head and the Bell had opened by 1848 among the cottages below the tinplate works.[81] The King's Head closed in the mid 20th century[82] and the Bell remained in 1992 (but closed and awaiting a new tenant). About 1887 the Redbrook Tinplate Co. built its workers an institute, including a meeting room and billiard room, on the north side of the works, adjoining the National school. In 1955 the company transferred the building to the parochial church council for use as a village hall. From c. 1963 it was run by the Redbrook community association, which also managed a recreation ground[83] that had been opened before 1920 at the riverside.[84]

By 1792 the Cross Keys inn had opened in Bream village at a house on the west side of the road leading into the Forest, and by 1814 the New Inn had opened in an early 17th-century house on the opposite side of the road.[85] Both closed in the mid 20th century, the sign of the Cross Keys being transferred to a public house in Bream's Eaves beyond the former parish boundary.[86] In 1864 a village wake was held in Whit week, at which the villagers competed in games for prizes strung on a rope across the roadway between the two inns. The wake later lapsed and was briefly revived in the 1920s. Until c. 1926 a maypole stood near the inns at the junction of the old village street and the Forest road.[87]

MANORS AND OTHER ESTATES. Although the parish of Newland was formed by

assarting after the Norman Conquest, it included one or more earlier estates that had been returned to or had reverted to the Forest woodland and waste. A six-hide manor called WYEGATE (Wigheiete) in Lydney hundred was held in Edward the Confessor's reign by Aleston and after the Conquest by Ralph de Limesi and William de Eu in succession. Before 1086, however, on William I's order it was included in the Forest. That evidently involved removing the population and taking the land out of cultivation, not merely the imposition of Forest law: Wyegate was valued at 60s. in 1066 but in 1086 a fishery worth 10s. was the only asset recorded.[88] The manor was presumably centred on Wyegate Green, at the south boundary of the later parish, with its lands on the high ground to the north and east and, perhaps, in the Mork brook valley in the later St. Briavels parish. Land in the area was being returned to cultivation by 1338, when licence to assart lands at Wyegate was granted to Grace Dieu abbey (Mon.), the owner of Stowe manor in St. Briavels;[89] in 1608 Stowe manor included c. 80 a. lying east of Wyegate Green.[90] 'Brocote', where two manors formed part of the Herefordshire hundred of Bromsash and which Domesday Book appears to place near Staunton, has been identified speculatively as Redbrook. The manors at Brocote had already become waste by 1066 and were described as within the Forest ('the king's wood') in 1086.[91]

As land was cleared and settled during the 12th and 13th centuries a royal manor of NEWLAND was established. In the early modern period it comprised only the chief rents and heriots charged on the principal estates of the parish, such as Clearwell, Breckness Court (in Coleford tithing), Wyeseal, and Upper and Lower Redbrook farms, and on cottages and small holdings in Lea Bailey tithing; Whitemead park was the only part of the parish that the Crown is recorded as holding as demesne.[92] Newland manor formed part of a royal estate, including also St. Briavels castle and manor and the profits of the Forest, that was farmed by the constables of St. Briavels in the 13th and 14th centuries[93] and was later held on lease under the Crown.[94]

WHITEMEAD PARK, the detached part of the parish near Parkend, was presumably inclosed from the Forest by the Crown itself. Land called the meadow of Whitemead was held by the constable of St. Briavels in 1283,[95] and Whitemead was termed a park in 1435 when the duke of Bedford held it as part of his St. Briavels castle estate.[96] The Crown appointed keepers of the park between 1464 and 1502,[97] and it may

75 Glos. R.O., Q/RSf 2.
76 Kelly's Dir. Glos. (1870), 524.
77 Glos. R.O., D 3168/8/3.
78 P.R.O., HO 107/2444.
79 Licensed Houses in Glos. 1891, 56; cf. Glos. Colln. (H) G 5.1 (8).
80 Kelly's Dir. Glos. (1856), 334; O.S. Map 6", Glos. XXXVIII. NW. (1887 edn.).
81 Glos. R.O., D 639/14.
82 Kelly's Dir. Glos. (1939), 274.
83 Glos. R.O., D 3168/4/7/66.
84 O.S. Map 1/2,500, Glos. XXXVIII. 2 (1922 edn.).
85 Glos. R.O., Q/RSf 2; O.S. Map 6", Glos. XXXIX. SW. (1883 edn.).

86 Camm, Bream through the Ages, 43–4.
87 Ibid. 9, 20, 35; Glos. Chron. 6 Aug. 1864.
88 Dom. Bk. (Rec. Com.), i. 166v.
89 Cal. Fine R. 1337–47, 65.
90 P.R.O., MR 879; Glos. R.O., D 608/8/2; cf. below, St. Briavels, manors.
91 Dom. Bk. (Rec. Com.), i. 181; Trans. B.G.A.S. cv. 123.
92 P.R.O., SC 6/858/14; Glos. R.O., D 2026/X 19; Berkeley Cast. Mun., General Ser. 16.
93 Cf. Pat. R. 1225–32, 477; Rot. Hund. (Rec. Com.), i. 176; Cal. Close, 1341–3, 153.
94 Below, St. Briavels, manors.
95 Cal. Close, 1279–88, 219.   96 P.R.O., E 101/141/1.
97 Cal. Pat. 1461–7, 361; 1476–85, 234, 457; 1494–1509, 272.

not again have been attached to the St. Briavels estate until the early 17th century. Sir Richard Catchmay held it as sub-lessee of the earls of Pembroke in 1627 and 1638,[98] and it was included in a renewal of the lease to the 4th earl in 1640.[99] Before 1653 it was taken in hand by the Commonwealth government which then sold it. The sale was opposed by local inhabitants, who claimed that Whitemead had never been imparked but was simply an inclosure made for use by the Crown and its lessees as a cattle pound for the Forest.[1] The sale was not recognized at the Restoration and in 1662 the Crown leased Whitemead to Henry, Lord Herbert,[2] later duke of Beaufort, and it then passed once more with the St. Briavels castle estate. After 1688, however, the duke's declining influence encouraged local inhabitants to challenge once more its status as a park[3] and mobs of commoners repeatedly broke its fences, so that the duke received no profit from it for c. 10 years.[4] During the 18th century tenants farmed the park under the Crown lessees, its c. 230 a. being divided into two farms after 1751.[5] In 1807 the lessee, the earl of Berkeley, surrendered it to the Crown, and in 1808, at the start of the programme of replanting the Forest, all but a few acres around Whitemead Park house at the the north-west corner were included in new plantations.[6] Whitemead Park house probably occupied the site of the farmhouse built in the park by an under-tenant before 1651,[7] and in the 18th century the farmhouse of the Barrow family, the principal under-tenants, was there.[8] In 1816 the house became the official residence of the deputy surveyor of the Forest, Edward Machen,[9] whose successors lived there until 1968.[10] In the mid 20th century it was also the local headquarters of the Forestry Commission, an office block being added in 1960. The house, which was rebuilt or extensively remodelled in the years 1810 and 1811, was sold with its grounds in 1970 to the Civil Service Motoring Association,[11] which demolished the house and established a clubhouse, camping ground, and caravan park for the use of its members; later a number of wooden holiday chalets was built.

In the Middle Ages the principal inhabitants of Newland were members of the Joce family

and their successors, who in the 14th and 15th centuries received chief rents from several hundred houses and plots of land in Newland village, Clearwell, Coleford, Whitecliff, Highmeadow, Bream, Mork, and other places in Newland and St. Briavels parishes.[12] Presumably the Joces had obtained a general grant from the Crown of new assarts or the rents from them in a wide area. The chief rents had effectively lapsed by 1868 when an attempt was made to levy some of them in St. Briavels.[13] The Joces and their successors also held the woodwardship of Bearse bailiwick,[14] which covered much of the area from which Newland and St. Briavels parishes were formed. The woodwardship was later thought to be attached to Clearwell,[15] the demesne estate of the holders, but a reference to William Joce as forester 'of St. Briavels' c. 1245[16] suggests that the bailiwick, too, originated in a wider grant of rights in the Newland and St. Briavels area.

Richard son of Joce, who was listed as one of the woodwards of Dean in 1223,[17] was presumably an early holder of Bearse bailiwick and the rights in assarted lands. William Joce, as mentioned above, was a forester c. 1245, and William Joce, also called William the woodward, held Bearse bailiwick in 1282.[18] He or another William gave lands in Newland to his son Philip in 1320,[19] and in 1338 John Joce, probably son and heir of Philip,[20] had licence to assart lands in Newland and St. Briavels.[21] John was claiming manorial rights in Newland in 1338,[22] and in 1349 he was receiving the chief rents mentioned above.[23] John Joce the elder and John Joce the younger were mentioned in 1365,[24] and the younger was presumably the man who with his wife Isabel made a settlement of a large estate in Newland and adjoining parishes in 1378.[25] John died before 1389,[26] and before 1395 Isabel married John Greyndour,[27] who died in 1415 or 1416.[28] Greyndour evidently secured an unrestricted title to his wife's estate, which from the early 15th century was known as the manor of CLEARWELL, the chief residence and most of the demesne lands being by then situated in Clearwell tithing. John was succeeded by Robert Greyndour, his son by his first wife Marion.[29] Robert Greyndour (d. 1443) was jointly enfeoffed of the estate with his wife Joan,[30] who

98 P.R.O., C 99/24; Hart, *Royal Forest*, 281; cf. below, St. Briavels, manors.
99 *Cal. S.P. Dom.* 1640, 232.
1 Ibid. 1653–4, 326, 405.   2 Ibid. 1663–4, 676.
3 Glos. R.O., D 2026/X 27; N.L.W., Mynde Park MS. 1666.
4 Badminton Mun. FmH 2/1/1.
5 Berkeley Cast. Mun., General Ser. T, box 25; General Ser. 16.
6 Hart, *Royal Forest*, 208–9; cf. G.D.R., T 1/128.
7 Glos. R.O., D 2026/X 14; P.R.O., E 317/Glos./20.
8 P.R.O., F 17/161; cf. Berkeley Cast. Mun., General Ser. T, box 25.
9 R. Anstis, *Warren James and Dean Forest Riots* (1986), 49–51.
10 Hart, *Royal Forest*, 213, 222, 226; *Kelly's Dir. Glos.* (1870 and later edns.), s.v. Parkend.
11 P.R.O., LR 4/20/9; LR 4/21; *Dean Forest Mercury*, 8 May 1970.
12 N.L.W., Dunraven MSS. 339; Glos. R.O., D 1677/GG 1225.   13 P.R.O., F 14/14.
14 *Trans. B.G.A.S.* xiv. 362; P.R.O., C 142/189, no. 82; *3rd Rep. Com. Woods* (1788), 76.

15 N.L.W., Dunraven MSS. 334, notes of inquisitions post mortem.
16 P.R.O., E 146/1/25.
17 *Rot. Litt. Claus.* (Rec. Com.), i. 533.
18 P.R.O., E 32/30, rot. 5; *Trans. B.G.A.S.* xiv. 362.
19 *Cal. Pat.* 1317–21, 431; cf. N.L.W., Dunraven MSS. 271.
20 Glos. R.O., D 33/26.
21 *Cal. Fine R.* 1337–47, 67.
22 N.L.W., Dunraven MSS. 325; cf. ibid. 326, deed 1342.
23 Ibid. 339.
24 Berkeley Cast. Mun., General Ser. 3573.
25 P.R.O., CP 25/1/78/78, no. 4.
26 N.L.W., Dunraven MSS. 325.
27 Ibid. 324; cf. *Cal. Pat.* 1441–6, 388.
28 *Cal. Fine R.* 1413–22, 144; P.R.O., PROB 11/2B (P.C.C. 37 Marche), f. 289v., his will, in which he is named as John Chin' (not otherwise found recorded as an alias and perhaps a clerical error) but refers to his son Rob. Greyndour and (half) brother Thos. Huntley.
29 *Cal. Close*, 1413–19, 338; cf. *Cal. Pat.* 1441–6, 388.
30 *Cal. Close*, 1441–7, 177–8; P.R.O., C 139/115, no. 34.

married before 1455[31] John Barre. John died in 1483[32] and Joan in 1484, when the Clearwell estate passed to Robert's heir Alice, the wife of Thomas Baynham[33] (d.1500)[34] and later of Sir Walter Dennis (d. 1505 or 1506). Alice (d. 1518) was succeeded by her son Sir Christopher Baynham,[35] and Sir Christopher was succeeded in the estate, apparently in his lifetime, by his son George Baynham.[36] George, who was knighted in 1546 and died that year,[37] left the estate to his son Christopher, who was a minor in the king's custody in 1548.[38] From Christopher (fl. 1555)[39] it passed, probably by 1558,[40] to his brother Richard (d. 1580), who was succeeded by another brother Thomas[41] (d. 1611).[42] Thomas Baynham settled his estates in Newland and the adjoining parishes on his elder daughter Cecily, wife of Sir William Throckmorton, Bt., while his younger daughter Joan, wife of John Vaughan, received estates that he owned elsewhere in the Forest area.[43]

Sir William Throckmorton (d. 1628) was succeeded in the Clearwell estate by his son Sir Baynham (d. 1664)[44] who paid a large fine to recover his estate from sequestration after the Civil War but forfeited it again later, buying it back in 1653. Before his death Sir Baynham apparently made the estate over to his son and heir, and the son, also Sir Baynham, was still in debt in 1672 as a result of the recovery of the estate.[45] The younger Sir Baynham Throckmorton died c. 1680, having provided for his estate to be sold for the benefit of his wife Catherine and his daughters. In 1684 James Stephens agreed to purchase the estate but died before completion, and in 1698 Catherine, her daughter Catherine Wild, her stepdaughter Carolina Scrymsher, and Stephens's widow Barbara sold Clearwell to Francis Wyndham.[46] From Francis Wyndham (d. 1716) the estate passed in the direct male line to John (d. 1725), Thomas (d. 1752),[47] and Charles. Charles Wyndham inherited the Glamorganshire estates of Dunraven Castle and Llanvihangel, and under the will of the uncle who left him the latter he took the surname Edwin. He died in 1801, when he was succeeded by his son Thomas Wyndham (d. 1814). Thomas was succeeded by his daughter Caroline, wife of Windham Henry Quin of Adare (co. Limerick), who took the additional surname Wyndham. W. H. Wyndham Quin, who had the courtesy title of Viscount Adare from 1822 and succeeded to the earldom of

Dunraven and Mount-Earl in 1824, died in 1850; Caroline, countess of Dunraven, retained Clearwell until her death in 1870.[48] Under family trusts the estate passed before 1876 to the countess's grandson Windham Henry Wyndham Quin, who with the trustees conveyed it c. 1882 to John Eveleigh Wyndham[49] (d. 1887).[50]

In 1893 the Wyndham trustees sold the estate to Henry Collins, whose mortgagees later secured possession[51] and in 1907 offered the estate for sale. It then comprised Clearwell Court and 14 farms in Newland and St. Briavels, a total of 2,300 a.[52] A large portion, comprising Noxon and Trowgreen farms and Noxon Park wood, was sold in 1907 to the Crown Commissioners of Woods, and a larger portion to Col. Alan Gardner, the tenant of Clearwell Court. Gardner died a few days after completing the purchase and his executors sold his estate in 1910 to James Lewis. Lewis sold the farms in 1912 to the Commissioners of Woods,[53] having sold the house and its park the previous year to Charles Vereker, later Col. Vereker, who died in 1947.[54] In 1992 the Crown's Clearwell estate covered 487 ha. (1,203 a.), formed of Noxon, Longley, Platwell, and Wainland farms in Newland and Bearse farm in St. Briavels.[55]

Philip Joce had a house at Clearwell in 1324[56] but John Greyndour had a house in Newland village in 1414,[57] and the owners of the estate may not have been consistently resident at Clearwell until the time of Robert Greyndour, the first to be styled of Clearwell rather than of Newland.[58] In 1443 Robert's house at Clearwell comprised hall, chapel, 12 chambers, buttery, pantry, and cellar, besides farm buildings.[59] It was presumably at the site of Clearwell Court, south-west of the village, which remained the principal residence of the owners of the estate until the early 19th century when the Wyndhams lived also at Adare and Dunraven.[60] Clearwell Court had 21 hearths in 1672,[61] and c. 1710 was a rambling structure, presenting a long multi-gabled front to the west. It was mainly of the 17th century but probably of several different builds within that period.[62] It was rebuilt by Thomas Wyndham c. 1728 from designs by Roger Morris[63] as a large mansion in castellated Gothic style. Initially it was of few rooms, with a two-storeyed centre recessed between short three-storeyed wings, all on a high basement. The windows of the principal floor have two-centred heads with simple **Y** tracery above

31   N.L.W., Dunraven MSS. 339.
32   P.R.O., C 140/84, no. 39.
33   Cal. Inq. p.m. Hen. VII, i, p. 47.
34   Trans. B.G.A.S. vi. 149; Cal. Close, 1485–1500, p. 175.
35   P.R.O., C 142/33, no. 69; Hockaday Abs. cxlvii, 1506.
36   Cf. P.R.O., C 142/113, no. 49.
37   Ibid. C 142/74, no. 91; Trans. B.G.A.S. vi. 150–1.
38   Hockaday Abs. ccxcv, 1548; Cal. Pat. 1548–9, 3.
39   Glos. R.O., D 33/146.   40   Cal. Pat. 1557–8, 306.
41   P.R.O., C 142/189, no. 82.
42   Ibid. C 142/340, no. 192.
43   N.L.W., Dunraven MSS. 260.
44   Glos. R.O., P 227/IN 1/1; for the Throckmortons, Burke, Extinct & Dorm. Baronetcies (1838), 527.
45   Cal. Cttee. for Compounding, ii. 1149–50; N.L.W., Dunraven MSS. 260, 270.
46   Glos. R.O., D 214/T 78; for Sir Baynham's daughters, cf. Bigland, Glos. ii. 261–2.
47   Glos. R.O., D 214/T 78; P 227/IN 1/2–3.

48   Complete Peerage, iv. 548–9; Earl of Dunraven, Dunraven Castle, Glam. (1926), 40–1, 61.
49   P.R.O., CRES 38/669, 672; Kelly's Dir. Glos. (1885), 430.
50   Inscr. in Clearwell cemetery.
51   P.R.O., CRES 38/672–3.
52   Glos. Colln. (H) G 5.1 (8).
53   P.R.O., CRES 38/669, 673.
54   Glos. Colln. RR 81.1, 3.
55   Inf. from asset manager (agric. est.), Crown Estate.
56   Glos. R.O., D 2244/9.
57   Ibid. D 2957/214.14.
58   e.g. N.L.W., Dunraven MSS. 325, deed 1419.
59   P.R.O., C 139/115, no. 34.
60   Dunraven, Dunraven Castle, 42, 45.
61   P.R.O., E 179/247/14, rot. 39.
62   Atkyns, Glos. plate at pp. 574–5.
63   Country Seat, ed. H. M. Colvin and J. Harris (1970), 145–9.

mullions and transoms, those of the first floor having square heads within mullions and transoms and all having hood mouldings. At the outer angles there are diagonal buttresses, and the roof is hidden by an embattled parapet bearing the Wyndham crest. In the mid 18th century additions, including a long axially-placed library, were made at the rear of the house. It is not known how the interior was fitted: a number of surviving fireplaces in early 18th-century style have been attributed both to Morris and to the mid 19th century when the interior was altered for the countess of Dunraven by John Middleton.[64] North-east of the house, a stable range with a central carriageway and a screen wall and road gate are probably by Morris, but the east end of the stables appears to incorporate part of the 17th-century stables, and the lodges at each end of the screen wall are 19th-century additions. The terracing of the gardens is probably contemporary with the mid 19th-century refurbishment of the house. The house, which was usually called Clearwell Castle in the 20th century, was gutted by fire in 1929 and was repaired by Col. Vereker. After his death in 1947 it was left empty for some years, and fittings were removed and the fabric badly damaged by vandals. In 1952 the house was bought by Frank Yeates,[65] son of a former gardener on the estate, who spent many years restoring the house, the work being done by himself and members of his family. The Yeates family sold the house in the early 1980s, when it became a hotel.[66]

An estate called *NOXON* in the south-east part of Clearwell tithing was established in 1317 when the Crown granted John of Wyesham, then constable of St. Briavels,[67] a fishpond and licence to assart 200 a. of Forest waste adjoining it. John took in 280 a. but the additional land was confirmed to him in 1321.[68] He died *c.* 1332, leaving as his heir a son John,[69] during whose minority Noxon was placed in the custody of Gilbert Talbot.[70] By the end of the 14th century Noxon had passed to William Wyesham, who leased it to Isabel, widow of John Joce, and in 1403 conveyed it in perpetuity to her and her second husband John Greyndour.[71] It then descended with the Clearwell estate, passing to the Crown in 1907.[72] There were farm buildings at Noxon in 1443,[73] but in the 16th and early 17th centuries most of the land was used as a park and in 1611 it had two lodges, a new one and an old one.[74] Later the south-western side of the

estate, adjoining the Lydney–Coleford road, was a tenant farm while the north-east side, chiefly comprising Noxon Park wood, was maintained as woodland and mined for iron ore.[75] Noxon Farm may occupy the site of one of the lodges, though the surviving house dates from the late 17th century. Its main range was probably built in two stages at that period, with the west end the earlier. During the 19th century the range was much altered and additions were made to its south side in three or more stages. The fishpond at Noxon in 1317 was probably on Oakwood brook on the north-east boundary;[76] a large pond that adjoins the farmhouse appears to have been made later, before 1840.[77]

A small manor called *WYESEAL* belonged to the bishop of Hereford in the early 13th century when it comprised a house called the Grange and lands extending along the Wye from Redbrook to the St. Briavels boundary. The narrow strip of riverside lands that later were tithe-free or tithable to the owner[78] evidently represented the original estate, and the house was presumably at the site of Wyeseal Farm. Successive tenants under the bishop were John of Newland and William, a priest, and in 1253 the bishop granted the estate in fee to Gay, a servant of William. It apparently passed to its later owners, the Bond family, through the marriage of Ellen, daughter of Thomas Gay.[79] Thomas Bond of Wyeseal was recorded in 1430,[80] and the same or another Thomas in 1462.[81] John Bond (d. by 1533) was succeeded at Wyeseal by his son George,[82] and John Bond owned Wyeseal manor in the 1580s[83] and was succeeded by his son Thomas. Thomas conveyed the estate in 1609 to William Catchmay (d. 1636), who devised a third of Wyeseal to his wife Tacy and the rest to his second son John.[84] Tacy leased her share in 1639 to George Bond of Redbrook,[85] and he or his heirs later acquired the freehold of the whole manor. Wyeseal then descended with Upper Redbrook farm[86] until 1800 when Lord Sherborne sold the estate, then *c.* 120 a., to the Revd. John Powell of Monmouth.[87] By 1840 it belonged to the Bigsweir estate in St. Briavels, with which it subsequently descended.[88] It may have been bought in the 1820s by George Rooke, who added Coxbury farm and other lands and woods nearby to his Bigsweir estate in 1826.[89] In 1919 the estate included over 300 a. in the west part of Newland.[90] In the later 17th century the Whitson family of Bristol, relatives of the Bonds, were tenants of the house at Wyeseal,[91]

64 Glos. Colln. RX 81.1; (H) G 5.1 (8).
65 Ibid. RR 81.3; for the ho., above, Plate 13.
66 Glos. Colln. RR 81.6.
67 Below, Forest of Dean, wardens.
68 *Cal. Fine R.* 1307–19, 330; 1319–27, 53; cf. N.L.W., Dunraven MSS. 335.
69 *Cal. Inq. p.m.* vii, p. 320.
70 *Cal. Fine R.* 1327–37, 335.
71 N.L.W., Dunraven MSS. 271.
72 Above, this section.
73 P.R.O., C 139/115, no. 34.
74 N.L.W., Dunraven MSS. 260.
75 G.D.R., T 1/128; Glos. Colln. (H) G 5.1 (8).
76 Cf. P.R.O., MR 879, which marks a pond on the brook N. of Noxon Park wood.
77 G.D.R., T 1/128.
78 Ibid.

79 Glos. R.O., D 2026/A 1, a later and probably inaccurate copy of the grant of 1253. A descent of the Bonds of Wyeseal, mainly without dates, is given in *Visit. Glos. 1682–3,* 16–17.
80 N.L.W., Dunraven MSS. 339.
81 Glos. R.O., D 1677/GG 1225.
82 Ibid. D 33/138.
83 Ibid. P 227/IN 1/1; P.R.O., C 3/215/31.
84 *Inq. p.m. Glos.* 1625–42, ii. 55.
85 Glos. R.O., D 2026/T 19.
86 Newland Valley est. deeds, Upper Redbrook fm. 1712–93; below, this section.
87 Heath, *Tintern Abbey,* [6]; Glos. R.O., D 637/I/76.
88 G.D.R., T 1/128; below, St. Briavels, manors.
89 Glos. R.O., D 1833/T 1, T 5, T 7.
90 Ibid. E 7.
91 Ibid. D 2026/T 19, T 39; cf. G.D.R. wills 1668/25.

which was later occupied as a farmhouse.[92] It was rebuilt in the mid 19th century.

Two farms called Upper and Lower Redbrook, with farmhouses beside Valley brook between Newland village and Lower Redbrook hamlet, formed the basis of what became known as the *NEWLAND VALLEY* estate in the 19th century. In 1608 *UPPER REDBROOK* farm belonged to Christopher Bond,[93] who had built up a large estate in Clearwell, Redbrook, and elsewhere in the parish.[94] Upper Redbrook passed to his son Richard (d. 1634), Richard's son George,[95] George's brother Christopher (d. 1668), and Christopher's nephew George Bond.[96] During the mid 17th century the Bonds acquired a number of other farms in and adjoining the valley,[97] and in 1712 George Bond settled his substantial estate on the marriage of his son Christopher (d. 1739), who was succeeded by his son Christopher (d. 1751). The last Christopher Bond left successive remainders to three sisters, two of whom died childless before 1754, leaving Jane, wife of James Lenox Dutton of Sherborne, in possession. Jane and James (both d. 1776) were succeeeded by their son James, created Lord Sherborne in 1784, who added Lower Redbrook farm and other lands to the estate.[98]

LOWER REDBROOK farm may have formed part of a substantial estate in Newland and adjoining parishes called Seward's and Ketford's lands in the 15th century. Thomas Elly (d. 1474), whose family was recorded at Redbrook from 1406,[99] owned that estate, and in 1490 his son Richard was said to have occupied it since his death,[1] but earlier that year John Lawrence of Bream was granted livery as heir of John Sampson of Redbrook.[2] Athanasius Elly owned Lower Redbrook farm in 1608,[3] and it later passed to Richard Elly, who sold it in the 1670s to John Bond,[4] a kinsman of the owner of Upper Redbrook. John Bond settled Lower Redbrook in 1698 on the marriage of his son Christopher (d. 1735), whose widow Alice surrendered her right to their son George (d. 1742 or 1743). George devised it to his brother John, whose son Christopher Bond of Walford (Herefs.) sold the farm, then 286 a., to Lord Sherborne in 1787.[5]

In 1800 Lord Sherborne's estate covered 1,235 a., comprising the farms called Wyeseal, Upper Redbrook (later renamed Valley House), Lower Redbrook (later Lodges), Birts, Clidden (later Glyn), Wrights (later Highbury), and Inwood.[6] It was split up in the first decade of the 19th century, the largest part, the main farms in the valley, being sold by Lord Sherborne in 1802 to William Cowley, who was lessee of ironworks at the foot of the valley. Cowley sold his estate in 1804 to Thomas Wightwick, who sold it in 1812 to James Garsed. Garsed or his assigns sold it in 1823 to Samuel Philips, who before his death in 1824 added several adjoining farms that Sherborne had sold separately, as well as Tanhouse farm at the head of the valley. By an agreement made between Samuel's heirs his whole Newland Valley estate passed to his nephew John Burton Philips of Teane (Staffs.).[7] J. B. Philips (d. 1847) was succeeded by his son John Capel Philips (d. 1907), whose second son John Augustus Philips[8] succeeded and sold the 1,121-acre estate in 1915 to W. R. Lysaght of Tidenham. In 1926 Lysaght made the estate over to his son D. R. Lysaght, who sold it in 1947 to the tenant of Lodges farm, E. F. White (d. 1961). The estate was later split up,[9] and in 1992 Lodges and Valley House farms, with *c.* 154 ha. (*c.* 380 a.), belonged to Mr. and Mrs. R. D. Vernon.[10]

Upper Redbrook Farm, long the home of one branch of the Bonds, was rebuilt or extensively remodelled in the early 19th century as a Regency villa,[11] probably for James Garsed who was resident on his estate from 1812 to *c.* 1821.[12] By 1831 it was known as Valley House.[13] It was demolished in 1956,[14] overgrown ruins and some outbuildings remaining in 1992. Lower Redbrook Farm was renamed Lodges Farm by 1831 after John Lodge, its late 18th-century tenant.[15] Part of the low northern range evidently survives from the substantial house that occupied the site in 1608[16] and incorporates on its south side a cross passage with a plank and muntin screen wall. In the late 17th century a tall main block was added south of the cross passage, with rooms ranged around a box-newel staircase. Its tall first-floor rooms had moulded plaster ceilings, of which only a fragment survives. In the early 18th century, probably in 1713,[17] the low north range of the house was extended westwards.

A substantial estate in Newland parish was acquired by the heirs of John Symons, a successful attorney of Clearwell,[18] who died in 1721. He left lands in the parish and £30,000 to his brother Richard, a London merchant, in trust to establish one of Richard's sons in a landed estate. Richard bought the Mynde Park estate in Herefordshire, where the family later lived, together with farms in Newland, settling the whole on the marriage of his eldest son John in 1735.[19] John Symons (d. 1763)[20] was succeeded by his nephew Richard Peers, who took the name

92 Glos. R.O., D 637/VII/22; D 1833/E 5/1.
93 P.R.O., MR 879.
94 Glos. R.O., D 2026/E 7, E 21, T 4.
95 Ibid. T 11; *Inq. p.m. Glos.* 1625–42, i. 206–8.
96 G.D.R. wills 1668/25; Bigland, *Glos.* ii. 260.
97 Glos. R.O., D 2026/T 39–41.
98 Newland Valley est. deeds, Upper Redbrook fm. 1712–93; ibid., abstracts of title, nos. 1–2.
99 Glos. R.O., D 1677/GG 150A, 190.
1 *Cal. Inq. p.m. Hen. VII*, i, pp. 244–5.
2 *Cal. Pat.* 1485–94, 315.
3 P.R.O., MR 879; cf. Glos. R.O., D 2026/X 19.
4 Glos. R.O., D 2026/T 58.
5 Newland Valley est. deeds, Lower Redbrook fm. 1698–1787; for death of the first Chris., Bigland, *Glos.* ii. 263.
6 Glos. R.O., D 637/VII/22.

7 Newland Valley est. deeds, *passim.*
8 Burke, *Land Gent.* (1898), ii. 1181–2; *Kelly's Handbook to Titled, Landed, and Official Classes* (1916), 1177.
9 Copies of deeds of Tanhouse Fm., in possession of Mr. and Mrs. Chamberlain.
10 Inf. from Mrs. Vernon.   11 Glos. Colln. RX 214.2.
12 Newland Valley est. deeds, Valley est. 1802–12; Glos. R.O., P 227/OV 1/1.
13 O.S. Map 1", sheet 43 (1831 edn.).
14 Inf. from Mrs. Chamberlain.
15 O.S. Map 1", sheet 43 (1831 edn.); Newland Valley est. deeds, Lower Redbrook fm. 1698–1787.
16 P.R.O., MR 879.   17 Date on fireplace.
18 N.L.W., Mynde Park MSS. 2289–2347.
19 Ibid. 1245, 1254.
20 Mon. in Much Dewchurch church (Herefs.); for the family, Burke, *Land. Gent.* (1846), 1345.

Symons and was made a baronet in 1774.[21] Sir Richard (d. 1796) was succeeded by a kinsman Thomas Raymond, who also took the name Symons, and in 1814 owned *c.* 460 a. in Newland parish, including Platwell, Wainland, Scatterford, Breckness Court, and Perrygrove farms (the last two situated in Coleford tithing). Thomas (d. 1818) was succeeded by his son Thomas Hampton Symons[22] (d. 1831). The younger Thomas was succeeded at Mynde Park by his son Thomas George Symons, but the Newland estate apparently belonged to other members of the family in 1840.[23] The Newland estate was split up after 1870, Platwell and Wainland farms being acquired before 1893 by the owners of Clearwell.[24]

Lands on the north side of Newland village which belonged in the mid 15th century to the Clearwell estate included a moated site at the head of Black brook, possibly the original residence of the Joce family.[25] In 1446 Joan Greyndour gave those lands as part of the endowment of a chantry she founded in honour of her husband Robert, assigning a house called Blackbrook, evidently at the moat, as the priest's residence.[26] The Crown sold the endowment of the chantry in 1559 to William Winter of Lydney,[27] whose son, Sir Edward, sold the land at Newland to Thomas Baynham, owner of Clearwell, in 1596.[28] Baynham's successors re-

tained it in 1653, when the house was called Chantry or Charter House.[29] About 1660 the land was acquired by William Probyn, and it passed to his descendants, owners of Newland House.[30] The site was described simply as the moat in 1757 and probably the house had by then been demolished.[31] The moat survived in 1992, partly obscured by farm buildings and a slurry tip.

In 1669 William Probyn owned and lived at Spout Farm in the village, and in 1671 he also bought other lands adjoining the former chantry estate. His lands passed at his death in 1703 to his son Edmund, knighted in 1726 on becoming a judge of King's Bench and from 1740 Lord Chief Baron of the Exchequer. Sir Edmund (d. 1742) devised his estate, which by then also included farms at Ellwood and in Coleford, to his nephew John Hopkins, who took the name Probyn.[32] John, who had acquired other property in Newland in 1726,[33] settled his estate in 1757 on the marriage of his son Edmund Probyn.[34] Edmund, though a considerable land-owner elsewhere in west Gloucestershire,[35] lived at Newland[36] in the house later called *NEWLAND HOUSE* at the south-west corner of the churchyard. He sold the house with Spout Farm and 156 a. in 1813 to Philip Ducarel,[37] but kept other property, including Millend farm, which at his death in 1819 he left to his daughters Sophia and Susan.[38] Philip Ducarel (d. 1855)

FIG. 9. NEWLAND HOUSE IN 1772

21 Cf. N.L.W., Mynde Park MS. 5260.   22 Ibid. 908.
23 P.R.O., PROB 11/1791B (P.C.C. 602 Tebbs), ff. 10v.–11v.; G.D.R., T 1/128.
24 *Kelly's Dir. Glos.* (1870), 524; P.R.O., CRES 38/673.
25 Above, this section.
26 N.L.W., Dunraven MSS. 325; *Reg. Spofford*, 28; for identification of the former chantry property, Glos. R.O., D 637/II/1/T 1, plan 1810 (notes 1810, in same bundle, wrongly identify the chantry house with Newland House).
27 *Cal. Pat.* 1558–60, 359.
28 N.L.W., Dunraven MSS. 271.   29 Ibid. 260.
30 Glos. R.O., D 23/T 25.   31 Ibid. D 637/II/1/T 1.
32 Ibid.; Bigland, *Glos.* ii. 262; for Sir Edm., *D.N.B.*
33 Glos. R.O., D 23/T 29.   34 Ibid. D 637/II/1/T 1.
35 Above, Abenhall, manor; *V.C.H. Glos.* viii. 62; x. 86; Rudder, *Glos.* 505, 533.
36 Rudder, *Glos.* 567; *Glouc. Jnl.* 3 May 1819.
37 Glos. R.O., D 637/II/1/T 1, T 4.
38 P.R.O., PROB 11/1616 (P.C.C. 233 Ellenbro'), f. 288; G.D.R., T 1/128; cf. *Trans. B.G.A.S.* vi. 194–7.

was apparently succeeded in his estate by his sister Jane Bevan, and by 1870 it belonged to his niece Julia Palmer (d. 1901).[39] Julia Palmer was succeeded in turn by her sons Charles Palmer (d. 1916) and Sir Frederick Palmer, Bt. (d. 1933). Most of the farmland may have been sold before 1923 when Sir Frederick offered Newland House for sale with just c. 26 a. of land; it was sold by his widow Lilian in 1945.[40] Their son Sir John Palmer lived in the village in another house until his death in 1963.[41]

The various houses in Newland village that the Probyns owned in the early 18th century included one described as a capital messuage in 1720 and another described then as new built,[42] but Newland House was apparently the house called Whitson's tenement that Sir Edmund Probyn held as lessee under the Highmeadow estate in 1726, when John Hopkins bought the freehold.[43] By 1772[44] Newland House was a long range of building with a west elevation of 10 irregular bays including a central, semicircular projection. The south part, which was of one tall storey and attics and contained the principal rooms, was probably built in the early 18th century; the main staircase, which survives in it, dates from c. 1725.[45] The north part of the house, of two storeys and attics and projecting eastwards beyond the line of the south part, was probably a later addition; it contained the service rooms. In the early 19th century the attics of the whole house were heightened to make a full new storey and some internal and external refitting was carried out. There were further alterations later that century, including a new east porch. The fittings of one room (including a fireback with the date 1748 and John Probyn's initials) were removed to a museum at Boston (Mass.) in the 1930s,[46] and the house was occupied by an evacuated school during the Second World War.[47] Later it was divided into flats, but it was unoccupied in 1992.

A manor called *YORKLEY*, presumably based on the two detached parts of Newland there, belonged by 1346 to Thomas, Lord Berkeley, who died in 1361.[48] It may have included land owned in 1310 by John ap Adam,[49] whose nearby Purton manor passed to the Berkeleys.[50] Lands in the Yorkley area later belonged to the Clearwell estate: in 1481 John and Joan Barre conveyed a house and 100 a. at Yorkley to Thomas Wall, and other lands, described as at Lydney, Gorsty field (in the east of

the detached part of Newland at Bream), and Badhamsfield (presumably land once of the ap Adams) to Thomas Kedgwin.[51] The western detached part at Yorkley later comprised Yorkley Court farm, which belonged by 1693 to the ironmaster Thomas Foley[52] (d. 1737), passing to his son Thomas and grandson Thomas (d. 1777), Lord Foley. Lord Foley's estates in the Forest area were sold soon after his death,[53] and in 1806 and 1821 Yorkley Court belonged to Thomas Packer.[54] By 1840 it belonged to Samuel Cholditch,[55] whose family still owned the farm in 1910.[56] In 1992, then c. 190 a., it was owned and farmed by Mrs. A. J. McBride. There were farm buildings, including a dovecot, and probably a dwelling on Lord Berkeley's manor in 1346.[57] The farmhouse at Yorkley Court was rebuilt in the early 19th century.

In the detached part of the parish at Bream the principal estate was based on a house called *PASTOR'S HILL*. In the late 16th century it belonged to a branch of the Hyett family, which sold it before 1608 to Warren Gough of Willsbury in St. Briavels. Warren (d. 1636) settled the estate, comprising 300 a., on his second son James[58] (d. 1691),[59] who devised it, subject to the life interest of his wife Mary (d. c. 1700), to his nephew William Gough of Willsbury, William's wife Mary, and their son James and his heirs. William held the estate in 1708,[60] and another William Gough owned it c. 1770.[61] Before 1803 it was bought by William Partridge of Monmouth,[62] and in 1840 the estate, comprising Pastor's Hill and Brockhollands farmhouses with 216 a., belonged to William Bagshaw.[63] In 1905 Pastor's Hill farm was bought by J. E. Hirst, whose granddaughter Mrs. E. B. Carpenter owned it with c. 80 a. in 1992.[64] The south range of the house dates from the early 17th century but has been altered on a number of occasions. In the later 17th century a porch was added to the south side, perhaps to emphasize a change from an earlier entry at the east end. In the early 18th century a central staircase was inserted, and in the early 19th century additions were made at the east end and the west end was remodelled. About 1910[65] a range of principal rooms in a suburban villa style was added to the north side of the old house.

Land in the north part of Newland tithing belonged to the Highmeadow estate, which is traced below with Staunton,[66] and land in Bream tithing to the Prior's Mesne (or Bream) Lodge

[39] Mons. in Newland church; Glos. R.O., D 637/II/1/E 1; *Kelly's Dir. Glos.* (1870), 607.
[40] Glos. R.O., D 2428/1/23/2; D 2299/4941; Burke, *Peerage* (1963), 1887–8.
[41] *Kelly's Handbook to Titled, Landed, and Official Classes* (1961), 1541; (1965), 1551.
[42] Glos. R.O., D 637/II/1/T 1.
[43] Ibid. D 3304; cf. ibid. D 637/II/1/T 1, plan 1810.
[44] Sketch 1772, at Boston Museum of Fine Arts (Mass.), reproduced above, Fig. 9.
[45] Cf. similar examples at the Victoria hotel, Newnham (dated 1726) and Hagloe House, Awre (house built c. 1725).
[46] *Bull. of Museum of Fine Arts, Boston*, June 1937, 35–8.
[47] Glos. R.O., D 2299/4941.
[48] Berkeley Cast. Mun., General Ser. acct. roll 326; *Berkeley MSS.* i. 302.
[49] B.L. Harl. Ch. 111, c. 32.
[50] Above, Lydney, manors.

[51] P.R.O., CP 25/1/79/94, nos. 48–9; for Gorsty field, Glos. R.O., D 2026/X 3 (bounds of Kidnalls coppice).
[52] N.L.W., Mynde Park MSS. 295, 345, 1132.
[53] Glos. R.O., D 2528; D 1833/T 13; cf. Burke, *Peerage* (1889), 556.
[54] Glos. R.O., SL 133; P 227/OV 1/1.
[55] G.D.R., T 1/128.
[56] Glos. R.O., SL 133; D 2428/1/23/2.
[57] Berkeley Cast. Mun., General Ser. acct. roll 326.
[58] *Inq. p.m. Glos.* 1625–42, ii. 63–8; cf. P.R.O., MR 879.
[59] Bigland, *Glos.* i. 241.
[60] G.D.R. wills 1691/187; 1699/29; cf. below, St. Briavels, manors.
[61] Rudder, *Glos.* 568.
[62] Rudge, *Hist. of Glos.* ii. 104.
[63] G.D.R., T 1/128.
[64] Inf. from Miss R. P. Hirst, of Pastor's Hill.
[65] Inf. from Miss Hirst.
[66] Staunton, manor.

estate, which is traced above with Aylburton in Lydney.[67]

In 1219 Henry III gave Robert of Wakering, the first rector of Newland, licence to assart 12 a. near the church.[68] Later a rectory glebe estate, probably also deriving from a royal gift of assarts, lay west of Clearwell village, between Rookery and Margery Lanes. The court, presumably meaning a house, of the rector of Newland in that area was mentioned c. 1300[69] and that of the bishop of Llandaff, owner of the rectory, in 1414;[70] the bishop's land there was mentioned in 1505.[71] In 1840 the bishop had 65 a. of land, together with a tithe barn standing beside Margery Lane. Adjoining land in private ownership then included fields called the Parsonage and a barn called Parsonage barn and may once have been part of the rectory glebe.[72] The rectory tithes and a barn were held on lease by Sir George Baynham of Clearwell in 1546.[73] In the late 17th century and the early 18th the rectory tithes, valued at c. £200, were leased to a branch of the Bond family, which sublet portions to others.[74] In 1840 the lessee of the tithes was Philip Ducarel of Newland House, who was awarded a corn rent charge of £1,080 for them.[75] In 1873 the bishop of Llandaff assigned his tithe rent charges from large areas of the parish to endow the separate benefices that had been established at Clearwell, Bream, and Coleford.[76]

ECONOMIC HISTORY. AGRICULTURE. The royal manor of Newland was formed almost entirely of freeholds owing only chief rents and heriots,[77] the rents charged when the original assarts were made or following compositions made with the Crown by the owners in the early 17th century. In the early 15th century some mills at Redbrook, mostly built fairly recently, were held on long leases,[78] but Whitemead park was the only land recorded as attached to the manor in demesne.[79]

The Joce family and their successors received chief rents from several hundred small holdings scattered throughout the parish and also acquired substantial demesne lands by assarting, mainly in the Clearwell area. In 1462 those demesnes, mostly then held on leases for terms of years, included Broadfields, lying between the Lydney–Coleford road and Bearse common, Callowalls fields, presumably the land later called Caudwell between the valley of Valley brook and Stowe, and Saunders fields north-east of Bream village. One smaller holding, held at will, owed six days' ploughing work. In 1462 demesne land of the estate held on lease brought in £26 a year, compared to £21 received as chief rents.[80] In the 16th century and the early 17th the lords of Clearwell held a considerable area in hand as parkland, sheep walk, and coney warren. In 1653 the emerging pattern of farms on the estate included one tenant's 108 a. at Great Caudwell and another's barn and seven closes in the area of the later Longley farm, and there were smaller tenant holdings based on houses at Stowe, Bream, and Clearwell.[81] In 1757 the estate comprised four large farms, based on Clearwell village, Trowgreen, Noxon, and Longley, and a number of smaller ones.[82]

A demesne farm was worked on Lord Berkeley's manor of Yorkley in the early 14th century. In 1346 116 a. of corn were reaped and there was a small stock of animals, principally a herd of 48 goats, the milk from which was sold. Four men working two ploughteams and a cowherd and goatherd were employed. The harvest work was done mainly by hired labour, and a few day-works owed by Berkeley tenants from Hinton, across the Severn, were also used, Yorkley presumably having no customary tenants.[83]

In the early 17th century much of the parish outside the Clearwell estate was held as substantial freehold farms, often of 100 a. or more. They included Upper and Lower Redbrook farms,[84] Inwood farm owned by the Sled family,[85] Platwell farm owned by the Skynn family,[86] and a large farm at Clearwell owned by the Worgan family.[87] Later, with the growth of the Valley estate under the Bonds and Lord Sherborne, the formation of an estate by the Symons family,[88] and lesser acquisitions by the Probyns of Newland House and the Probyns of Tanhouse Farm,[89] most of the farms were tenanted.

In the 15th century there were two small open fields in the north part of the parish, Hazlewell field on the slopes north-west of Newland village[90] and Blackbrook field lower down the hillside by the Black brook;[91] divisions of land in them were described in terms of 'day-works', presumably the number of days needed for ploughing.[92] The Newland freeholders, like those of the other parishes of the area, enjoyed common rights in the royal demesne land of the Forest.[93] They presumably exercised them mainly in the immediately adjoining areas, such as Bearse common in which the Clearwell estate claimed the largest right in the mid 19th century,[94] Clearwell Meend, and Horwell hill (later

67 Lydney, manors.
68 *Rot. Litt. Claus.* (Rec. Com.), i. 393.
69 Glos. R.O., D 33/4.
70 Ibid. D 1677/GG 161.
71 Ibid. GG 306.
72 G.D.R., T 1/128.
73 Hockaday Abs. ccxcv, 1548.
74 N.L.W., Mynde Park MSS. 5026, 5031; Atkyns, *Glos.* 573.
75 G.D.R., T 1/128.
76 Below, churches; Glos. R.O., P 93/IN 3/1.
77 Glos. R.O., D 2026/X 19; Berkeley Cast. Mun., General Ser. 16.
78 P.R.O., SC 6/858/14.
79 Above, manors.
80 Glos. R.O., D 1677/GG 1225; for lands mentioned, P.R.O., MR 879.

81 N.L.W., Dunraven MSS. 260.   82 Ibid. 339.
83 Berkeley Cast. Mun., General Ser. acct. roll 326.
84 Above, manors.
85 P.R.O., MR 879; cf. Glos. R.O., D 2026/T 39, deed 1670.
86 *Inq. p.m. Glos.* 1625–42, i. 231–2.
87 Ibid. 232; cf. Glos. R.O., D 654/III/76.
88 Above, manors.
89 Glos. R.O., D 637/II/1/T 1; D 608/8/2–3.
90 Ibid. D 1677/GG 172, 282; cf. ibid. D 637/II/1/T 1, plan 1810.
91 Ibid. D 2244/175; D 2957/214.62; N.L.W., Dunraven MSS. 325, deed 1446.
92 Glos. R.O., D 1677/GG 282; D 2244/175.
93 P.R.O., E 112/82, no. 300; F 14/13; Berkeley Cast. Mun., General Ser. 16.
94 Glos. R.O., Q/RI 121.

Bream's Meend). Large numbers of sheep were apparently pastured on the Clearwell estate in the 16th and early 17th centuries: 140 a. of Broadfields were in use as a sheep walk in 1611 and there were two sheephouses in that area and a third at the place later called Shop House near Clearwell village. All three were described as old sheephouses in 1637 and had presumably by then ceased to be used for that purpose.[95] A field on the Yorkley Court estate was named from a former sheephouse in the 18th century.[96] In 1625 Benedict Webb, a clothier of Kingswood (Wilts., later Glos.) who was promoting the use of home-grown rape seed oil in the manufacture of cloth, rented several hundred acres, including parts of the park and Broadfields, from the owner of Clearwell for growing rape.[97] The most productive meadow of the parish was probably along Valley brook, where in the 1630s the Bonds of Upper Redbrook farm made sluices and channels to water the meadows called Henbridge mead and Balls below Newland village.[98] In the mid 18th century the owners of Lower Redbrook farm, further downstream, also diverted water from the brook on to their meadows.[99] In 1801 in Newland parish as a whole large crops of wheat, barley, and oats were grown, with some turnips.[1] In 1840 in the parish as a whole arable greatly exceeded grassland.[2]

In 1840 the tithings of Newland, Clearwell, and Bream contained 28 farms of over 20 a. The largest were Longley (433 a.), Trowgreen (242 a.), and Noxon (204 a.) on the Clearwell estate, Lodges (314 a.) and Glyn (157 a.) on the Valley estate, Yorkley Court (182 a.), and Stowe Hall at Stowe (174 a.); a considerable acreage north of Newland village was attached to Cherry Orchard and Highmeadow farms, which lay partly in Staunton. Eight of the farms then had between 80 a. and 130 a., and twelve of them between 20 a. and 80 a.[3] In 1896 a total of 91 agricultural holdings was returned in the three tithings, and nine tenths of the land was then worked by tenant farmers.[4] In 1926 67 holdings were returned, comprising 10 of over 150 a., 28 others over 20 a., and 29 smallholdings; most of the smallholdings were in Bream tithing and were probably worked part-time by industrial workers. The larger farms then gave employment to a total of 93 farm labourers.[5] In 1988 in the residual Newland parish (comprising Newland and Clearwell tithings) 11 larger farms, over 50 ha. (124 a.), and 18 smaller ones, which were mostly worked part-time, were returned. Only about a quarter of the land, accounted for mainly by the farms of the Crown's Clearwell estate, was then held by tenants.[6]

In 1866 2,020 a. of the land of the three tithings were returned as arable compared with 1,489 a. of permanent grassland. Most of the farms practised sheep and corn husbandry, growing large crops of wheat, barley, roots, and grass seeds; fallows, of which 209 a. were returned, also played a part in the rotation. Over 3,000 sheep and lambs were returned, and c. 400 cattle, mostly kept for fattening.[7] The quantity of arable later fell, though less sharply than in the more lowland, Severnside parishes of the area: 1,779 a. were returned in 1896[8] and 841 a. in 1926. Sheepraising, stockrearing, and dairying all increased during the same period, with 3,996 sheep and lambs and 979 cattle returned in 1926.[9] In 1988 the residual parish was largely pastoral in character, with 934 ha. (2,308 a.) of permanent grassland, 272 ha. (672 a.) of arable, mainly growing barley, 1,107 cattle, and 5,365 sheep and lambs returned. Only one of the principal farms was a specialist arable enterprise, while six were concerned mainly with cattle and sheepraising and four mainly with dairying.[10]

MILLS, IRONWORKS, AND COPPER WORKS. In 1437, when 8 forges were listed at Newland and 1 at Bream, the parish was among the main ironworking centres in the Forest area;[11] some of the forges were probably at Coleford and Whitecliff.[12] By the end of the Middle Ages several mills had been established in the valleys of the two Red brooks in the west of the parish, and later the hamlets where those brooks joined the Wye had concentrations of industrial sites. At Upper Redbrook hamlet corn milling, fulling, paper making, copper making, ironmaking, and tinplating were all carried on at various times, and other mills at Lower Redbrook hamlet were absorbed in a copper works, which later became a large tinplate works.

In 1608 an iron furnace stood just over the parish boundary in Staunton at Knockalls hill by the junction of the road down the Upper Redbrook valley and the road to Staunton. It was owned by William Hall of Highmeadow[13] and was presumably still working in 1635 when his successor Benedict Hall owned two furnaces in the Newland area.[14]

On the upper Red brook, a short way below the Staunton road at a site called Upper Mill in the late 19th century, Christopher Hall of Highmeadow built a mill shortly before 1557, provoking disputes over water supply with the owners of two mills further downstream. His son William owned it in 1608.[15] It evidently went out of use later, though there was a building at the site, described as the old mill house, in 1792.[16] It was in use again by 1836[17] and, as part of the Bengough family's Highmeadow and

95 N.L.W., Dunraven MSS. 260; cf. P.R.O., MR 879.
96 Glos. R.O., SL 133.
97 *Econ. H.R.* 2nd ser. x. 256–64; cf. Glos. R.O., D 2026/X 15; Glos. Colln., Smyth of Nibley MS. VIII/111.
98 Glos . R.O., D2026/T 39, agreement 1663; for the lands (from 1948 the site of a sewage disposal works), P.R.O., MR 879.
99 Glos. R.O., D 2026/E 26.
1 *List and Index Soc.* clxxxix, p. 175.
2 G.D.R., T 1/128.
3 Ibid.
4 P.R.O., MAF 68/1609/6.
5 Ibid. MAF 68/3295/6.

6 Agric. Returns 1988.
7 P.R.O., MAF 68/25/9; MAF 68/26/8.
8 Ibid. MAF 68/1609/6.
9 Ibid. MAF 68/3295/6.
10 Agric. Returns 1988.
11 Berkeley Cast. Mun., General Ser. acct. roll 426.
12 Glos. R.O., D 1677/GG 1224–5.
13 P.R.O., MR 879; for the Highmeadow est., below, Staunton, manor.
14 P.R.O., SP 16/282, f. 253.
15 Ibid. MR 879; Glos. R.O., D 2026/T 11; D 1677/GG 541.
16 P.R.O., F 17/117(2), p. 39; MR 691 (LRRO 1/240).
17 Glos. R.O., D 637/VII/31.

Cherry Orchard estate,[18] continued working as a corn mill until shortly before 1918.[19]

Downstream, at the junction with the tributary stream that forms the county boundary with Monmouthshire, Elly's Mill, later called Redbrook mill, was recorded from 1438. Described as a new-built corn mill it was then owned by Thomas Elly[20] and it later passed from the Elly family to Christopher Bond (fl. 1567) and his son Richard, owners of Upper Redbrook farm.[21] It was later acquired by the Highmeadow estate and in the late 18th century was worked as a corn mill by the Ansley family.[22] It too passed with the Bengough's estate[23] and was worked until the early 20th century.[24]

The second furnace belonging to the Highmeadow estate in 1635 was probably the one which it later owned beside the upper Red brook on the west side of Furnace grove. It was presumably that Redbrook furnace that the parliamentary officers Robert Kyrle and John Brayne seised from Benedict Hall before 1646 and were working in 1649.[25] From 1671 until the early 19th century the furnace at Furnace grove was leased and worked in conjunction with forges owned by the Highmeadow estate at Lydbrook.[26] In 1792, when the estate owned another ironworks at the foot of the stream, the site was called Upper forge, but the furnace[27] continued in use until c. 1816.[28] From c. 1828 part of the site was used as an iron foundry by Thomas Burgham, who was in partnership with James Harris in 1840, when another part was used as a corn mill.[29] Burgham's foundry was worked until c. 1880[30] and the corn mill, known as Furnace Mill, until shortly before 1900.[31]

King's Mill, downstream near the site of the later tramroad incline,[32] was a new-built corn mill c. 1432 when the duke of Bedford as lord of the manor granted it in fee to John Wyrall.[33] The Wyralls of English Bicknor remained owners until 1712. They leased it from 1692 to the copper maker John Coster,[34] and part of the site was later used in connexion with a copper works just below, but the mill continued as a corn mill in possession of the Quick family, heirs of John's son Thomas. It was rebuilt before 1793, when it was leased to David Tanner,[35] who then had ironworks below, at the foot of the stream. Henry Courteen, miller and barge owner, later

worked the mill, probably by 1825,[36] and Ann Courteen owned it in 1840.[37] The Courteen family put up extensive new buildings, called Wye Valley Mills, on the site in 1873[38] and it became the principal flour mill of the area. Steam power was installed before 1885. The mill closed following a serious fire in 1925.[39]

A fulling mill below King's Mill was recorded from 1334,[40] and in 1435 was on lease from Newland manor to John Yevan and a partner.[41] It remained a fulling mill in 1490,[42] and in 1602, when it was bought by William Hall of Highmeadow, there was both a fulling mill and a corn mill at the site.[43] The corn mill was converted as a paper mill before 1680 when it was leased with the fulling mill to Charles Cony.[44] The lowest site on the upper Red brook may also have included the mill for sharpening instruments that was built at Redbrook c. 1400,[45] for Benedict Hall of Highmeadow owned a former grinding mill besides his fulling and corn mills in 1623.[46]

About 1692 John Coster took a lease of the paper mill and fulling mill at the bottom of Upper Redbrook and converted them to a copper works, building new ponds to provide power.[47] The works, with others built at Lower Redbrook, were established with the help of Swedish expertise and played an important role in the revival of the copper industry in England. Redbrook was possibly chosen because copper was then mined in the Forest but, if so, the veins were worked out by 1698, and the works were later supplied with ore from Cornwall.[48] John Coster, whose epitaph describes him as 'the restorer of the art of copper in Britain', was succeeded at his death in 1718 by his son Thomas, who had 26 copper furnaces at work in 1725.[49] The Coster family later assigned their lease of the works to the Bristol Brass Co., which, it was said, intended merely to close them down and stifle competition. By 1737 the works were ruinous and partly demolished and the owner, Lord Gage, began proceedings for waste.[50] They were in use again for copper making in 1756 when Joseph Jackson was the tenant.[51] By 1774 they had evidently been converted to ironworking, for a lease under the Highmeadow estate of two forges and a grinding mill close to the river bank was then offered for sale.[52] The ironworks were producing spades,

[18]   Below, Staunton, manor; G.D.R., T 1/128.
[19]   O. S. Map 1/2,500, Glos. XXXVIII. 3 (1902, 1922 edns.); Glos. R.O., D 1405/4/136.
[20]   Glos. R.O., D 33/103.
[21]   Ibid. D 2026/T 11; P.R.O., MR 879; *Inq. p.m. Glos.* 1625–42, i. 207; cf. above, manors.
[22]   Glos. R.O., D 1677/GG 1545, no. 54; P.R.O., F 17/117(2), p. 39; MR 691.
[23]   Glos. R.O., D 637/VII/31; D 1405/4/136.
[24]   O.S. Map 1/2,500, Glos. XXXVIII. 2 (1902, 1922 edns.).
[25]   Glos. R.O., D 421/E 9; P.R.O., LRRO 5/7A, depositions 1649.
[26]   *Trans. B.G.A.S.* lxxii. 136–7; Glos. R.O., D 1677/GG 1557; GG 1545, nos. 7, 47–51, 59, 116; below, Forest of Dean, industry (ironworks).
[27]   P.R.O., F 17/117(2), p. 45; MR 691; Glos. R.O., Q/RUm 30.
[28]   Hart, *Ind. Hist. of Dean*, 103.
[29]   Ibid. 167; G.D.R., T 1/128.
[30]   *Kelly's Dir. Glos.* (1856 and later edns.).
[31]   O.S. Maps 6", Glos. XXXVIII. NW (1887 edn.); 1/2,500, Glos. XXXVIII. 2 (1902 edn.).

[32]   P.R.O., MR 879.
[33]   Ibid. SC 6/858/14.
[34]   Glos. R.O., D 33/124, 196A; D 1677/GG 1560; P.R.O., CP 25/2/927/10 Anne Hil. no. 13.
[35]   Newland Valley est. deeds, mill at Redbrook 1716–1824; Glos. R.O., D 2166, lease 1793; plan c. 1830.
[36]   Farr, *Chepstow Ships*, 93.   [37]   G.D.R., T 1/128.
[38]   *Glouc. Jnl.* 15 Nov. 1873.
[39]   Harris, 'Wye Valley Ind. Hist.' Upper Redbrook, 22–4; *Kelly's Dir. Glos.* (1885), 536.
[40]   Glos. R.O., D 2957/214.3.
[41]   P.R.O., SC 6/858/14.
[42]   Glos. R.O., D 33/124.
[43]   Ibid. D 1677/GG 579.   [44]   Ibid. GG 1010.
[45]   P.R.O., SC 6/858/14.
[46]   Glos. R.O., D 2026/X 19.
[47]   Ibid. D 1677/GG 1560.
[48]   R. Jenkins, 'Copper Works at Redbrook and Bristol', *Trans. B.G.A.S.* lxiii. 145–67.
[49]   Ibid. 150–6.
[50]   Glos. R.O., D 1677/GG 1354–5, GG 1357.
[51]   Ibid. GG 1358.
[52]   *Glouc. Jnl.* 16 May 1774.

locks, hinges, and edge tools in 1780.[53] By 1792 they were held with the iron furnace upstream near Furnace grove,[54] and the two sites remained in the same occupation until the 1820s. The tenants James Davies and Co. were planning to establish tinplate works at Redbrook in 1805[55] and the riverside site was in use for that purpose by 1808.[56] The tenant Henry Davies bought both sites from the Crown's Highmeadow estate in 1823.[57]

In the late Middle Ages there were mills on the lower Red brook (later Valley brook) at Millend, east of Newland village. In 1360 John Long conveyed to John Joce and his wife Joan land on which a fulling mill had recently been built[58] and in 1430 the Clearwell estate included a fulling mill, occupied by John Erley, and an adjoining mill called Pool Mill, in a separate tenancy.[59] In 1444 the lady of Clearwell granted a lease of Pool Mill, together with a mill called Birchover Mill.[60] The site of Pool Mill and the adjoining fulling mill was probably beside Millend Lane c. 400 m. south of the junction with the Whitecliff–Highmeadow road: a field there was called Tuckmill mead in 1840.[61] Birchover Mill, named from the hill (later Bircham) above Millend, was recorded from 1275[62] and was listed as a leasehold under the Clearwell estate until 1478. In 1430 and 1478, however, another mill, described as under Birchover, was held freely from the estate.[63] One or both of those mills was presumably at Millend Farm, west of Millend Lane, where there was a mill in 1818,[64] which had ceased working by 1840.[65] By the late 18th century there was a corn and bark mill on Valley brook by Tanhouse Farm south of Newland village.[66]

Another group of mills stood at Lower Redbrook hamlet at the foot of Valley brook, at least two of which were absorbed into copper works in the late 17th century or the early 18th. In 1748 the works included a former grist mill or tuck mill and the site of another former corn mill, and a third mill standing nearby was also mentioned.[67]

The copper works at Lower Redbrook were established by the Governor and Company of Copper Miners in England, who were incorporated in 1691 and bought land at the hamlet in 1692. Thomas Chambers, one of the company, also built works nearby to operate on his own account, and his nephew and successor Thomas Chambers was also lessee of the company's works from 1716 until 1720, when the company was re-formed.[68] The company later took over Chambers's works, buying the freehold from his

heirs in 1748, and it bought other property in 1750 and 1762, presumably in order to enlarge its works.[69] The Lower Redbrook works continued under the Copper Miners Co. until 1790 when they were sold to the ironmasters David and William Tanner. The Tanners converted them to ironworks and later, probably from 1792, made tinplate there. In 1798, shortly before David's bankruptcy, they leased the works to William Cowley of Stourbridge (Worcs.), who built a new forge in the valley above the works soon after buying the Newland Valley estate in 1802. By 1803 Cowley had formed a partnership with John James,[70] who made tinplate at the works until c. 1819.[71]

In 1824 the freehold of the Lower Redbrook works was bought by Philip Jones, a banker, who spent over £8,000 on improvements, including an aqueduct bringing water from the upper Red brook to augment the supply. In 1825 Philip Jones leased the works to Benjamin and Henry Whitehouse, who agreed to make further improvements.[72] In 1848 the works comprised a large group of buildings, filling the foot of the valley.[73] Part of the stock of the Whitehouse family's business was put up for sale in that year,[74] and in 1851, when six tinplate manufacturers, including Edwin Whitehouse, were listed at Redbrook, the works were perhaps divided among several concerns. The works then employed c. 50 other inhabitants of Redbrook.[75] By 1870 they were carried on under the Redbrook Tinplate Co.,[76] which was re-formed in 1883 under directors of the firm of Coventry and Robinson. In the 20th century, when much of the products went for export, the works produced the finest grades of tinplate, used in tobacco and confectionery tins, besides thicker grades, used for canning. The Tinplate Co. was again re-formed in 1948 and the works were rebuilt as one large factory housing all the plant. At that period up to 500 men were employed, many of them coming from Monmouth. The factory, said to be the last tinplate works of its type to operate, closed in 1962[77] and the site was being cleared for redevelopment in 1992.

OTHER INDUSTRY AND TRADE. In the 15th and 16th centuries an unofficial market was held at Newland village, the traders taking advantage of the large numbers congregating at the parish church on Sundays and feast days. In 1426 huts and booths erected in the churchyard at festivals were ordered to be removed,[78] and in the 16th century shambles, called the butchers' row, adjoined the churchyard.[79] In 1563 a group of

53 Ibid. 18 Dec. 1780.
54 Ibid. 17 Dec. 1792; cf. P.R.O., F 17/117(2), p. 45.
55 Glos. R.O., D 1677/GG 1545, nos. 92, 104A, 113.
56 Ibid. Q/RUm 30.
57 5th Rep. Com. Woods (1826), 108; cf. Hart, Ind. Hist. of Dean, 103, 113, 167.
58 N.L.W., Dunraven MSS. 324.
59 Ibid. 339.   60 Ibid. 324.
61 G.D.R., T 1/128.   62 Glos. R.O., D 2244/11.
63 N.L.W., Dunraven MSS. 339; Glos. R.O., D 1677/GG 1224-5.
64 P.R.O., PROB 11/1616 (P.C.C. 233 Ellenbro'), f. 288.
65 G.D.R., T 1/128.
66 Below (other ind. and trade).
67 Glos. R.O., D 2166, deed 1748.

68 Trans. B.G.A.S. lxiii. 156-9.
69 Glos. R.O., D 2166, deeds 1748, 1750, 1762.
70 Ibid. D 639/11-12; Newland Valley est. deeds, deeds of forge 1814-25.
71 Glouc. Jnl. 8 Nov. 1819.
72 Glos. R.O., D 639/11; for Jones, cf. ibid. D 2166, deeds 1821, 1823, 1827.
73 Ibid. D 639/14, a sketch of the works, detail reproduced above, Plate 33.
74 Ibid. D 637/I/81.   75 P.R.O., HO 107/2444.
76 Kelly's Dir. Glos. (1870), 607.
77 Harris, 'Wye Valley Ind. Hist.' Lower Redbrook, 11-15; The Times, 1 Dec. 1961.
78 Reg. Spofford, 96-7; cf. ibid. 231.
79 Glos. R.O., D 2957/214.67; D 34/9/2; D 1677/GG 348.

butchers and other tradesmen from Newland and neighbouring parishes was cited for trading there during service times,[80] and the Sunday market was mentioned again in 1596.[81] It presumably lapsed during the 17th century when Coleford became a more frequented trading centre.

In 1608 the muster for Newland tithing (which comprised the Newland village area and the Redbrook valleys) included 26 tradesmen and craftsmen. There were five tanners,[82] most probably working tanneries on Valley brook near Newland village, where they were conveniently placed for the Bristol trade by means of the Wye and for a supply of bark from the Forest woodlands. In 1587 a Newland tanner, Edward Whitson, took a cargo of calfskins from Brockweir to put on board a French ship in the Kingsroad, in the Bristol Channel, provoking a violent confrontation with Bristol merchants who claimed a monopoly of the export of calfskins.[83] In the late 17th century and the early 18th two tanneries were worked near the village. One, known as the upper tanhouse and recorded until the 1750s, was probably sited just above the crossing of Valley brook by the Clearwell road,[84] while the other was lower down the brook at Tanhouse Farm. A house called Bark House in 1665, standing above Tanhouse Farm and south of Barkhouse Lane (later Laundry Road), was evidently also used in the trade.[85] A branch of the Probyn family were tanners at Newland for at least six generations. In 1636 Thomas Probyn took a lease of a Newland tanhouse,[86] and his successors, who were evidently at Tanhouse Farm by the end of the century, later acquired considerable freehold property adjoining the village and near Stowe. The last of the family to live at Tanhouse Farm, Edmund Probyn,[87] gave up working the tannery in 1773 and let it. It then included a water mill on Valley brook, which was used both as a corn mill and for grinding bark,[88] and in 1817 it included the corn mill, water-powered bark mills, and 100 tan pits.[89] The lessee James Rogers bought the freehold of the house and tannery in 1807, and tanning probably ceased there at his bankruptcy c. 1818.[90]

In the late medieval and early modern periods Newland tithing had a small clothmaking industry based on the fulling mills, mentioned above, at Redbrook and Millend. A weaver was recorded in 1501[91] and two tuckers and two weavers in 1608. Two tankard makers (probably making tankards of wood staves and iron hoops)

and two coopers were living in the tithing in 1608. There were then also two millstone hewers,[92] probably working quarries by the Wye near Lower Redbrook hamlet; millstones were reserved in a lease of land on the slopes there in 1675,[93] and a number of sites of millstone working have been identified in the area.[94] A maker of cider mills and millstones had quarries near Lower Redbrook in 1812,[95] and the trade was carried on there and at Penallt, on the Monmouthshire bank opposite, until the end of the 19th century.[96]

The two Redbrook hamlets played a part in the Wye carrying trade, providing a connexion between the Newland area and Bristol. In the later 17th century and early 18th much wood for the use of coopers was shipped to Bristol by the Bonds, owners of the Wyeseal estate, who also traded in cinders from old ironworkings.[97] In the early 18th century the copper works made regular use of a wharf at Wye's Green at Lower Redbrook for landing copper ore and other materials.[98] The hamlet was also a place where oak bark was stored for shipment to Bristol and elsewhere: there were at least two barkhouses there at the beginning of the 19th century, when they went out of use and were converted as chapels.[99] In 1800 boats ran to Bristol every spring tide,[1] and in the following years several local tradesmen, including ironmasters, a miller, and a timber merchant, owned barges.[2] River craft were built at Wye's Green in the early 18th century,[3] and the Hudson family and others built trows and barges of up to c. 50 tons at Redbrook in the early 19th century.[4]

A brewery was established at the bottom of Upper Redbrook hamlet in 1825 and was later run by members of the Burgham family until it closed in the 1920s. In 1904 it owned or had tied to it 22 public houses.[5] In the 19th century the two Redbrook hamlets had many tradesmen and craftsmen, a total of 32 being enumerated in 1851 in addition to the larger number of inhabitants employed at the tinplate works and mills.[6] An agricultural implement maker, a timber dealer, and several shopkeepers were among inhabitants in the early 20th century, and a garage had opened on the main Wye Valley road by 1931.[7]

In Clearwell tithing iron mining, quarrying, and stoneworking provided employment, and Clearwell village was well supplied with the usual rural trades, particularly during the 18th and early 19th centuries when the neighbouring Newland village adopted a mainly residential

80 Hockaday Abs. ccxcvi.
81 B.L. Harl. MS. 4131, f. 490v.
82 Smith, *Men and Armour*, 40–1.
83 *Adams's Chron. of Bristol*, ed. F. F. Fox (Bristol, 1910), 121.
84 Glos. R.O., D 2026/E 18; D 23/T 29; D 637/II/1/T 1, marr. settlm. 1757.
85 Ibid. D 2026/T 49.   86 Ibid. D 1677/GG 811.
87 Ibid. D 608/2–3; cf. ibid. D 2026/E 18, F 16; P 227/VE 2/1, min. 1729.
88 *Glouc. Jnl.* 21 June 1773; for the mill site, cf. G.D.R., T 1/128.
89 *Glouc. Jnl.* 13 Jan. 1817.
90 Glos. R.O., D 608/8/3.
91 Ibid. D 1677/GG 298.
92 Smith, *Men and Armour*, 40–1.

93 Glos. R.O., D 23/T 25, sale of lease 1750.
94 *New Regard of Forest of Dean*, vi. 33–6.
95 *Glouc. Jnl.* 6 July 1812.
96 *Glos. Soc. Ind. Arch. Jnl.* (1973), 11–12.
97 Glos. R.O., D 2026/A 1–2, A 4–5, E 23.
98 Ibid. T 64.
99 Below, churches; nonconf.; for the two bldgs., Glos. R.O., D 639/14.
1 *Glouc. Jnl.* 22 Sept. 1800.
2 Farr, *Chepstow Ships*, 90, 93–4, 114.
3 Glos. R.O., D 2026/T 64.
4 Farr, *Chepstow Ships*, 77, 80, 96, 140, 152, 158.
5 Harris, 'Wye Valley Ind. Hist.' Upper Redbrook, 18–19; Glos. R.O., D 2299/392.
6 P.R.O., HO 107/2444.
7 *Kelly's Dir. Glos.* (1906), 257; (1931), 268.

character. Twenty two tradesmen and craftsmen recorded in Clearwell tithing in 1608 included 3 miners, 3 masons, 2 grindstone hewers, 2 nail-makers and a lime burner.[8]

Deposits of iron ore under Noxon Park wood were some of the most productive in the Forest area. In the 13th century, when Noxon still belonged to the royal demesne as part of Bearse bailiwick, Bearse provided the Crown with greater mining royalties than any of the other bailiwicks.[9] In 1320 the bishop of Llandaff, to whose church of Newland Noxon became tithable in 1317 as an assart from the royal demesne, secured a grant of the tithes of all iron mines in the parish. Later that century, in the face of opposition from the constable of St. Briavels, successive bishops were at pains to uphold their right to what was evidently a valuable asset.[10] In 1415 John Greyndour devised his shares in mines in the parish, probably at Noxon (which he owned from 1403), and his stock of ore to his wife Isabel.[11] In the late 17th century Clearwell was the most usual venue for the Forest mine law court,[12] presumably because of the number of inhabitants working mines at Noxon and in adjoining parts of the royal demesne. Five or six small pits were worked at Noxon in the mid 18th century. The iron there was then taken by free miners on the same basis as other deposits in St. Briavels hundred, but in 1798 the owner Charles Edwin laid claim to all the rights and made the miners pay him a royalty instead of gale money to the Crown's gaveller. The claim, never accepted by the Crown, was enforced by Edwin's successors until 1907[13] when the Crown itself became the landowner. Between the 1830s and the 1890s the Noxon iron mines were leased to leading local ironmasters, including the owners of the works at Parkend and Cinderford,[14] and were said to produce up to £800 a year in royalties for the countess of Dunraven in the 1860s.[15] In 1910 a new company took an option to mine ore under part of Noxon by a level driven from the neighbouring part of the Forest, but the project failed in 1924 with nothing done.[16]

During the 19th century many inhabitants of the east part of Clearwell tithing gained their livelihood as miners, quarrymen, and stone cutters, the last probably employed at stoneworks within the Forest. In 1851 Clearwell village had c. 70 industrial workers, tradesmen, and craftsmen, twice as many as it had agricultural labourers; among them were 10 iron miners, 7 quarrymen, 6 stonemasons, 2 lime burners, and a stone merchant.[17] Several of the tithing's in-

habitants, including some of its farmers, traded as stone merchants in the later 19th century.[18] At the same period limekilns and quarries were worked in the south part of the tithing, where Stowe hamlet had three lime burners in 1851.[19] In the later 20th century two quarries at Stowe, worked for roadstone, were much enlarged.[20] Nailmaking was a trade carried on in Clearwell village throughout the 19th century, employing six men in 1851, and in 1851 there was also a tannery in the village.[21]

In Bream tithing eight tradesmen were recorded in 1608, including two miners.[22] In the 19th century and the early 20th the mining industry dominated the tithing. By 1851 the great majority of those living in the parochial parts of Bream and Yorkley worked as coal miners, and there were also some iron miners and quarrymen, together with a number of inhabitants following the usual village crafts.[23] Some small drift mines were worked in the tithing in the late 19th century and the early 20th,[24] but most of the inhabitants were then employed at pits in the adjoining parts of the Forest, with the large Princess Royal colliery, near Whitecroft, dominating employment by 1910.[25]

A fishery in the Wye belonged to Wyegate manor at the time of the Norman Conquest and was the only source of revenue there in 1086.[26] The owners of Wyeseal manor claimed a fishery in 1656, challenging a claim by Thomas Foley of London to all rights in the river between Upper Redbrook hamlet and Bigsweir, in St. Briavels.[27] In 1709, when George Bond, owner of Wyeseal, granted a lease to a London fishmonger, he himself was making the unrealistic claim to all the rights in the stretch of river between Redbrook and Brockweir,[28] in the lower parts of which the Bigsweir estate and the duke of Beaufort had fisheries.[29] In 1800, however, the owner, Lord Sherborne, claimed only about a mile of the river below Redbrook.[30] His lessee was then supplying salmon regularly to Bristol and London.[31] The Wyeseal fishery passed with the manor to the owners of the Bigsweir estate, who by 1895 were leasing it with their St. Briavels fishery.[32] The earl of Pembroke, constable of St. Briavels, had a fishing weir on the Wye at Redbrook in 1570,[33] but no later record of it has been found.

LOCAL GOVERNMENT.
Court baron and leet jurisdiction was exercised by a court held at St. Briavels castle for St. Briavels hundred and manor and Newland manor.[34] The office of ale

8 Smith, *Men and Armour*, 37–8.
9 P.R.O., E 32/31, m. 17; for Noxon, above, manors.
10 *Cal. Pat. 1381–5*, 395; *Cal. Close, 1327–30*, 293; 1354–60, 165; 1396–9, 243.
11 P.R.O., PROB 11/2B (P.C.C. 37 Marche), f. 289v.
12 Hart, *Free Miners*, 142.
13 *4th Rep. Dean Forest Com.* 34–5, 39–43; Glos. Colln. (H) G 5.1 (8).
14 N.L.W., Dunraven MSS. 335.
15 Glos. Colln. (H) G 5.1 (8).
16 P.R.O., F 3/1164.   17 Ibid. HO 107/2444.
18 *Kelly's Dir. Glos.* (1856 and later edns.).
19 P.R.O., HO 107/2444; O.S. Map 6", Glos. XXXVIII. SE. (1884 edn.).
20 O.S. Map 1/25,000, SO 50 (1951, 1978 edns.).

21 Glos. R.O., P 227/IN 1/6; *Kelly's Dir. Glos.* (1894), 122; P.R.O., HO 107/2444.
22 Smith, *Men and Armour*, 39.
23 P.R.O., HO 107/2444.
24 O.S. Maps 6", Glos. XXXIX. SW.; XLVII. NW. (1883 edn.); Glos. R.O., D 2428/1/23/2.
25 *Kelly's Dir. Glos.* (1910), 52.
26 *Dom. Bk.* (Rec. Com.), i. 166v.
27 Glos. R.O., D 2026/E 22.
28 Ibid. E 19.   29 Cf. below, St. Briavels, econ. hist.
30 Glos. R.O., D 637/VII/22.
31 Heath, *Tintern Abbey*, [4].
32 Glos. R.O., D 1833/E 5/1; T 13, lease 1900.
33 P.R.O., E 310/14/50, f. 36.
34 Above, St. Briavels hundred.

conner of Newland, for enforcing the assize of ale under the leet,[35] had become a direct Crown appointment by 1455;[36] in the late Middle Ages it was held with the office of rider of the Forest.[37] John Joce apparently held a court for his numerous free tenants in Newland in the mid 14th century,[38] but, with no customary tenancies or communal agriculture to administer, no court appears to have been held by his successors after the Middle Ages.

Surviving records of parish government in Newland include churchwardens' accounts for the years 1655–1786 and 1821–55[39] and vestry minutes for 1722–73 and 1786–96.[40] The parish had three churchwardens in 1576[41] and in the mid 17th century; later, one was appointed for Newland tithing, one for Coleford tithing, and one for Clearwell and Bream tithings together. For each of the four tithings, often termed 'beams' at Newland, an overseer of the poor, a highway surveyor, and a petty constable were appointed.[42] The ratepayers of a tithing were occasionally allowed to hold a separate meeting to determine cases relating to it, and in 1729 a differential rate was levied among the tithings, but the poor of all four were relieved together,[43] and the information given below applies also to Coleford tithing. The distant, scattered tithing of Lea Bailey appears never to have been rated to Newland and it was said that none of its poor were relieved by the parish until c. 1680. In the 1690s, with the expense of the tithing's poor increasing and no rates being levied, the Newland parish officers obtained an order from quarter sessions that Lea Bailey should maintain its own poor,[44] which it continued to do in the early 19th century.[45]

In 1664 a committee of parishioners was formed to provide employment for the poor and it made plans, possibly not implemented, for opening workhouses at Clearwell and Coleford.[46] In 1679 a serge manufacturer of Lacock (Wilts.) contracted with the parish to employ up to 60 paupers in spinning and other work.[47] From the mid 18th century there was a growing concern about the burden of the poor, with enquiries to identify residents who were without settlement in 1750 and 1755, a scheme for employing poor women at spinning flax in 1756, and general measures for tightening poor-law administration in 1759. Efforts were made regularly to persuade parishioners to take apprentices: 15 children were placed out in 1767 and 26 in 1787. In 1751 c. 45 adults and children were on permanent weekly relief and in 1771 c. 80.[48] A workhouse was established at Coleford town in or shortly before 1786 under a committee of the parish

officers and leading ratepayers,[49] and a workhouse master capable of supervising hemp, flax, and wool manufacture was advertized for in 1788.[50] By 1788 a salaried assistant overseer had been appointed.[51]

The parish's problems were caused mainly by the developing hamlets of the extraparochial Forest on its borders. In 1832 the Newland vestry claimed that over half the annual disbursements for relief were to inhabitants of the extraparochial areas. It said that many Foresters when disabled or too old to work came into the parish to seek relief; many of them had legal settlement in it, while the others burdened it with the cost of casual relief, removals, and lawsuits. The number of children who had to be supported was increased by the practice of unmarried women going to Forest hamlets to give birth, so that their children could not be affiliated by the parish officers.[52] Total expenditure on the poor averaged £768 in the years 1783–5, and it was £705, including £62 spent on lawsuits, in 1803 when there were 54 paupers in the workhouse and another 24 on permanent relief outside it.[53] In 1812–13 expenditure reached £1,741, and in 1813–14 it reached £2,294, with 58 paupers then maintained in the workhouse, 96 given permanent relief, and 174 given casual relief.[54] A contractor took all the poor at the sum of £1,200 a year in 1821,[55] and in the years 1825–34 the cost of relief varied between £980 and £1,319.[56]

The strength of nonconformity at Coleford made church rates an issue of controversy in the parish for some years after the mid 1830s, but the compulsory system was ended in 1858 when the dissenters expressed their willingness to contribute to the upkeep of the church fabric on a voluntary basis.[57]

In 1836 Newland parish, except for Lea Bailey, became part of the Monmouth poor-law union.[58] In 1894, when Coleford became a separate civil parish and urban district, Newland, Clearwell, and Bream tithings were included in the West Dean rural district,[59] with which they were transferred to the new Forest of Dean district in 1974.

CHURCHES. A new church to serve the assarted lands that became Newland parish was founded shortly before 1216. Robert de Wakering held it as rector in 1219 by appointment of King John and was said to have recently built the church. Henry III licensed Robert to assart 12 a. of land near it[60] and in 1221 and 1223 gave him oaks from the Forest to continue the build-

35 P.R.O., REQ 2/4/306.
36 Cal. Pat. 1452–61, 276.
37 Ibid. 1476–85, 503; L. & P. Hen. VIII, i, p. 67; viii, p. 118.
38 N.L.W., Dunraven MSS. 325, deed 1338; 326, deed 1342.
39 Glos. R.O., P 227/CW 2/1–2.
40 Ibid. VE 2/1–4.
41 Hockaday Abs. xlvii, 1576 visit. f. 124.
42 Glos. R.O., P 227/CW 2/1; VE 2/1, mins. 2 Nov. 1725; 1 Feb. 1726; East. 1739. For the term 'beam', cf. Smith, Men and Armour, 40; L. & P. Hen. VIII, xvii, p. 499.
43 Glos. R.O., P 227/VE 2/1, mins. 3 Sept. 1728; 4 Nov. 1729.
44 Ibid. D 2026/R 6.
45 Poor Law Abstract, 1804, 172–3; Poor Law Returns (1830–1), p. 67.

46 Glos. R.O., D 34/2/1.   47 Ibid. D 2026/R 4.
48 Ibid. P 227/VE 2/2–4.
49 Ibid. VE 2/4; OV 9/1.
50 Glouc. Jnl. 12 May 1788.
51 Glos. R.O., P 227/VE 2/4.
52 3rd Rep. Dean Forest Com. 16.
53 Poor Law Abstract, 1804, 172–3.
54 Ibid. 1818, 146–7.   55 Glos. R.O., P 227/OV 9/2.
56 Poor Law Returns (1830–1), p. 67; (1835), p. 65.
57 Glouc. Jnl. 26 Aug. 1837; 15 June 1850; 6 Aug. 1859.
58 Poor Law Com. 2nd Rep. pp. 526, 535.
59 Census, 1901.
60 Rot. Litt. Claus. (Rec. Com.), i. 393, 413; Pleas of the Crown for Glos. ed. Maitland, p. 48.

ing work.[61] In 1286 Edward I gave the advowson to the bishop of Llandaff,[62] who was allowed to appropriate the church in 1303, and a vicarage was ordained in 1304.[63] In 1283 Edward I had given the rector John of London the tithes of Whitemead park and his other new inclosures in the Forest.[64] In 1305 he gave the bishop of Llandaff the tithes from all recent or future assarts in the Forest.[65] The bishop of Llandaff remained patron of the vicarage, though the Crown attempted presentations to it on several occasions in the 15th century,[66] the earl of Pembroke presented under a grant from the bishop in 1562,[67] and William Hall of Highmeadow made unsuccessful presentations under a grant from the bishop in 1602.[68] In 1861 the advowson was transferred from the bishop of Llandaff to the bishop of Gloucester.[69]

Within the large parish Coleford and Bream had chapels by the late Middle Ages and one was built at Clearwell in 1830. The two older chapels appear to have usually been independent of the Newland incumbents, and all three places became separate ecclesiastical districts in the mid 19th century.[70] The living of Clearwell was united with that of Newland in 1981.[71]

At the ordination of the vicarage in 1304 the vicar was awarded the small tithes and offerings and a third of the hay tithes.[72] By the early 19th century, presumably in place of the share of the hay tithes, he took all the great tithes from an area of the parish immediately adjoining Newland village.[73] The tithes of iron mines in the parish were assigned to the appropriator's portion in 1320.[74] The first rector had a grant of 2 a. on which to build a house in 1220[75] and a successor had 10 oaks for the same purpose in 1238.[76] That house was presumably retained by the appropriator, for under the ordination of 1304 the vicar was to have a site on which to build a house.[77] The vicarage house was mentioned in 1385[78] and stood south-east of the churchyard. It was claimed that it was unfit for residence in 1823, and it was usually occupied by curates in the mid 19th century when the vicar George Ridout lived at a house which he held as lecturer of Newland.[79] The vicarage house, which was probably rebuilt in the 17th century and altered and extended later, was demolished c. 1871 and replaced by a building in Tudor style.[80]

Newland church was valued at £26 13s. 4d. in 1291,[81] and the vicarage was valued at £18 6s. 10d. in 1535.[82] The living was worth £60 in 1650,[83] £50 in 1710,[84] and £80 in 1750.[85] The vicarage tithes were commuted for a corn rent charge of £525 in 1840,[86] and the living was valued at £504 in 1856.[87]

Walter Giffard, later bishop of Bath and Wells and archbishop of York, became rector of Newland in 1247, succeeding his brother Hugh in the cure. Walter was succeeded in 1264 by John of London,[88] who held the cure until 1302 and was possibly the man of that name who later wrote a tribute and lament on the death of Edward I.[89] The medieval vicars included Henry Fouleshurst who exchanged the chancellorship of Llandaff cathedral for the living in 1394.[90] A parochial chaplain was mentioned in 1420,[91] and to serve the church and the large parish the vicar had the assistance of three chantry priests by the late Middle Ages.[92] In 1539 proceedings were taken against a Newland man William Lovell for denying the doctrine of transubstantiation.[93] In 1551 the vicar John Quarr was found unable to repeat the Ten Commandments.[94] Thomas Godwin was vicar 1613–15 on the presentation of his father, the bishop of Llandaff.[95]

A charity founded by William Jones in 1615 and administered by the Haberdashers' Company supported a lecturer at Newland.[96] The first lecturer Lawrence Potts, evidently a man of puritan views, antagonized some of the parishioners and attempts were made to remove him. His successor Peter Symonds, appointed in 1627, had similar views, leading the diocesan bishop, Godfrey Goodman, to attempt to obtain the right of appointment to the lectureship.[97] In 1631 Symonds was accused of involvement with the riots against the inclosure of Mailscot wood in the Forest.[98] After the outbreak of the Civil War he was forced to leave the parish for London but he returned in 1646. The following year William Hughes, vicar of Newland, complained that Symonds was trying to have the vicarage sequestrated and attached to the lecturer's post[99] and Symonds had obtained that object by 1650; a parliamentary survey then described him as a godly, able, and faithful preaching minister.[1] In 1651 he was granted an augmentation of £30 a year by the trustees for the maintenance of ministers. In 1654 Francis Ford was appointed to serve Newland, and he was given an augmentation of £20 a year in 1657.

61 Rot. Litt. Claus. i. 469, 530.
62 Cal. Chart. R. 1257–1300, 337.
63 Reg. Swinfield, 393–4, 411–12.
64 Cal. Close, 1279–88, 219.
65 Cal. Pat. 1301–7, 319.
66 Ibid. 1416–22, 55, 104, 260; cf. Reg. Lacy, 89–90; Cal. Pat. 1441–6, 466.
67 Hockaday Abs. ccxcvi.   68 Ibid.; cf. Eccl. Misc. 99.
69 Lond. Gaz. 26 July 1861, p. 3118.
70 Below, this section; above, Coleford, churches.
71 Glouc. Dioc. Dir. (1991–2), 57.
72 Reg. Swinfield, 411–12.
73 G.D.R., V 5/214T 4; T 1/128.
74 Cal. Pat. 1381–5, 395.
75 Rot. Litt. Claus. (Rec. Com.), i. 413.
76 Close R. 1237–42, 80.
77 Reg. Swinfield, 411–12.   78 Glos. R.O., D 2244/78.
79 Hockaday Abs. ccxcvii, 1823, 1835, 1840, 1843; G.D.R. vol. 384, f. 148.
80 Watercolour of old vicarage (in village meeting room

1992); Glos. R.O., P 227/IN 3/1.
81 Tax. Eccl. (Rec. Com.), 161.
82 Valor Eccl. (Rec. Com.), ii. 501.
83 Trans. B.G.A.S. lxxxiii. 98.
84 Hockaday Abs. ccxlvii.
85 G.D.R. vol. 381A, f. 5.   86 Ibid. T 1/128.
87 Ibid. vol. 385, p. 154.
88 Cal. Pat. 1232–47, 510; 1258–66, 319; cf. D.N.B.
89 Trans. B.G.A.S. lxi. 188–95.
90 Reg. Trefnant, 178, 189.
91 Reg. Lacy, 87.   92 Below, this section.
93 Reg. Bothe, 381; Hockaday Abs. ccxcv.
94 E.H.R. xix. 120.
95 Hockaday Abs. ccxcvi; D.N.B. s.v. Godwin, Francis.
96 Below, char.
97 W. M. Warlow, Hist. of Charities of Wm. Jones (Bristol, 1899), 265–70.
98 Cal. S.P. Dom. 1631–3, 36.
99 Warlow, Char. of Wm. Jones, 270–2.
1   Trans. B.G.A.S. lxxxiii. 98.

Ford died in 1657, when the trustees appointed as vicar Samuel Fawcett,[2] who had succeeded Symonds as lecturer in 1652. Fawcett conformed at the Restoration and retained the lectureship until 1666, but the vicarage was recovered by William Hughes,[3] who held it until 1679, at first in plurality with Staunton and later with English Bicknor.[4]

The 18th-century vicars were usually pluralists and included Morgan Evans, 1710–37, also vicar of Weobley (Herefs.), and Peregrine Ball, 1746–94, also vicar of Trelleck (Mon.). Curates were regularly appointed at Newland.[5] Payler Matthew Procter, vicar 1803–22,[6] also served Coleford chapel at the start of his incumbency and was one of the first of the local clergy to concern themselves with the inhabitants of the extraparochial Forest.[7] In 1832 George Ridout, the lecturer since 1813, was instituted vicar and held both offices until his death in 1871.[8]

The lecturers of Newland received a salary of £33 6s. 8d. from 1714 after the resolution of financial problems of the Jones charity and litigation between the parish and the Haberdashers' Company, and the salary had been doubled by 1739. The lecturers had been provided with a dwelling since the foundation of the charity.[9] Their duties in the early 19th century, and presumably from the beginning, included preaching in the church each Sunday,[10] and several of the lecturers also served as curate at Bream chapel.[11] Under a Scheme of 1922 the lecturer's salary was fixed at £80, for which he was required to preach each Sunday, subject to the vicar's consent, and to supervise and serve as chaplain the almspeople supported by the charity. The same duties were required under a Scheme of 1973, and a lecturer was still maintained by the Haberdashers at a modest stipend in 1992.[12]

In 1825 a former barkhouse near the river at Lower Redbrook hamlet was converted as a mission chapel and schoolroom for that part of the parish, and in 1851 one service was held there each Sunday.[13] It was replaced in 1873 by a new chapel of ease, dedicated to St. Saviour, standing on the east side of the road between the hamlets of Upper and Lower Redbrook. Designed by J. P. Seddon,[14] the chapel is aligned north–south and comprises chancel with west transept and nave with south-west bell turret and west porch. In 1992 one Sunday service was held in each of the three buildings of the united benefice, the parish church, Clearwell church, and Redbrook chapel.[15]

When granting the tithes of new assarts to the bishop of Llandaff in 1305 Edward I required him to establish a chantry at Newland for the benefit of the king and his ancestors.[16] The chantry, called King Edward's service, continued until the dissolution of chantries in 1548, when the chantry priest was said to be required to assist the vicar in his duties when necessary. The annual income, in the form of a stipend paid by the bishop or his lessee of the rectory tithes, was then £5 6s. 8d.[17] A chantry dedicated to the Virgin Mary had been established in the church by 1458 when lands and rents, apparently its endowment, were transferred to feoffees.[18] In 1548, when its endowment was worth £7 17s. 6d. a year, the priest was required as part of his duties to visit the forges and mines in the parish twice a week and read the Gospel there.[19] No evidence has been found to support the suggestion that its founder was John Greyndour (or Chin)[20] whose new chapel in the church was mentioned in 1415, but in view of his ownership of mines in Noxon that is a possibility.[21]

In 1446 Joan Greyndour founded a chantry, called Robert Greyndour's chantry, for the benefit of her late husband and other members of his and her families. It was housed in the family chapel of St. John the Baptist and St. Nicholas in the parish church and endowed with over 200 a. of land in Newland and Lydney, including the house called Blackbrook as the priest's residence. Joan made detailed regulations for the observance of the priest, who was also to teach a school,[22] and she continued to exercise a close supervision, altering the regulations at least twice.[23] Her many pious donations at her death in 1485 included a cross, chalice, and other equipment for use in the chapel.[24] The patronage was exercised by her successors to the Clearwell estate.[25] The Greyndour chantry's lands, valued at £11 14s. 6d. in 1548,[26] were sold by the Crown to (Sir) William Winter of Lydney in 1559;[27] the descent of those in Newland is traced above.[28]

The parish church of *ALL SAINTS*, which bore that dedication by 1305,[29] is a large, prominently sited building. It is built of coursed rubble and ashlar and comprises chancel with side chapels, an aisled and clerestoried nave with south chapel and south porch, and a west tower.

There are no obvious remains of the original, early 13th-century church,[30] but a weathering on the east face of the tower probably indicates its roof line and the relatively short nave may preserve its length. The tower was begun in the

2 Hockaday Abs. ccxcvi.
3 Warlow, *Char. of Wm. Jones*, 273–4, 277; Hockaday Abs. ccxcvi, 1662.
4 Hockaday Abs. ccxcvi.
5 Ibid. ccxcvii.
6 Ibid.
7 Above, Coleford, churches; below, Forest of Dean, churches (Christ Church).
8 Warlow, *Char. of Wm. Jones*, 286–8.
9 Ibid. 54, 62–5, 266–7, 282–3.
10 G.D.R. vol. 383, no. cxxiii.
11 Below, this section.
12 Glos. R.O., D 3469/5/112; inf. from char. assistant, Haberdashers' Co.
13 P.R.O., HO 129/577/1/3/5; Glos. R.O., D 637/I/87; D 639/14.
14 *Kelly's Dir. Glos.* (1889), 851; *Glouc. Jnl.* 26 Aug. 1873.

15 Notice at Newland ch.
16 *Cal. Pat.* 1301–7, 319.
17 *Trans. B.G.A.S.* viii. 292; Hockaday Abs. ccxcv, 1548.
18 Glos. R.O., D 1677/GG 251.
19 *Trans B.G.A.S.* viii. 292; for its endowment, P.R.O., E 310/14/50, f. 33.
20 *Trans. B.G.A.S.* lv. 221.
21 P.R.O., PROB 11/2B (P.C.C. 37 Marche), f. 289v.
22 *Reg. Spofford*, 281–8; *Cal. Pat.* 1441–6, 388, 446–7.
23 *Reg. Stanbury*, 21–33, 105–10.
24 Hockaday Abs. ccxcv.
25 *Reg. Bothe*, 334, 382.
26 *Trans. B.G.A.S.* viii. 292.
27 *Cal. Pat.* 1558–60, 359; Glos. R.O., D 421/19/21.
28 Above, manors.
29 *Reg. Swinfield*, 417.
30 Above, this section.

late 13th century, and the chancel, the chapel south of it, the arcades and aisles, and the south porch are mainly the product of a major rebuilding programme in the earlier 14th. A licence granted in 1332 to the bishop of Llandaff to dedicate two altars when the parishioners required him to do so presumably marks a stage in the rebuilding.[31] The upper stages of the tower, surmounted by corner pinnacles with a larger pinnacle at the head of the stair-turret, are of the late 14th century or early 15th. The north chapel and that east of the porch were added in the 15th century, when the east window and windows in the south aisle were remodelled. The north arcade appears to have been reconstructed in the early 16th century, when the piers were heightened and a rood stair incorporated in the east respond. The original, low clerestory, which included windows over the chancel arch,[32] may also have been added then. Before its mid 19th-century restoration the church was described as having principal features of the Third Pointed (or perpendicular) period.[33] A small building with a chimney that was attached to the north-east corner of the chancel by the late 18th century was presumably a post-medieval vestry.[34] It was replaced in the early 19th century by a new vestry occupying the angle of the chancel and north chapel.[35]

Between 1861 and 1863 a very thorough restoration of Newland church was carried out under William White, who renewed many of its features in the appropriate early 14th-century and 15th-century styles. Apart from the tower, the building was in a poor condition and it was thought necessary to reconstruct much of the chancel, the chancel arch, parts of both arcades, and the north aisle wall. Buttresses were added, new roofs were put on, and the clerestory was heightened. The north-east vestry was demolished, and a west gallery, probably that installed in 1686, a gallery pew in the north chapel, and other post-medieval fittings were removed.[36]

Of the church's three chapels, that of the earlier 14th century on the south side of the chancel was by tradition built by John Joce (fl. 1338, 1349),[37] and in 1446, when it bore the dedication to St. John the Baptist and St. Nicholas, a successor to his estate, Joan Greyndour, founded the Greyndour chantry there.[38] After the dissolution of the chantry, it remained the private chapel and burial place of the owners of the Clearwell estate.[39] A table tomb in the south

aisle with effigies of an armoured knight and a lady is evidently for Joce and his wife and may have been moved from the chapel when it became a chantry. The head of the male effigy rests on a helm surmounted by a saracen's head, the Joce family crest.[40] A tomb in the chapel has brasses representing Robert Greyndour (d. 1443) and his wife Joan. The tomb was later inscribed with the name of Sir Christopher Baynham, a mid 16th-century owner of Clearwell, and a small brass with a heraldic crest, usually known as the 'miner's brass', was inserted. The crest depicts, standing on a helm, a Forest of Dean miner with a candle-holder clenched in his teeth, a mattock in his hand, and a hod on his back.[41] Its significance is not clear but it may have been used as a crest by the Baynhams in the 16th century, the subject chosen because of their mining interests in Noxon and elsewhere: there was once a similar device in a window at the manor house of Bledisloe, in Awre, which the family also owned.[42]

The origins of the chapels north of the chancel and east of the south porch are obscure. On architectural grounds either could be the new chapel of John Greyndour mentioned in his will of 1415,[43] and no firm evidence has been found to support the suggestion that the former housed St. Mary's chantry and the latter King Edward's.[44] By the mid 17th century the north chapel belonged to the Highmeadow estate and members of the Hall family were buried there.[45] The chapel by the porch belonged to the Probyns of Newland House by 1733 and Sir Edmund Probyn (d. 1742) was buried there,[46] commemorated by a bust.[47] The Probyns retained their right to it after 1813 when they sold Newland House, whose new owner Philip Ducarel leased,[48] and in 1822 bought, the right to the Highmeadow estate chapel.[49]

Apart from the Joce and Greyndour tombs, mentioned above, the church contains a collection of early effigies, most moved from their original sites. In relief on slabs are effigies of a lady of the late 13th century, a pair of civilian figures of the 14th century, a priest of the 14th century, and a priest of the 15th century.[50] Two monuments brought into the church from the churchyard in the mid 20th century commemorate holders of Forest offices. The tomb of John Wyrall (d. 1457), a forester who held one of a group of serjeanties attached to St. Briavels manor,[51] depicts him in effigy with the accoutre-

[31] *Reg. T. de Charlton*, 14.
[32] Photog. of ch. before restoration (at Newland ch. in 1992), reproduced above, Plate 35.
[33] *Glos. Ch. Notes*, 65–6.
[34] Bigland, *Glos.* ii, plate at pp. 256–7; cf. Glos. R.O., P 227/VE 2/1, min. 1735.
[35] Photog. of ch. before restoration.
[36] *Trans. R.I.B.A* (1863–4), 29–42; for the gallery, Glos. R.O., P 227/CW 2/1, acct. 1686.
[37] Atkyns, *Glos.* 573; for Joce and his successors, above, manors.   [38] *Reg. Spofford*, 281–2.
[39] Atkyns, *Glos.* 573; Bigland, *Glos.* ii. 258, 261.
[40] Roper, *Glos. Effigies*, 446–8; for the crest, cf. seals on Glos. R.O., D 1677/GG 113; D 2244/60.
[41] For a full description of the tomb, J. Maclean, 'Notes on the Greyndour Chapel and Chantry', *Trans. B.G.A.S.* vii. 117–25; for the miner's brass, above, Plate 26.
[42] Bodl. MS. Rawl. B. 323, f. 101, which describes 'a tawny or ore coloured man with a stick in his mouth, cleft

at one end, a flaming candle in the cleft'.
[43] P.R.O., PROB 11/2B (P.C.C. 37 Marche), f. 289v.
[44] Modern acounts of the ch. are often based on C. Fortescue–Brickdale, 'Newland in the Middle Ages', *Trans. B.G.A.S.* lv. 204–27, which makes unsupported assumptions about its hist., fails to identify the testator of 1415 as Greyndour, and misinterprets the will's mention of a chamber over the gate of Greyndour's house as referring to the ch. porch.
[45] Bigland, *Glos.* ii. 258, 263; Atkyns, *Glos.* 574.
[46] Glos. R.O., D 23/F 1; Bigland, *Glos.* ii. 258, 262.
[47] Roper, *Glos. Effigies*, 456–7.
[48] Glos. R.O., D 2091/E 2, acknowledgment about ownership of a pew 11 Nov. 1816; cf. above, manors.
[49] Glos. R.O., D 34/9/64.
[50] Roper, *Glos. Effigies*, 444–5, 449–50, 453–4.
[51] *Cal. Pat.* 1446–52, 415; cf. below, St. Briavels, manors. A rhyming couplet, naming him as Jenkin Wyrall and perhaps added later, no longer survives: Atkyns, *Glos.* 574.

ments of his office including a short sword, a hunting horn, and at his feet a hound.[52] A slab incised with the figure of a man in mid 17th-century dress with a longbow and arrow[53] probably depicts a holder of the office of bow-bearer; the office was attached to the chief forestership that the owners of Clearwell held in right of Hathaways manor, in St. Briavels.[54]

The font is dated 1661 and has an octagonal bowl and base of stone, its panels decorated with shields and other devices in a rustic style.[55] The church has a brass chandelier, apparently acquired in 1724 or 1725.[56] The reredos in the chapel south of the chancel was painted c. 1930 by the artist Eleanor Fortescue-Brickdale (d. 1945), whose family lived in the village.[57] The church's five bells were increased to six in 1701.[58] In 1992 the ring comprised: (i) recast by William Blews & Sons of Birmingham 1875; (ii) by John Pennington 1660; (iii) by Abraham Rudhall 1701, recast by the Loughborough foundry 1936; (iv, v, and tenor) recast by Abraham Rudhall 1728.[59] The plate includes a chalice and paten cover of 1606 and a tankard flagon of 1802.[60] The parish registers survive from 1560, except that baptisms and burials for the years 1753–82 are missing.[61] In the churchyard the steps and socket of a substantial 14th-century cross may be the remains of the village cross that once stood in the roadway by the north-east entrance to the churchyard.[62] In 1864 a new socket, copied from the original, and shaft and head were placed on the steps.[63] The extensive collection of carved headstones includes an unusual number of small, late 17th-century stones, as well as a wide variety from the Georgian period in the local Forest styles.

A chapel at Bream, which had the dedication to *ST. JAMES* by 1742,[64] was recorded from 1505 when it was being served by a chaplain.[65] In 1618 the chapel and its yard, called Chapel Hay, were in private ownership, that of Thomas Donning, who later conveyed them to trustees to hold as an independent chapel for the use of the inhabitants of Bream tithing. James Gough (d. 1691), owner of the Pastor's Hill estate, gave land at Stroat, in Tidenham, from the deaths of himself and his wife Mary (d. c. 1700) for the poor of the tithing and to provide 5s. each Sunday for a preacher in the chapel. William Powlett (d. 1703), owner of the Prior's Mesne Lodge estate, gave leasehold lands in Aylburton to provide 2s. 6d. each Sunday for a deacon to

read prayers and, if necessary, preach, but gave his trustees the option of applying the gift with Gough's. The three gifts were later administered by a single body of trustees[66] who allowed the curate serving the chapel to receive all the rents of the land until 1816 when, in a more correct performance of their trusts, the surplus of Gough's gift was assigned to the poor and the rent of Chapel Hay was applied as a repair fund for the chapel. That left the curate with an annual income of £34 from the charities.[67] In addition two augmentations to the living had been given by Queen Anne's Bounty, £200 in 1752 and £200 to meet a like benefaction in 1786.[68] The living was described as a perpetual curacy in 1801.[69] After being rebuilt in 1824 the chapel was conveyed by the trustees to the vicar of Newland, and in 1826 the chapel and yard were consecrated by the bishop.[70]

In 1854 a consolidated chapelry of Bream was formed, comprising the principal part of Bream tithing and an adjoining part of the Forest ecclesiastical district of St. Paul's.[71] The living, which was later styled a vicarage, was worth £53 a year in 1856.[72] Between 1861 and 1863 it was augmented by private benefactions and grants from the Ecclesiastical Commissioners' common fund,[73] and in 1873 the bishop of Llandaff released to it the rectorial tithe rent charges of the part of Newland included in the chapelry.[74] In 1887 the living was worth £320.[75] A glebe house was built in 1861.[76]

James Gough evidently intended that the preacher at Bream should remain independent of Newland church, providing that the whole proceeds of his gift should go to the poor if the vicar of Newland attempted to interfere in the appointment of the preacher; it was said, however, that Mary Gough gave 5s. a week during her lifetime to the vicar so that his curate could do the duty.[77] The chapel trustees and the vicar were disputing the right of nomination in 1743 when the diocesan bishop licensed a curate to serve the chapel.[78] The surviving chapel trustee nominated to the living in 1801, but the vicar nominated in 1813 and 1819.[79] In 1854 the advowson of the consolidated chapelry was assigned to the bishop.[80]

In the 17th century some of the lecturers of Newland served Bream chapel on an occasional basis.[81] Thomas Jekyll, lecturer from 1676, preached there and his successor in 1681, Humphrey Jordan, undertook to preach there as often as he could.[82] In 1743 the lecturer James Birt was licensed to the chapel, which he served until

52 Roper, *Glos. Effigies*, 450–3, which is mistaken in saying that he held a woodwardship of one of the Forest bailiwicks.
53 Ibid. 454–5, where he is identified, with no supporting evidence, as a member of the Wyrall fam.
54 Below, St. Briavels, manors.
55 *Trans. B.G.A.S.* xlvii. 189.
56 Ibid. lxxxi. 123–4.
57 Ibid. lv. 223; cf. *Who Was Who, 1941–50*, 402; *Glos. Countryside*, July 1932, 50.
58 Glos. R.O., P 227/CW 2/1.
59 *Glos. Ch. Bells*, 446–7.
60 *Glos. Ch. Plate*, 155.
61 Glos. R.O., P 227/IN 1/1–10.
62 Above, intro.
63 Pooley, *Glos. Crosses*, 65–7.
64 Glos. R.O., D 33/349.
65 *Reg. Mayew*, 68.
66 Glos. R.O., D 33/349; for the Goughs, above, manors;

for Powlett, above, Lydney, manors.
67 *19th Rep. Com. Char.* 104.
68 Hodgson, *Queen Anne's Bounty* (1845), p. cclxxxiii.
69 Hockaday Abs. cxxxii.
70 G.D.R. vol. 351, pp. 49–53.
71 *Lond. Gaz.* 16 June 1854, p. 1863; cf. Glos. R.O., P 348/CW 3/1.
72 G.D.R. vol. 384, f. 28.
73 *Lond. Gaz.* 15 Oct. 1861, p. 4067; 22 July 1862, p. 3653; 12 June 1863, p. 3023.
74 Glos. R.O., P 57/IN 3/2.
75 *Crockford* (1887), 306.
76 *Kelly's Dir. Glos.* (1889), 681.
77 Glos. R.O., D 33/349.
78 G.D.R. vol. 381A, f. 5; Hockaday Abs. cxxxii.
79 Hockaday Abs. cxxxii.
80 *Lond. Gaz.* 16 June 1854, p. 1863.
81 Glos. R.O., D 33/349.
82 Warlow, *Char. of Wm. Jones*, 280–1.

his death in 1801, when his son Thomas (d. 1813), who had succeeded him in the lectureship, was licensed.[83] In 1750 a single service was being held in the chapel each Sunday[84] and there were apparently no communion services until c. 1819 when Bishop Ryder ordered that they should be held at the three main festivals.[85] The chapel was used for baptisms, including from the late 18th century many for inhabitants of the adjoining part of the Forest. Some burials took place in the 1790s, presumably in the chapel itself rather than its yard,[86] which was made a burial ground after the consecration of the chapel in 1826.[87] Marriages were not performed until the creation of the consolidated chapelry.[88] Henry Poole, who was founder and first incumbent of St. Paul's church at Parkend,[89] also held the cure of Bream from 1819 until 1854. He and Cornelius Witherby, appointed to the cure in 1858,[90] provided schools and improved church accommodation for the inhabitants of the Newland and Forest parts of the Bream area.[91]

Bream chapel was rebuilt in 1824 to the designs of the curate Henry Poole.[92] Funds were collected by means of a brief licensed by the Crown, which itself contributed £250.[93] The small stone building included a tower with a cupola.[94] It was partly rebuilt in 1861, when a new chancel, north aisle, south porch, and south-west bellcot were added to the original nave. Much of the cost was met by Alice Davies,[95] sister of the former deputy surveyor of the Forest of Dean, Edward Machen.[96] In 1891 a north chapel was added to the chancel and the south porch was moved from the centre to near the west end of the nave.[97] The font has an octagonal bowl on a slender pillar and apparently dates from the 17th century.[98] The single bell in the bellcot was replaced or recast in 1901.[99] The plate includes a chalice and paten cover given to the old chapel by James and Mary Gough in 1680, and a set of 1854 by John Keith, given by Edward Machen in 1855.[1] The registers survive from 1751 for baptisms, 1827 for burials, and 1855 for marriages.[2]

At Clearwell a chapel of ease, dedicated to *ST. PETER*, was built in 1830 through the efforts of the vicar Henry Douglas and the lecturer George Ridout,[3] and the site at the east end of the village was given by Kedgwin Hoskins of Platwell.[4] The cost was met by a grant of £400 from the Church Building Society and £950 raised by subscription. A small endowment of land brought in an income of £15 a year in 1851.[5] In 1856 a consolidated chapelry of Clearwell was formed, including also an adjoining part of the ecclesiastical district of St. Paul in the Forest.[6] The endowments of the new living included part of the vicar of Newland's tithe rent charge[7] and £800 raised by subscription,[8] and a further £1,000 was donated in 1860.[9] The patronage was assigned to the countess of Dunraven and reverted to the bishop of Gloucester at her death in 1870.[10] In 1866 a new church was built at the cost of the countess near the gate of Clearwell Court, and the old church was demolished and a small mortuary chapel built on part of the site,[11] which remained in use as a burial ground. The living was declared a vicarage in 1866,[12] and in 1873 was augmented by the remainder of the vicarage tithe rent charges for the area and those of the rectory.[13] It had a net annual value of £300 in 1887.[14] A vicarage house was built before 1870[15] and was sold after the union of the benefice with Newland in 1981.[16]

The chapel built in 1830 was a small brick building,[17] designed by George Maddox of Monmouth.[18] The new church of 1866 was designed in the high Victorian style by John Middleton of Cheltenham[19] and is built of dark Forest sandstone with Bath stone dressings. It comprises chancel with north organ chamber, aisled and clerestoried nave with a timber south porch, and south-west tower with spire. The interior is richly decorated and furnished. A ring of four bells was provided in 1869 by John Warner & Sons of London.[20] A set of new plate and an almsdish of c. 1755 were given to the old chapel by the countess of Dunraven in 1855.[21] The organ installed in the new church in 1866 was brought from her family's house at Adare (co. Limerick) and was made c. 1820 by a Dublin firm.[22] The registers survive for baptisms from 1830 and for marriages and burials from 1856.[23]

NONCONFORMITY. Within the ancient parish of Newland the main seat of nonconformity was Coleford town.[24] Meetings recorded in the parochial lands at Bream and Yorkley in the early 19th century[25] presumably drew part of

83 Ibid. 283–5; Hockaday Abs. cxxxii.
84 G.D.R. vol. 381A, f. 5.   85 Ibid. 382, f. 21.
86 Glos. R.O., P 57/IN 1/1.
87 Ibid. IN 1/17; G.D.R. vol. 351, p. 53.
88 Glos. R.O., P 57/IN 1/8.
89 Below, Forest of Dean, churches.
90 Hockaday Abs. cxxxii.
91 Below, Forest of Dean, educ. (elem. schs.); below, this section.
92 P.R.O., HO 129/577/1/1/1; Colvin, *Biog. Dict. Brit. Architects* (1978), 650.
93 Hockaday Abs. cxxxii, 1820; *3rd Rep. Dean Forest Com.* 6.   94 *Kelly's Dir. Glos.* (1856), 233.
95 Ibid. (1889), 681.
96 *Trans. B.G.A.S.* lxiv, pedigree at pp. 96–7; cf. below, Forest of Dean, educ. (elem. schs.: Parkend; Bream).
97 *Kelly's Dir. Glos.* (1923), 53.
98 *Trans. B.G.A.S.* xlvii. 179, 184.
99 *Kelly's Dir. Glos.* (1889), 681; *Glos. Ch. Bells*, 163.
1 *Glos. Ch. Plate*, 28.
2 Glos. R.O., P 57/IN 1/1–19.

3 *Glouc. Jnl.* 30 Jan. 1830; P.R.O., HO 129/577/1/2/4.
4 Glos. R.O., P 88/IN 1/1, note at front; G.D.R., T 1/128.   5 P.R.O., HO 129/577/1/2/4.
6 *Lond. Gaz.* 18 Apr. 1856, pp. 1464–5.
7 Glos. R.O., P 88/IN 3/1, deed 29 Sept. 1873.
8 Hodgson, *Queen Anne's Bounty* (suppl. 1864), pp. xli, lxvi.   9 Glos. R.O., P 88/IN 3/5.
10 *Lond. Gaz.* 18 Apr. 1856, p. 1465.
11 *Kelly's Dir. Glos.* (1870), 524; Glos. R.O., P 88/CW 3/1.
12 *Lond. Gaz.* 29 June 1866, p. 3740.
13 Glos. R.O., P 88/IN 3/1.
14 *Crockford* (1887), 934.
15 *Kelly's Dir. Glos.* (1870), 524.   16 Above, this section.
17 *Kelly's Dir. Glos.* (1856), 269.
18 Colvin, *Biog. Dict. Brit. Architects*, 534.
19 *Illustrated Times*, 16 Feb. 1867, p. 99.
20 *Glos. Ch. Bells*, 231–2.   21 *Glos. Ch. Plate*, 54–5.
22 *Trans. B.G.A.S.* xciii. 171.
23 Glos. R.O., P 88/IN 1/1–8.
24 Above, Coleford, prot. nonconf.
25 Hockaday Abs. cxxxii, 1821, 1827, 1833; ccxcvii, 1815, 1827.

their congregations from the growing hamlets in the adjoining Forest.[26]

At Clearwell a Congregational meeting was licensed in 1672 at the house of John Skinner, who had been ejected from the livings of Weston under Penyard and Hope Mansell (both Herefs.).[27] The Baptists of Coleford registered houses in Clearwell village in 1818 and 1819[28] but their cause does not seem to have long survived there. A Primitive Methodist preaching room was built in the village in 1836. In 1851 it was served by a minister from Monmouth and the congregations at morning, afternoon, and of evening services averaged 40, 64, and 80 respectively.[29] A new chapel was built in 1852[30] and continued in use as a Methodist chapel until c. 1977.[31]

At Lower Redbrook hamlet a former barkhouse, which was bought by John Taylor in 1808 and converted as a chapel before 1814,[32] was probably the building below the tinplate works that was used as a Wesleyan Methodist chapel in 1848.[33] In 1851 the Wesleyan chapel had average congregations of 80 in the morning and 150 in the evening.[34] It closed before 1895,[35] but it had apparently reopened by 1920[36] and a Methodist group was meeting in the hamlet between c. 1950 and c. 1971.[37]

EDUCATION. A grammar school was attached to the chantry founded in Newland church in 1446 by Joan Greyndour for her husband Robert. She directed that the chaplain and a suitably qualified clerk employed by him should instruct pupils, of whom those learning Latin grammar were to pay 8d. a quarter and those learning the alphabet, the service of matins, and the psalter 4d. a quarter. Roger Ford, the chaplain at the dissolution of the chantry in 1547, enjoyed a good reputation as a teacher and his school was well attended. It was continued for some years at least, Ford receiving a stipend from the Court of Augmentations until 1553 or 1554.[38]

A schoolmaster recorded at Newland in 1576[39] was presumably teaching a school supported by Edward Bell, who by his will in that year gave funds to finish building the school which he had begun.[40] Another schoolmaster, a graduate, died at Newland in 1592.[41] A trust deed secured Bell's charity in 1627, assigning £10 a year as the salary of a master to teach grammar,[42] and the school continued in a house on the west side of Newland churchyard. Regulations in 1658 laid down a basic curriculum comprising only reading, writing, and the catechism, but further studies,

to be pursued in accordance with the ability of individual pupils, evidently included Latin, as candidates for the mastership had to be competent to teach 'a free grammar school'. Entrants to the school had to show that they could already read a chapter of the bible, but, after complaints that that qualification excluded many poor children, it was changed in 1663 to the reading of a psalm.[43] A gift from John Whitson, which became payable in 1663, added £10 to the master's salary.[44] John Symons (d. 1721) of Clearwell, intending to discourage beneficed clergymen or curates from taking the post, gave £100 to buy land to augment the salary, with a proviso that the profits should go to the almspeople of Bell's charity if a clergyman was appointed.[45] The masters were usually laymen during the late 17th century and the early 18th, but from c. 1800 clergymen were usually appointed and were allowed to supplement their salary by taking private pupils.[46] Regulations of 1817 fixed the number of boys to be educated on the foundation at 15, aged between 7 and 14 years, with private pupils to be taken only in such numbers as would not unduly divert the master's attention. The curriculum was to include Latin grammar, the catechism, and the principles of religion, with English grammar, writing, and arithmetic to be taught if the parents so wished, and public examination of the pupils was introduced. From 1814 the master's salary was £30 and from 1835 £75. In 1836, because of a dwindling demand for charity places, there was an abortive scheme to turn the school into a fee-paying academy offering commercial education. Only 5 charity boys were attending in 1837 and there were 12 in 1847.[47] The school suffered as a result of the financial and administrative problems of the charity during the mid 19th century, and in 1876 it was transferred to new premises at Coleford. The school building beside Newland churchyard, later called the Old School House, had been sold the previous year.[48]

In 1712 there were six charity schools at Newland, presumably dispersed among its various hamlets. The schools were supported by subscriptions, which paid for teaching a total of c. 108 children and clothing 25 of the poorest.[49] Probably they had been founded through the efforts of Francis Wyndham, owner of the Clearwell estate, who was an early supporter of the S.P.C.K.[50] It is not known how long the charity schools survived, but there was a parish school or dame school at Newland village in 1735 when a woman was given permission to teach in the vestry room of the church.[51]

26 Below, Forest of Dean, prot. nonconf.
27 *Calamy Revised*, ed. A. G. Matthews, 444.
28 Hockaday Abs. clviii; cf. C. E. Hart, *Coleford* (1983), 10–11.
29 P.R.O., HO 129/577/1/2/3.   30 Date on bldg.
31 Glos. R.O., D 2598/16/7.
32 Newland Valley est. deeds, abs. of title of John Taylor 1824; cf. Hockaday Abs. cxcvii, 1811.
33 Glos. R.O., D 639/14.
34 P.R.O., HO 129/577/1/3/8.
35 G.R.O. Worship Reg. no. 5346.
36 O.S. Map 1/2,500, Glos. XXXVIII. 6 (1921 edn.).
37 G.R.O. Worship Reg. no. 62634.
38 For a fuller account, *V.C.H. Glos.* ii. 409–16, where the writer did not know of the foundation deed, in *Reg.*

Spofford, 281–8.
39 Hockaday Abs. xlvii, 1576 visit. f. 124.
40 For the general hist. of Bell's char., below, char.
41 Glos. R.O., P 227/IN 1/1.
42 Ibid. D 34/9/1.   43 Ibid. 2/1.
44 Ibid.; G.D.R., V 5/214T 3; cf. below, char.
45 N.L.W., Mynde Park MS. 1245.
46 Glos. R.O., D 34/2/1; *Glouc. Jnl.* 4 Jan. 1808.
47 Glos. R.O., D 34/2/1.
48 Ibid. 2/5; cf. ibid. D 2091/T 2. For the school's later hist., above, Coleford, educ.
49 *Glos. N. & Q.* i. 294.
50 *A Chapter in Church Hist.: Mins. of S.P.C.K. 1698–1704*, ed. E. McClure (1888), 1, 6, 12, 162.
51 Glos. R.O., P 227/VE 2/1.

Mary Gough, widow of James Gough of Pastor's Hill, by will proved 1700 gave £50 to buy land, the profits of which were to be used to teach poor children of Bream tithing and apprentice one or more child each year.[52] By 1712 another benefaction had been applied with her gift and 23 children were being taught.[53] It was evidently in respect of Mary Gough's gift that in the mid 1820s a rent charge of £2 10s. was being paid to the chapel clerk of Bream, who taught 12 children.[54] Later the charity was applied to the National school established at Bream Tufts in the adjoining part of the Forest. The history of that school and a successor at Bream's Eaves is given below.[55]

In the early 19th century the parish had a number of small dame schools, most of them apparently at Coleford. Sunday schools held at the various villages in 1833 included one in Newland village run by the daughters of Mrs. Yorke of Birchamp House, who also taught girls needlework on weekdays.[56] The history of Newland National school, which was at Whitecliff, is given above under Coleford.[57]

At Clearwell village a National day and Sunday school for infants had been started by 1847 and had a weekday attendance of 42. It was supported by subscriptions and pence.[58] In 1859 a new National school in the road later called Church Road was opened, built mainly at the cost of the countess of Dunraven. As its annual income was supplemented by a small grant from the Commissioners of Woods,[59] it presumably drew some of its pupils from the adjoining Forest. In 1885 the average attendance was 63 in mixed and infants' departments.[60] The school was enlarged in 1867 and 1900,[61] and in 1910, when it was called Clearwell C. of E. school, it had accommodation for 159. The average attendance in 1910 was 135[62] and in 1938 89.[63] In 1992 there were 52 children on the roll.[64]

A building at Lower Redbroook hamlet opened as a chapel of ease in 1825[65] also housed a day and Sunday school. By 1847 it had been affiliated to the National Society, was supported by subscriptions and pence, and taught 25 children on weekdays.[66] In 1861, when about half the cost was met by a grant of £24 a year from the Redbrook Tinplate Co., the average attendance was 55. In 1873 a new National school, built on the south side of the new Redbrook chapel of ease, was opened.[67] The school building was enlarged in 1877, and in 1885 there was an average attendance of 70, forming a single department.[68] In 1910, as the Redbrook C. of E.

school, it had accommodation for 104 and an average attendance, in mixed and infants' departments, of 91.[69] By 1938 the average attendance had fallen to 57,[70] and in 1992 there were 30 children on the roll.[71]

CHARITIES FOR THE POOR. Edward Bell, a native of Newland parish who had become steward to the politician Sir William Petre, by will dated 1576 left funds to complete a school and almshouses which he had begun to build at Newland.[72] His intended endowment was later said to be a rent charge of £20, of which £10 was to pay a schoolmaster, £8 to support four almsmen and four almswomen, and £2 to maintain the buildings, but the endowment was not secured, and the parishioners later took proceedings against Bell's sons and in 1603 obtained a Chancery decree for the payment of the charge. In 1627 Bell's son Edward conveyed a substantial but scattered estate in the parish to trustees to support the payments.[73] The endowment was later augmented by several other gifts, those for the benefit of the almspeople being a meadow devised by Christopher Bond (d. 1668) of Redbrook in respect of a bequest of £50 made by his brother George,[74] a house given by William Bromwich (d. by 1672) of Scatterford,[75] £100 given by a Mrs. Williams before 1786,[76] and £800 bequeathed by Kedgwin Hoskins (d. 1834) of Platwell to be invested in stock.[77] In 1779 the charity owned 101 a. of land, with the almshouses and the schoolhouse;[78] in 1823 the trustees enlarged the endowment by buying Owen farm in Coleford with £1,300 raised by a sale of timber.[79] Under regulations of 1658 the trustees held quarterly meetings and appointed one of their number as 'renter' to carry out the day-to-day administration.[80] The almshouses were rebuilt or enlarged in 1662 and in the following year comprised an old building housing the four men and a new building housing the four women. From 1755 each inmate received 16s. a quarter, raised in 1792 to £1 6s. a quarter. From 1835 each inmate was paid 5s. 7½d. a week and was given a cloak every two years.[81]

In 1858 financial problems of Bell's charity led to a reduction in the pay of the almspeople, and in the mid 1860s dissension among the trustees was followed by the appointment of a new body, including the incumbents of the four churches in the parish, and tighter control of the management of the estate, which had been left almost entirely in the renter's hands, was instituted.[82]

52 G.D.R. wills 1699/29.
53 *Glos. N. & Q.* i. 292–3.
54 *19th Rep. Com. Char.* 104.
55 Forest of Dean, educ. (elem. schs.).
56 *Educ. of Poor Digest,* 304; *Educ. Enq. Abstract,* 322; for Mrs. Yorke, Glos. R.O., D 637/VII/22.
57 Coleford, educ.
58 Nat. Soc. *Inquiry, 1846–7,* Glos. 12–13.
59 P.R.O., ED 7/35/233; *Kelly's Dir. Glos.* (1870), 524.
60 *Kelly's Dir. Glos.* (1885), 430.
61 Ibid. (1923), 133.
62 *Bd. of Educ., List 21, 1911* (H.M.S.O.), 165.
63 Ibid. *1938,* 128.
64 *Schools and Establishments Dir. 1992–3* (co. educ. dept.), 12.
65 Above, churches.
66 Nat. Soc. *Inquiry, 1846–7,* Glos. 13.

67 P.R.O., ED 7/35/234.
68 *Kelly's Dir. Glos.* (1885), 536; (1894), 247.
69 *Bd. of Educ., List 21, 1911,* 165.
70 Ibid. *1938,* 128.
71 *Schools and Establishments Dir. 1992–3,* 28.
72 *Trans. B.G.A.S.* lxxxv. 147–55.
73 Glos. R.O., D 34/9/22; 1/2–4.
74 G.D.R. wills 1668/25.
75 Glos. R.O., D 34/9/25.
76 *19th Rep. Com. Char.* 99.
77 Glos. R.O., D 1896, deeds of Lindors est. 1735–1850, copy of will.
78 Ibid. D 34/6/1.
79 Ibid. 9/69.
80 Ibid. 2/1.
81 Ibid.
82 Ibid. 2/5.

In 1891 the annual income from land and stock was £199.[83] A Scheme of 1908 divided the foundation into the Educational Charity of Edward Bell and Others which managed the endowment and ran the school, by then based at Coleford, and the Pension Charity of Edward Bell and Others which was given the almshouses and £65 a year from the endowment. The Educational Charity sold the charity lands c. 1919 and invested the proceeds in stock. In 1908 it was intended that the Pension Charity should dispose of the almshouses and provide pensions for poor people of the ancient parish, but instead it continued to maintain the almshouses, and that application was confirmed by a Scheme of 1961. Under a Scheme of 1968, however, the building was sold and the proceeds and the £65 a year were applied as a general 'relief in need' charity for the ancient parish.[84] The almshouses, a two-storeyed building on the north side of the churchyard, apparently date mainly from an 18th-century rebuilding. Each storey originally had four almsrooms, but in 1992 the building was occupied as a single private house.

William Jones, a Hamburg merchant and probably a native of Newland, by will proved 1615 gave £5,000 to the Haberdashers' Company for the use of the poor of Newland and for the maintenance of a lecturer there. Almshouses were built in Newland village in 1617 and letters patent securing the charity in 1620 ordained that 16 almspeople should be maintained.[85] Under statutes drawn up in 1655 the almspeople were to be supervised by the lecturer and given 2s. a week and cloth for a gown every other year.[86] The Haberdashers' Company bought two farms at Eynesbury (Hunts.) as an endowment for the charity but in 1675, when the company was in severe financial difficulties, it sold them and used the proceeds to buy in leases of its estate of Hatcham Barnes (Kent), which was intended to be applied to support the charity and a similar one founded by Jones at Monmouth. Payments to Newland later lapsed and in 1701 the parishioners obtained a Chancery decree that the Haberdashers should provide £200 a year to support the almshouses and lecturer. Payments were not regularly resumed until 1714 when it was agreed that the alsmspeople should receive 1s. a week. At the instance of Judge Edmund Probyn of Newland the Haberdashers later increased their support and the almspeople received 2s. a week from 1739. Their pay was raised to 3s. in 1813[87] and 7s. in 1893.[88] A Scheme of 1922 provided for between 10 and 16 almspeople to be chosen by the Haberdashers on the nomination of a local committee and supervised by the lecturer; married couples were to be allowed.[89] A Scheme of 1973 widened the qualification to include those who had lived for at least two years in the civil parishes of Newland, Coleford, West Dean, and Lydbrook. In 1992 there were 11 almspeople, who made weekly contributions in aid of their maintenance.[90]

The almshouses of the Jones charity comprise a long, single-storeyed range on the south side of Newland churchyard. By 1840 they were divided as 10 dwellings[91] and presumably, as in the 1890s, six each housed two almspeople. By tradition there was once a full set of 16 almshouses until some were destroyed in a fire. A slightly larger dwelling attached to the west end of the range was apparently built to house the charity's lecturer,[92] but by 1840 he occupied a substantial early 18th-century house, later called the Lecturage, standing near the east end of the almshouses. Whether it was built by the charity, which seems unlikely in view of the financial problems of the early 18th century, or given to it is not known. The Lecturage was sold by the Haberdashers in 1963,[93] and in 1992 the lecturer occupied the dwelling at the west end of the almshouses.

By will dated 1611 Thomas Baynham, owner of the Clearwell estate, allowed two women to continue to live rent-free in a house which he owned, giving it from their deaths as an almshouse for two poor widows.[94] How long it remained in use is not known, but c. 1700 a later owner of the estate, Francis Wyndham, built an almshouse for four widows, to each of whom he made an allowance of 1s. a week and a set of clothes every other year.[95] Wyndham's almshouse was presumably that in four occupations owned by the estate in the 19th century at the north-west end of Clearwell village near Stank Farm.[96] It went out of use in the early 20th century, and in 1918 trustees were appointed to sell it. In 1939 £25 in stock and bonds were held in respect of it, the income from which was assigned to be distributed to two widows.[97]

The poor of Newland received £20 a year from a charity founded for Newland and Staunton by Henry Hall (d. 1645).[98] In the 1820s it was distributed to old people in sums of 10s.–12s., two thirds of it in Clearwell tithing and a third in Newland tithing.[99] John Whitson (d. 1629), a Bristol alderman and merchant venturer, charged property in Bristol with £12 a year for the poor of Clearwell, his birthplace, and with the bequest for Bell's grammar school mentioned above.[1] In the 1820s his gift to the poor was distributed in sums of 3s.–14s. William Hoskins by will dated 1661 charged his Stowe Grange estate in St. Briavels with 40s. a year for old people of Newland parish. In the 1820s, however, the distribution was confined to Clearwell tithing.[2] In 1681 a small farm called Old Box in Awre parish was bought with an accu-

83 Glos. R.O., D 34/1/9.
84 Ibid. D 3469/5/112.
85 Warlow, *Char. of Wm. Jones*, 53–4, 265–7.
86 Ibid. 364–7.
87 Ibid. 55–65.
88 Ibid. 288–9.
89 Glos. R.O., D 3469/5/112.
90 Inf. from char. assistant, Haberdashers' Co.
91 G.D.R., T 1/128.
92 Warlow, *Char. of Wm. Jones*, 54, 265, 289, 293.
93 Inf. from archivist, Haberdashers' Co.
94 N.L.W., Dunraven MSS. 271.
95 Bodl. MS. Top. Glouc. c. 3, f. 192v.
96 G.D.R., T 1/128; O.S. Map. 1/2,500, Glos. XXXVIII. 8 (1881 edn.).
97 Glos. R.O., D 3469/5/112.
98 Below, Staunton, char.
99 *19th Rep. Com. Char.* 100.
1 G.D.R., V 5/214T 3; *D.N.B.*
2 *19th Rep. Com. Char.* 88, 100–1.

mulation of funds from the Hall charity, with which the land was later administered. In the mid 1820s it was rented for £50 a year, which, with additional income from the proceeds of a sale of timber, was distributed to the poor of Bream and Coleford tithings.[3]

In 1973 the Hall charity and the charity endowed with Old Box farm were united to to form a general 'relief in need' charity for inhabitants of the ancient parish. In 1975 the Baynham, Whitson, and Hoskins charities were formed into the Clearwell Combined Charity, a relief in need charity for inhabitants of Clearwell.[4]

James Gough (d. 1691), who gave lands in Tidenham to support a payment to a preacher at Bream chapel, gave the surplus income from the lands to the poor of Bream tithing.[5] The whole of the rent was given to the preacher for some years before 1816 when the surplus, then c. £31 a year, was redirected to the poor together with the income from the proceeds of a timber sale.[6] In 1906, when the land produced a total of £51 a year, the two parts of the charity were divided into ecclesiastical and non-ecclesiastical charities. Thomas Hill by deed of 1877 gave a cottage and garden for the poor of the part of Bream ecclesiastical parish that lay in the Forest of Dean. In 1973 the Gough non-ecclesiastical charity and the Hill charity, both by then drawing their income from stock and bonds, were amalgamated into a general relief in need charity for the inhabitants of Bream ecclesiastical parish.[7]

RUARDEAN

RUARDEAN, a largely rural parish but much affected by mining and other industrial activity, lies on the boundary with Herefordshire 7 km. SSE. of Ross-on-Wye (Herefs.). Accounted part of the Herefordshire hundred of Bromsash in 1086[8] but later in Gloucestershire and part of the Forest of Dean,[9] Ruardean was, as a parish, roughly rectangular in shape, extending eastwards from the river Wye to a stream called Dry brook and having extraparochial land of the Forest to the south and east.[10] The river Wye marked the parish boundary downstream to the village of Lydbrook, the lowest part of which was divided between Ruardean and English Bicknor by a tributary stream. At Lydbrook Ruardean included most of a small island in the river, which disappeared in the mid 19th century,[11] and had a small detached piece to the south bounded partly by extraparochial land. Ruardean's northern boundary followed a track running westwards from Dry brook and then turning northwards for a short distance to Bartley's (formerly Bereslys) Oak, which in 1787 marked the county boundary.[12] Land to the north between Dry brook and Bartley's Oak, part of the Crown's ancient demesne woodland,[13] was sometimes said to be in Ruardean[14] but, although it was still regarded as part of the royal forest in 1833,[15] it was later in Hope Mansell parish (Herefs.).[16] Further west the Ruardean boundary followed Lodgegrove (formerly Bishop's) brook, which rose at a place called Ashwell in the 13th century and flowed into the Wye at Bishopswood.[17] Ruardean's long southern boundary, less regular than the others, was marked in places by tracks and old banks along the edge of the extraparochial land,[18] on which the settlements of Ruardean Woodside and, to the east, Ruardean Hill, grew up. In 1787 and 1833 the lords of the manor of Ruardean claimed rights within the Forest at Ruardean Hill.[19]

In the later 1870s, after some minor adjustments in the Forest's boundaries, Ruardean's area was 1,593 a.[20] The detached piece at Lydbrook was consolidated with the rest of the parish in 1884 when Ruardean absorbed two detached pieces of Newland, one containing 22 a. at Lydbrook and the other 14 a. on the southern boundary at Reddings.[21] In 1935 Ruardean lost 142 a. at the south-western corner to the new civil parish of Lydbrook and gained 4 a. from East Dean civil parish. In 1957 Ruardean's boundaries with Drybrook civil parish were adjusted by transferring 21 a. in the east to Drybrook and 95 a. in the south at the Pludds and Knights Hill to Ruardean, which was left with 1,567 a. (634 ha.).[22] The following account deals with the parish as it was constituted before 1884 except for those areas in the east and west forming parts of the villages of Drybrook and Lydbrook, which are treated as part of the Forest of Dean. It does not entirely respect the northern boundary for it includes the history of the Bishopswood ironworks, which were partly in Walford (Herefs.).

The land rises steeply from the river Wye to over 250 m., reaching 290 m. in the south-east near Ruardean hill, and falls at the eastern end to 180 m. Most of the parish is drained by

3   Ibid. 101; G.D.R., V 5/214T 3.
4   Glos. R.O., D 3469/5/112.
5   Ibid. D 33/349.
6   *19th Rep. Com. Char.* 104.
7   Glos. R.O., D 3469/5/112.
8   *Dom. Bk.* (Rec. Com.), i. 185v.; this account was written in 1990.
9   *Trans. B.G.A.S.* lviii. 109; lxvi. 176.
10   P.R.O., MR 415 (F 16/47); *2nd Rep. Dean Forest Com.* 31.
11   Cf. G.D.R., T 1/151; O.S. Map 6", Glos. XXXI. NW. (1883 edn.).
12   P.R.O., MR 415; G.D.R., T 1/151.
13   *Trans. B.G.A.S.* xiv. 365; *Hist. & Cart. Mon. Glouc.* (Rolls Ser.), iii. 234–6.

14   Cf. Glos. R.O., D 1677/GG 556.
15   P.R.O., F 17/17; cf. ibid. MR 415.
16   Glos. R.O., Q/RGf 1/8.
17   *Trans. B.G.A.S.* lxvi. 178–80; cf. N.L.W., Courtfield MSS. 107, ct. 25 Sept. 1647.
18   *2nd Rep. Dean Forest Com.* 30–1.
19   P.R.O., MR 415; *2nd Rep. Dean Forest Com.* 37.
20   O.S. *Area Bk.* (1878); cf. G.D.R., T 1/151; O.S. Maps 6", Glos. XXIII. SE., SW. (1883 edn.); XXXI. NE., NW. (1883–4 edn.).
21   L.G.B. Prov. Orders Conf. (Poor Law) Act, 1883, 46 & 47 Vic. c. 80 (Local); above, Newland, intro. (Table I).
22   *Census*, 1931 (pt. ii); 1961.

streams flowing in deep valleys north-westwards to the Wye or Lodgegrove brook, and the eastern end is drained by Dry brook. The southern part of the parish, where the land falls slightly towards the Forest at Ruardean Woodside, lies on the beds of sandstone and shale forming the Forest of Dean coalfield, of which one of the deepest and most productive seams, the Coleford High Delf, forms an outcrop running through Ruardean from Ruardean hill to Lydbrook. Elsewhere the land is formed mainly by various strata of carboniferous limestone but the underlying Old Red Sandstone outcrops in an area of lower ground at Bishopswood.[23] The coal and limestone have been extensively exploited and deposits of iron ore near Drybrook[24] have also been mined. Clearance of land in Ruardean for cultivation was piecemeal and much land, notably in the east and the south-west, remained uncultivated in the late 13th century.[25] The pattern of small closes in which the land was farmed was completed before 1608.[26] Most of the surviving woodland, extended at 42 a. in 1847[27] and 59 a. in 1905,[28] is in the valley of Lodgegrove brook, and at Bishopswood it includes Catshill wood, recorded from 1647.[29] An area of woodland known in the later 14th century as Goldfinch's grove was also in the north.[30] Some woods also remain in the south-west near Lydbrook. The existence of medieval parkland next to a castle north of Ruardean village is suggested by a field name recorded from 1607.[31]

The village, on a hillside in the centre of the parish, grew up along a route linking Mitcheldean with Lydbrook and Monmouth.[32] Several ancient tracks crossed Dry brook to combine east of the village. One, marking a section of Ruardean's northern boundary, was joined south of Bartley's Oak by another, which was the old county boundary,[33] and east of the village at Varnister by a road which linked the village with Ross-on-Wye in the 15th century.[34] Further south Morse (formerly Haseley) Lane,[35] running west from Drybrook village, had become the principal route from Mitcheldean to Ruardean village by the later 15th century.[36] The route from Ruardean to Lydbrook once followed a track descending past Ragman's Slade to the Wye,[37] where it joined a road running beside the river. That road was also joined by Vention Lane, which emerged from the woodland near Moorwood[38] and apparently took its name from a coal mine known in the later 17th century as New Invention.[39] In the south several ancient routes lead into the Forest. One, running south-west from Ruardean village to the Pludds, was known in 1282 as the smiths' way[40] and, at its southern end, in 1833 as Eddy's Lane.[41] The road running south from the village to Ruardean Woodside (formerly Hanway Eaves)[42] was called Hanway in 1282.[43] At Turner's Tump it was crossed by a track which led south-east to the Forest and was joined below Ruardean hill by a route from the village and Varnister by way of Crooked End,[44] known in 1598 as Diggins (later Walker's) Lane.[45]

In the late 18th century the road beside the river Wye was part of a route between Ross-on-Wye and Coleford.[46] From 1827 the Ruardean section, from Bishopswood to Lydbrook, was maintained by the Dean Forest turnpike trustees,[47] who improved it. In 1841 the trustees built a new road across the parish to link Bishopswood with Nailbridge to the south-east. The road, which incorporated parts of old roads, ran by way of Marstow, the village, and Crooked End and provided a new route from the village to Ross.[48] By that time the track past Ragman's Slade had been replaced as the principal route from the village to Lydbrook by a road branching from the Pludds road for Moorwood and Vention Lane,[49] and a more direct route to Lydbrook opened in 1909 on the completion of a road at Joy's Green.[50] Tollgates were placed near Bishopswood on the Lydbrook and Nailbridge roads,[51] which ceased to be turnpikes in 1888.[52] In the 19th century several mineral railways were laid down in Ruardean.[53] One crossing the eastern end of the parish also carried passengers from Newnham and Cinderford to Drybrook between 1907 and 1930.[54] Waterscross, on the Wye at the foot of Vention Lane, was mentioned by that name from 1642[55] and may have been the site of an ancient river crossing, but its use is not recorded until 1852 when a ferry operated there.[56] Later there was a ferry downstream, just above Lydbrook, to

23 Geol. Surv. Map 1/50,000, solid and drift, sheet 233 (1974 edn.); cf. Geol. of Forest of Dean Coal and Iron-Ore Field (H.M.S.O. 1942), 2.
24 Atkinson, Map of Dean Forest (1847).
25 Trans. B.G.A.S. xiv. 365–6; lviii. 151–4.
26 P.R.O., MR 129 (SP 14/40, no. 88).
27 G.D.R., T 1/151.
28 Acreage Returns, 1905.
29 N.L.W., Courtfield MSS. 107.
30 Heref. R.O., F 8/II/23; Glos. R.O., D 2244/85.
31 N.L.W., Courtfield MSS. 422, 466; G.D.R., T 1/151 (no. 297).
32 Glos. R.O., D 1677/GG 91, 183; Heref. R.O., F 8/II/31, 85.
33 P.R.O., MR 415.
34 Heref. R.O., F 8/II/28; cf. Glos. R.O., Q/RUm 152; O.S. Map 6", Glos. XXXI. NW. (1883 edn.).
35 P.R.O., MR 129.
36 Glos. R.O., D 4431, deed 30 Aug. 22 Edw. IV; cf. ibid. D 1677/GG 594, 881.
37 Ibid. D 1677/GG 91; Heref. R.O., F 8/II/30.
38 Taylor, Map of Glos. (1777).
39 P.R.O., F 17/7.
40 Trans. B.G.A.S. xiv. 365; P.R.O., MR 129.
41 2nd Rep. Dean Forest Com. 30; Glos. R.O., Q/RGf 1/8.
42 Glos. R.O., D 892/T 69; D 1229, Ruardean deeds 1642–1853, deed 18 Oct. 1676.
43 Trans. B.G.A.S. xiv. 365; P.R.O., MR 129.
44 Taylor, Map of Glos. (1777); O.S. Map 6", Glos. XXXI. NW. (1883 edn.).
45 Glos. R.O., D 829/T 69; cf. ibid. D 1677/GG 614; P.R.O., MR 129.
46 Taylor, Map of Glos. (1777).
47 Dean Forest Roads Act, 7 & 8 Geo. IV, c. 12 (Local and Personal).
48 Nicholls, Forest of Dean, 196–7; the new road's route varied from that specified in Dean Forest Roads Act, 1 & 2 Vic. c. 38 (Local and Personal); cf. Glos. R.O., Q/RUm 107, 152.
49 Taylor, Map of Glos. (1777); Greenwood, Map of Glos. (1824).
50 Glos. R.O., DA 24/100/5, pp. 52, 294.
51 G.D.R., T 1/151; P.R.O., HO 107/365.
52 Dean Forest Turnpike Trust Abolition Act, 51 & 52 Vic. c. 193.
53 Below, econ. hist. (other ind. and trade).
54 Below, Forest of Dean, industry (tramroads and railways).
55 N.L.W., Courtfield MSS. 107.
56 Glouc. Jnl. 3 July 1852.

Courtfield, in Welsh Bicknor (Herefs., formerly Mon.), the seat of the Vaughan family and the site of a Roman Catholic chapel.[57] Both ferries no longer operated in 1990.

Ruardean church, dating from the 12th century, stands near the top of the village.[58] Some distance to the north-west was a manor house, which was replaced in the 14th century by a castle. The early cottages were built along the road west of the church and by the 17th century they extended beyond the junction of Caudle Lane,[59] which led southwards to a spring providing a public water supply until the 20th century.[60] Among buildings near the church in 1591 were a former church house, west of the churchyard, and the church house then in use, between the churchyard and the street. That house had been replaced by 1667 by a new cottage,[61] which was probably pulled down for an enlargement of the churchyard in 1743.[62] A few cottages on the north side of the churchyard[63] were removed in the 1870s.[64] At the west end of the village a medieval house known as Hathaways Hall was used in the 17th century as a court house[65] and in 1667 there was a dwelling at the place called Cinder Hill, north of the main street.[66] Many early buildings in the village were replaced in the 19th and 20th centuries. A cottage near the church bears the date 1728 and the initials of the innholder Richard Bennett and his wife Grace.[67] Midway along the village street a former chapel, dating from 1798,[68] is set back behind the sites of a pond and a pound.[69] Further west the street broadens at the junction of Caudle Lane to form an area known by 1823 as the Square.[70] At the west end of the village, known as Townsend, one house bears the date 1770 and the initials of the carpenter John Bennett and his wife Ann,[71] and further west another house is dated 1835.[72] Above the village to the south one or two cottages stood at Turner's Tump in 1608.[73] In the mid 1820s there were several houses there and at Shot hill, to the west,[74] where a new village school was built in the early 1870s. To the south a street of five houses was laid out at Petty Croft in the late 1860s.[75] In 1935 five pairs of council houses were built at Townsend.[76]

After the Second World War the village was much enlarged by council and private housing. Most of the new houses were at the eastern end along the Drybrook and old Ross roads. Earlier building on the Drybrook road included one or more houses at Crossways, just beyond the junction of the Ross road,[77] and a few farmsteads and cottages and a chapel at Crooked End, to the east by a small green known in 1609 as Darby's green.[78] At Varnister (formerly le Vernhurst)[79] several cottages clustering around a green, perhaps that called Dymock's green in 1603,[80] were apparently pulled down in 1722,[81] and settlement comprised two or three cottages east of the green in the early 19th century.[82] Among the first dwellings built after 1945 were those on a council estate created at Crossways in the early 1950s.[83] It was enlarged in the early 1970s and the roads linking the village, Crooked End, and Varnister were filled with private houses from the 1960s.[84]

In the early 17th century there were scattered farmsteads and cottages throughout the parish. Some stood at intervals along the Forest boundary[85] and some on waste ground in other parts of the parish.[86] All the early buildings, including five houses built shortly before 1656 by William Roper, lord of Ruardean manor,[87] appear to have been replaced. In the east a few dwellings on Morse Lane included Ash Farm, purchased in the 1720s for several Mitcheldean charities.[88] At White Hill, known sometimes as Morse or Hazle Farm,[89] the house was rebuilt on a larger scale in the 18th or 19th century and was unoccupied in 1990. In the south-eastern corner of the parish, part of an area known as the Morse,[90] there was a farmstead at Ground Farm in 1749[91] and a few cottages were later built on the Nailbridge road (Morse Road) constructed in 1841.[92] In the 16th and 17th centuries there were a few cottages in the north-eastern corner of the parish at the place known as Haseley[93] (later Hawthorns).[94] On Ruardean's northern boundary the farmstead at Barrellhill was recorded from 1709.[95] In the south a farmstead west of Ruardean hill, evidently

[57] O.S. Map 1/2,500, Glos. XXXI. 1 (1923 edn.); W.I. hist. of Lydbrook (c. 1959, TS. in Glos. Colln.), 12–13.
[58] Above, Plate 18.
[59] P.R.O., MR 129.
[60] Heref. R.O., F 8/II/11; Richardson, Wells and Springs of Glos. 139–40.
[61] Glos. R.O., P 275/CH 1.
[62] Date on gateway to churchyard.
[63] G.D.R., T 1/151.
[64] Glos. R.O., P 275/VE 2/1; cf. O.S. Map 6", Glos. XXXI. NW. (1883 edn.).
[65] Below, manors; N.L.W., Courtfield MSS. 790, ct. 19 Oct. 2 Chas. I; Glos. R.O., D 23/T 1.
[66] Heref. R.O., F 8/III/66; cf. Taylor, Map of Glos. (1777).
[67] G.D.R. wills 1742/222.
[68] Below, nonconf.
[69] G.D.R., T 1/151; Glos. R.O., P 275/VE 2/1, min. 2 Aug. 1889.
[70] G.D.R. vol. 344, f. 113v.
[71] Ibid. wills 1799/99; Glos. R.O., P 275/IN 1/6, burial 5 Feb. 1799.
[72] The ho. also bears the inits. 'J. M. G.'
[73] P.R.O., MR 129.
[74] Greenwood, Map of Glos. (1824); cf. O.S. Map 6", Glos. XXXI. NW. (1883 edn.).
[75] Glos. R.O., D 5851/2/3; P 275/VE 2/1, min. 2 Nov. 1870.

[76] Ibid. DA 24/100/12, pp. 32, 58.
[77] Ibid. D 5301; G.D.R., T 1/151.
[78] Glos. R.O., D 1677/GG 614; Taylor, Map of Glos. (1777).
[79] Heref. R.O., F 8/II/16, 28.
[80] Glos. R.O., D 1677/GG 581.
[81] Glos. Colln. RV 254.1 (5–6).
[82] Greenwood, Map of Glos. (1824); O.S. Map 1", sheet 43 (1831 edn.).
[83] Glos. R.O., DA 24/602/1.
[84] Cf. O.S. Map 1/2,500, SO 6217 (1961, 1973 edns.); Dean Forest Mercury, 7 May 1971.
[85] P.R.O., MR 129; F 17/7.
[86] Heref. R.O., F 8/I/1.
[87] Glos. R.O., D 2026/X 14, f. 7v.
[88] Ibid. P 220/CH 3/1; G.D.R., T 1/151 (no. 657).
[89] Glos. R.O., D 1388, sale papers, Ruardean abstracts of title; cf. below, manors.
[90] Glos. R.O., D 4431, deed 30 Aug. 22 Edw. IV; O.S. Map 6", Glos. XXXI. NE. (1884 edn.).
[91] Glos. R.O., D 36/T 49; D 2123, pp. 97, 101.
[92] O.S. Maps 6", Glos. XXXI. NE., NW. (1883–4 edn.).
[93] Glos. R.O., D 1677/GG 422, 430, 742, 753; D 332/T 15/1–2; cf. P.R.O., MR 129; MR 415.
[94] O.S. Map 6", Glos. XXIII. SE. (1883 edn.).
[95] G.D.R. wills 1709/55.

established by the later 17th century,[96] became known as Hill Farm.[97] On the road to Ruardean Woodside a house (formerly Meend Farm) on the site of a dwelling recorded in 1608[98] incorporates a range bearing the date 1737 and the initials of John Cradock and his wife Grace.[99] Smithers Cross, near the road to the Pludds, belonged to Thomas Terrett in 1723[1] and remained in his family in the mid 19th century, when it was one of Ruardean's principal farmsteads.[2] To the south the farmstead at Smithway was built by the Eddy family in the early 17th century on land called Smithway Meend.[3] To the east the earliest building at Knights Hill was a farmstead established within Ruardean parish by 1608.[4]

In the west there was a dwelling at Marstow before 1293 when a man surnamed of Marstow lived in the parish.[5] His dwelling may have been at Great Marstow Farm, where there was a farmstead in the mid 17th century.[6] Also by the mid 17th century the small farmsteads to the south at Little Marstow Farm, Ragman's Slade, and Glasp Farm had all probably been established.[7] Further south there were a few houses within Ruardean at Moorwood in the early 18th century.[8] Waterscross had a farmhouse by the mid 18th century[9] and several houses were later built at the bottom of Vention Lane near wharves on the river Wye.[10] Some were in ruins in 1959 and a row of mid 19th-century cottages was demolished after that.[11] Further north houses were built at intervals along the Ross road by the river in the 19th and 20th centuries. One known as Wyelands, occupied in the 1820s by a partner in a firm trading from an adjoining wharf,[12] was demolished in the 1970s and its grounds used for a pumping station constructed to supply water from the Wye to a large part of the county.[13] In the north-eastern corner of Ruardean a few houses by the river were part of the settlement of Bishopswood.[14] Most of those surviving were built in the 19th century by John Partridge, whose mansion nearby was destroyed

in 1873.[15] Beverley House (formerly Beechgrove), built in the early 1840s,[16] was in 1901 the residence of the vicar of Bishopswood.[17]

Four inhabitants of Ruardean were recorded in 1086[18] and 18 persons were assessed there in 1327 for the subsidy.[19] The muster roll of 1539 gives 40 names for Ruardean[20] and in 1563 there were said to be 54 households in the parish.[21] The number of communicants was estimated at 160 in 1551[22] and at 250 in 1603,[23] and there were said to be 80 families in Ruardean in 1650.[24] The population, estimated c. 1710 at 500 in 100 houses,[25] grew considerably during the 18th century[26] and was estimated at 758 c. 1775[27] and enumerated at 845 in 1801. It fell to 729 by 1821 and then rose steadily to 1,295 by 1881, before falling again to 1,096 by 1901. The decline was reversed in the mid 20th century, the change being partly accounted for by the boundary changes of 1957, and Ruardean had 1,420 residents in 1981.[28]

The sites of two Ruardean inns named in the early 18th century are unknown[29] but in the village Caudle Lane had the Crown in 1756[30] and the south side of the main street had the Angel, the Malt Shovel, and the Bell, recorded from 1760, 1774, and 1780 respectively.[31] The Bell, opposite the church,[32] was for a time the principal meeting place in the parish;[33] it was closed after 1939.[34] The Crooked Inn, recorded in 1775,[35] may have given its name to Crooked End. Inns and alehouses were opened elsewhere in Ruardean in the 19th century.[36] Waterscross had the New Inn in Vention Lane by 1829.[37] Known later as the King's (or Queen's) Head[38] it was closed c. 1890.[39] A beerhouse on the parish boundary at Ruardean Woodside in 1841[40] was known later as the Jovial Colliers; it closed after 1959.[41] At the Morse the Nelson (later the Nelson Arms) had opened in Morse Road by 1868 and the Rose in Hand in Morse Lane by 1876.[42] They, together with the Angel and the Malt Shovel in the village, survived in 1990.

Between 1760 and 1817 five friendly societies,

96 P.R.O., F 17/7.
97 Glos. R.O., D 2318/I/14; D 2428/1/49.
98 P.R.O., MR 129; O.S. Map 6", Glos. XXXI. NW. (1883 edn.).
99 Glos. R.O., D 3304, will of John Cradock 1759; cf. G.D.R., T 1/151 (no. 563).
1 Glos. R.O., P 275/CW 3/1.
2 Ibid. D 3304; G.D.R., T 1/151.
3 N.L.W., Courtfield MSS. 339, 430.
4 P.R.O., MR 129.   5 Heref. R.O., F 8/II/5, 17.
6 Glos. R.O., D 36/T 52.
7 Ibid. M 2, f. 23 and v.; N.L.W., Courtfield MSS. 107; Heref. R.O., F 8/II/115.
8 Glos. R.O., P 275/CW 3/1.
9 N.L.W., Courtfield MSS. 547, 549.
10 G.D.R., T 1/151; O.S. Map 1/2,500, Glos. XXXI. 1 (1881 edn.); below, econ. hist. (other ind. and trade).
11 O.S. Map 1/2,500, SO 6116 (1961 edn.); W.I. hist. of Lydbrook, 8.
12 Paar, Severn and Wye Railway, 58-61; O.S. Map 6", Glos. XXXI. NW. (1883 edn.).
13 Pearce, 'Water Supply in Dean', 107-17.
14 Cf. Glos. R.O., P 275/CW 3/1; Q/RUm 14; Taylor, Map of Glos. (1777).
15 Below, manors.
16 Glos. R.O., D 1388/SL 3, no. 73; O.S. Map 6", Glos. XXIII. SW. (1883 edn.).
17 O.S. Map 6", Glos. XXIII. SW. (1905, 1924 edns.); Glos. R.O., D 2428/1/49; cf. Kelly's Dir. Herefs. (1885),

1240.
18 Dom. Bk. (Rec. Com.), i. 185v.
19 Glos. Subsidy Roll, 1327, 44.
20 L. & P. Hen. VIII, xiv (1), p. 271.
21 Bodl. MS. Rawl. C. 790, f. 28v.
22 E.H.R. xix. 120.
23 Eccl. Misc. 99.   24 Trans. B.G.A.S. lxxxiii. 97.
25 Atkyns, Glos. 631.
26 Cf. G.D.R., V 5/254T 5; Hockaday Abs. cccxxvi, 1776.
27 Rudder, Glos. 635.   28 Census, 1801–1981.
29 Glos. R.O., P 275/CW 3/1; Glos. Colln. RV 254.1 (16).
30 Glos. R.O., D 543, misc. deeds 1694–1876.
31 Ibid. Q/RSf 2; P 275/CW 2/2.
32 O.S. Map 1/2,500, Glos. XXXI. 2 (1923 edn.).
33 Glos. R.O., P 275/CW 2/2; ibid. VE 2/1; ibid. Q/RSf 2.
34 Cf. Kelly's Dir. Glos. (1939), 301.
35 Hockaday Abs. cccxxvi.
36 Cf. Kelly's Dir. Glos. (1856 and later edns.), s. vv. Ruardean, Lydbrook, East Dean.
37 Glos. R.O., P 275/OV 1/1; G.D.R., T 1/151.
38 O.S. Map 6", Glos. XXXI. NW. (1883 edn.); Kelly's Dir. Glos. (1879), 697.
39 Cf. Kelly's Dir. Glos. (1889), 834; Licensed Houses in Glos. 1891, 156-7.
40 Glos. R.O., Q/FR 4/1, f. 107; Q/RGf 1/8; P.R.O., HO 107/365.
41 O.S. Maps 6", Glos. XXXI. NW. (1883 edn.); 1/2,500, SO 6216 (1961 edn.).
42 Glouc. Jnl. 5 Sept. 1868; Morris's Dir. Glos. (1876), 563.

meeting in inns in Ruardean village, were established.[43] Two societies existed in 1803 and just over 100 parishioners belonged to societies in 1813.[44] The earliest known society was the club which lent money to the parish overseers before 1769.[45] By 1800 one local society owned property in the parish,[46] perhaps at Varnister where a friendly society had two cottages in 1847.[47] Other societies were formed in Ruardean in the mid 19th century, including in 1841 a branch of the Odd Fellows.[48] A hut, used in the later 1930s as a centre for unemployed villagers, became the village hall. It was replaced by a brick hall built in 1956 on a corner of land near Crossways acquired by the parish in 1947 for a playing field. Earlier the Forest of Dean miners' welfare committee had provided a playing field in the village.[49] In the 20th century annual brass band and choir contests were held in Ruardean; the band competition, established before 1910, was abandoned in the late 1970s. A mock court presided over by a mayor, an office dating from well before 1908 and supposedly held by the village's tallest man, met in the Angel inn in the 1980s.[50]

In the 17th century Ruardean had a number of Roman Catholic families, notably the Vaughans who were landowners. From the early 18th century the parish was without resident gentry, and until 1842 it lacked its own incumbent clergyman. Among natives of Ruardean, James Horlick (1844–1921) amassed a fortune in the United States of America from a malted milk drink bearing his surname and was given a baronetcy in 1914.[51] Ruardean featured in Mayne Reid's historical romance *No Quarter*,[52] and gained local notoriety in 1889 when two performing bears, belonging to a troupe of Frenchmen, were killed there after a hostile mob had pursued them from Cinderford.[53]

MANORS AND OTHER ESTATES. An estate of 4 hides in Ruardean, held in 1066 by Hadwig, had passed by 1086 to William son of Baderon, under whom it was held by Solomon.[54] Robert of Aumale (fl. 1176)[55] was perhaps the man with that name who claimed the advowson of Ruardean church in 1200[56] and held land in

Ruardean from the Crown by the serjeanty of guarding the bailiwick of Ruardean in the Forest. He was succeeded by his son William of Aumale, who obtained seisin of the land in 1233.[57] William, from whom the bailiwick was taken in hand for the Crown in 1250,[58] held the manor of *RUARDEAN* at his death c. 1256 by a cash rent, the service of attending the constable of St. Briavels with a horse and hauberk in the Forest, and suit to the Forest court. The manor was divided between his sisters or their sons, Thomas d'Evercy, Isabel of Aumale, Richard of Stalling, Maud of Aumale, and William Hathaway.[59] Some rents passed to Robert of Stalling, who died c. 1296 leaving an infant son John.[60] Although Thomas d'Evercy's share was said to be held by the service of guarding Ruardean bailiwick and paying a cash rent of 20s. at St. Briavels castle,[61] the Crown entrusted the bailiwick in 1301 to two men.[62] The Crown also made grants of the bailiwick in 1376 during the minority of the heirs of Thomas Hathaway, who was said to have held it in fee,[63] and in 1385.[64] Custody of the bailiwick had been restored to Ruardean manor by 1428[65] and was held with it until the late 18th century.[66]

Thomas d'Evercy's share of the estate, which continued to be called the manor of Ruardean,[67] passed at his death c. 1293 to his grandson Thomas d'Evercy.[68] William of March, bishop of Bath and Wells, who was apparently the latter's guardian,[69] had given the manor by 1302 to Robert Urry, possibly a relative of the d'Evercys, and Robert had sold it by 1306 to Alexander of Bicknor.[70] Alexander, a clerk who was appointed treasurer of Ireland in 1307,[71] agreed in 1311 to settle the manor on the marriage of his niece Margery and Geoffrey of Langley[72] but he retained it in 1325 when the reversion was granted to Richard of Carrant and his wife Margery, presumably the niece.[73] Alexander Carrant died seised of the estate in 1375 leaving his son John, a minor, as his heir.[74] John (d. 1382) was succeeded by his brother Edward, also a minor, whose father-in-law Thomas of Manston[75] had been custodian of the estate from 1376.[76] By 1415 it had apparently passed to Thomas Carrant[77] and in 1428 Thomas Carrant of Gloucester quitclaimed it to Robert Baynham of Mitcheldean.[78] At his death in

43 Glos. R.O., Q/RSf 2.
44 *Poor Law Abstract, 1804*, 172–3; *1818*, 146–7.
45 Glos. R.O., P 275/CW 2/2.
46 Ibid. Q/REl 1A, St. Briavels.
47 G.D.R., T 1/151.
48 Glos. R.O., Q/RZ 1; *Glouc. Jnl.* 15 July 1843; 11 June 1853.
49 Glos. R.O., D 3168/3/8; 4/7/68.
50 Mullin, *Forest in Old Photog.* 62, 66; H. Phelps, *Forest of Dean* (1982), 94; *Glos. & Avon Life*, Aug. 1984, 55.
51 Burke, *Peerage* (1963), 1252; *Glos. & Avon Life*, Aug. 1984, 55.
52 1888 edn. in Glos. Colln. 25740.
53 *Glouc. Jnl.* 4 May 1889; Glos. Colln. RR 254.2.
54 *Dom. Bk.* (Rec. Com.), i. 185v.; cf. *Trans. B.G.A.S.* cv. 121.
55 *Pipe R.* 1176 (P.R.S. xxv), 127.
56 *Cur. Reg. R.* i. 213, 315–16.
57 *Ex. e Rot. Fin.* (Rec. Com.), i. 240; cf. *Pipe R.* 1199 (P.R.S. N.S. x), 32; *Rot. Litt. Claus.* (Rec. Com.), i. 442–3.
58 *Trans. B.G.A.S.* xxxiii. 203.
59 *Inq. p.m. Glos.* 1236–1300, 17–19.
60 Ibid. 184–5.
61 *Cal. Inq. p.m.* iii, p. 58; P.R.O., C 143/62, no. 8.

62 *Cal. Pat.* 1301–7, 4.
63 Ibid. 1374–7, 234; Thos. was also chief forester (or serjeant-in-fee) by virtue of tenure of an estate in St. Briavels: *Inq. p.m. Glos.* 1359–1413, 116–17; below, St. Briavels, manors (Hathaways).
64 *Cal. Pat.* 1381–5, 559.
65 *Cal. Close*, 1422–9, 459; P.R.O., E 134/36 Eliz. I Hil./21; C 142/335, no. 32.
66 Glos. R.O., D 2026/X 3; D 36/Q 2; Heref. R.O., F 8/III/215; *3rd Rep. Com. Woods* (1788), 76.
67 Cf. *Cal. Pat.* 1301–7, 43.
68 *Inq. p.m. Glos.* 1236–1300, 161; *Cal. Inq. p.m.* iii, p. 58, gives Thomas's heir as his son Thos.
69 Cf. J. Maclean, 'Hist. of Parish and Manor of Ruardean', *Trans. B.G.A.S.* viii. 127.
70 *Cal. Pat.* 1301–7, 43, 446; cf. *Berkeley MSS.* iii. 357.
71 *Trans. B.G.A.S.* viii. 130.
72 *Langley Cart.* (Dugdale Soc. xxxii), p. 21.
73 *Trans. B.G.A.S.* viii. 131–2.
74 *Inq. p.m. Glos.* 1359–1413, 100.
75 *Cal. Inq. p.m.* xv, pp. 290–1.
76 *Cal. Fine R.* 1368–77, 335–6; 1377–83, 92, 329.
77 B.L. Add. Ch. 32998; cf. Heref. R.O., F 8/II/29.
78 *Cal. Close*, 1422–9, 459.

1436[79] Robert settled the manor on his daughter Anne. She later married Thomas Deerhurst[80] and the manor passed to their son John.[81] He died in 1484 leaving Thomas Deerhurst, an infant, as his heir.[82] Of Robert Baynham's direct descendants Sir Alexander Baynham died seised of land in Ruardean in 1524[83] and William Baynham held the manor at his death in 1568. William was succeeded in turn by his sons Robert[84] (d. 1572) and Joseph (d. 1613), whose son Alexander[85] retained the manor at least until 1617.[86] The descent of the manor after 1617 is obscure. Joan Vaughan, owner of Hathaways in Ruardean, claimed ownership in and before 1634[87] but Thomas Roper evidently owned the manor in 1645. Thomas, a Roman Catholic,[88] died in 1647[89] and his son William recovered part of the manor sequestered for his own recusancy.[90] William (d. 1685) was succeeded by his son John but in 1703 the manor was held by Benjamin Hyett, a Gloucester attorney, who was apparently among John's creditors.[91] Just before his death in 1709 John Roper appointed trustees to sell the manor and in 1717, the sale having been delayed by his protestant heir Edward Roper of Eltham (Kent), it was purchased by Edward's son-in-law Charles Henshaw, who paid off John's debts.[92] Charles (d. 1726) was succeeded by his daughters Elizabeth, Katherine, and Susanna,[93] and in 1738 Katherine and the baronets Edward Dering and Rowland Wynne, the respective husbands of Elizabeth and Susanna, sold the manor to Stephen Ashby of Worcester.[94] Ashby, who had acquired Hathaways manor and other land in Ruardean, died in 1743 leaving his Ruardean estate to his cousin Richard Clarke of New Hill Court (later Hill Court) in Walford (Herefs.).[95] Richard (d. 1748) was succeeded by his brother John (d. 1759) and John by his sisters Alicia (d. 1779), Jane (d. 1806), and Mary (d. 1789) as joint owners.[96] After Jane's death much of her Ruardean land was sold off in lots[97] but the Hill Court estate, which she left to Kingsmill Evans,[98] retained a small part of it.[99] The manorial rights and some land were bought by James Pearce of Lydbrook.[1] He died in 1827 leaving his estate to his wife Ann for life, and in 1856, when she was still alive, his surviving son John sold the manorial rights and a little land to John Francis Vaughan of Courtfield,[2] whose family had held land in Ruardean since 1635 or earlier.[3] From J. F. Vaughan (d. 1880) the manorial rights passed in the direct line to Francis (d. 1919), Charles[4] (d. 1948), and Joseph (d. 1972),[5] and trustees acting for Joseph's son Mr. Patrick Vaughan held them in 1990.[6]

In the later Middle Ages the manor included a castle[7] built under the licence granted in 1311 to Alexander of Bicknor to crenellate his house at Ruardean.[8] The castle, on a spur north-west of the church, was defended by a perimeter wall and included a substantial earthwork. It may have been still standing in 1611[9] but most of its masonry had been removed by 1831.[10] In the 1930s, when the site was investigated by local treasure hunters, remains of a small chamber were uncovered and in 1990 the surviving fabric included part of a doorway.[11]

William Hathaway, one of the lords of Ruardean in the early 14th century,[12] had probably inherited part of William of Aumale's estate as a minor.[13] Hathaway's estate, later called *HATHAWAYS* or *HATHAWAYS COURT* manor,[14] was held from Alexander of Bicknor for a cash rent. It passed from William (d. c. 1317) to his son William[15] and by 1355 to the latter's son Walter. Thomas Hathaway, the owner in 1366,[16] held land in Ruardean from the Crown for a cash rent paid at St. Briavels castle and at his death in 1376 his heirs were his infant daughters Isabel, Sibyl, and Ellen.[17] His estates in Ruardean and St. Briavels were divided between them in 1382, when Isabel and her husband Thomas Walwyn received her share.[18] The Crown retained the other shares until Sibyl, who married Nicholas Hyde, and Ellen came of age.[19] Thomas Walwyn, of Much Marcle (Herefs.), died in 1415 and was survived by Isabel and several sons, of whom Richard was his heir.[20] In 1445 Ellen, the widow of William Walwyn, quitclaimed rents in Ruardean to John Hickox and his wife Isabel, and in 1450 Isabel quitclaimed land which she had inherited from

79 P.R.O., C 139/79, no. 15.
80 Ibid. C 1/39, no. 101.
81 Ibid. C 1/56, no. 231; cf. *V.C.H. Glos.* x. 184.
82 *Cal. Inq. p.m. Hen. VII*, i, p. 50.
83 P.R.O., C 142/42, no. 112; for the Baynhams, *Trans. B.G.A.S.* vi. 184.
84 P.R.O., C 142/149, no. 129; cf. Glos. R.O., D 1677/GG 384.
85 P.R.O., C 142/164, no. 62; C 142/335, no. 35.
86 Ibid. CP 25/2/298/15 Jas. I East. no. 37.
87 Glos. R.O., D 3921/I/42; P.R.O., E 178/5304, mm. 10, 20.
88 P.R.O., LRRO 5/7A, inquisition 1645.
89 For the Ropers, *Genealogist*, N.S. xiii. 140–4.
90 *Cal. Cttee. for Compounding*, v. 3192; P.R.O., CP 25/2/656/17 Chas. II Trin. no. 7.
91 Heref. R.O., F 8/I/1, 13–16; III/217; cf. *V.C.H. Glos.* iv. 105.
92 Heref. R.O., F 8/II/110; III/215.
93 Glos. Colln. RV 254.1 (12).
94 Heref. R.O., F 8/II/111.
95 Ibid. 67; P.R.O., PROB 11/731 (P.C.C. 27 Anstis), ff. 211v.–214v.; V. Green, *Hist. of Worc.* (1796), ii, app. p. cxix.
96 N.L.W., Courtfield MSS. 319.
97 Cf. Glos. R.O., D 608/13/2; Heref. R.O., F 8/II/89.
98 J. Duncumb, *Hist. and Antiquities of Herefs.* (edn. by W. H. Cooke, 1882), iii. 188.
99 Glos. R.O., D 5844/1; cf. Burke, *Land. Gent.* (1937), 1838–9.
1 N.L.W., Courtfield MSS. 319.
2 Ibid. 321–2; Glos. R.O., D 5844/1.
3 N.L.W., Courtfield MSS. 452, 465; Glos. R.O., D 637/I/70; III/8; Q/RNc 1, pp. 40–2, 60–7; 2/1, pp. 22–3; G.D.R., T 1/151.
4 *Kelly's Dir. Glos.* (1879 and later edns.); Burke, *Land. Gent.* (1937), 2323–4.
5 M. Vaughan, *Courtfield and the Vaughans* (1989), 186.
6 Inf. from Mr. P. Vaughan.
7 Cf. Heref. R.O., F 8/II/24, 28; Glos. R.O., D 2244/85.
8 *Cal. Pat.* 1307–13, 355.
9 Glos. R.O., D 33/271; cf. P.R.O., MR 129.
10 *Gent. Mag.* ci (1), 403, 487–8.
11 Glos. R.O., D 3921/III/25.
12 *Feud. Aids*, ii. 275.
13 *Inq. p.m. Glos.* 1236–1300, 17–19.
14 P.R.O., C 142/33, no. 69; N.L.W., Courtfield MSS. 787, 790.
15 *Inq. p.m. Glos.* 1302–58, 164; *Cal. Close*, 1307–13, 437.
16 Heref. R.O., F 8/II/19–21.
17 *Inq. p.m. Glos.* 1359–1413, 116–17.
18 Ibid. 122; *Cal. Fine R.* 1377–83, 287–8.
19 *Cal. Fine R.* 1383–91, 323; *Cal. Close*, 1389–92, 260.
20 *Trans. B.G.A.S.* viii. 134; B.L. Add. Ch. 32998.

her mother Sibyl Hyde to William Walwyn of Bickerton in Much Marcle.[21] William held a manor court in 1454,[22] when he was also described as of Ruardean,[23] and at his death in 1471 Hathaways, held from Ruardean manor for 1d., passed to his daughter Alice, wife of Thomas Baynham[24] (d. 1500). Alice, who later married Sir Walter Dennis (d. 1505 or 1506),[25] died in 1518 and the estate passed to her son Sir Christopher Baynham[26] (fl. 1534).[27] His son George, who held it in 1541,[28] was knighted in 1546 and died later that year leaving the manor for life to his wife Cecily, who later married Sir Charles Herbert.[29] From Cecily, whose son Richard Baynham may have held the manor court in the 1550s, it passed in 1585 to another son Thomas Baynham,[30] who was succeeded in 1611 by his daughter Joan and her husband John Vaughan of Kinnersley (Herefs.).[31] John, a Roman Catholic, was outlawed and in 1612 the manors he held in Joan's right were confiscated.[32] Joan recovered her estates but forfeited them, temporarily, on her conviction for recusancy in 1619. John died later that year and Joan, who continued to support the Roman Catholic cause and resided in Ruardean, in 1642. Her son and heir Baynham Vaughan[33] died in 1650,[34] his estates having been sequestered for his recusancy.[35] Hathaways, which in 1658 was held by Thomas Frewen and John Monger, was eventually recovered by John Vaughan,[36] Baynham's eldest son, who died in 1694.[37] The estate passed to John's cousin Thomas Vaughan, a lunatic by 1703, and reverted at his death c. 1727 to Sir John Gifford, Bt., of Burstall (Leics.).[38] In 1736 Joseph Clarke bought the manor from Gifford for his nephew Stephen Ashby,[39] and in 1738 it was united with Ruardean manor, with which it passed to the Clarke family on Ashby's death.[40]

A house called Hathaways Hall, presumably the residence of the Hathaways in the 1350s,[41] was recorded from 1482.[42] Its site, known in 1438 as the Court Place,[43] was at the west end of the village by a lane to Marstow.[44] The house,

which was occupied by tenants in the 16th century, was used for holding courts in 1616 and possibly much later.[45] Another house in the village became the home of Joan Vaughan before 1623,[46] and John Vaughan was assessed on 10 hearths in Ruardean in 1672.[47] In the early 18th century the Vaughans' house was the home of Roger Vaughan (d. 1719),[48] brother of Thomas.[49] The house, which was by the road to Turner's Tump, passed with the manorial rights.[50] It was unoccupied by 1847[51] and its remains had been demolished by 1878.[52]

Flaxley abbey granted a lease of land at the Morse for 99 years to George Baynham in 1535.[53] After the Dissolution the abbey's lands in Ruardean, which were sometimes known as the manor of *RUARDEAN*, remained part of the Flaxley Abbey estate until 1749[54] when Thomas Crawley-Boevey conveyed them to Maynard Colchester.[55] The land, which in 1785 covered 34 a. centred on Ground Farm,[56] descended with the Colchesters' Wilderness estate until c. 1918.[57]

An estate in the east part of Ruardean was known in the late 18th century as the manor of the *MORSE* or the *HAZLE*.[58] It included land which belonged in 1647 to Benedict Hall[59] and descended with his Highmeadow estate[60] until 1726 when Thomas Gage, Viscount Gage, sold over 130 a. in Ruardean to John Hopkins.[61] By 1755 some land, known as Hazle farm, had passed to William Harrison[62] (d. 1759) of Newnham, who left it to his granddaughter Elizabeth Harrison. She died in 1774[63] and her husband Charles Jones in 1796,[64] the farm then passing to their daughters Margaret and Elizabeth. Elizabeth and her husband Samuel Damsell relinquished their interests in 1797 when they separated and Elizabeth secured an annuity from the estate. Margaret, the widow of Joseph Jackman, twice remarried, the second time to Thomas Smith, and was succeeded at her death in 1827 by her son Robert Jackman,[65] who owned 84 a. including the homestead at White

21 Heref. R.O., F 8/II/36–9, 41.
22 N.L.W., Courtfield MSS. 787.
23 *Trans. B.G.A.S.* viii. 135.
24 P.R.O., C 140/37, no. 26; cf. ibid. C 1/56, no. 231.
25 *Trans. B.G.A.S.* vi. 149; Hockaday Abs. cxlvii, 1506.
26 P.R.O., C 142/33, no. 69.
27 Glos. R.O., D 1677/GG 370.
28 N.L.W., Courtfield MSS. 790.
29 *Trans. B.G.A.S.* vi. 150–1.
30 N.L.W., Courtfield MSS. 787; *Trans. B.G.A.S.* vi. 185–7; Ric. died in 1580 owning the reversion of half the manor: P.R.O., C 142/189, no. 82.
31 P.R.O., C 142/340, no. 192.
32 *Trans. B.G.A.S.* vi. 152–3; *Cal. S.P. Dom. 1580–1625*, 545.
33 Heref. R.O., F 8/II/101, 130; P.R.O., E 134/22 Jas. I Hil./3; cf. Glos. R.O., D 36/M 2; *Misc.* viii (Cath. Rec. Soc. xiii), 150–6.
34 Bigland, *Glos.* iii, no. 222.
35 *Cal. Cttee. for Compounding*, iii. 2360–2; iv. 2536; v. 3182.
36 N.L.W., Courtfield MSS. 107, 790.
37 Bigland, *Glos.* iii, no. 222.
38 Heref. R.O., F 8/II/93, 115; III/248; Glos. R.O., Q/RNc 2/6; G. E. C. *Baronetage*, iii. 129.
39 Heref. R.O., F 8/III/214; Glos. R.O., D 332/T 17; cf. P.R.O., PROB 11/731 (P.C.C. 27 Anstis, will of Steph. Ashby), ff. 211v.–214v.
40 Above, this section.
41 Heref. R.O., F 8/II/19–21.

42 N.L.W., Courtfield MSS. 787.
43 Heref. R.O., F 8/II/32.
44 Glos. R.O., D 2244/85; N.L.W., Courtfield MSS. 790, ct. 19 Oct. 2 Chas. I.
45 N.L.W., Courtfield MSS. 787; Glos. R.O., D 23/T 1.
46 G.D.R. vol. 152; P.R.O., E 134/22 Jas. I Hil./3.
47 P.R.O., E 179/247/14, rot. 39d.
48 Glos. R.O., Q/SO 4; Bigland, *Glos.* iii, no. 222.
49 Heref. R.O., F 8/II/115.
50 N.L.W., Courtfield MSS. 319, 322; Glos. R.O., P 275/SP 1, min. 23 Oct. 1857.
51 G.D.R., T 1/151 (nos. 460–2).
52 O.S. Map 6", Glos. XXXI. NW. (1883 edn.).
53 Glos. R.O., D 1677/GG 557.
54 *L. & P. Hen. VIII*, xii (1), p. 353; xviii (1), p. 124; xix (1), p. 379; above, Flaxley, manor.
55 Glos. R.O., D 36/T 49.
56 Ibid. D 2123, pp. 97, 101.
57 Ibid. D 177/VI/4; D 543, sale partics. 21 Dec. 1918; above, Mitcheldean, manor.
58 Glos. R.O., D 1388, sale papers, Ruardean abstracts of title.
59 Ibid. D 1677/GG 881.
60 Cf. ibid. GG 594; D 421/Z 4; Q/RNc 2/3, pp. 5–8; cf. Rudder, *Glos.* 567, 569, 690.
61 Glos. R.O., D 23/T 29; D 3304, deed 16 July 1726.
62 Ibid. D 543, Ruardean deed 20 Sept. 1755.
63 G.D.R. wills 1759/150; Glos. R.O., P 228/IN 1/3.
64 Glos. R.O., P 228/IN 1/4; cf. ibid. 6, marriage 1 July 1762.
65 Ibid. D 1388, sale papers, Ruardean abstracts of title.

Hill in 1847.[66] Most of that land was owned in 1870 by Charles Wadley[67] and in 1906 by James Brain of Drybrook.[68]

In the early 19th century a large estate was created at *BISHOPSWOOD* by the Monmouth ironmaster William Partridge. It included woodland in Walford (Herefs.) formerly belonging to Ross Foreign manor, ironworks and land in Walford and Ruardean formerly belonging to the Foley family,[69] and from 1809 land in Ruardean formerly belonging to the Clarke family.[70] William Partridge (d. 1819) was succeeded by his son John, who built a mansion just within Ruardean. He sold the estate, which covered *c.* 1,300 a., mostly in Walford, in 1874 following the house's destruction to Jacob Chivers.[71] Jacob died in 1883 leaving his estates in trust for his son Thomas.[72] The Bishopswood estate was acquired by 1889 by H. L. B. McCalmont[73] and was bought in 1901 by W. O. N. Shaw, in 1906 by Sir George Bullough, and in 1910 by R. H. Storey. Storey, who sold off some farms in Ruardean,[74] retained the estate until the late 1940s. From 1950 land which had belonged to the estate was bought piecemeal by T. S. Chambers and at his death in 1978 it passed to Mr. William F. Brooks, the owner in 1990 of *c.* 530 a. (*c.* 214.6 ha.), mostly woodland in Walford and Ruardean.[75] Bishopswood House was built for John Partridge in the early 1820s to designs in an Elizabethan style by Jeffry Wyatt.[76] It stood by Lodgegrove brook in wooded grounds incorporating ponds originally formed for ironworks there.[77] In 1873 the house was destroyed by fire except for two rear wings,[78] and a partial restoration, begun by Jacob Chivers, was completed after 1885.[79] The restored house was pulled down following a fire *c.* 1918.[80] Some outbuildings in Walford were retained and converted as dwellings.[81] Among outlying buildings in the grounds belonging to Ruardean are an entrance lodge on the Lydbrook–Ross road[82] and a gamekeeper's lodge to the east. The latter incorporates a castellated tower of three storeys providing extensive views of the river Wye and surrounding countryside and used by 1844 as a summer house.[83]

Corn and hay tithes in Ruardean belonged to the precentor of Hereford cathedral as appropriator of Walford church, of which Ruardean was a chapelry, and small tithes to the vicar of Walford.[84] The vicarial tithes, which sometimes were held under a lease[85] and in the mid 18th century were paid to a curate serving Ruardean,[86] were given to the new benefice of Ruardean in 1842.[87] The precentor's tithes, which usually were farmed by a lessee[88] and in 1847 were commuted for a corn rent charge of £135,[89] later passed to the Ecclesiastical Commissioners and in 1875 were used to augment the Ruardean benefice.[90]

ECONOMIC HISTORY. AGRICULTURE. In 1086 the Ruardean estate of William son of Baderon had 3 ploughteams in demesne and his tenants there, a bordar, 2 *villani*, and a Welshman, shared 3 teams.[91] In 1220 five teams were recorded in Ruardean[92] and in 1256 the manor, to which some customary services were owed, included two ploughlands and assized rents worth just over £10.[93] That value indicates that many freehold estates had been established. Ruardean manor in 1293 included 60 a. and rents from free and customary tenants valued at £5 5s. 6d. and 10s. respectively[94] and in 1306 thirty free tenants paid rents worth 6 marks.[95] Robert of Stalling's estate in 1297 comprised rents and other payments from customary tenants worth 32s. 4d. and 18d. respectively.[96] Hathaways manor included 30 a. of arable and 20s. in rents from free tenants in 1317,[97] and 80 a. of arable and 26s. 8d. in assized rents in 1376.[98] Leases for lives or years had been introduced on that manor by 1481, and 11 free tenants owed reliefs, heriots, and suit of court besides cash rents in 1519.[99]

In the 17th century there were many small freeholds and leaseholds in Ruardean. Most parishioners had only a few acres or a garden[1] and did not depend primarily on agriculture for a living. Of 72 parishioners listed in 1608 only 2 were described as yeomen and 9 as husbandmen.[2] On Hathaways manor, to which 15 freeholders owed suit of court and from which 42 holdings were held by lease in 1620,[3] several leaseholds remained burdened with heriots and

66 G.D.R., T 1/151.
67 Glos. R.O., Q/RUm 373; *Kelly's Dir. Glos.* (1870), 624.
68 *Kelly's Dir. Glos.* (1906), 283–4; Glos. R.O., D 2428/1/49.
69 Duncumb, *Hist. Herefs.* (1882), iii. 181, 194; cf. Glos. R.O., Q/REl 1A, St. Briavels.
70 Glos. R.O., D 608/13/2; Heref. R.O., F 8/II/89.
71 Duncumb, *Hist. Herefs.* (1882), iii. 194, 205; Glos. R.O., D 1388/SL 3, no. 73; cf. G.D.R., T 1/151.
72 Heref. R.O., AH 87/2.
73 *Kelly's Dir. Glos.* (1889), 873; Burke, *Land. Gent.* (1898), i. 955–6.
74 Glos. R.O., D 936/Y 121; cf. *Kelly's Dir. Glos.* (1897 and later edns.).
75 Inf. from Mr. Brooks, of Bishopswood Ho., Walford.
76 Colvin, *Biog. Dict. Brit. Architects* (1978), 962; cf. Glos. R.O., P 275/CW 2/3, church rate 15 Apr. 1823; T. D. Fosbroke, *Wye Tour* (1826), 34.
77 Glos. R.O., D 1388/SL 3, no. 73; below, econ. hist. (mills and ironworks).   78 *Glouc. Jnl.* 6 Dec. 1873.
79 Littlebury, *Herefs. Dir.* (1876), 638; *Kelly's Dir. Herefs.* (1879), 1048; (1885), 1239; cf. O.S. Map 6", Glos. XXIII. SW. (1883, 1903 edns.).
80 Inf. from Mrs. Brooks; cf. O.S. Map 6", Glos. XXIII.

SW. (1924 edn.).
81 Cf. O.S. Map 1/2,500, SO 6018 (1961 edn.).
82 Glos. R.O., Q/SRh 1827 B/4.
83 Ibid. D 1388/SL 3, no. 73; *Kelly's Dir. Herefs.* (1870), 383.
84 G.D.R., B 4/3/1037; T 1/151; V 5/254T 1, 3.
85 Ibid. B 4/3/1039.
86 Hockaday Abs. cccxxvi, 1737; G.D.R. vol. 381A, f. 7; Rudder, *Glos.* 635.
87 G.D.R. vol. 361, ff. 51v.–53v.; below, church.
88 G.D.R., B 4/3/1037; Glos. R.O., Q/RNc 2/3, pp. 9–10; D 936/Y 46.
89 G.D.R., T 1/151.
90 *Lond. Gaz.* 7 May 1875, p. 2457; below, church.
91 *Dom. Bk.* (Rec. Com.), i. 185v.
92 *Bk. of Fees*, i. 308.
93 *Inq. p.m. Glos.* 1236–1300, 18–19.   94 Ibid. 161.
95 P.R.O., C 143/62, no. 8.
96 *Inq. p.m. Glos.* 1236–1300, 184–5.
97 Ibid. 1302–58, 164.
98 *Cal. Inq. p.m.* xiv, pp. 237, 303.
99 N.L.W., Courtfield MSS. 787.
1 Glos. R.O., D 36/M 2, ff. 14–20; Q/RNc 1, pp. 40–2, 60–7; N.L.W., Courtfield MSS. 107, 790; Heref. R.O., F 8/I/2.
2 Smith, *Men and Armour*, 43–4.
3 Glos. R.O., D 36/M 2, ff. 14–20.

additional rents of hens and capons at the end of the century.[4] A few other holdings, including several of Ruardean manor, also owed rents of a customary nature.[5] By the later 18th century most leases granted in the parish were for 21-year terms.[6]

Clearance of land for cultivation at Ruardean began before 1066[7] and continued well into the Middle Ages. An assart apparently next to the Wye was recorded in 1199;[8] some small parcels of land were described as old assarts in 1270[9] and others as new assarts in 1282.[10] The eastern half and the southern and south-western parts of Ruardean remained uncultivated at that time[11] and the area between the Crown demesne in the Forest and Bishopswood was described in 1354 as a wilderness.[12] Farmland and woodland at the Morse, where there was pasture in 1482,[13] was regarded as new assart in 1535.[14] In 1608, when the pattern of closes was complete, the Crown claimed those west of the road to Ruardean Woodside as former assarts,[15] accepting a composition for them in or soon after 1618.[16] The place-name element 'meend' indicating waste or open ground in forest land was applied to much land in Ruardean,[17] where the survival of waste ground and a number of greens[18] also reflected the parish's origins. The waste ground, which was regarded as the property of the lords of Ruardean and Hathaways manors, was used for the tipping of cinders or slag from early ironworks and for common pasture.[19] Occupiers of land had pasture rights on the extraparochial land of the Forest, for which the parish paid 3s. 4d. in herbage money in the early 1680s,[20] and 16 people exercised those rights in 1860.[21] Sheep were being kept at Ruardean in 1222 when Henry III granted the monks of Flaxley a sheephouse nearby during his minority,[22] and in 1306 a Ruardean man was accused of stealing sheep.[23]

Most agricultural holdings in Ruardean were small and in the late 18th century and the 19th inhabitants sometimes combined husbandry with coal mining or a trade such as carpentry, haulage, or malting.[24] In 1831, when about a third of families depended chiefly on agriculture, 32 farmers lived in the parish and 29 of them employed labour, mostly one or two farmhands each.[25] In 1806 the largest farms on Jane Clarke's estate comprised 80 a., 70 a., 62 a., and 56 a.[26]

and in 1820 the largest of ten holdings on Kingsmill Evans's estate was a farm of 46 a. at Moorwood.[27] By 1837 two of the principal farms, Marstow and Ragman's Slade on the Bishopswood estate, had been amalgamated to create a holding of 152 a.[28] and in 1847 there were also six farms with 60–100 a. and another eight with 20–60 a. in the parish.[29] In 1880 Marstow farm, from which Ragman's Slade had been detached, contained 212 a. and was in hand.[30] The number of agricultural occupiers recorded in 1896 and 1926 was 38. A majority of them were tenant farmers and at the latter date most had under 50 a.[31] The pattern of landholding remained much the same in 1988, when of 30 agricultural holdings returned for the parish 21 had 20 ha. (c. 50 a.) or less and only 2 had 40 ha. (c. 100 a.) or more. Most were worked on a part-time basis.[32]

In the early 19th century farmland in Ruardean was used chiefly as pasture.[33] Stock raising, sheep farming, and dairying were all presumably represented in the local economy in 1802 when it was announced that a toll-free fair would be held each year in late June at Ruardean for the sale of livestock, wool, and cheese.[34] In 1801 arable crops were said to cover 360 a., of which barley and wheat accounted for all but 20 a. devoted to potatoes,[35] but in 1847 the parish contained 643 a. of arable and 796 a. of meadow and pasture.[36] In 1866, when the arable area was smaller, wheat, barley, turnips, and grass leys were grown in rotation and 618 a. were permanently under grass.[37] Sheep farming remained a significant activity, 1,136 sheep being recorded that year, and beef and dairy cattle and pigs were kept.[38] A village publican was a cattle dealer and a farmer was a butcher in 1870,[39] and one farmer dealt in wool and another in manure in 1876.[40] In the late 19th century and the early 20th some arable land was turned permanently to grass and by 1926, when permanent grassland covered some 831 a., the amount of cereals and root crops grown was much reduced. Orchards covered 34 a. in 1896. The dairy herds were enlarged during that period and the flocks, which had decreased in size by 1896, and the beef herds were also enlarged in the early 20th century, 1,343 sheep and 212 cattle, including dairy cows, being returned in 1926 compared with 808 and 133 respectively in 1896.[41] An annual sheep and

4 Ibid. Q/RNc 2/6–7.
5 Ibid. D 421/Z 4; Glos. Colln. RV 254.1 (4–6).
6 Heref. R.O., F 8/III/1–76; Glos. R.O., D 637/III/8.
7 Dom. Bk. (Rec. Com.), i. 185v.
8 Pipe R. 1199 (P.R.S. N.S. x), 32.
9 P.R.O., E 32/29, rot. 7.
10 Ibid. E 32/30, rot. 19 and d.
11 Trans. B.G.A.S. xiv. 365–6.
12 Reg. Trillek, 224–5.
13 Glos. R.O., D 4431, deed 30 Aug. 22 Edw. IV.
14 Ibid. D 1677/GG 557.
15 P.R.O., MR 129; Cal. S.P. Dom. Addenda 1623–5, 570.
16 Glos. R.O., D 1229, Ruardean deeds 1642–1853, deed 14 Jan. 1642; cf. Hart, Royal Forest, 100.
17 P.N. Glos. (E.P.N.S.), iii. 218; cf. Glos. R.O., D 36/M 2, ff. 16v.–17; D 1677/GG 884; D 4431, deed 16 July 10 Eliz. I; P 275/CH 5; Heref. R.O., F 8/II/34, 78, 91; N.L.W., Courtfield MSS. 107, 339, 790.
18 Cf. Trans. B.G.A.S. xiv. 365.
19 Heref. R.O., F 8/I/13; II/93.
20 5th Rep. Dean Forest Com. 65 and nn., 67; Glos. R.O., P 275/CW 2/1–2.

21 P.R.O., F 3/128, letter 29 Nov. 1860.
22 Rot. Litt. Claus. (Rec. Com.), i. 490.
23 P.R.O., JUST 1/286, rot. 8d.
24 G.D.R. wills 1767/72; 1780/27; 1786/110; Glos. R.O., D 185/IV/41/8; P 275/IN 1/7; Morris's Dir. Glos. (1876), 563.
25 Census, 1831.   26 Glos. R.O., D 608/13/2.
27 Heref. R.O., F 8/III/248.
28 Glos. R.O., P 275/OV 1/1; D 1388/SL 3, no. 73.
29 G.D.R., T 1/151.
30 Heref. R.O., AH 87/1.
31 P.R.O., MAF 68/1609/16; MAF 68/3295/16.
32 Agric. Returns 1988.
33 Rudge, Hist. of Glos. ii. 106.
34 Glouc. Jnl. 21 June 1802; cf. ibid. 6 June 1803; 18 June 1804.
35 List & Index Soc. clxxxix, p. 177.
36 G.D.R., T 1/151.
37 P.R.O., MAF 68/26/9.
38 Ibid. MAF 68/25/20.
39 Kelly's Dir. Glos. (1870), 624.
40 Morris's Dir. Glos. (1876), 563.
41 P.R.O., MAF 68/1609/16; MAF 68/3295/16; cf. Acreage Returns, 1905.

cattle fair was held in the village in the 1890s.[42] A dairyman lived in the parish in the early 1930s.[43] Some land was made unsuitable for agriculture by subsidence and tipping connected with coal mining.[44] At Hill Farm below Ruardean hill the site of an opencast mine worked in the late 1970s had been returned to agricultural use by the mid 1980s.[45] In 1988 most of the land in the parish remained under grass and four of the larger farms specialized in dairying and another kept a large flock of sheep. Some beef cattle were also reared and one holding was devoted primarily to egg production.[46]

MILLS AND IRONWORKS. Robert of Aumale had one or more itinerant forges working in woodland within the Forest by the late 12th century.[47] Up to five such forges operated in or near Ruardean at any time in the mid 13th century[48] and more than five, possibly including one owned by a ploughmaker, worked in the area later that century.[49] Smiths and forges were frequently recorded in the later Middle Ages[50] and a parishioner was described as a tongholder in 1579.[51] At least five smiths and the son of another lived in Ruardean in 1608[52] and a founder was resident in 1664.[53] A furnace presumably operated east of Ruardean village in a field by the Drybrook road known in 1685 as Furnace meadow.[54] A forge producing anvils in the late 17th century[55] was perhaps that, in the western part of the village, belonging in 1792 to the Highmeadow estate.[56]

Among the earliest mills known to have belonged to Ruardean were several at Lydbrook, which became an industrial centre with corn and cloth mills and ironworks; its history is treated below.[57] In 1336 Richard Talbot obtained permission to construct a mill on Lodgegrove brook.[58] It was perhaps that later called Diggins Mill,[59] an ancient grist mill which remained in use in 1706.[60] Downstream in Walford (Herefs.) stood New Mill, which belonged to Robert Devereux (d. 1646), earl of Essex.[61] Two furnaces at Bishopswood, evidently the property of Robert's father Robert,

earl of Essex, were worked from 1600 by George Catchmay together with forges at Lydbrook.[62] Both furnaces were abandoned before 1617[63] and the younger Robert Devereux later built a furnace at Bishopswood on Lodgegrove brook, which he diverted for that purpose.[64] In 1633 that furnace may have been worked together with a forge at Lydbrook by Sir John Kyrle, Bt.,[65] and by 1638 it may have been shut down by the lessees of the king's ironworks in the Forest of Dean.[66] George Williams, a founder employed at the furnace at least until 1675,[67] produced castings, perhaps including ordnance, for John Hannis in 1639.[68] The furnace, above the Ross road,[69] was controlled by Robert Kyrle in the late 1640s.[70] Later it was operated by Paul Foley in partnership from 1674 with his brother Philip and from 1685 with Richard Avenant and John Wheeler.[71] The Foley family worked the furnace with forges at Lydbrook in the late 1720s[72] and built a forge upstream of the furnace probably in the late 1740s.[73] The forge, which produced blooms for conversion to bar iron at the Foleys' forge at Lower Lydbrook,[74] had changed hands by 1787 when it was operated by the Monmouth ironmaster William Partridge.[75] William and his brother John (d. 1810) later purchased the Bishopswood ironworks,[76] which included stamping machines for crushing cinders.[77] Most of the works closed c. 1815 but James Pearce operated the forge for a few years until the early 1820s,[78] when John Partridge used the ironworks' site for a new mansion and its grounds.[79] The lowest pond made for the ironworks disappeared[80] and the forge, described in 1878 as an old corn mill, fell into ruin. A pumping station was built there in the 1960s.[81]

Other mills in or near Ruardean included several of unknown or uncertain location. One existed in the later 13th century,[82] when a route probably south of the village was called Mill Way.[83] In 1419 there was a post mill near Diggins Lane,[84] land to the east of which was later known as Windmill hill.[85] In 1617 there was a new mill apparently south-west of Ragman's

42 J. Gibbs, 'Development of Educ. in Two Forest of Dean Schs. 1870–1903' (Bristol Univ. Dip. Ed. thesis, 1967), 79.
43 Kelly's Dir. Glos. (1931), 296; (1935), 295.
44 Dean Forest Mercury, 9 Nov. 1973; 16 May 1975.
45 M. V. Bent, Highest Point of Dean (1985), 81–2.
46 Agric. Returns 1988.
47 Rot. Litt. Claus. (Rec. Com.), i. 334–5, 442–3.
48 P.R.O., E 146/1/25.
49 Ibid. E 32/29, rot. 2; E 32/30, rot. 23d.; E 32/31, m. 16; Nicholls, Iron Making, 24.
50 Glos. Subsidy Roll, 1327, 44; Hart, Royal Forest, 69; Glos. R.O., D 1677/GG 103, 316; Hockaday Abs. cccxxvi, 1508, 1542, 1545, 1546; Heref. R.O., F 8/II/83, 85.
51 Heref. R.O., F 8/II/94.
52 Smith, Men and Armour, 44.
53 Glos. R.O., D 4431, deed 18 July 16 Chas. II.
54 Ibid. D 1677/GG 594.
55 Ibid. P 275/IN 1/1, burials 25 June 1683, 25 July 1699; Bodl. MS. Top. Glouc. c. 3, f. 137.
56 P.R.O., F 17/117(2), p. 44; MR 691 (LRRO 1/240).
57 Forest of Dean, industry (ironworks; mills).
58 Cal. Pat. 1334–6, 266.
59 N.L.W., Courtfield MSS. 107.
60 Glos. R.O., D 5851/2/1.
61 N.L.W., Courtfield MSS. 107, 452; Duncumb, Hist. Herefs. (1882), iii. 105.
62 P.R.O., E 134/44 Eliz. I Trin./3.
63 Glos. R.O., D 1677/GG 654.

64 N.L.W., Courtfield MSS. 107; cf. P.R.O., E 178/5304, m. 34.
65 Glos. R.O., D 1677/GG 784; P.R.O., SP 16/282, f. 253.
66 P.R.O., E 134/14 Chas. I Mich./42.
67 Heref. R.O., F 8/II/92; Glos. R.O., P 275/CW 3/1.
68 Cal. S.P. Dom. 1639, 509, 543.
69 I. Taylor, Map of Herefs. (1786); Taylor, Map of Glos. (1777); cf. Trans. Woolhope Naturalists' Field Club, xxviii. 89.
70 P.R.O., LRRO 5/7A, depositions 25 Sept. 1649.
71 Hart, Ind. Hist. of Dean, 24, 45, 93; Glos. R.O., D 3921/II/12.
72 P.R.O., E 134/4 Geo. II East./11.
73 Hart, Ind. Hist. of Dean, 64; Taylor, Map of Glos. (1777).
74 Trans. B.G.A.S. lxxii. 143.
75 Glos. R.O., P 275/CW 2/2; Q/REl 1A, St. Briavels.
76 Duncumb, Hist. Herefs. (1882), iii. 194.
77 H. R. Schubert, Hist. Brit. Iron and Steel Ind. (1957), 368.
78 Hart, Ind. Hist. of Dean, 95; Glos. R.O., P 275/CW 2/3; Q/REl 1A, St. Briavels.
79 Above, manors.
80 Cf. G.D.R., T 1/151 (nos. 215, 216A, 218); Glos. R.O., D 936/Y 118; Q/RUm 14.
81 O.S. Maps 6", Glos. XXIII. SW. (1883 edn.); 1/2,500, SO 6018 (1961 edn.); Bull. Hist. Metallurgy Group, ii (1), 31.
82 P.R.O., E 32/29, rot. 7.
83 Heref. R.O., F 8/II/11.
84 Glos. R.O., D 1677/GG 167; cf. ibid. D 892/T 69; P 275/CH 2.
85 G.D.R., T 1/151 (no. 593).

Slade,[86] and in or before 1658 Henry Rudge conveyed a paper mill possibly on Lodgegrove brook to his son Henry.[87] In 1698 John Vaughan of Huntsham (Herefs.) owned a paper mill, which passed in 1721 to John Vaughan of Courtfield.[88] It was presumably among several paper mills at Ragman's Slade,[89] which continued in use in 1733.[90] Two water mills in Ruardean were acquired in 1690 by Samuel Brewster and Thomas Stone.[91] A mill recorded in 1778[92] was presumably that, on the stream north of the village,[93] which in 1795 had a pump downstream to draw water back to its pond.[94] The mill was unoccupied in 1829.[95]

OTHER INDUSTRY AND TRADE. The iron industry generated much economic activity in Ruardean. Charcoal burners, who supplied the fuel for the forges, worked in or near the parish in the later 13th century.[96] Among metal trades nailmaking, established in Ruardean by 1509,[97] was represented by six nailers in 1608[98] and continued well into the 19th century.[99] In 1667 and 1678 pins were apparently also made in the parish.[1] The cinders left by the early forges, many of which were scattered near the village,[2] were being removed for resmelting at nearby ironworks in the late 17th century. In 1702 the lord of Hathaways manor agreed to end digging at Cinder Hill where building had taken place[3] and in 1722 the lord of Ruardean manor evicted four cottagers to enable cinders at Varnister green to be mined.[4] Many horses were kept in the parish in the early 18th century to transport cinders and charcoal to ironworks and coal from the Forest to the surrounding countryside.[5] Cinder mining and charcoal burning continued in Ruardean in the mid 1760s.[6]

Land in Ruardean was mined and quarried over a long period. Colliers were recorded in the parish from 1608[7] and some inhabitants worked or had interests in mines within the Crown's demesne woodland of the Forest.[8] The coal outcrops south of the village were mined before 1720[9] and two pits, called True Blue[10] and Windrills, the latter by the road to the Pludds,

were in production in 1788.[11] True Blue was owned by a partnership[12] and by the early 19th century its workings honeycombed the ground as far south as Ruardean Woodside.[13] In 1835 the workings nearest Ruardean Woodside belonged to Newham Bottom colliery, which had the same owners as True Blue, and those southwest of the village to Reddings Level colliery, and in 1841 the right of two other collieries to exploit seams near Ruardean Woodside and Ruardean Hill was confirmed.[14] Coal mining was much the largest source of employment in Ruardean at that time,[15] and the Forest branch of the Amalgamated Association of Miners established a lodge in the parish in 1872 or 1873.[16] True Blue and Newham Bottom collieries, acquired in 1884 by a syndicate of free miners and in 1889 by the Brain family, were abandoned c. 1910.[17] True Blue mine was reopened in the 1920s[18] and employed 35 men at the outbreak of the Second World War.[19] It closed in the 1950s.[20] Reddings Level colliery, which came into the same hands as True Blue, had closed by 1901.[21] Little more coal was mined in that area[22] until 1955 when a drift mine was opened near the Lydbrook road. It employed 10 men in 1966[23] and continued in production until the late 1980s.[24] After the Second World War several smaller drifts were opened near Hill Farm. They were abandoned in the late 1950s but mining was resumed later and the remaining coal there was extracted by the opencast method in the later 1970s.[25] The Brains also mined iron ore near Drybrook. Their mine, north of Morse Lane, opened before 1869 and was linked by 1877 to a narrow-gauge railway serving Trafalgar colliery in the Forest. The mine proved unprofitable[26] but, although the railway lines had been removed by 1901,[27] it was not finally abandoned until 1923.[28]

Stoneworking in Ruardean was represented by a mason in 1608,[29] and in the 18th century and the early 19th several stonecutters, quarrymen, and masons lived there.[30] Two lime burners were recorded in 1608[31] and a limekiln was built by the river Wye shortly before 1635.[32]

[86] Glos. R.O., D 4431, deed 17 Jan. 14 Jas. I.
[87] N.L.W., Courtfield MSS. 107.
[88] Glos. R.O., Q/RNc 1, pp. 40–2; 2/1, pp. 22–3.
[89] Bodl. MS. Top. Glouc. c. 3, f. 137.
[90] Glos. R.O., D 892/T 69.
[91] P.R.O., CP 25/2/831/2 Wm. and Mary East. no. 7.
[92] Glos. R.O., P 275/CW 2/2.
[93] Bryant, Map of Glos. (1824).
[94] S. D. Coates and D. G. Tucker, Water Mills of Middle Wye Valley (Monmouth District Mus. Service, 1983), 64–6.
[95] Glos. R.O., P 275/OV 1/1.
[96] Hart, Royal Forest, 45.   [97] Hockaday Abs. cccxxvi.
[98] Smith, Men and Armour, 44.
[99] Glos. R.O., D 4431, deed 20 Apr. 4 Chas. I; P 275/CH 1, 6; ibid. IN 1/7; Slater's Dir. Glos. (1868), 235.
[1] Glos. R.O., Q/SIb 1, f. 153v.; Q/SO 1, f. 172v.
[2] Rudge, Hist. of Glos. ii. 106.
[3] Heref. R.O., F 8/II/93.
[4] Glos. Colln. RV 254.1 (5–6).   [5] G.D.R., V 5/254T 3.
[6] Heref. R.O., F 8/III/152, 199, 226, 257.
[7] Smith, Men and Armour, 44; P.R.O., E 178/5304, m. 11v.; Glos. R.O., P 275/IN 1/1; Heref. R.O., F 8/II/59; III/60.
[8] Glos. R.O., D 2957/254.11; G.D.R. wills 1742/222; 1766/54; 1767/72.
[9] Heref. R.O., F 8/I/19; III/15.
[10] Opened perhaps in 1743: Nicholls, Forest of Dean, 235.
[11] 3rd Rep. Com. Woods (1788), 89, 91; G.D.R., T 1/151 (no. 499).
[12] G.D.R. wills 1799/99.

[13] Glos. R.O., D 3304, will of John Cradock 1806; cf. G.D.R., T 1/151 (nos. 547, 553).
[14] Award of Dean Forest Mining Com. (1841), 42–4, 59, 71–3, 79, 153–4, map at pp. 40–1; Glos. R.O., Q/RUm 173/1, plans A 3–4.
[15] P.R.O., HO 107/365; HO 107/1976.
[16] Fisher, Custom and Capitalism, 75, 186.
[17] Glos. R.O., D 543, True Blue deeds.
[18] Cf. O.S. Map 1/2,500, Glos. XXXI. 2 (1923 edn.); Glos. R.O., DA 24/100/10, p. 617.
[19] Glos. R.O., AP/R 1/SE 2A/F, no. 12.
[20] Cf. B. Waters, Forest of Dean (1951), 134.
[21] Glos. R.O., D 3304, sale partics. 1905; O.S. Map 6", Glos. XXXI. NW. (1903 edn.).
[22] Cf. Glos. R.O., D 543, True Blue deeds; O.S. Map 1/2,500, Glos. XXXI. 2 (1923 edn.).
[23] Glos. R.O., D 3921/II/26.
[24] Glos. & Avon Life, Aug. 1984, 54; local inf.
[25] Dean Forest Mercury, 9 Nov. 1973; 16 May 1975; Bent, Highest Point of Dean, 81–2.
[26] J. G. Wood, Laws of Dean Forest (1878), 435; Glos. R.O., D 262/T 1; D 177/VI/4.
[27] Cf. O.S. Map 6", Glos. XXXI. NE. (1884, 1903 edns.).
[28] Paar, G.W.R. in Dean, 145–8.
[29] Smith, Men and Armour, 44.
[30] Heref. R.O., F 8/III/51; Glos. R.O., P 275/CH 6; ibid. IN 1/5–7.   [31] Smith, Men and Armour, 44.
[32] N.L.W., Courtfield MSS. 452.

One or more kilns were operating near Bishopswood in 1818.[33] A brickmaker living within the parish at Moorwood in 1803 opened a quarry and built a limekiln there before 1829.[34] In the mid 19th century quarries were opened elsewhere in the parish[35] and cranes and a shed were provided for working sandstone beds south of the village at Petty Croft.[36] Many quarries and kilns had been abandoned by the late 1870s but limestone was still worked north of Drybrook.[37] One quarry there was served by a railway in 1870[38] and was worked by the county council in 1910.[39] The Drybrook quarries, which were idle in the mid 1920s,[40] were served by the Forest's railway system from 1928 until 1953[41] and included tarmacadam works by 1942.[42] The main quarry was enlarged considerably by Amey Roadstone Corporation after 1960[43] and in 1989 it employed 25 men and produced among other things crushed aggregates for the building industry and lime for agricultural use.[44]

Trade on the river Wye gave work to sailors in 1608 and 1743.[45] Forest coal destined for Herefordshire was loaded into barges from the river bank above Lydbrook before 1680[46] and there were several wharves on that section of the bank in the later 18th century.[47] More were provided to handle the increase in the coal and stone trades following the construction in the early 19th century of the Severn & Wye tramroad to Lydbrook and of a branch line from Lydbrook to Bishopswood. At Bishopswood the tramroad, completed in 1814, had sidings to wharves near the Ruardean boundary and was linked by an inclined plane with the forge on Lodgegrove brook.[48] In 1820 E. J. Scott, a London solicitor, built a tramroad to link a colliery at Moorwood with the Wye at Waterscross. The line, which incorporated an inclined plane running down Vention Lane and crossing the Bishopswood tramroad, was opposed by the Severn & Wye company and was taken up c. 1823.[49] At that time a Lydney firm traded at a wharf midway between Waterscross and Bishopswood,[50] and in the mid 1830s the partnership of William Montague and Charles

Church of Gloucester occupied four of the coal wharves at Bishopswood.[51] By the late 1840s the only wharves in use above Lydbrook were those at Waterscross and midway between Waterscross and Bishopswood[52] and few if any of the Ruardean men living outside Lydbrook and Bishopswood worked as bargemen or watermen.[53] The Lydbrook–Bishopswood tramroad, the northern end of which was removed after the closure of the Bishopswood ironworks, ran as far as the Ross road in 1833. It carried little traffic and the track was taken up in 1874.[54] The line's course to the road, winding to maintain a steady gradient, was still clearly visible in 1990.

Osiers growing by the river Wye have supplied basket makers in Ruardean. One maker active in 1608[55] was granted a lease of osier beds on both river banks in 1640,[56] and his craft continued to be practised in the parish at least until 1803.[57] The Wye fishery adjoining Ruardean belonged to John Vaughan of Huntsham in 1698, when he leased a right to take small fish to Richard Wheatstone.[58] The Wheatstones of Lydbrook retained the right, under the Vaughans of Courtfield, to fish for eels and small fish with nets, poles, and wheels until the later 18th century.[59]

Personal names suggest that cloth was made in Ruardean in the later 13th century.[60] Flax and hemp were worked there in 1482,[61] and in 1608, when a fuller and two weavers were recorded in the parish,[62] the local cloth industry was centred on Lydbrook.[63] A weaver lived in the parish in 1791[64] and another in Ruardean village in 1841.[65] In the 17th century several Ruardean men worked as woodcutters or sawyers[66] and others used timber in making shovels,[67] trenchers, barrels, cabinets, and saddletrees.[68] In later centuries a number of timber merchants was recorded.[69] A local tanning industry established by 1608, when three glovers also lived in the parish,[70] was based on Lydbrook.[71] In the 1620s Hathaways manor court sought to regulate the leather trade.[72] Ruardean had a baker and several butchers in 1276[73] and the usual village crafts and trades were later fairly well represented.[74] Inhabitants included soapboilers and tallow-

33 Glos. R.O., P 275/CW 2/3.
34 Ibid. D 637/II/T 1, L 3.
35 Ibid. P 275/VE 2/1, min. 23 Apr. 1841.
36 Ibid. D 1229, Ruardean deeds 1854–8.
37 O.S. Maps 6", Glos. XXIII. SE., SW. (1883 edn.); XXXI. NE., NW. (1883–4 edn.).
38 Glos. R.O., Q/RUm 373.
39 Ibid. D 2428/1/49. 40 Hart, Ind. Hist. of Dean, 308.
41 Paar, G.W.R. in Dean, 57.
42 Glos. R.O., AP/R 1/SE 2A/F, no. 8.
43 Cf. O.S. Maps 1/2,500, SO 6417 (1961, 1973 edns.); SO 6418 (1961 edn.).
44 Dean Forest Mercury, 5 Mar. 1989.
45 Smith, Men and Armour, 44; Glos. R.O., D 3304.
46 Hart, Free Miners, 105, 123.
47 Glos. R.O., D 637/III/8; Q/REl 1A, St. Briavels, 1788, 1800; Q/RUm 14.
48 Paar, Severn and Wye Railway, 19–22, 57–9; Severn and Wye Railway and Canal Act, 50 Geo. III, c. 215 (Local and Personal); Bryant, Map of Glos. (1824).
49 Paar, Severn and Wye Railway, 61; R. Anstis, Ind. Teagues and Forest of Dean (1990), 125; cf. Bryant, Map of Glos. (1824).
50 Paar, Severn and Wye Railway, 59; Bryant, Map of Glos. (1824).
51 Glos. R.O., P 275/CW 2/3; ibid. OV 1/1; cf. V.C.H. Glos. iv. 139; for Montague, below, Forest of Dean, industry

(ironworks).
52 G.D.R., T 1/151.
53 P.R.O., HO 107/365; HO 107/1976; cf. Glos. R.O., P 275/IN 1/7.   54 Paar, Severn and Wye Railway, 58–9.
55 Smith, Men and Armour, 44.
56 N.L.W., Courtfield MSS. 465.
57 Glos. R.O., D 1677/GG 937; P 275/IN 1/1, 6.
58 Ibid. Q/RNc 1, pp. 40–2; 2/1, pp. 22–3.
59 Ibid. D 637/III/8.
60 Heref. R.O., F 8/II/1–2, 5–7, 10–14, 17.
61 N.L.W., Courtfield MSS. 787.
62 Smith, Men and Armour, 44.
63 Below, Forest of Dean, industry (mills).
64 Heref. R.O., F 8/III/71.   65 P.R.O., HO 107/365.
66 Ibid. E 178/3837; E 178/5304, mm. 10, 42.
67 Smith, Men and Armour, 43–4.
68 P.R.O., E 178/3837; Heref. R.O., F 8/III/39; Glos. R.O., P 275/IN 1/1.
69 Heref. R.O., F 8/II/63; Kelly's Dir. Glos. (1906), 284; (1914), 295–6.
70 Smith, Men and Armour, 43–4; cf. P.R.O., E 178/3837.
71 Below, Forest of Dean, industry (other ind. and trade).
72 N.L.W., Courtfield MSS. 790.
73 Rot. Hund. (Rec. Com.), i. 182.
74 Smith, Men and Armour, 44; Glos. R.O., P 275/IN 1/5–7; Q/SIb 1, ff. 3v.–4, 16, 153v.; Heref. R.O., F 8/III/40, 42, 46; Kelly's Dir. Glos. (1856 and later edns.).

chandlers in 1523[75] and 1781[76] and a musician in 1793. Ropemaking, introduced by 1818, continued in 1851.[77]

Ruardean, where 67 of the 187 families resident in 1831 depended chiefly on trades or crafts and 60 on agriculture,[78] was generally impoverished in the 19th century and the early 20th.[79] Few professional people apart from a surgeon at Bishopswood in 1851[80] and another in the village in 1876[81] lived there. In the mid 19th century building trades and haulage provided some employment. The village had several shops, mostly grocery and drapery stores,[82] and in the later 19th century outlying places such as Waterscross and the Morse also had shops. The Cinderford co-operative society had opened branches at the Morse and in the village by 1894 and 1906 respectively.[83] In the 1920s and 1930s many traditional trades and crafts disappeared.[84] One of the last blacksmiths worked a smithy, built by the Lydbrook–Ross road in the mid 19th century[85] and occupied by a joiner and furniture maker in 1990. A bacon-curing factory in the centre of Ruardean closed in 1928,[86] and the parish, which continued to depend heavily on the mining industry,[87] suffered much unemployment in the early 1930s.[88] Mining jobs were lost with the gradual cessation of deep mining in the Forest coalfield, completed in 1965.[89] In 1990 the village had half a dozen small shops.

LOCAL GOVERNMENT.

William of Aumale's profits from a manor court in Ruardean were mentioned in 1256.[90] Later the courts of Ruardean and Hathaways manors exercised view of frankpledge. For Hathaways manor there survive a court book of 1620–1,[91] court rolls of 1642, 1647, and 1658, and court papers, mostly records of presentments, for many years in the periods 1454–82, 1519–89, and 1603–38 and for a few years between 1642 and 1715.[92] The court assembled twice a year as a court leet and a court baron. It sometimes sat as a court of survey and in the mid 17th century sometimes only as a court baron. It heard pleas of assault, affray, and bloodshed and enforced the assize of ale until the mid 17th century. In addition to tenurial and estate matters it supervised the repair and maintenance of roads and watercourses and regulated encroachments on the lord's waste. In 1530 it appointed two constables, two aletasters, two bread weighers, and two water bailiffs and in the

1620s, by which time the offices of aletaster and bread weigher had been merged, it chose a searcher and sealer of leather. The court was held until 1735 or later.[93] For Ruardean manor court papers survive for most years between 1692 and 1707 and for 1720, 1723, and 1725.[94] It met twice a year, combining view of frankpledge with a court baron, and dealt with the repair and maintenance of roads and watercourses and with encroachments on the lord's waste besides tenurial and other estate matters. The lord's failure to provide a pound was presented in 1698 and the pulling down of cottages on the waste by the lord of Hathaways without the freeholders' consent in 1700. The court met until 1730 or later.[95]

Ruardean had at least one churchwarden in 1446[96] and two churchwardens (*procuratores ecclesie*) were recorded in 1523.[97] They derived some income from land and buildings belonging to the parish.[98] Poor relief was administered by two overseers[99] and highway repairs by two surveyors, who were reported to Ruardean manor court in 1702 for failing to cleanse ditches alongside the parish roads.[1] The parish provided stone water troughs at Caudle well in 1779. In the later 18th century, when the overseers each served in turn for six months, poor relief took the usual forms. Paupers were badged and some were employed to spin flax and make cloth, which was occasionally given to the needy. The parish subscribed to the Gloucester infirmary by 1770 and had several poorhouses.[2] Other cottages built at the parish's expense on waste land had been pulled down c. 1700.[3] A parish workhouse had been established by 1803, when it had 7 inmates and 21 children attended one or more schools of industry.[4] The workhouse was managed by a married couple in 1816.[5] In the late 18th century many people living in the extraparochial Forest of Dean had legal settlement in Ruardean[6] and among parishes adjoining the Forest the burden of relief was greater only in Newland. Ruardean's annual expenditure on the poor rose from £117 in 1776 to £377 in 1803, when 66 people were on relief, all of them permanently,[7] and to £699 in 1813, when the numbers receiving regular and occasional help were 50 and 25 respectively.[8] Much less was spent in the later 1820s.[9] In 1831 a local butcher agreed to administer relief and the following year an outsider farmed the poor for £310.[10] At that time the parish was responsible for c. 166 families

75 Hockaday Abs. cccxxvi.   76 Glos. R.O., P 275/CH 3.
77 Ibid. IN 1/6–7; P.R.O., HO 107/1976.
78 *Census*, 1831.   79 Nat. Soc. files, Ruardean.
80 P.R.O., HO 107/1976.
81 *Morris's Dir. Glos.* (1876), 563.
82 Glos. R.O., P 275/IN 1/7; P.R.O., HO 107/365; HO 107/1976.
83 *Morris's Dir. Glos.* (1876), 563; *Kelly's Dir. Glos.* (1856–1906 edns.), s.vv. East Dean, Lydbrook, Ruardean.
84 *Kelly's Dir. Glos.* (1914 and later edns.), s.vv. Lydbrook, Ruardean.
85 Glos. R.O., P 275/VE 2/1, min. 29 Apr. 1859; D 1251/A/1.   86 Ibid. D 2299/4078.
87 Cf. Nat. Soc. files, Ruardean.
88 Glos. R.O., D 3168/4/7/68.
89 Below, Forest of Dean, industry (mining from 1770s).
90 *Inq. p.m. Glos.* 1236–1300, 18.
91 Glos. R.O., D 36/M 2.
92 N.L.W., Courtfield MSS. 107, 787, 790.

93 Heref. R.O., F 8/III/214.
94 Ibid. I/1–16, 18–21; III/217.
95 Glos. Colln. RV 254.1 (16).
96 Hockaday Abs. cccxxvi.
97 Heref. R.O., F 8/II/58; cf. Hockaday Abs. cccxxvi, 1563.
98 Below, church. Churchwardens' accts. for the periods 1673–82, 1767–88, and 1813–69 are included in Glos. R.O., P 275/CW 2/1–3; cf. G.D.R., B 4/1/2119; *Trans. B.G.A.S.* viii. 143–6.
99 Glos. R.O., Q/SIb 1, f. 8v.   1 Heref. R.O., F 8/I/12.
2 Glos. R.O., P 275/CW 2/2–3.
3 Heref. R.O., F 8/I/10.
4 *Poor Law Abstract, 1804*, 172–3.
5 Glos. R.O., P 275/CW 2/3.
6 Ibid. D 421/X 5/2.
7 *Poor Law Abstract, 1804*, 170–3.
8 Ibid. *1818*, 146–7.
9 *Poor Law Returns* (1830–1), p. 67; cf. ibid. (1835), p. 65.
10 Glos. R.O., P 275/CW 2/3.

in the Forest and continued to experience great difficulty in financing relief.[11] In 1837 Ruardean parish was added to the Herefordshire poor-law union of Ross[12] but following the implementation of the 1894 Local Government Act it became part of East Dean and United Parishes rural district.[13] East Dean rural district as constituted in 1935 included Ruardean except for the area transferred that year to the new civil parish of Lydbrook, which was part of West Dean rural district.[14] Both Ruardean and Lydbrook were included in the new Forest of Dean district in 1974.

CHURCH. In 1200 Hugh of Walford disputed the advowson of Ruardean church with Robert of Aumale.[15] In 1291 Westbury-on-Severn church received an annual render of 1 lb. of incense from Ruardean church but the latter was a chapel of Walford (Herefs.), of which the precentor of Hereford cathedral was appropriator[16] and patron of the vicarage.[17] The precentor appointed a curate or chaplain for Ruardean chapel in the early 16th century but the vicar of Walford apparently claimed that right in 1523.[18] The dispute was evidently resolved after 1535[19] and the vicars of Walford or, more usually, their curates served the chapelry.[20] Although its church had acquired burial rights by 1472,[21] Ruardean remained a chapelry of Walford until 1842 when it was constituted a separate benefice in the precentor's gift. The new benefice, endowed with the income that the vicar of Walford had enjoyed from Ruardean, was a perpetual curacy[22] (later a vicarage)[23] and following a fuller endowment in 1875 was styled a rectory.[24] The patronage was exercised by the bishop of Gloucester and Bristol in 1846 by reason of lapse[25] and passed to the bishop after the precentor's death in 1855.[26] Bishopswood House was included in the ecclesiastical district assigned in 1845 to a church which John Partridge had built on the Walford side of his estate,[27] and the south-western corner of Ruardean was part of the district given in 1852 to a new church at Lydbrook.[28]

The profits of Ruardean church, farmed by two men in 1397,[29] comprised tithes, including those of milk, lambs, and wool, and offerings valued at £5 5s. 4d. in 1535, when the precentor of Hereford and the vicar of Walford disputed their ownership.[30] Later they belonged to the vicar[31] and were worth £15 in the mid 18th century, when they were paid to his curate,[32] and £60 in 1842, when they were assigned to the new benefice of Ruardean.[33] The tithes were commuted in 1847 for a corn rent charge of £100[34] and the Ecclesiastical Commissioners increased the benefice's value, £150 in 1856,[35] by annual grants of £5 from 1857 and, in response to a gift of £200, of £6 13s. 4d. from 1869.[36] The £5 was replaced in 1875 by the tithe rent charge of £135 in Ruardean formerly awarded to the precentor of Hereford.[37] In 1842 Ruardean was said to have a glebe house unfit as a residence[38] but no other mention of it has been found[39] and in 1851 the perpetual curate had lodgings in the village.[40] A subscription for building a parsonage house was opened in 1857[41] and, following a grant from the Ecclesiastical Commissioners in 1871,[42] a small house at the east end of the village was purchased together with 3 a. The house, which was remodelled and enlarged in the early 1880s,[43] was sold c. 1980 when a bungalow was built for the rector in its grounds.

It was reported that no quarterly sermons were preached in Ruardean in 1548[44] and again in 1576; at the latter date only one annual communion service was held.[45] The curate serving the church in 1551 had a satisfactory knowledge of doctrine[46] and the curate in 1593 was deemed unlearned but of honest life.[47] A later curate may have been the Ruardean minister involved in inclosure riots at Mailscot, near English Bicknor, in 1631.[48] Of the Walford vicars who served Ruardean in person Richard Greenaway, vicar 1681–1745,[49] was suspended in 1739 for failing to attend an episcopal visitation.[50] Edward Kidley, rector of Welsh Bicknor (Mon., later Herefs.) across the river Wye, was employed as curate in Ruardean between 1737 and 1754.[51] From 1811 and until his death in 1842 Ruardean was served by the antiquary and county historian Thomas Dudley Fosbrooke, curate and later vicar of Walford. His writings published during

11 3rd Rep. Dean Forest Com. 6, 12, 29.
12 Heref. R.O., K 42/406, pp. 82, 167, 171.
13 Glos. R.O., DA 24/100/1, pp. 15, 47; Glos. Colln. (H) F 5.19 (14).
14 Census, 1931 (pt. ii).   15 Cur. Reg. R. i. 213, 315–16.
16 Tax. Eccl. (Rec. Com.), 157, 161; cf. Inq. Non. (Rec. Com.), 147.
17 Reg. Swinfield, 539; Reg. Gilbert, 120; Reg. Spofford, 363.
18 Hockaday Abs. cccxxvi; Glos. R.O., D 2957/254.8.
19 Valor Eccl. (Rec. Com.), iii. 7, 25.
20 Hockaday Abs. cccxxvi; xxx, 1544 stipendiaries, f. 7; xxxi, 1548 clergy, f. 46; xliv, 1572 visit. f. 7; Glos. R.O., P 275/IN 1/1–7.
21 Heref. R.O., F 8/II/51; cf. Glos. R.O., D 1677/GHe 7.
22 G.D.R. vol. 361, ff. 51v.–53v.
23 Kelly's Dir. Glos. (1870), 624.
24 Ibid. (1879 and later edns.); cf. Lond. Gaz. 7 May 1875, p. 2457.
25 Hockaday Abs. cccxxvi.
26 Morris's Dir. Glos. (1876), 563; cf. Cathedrals Act, 3 & 4 Vic. c. 113, s. 41; Hockaday Abs. ccli. Slater's Dir. Glos. (1868), 233, names the Eccl. Com. as patrons.
27 G.D.R., V 6/101.
28 Lond. Gaz. 20 Apr. 1852, pp. 1118–19.
29 E.H.R. xliv. 446.

30 Valor. Eccl. (Rec. Com.), iii. 25.
31 Hockaday Abs. cccxxvi, 1549; above, manors.
32 G.D.R. vol. 381A, f. 7; Rudder, Glos. 635; cf. Hockaday Abs. cccxxvi, 1737.
33 G.D.R. vol. 361, ff. 51v.–53v.
34 Ibid. T 1/151.
35 Ibid. vol. 384, f. 168.
36 Lond. Gaz. 8 Sept. 1857, pp. 3034–6; 23 Sept. 1869, p. 2435.
37 Ibid. 7 May 1875, p. 2457; above, manors.
38 G.D.R. vol. 361, ff. 51v.–53v.
39 Cf. ibid. V 5/254T 1, 3; ibid. vol. 381A, f. 7.
40 P.R.O., HO 107/1976.
41 Glos. R.O., P 275/SP 1; ibid. VE 2/1.
42 Lond. Gaz. 12 May 1871, p. 2270.
43 Trans. B.G.A.S. viii. 138–9; Glos. R.O., D 1381/6v; 129; O.S. Map 6", Glos. XXXI. NW. (1883 edn.).
44 Hockaday Abs. cccxxvi.
45 G.D.R. vol. 40, f. 250v.   46 E.H.R. xix. 120.
47 Hockaday Abs. lii, state of clergy 1593, f. 13.
48 Acts of P.C. 1630–1, 290.
49 Duncumb, Hist. Herefs. (1882), iii. 198–9; G.D.R., V 1/200.
50 G.D.R., B 4/1/2134.
51 Hockaday Abs. cccxxvi; G.D.R., V 1/200; ibid. vol. 397, f. 7; Glos. R.O., P 275/IN 1/3.

that time included a guide to the river Wye.[52] In 1822 Fosbrooke allowed Isaac Bridgman, the curate of Holy Trinity near Drybrook, to deliver a weekly lecture in the church, which Bridgman opened on one occasion to the evangelical preacher Rowland Hill.[53] In his later years Fosbrooke sometimes employed a curate at Ruardean.[54] Henry Formby, the first holder of the separate benefice of Ruardean, was, by his support for the Oxford Movement, soon unpopular with parishioners and he resigned in 1845.[55] During the ministry of William Penfold, 1850–81,[56] who was poverty-stricken and frequently at odds with parishioners, a lead in church matters was often taken by John Burdon, rector of English Bicknor.[57]

In 1442 there was a chantry of St. Mary in Ruardean served by a chaplain[58] but no other record of it has been found. Property owned by the parish, presumably including a house left for the church by a Ross man in 1504,[59] produced an income used to repair the church, acquire ornaments and books, and provide other benefits for the parish, besides helping to equip parishioners for militia service. In 1591 feoffees were appointed to administer the property[60] and later the income was applied solely to church repairs and the trust became known as the Church Lands charity.[61] Two thirds of the income were assigned to the church in 1898, when the parish charities were reorganized,[62] and were worth £122 in 1989.[63]

The church, which was dedicated to *ST. JOHN THE BAPTIST* by the 14th century,[64] is built of sandstone rubble and ashlar and has a chancel, a nave with a north organ chamber and a south aisle and porch, and a west tower with a spire. The aisle was probably the 12th-century church, and the tympanum over its south doorway has a carving of that period representing St. George and the Dragon.[65] The chancel and nave, which had no division between them, and the porch were built in the 13th century and the tower was added in the 14th, presumably beginning in 1364 when the foundations of a belfry were laid.[66] Many windows in the chancel and nave and the west window of the tower were renewed in the 15th century. In 1563 the whole church was in need of repair and a parish rate had been levied for repairing the spire.[67] The north doorway had been blocked

and the pulpit placed against the north wall of the nave by 1721 when the church was repewed by order of the parish vestry and seating for the singers was provided in the chancel.[68] By 1754 more pews had been installed[69] and in 1776 a west gallery was erected in the nave against the tower to provide more accommodation for the singers, the chancel seats being sold to parishioners to help defray the cost.[70] The space under the tower was ceiled for use as a vestry room.[71] On the advice of Joseph Bryan of Gloucester the spire was rebuilt in 1768, the cost being borne by a church rate and voluntary contributions, including payments from 37 cottagers and young men apparently living on extraparochial waste land adjoining Ruardean.[72] For a time a side of the tower was whitewashed to serve as a fives court; the game was discontinued in the churchyard in the early 19th century.[73] The church had fallen into serious disrepair by the mid 19th century. Some restoration work was carried out, notably on the south aisle, and in 1866 and 1867 the spire was rebuilt under the supervision of the Revd. John Burdon, who paid for the addition of pinnacles and flying buttresses.[74] The chancel east wall was also rebuilt but in 1889 the church, its walls and nave arcade leaning dangerously, was closed as unsafe. It reopened the following year after much of it had been rebuilt to designs by Waller & Son of Gloucester. During that work many windows were renewed or replaced, new seats were installed, the gallery and the ceiling under the tower were removed, screens were placed in the tower arch and between the chancel and nave, the organ chamber was built, a concrete floor was laid, sealing the vaults below, and the ground around the church was lowered to improve drainage.[75] A small carving of two fishes, probably a jamb of the south doorway, was discovered in a house in Ruardean in the mid 1950s and was reset in the aisle south wall in the mid 1980s.[76]

Of the fittings the font and the wooden pulpit date from the 17th century, the font having an octagonal bowl dated 1657.[77] Tombchests in the nave for Baynham Vaughan (d. 1650) and members of his family, Roman Catholics, were removed in the 19th century, before 1872.[78] By deed of 1590 Anthony Sterry, vicar of Lydney, gave a rent charge of 5s. for the repair of the church bells and the ringing of a peal at Christmas.[79] Later

52 Glos. R.O., P 275/IN 1/4; *Trans. B.G.A.S.* xxxvii. 135–84; I. Gray, *Antiquaries of Glos. and Bristol* (B.G.A.S. 1981), 87–90.
53 Glos. Colln. L 9.3–4.
54 Hockaday Abs. cccxxvi; Glos. R.O., P 275/IN I/7.
55 Hockaday Abs. cccxxvi; *Glouc. Jnl.* 13 July, 9 Nov. 1844.
56 Glos. R.O., P 275/IN 1/7, 13.
57 Nat. Soc. files, Ruardean.
58 Hockaday Abs. cccxxvi.
59 Glos. R.O., D 1677/GHe 7; cf. Heref. R.O., F 8/II/58.
60 Glos. R.O., P 273/CH 1.
61 *Trans. B.G.A.S.* viii. 147–8; *19th Rep. Com. Char.* 105.
62 Glos. R.O., D 3469/5/128.
63 Inf. from the rector.
64 Heref. R.O., F 8/II/4; cf. Hockaday Abs. cccxxvi, 1508; G.D.R. vol. 397, f. 7. A dedication to St. Luke was recorded in 1851: P.R.O., HO 129/347/2/7/13.
65 Verey, *Glos.* ii. 330; *Trans. B.G.A.S.* lxxvi, plate between pp. 70–1; viii. 139–40, which dismisses the opinion that it depicted St. Michael. For the ch., above, Plate 18.
66 *Inq. p.m. Glos.* 1359–1413, 122.
67 Hockaday Abs. cccxxvi.

68 Glos. R.O., P 275/CW 3/1; part of the cost may have been met by a legacy of £20 from Sarah Reeve of Gloucester: Bigland, *Glos.* iii, no. 222. A pew said to have been built for John Vaughan in 1694 remained until 1890: *Trans. B.G.A.S.* viii. 141; Glos. R.O., P 275/VE 2/1.
69 G.D.R., V 5/254T 4–5.
70 Glos. R.O., D 3304; Hockaday Abs. cccxxvi.
71 *Trans. B.G.A.S.* viii. 141.
72 Glos. R.O., P 275/CW 2/2; cf. Colvin, *Biog. Dict. Brit. Architects*, 155.
73 Nicholls, *Forest of Dean*, 152; Bright, *Nonconf. in Dean*, 28.
74 Glos. R.O., P 275/VE 2/1; *Glos. Ch. Notes*, 168–70.
75 Glos. R.O., P 275/VE 2/1; *Glouc. Jnl.* 27 Sept. 1890.
76 Verey, *Glos.* ii. 330; *Trans. B.G.A.S.* lxxvi. 70–4; *Glos. & Avon Life*, Mar. 1985, 68–9.
77 Cf. *Trans. B.G.A.S.* xlvii. 176, 190.
78 Bigland, *Glos.* iii, no. 222.
79 Glos. R.O., P 275/CH 4; by 1680 the rent was used only to pay for the Christmas peal: ibid. CW 2/1–3; *19th Rep. Com. Char.* 105.

the church had six bells, of which three were recast at the Whitechapel foundry in 1866, and in 1905 the peal was enlarged by the gift of two trebles from the same foundry by Francis Brain and the Horlick family. Of the bells untouched in 1866 one was cast by Abraham Rudhall the younger in 1725, another was recast in 1926, and one dating from the late 16th century was replaced in 1929 and was kept in the church in 1990.[80] The church had a clock in 1680.[81] Among the plate is a chalice of 1744 acquired in 1746.[82] The parish registers survive from 1538 but most marriages between 1690 and 1735 took place at Walford. From the later 18th century the registers distinguish some entries for inhabitants of the extraparochial Forest of Dean.[83]

NONCONFORMITY. Several parishioners did not attend church in 1582[84] and a clerk performed a marriage in a house in the late 1580s.[85] The Vaughans, landowners in the parish from 1611,[86] were a prominent Roman Catholic family and Joan Vaughan's employment by 1623 of the priest John Broughton (or Crowther) as her steward suggests that she had a private chapel. Broughton was still at Ruardean in 1641 when his patroness was imprisoned for sheltering him.[87] In the later 17th century several households included Roman Catholics[88] and in 1676 eight papists were recorded in Ruardean.[89] Five papists were said to live there c. 1720[90] but only one was recorded in 1735,[91] after the Vaughans' departure from the parish. In the early 19th century a few parishioners belonged to the congregation of a Roman Catholic chapel across the river Wye at Courtfield.[92]

Among protestant dissenters living in Ruardean in 1668 were John Chapman and Thomas Bradley,[93] whose houses were licensed for worship in 1672. Bradley belonged to a congregation with Thomas Smith, formerly vicar of Longhope, as its minister.[94] Four protestant nonconformists were in Ruardean in 1676[95] and Chapman's house was being used for meetings in 1679.[96] Two Presbyterians were recorded in 1735.[97] From 1775 the Mitcheldean Independent church under its pastor Benjamin

Cadman used the Crooked Inn for a mission to Ruardean.[98] Another house was licensed for the mission in 1782[99] and a chapel was built in the village in 1798.[1] During the ministry of John Horlick, 1801–51, who also served Mitcheldean, the congregation grew; in 1804 a gallery was erected in the chapel and in 1813 the building was enlarged.[2] Horlick, who in 1808 registered a collier's house for worship,[3] claimed an average congregation of 130 for the chapel in 1851.[4] The meeting, later called Congregational,[5] had 25 members in 1900.[6] The chapel closed after 1960[7] and was used as a carpenter's store and was in disrepair in the late 1980s.

In 1824, about the time a Wesleyan Methodist preacher visited Ruardean,[8] a house in the village was registered for worship.[9] In 1828 Mary Cook built a small Bible Christian chapel at Crooked End.[10] The chapel, the Bible Christians' first in west Gloucestershire,[11] was known as Ebenezer[12] and had congregations of up to 80 in 1851.[13] It was enlarged in 1873[14] and became part of the United Methodist Church formed in 1907.[15] The chapel closed in the early 1980s[16] and was in bad repair in 1990. A few people continued to worship in an adjoining house.[17] In the mid 19th century Bible Christians and Primitive Methodists both attempted to establish meetings in the village and below Ruardean hill at Hill Farm.[18] A group of Christadelphians, which in 1914 moved its meeting from the Pludds to Morse Lane,[19] has not been traced later.

EDUCATION. John Broughton, the Roman Catholic priest whom Joan Vaughan was harbouring by 1623, sometimes acted as a schoolmaster[20] and in 1631 William Browne, his co-religionist, was teaching in Ruardean without a licence.[21] One of them presumably was the 'notorious popish schoolmaster' suspended in 1635 by Archbishop Laud's vicar general.[22] In 1704 Thomas Wade, a member of Gloucester's Independent church, was paying a schoolmistress £5 a year for teaching 12 poor children to read and recite a nonconformist catechism.[23] The Revd. Richard Greenaway by will proved 1745 left £60 to pay a master to teach 15 poor children to read the bible and say the church

80 *Glos. Ch. Notes*, 169; *Glos. Ch. Bells*, 526–30.
81 Glos. R.O., P 275/CW 2/1.
82 *Glos. Ch. Plate*, 176–7.
83 Glos. R.O., P 275/IN 1/1–14; cf. G.D.R., V 1/200; Heref. R.O., AO 19/1.
84 Glos. R.O., D 2052.
85 G.D.R. vol. 68, f. 64.
86 Above, manors.
87 Glos. R.O., D 2052; P.R.O., E 134/22 Jas. I Hil./3; *Misc.* viii (Cath. Rec. Soc. xiii), 150–6.
88 Glos. R.O., D 2052; cf. G.D.R. vol. 251, f. 38 and v.
89 *Compton Census*, ed. Whiteman, 544.
90 Glos. R.O., Q/SO 4.   91 G.D.R. vol. 285B(1), f. 7.
92 *Misc.* iv (Cath. Rec. Soc. iv), 416, 424, 427.
93 G.D.R. vol. 217.
94 *Cal. S.P. Dom.* 1672, 71, 118, 196, 216, 577; *Calamy Revised*, ed. A. G. Matthews, 449; cf. Turner, *Orig. Rec. of Early Nonconf.* ii, 815, 820; iii. 540–1.
95 *Compton Census*, ed. Whiteman, 544.
96 G.D.R. vol. 230.
97 Ibid. 285B(1), f. 7.
98 Hockaday Abs. cccxxvi; Glos. R.O., D 2297.
99 Glos. R.O., Q/SO 10, ff. 38v.–39.
1 Hockaday Abs. cccxxvi; cf. J. Stratford, *Good and Great Men of Glos.* (1867), 409.

2 Glos. R.O., D 2297; cf. Stratford, *Good and Great Men*, 412–13.
3 Hockaday Abs. cccxxvi.
4 P.R.O., HO 129/347/2/7/15.
5 *Kelly's Dir. Glos.* (1879), 730.
6 Glos. R.O., D 2052.
7 O.S. Map 1/2,500, SO 6117 (1960 edn.).
8 Bright, *Nonconf. in Dean*, 35.
9 G.D.R. vol. 344, f. 113v.
10 Hockaday Abs. cccxxvi; G. E. Lawrence, *Bible Christians of Forest of Dean*, ed. H. R. Jarrett (1985), 23; it was described as Primitive Methodist in G.D.R., T 1/151 (no. 327).
11 Cf. *V.C.H. Glos.* x. 117.
12 Glos. R.O., D 2598/5/8.
13 P.R.O., HO 129/347/2/7/16.
14 *Forest of Dean Examiner*, 25 Sept. 1874.
15 Lawrence, *Bible Christians*, 37.
16 Glos. R.O., D 2598/26/4.
17 *Citizen* (Glouc.), 7 Feb. 1989.
18 Glos. R.O., D 2598/4/6; 5/2, 8.
19 *Dean Forest Mercury*, 16 Aug. 1968.
20 P.R.O., E 134/22 Jas. I Hil./3; cf. *Misc.* viii (Cath. Rec. Soc. xiii), 150–6.
21 G.D.R. vol. 176, p. 162.   22 *Cal. S.P. Dom.* 1635, p. xli.
23 *Trans. B.G.A.S.* viii. 148; cf. Glos. R.O., D 4270/4/1/2–5.

catechism.[24] The principal, at first lent out, was used to open a free school in 1774, the master having a salary of £3.[25] A legacy from Thomas Richards (d. 1766)[26] of £25 to teach poor children reading and to buy them books was not applied as intended but by 1812 £1 5s. had been added to the salary of the free school's teacher in respect of it.[27] In 1819, although other day schools supplemented the 15 places in the free school, many children were without schooling.[28] In 1833, when the free school was funded partly by subscriptions, a benefactor supported a day school teaching 43 children and the parents of 10 children in another day school paid fees; there were also 16 children in a boarding school begun in 1830.[29] Sunday schools were started in the early 19th century by the curate T. D. Fosbrooke[30] and, evidently without success, by the Independents under John Horlick.[31]

The departure of the curate Henry Formby in 1846 occasioned the closure of a school[32] but in 1851 the inhabitants included a schoolmaster and a schoolmistress.[33] The salary of the free school's teacher, which was paid during that period, was used from 1851 by the incumbent[34] to support a mixed school, opened perhaps as early as 1848, in a cottage north of the churchyard. That school, which also had a small income from voluntary contributions and pence, was run on the National plan but its premises were unsuitable and in 1872 it moved to a new building at Shot hill. The new school, built with the help of the Revd. John Burdon, started with an average attendance of 55.[35] It had separate mixed and infants' departments from 1874 and lost some children to a new board school at Ruardean Woodside in 1878. The National school, in which evening classes were held in 1878, was enlarged in 1882[36] and had an average attendance exceeding 200 before the end of the

century,[37] falling after 1910 to 85 in 1938.[38] It accepted controlled status in 1947[39] and, as Ruardean C. of E. Primary school, had 79 children on its roll in 1990.[40] After 1898, when they were directed to provide prizes for schoolchildren, the Greenaway and Richards charities paid small sums to the church's Sunday school and the primary school respectively.[41]

CHARITIES FOR THE POOR. Richard Poole (d. 1618) by nuncupative will gave 40s. for the poor and the church. Although the churchwardens received the gift[42] no evidence for its distribution has been found. John Williams by deed of 1674 gave land, yielding 15s. in 1683, for a cash distribution[43] and Godfrey Taylor, a London gunmaker, by deed of 1697 a house with 2 a. to pay 28 Ruardean inhabitants, preferably his relatives or widows of parishioners, 1s. each and to provide 2s.-worth of refreshment for the trustees.[44] The charities were distributed together in the later 18th century.[45] A gift of £30 from Thomas Richards (d. 1766)[46] by will for a cash dole to widows and householders was not used as intended at least until 1803. In the later 1820s it was represented by a distribution of 30s. with Taylor's charity,[47] but it has not been traced later. Elizabeth Moore (d. c. 1780) gave a house yielding 15s. for the poor but the charity's income had fallen to 6s. or less by the 1820s, when the incomes of the Williams and Taylor charities remained at 15s. and 30s. respectively.[48] In 1898, when the parish charities were reorganized, the Williams, Taylor, and Moore charities and a third of the income of the Church Lands charity were assigned for general eleemosynary purposes,[49] and in 1989 the income available for the needy was £74, of which £61 came from the Church Lands charity.[50]

ST BRIAVELS

ST. BRIAVELS[51] lies on the east bank of the river Wye 11 km. (6¾ miles) upstream from Chepstow (Mon.). In 1086 and until the 1160s or later it was called Lydney or Little Lydney, having presumably had an ancient tenurial connexion with the nearby place still called Lydney,[52] but the name St. Briavels, thought to derive from the Celtic saint Brieuc,[53] was also in use by

1130.[54] Parts of St. Briavels parish were formed by assarting from the royal demesne land of the Forest of Dean in the early Middle Ages, and it was enlarged by the addition of detached parts of the extraparochial Forest in 1842. A royal castle built in the village before 1130, on a commanding site above the Wye, became the administrative centre of the Forest. In the 13th

24 P.R.O., PROB 11/740 (P.C.C. 168 Seymer), ff. 170–1.
25 Glos. R.O., P 275/CW 2/2.
26 Ibid. IN 1/5; Richards may have been resident in Hope Mansell (Herefs.): cf. ibid. D 3304, notice 18 June 1803.
27 19th Rep. Com. Char. 105; Glos. R.O., P 275/CW 2/3.
28 Educ. of Poor Digest, 307.
29 Educ. Enq. Abstract, 325; the benefactor may have been Thos. Griffiths, a Bristol cabinet maker, who by will proved 1834 left land and £400 to found a school in or near Ruardean: Glos. R.O., D 543, will.
30 Trans. B.G.A.S. xxxvii. 168.
31 Bright, Nonconf. in Dean, 2–3.
32 Nat. Soc. Inquiry, 1846–7, Glos. 14–15; cf. Glos. R.O., P 275/IN 1/7.
33 P.R.O., HO 107/1976.   34 Glos. R.O., P 275/CW 2/3.
35 P.R.O., ED 7/35/274; Nat. Soc. files, Ruardean.
36 Gibbs, 'Educ. in Two Forest of Dean Schs.' 12–13, 19, 28–9, 67.
37 Kelly's Dir. Glos. (1885–1914 edns.); Public Elem. Schs.

1906, 188.
38 Bd. of Educ., List 21, 1911 (H.M.S.O.), 166; 1922, 107; 1932, 117; 1938, 129.
39 Glos. R.O., CE/M 2/30, f. 83.
40 Educ. Services Dir. 1990–1 (co. educ. dept.), 28.
41 Glos. R.O., D 3469/5/128; CH 21, E. Dean rural district, p. 15.   42 Glos. R.O., P 275/IN 1/1.
43 19th Rep. Com. Char. 105; Trans. B.G.A.S. viii. 147 and n.   44 Glos. R.O., P 275/CH 5.
45 Ibid. CW 2/2.   46 Ibid. IN 1/5.
47 Ibid. D 3304, notice 18 June 1803; 19th Rep. Com. Char. 105.   48 19th Rep. Com. Char. 104–5.
49 Glos. R.O., D 3469/5/128.
50 Inf. from the rector.
51 This account was written in 1991.
52 Dom. Bk. (Rec. Com.), i. 167; Dugdale, Mon. vi (2), 1094; Pipe R. 1167 (P.R.S. xi), 144; cf. below, manors.
53 P.N. Glos. (E.P.N.S.), iii. 243.
54 Pipe R. 1130 (H.M.S.O. facsimile), 76.

century St. Briavels was also one of the sites of the Forest iron industry.

This account covers the history of the parish within its modern boundaries, which are the product of a complex history. In 1066 St. Briavels probably comprised a small manor based on the village, closely surrounded by the Forest woodland and waste. A manor called Wyegate, which William I afforested and took out of cultivation before 1086, may have included land in the north part of the later parish,[55] and by the early 13th century a royal estate called Stowe, including a hermitage, occupied land on the north boundary.[56] Assarting later increased the area of St. Briavels, much of the north and east parts of which was claimed by the Crown as ancient assart in the early 17th century.[57] In 1361 200 a. adjoining the Stowe estate were found to have been assarted since 1226.[58] Land called Rodmore near the east boundary of the later parish was being encroached by 1231,[59] and the king's reeve of St. Briavels, apparently acting without royal sanction, built a house on land at Willsbury in the same area before 1270.[60] In 1282, however, the eastern end of the later parish was probably still within the royal demesne of the Forest, for part of the west boundary of the Forest bailiwick called Bearse was then described as running from Stowe along the edge of the cultivated land of St. Briavels past Rodmore to Cone brook;[61] the boundary presumably included the land that became known as Bearse common, later a detached part of the Forest waste, and may then have turned southwards, following Rodmore Lane from the site of Great Hoggins Farm down to the Cone. By 1294 an estate at Rodmore, with land east of Rodmore Lane, was in private ownership and Willsbury probably was by 1300.[62] A new assart of 60½ a. described as at 'le Horestone' in 1316 probably adjoined the stone called the Long stone,[63] north of the road from Bream to St. Briavels on the later Closeturf farm, and 33 a. which Osbert Malemort was licensed to assart in 1306 and which his son William Gainer held in 1361[64] can probably be identified with Gainer's Mesne, lying on the later parish boundary, east of Closeturf.[65] The tithes from some of the new land were disputed by the dean and chapter of Hereford, owners of St. Briavels chapel, and the bishop of Llandaff, who was granted the tithes from new assarts in the Forest for his church of Newland in 1305. By arbitration in 1310 the boundary between the chapelry and Newland on the north-east was fixed on or close to its modern course: from an old castle at Stowe, the earth-

works of which still survive, it was traced past unidentified landmarks, which presumably took it west and south of Bearse common, along a portway, evidently the lane between Bearse Farm and Bream Cross, to the Coleford–Aylburton road ('Aylburton way'), and along that road to the Pailwell oak, which probably stood at the place near the head of Pailwell (later Park) brook where the boundaries of St. Briavels, Bream tithing of Newland, and Aylburton tithing of Lydney met.[66] In the north-west part of the later parish the valley between the village and the Wye was being cleared for cultivation by 1199 when an assart of 6 a. at Lindhurst (later the site of Lindors farm) was recorded.[67]

The progress of assarting left detached parts of the extraparochial Forest[68] within or adjoining St. Briavels parish. In 1608 St. Briavels Mesne, an area of 81 a. on the hillside below the village, was extraparochial,[69] but in 1787 only 24 a. in its western part, known as Mocking (or Mawkins) Hazel wood, was surveyed as part of the extraparochial Forest. The status of the eastern part, called Lower Meend, was in doubt in the early 19th century,[70] when it had been encroached by cottagers, but it was later assumed to be part of the parish. In 1787 the Fence, on the north boundary of the parish, probably the land called in 1282 'le defens', meaning an inclosure, was an extraparochial area of 44 a., and Bearse common, which retains the name of the Forest bailiwick dismembered by assarting in the St. Briavels and Newland area, was an extraparochial area of 102 a. adjoining the north-east boundary. To the south-west St. Briavels was bounded by a great tract of extra-parochial land called Hudnalls.[71] Extended at 1,205 a. in 1608 and 1,010 a. in 1641,[72] it comprised the land later distinguished separately by the names Hudnalls and St. Briavels common and the north and west parts of the land later called Hewelsfield common.[73] Although encroached upon, the extraparochial areas remained part of the royal demesne of the Forest until the 19th century.[74] In 1827 the Crown sold its rights in Hudnalls, Mocking Hazel wood, and the Fence to the owner of the Bigsweir estate, and later in the century its rights in Bearse common passed to the owner of the Clearwell estate.[75]

In 1840 St. Briavels parish was said to contain 3,312 a. Its principal part was bounded on the west by the river Wye, on the north mainly by field boundaries and the ancient portway mentioned above, on the east partly by the Coleford–Aylburton road and Colliers brook,

55 Above, Newland, manors.
56 Below, manors.
57 Glos. R.O., D 33/188A; D 177, Aylesmore est. deeds abs. of title to Batmore; Suff. R.O., HA 49/A III(b)/2, deeds 1618.
58 *Cal. Pat.* 1361–4, 11.
59 *Close R.* 1227–31, 521; *Cal. Chart. R.* 1226–57, 366.
60 P.R.O., E 32/29, rot. 6d.
61 Ibid. E 32/31, m. 12.
62 Below, manors.
63 *Cal. Inq. p.m.* v, p. 417; cf. below, this section.
64 Hist. MSS. Com. 55, *Var. Colln. IV, Glemham Hall,* pp. 178–9.
65 P.R.O., MR 879 (F 17/1).
66 B.L. Harl. Ch. 111, c. 32.
67 *Pipe R.* 1199 (P.R.S. N.S. x), 32.

68 For their boundaries and acreage in 1787, P.R.O., MR 415 (F 16/47); G.D.R., T 1/153.
69 P.R.O., MR 879; cf. Glos. R.O., D 2026/X 14 (s.v. purprestures within waste soil of Forest).
70 Glos. R.O., D 1833/T 18, deeds 1824, 1825, 1835; G.D.R., T 1/153–4; *Census,* 1841.
71 *Trans. B.G.A.S.* xiv. 362–3.
72 P.R.O., MR 879; LRRO 5/7A, f. 1v.
73 G.D.R., T 1/153; for the modern names, *Census,* 1841; G.D.R., T 1/154; O.S. Maps 1", sheet 35 (1830 edn.); 6", Glos. XLVI. NW., NE. (1884 edn.). For Hewelsfield common, above Hewelsfield, intro.
74 P.R.O., MR 415; Crown Land Revenue Act, 54 Geo. III, c. 70, s. 10.
75 Below, this section; econ. hist. (agric.).

and on much of the south by Aylesmore brook and the steep hillside north of Hudnalls. A detached part of the parish, mainly a narrow strip of meadowland, bordered the Wye below and west of Hudnalls, extending from near the principal part at Bigsweir southwards to Brockweir village.[76] In 1842 the civil parish was enlarged to include Mocking Hazel wood, the Fence, Bearse common, and most of Hudnalls, the rest of Hudnalls going to Hewelsfield civil parish.[77] The new parish boundary with Hewelsfield was fixed on the brook running down the hillside through Hudnalls between St. Briavels common and Hewelsfield common. The brook was called Mere (or Meer) brook by 1608,[78] a name which suggests that it delimited the areas over which St. Briavels and Hewelsfield had respectively exercised rights, and even before 1842 the north and south-west parts of Hudnalls were sometimes popularly regarded as being within St. Briavels parish.[79] After 1842 the civil parish comprised 4,798 a. (1,942 ha.).[80]

Much of the enlarged parish lies on a plateau high above the Wye Valley. In the south-west Hudnalls rises to just over 260 m. (853 ft.), steep sided on the north and towards the river on the west and sloping more gently towards the Brockweir valley on the south. In the north-west the land also rises steeply from the river to the top of Wyegate hill at over 210 m. (689 ft.). Between Hudnalls and Wyegate hill a horseshoe-shaped valley, perhaps formed by a vanished meander of the river, breaks into the high ground, and side valleys, formed by Mork brook and its tributary, Slade brook, combine to enter the main valley from the east. In the east part of the parish the land is open and gently rolling, mostly at c. 200 m. (656 ft.), while to the south-east Aylesmore brook joins the headwaters of Cone brook to form a deep valley draining to the Severn. The west part of the parish lies on the Old Red Sandstone and the east part on carboniferous limestone.[81]

In 1086 St. Briavels manor included a wood measuring 1 league by ½ league,[82] and the steep slopes of the Wye Valley have remained thickly wooded. Woods in those areas, owned by the Bigsweir estate, accounted for most of c. 500 a. of woodland recorded on the parochial land in 1840. Rodmore grove (70 a.) on the east boundary was then the only large wood in the upland areas.[83] Hudnalls was said to contain 710 a. of underwood and 300 a. of cleared ground in 1641.[84] On its high land and southern slopes the woodland was cleared by the exercise of commoning rights and rights to take timber, and from c. 1800[85] encroachments produced a pattern of tiny fields. In 1991 the woodland on the steep slopes remained native hardwoods, mostly coppiced but including some large oaks and beeches on the northern edge of Hudnalls. On Bearse common, in the Slade brook and Aylesmore brook valleys, and elsewhere conifer plantations were established in the 20th century. Some small open fields once lay around St. Briavels village, while in the east of the parish assarting in the early Middle Ages produced a pattern of compact, inclosed farms.

Offa's Dyke[86] descends Wyegate hill to the floor of the horseshoe valley, where it appears prominently in St. Margaret's grove, north of Mork brook. It is discernible again south of Lindhurst, where it was recorded by name ('Offedich') in 1321,[87] and it crosses the high land of Hudnalls as a reduced but fairly continuous feature. The ancient megalith called the Long stone, 10 ft. high, which stood in a field near Closeturf Farm,[88] was blown to pieces with gunpowder by a farmer in 1875.[89]

The principal ancient route through the parish was probably that which linked several of the early settlements on the east side of the Wye. From Hewelsfield village it ran past the site of Aylesmore Court to St. Briavels village, descended Mork hill to a ford on Mork brook, climbed the opposite side of the valley to Wyegate Green, which is probably the site of the manor depopulated in the late 11th century, and continued through Newland parish to the riverside at Redbrook. The road became known as Hewelsfield Lane south of St. Briavels village and Mork Lane north of it, and the section up to Wyegate Green was called Wyegate's way in 1376.[90] The road from Chepstow, west of Hewelsfield Lane and meeting it at the village, was in existence by 1448.[91] Another ancient route, recorded in 1445 as the Monmouth to Brockweir road,[92] followed the east bank of the Wye below Wyegate hill and Hudnalls. At Bigsweir, where shallows and a group of tiny islets were used as the basis of a fishing weir, the river was fordable:[93] Passage Lane was mentioned in that area in 1445[94] and Passage mead, upstream of the ford, was so called by 1787.[95] The road leading from the ford up the Mork brook valley towards the Forest was evidently a significant route in the early Middle Ages, for a castle was built at Stowe to command the head of the valley and two chapels stood by the road, one at Stowe and one at Mork hamlet.[96] St. Briavels village was linked to the ford and the Monmouth–Brockweir road by a steep track down through Lindhurst.[97] The principal ancient road from the village eastwards into the extraparochial Forest was that called the portway in 1310.[98] It

76 G.D.R., T 1/153; O.S. Map 1", sheet 35 (1830 edn.).
77 Dean Forest Poor-Relief Act, 5 & 6 Vic. c. 48.
78 P.R.O., MR 879; Taylor, Map of Glos. (1777).
79 3rd Rep. Dean Forest Com. 26–7.
80 O.S. Area Bk. (1881).
81 Geol. Surv. Map 1", solid, sheet 35 (1845 edn., revised to 1872).
82 Dom. Bk. (Rec. Com.), i. 167.
83 G.D.R., T 1/153.
84 P.R.O., LRRO 5/7A, f. 1v.
85 Below, econ. hist. (agric.).
86 C. Fox, Offa's Dyke (1955), 188–91.
87 N.L.W., Dunraven MSS. 271.
88 Rudder, Glos. 307; O.S. Map 1", sheet 35 (1830 edn.).
89 Trans. B.G.A.S. i. 105–6.
90 Hist. MSS. Com. 55, Glemham Hall, p. 179; cf. Glos. R.O., D 1677/GG 1224. For Pickentree fields and grove named in those sources, P.R.O., MR 879.
91 Glos. R.O., D 2244/140.
92 N.L.W., Dunraven MSS. 271.
93 Glos. R.O., Q/SRh 1830 B.
94 N.L.W., Dunraven MSS. 271.
95 Glos. R.O., D 1833/E 1.
96 Below manors (Stowe); church.
97 P.R.O., MR 879.
98 Above, this section.

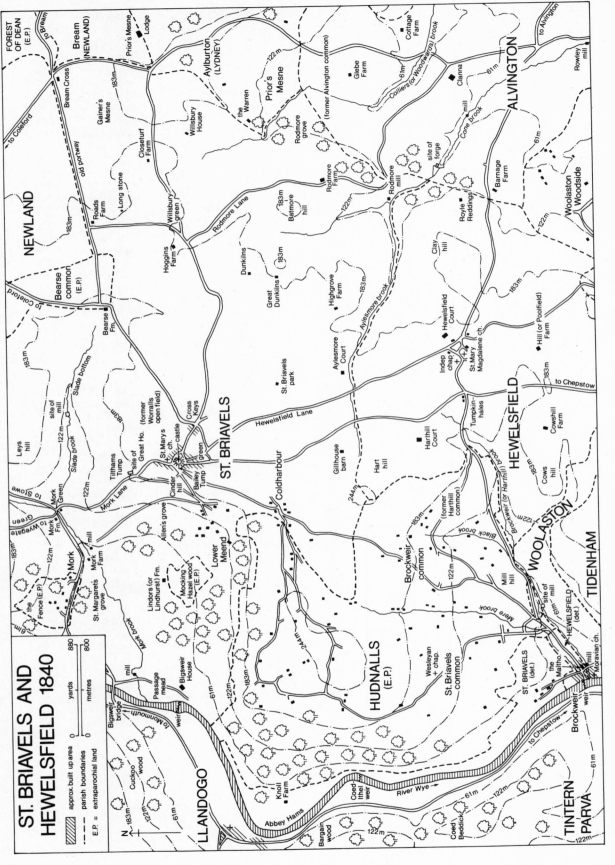

FIG. 10

ran on the line of the modern Coleford road to Bearse common, beyond which it followed the parish boundary to the place called Bream's gate cross in 1464 (later Bream Cross).[99] In 1625 William Whittington of St. Briavels left £5 for a causeway on part of the road[1] and the remains of pitching were visible on a stretch east of Roads House in 1991. Around the village and the hamlet of Coldharbour, to the south-west, a complex pattern of minor lanes was in place by 1608,[2] and a similarly complex pattern evolved in the early 19th century to serve the scattered dwellings on Hudnalls.

Under an Act of 1824 a new turnpike road was built up the Wye Valley to link Chepstow and Monmouth. It crossed from the Monmouthshire bank by a new bridge, called Bigsweir bridge, a single cast-iron span with stone abutments, which was opened in 1827, and it incorporated most of the old riverside road in the north of St. Briavels parish. The same Act turnpiked the road from Bigsweir bridge up the Mork valley and authorized a branch from that road up to St. Briavels village.[3] The road to the village was built in 1829 and, although it was later taken over by the turnpike trust, the cost was met by the parish and George Rooke, owner of the Bigsweir estate. It replaced an old lane, which had partly followed a more westerly course through Allen's grove, and a new bridge was built for it over Mork brook. Turnpike gates were set up near the foot of the new road to the village[4] and at Mork Green, where the Mork valley road crossed the old road to Wyegate.[5] In 1830, by agreement of the parish vestry and George Rooke, the old riverside road south of Bigsweir bridge was closed.[6] The Wye Valley and Bigsweir roads remained turnpikes until 1879.[7] The short stretch of the Chepstow–Coleford road north of Bearse Farm, where it branched from the line of the old portway to cross the extraparochial Bearse common, was repaired under the Forest turnpike trust established in 1796.[8] A tollbooth was sited at Bearse Farm.[9] Within St. Briavels the Chepstow–Coleford road was repaired by the parish under indictment in 1813,[10] and in 1837 it was described as equal in condition to a turnpike road.[11] The use of the other old main roads declined following the improvements of the 1820s. That from Hewelsfield to Wyegate Green was closed as a highway south of St. Briavels village in 1837.[12] In 1991 most of it survived as an unmade bridle way between high hedges, as did the old portway, which the parish had tried to get Clearwell tithing to join in repairing and widening in 1876.[13]

After 1876 when the Wye Valley railway was built along the Monmouthshire bank of the river the parish was served by a station, called St. Briavels, in Llandogo parish near the west end of Bigsweir bridge. The line was closed to passenger traffic in 1959 and to freight in 1964.[14]

A market was founded at St. Briavels in 1208, and the villagers were termed burgesses in 1352. The attempt to establish St. Briavels as a market centre ultimately failed,[15] but the village, with its role at the centre of the Forest administration, was probably fairly large in the Middle Ages. It stands high on the eastern rim of the horseshoe valley on the ancient route between Hewelsfield and Wyegate Green, which perhaps formed its main street in the Anglo-Saxon period. The parish church stands beside that route and probably pre-dated St. Briavels castle, which was founded before 1130[16] to the south of the church, astride the ancient route. The castle became and remains the dominant feature of the village, with a network of lanes centred on it. A lane circling the castle earthworks was joined on the south side by Hewelsfield Lane in the village, which becomes Pystol Lane in the village, and by the Chepstow road, called High Street. In 1608 there was a continuous green or open market place between the two streets and High Street had houses only on its west side.[17] Only a small open space called the Square later survived at the north end near the castle, but further south, where the two roads entered the village near the 19th-century school, a patch of green remained in 1991. The other main streets are Mork Lane, on the ancient route north of the castle, Church Street, called Venny Street in 1388,[18] which runs east of the castle and in 1608 continued east of the churchyard to join Mork Lane, and East Street, by which the route to Coleford left the village, running south-eastwards from the central ring of lanes. West of the castle, where the ground falls steeply away, lanes from the settlements of the west part of the parish meet below a triangular spur of waste ground that was called Bailey green in 1619 and later Bailey Tump.[19] In that area of the village, which became known as Cinder hill, the lanes traversing the hillside formed an even more complex pattern before the 1830s than survived there in 1991.[20] On the south side of the village, Barrowell Lane,[21] named from Barrow (anciently Barrel) well,[22] linked Hewelsfield Lane and the Coleford road.

In 1608 the most concentrated groups of houses in the village, probably cottages or other small dwellings, were near the castle, some on the east side of Church Street and others extend-

[99] Glos. R.O., D 1677/GG 257.
[1] Trans. B.G.A.S. x. 311. [2] P.R.O., MR 879.
[3] Abbey Tintern and Bigsweir Roads Act, 5 Geo. IV, c. 29; Glouc. Jnl. 11 Aug. 1827; Glos. R.O., Q/SRh 1830 B. The Forest trust of 1796 had included the part of the Mork valley road skirting the Fence: Dean Forest Roads Act, 36 Geo. III, c. 131.
[4] Glos. R.O., P 278/CW 2/2, mins. 11 Dec. 1828; 28 Jan. 1830; Q/SRh 1830 B; 1876 D.
[5] Ibid. D 1896, Mork fm. deeds 1709–1867, plan on deed 1840.
[6] Ibid. P 278/CW 2/2, min. 1 Dec. 1828; Q/SRh 1830 B.
[7] Annual Turnpike Acts Continuance Act, 37 & 38 Vic. c. 95.
[8] Dean Forest Roads Act, 36 Geo. III, c. 131. The Act, but not its later renewals, also included the part of the

portway crossing Bearse common.
[9] Bryant, Map of Glos. (1824); Glouc. Jnl. 11 Aug. 1827.
[10] Glos. R.O., Q/SR 1813. [11] Ibid. Q/SRh 1837 C/2, 4.
[12] Ibid. C/2. [13] Ibid. P 278/VE 2/1.
[14] O.S. Map 1/25,000, SO 50 (1951 edn.); Paar, G.W.R. in Dean, 113, 121.
[15] Below, econ. hist. (other ind. and trade); Cal. Chart. R. 1341–1417, 125.
[16] Below, manors; for the castle and village, above, Plate 8.
[17] For the village in 1608, P.R.O., MR 879; below, Fig. 11. [18] N.L.W., Dunraven MSS. 324.
[19] Ibid. 327; O.S. Map 1/2,500, Glos. XLVI. 3 (1881 edn.).
[20] Glos. R.O., Q/SRh 1830 B; 1837 C/1, 3. [21] Ibid. D 34/6/1.
[22] N.L.W., Dunraven MSS. 339, rental of est. of John Joce; 327, lease 1733.

ing along the south side of the castle earthworks from Church Street down to Cinder hill. High Street then had *c.* 7 larger houses spaced at regular intervals along its west side, with the southernmost one at or near the site of the later farmhouse called New House; possibly they originated as the dwellings of a group of Forest officers called serjeants-in-fee who were based at St. Briavels in the 13th century.[23] In 1608 there were a few houses near the south end of Pystol Lane near Barrow well, while north of the castle small farmhouses were scattered along Mork Lane as far as a place called Tilthams Tump, where the lane dips down Mork hill. The village was later reduced in extent. At the beginning of the 18th century the sites of demolished houses were visible,[24] and by 1840 the houses between the Square and Cinder hill and most of those near Barrow well and on Mork Lane had gone. Most of the houses on the west side of High Street had also been demolished and those near the north end had been replaced by a more continuous row. A few houses had been built on the east side of Pystol Lane and others, one dated 1829, had been added recently near a place known as Cross Keys at the junction of East Street, Barrowell Lane, and the Bream and Coleford roads.[25]

The older parts of the village are formed mainly of modest, two-storeyed, stone-built dwellings of the late 18th century and the early 19th. Church (formerly Churchyard) Farm, near the south end of Mork Lane, dates in part from the late 16th century and had a cross passage flanked by two large rooms. The south end of the house was added or rebuilt in the 18th century and a new cross passage was formed in the end of the older part. A small gabled building opposite the entrance to Church Street, by tradition once the home of the priests who served a chantry in the church,[26] dates in part from the 17th century but was much altered later, and the George inn south-east of the castle is also 17th-century in origin. Cinderhill, below Bailey Tump, is an **L**-shaped 17th-century farmhouse, restored and remodelled in the 20th. In 1698 it was owned, with a small estate in the parish, by the Birkin family and in 1760 it passed by marriage to James Davies[27] (d.1781), curate of St. Briavels.[28] St. Briavels House on the east side of Pystol Lane is a moderate-sized 19th-century residence, perhaps built for Charles Lord Denton, a prominent inhabitant and benefactor to the village.[29] A few small 18th- and early 19th-century farmhouses in and adjoining the village include Patchwell Farm in East Street, which in 1991 was being restored and its buildings converted

as dwellings, and New House Farm on the Chepstow road south of the school.

In 1931 the Lydney rural district built eight council houses at Cross Keys on the east side of the village,[30] and the council estate there was enlarged in the 1950s and 1960s, partly by a small group of old people's bungalows.[31] In the late 1960s and early 1970s[32] a substantial estate of private houses was formed in the south-east part of the village, filling the area between Pystol Lane and East Street and partly based on Barrowell Lane, which was improved and extended south-westwards to enable Coleford–Chepstow traffic to bypass the village centre. A few small housing developments in the late 1980s included one on the Bream road, east of Cross Keys.

In the horseshoe valley below St. Briavels village a place called Lindhurst was settled by 1310,[33] and in 1608 apparently comprised a number of dwellings.[34] Later there was only a single farmstead, the name of which by the 19th century was corrupted to Lindors Farm.[35] Further north a hamlet called Mork, of which little survived by the 20th century, grew up on the Bigsweir–Stowe road around the junction with the old road descending from St. Briavels village through Allen's grove. By the mid 14th century it had three or more houses, a mill, and a roadside chapel,[36] and in 1608 it comprised *c.* 13 small dwellings, most of them grouped loosely around a green on the Stowe road east of the junction.[37] A farmhouse called Mork Farm below the junction belonged during the 17th and 18th centuries to the Dale family, whose enlargement of their farm caused the disappearance of at least some of the other houses of the hamlet.[38] In 1846 the farm was bought by James White (d. 1871), a land agent of Coleford, who replaced the house with a large residence in an elaborate Tudor style, named Lindors, and formed a garden with an ornamental pond on Mork brook below.[39] A smaller house in a similar style, called Woodlands, was built nearby, on the north side of the road, *c.* 1850.[40] Further up the road to Stowe, where the road and the brook were crossed by the St. Briavels–Wyegate road, a settlement was established near another small green. In 1608, when the place was known as Mork Green, there were three or four houses there.[41] A farmhouse standing close to the road junction and known as Mork Farm by 1880[42] apparently occupies the site of a dwelling recorded in 1376.[43] It is a gabled, stone building of the early 17th century, built on an **L**-shaped plan and entered beneath a newel-stair turret in the angle of its two ranges. Internally many of the original fittings survive. At the head of the valley St. Briavels included two farmhouses

23   Below, manors.
24   Bodl. MS. Rawl. B. 323, f. 111.
25   G.D.R., T 1/153.
26   O.S. Map 1/2,500, Glos. XLVI. 3 (1881 edn.).
27   Glos. R.O., D 33/330; D 1833/T 6.
28   Ibid. P 278/IN 1/3–4.
29   W. J. Creswick, *Where I was Bred* (Coleford, *c.* 1970), 15; inscr. in ch.
30   Glos. R.O., DA 28/100/10, pp. 263–4, 274, 333.
31   Ibid. 15, pp. 464–5; 17, mins. 28 May 1957; 15 Aug. 1961; 22 Oct. 1963.
32   Inf. from Mrs. M. Cope, a St. Briavels par. councillor.
33   N.L.W., Dunraven MSS. 325.

34   P.R.O., MR 879.
35   Glos. R.O., D 1833/E 1; O.S. Maps 1", sheet 35 (1830 edn.); 6", Glos. XLVI. NE. (1884 edn.).
36   N.L.W., Dunraven MSS. 339; below, church.
37   P.R.O., MR 879.
38   Glos. R.O., D 1440, St. Briavels deeds 1560–1827; D 1896, Mork fm. deeds 1709–1867.
39   Ibid. D 1896, Mork fm. deeds 1709–1867; deeds of Lindors est. 1852–1927; D 637/VII/28.
40   Ibid. D 1896, Woodlands deeds 1847–76.
41   P.R.O., MR 879.
42   O.S. Map 6", Glos. XXXVIII. SE. (1884 edn.).
43   Hist. MSS. Com. 55, *Glemham Hall*, p. 179.

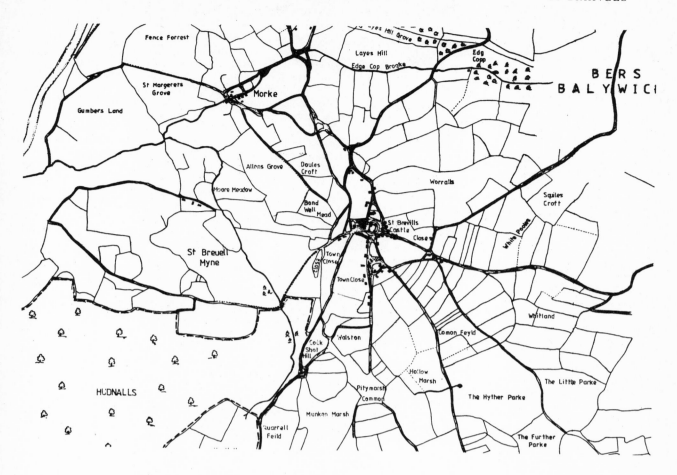

FIG. 11. ST BRIAVELS VILLAGE AREA, 1608

attached to the hamlet of Stowe, which is otherwise in Newland parish. Stowe Grange, on the south-east side of the road, is on the site of a medieval manor.[44] There was a farmhouse at Stowe Farm, further down the hill on the other side of the road, by 1608 when the farm belonged to the Clearwell estate;[45] in the late 17th century and until c. 1780 it was part of a scattered estate that the Foley family of Stoke Edith (Herefs.) owned in the parish.[46]

Only a few early dwellings were established on the banks of the Wye beside the old Monmouth–Brockweir road. A house called the Florence stood near the north boundary of the parish by 1588.[47] Its name, recorded as that of a wood in 1253,[48] possibly derived from St. Florent abbey (Saumur), which had a claim to St. Briavels church in the 12th century.[49] The Florence descended with the adjoining Wyeseal manor, in Newland,[50] and in 1800 was occupied by the woodman of Lord Sherborne's large Newland estate.[51] It was rebuilt in an ornamental style c. 1900 and was a hotel in 1991. Bigsweir House, built beside the weir of that name and the ford,

was the centre of one of principal estates of the parish.[52] Knoll Farm, on the ancient parochial land on the promontory below Hudnalls, is possibly the successor of a house built in that area by John Williams, a mariner, c. 1750.[53] In the early 19th century a few cottages were built at the riverside in St. Briavels parish close to Brockweir, most of them occupied by watermen employed in Brockweir's trade.[54] In the 20th century they were demolished or else incorporated in larger dwellings. Further north the lower slopes of the wooded hillside were settled with private houses in the late 19th century, one of them, a substantial dwelling called Brockweir House, with its own boathouse on the river bank below.

Farmsteads are scattered fairly evenly across the high ground of the east and south parts of the ancient parish. Willsbury and Rodmore were established in the early Middle Ages and Aylesmore Court by the late 17th century.[55] Great Hoggins Farm, at a place called Willsbury green[56] where the Bream road meets Rodmore Lane, was owned and farmed by the Allen family

44 Below, manors.   45 P.R.O., MR 879.
46 Glos. R.O., D 1833/T 13; D 2528.
47 Ibid. D 2026/E 7.   48 Ibid. A 1.
49 Below, church.
50 Glos. R.O., D 2026/E 7; D 1833/T 8; G.D.R., T 1/153;
cf. above, Newland, manors.

51 Glos. R.O., D 637/VII/22.
52 Below, manors.
53 Glos. R.O., D 1833/T 11.
54 O.S. Map 1", sheet 35 (1830 edn.); cf. P.R.O., HO 107/2443.
55 Below, manors.   56 P.R.O., MR 879.

from the early 18th century to the mid 19th.[57] It is a late 17th-century stone farmhouse of two storeys and attics, which had a symmetrical plan with central entrance and end-gable stacks. A back wing was added in 1767,[58] displaced windows being reset in it, and by the 19th century a lean-to occupied the angle between the new and old ranges. In the mid 19th century the main range was extended eastwards and the dormers and ground-floor windows of the old part of that range were made uniform with those of the extension. The other farmhouses are mainly small buildings in the plain vernacular style of the 18th century and early 19th, though a number occupy earlier sites. Bearse Farm, where the Coleford road leaves the old portway, was established by the mid 17th century,[59] as was Bream Cross Farm, at the east end of the portway; Bream Cross had the alternative name of Brockets in 1659.[60] Roads Farm (later Roads House), on the portway at the junction with a lane from Willsbury green, was mentioned in 1704. Lands called Closeturf, north-east of the green, then contained only a barn,[61] Closeturf Farm being built beside the Bream road in the mid 18th century. One of two farmhouses called Dunkilns, standing close together south of the Bream road, existed by 1723. The more southerly of the two was later distinguished as Great Dunkilns,[62] and the northern one was called Severn View in the 20th century.[63] Highgrove, further south, is a house of c. 1820 and was probably newly established then as the principal farmhouse on the Aylesmore estate.[64] A residence called Ghyll House was built on the site of a barn west of the Chepstow road c. 1910.[65]

The former extraparochial common lands in the west part of St. Briavels were populated by squatters during the late 18th century and the early 19th. Three cottages recorded on Hudnalls in 1656[66] may not have survived the government's expulsions of illegal settlers from Forest lands in the following years.[67] The parishioners of St. Briavels were later active in preventing encroachments,[68] but attempts to prevent cottagers settling were apparently abandoned at the start of the 19th century, when Hudnalls rapidly became studded with cottages and small farmhouses.[69] By 1841 the parts that were added to St. Briavels civil parish the next year—the high plateau in the north and St Briavels common on the southern slopes—contained more than 130 houses,[70] many of them with closes of cultivated

land around them; in 1832 most of the settlers were said to be former inhabitants of the parish.[71] Some of the small dwellings on Hudnalls were evidently abandoned and demolished later in the 19th century, following the onset of the agricultural depression. Losses there presumably accounted largely for the fall in the total number of inhabited houses in St. Briavels parish from 299 in 1871 to 260 in 1881 and 251 in 1891; 15, 48, and 38 unoccupied dwellings respectively were recorded at those dates.[72] By the end of the century, however, the decline in the number of houses was halted[73] as the Hudnalls area began to attract wealthier private residents, who enlarged some of the cottages and built new houses.[74] New building continued in the 1930s,[75] when a number of bungalows and other small dwellings were put up in the area, and in the later 20th century, when some more substantial houses were built and the surviving older cottages were modernized and extended.

At Coldharbour, where a number of lanes meet at the north-east corner of Hudnalls, a small hamlet was established on parochial land in the early 19th century and comprised c. 5 cottages in 1840.[76] At Lower Meend, the common below St. Briavels village, three cottages were recorded in 1656,[77] but they possibly did not long survive, and the main period of settlement there began c. 1770.[78] By 1840 there was a total of c. 20 small stone cottages, scattered on the steep hillside around a stream.[79] At the Fence, on the slopes north of Mork brook, a similar settlement grew up, containing 6 cottages by 1788 and 11 by 1841.[80]

In 1327 22 inhabitants of St. Briavels and Hewelsfield were assessed for the subsidy.[81] There were said to be c. 170 communicants in St. Briavels in 1551[82] and 49 households in 1563,[83] and in 1650 the population was said to comprise 80 families.[84] About 1710 the population was estimated at 400 in 80 houses,[85] and c. 1775 at 766 in 122 houses,[86] though there is little other indication of such a substantial rise over the period and the second figure is probably an overestimate. In 1801 670 inhabitants in 144 houses were enumerated, the figures evidently including the settlements that were beginning to form in the adjoining extraparochial areas. In 1841 the parish contained 585 people in 105 houses, while Lower Meend, the Fence, and the parts of Hudnalls that were added to the parish

57 Glos. R.O., D 892/T 70, deed 1729; P 209/MI 1, p. 133; G.D.R., T 1/153.
58 Date and initials (T. and E. A.) on bldg.
59 Below, manors (Great Ho.).
60 Glos. R.O., D 33/317.
61 Ibid. 315, 321, 331–2.
62 Ibid. D 1440, St. Briavels deeds 1560–1827; O.S. Map 6", Glos. XLVI. NE. (1884 edn.).
63 O.S. Map 1/25,000, SO 50 (1951 edn.).
64 G.D.R., T 1/153.
65 Creswick, Where I was Bred, 16; O.S. Map 6", XLVI. NE. (1884 edn.).
66 Glos. R.O., D 2026/X 14.
67 Hart, Royal Forest, 151, 179.
68 Below, econ. hist. (agric.).
69 Trans. B.G.A.S. ix. 100 n.; Bryant, Map of Glos. (1824); Greenwood, Map of Glos. (1824).
70 Census, 1841, where 159 houses (9 of them uninhab-

ited) were enumerated in those areas with Lower Meend; cf. below, this section.
71 3rd Rep. Dean Forest Com. 17.
72 Census, 1871–91.
73 Ibid. 1901–11.
74 Cf. above, Hewelsfield, intro.
75 Cf. Glos. R.O., DA 28/100/11, p. 345; 13, pp. 200, 243.
76 G.D.R., T 1/153.
77 Glos. R.O., D 2026/X 14.
78 Ibid. D 1833/T 18, affidt. 1835.
79 G.D.R., T 1/153.
80 3rd Rep. Dean Forest Com. 112; Census, 1841.
81 Glos. Subsidy Roll, 1327, 5–6.
82 E.H.R. xix. 121.
83 Bodl. MS. Rawl. C. 790, f. 28.
84 Trans. B.G.A.S. lxxxiii. 97.
85 Atkyns, Glos. 296.
86 Rudder, Glos. 309.

the next year contained 702 people in 161 houses. In 1851 the enlarged parish had a population of 1,194, which rose to 1,315 by 1871 but then fell to 1,065 by 1901. In the first 70 years of the 20th century the population fluctuated at around 1,100, and between 1971 and 1991 it rose from 1,140 to 1,331.[87]

In 1600 there were three victualling houses at St. Briavels, whose owners were presented for allowing disorderly behaviour and illegal gaming.[88] By 1721 the George inn, south-east of the castle, had opened,[89] and it was possibly the inn that was called the Castle in 1799,[90] though in 1702[91] and until the early 19th century an alehouse was kept in the castle itself by the gaoler of the debtors' prison there.[92] By 1818 the Plough inn had opened on the west side of High Street and by 1840 there was a beerhouse, called the Crown, near Barrow well at the south end of the village.[93] The Plough had closed by 1880,[94] and the George and the Crown remained open in 1991.

An ancient ceremony, first found recorded at the start of the 18th century, involved the distribution of bread and cheese to the poor in St. Briavels church at Whitsun. By tradition it was instituted in connexion with a grant of a right of taking wood in Hudnalls, each parishioner contributing 1d. (later 2d.) in acknowledgment of the right.[95] The ceremony was rowdy in the early 19th century: the dole of bread and cheese was thrown from the galleries and the congregation scrambled for it on the church floor,[96] sometimes using it to pelt the curate. The rowdiness led to the ceremony being transferred to the churchyard c. 1857 and later to the road outside, where it was accompanied with drunkenness and fighting until c. 1890.[97] In the early 1990s the distribution of the bread and cheese, which for many years had been organized by one family, the Creswicks, was made at the old manor pound near the north end of Bailey Tump.[98] Also contributing to the villagers' reputation for unruly behaviour in the early 19th century was a gathering for cockfighting held on Whit Monday until suppressed by the curate c. 1845.[99] A village wake, including sports and maypole dancing, continued in Whit week in the 1850s.[1] It presumably took place on Bailey Tump, where a maypole stood in 1880.[2]

In 1826 a friendly society held its meetings at the George inn,[3] and by 1846 there was a separate society for women.[4] The vicar W. T. Allen, who served the cure from 1867, started a sick and burial society.[5] In 1854 C. L. Denton founded a village reading room and library in a building at the west end of East Street and he later provided a billiard and recreation room there.[6] At his death in 1892 Denton left legacies for the benefit of the village. His nephew and heir O. W. Andrews[7] gave a site adjoining the reading room for an assembly room, which was built in 1924.[8] The reading room was closed c. 1960 but the assembly room, recently modernized, remained in use in 1991.[9] The village had a cricket club by 1897,[10] and a village playing field was opened on the north side of East Street c. 1947.[11]

MANORS, CASTLE, AND OTHER ESTATES.

A manor at St. Briavels was known as *LYDNEY* in 1086 and *LITTLE LYDNEY* in the 1160s[12] but from the 13th century was generally called the manor of *ST. BRIAVELS*. It formed part of Lydney hundred in the 11th century and had presumably had a tenurial connexion with Lydney. Alfer held it in 1066,[13] and it was possibly among estates given at the Conquest to William FitzOsbern: his foundation Lire abbey (Eure) later claimed St. Briavels church and tithes as an adjunct to Lydney church. Wihanoc, lord of Monmouth, may have later acquired the manor, and in 1086 his nephew and successor William son of Baderon held it, extended at six hides. In 1144 William's son and successor to the lordship of Monmouth, Baderon of Monmouth, confirmed St. Briavels church to Wihanoc's foundation Monmouth priory, against which Lire had later to establish its right, and at the same period the place was named as Lydney Baderon.[14] No certain evidence has been found, however, that Baderon was in possession of St. Briavels in 1144, and it is likely that the manor had already passed from his family to the Crown, for in 1130 St. Briavels castle was recorded as a royal castle. Castle and manor later became established as the administrative centre of the Forest and as the head of a hundred or liberty of St. Briavels.[15]

In 1130 the hereditary sheriff of Gloucestershire, Miles of Gloucester, later earl of Hereford, accounted for the wages of a knight and other officers

[87] *Census*, 1801–1991.
[88] B.L. Harl. MS. 4131, f. 553.
[89] Glos. R.O., P 278/CW 2/1.
[90] *Glouc. Jnl.* 24 June 1799.
[91] Badminton Mun. FmH 2/1/1, affidt. of Thos. Davies.
[92] *Trans. B.G.A.S.* iii. 334–5; *1st Rep. Dean Forest Com.* 16.
[93] G.D.R., T 1/153; Glos. R.O., P 175/IN 3/1, f. 39.
[94] O.S. Map 1/2,500, Glos. XLVI. 3 (1881 edn.).
[95] Bodl. MS. Top. Glouc. c. 3, f. 138v.; Rudder, *Glos.* 307.
[96] *Glouc. Jnl.* 1 June 1807.
[97] *Trans. B.G.A.S.* xviii. 82–3.
[98] Creswick, *Where I was Bred*, 5; inf. from Mrs. Cope.
[99] *Glos. Chron.* 6 Aug. 1864.
[1] *Glouc. Jnl.* 2 June 1855.
[2] O.S. Map 1/2,500, Glos. XLVI. 3 (1881 edn.).
[3] Glos. R.O., Q/RSf 2.
[4] Ibid. Q/RZ 1.

[5] Creswick, *Where I was Bred*, 11; G.D.R. vol. 384, f. 28.
[6] O.S. Map 1/2,500, Glos. XLVI. 3 (1881 edn.); *Kelly's Dir. Glos.* (1885), 557; (1935), 296.
[7] Inscr. in ch.
[8] Glos. R.O., P 278/CH 4/1; Creswick, *Where I was Bred*, 15–16.
[9] Inf. from Mrs. Cope.
[10] *Kelly's Dir. Glos.* (1897), 278.
[11] Inf. from Mrs. Cope.
[12] The identification, first made in G. Ormerod, *Strigulensia* (1861), 109–13, is established by 12th-cent. documents concerning St. Briavels ch.: Dugdale, *Mon.* vi (2), 1094; *Cal. Doc. France*, pp. 403–4, 409–13.
[13] *Dom. Bk.* (Rec. Com.), i. 167.
[14] Ibid.; *Cal. Doc. France*, pp. 409–13; *Trans. B.G.A.S.* iv. 129–30.
[15] Below, Forest of Dean, forest admin. (early hist.); above, St. Briavels hundred.

of St. Briavels castle.[16] He presumably then had custody of the castle under the Crown, and is by tradition credited with building it.[17] In 1139 Empress Maud granted the castle together with the Forest of Dean to Miles in fee.[18] The grant presumably included the manor adjoining the castle: by tradition it was Miles who gave rights in Hudnalls to the men of St. Briavels,[19] and he made a grant of a forge at St. Briavels between 1141 and his death in 1143.[20] The castle and the Forest were exempted from lands that Henry II confirmed to Miles's son, Roger, earl of Hereford, in 1154 or 1155,[21] and from 1160 the castle was recorded in possession of the Crown's custodians of the Forest.[22] During the next two centuries the castle and manor of St. Briavels,[23] together with Newland manor and the profits of the Forest, were appurtenant to the offices of constable of St. Briavels and warden of the Forest, held during royal pleasure at an annual farm.[24] In 1341 the constable Guy Brian was given tenure of his office for life. On his death in 1390[25] castle, manors, and Forest, which for convenience will be here termed the St. Briavels castle estate, passed under a reversionary grant, quit of the farm, to Thomas, duke of Gloucester, whose grant was converted to one in tail male in 1391.[26] After the duke's death and forfeiture in 1397 the estate was granted for life at farm to Thomas le Despenser, earl of Gloucester,[27] who forfeited it in 1399.[28] Henry IV then gave it in fee to his son John, later duke of Bedford, who died without issue in 1435.[29] From that time the St. Briavels castle estate was separated tenurially from the constableship and wardenship, though for much of the 17th and 18th centuries the same people held the lease of the estate and, under a separate royal patent, the two offices.[30]

In 1437 the Crown assigned one third of the St. Briavels castle estate as dower to the duke of Bedford's widow Jacquette of Luxembourg, who had married Richard Woodville,[31] later Lord Rivers. She surrendered her right c. 1466, when it was granted to William Herbert, later earl of Pembroke, who was executed in 1469.[32] The remainder of the estate was granted for

seven years from 1436 to Richard Beauchamp, earl of Warwick, and at his death in 1439 to Ralph Botiller and John Beauchamp for their lives.[33] In 1445 the reversion of the whole estate was granted in fee to Henry Beauchamp, duke of Warwick (d. 1446),[34] whose sister and heir Anne and her husband Richard Neville, earl of Warwick, were dealing with the estate in 1466.[35] Anne released her right to the Crown in 1488[36] but other evidence suggests that the Crown had the whole estate in hand from 1476 or earlier.[37]

In 1490 the Crown leased the St. Briavels castle estate to Thomas Baynham, and the lease was renewed to him and his son Christopher for 30 years in 1498.[38] The Baynhams remained in possession to the end of their term in 1528[39] when a lease was granted to Sir William Kingston[40] (d. 1540). Sir William's son, Sir Anthony Kingston, had a 21-year lease from 1547,[41] which he immediately assigned to William Guise of Elmore. Guise renewed the lease,[42] and at his death in 1574 was succeeded by his son John (d. 1588),[43] who secured an assignment of a 30-year lease granted in 1583 to the Lord Chancellor, Sir Thomas Bromley.[44] In 1591 the estate was held by John Guise's eldest son William during the minority of a younger son John.[45] In 1611 a 40-year lease was granted to William Herbert, earl of Pembroke,[46] and he assigned some of his rights in 1612 to Sir Richard Catchmay, who remained in possession of them in 1638.[47] The earl (d. 1630) was succeeded by his brother Philip, who renewed the lease for 40 years in 1640; Newland manor was then specified as part of the estate for the first time, but it had probably been included since 1490. Philip, earl of Pembroke, who sided with parliament in the Civil War, died in 1650,[48] and his assignees apparently retained the lease until the Restoration when one of them conveyed it to Henry Somerset, Lord Herbert. Somerset, later marquess of Worcester and duke of Beaufort, held the St. Briavels castle estate until his death in 1700, securing a renewal of the lease from Queen Catherine, who had been given the estate as part of her dower in 1665. The duke's widow Mary retained the estate[49] until 1706 or later and apparently sold

16 *Pipe R.* 1130 (H.M.S.O. facsimile), 76.
17 Atkyns, *Glos.* 294.
18 B.L. Lansdowne MS. 229, f. 123v.
19 Bodl. MS. Top. Glouc. c. 3, f. 138v.
20 *Camd. Misc.* xxii. 15, 28–9.
21 *Rot. Chart.* (Rec. Com.), 53, 61.
22 *Pipe R.* 1160 (P.R.S. ii), 123.
23 The earliest mention found of the man. in possession of the constable as an adjunct of the cast. is in 1232: *Pat. R. 1225–32*, 477; cf. *Cal. Pat. 1258–66*, 87.
24 P.R.O., SC 6/850/18–19; *Cal. Close, 1341–3*, 153; cf. below, Forest of Dean, wardens.
25 *Cal. Fine R. 1337–47*, 243; *Trans. B.G.A.S.* lxii. 23–4.
26 *Cal. Pat. 1381–5*, 579; *1388–92*, 297, 360, 406.
27 Ibid. *1396–9*, 224.
28 *Complete Peerage*, v. 729; *Cal. Fine R. 1399–1405*, 14.
29 *Cal. Pat. 1399–1401*, 159; P.R.O., SC 6/858/14; SC 6/1116/11; E 101/141/1.
30 Cf. below, Forest of Dean, wardens.
31 P.R.O., C 139/84, no. 76.
32 *Cal. Pat. 1461–7*, 169, 533; *Complete Peerage*, x. 400–1.
33 *Cal. Fine R. 1430–7*, 314; *Cal. Pat. 1436–41*, 407; Berkeley Cast. Mun., General Ser. acct. roll 426; the earl's grant was made in Feb. 1437 to run from the preceding

Michaelmas. For the earls of Warwick, *Complete Peerage*, xii (2), 379–93.
34 *Cal. Pat. 1441–6*, 400–1.
35 P.R.O., CP 25/1/294/74, no. 41. A grant was made to Geo., duke of Clarence, in 1464: *Cal. Pat. 1461–7*, 329.
36 P.R.O., CP 25/1/294/79, no. 7.
37 Glos. R.O., D 33/120; cf. *Cal. Fine R. 1471–85*, pp. 206, 310–11.
38 *Cal. Fine R. 1485–1509*, pp. 129, 205, 277.
39 N.L.W., Dunraven MSS. 324.
40 P.R.O., C 60/338, m. 14.
41 *L. & P. Hen. VIII*, xxi (2), p. 241; cf. *Trans. B.G.A.S.* vi. 292.
42 P.R.O., E 112/15, no. 58; C 60/379, m. 19.
43 Ibid. E 112/15, no. 9; cf. *Trans. B.G.A.S.* iii. 70. A lease granted in 1571 to Rog. Taverner, deputy surveyor general of Crown woods, and cancelled in 1583, was evidently not implemented: P.R.O., C 60/387, m. 3; E 112/15, no. 58.
44 P.R.O., C 60/401, m. 43.   45 Ibid. E 112/16, no. 120.
46 Ibid. C 66/1904, mm. 10–11.
47 Ibid. C 99/36; cf. ibid. C 99/24; Glos. R.O., D 1677/GG 1220; Hart, *Royal Forest*, 281.
48 *Cal. S.P. Dom. 1640*, 232; *Complete Peerage*, x. 412–18.
49 Badminton Mun. FmH 2/1/1; *Complete Peerage*, ii. 51–2.

the lease to James Berkeley (d. 1736), earl of Berkeley, who had a new lease from the Crown in 1727. The earl's descendants, Augustus (d. 1755), earl of Berkeley, Frederick Augustus (d. 1810), earl of Berkeley, and William FitzHardinge Berkeley, Lord Segrave, remained lessees[50] until 1838. Lord Segrave was then succeeded as lessee by the former steward of the estate William Roberts, a Coleford solicitor, who held the estate until 1858.[51] From then the manorial rights of St. Briavels and Newland were kept in hand by the Crown,[52] but in 1991 were managed for it by the Forestry Commission.[53]

The only land in the parish held in demesne with the castle and manor in the modern period was that called St. Briavels park, which was recorded from 1437 when it was extended at 100 a.[54] The main part of the park was a group of closes south-east of the village, adjoining Hewelsfield Lane, and it also included land called Just Reddings adjoining the Bream road.[55] On the main part a barn was built in 1751–2 and, before 1795, a small farmhouse known as Park Farm, which was rebuilt in 1825. In the late 17th century and the 18th the park, comprising 106 a., was held on 21-year leases under the Crown's lessees.[56] It was sold by the Crown in the mid 19th century, before 1875,[57] most of it becoming part of Highgrove farm.[58] The farmhouse was replaced by a group of private houses in the 1980s. The other main assets of the St. Briavels castle estate in the modern period were drawn from the Forest area as a whole and comprised chief rents paid for the manors and assarted lands of the liberty of St. Briavels, herbage money owed by bordering parishes and tithings for rights of common in the Forest, and a customary payment from quarry owners. The lessees gave up collecting the quarry rents in 1819[59] and the herbage money c. 1835,[60] and the chief rents were redeemed between the 1860s and the 1930s.[61]

St. Briavels castle[62] stands in the village on the edge of a ridge at c. 200 m. above the river Wye. The earliest part of the defences was evidently the low motte at the south. It presumably carried a stone or timber tower by 1130, but later in the 12th century a square stone keep, said to have been c. 100 ft. high,[63] was built on the motte. Probably by the early 13th century a curtain wall was built, raised on an earth bank and surrounded by a broad

moat. An area of 1½ a., roughly oval-shaped, was enclosed by the defences, but Bailey Tump, the triangular spur of ground projecting towards the valley west of the moat, and a similar-shaped area on the level ground to the east, on which side the original main entrance into the castle is thought to have been, appear to have once formed part of the castle grounds. The castle site was extraparochial until the mid 19th century.[64]

Substantial expenditure on the castle in the years 1209–11 may have included the cost of the two-storeyed, domestic range on the north-west. It included two principal first-floor rooms, which were probably the royal apartments that were mentioned in 1227 and 1255.[65] King John stayed at the castle at least five times in his reign,[66] Henry III was there four times in the 1220s and 1230s and visited again in 1256,[67] and Edward II came there in 1321 when his baronial opponents were levying forces in the Marches.[68] The castle's main functions in the early Middle Ages, however, were as the headquarters of the constable-warden, a prison for those attached and awaiting bail for forest offences,[69] and an arsenal for locally manufactured weapons.[70] North of the domestic range, a strong keep-like gatehouse, the principal surviving feature of the castle,[71] was built in 1292–3 on the orders of Edward I. It comprises a pair of three-storeyed towers, which project into the moat beyond the curtain wall and original north gateway, and a long central passage to which access was controlled by a drawbridge and portcullis at the front entrance and by internal portcullisses at the entrances to the rooms leading from it. Soon afterwards a two-storeyed chapel block, possibly replacing a wooden chapel that was ordered to be built adjoining the king's chamber in 1237, was added to the east of the domestic range across the axis of the entrance passage. At the same period, possibly c. 1310 when a 'peel' was ordered for the added security of the castle, the curtain wall was extended to take in a small area south of the keep. There was a small tower or bastion where the new wall rejoined the original curtain at the south-east corner of the castle. Other buildings adjoining the curtain wall on the east included a hearth or forge, possibly that used for the manufacture of crossbow bolts during the 13th century. A tall chimney rising from the buildings on that side had a cap in the form of a forester's horn, which in the late 18th

[50] Berkeley Cast. Mun., General Ser. T, box 25; for the Berkeleys, Burke, *Peerage* (1963), 228.
[51] P.R.O., F 3/128, letter 29 Jan. 1859; Berkeley Cast. Mun., General Ser. letters 9; Roberts's lease was backdated to Mich. 1837.
[52] P.R.O., F 3/587; F 14/14.
[53] Inf. from asset manager (agric. est.), Crown Estate.
[54] P.R.O., C 139/84, no. 76; cf. *Cal. Pat.* 1461–7, 169; *Cal. Fine R.* 1471–85, pp. 206, 310–11.
[55] P.R.O., E 317/Glos./2; F 17/165.
[56] Berkeley Cast. Mun., General Ser. 16; ibid. General Ser. T, box 25; Glos. R.O., D 2700/QC 7/6.
[57] *Trans. B.G.A.S.* iii. 356.
[58] Glos. R.O., D 177, Highgrove fm. papers 1919–20.
[59] Berkeley Cast. Mun., General Ser. 16; P.R.O., F 3/587, surv. 1835; F 14/13.
[60] P.R.O., F 3/128, letters 1 Jan., 4 Feb. 1861.
[61] Ibid. F 3/128, 586, 1032.

[62] Account based on P. E. Curnow and E. A. Johnson, 'St. Briavels Castle', *Chateau Gaillard*, xii. 91–114. For the medieval documentary evidence for the building, *Hist. of the King's Works*, ii. 821–3, and for another, detailed account, W. T. Allen, 'St. Briavels Castle', *Trans. B.G.A.S.* iii. 325–67.
[63] Bigland, *Glos.* i. 235; P.R.O., F 17/165.
[64] *1st Rep. Dean Forest Com.* 4, 18.
[65] *Cal. Lib.* 1226–40, 13; 1251–60, 207.
[66] T. D. Hardy, *Description of Patent Rolls and Itin. of King John* (1835), index.
[67] 'Itin. of Hen. III' (1923, TS. at P.R.O.).
[68] *Cal. Pat.* 1317–21, 574; cf. *Cal. Close,* 1318–23, 364; M. McKisack, *Fourteenth Cent.* (1959), 61.
[69] P.R.O., E 32/33; *Cal. Pat.* 1281–92, 168; *Cal. Close,* 1341–3, 453.
[70] Below, econ. hist. (mills and ironworks).
[71] Above, Plates 8, 40.

or early 19th century was moved to the west domestic range.[72]

In the modern period the castle was used for holding the hundred leet and a court for civil actions in St. Briavels hundred and as a gaol for debtors imprisoned by the latter. The courts and the gaol, which continued until 1842, were among the responsibilities of the constable of St. Briavels, while the castle and the obligation of its upkeep were vested in the Crown lessee, but as the office and the lease were for so long held by the same people the distinction became blurred.[73] The courts were held in parts of the west range: in 1804 the former chapel served as the courtroom and the southernmost room of the former royal apartments as a jury room, while the west tower of the gatehouse housed the gaol and the gaoler and his family.[74] The north part of the royal apartments was roofless by the late 18th century[75] and was used to impound cattle illegally pastured in St. Briavels and Newland manors[76] until 1866 when the Crown built a new manor pound outside the castle.[77] Unused parts of the castle were allowed to decay, and in 1680 much was said to have been demolished.[78] The keep survived in a ruined state in 1732[79] but part fell in 1752 and the remainder c. 1774.[80] In 1777 the decrepit state of the surviving buildings caused the Crown to allow Lord Berkeley £372 for repairs out of the fine for renewing his lease; parts later repaired[81] included the top of the east tower of the gatehouse, which was in ruins in 1732 and 1775 but had been reroofed by 1807.[82] In 1798, however, Thomas James, who held the courts in the castle as Lord Berkeley's deputy constable and steward, complained that the state of the roof and windows was a danger to his health in the winter months.[83]

After the Crown took the castle in hand in the mid 19th century the courtroom was used for some years as the parish school and other parts were let as a dwelling, one tower of the gatehouse being occupied in 1879.[84] About 1898,[85] to form a more substantial residence, the gatehouse and the west domestic range were restored and partly remodelled, though some of the original internal features were preserved. The castle was let as a private house until 1939, and, after housing an evacuated school during the war, it was let in 1948 to the Youth Hostels Association. It remained in use as a youth hostel in 1991, management of the property having been transferred from the Crown Estate to the Department of Environment in 1982.[86] The moat was drained in the mid 19th century,[87] and after 1961 a Moat Society, formed by the villagers, cleared it of undergrowth and laid it out as a public garden.[88]

A small estate at St. Briavels, later called *HATHAWAYS* manor, was held from the Crown by the service of chief serjeant-in-fee, or chief forester, of Dean. The obligations of the holders included the maintenance of an under-forester, styled the bowbearer, to patrol the Forest on foot, and their perquisites included the right to course with dogs outside the covert and an allowance of venison, interpreted from the early 17th century as the shoulder of every deer killed and 10 fee bucks and 10 fee does annually.[89] The manor and forestership were presumably held by Nigel Hathaway, who was named first among the serjeants-in-fee of the Forest in 1220,[90] and by William Hathaway, apparently Nigel's son, who died before 1250. William's widow married Philip Wyther, who bought the wardship of his land and heir.[91] In 1282 the chief forester was another William Hathaway,[92] who was also constable of St. Briavels from 1287 to 1291.[93] At his death c. 1317 William held a house, 24 a. of land, and 30s. free rent by his service as chief forester and, an obligation not found mentioned later, of finding an armed horseman to serve at the castle in wartime. He was succeeded by his son William,[94] (fl. 1338).[95] The manor may have passed by the 1350s to Walter Hathaway,[96] and Thomas Hathaway died holding it in 1376. Thomas's heirs were three daughters,[97] among whom his estates were partitioned in 1382, when Isabel, who married Thomas Walwyn, received her share and shares were allotted to Sibyl and Ellen to await their coming of age.[98] By 1431 Hathaways manor had passed to Robert Greyndour,[99] and it then descended with his Clearwell estate[1] until 1680 when Sir Baynham Throckmorton settled it on three of his daughters, Elizabeth and Mary (both d. 1684) and Carolina.[2] In 1710 Carolina and her husband James

72   Glos. R.O., A 278/2; *Trans. B.G.A.S.* iii. 331.
73   Above, St. Briavels hundred; Hart, *Royal Forest*, 299; cf. P.R.O., F 3/587, surv. 1835.
74   P.R.O., F 17/165; *1st Rep. Dean Forest Com.* 4, 16.
75   F. Grose, *Antiquities of Eng. and Wales,* ii (2nd edn. c. 1783), plate facing p. 141, reproduced above, Plate 40.
76   P.R.O., F 17/165; *1st Rep. Dean Forest Com.* 17, where 'Newnham' is evidently a misprint for 'Newland'.
77   P.R.O., F 14/14; O.S. Map 1/2,500, Glos. XLVI. 3 (1881 edn.).
78   Hart, *Royal Forest*, 299.
79   Glos. R.O., A 278/2.
80   Bigland, *Glos.* i. 235; Grose, *Antiquities*, ii. 144; P.R.O., F 17/165.
81   Berkeley Cast. Mun., General Ser. T, box 25, letters patent 1777; contract with builder 1783.
82   Glos. R.O., A 278/1–2; Grose, *Antiquities*, ii. 144, plate facing p. 141.
83   Berkeley Cast. Mun., General Ser. T, box 25, letter 1798.
84   *Trans. B.G.A.S.* iii. 359–60.

85   P.R.O., F 16/67; *Kelly's Dir. Glos.* (1906), 285.
86   Inf. from asset manager (agric. est.), Crown Estate.
87   *Trans. B.G.A.S.* iii. 332.
88   Notice in garden.
89   For the office, P.R.O., E 32/32, m. 8; C 99/20, no. 120; Glos. R.O., D 2026/X 3; N.L.W., Mynde Park MS. 5158.
90   *Rot. Litt. Claus.* (Rec. Com.), i. 442–3.
91   *Ex. e Rot. Fin.* (Rec. Com.), ii. 85–6; *Cal. Inq. Misc.* i, pp. 31–2.
92   P.R.O., E 32/30, rot. 5; E 32/32, m. 8.
93   *Trans. B.G.A.S.* xxxiii. 177.
94   *Cal. Inq. p.m.* vi, p. 16.
95   *Hist. & Cart. Mon. Glouc.* (Rolls Ser.), iii. 235.
96   Cf. above, Ruardean, manors (Hathaways).
97   *Cal. Inq. p.m.* xiv, p. 237.
98   *Cal. Close, 1389–92*, 260.
99   N.L.W., Dunraven MSS. 339; P.R.O., C 139/115, no. 34.
1   Above, Newland, manors; Glos. R.O., D 36/M 1, rot. 2d.; P.R.O., C 142/189, no. 82; *Cal. S.P. Dom. 1676–7*, 27–8.
2   N.L.W., Dunraven MSS. 271; Bigland, *Glos.* ii. 261–2.

Scrymsher sold the manor to Francis Wyndham, and Hathaways then descended once more with Clearwell.[3]

In the early 18th century Hathaways manor comprised only chief rents and two closes, one of which, Hathaways orchard north-east of the churchyard, had presumably been the site of the house.[4] By 1787 the post of bow-bearer had come to be regarded as a distinct office held by the chief forester, then Charles Edwin of Clearwell, in person; Edwin's statement then that as bowbearer he was required to attend, accompanied by six men clothed in green, when the sovereign came to hunt in Dean may have included a degree of romantic embellishment. The chief foresters continued to claim their fee venison[5] until the deer were cleared from the Forest in the early 1850s but in the last years only one buck was taken annually.[6]

A group of small estates at St. Briavels, each originally a house and 12 a., was held by other serjeants-in-fee of the Forest, who performed their office on foot, whereas the chief forester went on horseback. The king's serjeants of St. Briavels were mentioned in 1216.[7] At various times during the 13th century between 6 and 11 serjeanties-in-fee of the Forest (apart from the chief forestership) were listed,[8] though only 5 are known for certain to have been attached to estates at St. Briavels, and most of those holding them in the 13th century and the early 14th had other estates, in Newnham, Lydney, or Awre, and possibly did not actually reside. In later centuries the holders were usually called foresters-in-fee,[9] but, to avoid confusion with the woodwards of the Forest's bailiwicks who had that style in the Middle Ages, they are termed serjeants-in-fee in this account.

One serjeanty at St. Briavels was held by William of Lasborough (d. c. 1261), passing to his daughter Agatha and her husband Henry of Dean[10] (d. c. 1292).[11] In 1297 Agatha gave 10 a. of her 12 a. to Richard of Dean,[12] and Henry of Dean apparently held a serjeanty in 1338.[13] Another Richard of Dean gave the land and serjeanty to John of Monmouth in 1342.[14] Roger and Richard Wyther were among the serjeants-in-fee listed in 1220,[15] and Richard's

son Walter[16] held one of the St. Briavels serjeant-ies in 1252.[17] Walter Wyther (d. 1270) was succeeded by his son-in-law William Boter[18] (d. c. 1285),[19] and Philip Boter was apparently a serjeant-in-fee in 1338.[20] Alexander of Stears was a serjeant in 1220 and 1250, and in the early 14th century a family of that name, who owned Stears manor in Newnham, held one of the St. Briavels estates.[21] It was evidently that serjeanty that passed to William Aylburton, who owned land at St. Briavels and Stears manor at his death in 1539.[22] Another estate, probably held by Robert son of Warren before 1250,[23] passed to Thomas Warren (fl. 1282), to William Warren (d. 1348), to William's son John (fl. 1364), and to William Warren (d. 1419).[24] A fifth estate was possibly held by Martin of Box (fl. 1220) and by William and Geoffrey of Box cliff, who were mentioned as serjeants at different times in the early 13th century.[25] It passed to Ellen of Box, who was succeeded before 1276 by Robert of Awre.[26] That or another Robert of Awre died holding it before 1326 and was succeeded by his son John[27] (fl. 1338).[28] One estate was evidently represented c. 1451 by 8s. 4d. rent in St. Briavels acquired with a serjeanty by John Wyrall,[29] who is depicted with his accoutrements of office on a tomb at Newland.[30]

The houses and estates of the serjeants-in-fee have not been identified and their later history is obscure. The owners of Box manor in Awre, a former estate of William of Lasborough,[31] were serjeants-in-fee in 1637 and later, suggesting that some of the serjeanties had become annexed by association to estates outside the parish, but most of the eight serjeanties listed until the late 18th century apparently descended by inheri-tance rather than tenure.[32]

An estate called the manor of *STOWE* was based on a hermitage and a castle on the ridge in the north part of St. Briavels between the Stowe valley and the valley of Slade brook. The hermitage was recorded in 1220 when it was served by chaplains appointed by the Crown.[33] In 1226 Henry III granted it with 2 ploughlands and pasture rights to Grace Dieu abbey (Mon.), then newly founded by John of Monmouth, who was constable of St. Briavels from 1216 to c. 1224. The abbey undertook to establish a chan-try of three monks at the hermitage to celebrate

[3] N.L.W., Dunraven MSS. 334. Wyndham also had a conveyance from Carolina's half-sister Catherine and her husband Thos. Wild in 1711; cf. Burke, *Ext. & Dorm. Baronetcies* (1838), 527.
[4] N.L.W., Dunraven MSS. 334; cf. G.D.R., T 1/153.
[5] *3rd Rep. Com. Woods* (1788), 81.
[6] P.R.O., F 16/52.
[7] *Rot. Litt. Claus.* (Rec. Com.), i. 334–5.
[8] Ibid. i. 442–3; ii. 126; P.R.O., C 60/47, m. 13; E 32/30, rott. 33, 35; E 32/32, m. 4; those sources support parts of the descents which follow.
[9] Glos. R.O., D 2026/X 3; *3rd Rep. Com. Woods* (1788), 76.
[10] *Cal. Inq. p.m.* i, p. 139.
[11] Ibid. iii, p. 37.
[12] *Cal. Pat.* 1292–1301, 293.
[13] *Hist. & Cart. Mon. Glouc.* iii. 235.
[14] *Cal. Pat.* 1340–3, 429.
[15] *Rot. Litt. Claus.* (Rec. Com.), i. 442–3.
[16] *Ex. e Rot. Fin.* (Rec. Com.), i. 258.
[17] *Cal. Chart. R.* 1226–57, 377.

[18] *Cal. Inq. p.m.* i, pp. 235–6; *Cal. Chart. R.* 1257–1300, 165–6.
[19] *Cal. Inq. p.m.* ii, p. 335.
[20] *Hist. & Cart. Mon. Glouc.* iii. 235.
[21] *Cal. Inq. p.m.* v, p. 52; vi, p. 278; cf. *V.C.H. Glos.* x. 38.
[22] P.R.O., C 142/90, no. 111.
[23] *Ex. e Rot. Fin.* (Rec. Com.), ii. 85–6.
[24] *Cal. Inq. p.m.* xi, p. 467; *Cal. Close*, 1364–8, 18–19; P.R.O., C 138/40, no. 52.
[25] *Pipe R.* 1204 (P.R.S. N.S. xviii), 152; *Bk. of Fees*, i. 343.
[26] *Rot. Hund.* (Rec. Com.), i. 176.
[27] *Cal. Inq. p.m.* vi, p. 411.
[28] *Hist. & Cart. Mon. Glouc.* iii. 235.
[29] *Cal. Pat.* 1446–52, 415.
[30] Roper, *Glos. Effigies*, 450–3.
[31] Cf. above, Awre, manors.
[32] Glos. R.O., D 2026/X 3; D 4431, swanimote roll; D 36/Q 2; *3rd Rep. Com. Woods* (1788), 76; cf. Rudge, *Hist. of Glos.* ii. 22.
[33] *Rot. Litt. Claus.* (Rec. Com.), i. 427.

for the king's ancestors, and the gift, made during pleasure, was converted to a grant in free alms in 1227.[34] In 1338 Edward III added 36 a. of his demesne waste at Wyegate and 'Long field' to the endowment,[35] some of it evidently within Newland parish, where land on the east side of Wyegate Green belonged to the owner of Stowe manor in 1608.[36] In 1361 Grace Dieu abbey claimed that it was unable to maintain the chantry because of the loss of common pasture in adjoining lands which had been taken into cultivation; the Crown allowed the chantry, then said to be served by two monks, to be transferred to the abbey itself.[37] The estate at Stowe remained a grange of the abbey.[38]

In 1554 the Crown sold Stowe manor to Thomas Carpenter and William Savage,[39] and in 1556 Carpenter conveyed it to William Warren and his wife Marian,[40] whose family, the Catchmays, had been lessees of the site of the manor from 1488 or earlier. In 1559 Warren granted a 40-year lease to William Wyrall of English Bicknor.[41] William Warren died in 1573,[42] having settled Stowe on the marriage of his daughter Joan with George ap Robert (or Probert). In 1582 Joan, by then a widow, had a release of right from Thomas James of Bristol, son of her sister Margaret, and in 1584 she had a similar release from George Gough of Hewelsfield, who had married a third sister, Mary.[43] Joan later married William Carpenter, whom she survived, and died in 1617. Her son William Probert succeeded to Stowe,[44] and he and his son Henry conveyed the manor house called Stowe Grange and the bulk of the estate to William Hoskins in 1627 and outlying parts to others in 1629.[45] William Hoskins (d. 1661 or 1662), a cooper of Southwark (Surr.), left his Stowe estate to a cousin Kedgwin Hoskins,[46] whose son Kedgwin (d. 1685 or 1686) devised to his wife Mary the reversion, after his father's death.[47] The son of the younger Kedgwin, also called Kedgwin, had succeeded by 1696[48] and in 1735 added a farm (later called Mork farm) at Mork Green. He died in 1743[49] and his widow Alice apparently held Stowe until her death in 1756.[50] Their son Kedgwin (d. 1764) and his son Kedgwin (d. 1834), both of whom lived at Platwell in Clearwell, held the estate in succession. The latter left it to his brother-in-law, the Revd. John Hoskins,

and then to John's son Kedgwin Hoskins[51] who had succeeded by 1840.[52] That Kedgwin (d. 1852) used his estate as security in his banking business, carried on with partners at Hereford and Ross-on-Wye (Herefs.), and his mortgagees and trustees sold Mork farm to James White of Lindors in 1855 and Stowe Grange with 190 a. to Edwin Cook in 1857.[53] Cook sold his estate c. 1867 to the owners of the Clearwell estate[54] and it was among farms of that estate that were bought by the Crown Commissioners of Woods in 1912.[55] In 1991 the land was farmed by the Crown's tenant of the adjoining Longley farm, in Newland, Stowe Grange having been sold in 1971.[56]

The site of the castle, at the north end of the estate commanding a route up the Stowe valley from the Wye, is a substantial circular rampart. Much rubble stonework is strewn around but may derive from quarrying rather than from buildings. Presumably built for the Crown soon after the Conquest, the castle may have been occupied only for a short period until the establishment of St. Briavels castle on a stronger site and one more effective for controlling the Wye crossing at Bigsweir. In 1310, in the only early reference found to it, the castle at Stowe was called the 'old castle'.[57] The hermitage stood on the ridge to the south-west.[58] The bases of the walls of a small single-celled building, which had a chamfered doorway on the north-west side, survive there among later farm buildings. The site probably included a graveyard for those serving the chapel, for skeletons were discovered during foundation work for a barn built in 1912.[59] Under a lease granted by Grace Dieu abbey in 1418 the lessee agreed to build a suitable house on the grange[60] and perhaps from that date there was a house at the site of Stowe Grange, which stands by the road below the chapel at the foot of a steep bank. A low wing towards the road incorporates a late 16th-century doorway and trusses, which are probably in situ, but the rest of the house dates from the late 17th century and has a short main range with central three-storeyed porch and a stair projection at the rear.

About 1350 John Joce of Newland owned an estate called the manor of *ST. BRIAVELS*, comprising numerous small tenant holdings at Mork and elsewhere. The manor later descended

34 Ibid. ii. 132, 170; for the abbey, *Mon. Antiquary*, i. 85–106.
35 P.R.O., C 143/239, no. 21; *Cal. Fine R. 1337–47*, 65.
36 P.R.O., MR 879 (F 17/1).
37 *Cal. Pat. 1361–4*, 11.
38 P.R.O., SC 6/Hen. VIII/2496.
39 *Cal. Pat. 1553–4*, 162–3.
40 Ibid. 1555–7, 89.
41 Hist. MSS. Com. 55, *Glemham Hall*, pp. 185–6; Glos. R.O., D 33/149; for Marian, cf. *Berkeley MSS.* iii. 135.
42 P.R.O., PROB 11 (P.C.C. 26 Peter), f. 192 and v.
43 Ibid. C 142/185, no. 94; Hist. MSS. Com. 55, *Glemham Hall*, p. 186.
44 P.R.O., C 142/377, no. 92; C 60/489, mm. 16–17.
45 Ibid. CP 25/2/420/3 Chas. I Trin. no. 18; Suff. R.O., HA 49/A III(b)/7, deed 1629; Glos. R.O., D 608/8/2.
46 P.R.O., PROB 11/309 (P.C.C. 116–17 Land), ff. 72–73v.
47 G.D.R. wills 1685/253.

48 Glos. R.O., D 329/T 6.
49 Ibid. D 1896, deeds of Lindors est. 1735–1850.
50 Bigland, *Glos.* i. 241; Glos. R.O., P 278/CW 2/1, rate 1748.
51 Glos. R.O., D 1896, deeds of Lindors est. 1735–1850; cf. Bigland, *Glos.* i. 241; Rudge, *Hist. of Glos.* ii. 110; Burke, *Land. Gent.* (1846), i. 596.
52 G.D.R., T 1/153.
53 Glos. R.O., D 1896, deeds of Lindors est. 1852–1927; P.R.O., CRES 38/672.
54 *Trans. B.G.A.S.* ix. 91.
55 P.R.O., CRES 38/672–3.
56 Inf. from asset manager (agric. est.), Crown Estate.
57 B.L. Harl. Ch. 111, c. 32.
58 O.S. Map 6", Glos. XXXVIII. SE. (1884 edn.), on what grounds are not clear, calls it St. Margaret's chapel and also marks 'St. Margaret's hermitage' at the nearby Stowe Hall (in Newland par.).
59 Glos. R.O., D 3921/III/28.
60 Ibid. D 33/82A.

to Joce's descendants, owners of the Clearwell estate; Robert Greyndour held a court for it in the early 1440s.[61] In the late 15th century it was composed mainly of small freeholds owing chief rents,[62] and it has not been found separately recorded among the estates of the owners of Clearwell after 1669.[63] Several other estates in St. Briavels which descended with Clearwell at various periods are traced above and below.

An estate called RODMORE on the east side of the parish was recorded from 1294, having evidently been formed by assarting. It was called a manor in 1294, a status not accorded it later, and was held by Ralph Hathaway, who had licence to establish a chantry in a chapel he had built there.[64] Ralph died c. 1316, holding a house and 30 a. at Rodmore, for which he owed rent and suit of court at St. Briavels castle. He also then had 60½ a. of new assart land at 'le Horestone', which was probably further north near the Long stone on the later Closeturf farm, where his successors owned land in the early 16th century. Ralph was succeeded by his son William,[65] and Ralph, son and heir of William Hathaway of Rodmore, was mentioned in 1374.[66] In 1498 Rodmore was apparently owned by another William Hathaway, who settled lands on his wife Joan for her life in 1509. His heir Richard Hathaway confirmed the settlement in 1514.[67] In 1608 Rodmore belonged to Thomas James[68] of Soilwell, Lydney, and it remained in possession of the Jameses of Soilwell[69] until 1689, when they sold it to Thomas Morgan of Tintern (Mon.).[70] It was apparently sold to William Ford in 1711,[71] and he owned it at his death in 1733, his widow Mary retaining it to c. 1746.[72] Thomas James owned it in 1791[73] and he or a later Thomas James owned Rodmore Farm with 205 a. in 1840.[74] A Thomas James died in possession of Rodmore and the adjoining Willsbury farm c. 1885, and his son William sold the two farms in 1892 to W. B. Marling of Clanna, Alvington. Marling added Highgrove farm to his estate the same year, giving him c. 560 a. of farmland in St. Briavels parish.[75] Rodmore was part of the Clanna estate until 1939 or later.[76] In 1991, comprising 170 a., it was owned and farmed by Mr. R. W. James. The farmhouse was rebuilt c. 1700 as a tall,

single-depth range with a projecting stair turret at the rear and a front with a pediment and an elaborate stone doorcase. The interior was extensively refitted and modernized c. 1970.[77] Hathaways fields and Hathaways barn, which form part of the farm,[78] were presumably named from its earliest owners, but they were in a different ownership during the 17th and 18th centuries.[79]

At WILLSBURY, adjoining Rodmore to the north-east, Adam, the reeve of St. Briavels manor, apparently acting illegally, built a house shortly before 1270.[80] John Malemort, son of Richard Malemort of Willsbury, was mentioned c. 1300.[81] John Gainer of Willsbury was mentioned in 1385[82] and another John Gainer of Willsbury in 1462.[83] Christopher Gainer sold a house and land there to John ap Gwyllym in 1539.[84] Willsbury was possibly acquired later by William Warren (d. 1573), passing to his daughter Mary and her husband George Gough of Hewelsfield.[85] Their son Warren Gough (d. 1636) settled a capital messuage and lands at Willsbury on his wife Dorothy with reversion to trustees for his son Richard's children.[86] William Gough, Richard's son, owned Willsbury in 1689 when he settled it, reserving a life interest in some lands and part of the house, on the marriage of his son Charles. William was living on his Pastor's Hill estate, in Bream, in 1708, and in 1724 Charles settled Willsbury on his own son William.[87] William Gough (d. 1773)[88] was succeeded by his son the Revd. James Gough or Aubrey, who sold Willsbury in 1791 to Thomas Evans. Evans (d. 1832) left the estate in trust to provide an annuity for his son Thomas, who was living at Willsbury in 1845. On the younger Thomas's death the trustees were to convey Willsbury to his daughter Eleanor, and she and her husband, Dr. Symeon Bartlett, owned Willsbury House and 140 a. in 1853. The Bartletts sold the estate in 1864 to Thomas James,[89] with whose Rodmore farm it passed to the Clanna estate; W. B. Marling sold the farm in 1920 to the tenant E. W. Miles.[90] The house later passed into separate ownership from the land, which in 1991 was owned and farmed, with Great Dunkilns and Severn View farms, by N. & K. Cooke and Sons.[91]

61 N.L.W., Dunraven MSS. 339.
62 Glos. R.O., D 1677/GG 1224.
63 P.R.O., C 142/340, no. 192; N.L.W., Dunraven MSS. 260, 270.
64 Chart. and Rec. of Heref. Cath., ed. W. W. Capes (Heref. 1908), 167–8.
65 Cal. Inq. p.m. v, p. 417; Cal. Fine R. 1307–19, 316; for the land at Closeturf, N.L.W., Dunraven MSS. 271, deed 1514.
66 Glos. R.O., D 2244/66.
67 N.L.W., Dunraven MSS. 271.
68 P.R.O., MR 879.
69 Inq. p.m. Glos. 1625–42, i. 111; above, Lydney, manors.
70 Glos. R.O., D 247/30B.
71 Ibid. P 278A/OV 2/1; P.R.O., CP 25/2/926/9 Anne Hil. no. 1.
72 Glos. R.O., P 278/CW 2/1; Bigland, Glos. i. 241.
73 Glos. R.O., P 209/MI 1, p. 130.
74 G.D.R., T 1/153.
75 Glos. R.O., D 177, Highgrove fm. papers 1919–20;

sched. of deeds of Rodmore, etc.
76 Ibid. Clanna est. sale papers 1919–20; Kelly's Dir. Glos. (1939), 302.
77 Inf. from Mr. James.
78 Cf. G.D.R., T 1/153.
79 P.R.O., MR 879; Glos. R.O., D 2528.
80 P.R.O., E 32/29, rot. 6d.
81 N.L.W., Dunraven MSS. 326.
82 Hist. MSS. Com. 55, Glemham Hall, pp. 178–9, where a Wm. Gainer, son of Osbert Malemort, is also mentioned.
83 Glos. R.O., D 1677/GG 1225.
84 P.R.O., CP 40/1103, Carte rott. 12d.–13.
85 Rudge, Hist. of Glos. ii. 109; above, this section (Stowe); for the Goughs, Visit. Glos. 1682–3, 74–5.
86 Inq. p.m. Glos. 1625–42, iii. 63–8.
87 Glos. R.O., D 177, Gough fam. deeds.
88 Bigland, Glos. i. 239.
89 Glos. R.O., D 177, Willsbury est. papers.
90 Ibid. Clanna est. sale papers 1919–20.
91 Inf. from Mr. R. Cooke.

At Willsbury House a three-storeyed, early 17th-century porch on the west front marks the division between the tall, originally gabled, principal rooms at the north end of the house and the lower, service rooms at the south end. In the late 18th century or the early 19th the house was remodelled: the gables on the east and west fronts were replaced by a full storey, most of the windows were replaced by sashes, a new staircase was inserted, and additions were made at the service end. Considerable internal alterations were made in the mid and later 20th century. An octagonal lodge in Tudor style was built on the Bream road in 1850[92] and was later extended. At the south end of the farm, near Rodmore grove, the owners had a large fishpond in 1689.[93] By the mid 19th century it had been filled in.[94]

An estate by the river Wye called *BIGS-WEIR* had its origin in lands belonging to the bishop of Hereford, presumably once forming part of his Wyeseal estate, based in the adjoining part of Newland.[95] In 1310 Thomas Mushet sold to William Joce a house and lands by the Wye, held from the bishop, together with lands nearby, at Lindhurst, that Thomas had recently acquired from William Hathaway.[96] In 1320 William Joce conveyed the lands to his son Philip, and they later descended with the Clearwell estate. In 1445 Joan Greyndour leased them, including a house called Philip Joce's Place which was perhaps at the site of Bigsweir House, to Thomas Catchmay. Catchmay already held other lands in the same part of the parish[97] and he or one of his successors acquired the freehold of Joan's land.[98] John Catchmay of Bigsweir was mentioned in 1509[99] and Thomas Catchmay of Bigsweir in 1555.[1] By 1608 the Bigsweir estate was held by George Catchmay,[2] who then employed at least eight servants.[3] George (d. *c.* 1617) was succeeded by his son Sir Richard Catchmay (fl. 1638),[4] and by 1649 Bigsweir had passed to Sir William Catchmay,[5] who was succeeded by his son Tracy Catchmay[6] (d. 1708).[7] Tracy's widow Barbara held the estate during the minority of his son William,[8] who died in 1743. William was succeeded by his sister Jane and her husband James Rooke (d. 1773).[9] The estate, which in 1787 comprised

Bigsweir House, Lindors Farm, and 430 a. of farmland and woodland,[10] descended in direct line to James Rooke (d. 1805), who reached the rank of general in his military career, James (d. by 1823), and George.[11] George Rooke much enlarged the estate by purchases of land and woods in St. Briavels and Newland[12] and died in 1839, leaving it for life to his aunt Hannah, wife of George Worrall. She assumed the name and arms of Rooke after her husband's death in 1840, and sold her interest in 1848 to Willoughby Sandilands Rooke, later Colonel Rooke, who had the reversion under George Rooke's will.[13] W. S. Rooke died in 1891 and the estate, which also included Pilstone House and lands in Llandogo on the Monmouthshire bank of the river, passed to his son George Douglas Willoughby Rooke (fl. 1953).[14] George was succeeded by his grandson J. C. O. R. Hopkinson, later Major-General Hopkinson, the owner in 1991.[15] Bigsweir House, which stands on the river bank by the site of the weir and ford, was rebuilt in the early 18th century as a stone house of two storeys and attics with a symmetrical five-bayed front. Additions were made later to the south-west end and at the rear.

A house called *GREAT HOUSE*, at Tilthams Tump on Mork Lane, and an estate lying in and around the Slade brook valley belonged to the Whittington family in the early 17th century. In 1609 Richard Whittington conveyed the estate to his son Thomas,[16] who sold it piecemeal between 1610 and 1619 to John Gonning, a merchant and later mayor of Bristol.[17] Gonning added other lands during the next 20 years, including in 1629 a farmhouse and lands bought from William Probert, former owner of Stowe. His later purchases were made in conjunction with his son John[18] and in 1645, shortly before his death, he released all his right to John.[19] The younger John Gonning, also mayor of Bristol, died in 1662[20] and was succeeded by his son Robert. Robert, who was knighted, added other lands. At his death *c.* 1679[21] he owned *c.* 500 a. in St. Briavels and adjoining parishes, most of the St. Briavels land forming a compact block with Great House at its west end and Bearse Farm at the east.[22] Sir Robert Gonning's widow Anne, who married Sir Dudley North (d.

92 Glos. R.O., D 177, Willsbury est. papers.
93 Ibid. Gough fam. deeds; cf. ibid. D 421/L 4.
94 Ibid. D 177, Willsbury est. papers.
95 Above, Newland manors. The original est. in St. Briavels was evidently represented by riverside lands that were tithe free or tithable to the owner in 1840: G.D.R., T 1/153, which attributed the tithe-free status to ownership by Llanthony priory.
96 N.L.W., Dunraven MSS. 325.
97 Ibid. 271; cf. above, Newland, manors.
98 Cf. Glos. R.O., D 1833/E 1.
99 N.L.W., Dunraven MSS. 271.
1   Glos. R.O., D 33/302.
2   Ibid. P 278A/PC 3/2; cf. P.R.O., E 137/13/4.
3   Smith, *Men and Armour*, 39.
4   P.R.O., PROB 11/130 (P.C.C. 118 Weldon), ff. 436–7; C 3/405/97; Hart, *Royal Forest*, 281.
5   Glos. R.O., D 33/312.
6   Atkyns, *Glos.* 296; for the Catchmays, *Visit. Glos. 1682–3*, 74–5.
7   Glos. R.O., P 278/IN 1/1.

8   P.R.O., PROB 11/509 (P.C.C. 165 Lane), ff. 260v.–262; Glos. R.O., P 278A/OV 2/1.
9   Bigland, *Glos.* i. 238–9.
10 Glos. R.O., D 1833/E 1.
11 Ibid. E 2; P.R.O., PROB 11/1445 (P.C.C. 508 Pitts), ff. 159–61.
12 Glos. R.O., D 1833/T 3, T 6, T 11, T 14–18.
13 Ibid. D 1833/E 5/2.
14 Ibid. E 5/1; *Kelly's Handbook to Titled, Landed, and Official Classes* (1953), 1792.
15 *Who's Who* (1992), 905.
16 Suff. R.O., HA 49/A III(b)/13.
17 Ibid. 2.   18 Ibid. 7, 10–11.
19 Ibid. 6; A IV(h)/3.
20 *Deposition Books of Bristol, 1643–7*, i (Bristol Rec. Soc. vi), 247–8.
21 N.L.W., Dunraven MSS. 270, petition to Exchequer *c.* 1672; Suff. R.O., HA 49/A III(b)/13, deed 1664; A IV(h)/7.
22 Suff. R.O., HA 49/A III(b)/28; cf. N.L.W., Dunraven MSS. 334, deed 1732.

1691),[23] retained the estate until her death after 1713, when it reverted to members of the Strode and Langton families, heirs of Sir Robert's sisters.[24] One of the heirs, Mercy Strode, had married Francis Wyndham of Clearwell, whose grandson Thomas acquired the rest of the Strodes' share in 1730 and the Langtons' share in 1732.[25] The Great House estate then descended with Clearwell, passing in 1912 to the Crown, which retained it in 1991.[26] In the late 17th century Great House was a substantial gabled building,[27] and in 1732 it was described as a large old mansion.[28] It was in use as the principal farmhouse of the estate in 1760.[29] It was later demolished, perhaps before 1791 when the bulk of the land was being farmed from Bearse Farm,[30] which remained the farmhouse in 1991.

The *AYLESMORE* estate in the south part of the parish belonged in 1670 to Edmund Bond of Walford (Herefs.) who settled it on the marriage of his second son Edmund. Mary, widow of the younger Edmund, sold her interest in 1707 to their son Edmund,[31] who was said to have a good house and estate c. 1710.[32] Edmund (d. 1743) devised it to his niece Mary, the wife of Richard Bond of Brockweir. Richard died in 1754[33] and Mary before 1771, the Aylesmore estate passing to her daughters Frances, wife of John Prosser, and Elizabeth Eleanor Bond. The sisters sold it in 1797 to John Mudway, whose mortgagee Robert Williams gained possession in 1814 and sold the estate, then comprising c. 170 a., to Lawrence Peel of Manchester in 1820. Peel bought Aylesmore for his son William Henry Peel,[34] who enlarged it to an estate of over 1,000 a. by purchases in St. Briavels and Hewelsfield. By 1840 he owned Aylesmore Court with Highgrove, Dunkilns (later Severn View), and New House farms in St. Briavels and Hewelsfield Court and Cowshill farms in Hewelsfield.[35] W. H. Peel died in 1872, and in 1876 his trustee sold the estate to Augustus Smith, whose mortgagee gained possession before 1881 and split up the estate. Highgrove farm with 197 a. in St. Briavels was bought by Robert Parnall, who sold it in 1892 to W. B. Marling of Clanna. Aylesmore Court with the adjoining Hewelsfield Court farm was bought by John Macpherson and during the remainder of the 1880s and the early 1890s passed through a rapid succession of owners and their mortgagees.[36] Before 1906 Aylesmore Court with a remnant of its estate was acquired by P. N. Palin[37] (d. 1933), whose widow Edith retained it[38] and was succeeded by

her nephew Roger Fleetwood Hesketh. He sold it in 1952 to Mr. J. Arnott, who owned the house with c. 120 a. of land in 1991.[39] Aylesmore Court, which stands at the south boundary of the parish, on the east side of Hewelsfield Lane, is a plain, square villa of the early 19th century, presumably built by the Peels soon after 1820. It was enlarged to the west by a service wing in the late 19th century. The substantial coach house and stable block (converted to dwellings in the 1980s) and the planting of the land to the south and west to form a small park evidently date from the rebuilding of the house, and there is a late 19th-century entrance lodge on the Chepstow road.

In 1219 when Lire abbey granted Lydney church and its chapel of St. Briavels to the dean and chapter of Hereford it reserved to itself a tenement at St. Briavels held by Hugh Wyther;[40] no later record of that land has been found. The dean and chapter as impropriators of Lydney owned the corn tithes of St. Briavels parish, granting them out on long leases. Those tithes were valued at £50 c. 1710[41] and were commuted for a corn rent charge of £215 in 1840. The tithes, both great and small, from certain riverside lands then belonged to the landowners Hannah Rooke of Bigsweir and Warren Jane of Chepstow, who were each awarded a corn rent charge of £4 for them. Parochial land that was found to be exempt from tithes in 1840[42] included some riverside land of the Bigsweir estate, which presumably had once belonged to the bishop of Hereford,[43] Abbey Hams opposite Llandogo, which the duke of Beaufort owned, evidently as former property of Tintern abbey (Mon.),[44] and Rodmore grove, formerly a demesne wood of Llanthony priory's manor of Alvington.[45] In 1850 it was decided, on grounds which are not clear, that 142 a. of the extraparochial land in Hudnalls, Mocking Hazel wood, and the Fence were tithable to the landowner, and a corn rent charge of £3 was assigned to the Rookes of Bigsweir,[46] who had bought the Crown's rights in those lands.[47]

ECONOMIC HISTORY. AGRICULTURE. In 1086, when probably only a small part of the later parish was under cultivation, William son of Baderon's manor had 2 teams in demesne and 3 *servi*, while 3 *villani* and 5 bordars had 2 teams between them.[48] In 1224 and in 1246 oxen, ploughs, and seed were to be provided for

23 Burke, *Peerage* (1963), 1084.
24 Suff. R.O., HA 49/A III(a)/2, lease 1683; ibid. 3.
25 N.L.W., Dunraven MSS. 334.
26 Glos. R.O., P 209/MI 1, pp. 123, 154-7; G.D.R., T 1/153; P.R.O., CRES 38/673; above, Newland, manors.
27 Suff. R.O., HA 49/A III(b)/28.
28 N.L.W., Dunraven MSS. 334.
29 Ibid. 339.
30 Ibid. 327; Glos. R.O., P 209/MI 1, p. 123.
31 Glos. R.O., D 177, Aylesmore deeds.
32 Atkyns, *Glos.* 296.
33 Glos. R.O., D 177, Aylesmore deeds; Bigland, *Glos.* ii. 86.
34 Glos. R.O., D 177, Aylesmore deeds; for the est. before 1820, ibid. P 175/IN 3/1, f. 35.
35 G.D.R., T 1/100, 153.
36 Glos. R.O., D 177, Hewelsfield Ct. and Highgrove

papers 1892.
37 *Kelly's Dir. Glos.* (1906), 285; Glos. R.O., D 2428/1/40.
38 *Kelly's Dir. Glos.* (1939), 302; Burke, *Land. Gent.* (1937), 1103.
39 Inf. from Mr. Arnott.
40 B.L. Harl. MS. 6203, pp. 70-1.
41 G.D.R., V 5/256T 1; Atkyns, *Glos.* 296; Glos. R.O., D 326/L 16.
42 G.D.R., T 1/153; cf. ibid. V 5/256T 5.
43 Cf. above, this section.
44 Cf. Glos. R.O., D 2700/QC 7/5; below, econ. hist. (fisheries).
45 P.R.O., SC 6/Hen. VIII/1224; G.D.R. vol. 89, deposition of John Sledd 9 Mar. 1601/2.
46 G.D.R., T 1/154.
47 Above, intro.
48 *Dom. Bk.* (Rec. Com.), i. 167.

cultivating the demesne land on the royal manor.[49] About 1250 the manor had 2 plough-lands in demesne,[50] and in 1280 arable and meadowland were worked by salaried farm servants.[51] The pasture and meadow recorded on lease from the manor in the 1430s were probably in St. Briavels park, which was later the only demesne attached to the St. Briavels castle estate. Rents of assize and some payments for assarts were the only other profits from land accounted for in the 1430s[52] and it is probable that freeholders, holding by rent and fealty, and the serjeants-in-fee, holding by their office, constituted the whole tenantry. In the 18th and 19th centuries all the tenants were freeholders, owing chief rents and heriots.[53] Most of the land on the St. Briavels manor belonging to the Clearwell estate was held freely in 1431,[54] and in 1536 Stowe manor received rents from six free tenements as well as from its demesne held at farm.[55]

The land earliest in cultivation was evidently in the central part of the parish around the village, Coldharbour, and St. Briavels park. There was open-field land in that area, and the general pattern of land ownership there in the early 17th century was a fragmentary one in contrast to the more compact farms of the east and north-east parts of the parish.[56] Colpatch common field adjoining St. Briavels park was mentioned in 1322,[57] and in 1608, when an open field of 7 a. called the Rye field survived beside Hewelsfield Lane, much of the area east of the village, bounded by the park, Hewelsfield Lane, and the Coleford road, was occupied by small, regularly-shaped closes, perhaps the result of a planned inclosure.[58] Over and Nether Wyralls (later Woralls) common fields, mentioned in 1478,[59] lay north-east of the village by the Coleford road and still contained 35 a. of open land in 1608.[60]

The tenants' right to common pasture in the royal demesne of the Forest[61] was exercised mainly in the detached areas that adjoined their parish. In Hudnalls they also claimed an ancient right to cut and take wood at will. Their claim, which later tradition ascribed to a grant by Miles of Gloucester, earl of Hereford,[62] was recorded in 1282 when they were said to be destroying the woodland,[63] and the right was confirmed, but not clearly defined, by the Dean re-afforestation Act of 1668.[64] It was evidently interpreted as more extensive than the estovers (firebote, housebote, and hedgebote) claimed by the ten-

ants in other parishes adjoining the Forest;[65] probably Hudnalls supplied some of the regular trade from that part of the Wye Valley to Bristol in wood for coopers and other craftsmen.[66] The men of St. Briavels probably only ever exercised the right in the north and south-western parts of Hudnalls, for in the south-eastern part, the later Hewelsfield common, the men of Hewelsfield appear to have exercised exclusive rights.[67]

In 1696 and for a few years afterwards the parish vestry paid a keeper of Hudnalls a salary of £2, presumably to safeguard the rights to wood and common pasture.[68] Unidentified encroachments thrown down at the parish's expense in 1740 or 1741 were probably in Hudnalls, for legal action against 'offenders in Hudnalls' was planned or in progress at the same time.[69] In the early 19th century, however, the clearing of land for cultivation and the building of cottages proceeded unchecked,[70] so that by 1850 less than 300 a. of the original c. 1,000 a. in the whole of Hudnalls remained woodland and waste.[71] Of the smaller parts of the Forest demesne surviving in the St. Briavels area in 1787, 10 a. of the Fence had been taken by cottagers and 15 a. of Mocking Hazel wood had been encroached by the owner of the Bigsweir estate.[72] In 1827 George Rooke, owner of Bigsweir, bought the Crown's rights in Hudnalls, the Fence, and Mocking Hazel wood, subject to the parishioners' rights to wood and common pasture,[73] which they continued to exercise in the surviving woodland in the north and west parts of Hudnalls. In 1904 the parish council tried to prevent G. D. W. Rooke from cutting and selling underwood there and it was later agreed that he and the parishioners could take wood for their own use but not for sale.[74] The right to herbage, pannage, and estovers in 150 a. of woodland in Hudnalls was registered in 1977 under the Commons Act of 1965.[75] Bearse common did not suffer encroachment, and in 1871 the Crown enclosed 83 a. for its exclusive use, leaving 24 a. at the south end for those claiming commoning rights, namely 16 adjoining landowners.[76] In 1876 W. H. Wyndham Quin, owner of the Clearwell estate, bought out the rights of his fellow commoners, and before 1882 he also bought the Crown's part; the Crown regained the whole of Bearse common as part of the Clearwell estate in 1912.[77]

In the late 18th century[78] and the earlier 19th the parish had c. 17 principal farms. In 1818 the

49 *Rot. Litt. Claus.* (Rec. Com.), i. 588; *Cal. Lib.* 1245–51, 79.
50 P.R.O., E 146/1/26.
51 Ibid. SC 6/850/19.
52 Ibid. E 101/141/1; SC 6/850/20; Berkeley Cast. Mun., General Ser. acct. roll 426. For the park, above, manors.
53 Berkeley Cast. Mun., General Ser. 16; P.R.O., F 3/587, surv. 1835.
54 N.L.W., Dunraven MSS. 339; cf. Glos. R.O., D 1677/GG 1224.
55 P.R.O., SC 6/Hen. VIII/2496.
56 Ibid. MR 879.
57 Glos. R.O., D 33/16.
58 Ibid. 184; P.R.O., MR 879.
59 Glos. R.O., D 1677/GG 1224.
60 P.R.O., MR 879.
61 Ibid. E 112/82, no. 300; Rudder, *Glos.* 307.
62 Bodl. MS. Top. Glouc. c. 3, f. 138v.; cf. Rudder, *Glos.* 307.
63 *Trans. B.G.A.S.* xiv. 363.
64 Dean Forest Act, 19 & 20 Chas. II, c. 8.
65 Cf. P.R.O., E 112/82, no. 300.

66 C. Heath, *Hist. and Descriptive Accounts of Tintern Abbey* (Monmouth, 1801), [10].
67 Above, Hewelsfield, intro.
68 Glos. R.O., P 278A/OV 2/1.
69 Ibid. P 278/CW 2/1.
70 *Trans. B.G.A.S.* ix. 100 n; above, intro.
71 G.D.R., T 1/154, where the 109 a. described as 'common land' was presumably Bearse common and the 300 a. described as 'rough ground' was presumably in Hudnalls, Mocking Hazel, and the Fence: cf. above, intro.
72 Glos. R.O., photocopy 412/4; D 1833/E 1.
73 *6th Rep. Com. Woods,* H.C. 317, p. 152 (1829), xiv; cf. Crown Land Revenue Act, 54 Geo. III, c. 70.
74 Glos. R.O., P 278A/PC 1/1; P.R.O., F 3/587.
75 Reg. of Common Land (Glos. co. legal services dept.), no. CL 333.
76 Glos. R.O., Q/RI 121.
77 P.R.O., CRES 38/669, 672–3.
78 Glos. R.O., P 209/MI 1, pp. 120–36.

largest ones, which apart from Lindors farm were on the high, open land in the east and north-east, were Aylesmore (167 a.), Bearse farm (160 a.), Rodmore (156 a.), Willsbury, Lindors farm, and Great Hoggins (each with c. 140 a.), Stowe Grange (112 a.), and one of the farms called Dunkilns (101 a.); 115 a. on the east boundary belonged to the Prior's Mesne Lodge estate in Lydney parish. Another 7 farms had between 50 a. and 100 a. By 1840 Bearse farm had been enlarged to 273 a. and Rodmore and Stowe Grange to c. 200 a., and the new High-grove farm (149 a.) had been established on the Aylesmore estate. In the earlier 19th century most of the land was tenanted, few of the owners of the substantial freehold estates farming their land.[79] The inclusion of Hudnalls later gave the parish a large number of independent smallhold-ers, and a total of 100 agricultural occupiers was returned in 1896[80] and 89 in 1926. The pattern of principal farms remained much the same, however, with in 1926 3 returned as 150–300 a. and 13 as 50–150 a.[81]

The parish had a growing proportion of land under crops in the late 18th century and the early 19th. The tithable arable land was measured at 785 a. in 1791,[82] at 1,169 a. (out of a total of 2,619 a. of tithable farmland) in 1818,[83] and 1,292 a. (out of a total of 2,691 a.) in 1840.[84] In 1850 as much as 400 a. of the land encroached in Hud-nalls and the other former extraparochial areas was under the plough.[85] In 1818 the 16 farms in the parish that had over 50 a. of land mostly grew wheat, barley, and oats, rotated with tur-nips, clover, or grassland leys as the fodder crops; almost all of the farms still fallowed some land each year and on several a fallow was evidently one whole course in the rotation.[86] In 1866 in the enlarged parish 1,489 a. were re-turned as under crops compared with 1,243 a. of permanent grassland; wheat (453 a.) was the principal crop, with barley, roots, and clover and leys, the other main elements in the rotation.[87] Totals of 458 cattle, including 143 dairy cows, and 1,386 sheep were returned.[88] The general slump in cereals had reduced the total area returned as under crops to 895 a. by 1896[89] and to 408 a. by 1926, when only 53 a. of wheat and 12 a. of barley were returned. Dairying and stock raising became a significant activity over the period, with a total of 826 cattle, including 267 cows in milk, being returned in 1926.[90] St. Briavels had a reputation for producing good cider in the late 18th century,[91] and 125 a. of orchards were returned in 1896.[92] Almost all had been grubbed up by 1991.

By 1991 many of the smallholdings and small farms in the Hudnalls area and in and around the village had gone. In the east and north-east of the parish some amalgamations of farms had occurred and some farmhouses had been sold away from their lands, but the pattern of me-dium-sized family-run farms remained largely intact. In 1988 a total of 34 agricultural holdings, worked by 74 people, was returned in the parish, though 19 of the smaller ones were worked on a part-time basis. Dairying was then the principal enterprise, ten of the larger farms being mainly so used; a total of c. 650 cows in milk was returned. Sheep and cattle were raised, and 263 ha. (650 a.) were cropped with wheat, barley, or maize.[93] Two large battery egg units, one on the old portway near Bearse common and the other south of the Bream road, were built in the mid 1960s by Sterling Poultry Products[94] and re-mained in production in 1991.

MILLS AND IRONWORKS. In the era of bloomery forges St. Briavels was one of the centres of ironworking in the Forest area. Miles, earl of Hereford, granted a forge at St. Briavels to Tintern abbey (Mon.) before 1143.[95] In 1216 a royal order for the removal of all forges from the Forest exempted those belonging to St. Briavels castle and others held by the serjeants-in-fee, presumably worked in and around St. Briavels.[96] About 1250 the king's great forge belonging to the castle was found to be an uneconomic enter-prise, because more profit could be realized by selling the wood used to fuel it;[97] the forge was reserved in the grant of the castle to an incoming constable in 1255[98] and it was destroyed by royal order soon afterwards.[99] Eight men of St. Briav-els in 1270[1] and at least 13 in 1282 had movable forges at work in the Forest, presumably in the parish or its immediate area.[2] Among them was Adam, the king's reeve of the manor, who in 1270 was reported to employ eight charcoal burners and to have destroyed much woodland, even burning timber that had been assigned for repairing the castle.[3] Possibly St. Briavels was largely deserted by the industry in the latter part of the bloomery era: it did not figure in a list of forges in the Forest parishes owing rent to the Crown in 1437.[4] The steep hillside immediately below the village on the west, where waste from the ironworks was tipped, became known as Cinder hill[5] and in 1683 two men paid a land-owner in that area £30 a year for licence to dig cinders.[6]

In the 13th century and the early 14th iron produced in the area was used to manufacture

79 Ibid. P 175/IN 3/1, ff. 21–43; G.D.R., T 1/153.
80 P.R.O., MAF 68/1609/6.
81 Ibid. MAF 68/3295/6. 82 Glos. R.O., P 209/MI 1, p. 136.
83 Ibid. P 175/IN 3/1, f. 51.
84 G.D.R., T 1/153.
85 Ibid. 154.
86 Glos. R.O., P 175/IN 3/1, ff. 21–43.
87 P.R.O., MAF 68/26/8.
88 Ibid. MAF 68/25/9.
89 Ibid. MAF 68/1609/6.
90 Ibid. MAF 68/3295/6.
91 Bigland, Glos. i. 235.
92 P.R.O., MAF 68/1609/6.
93 Agric. Returns 1988.

94 Inf. from Mrs. Cope.
95 Cal. Chart. R. 1300–26, 96.
96 Rot. Litt. Claus. (Rec. Com.), i. 334–5; cf. ibid. 442–3, which mentions itinerant forges in the Forest held by 10 serjeants-in-fee.
97 P.R.O., E 146/1/26.
98 Cal. Pat. 1247–58, 450.
99 Cal. Close, 1341–3, 153; cf. Trans. B.G.A.S. xiv. 369.
1 P.R.O., E 32/29, rot. 2.
2 Ibid. E 32/30, rot. 23; E 32/31, m. 15.
3 Ibid. E 32/29, rot. 6d.
4 Berkeley Cast. Mun., General Ser. acct. roll 426.
5 Glos. R.O., Q/SRh 1837 C/2.
6 Suff. R.O., HA 49/A III(a)/2.

crossbow bolts (quarrels) for the royal armies and castle garrisons.[7] Bolts were being made at St. Briavels under the constable's supervision in 1223,[8] and in 1228 Henry III sent John de Malemort, John's brother called William the smith, and a fletcher to St. Briavels to manufacture them.[9] John operated there for many years, provided with his equipment and wages by the constable.[10] In 1265 he undertook to produce 25,000 bolts each year.[11] Large stocks were stored at the castle and distributed all over England: in 1237, for example, 20,000 went to Dover castle[12] and in 1257 30,000 were sent to Chester for Henry III's Welsh expedition.[13] A John de Malemort, possibly the son of the man sent in 1228, remained at work at St. Briavels in 1278,[14] and the family became well established locally.[15] The last record found of the manufacture of bolts at St. Briavels was in 1335 when the king's fletcher and ten other fletchers were employed there.[16]

William son of Baderon's manor included a mill in 1086.[17] The constable of St. Briavels had orders to build one in 1283[18] and one belonged to the castle and manor in 1331.[19] There was a mill at Mork, paying rent to the Joce family, by c. 1350.[20] It was perhaps at the site of the later Mork mill, just above the crossing of Mork brook by the old road from St. Briavels village, but there may have been more than one mill at Mork in the Middle Ages: in the 1430s both the Clearwell estate[21] and the royal manor were receiving chief rents from mills in the hamlet.[22] A fulling mill and a dyehouse were built at or immediately adjoining the site of Mork mill shortly before 1688, when they were sold to Thomas Dale, owner of the nearby Mork Farm. The mill and dyehouse were worked in 1688[23] and until 1709 or later by Thomas Hunt, dyer.[24] By 1775 Mork mill was part of an estate of the Foley family in the parish,[25] and in 1789 it was owned and worked as a corn mill by John Ansley.[26] It continued to grind corn until 1874 when it was bought by the owner of Lindors, the new house built on the site of Mork Farm.[27] The stone-built mill and millhouse became outbuildings to the house, and by 1991 had been restored and altered to form a dwelling.

A mill further down Mork brook, just above the old Monmouth–Brockweir road, was called Stert Mill in 1320 and later Wye's Mill. It was included in a lease of land at Bigsweir that Joan Greyndour made to Thomas Catchmay in 1445, and in 1648 it was on lease to Sir William Catchmay, who may have acquired the freehold from the Throckmortons of Clearwell in that year.[28] It remained part of the Bigsweir estate,[29] and was recorded until 1830.[30]

A water corn mill at an unidentified site stood on lands owned by Warren Gough of Hewelsfield c. 1630; it had been demolished by the later 17th century.[31] A mill, sometimes called Nedgetop Mill, stood on Slade brook in Slade bottom.[32] It belonged to the Whittingtons' Great House estate in 1609[33] and was sold to John Gonning in 1616.[34] No record has been found of it after 1688.[35]

On Cone brook at the south-east corner of the parish a mill called Wood Mill,[36] later Rodmore mill, was recorded from 1349. In the 15th century it was owned by the Clearwell estate and was worked as a fulling mill in 1431 and 1478.[37] In 1628 it was a corn mill and belonged to the adjoining Rodmore estate.[38] An iron furnace was later built on land adjoining the mill, and Sir John Winter of Lydney was working it in 1635.[39] In 1646 two parliamentary officers Robert Kyrle, governor of Monmouth, and John Brayne of Littledean became partners to work the furnace with several other ironworks in the neighbourhood.[40] The furnace went out of use later in the century, but in 1689 the Rodmore estate included the corn mill and two iron forges.[41] The forges at Rodmore were occupied by John Hanbury in 1719 and remained in his family's possession in 1746, probably going out of use then.[42] The corn mill probably passed from the Rodmore estate in 1754 when members of the Ford family conveyed an unidentified mill to Samuel Stokes.[43] By 1774 it had been converted to make paper, and in 1789 it was let as a paper mill[44] to James Stevens, whose family bought the freehold in 1805[45] and made paper there until 1842.[46] By 1863 Rodmore mill was a corn mill again. It became part of the Clanna estate in 1903,[47] and had ceased working by 1919 when it was let with a small farm.[48] The millhouse dates from the 17th century and is

7 For full details of the quarrel making, Hart, *Royal Forest*, 267–72.
8 *Rot. Litt. Claus.* (Rec. Com.), i. 576.
9 *Cal. Lib. 1226–40*, 61.
10 Ibid. 240; *1245–51*, 41, 380.
11 *Close R. 1254–61*, 260.
12 *Cal. Lib. 1226–40*, 258.
13 Ibid. *1251–60*, 390.
14 *Cal. Close, 1272–9*, 438.
15 P.R.O., E 32/30, rot. 23; *Glos. Subsidy Roll, 1327*, 5; Hist. MSS. Com. 55, *Glemham Hall*, pp. 175–6.
16 *Cal. Close, 1337–9*, 11.
17 *Dom. Bk.* (Rec. Com.), i. 167.
18 *Cal. Close, 1279–88*, 204.
19 Ibid. *1330–3*, 229.
20 N.L.W., Dunraven MSS. 339.
21 Ibid.; cf. Glos. R.O., D 1677/GG 1224.
22 Berkeley Cast. Mun., General Ser. acct. roll 426.
23 Glos. R.O., D 1440, St. Briavels deeds 1560–1827.
24 Ibid. D 1896, Mork fm. deeds 1709–1867.
25 Ibid. D 2528.
26 Ibid. D 1896, Mork mill deeds 1789–1874.
27 Ibid. deeds of Lindors est. 1852–1927; cf. *Kelly's Dir. Glos.*

(1870), 625; O.S. Map 6", Glos. XXXVIII. SE. (1884 edn.).
28 N.L.W., Dunraven MSS. 271; cf. above, manors (Bigsweir).
29 Glos. R.O., P 278A/OV 2/1; D 1833/E 1.
30 O.S. Map 1", sheet 35 (1830 edn.).
31 Glos. R.O., D 2026/L 8; cf. *Visit. Glos. 1682–3*, 74–5.
32 Glos. R.O., D 2026/X 19; Suff. R.O., HA 49/A III(b)/28.
33 Suff. R.O., HA 49/A III(b)/13.
34 Ibid. A III(b)/2.
35 Ibid. A III(a)/1.
36 P.R.O., MR 879.
37 N.L.W., Dunraven MSS. 339; Glos. R.O., D 1677/GG 1224.
38 *Inq. p.m. Glos. 1625–42*, i. 111.
39 P.R.O., SP 16/282, f. 253.
40 Glos. R.O., D 421/E 9.   41 Ibid. D 247/30B.
42 Ibid. P 278/CW 2/1.   43 Ibid. D 637/III/10.
44 *Glouc. Jnl.* 12 Dec. 1774; 15 June 1789.
45 Glos. R.O., D 637/II/9/E 2.
46 *Trans. B.G.A.S.* xciv. 131.
47 Glos. R.O., D 177, Rodmore mill papers 1903.
48 Ibid. Clanna est. sale papers 1919–20.

adjoined by a substantial stone mill building, which in 1991 was being converted to form part of the house.

FISHERIES. Fishing rights in the Wye adjoining St. Briavels were recorded from 1086 when half a fishery belonged to William son of Baderon's manor.[49] Bigs weir, on the river near Bigsweir House, was mentioned c. 1287 when half of it, possibly the half adjoining the Welsh bank, was leased by the bishop of Llandaff to the constable of St. Briavels; the bishop regained possession from the constable in 1322.[50] Half of a weir that Edward II alienated from the castle and manor to Tintern abbey[51] may have been the part of Bigs weir on the St. Briavels side, for Tintern held Bigs weir in 1331.[52] In 1437, however, the farm of Bigs weir was accounted for as part of the St. Briavels castle estate, but nothing was received from it as the weir was in ruins.[53] Ithel weir, later called Coed-Ithel weir, further downstream, belonged to the earl marshal's Tidenham manor but was alienated by him before 1289,[54] probably to Tintern which held it in 1331. In 1331 Bigs weir and Ithel weir and others owned by Tintern on the Wye were reported to have been heightened so that they impeded navigation; when the bailiff of St. Briavels manor tried to enforce a royal order to lower the weirs he was resisted forcibly by the abbot and monks.[55] In 1398 the abbot was censured for taking salmon fry in his fish traps at Ithel weir.[56] Ithel weir passed with other property of Tintern to the earl of Worcester in 1537[57] and the earl's successors, the dukes of Beaufort, later had the fishing rights on the lower part of the river, adjoining the detached part of St. Briavels. The owners of the Bigsweir estate later had the rights in the upper part of the river, adjoining the main part of the parish, having presumably become owners of Bigs weir as well as of fishing rights which in 1310 belonged to the estate held from the bishop of Hereford.[58] New weir, near the Florence just within the north boundary, was apparently part of a fishery that belonged to Wyeseal manor, in Newland. After the Rookes of Bigsweir bought that manor in the early 19th century[59] they had all the fishing rights on the Gloucestershire bank from Redbrook to a point opposite Llandogo, and in 1900 they also had rights on the Monmouthshire bank between Whitebrook and Llandogo in respect of lands they owned there.[60]

During the 17th century and the early 18th Acts of parliament for improving the Wye navigation provided for the dismantling of the weirs on the river.[61] In 1791 a ruined fish house stood on the duke of Beaufort's land called Abbey Hams just north of Ithel weir,[62] and the rights confirmed to the duke in 1866 as part of his extensive fishery in the lower Wye included, on the bank adjoining St. Briavels, a crib at a place called Turk's Hole, apparently near Abbey Hams, and a boat and stop net used at Coed-Ithel.[63] The Rookes of Bigsweir used cribs and stop nets adjoining their estate in the 19th century until 1866 when an inquiry declared the practice illegal.[64] In the 1890s the Bigsweir fishery was leased to Miller Bros. of Chepstow, who were also tenants of the duke of Beaufort's Wye fisheries. The duke sold his fishing rights to the Crown Commissioners of Woods in 1901,[65] and they passed in the 1920s to the Wye Board of Conservators. In 1991 the National Rivers Authority, as successor to the board, held them, while the Bigsweir estate still owned its rights.[66]

OTHER INDUSTRY AND TRADE. In 1208 the Crown established a market at St. Briavels on Saturdays.[67] In 1232 the day was changed to Tuesday and then to Monday[68] and in 1309 it was changed again to Tuesday. A fair at Michaelmas was granted in 1309 but moved to the Nativity of St. Mary in 1318.[69] In the mid 1430s the manor claimed two fairs, at St. John before the Latin Gate and at St. Clement, but they were not then being held, nor apparently was any market.[70] The alterations to the dates suggest that it was found difficult to establish St. Briavels as a trading centre. Its central role in the Forest administration and its ironworking industry doubtless encouraged some trade in the early Middle Ages, but later there was little to counteract the relative inaccessibility of the place. The market and fairs had certainly lapsed by c. 1700.[71] The only later revival appears to have been the Midsummer pleasure fair that was held in the village streets at the start of the 20th century; it was moved to an outlying site c. 1905 and had lapsed by the 1960s.[72]

In 1608 11 tradesmen and craftsmen were mustered from the parish, including a mercer, a weaver, and a miner, who possibly worked in an adjoining area, as no iron or coal workings have been found recorded within the parish. Four watermen also listed were probably employed on vessels trading from Brockweir.[73] Village craftsmen were mentioned with reasonable regularity later.[74] In 1811, in an enumeration that evidently included the outlying extraparochial areas, 11 families were supported by trade compared with

---

[49] *Dom. Bk.* (Rec. Com.), i. 167.
[50] *Cal. Close, 1318–23*, 472–3.
[51] Ibid. *1341–3*, 153.　　　[52] *Cal. Close, 1330–3*, 370–1.
[53] Berkeley Cast. Mun., General Ser. acct. roll 426.
[54] *V.C.H. Glos.* x. 71.
[55] *Cal. Close, 1330–3*, 370–1.
[56] *Public Works in Med. Law*, i (Selden Soc. xxxii), 166.
[57] *L. & P. Hen. VIII*, xii (1), pp. 350–1.
[58] N.L.W., Dunraven MSS. 325.
[59] Above, Newland, manors; econ. hist.
[60] Glos. R.O., D 1833/E 5/1, rep. of inspector of fisheries 1901; T 13, lease 1900.
[61] I. Waters, *About Chepstow* (Chepstow, 1952), 20.
[62] Glos. R.O., D 2700/QC 7/5.
[63] Ibid. Q/RF.　　　　　　[64] Ibid. D 1833/E 5/1.

[65] Ibid.; ibid. T 13, lease 1900; cf. Waters, *About Chepstow*, 33.
[66] Inf. from National Rivers Authority (Welsh Region), Monmouth.
[67] *Rot. Litt. Claus.* (Rec. Com.), i. 107.
[68] *Close R. 1231–4*, 95, 115.
[69] *Cal. Close, 1307–13*, 105; *1318–23*, 5.
[70] P.R.O., E 101/141/1; SC 6/858/15; Berkeley Cast. Mun., General Ser. acct. roll 426.
[71] Bodl. MS. Rawl. B. 323, f. 111.
[72] Creswick, *Where I was Bred*, 14–15.
[73] Smith, *Men and Armour*, 39–40. For Brockweir, above, Hewelsfield, econ. hist.
[74] e.g. Glos. R.O., D 1833/T 3, T 6; P 278/CW 2/1, rota of par. officers 1745.

160 by agriculture, and the number of families suported by trade rose to 30 by 1831.[75] In 1851 *c.* 95 men in the enlarged parish followed non-agricultural occupations, about a third of them living in St. Briavels village and the rest inhabiting the cottages of Lower Meend, Hudnalls, St. Briavels common, and the part of the riverside adjoining Brockweir. St. Briavels village was then well supplied with craftsmen, among them 5 blacksmiths, but it had only a few shopkeepers and only one professional man, a surgeon. Among the cottagers of the outlying areas the woodworking trades were particularly well represented, with 9 carpenters, 2 hoopmakers, 2 hurdlemakers, and a maker of chairs enumerated, and more directly the woodlands gave employment to 8 woodmen and woodcutters and 2 wood dealers. The stoneworking trades were also well represented, with 8 masons and 3 tilers living in the outlying areas.[76] In those two trades the Hulin family predominated in the earlier 19th century. Members of the family had worked stone at St. Briavels since 1713 or earlier,[77] and in the early 1820s at least six were masons or tilers there.[78] Thirteen men, classed as mariners, sailors, or watermen, lived in the outlying parts of the parish in 1851, all presumably employed in Brockweir's trade.[79]

Stone has been quarried extensively in the parish, and lime burning, recorded from the early 18th century,[80] became a significant trade in the 19th century, usually carried on by farmers as a sideline. By 1840 there were limekilns at a number of sites, including two at Willsbury green near Great Hoggins Farm, whose owner William Allen[81] had traded as a builder in 1830 when he was one of the contractors for the new tower of the parish church.[82] By 1880 kilns and small quarries were scattered over the eastern, upland part of the parish.[83] Lime burning had by then been further encouraged by the opening of the Wye Valley railway, and the lime was carted to the station on the other side of Bigsweir bridge. Lime burning came to an end in the early 20th century,[84] but quarrying continued, and a large quarry at Stowe on the north boundary of the parish was being worked for roadstone in 1991.

The parish retained a fairly substantial body of craftsmen in the early 20th century, with 6 masons and 4 carpenters among those listed in 1906.[85] By 1939 most of the traditional crafts had died out but 10 sellers of provisions and other shopkeepers were listed, together with builders, motor engineers, and a haulage contractor.[86] St. Briavels village had a post office with general

store and a butcher's shop in 1991. The number of visitors attracted there by the castle and the Wye Valley scenery had encouraged the establishment of a pottery.

LOCAL GOVERNMENT.

In 1276 return of writs, assize of bread and ale, gallows, and pleas of *vee de naam* were claimed for the royal manor of St. Briavels.[87] The manor court was held at St. Briavels castle with the courts for St. Briavels hundred, which are described above.[88] In the 1440s a court was being held for the St. Briavels manor that belonged to the owners of the Clearwell estate.[89] A lease of the site of Stowe manor in 1559 referred to a court being held there, although in practice it may already have lapsed.[90]

The accounts of the two churchwardens of St. Briavels survive for the years 1719–59 and from 1811[91] and those of the two overseers of the poor for 1692–1725,[92] and there are vestry minutes from 1833.[93] In 1745 a rota by houses was made for filling the offices of churchwarden and overseer.[94] The parish had two constables in 1718. In the early 18th century there were usually *c.* 10 people receiving a weekly dole from the overseers, and other parishioners were helped with the payment of house rent.[95] Payments to vagrants were causing concern in 1723 and were ordered to be discontinued.[96] In 1813 and 1814 the parish gave 26 people regular weekly pay and more than 40 occasional relief; the total annual expenditure was *c.* £460, a sum similar to that in much more populous parishes like Lydney and Awre.[97] In the late 1820s expenditure reached another peak, at just over £300.[98] Poor cottagers living in Hudnalls and other extraparochial areas were then receiving relief from the parish, and in 1835 it was said that most of the inhabitants of Hudnalls had their legal settlement in St. Briavels.[99] By 1828 a workhouse had been built on Mork Lane at the north end of the village, and the poor there were farmed out that year.[1] By 1833 a select vestry had been formed and an assistant overseer appointed. In 1836 the parish gave 19 people weekly pay and housed another 10, mostly disabled and infirm, in the workhouse. In that year the parish became part of the Chepstow poor-law union, which the ratepayers voted to join in preference to the Monmouth union.[2]

In the mid 1840s, following the addition of the extraparochial areas, the parishioners became concerned about high rates. In 1846 payers to the highway rates owning two or more horses were allowed to contribute part of their assess-

75 *Census*, 1811, 1831.   76 P.R.O., HO 107/2443.
77 Glos. R.O., D 34/9/75; P 278/CW 2/1, accts. 1736–7, 1742–3.   78 Ibid. D 1833/T 17.
79 P.R.O., HO 107/2443.
80 Glos. R.O., D 33/337; N.L.W., Dunraven MSS. 334, deed 1732.
81 G.D.R., T 1/153 (nos. 14, 45, 130, 132–3, 262).
82 Glos. R.O., P 278/CW 2/2.
83 O.S. Maps 6", Glos. XXXVIII. SE.; XLVI. NE. (1884 edn.).
84 Creswick, *Where I was Bred*, 13–14.
85 *Kelly's Dir. Glos.* (1906), 285.
86 Ibid. (1939), 302–3.
87 *Rot. Hund.* (Rec. Com.), i. 176.

88 St. Briavels hundred.
89 N.L.W., Dunraven MSS. 339.
90 Glos. R.O., D 33/149; cf. P.R.O., SC 6/Hen.VIII/2496.
91 Glos. R.O., P 278/CW 2/1–3.
92 Ibid. P 278A/OV 2/1.
93 Ibid. P 278/VE 2/1.   94 Ibid. P 278/CW 2/1.
95 Ibid. P 278A/OV 2/1.   96 Ibid. P 278/CW 2/1.
97 *Poor Law Abstract, 1818*, 146–7; cf. ibid. 144–5.
98 *Poor Law Returns* (1830–1), p. 66.
99 *3rd Rep. Dean Forest Com.* 17; cf. Glos. R.O., P 278/VE 2/1, min. 24 Oct. 1836.
1 Glos. R.O., P 278A/OV 9/1; P 278/VE 2/1, min. 11 May 1837; for its site, Creswick, *Where I was Bred*, 6.
2 Glos. R.O., P 278/VE 2/1.

ment by hauling stone and in 1849 all payers were permitted to meet a third of their assessment by haulage.[3] That system, which was evidently adopted because several of the farmers owned small quarries, probably continued after 1867, when the parish opted not to join the Lydney highway district that was formed from the Gloucestershire parishes of the Chepstow union.[4] St. Briavels continued to repair its lesser roads until 1898 when they were taken over by the Lydney rural district, in which the parish had been included for other purposes from 1894.[5] With the rest of the rural district it passed into the new Forest of Dean district in 1974.

CHURCH. St. Briavels church was a chapel to Lydney church for much of its history. It was probably included in a grant of Lydney church to Lire abbey (Eure) by William FitzOsbern (d. 1071),[6] but in 1144 Baderon of Monmouth confirmed St. Briavels church to Monmouth priory, a cell of St. Florent abbey (Saumur), and it was then claimed to have been part of the endowment of the priory by its founder Wihanoc of Monmouth in William I's reign.[7] That confirmation was approved by the bishop of Hereford, and St. Florent secured papal confirmations in 1146 and 1157,[8] but the claim had presumably been challenged by Lire abbey for many years, and between 1164 and 1166 the bishop of Worcester, arbitrating between Lire and St. Florent, confirmed Lire's right to the church. St. Florent was able only to establish its right to two sheaves out of the demesne tithes of St. Briavels, and it released those to Lire under the settlement. At the same period, probably also in the 1160s, the bishop of Hereford dedicated the church and confirmed it to Lire as a chapel of Lydney church.[9] In 1186 a papal bull once more confirmed the church to St. Florent,[10] but there is no evidence that the claim was resumed. St. Briavels was included as a chapel to Lydney in the grant of Lydney church by Lire abbey to the dean and chapter of Hereford in 1219.[11]

St. Briavels had burial rights by 1282[12] but in other respects remained a chapel of ease, the tithes being taken by the impropriator and vicar of Lydney.[13] Priests, styled curates or chaplains, were assigned by the vicar to serve it, and from the mid 17th century they usually also had charge of the neighbouring chapelry of Hewelsfield.[14] in 1750 the curate had a salary of £25 and was allowed the surplice fees and a sermon

charity founded by William Whittington.[15] In 1825 the curate received £100 a year.[16]

In 1859 a separate benefice was created, endowed with the vicar of Lydney's tithe rent charge from the parish. The living, a perpetual curacy but styled a vicarage from 1866, was placed in the gift of the dean and chapter of Hereford, patrons of Lydney.[17] The first incumbent, Horatio Walmsley, bought a cottage at the south-east corner of the churchyard and in 1864 assigned it for use as a vicarage house; the building was enlarged and remodelled in two stages in a Tudor style. The gift of the vicarage house was matched by £200 granted by Queen Anne's Bounty in augmentation of the benefice,[18] which was worth £150 a year in 1879.[19] The ecclesiastical parish comprised only the ancient parish of St. Briavels until 1932: it was then extended to include most of the former extraparochial areas of the civil parish, but the south part of St. Briavels common and the part of the ancient parish adjoining Brockweir were added then to Hewelsfield ecclesiastical parish.[20] In 1963 the benefice was united with that of Hewelsfield. The incumbent continued to live at St. Briavels, where a new vicarage house was acquired in 1981.[21]

Two of the stipendiary curates who served the longest were James Davies, appointed before 1731, and Thomas Edmunds, who succeeded Davies in 1769 and died in the post in 1804.[22] In 1750 Davies held only one service each Sunday, in the morning or afternoon by alternation with Hewelsfield chapel,[23] and the same arrangement was followed in 1825.[24]

The history of the hermitage chapel at Stowe is given above.[25] A chapel dedicated to St. Margaret stood beside the road at Mork between St. Margaret's grove, with which the chapel was endowed, and Mork Farm (the house later replaced by Lindors).[26] The chapel was possibly established as a hospital in connexion with the route from the river crossing at Bigsweir, for a warden of St. Margaret's hospital at St. Briavels was granted protection by the Crown in 1256.[27] No later record has been found until 1522 when an indulgence was issued to help finance repairs at the chapel.[28] It was later said that, before its dissolution under the Act of 1547,[29] a lease of the chapel was granted by the parishioners of St. Briavels; perhaps they had communal responsibility for its management.[30] The building was in private ownership in 1642,[31] though the Commonwealth government aparently laid claim to

3 Ibid.
4 Ibid. min. 7 Mar. 1867; D 1219/3.
5 Ibid. DA 28/100/1, pp. 98, 107, 110, 212.
6 Above, Lydney, churches.
7 Cal. Doc. France, pp. 409–10. The church was not, however, mentioned in Wihanoc's endowment as given in Dugdale, Mon. iv. 596.
8 Cal. Doc. France, pp. 403–4, 409–10.
9 Dugdale, Mon. vi (2), 1094.
10 Cal. Doc. France, p. 404.
11 B.L. Harl. MS. 6203, pp. 70–3; cf. Close R. 1227–31, 76. Two years later the ch. was said to be in the king's gift but no later evidence has been found of a claim by the Crown: Cur. Reg. R. x. 260.
12 Reg. Swinfield, 3–4.
13 G.D.R., V 5/256T 1; T 1/153.
14 Cal. Lib. 1245–51, 301; Hockaday Abs. cccxxviii;

Trans. B.G.A.S. lxxxiii. 97; G.D.R. vol. 381A, f. 4.; vol. 321.
15 G.D.R. vol. 381A, f. 4; cf. below, this section.
16 G.D.R. vol. 383, no. cxix.
17 Ibid. 384, f. 28; Trans. B.G.A.S. ix. 78.
18 Glos. R.O., P 278/IN 3/1; IN 1/7, mem. at end.
19 Kelly's Dir. Glos. (1879), 731.
20 Glos. R.O., P 278/IN 3/5.
21 Ibid. 6–7.
22 Ibid. IN 1/1, 3–4.   23 G.D.R. vol. 381A, f. 4.
24 Ibid. 383, no. cxix.   25 Manors.
26 For its site, Glos. R.O., D 1440, St. Briavels deeds 1560–1827, deeds 1664, 1666; D 1896, Mork fm. deeds 1709–1867, deed 1840.
27 Cal. Pat. 1247–58, 490.   28 Reg. Bothe, 360.
29 Cf. P.R.O., E 310/14/53, f. 27.
30 Hockaday Abs. cccxxviii, 1553.
31 Suff. R.O., HA 49/A III(a)/4; A III(b)/9, 12.

the freehold in 1652.[32] In 1664 the chapel was bought by the Dale family of Mork Farm.[33] It was later demolished, probably before 1709.[34]

A chantry chapel in St. Briavels church, dedicated to St. Mary, was said at its dissolution to have been endowed by a group of donors.[35] It was presumably served by one of the three chaplains recorded at St. Briavels in 1475,[36] and in 1518 an apostate monk of Grace Dieu abbey was said to serve a chantry in the church.[37] In the 1540s the priest serving the chantry also taught children of the parish.[38] The chantry property, which included a number of houses in the village, was sold by the Crown in 1549.[39]

William Whittington (d. 1625) gave 26s. 8d. a year for sermons to be preached each quarter in St. Briavels church and 20s. to provide furnishings and ornaments.[40] The sermons were being preached as directed in the 1820s,[41] and in the 1960s the fund was used for the expenses of a visiting preacher at Whitsun.[42] A newly built mission chapel standing at Mork, near Lindors, was licensed in 1887 and remained in use in the early 20th century.[43]

The church of *ST. MARY*, which was known by that dedication by 1471[44] but was apparently dedicated to St. Briavels in the 12th century,[45] is built of rubble with ashlar dressings. It comprises chancel with north vestry, central crossing with north and south transepts, aisled and clerestoried nave, and south tower incorporating a porch. The south aisle and its five-bayed arcade are of the 12th century. The crossing, which carried a low, broad tower, and the north transept are of *c.* 1200, and the reconstruction of the east end was completed by the addition of a long chancel in the 13th century.[46] The north aisle was built *c.* 1300 and there may then have been some widening of the nave, which is not central to the western crossing arch. The south transept was remodelled in the 14th century and a rood stair was later built against its west side. Instability of the foundations made necessary the removal of the central tower in 1829, and a new tower, its ground floor forming a porch, was built against the south aisle in 1830–1 in place of an old porch. The new tower was designed by John Briggs of Chepstow.[47] In 1861 the chancel was rebuilt in shortened form with a vestry adjoining it on the north, the west window and the north aisle windows were replaced, and a ceiling, inserted in 1756, was removed from the nave.[48]

The Norman stone font has a plain tub-shaped bowl with a projecting waistband of scallops.[49] A canopied monument in the chancel with effigies of William Warren (d. 1573) and his wife[50] was taken down at the rebuilding of the chancel in 1861; the broken parts were preserved in the church[51] and in 1974 the effigies were reassembled on a new base in the south aisle.[52] A 13th-century tomb recess in the south transept was uncovered and restored in the late 19th century and an ancient coffin lid, which has an early 14th-century carved head inserted in it, was placed in the recess. A 13th-century piscina, presumably once used by the chantry priest, was moved from the north transept to the new chancel in 1861.[53] A brass chandelier given to the church in 1732 was removed in 1861.[54] The church had five bells before 1764 when William Evans of Chepstow recast them and added a sixth. The ring was augmented to eight when it was transferred to the new tower in 1831, the two new bells being cast by John Rudhall; the new treble was recast in 1905.[55] The plate includes a chalice and paten cover given to the church in 1795 and a mid 19th-century paten and flagon given by the trustees of Whittington's charity in 1860.[56] An ancient embroidered altar frontal is preserved in the church.[57] The registers survive from 1660.[58]

NONCONFORMITY. A house was licensed for use by Presbyterians in 1746[59] but no other record of the group has been found. Wesleyan Methodists, under a Chepstow minister, met at Green Farm in the village in 1819.[60] A Wesleyan Methodist chapel in the part of Hudnalls that became known as St. Briavels common[61] was built *c.* 1818; in 1851 it had congregations of up to 18 in the morning and up to 40 in the afternoon.[62] It remained open as a Methodist chapel until the mid 20th century[63] and had been converted as a house by 1991. Bible Christians (Bryanites) were meeting in the parish in 1825[64] but are not recorded later. Baptists, under a minister of Llandogo (Mon.), registered a house in 1828[65] and were again meeting in the parish in 1854,[66] but did not establish a church there.[67]

---

32 P.R.O., E 317/Glos./4.
33 Glos. R.O., D 1440, St. Briavels deeds 1560–1827.
34 Ibid. D 1896, Mork fm. deeds 1709–1867.
35 *Trans. B.G.A.S.* viii. 295.
36 *Reg. Myllyng*, 11.   37 Hockaday Abs. cccxxviii.
38 *Trans. B.G.A.S.* viii. 295–6.
39 *Cal. Pat.* 1548–9, 399; *Trans. B.G.A.S.* ix. 80–4.
40 *Trans. B.G.A.S.* x. 308–11.
41 *19th Rep. Com. Char.* 89.
42 Glos. R.O., D 3469/5/112, letter 30 Apr. 1971.
43 Ibid. P 278/IN 2/1; inf. from Mrs. Cope.
44 Hockaday Abs. cccxxviii.
45 Dugdale, *Mon.* vi (2), 1094.
46 For the ch. before the 19th-cent. alterations, Bigland, *Glos.* i, plate facing p. 235.
47 Glos. R.O., P 278/CW 2/2.
48 *Trans. B.G.A.S.* ix. 75–6; cf. Glos. R.O., P 278/CW 2/1; Bigland, *Glos.* i. 235.
49 *Trans. B.G.A.S.* xxxiv. 195.
50 Bigland, *Glos.* i, plate facing p. 235; Rudder, *Glos.* 309.

51 *Trans. B.G.A.S.* vi. 33.
52 Church guide (*c.* 1985).
53 *Trans. B.G.A.S.* v. 32–3.
54 Glos. R.O., P 278/CW 2/1, acct. 1732–3; CW 3/12.
55 *Glos. Ch. Bells*, 530–3.
56 *Glos. Ch. Plate*, 177–8.
57 *Trans. B.G.A.S.* ix. 76; xi. 259.
58 Glos. R.O., P 278/IN 1/1–4.
59 Ibid. Q/SO 3.
60 Hockaday Abs. cccxxviii.
61 O.S. Map 6", Glos. XLVI. NW. (1884 edn.).
62 P.R.O., HO 129/576/3/6/14, where it was described as at Brockweir common in St. Briavels par.; cf. Hockaday Abs. ccxliii, 1819, where, before the new par. boundary was established, it was described as at Brockweir common in Hewelsfield par.
63 *Kelly's Dir. Glos.* (1939), 302.
64 G.D.R. vol. 383, no. cxix.   65 Hockaday Abs. cccxxviii.
66 G.R.O. Worship Reg. no. 2109.
67 *Glouc. Jnl.* 24 Aug. 1861.

Independents and Congregationalists met in houses in the parish in 1824[68] and in the 1850s[69] and became permanently established in 1861 when a chapel was built on the east side of High Street.[70] In 1908 the Congregational church at St. Briavels had 25 members and had outlying mission stations at Mork and at 'the Common'.[71] The latter was evidently a small chapel near Chapel Farm in the north part of Hudnalls, which had been built by 1880, when it was styled Independent.[72] In 1991 the chapel in the village, which was then under a lay pastor and affiliated to the Evangelical Fellowship of Congregational Churches, had morning congregations of c. 40 and evening congregations of c. 25. The chapel at Hudnalls, known as the Gideon chapel, was then used mainly as a youth centre by young members of the St. Briavels congregation and by visiting groups from other churches.[73]

EDUCATION. There were two small private day schools and a church Sunday school at St. Briavels in 1818.[74] A National school had been established by 1847 when it had an attendance of 54. School pence were charged at a rate of more than 1d. a week because little supplementary income could be raised by subscriptions; some of the poorest children could not afford to attend. The unsecured schoolroom where it was held[75] was presumably, as in 1858 and until 1872, a room in the castle.[76] A new church school, on the Chepstow road at the south end of the village, was opened in 1872. It was built at the instigation of the vicar W. T. Allen, whose architect son designed the building, and the site was given by W. H. Peel of Aylesmore.[77] The average attendance was 135 in 1885,[78] and in 1910, when it was called St. Briavels Parochial school, the average attendance was 164 in mixed and infants' departments. Attendance fell during the early 20th century to 97 in 1938.[79] In 1991, as the St. Briavels Parochial C. of E. school, it had 64 children on its roll.[80]

Children from the south part of the parish attended schools in or near Brockweir, whose history is given above under Hewelsfield.[81] An outlying nonconformist chapel, probably the Wesleyan chapel at St. Briavels common, was being used for a small day school under an untrained teacher in 1867.[82]

CHARITIES FOR THE POOR. William Whittington (d. 1625) gave lands in St. Briavels parish to support ecclesiastical bequests, payments of £3 a year to 12 poor people, and £3 a year for apprenticeships.[83] John Gonning (d. 1662) charged his Great House estate with £5 for the poor; William Hoskins by will dated 1661 gave 20s. charged on his Stowe Grange estate; and John Braban by will dated 1684 gave 40s., which was later charged on Cinderhill house. A bequest of 40s. charged on one of the Dunkilns farms by Thomas Evans by will dated 1820 was apparently never implemented. In the 1820s the various eleemosynary bequests were distributed to the poor in the church at Easter.[84] Under the Whittington charity an apprenticeship was made every one or two years in the 18th century and the early 19th and at longer intervals later.[85]

Caroline Ironside by will proved 1879 gave a legacy to provide the poor of St. Briavels and Llandogo (Mon.) with clothes and other necessities. In 1900 when the endowment was £57 stock, producing an income of under £2, it was divided to form separate charities for each parish.[86]

In 1915 all the charities except Whittington's were placed under a single body of trustees, as the United Charities. In 1971 the Whittington charity was placed under the trustees of the United Charities and part of its income was applied, with that of the other charities, to relieve the poor in cash or kind and another part to aid young people entering a trade or profession. In 1991 the charities distributed c. £30 in sums of £3 to ill and handicapped people and, under the separate provision for the Whittington charity, small items of equipment were occasionally purchased for young people starting work. All the income was then drawn from investments, the Whittington land having been sold in 1878 and the Hoskins, Braban, and Gonning rent charges redeemed in 1916, 1945, and 1973 repectively.[87]

C. L. Denton (d. 1892)[88] left an endowment to establish an almshouse for three elderly men and three elderly widows. It was built on the south side of East Street in 1895 by his heir O. W. Andrews.[89] The almshouse was modernized in the late 1960s,[90] and in 1991 the six occupants paid a low rent for their accommodation.[91]

A customary distribution of bread and cheese to the poor at St. Briavels is described above.[92]

68 Hockaday Abs. cccxxviii.
69 G.R.O. Worship Reg. nos. 1383, 7057, 9443.
70 Glouc. Jnl. 24 Aug. 1861.
71 Glos. Colln. J 11.48 (13, 16).
72 O.S. Map 6", Glos. XLVI. NE. (1884 edn.).
73 Inf. from Mr. M. F. James, lay pastor.
74 Educ. of Poor Digest, 308.
75 Nat. Soc. Inquiry, 1846–7, Glos. 4–5.
76 P.R.O., ED 7/35/275; Trans. B.G.A.S. iii. 359.
77 Glos. R.O., P 278/VE 2/1, mins. 13 Oct. 1870; 15 Aug. 1872; ibid. IN 1/7, mem. at end.
78 Kelly's Dir. Glos. (1885), 557.
79 Bd. of Educ., List 21, 1911 (H.M.S.O.), 166; 1922, 107; 1932, 117; 1938, 129.
80 Schools and Establishments Dir. 1991–2 (co. educ. dept.), 29.
81 Hewelsfield, educ.
82 Glos. R.O., P 278/SC 1/2.
83 Trans. B.G.A.S. x. 304–12.
84 19th Rep. Com. Char. 87–9; Glos. R.O., P 278/CH 3/1; for Gonning and Hoskins, cf. above, manors. After the demolition of Great Ho., Gonning's charge was transferred to Church Fm.
85 Glos. R.O., D 1440, St. Briavels deeds 1560–1827; P 278/CH 1/6–7.
86 Ibid. D 3469/5/112.
87 Ibid.; inf. from Mrs. Cope.
88 Plaque in ch.
89 Creswick, Where I was Bred, 15.
90 Glos. R.O., D 3469/5/112.
91 Inf. from Mrs. Cope.
92 Intro.

STAUNTON

STAUNTON[93] is situated high above the river Wye on the north-west fringes of the Forest of Dean, 2.5 km. east of Monmouth. From the 1820s when much of its farmland was converted to timber plantations two thirds of the small parish comprised woodland. Staunton included part of Highmeadow, which was a considerable hamlet before becoming the site of a large mansion. The other part of Highmeadow was in Newland parish (mainly in its Coleford tithing) but its history is included wholly under Staunton. Also included in this account is Cherry Orchard farm at a place formerly called Ashridge on the Newland boundary west of Highmeadow.

A manor established at Staunton in Anglo-Saxon times had become part of the Forest waste by 1066, but the settlement was re-established before the 1140s when a church had been built.[94] Additional land was probably added throughout the early Middle Ages. An assart of 120 a. that Ralph of Willington was licensed to make in 1225, described as lying to the right of Staunton and the road leading to the Wye and Monmouth,[95] may have been in the north part of the later parish, though Ralph is not otherwise found recorded in connexion with Staunton. In 1258 22 inhabitants of Staunton were listed at the Forest eyre as holding small assarts of one or two acres each,[96] and in 1339 the lord of the manor John of Staunton (or Walding) held 30 a. of new assart.[97] Lands in the west part of the parish at Knockalls, described as 'the king's common' in 1536,[98] and at Staunton Meend remained outlying parts of the royal demesne land of the Forest until the Crown alienated them in 1629.[99] The whole parish remained within the jurisdiction of the Forest while that jurisdiction was enforced.[1]

Staunton parish was compact in shape and covered 1,530 a.[2] (619 ha.). The south part of its east boundary followed an old road leading from Highmeadow towards Staunton village, and the north part of that boundary descended Whippington brook, recorded as 'Wybaltunes' brook in 1282.[3] The north boundary left the brook above its confluence with the Wye to run westwards to an oak tree, called Bellman's Oak in 1653,[4] and the west boundary, adjoining land that until the 16th century formed part of the marcher lordship of Monmouth and thereafter was in Monmouthshire, climbed a track to the old course of the Gloucester–Monmouth road at a place that was called Staunton gate in 1300. The boundary then followed the road down to

a stone called the Broad stone and descended a brook, called Threbrook in 1300[5] and later Try mouth brook or Grange brook,[6] to its confluence with the upper Red brook. The south boundary of the parish followed the Monmouth–Newland road up towards Highmeadow.

The parish is on part of an irregular spur of land, formed of carboniferous limestone,[7] and is mostly at over 150 m.; Staunton village is situated at c. 210 m. and the highest point of the parish, a ridge on the west crowned by the stone called the Buck stone, reaches 279 m. In the south part of the parish a narrow valley divides the Buck stone ridge on the west from a slightly lower ridge on the east and runs down into the deep valley of the upper Red brook.

In 1608 much of the high west ridge was waste land called Staunton Meend, covering 123 a.[8] A part of it, or possibly the whole, was evidently the land called Staunton Meend Ridges which, with other land called Knockalls further south, was granted by the Crown in fee in 1629 to the Hall family,[9] owners of Staunton manor and the large Highmeadow estate. Later the western slopes, towards Monmouthshire, belonged to the estate as a several wood called Rodge wood, while the eastern slopes, above the village and central valley, retained the name Staunton Meend and were manorial waste, commonable to the tenants. The common covered 42 a. in 1792.[10] Considerable areas of the parish were too steep for cultivation and remained woodland.[11] In 1792 there were 455 a. of woods in the parish, all belonging to the Highmeadow estate; the main woods were then Rodge wood, Patches wood at the north end of the parish, Bunjups, Knockalls, and Birchen groves on the south-west slopes above the upper Red brook, and the Hoods on the east side of the central valley. The owner of the estate then had a dwelling for his woodman at Reddings, on the north-west boundary between Patches wood and his large Hadnock wood in Monmouthshire.[12] Less steep ground, north of the village, on the ridge south-east of it, and in the valley south of it, was farmland and included some open fields until the early 17th century.[13]

Between 1823 and 1827 the Crown Commissioners of Woods, who had bought the Highmeadow estate, planted c. 550 a. of Staunton's farmland as part of the policy of raising oaks for future naval requirements. The ancient woods at Patches and above the Red brook valley were considerably enlarged but the principal

93 This account was written in 1994.
94 Below, manor.
95 *Rot. Litt. Claus.* (Rec. Com.), ii. 62.
96 P.R.O., E 32/28, rot. 7 and d.
97 *Cal. Inq. p.m.* xvi, pp. 64–5.
98 Glos. R.O., D 1677/GG 590.
99 Below, this section.
1 Below, Forest of Dean, bounds.
2 *O.S. Area Bk.* (1881).
3 P.R.O., E 32/31, m. 13.
4 Glos. R.O., D 1677/GG 1558; O.S. Map 6", Glos. XXX. SE. (1884 edn.).

5 *Trans. B.G.A.S.* lxvi. 178.
6 P.R.O., MR 879 (F 17/1); Taylor, *Map of Glos.* (1777); *Trans. B.G.A.S.* vii. 241; Glos. R.O., P 310/MI 1.
7 Geol. Surv. Map 1", solid, sheet 43 (1845 edn.).
8 P.R.O., MR 879.
9 Glos. R.O., D 421/E 5, letters patent 1640; cf. ibid. D 2026/X 14, s.v. purprestures within Lord Protector's waste.
10 P.R.O., MR 691 (LRRO 1/240); F 17/117(2), p. 45.
11 For the woodland in 1608, ibid. MR 879.
12 Ibid. MR 691; F 17/117(2).
13 Below, econ. hist.

new plantations were on the high ground of the east part of the parish[14] where the old fields such as Blakes, Windmill field, Shobleys, and High Reddings were lost. The Crown woodlands were later administered as Reddings Inclosure, comprising the north end of the parish and the adjoining Hadnock wood with a woodman's lodge at the old building, Knockalls Inclosure, in the south of the parish with a lodge at the south end of Staunton Meend, and Marian's Inclosure, in the east of the parish and including also land in Coleford tithing.[15] In 1843 Staunton parish comprised 1,015 a. of old woods and new plantations, 407 a. of farmland, and 62 a. of commonable waste.[16] A quarry worked on the edge of the plantations north of Highmeadow removed a large part of the ridge there during the later 20th century.[17]

The first element in the name of the parish (O.E. *stan*)[18] probably refers to a rocky outcrop, called the Cliff or Toad's Mouth,[19] by the Gloucester–Monmouth road at the west end of Staunton village, but it is also appropriate to an area with several megaliths. The Long stone, so called by 1336,[20] is a pillar of rock beside the Gloucester–Monmouth road near the east boundary of the parish. The Broad stone, which as mentioned above was a boundary mark in 1300,[21] is the largest of several lumps of rock lying in the fields of Broadstone farm at the west side of the parish. The celebrated local landmark called the Buck stone[22] surmounts the ridge above Staunton Meend at a popular viewpoint over the Wye Valley. The stone tapers to a narrow base, which once enabled it to be rocked, though that was said to be no longer possible *c.* 1775.[23] Later the stone attracted attempts to topple it, a feat that was achieved in 1885 by a party of five travelling actors and a Monmouth innkeeper, with whom they were lodging. The stone split into several pieces, but at the expense of the Crown, the landowner, it was cemented together and secured in its place with an iron bar.[24]

The road from Coleford town to Monmouth, passing through the village, was included by Ogilby in 1675 as part of the main London to South Wales road.[25] From the mid 18th century, because of the difficulties of negotiating the long hill between the village and Monmouth bridge over the Wye, a road at the south edge of Staunton parish, running down the upper Red brook valley to the Wye, was the coaching route to Monmouth.[26] That road was made a turnpike west of the end of Highmeadow hamlet in 1755,[27] and the Forest of Dean turnpike Act in 1796 covered the road leading from Coleford town through Whitecliff and up Highmeadow's main street.[28] Under an Act of 1831,[29] however, the Monmouth trust turnpiked the road through Staunton village and much improved it. In the village, where the old course made two awkward, right-angled bends, it was replaced by a new line from south of the parish church to the more westerly of the bends. Also, as part of a new line down the long hill to the Wye, a higher and slightly more southerly course replaced the old hollow way that had followed the parish boundary as far as the Broad stone.[30] An improvement had already been made at the expense of the parish in 1824 when part of the crag called the Cliff at the west end of the village was blown up.[31] East of the village the road was turnpiked in 1831 by the Forest of Dean trust,[32] and in 1841 that trust built a new line via Berry Hill, replacing the route through Coleford town; it joined the old road near the Long stone just within Staunton's boundary.[33] The Monmouth trust, which had a tollhouse near the west end of the village,[34] was discontinued in 1878[35] and the Forest trust in 1888.[36]

A road from Staunton village to English Bicknor, recorded in 1282,[37] led from near the church to cross Whippington brook near Coalpit Hill, and another, recorded from 1348, ran south-eastwards from the church over the ridge to Highmeadow. Another road branched from the Highmeadow road at a place on the ridge where a windmill stood and ran south by way of Ashridge Cross (at the later Cherry Orchard Farm) to Newland village;[38] it appears to have been abandoned north of Cherry Orchard by the late 18th century.[39] A road leading from Staunton village down the central valley to the upper Red brook valley was called Mill way in 1348 and later Mill Lane.[40] During 1823 and 1824 the parish considerably improved Mill Lane, which then gave the villagers access to the Monmouth turnpike.[41] Under an Act of 1856 the Monmouth trust built a new road branching out of Mill Lane and leading along the east side of the central valley to Cherry Orchard Farm.[42] Of the old roads, the Bicknor road remained in use only as a track for forestry vehicles in 1994, while the

[14] P.R.O., F 17/117(1); Glos. R.O., P 310/SU 2/1; IN 3/1.
[15] O.S. Maps 6", Glos. XXX. SW., SE.; XXXVIII. NE. (1883–4 edn.).
[16] G.D.R., T 1/170.
[17] Cf. O.S. Map 1/25,000, SO 51 (1949, 1989 edns.).
[18] *P.N. Glos.* (E.P.N.S.), iii. 247.
[19] G.D.R., T 1/170; A. O. Cooke, *Forest of Dean* (1913), 265–6.
[20] Glos. R.O., D 1677/GG 53; cf. P.R.O., MR 879.
[21] *Trans. B.G.A.S.* lxvi. 178.
[22] Bodl. MS. Rawl. B. 323, f. 123v; above, Plate 1.
[23] Rudder, *Glos.* 689.
[24] E. G. Fraser, *Notes on Staunton Topics* (Monmouth, priv. print. 1906), 48–9; cf. *Glouc. Jnl.* 19 Dec. 1885.
[25] Ogilby, *Britannia* (1675), p. 30.
[26] Cf. Glos. R.O., Q/RUm 98/1; Bryant, *Map of Glos.* (1824).
[27] Monmouth Roads Act, 28 Geo. II, c. 31.
[28] Dean Forest Roads Act, 36 Geo. III, c. 131; cf. Glos. R.O., D 1677/1545, no. 16.

[29] Monmouth Roads Act, 1 & 2 Wm. IV, c. 18 (Local and Personal).
[30] Glos. R.O., Q/RUm 126.
[31] Ibid. P 310/SU 2/1.
[32] Dean Forest Roads Act, 1 & 2 Wm. IV, c. 42 (Local and Personal).
[33] Nicholls, *Forest of Dean*, 197; Glos. R.O., Q/RUm 152.   [34] G.D.R., T 1/170.
[35] Annual Turnpike Act Continuance Act, 1878, 41 & 42 Vic. c. 62.
[36] Dean Forest Turnpike Trust Abolition Act, 51 & 52 Vic. c. 193.
[37] P.R.O., E 32/31, m. 13; cf. Glos. R.O., D 1677/GG 83.
[38] Glos. R.O., D 1677/GG 66, 96; *Trans. B.G.A.S.* vii. 239, 241; cf. P.R.O., MR 879.   [39] P.R.O., MR 691.
[40] Glos. R.O., D 1677/GG 66; *Trans. B.G.A.S.* vii. 238, 241.
[41] Glos. R.O., P 310/SU 2/1; Q/SRh 1823 C/4.
[42] Monmouth Roads Act, 19 & 20 Vic. c. 89 (Local and Personal); Glos. R.O., D 637/I/97.

Highmeadow road could be traced only as a woodland ride and part, north of Highmeadow, had been quarried away.

A tramroad opened in 1812 to supply Forest coal to Monmouth followed the road from Newland village to Cherry Orchard and turned down the valley to Upper Redbrook hamlet. Most of its course was later followed by the Coleford–Monmouth railway, which operated between 1883 and 1916. A small station to serve Newland village was built just east of Cherry Orchard Farm[43] and adapted to form a house in the mid 20th century.

The old irregular course of the Gloucester–Monmouth road formed the main street of Staunton village. At the east end of the village, by the junction with the old roads from English Bicknor and Highmeadow, there was a village green, broadening towards its northern end, where it was known as the Butts.[44] The parish church and rectory stood on the east side of the green and at its south end was a cross, of which the stepped base survives.[45] The cross was mentioned in 1393,[46] and it was called the high cross in 1511[47] in distinction from a cross which in 1608 stood further west at the first right-angled bend in the village street.[48] The western cross was later removed but the place was known as Lower Cross during the 18th and 19th centuries.[49] The village pound stood on the south-west part of the green until 1828 when a school was built on its site;[50] a new stone-walled pound was built south of the main street and survived in 1994. The medieval manor house, abandoned

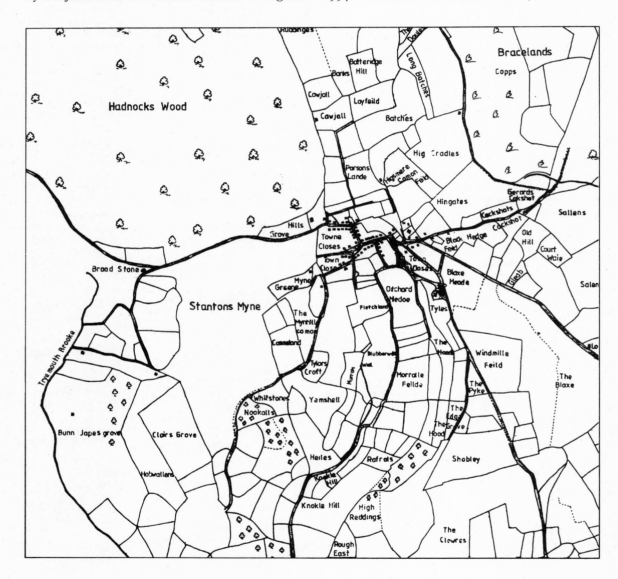

FIG. 12. STAUNTON VILLAGE AREA, 1608

43 Above, Newland, intro.; O.S. Map 1/2,500, Glos. XXXVIII. 3 (1881, 1902 edns.).
44 P.R.O., MR 879.
45 Pooley, *Glos. Crosses*, 16–17.

46 Glos. R.O., D 2244/89.
47 Ibid. D 1677/GG 313.   48 P.R.O., MR 879.
49 Glos. R.O., P 310/MI 1; D 637/II/4/T 7.
50 Fraser, *Staunton*, 30.

and ruined by the late 16th century, stood south of the green on land called Court Orchard,[51] and Staunton Farm, the village's principal farmhouse in modern times, was later built nearby, within the angle formed by the main street and the Highmeadow road.

In 1608 the village comprised c. 50 houses: the street was closely built up between the green and the Cliff at the parish boundary and there were a few scattered dwellings east of the green.[52] During the 17th and 18th centuries the village contracted, losing most of its western houses and becoming concentrated in the part of the street between the green and Lower Cross;[53] nine houses were in decay in 1653[54] and in 1769 there were 12 decayed houses or empty sites.[55] About 1710 Staunton parish, including also the few houses then remaining within it at Highmeadow or at other outlying sites, was said to contain 54 houses,[56] but in 1801 only 42 inhabited houses and four uninhabited were enumerated in the parish.[57] The new line of road built in 1831, bypassing the main part of the street, altered the pattern of the east end of Staunton village by removing part of the green and dividing the church and rectory and the Butts from the rest of the village. The new road was not built up, but a few houses were added to the village during the 19th century and the early 20th, including some on the main road west of the junction with the new road and others on a lane leading from Lower Cross towards Staunton Meend.

Staunton Farm is a small late 17th-century farmhouse, rubble built and gabled. Part of a cottage west of the old school is dated 1719, and a 17th-century cottage adjoins it. The east part of Staunton House, at Lower Cross, is of the late 18th century, and in the mid 19th century, probably when it was the home of Alexander Gibbon (d. 1870), a prominent resident of the village,[58] it was enlarged to form a long, low range of building. The other houses which survived until the 19th century were all rebuilt or remodelled. The Elms, a house built in the late 19th century, was a home for the elderly in 1994 and had a large recent extension. Whippington's Corner, a small estate built by West Dean rural district east of the church, was begun in 1950 and enlarged in 1956.[59] A small private estate was added on the north side of the village in the late 1980s.

The few outlying dwellings recorded in the north part of the parish included Broadstone (or Broadstones) Farm, a farmstead established before 1653 in a group of closes on the Monmouthshire boundary below Rodge wood.[60] The small farmhouse was altered and heavily restored in the mid 20th century. In 1622 another small farmstead called Hobwaldings[61] stood further south, between the farmland of Broadstone farm and Bunjups grove. The house was demolished before 1769[62] and its site and lands were included in the new plantations in the 1820s.

The hamlet of Highmeadow, partly within the south boundary of Staunton and partly in the ancient parish of Newland, was established on the road between Whitecliff and Staunton village, where it runs up a coomb to emerge on the high ridge above the head of the upper Red brook valley. Highmeadow was settled by the beginning of the 14th century,[63] and three houses at Highmeadow Street were mentioned in 1368.[64] In the 1560s there were 14 or more families living at Highmeadow,[65] and in 1608[66] the hamlet comprised 18 houses, straggling down the road from the crossroads at its higher, north-western end as far as a point marked in 1994 by the remains of a bridge of the Monmouth tramroad. From the higher part of the hamlet a lane, recorded from 1369[67] and called Highmeadow way in 1608, ran down the hill to Newland village. From lower down the street another lane, which was once part of the main route betwen Coleford town and Newland village,[68] branched off to join Highmeadow way at a wayside cross called Hodgeway Cross. The Hall family had a large house at the junction of the main street and Highmeadow way in 1608, and the lower part of the hamlet included the home of another fairly prosperous family called Bell,[69] which gave its name to an adjoining small wood, Bell's grove.[70]

Highmeadow was transformed during the 17th century by the Hall family, which became owners of the whole hamlet. The Halls acquired several houses as part of a substantial purchase in 1599 and at least nine others by individual purchases between 1606 and 1641.[71] About 1670 Henry Benedict Hall built a large mansion at the top of the hamlet north-west of his old house, and it was perhaps then that the main street above the junction with the Coleford–Newland road was moved north-eastwards so that it ran clear of the buildings of the old house and made more room for a forecourt for the new mansion.[72] The mansion and its grounds covered the sites of several of the old houses and most of the others were evidently demolished or abandoned to decay at the same period, all the land around being formed into a large home farm.[73] In 1792 apart from the mansion and the Halls' old house and outbuildings the only houses in the street were one at the junction with the old Coleford–Newland road and one north of the mansion.[74] The mansion was demolished at the beginning

51 Below, manor.
52 P.R.O., MR 879; cf. above, Fig. 12.
53 Cf. ibid. MR 691.
54 Glos. R.O., D 1677/GG 1558.
55 Ibid. P 310/MI 1.   56 Atkyns, Glos. 689.
57 Census, 1801.
58 G.D.R., T 1/170; Kelly's Dir. Glos. (1870), 639; tombstone in churchyard.
59 Glos. R.O., DA 25/600/2.
60 Ibid. D 1677/GG 1558; cf. ibid. P 310/MI 1.
61 N.L.W., Mynde Park MS. 70.
62 Glos. R.O., P 310/MI 1; cf. P.R.O., MR 691; F 17/117(2).

63 Glos. R.O., D 1677/GG 2, 20.
64 Ibid. GG 96.
65 Ibid. P 227/IN 1/1.
66 For the hamlet in 1608, P.R.O., MR 879.
67 Glos. R.O., D 1677/GG 97.
68 Ibid. GG 208, 436, 461.
69 Ibid. GG 409, 436, 604, 627, 952, 1539; Trans. B.G.A.S. lxxxv. 148–9.   70 P.R.O., MR 691.
71 Glos. R.O., D 1677/GG 601, 604, 627, 708, 744, 874, 1539.
72 Below, manor; cf. Glos. R.O., GPS 227/2.
73 Glos. R.O., D 1677/GG 925, 1097.
74 P.R.O., MR 691; F 17/117(2).

of the 19th century. In 1994 part of the Halls' old house survived among the buildings of Highmeadow farm,[75] but a bungalow occupied by the farmer was then the only inhabited house.

Below Highmeadow, at the top of the upper Red brook valley, there was a small hamlet called Ashridge, possibly containing no more than three or four houses. The name Ashridge was used generally for the whole of the valley and the lower part, at Upper Redbrook hamlet, was once known as Ashridge Slade,[76] but as a settlement name Ashridge seems to have been limited to the area around the junction of the valley road with the road to Newland village. Two inhabitants of Ashridge were mentioned in 1309 and there were three or more houses in the 1440s, one of them described as at Ashridge Cross,[77] which was the name of the junction in 1653.[78] In the modern period the only dwelling there was a farmstead of the Highmeadow estate, known by 1738 as Cherry Orchard Farm. Its farmhouse, which stood south-west of the junction,[79] was a large range of building dating in part from the 17th century or earlier.[80] At the end of the 19th century,[81] however, a new square farmhouse was built further east, adjoining the Newland village road. The old farmhouse was occupied as farm buildings and a labourer's cottage in 1918,[82] and it was later demolished.

Staunton parish was said to contain c. 100 communicants in 1551,[83] 25 households in 1563,[84] and 40 families in 1650.[85] About 1710 the population was estimated at c. 220.[86] A population of only 159 was enumerated in 1801, rising to 204 by 1831. Numbers remained fairly static during the mid 19th century, but fell during the 1870s to 121 in 1881, the cause presumably as much a reduction of work in the maturing timber plantations as the onset of the agricultural depression. During the next 50 years the population fluctuated between 120 and 170, but there was a rise in the mid and later 20th century to reach 267 by 1991.[87]

In 1799 Staunton village had an inn called the Ostrich[88] on the west of Lower Cross. By 1832 its sign had changed to the Royal Oak,[89] under which it remained open until 1890 or later.[90] By 1813 the White Horse had opened in the west part of the village street,[91] which remained the main road after 1831. The White Horse, rebuilt in the late 19th century, was the only public house in 1994. The village schoolroom was used as a reading room after the school closed in 1911,[92] and it remained in use as the village hall in 1994.

From the 17th century Staunton parish was dominated by the Highmeadow estate, which was owned successively by the Hall and Gage families before being sold to the Crown in 1817.[93] In 1816 just after the duke of Wellington had visited Monmouth a rumour was current that the government might buy the estate as his reward from the nation. If a later anecdote, that the duke looked at the view over the Wye from Staunton and declared it too reminiscent of the Pyrenees, is true, the incident presumably occurred during the same visit.[94]

MANOR AND OTHER ESTATE. In Edward the Confessor's reign Earl Godwin held a manor at Staunton, assessed at 1 hide and forming part of the Herefordshire hundred of Bromsash. Another manor of 1 hide in the same hundred, held by Brictric, appears to be associated by the Domesday account with Godwin's manor and may also have been at Staunton. By 1066 both those manors had reverted to waste and they remained so, as part of the Crown's Forest of Dean, in 1086.[95]

A new manor of STAUNTON later emerged from the Forest waste, possibly as part of the lordship of Monmouth, whose holder Baderon of Monmouth confirmed Staunton church to Monmouth priory in 1144.[96] By the 13th century Staunton formed part of the royal hundred or liberty of St. Briavels, its owners paying a chief rent to St. Briavels castle and having custody of a bailiwick in the demesne woodlands of the Forest.[97] The lords of Staunton were deprived of the bailiwick from 1250 until 1265[98] and again from c. 1281 to 1290,[99] but afterwards Staunton bailiwick remained with the owners of the manor.[1]

A family which took its name from the place but during the 13th and 14th centuries used the alternative surname of Walding held Staunton manor during the Middle Ages. Henry of Staunton, who held a Forest bailiwick in 1199,[2] was evidently lord of the manor, and in 1220 and 1223 manor and bailiwick were held by Philip of Bampton[3] during the minority of Henry's heir.[4] The heir was presumably Richard of Staunton (or Walding) who had succeeded by 1234[5] and died before 1265. During the minority of his grandson and heir Thomas, Richard's lands were granted to Walter Wyther, who granted his right in 1266 to Richard de la More.[6] Thomas of Staunton died seised of the manor in

75 Below, manor.
76 P.R.O., MR 879; above, Newland, intro.
77 Glos. R.O., D 1677/GG 26, 40, 234, 236.
78 Ibid. GG 1558.
79 Ibid. P 227/IN 1/2, burials 1738; P.R.O., MR 691.
80 Glos. R.O., D 1405/4/136.
81 O.S. Map 1/2,500, Glos. XXXVIII. 3 (1881, 1902 edns.).
82 Glos. R.O., D 1405/4/136.
83 E.H.R. xix. 120.
84 Bodl. MS. Rawl. C. 790, f. 27.
85 Trans. B.G.A.S. lxxxiii. 97.
86 Atkyns, Glos. 689.
87 Census, 1801–1991.
88 Glos. R.O., Q/RSf 2. The sign was the crest of the Probyn fam., which is not, however, known to have been connected with the village: cf. above, Newland, intro.
89 Glos. R.O., D 637/II/4/T 4; G.D.R., T 1/170.

90 Kelly's Dir. Glos. (1870), 639; Glos. R.O., D 637/II/4/T 9, insurance policy.
91 Glos. R.O., P 310/SU 2/1.
92 Below, educ.   93 Below, manor.
94 Glouc. Jnl. 29 July 1816; Cooke, Forest of Dean, 254.
95 Dom. Bk. (Rec. Com.), i. 181.
96 Below, church.
97 Cal. Inq. p.m. iii, pp. 195–6; Glos. R.O., D 2026/X 19; P.R.O., F 14/13.
98 P.R.O., C 60/47, m. 13; Cal. Pat. 1258–66, 472.
99 Cal. Close, 1288–96, 86; cf. Trans. B.G.A.S. xiv. 363.
1 e.g. Glos. R.O., D 1799/T 34; Hart, Royal Forest, 274; 3rd Rep. Com. Woods (1788), 76.
2 Pipe R. 1199 (P.R.S. N.S. x), 32.
3 Rot. Litt. Claus. (Rec. Com.), i. 442–3, 553.
4 Bk. of Fees, ii. 1338.   5 Close R. 1231–4, 528.
6 Cal. Pat. 1258–66, 472, 595.

1292, leaving his son John, a minor whose lands were later taken into the custody of John Botetourt, the constable of St. Briavels.[7] John of Staunton was lord in 1307[8] and died in 1339, when his son Thomas, who was enfeoffed of part of the manor in his father's lifetime, succeeded.[9] Thomas (d. 1361) left a son John of Staunton, a minor, whose lands were in the custody of Richard des Armes for a few years from 1362.[10] John of Staunton held the manor in 1393 and 1420.[11] Richard Staunton held it in 1428 and 1443[12] and was succeeded before 1454[13] by his son Thomas Staunton (d. 1473); Thomas's widow Joan, who married Hugh Amondesham, retained it until 1487 or later. Thomas's son John, a minor at his father's death,[14] later succeeded and died in 1526, when the manor passed to his brother Thomas Staunton[15] (d. 1528). Thomas left an infant daughter Margaret,[16] and it was presumably the same Margaret who with her husband Robert Saunders sold the manor in 1539 to Henry Brayne of Bristol.[17]

Henry Brayne (d. 1558) was succeeded by his son Robert[18] (d. 1570) who settled Staunton on his wife Goodith as jointure.[19] Goodith married John Seymour (d. by 1601) and retained the manor until 1608 or later.[20] It passed in moieties to Charles Gerrard, grandson of Sir Charles Somerset and his wife Emme, and John Winter, son of George Winter and his wife Anne; Emme and Anne were sisters and coheirs of Robert Brayne.[21] Charles Gerrard, who was knighted, sold his moiety in 1620 to Benedict Hall of Highmeadow,[22] and John Winter (d. 1619) was succeeded by his son George,[23] who sold his moiety to Hall in 1620.[24] Staunton manor then descended as part of the Highmeadow estate. The manorial rights belonged to the Crown from its purchase of that estate in 1817,[25] and in 1994 they were under the management of the Forestry Commission.[26]

The manor house of the Staunton family, recorded in 1295,[27] stood in the village on land later called Court Orchard, south of Staunton Farm by the entrance of the Highmeadow road. It was in ruins by 1579,[28] and some remains were still visible c. 1710.[29] A feature known as Castle ditch in 1698, near the west end of Court Orchard, was possibly the remains of a moat.[30] In the mid 17th century Court Orchard became part of the glebe by an exchange of land between the Halls and the rector.[31]

The *HIGHMEADOW* estate, which became one of the largest in the Forest area, was built up by the Hall family. The Halls were recorded at Highmeadow from the 13th century,[32] and they acquired land in the area throughout the 16th century and the early 17th, their largest purchases being in the 1620s and 1630s.[33] Henry Hall of Highmeadow died in 1518.[34] William Hall (d. 1545) of Highmeadow was succeeded by his son Christopher[35] (fl. 1595)[36] and Christopher by his son William. William's purchases included an estate bought from Richard Hyett in 1599,[37] which was probably that in Newland and Staunton once owned by Alexander Baynham (d. 1524) and his son John,[38] lords of Mitcheldean; Alexander's grandfather Robert Baynham had owned property at Highmeadow in 1423.[39]

William Hall died in 1615 and his son and successor Benedict[40] was said to have 800 a. in Newland and Staunton parishes in 1619.[41] He added Staunton manor in 1620[42] and English Bicknor manor in 1633.[43] Benedict Hall was a Roman Catholic and was sequestrated for recusancy before 1650 and did not recover his estates until 1656 or later.[44] He died in 1668 and was succeeded by his son Henry Benedict Hall[45] (d. 1691), whose son and successor Benedict[46] died c. 1720. Benedict's heir was his daughter Benedicta Maria Theresa, the wife of Thomas Gage.[47] Gage, who was created Viscount Gage in the peerage of Ireland in 1720, sat as M.P. for Tewkesbury 1721–54. He was succeeded at his death in 1754 by his son William Hall Gage, who added the barony of Gage of Highmeadow to his titles in 1790. William (d. 1791) was succeeded by his nephew Henry Gage (d. 1808) and Henry by his son Henry Hall Gage.[48] The 4th Viscount sold the Highmeadow estate to the Crown Commissioners of Woods in 1817. It then covered 4,257 a., including seven farms in Staunton, Newland, and English Bicknor parishes, the woods of Hadnock, Monmouthshire, and of Mailscot, and mills and ironworks at Lydbrook

7 *Cal. Inq. p.m.* iii, pp. 195–6.
8 Glos. R.O., D 1677/GG 25, 35; cf. *Feud. Aids*, ii. 275.
9 *Cal. Inq. p.m.* viii, pp. 246–7; cf. ibid. xvi, p. 65.
10 Ibid. xvi, pp. 64–5; *Cal. Pat. 1361–4*, 176.
11 Glos. R.O., D 1677/GG 128, 136, 145; *Reg. Lacy*, 117.
12 *Reg. Spofford*, 354; Glos. R.O., D 33/106.
13 Glos. R.O., D 1677/GG 244.
14 P.R.O., C 140/536, no. 65; *Cal. Fine R. 1471–85*, p. 162; *Reg. Myllyng*, 199.
15 P.R.O., C 142/45, no. 90.
16 Ibid. C 142/48, no. 84.
17 Ibid. CP 25/2/14/82, no. 17; cf. ibid. C 142/122, no. 76.
18 Ibid. C 142/122, no. 76.
19 Ibid. C 142/157, no. 74.
20 Ibid. C 142/266, no. 121; MR 879.
21 Glos. R.O., D 1799/T 34; P.R.O., C 142/199, no. 79; C 142/266, no. 121.   22 Glos. R.O., D 1677/GG 668.
23 P.R.O., C 142/386, no. 91.
24 Glos. R.O., D 1677/GG 666.
25 Below, this section; P.R.O., CRES 38/604; F 14/10; F 3/727–8.
26 Inf. from asset manager (agric. est.), Crown Estate.
27 *Cal. Inq. p.m.* iii, pp. 195–6.
28 Glos. R.O., D 1799/T 34; and for Court Orchard, P.R.O., MR 691.   29 Atkyns, *Glos.* 688.

30 G.D.R., V 5/285T 5; Glos. R.O., P 310/SU 2/1, and for Orchard meadow mentioned there, P.R.O., MR 691.
31 G.D.R., V 5/285T 3.
32 Glos. R.O., D 1677/GG 8, 19–20.
33 Ibid. GG 299, 332, 382, 410, 415, 498, 520, 590–865.
34 Hockaday Abs. ccxcv.
35 Ibid.; P.R.O., C 142/74, no. 81; for the Halls, *Trans. B.G.A.S.* vii. 264–6.
36 Glos. R.O., D 1677/GG 541.
37 Ibid. GG 566.
38 P.R.O., C 142/42, no. 112; C 142/48, no. 102.
39 Glos. R.O., D 33/85; D 2957/214.23; cf. above, Mitcheldean, manor.
40 P.R.O., PROB 11/125 (P.C.C. 45 Rudd), f. 353 and v.
41 Glos. R.O., D 1677/GG 657.
42 Above, this section.
43 Above, Eng. Bicknor, manor.
44 *Cal. Cttee. for Compounding*, i. 87, 739; ii. 2200–4.
45 P.R.O., PROB 11/327 (P.C.C. 65 Hone), ff. 62v.–63; Glos. R.O., D 1677/GG 952, 981.
46 P.R.O., PROB 11/407 (P.C.C. 191 Vere), ff. 13v.–14; Glos. R.O., D 1677/GG 1027–8, 1095.
47 Glos. R.O., D 1677/GG 1105, 1138.
48 Burke, *Peerage* (1935), 1014–15.

and Redbrook.[49] During the next few years the Crown sold parts of the estate,[50] retaining *c.* 3,400 a., comprising the old woods and farmland which it turned over to timber production. The Crown estate, usually known collectively as Highmeadow woods, was subsequently managed with the Forest of Dean and was transferred with the Forest to the Forestry Commission in 1924.[51]

The south end of the Highmeadow estate, comprising 395 a. of farmland based on Highmeadow and Cherry Orchard Farms, was sold by the Crown in 1825 to Sir Robert Inglis, Bt.[52] Inglis offered it for sale in 1836,[53] and it was bought then or soon afterwards by George Bengough, of the Ridge, Wotton under Edge.[54] George (d. 1856) was succeeded in turn by his sons George Henry (d. 1865) and John Charles (d. 1913), and it was among extensive Gloucestershire estates put up for sale by John's grandson, Nigel James Bengough, in 1918. It was bought then by the tenant H. J. Smith,[55] whose family remained owners until the mid 20th century when the two farms were sold as separate units.[56]

In 1608 the Halls' house at Highmeadow was a large dwelling with outbuildings at the junction of the Whitecliff–Staunton road and the lane from Newland village, near the higher end of what was then a considerable hamlet.[57] Before 1672 Henry Benedict Hall built a large mansion[58] north-west of the old house on the edge of a ridge which commanded wide views over the Wye Valley. The building of the mansion involved terracing the ground, and probably the demolition of several small houses at the upper end of the hamlet.[59] Highmeadow House, 164 ft. long and of two storeys with dormered attics and cellars below, was built on an **H** plan with a central double-depth range of nine bays and projecting end wings. Both the west front, facing the valley, and the east front to the road were given elaborate formal treatment and were approached by flights of steps extending across the full width of the recesses between the wings. On the ground floor a central entrance hall was entered from an axial screens passage built across the end of another hall-like room, and on the floor above the full depth of one of the side wings was occupied by a long gallery. On the east front a railed forecourt with a circular carriage drive was formed, with a walled outer

court.[60] During the 18th century the house was used ocasionally by the Gages, whose principal residence was at Firle (Suss.). By 1805 they had given up Highmeadow, which then or soon afterwards was dismantled and the materials sold piecemeal.[61] In 1994 the site was still marked by a turf-covered heap of rubble, and remains of the cellars survived below ground and remains of the forecourt walling above.

The Halls' old house remained in use as a farmhouse during the 18th century and was known as Highmeadow Lower House.[62] During the 19th and early 20th centuries when Highmeadow and Cherry Orchard farms were a single tenancy Cherry Orchard was the principal farmhouse, and by 1918 the old house at Highmeadow had been divided into two farm cottages.[63] From the early 1930s the two farms were managed separately and the farmers of Highmeadow lived in a bungalow built west of the farm buildings on the lane to Newland.[64] One range of the old house survived in use as a farm building in 1994. It retains some late-medieval windows, probably reset, and the massive, carved supports of a porch roof.

ECONOMIC HISTORY. In 1295 only 30 a. of arable, ½ a. of meadow, and 1½ a. of wood were recorded in demesne on Staunton manor,[65] but in 1342 the demesne was extended to 1 ploughland and 80 a., with 20 a. of meadow, 6 a. of pasture, and 12 a. of wood.[66] In 1579 the manor had a large demesne estate, mainly in closes in the area south of the village and old manor house but also including some large outlying groves and closes.[67] By 1608 the demesne estate was challenged in size by the expanding Highmeadow estate, whose owner William Hall was then also tenant of some parts of the demesne.[68] After Benedict Hall acquired the manor in 1620 most of the farmland of Staunton parish belonged to the Highmeadow estate.

In 1295 the manor received 24*s.* 1*d.* in rent from free tenants and 13*s.* for the rent, works, and fines of customary tenants,[69] and in 1342 the rent from its tenants amounted to 120*s.*[70] No customary tenancies were recorded after the Middle Ages, but only free tenancies, most of which comprised no more than houses, gardens, and orchards. In 1579 47 holdings, 38 of them including dwellings, owed chief rent to the

[49] P.R.O., CRES 38/604; Crown Land Revenues Act, 57 Geo. III, c. 97. The sale was effective from 1817 but not completed until the final instalment of the purchase price in 1821.

[50] *3rd Rep. Com. Woods* (1819), 19; *4th Rep. Com. Woods* (1823), 29, 96; *5th Rep. Com. Woods* (1826), 108, 110; cf. Glos. R.O., D 23/E 38, E 42.

[51] *Select Cttee. on Woods* (1849), 145–6, 482; *Lond. Gaz.* 25 Mar. 1924, pp. 2510–13; cf. below, Forest of Dean, forest admin. (replanting and reorganization; forest in 20th cent.).

[52] *5th Rep. Com. Woods* (1826), 110; cf. Glos. R.O., P 310/SU 2/1.

[53] Glos. R.O., D 637/VII/31.

[54] G.D.R., T 1/128, 170; for the Bengoughs, Burke, *Land. Gent.* (1937), 135–6.

[55] *Kelly's Dir. Glos.* (1870 and later edns.); Glos. R.O., D 1405/4/136.

[56] *Kelly's Dir. Glos.* (1939), 274; inf. from Mr. F. D. Morgan, of Highmeadow Fm.

[57] P.R.O., MR 879.

[58] Ibid. E 179/247/14, rot. 38; E 134/35 Chas. II

Mich./40, deposition of Thos. Palmer. Bigland, *Glos.* ii. 258–9, records a date 1633 over the doorway, presumably a misreading or misprint.

[59] Cf. P.R.O., MR 879.

[60] For the house, Glos. R.O., A 227/1–2; GPS 227/2, reproduced above, Plate 5.

[61] Glos. R.O., D 1677/GG 1545, nos. 95, 97, 101–2; *Glouc. Jnl.* 3 June 1805.

[62] Glos. R.O., D 1677/GG 1095, 1097, 1105, 1121.

[63] Ibid. D 637/VII/31; D 1405/4/136; cf. P.R.O., HO 107/2444; *Kelly's Dir. Glos.* (1870), 607.

[64] *Kelly's Dir. Glos.* (1931), 268; (1935), 268; inf. from Mr. Morgan.

[65] *Cal. Inq. p.m.* iii, pp. 195–6.

[66] Ibid. viii, pp. 246–7.

[67] *Trans. B.G.A.S.* vii. 238–43; for identification of the lands, P.R.O., MR 691; MR 879.

[68] P.R.O., MR 879.

[69] *Cal. Inq. p.m.* iii, pp. 195–6.

[70] Ibid. viii, pp. 246–7.

manor.[71] In 1653 there were 33 free tenants with between them a total of 43 houses, 9 of which were in decay. The manor also had some free tenants in a part of Coleford tithing that was claimed to belong to it and one or two others in adjoining parts of Hadnock.[72] By 1769 further amalgamations of holdings had reduced the number of free tenants to 23 and the number of inhabited houses to 25. Tenants with houses or sites of former houses owed a heriot, which might be commuted for two years' chief rent, and a relief of two years' chief rent was owed at an alienation. By 1769 a number of people occupied encroachments on Staunton Meend,[73] for which small rents were later levied. In 1817 a larger number of encroachments on the waste in Coleford also owed rents to the manor, and many more, not yet charged with rent, had been established there in the previous few years. The rents of all the free tenants of Staunton manor amounted to £2 15s. 5d. in 1817, with a further sum of £8–9 received for the encroachments.[74] Most rents and payments for encroachments in Staunton and Coleford were redeemed in the 1860s and 1880s,[75] and in 1891 there were said to be no more than three free tenants of the manor, only one of whom was resident.[76]

On the south boundary of the parish at Highmeadow and Ashridge there was a similar pattern of small freehold tenancies until the early 17th century.[77] After the Halls acquired all the surrounding land and most of the houses were demolished or left to decay, that area comprised only the two farms of Highmeadow and Cherry Orchard.[78]

In the 13th and 14th centuries the parish had a number of open fields, holdings in which were sometimes called *dietae*, presumably units of land that needed a day to plough.[79] Morewall (later Morrall) field lay in the valley, beside Mill Lane, Shobleys field lay in the fork of the roads leading to Highmeadow and Cherry Orchard on the high land (later planted) near the east side of the parish, and Windmill field adjoined the Highmeadow road north of Shobleys.[80] An open field called Clowers (or Clore) was apparently near the head of the upper Red brook valley, on the north side of the Newland–Redbrook road, though in the 17th century there was other land of the same name on the ridge south of Shobleys.[81] North of the village on the slopes descending to the Wye lay Heymere field, possibly that called Staunton field *c.* 1300, and further down the hill was Ley field.[82] Inclosure of the open fields was evidently well under way by 1579 when the manorial demesne included lands called the great piece in Morrall field and the great piece in Ley field.[83] In 1608 Morrall, Ley, and Windmill fields were closes on the

manorial demesne and Shobleys and Clowers were closes on the Highmeadow estate. Heymere then remained an open field,[84] and the sale of 9 a. there to Benedict Hall in 1632 may have marked the end of the process of inclosure.[85] The inhabitants of Staunton enjoyed common rights on Staunton Meend and other much smaller parcels of waste. With the other parishes of the area they also had common in the Crown demesne lands of the Forest.[86] The parishioners paid herbage money for the same to the lessee of the St. Briavels castle estate until the 1830s,[87] but their rights were perhaps little exercised after 1625 when the sale of Mailscot wood[88] deprived them of the use of the only large tract of demesne woodland adjoining the parish. Staunton Meend remained common land in 1994 when two villagers pastured horses there; the right of soil had been bought by the parish council from the Forestry Commission for a nominal sum.[89]

In the early 17th century much of the Halls' estate was kept in hand and used as sheep[90] and cow pasture. In 1655 the estate included a 100-acre sheep walk on the ridge above the Newland–Monmouth road and smaller sheep pastures at the former Windmill field and at the Hays, above and east of Highmeadow.[91] By the late 18th century most of the farmland of the estate in the Staunton area was organized as three tenant farms. In 1792 Staunton farm, based at the farmhouse in the village, had 280 a., mainly lying in the valley south of the village and on the ridge to the south-east. Cherry Orchard farm, with its farmhouse beside the Newland–Monmouth road at the south boundary of the parish, had 358 a. (including 145 a. in Newland), lying along the road and on the ridge to the north. The cherry orchard from which it took its name then covered 16 a. on the north side of the road. Highmeadow farm, based on the old house near the owner's mansion, had 291 a. (mainly within Newland), lying around Highmeadow hamlet and in Coleford tithing to the north. The three large farms and a few small holdings in Staunton were held on leases, which were renewed for 16 years from 1793. In the north part of Staunton parish there were also a few freehold farms, all of under 60 a. In 1792 the 929 a. on the three big farms included 392 a. of arable,[92] and in Staunton parish in 1801 239 a. were returned as under crops, mainly wheat and barley.[93]

Following the establishment of the new timber plantations in the 1820s, only *c.* 400 a. of farmland remained in Staunton parish. In 1843 the surviving farmland of the south part of the parish, 141 a., belonged to Cherry Orchard and Highmeadow farms,[94] which had another 175 a.

71 *Trans. B.G.A.S.* vii. 240, 242.
72 Glos. R.O., D 1677/GG 1558; cf. above, Coleford, manors.
73 Glos. R.O., P 310/MI 1.
74 Ibid. D 1677/GG 1545, no. 118A.
75 Ibid. P 310/IN 3/3–4; P.R.O., F 14/10.
76 P.R.O., F 3/727, letter 3 Oct. 1891.
77 Glos. R.O., D 1677/GG, *passim*.
78 Cf. P.R.O., F 17/117(2), pp. 35–6; MR 691.
79 Glos. R.O., D 1677/GG 121, 243.
80 Ibid. GG 9, 66–7; cf. P.R.O., MR 879.
81 Glos. R.O., D 1677/GG 10, 45, 464; P.R.O., MR 691; MR 879.

82 Glos. R.O., D 1677/GG 10, 66, 333, 498; cf. P.R.O., MR 879.
83 *Trans. B.G.A.S.* vii. 239, 241.   84 P.R.O., MR 879.
85 Glos. R.O., D 1677/GG 769.   86 Ibid. P 310/MI 1.
87 N.L.W., Mynde Park MS. 1629; P.R.O., F 3/587.
88 Above, Eng. Bicknor, manor; econ. hist.
89 Inf. from Mr. G. L. Clissold, of Staunton.
90 Cf. G.D.R. vol. 89, depositions 23 Feb. 1603.
91 Glos. R.O., D 1677/GG 925.
92 P.R.O., F 17/117(2), pp. 35–40, 49–55; MR 691.
93 *List & Index Soc.* clxxxix, p. 178.
94 G.D.R., T 1/170.

in Newland parish.[95] The two farms, which formed a single tenancy from the early 19th century to the early 20th,[96] had a preponderance of arable over pasture in the mid 19th century[97] and in 1851 employed 12 farm labourers, some of them living in at Cherry Orchard.[98] In 1918 about two thirds of the acreage was pasture and the buildings at both sites mainly cattlesheds.[99] In 1994, when they were separate freehold farms, Highmeadow supported a flock of over 1,000 sheep and Cherry Orchard had a dairy herd of 90 cows.[1]

Of the farms based in the village in 1843 only Staunton farm (then known as Hill farm), with 89 a., was more than a smallholding. Broadstone farm then had 114 a., lying around its farmhouse, below the woods on the Monmouthshire boundary, or in the central valley, where a barn became known as Partridge's barn from the mid 19th-century owners.[2] In 1866 on those two farms and the smaller holdings 119 a. of arable, rotating wheat, barley, roots, and clover, and 77 a. of permanent grass were returned. The livestock returned were 576 sheep and 23 cattle.[3] In 1926 in the north parts of the parish there remained only two farms of more than 50 a. and five smallholdings, employing between them a total of six farm labourers. The amount of arable returned had fallen to 70 a. and there had been an increase in the cattle kept for dairying.[4] In 1988 only 8 ha. (20 a.) of land was returned as cropped, and the one farm then worked full-time and four part-time holdings raised cattle and sheep.[5]

A windmill recorded on the manorial demesne from 1342[6] stood on the ridge near the Staunton–Highmeadow road and gave its name to Windmill field. It was in ruins in 1579.[7] The village was later served by corn mills on the upper Red brook at the south edge of the parish[8] and the lane leading to them became known as Mill Lane.[9]

Henry II licensed a forge at Staunton,[10] and in 1282 10 Staunton men were working movable forges in the area.[11] In 1437, however, only a single forge was recorded at Staunton among those in the Forest parishes owing payments to the Crown.[12] A building called an 'oresmith' stood in or near the village in 1484[13] and another adjoined a house at Highmeadow in 1521.[14] A smith-holder of Highmeadow leased land and the right to cut underwood for charcoaling from the lord of Staunton manor in 1553.[15] Heaps of

cinders left by the medieval ironworkers were later found in several parts of Staunton village.[16] A blast furnace which in 1608 stood near the Newland–Monmouth road within the parish boundary is mentioned above with the history of the ironworks of the Highmeadow estate at Upper Redbrook.[17]

Deposits of iron ore in the parish were presumably being dug in 1608 when four miners were recorded.[18] Small mines were worked during the 18th century and c. 1770 were said to provide the chief employment for the labouring class.[19] In 1859 a miner took a gale for working ore east of the village between the Coleford road and the old road to Bicknor and a mine opened there was worked until 1874.[20] Robinhood mine near the parish boundary south-west of the Coleford road, presumably so called because it was in the plantation called Marian's Inclosure,[21] was opened in 1871.[22] It was described as a colour mine in 1889[23] and for many years was worked mainly for red oxide. For several years before its closure in 1932, however, it produced iron ore only. It was worked again by the Ministry of Supply during the Second World War,[24] and ruins of buildings remained in 1994.

Lime burning was a trade in the parish by 1608.[25] In 1664 there was a limekiln on waste land near the church,[26] and in 1792 one stood at a quarry at Tillys, south-east of the village below the Staunton–Highmeadow road. Two others, belonging to Cherry Orchard farm, stood at a quarry on the ridge to the north-east of the farm in 1792,[27] and the exaggerated claim was made in 1803 that they supplied most of Herefordshire and Monmouthshire.[28] They had gone out of use by 1880 when there were other kilns on the farm's land beside the old tramroad near the head of the upper Red brook and others on Highmeadow farm east of Highmeadow's street.[29] Three limekilns were worked at Tillys in the late 19th century.[30] From the 1950s the quarry on the ridge above Cherry Orchard Farm was worked for roadstone.[31] By 1994, when it was operated by Tarmac Ltd., it had been greatly enlarged and a new access road, made through the woods to the Coleford–Monmouth road, carried constant lorry traffic.

During the 17th and 18th centuries much of the woodland of the Highmeadow estate in Staunton and adjoining parishes was probably managed as coppice, for it provided regular

95 Ibid. T 1/128.
96 Glos. R.O., P 310/IN 3/2; D 1405/4/136.
97 Ibid. D 637/VII/31.
98 P.R.O., HO 107/2444.
99 Glos. R.O., D 1405/4/136.
1 Inf. from Mr. F. D. Morgan of Highmeadow Fm. and Mr. J. R. R. Blanch of Cherry Orchard Fm.
2 G.D.R., T 1/170; cf. O.S. Map 6", Glos. XXX. SE. (1884 edn.).
3 P.R.O., MAF 68/25/9; MAF 68/26/8; in those agric. returns Cherry Orchard and Highmeadow farms were evidently included under Newland rather than Staunton.
4 Ibid. MAF 68/3295/6.
5 Agric. Returns 1988.
6 Cal. Inq. p.m. viii, pp. 246–7.
7 Trans. B.G.A.S. vii. 241; cf. P.R.O., MR 879.
8 Above, Newland, econ. hist. (mills and ironworks).
9 Trans. B.G.A.S. vii. 238; Glos. R.O., Q/SRh 1823 C/4.
10 Rot. Litt. Claus. (Rec. Com.), i. 320.

11 P.R.O., E 32/30, rot. 23d.
12 Berkeley Cast. Mun., General Ser. acct. roll 426.
13 Glos. R.O., D 1677/GG 284.
14 Ibid. GG 332.   15 Ibid. GG 419.
16 Ibid. GG 290; P 310/MI 1.
17 Above, Newland, econ. hist. (mills and ironworks).
18 Smith, Men and Armour, 36.
19 Atkyns, Glos. 689; Rudder, Glos. 689.
20 P.R.O., F 3/200.
21 O.S. Map 6", Glos. XXX. SE. (1884 edn.).
22 P.R.O., F 3/315.   23 Kelly's Dir. Glos. (1889), 891.
24 Hart, Ind. Hist. of Dean, 247.
25 Smith, Men and Armour, 36.
26 Glos. R.O., D 1677/GG 939.   27 P.R.O., MR 691.
28 Glouc. Jnl. 4 Apr. 1803.
29 O.S. Map 6", Glos. XXXVIII. NE. (1884 edn.).
30 Ibid. XXX. SE. (1884 edn.); 1/2,500, Glos. XXX. 15 (1902 edn.).
31 Inf. from Mr. Morgan.

allowances of cordwood to the lessees of the estate's ironworks at Redbrook and Lydbrook.[32] Wood for barrel making was also cut and sent by water to Bristol in the late 18th century.[33] There were, however, some large timber oaks in the woods at the beginning of the 19th century, when many were felled and sold to a Monmouth timber merchant.[34] From the 1820s, when the plantations for navy timber were made, until the early 20th century the Crown woodlands were the main source of employment in Staunton parish.[35] In 1851 the inhabitants included 2 woodwards, a woodman, and 11 woodcutters.[36]

Three smiths, a carpenter, and a tiler recorded at Staunton in 1608 were probably based in the village,[37] though Highmeadow hamlet also had a few tradesmen at the period: a blacksmith of Highmeadow was mentioned in 1560, two tailors later in the 16th century, and a carpenter in 1639.[38] In 1851, apart from those employed in the woods, 12 non-agricultural tradesmen were recorded in Staunton parish, including a grocer, a tailor, a blacksmith, and 3 shoemakers.[39] A boot repairer recorded in 1939 was one of the last representatives of traditional village trades. There were then two guest houses and a small hotel in the village,[40] which was situated on a main motoring route and in a popular tourist area. The village had one or two small shops during the later 19th century and the earlier 20th[41] but in 1994 its only shop was one attached to a petrol station.

LOCAL GOVERNMENT. Records of courts baron with courts of survey for Staunton manor survive for 1653[42] and 1769 and of courts baron for 1774 and 1780,[43] and there are records for courts held in the late 19th century and early 20th.[44] In 1774 the court met in Staunton village,[45] but in 1803 and later it was held at the Angel inn,[46] in the part of Coleford town that was claimed to belong to the manor. In the late 19th century and early 20th it was convened only every seven years, the last time apparently being in 1912. In those last sessions the deputy surveyor of the Forest usually acted as steward under the Crown and the business comprised a perambulation of the manor and some present-ments of encroachments and of the deaths of free tenants. The court styled itself a leet by the 1860s,[47] though leet jurisdiction over Staunton had earlier been exercised by the hundred court held at St. Briavels castle.[48]

The parish had two churchwardens in 1572,[49] and there were later also two overseers of the poor, whose accounts survive for the years 1803–18,[50] and two surveyors of the highways, whose accounts survive for 1774–1826.[51] The admini-stration of poor relief in the village was on a small scale, probably with no expedients necessary beyond weekly doles to the few disabled or unemployed villagers. At the beginning of the 19th century the annual cost rarely exceeded £100, with no more than c. 12 people receiving regular weekly pay,[52] and the cost rose only to a peak of £146 during the late 1820s and early 1830s.[53] Staunton was included in the Monmouth poor-law union in 1836.[54] In 1894 it became part of the West Dean rural district[55] and was included in the Forest of Dean district from 1974.

CHURCH. A church was recorded at Staunton from 1144 when Baderon of Monmouth confirmed it to Monmouth priory, a cell of St. Florent abbey (Saumur). The record of the confirmation in the abbey's cartulary implied that the church was given to the priory by its founder Wihanoc of Monmouth, who died or resigned his estates before 1086, but since Staunton was waste during the Conqueror's reign that seems unlikely.[56] The grantor, and perhaps builder of the church, was more likely Baderon himself or his immediate predecessor in the lordship of Monmouth, William son of Baderon.[57] The living of Staunton was a rectory in 1269[58] and has remained one. In 1922 it was united with the vicarage of Coleford.[59]

Monmouth priory's right to the church was confirmed by papal bull in 1186[60] but it was apparently challenged in King John's reign.[61] The priory successfully presented to the rectory in 1270 and 1303,[62] but the guardian of the heir to Staunton manor was claiming the advowson against the priory in 1269,[63] and in 1317 the lord of the manor, John of Staunton, presented.[64] In 1365 the Crown presented during the minority of the heir to the manor[65] and it presented again in 1383.[66] In 1394 John of Staunton (or Wald-ing), the lord of the manor, presented,[67] and the advowson later remained with the manor, al-though the bishop collated to the living in 1582,

[32] Glos. R.O., D 1677/GG 1545, no. 7; GG 1557.
[33] Ibid. GG 1172, bills 1768, 1797–9.
[34] Ibid. estate accts. 1807, 1813; for the merchant (Hezekiah Swift), Harris, 'Wye Valley Ind. Hist.' Mon-mouth (pt. 3), 11–13.
[35] Glos. R.O., P 310/IN 3/1, petitions 1843, c. 1857; W.I. hist. of Staunton (1958, TS. in Glos. Colln.), 4.
[36] P.R.O., HO 107/2444.
[37] Smith, Men and Armour, 36.
[38] Glos. R.O., D 1677/GG 436, 461, 521, 854.
[39] P.R.O., HO 107/2444.
[40] Kelly's Dir. Glos. (1939), 317.
[41] Ibid. (1856 and later edns.).
[42] Glos. R.O., D 1677/GG 1558.
[43] Ibid. P 310/MI 1.
[44] P.R.O., F 3/727–8; F 14/10.
[45] Glos. R.O., P 310/MI 1.
[46] Glouc. Jnl. 10 Oct. 1803; 14 Dec. 1807.
[47] P.R.O., F 3/727–8; F 14/10.
[48] e.g. Glos. Colln. 15930, ct. 5 Oct. 1719.

[49] Hockaday Abs. xliv, 1572 visit. f. 7.
[50] Glos. R.O., P 310/OV 2/1.
[51] Ibid. SU 2/1.
[52] Ibid. OV 2/1; Poor Law Abstract, 1804, 172–3; 1818, 146–7.
[53] Poor Law Returns (1830–1), p. 67; (1835), p. 65.
[54] Poor Law Com. 2nd Rep. p. 535.
[55] Census, 1901.
[56] Cal. Doc. France, pp. 409–10. Staunton was not among the churches included in Wihanoc's foundation charter to Monmouth: Dugdale, Mon. iv. 596.
[57] Cf. Trans. B.G.A.S. iv. 129–30.
[58] P.R.O., JUST 1/275, rot. 44.
[59] Lond. Gaz. 25 Apr. 1922, pp. 3223–4.
[60] Cal. Doc. France, p. 404.   [61] Dugdale, Mon. iv. 595.
[62] Cat. Anct. D. iii, D 328; Reg. Swinfield, 533–4.
[63] P.R.O., JUST 1/275, rot. 44.
[64] Reg. Swinfield, 544.
[65] Cal. Pat. 1364–7, 159.
[66] Reg. Gilbert, 117.
[67] Reg. Trefnant, 178.

and in 1655, while Benedict Hall's estate was in sequestration, the Lord Protector presented. The Halls, though Roman Catholics, exercised the advowson several times during the 1660s and 1670s.[68] The 4th Viscount Gage reserved the advowson when he sold his estate, and in 1830 sold it to Edward Machen (d. 1862). It passed to Edward's son Edward (d. 1893), rector of Staunton, and then to the Revd. Edward's son Charles (d. 1917), whose heir[69] transferred it in 1917 to the bishop.[70]

The rector of Staunton's glebe land, a few closes adjoining the village, was extended at 11½ a. in 1678[71] and at 12 a. in 1843.[72] By an arrangement made before 1655[73] and still in force in 1680, the Halls paid the rector a composition of £12 a year for the tithes from their demesne lands in the parish. The smaller occupiers paid most of their tithes in kind in 1680, though there were cash payments for gardens, cows, calves and colts, and for horses used to carry charcoal or iron ore.[74] In the 1820s when the Crown planted 550 a. of the farmland with timber the rector Richard Davies sought compensation for his tithes, estimated to be reduced from 5s. 6d. an acre to 1s. an acre,[75] and by 1828 he was receiving an annual payment from the Commissioners of Woods to cover the balance.[76] In 1843 the tithes of the parish were commuted for a corn rent charge of £147 5s. 2d., only £62 3s. of it coming from the two thirds occupied by the Crown's old woodland and new plantations.[77] The compensation was continued until Davies's death in 1857 but it was refused to his successor.[78] The tithe rent charge for the Crown woodlands was redeemed in 1920.[79]

The rectory house, standing on the north side of the churchyard, contained five rooms on the ground floor and five on the first floor in 1698.[80] The rector Thomas Mallet rebuilt it c. 1814,[81] and it was extended to the north-west in the late 1850s by the rector Edward Machen, using part of a legacy left for that purpose by his uncle and predecessor, Richard Davies.[82] It was sold and converted to flats after the union of the benefices in 1922, the incumbent living at Coleford.[83]

The rectory was valued at £6 13s. 4d. in 1291, and a portion valued at 4s., presumably awarded under a settlement of the dispute over the advowson, was held by the prior of Monmouth then[84] and until the Dissolution. In 1535 the rectory was valued at £6 11s.[85] It was worth £39 in 1650,[86] £70 in 1750,[87] £200 in 1814,[88] and £253 in 1856.[89]

Stephen Askeby, rector of Staunton in 1277, had licence to study for a year at Paris.[90] Roger Winter, rector 1538–82[91] and also vicar of Woolaston,[92] was found to be unable to repeat the Commandments in 1551, and though he could repeat the articles of the Creed he would not accept that they could be proved from Scripture but only by the authority of the Church.[93] His successor John Trubshaw, 1582–94,[94] was also a pluralist and in 1593 was among Gloucestershire incumbents categorized as 'slender scholars and of life suspected'.[95] Francis Hampton, rector from 1629, retained the living until his death in 1654.[96] Charles Godwin subscribed as rector in 1662 and was succeeded in 1664 by William Hughes,[97] who held the living in plurality with Newland[98] until 1670. In 1703, in the incumbency of William Harrison 1679–1724, the churchwardens reported that their rector was a man of sober life and orthodox principles, that there were no immoral or disorderly parishioners, and that the church was in good repair. Thomas Hill, rector 1727–64, was also vicar of Llanarth (Mon.).[99] William Barnes, rector c. 1765[1]–1813, resided at Monmouth in 1786 and in 1808, when he claimed that Staunton's exposed situation and cold climate would endanger his health.[2] Thomas Mallet, 1813–22, was also vicar of Dixton Newton (Mon.); his successor Richard Davies[3] served Dixton until 1833.[4] Davies, whose father James Davies of Eastbach Court, English Bicknor, had been Lord Gage's local agent,[5] had taken orders in expectation of the living of Staunton.[6] At his death in 1857 his brother Edward Machen, the new patron, presented his own son Edward, who served until 1874.[7]

A chapel of St. John the Baptist stood near the village in 1368,[8] but no further record of it has been found. Its site was presumably at or near St. John the Baptist's well on the north side of the main road, near the Monmouthshire boundary.[9]

The church of *ALL SAINTS* was so called by 1735[10] but had a dedication to St. Nicholas in 1144[11] and until 1403 or later.[12] It is built of rubble and ashlar and has chancel, central tower with transepts, and aisled nave with south porch.

68 Hockaday Abs. cccl.
69 *Trans. B.G.A.S.* vii. 250, 259; *Kelly's Dir. Glos.* (1906), 299; for the Machens, Burke, *Land. Gent.* (1937), 1469. 70 *Lond. Gaz.* 10 Aug. 1917, p. 8126.
71 G.D.R., V 5/285T 2. 72 Ibid. T 1/170.
73 Glos. R.O., D 1677/GG 923.
74 G.D.R., V 5/285T 3.
75 Glos. R.O., P 310/IN 3/1.
76 G.D.R., V 5/285T 10. 77 Ibid. T 1/170.
78 Glos. R.O., P 310/IN 3/1.
79 G.D.R., T 1/170. 80 Ibid. V 5/285T 5.
81 Hockaday Abs. cccl, 1814; Glos. R.O., P 310/IN 3/1, petition 1820.
82 Glos. R.O., D 637/II/4/T 9, notebook (letter 12 Sept. 1862); Fraser, *Staunton*, 31–2.
83 Glos. R.O., P 93/IN 3/2; W.I. hist. of Staunton, 7.
84 *Tax. Eccl.* (Rec. Com.), 160.
85 *Valor Eccl.* (Rec. Com.), ii. 502.
86 *Trans. B.G.A.S.* lxxxiii. 97.
87 G.D.R., vol. 381A, f. 8.
88 Ibid. 382, f. 20. 89 Ibid. 384, f. 188.

90 *Reg. Cantilupe*, 134–5.
91 Hockaday Abs. xlvii, 1576 visit. f. 124; cccl, 1582.
92 *V.C.H. Glos.* x. 116.
93 *E.H.R.* xix. 120; *Trans. B.G.A.S.* iv. 18.
94 Hockaday Abs. cccl.
95 Ibid. xlix, state of clergy 1584, f. 44; lii, state of clergy 1593, f. 13.
96 Ibid. cccl; Glos. R.O., D 1677/GG 923.
97 Hockaday Abs. cccl.
98 Ibid. ccxcvi. 99 Ibid. cccl.
1 Glos. R.O., P 310/MI 1.
2 Hockaday Abs. cccl; G.D.R. vol. 321.
3 Hockaday Abs. cccl; Bigland, *Glos.* iii, no. 251.
4 Glos. R.O., P 310/IN 3/2.
5 Ibid. D 1677/GG 1545. 6 Ibid. P 310/IN 3/1.
7 Hockaday Abs. cccl; G.D.R. vol. 385, p. 195.
8 Glos. R.O., D 2244/59.
9 Ibid. D 1677/GG 1558; O.S. Map 1/2,500, Glos. XXX. 15 (1902 edn.). 10 G.D.R. vol. 285B(1), f. 7.
11 *Cal. Doc. France*, pp. 409–11.
12 Glos. R.O., D 1677/GG 22, 66, 145.

The tower, nave, and north arcade are of the 12th century, and the chancel was rebuilt and the transepts and south aisle added in the 13th. In the 14th century the south aisle was widened to align with the south wall of the south transept, and there was a similar enlargement of the north aisle in the 15th century; the west walls of both transepts were removed to unite them with the aisles. In the 15th century the top stage of the tower was added and the nave was given a new west window. At an unknown date, presumably after the early 16th century, the three western bays of the north aisle were demolished and that part of the arcade incorporated in a new nave north wall.

By the late 17th century the south transept was screened off from the south aisle to form a manorial chapel,[13] but in the 1820s it was being used as a vestry and schoolroom.[14] The north transept was known as Higgins chancel in the late 18th century from a family of freehold tenants whose members were buried there.[15] In the early 19th century the church had the usual Georgian fittings, including lath and plaster ceilings, a three-decker pulpit, and Commandments boards on each side of the east window.[16] During alterations in the early 1860s, made mainly at the cost of a local resident, the Revd. James Hammond, stained glass was put into several windows and an organ was provided; at his death in 1871[17] Hammond left £100 stock to help provide a salary for the organist.[18] In 1872 the church was restored to the plans of J. W. Hugall, the cost met mainly by a legacy given to the parish by the former rector Richard Davies, supplemented by members of his family, and a grant from the Crown as lord of the manor.[19] The south transept was then remodelled: its roof, which had been ridged east–west, was rebuilt with a north–south ridge, its east and south windows were exchanged to fit the new form, and its south doorway was moved to the north side of the chancel to serve as a priest's door. At the same time the nave was reroofed, the columns of the south arcade were straightened and their bases renewed, the church was repewed and refitted, and the north transept was screened off to form a vestry. About 1905 the north transept was restored for use as a chapel, while the south transept became the vestry and organ chamber.[20]

A late 15th-century stone pulpit is incorporated in the rood stair at the east end of the north arcade. The Norman font is a cube of stone, once thought to have been a Roman altar, hollowed out and given a band of pellet decoration.[21] It was presumably replaced in the 14th century by the octagonal font of that period which also survives in the church.[22] About 1830 the early font was standing outside to catch rainwater from a roof-spout and was moved inside; it, and the ancient pulpit, were returned to use at the restoration of 1872.[23] The church had a ring of four bells at the beginning of the 18th century,[24] two of them medieval bells and one cast by John Pennington in 1623. In 1862, by G. Mears & Co. and at the cost of James Hammond, the Machen family, and another parishioner Samuel Harris, three of the old bells, which had cracked, were recast and two new bells were added to the ring. The fourth old bell was recast in 1915.[25] A set of plate dated 1684, comprising chalice, paten cover, and credence paten, was given to the church by the lord of the manor Henry Benedict Hall.[26] The parish registers survive from 1653.[27]

NONCONFORMITY. The Halls of Highmeadow were Roman Catholics and they presumably encouraged the survival of Catholicism in Staunton. Eleven Catholics, apart from Benedict Hall and two of his family, were listed there c. 1720.[28] A Jesuit priest lived at Cherry Orchard Farm in the late 1760s.[29]

In 1735 five Anabaptists were recorded at Staunton.[30] A Methodist society meeting at Coleford had adherents at Staunton from the late 1780s. It was probably that group that registered a house at Staunton in 1796, and in the early 19th century it met at the house of Richard Morgan.[31] There was perhaps another group of dissenters in the village c. 1825 when two houses were in use for worship,[32] but in the later 19th century local dissenters presumably attended chapels in Coleford.

EDUCATION. In the early 19th century a parish day school was held in the south transept of Staunton church.[33] In 1819 20 children attended, 8 of them paid for by their parents and the rest educated free by the rector Thomas Mallet. Mallet also ran a Sunday school, attended by c. 70 children in 1819.[34] In 1828 a small single-room school was built near the east end of the main village street on a piece of manorial waste that the Crown conveyed in trust to the rector and churchwardens in 1859.[35] The school was affiliated to the National Society by 1847. In the 1830s and 1840s it was attended by c. 30 children. Some of the parents paid, the rate being 1s. a quarter in 1833,[36] but in the year 1875 only 11s. of c. £46 that it cost came from pence, the bulk being supplied by voluntary contribu-

[13] Bodl. MS. Rawl. B. 323, f. 123v.; Bigland, *Glos.* iii, no. 251.
[14] Fraser, *Staunton*, 30.
[15] Bigland, *Glos.* iii, no. 251; cf. Glos. R.O., D 1677/GG 1558; P 310/MI 1.
[16] Fraser, *Staunton*, 30–2.
[17] Ibid. 32, 38, 44; Glos. R.O., D 637/II/4/T 9, notebook.
[18] Glos. R.O., D 3469/5/112.
[19] Ibid. P 310/CW 3/1; D 637/II/4/T 9, notebook.
[20] Fraser, *Staunton*, 32–3.
[21] *Trans. B.G.A.S.* xxxii. 310–12.
[22] Ibid. xxxix. 84.
[23] Fraser, *Staunton*, 31–2.
[24] Bodl. MS. Rawl. B. 323, f. 123v.
[25] *Glos. Ch. Bells*, 574–7; Glos. R.O., D 637/II/4/T 9, notebook.

[26] *Glos. Ch. Plate*, 193–4.
[27] Glos. R.O., P 310/IN 1/1–5.
[28] Ibid. Q/SO 4, at end.
[29] *Misc.* viii (Cath. Rec. Soc. xiii), 188 and n.
[30] G.D.R. vol. 285B(1), f. 7.
[31] Bright, *Nonconf. in Dean*, 37–9, 46; Hockaday Abs. cccl, 1796, 1814, 1824, 1832.
[32] G.D.R. vol. 383, no. cxxxii.
[33] Fraser, *Staunton*, 30.
[34] *Educ. of Poor Digest*, 312.
[35] P.R.O., ED 7/37; Glos. R.O., P 310/SC 1.
[36] *Educ. Enq. Abstract*, 327; Nat. Soc. *Inquiry*, 1846–7, Glos. 16–17.

tions.[37] During the last 20 years of the 19th century and the first decade of the 20th attendance was rarely more than *c.* 20 children, and the school was closed in 1911.[38] The village children subsequently went to school in Coleford, and the school building, which reverted to the Commissioners of Woods, became a village reading room.[39]

CHARITIES FOR THE POOR.

A house and 4 a. of land, the donor unknown, were applied to the use of the poor of Staunton parish. About 1820, by which time the house had fallen down, the land was exchanged with the Crown for a piece of manorial waste called Meend green, which produced a rent of £5 2s.[40]

Henry Hall (d. 1645), a son of William Hall of Highmeadow, left £40 a year, half for the poor of Staunton and half for the poor of Newland. His brother Benedict and nephew John Hall,[41] who were later credited as founders of the charity, charged the sum in 1657 on a farm at St. Weonards (Herefs.).[42] Staunton's share was presumably not distributed for some years, for by 1683 an accumulation of the charge, £100, was out on loan, and before 1705 £140, apparently from the same source, was secured on land called Braceland in English Bicknor. Another accumulation of the £20 a year was used before 1683 to buy a small house near the cross at the east end of the village for use as an almshouse.[43] In the mid 1820s the £20 and £7 a year charged on Braceland were distributed to the poor of the parish in general and the almshouse, which was managed by the same trustees, housed four people. It was then planned to apply the rent charges and the rent from Meend green to the maintenance of the almspeople,[44] and that was being done in 1896 when the whole was administered as a single charity.[45] In 1961 the trustees of the Hall charity mortgaged the almshouse to raise funds to renovate it, and in 1971 most of their income was applied to paying the interest, though some cash was distributed to poor widows. The two occupants of the almshouse then paid 5s. a week rent.[46]

Sarah Richards by will proved 1845 gave £100 to be invested in stock and the proceeds distributed to poor widows and widowers. In 1971 the £2 a year received was divided among four people.[47]

Plans made in 1976 to amalgamate the Staunton charities were not implemented, but they were administered as one in 1994. The almshouse, which was then occupied by a single tenant for a rent set at half the sum appropriate under the 'fair rent' scheme, was then undergoing further extensive repairs financed mainly by a local authority grant and an interest-free loan from the Almshouse Association. All the charity income, including also the small sum received for the Richards charity, the interest on £280 which had apparently been acquired with an accumulation of one of the Hall rent charges, and £200 rent for Meend green, was then being applied to the renovation project.[48]

37 P.R.O., ED 7/37.   38 Glos. R.O., P 310/SC 2.
39 Ibid. P 310/SC 1; *Kelly's Dir. Glos.* (1914), 310.
40 *19th Rep. Com. Char.* 106.
41 Rudder, *Glos.* 569.   42 *19th Rep. Com. Char.* 100.
43 G.D.R., V 5/285T 4, 7.

44 *19th Rep. Com. Char.* 106.
45 Glos. R.O., P 310/CH 1.
46 Ibid. D 3469/5/112.   47 Ibid.
48 Inf. from Mr. G. Jones, of Staunton, a trustee; cf. Glos. R.O., D 3469/5/112.

THE FOREST OF DEAN

HE FOREST of Dean lies in west Gloucestershire in the angle formed by the rivers Severn and Wye as they approach their confluence. A large tract of woodland and waste land there was reserved for royal hunting before 1066 and survived into the modern period as one of the principal Crown forests in England, the largest after the New Forest. The name Forest of Dean was recorded from c. 1080[1] and was probably taken from the valley on the north-east of the area, where a manor called Dean was the Forest's administrative centre in the late 11th century.

In modern times the name Forest of Dean was sometimes used loosely for the part of Gloucestershire between the Severn and Wye, but all that land belonged to the Forest (used in the specific sense of the area subject to the forest law) only for a period in the early Middle Ages. In the 13th century the Forest's bounds were the two rivers and it extended northwards as far as Ross-on-Wye (Herefs.), Newent, and Gloucester; it then included 33 Gloucestershire and Herefordshire parishes, besides a central, uncultivated area which the Crown retained in demesne. Revised bounds, perambulated in 1300 and accepted by the Crown in 1327, reduced the extent of the Forest to the royal demesne and 14 parishes or parts of parishes, most of them, like the demesne itself, in St. Briavels hundred. After 1668 in practice, and after 1833 officially, the Forest comprised the royal demesne only. The changes in the bounds over the centuries are described below.[2] The royal demesne remained extraparochial until the 1840s when, villages and hamlets having grown up within it, it was formed into the civil townships (later parishes) of East Dean and West Dean and into ecclesiastical districts. After mid 20th-century changes the bulk of the former demesne land belonged in 1994 to the civil parishes of West Dean, Lydbrook, Cinderford, Ruspidge, and Drybrook.[3]

This part of the volume relates the history of the central block of royal demesne land as constituted after 1668, an area of c. 23,000 a. (c. 9,308 ha.).[4] For convenience of treatment, the account also covers a number of detached parts of Newland parish and its tithing of Lea Bailey, which were islands within the extraparochial Forest or bordered it,[5] a detached part of Mitcheldean called Blackwell meadows, and the whole of Lydbrook village, which was divided between the extraparochial Forest, Newland, English Bicknor, and Ruardean. Some parts of the extraparochial Forest which lay detached from the main block are treated with the histories of parishes which adjoined them: the largest, lying near the Wye and called Hudnalls, is included in part with St. Briavels and in part with Hewelsfield, while Mocking Hazel wood, Bearse common, and the Fence in the same area are included with St. Briavels, the Glydden, also in the Wye Valley, with Newland, and Walmore common and Northwood green, to the north-east of the main block, with Westbury-on-Severn in another volume. Woods at Mailscot, near English Bicknor parish, and at Kidnalls and the Snead, north of Lydney parish, removed from the royal demesne by 1668 but remaining extraparochial, are treated above with the histories of those parishes.

---

[1] *Hist. & Cart. Mon. Glouc.* (Rolls Ser.), ii. 186. This account of the Forest of Dean was written between 1992 and 1994.
[2] Bounds.
[3] Below, Local Govt.
[4] Below, Bounds.
[5] Fig. 13; above, Newland, intro (table I); the detached parts of Newland covered in this account are those numbered 1–11, 16, 19, 21–2.

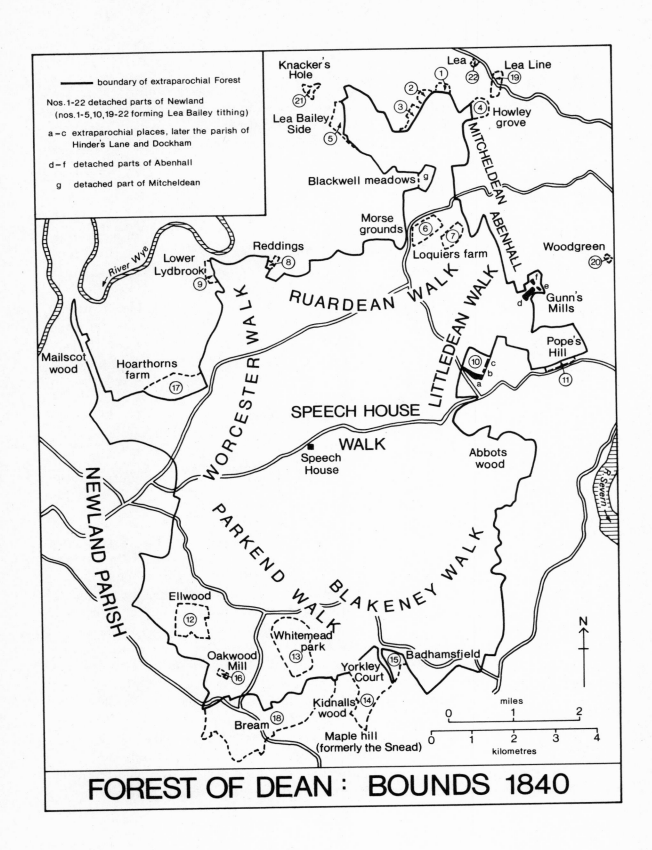

Nos.1-22 detached parts of Newland
(nos.1-5,10,19-22 forming Lea Bailey tithing)

a-c extraparochial places, later the parish of
Hinder's Lane and Dockham

d-f detached parts of Abenhall

g detached part of Mitcheldean

— boundary of extraparochial Forest

FOREST OF DEAN : BOUNDS 1840

Fig. 13

286

The formerly extraparochial land of the Forest of Dean lies mainly at over 200 m. (656 ft.), reaching its highest point, 290 m. (951 ft.), at Ruardean hill in the north. Sometimes described as a plateau but actually comprising steep ridges and the valleys of streams draining to the Severn and Wye, its boundaries with the surrounding cultivated and ancient parochial lands are in most places defined by a scarp where the underlying carboniferous limestone of the region outcrops. On the west, however, the limestone outcrops at a shallower angle and there is a less obvious distinction in height between the Forest and the cultivated land of the large ancient parish of Newland. The long valley of Cannop brook, earlier called the Newerne stream,[6] crosses the west part of the Forest from north to south, and a stream called in its northern part Cinderford brook and in its southern Soudley brook forms a long winding valley through the east part. Blackpool brook, so called by 1282,[7] carves another deep valley through the south-eastern edge of the high land to meet Soudley brook at Blakeney below the Forest's scarp, and at the Forest's northern edge Greathough brook, formerly Lyd brook,[8] descends a valley to the Wye. The streams were dammed in places for ironworks, notably in the Cannop valley where two large ponds were made in the 1820s to provide power for works at Parkend.[9] Other large ponds on a tributary stream of Soudley brook at Sutton bottom, near Soudley, were built as fishponds in the mid 19th century for a privately-owned estate in that part of the Forest called Abbots wood.[10] In the late 20th century the Forestry Commission maintained the Forest's ponds as nature reserves and as a public amenity; new ones were made at Woorgreen, near the centre of the Forest, as part of landscape restoration following opencast coal mining in the 1970s,[11] and at Mallards Pike, near the head of Blackpool brook, in 1980.[12]

Geology has given the Forest its rich industrial history. The land is formed of basin-shaped strata of the Carboniferous series. Underlying and outcropping at the rim are limestones which, especially the stratum called Crease Limestone, contain deposits of iron ore. Above are beds of sandstone, shale, and coal. The lowest bed of sandstone is known by the local name of Drybrook Sandstone, and the highest is the Pennant Sandstone. There are over 20 separate coal seams, varying in thickness from a few inches to 5 ft., the highest yielding being the Coleford High Delf which rises close to the surface near the rim of the Forest.[13] Surface workings, shallow pits, or levels driven into the hillsides were the means of winning the iron ore and coal until the late 18th century when deeper mines were sunk. There were also numerous quarries, notably those in the Pennant Sandstone at Bixhead and elsewhere on the west side of the Cannop valley; that stone, which varies in colour but is mainly dark grey, was the principal building material used in the Forest's 19th-century industrial hamlets.

The Forest was most significant as a producer of oak timber, which was the principal reason for its survival in the modern period. Until the early 17th century, however, there was as much beech as oak among its large timber trees,[14] and chestnut trees once grew in profusion on the north-east side of the Forest near Flaxley[15] and gave the name by 1282 to a wood called the Chestnuts.[16] The

[6] P.R.O., E 32/31, m. 12.　　　[7] Ibid. m. 11.
[8] Ibid. m. 13.　　　[9] Below, Industry, ironworks.
[10] New Regard of Forest of Dean, vi. 40.
[11] Glos. R.O., D 6993/1/2, mins. 13 Jan. 1977; 29 Mar. 1978; 10 Oct. 1980.
[12] Dean Forest Mercury, 4 Jan. 1980.
[13] F. B. A. Welch and F. M. Trotter, Geol. of Country

around Mon. and Chepstow (Memoirs of Geol. Surv. 1960), 66–71, 86–105; Bull. of Hist. Metallurgy Group, ii (1), 16–26.
[14] Badminton Mun. FmE 2/3/1, f. 4; Hart, Royal Forest, 280–2.
[15] Above, Flaxley, intro.
[16] P.R.O., E 32/31, m. 9; Glos. R.O., D 2026/X 3.

underwood was composed of a variety of small species such as hazel, birch, sallow, holly, and alder.[17] The ancient forest contained many open areas. In 1282 various 'lands', or forest glades, maintained by the Crown presumably as grazing for the deer, included several with names later familiar in the Forest's history, Kensley, Moseley, Cannop, Crump meadow, and Whitemead (later a part of Newland parish). Numerous smaller clearings called 'trenches' had also been made[18] as corridors alongside roads for securing travellers against ambush[19] or for the grazing and passage of the deer.[20] Larger areas of waste, or 'meends', such as Clearwell Meend and Mitcheldean Meend, lay on the borders adjoining the manorial lands, whose inhabitants used them for commoning their animals.

Much ancient woodland was destroyed to make charcoal for the iron industry in the 16th and 17th centuries, but the re-establishment of the woods was encouraged by a policy of inclosure begun in the 1660s and designed to produce shipbuilding timber. The policy faltered during the 18th century but in the early 19th century large new inclosures were again formed and planted almost entirely with oak. A few Weymouth pines planted before 1787[21] were apparently the first conifers introduced to the Forest, and conifers were widely planted in the 19th century to shelter the young oak plantations. Large plantations of pure conifer were made during the 20th century and threatened to dominate the woodlands before 1971 when a policy of keeping equal proportions of coniferous and broadleaved trees was adopted. In 1994, when the Forest was more thickly planted than for several centuries, it included isolated late 17th-century oaks, park-like areas of early 19th-century oak preserved mainly as an amenity, and large plantations of oak, beech, fir, and spruce managed for commercial purposes.[22]

Although the royal demesne land was without permanent habitation until the early modern period, it was crossed by many ancient tracks, used by ironworkers, miners, and charcoal burners; large numbers, many termed 'mersty' (meaning a boundary path), were recorded in 1282 in a perambulation of the Forest bailiwicks, its administrative divisions.[23] One of the more important ancient routes, known as the Dean road, had a pitched stone surface and borders of kerbstones. It ran between Lydney and Mitcheldean across the eastern part of the demesne by way of Oldcroft, a crossing of Blackpool brook, recorded as Blackpool ford in 1282,[24] and a crossing of Soudley brook at Upper Soudley. The survival of much pitching and kerbing after the road went out of use in the turnpike era, and the possibility that it had linked two important Roman sites at Lydney and Ariconium, in Weston under Penyard (Herefs.), has led to the suggestion that it was a Roman road,[25] though much of the stonework probably dates from the medieval and early modern periods; an estimate was made for renewing long stretches of the road, including the provision of new border stones, as late as the 1760s.[26] Much remained visible in the 1930s, but recent damage by timber wagons and other vehicles was recorded then[27] and continued later. A short stretch near Blackpool brook,[28] including part

17 Hart, *Royal Forest*, 276, 298; Glos. R.O., D 1677/GG 1223.
18 P.R.O., E 32/31, mm. 8–14.
19 *Close R.* 1234–7, 1, 248; *Cal. Pat.* 1247–58, 435; cf. Statute of Winchester, 13 Edw. I, s. 5.
20 *Cal. Fine R.* 1307–19, 37.
21 *3rd Rep. Com. Woods* (1788), 113.
22 For hist. of woodland management, below, Forest Admin.

23 P.R.O., E 32/31, mm. 9–14; *P. N. Glos* (E.P.N.S.), iv. 174.
24 P.R.O., E 32/31, m. 11.
25 I. D. Margary, *Roman Roads in Britain* (1973), 332–3.
26 Berkeley Cast. Mun., General Ser. T, box 25, representation by verderers to Treas. 1768.
27 A. W. Trotter, *Dean Road* (Glouc. 1936), a detailed, illustrated surv. of the road. For an excavation of a section, *New Regard of Forest of Dean*, i. 5–9.
28 Above, Plate 43.

of a side branch across a bridge beside the ford, was preserved and open to view in 1994.

Two main routes crossed the extraparochial Forest from north-east to south-west and on them were sited the principal points of reference in a terrain with few landmarks. A route from the Severn crossing at Newnham to Monmouth recorded in 1255, when 'trenches' were ordered to be made beside it,[29] was presumably that through Littledean, the central Forest, and Coleford. It entered over a high ridge west of Littledean, where a hermitage of St. White had been founded by 1225,[30] and crossed Soudley (or Cinderford) brook at the place called Cinder ford in 1258,[31] long before its name was taken by the principal settlement of the extraparochial Forest that formed on the hillside to the north-east of the crossing. Further west, near the centre of the Forest, the road passed the clearing called Kensley, where a courthouse stood by 1338 close to the site of the later Speech House,[32] and crossed Newerne (or Cannop) brook at Cannop, which for a few years in the mid 17th century was the centre of a large private estate established within the Forest.[33] The road emerged into the cultivated land of Coleford tithing at a place later called Broadwell Lane End, where a tree called Woolman oak in 1608[34] was probably the 'W(o)lfmyen' oak which in 1282 was a landmark at the boundary of four of the Forest's bailiwicks.[35] The other main route, recorded in 1282 as the high road to Monmouth,[36] was that crossing the high north-western part of the extraparochial land from Mitcheldean, by way of Nailbridge, Brierley, Mirystock, where it crossed a tributary of Cannop brook above Lydbrook, to Coleford. The two remained the principal routes through the Forest but the northern one, described in the 1760s as the great road through the Forest from Gloucester to South Wales, was much altered in its course by later improvements.[37]

The rivers Severn and Wye played a vital role in the development of Dean's industry but few of the various tracks and hollow ways that led from the central Forest to riverside landing-places and ferries were usable other than by packhorses before the 19th century. One of the few routes negotiable by wagons and timber rigs was the central main road out to Littledean with its branch down to Newnham; that was the usual route for carrying timber out of the Forest in 1737 when the Crown was asked to assist Newnham parish to repair part of it.[38] Later in the 18th century a road leading from the south part of the woodlands by way of Parkend and Viney Hill to Gatcombe and Purton on the Severn became the principal route for timber destined for the naval dockyards.[39] The repair of the roads, which was the responsibility of turnpike trustees from 1796, and the development of a network to serve the new Forest settlements are discussed below,[40] as are the tramroads and railways which were built in the 19th century to serve the Forest's industry.[41]

The Crown's hunting rights, which provided the original motive for the Forest's preservation, were much used in the 13th century. The frequent orders made at the period for taking deer for gifts by the Crown and to meet the needs of the royal household suggest that fallow deer were the majority species in Dean, with red deer and roe present in smaller numbers.[42] In 1278 the Forest was sufficiently well

[29] Cal. Pat. 1247–58, 435.
[30] Above, Flaxley, intro.; church.
[31] Cal. Chart. R. 1257–1300, 11.
[32] Below, Settlement, forest lodges.
[33] Below, Forest Admin., exploitation 1603–68.
[34] P.R.O., MR 879 (F 17/1).
[35] Ibid. E 32/31, mm. 12–14.
[36] Ibid. m. 13.
[37] Badminton Mun. FmS/G 2/4/4, 6; 3rd Rep. Com.

Woods (1788), 109; below, Settlement, intro.
[38] Berkeley Cast. Mun., General Ser. T, box 25, representation by verderers to Treas. 1737.
[39] 3rd Rep. Com. Woods (1788), 109; Dean Forest Roads Act, 36 Geo. III, c. 131.
[40] Settlement, intro.; Local Govt.
[41] Industry, tramroads and railways.
[42] Trans. B.G.A.S. xxxiii. 165.

stocked for royal huntsmen to take 100 fallow bucks.[43] At that period all three species of deer were classed as beasts of the forest, reserved for the exclusive use of the Crown, but roe were not classified as such after 1340.[44]

During the 17th century felling of the woods reduced the numbers of deer. The reafforestation Act of 1668, referring to a possible 'restoration' of the king's deer, set an upper limit of 800 animals, so as not to threaten the new inclosures made for navy timber.[45] Preservation of the deer remained a role of the re-invigorated Forest administration following the Act,[46] and lax administration during the 18th century allowed poaching to reduce the numbers. In 1751 the scarcity of the deer made advisable a three-year moratorium on taking venison under royal warrants.[47] In 1788 the keepers estimated that the woods contained *c.* 500,[48] but twenty years later there were said to be hardly enough to meet the Crown's usual annual demand of 4 bucks and 4 does.[49] Tighter administration introduced then to protect extensive new plantations encouraged an increase by 1839 to *c.* 800 and, in spite of losses in the hard winter of 1840–1, *c.* 600 remained in the late 1840s and 20 or 30 a year were killed under warrant. In 1849 the Crown Commissioners of Woods ordered the destruction of the deer, on the grounds of the 'demoralizing effects' on the local population of the opportunities for poaching, and all, or almost all, were killed before 1855. At the beginning of the 20th century, however, a small herd of fallow lived in Highmeadow woods, a large Crown estate adjoining the Forest, possibly descendants of some given to the Crown in 1846 and released there;[50] by mid century another herd had become established in the centre of the Forest woodland, near the Speech House. In 1969 there were *c.* 65 animals in the Highmeadow herd and *c.* 50 near the Speech House,[51] and *c.* 250 fallow deer grazed the Forest and adjoining woodlands in 1994.[52]

Of the other beasts of the forest, wild boar were numerous in Dean in the early Middle Ages, with, for example, 100 boars and sows ordered for a Christmas feast in 1254.[53] Boar still roamed the Forest in the 1280s, like the deer a prey both of royal huntsmen and poachers.[54] In 1282 eyries of falcons and sparrowhawks were among the perquisites claimed by woodwards of several Forest bailiwicks,[55] and there were eyries of goshawks in the woods in 1565.[56] Some traditional nesting places were lost by the indiscriminate felling of great trees in the early and mid 17th century, including eyries reserved for the king's use in a wood called the Bourts, at the northern rim of the demesne above English Bicknor,[57] but peregrine falcons continued to nest later in cliffs above the Wye adjoining the Forest near Symonds Yat.[58] Until the 1280s or later the Forest's woods sheltered packs of wolves.[59]

The commoning of pigs, sheep, and cattle in the royal demesne land of the Forest is described below as an integral, and often contentious, part of the story of the Forest's administration and management.[60] From the mid 18th century encroach-

43 P.R.O., E 32/30, rot. 16.
44 *Select Pleas of the Forest* (Selden Soc. xiii), pp. x–xiv.
45 Dean Forest Act, 19 & 20 Chas. II, c. 8, s. 7.
46 Badminton Mun. FmS/G 2/4/4.
47 Berkeley Cast. Mun., General Ser. T, box 25, papers about keepers' misdemeanours 1742; order by chief justice of forests S. of Trent to officers 1751.
48 *3rd Rep. Com. Woods* (1788), 86.
49 Rudge, *Hist. of Glos.* ii. 10–11.
50 P.R.O., F 16/52; Hart, *Verderers*, 180–1, 183–4.
51 Glos. R.O., D 6993/1/1, mins. 21 Dec. 1964; 20 Aug. 1969.

52 Inf. from Mr. J. E. Everard, deputy surveyor, Forest Enterprise, Coleford.
53 *Trans. B.G.A.S.* xxxiii. 165.
54 P.R.O., E 32/30, rott. 10d., 16.
55 Ibid. E 32/32, mm. 1–2, 5.
56 Badminton Mun. FmE 2/3/1, f. 4.
57 P.R.O., E 178/3837, depositions 1614; Glos. R.O., D 421/E 4.
58 Above, English Bicknor, intro.
59 *Hist. & Cart. Mon. Glouc.* ii. 184; P.R.O., E 32/30, rot. 7.
60 Forest Admin.

ment of land on the fringes of the royal demesne created numerous smallholdings. Their occupants, often miners or quarrymen, pastured sheep on the Forest waste and worked small arable plots, gardens, and orchards. In 1896 in the parishes of East and West Dean, in which most of the formerly extraparochial Forest land was then included, 338 occupiers of land were returned. They held a total of c. 2,200 a., including 416 a. of arable, mainly growing potatoes and oats, turnips, and other fodder crops, and 163 a. of orchard; their stock was 6,514 sheep, 379 cattle, and 590 pigs.[61] The sheep were part of a larger number in the Forest, where a survey found 10,851 in 1898,[62] though sheep were of dubious legality and were commoned only on sufferance of the Forest authorities until 1980 when a limit of 5,000 was accepted.[63] In 1926 when 222 occupiers of land in East and West Dean made returns only 14 had more than 20 a.[64] The few larger farms included some, like Hoarthorns farm, near English Bicknor, and Loquiers farm, near Drybrook, in former detached parts of Newland that had been added to the two parishes. In the late 20th century smallholdings, usually worked part-time, were still characteristic of the cleared and settled area on the Forest fringes,[65] and the commoners' sheep, roaming the wastes and roadside verges, remained a familiar feature of the Forest scene.

The history of the royal demesne land of the Forest of Dean in the Middle Ages is that of the administration established to enforce the forest law in defence of the vert and venison and of the mining and ironmaking industries. The administration operated in its fullest form between the late 12th century and the early 14th, a period when it had jurisdiction over a wide tract of manorial and parochial land as well as the royal demesne. It was centred on St. Briavels castle and manor, headed by a royal appointee of considerable standing who was styled constable of St. Briavels castle and warden of the Forest of Dean, and staffed by various categories of foresters, the principal ones holding office by tenure of surrounding manors. The forest system was enforced by an attachment court, presided over by verderers, and by the regular forest eyres with their wide judicial and investigative functions. Even with the full apparatus of a royal forest in place, however, there was corruption by officials and much poaching and timber stealing by local inhabitants. Mining, which in the Middle Ages was mainly for iron ore, and the associated ironmaking industry were anciently established in Dean. A body of mining law, codified in the 13th or 14th century, and protected, enforced, and amended by a mine law court and a Crown-appointed gaveller, restricted the digging, carrying, and sale of ore, coal, and stone to the 'free miners' of St. Briavels hundred. By the 13th century the mines and numerous charcoal pits supplied and fuelled small bloomery forges, which were moved from place to place in the woodlands of the royal demesne and surrounding parishes; the inefficient working of the bloomeries left a legacy of mounds of 'cinders' (slag rich in ore) to be reprocessed later by the water-powered blast furnaces, first introduced to surrounding parishes in the late 16th century.

In the early modern period the Forest administration's basic aim shifted from the defence of the royal hunting rights, and the associated gathering of revenue in the form of fines on offenders, to the preservation and management of the woods

[61] P.R.O., MAF 68/1609/6.
[62] Fisher, *Custom and Capitalism*, 148.
[63] Below, Forest Admin., woodland management and commoning 1820–1914; Forest in 20th cent.
[64] P.R.O., MAF 68/3295/6, 16.
[65] Agric. Returns 1988, s.vv. Drybrook, Lydbrook, Ruspidge.

for shipbuilding timber. As a result it came into conflict even more markedly with the ironworkers and miners who needed wood for charcoaling and for shoring mines, with the larger numbers of local inhabitants who claimed, and jealously guarded, the right to pasture animals on the demesne, and with squatters who established themselves there in makeshift cabins and stole wood for a variety of trades. The later history of Dean had a cyclical pattern: the pressures tending to the destruction of its woods gained ground in times of weak and inefficient administration and were restricted again in times when the government pursued determinedly its aim to preserve the Forest as a nursery of timber.

In the early 17th century the Stuart kings, seeking short-term profit from their assets, allied themselves with the destructive forces. From 1612 they allowed ironmasters to set up furnaces and forges on the demesne and assigned to them a large annual quota of coppice wood and offal wood for charcoaling; the exercise of those concessions was accompanied by embezzlement of wood, the introduction of cabiners to the demesne, and, though great trees were supposed to be preserved, the destruction of much potential shipbuilding timber. Charles I leased or sold large parts of the demesne in the 1620s. At the same time his search for revenue led him to reimpose the forest law on the local inhabitants in its full rigour by an eyre in 1634. His policy culminated in the sale of the bulk of the demesne to Sir John Winter of Lydney in 1640 but the Long Parliament's assault on the royal prerogative made that arrangement short lived. In the Civil War local royalists, led by Winter, contested control of the Forest and surrounding parishes with the parliamentary garrison at Gloucester. There were numerous skirmishes in the Forest area and some larger incursions, including the advance of Welsh levies against Gloucester under the command of Lord Herbert in February 1643 and the arrival of a destructive force under Prince Rupert in the spring of 1645.[66] Following the war, with the forest administration enfeebled by the sanctions imposed on the royalist gentry, a group of army officers took control of the ironworks and did further damage to the woodlands.

Under the Protectorate the Forest was more efficiently administered, and after the Restoration Charles II's government, committing itself to a policy of preservation to raise ship timber, inclosed over half the demesne under an Act of 1668, removed the ironworks and illegal squatters, and added more effective elements to the cumbersome administrative apparatus. During the 18th century, however, governmental control was relaxed and the local administration, vitiated by a system of fees which put a premium on abuse and neglect, allowed wood stealing and encroachment to become rife. Squatters began to establish hamlets around the fringes of the demesne, which contained almost 600 dwellings by 1787. The new settlers lived in primitive conditions in roughly-built cottages, and evangelical clergy and nonconformist preachers, who began to minister to them c. 1800, equated the task with missions to the heathen. Three Anglican churches built between 1816 and 1822, at Berry Hill, Harrow Hill near Drybrook, and Parkend, were among signs that the new settlements had become accepted as permanent features of the demesne.

A regular supply of good quality timber produced for the naval dockyards from the late 17th-century inclosures encouraged the government to embark on a fresh programme of inclosing and planting at the end of the Napoleonic Wars, and,

66 *Bibliotheca Glos.* ii. 1–152 (*passim*); *Trans. B.G.A.S.* xviii. 94–106.

under the Crown Commissioners of Woods and a long-serving local deputy surveyor, Edward Machen, the efficiency and reputation of the forest administration were restored. The Forest's industry was also transformed in the early 19th century as outsiders invested in it and formed partnerships with local men. Edward Protheroe of Bristol was the most notable of the 'foreign' capitalists at the period, and later the Crawshay family of Merthyr Tydfil (Glam.) played a leading role. Coal mining especially was developed by building tramroads to carry the coal to shipping points on the Severn and Wye and by installing more steam pumps and new equipment to enable mines to be sunk to the deeper and higher quality seams; the iron industry was revived by the introduction of coke-fired blast furnaces, and quarrying was also much expanded. Many of the poorer inhabitants felt threatened by the changes, in their role as free miners by the erosion of the old protective customs and in their role as commoners by the restrictions imposed under the replanting programme. Their antagonism culminated in riots against the new inclosures in 1831. A detailed enquiry into the Forest, begun the following year, led to statutory measures for regulating the mines, regularizing the Foresters' tenure of their cottages and encroachments, and parochializing the Forest.

In the later 19th century and the early 20th the Forest was a complex industrial region, including deep coal mines and iron mines, iron and tinplate works, foundries, quarries and stone-dressing works, wood distillation works producing chemicals, a network of railways, and numerous minor tramroads. The Forest population grew rapidly: Cinderford was laid out in the mid 19th century on a fairly conventional urban plan and Lydbrook, Parkend, and Drybrook became minor centres, but the characteristic form of settlement remained the sprawling hamlets of haphazardly placed cottages on the periphery. There were substantial accumulations on the hillsides above Ruardean on the north side, along the Soudley valley on the east, above Blakeney on the south-east, in the Yorkley and Bream area above Lydney on the south, and in the Lane Ends and Berry Hill areas adjoining Coleford on the west. Altogether the Forest came to contain c. 20 villages and hamlets, and its population rose from 7,014 in 1831 to 26,624 in 1921.

As part of the infrastructure of the new settlements, more Anglican churches were built, and numerous small nonconformist chapels were founded as nonconformity, particularly the fundamentalist Bible Christian and Primitive Methodist sects, gained a firm hold. Education was provided mainly by church schools until the 1870s when a school board, dominated by nonconformists, undertook a major building programme. From the 1870s the need of the new settlements for water-supply and sewerage schemes began to be addressed, and a proper system of minor roads was formed in the early 20th century. The Foresters' origins as illegal squatters and their struggle to defend their commoning and mining rights gave them a strong sense of community, as well as a reputation for surliness and suspicion towards outsiders. Characteristics shared with other British coalfields, such as a devotion to sport, the central role of miners' clubs, and the formation of brass bands, also helped to create a distinct identity.

The demise of wooden navies long before the early 19th-century plantations matured led to a period of uncertainty about the role of the Forest's administration, but its timber later proved of great national value in the two world wars. In 1924 the Commissioners of Woods transferred control to the Forestry Commission, which during the rest of the 20th century managed the Forest, together with large tracts of woodland in surrounding areas, as primarily a commercial enterprise but with increasing stress on the provision of amenities for leisure; in 1994 the two buildings which had played the principal roles in the administration of the Forest both served tourism, the Speech House in the centre as a hotel and St. Briavels castle in an adjoining parish as a youth hostel. The gradual loss of jobs in traditional industries in the 20th century, ending with the closure of the last deep mines in the 1960s, made necessary the provision of new sources of employment, found mainly in surrounding parishes and towns. Those changes and other modern pressures began to dilute the character of the people and, with the reclamation of industrial sites and more intensive planting, soften the appearance of the landscape, though features such as the continuing use of the rights of free miners and commoners and the survival from the old forest administration of the office of verderer helped to preserve the memory of the area's distinctive history. In 1994 enough remained of the traditional character of the Forest of Dean for it to be seen by outsiders and by its inhabitants as very different from the rest of Gloucester-shire.

For much of its history the Forest of Dean, using the term in the particular sense of the area subject to forest law, included two distinct sorts of land: on the one hand there was land held by the Crown in demesne, mainly extraparochial and uninhabited woodland and waste, and on the other manorial and private freehold land, mainly cultivated, settled, and formed into parishes.

The extent of the Forest[1] at the time of the Norman Conquest is uncertain. Domesday Book refers to it only indirectly, though the disposition of the manors which it records in the area enables a rough idea of the late 11th-century extent to be gained.[2] The only lands referred to in 1086 as being in 'the king's forest' or 'the king's wood' were a group of manors that had gone out of cultivation before the Conquest, two other manors which had been recently placed in the Forest and had apparently been cleared of population, and some isolated parcels of land, also apparently unpopulated. Domesday Book suggests, therefore, that no settled or manorial land was then within the Forest bounds. If that was so, the late 11th-century Forest was confined to an area not unlike its modern bounds,[3] except that to the north-west and west it bordered the river Wye for much of the river's course between English Bicknor and Brockweir.

To the south-east it was probably confined to the high land away from the river Severn, for the Severn shore between Highnam, near Gloucester, and the confluence with the Wye in Tidenham, near Chepstow, was occupied in 1066 by a string of 25 manors in the nine later parishes bordering the river. On the west the more rugged lands bordering the Wye were much less heavily populated in 1066 and in some areas cultivation had been abandoned. Staunton, opposite Monmouth, 'Whippington', an estate nearby, and possibly a third manor in the same area had reverted to waste by 1066, as also had two manors at a place called 'Brocote', which almost certainly adjoined the Wye in the Forest area and has speculatively been identified with Redbrook. Those manors (then all part of Herefordshire) remained waste in 1086 and four of them were described as 'still in the king's wood'.[4]

Along the Wye below Ross-on-Wye (Herefs.) the inhabited manors in 1066 were Cleeve (Herefs.), Walford (Herefs.), Ruardean (then Herefs., later Glos.), English Bicknor, Wyegate on the borders of the later parishes of Newland and St. Briavels, St. Briavels, Hewelsfield, Madgett, and part of Tidenham. Of those, Wyegate and Hewelsfield, though acquiring new

Norman lords after the Conquest, were placed within the Forest by King William's command before 1086. For neither was owner, tenantry, or current value recorded, only a fishery at Wyegate,[5] and the implication is that they had been cleared and added to the waste. On the northern edge of the later Forest, from Ross to Highnam, another 10 Herefordshire and Gloucestershire manors existed in 1066, forming a fairly compact wedge of land along and south of the line of the Ross–Gloucester road. The most southerly manor of that area, then called Dean and evidently comprising land in and around the later Mitcheldean parish, was held by the service of custody of the Forest.[6] In 1086 a yardland in Taynton, some way north of the Ross–Gloucester road, and land at Cleeve, used to raise sheep and produce honey, were both said to be forest land, while woodland in Ross was stated to be in the 'king's enclosure' (*defensu regis*).[7] Those references and a mention of woodland adjoining Churcham as being within the bounds of the Forest of Dean *c.* 1080[8] have led to the suggestion that the Forest included detached parcels of woodland and waste north of the main area.[9]

Between 1086 and 1228 the bounds of the juridical Forest were enlarged to include all the Gloucestershire and Herefordshire manors and villages in an area bounded on the south-east by the Severn from Over bridge, adjoining Gloucester, to the mouth of the Wye, on the west by the Wye from its mouth up to a ford between Goodrich castle and Walford (Herefs.), on the north-west by bounds, mainly trackways, running from the ford by way of Weston under Penyard (Herefs.) and Gorsley to Oxenhall bridge on Ell brook near Newent, and on the north-east by the main road from Newent to Gloucester.[10] An early stage of that enlargement was evidently the inclusion of the Domesday manors of St. Briavels, English Bicknor, Ruardean, and 'Dean'. Those manors together with the manors of Flaxley, Newland, Blakeney, and Walmore, at Northwood in Westbury, which were formed from the demesne woodland and waste during the 12th century, and the reconstituted manors of Staunton and Hewelsfield later comprised the hundred or liberty of St. Briavels,[11] which was regarded later as the core of the Forest. About 1245 three other Gloucestershire hundreds, Bledisloe, Westbury, and Botloe, which by then were wholly or partly included in the Forest, were termed 'the three foreign hundreds' in distinction from St. Briavels hundred,[12] and certain Forest customs

---

[1] For discussions of the early boundaries, C. E. Hart, 'Metes and Bounds of the Forest of Dean', *Trans. B.G.A.S.* lxvi. 166–207; M. L. Bazeley, 'Forest of Dean in its Relations with the Crown during the 12th and 13th Centuries', ibid. xxxiii. 153–64. G. B. Grundy, 'Ancient Woodland of Glos.' ibid. lviii. 65–155, fails to appreciate the distinction between the demesne and manorial lands, confuses the dating of the perambulations, and misidentifies many landmarks.
[2] For the Domesday manors, cf. maps in *Dom. Bk.: Glos.* ed. J. S. Moore (1982); *Herefs.* ed. F. and C. Thorn (1983); but 'Newarne' is more likely to be the place of that

name in Lydney, and other identifications are necessarily speculative.
[3] Below, this chapter.
[4] *Dom. Bk.* (Rec. Com.), i. 181–2.
[5] Ibid. 166v.–167.
[6] Ibid. 167v.
[7] Ibid. 167v., 179v., 182.
[8] *Hist. & Cart. Mon. Glouc.* (Rolls Ser.), ii. 186.
[9] *Trans. B.G.A.S.* xxxiii. 157.
[10] Ibid. lxvi. 176–8; *Close R.* 1227–31, 98–9.
[11] Above, St. Briavels hundred.
[12] P.R.O., E 146/1/25.

FOREST OF DEAN

Bounds in the 13th and 14th Centuries

◇ Places excluded from the Forest before 1300

○ Excluded by the 1300 perambulation, confirmed in 1327

● Remaining in the Forest after 1327

Rodley manor comprised Rodley, Adsett, Bollow, Chaxhill, Cleeve, Elton, and Stantway tithings

Principal identifiable landmarks
in 1228 and 1282 perambulations

A ford at Goodrich castle
B Striguil bridge
C Gloucester (Over) and Leadon bridges
D Gloucester–Newent road
E Oxenhall bridge
F Gorsley ford
G ?'Luce cross' (Aston Crews)
H Bromsash
I Bollitree
J Alton

in 1300 perambulation

1 Bishop's brook
2 ? 'Jutelynde' (Symonds Yat rock)
3 Broad stone
4 'Thre' brook
5 Brockweir brook
6 Harthill wood
7 confluence of Aylesmore and Cone brooks
8 Newerne stream at the Snead
9 Lanes brook
10 ? John of Box's fishery (Hamstalls Pill)

11 Ayleford brook
12 ? brook below Newnham (Collow Pill)
13 ? Crolingham
14 Piper's grove
15 Denny hill
16 Birchen grove
17 Brimstones
18 Elton marsh
19 confluence of Garne (Longhope) brook and Timbridge sike
20 Hope well

FIG. 14

relating to mining and quarrying later applied only within St. Briavels hundred.[13] Whether the enlargement was the work of one of the early Norman kings or of Miles, earl of Hereford, and his son Roger, who ruled the Forest betweeen 1139 and 1154, is not known. It almost certainly dated from before 1154: apart from Hewelsfield, which may not have become part of the hundred until the late 13th century, the inclusion of the manors of St. Briavels hundred was not challenged under the terms of the Charter of the Forest of 1217.

The dates of the other extensions are also uncertain, with two perambulations making contradictory statements. A jury stated in 1228 that the wider bounds of the Forest, including all the land between the Severn and Wye and Newent, had been reached before 1154, while in 1300 another maintained that most of the extensions beyond St. Briavels hundred were the work of King John.[14] There is no definite evidence by which those statements can be judged, but possibly both were incorrect and the extensions were made under Henry II. In 1167, when heavy fines for forest offences were levied in many English counties by the chief justice of the forests, the 19 Gloucestershire places west of the Severn represented were all within the wider bounds of Dean recorded in 1228. The places fined were not necessarily then within the Forest, for some offences, such as poaching and wood stealing, may have been committed elsewhere than in the offenders' own township, but the coincidence and the absence of places outside the wider bounds is suggestive, as is the inclusion on the Gloucestershire list of Hope Mansell (Herefs.) and Hadnock in the lordship of Monmouth, both also within the wider bounds.[15] A fine in 1199 for waste in woodland within Aylburton provides more definite evidence for the inclusion of a part of Bledisloe hundred by the start of King John's reign. The same year the inclusion of part of Herefordshire and part of Botloe hundred are suggested by a fine on the reeve of Ross for making large assarts from the Forest and by a mention of Walter of Huntley in the capacity of a Forest official, probably a regarder.[16]

The date of the enlargements later became obscured by the long dispute between the Crown and the barons over forest boundaries and over the implementation of the Charter of the Forest which the barons secured with the reissue of Magna Carta in 1217. By the Forest Charter all land afforested in the years 1154–1216 was to be disafforested unless it was demesne of the Crown at the time of the afforestation. As with other forests,[17] new perambulations carried out in 1219 appear to have disafforested large areas on those grounds, but in 1227 Henry III, asserting his personal rule and questioning measures taken during his minority, ordered inquiries into those decisions and those who made them. New perambulations to revise the work were ordered,[18] and in 1228 a jury of knights of Gloucestershire produced a verdict in line with what the Crown expected of them, one that put the wider bounds outside the terms of the Forest Charter.[19] Although some places effectively became free of the jurisdiction, the wider bounds remained the official bounds of the Forest throughout the 13th century and were confirmed by a perambulation of 1282.[20] Under baronial pressure, Edward I reissued the Forest Charter in 1297 and ordered new perambulations, one for Dean being made in 1300. In a very different climate from that of 1228 the jury attributed the extensions to King John, though, as suggested above, it is doubtful whether he was responsible; the jurors appear to have produced no documentary evidence for their statement, merely citing local tradition.[21]

The perambulation of 1300 excluded from the Forest 17 Gloucestershire vills, mostly bordering the Severn or in the north-east, besides the whole Herefordshire part, comprising c. 10 vills in the area between the county boundary and Ross.[22] The Forest was left as the royal demesne and the parishes of St. Briavels hundred (except for Hewelsfield), together with Minsterworth, the large part of Westbury-on-Severn parish that formed the manor of Rodley, Newnham parish except for Ruddle manor, and Awre parish except for Box manor.[23] The terms of the Forest Charter appear to have been generally correctly applied, for, of the manors outside St. Briavels hundred that were left within the Forest, Minsterworth, Rodley, Newnham, and Awre were recovered by Henry II from Roger, earl of Hereford, or his brother Walter, in the first years of his reign and remained demesne manors of the Crown until the 13th century.[24] Edward I confirmed the perambulation of 1300 in 1301. Later, however, he challenged the conclusions of the perambulations made for Dean and other forests and annulled them in 1305. The wider bounds of Dean were reinstated until 1327, when Edward III confirmed the perambulation of 1300.[25] In the intervening period the return to the wider bounds was more than nominal: Forest officers attempted to restrict the woodland management of the prior of Newent at Yartleton wood, in Newent,[26] and that of the abbot of Gloucester at Birdwood, in Churcham, and at Hope Mansell.[27]

[13] *4th Rep. Dean Forest Com.* 7, 65–6; Dean Forest Mines Act, 1 & 2 Vic. c. 43. [14] Below, this chapter.
[15] *Pipe R.* 1167 (P.R.S. xi), 143–5, where Baderon's Hope is Longhope, Monk's Rodela is Ruddle, the two places called Abbot's Ham are Churcham and Highnam, and St. Briavels appears as Little Lydney.
[16] Ibid. 1199 (P.R.S. N.S. x), 33.
[17] For the political background, *Select Pleas of the Forest* (Selden Soc. xiii), pp. xciii–xcix, cxxxv; M. Powicke, *Thirteenth Cent.* (1962), 682–3, 699–703.
[18] *Rot. Litt. Claus.* (Rec. Com.), i. 434–5; ii. 212–13; *Pat. R. 1216–25,* 569.
[19] *Close R. 1227–31,* 98–9.

[20] *Trans. B.G.A.S.* lxvi. 175–6.
[21] Ibid. 176–83. [22] Ibid.
[23] Fig. 14. The plan in *Trans. B.G.A.S.* lxvi. 189 misreads the landmarks to exclude Minsterworth and (apparently) Newnham town.
[24] *Rot. Chart.* (Rec. Com.), 53; *Pipe R.* 1160 (P.R.S. ii), 28; 1169 (P.R.S. xiii), 114; 1174 (P.R.S. xxi), 24; cf. above, Awre, manors; *V.C.H. Glos.* x. 36, 89 (where the inclusion of Rodley among the manors that Henry II confirmed to Earl Roger is not mentioned).
[25] *Select Pleas of the Forest,* pp. cv–cvi.
[26] *Trans. B.G.A.S.* xxix. 298–300.
[27] *Cal. Close, 1323–7,* 70.

During the 13th century some areas, though included within the Forest by the perambulations, had managed to assert their freedom or partial freedom from forest law. Three private chases had been created on the fringes of the Forest by 1228.[28] The largest was Tidenham chase belonging to the Earl Marshal's lordship of Striguil and covering the parishes of Tidenham and Woolaston in the angle of the Severn and Wye. By the 1260s the limits of the chase, including on the north Brockweir brook running into the Wye and on the north-east Cone brook running into the Severn, were recognized as the de facto Forest boundary by the officers of the Forest, who were principally concerned with the chase as the origin of poaching expeditions into Dean.[29] The vills in the chase were summoned to the Forest regard of 1282 but failed to appear.[30] In the enclave that later formed a part of Monmouthshire on the east bank of the Wye, comprising the hamlets of Hadnock and Wyesham, King John granted John of Monmouth, lord of Monmouth, licence to impark part of Hadnock woods. By 1282 the later lords of Monmouth and other landowners in the area had effectively freed themselves from the restrictions of forest law.[31] Penyard park, on a high wooded hill in the north part of the Forest, in Herefordshire, was a chase of the bishops of Hereford by 1228, and in 1286, when the activities of the bishop's huntsman there were challenged by Forest officers, a jury declared it to be outside the Forest.[32] The inhabitants of Huntsham tithing (Herefs.), in the loop of the Wye between English Bicknor and Symonds Yat, had also effectively excluded themselves by 1282 when they were reported to have ceased attending inquisitions and eyres.[33] Exclusion of those four areas had been accepted by 1300 and was confirmed by the new perambulations.

After 1327 there was little or no change in the composition of the Forest until 1597 when Minsterworth parish was excluded. Its inhabitants then cited their membership of the Forest in support of a claim to commoning rights in the demesne woodland, but commoners from the other parishes, who were attempting to exclude their animals, manipulated the evidence and secured a judgement that Minsterworth was outside the Forest. The revised bounds of 1300 had, from Newnham, ascended the Severn as far as a meadow called Crolingham at the boundary of Minsterworth and Highnam and then turned inland to Piper's grove, at the parting of the roads from Gloucester to Ross-on-Wye and Chepstow. Witnesses were found, however, to depose that Crolingham was just above Newnham town and Piper's grove inland from there, near the Newnham-Littledean boundary; the difficulty of connecting the supposed landmarks with what followed in the perambulation was left unresolved.[34] By 1623 Rodley manor had also ceased to be accepted as part of the Forest,[35] possibly as a result of the same judgement. Both it and Minsterworth were in the duchy of Lancaster[36] and on that ground they may earlier have ceased to be subject to some aspects of the Forest jurisdiction.

In 1634 during a forest eyre, held as part of Charles I's attempt to reassert ancient Crown privileges, the justices and royal officials revived the wider bounds of Dean and secured a judgement that the perambulations of 1228 and 1282 were valid. In view of long usage, however, forest offences in the outlying areas were not proceeded with at the eyre,[37] and an Act of 1641 restored the bounds of all forests to those in accepted use in 1623.[38] An Act of 1657 lifted the heaviest burdens of the forest law from the manorial lands of Dean,[39] and an Act of 1668, while confirming the bounds of 1623 and re-applying the forest law to the royal demesne, confirmed the mitigation of the law in the manorial lands; manorial owners and freeholders were subsequently free to fell and manage their woodlands and inclose and otherwise improve their lands as they wished and also to enjoy hunting rights in them.[40] During the late 17th century and the 18th the bounds of 1623 continued to define the Forest, with, for example, all the parishes of St. Briavels hundred (except Hewelsfield), the bulk of Newnham and Awre, and Northwood tithing, in Westbury, sending representatives to the swanimote.[41] For practical purposes, however, the Forest administration was then only concerned with the royal demesne, and the demesne was accepted as constituting the Forest in 1833 when the Dean Forest commissioners cited the bounds of 1300 but perambulated and reported only on the royal demesne.[42]

The royal demesne land of the Forest as it existed in the 19th century was the residue of a much larger area of woodland and waste that had been reduced over the centuries by assarting and by royal grants. The earliest and most significant encroachments upon it occurred largely unrecorded during the 12th century. They included the formation from many individual assarts of the bulk of Newland, which gained the status of a separate manor and parish at the start of the 13th century, the creation of Flaxley by a gift of Roger, earl of Hereford, to his foundation Flaxley abbey c. 1150, the reconstitution of Staunton and Hewelsfield, and on the south-eastern fringes of the demesne the emergence of the small manors of Blakeney, added to Awre parish,[43] Walmore at Northwood, added to Westbury parish,[44] and probably Blythes Court

28 Close R. 1227–31, 98–9.
29 V.C.H. Glos. x. 51; P.R.O., E 32/29, rot. 7d.; E 32/30, rott. 12, 14d., 21d. 30 P.R.O., E 32/31, m. 5.
31 Ibid. E 32/30, rot. 8d.; E 32/31, m. 15.
32 Trans B.G.A.S. xxix. 301. 33 P.R.O., E 32/31, m. 9.
34 Ibid., E 123/19, ff. 151–152v.; E 134/36 Eliz. I Hil./21; Glos. R.O., D 2026/X 5; cf. P.R.O., MR 397 (E 178/7035), evidently the map mentioned as made during the suit. For Piper's grove, cf. Glos. R.O., D 326/E 1, f. 5; O.S. Map 1", sheet 43 (1831 edn.). A perambulation of c. 1680 repeated the supposed bounds: Rudder, Glos. App. III.
35 Below, this chapter. 36 V.C.H. Glos. x. 1.
37 3rd Rep. Com. Woods (1788), 59–60.
38 Forest Metes and Bounds Act, 16 Chas. I, c. 16.
39 Acts & Ords. of Interr. ed. Firth & Rait, ii. 114–15.
40 Dean Forest Act, 19 & 20 Chas. II, c. 8.
41 Glos. R.O., D 36/Q 2; N.L.W., Dunraven MSS. 330.
42 2nd Rep. Dean Forest Com. 23–37.
43 Above, Awre, Flaxley, Hewelsfield, Newland, and Staunton (intro. and manors sections). 44 V.C.H. Glos. x. 80, 91.

in Newnham[45] and Soilwell in Lydney.[46] The continuing pressure on land in the 13th century is reflected, among other examples, by encroachments on the demesne on the east side of St. Briavels parish,[47] considerable assarts made by the lords of Littledean,[48] 180 a. of assart, probably on the hillsides above Newnham, held by the woodward of Blaize bailiwick in 1306,[49] and, in one of the areas only nominally attached to the Forest, 200 a. assarted from Tidenham chase before 1282 by Tintern abbey (Mon.), owner of Woolaston manor.[50] In most cases the Crown gave retrospective sanction to the assarts by levying small rents, and it followed a more deliberate policy for all forests in the early 14th century, appointing commissioners in 1303[51] and 1313[52] to dispose of unwanted land to interested parties at fee-farm rents, and presumably for initial fines. Bearse bailiwick on the west side of the demesne was dismembered at the period, with 212 a. at Prior's Mesne added by Llanthony priory to its Aylburton estate in 1306,[53] John of Wyesham, constable of St. Briavels, obtaining a substantial estate at Noxon, near Clearwell, in 1317, and John Joce, the woodward of the bailiwick, securing large tracts of land in the same area.[54]

Detached parts of Newland parish on the fringes of the demesne or forming islands within it[55] were probably mostly taken out of the demesne between 1305, when the impropriator of Newland church was given the tithes from all recent and future assarts in the Forest,[56] and the Black Death in 1349, when the era of pressure on land ended. Detached parts near the main body of Newland parish, at Bream, Yorkley, and Ellwood, had certainly been wholly or partly created by the mid 14th century,[57] and some more distant parts at Lea Bailey, on the Herefordshire border, were recorded from the early 15th century.[58] Small detached parts at Lower Lydbrook and in the Oakwood brook valley were apparently made in the early 15th century in connexion with the building of mills on parcels of waste.[59]

An island called Whitemead park, inclosed before 1283 and added to Newland parish, remained in Crown ownership and was sometimes accounted a part of the Forest demesne later.[60] Abbots wood, covering c. 880 a. on the east side of the Soudley brook valley, also had an anomalous status after the Crown granted it to Flaxley abbey in 1258 quit of forest law but with the

herbage, hunting, and mineral rights reserved. The wood later remained the freehold of the owners of the Flaxley estate but for some purposes it was administered with the royal demesne.[61]

Gifts, sales, and leases made by Charles I in the 1620s effectively disafforested c. 3,000 a. of the royal demesne, and the bulk of the remainder was disafforested when sold to Sir John Winter in 1640, though that sale was rescinded in 1642.[62] The Act of 1668 reafforested the demesne and applied it to producing timber for the navy and most of the alienated lands were recovered,[63] but woods called the Snead and Kidnalls, covering c. 280 a. near Lydney, and Mailscot, c. 800 a. on the north-west of the demesne between English Bicknor and Staunton, remained outside the Forest and became parts of the Lydney and Highmeadow estates respectively.[64] Although severed from the royal demesne, the Snead, Kidnalls, and Mailscot remained extraparochial land until parochialized with the demesne in 1842.[65]

In 1668 the surviving royal demesne land was estimated at c. 23,000 a.,[66] and in 1788 it was surveyed as 23,250 a.[67] Its main portion was by then confined to the higher ground at the centre of the old Forest area. On the north, east, and south its bounds mostly followed steep ridges, but the boundary with the Wyeside parishes to the west was less clearly defined by the lie of the land. The chief irregularities in the shape of the main part of the demesne, apart from the islands of Newland parish within it, were to the north, where a spur included the Lea Bailey woods on the Herefordshire boundary, and on the north-west, where, following the exclusion of Mailscot wood, a narrow strip of waste extended along the road from Berry Hill to Symonds Yat rock. Detached parts of the royal demesne were Walmore common (240 a. in 1788) and a small parcel called Northwood green, both within Westbury, Hudnalls covering c. 1,200 a. above the Wye Valley adjoining St. Briavels and Hewelsfield parishes, Bearse common, the Fence, and Mocking Hazel wood, within or adjoining St. Briavels, and the Glydden, within Newland parish near Lower Redbrook.[68]

The royal demesne was further reduced in 1827 when the Crown sold its rights in Hudnalls, which was by then much encroached, Mocking Hazel, and the Fence.[69] In 1869 it sold

45 Ibid. 39; above, St. Briavels hundred.
46 Above, Lydney, manors.
47 Above, St. Briavels, intro.
48 Above, Littledean, manors.
49 Cal. Inq. p.m. iv, p. 236.
50 V.C.H. Glos. x. 103, 107.
51 Cal. Pat. 1301–7, 156, 310, 429, 531; cf. P.R.O., C 115/K 2/6683, f. 89.
52 Cal. Fine R. 1307–19, 164, 183.
53 Above, Lydney, manors.
54 Above, Newland, intro.; manors.
55 For Newland's detached parts, ibid. intro. (Table I); above, Fig. 13.
56 Cal. Pat. 1301–7, 319. Although intended, to an unspecified extent, as retrospective, the grant met opposition from tithe owners of other parishes and it is unlikely that many pre-1305 assarts were secured to Newland: ibid. 547; Cal. Close, 1307–13, 85; Rot. Parl. i. 200, 317; Reg. Orleton, 319–20.
57 Above, Newland, intro.
58 In 1437 land formerly held by a man of Lea, land held by a man of Hope Mansell, land 'at Pontshill', and land at Meryvale (probably the later Merryfold farm) paid rents to the Crown's lessee: Berkeley Cast. Mun., General Ser. acct. rolls 426; for Merryfold, cf. below, Settlement (other villages: Lea Bailey).
59 Below, Industry, mills.
60 Above, Newland, manors.
61 Cal. Chart. R. 1257–1300, 11; 3rd Rep. Com. Woods (1788), 111–12.
62 Below, Forest Admin., exploitation 1603–68.
63 Ibid. reformed admin.
64 Above, Lydney, intro.; Eng. Bicknor, intro.
65 Dean Forest Poor-Relief Act, 5 & 6 Vic. c. 48.
66 Dean Forest Act, 19 & 20 Chas. II, c. 8.
67 3rd Rep. Com. Woods (1788), 111–12; the figure excludes Abbots wood and Whitemead park.
68 Ibid. 112; for the bounds, P.R.O., MR 415 (F 16/47); Atkinson, Map of Dean Forest (1847); above, Fig. 13.
69 Above, St. Briavels, intro.; econ. hist.

its rights in Abbots wood, which was disafforested under an inclosure award of 1872;[70] the freehold was bought back by the Crown in 1899.[71] In 1871 when the Crown inclosed the bulk of Walmore and Bearse commons both were disafforested.[72]

From the mid 18th century encroachments by cottagers removed from Crown control other land on the fringes of the central block of royal demesne, where new hamlets were formed. In 1838 the Crown conceded ownership of encroachments made before 1787 and later sold many others to the occupants;[73] by 1874 2,100 a. had been removed from the demesne in that

way. During the later 19th and the 20th centuries the Forest of Dean still constituted the whole 23,000–24,000 a. of the former royal demesne, but the land that was owned by the Crown and administered by the Commissioners of Woods, mainly inclosed timber plantations and commonable waste, was restricted to c. 19,200 a. by 1874,[74] and the area transferred to the Forestry Commission in 1924 was 19,347 a. Highmeadow woods, on the north-west of the Forest, bought by the Commissioners of Woods in 1817, and other local woodlands acquired by the Forestry Commission in the 20th century were administered with Dean but not part of it.[75]

SETTLEMENT

ON the royal demesne land of the Forest of Dean settlement before the 18th century was in the form of makeshift cabins inhabited by ironworkers, charcoal burners, and others while their operations were in progress or until they were expelled by the Forest authorities. Permanent villages and hamlets did not begin to form until the mid 18th century, and the one small town, Cinderford, was largely a creation of the mid 19th century. In the area treated in this account, however, some of the detached parts of Newland within or adjoining the north-east part of the demesne, including those which formed Lea Bailey tithing, had small farmsteads and a few cottages from an earlier period.

Some people were settled within the bounds of the royal demesne at Hillersland, north of Coleford, in the later 16th century.[76] There was a more significant movement of people into the Forest woodlands and waste after the establishment of the king's ironworks on the demesne in 1612 and the licensing of the lessees and other local ironmasters to take cordwood for their works. Leases of the king's ironworks to the earl of Pembroke in 1612[77] and to Sir Baynham Throckmorton and his partners in 1636 permitted the building of cabins necessary for the workmen,[78] but during that period many others took advantage of the felling and charcoaling operations to establish themselves illegally in the woodlands, often using stolen timber to make barrel staves, trenchers, and cardboard. In 1616 it was reported that 79 cabins inhabited by 346 people had been set up in the coppices where royal commissioners empowered to supply the ironmasters were felling,[79] and in 1628 44 cabins were enumerated in Bicknor bailiwick, most of them in Mailscot wood, and 41 in Blakeney bailiwick.[80] In 1637 John Broughton claimed that the lessees of the ironworks, whom he was trying to discredit so as to obtain a lease for himself, had allowed 160 cabins to become es-

tablished, whereas no more than 20 were needed for the works.[81] A peak of illegal settlement was apparently reached in the late 1640s when a group of parliamentary army officers carried on ironworks both within and outside the demesne with little control from the government or Forest officials. In 1649 the ironmasters were employing numerous cabiners, whose dwellings were largely built of timber and who further contributed to the destruction of the woods by keeping large herds of goats.[82] Moseley Green near Parkend, Oldcroft above Lydney, Whitecroft near Bream, Mirystock above Lydbrook, and 'Coleford's Eaves' were among the places inhabited by cabiners at the period.[83] At the justice seat of 1656 c. 80 dwellings on the royal demesne, including some on the outlying tracts near St. Briavels and at Walmore near Westbury, were presented; by then the needs of the ironworks had also attracted numbers of settlers to parochial lands situated close to the blast furnaces, including Whitemead park and Yorkley near Parkend.[84]

The first major expulsion of the illegal settlers was carried out by John Wade, who managed the ironworks and woodland for the Commonwealth government from 1653:[85] in 1662 royal commissioners stated that he had demolished as many as 400 cabins and cottages. The commissioners claimed that only five remained,[86] but either their inquiry was less than rigorous or, during the continuing uncertainty about government intentions for the Forest in the early 1660s, more squatters slipped back, and further measures were necessary. In 1671 the marquess of Worcester, warden of the Forest, ordered the demolition of all cabins except those necessary for the officially sanctioned cording and charcoaling operations of the ironmaster Paul Foley,[87] and in 1678 quarter sessions ordered the magistrates of the Forest division to remove all poor people from the waste and settle them in

---

70 Abbots Wood (Dean Forest) Act, 1870, 33 & 34 Vic. c. 8 (Local); Glos. R.O., Q/RI 52.
71 *Rep. Dean Forest Cttee.* (1958), 7.
72 Walmore and Bearse Common Inclosure Act, 29 & 30 Vic. c. 70 (Local and Personal); Glos. R.O., Q/RI 121, 153.
73 Below, Settlement.
74 *Dean Forest Select Cttee.* (1874), 2.
75 *Rep. Dean Forest Cttee.* (1958), 9, 11, plan at end.
76 G.D.R. wills 1568/152; Glos. R.O., D 1677/GG 529; P.R.O., MR 879 (F 17/1).

77 P.R.O., C 99/34.   78 Ibid. C 66/2740, no. 18.
79 Ibid. E 178/3837.   80 Ibid. E 178/5304, mm. 18–19.
81 *Cal. S.P. Dom.* 1637, 205.
82 P.R.O., LRRO 5/7A, inq. 1649; Hart, *Royal Forest*, 289.
83 P.R.O., E 178/5304, m. 11d.; LRRO 5/7A, inq. 1641; presentments 1649.
84 Glos. R.O., D 2026/X 14.
85 Cf. below, Forest Admin., exploitation 1603–68.
86 Hart, *Royal Forest*, 289.
87 Glos. R.O., D 2026/X 22.

adjoining parishes.[88] In 1680 a new government commission found *c.* 30 cabins, home to *c.* 100 people, many of whom were said to have lived all their lives within the royal demesne. The commissioners demolished the cabins and the encroachments around them and took steps to find the occupants legal settlement elsewhere.[89] In the following year a perambulation found only 8 cottages on the royal demesne of the Forest, in Chestnuts wood near Flaxley, at 'Bicknor's Lane End', and at a place called Buttocks End.[90]

Some of the cabiners removed at various times in the later 17th century settled on waste land in the north part of Littledean[91] and some in parts of Lea Bailey tithing,[92] and others may have included the small groups of new cottagers recorded in 1680 on a Lydney common[93] and on a Woolaston common.[94] The resettlement of *c.* 1680 was apparently made with the co-operation and active involvement of the local manorial owners: Sir Baynham Throckmorton of Clearwell, Sir Duncombe Colchester of Westbury, and Charles Winter of Lydney were among the magistrates making the order of 1678,[95] while the commission of 1680 included Throckmorton and was headed by the marquess of Worcester, owner of Tidenham and Woolaston manors and lessee of the Crown manors of Newland and St. Briavels.[96]

The late 17th century and the early 18th was a period when apparently the royal demesne was virtually uninhabited, though the statement *c.* 1710 that the six keepers' lodges, built in the 1670s, were the only dwellings on it[97] seems unreliable. By the mid 18th century the increasing slackness of the administration had allowed squatters to creep back once more, and the permanent establishment of settlements within the Forest was under way as miners and quarrymen built cottages, took in land for gardens, and raised animals around the perimeter of the extraparochial area. The encroachments, on which there were at least 134 dwellings in 1752,[98] were small and numerous and by 1788, when their number had grown to 1,771 covering 1,358 a., they contained 578 cottages.[99] The cottages were scattered randomly among the mines and quarries and were often in remote places. Many were in Worcester walk where much early building took place in the Berry Hill and Lydbrook areas. The cottages of the period, still often termed cabins, remained primitive low dwellings, sometimes erected hastily in the widespread belief, recorded in the mid 19th century, that the Forest authorities had no power to pull down those built overnight. Some were

TABLE II: COTTAGES AND ENCROACHMENTS ON CROWN LANDS 1752–1834

Walk	1752	1787		1811–12		1834	
	cottages	cottages	encroach-ments (acres)	cottages (1811)	encroach-ments (acres, 1812)	cottages	encroach-ments (acres)
Blakeney	24	98	196	136	244	251	246
Littledean	13	54	123	114	278	196	283
Parkend	19	115	418	160	517	304	532
Ruardean	29	95	326	188	553	290	555
Speech House	0	1	0.1	5	0.5	0	0.5
Worcester	49	222	296	276	491	421	491
TOTAL	134	585	1,359.1	879	2,083.5	1,462	2,107.5

Notes. Blakeney walk included the Lydney road at Yorkley, Worcester walk included Hillersland, and Littledean walk in 1752 included Jas. Lloyd's ho. at Gunn's Mills, later accounted part of Abenhall parish: above, Abenhall. The returns on which the survey of 1752 was based gave slightly different figs. for some walks and listed 15 cottages in an unidentified part of the Forest: Berkeley Cast. Mun., General Ser. T, box 25. The areas given as encroachments in 1812 and 1834 include a few acres granted by the Crown in the 1830s in fee simple or in exchange for old encroachments: cf. *2nd Rep. Dean Forest Com.* 24.

Sources: Berkeley Cast. Mun., General Ser. T, box 25, partic. of cottages 1752; P.R.O., F 16/31, ff. 2–62 (surv. of Dean Forest by A. and W. Driver 1787); *Census,* 1811; *2nd Rep. Dean Forest Com.* 37–84.

88 Ibid. Q/SO 1, f. 181.   89 Hart, *Royal Forest,* 300.
90 Glos. R.O., D 1677/GG 1223.   91 Above, Littledean, intro.
92 Glos. R.O., D 2026/R 6.   93 Above, Lydney, intro.
94 Glos. R.O., D 2700/MF 3/1.
95 Ibid. Q/SO 1, ff. 180–1; cf. ibid. D 2026/R 6.
96 Hart, *Royal Forest,* 178.

97 Atkyns, *Glos.* 384; cf. below, forest lodges.
98 Table II.
99 *3rd Rep. Com. Woods* (1788), 111–12: figures exclude encroachments and cottages in detached parts of the Forest such as the Fence, near St. Briavels, and Northwood green and Walmore common, near Westbury-on-Severn.

of turf and a few of wood, mud, or rushes, but most had dry stone walls and turf roofing. They were generally windowless with a paved floor and, at one end, a fireplace and a chimney.[1]

The process of encroachment continued well into the 19th century. From 1808, when it was rigorously opposed by the Crown, hedges or palings were often moved forward surreptitiously, but that ruse resulted in only a small increase in the total area of the encroachments,[2] which was over 2,000 a. in 1834.[3] In 1838 the Crown conceded freehold status to the older encroachments on its demesne and gave holders of land inclosed between 1787 and 1834 the choice of purchasing it within 10 years or of leasing it.[4] Many Foresters opted to purchase in the period 1840–5. After 1834 encroachment, which was mainly in the form of minor incursions over the boundaries of existing plots, continued to be resisted firmly by the Forest administration, acting through a revived verderers' court.[5] Encroachment and building also occurred in Abbots wood, an estate on the east side of the Forest acquired by William Crawshay from the Crawley-Boeveys in 1836,[6] and titles to property there were not secured until 1872 when commoning rights on the estate were extinguished. The Crown, which had released its remaining rights in the estate to Henry Crawshay in 1869,[7] purchased back most of the land in 1899.[8]

With the expansion of the mining and ironworking industries in the early 19th century many new cottages were built in the Forest. By 1841 there were 1,873 dwellings there, 1,770 being on Crown land and the remainder on the Abbots wood estate in the Cinderford bridge, Ruspidge, and Soudley areas.[9] During that period two-storeyed cottages, mainly of local sandstone and of rusticated appearance, were built, some of them replacing cabins. A few employers provided terraced cottages and some poorer families made their homes in abandoned drift mines.[10] After the 1830s the pattern of settlement was severely circumscribed by the halting of the process of encroachment. Most new building took place on closes of land formed before 1834 and made freehold by 1845. The Crown, which released land for endowing churches and building church schools, sold many small strips of land mixed up with the freehold plots after 1855 but the high prices it demanded discouraged many Foresters from enlarging their holdings lawfully and potential new settlers from buying land. As a result only part of the rapid population increase accompanying industrial growth in the mid 19th century was housed within the Forest waste and, to meet the demand for accommodation, land societies developed from the 1850s a few small estates

on ancient parochial land adjoining the Forest, notably on the east side at Cinderford and on the west side near Coleford. Within the Forest, where there were 4,232 inhabited dwellings in 1871,[11] many semi-detached cottages were built next to older dwellings and several disused industrial buildings became dwellings. Little building took place in the central area, where there had been few encroachments before 1834 and where the provision of houses near the larger industrial concerns was inhibited by the reluctance of the Crown to surrender land for terms longer than 31 years and by the lack of roads.[12]

By the end of the century settlement sprawled haphazardly over the hillsides around the edge of the Forest. Villages and hamlets merged into one another and many lacked clear focal points. The small town of Cinderford was an exception. Much building had taken place with scant regard to sanitation[13] and the replacement or demolition of the old cabins, which had accelerated after 1838 when many Foresters became freeholders, had not been completed in some of the remoter districts.[14] Many dwellings were no better than hovels[15] and from the 1920s, when the shortage of habitable cottages forced families to take up residence in huts and other temporary buildings on Crown land,[16] local councils provided new houses. The compulsory demolition of ramshackle and insanitary cottages was under way by the later 1930s,[17] and during the later 20th century many settlements came to be dominated by estates of council houses and bungalows. Piecemeal private building and rebuilding continued and produced many new houses and bungalows in a wide variety of styles.

The rapid increase in the Forest's population had begun by 1788 when c. 2,000 people lived on Crown land.[18] In 1811 the population of the extraparochial area, presumably including Abbots wood but not extraparochial land on Littledean hill later forming the parish of Hinder's Lane and Dockham, was 4,073. Between 1811 and 1881 the extraparochial area saw a more than fivefold increase in its population and, whereas in the later 18th century the north-west side of the Forest had been more heavily populated than other places, new villages and hamlets sprang up elsewhere and Cinderford, on the east side, became a town. Cinderford and some of the villages, including Lydbrook, lay partly outside the Forest, so their growth is not fully reflected in Table III. Over the Forest as a whole, as represented by the townships of East and West Dean, the rate of population increase slackened after 1881 and a small decline in East Dean in the 1890s was presumably caused by the closure of local ironworks. In the early 20th

1 Nicholls, *Forest of Dean*, 151–2; P.R.O., F 16/31, ff. 2–62.
2 Fisher, *Custom and Capitalism*, 23, 35.
3 Above, Table II.
4 Dean Forest Encroachments Act, 1 & 2 Vic. c. 42.
5 Fisher, *Custom and Capitalism*, 107–9; below, Forest Admin., replanting and reorganization.
6 *New Regard of Forest of Dean*, vi. 40.
7 Glos. R.O., Q/RI 52.
8 *78th Rep. Com. Woods*, H.C. 242, p. 24 (1900), xvii.
9 Glos. R.O., Q/FR 4/1, f. 144.

10 Nicholls, *Forest of Dean*, 151–2.
11 *Census*, 1871, s.vv. E. and W. Dean.
12 *Dean Forest Select Cttee.* (1874), *passim*; Fisher, *Custom and Capitalism*, 107–9.
13 *Dean Forest Select Cttee.* (1874), p. iii.
14 *Glouc. Jnl.* 18, 25 Dec. 1897.
15 P.R.O., F 3/1275.
16 Glos. R.O., DA 24/950/2, pp. 228, 239.
17 Ibid. DA 24/100/12, pp. 13–14.
18 *3rd Rep. Com. Woods* (1788), 41.

Walk	1801	1811	1821	1831	1841
Blakeney	592	598	857	1,107	1,307
Littledean	355	513	773[a]	1,227	2,597[b]
Parkend	656	761	1,214	1,566	2,298
Ruardean	620	908	1,060	1,343	2,365
Speech House	9	20	43	50	66
Worcester	1,093	1,273	1,588	1,721	2,059
TOTAL	3,325	4,073	5,535	7,014	10,692

Township	1851	1861	1871	1881	1891	1901	1911	1921	1931
East Dean	7,482	9,547	11,270	12,909	13,298	13,160[c]	14,594	15,010	14,678
West Dean	6,084	8,254	9,591	9,289	9,106	9,995[d]	10,570	11,614	11,432
TOTAL	13,566	17,801	20,861	22,198	22,404	23,155	25,164	26,624	26,110

Civil parish (with date of creation)	1951	1961	1971	1981	1991
Cinderford (1953)	6,982	6,918	6,939	7,224	7,658
Drybrook (1953, altered 1957)	2,852	2,832	2,905	2,719	2,745
Lydbrook (1935)	2,562	2,465	2,310	2,392	2,329
Ruspidge (1953)	2,025	2,108	2,201	2,394	2,420
West Dean (altered 1935)	10,783	9,939	10,501	10,872	12,155
TOTAL	25,204	24,262	24,856	25,601	27,307

Notes. The figures for 1851–1901 are for the townships before boundary changes of the 1880s and 1890s; those for 1911–91 are for the townships and later civil parishes covering most of the former extraparochial area. The detached parts of Newland parish which made up Lea Bailey tithing had a population of 86 in 1801, rising to 279 by 1881, an increase mainly accounted for by new building in part of Cinderford. The figures for East Dean include for 1851 extraparochial land on Dean hill and for 1851–1901 extraparochial land on Littledean hill which became the parish of Hinder's Lane and Dockham in 1869: P.R.O., HO 107/1959; below, Local Government.

a   The return for Littledean included 123 people living on extraparochial land, presumably on Littledean and Dean hills, adjoining the parish.

b   Including people living on the Abbots wood estate and on the extraparochial land on Littledean and Dean hills: P.R.O., HO 107/364.

c   14,588 in the township as constituted in 1911.

d   10,037 in the township as constituted in 1911.

Source: Census, 1801–1991

century the population rose to 26,624 by 1921 but later it declined as the mining industry waned and people emigrated. The creation of new civil parishes and other boundary changes in the mid 20th century obscured population trends in the former extraparochial Forest after the Second World War but it appears that, with the exception of the Lydbrook area, the general decline halted in the 1960s and that the number of residents grew in the 1980s to exceed what it had been in 1921.

[19] Glos. R.O., Q/SO 1, ff. 71, 182v.

The evolution of settlement in the 18th and 19th centuries gave rise to an intricate network of lanes and paths between encroachments on the edge of the Forest, and in only a few places did those lanes follow the major roads that crossed the royal demesne. In the later 17th century three important roads ran westwards to converge on Coleford.[19] The road from Mitcheldean, used by traffic between Gloucester and South Wales in the 1670s, climbed Plump hill[20] but by the mid 18th century it took a

[20] Ogilby, *Britannia* (1675), p. 30, plate 15.

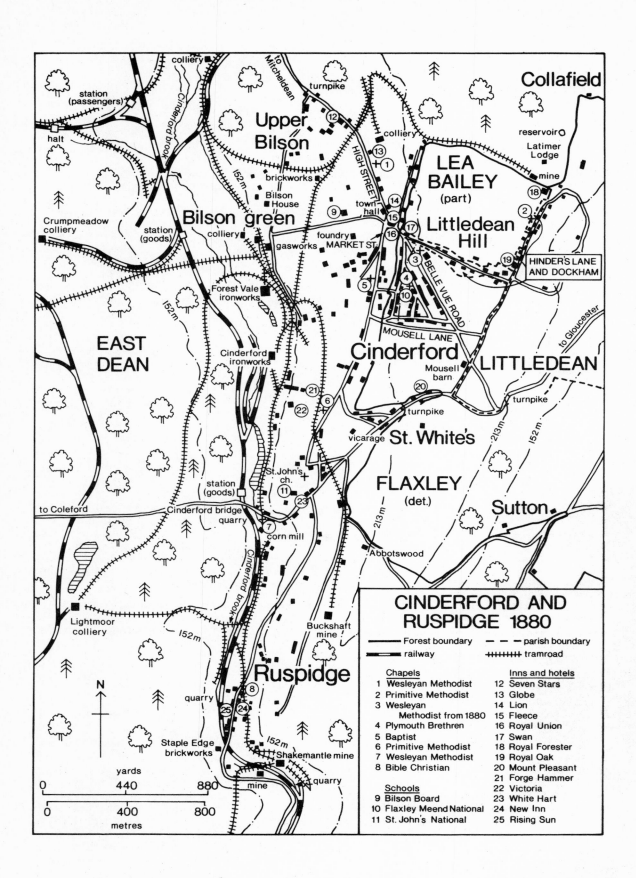

CINDERFORD AND RUSPIDGE 1880

—— Forest boundary   – – – parish boundary
▬▬▬ railway   ++++++ tramroad

Chapels
1 Wesleyan Methodist
2 Primitive Methodist
3 Wesleyan
    Methodist from 1880
4 Plymouth Brethren
5 Baptist
6 Primitive Methodist
7 Wesleyan Methodist
8 Bible Christian

Schools
9 Bilson Board
10 Flaxley Meend National
11 St. John's National

Inns and hotels
12 Seven Stars
13 Globe
14 Lion
15 Fleece
16 Royal Union
17 Swan
18 Royal Forester
19 Royal Oak
20 Mount Pleasant
21 Forge Hammer
22 Victoria
23 White Hart
24 New Inn
25 Rising Sun

FIG. 15

different route, entering the Forest at Stenders and running over Harrow hill.[21] The road from Littledean, which entered the Forest at St. White's and crossed the Cinderford and Cannop brooks by small bridges, was also used by traffic between Gloucester and South Wales in the later 18th century. The road from Purton passage on the Severn ran over Viney hill and through Parkend where it crossed Cannop brook by a bridge near the north end of Whitemead park. The road was used in the later 18th century for taking timber out of the Forest to the river at Purton and Gatcombe.[22] Also still in use in the later 17th century and kept in repair until 1768 or later was the ancient pitched road called the Dean road, supposedly Roman, which linked Mitcheldean and Littledean with Lydney by way of bridges at Soudley and over Blackpool brook near Blakeney hill.[23] In the mid 18th century a road between Ross-on-Wye (Herefs.) and Chepstow (Mon.) crossed Blackpool brook east of Moseley Green.[24] In the later 18th century several roads were improved[25] and in 1796 turnpike trustees were appointed to look after those forming parts of the routes to Coleford from Mitcheldean, Littledean, and Purton and Gatcombe, the route between Mitcheldean and Littledean, and a road to Lydbrook branching from the Mitcheldean–Coleford route at Mirystock.[26] The trustees built several new roads, including in the late 1820s those from Parkend to Bream and from Littledean to Nailbridge and in 1841 those leading from the Mitcheldean–Coleford road at Edge End towards Staunton and Monmouth, from Parkend to Blakeney, from Mitcheldean to Nailbridge by way of Plump hill, from Nailbridge to Bishopswood, and from Drybrook to Bailey Lane End.[27] The road between Yorkley and Bream was constructed after 1859.[28] Those roads attracted some new building at the edge of the Forest, notably the Littledean–Nailbridge road which influenced the shape of Cinderford town. The most important roads made after the turnpike trust was abolished in 1888[29] were those linking Cinderford with Blakeney, completed in 1890,[30] and Lydbrook with Lydney, built 1902–5.[31] The Cinderford–Blakeney road encouraged new building at Ruspidge and Soudley and the Lydbrook–Lydney road, which ran southwards from Mirystock alongside Cannop brook, encouraged building at Cannop, Parkend, and Whitecroft. A number of local roads constructed

before the First World War and in the later 1920s[32] attracted some new building in established settlements.

CINDERFORD AND RUSPIDGE.

The town of Cinderford grew up in the 19th century to become the main settlement on the east side of the Forest. It took its name, recorded in 1258,[33] from the slag of early ironworks in the valley bottom at or near the place where the Littledean–Coleford road crossed the Cinderford (or Soudley) brook; a bridge had been built there by 1674.[34] Industrial development in that part of the Forest in the early 19th century, particularly the revival of the Cinderford ironworks in the late 1820s,[35] was accompanied by the building of many cottages and a substantial growth in population,[36] and in the 1840s the area near the bridge was chosen as the site for a school and a church. Later in the century the settlement grew into a small town with many of its shops, inns, and other meeting places to the north on or near the Littledean–Nailbridge road. The town continued to expand in the 20th century and extensive industrial development took place there after the Second World War.

In 1832 there were c. 51 dwellings east of the brook at Cinderford bridge, in the area then called Lower Cinderford.[37] Most were south of the road (St. White's Road) on Ruspidge Meend, which belonged to the Abbots wood estate[38] and where Edward Protheroe built cottages, including several terraces, for miners in his employment.[39] In 1841 the settlement at the bridge included a chapel and two beerhouses.[40] On the hillside to the north-east, known as Cinderford Tump, the White Hart inn had opened by 1834[41] and, to the west, a school was built by Edward Protheroe in 1840 and the church of St. John the Evangelist was opened in 1844.[42] At the ironworks, which stood 800 m. north of Cinderford bridge, cottages were built at the bottom of the later Victoria Street to the south-east. In 1832 the area, known as Upper Cinderford, included c. 38 houses,[43] mostly terraced cottages provided by the ironworks' owners, and a beerhouse called the Forge Hammer.[44] By the mid 19th century a few houses had been built further north on Bilson (formerly Cartway) green,[45] which later became the main industrial area of Cinderford. One house, next to Bilson colliery, was occupied by Edward

[21] Badminton Mun. FmS/G 2/4/4; P.R.O., MR 415 (F 16/47).   [22] *3rd Rep. Com. Woods* (1788), 83; P.R.O., MR 415.
[23] Glos. R.O., Q/SO 1, f. 71; P.R.O., MR 415; Berkeley Cast. Mun., General Ser. T, box 25, mem. to Treasury about road repairs 1768; A. W. Trotter, *Dean Road* (1936), *passim*.
[24] P.R.O., F 17/2.
[25] Badminton Mun. FmS/G 2/4/4; Nicholls, *Forest of Dean*, 194.   [26] Dean Forest Roads Act, 36 Geo. III, c. 131.
[27] Nicholls, *Forest of Dean*, 196–7; Dean Forest Roads Acts, 7 & 8 Geo. IV, c. 12 (Local and Personal); 1 & 2 Vic. c. 38 (Local and Personal).
[28] P.R.O., F 16/64; Dean Forest Roads Act, 21 & 22 Vic. c. 86 (Local and Personal).
[29] Dean Forest Turnpike Trust Abolition Act, 51 & 52 Vic. c. 193.
[30] P.R.O., LRRO 5/7B; Glos. R.O., DA 40/100/3, pp. 115–16; 4, pp. 2–3, 66–7.
[31] *80th Rep. Com. Woods*, H.C. 247, p. 3 (1902), xxi; *81st*

Rep. Com. Woods, H.C. 232, p. 3 (1903), xviii; *83rd Rep. Com. Woods*, H.C. 221, p. 3 (1905), xxii.
[32] Glos. R.O., DA 24/297; DA 25/701/1.
[33] *Cal. Chart. R.* 1257–1300, 11.
[34] Glos. R.O., Q/SO 1, ff. 71, 182v.
[35] Below, Industry, ironworks.
[36] Above, Tables II and III, s.v. Littledean walk.
[37] *3rd Rep. Dean Forest Com.* 11.
[38] Glos. R.O., Q/RGf 1/7; P.R.O., F 17/76.
[39] Glos. R.O., Q/RUm 160; Mountjoy, *Dean Collier*, 19.   [40] Glos. R.O., Q/FR 4/1, ff. 79, 136.
[41] *Glouc. Jnl.* 6 Sept. 1834.
[42] Nicholls, *Forest of Dean*, 171–2.
[43] *3rd Rep. Dean Forest Com.* 11.
[44] Glos. R.O., Q/RGf 1/7; *2nd Rep. Dean Forest Com.* 65; *Reg. Electors W. Division Glos. 1832–3*, 112.
[45] Glos. R.O., Q/RGf 1/7; Atkinson, *Map of Dean Forest* (1847).

Protheroe's agent Aaron Goold in 1831, when the fences around its enclosure were destroyed by rioters.[46] Known later as Bilson House, it was demolished after 1973, during redevelopment of the area.[47]

In the later 19th century Cinderford's development centred on the hillside east of Bilson in the area known at that time as Woodside,[48] Littledean Woodside, or Bilson Woodside.[49] Building had begun there before 1782, when eight cottages were standing on encroachments on the edge of the royal demesne in the area of the later Heywood Road.[50] At the same time cottages were built on extraparochial land to the east in Dockham Road (formerly Hinder's Lane) and higher up on Littledean hill,[51] and in 1832 there were c. 86 cottages at and above Woodside.[52] The settlement of Littledean Hill, on a ridge overlooking Littledean to the east, also included cottages on land belonging to Littledean parish and Lea Bailey tithing.[53] The Royal Forester inn near the Forest keeper's lodge called Latimer Lodge was recorded from 1838[54] and, further south, a chapel was built in 1824[55] and an inn called the Royal Oak had opened by 1838.[56] The oldest dwelling on the hill was possibly a farmhouse standing at the east end of Dockham Road in 1797, in the area known later as Dockham and within Flaxley parish.[57] To the south at St. White's there were one or two cottages on Crown land adjoining the Littledean–Coleford road by the late 1760s[58] and a public house had opened there, in the area called Mount Pleasant, by 1841.[59]

In the mid 19th century houses were built at Woodside on land adjoining the Littledean–Nailbridge road. The road, made in the late 1820s,[60] descended north-westwards from Mousell barn, near St. White's, along Belle Vue Road across Flaxley Meend, and along High Street within the Forest.[61] By the mid 1830s there was a cluster of cottages at the top of High Street by a tollgate west of the junction of Dockham Road with the new route[62] and a few cottages had been built on Mousell Lane, an old route over Flaxley Meend.[63] Several more cottages had been erected near the tollgate by the mid 1850s,[64] and much new building had taken place in that area by the late 1860s. On the north-east side of High Street the

Swan hotel, at the bottom of Dockham Road, was built as a posting house in 1867 on the site of an earlier inn[65] and the Lion (formerly the Dolphin) inn, lower down, was built several years earlier.[66] In the late 1860s a town hall was built opposite the Lion on land formerly used for holding fairs.[67] Opened in 1869,[68] the hall had a large room on the first floor for concerts, meetings, and lectures and rooms on the ground floor for the sale of market produce and for offices.[69] In 1885 the lower floor accommodated a furniture shop[70] and later markets were held next to the Lion.[71] Lower down High Street empty spaces were filled and by the late 1870s new building had extended settlement north-west to the junction with Valley (formerly Upper Bilson) Road, to which point the tollgate had been moved. In the area south of the top end of High Street much of Market Street, which ran south from the town hall, and the northern ends of Commercial Street and Victoria (formerly Station) Street, into which Market Street divided, were built up between the mid 1850s and the late 1870s.[72] In 1877 a police station was built west of the town hall by the road to Bilson (later Station Street).[73] The area around the town hall became Cinderford's main shopping area.

An important factor in the development of the town centre was new building in Flaxley Meend, part of the Flaxley Abbey estate, to the south-east.[74] Wesley, a large chapel at the bottom of Belle Vue Road, was built in 1849[75] by Aaron Goold, who a few years later built St. Annals (formerly Belle Vue House) to the south-east as his residence.[76] Both buildings were set originally in wooded grounds and gardens.[77] The house became an institute in the early 20th century[78] and was used as offices by East Dean and United Parishes rural district council and its successors from 1929 until 1991.[79] Two cottages north-west of the chapel were converted c. 1880 by the industrialist Jacob Chivers as his residence, which became a manse in 1912 and was demolished in 1990.[80] The northern end of Woodside Street, running south from the junction of Belle Vue Road and Dockham Road, had been formed by 1859, when building was under way on its west side, and the area to the south, extending to Mousell Lane and bounded on the

46 P.R.O., F 16/63 (no. 2425); F 16/70; R. Anstis, *Warren James and Dean Forest Riots* (1986), 120.
47 O.S. Maps 6", Glos. XXXI. SE. (1883 edn.); 1/2,500, SO 6514 (1974, 1991 edns.).
48 G.D.R., T 1/128.
49 Glos. R.O., DA 6/100; D 2516/6/1; DC/H 29; *Glouc. Jnl.* 29 June 1867.
50 P.R.O., F 17/4; cf. ibid. MR 415.
51 Cf. surv. of Sir Thos. Crawley-Boevey's estates 1797 (no. 8): copy in Glos. R.O., MF 285; O.S. Map 1/2,500, Glos. XXXI. 11 (1881 edn.).
52 *3rd Rep. Dean Forest Com.* 11.
53 O.S. Map 6", Glos. XXXI. SE. (1883 edn.).
54 Glos. R.O., Q/RZ 1; G.D.R., T 1/128 (no. 2703).
55 Glos. R.O., D 2297; Q/RUm 107.
56 Ibid. Q/RZ 1; O.S. Map 6", Glos. XXXI. SE. (1883 edn.).
57 Surv. of Crawley-Boevey est. 1797 (no. 8); O.S. Map 6", Glos. XXXI. SE. (1883 edn.).
58 Glos. R.O., Q/SO 9, ff. 64v., 92; cf. P.R.O., MR 415.
59 P.R.O., HO 107/364, s.v. Littledean walk.
60 Nicholls, *Forest of Dean*, 197.
61 O.S. Map 1", sheet 43 (1831 edn.).

62 Glos. R.O., Q/RGf 1/7.
63 *Reg. Electors W. Division Glos. 1832–3*, 107, 111.
64 P.R.O., F 16/63.   65 *Glouc. Jnl.* 29 June 1867.
66 Ibid. 5 Sept. 1868; Mountjoy, *Dean Collier*, 26.
67 *Glos. Chron.* 29 June 1867; O.S. Map 1/2,500, Glos. XXXI. 11 (1881 edn.).
68 *Glouc. Jnl.* 15 May 1869.
69 *Morris's Dir. Glos.* (1876), 466.
70 *Kelly's Dir. Glos.* (1885), 420–1.
71 O.S. Map 1/2,500, Glos. XXXI. 11 (1902 edn.).
72 P.R.O., F 16/63; O.S. Maps 6", Glos. XXXI. NE., SE. (1883–4 edn.); 1/2,500, Glos. XXXI. 11 (1881 edn.).
73 Date on bldg.
74 Glos. R.O., D 4543/2/2/3.
75 Date on bldg.
76 *Glouc. Jnl.* 28 July 1849; 6 July 1850; 21 June 1862; in 1851 Goold's fam. still lived at Bilson Ho.: P.R.O., HO 107/1959, s.v. E. Dean.
77 O.S. Map 1/2,500, Glos. XXXI. 11 (1881 edn.).
78 P.R.O., F 3/1272.
79 Glos. R.O., DA 24/100/10, pp. 677–9; *Dean Forest Mercury*, 11 Jan. 1991.
80 *Dean Forest Mercury*, 23 Mar. 1990.

north-east by Belle Vue Road, was laid out for housing by a land society.[81] Building in the new streets, based on the triangle formed by Woodside Street, Abbey Street, and Flaxley Street, was piecemeal and continued in the mid 1870s[82] when the area was known as New Town.[83] To the north the east side of Woodside Street and the south-west side of Belle Vue Road were filled with houses later in the century.[84] The number of houses in Flaxley Meend, where the population grew by over 800 in the 1860s,[85] increased from 14 in 1851 to 234 in 1891.[86]

Elsewhere in Cinderford building continued in a haphazard fashion after 1840 and was mainly confined to scattered encroachments made before 1834.[87] At Bilson industrial development included gasworks erected in 1860,[88] and a large school was built north of the road to the town centre (later Station Street) in 1877.[89] To the north at Upper Bilson, at the north-west end of the town, where there were eight cottages including a beerhouse in 1841,[90] most houses were built after 1856.[91] On the east side of the town Ladywell Manor (formerly St. Annal's Lodge), north of Dockham Road, was probably built by Aaron Goold.[92] In the later 19th century Cinderford's population more than trebled. In the area north of St. White's Road including Bilson, Upper Bilson, Flaxley Meend, and Littledean Hill it rose from 1,730 to 5,920 and the number of houses increased from 344 to 1,184 between 1851 and 1891.[93]

The development of the west side of the town was greatly influenced by the construction in the late 1890s of Valley Road, which followed the line of an abandoned tramroad north from Cinderford bridge and crossed the site of the Cinderford ironworks.[94] Two ranges, the only buildings of the ironworks to survive, were converted as terraced cottages.[95] In 1897 and 1898 the Crown improved two routes leading down to the new road, one westwards from High Street to the Bilson gasworks by way of Wesley Road and part of Station Street and the other south-westwards along Victoria Street.[96] At the bottom of Station Street the terminus of a new stretch of railway was opened on the north side and a hotel was built opposite it in 1900.[97] Piecemeal development continued on all sides of Cinderford in the early 20th century and on the Double View estate at the top of Belle Vue Road, south of Littledean Hill, it had begun by 1896.[98] In 1924 East Dean and United Parishes rural

district council built 10 houses in Church Road, the continuation southwards of Commercial Street to St. White's Road. Council houses were built later in Victoria Street and on the site of Mousell barn at the top of Belle Vue Road, and the demolition of older dwellings deemed uninhabitable had begun by 1937, when an estate of 46 council houses was completed north of St. White's Road.[99] After the Second World War two large council estates grew up on the north side of the town. The Hilldene estate, in the Heywood Road area north-east of the town centre, was started in 1948. The first houses on the Denecroft estate, also begun in 1948, were at Upper Bilson and by the 1980s the estate had spread south-westwards to fill much of the area, including former railway land, bounded by Station Street and Valley Road. Council houses and bungalows were also built in the Victoria Street area in the 1960s.[1] After 1945 many small bungalows were built privately in Cinderford, some in place of older stone cottages, and from the 1960s a number of private housing estates were also built.[2] By 1992, as a result of infilling, the town's housing estates stretched as far as Littledean Hill on the east and St. White's Road on the south-east. The west side of the town remained its principal industrial area, although a large engineering factory dating from the late 1940s[3] at the bottom of Station Street was disused in 1992. From the late 1960s there was considerable redevelopment around the north end of Valley Road with the laying out of new industrial estates and roads and the building of new factories.[4] Further south some houses were built east of Valley Road in the 1980s.

Alterations to the town centre in the 20th century included the removal before the First World War of a building at the centre of the area known later as the Triangle, on the east side of Market Street near the entrance to Station Street.[5] A memorial to townsmen killed during the war was unveiled there in 1923.[6] In an extensive redevelopment in the late 1950s and early 1960s to widen the streets and form a larger open space in the centre, the buildings on the south-west side of High Street, down to and including the town hall, and on the east side of the north end of Market Street were demolished.[7] South-east of the new centre a row of shops was built in High Street in 1965.[8] The west end of Dockham Road was remodelled later to accommodate a bus station and was further

[81] Glos. R.O., D 4543/2/2/3; *Dean Forest Select Cttee.* (1874), 36.
[82] Glos. R.O., D 543, deeds 18 May 1867; 6 Mar. 1875.
[83] *Forest of Dean Examiner*, 28 May 1875.
[84] O.S. Map 1/2,500, Glos. XXXI. 11 (1881, 1902 edns.).
[85] *Census*, 1861–71, s.v. Flaxley.
[86] P.R.O., HO 107/1959, s.v. Flaxley; RG 12/2006, s.v. E. Dean.
[87] Glos. R.O., Q/RGf 1/7; P.R.O., F 16/63; O.S. Map 6", Glos. XXXI. SE. (1883 edn.).
[88] Glos. R.O., D 2516/6/1.　　[89] *Glouc. Jnl.* 8 Dec. 1877.
[90] Glos. R.O., Q/FR 4/1, ff. 85–6.
[91] P.R.O., F 16/63; O.S. Map 6", Glos. XXXI. SE. (1883 edn.).
[92] *Kelly's Dir. Glos.* (1863), 254; O.S. Map 6", Glos. XXXI. SE. (1883 edn.).
[93] P.R.O., HO 107/1959, s.vv. E. Dean, Flaxley, extra-par. place in Littledean walk; HO 107/1976, s.v. Lea Bailey hamlet; RG 12/2005–6, s.v. E. Dean.
[94] O.S. Map 6", Glos. XXXI. SE. (1883, 1903 edns.).
[95] Ibid. 1/2,500, Glos. XXXI. 11 (1881, 1902 edns.); one range was demolished in 1960: Hart, *Ind. Hist. of*

Dean, 127.
[96] Inscr. on markers at both ends of both routes.
[97] Glos. R.O., DA 24/100/2, pp. 214–15; 3, p. 204; Paar, *Severn and Wye Railway*, 83.
[98] Glos. R.O., DA 24/100/1, pp. 42, 141; cf. O.S. Map 6", Glos. XXXI. SE. (1903, 1924 edns.).
[99] Glos. R.O., DA 24/100/9–12, *passim*; DA 24/600/1.
[1] Ibid. DA 24/602/1–3; O.S. Map 1/2,500, SO 6514 (1960 and later edns.).
[2] W.I. portrait of Cinderford (1965, copy in Cinderford libr.).
[3] D. E. Evans, *Lister's: The First Hundred Years* (Glouc. 1979), 184.
[4] O.S. Maps 1/2,500, SO 6413–14, 6513–14 (1960 and later edns.); Glos. R.O., K 193/48.
[5] Phelps, *Forest in Old Photog.* (1983), 62; O.S. Map 1/2,500, Glos. XXXI. 11. (1902, 1922 edns.).
[6] *Glouc. Jnl.* 24 Nov. 1923.
[7] Glos. R.O., DA 24/132/75.
[8] W.I. portrait of Cinderford.

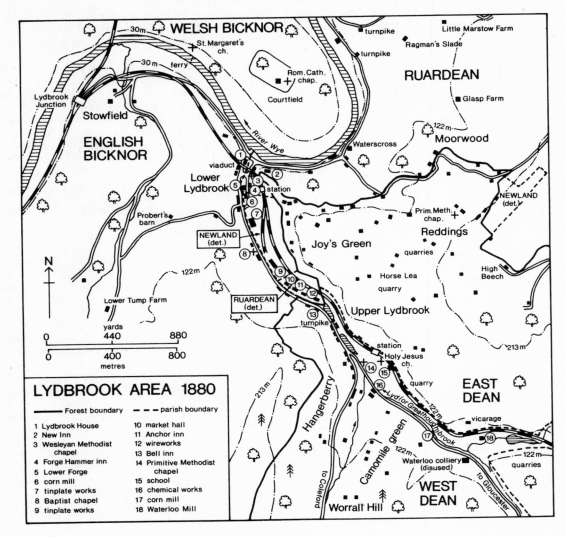

FIG. 16

redeveloped *c.* 1990 when a health centre and a supermarket were built on the north side.[9]

Before it became a suburb of Cinderford in the 20th century Ruspidge (formerly Ruspidge Meend), the area south of St. White's Road and east of Cinderford brook,[10] contained scattered cottages. Building presumably began before the 19th century, when Ruspidge belonged to the Abbots wood estate, and there were 45 inhabited cottages to the south of the settlement at Cinderford bridge in 1841.[11] William Crawshay, who worked mines there from the late 1820s and purchased the Abbots wood estate in 1836,[12] owned two rows of cottages near Buckshaft mine in 1838.[13] The Crawshays provided other dwellings, including *c.* 1864 Forest Lodge, a large house off St. White's Road.[14] Abbotswood, the

principal house in Ruspidge, stood in grounds higher up to the east and dated from a rebuilding of the 1840s for the Crawshays.[15] Henry Crawshay lived there in 1851 and his son Edwin[16] until the late 1870s.[17] A chapel was added soon after the house became a Church of England temperance home in 1907[18] and the house was remodelled after 1917 for A. J. Morgan[19] (d. 1936), a partner in the Crawshays' mining business.[20] Abbotswood, which became a convent and nursing home in 1939,[21] was demolished after 1960[22] but an entrance lodge dating from the 1870s[23] survived as part of a housing estate in 1992. Building continued in Ruspidge in a piecemeal fashion throughout the 19th century, including on Ruspidge Road, which in 1889 became part of a new road from Cinderford to

9   O.S. Map 1/2,500, SO 6514 (1960 and later edns.).
10   P.R.O., MR 415.
11   Glos. R.O., Q/FR 4/1, ff. 136–41.
12   Below, Industry, mining from 1770s; *New Regard of Forest of Dean*, vi. 40.
13   P.R.O., F 17/76; F 16/63 (nos. 2906–12, 2916–20); F 16/70.
14   Glos. R.O., Q/RI 52.
15   Sopwith, *Map of Dean Forest* (1835); P.R.O., F 17/76; F 16/63 (no. 2850); F 16/70.
16   P.R.O., HO 107/1959, s.v. E. Dean.

17   *Kelly's Dir. Glos.* (1863), 256; *Forest of Dean Examiner*, 14 Nov. 1873; *V.C.H. Glos.* x. 8.
18   *Glouc. Jnl.* 15 June 1907; Glos. Colln. (H) C 26.26.
19   Glos. R.O., D 2299/6296, 9567.
20   Ibid. P 85/CW 3/4; M. V. Bent, *Last Deep Mine of Dean* (1988), 20.
21   Glos. R.O., D 5467/6/1.
22   O.S. Map 1/2,500, SO 6512 (1960, 1991 edns.).
23   Glos. R.O., Q/RI 52; O.S. Map 6", Glos. XXXI. SE. (1883 edn.).

Soudley and Blakeney.[24] At the south end of Ruspidge a dozen cottages, among them a row owned by Edward Protheroe, stood on the hillside east of the Bullo Pill tramroad in 1838,[25] and a chapel was built in 1857.[26] West of the brook on Crown land below Staple Edge there were six cottages by 1856.[27] The first council houses in Ruspidge were 20 built in 1935 at the south end of Buckshaft Road to replace older cottages nearby.[28] Council houses built after the Second World War included a group of 26 at the north end of Ruspidge Road begun in 1956.[29] Several estates of private houses and bungalows were laid out from the 1960s, one of them in the former grounds of Abbotswood.[30]

LYDBROOK. The industrial village of Lydbrook on the northern side of the Forest forms a straggling settlement along a narrow valley formed by Greathough (or Lyd) brook as it descends to the river Wye.[31] A mill was working there in the mid 13th century[32] and an inhabitant of Lydbrook was recorded in 1282.[33] The earliest building was in the lower part of the valley, on parochial land divided between English Bicknor, Ruardean, and Newland,[34] where there was a succession of mills and forges by the late 16th century.[35] The road from Coleford to Ross-on-Wye ran west of the brook down to the village of Lower Lydbrook by the Wye; there it turned east and a lane to Stowfield, to the north-west, branched from it.[36] The Priory, a house at the corner of the old road to English Bicknor, has at its centre a three-bay cross wing of the 16th century. To its north is one bay of a contemporary main range, which may have been an open hall, and to the south a taller block of the early 17th century has a short chimney bay and a one-bay parlour. The earlier ranges appear to have been entirely timber framed with close studding of high quality but the ground-floor wall has mostly been rebuilt in rubble. The later block is of similar construction on a stone basement. The northern end of the 'hall' range was replaced in the later 18th century by a service range of two storeys. A dwelling called Boxbush House, recorded in 1597[37] and acquired later by the Vaughan family of Courtfield,[38] may have been on the site where in 1759 Richard Wheatstone built a house facing across the Ross road to a coal wharf on the Wye.[39] By 1806 that house had

become the New Inn[40] (later the Courtfield Arms), which was enlarged in the early 20th century.[41]

In the 18th and 19th centuries the expansion of the ironworks and the establishment of tinplate works above Lower Lydbrook[42] stimulated much new building in the valley. The ironmasters provided a number of cottages near their works[43] and in 1832 Lydbrook, including Upper Lydbrook, contained 256 cottages, 210 of them on the extraparochial land of the Forest.[44] In Lower Lydbrook cottages were built on both sides of the brook[45] and by the 1780s there were scattered dwellings higher up to the east within the extraparochial area.[46] Lydbrook House, one of two early 19th-century brick houses at the bottom of Lower Lydbrook, was built for James Pearce (d. 1827), the owner of an adjoining malthouse.[47] About 1840 it was the home of the ironmaster William Allaway.[48] To the north-west houses on or overlooking the Stowfield road, formed along the river bank in 1853,[49] include one built in 1872.[50] Higher up the Lydbrook valley, near the sites of the highest ironworks,[51] stands a 17th-century timber-framed house with a small early 18th-century wing; it is reputed to have been the childhood home of the actress Sarah Siddons (née Kemble in 1755).[52] In the same area there was a scattering of cottages, some of them on Crown land, by the 1750s[53] and an inn called the Bell in 1792.[54] East of the road the Anchor inn had opened by 1807[55] and a wooden market hall was built next to it in 1873.[56] From 1874 a viaduct carrying the Severn & Wye railway high across the Lydbrook valley was a dominant feature of Lower Lydbrook;[57] after its demolition in 1965[58] several buildings near the feet of its piers were removed to improve the Ross road and some new houses were built nearby. Although the ironworks and tinplate works closed before 1930,[59] the industrial character of the lower part of the Lydbrook valley was retained through the construction of new factories on some of their sites.

The earliest cottages in Upper Lydbrook, above Lower Lydbrook, were built in the 18th century. The pattern of settlement, on Crown land, was random.[60] By the 1820s, when Anglican and nonconformist chapels were erected there,[61] it extended some way up the valley and included small groups of cottages clinging to the hillsides to the south above a tributary of Greathough brook at the place called Hangerberry and on

24 P.R.O., LRRO 5/7B; Glos. R.O., DA 40/100/4, pp. 2–3.
25 P.R.O., F 17/76; Glos. R.O., Q/RUm 160.
26 Inscr. on bldg.
27 P.R.O., F 16/63 (nos. 3080–9); F 16/70.
28 Glos. R.O., DA 24/100/11, pp. 259–63, 273, 335, 348; DA 24/600/1.
29 Ibid. DA 24/602/1–3.
30 O.S. Maps 1/2,500, SO 6511 (1959, 1983 edns.); SO 6512 (1960, 1991 edns.).
31 P.R.O., F 17/96.
32 Cal. Pat. 1247–58, 524.
33 P.R.O., E 32/30, rot. 19.
34 G.D.R., T 1/25, 128, 151.
35 Below, Industry, ironworks; mills.
36 Glos. R.O., D 23/E 35.
37 N.L.W., Courtfield MSS. 116.
38 Glos. R.O., Q/RNc 1, pp. 40–2; 2/1, pp. 22–3.
39 Ibid. D 637/I/70; D 892/T 69; date and inits. on bldg.
40 Glouc. Jnl. 7 Apr. 1806.
41 O.S. Map 1/2,500, Glos. XXXI. 1 (1881 and later edns.).

42 Below, Industry, ironworks.
43 Glouc. Jnl. 9 Feb. 1818; G.D.R., T 1/25, 128, 151; P.R.O., F 16/64 (nos. 125–32); F 16/71.
44 3rd Rep. Dean Forest Com. 11.
45 G.D.R., T 1/25, 151.
46 P.R.O., MR 415.
47 Glos. R.O., D 5844/1.   48 G.D.R., T 1/25.
49 Glos. R.O., Q/SRh 1852 C/1; 1853 D.
50 Date on ho.
51 Cf. P.R.O., F 17/117(2), p. 44; MR 691 (LRRO 1/240).
52 Nicholls, Personalities of Dean, 83–4; D.N.B.
53 P.R.O., F 17/96.   54 Ibid. MR 691.
55 Glouc. Jnl. 30 Nov. 1807.
56 Forest of Dean Examiner, 20 Sept. 1873.
57 Paar, Severn and Wye Railway, 79; above, Plate 30.
58 Dean Forest Mercury, 30 July 1965.
59 Below, Industry, ironworks.
60 Cf. P.R.O., MR 415.
61 Below, Churches (Holy Jesus); Prot. Nonconf., Prim. Methodists.

Camomile green.[62] In 1743, when Viscount Gage, lord of English Bicknor manor, claimed ownership of Hangerberry, it was said that the Bicknor overseers had built a cottage and that an alehouse had been licensed[63] and in 1782 seven cottages were recorded there.[64] The road south-east up the main valley to Mirystock, part of the route to Mitcheldean, had little early building.[65] Random building continued from the 1840s in Upper Lydbrook, where in 1874 there were well over 197 houses with a population of 890.[66] Some of the new houses were on the Mirystock road and on the road to Coleford, which ran south through Hangerberry[67] and had been rebuilt in the late 1820s.[68] The church of Holy Jesus, which stands high up on the north-east side of the main valley, was opened in 1851.[69] New building at Upper Lydbrook in the early 20th century included a chapel and a school,[70] and West Dean rural district council built three pairs of houses at Hangerberry in 1923 and eleven pairs on Camomile green in the early 1930s.[71]

PARKEND. The village of Parkend in the south of the Forest lies in a basin formed by Cannop brook and several of its tributaries and takes its name from the ancient inclosure of Whitemead park, in a detached part of Newland parish, to the south-west. A dwelling recorded at Parkend in 1725 was possibly in the mid 1770s the solitary cottage standing west of a bridge,[72] which in the 1670s carried the road linking Coleford with Purton and Gatcombe by way of Yorkley across the brook.[73] The site of the cottage was occupied by the Fountain inn in 1841.[74] To the west the Coleford road, which ran north-westwards past York Lodge in 1787,[75] was evidently diverted along the valley south of Bostonbury and Birch hills after it was turnpiked in 1796.[76] Parkend grew as an industrial settlement in the early 19th century when, following the establishment of ironworks there and the construction of the Severn & Wye tramroad alongside Cannop brook, it became the focal point for several mineral railways.[77] In the early 1820s the Revd. Henry Poole built a church and a school to the east. Later he added a parsonage and lodge next to the church, and the school, to the north on the Yorkley road, was rebuilt on a different site.[78] Most building in

Parkend took place after the ironworks, which stood east of the brook and north of the Yorkley road, reopened in the mid 1820s,[79] and the village's development was influenced by the construction in 1841 of the Blakeney road branching north-eastwards from the Coleford road 400 m. west of Parkend bridge.[80] In 1841 the ironworks included eight cottages standing under a bridge spanning the Severn & Wye tramroad,[81] and in or soon after 1847 their owners built 12 cottages to the north-east at Mount Pleasant.[82] In the early 1850s the area north-west of the ironworks was filled with tinplate works and 24 houses for the workmen.[83] Those houses, in two three-storeyed ranges set at right angles to one another, became known as the Square.[84] By 1859 there were three houses on the north-west side of the Blakeney road, including the residence of Thomas and William Allaway, owners of the tinplate works. A row of cottages was built west of the road in 1859[85] and more houses and a chapel had been added to the north-west side of the road by the late 1870s.[86] In 1874 Parkend, together with Moseley Green to the north-east, had a population of 791 living in 143 houses.[87] On the east side of the village Parkend House, by the Yorkley road, dates from a rebuilding of a house belonging in 1834 to a colliery company.[88] It became the home of the mine owner T. H. Deakin (d. 1935)[89] and in 1992 was a hotel. Colliery offices and workshops north of the road were converted as a house known as Castlemain Mill in the mid 20th century.[90]

Most of the buildings of the ironworks and tinplate works were demolished in the 1890s[91] and Parkend's triangular plan was consolidated in 1903 when the Lydney road, part of a new route from Lydbrook and running south-east from the Blakeney road, was constructed over the sites of both works. A few houses were built on the north-east side of the new road[92] and the engine house of the ironworks was converted as a forestry school and institute in 1908.[93] A playing field laid out by the 1950s occupied most of the land within the triangle formed by the principal roads.[94] In the early 20th century the village expanded southwards along the Lydney road and after the First World War houses were built on the Blakeney road, at the junction with the Lydbrook road. Further along the Blakeney road eight council houses in a terrace were built in

62 Bryant, *Map of Glos.* (1824); O.S. Map 6", Glos. XXXI. NW. (1883 edn.).
63 Glos. R.O., D 23/E 35.
64 P.R.O., F 17/4.
65 Glos. R.O., Q/RGf 1/4.
66 *Dean Forest Select Cttee.* (1874), 30, where the Lydbrook figures are only for that part in W. Dean.
67 P.R.O., F 16/64; O.S. Maps 1/2,500, Glos. XXXI. 1, 5 (1881 and later edns.).
68 Nicholls, *Forest of Dean*, 197; Dean Forest Roads Act, 7 & 8 Geo. IV, c. 12 (Local and Personal).
69 Below, Churches.
70 *Glouc. Jnl.* 4 Sept. 1909; 21 Sept. 1912.
71 Glos. R.O., DA 25/603.
72 Ibid. P 227/IN 1/2; P.R.O., F 17/161.
73 Glos. R.O., Q/SO 1, f. 182v.
74 Ibid. Q/FR 4/1, f. 55.
75 P.R.O., MR 415.
76 Dean Forest Roads Act, 36 Geo. III, c. 131; Bryant, *Map of Glos.* (1824). 77 Paar, *Severn and Wye Railway*, 47.
78 Below, Churches (St. Paul); Educ., elementary schs.; P.R.O., F 16/64 (nos. 2006–10); F 16/71.

79 Below, Industry, ironworks.
80 Nicholls, *Forest of Dean*, 197; for the village, below, Fig. 18.
81 Glos. R.O., Q/RUm 175.
82 Hart, *Ind. Hist. of Dean*, 128; P.R.O., F 16/64 (no. 1990); F 16/71.
83 Nicholls, *Forest of Dean*, 227.
84 O.S. Map 6", Glos. XXXIX. SW. (1883 edn.); Hart, *Ind. Hist. of Dean*, plate at p. 84.
85 P.R.O., F 16/64 (nos. 1954–82); F 16/71.
86 O.S. Map 6", Glos. XXXIX. SW. (1883 edn.).
87 *Dean Forest Select Cttee.* (1874), 30.
88 Glos. R.O., Q/RGf 1/5; *2nd Rep. Dean Forest Com.* 57.
89 *Glouc. Jnl.* 14 Aug. 1886; 3 Aug. 1935.
90 Local inf.
91 Hart, *Ind. Hist. of Dean*, 129, 199; O.S. Map 6", Glos. XXXIX. SW. (1883, 1904 edns.).
92 *81st Rep. Com. Woods* (1903), 3; O.S. Map 1/2,500, Glos. XXXIX. 10 (1903, 1922 edns.).
93 P.R.O., F 3/1120; F 3/1162.
94 O.S. Maps 1/2,500, SO 6107–8 (1960 edn.).

1923 and several pairs of council houses in 1933;[95] the estate was much enlarged in the 1950s and 1960s.[96] Private building continued in the village in the mid 20th century and two factories were built on the Lydbrook road. Among buildings demolished during that period were the Square in the mid 1950s[97] and a house near the Yorkley road, formerly the British Lion inn, and cottages adjoining it.[98] West of the village, in the fork of the Coleford and Bream roads, a single-storeyed tollhouse recorded in 1834[99] was rebuilt by the Crown in 1906 as a two-storeyed house.[1]

OTHER VILLAGES AND HAMLETS. The other settlements of the Forest are generally less well defined. Those on the fringes of the formerly extraparochial area are treated here in a roughly clockwise progression, beginning near Lydbrook, and are followed by a description of hamlets further within the Forest.

The hillsides east of Lydbrook,[2] where 44 cottages were recorded in 1782 in the area then known as Moorwood, remained sparsely settled in the 19th century and lacked easy access until a new road from Lydbrook to Ruardean was completed in 1909.[3] Some of the early cottages were at JOY'S GREEN, east of Lower Lydbrook,[4] where a school was built in the early 1880s.[5] From 1938, after the area had been transferred to West Dean rural district,[6] the land west of the school was filled with council houses and bungalows, a process that continued in the early 1970s.[7] South of the school a number of houses were built by the Lydbrook–Ruardean road in the later 20th century. To the south-east at Horse Lea (or Hawsley)[8] a solitary cottage, built before 1787[9] and enlarged in the mid 19th century, had become a beerhouse by 1870[10] and was the Masons' Arms inn in 1992. Many of the early cottages in the Moorwood area were to the north-east adjoining Ruardean parish, including a row, recorded in 1834, by a track to Ruardean at High Beech.[11] Further west at Vention a cottage built before 1834[12] was a beerhouse called the Royal Spring in 1869.[13]

Crown land south of Ruardean, extending from Astonbridge hill to Ruardean hill, contained 44 scattered dwellings in 1782.[14] A few were below Smithway in the area known by 1787 as THE PLUDDS.[15] One of the oldest surviving

houses there, Pludds Court at the west end, dates from the late 18th century or the early 19th. Random building continued at the Pludds after 1840[16] and a beerhouse called the Royal Oak had opened by 1891.[17] Among buildings erected after the Second World War were two pairs of council houses completed in 1947[18] and several private bungalows. To the north-east the small hamlet of Knights Hill had been established by 1787 east of an ancient farmstead belonging to Ruardean.[19] It stands on the west side of a deep valley, known as Newham bottom, in which new cottages were built in the 19th century. More extensive settlement took place on the bleak hillside east of that valley at RUARDEAN WOOD-SIDE, in the area once known as Hanway Eaves,[20] where the number of cottages rose from c. 10 in 1787[21] to c. 46 in 1832.[22] Some buildings clustered where an ancient route from Ruardean entered the Forest.[23] To the east a beerhouse called the Roebuck, opened by 1862, acquired new premises closer to the Ruardean Hill road[24] after that road was completed in 1900.[25] To the south the Denecroft estate, developed by East Dean rural district council from 1954, comprised 27 houses in 1960.[26]

On RUARDEAN HILL, the summit of which is at 290 metres the highest point in the Forest, random building on waste land produced a hillside settlement typical of many on the fringes of the Crown demesne. There were c. 14 cottages on the hill in 1787[27] and c. 63 in 1832.[28] From 1854 the settlement had a chapel on its south side.[29] The first road over the hill ran from Ruardean Woodside on the west and to a junction with Morse Road, in Ruardean, on the north. After its completion in 1900[30] a building nearby, used in 1910 as the Nag's Head inn, was rebuilt.[31] Little new building took place on the south side of the hill, where a road leading to the Mitcheldean–Coleford road was constructed in 1930,[32] but from the 1960s several houses, some of them forming a small estate, were built at the top and on the north side. Lower down to the east there was scattered building on Morse Road, formed in 1841 as part of the road from Nailbridge to the Wye at Bishopswood through Ruardean.[33]

NAILBRIDGE, in the Dry brook valley, took its name from a bridge carrying the Mitcheldean–Coleford road over the brook.[34] In the later 1790s

95 Glos. R.O., DA 25/603.
96 Ibid. DA 25/600/2.
97 R. Anstis, *Story of Parkend* (1982), 49.
98 O.S. Maps 1/2,500, Glos. XXXIX. 10 (1878 edn.); SO 6108 (1960 edn.).
99 Glos. R.O., Q/RGf 1/5; Hart, *Ind. Hist. of Dean*, plate at p. 373.   1 Inscr. on bldg.
2 For the northern edge of the Forest, below, Fig. 23.
3 P.R.O., F 17/4; Glos. R.O., DA 24/100/5, p. 295.
4 P.R.O., MR 415.   5 Inscr. on bldg.
6 Glos. R.O., DA 24/100/12, p. 18.
7 Ibid. DA 25/600/1–2; DA 25/602.
8 O.S. Map 6", Glos. XXXI. NW. (1883 edn.); P.R.O., RG 12/2004, s.v. E. Dean.   9 P.R.O., MR 415.
10 *Kelly's Dir. Glos.* (1870), 532.
11 Glos. R.O., Q/RGf 1/8.   12 Ibid. 4.
13 *Glouc. Jnl.* 18 Sept. 1869; O.S. Map 1/2,500, Glos. XXXI. 1 (1881 edn.).
14 P.R.O., F 17/4.   15 Ibid. MR 415.
16 Glos. R.O., Q/RGf 1/8; O.S. Map 6", Glos. XXXI. NW. (1883 edn.).
17 *Licensed Houses in Glos. 1891*, 150–1; P.R.O., RG

12/2004, s.v. E. Dean.
18 Glos. R.O., DA 24/602/1.
19 P.R.O., MR 415.
20 Glos. R.O., D 892/T 69; D 1229, Ruardean deeds 1642–1853, deed 1676.
21 P.R.O., MR 415.   22 *3rd Rep. Dean Forest Com.* 11.
23 Glos. R.O., Q/RGf 1/8.
24 P.R.O., FS 2/3; O.S. Map 1/2,500, Glos. XXXI. 2 (1881 and later edns.).
25 Inscr. on road marker at Ruardean Woodside; cf. Glos. R.O., DA 24/100/3, pp. 26, 251–2.
26 Glos. R.O., DA 24/602/1–2.
27 P.R.O., MR 415.   28 *3rd Rep. Dean Forest Com.* 11.
29 *Ruardean Hill Bapt. Ch. 1854–1954* (copy in Glos. R.O., NC 75), 1.
30 Inscr. on road marker at Ruardean Woodside; Glos. R.O., DA 24/100/3, pp. 26, 251–2.
31 Glos. R.O., D 2428/1/28; O.S. Map 1/2,500, Glos. XXXI. 3 (1903, 1923 edns.).
32 Glos. R.O., DA 24/100/10, p. 658; DA 24/711.
33 Nicholls, *Forest of Dean*, 197.
34 P.R.O., MR 415.

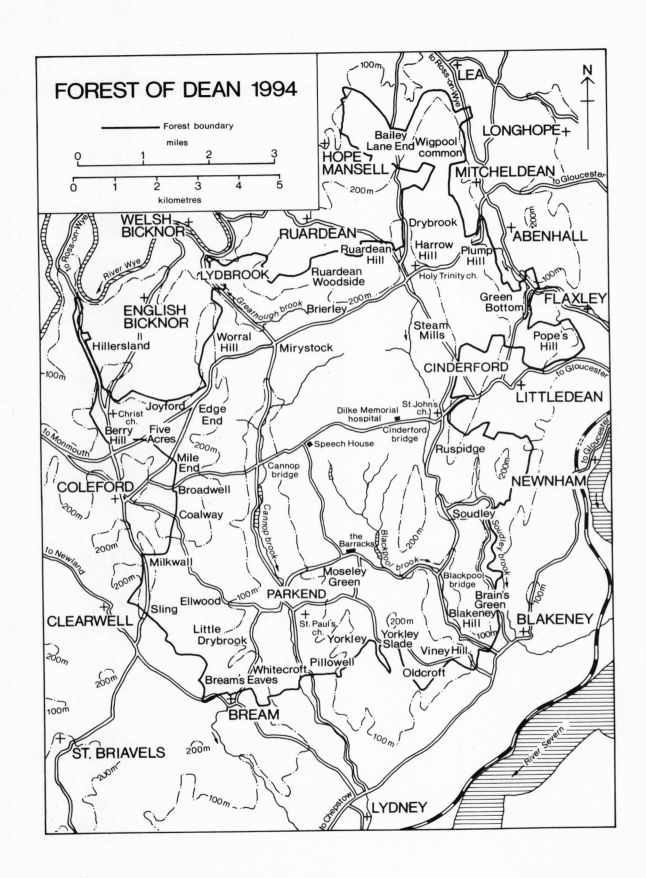

FIG. 17

the section of the road over Harrow hill from Stenders, to the north-east, was diverted through Drybrook village to cross the brook at Teague's (or Pluckpenny) bridge, upstream of Nail bridge, and run south-eastwards to a junction with the Coleford road, from where new roads were built to Littledean to the south-east in the late 1820s and to Mitcheldean, over Plump hill, in 1841.[35] In 1834 there were five cottages west of the brook near Teague's bridge.[36] Some later buildings in that area, where two engine houses were used as dwellings in 1856,[37] were on Morse Road, constructed in 1841 as a continuation north-westwards of the road from Littledean.[38] To the south-east an area alongside the road filled with mines and railways was covered after 1960 with the extensive yards and buildings of a timber and builders' merchant,[39] and at the junction of the Coleford road a beerhouse, opened by 1841[40] and known as the Railway inn in 1856,[41] was demolished after 1960.[42] To the south-west on the north side of the Coleford road a terrace of 15 cottages, later called Hawkwell Row, was built in the 1880s or 1890s by Jacob Chivers or A. C. Bright, successive owners of a nearby colliery and tinplate works,[43] and several houses and bungalows were built in the mid 20th century. Building on Harrow (or Harry) hill began on the north side towards Drybrook before 1787[44] and the hamlet of Harrow Hill contained c. 24 cottages in 1832.[45] Holy Trinity church, standing to the south-west on Quarry hill, was opened in 1817[46] and a parsonage house was completed, to the south-east, a few years later.[47] Cottages were built in old inclosures on the main part of Harrow hill from the mid 19th century[48] and scattered houses and bungalows were built in the area in the later 20th century.

DRYBROOK, a village north of Cinderford, grew up at a crossing of Dry brook by an old route from Mitcheldean to Ruardean,[49] called Morse Lane west of the village. East of the brook, which marked the eastern boundary of Ruardean,[50] two small farmsteads were established in the Morse grounds, an area belonging to Newland.[51] One, later Drybrook Farm, was near the brook and was described as new-built in 1749 when ownership of the Morse grounds passed from the Crawley-Boeveys of Flaxley Abbey to the Colchesters of the Wilderness.[52] In 1840 the farmstead further east was called the Morse and occupied by William Manning,[53] and later it was called Manning's Farm.[54] In 1782 there were also 12 cottages at Drybrook on the extraparochial Forest waste bordering Ruardean[55] and by 1832 their number had risen to c. 38, including several to the north at Hawthorns.[56] The route from Mitcheldean, by way of Stenders to the east, had been improved in 1766[57] and incorporated in the later 1790s in a new road to Coleford, which branched south to follow a track past Drybrook Farm to Nailbridge. A lane running northwards to Hawthorns was included in 1841 in a new road to Bailey Lane End on the Forest boundary.[58] The junction of the Mitcheldean–Nailbridge road with the roads to Ruardean and Bailey Lane End became the focal point of the village and was the site of several inns in the later 19th century[59] and of several shops in 1992. The Hearts of Oak (formerly the New Inn),[60] a short distance to the south-west, was built as a beerhouse in 1838.[61] Most of the early cottages were north-west of the crossroads[62] and in 1836 a chapel was erected on the Hawthorns road.[63] On the south-west side of the village Quabbs House (formerly the Quabbs) belonged to Ruardean and in 1847 was the residence of the mine owner Cornelius Brain.[64] A school was built on the Nailbridge road in 1862.[65] From 1907 Drybrook had a passenger railway service to Gloucester from a halt[66] on the west side of the village, and in the early 20th century a few houses were built on the east side by the Mitcheldean road.[67] The village was much enlarged after the Second World War and it became the centre of the new civil parish of Drybrook created in 1953 for the surrounding hamlets.[68] Most of the new houses were north of the Mitcheldean road in the large Sunnymeade estate, which was developed piecemeal by East Dean rural district council from 1948. The estate, which included several blocks of flats, was extended eastwards in 1969.[69] Some private houses were also built in the village during that period.

North of Drybrook there were 11 cottages on Dean (or Mitcheldean) Meend in 1782.[70] A small settlement on the road to Hope Mansell (Herefs.), known as Hawthorns in the 1830s, straddled the boundary between the extraparochial Forest and the parishes of Ruardean and Hope Mansell to the west[71] and originated as a

35 Nicholls, *Forest of Dean*, 195–7; Glos. R.O., Q/RUm 107.
36 Glos. R.O., Q/RGf 1/8, where the bridge is incorrectly called Nail bridge.
37 Ibid. Q/RUm 269.
38 Nicholls, *Forest of Dean*, 197.
39 O.S. Maps 1/2,500, Glos. XXXI. 3 (1878 and later edns.); SO 6416 (1961 edn.).
40 Glos. R.O., Q/FR 4/1, f. 133; DC/H 137.
41 Ibid. Q/RUm 269.
42 O.S. Map 1/2,500, SO 6416 (1961 edn.).
43 P.R.O., F 3/416.
44 Ibid. MR 415.
45 *3rd Rep. Dean Forest Com.* 11.
46 *Glouc. Jnl.* 10 Feb. 1817.
47 Glos. R.O., Q/RGf 1/8; *2nd Rep. Dean Forest Com.* 83.
48 Glos. R.O., Q/RGf 1/8; P.R.O., F 16/63.
49 Glos. R.O., D 2957/303.2; D 4431, deed 30 Aug. 22 Edw. IV.
50 *2nd Rep. Dean Forest Com.* 31; G.D.R., T 1/151.
51 Glos. R.O., D 2123, pp. 98–9, 101; Q/RGf 1/8.
52 Ibid. D 36/T 49.
53 G.D.R., T 1/128 (no. 2716).
54 O.S. Map 6", Glos. XXXI. NE. (1903 edn.).
55 P.R.O., F 17/4.
56 *3rd Rep. Dean Forest Com.* 11; cf. O.S. Map 6", Glos. XXIII. SE. (1883 edn.).
57 Badminton Mun. FmS/G 2/4/6.
58 Nicholls, *Forest of Dean*, 195, 197; Glos. R.O., Q/RUm 107, 152.
59 O.S. Map 1/2,500, Glos. XXXI. 3 (1878 edn.); Glos. R.O., D 543, Mitcheldean brewery, True Heart inn deed 1887.
60 O.S. Map 6", Glos. XXXI. NE. (1884 edn.).
61 Date on bldg.; Glos. R.O., Q/FR 4/1, f. 115.
62 Glos. R.O., Q/RGf 1/8.
63 Below, Prot. Nonconf., Bible Christians; for site, P.R.O., F 16/63 (no. 436); F 16/70.
64 G.D.R., T 1/151.
65 Date on bldg.
66 Paar, *G.W.R. in Dean*, 59–60.
67 O.S. Map 1/2,500, Glos. XXXI. 3 (1903, 1923 edns.).
68 *Census*, 1961.
69 Glos. R.O., DA 24/602/1–3.
70 P.R.O., F 17/4.
71 *Reg. Electors W. Division Glos. 1832–3*, 105, 110; O.S. Map 6", Glos. XXIII. SE. (1883 edn.).

cluster of buildings on the parochial land in the 16th century at the place then called Haseley.[72] In 1851 the hamlet included an inn known as the Crown.[73] In the late 1870s T. B. Brain had gasworks at Puddlebrook, to the north-east,[74] supplying Euroclydon, his large house on a prominent site nearby, in Hope Mansell parish.[75] Some of the dwellings recorded on Mitcheldean Meend in 1782 may have stood on the edge of Wigpool common, to the north, where settlement remained widely scattered in 1834.[76] Among the houses there in 1992 was one built in the late 19th century at an iron-ore mine.[77] In 1782 there was also a cottage to the east in Lining wood,[78] overlooking the Mitcheldean–Lea road. South-west of Wigpool at Blackwell meadows, a detached part of Mitcheldean parish,[79] a cottage or small farmhouse built by 1583[80] was one of two dwellings there in 1785.[81] It was apparently rebuilt as two cottages in the mid 19th century and three or four more houses had been built near it by the later 20th century.

There was also early settlement below Wigpool in scattered parts of LEA BAILEY tithing of Newland adjoining Forest woodland known as Lea Bailey.[82] The tithing, which also comprised land on Littledean hill adjoining Cinderford and at Lea Line and Blaisdon,[83] contained a number of dwellings in the early 17th century[84] and one at Lea Line had been a victualling house in 1596.[85] By the 18th century several small farmsteads or cottages had been built north and north-west of Wigpool on parts of the tithing which overlooked Weston under Penyard (Herefs.) and Lea (Glos. and Herefs.) and included many of the cottages strung out along a road to Lea in the mid 19th century.[86] Merryfold, a small farmhouse recorded from 1659,[87] stood on the site of Lea Bailey (formerly Merefold or Mereford) Farm, north-west of Wigpool.[88] To the south-west, where a cottage was recorded in 1705 and a new one was built c. 1818,[89] a pound was established within the Forest before 1788[90] and there was a small group of cottages, some in Lea Bailey tithing and some on extraparochial land, in 1834.[91] Some way north-east of Lea Bailey Farm, a small farmhouse, known in 1992 as Pound Farm, dates from the 18th century. Some cottages had been built within the Forest at Lea Bailey by the mid 18th century, 5 being recorded there in 1752[92] and 13 in 1782.[93] The largest

group in the 1780s clung to the hillside at Lea Bailey Hill, north of Wigpool.[94] A few early cottages within the Forest were on or near the Lea road, to the south-west,[95] where a nonconformist chapel was built in 1836 and an inn called the Yew Tree was open in the late 1870s.[96] To the south-west at Bailey Lane End, where one or two cottages had been built by a lane from the Rudge in Weston under Penyard by 1787,[97] a small hamlet was formed after 1841, when a road linking Drybrook, to the south, with Ross-on-Wye was built there.[98] Little building took place west of the road until the later 20th century when several new houses and bungalows were built in the hamlet.

By the 1780s there were also scattered cottages on the edge of the Forest in the main part of Lea Bailey, which occupied a promontory extending north-westward from Bailey Lane End to a place called Hell Gay Gate. Several were in the area known by 1841 as the Dancing green and several were to the north-west, where a lane from Pontshill in Weston under Penyard entered the Forest. In 1787 there were a few cottages south of Hell Gay Gate on the hillside then known as Palmer's hill,[99] where by 1834 a small group had formed at Palmer's Flat, on the boundary of Weston under Penyard.[1] Nearby to the south, where a part of Lea Bailey tithing adjoined the Forest on the hillside above Hope Mansell[2] in the area once known as Lea Bailey Side, one or two small farmsteads or cottages had been built by 1625[3] and a small group of cottages straddled the Forest boundary in the early 19th century.[4] Most of those in Lea Bailey tithing were said in 1812 to belong to a Mr. Palmer.[5] Further south at Baileybrook, where an early cottage by Bailey brook belonged to Lea Bailey tithing,[6] there were cottages higher up within the Forest by the 1780s. Upstream within the Forest at Newtown, to the south-east, there was a cottage by the brook in 1787[7] and several more cottages were built after 1834.[8] On the opposite, western, side of the Hope Mansell valley, Knacker's Hole, occupying the end of a ridge above the buildings called Bill Mill, was formerly a detached part of Lea Bailey tithing. In 1812 it contained three cottages,[9] one on the crest of the ridge and the others presumably lower down to the north-east, where three cottages, including a pair, stood in 1840.[10]

72 Above, Ruardean, intro.
73 P.R.O., HO 107/1976, s.v. Hope Mansell.
74 O.S. Map 6", Glos. XXIII. SE. (1883 edn.); Glos. R.O., DA 24/100/3, pp. 435–7.
75 Kelly's Dir. Herefs. (1879), 992.
76 Glos. R.O., Q/RGf 1/8.
77 O.S. Map 6", Glos. XXIII. SE. (1883 edn.).
78 P.R.O., F 17/4.
79 G.D.R., T 1/123.
80 Glos. R.O., D 4431, deed 6 Feb. 25 Eliz. I.
81 Ibid. D 2123, pp. 85–7.
82 G.D.R., T 1/128; O.S. Maps 6", Glos. XXIII. SE., SW. (1883 edn.).
83 Above, Newland, intro. (Table I).
84 Glos. R.O., P 227/IN 1/1.
85 B.L. Harl. MS. 4131, f. 500.
86 G.D.R., T 1/128; O.S. Maps 1/2,500, Glos. XXIII. 7, 11 (1881 edn.).
87 Glos. R.O., D 36/T 48.
88 Ibid. Q/RGf 1/8; P.R.O., MR 415; O.S. Map 6", Glos. XXIII. SE. (1883 edn.).
89 Glos. R.O., D 23/T 22.
90 P.R.O., F 17/6.
91 Glos. R.O., Q/RGf 1/8; G.D.R., T 1/128.
92 Berkeley Cast. Mun., General Ser. T, box 25, partic. of cottages 1752.
93 P.R.O., F 17/4.
94 Ibid. MR 415.
95 Glos. R.O., Q/RGf 1/8.
96 Ibid. D 2297; O.S. Map 6", Glos. XXIII. SE. (1883 edn.).
97 P.R.O., MR 415.
98 Nicholls, Forest of Dean, 197; O.S. Map 6", Glos. XXIII. SE. (1883 edn.).
99 P.R.O., MR 415; HO 107/364, s.v. Herbert walk.
1 Glos. R.O., Q/RGf 1/8.
2 O.S. Map 6", Glos. XXIII. SW. (1883 edn.).
3 P.R.O., E 137/13/4; cf. Glouc. Jnl. 8 May 1809.
4 Glos. R.O., Q/RGf 1/8.
5 P.R.O., F 14/13.　6 G.D.R., T 1/128 (no. 2750).
7 P.R.O., MR 415.
8 Glos. R.O., Q/RGf 1/8.
9 P.R.O., F 14/13; O.S. Map 1/25,000, SO 62 (1957 edn.).
10 Glouc. Jnl. 23 Oct. 1815; G.D.R., T 1/128 (nos. 2767–9, 2773).

North-east of Wigpool on Mitcheldean common a cottage on the west side of the Mitcheldean–Lea road was the Rising Sun beerhouse in 1838.[11] East of the road a farmstead in Lea Bailey tithing was part of Maynard Colchester's estates in 1785[12] and its house was rebuilt in the mid 19th century. To the southeast, at the south-east corner of Howley grove, Laine's Farm is a small early 19th-century farmhouse at the site of a barn recorded from 1772.[13] To the north-east at Lea Line settlement on land belonging to Lea Bailey tithing comprised in 1840 a cottage on the Gloucester–Ross road and a farmhouse, rebuilt later in the century, and a tollhouse by the road to Aston Crews (Herefs.).[14]

On the east side of the Forest there were 10 cottages in 1782 in the area then known as Edge Hills.[15] One may have been the small isolated farmhouse west of Plump hill which Thomas Crawley-Boevey granted under lease to Giles Loquier in 1729. The farmhouse, part of the Colchester family's estates from 1749,[16] became known as Loquiers Farm[17] and by 1840 a barn had been built to the east in a detached part of Newland parish where the farmland lay.[18] In the 1780s there were apparently three cottages at the bottom of Plump hill, south-west of Mitcheldean.[19] By 1832 the number of dwellings in the hamlet of PLUMP HILL had risen to c. 32,[20] and the development of Westbury Brook mine and other industrial activity stimulated more random building there later in the century.[21] Some new buildings faced the Mitcheldean–Coleford road, constructed over the hill in 1841.[22] One of the first, half way up the hill, was a beerhouse in 1851.[23] Later called the Point inn, it was demolished during road improvement after 1960.[24] Higher up the road a pair of small houses was built in 1876 by the quarrymaster Aaron Simmonds.[25] Much further along the road on Merring Meend a pair of houses built near Fairplay mine in 1856[26] was later converted as four cottages.[27] Most houses built at Plump Hill in the 20th century were on the lower part of the hill. Cottages dotting the steep wooded hillsides further south, near Abenhall, include an early group in Horsepool bottom.[28]

Further south in the Edge Hills area, where there were c. 12 cottages in 1832,[29] several small dispersed settlements, including Collafield, had

been established by the 1780s.[30] At Shapridge there were four cottages on Crown land above Gunn's Mills in 1782,[31] and south of Shapridge the hamlet of Green Bottom, in a remote valley west of the Mitcheldean–Littledean road, contained two or three cottages in 1787.[32] Later buildings include a house built in 1877 as part of the new Cinderford waterworks west of Green Bottom.[33] To the south, on the Littledean road, a house built in 1859[34] became a nurses' home in 1908 when an isolation hospital, an iron building put up nearer Green Bottom in 1896, was re-erected in its garden.[35]

East of the Mitcheldean–Littledean road there were 15 cottages on the lower slopes of Chestnuts hill in 1782.[36] Some were on the south-western side at Waterend Lane,[37] on the Littledean boundary, where six cottages stood on Crown land in 1834.[38] More extensive squatter settlement took place east of the hill at POPE'S HILL, where in 1787 there were c. 10 cottages scattered over a wide area including Hangman's hill to the north and Blackmore's Hale to the south-east, on the boundary of Westbury-on-Severn.[39] The population of Pope's Hill in the early 1830s was c. 150.[40] To the south, near the Westbury–Littledean road, a cottage on the old Littledean road had become a beerhouse (in 1992 the Greyhound inn) by 1841.[41] Further west on the Westbury–Littledean road a pair of small brick houses called Model Cottages is dated 1863. South of Littledean village on the Soudley road a lodge was built on Crown land at Sutton in 1904.[42] Further east settlement above Newnham in Blaize Bailey comprised two cottages in 1782.[43]

The village of SOUDLEY, lying in the Cinderford brook valley downstream from Ruspidge, grew up north of the brook on the Abbots wood estate. Some of the first dwellings were in a remote spot known as Scilly Point,[44] to the west of Soudley bridge[45] which had been built before 1674 to carry the Dean road.[46] Many, if not all, of the early cottages, which in 1841 numbered 19[47] and included a row of three owned by Edward Protheroe,[48] were built following the construction of the Bullo Pill tramroad along the valley in the early 19th century. The tramroad became a road after a railway opened there in 1854[49] and the road was incorporated in the new Cinderford–Blakeney road in 1889.[50] In Upper

11 Glos. R.O., Q/RGf 1/8; *2nd Rep. Dean Forest Com.* 79; *Reg. Electors W. Division Glos. 1838–9*, 144.
12 Glos. R.O., D 2123, pp. 112, 115, 117; O.S. Map 6", Glos. XXIII. SE. (1883 edn.).
13 Glos. R.O., D 36/T 36; D 543, Laine's Farm deeds 1814–1865; G.D.R. wills 1772/150B.
14 G.D.R., T 1/128 (nos. 2825–8, 2834).
15 P.R.O., F 17/4.   16 Glos. R.O., D 36/T 49.
17 Ibid. D 2123, pp. 103, 105; P.R.O., F 16/63.
18 G.D.R., T 1/128 (no. 2711).   19 P.R.O., MR 415.
20 *3rd Rep. Dean Forest Com.* 11.
21 Glos. R.O., Q/RGf 1/7–8; P.R.O., F 16/63; O.S. Map 6", Glos. XXXI. NE. (1903 edn.).
22 Nicholls, *Forest of Dean*, 197.
23 P.R.O., HO 107/1959, s.v. E. Dean; F 16/63 (no. 662); F 16/70.
24 O.S. Map 1/2,500, SO 6617 (1961 edn.).
25 Date and inits. on bldg.; *Kelly's Dir. Glos.* (1879), 629.
26 P.R.O., F 16/63 (nos. 845–6); F 16/70.
27 O.S. Map 1/2,500, Glos. XXXI. 3 (1878 edn.).
28 Glos. R.O., Q/RGf 1/7.

29 *3rd Rep. Dean Forest Com.* 11.
30 P.R.O., MR 415.
31 Ibid. F 17/4.   32 Ibid. MR 415.
33 Pearce, 'Water Supply in Dean', 19–20.
34 Date on ho.
35 Glos. R.O., DA 24/100/5, pp. 114–15, 124, 204.
36 P.R.O., F 17/4.   37 Ibid. MR 415.
38 Glos. R.O., Q/RGf 1/7.
39 P.R.O., MR 415; for Blackmore's Hale, *V.C.H. Glos.* x. 84.
40 *3rd Rep. Dean Forest Com.* 4.
41 Glos. R.O., Q/RGf 1/7; Q/FR 4/1, f. 90.
42 Date on bldg.   43 P.R.O., F 17/4.
44 Ibid. F 17/76; O.S. Map 1", sheet 43 (1831 edn.).
45 Greenwood, *Map of Glos.* (1824).
46 Glos. R.O., Q/SO 1, f. 71.
47 Ibid. Q/FR 4/1, ff. 139–41.   48 Ibid. Q/RUm 160.
49 Paar, *G.W.R. in Dean*, 21, 34–5, 46, 54; Glos. R.O., Q/RI 52.
50 P.R.O., LRRO 5/7B; Glos. R.O., DA 40/100/4, pp. 2–3, 6–7.

Soudley, the part of the village near Soudley bridge, a school-chapel provided in 1875 was replaced later by separate and more substantial buildings.[51] The White Horse inn, near the junction of the Littledean road, dates from c. 1898.[52] In 1931 East Dean and United Parishes rural district council built three pairs of houses west of the church.[53] More council houses were provided after the Second World War, most of them between 1954 and 1968 in a small estate east of the Littledean road, and private houses were built at the west end of the village after 1960.[54] South of the brook some early cottages were built on Bradley hill,[55] at the foot of which two cottages were built after 1787[56] on the site occupied in the late 1870s by Brook Farm.[57] Higher up are a chapel built in 1846[58] and a building of the late 1830s used until c. 1898 as the White Horse beerhouse.[59] Downstream of Upper Soudley towards Lower Soudley, industrial buildings at Camp Mill, dating from the 19th century, were adapted as the Dean Heritage museum in 1983.[60]

There was scattered building downstream of Soudley where the valley of the brook became a centre of ironworking in the later 18th century. While the ironworks were east of the brook within Newnham parish,[61] many of the cottages built before the mid 19th century were on the west side of the valley on extraparochial land in the areas known as Bradley and Ayleford.[62] At Bradley, sometimes called Ayleford in the mid 19th century,[63] there were in 1782 five cottages including those on Bradley hill to the west.[64] By the brook Bradley House was presumably built for Samuel Hewlett, an ironfounder who was the occupant in 1834.[65] To the south are two mid 19th-century houses, one, Ayleford House, dated 1866. Downstream, nearer the hamlet of Ayleford, a row of four cottages north-west of Two Bridges, owned by Samuel Hewlett in 1834,[66] was partly derelict in 1992. Further south at Brain's Green on the boundary with Awre parish scattered settlement included c. 16 dwellings on Crown land in 1834.[67] One, a three-storeyed house, is dated 1785 with the initials of George Gwilliam, a carpenter, and his wife Mary.[68]

Many of the cottages and gardens in Blakeney walk in 1752[69] were presumably at BLAKENEY HILL, at the south-east corner of the Forest, on a steep hillside above Blakeney village.[70] The hill, on which 34 cottages were recorded in 1782,[71] has been extensively quarried and the east side was known as Gibralter in the early 19th century.[72] Many of the early cottages were on the south- west side in the Blackpool brook valley,[73] the floor of which was known as Old Furnace bottom from early ironworks.[74] By 1834 there were c. 80 cottages, including one dated 1830, on the hill and in the valley,[75] and later there was much new building and rebuilding there, typical cottages being dated 1848 and 1850. On the south-west side of the hill, which became known as Blakeney Woodside, some houses and bungalows were built in the later 19th and the 20th centuries on the Blakeney–Coleford road, constructed along the valley in 1841.[76] A school was provided, at Blakeney Woodside, in 1851[77] and a nonconformist chapel, in a prominent position at the top of the hill, in 1874.[78]

Further south random settlement began on VINEY HILL before 1787,[79] and c. 30 cottages had been built there by 1834.[80] The earliest dwellings were on the east side of the hill, just within the extraparochial Forest and north of a road descending to the river Severn at Gatcombe.[81] The road's course over the hill was diverted northwards after it was turnpiked in 1796.[82] Much rebuilding and new building took place on the hill after 1840, and several large houses and bungalows commanding extensive views across the Severn were built in the later 20th century. The New Inn, north of the Gatcombe-Yorkley road, had opened by 1876.[83] In 1834 there was a number of cottages to the west in the Hay End area.[84] Old Albion House, on the Yorkley road, was originally an inn built before 1855[85] to replace a beerhouse to the south-east.[86] To the west a school and schoolhouse were built on the Yorkley road in 1850,[87] and All Saints' church and its parsonage were built nearer Viney Hill hamlet in the mid 1860s.[88] Early squatter settlement south of the Yorkley road in Oldcroft, where Crown land formed a wedge on high ground above Lydney, included the 13 cottages

[51] O.S. Map 6", Glos. XXXIX. NE. (1884 edn.); *Glouc. Jnl.* 14 May 1910; below, Educ., elementary schs.
[52] Glos. R.O., DA 24/100/2, p. 142.
[53] Ibid. DA 24/600/1.
[54] Ibid. DA 24/602/1–3; O.S. Map 1/2,500, SO 6510 (1958, 1978 edns.).
[55] P.R.O., F 17/4.
[56] Glos. R.O., Q/RGf 1/6; *2nd Rep. Dean Forest Com.* 57; G.D.R. wills 1837/108.
[57] O.S. Map 6", Glos. XXXIX. NE. (1884 edn.).
[58] Inscr. on bldg.
[59] Glos. R.O., Q/RGf 1/6; Q/FR 4/1, f. 58; DA 24/100/2, p. 142; O.S. Map 6", Glos. XXXIX. NE. (1884 edn.).
[60] Below, Industry, ironworks; mills; *Dean Forest Mercury,* 29 Apr. 1983.
[61] Below, Industry, ironworks; Glos. R.O., D 3921/III/6; *V.C.H. Glos.* x. 42.
[62] P.R.O., MR 415; Glos. R.O., Q/RGf 1/6.
[63] Glos. R.O., D 3921/III/6.
[64] P.R.O., F 17/4.
[65] Glos. R.O., Q/RGf 1/6; *2nd Rep. Dean Forest Com.* 57; for Hewlett, below, Industry, ironworks; other ind. and trade.
[66] Glos. R.O., Q/RGf 1/6; *2nd Rep. Dean Forest Com.* 57.
[67] Glos. R.O., Q/RGf 1/6.

[68] G.D.R. wills 1814/201.
[69] Above, Table II.
[70] For the hamlet, above, Plate 19.
[71] P.R.O., F 17/4.
[72] Bryant, *Map of Glos.* (1824); J. Atkinson, *Plan of Forest of Dean with High Meadow and Great Doward Woods* (1845).
[73] P.R.O., MR 415.
[74] O.S. Map 6", Glos. XXXIX. SE. (1886 edn.); above, Awre, econ. hist.
[75] Glos. R.O., Q/RGf 1/6.
[76] Nicholls, *Forest of Dean,* 197.
[77] Ibid. 170.
[78] Inscr. on bldg.
[79] P.R.O., MR 415.
[80] Glos. R.O., Q/RGf 1/6.   [81] P.R.O., MR 415.
[82] Dean Forest Roads Act, 36 Geo. III, c. 131; Bryant, *Map of Glos.* (1824).
[83] *Forest of Dean Examiner,* 7 July 1876.
[84] Glos. R.O., Q/RGf 1/6.
[85] *Glouc. Jnl.* 21 July 1855; G.D.R. wills 1857/126.
[86] Glos. R.O., Q/FR 4/1, f. 71; Q/RGf 1/6; *2nd Rep. Dean Forest Com.* 62.
[87] Nicholls, *Forest of Dean,* 170; Glos. R.O., A 111/1/2.
[88] *Glouc. Jnl.* 27 Apr. 1867; Glos. R.O., P 348/MI 3.

recorded in 1782 at Deadman's Cross,[89] where the road crossed the Dean road linking Littledean and Lydney.[90] In 1834 Oldcroft contained *c.* 35 scattered cottages,[91] and later new houses were put up and some older ones replaced. In the later 20th century several cottages were enlarged and some large houses were built, especially on the south-east side of the hamlet. On the north-west side, at a place known as the Tuft of Beeches,[92] a public house called the Loyal Forester closed before 1893.[93]

By the early 20th century a string of mining villages had grown up along the southern edge of the Forest from Yorkley Slade in the east to Bream in the west. The earliest buildings at YORKLEY were on detached parts of Newland comprising Badhamsfield and Yorkley Court farms.[94] In 1782 there were also 18 cottages scattered widely on extraparochial land in the Bailey hill area.[95] Some were on the lower ground to the east at Yorkley Slade, formerly the Slade, where four dwellings stood in a clearing north of the Gatcombe–Coleford road in 1787.[96] There were *c.* 14 cottages in the clearing in 1834[97] and their number increased later.[98] Some way to the north-east, within the woodland at Tomlin, there were at least three cottages in the early 1770s[99] but only a single abandoned house in 1958.[1] The Nag's Head inn, south of the Gatcombe–Coleford road in Newland parish,[2] was recorded from 1788[3] and was enlarged *c.* 1850 by the addition of a range with two cottages at the north end.[4] From the later 19th century a few houses, including one dated 1874, were built on the Gatcombe road. West of Yorkley Slade, five houses were built on the south side of the Coleford road between 1834 and 1859[5] and several houses on the north side in the early 20th century.[6] From 1930 a large estate of council houses was formed on the hillside to the north.[7]

Further west in Yorkley in the late 1780s there were *c.* 16 fairly widely scattered cottages on high ground overlooking a valley to the south-west. Half of them were on Crown land and the rest on the Yorkley Court estate.[8] In 1834 there were *c.* 40 cottages in that area.[9] In the mid 19th century much rebuilding and new building took place at Yorkley, some of it by employees at the Parkend ironworks, and in 1874 Yorkley together with Pillowell, to the south-west, had 224

houses spread haphazardly over a wide area and a population of 1,172.[10] Crossroads at the top of Bailey hill, where the Gatcombe–Coleford road turned northwards and was joined by other routes, became a focal point. An inn there was known as the Royal Oak in 1910[11] and as the Bailey inn in 1992. On the Lydney road running southwards from the crossroads are a house dated 1811 and, at the corner of a lane to Yorkley Wood, a cottage dated 1796. Further along the Lydney road two cottages were built on Crown land before 1834.[12] North of the crossroads building on the west side of the Coleford road began in the mid 19th century and by 1859 a new tollhouse had been erected some distance from the village. The Bream road, which descends south-westwards to Pillowell from the Coleford road, was constructed after 1859[13] and attracted some new building, notably at the bottom of Yorkley where a few council houses were provided in 1923[14] and the 1950s.[15] A large house on Captain's green, north-west of the road, was built in 1930 as the parsonage for an intended church and was later converted to accommodate a mission church.[16] Among houses built after the Second World War were a few in the 1980s forming a small private estate on the road descending westwards from the crossroads on Bailey hill.

Settlement at PILLOWELL, on the side of the valley below Yorkley, began before 1742 on land belonging to Newland parish[17] and the village included in 1787 *c.* 10 cottages on Crown land to the north-west. Most dwellings were at the lower end, to the south-west,[18] near the well which gave the village its name[19] and where a cottage was built *c.* 1784 on the north side of Kidnalls wood.[20] By 1835, when a chapel was built on the hillside,[21] the number of cottages had increased to *c.* 30[22] and in 1851 the houses within Newland parish numbered seven.[23] In the mid 19th century new houses were built on the hillside and some older ones were rebuilt, two cottages just below Yorkley being dated 1842 and one at the bottom of the Yorkley Wood road 1849, and in 1877 a large school and a pair of schoolhouses were built on the valley floor.[24] A few houses were later built on the Yorkley–Bream road, constructed after 1859,[25] and eight council houses were provided in the village in 1940.[26] In a valley to the north-west the hamlet of Phipps Bottom comprised five or six cottages

89　P.R.O., F 17/4.
90　O.S. Map 6", Glos. XXXIX. SE. (1886 edn.).
91　Glos. R.O., Q/RGf 1/6.
92　O.S. Map 6", Glos. XXXIX. SE. (1886 edn.).
93　Photocopy of deed 9 Dec. 1893, in possession of Mrs. A. Kear, of Oldcroft.
94　Above, Newland, intro. (Table I); cf. Glos. R.O., P 209/IN 1/1.
95　P.R.O., F 17/4.
96　Ibid. MR 415.
97　Glos. R.O., Q/RGf 1/6.
98　P.R.O., F 16/64; O.S. Map 6", Glos. XXXIX. SE. (1886 edn.).
99　G.D.R. wills 1774/25; 1776/193; P.R.O., MR 415.
1　O.S. Map 1/2,500, SO 6407 (1959 edn.).
2　G.D.R., T 1/128 (no. 2530).　　3　P.R.O., F 17/6.
4　G.D.R., T 1/128; ibid. wills 1856/175.
5　Glos. R.O., Q/RGf 1/6; P.R.O., F 16/64.
6　O.S. Map 1/2,500, Glos. XXXIX. 3 (1903, 1922 edns.).
7　Glos. R.O., DA 25/600/1–3; DA 25/602.

8　P.R.O., MR 415; Glos. R.O., D 2528, pp. 20–1, plan G.
9　Glos. R.O., Q/RGf 1/5–6; G.D.R., T 1/128.
10　*Kelly's Dir. Glos.* (1870), 533; *Dean Forest Select Cttee.* (1874), 30.
11　Glos. R.O., D 2428/1/23/2; annotated copy of O.S. Map 1/2,500, Glos. XXXIX. 11 (1903 edn.).
12　Glos. R.O., Q/RGf 1/6; *2nd Rep. Dean Forest Com.* 63.
13　P.R.O., F 16/64.
14　Glos. R.O., DA 25/603.
15　Ibid. DA 25/600/2.
16　*Christian Herald*, 8 June 1974.
17　G.D.R. wills 1742/148.　　18　P.R.O., MR 415.
19　Cf. O.S. Map 6", Glos. XXXIX. SW. (1883 edn.).
20　Glos. R.O., D 421/E 29.
21　Below, Prot. Nonconf., Prim. Methodists.
22　Glos. R.O., Q/RGf 1/5.
23　P.R.O., HO 107/2444, s.v. Newland (Bream); O.S. Map 6", Glos. XXXIX. SW. (1883 edn.).
24　*Glouc. Jnl.* 8 Dec. 1877; above, Plate 38.
25　P.R.O., F 16/64.
26　Glos. R.O., DA 25/600/2.

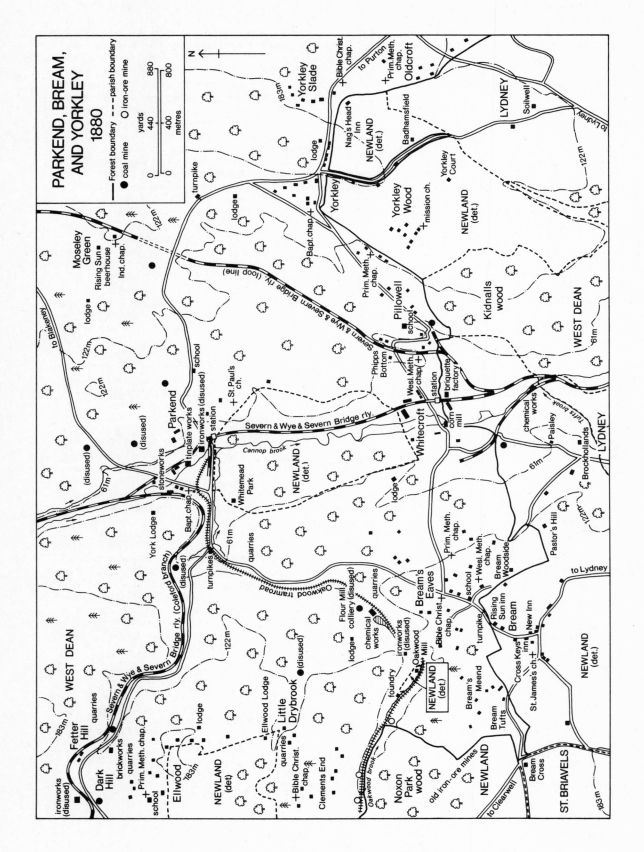

PARKEND, BREAM,
AND YORKLEY
1880

—— Forest boundary --- parish boundary
● coal mine   ○ iron-ore mine

FIG. 18

in 1834,[27] and a beerhouse called the Swan opened there by the Bream road before 1891.[28]

The hamlet of Yorkley Wood (formerly Jones's Wood),[29] high above Yorkley and Pillowell in the detached part of Newland parish, was established in the 1840s when a small wood formerly belonging to the Yorkley Court estate was cleared.[30] Twenty small houses had been built by 1851[31] and a few more were added later. To the south Shaphouse Farm (formerly Grove Cottage),[32] at the site of two cottages recorded in 1840,[33] includes late 20th-century buildings provided for an equestrian centre.

The village of WHITECROFT, at a crossing of Cannop brook, grew up on extraparochial land and an adjoining part of Bream tithing of Newland.[34] There was at least one cottage within the tithing in the late 17th century[35] but most of the original dwellings, including 16 cottages recorded in 1782,[36] were placed randomly on Crown land.[37] To the north, terraces containing 30 cottages were built before 1834 on either side of the Severn & Wye tramroad (later railway) for employees in the Parkend collieries.[38] They were demolished in the 20th century, one row surviving until the mid 1970s.[39] On the east side of Whitecroft a chapel on the hillside opposite Pillowell dates from 1824[40] and some building had taken place on the north side of the new Bream–Yorkley road by 1878.[41] In 1874 the main part of the village including Parkhill had 116 houses with a population of 610.[42] To the north on the Parkend road, completed in 1903 as part of the route linking Lydney and Lydbrook,[43] there was little building before the mid 20th century when several industrial workshops were erected.[44] On the south side of Whitecroft, where a factory was built in 1866,[45] industrial sites developed on both sides of the Lydney road in the later 20th century. During that period small estates of private and council houses grew up on both sides of the Yorkley road, and in the late 1980s a few private houses were built east of the Parkend road. At Parkhill, on the west side of Whitecroft where some of the early cottages on Crown land stood,[46] there were 18 houses in 1851.[47] In the early 20th century several houses were built to the north-west[48] and in 1923 West Dean rural district council built seven pairs of houses north of the

Bream road.[49] More council houses were built in the 1930s and the council estate was extended northwards in 1949.[50] Further along the Bream road several brick buildings put up in the early 20th century for Princess Royal colliery survived in 1992.[51]

South-west of Whitecroft there were half a dozen cottages on Saunders green in 1834.[52] Later the small hamlet of Brockhollands, on a hillside above Cannop brook, was formed north-west of an ancient farmstead within Newland parish.[53] A row of brick cottages had been built near the road from the Tufts to Bream by the early 1870s when, following the diversion of a new road to Whitecroft, a land society sponsored by a Conservative building society laid out roads for a housing estate lower down the valley side.[54] Two pairs of houses had been built at Paisley (or Peaseley) by the late 1870s[55] but the venture was abandoned and most of the roads have disappeared. A row of stone cottages was built on the Bream road in the 1880s or 1890s[56] and later buildings there included a few houses and bungalows. Further along the road several cottages were built near Pastor's Hill, another farmstead of Newland parish, before 1840.[57]

The village of Bream, in the north-west part of a large detached part of Newland, grew northwards to include the area around BREAM'S EAVES on extraparochial land.[58] There 10 cottages had been built on encroachments on Crown land by 1752[59] and settlement, which contained 29 cottages in 1782,[60] remained widely scattered in the early 19th century.[61] Just outside the extraparochial area, on the Parkend road north of the old part of Bream village, a stone house dated 1729 was the Rising Sun inn by 1787.[62] It has been enlarged and in 1992 was known as the Village Inn. To the south-west a row of cottages had been built by the roadside by 1840.[63] Between 1840 and 1880 many cottages, several of them in pairs, were built on the former encroachments around Bream's Eaves,[64] which in 1874 had 301 houses and a population of 1,519.[65] Settlement remained scattered and until after the First World War most new building was confined to those plots. Buildings on the Parkend road included, on the east side, a school at the junction of the lane to Pastor's Hill in 1862.[66] In the early 20th century the road took on the appearance of

27 Ibid. Q/RGf 1/5.
28 *Licensed Houses in Glos. 1891*, 58; *Kelly's Dir. Glos.* (1894), 260.
29 P.R.O., HO 107/2444, s.v. Newland (Bream).
30 Glos. R.O., D 2528, pp. 20–1, plan G; G.D.R., T 1/128 (no. 2568).
31 P.R.O., HO 107/2444, s.v. Newland (Bream).
32 O.S. Map 6", Glos. XXXIX. SW. (1883 edn.).
33 G.D.R., T 1/128 (nos. 2554–5).
34 O.S. Map 6", Glos. XXXIX. SW. (1883 edn.).
35 Glos. R.O., P 209/IN 1/1.
36 P.R.O., F 17/4.   37 Ibid. MR 415.
38 Glos. R.O., Q/RGf 1/5; *2nd Rep. Dean Forest Com.* 51.
39 O.S. Map 1/2,500, Glos. XXXIX. 14 (1881 and later edns.); G. E. Lawrence, *Kindling the Flame* (1974), 26: copy in Glos. R.O., D 2598/23/1.
40 Below, Prot. Nonconf., Wesleyan Methodists.
41 O.S. Map 6", Glos. XXXIX. SW. (1883 edn.).
42 *Dean Forest Select Cttee.* (1874), 30.
43 *81st Rep. Com. Woods* (1903), 3.
44 Cf. O.S. Map 1/2,500, SO 6106 (1960 edn.).
45 Glos. R.O., D 2299/584; *Kelly's Dir. Glos.* (1870), 534; O.S. Map 6", Glos. XXXIX. SW. (1883 edn.).

46 Glos. R.O., Q/RGf 1/5.
47 P.R.O., HO 107/2444, s.v. W. Dean.
48 O.S. Map 1/2,500, Glos. XXXIX. 14 (1903, 1922 edns.).
49 Glos. R.O., DA 25/603.
50 Ibid. DA 25/600/1–3; O.S. Map 1/2,500, SO 6106 (1960 edn.).   51 Glos. R.O., DA 25/711/11.
52 Ibid. Q/RGf 1/5; O.S. Map 6", Glos. XXXIX. SW. (1883 edn.).
53 Cf. G.D.R., T 1/128 (no. 2431); above, Newland, intro. (Table I).
54 Glos. R.O., D 3488; Q/SRh 1869 D/1; Fisher, *Custom and Capitalism*, 117.
55 O.S. Map 6", Glos. XXXIX. SW. (1883 edn.).
56 Ibid. (1904 edn.).   57 G.D.R., T 1/128 (nos. 2414–15).
58 For the old village, Newland, intro.
59 Berkeley Cast. Mun., General Ser. T, box 25, partic. of cottages 1752.
60 P.R.O., F 17/4.   61 Glos. R.O., Q/RGf 1/5.
62 Ibid. Q/RSf 2; Q/RUm 107.
63 G.D.R., T 1/128 (nos. 2631–14).
64 Glos. R.O., Q/RGf 1/5; O.S. Map 6", Glos. XXXIX. SW. (1883 edn.).   65 *Dean Forest Select Cttee.* (1874), 30.
66 Below, Educ., elementary schs.

a main street (later High Street) with the building, beyond the school, of several shops and houses,[67] one of which later became the Cross Keys inn. South-west of the school and opposite the Rising Sun, land called Sun green became a recreation ground c. 1887[68] and at the junction of the road to Bream's Meend, known in 1788 as St. Ann's Cross,[69] a cenotaph to villagers killed in the First World War was raised in the early 1920s.[70] At Bream Woodside, by the lane to Pastor's Hill, there were over a dozen cottages, half of them within Newland parish, in 1834[71] and one later building was the King's Head inn in 1876.[72] To the north more cottages appeared east of Hang hill in the mid 19th century and lower down to the east, where there was a beerhouse called the Masons' Arms in 1879,[73] several houses were built in the early 20th century.[74] In the west in the Mill hill area, where there were less than a dozen cottages in 1834,[75] later buildings included a few cottages on the north-west side of Sun green, one of which is dated 1863. Some new building also took place at Bream's Meend, to the south-west, where there had been c. 12 cottages in 1834, and at Bream Tufts, by the Bream–Coleford road, where a school dating from 1830 and three cottages had stood in 1834.[76]

After the First World War there was much new building in the Bream area. From 1923 houses were built by West Dean rural district council, and by the Second World War dwellings, including 64 council houses, lined the Parkend road[77] as far as Knockley Cottages, a pair of houses to the north-east built by the Crown in 1909 for the Princess Royal Colliery Co.[78] Later council houses were on the east side of Bream's Eaves. There development of the Hillside estate, south of the Yorkley road, began in 1948 with the provision of 20 bungalows (later replaced)[79] and continued in 1992 with the construction of 14 houses under the sponsorship of the district council and a housing association. To the south-west the Highbury estate, which included 16 council houses built off the south part of High Street in 1923,[80] was enlarged from 1955 to cover an area reaching eastwards to Bream Woodside.[81] Many houses and bungalows were built privately in the 20th century, usually as small infill schemes among groups of older cottages, and as a result in 1992 the built-up area extended

from Pastor's Hill in the east to Bream Tufts in the west.

North-west of Bream a few, mainly industrial, buildings were put up from the 1840s in the Oakwood valley near an ancient corn mill in a detached part of Newland parish.[82] Further west at Clements End, near the south-western boundary of the Forest, there were several groups of scattered cottages by 1787.[83] One group, in the areas known in the 1820s as Clements Tump and Cleverend Green,[84] comprised six cottages in 1834[85] and was represented by the 16 houses recorded at 'Elwall' in 1851.[86] It included a nonconformist chapel from 1869.[87] To the north-west there were ten cottages on Clements End green in 1834[88] and among later buildings there one, in 1878 a beerhouse,[89] was the Montague inn in 1992. By 1787 there were also a few dwellings north-east of Clements End at Little Drybrook, in a secluded valley below an old farmhouse (later Ellwood Lodge) in an adjoining detached part of Newland.[90] The hamlet comprised six cottages in 1834,[91] among them a two-storeyed dwelling dated 1805 with the initials of William Taylor, a quarry owner, and his wife Hannah.[92] Building had also begun in the Marsh Lane area, to the north-west, by 1787.[93] There were 11 cottages scattered along the lane, which ran northwards to Ellwood, in 1834[94] and a few more were erected later in the century.

Some early building was done at ELLWOOD within the detached part of Newland[95] and there were also 11 cottages on extraparochial land to the north and north-east by 1782. A few were at Dark Hill and Fetter Hill.[96] Ellwood, where a nonconformist chapel was built in 1841[97] and a school in 1878,[98] had 20 houses, 7 of them within Newland, in 1851.[99] Later houses included one provided by the Crown in the 1900s,[1] and in the mid and later 20th century the hamlet grew with the addition of several new houses and bungalows, among them four council houses in 1968.[2] The areas north and west of Ellwood have been much disturbed by mining and quarrying and have remained sparsely settled.[3] One cottage among quarries at Dark Hill was known in 1837 as the Vine Tree.[4] At Fetter Hill, where there were a few cottages near the Coleford–Parkend road in 1834,[5] several new houses were built in the 19th and 20th centuries,[6] and some of the early cottages had been demolished by 1960.[7] A

67 O.S. Map 1/2,500, Glos. XXXIX. 13 (1903, 1922 edns.).
68 P.R.O., F 3/473.   69 Ibid. F 17/6.
70 Ibid. F 3/1484.   71 Glos. R.O., Q/RGf 1/5.
72 Morris's Dir. Glos. (1876), 476; O.S. Map 6", Glos. XXXIX. SW. (1883 edn.).
73 Glos. R.O., Q/RGf 1/5; O.S. Map 6", Glos. XXXIX. SW. (1883 edn.).
74 They include hos. dated 1902, 1912, and 1913.
75 Glos. R.O., Q/RGf 1/5.
76 Ibid.; O.S. Map 6", Glos. XXXIX. SW. (1883 edn.); below, Educ., elementary schs.
77 Glos. R.O., DA 25/603; DA 25/600/1.
78 P.R.O., F 3/1077.
79 Glos. R.O., DA 25/600/2; O.S. Map 1/2,500, SO 6006 (1960 edn.).
80 Glos. R.O., DA 25/603.
81 Ibid. DA 25/600/2; DA 25/602; O.S. Map 1/2,500, SO 6005 (1960, 1971 edns.).
82 G.D.R., T 1/128; P.R.O., F 16/64; O.S. Map 6", Glos. XXXIX. SW. (1883 edn.).

83 P.R.O., MR 415.   84 Glos. R.O., P 227/IN 1/16.
85 Ibid. Q/RGf 1/5.
86 P.R.O., HO 107/2444, s.v. W. Dean.
87 Date on chapel.   88 Glos. R.O., Q/RGf 1/5.
89 O.S. Map 1/2,500, Glos. XXXVIII. 12 (1881 edn.).
90 P.R.O., MR 415.
91 Glos. R.O., Q/RGf 1/5.   92 G.D.R. wills 1830/116.
93 P.R.O., MR 415.   94 Glos. R.O., Q/RGf 1/5.
95 G.D.R., T 1/128; above, Newland, intro. (Table I).
96 P.R.O., F 17/4; cf. Glos. R.O., Q/RGf 1/5.
97 Inscr. on bldg.   98 Below, Educ., elementary schs.
99 P.R.O., HO 107/2444, s.vv. W. Dean, Newland (Clearwell).   1 Inscr. on bldg.
2 Glos. R.O., DA 25/600/2.
3 Cf. O.S. Map 6", Glos. XXXIX. NW. (1883 edn.).
4 Glos. R.O., D 5377/7/1.
5 Ibid. Q/RGf 1/5.
6 P.R.O., F 16/64; O.S. Map 6", Glos. XXXIX. NW. (1883 and later edns.).
7 O.S. Map 1/2,500, SO 5908 (1960 edn.).

few houses were built further along the Parkend road in the mid 19th century.[8]

In 1752 there were several dwellings on Clearwell Meend, on the Forest boundary east of Clearwell in Newland,[9] and in 1782 there were 23 cottages scattered over a wide area extending to Clements End green and Marsh Lane.[10] The remains of a cross known in the later 17th century as Gattle's cross stood east of the Lydney–Coleford road in 1992.[11] On the south side of Clearwell Meend at Clay Lane End, where the hamlet called SLING developed in the 20th century, the area east of the Lydney–Coleford road contained an ancient farmstead just within Newland parish and a few scattered cottages in 1834, and there was a tollhouse west of the road. Two of the cottages, in the fork of a road to Parkend,[12] were later occupied by a beerhouse called the Miners' Arms.[13] Several more cottages were built before the 1920s when the growth of Sling, named from a local mine,[14] began around crossroads formed by routes from St. Briavels to Parkend and from Bream's Eaves to Coleford. Four pairs of council houses were built on the Coleford road in 1923 and a few more council houses were completed in 1931.[15] Later, engineering works were established north of the hamlet, which grew considerably after the Second World War with the building of large numbers of council and private houses and bungalows.[16] Many of the new houses, including an estate formed in the late 1980s, were on the road to Bream's Eaves, along which the hamlet extended south-eastwards to Clements End in 1992.

On the western side of the Forest a line of continuous settlement developed along the boundary of Coleford tithing of Newland. The earliest houses at MILKWALL were within Coleford,[17] north of Clearwell Meend, and in 1834 there were only three dwellings on the extraparochial Crown land there. The westernmost, standing near the Coleford–Chepstow road, was known as Perrygrove House in 1841[18] and was apparently enlarged for the ironmaster W. H. Jackson in the early 1840s.[19] Among houses built within the extraparochial area after 1834 was one used in the late 1870s as a beerhouse,[20] later the Tufthorn inn. By 1865 building had begun on new roads within Coleford at Tufthorn laid out

by the British Land Society[21] and by the late 1870s there were over 20 houses on them. Building continued there into the 20th century,[22] and the built-up area later spread north-west towards Coleford town and south into the Forest. Most of the new houses and bungalows within the Forest, some of them built before 1960, were on the Lambsquay and Ellwood roads,[23] the second of which had been made in 1906.[24] A church was built at Milkwall in 1935.[25] In 1834 there were a few 18th- and early 19th-century cottages on Gorsty knoll and at Palmer's Flat, east and north-east of Milkwall respectively.[26] At Palmer's Flat the land society mentioned above had acquired a plot of land near the road to Coalway Lane End by 1859 and c. 20 houses had been built on it by the late 1870s.[27] Piecemeal building continued there later.[28] Lower down to the east, where a small group of cottages was formed near the Coleford–Parkend road in the mid 19th century,[29] several houses were replaced after 1960.[30]

Scattered encroachments on Coleford Meend, east of Coleford tithing and perhaps including some at Palmer's Flat, contained 2 cottages in 1752[31] and 21 in 1782.[32] Later building was both within and outside the extraparochial Forest[33] and in 1874 the area, the Lane End district, contained 349 houses and a population of 1,638 within the Forest.[34] Four of the cottages on extraparochial land in 1782 were the first dwellings of the hamlet of COALWAY LANE END. Early building at Coalway was on or near the road between Coleford and Parkend,[35] which was diverted southwards after it was turnpiked in 1796.[36] On the road within Coleford are two late 18th-century houses and a cottage dated 1828, and an inn called the Plough had opened there by 1851.[37] A road to Five Acres, which branched north-eastwards from the Coleford–Parkend road at the Forest boundary, was diverted c. 1858 to form a continuation northwards of the route from Palmer's Flat,[38] and in the late 19th century and the early 20th several houses were built on it and near the crossroads it made with the Coleford–Parkend route.[39] There was much new building at Coalway in the later 20th century, particularly within Coleford. In 1955 an estate of 12 council houses was built north of the Coleford road[40] and in 1966 and 1977 schools

[8] Glos. R.O., Q/RGf 1/5; O.S. Map 6", Glos. XXXIX. SW. (1883 edn.).
[9] Berkeley Cast. Mun., General Ser. T, box 25, partic. of cottages 1752.
[10] P.R.O., F 17/4; MR 415.
[11] Ibid. F 17/7.
[12] Glos. R.O., Q/RGf 1/5; G.D.R., T 1/128.
[13] O.S. Map 6", Glos. XXXVIII. SE. (1883 edn.).
[14] O.S. Map 1/2,500, Glos. XXXVIII. 12 (1902, 1922 edns.).
[15] Glos. R.O., DA 25/603.
[16] Ibid. DA 25/600/2; DA 25/602; O.S. Maps 1/2,500, SO 5807 (1978 edn.); SO 5808 (1972 edn.).
[17] Above, Coleford, intro.
[18] Glos. R.O., Q/RGf 1/5; Q/FR 4/1, f. 51.
[19] Ibid. P 93/IN 1/5, entry 26 Mar. 1844; P.R.O., HO 107/364, s.v. Parkend walk (Perrygrove): HO 107/2444, s.v. W. Dean (Perrygrove).
[20] O.S. Map 6", Glos. XXXVIII. NE. (1884 edn.).
[21] Glos. R.O., D 661; one ho. is dated 1868.
[22] O.S. Map 6", Glos. XXXVIII. NE. (1884 and later edns.).
[23] O.S. Map 1/2,500, SO 5809 (1960, 1978 edns.).
[24] Inscr. on road marker at Milkwall; cf. Glos. R.O., DA 25/701/1.

[25] Glouc. Jnl. 30 Nov. 1935.
[26] Glos. R.O., Q/RGf 1/5; cf. P.R.O., MR 415.
[27] Bristol R.O. 35721, Coleford papers 1855–96; O.S. Map 6", Glos. XXXVIII. NE. (1884 edn.).
[28] One ho. is dated 1919.
[29] Glos. R.O., Q/RGf 1/5; P.R.O., F 16/64; O.S. Map 6", Glos. XXXIX. NW. (1883 edn.).
[30] O.S. Map 1/2,500, SO 5809 (1960, 1978 edns.).
[31] Berkeley Cast. Mun., General Ser. T, box 25, partic. of cottages 1752.
[32] P.R.O., F 17/4; MR 415.
[33] Glos. R.O., Q/RGf 1/4–5.
[34] Dean Forest Select Cttee. (1874), 30.
[35] P.R.O., F 17/4; MR 415.
[36] Dean Forest Roads Act, 36 Geo. III, c. 131; Bryant, Map of Glos. (1824).
[37] Reg. Electors W. Division Glos. 1851–2, 49; O.S. Map 6", Glos. XXXVIII. NE. (1884 edn.).
[38] Glos. R.O., Q/RUm 271; P.R.O., F16/64; Dean Forest Roads Act, 21 & 22 Vic. c. 86 (Local and Personal).
[39] Some hos. are dated 1890, 1903, and 1910.
[40] Glos. R.O., DA 25/600/2; O.S. Map 1/2,500, SO 5810 (1960 edn.).

were opened there.[41] Private houses were built west of the Five Acres road after 1960 and, further north at Wynols Hill, the site of a large camp established early in the Second World War and occupied from 1942 by Italian prisoners, was covered with houses in the 1970s.[42] To the north, near Broadwell, an estate of 64 council houses was built in the mid 1950s and enlarged in the early 1960s.[43]

Settlement at BROADWELL LANE END principally followed the Forest boundary and the road from Coalway to Five Acres. In 1787 it contained c. 12 cottages on Crown land.[44] Some cottages built before 1834 were on the Coleford–Littledean road including a group within Coleford at Littledean (formerly Poolway) Lane End.[45] In the north-eastern angle of the crossroads formed by the two roads a school was built in 1863[46] and a church in 1938.[47] Further north the British Land Society laid out new roads north of Broadwell Farm, an old farmstead within Coleford, in 1859 and several houses had been built on them by the late 1870s.[48] Many of Broadwell's 20th-century houses were provided by West Dean rural district council, which between 1923 and 1934 built 44 east of the Five Acres road, in 1948 filled the area to the south with prefabricated bungalows, most of which were replaced later in the century, and in 1968 and 1970 built 58 houses on an estate to the north.[49] South-east of the Littledean road in the Barnhill area there were 12 cottages in 1851[50] and five pairs of council houses were built in 1936 and 1938.[51] Piecemeal private building continued at Broadwell in the late 1980s. Further north on the Five Acres road at Mile End the earliest cottages on Crown land, numbering five in 1787, were north-west of the Coleford–Mitcheldean road.[52] Among those built there before 1834 were a few on the Mitcheldean road within Coleford at the place known as Mitcheldean (formerly Dark Stile) Lane End.[53]

In the north-western corner of the Forest there was much early building around BERRY HILL, where the extraparochial land formed a peninsula to the north of Coleford, and in 1836 the settlement was called Upper Berry Hill to distinguish it from Lower Berry Hill in Coleford.[54] Several farmsteads were established on the Forest boundary at Berry Hill and at Five Acres, to the east,[55] and by 1782 there were 23 cottages

scattered over the extraparochial land.[56] Most of the cottages, including several built before 1758, were in the south-west on or near the road from Coleford to English Bicknor.[57] In that area, known in 1851 as Brooming knoll,[58] a house built c. 1830 had become the King's Head beerhouse by 1856.[59] To the north-west a small farmhouse recorded in 1758[60] and known later as Whitehall[61] was derelict in 1992. To the north on the Bicknor road Christ Church, the first church to be built in the extraparochial Forest, dates from 1812.[62] Some of the encroachments containing 18th- or early 19th-century cottages were at Five Acres[63] and one cottage there became the Rising Sun inn after the construction of the Monmouth–Mitcheldean road past its south side in 1841.[64] After 1840 many new cottages and houses were built at Berry Hill and Five Acres, and in 1874 the area, including nearby Joyford and Short Standing, had 295 houses and a population of 1,311.[65] A chapel was built at Five Acres in 1851.[66] A few of the early 20th-century houses at Five Acres were on the Mitcheldean road where a school built in 1914[67] was the oldest part of a large college campus in 1992.[68] The first council houses in the area, 16 built between Berry Hill and Five Acres in 1923, formed the Coverham estate,[69] which was enlarged in the 1930s and 1950s. Other council estates were developed there after the Second World War, including one north of the Rising Sun in the 1960s, and private building continued during that period.[70]

Early settlement on the hillside at JOYFORD, north-east of Berry Hill, included by 1758 several cottages on Crown land[71] overlooking buildings belonging to English Bicknor and a detached part of Newland.[72] In 1782 there were 40 cottages within the Forest at Joyford, including 12 up the hill[73] in the area known in 1804 as the Lonk.[74] On the lower part of the hill a beerhouse, later called the Dog and Muffler, opened before 1838.[75] In 1851 there were eight houses to the east in Ninewells bottom, then known as the Mire.[76]

North of Berry Hill, cottages had appeared within the Forest at Short Standing, near a farmstead belonging to English Bicknor, by 1758[77] and there were 12 there in 1782.[78] Northwest of Short Standing at Hillersland, on the

41 Below, Educ., elementary schs.
42 *Lessons of a Lifetime*, ed. B. Rendell and K. Childs (1984), 77–8; O.S. Map 1/2,500, SO 5810 (1960, 1973 edns.).
43 Glos. R.O., DA 25/600/2.
44 P.R.O., MR 415.
45 Glos. R.O., Q/RGf 1/4–5; O.S. Map 6", Glos. XXXVIII. NE. (1884 edn.); Dean Forest Roads Act, 36 Geo. III, c. 131.   46 Inscr. on bldg.
47 Glos. R.O., D 3921/II/6.
48 Bristol R.O. 35721, Coleford papers 1855–96; O.S. Map 6", Glos. XXXVIII. NE. (1884 edn.).
49 Glos. R.O., DA 25/600/2; DA 25/602–3; O.S. Map 1/2,500, SO 5811 (1960, 1974 edns.).
50 P.R.O., HO 107/2444, s.v. W. Dean.
51 Glos. R.O., DA 25/600/1.
52 P.R.O., MR 415.
53 Glos. R.O., Q/RGf 1/4; O.S. Map 6", Glos. XXX. SE. (1884 edn.); Dean Forest Roads Act, 36 Geo. III, c. 131.
54 Glos. R.O., Q/RUm 152; O.S. Map 6", Glos. XXX. SE. (1884 edn.).
55 Above, Coleford, intro.   56 P.R.O., F 17/4.
57 Ibid. F 17/96; MR 415.
58 Ibid. HO 107/2444, s.v. W. Dean; cf. ibid. F 16/64

(no. 897); F 16/71.
59 Glos. R.O., D 637/I/58; *Kelly's Dir. Glos.* (1856), 271.
60 P.R.O., F 17/96.
61 Ibid. HO 107/364, s.v. Worcester walk; O.S. Map 6", Glos. XXX. SE. (1884 edn.).
62 Below, Churches.
63 P.R.O., MR 415; Glos. R.O., Q/RGf 1/4.
64 *Kelly's Dir. Glos.* (1870), 533; Nicholls, *Forest of Dean*, 197.
65 *Dean Forest Select Cttee.* (1874), 30.
66 Inscr. on bldg.
67 *Glouc. Jnl.* 4 Apr. 1914.
68 Below, Educ., secondary schs.; technical schs. and colleges.
69 Glos. R.O., DA 25/603.
70 Ibid. DA 25/600/1–3; O.S. Map 1/2,500, SO 5712 (1960, 1971 edns.).
71 P.R.O., F 17/96.   72 G.D.R., T 1/25, 128.
73 P.R.O., F 17/4; MR 415.
74 Glos. R.O., P 93/IN 1/3.
75 Ibid. Q/FR 4/1, f. 11; *Reg. Electors W. Division Glos. 1838–9*, 135.
76 P.R.O., HO 107/2444, s.v. W. Dean.
77 Ibid. F 17/96.   78 Ibid. F 17/4.

road from Coleford to Goodrich (Herefs.), several cottages were recorded from 1565 on a green,[79] where an inn or beerhouse called the Cock in 1748[80] was renamed the Rock in the mid 19th century.[81] There were a few cottages strung out along the road in 1787[82] and their number had increased to 17 by 1834.[83] Further north at Redinhorne, near Symonds Yat rock, there was a cottage on the road in 1608.[84] Three cottages were recorded there in 1792[85] and the few houses there in 1992 included a wooden bungalow used as the Symonds Yat post office.[86]

To the east of Joyford at EDGE END two cottages or cabins stood apart in 1787 on encroachments on Crown land, high up on a hillside overlooking Hoarthorns Farm (in the detached part of Newland).[87] By 1834 two small groups of cottages had formed on those encroachments,[88] and in 1859 they contained 12 dwellings.[89] Both groups were enlarged by later building. The group to the north-east, where an iron chapel was erected in 1894,[90] was extended in the early 20th century by the building of several houses facing the Mitcheldean road to the south-east,[91] and by 1992 a few bungalows filled the north side of the road between the two groups of cottages. To the south-west, in the area around the junction of the roads from Monmouth and Coleford to Mitcheldean, four pairs of council houses were built in 1923 and several council houses and bungalows added in 1971.[92] Further north the small hamlet of Carterspiece, straddling the boundary between the Forest and English Bicknor, included a cottage on Crown land in 1758.[93]

The settlement of WORRALL HILL, mainly of 20th-century growth, comprised four cottages high on the hillside above Lydbrook in 1782.[94] A few more houses were built in the 19th century and a small nonconformist chapel in 1884.[95] In 1923 West Dean rural district council built 20 houses there,[96] most of them by the Coleford–Mitcheldean road where there was infilling with new houses in the mid 1960s. Most building in the hamlet in the later 20th century took place down the hill to the north-east where several roads were formed for new estates of council and private houses and bungalows.[97]

The central areas of the Forest remained sparsely populated during the 19th and 20th centuries, with few dwellings apart from the Speech House at Kensley, beside the main Cinderford–Coleford road, and the other Crown lodges.[98] In the mid 19th century some mines, quarries, and other industrial sites had one or two small cottages nearby.[99] At Lightmoor colliery there was a row of four cottages in 1856[1] and, among other large collieries, Crump Meadow had two houses in 1874[2] and Trafalgar had several, including one for its manager, in 1878.[3]

Settlement at MOSELEY GREEN, north-east of Parkend between the roads to Blakeney and Yorkley, comprised one dwelling on an encroachment in 1787[4] and two cottages in 1834.[5] In 1859 the hamlet also included a row of three cottages owned by the main Parkend colliery company.[6] Later buildings were a nonconformist chapel converted as two dwellings at the turn of the century and one to the north occupied by the Rising Sun beerhouse in the late 1870s.[7] Further north a row of miners' cottages, known as the Barracks, was built on the road from Parkend to Blakeney in the late 1840s.[8] The cottages, numbering 20 in five identical blocks, were leased to local colliery owners by the Crown,[9] which in 1908 erected a row of four cottages to the west and in 1910 and 1911 rebuilt the original dwellings as four ranges containing 16 cottages.[10] Scattered houses nearby include one on the Blakeney road created by enlarging the remains of a chapel built in 1907.[11]

A few houses were built at CANNOP in the valley south-west of the Speech House. The earliest, a pair of mid 19th-century cottages at chemical works[12] north of the Littledean–Coleford road and west of Cannop brook, were occupied in 1859 as four dwellings[13] and were later remodelled. They were demolished in 1966.[14] Nearby two or three cottages were built at the crossroads formed in 1903 on the completion of the Lydbrook–Lydney road,[15] and in 1913 the Crown built three pairs of cottages on the Lydbrook road for employees at wood distillation works which it then established at Cannop.[16] Further along the Lydbrook road, at the bottom of Wimberry Slade, the

79 G.D.R. wills 1568/152; Glos. R.O., D 1677/GG 529; P.R.O., MR 879 (F 17/1).
80 Glos. R.O., D 2926/2.
81 Reg. Electors W. Division Glos. 1850–1, 55; Kelly's Dir. Glos. (1870), 533.   82 P.R.O., MR 415.
83 Glos. R.O., Q/RGf 1/4; 2nd Rep. Dean Forest Com. 49.
84 P.R.O., MR 879.
85 Ibid. F 17/117(2), pp. 6–7, 19; MR 691.
86 Cf. Kelly's Dir. Glos. (1910 and later edns.), s.v. Eng. Bicknor.
87 P.R.O., MR 415; O.S. Map 6", Glos. XXXI. SW. (1883 edn.).
88 Glos. R.O., Q/RGf 1/4.   89 P.R.O., F 16/64.
90 Below, Prot. Nonconf., Prim. Methodists.
91 O.S. Map 1/2,500, Glos. XXXI. 9 (1903, 1922 edns.).
92 Glos. R.O., DA 25/602–3; O.S. Map 1/2,500, SO 5913 (1960 edn.).
93 P.R.O., F 17/96; MR 691.
94 Ibid. F 17/4.
95 Date on chapel.   96 Glos. R.O., DA 25/603.
97 Ibid. DA 25/600/2; DA 25/602; O.S. Map 1/2,500, SO 6014 (1961, 1974 edns.).
98 Below, forest lodges.
99 P.R.O., F 16/63; F 16/64; HO 107/1959, s.v. E. Dean;

HO 107/2444, s.v. W. Dean.
1 Ibid. F 16/63 (nos. 2997–3000); F 16/70.
2 Dean Forest Select Cttee. (1874), 48.
3 O.S. Map 1/2,500, Glos. XXXI. 10 (1878 edn.); cf. Dean Forest Mercury, 14 Mar. 1986.
4 P.R.O., MR 415.   5 Glos. R.O., Q/RGf 1/6.
6 P.R.O., F 16/64 (nos. 2093–5); F 16/71.
7 O.S. Map 6", Glos. XXXIX. NW. (1883, 1903 edns.); below, Prot. Nonconf., Congregationalists; Prim. Methodists.
8 Atkinson, Map of Dean Forest (1847); P.R.O., HO 107/2444, s.v. W. Dean; cf. 25th Rep. Com. Woods, H.C. 753, pp. 13, 85 (1847–8), xxxvii; Glos. R.O., Q/RUm 254.
9 P.R.O., F 16/64 (nos. 2041–61); F 16/71; 36th Rep. Com. Woods, H.C. 380, p. 88 (1857–8), xxxi; 37th Rep. Com. Woods, H.C. 54, p. 74 (1859 Sess. 2), xi.
10 Dates on bldgs.; P.R.O., F 3/1130; O.S. Map 6", Glos. XXXIX. NW. (1904, 1924 edns.).
11 Inscr. on bldg.; cf. Citizen (Glouc.), 31 Oct. 1986.
12 Glos. R.O., Q/RUm 175, p. 6.
13 P.R.O., F 16/64 (nos. 1078–81); F 16/71.
14 Hart, Ind. Hist. of Dean, 346.
15 O.S. Map 1/2,500, Glos. XXXI. 13 (1903, 1922 edns.); 81st Rep. Com. Woods (1903), 3.
16 Dates on bldgs.; P.R.O., F 3/1266.

Crown built five pairs of cottages in 1907 and 1911 for workers at Cannop colliery.[17]

South of the Speech House, on the Moseley Green road, a building known as Old Dean Hall was built by the Crown for a forestry school in 1915[18] and was part of a special school in 1992. East of the Speech House, on the Littledean road near Cinderford, a hospital was opened in 1923.[19]

The hamlet of BRIERLEY, sometimes called Brierley Hill,[20] on the main Coleford road southwest of Nailbridge, grew in the mid 19th century. The earliest cottages, built between 1787 and 1834, were one at a quarry on the north side of the road and three on a steep hillside to the north-east.[21] The cottage by the road[22] had become an inn under the sign of the Swan by 1859[23] and a house to the east is dated 1864. More cottages appeared on the hillside to the north-east in the mid 19th century[24] and a small chapel opened in the hamlet in 1884.[25] The hamlet expanded westwards in the early 20th century with the building of houses and bungalows, some of timber, on the north side of the Coleford road.[26] At the west end three pairs of council houses were built in 1931.[27]

The settlement of STEAM MILLS, on the Littledean road between Nailbridge and Cinderford, came into being in the 1840s when Timothy Bennett built a steam-powered corn mill west of the road[28] near a mine called Old Engine.[29] In 1856 there were seven cottages to the north and an inn or beerhouse called the Old Engine to the south.[30] By 1878 the buildings north of the mill included a row of ten cottages and new premises for the Old Engine.[31] The collection of cottages at New Town, south of Steam Mills towards Broadmoor, was formed between 1856 and 1878,[32] and Steam Mills acquired a nonconformist chapel and a school in the early 1880s.[33]

FOREST LODGES. One of the earliest buildings put up on the royal demesne was used by the Forest's attachment (or speech) court. Recorded from 1338, the courthouse stood at Kensley,[34] beside the Cinderford–Coleford road on the eastern edge of the Cannop valley, and

was at or very close to the site of its late 17th-century successor, the Speech House.[35] The court met at Kensley in 1566 and 1608,[36] but the courthouse had evidently been demolished or fallen into disrepair by 1623 when a house at Cannop, built c. 1619 by lessees of the Crown's ironworks, was used by the court[37] and was called the new speech house.[38] In 1628 the house at Cannop was said to be the only building suitable for Forest business, but the Forest officers were then being prevented from using it,[39] perhaps a consequence of the Crown's recent alienation of an estate based on Cannop;[40] in 1637 the attachment court met at Littledean.[41]

In the 1670s when the royal demesne was divided into six walks a keeper's lodge was provided for each.[42] For King's (later Speech House) walk a new lodge and courthouse, at first called the King's Lodge but later the Speech House,[43] was built at Kensley c. 1670.[44] It was said to have been very poorly constructed,[45] and it was altered and improved later: the date 1676 was placed above its side door and the date 1680 on its main front,[46] and further work was needed after it was severely damaged by rioters at the Revolution of 1688.[47] The Speech House was a keeper's lodge until shortly before 1841,[48] by which year it was leased as an inn;[49] it remained, however, the meeting place of the attachment court (usually by then called the verderers' court).[50] By the late 19th century the Speech House was a hotel frequented by tourists[51] and it was enlarged to provide additional accommodation c. 1882.[52] It was still a hotel in 1994, when it was leased by Forte Ltd. from the Forestry Commission. The late 17th-century building, which faces westwards over the Cannop valley, is a plain block of two storeys and attics and is built of the local sandstone with, internally, massive oak beams. Its south end contains two principal rooms, the upper one described as a dining room in 1854 and the lower one, which has a dais against the south wall, used as the courtroom.[53] The block added c. 1882 was on the east side of the building and gave the Speech House a new main front to the Cinderford–Coleford road; designed by George Pearson of Ross-on-Wye (Herefs.),[54] it

17 Dates on bldgs.; P.R.O., F 3/1079; F 3/1217.
18 93rd Rep. Com. Woods, H.C. 285, p. 37 (1914–16), xxxvii; 95th Rep. Com. Woods, H.C. 104, p. 19 (1917–18), xviii; O.S. Map 1/2,500, Glos. XXXI. 14 (1922 edn.).
19 Glouc. Jnl. 30 June 1923.
20 Kelly's Dir. Glos. (1870), 532.
21 P.R.O., MR 415; Glos. R.O., Q/RGf 1/8.
22 Cf. G.D.R. wills 1824/162.
23 Glouc. Jnl. 19 Mar. 1859; Glos. R.O., reg. wills 1874, ff. 274v.–277v.
24 Stone dated 1860 reset on one cottage.
25 Date on chapel.
26 O.S. Map 1/2,500, Glos. XXXI. 6 (1902, 1922 edns.); W. Foley, Child in the Forest (1974), 46.
27 Glos. R.O., DA 24/600/1.
28 Below, Industry, mills; O.S. Map 6", Glos. XXXI. NE. (1884 edn.).
29 Glos. R.O., Q/RUm 107; the area was called Old Engine in the mid 19th cent.: P.R.O., HO 107/1959, s.v. E. Dean.
30 P.R.O., F 16/63 (nos. 1819–32); F 16/70; Kelly's Dir. Glos. (1856), 278.
31 O.S. Map 1/2,500, Glos XXXI. 7 (1878 edn.).
32 P.R.O., F 16/63; O.S. Map 1/2,500, Glos. XXXI. 7 (1878, 1903 edns.).
33 Below, Prot. Nonconf., Baptists; Educ., elementary schs.
34 P.R.O., E 32/33, m. 3.

35 Cal. Treas. Bks. 1669–72, 380.
36 P.R.O., E 146/1/31; E 137/13/4.
37 Ibid. E 137/13/4; B.L. Lansd. MS. 166, f. 380.
38 Glos. R.O., P 138/IN 1/1, burial 27 Feb. 1623/4.
39 P.R.O., E 178/5304, m. 13.
40 Below, Forest Admin., exploitation 1603–68; it was possibly 'Cannop House' mentioned as part of the alienated est. in 1661: Cal. S.P. Dom. 1660–1, 588; cf. Hart, Verderers, 133–4.
41 P.R.O., E 146/3/29.
42 Below, Forest Admin., reformed admin.
43 Glos. R.O., D 36/Q 2.
44 Cal. Treas. Bks. 1669–72, 372–3, 380, 429; a plan to build it at Coleford was abandoned: ibid. 112–13, 524.
45 Glos. R.O., D 1677/GG 1223.
46 Hart, Verderers, 131–2.
47 Cal. Treas. Bks. 1689–92, 40, 586–7, 1496.
48 Select Cttee. on Woods (1849), 128; P.R.O., F 3/455, superannuation of keeper of Worc. walk 1895.
49 P.R.O., HO 107/364, s.v. Speech Ho. walk; Hart, Verderers, 147.
50 P.R.O., F 16/21–2.
51 Kelly's Dir. Glos. (1889), 863; Glos. Colln. prints 125A.16.
52 P.R.O., F 17/144.
53 Ibid. F 17/143; for the courtroom, above, Plate 41.
54 P.R.O., F 17/144.

matched the earlier block in style and stone-work.[55] Internal restoration in 1956 included the renewal of the roof beams in the courtroom,[56] which in 1994 was the hotel dining room but also used for the meetings of the Forest's verderers.

Sites for lodges in the other five walks were being chosen in 1675.[57] By 1677 lodges for the walks called Worcester, Danby, and Latimer had been built under the direction of the marquess of Worcester, constable of St. Briavels and warden of the Forest, and for York walk a house at Parkend, formerly used by lessees of ironworks there, had been bought; for Herbert walk the purchase of another conveniently sited house was in hand.[58] Each of the lodges, including the Speech House, was assigned an inclosure of c. 30 a., which its keeper farmed,[59] and by the mid 18th century the outbuildings at the lodges included cattle pounds and kennels for hounds.[60] York Lodge ceased to house a keeper c. 1840,[61] and from 1859 or earlier was leased as a residence to Parkend industrialists,[62] and Latimer Lodge and its land were leased as a smallholding from 1882.[63] Worcester, Danby, and Herbert lodges were occupied by keepers until 1914 or later.[64] All five were sold by the Forestry Commission in the late 20th century.[65]

Sites commanding wide views[66] were chosen for the lodges, so that the keepers could watch for fires, timber stealing, or other damage to the plantations. Worcester Lodge is on high ground on the west side of the Cannop valley, Danby Lodge at the summit of a high ridge on the west side of the Blackpool brook valley, and Herbert Lodge faces into the Forest from the south side of Ruardean hill. Latimer Lodge, where a new lodge built on a different but nearby site between 1731 and 1735 replaced the original,[67] stands high on Littledean hill at the north-east rim of the Forest. York Lodge, on a hillside west of Parkend village, is rather less prominently sited. Worcester Lodge is dated 1675, though it was repaired after 1688 when, with the Speech House and York Lodge, it was badly damaged by the rioters.[68] The late 17th-century stone range, similar to a medium-sized farmhouse of the period, has external stacks at each end and a moulded stone doorway in the centre of the

east front. In the 19th century low additions were made at each end, and in 1911 a twin-gabled extension, incorporating an existing single-storeyed back kitchen, was made on the west.[69] Danby Lodge, probably built on a plan similar to Worcester Lodge, was remodelled and extended in the 19th century, York Lodge was rebuilt in the 19th century and a new room added at its north end in 1914,[70] and Herbert Lodge was rebuilt or remodelled in the 19th century and again much altered in the late 20th. At Latimer Lodge the building of the early 1730s is a long, symmetrical range with a hipped roof and dormered attics; it was refitted internally in 1906[71] and later in the 20th century, and the house was converted as four flats c. 1990. The keepers' inclosures of pasture land adjoining the six lodges were largely intact in 1994, that at Worcester Lodge still in Forestry Commission ownership and used as a holiday campsite.

In the early 19th century, when the royal demesne of the Forest was replanted, 24 small lodges were established to house woodmen to guard and maintain the new inclosures.[72] For Shutcastle Inclosure, near Ellwood, a cottage on an old encroachment was bought, and the lodge for Oakenhill Inclosure, near Yorkley, was apparently a cottage that had housed a watchman[73] appointed by the Forest administration c. 1780.[74] The other lodges were new buildings put up between 1806 and 1815,[75] often, like those at Lea Bailey, Serridge, Barnhill, Staple Edge, and Chestnuts, at high and isolated sites in the middle of the inclosures.[76] The small two-storeyed cottages, built of local stone, were identified by an inscription on a window lintel, recording the name, date, and acreage of the inclosure and, usually, the name of the Crown's surveyor general of woods, Lord Glenbervie.[77] The staff of woodmen employed in the Forest was reduced during the 19th century, and by 1897 nine of the cottages were no longer occupied for their original purpose, some being let to forestry workers.[78] During the 20th century several of the cottages were demolished or abandoned to decay, while others, mainly those at the more accessible sites, were sold by the Forestry Commission in the 1960s and early 1970s.[79]

[55] Above, Plate 39; for the building before enlargement, Nicholls, *Forest of Dean*, 51; Phelps, *Forest in Old Photog.* (1983), 122.
[56] Hart, *Verderers*, 168.
[57] *Cal. Treas. Bks.* 1672–5, 307.
[58] Glos. R.O., D 1677/GG 1223.
[59] *Cal. Treas. Bks.* 1672–5, 307; *3rd Rep. Com. Woods* (1788), 84.
[60] *Glouc. Jnl.* 22 July 1735; Berkeley Cast. Mun., General Ser. T, box 25, papers about keepers' misdemeanours.
[61] *Select Cttee. on Woods* (1849), 128; P.R.O., F 3/455, superannuation of keeper of Worc. walk 1895.
[62] P.R.O., F 3/221.
[63] Ibid. F 3/459.
[64] Ibid. F 3/455; F 3/1184.
[65] Inf. from Mr. J. E. Everard, deputy surveyor, Forest Enterprise, Coleford.
[66] For the sites, P.R.O., F 16/47; Atkinson, *Map of Dean Forest* (1847).
[67] P.R.O., LR 4/3/59; F 17/7.

[68] *Cal. Treas. Bks.* 1689–92, 1496.
[69] P.R.O., F 3/1224.
[70] Ibid. F 3/1099.
[71] Ibid. F 3/459.
[72] Ibid. LR 4/20/25; cf. *Select Cttee. on Woods* (1849), 163.
[73] P.R.O., LR 4/21; cf. ibid. F 16/47.
[74] *3rd Rep. Com. Woods* (1788), 84.
[75] P.R.O., LR 4/20/6; LR 4/21–5.
[76] O.S. Maps 6", Glos. XXIII. SW.; XXXI. NW., SE., SW.; XXXIX. NE., NW., SE., SW. (1883–4 edn.) mark 20 of the lodges, and others were in the inclosures at Haywood, Edgehills, Ruardean hill, and Lea Bailey (a second one, perhaps at Lower Lea Bailey): P.R.O., LR 4/20/6; LR 4/21, 30; Atkinson, *Map of Dean Forest* (1847).
[77] Inscrs. visible in 1994 included those at Yew Tree Brake, Sallow Vallets, Cockshoot, Nagshead hill, and Blakeney hill. The lintels from Barnhill and Crabtree hill lodges were at Dean Heritage mus., Soudley.
[78] P.R.O., F 3/319; cf. ibid. F 3/37.
[79] Inf. from Mr. Everard and residents of former lodges.

INDUSTRY

ITS timber and mineral resources have given the formerly extraparochial Forest of Dean a rich and distinct industrial history. The Forest lies in a basin formed by carboniferous strata and is almost coterminous with fields of coal and iron ore. The coal measures, which outcrop in three roughly concentric circles near the edge of the Forest, are mostly thin but some 14 seams have proved workable. The ore, found in the sandstone and the limestone formations beneath and around the coalfield, has also been mined together with associated deposits of ochres and oxides, used as colouring agents.[80]

Ore mining and ironmaking, the latter sustained for many centuries by charcoal burning, began in early times. Later much iron ore and coal was taken away by road and river and Forest stone was also quarried and dressed for local and distant markets. Mining, which was long regulated by custom and limited by flooding in the basin, was largely confined to the edge of the coalfield until the 19th century. The mining and ironmaking industries were at their peak in the 19th century when they spawned an intricate network of tramroads and railways and a number of related industries, including engineeering. In the 20th century deeper mining was abandoned as reserves of ore and coal became uneconomic to work, and jobs in mining and heavy industry disappeared to be replaced by other forms of employment.

MINING TO THE 18TH CENTURY. There is little direct documentary evidence of Dean's mining industry before the mid 13th century. The rich deposits of iron ore were exploited by the Romans[81] and supplied ironworkers operating in Dean by the later 11th century.[82] Coal was being dug in several of the Forest's bailiwicks in the mid 1240s[83] but its extraction was of secondary importance to ore mining until the 17th century. Red oxide and yellow ochre were also mined before the 15th century.[84]

About 1250 the Crown received rents from some ore and coal mines and ½d. for every load of coal carried on the river Severn, the toll, which was apparently also levied on ore carried on the river, being farmed to Pain of Lydney for £24. Other royal revenue came from a toll on traffic using the road to Gloucester and from cinders,[85] the slag produced by early ironworking which was rich in iron.[86] Control over the digging of ore differed in the various bailiwicks. In 1282, when the Crown farmed its revenues from ore mining for £46 and was entitled to ½d.

for every load of ore taken out of the Forest, perhaps excepting Lea bailiwick, the woodwards of Abenhall, Bicknor, and Blakeney bailiwicks took or claimed the ore within their jurisdictions and Richard Talbot took the ore in Lea bailiwick. Miners in Bearse and Mitcheldean bailiwicks paid the Crown 1d. a week and, like those in Staunton bailiwick who owed ½d., had to sell ore to sustain one royal forge at a fixed price. In each productive ore mine in Mitcheldean and apparently in Bearse and Staunton bailiwicks the king employed a man alongside the miners and took his share of the profits. In those three bailiwicks and apparently in Abenhall bailiwick the king also bought a fixed amount of ore each week known as 'law ore', the amount in Bearse bailiwick, which had greater reserves of ore, being four times larger than in each of the others.[87] The regulation of coal mining similarly varied. In the mid 1240s the constable of St. Briavels castle and the woodwards of Blakeney and Staunton bailiwicks seem to have shared payments from colliers working in those areas, while the woodward of Abenhall bailiwick received 1d. for each horse-load of coal.[88] In 1282 coal found in Bearse, Littledean, Mitcheldean, and Ruardean bailiwicks belonged to the Crown and that in Abenhall, Bicknor, Blakeney, Lea, and Staunton bailiwicks was taken or claimed by the respective woodwards.[89] The woodward of Blakeney continued to claim all mines within his bailiwick in 1634.[90]

The techniques of medieval mining were necessarily primitive. Ore was extracted from the limestone outcrops to the west and east of the coalfield by surface workings, often known locally as scowles.[91] Such workings usually left behind winding trenches and some reached great depths to win ore found in chambers or 'churns' varying considerably in size. The coal outcrops were mined by short drifts or levels and by small pits.[92] Dean's miners with their expertise in excavating and burrowing were valued by the Crown as sappers and by the 1220s they were frequently conscripted for military service. In 1253 twenty of them were impressed to accompany the king on a Gascon expedition and later many served in Scotland under Edward II and Edward III and in France under the latter. In 1319 twelve miners were also conscripted to work the iron mines of Hugh le Despenser the younger in South Wales. The call for Dean's miners to serve in armies overseas was renewed in 1419, 1522,[93] and 1577.[94]

The Dean miners enjoyed privileges which

80 Geol. of Forest of Dean Coal and Iron Field (H.M.S.O. 1942), passim; Fisher, Custom and Capitalism, 8.
81 C. E. Hart, Ind. Hist. of Dean (1971), 216; New Regard of Forest of Dean, iv. 5–11. Hart's hist. is a detailed and comprehensive account of ind. sites based on original research. 82 Below, ironworks.
83 P.R.O., E 146/1/25.
84 Hart, Ind. Hist. of Dean, 244.
85 P.R.O., E 146/1/26; cf. C. E. Hart, Free Miners of Royal Forest of Dean and Hundred of St. Briavels (1953),

158–9. Hart's account of the free miners includes extracts from many original documents. 86 Below, ironworks.
87 V.C.H. Glos. ii. 219; Trans. B.G.A.S. xiv. 368–9.
88 P.R.O., E 146/1/25. 89 Hart, Free Miners, 14–15.
90 Ibid. 183. 91 For an example, above, Plate 2.
92 Inf. from Mr. I. J. Standing, curator, Dean Heritage mus., Soudley; cf. V.C.H. Glos. ii. 219; New Regard of Forest of Dean, iv. 5; Fisher, Custom and Capitalism, 8; Hart, Ind. Hist. of Dean, 254. 93 Hart, Free Miners, 19, 21–4.
94 Acts of P.C. 1575–7, 335.

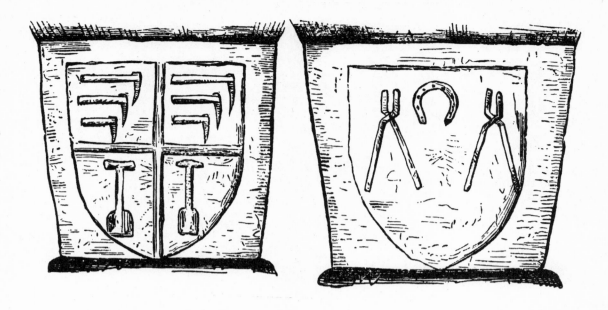

FIG. 19. CARVINGS OF MINERS' AND SMITHS' TOOLS ON ABENHALL CHURCH FONT

included a code of customary mining law. Tradition states that they acquired those privileges from the Crown in return for their services in the Scottish wars of the 14th century, and particularly at sieges of Berwick.[95] The earliest surviving records, of the 17th century, attribute the laws to Edward III but their reference to the wider bounds of the Forest,[96] in force from some time before 1228 until 1301 and from 1305 to 1327,[97] indicates an earlier origin. Later the miners' franchises and laws, which by the mid 19th century had become known as the 'Book of Dennis',[98] applied only to St. Briavels hundred, which covered a smaller area than the reduced bounds of the Forest confirmed in 1327. The franchises were evidently gained by long usage in respect of ore mining and in time were applied to the winning of coal and ochre.[99] The Crown's right, recorded in 1282, to buy 'law ore' from miners in at least three bailiwicks[1] implies the existence of a mining court. Such a court met in 1469 at a place called Hill pit and was later known as the mine law court. It had exclusive jurisdiction over the miners and their workings and protected their privileges and customs. Disputes, including pleas of debt, were tried by a jury of 12 miners and appeals were allowed to a jury of 24 miners and, in the last resort, to one of 48.[2] Among their privileges the miners were taking wood to shore up their works in 1282.[3] They also enjoyed free access to their works from highways,[4] and carrying rights were possibly at the heart of a dispute with the ironworkers in 1375.[5]

By the later Middle Ages the Crown also regulated mining in Dean through the office of gaveller or keeper of the 'gale'. The office had been created by 1464, when it was granted, together with the Crown's mining revenues, to Robert Hyett for life, and by 1484 it was held by two men in charge respectively of the eastern and western halves of the Forest.[6] The division existed by 1435 when the Crown farmed its mining revenues, known as the gavel, in the area 'under the wood' to two men for £22 and in the area 'above the wood' to one man for £20 3s. 4d.[7] The area 'under the wood', comprising the eastern part of the royal demesne woodland with Flaxley, Littledean, Mitcheldean, Ruardean, and parts of Awre and Lea, was sometimes called the gale of Mitcheldean. That 'above the wood', comprising the western part of the royal demesne with English Bicknor, St. Briavels, Newland, and Staunton, was sometimes called the gale of Newland.[8] In the early 17th century there was a single gaveller and many of his duties, notably the collection of royal mining revenues, were carried out by deputies. At the Restoration the Crown apparently reverted to the practice of appointing a gaveller for each half of the Forest, Sir Baynham Throckmorton the younger of Clearwell being granted the keepership of the gale above the wood, but by 1681 the two keeperships were again vested in a single person.[9] The number of deputy gavellers is known to have varied from two to six in the 17th and 18th centuries.[10]

Iron ore, cinders, and coal were presumably exploited throughout the later Middle

95 Hart, *Free Miners*, 17; *V.C.H. Glos.* ii. 219.
96 Hart, *Free Miners*, 19, 34–47.
97 Cf. above, Bounds.
98 Hart, *Free Miners*, 35–6.
99 Ibid. 43.
1 Above, this section.
2 Glos. R.O., D 6177/1–2; cf. Hart, *Free Miners*, 72–4.

3 *Trans. B.G.A.S.* xiv. 369.   4 Hart, *Free Miners*, 40.
5 *Cal. Pat.* 1374–7, 155.
6 Hart, *Free Miners*, 52–3.
7 P.R.O., E 101/141/1.
8 Hart, *Free Miners*, 51; N.L.W., Dunraven MSS. 324.
9 Hart, *Free Miners*, 55–8.
10 Ibid. 3 n., 58–60, 225; *3rd Rep. Com. Woods* (1788), 91.

Ages.[11] From the late 16th century the Forest produced considerable amounts of ore and cinders for blast furnaces operating in an area extending into Herefordshire and Monmouthshire.[12] In 1612 the Crown, by the agency of the earl of Pembroke, attempted to divert all the ore and cinders to new ironworks established on the royal demesne of the Forest but the miners continued to sell ore and cinders elsewhere. By 1614 over 35 of them had formed an association pledged to supply ironworks outside the Forest. Some had contracts with agents of William Chesshall, a London merchant,[13] who under a licence of 1606 traded in ore and cinders to Ireland.[14] The miners responded to the Crown's interference in their customary rights in 1612 by rioting.[15] Lessees of the king's ironworks also attempted to restrain the mining and sale of ore and cinders but the miners refused to give up their privileges. Coal miners were as equally adamant in 1637 when Edward Terringham secured a lease for 31 years of all coal mines and quarries in the Forest. More than 100 families then depended on mining ore or coal. Terringham mined coal in several places but his works were destroyed and he relinquished the lease in 1640. By that time Sir John Winter of Lydney owned the ore and coal mines in most of the Forest by virtue of a royal grant. The miners worked their own pits and levels throughout the period,[16] as they did after 1668 when Terringham's son Francis (d. by 1675) acquired a new lease of the collieries and quarries.[17] Ore and cinders continued to be sent to furnaces outside the extraparochial Forest after those within it were demolished in 1674 and the Irish trade remained important.[18] Although experiments in the 1650s to use Forest coal for smelting ore failed,[19] the coalfield in the later 17th century had markets in parts of Gloucestershire, Herefordshire, and Monmouthshire for three grades of coal, used as fuel in houses, forges, and limekilns respectively.[20] Grading was according to size by means of sieves made in places such as Mitcheldean, Newnham, and Tidenham.[21]

Ochre mining also continued in the 17th century. About 1611 Robert Treswell, the surveyor of Crown woods, sought permission to dig for yellow ochre[22] and in 1634 Henry Hippon and Edward Lassells wanted, in return for taking timber to a Kent shipyard, a monopoly in mining yellow ochre on the edge of the Forest above Littledean.[23] In that area, and particularly in Abbots wood, were rich deposits of red oxides and yellow ochres,[24] and in 1650 a mine known as Maple pit or the Yellowshraft was possibly supplying two London merchants with ochre.[25]

The mine law court, customarily summoned by the gavellers when need arose or when three actions were pending, met in the presence of the deputy constable of St. Briavels castle, the castle clerk who was the court steward, and the deputy gavellers in the early 17th century. Having no fixed meeting place, it was convened in the open, under a hedge or tree, or in a house, and at times it employed a crier.[26] In 1656 it held a session in Littledean and later it met often at Clearwell and also at Coleford, Mitcheldean, and Ruardean. In 1680 it assembled at the Speech House, which became its usual venue in the 18th century.[27] During that period the court acted like a corporation for a society or fellowship of miners. It settled disputes between miners and sought to preserve the system of mining shaped by customs established in the Middle Ages. Fines for breaches of custom, paid in ore or coal and sometimes in cash, were divided between the Crown and plaintiffs. The customary system, born of a need to support small-scale co-operative ventures, stifled individual enterprise and it was increasingly challenged, sometimes with the connivance of Crown officials.[28] The court modified customs when change was desirable or consistent with the miners' interests.[29] The customs, which in 1634 were apparently declared to have no legal basis,[30] centred on an exclusive right to win ore, ochre, and coal in the Forest and to carry and sell those minerals in the surrounding countryside. The right to mine originally extended to all land but was later banned in gardens, orchards, and curtilages and in the extensive inclosures for the growth of timber created in the Forest under the reafforestation Act of 1668. That Act confirmed the miners' privileges in a general way without specifying what they were, and an attempt, immediately after its enactment, to make miners pay for the wood required for their works was soon abandoned. To provide legal defence of the customs, as was needed in 1675, and relief for injured miners the mine law court levied rates on the miners, and in 1685 it ruled that any jury making a rate was to represent equally the colliers and ore miners.[31]

The right or freedom to mine was restricted to native residents of St. Briavels hundred and came to be reserved to those who were sons of free miners. By custom aspirants to the freedom worked for a year and a day in the mines and usually provided a dinner for the miners' fellowship. The freedom was forfeit for breaches of mining custom and for perjury in the mine law court. In 1668 the court ruled that natives might acquire the freedom by an apprenticeship of six

11 Cf. Hart, *Ind. Hist. of Dean*, 7; Leland, *Itin.* ed. Toulmin Smith, ii. 64.
12 Hart, *Ind. Hist. of Dean*, 219, 222.
13 Hart, *Free Miners*, 166–73; below, ironworks.
14 *Cal. S.P. Dom.* 1603–10, 306.
15 Hart, *Free Miners*, 165.
16 Ibid. 184–97, 206.
17 Ibid. 218–26.
18 Hart, *Ind. Hist. of Dean*, 220, 222; *Trans. B.G.A.S.* lxxii. 135, 141.
19 Below, ironworks.
20 Hart, *Free Miners*, 82, 105; Hart, *Ind. Hist. of Dean*, 257.
21 Hart, *Ind. Hist. of Dean*, 259; Smith, *Men and Armour*, 33, 48, 51.
22 *Cal. S.P. Dom.* 1611–18, 107.
23 Ibid. 1634–5, 301.
24 Bodl. MS. Top. Glouc. c. 3, f. 193.
25 Hart, *Free Miners*, 199, 206. 26 Ibid. 66–71, 73.
27 Ibid. 142; for Speech Ho., above, Settlement, forest lodges.
28 Hart, *Free Miners*, 10–11, 72–4; cf. Fisher, *Custom and Capitalism*, 6–7.
29 *Award of Dean Forest Mining Com.* (1841), 11–20.
30 *3rd Rep. Com. Woods* (1788), 12; Hart, *Free Miners*, 184, 206.
31 Hart, *Free Miners*, 3, 38, 40, 86–7, 108–9, 216–17, 222; *Award of Dean Forest Mining Com.* (1841), 14–15.

years to a free miner and that cabiners or squatters born in the Forest might obtain them by working seven years in the mines. In 1680 it restricted the freedom to men who had been apprenticed for five years to their fathers or other free miners and had reached the age of 21. From 1737 sons of 'foreigners', persons not born in the hundred, were allowed to qualify by serving a seven-year apprenticeship to a free miner.[32]

In the early 17th century miners prospected for ore and coal at will without seeking land-owners' permission. After they had opened up the ground and dug three steps they summoned the gaveller to 'gale' or license that mine to them and assign a right of way to the nearest highway, each miner paying 1d. Each mine was developed by a partnership of up to five miners, and the partners, known as 'verns', were helped some-times by sons and apprentices. The Crown, acting through the gaveller, was entitled to instal a miner in each mine to win for it a share of the ore or coal raised, and private landowners also had the same right in mines on their land. The king's man was long regarded as the third most important member of any company of miners. Active miners paid the Crown 1d. a week and 'law ore'. The latter, a quarterly payment for the mine law court in ore or coal, was sometimes commuted for 3d. and many miners com-pounded for an annual sum to cover all their dues.[33] By custom a miner was free to dispose of his share or 'dole' in a mine to whom he chose;[34] c. 1650 six miners leased an ochre mine near Littledean to John Brayne for 21 years.[35]

Where possible miners drove adits or levels upwards on hillsides to assist drainage and the removal of coal. Drains were occasionally im-peded by the sinking of new pits, a problem which the mine law court sought to remedy in 1674 by obliging miners opening works within 100 yd. of a drain to obtain the consent of its owners. Much mining was on a larger scale than had been permitted by ancient custom, which had protected a mine within the radius in which the spoil from it could be thrown. The mine law court attempted to inhibit the growth in the size of mines. In 1668 it restricted each miner's output to the amount of ore or coal that four horses could carry away, but in 1754 it extended to 1,000 yd. the distance within which a working level had protection from new pits.[36] Horses worked inside some mines, presumably drifts, by 1687.[37] With the growth in coal mining in the later 17th century there was greater damage to the woodland as miners took wood to shore up their workings, and some Newland residents, alarmed at the destruction, formed an associa-tion to work a drift at Milkwall and buy the wood needed for its support from elsewhere.[38] Some of the largest and deepest mines were created by exploiting the iron ore on the eastern and south-

western sides of the coalfield. Many centuries of ore mining had exhausted deposits near the surface and in the 17th century miners dug below abandoned labyrinths of workings to form large caverns, some of them over 450 ft. under-ground.[39]

Minerals were carried out of the Forest by horses, donkeys, and mules[40] and loaded on boats and barges plying on the rivers Wye and Severn. There were numerous pitching places on the banks of the Wye, including Monmouth and, in Newland parish, Redbrook, and in the later 17th century Brockweir handled ore bound for Ireland.[41] On the Severn some ore was shipped at Lydney Pill in the 1650s, and Newn-ham, which conducted trade with Ireland, handled ore and coal in the 1660s.[42] The carrying trade gradually came under the control of for-eigners. The miners' exclusive right to deliver ore and coal outside St. Briavels hundred was sanctioned by the mine law court in 1668 but it proved prejudicial to the interests of friends and tenants of the marquess of Worcester, constable of St. Briavels, in Monmouthshire and Here-fordshire and it was rescinded in 1674 to allow foreigners to purchase coal at the mines for their own use.[43] The demand for Forest coal grew to the point when in 1687 the residents of the hundred could not buy enough for their house-hold needs. Merchants and agents from Monmouthshire and Herefordshire removed large amounts and in 1719 the miners attempted, albeit with little success, to regain control of the carrying trade by allowing only inhabitants of adjoining parts of Gloucestershire, including Newent and Westbury-on-Severn, access to the mines to collect coal for their own use.[44]

The miners' loss of the carrying trade was almost certainly brought about by controls to prevent them from underselling one another.[45] To that end the mine law court set the minimum prices they were to charge at the mines and outside the Forest and entrusted negotiations with their customers to a few of their number. Ore sales were conducted in that fashion until 1676.[46] Some colliers ignored price regulation and in 1680 the court attempted to support the coal price in and around Monmouth by fixing the minimum prices to be paid at pitching places on the river banks above the town. For some reason all price controls were lifted in 1687 but they were reintroduced from 1693 and the prac-tice of appointing bargainers to act for the miners resumed. In 1699 the court imposed a ban on the carriage of coal on the Wye below Welsh Bicknor (Mon., later Herefs.), presum-ably to maintain prices at Monmouth by diverting its trade overland.[47] By 1719 the court was regulating traffic on the river in a way that divided the Herefordshire and Monmouthshire markets between the mines of the east and west

[32] Hart, *Free Miners*, 2, 43, 81, 104, 127–8, 193, 222; *4th Rep. Dean Forest Com.* 4; *Award of Dean Forest Mining Com.* (1841), 13–17.
[33] Hart, *Free Miners*, 5–7, 38, 40, 50, 171, 176–7, 180.
[34] Ibid. 42.   [35] Ibid. 199.
[36] Ibid. 43, 82–3, 85, 112, 125, 136; Hart, *Ind. Hist. of Dean*, 255–9.
[37] Hart, *Free Miners*, 111.
[38] *3rd Rep. Com. Woods* (1788), 17.

[39] *Trans. B.G.A.S.* ii. 231; Hart, *Ind. Hist. of Dean*, 225.
[40] Hart, *Free Miners*, 79–80; G.D.R., V 5/254T 3.
[41] Hart, *Free Miners*, 90, 103, 105, 114.
[42] Ibid. 79–80, 83, 206.
[43] Ibid. 81, 84.
[44] Ibid. 110, 122–3, 126.
[45] *Award of Dean Forest Mining Com.* (1841), 17.
[46] Hart, *Free Miners*, 73, 79–82, 97.
[47] Ibid. 105, 110–16.

FIG. 20. FOREST OF DEAN IRON MINERS EQUIPPED FOR WORK, c. 1855

sides of the Forest respectively and in 1741 it gave free miners with barges on the river preference in carrying that traffic.[48] Much trade went through Lydbrook, where the main wharf was busy in 1770, with cranes loading coal destined for Hereford and elsewhere into barges.[49] Outlets for Forest coal on the river Severn in the 18th century included Lydney Pill, Purton Pill, Gatcombe, and Newnham.[50]

MINING FROM THE 1770s. In the 18th century furnaces near the Forest, which needed a supply of cinders to produce good iron from local ore,[51] depended increasingly on ore from Lancashire. As a result regular ore mining in Dean ceased, leaving abandoned chambers,[52] known as 'old men's workings', to be rediscovered in the following century.[53] In 1787 about 22 men, each paying the gaveller 4s. a year, dug ore occasionally in old workings,[54] and in 1788 Parkend walk was said to have 8 ore mines employing c. 20 free miners and 3 boys or apprentices.[55] The coal industry on the other hand expanded in the 18th century. New pits and levels were frequently opened. Some of their names, such as Long Looked For, Pluck Penny, and Small Profit, reflected the speculative nature of the industry, which until David Mushet published a survey of the strata in 1824 relied on personal knowledge of the geology of the outcrop.[56] In 1787 the Forest was found to have 121 coal mines, of which 90 were at work producing 1,816 tons a week and employing 662

free miners.[57] The following year 106 collieries were noted employing over 442 miners, including many boys and 6 women; the bulk of the mines were in Parkend and Ruardean walks. The outcrops most intensively worked were those running northwards from Cinderford to Nailbridge and thence south-westwards across Serridge green to Beechenhurst hill, those running northwards from Whitecroft to Moseley Green and Staple Edge, and those on the west side of the Forest towards Coleford.[58]

With the expansion of coal mining and the growth in the size of mines disputes in the coalfield became more frequent. Deeper working increased the risk of flooding from adjacent mines, a hazard that Churchway (or Turnbrook) colliery had experienced by 1748.[59] The free miners, often at odds with one another, became embroiled with foreigners, who participated in the industry in greater numbers. The growth of the industry and the intervention of foreigners sealed the collapse of the customary system of mining. The breakdown had been manifested in the early 18th century by the conferring of free miners' privileges on local landowners; earlier the mine law court had been more sparing in granting those rights to Crown officials and others.[60] Ownership of coal mines became unevenly distributed. Of 66 partnerships reported in 1787 as working 98 mines about a third controlled more than one colliery and one as many as seven.[61] The mine law court became ineffective, its proceedings marred by disorder and violent arguments and its decisions ignored.

48 Ibid. 123, 129–30.
49 W. Gilpin, *Observations on River Wye in 1770* (1789), 35–6.
50 Hart, *Free Miners*, 132; Rudder, *Glos.* 572; Glos. R.O., D 421/E 49.
51 Hart, *Ind. Hist. of Dean*, 222.
52 *Trans. B.G.A.S.* ii. 231–3; Rudge, *Hist. of Glos.* ii. 17–18.
53 Nicholls, *Iron Making*, 62.

54 *3rd Rep. Com. Woods* (1788), 91.
55 Ibid. 88.
56 Nicholls, *Forest of Dean*, 235; Fisher, *Custom and Capitalism*, 8.
57 *3rd Rep. Com. Woods* (1788), 91.
58 Ibid. 88, 108–9.
59 Nicholls, *Forest of Dean*, 283–4.
60 Hart, *Free Miners*, 10–11, 84–5, 125, 127–8, 135–7, 141–4.
61 Fisher, *Custom and Capitalism*, 9.

In 1775 it tried to prevent foreigners from owning or working mines. That year its papers disappeared from the Speech House, being removed allegedly by John Robinson, a deputy gaveller, who had opened a number of mines in partnership with foreigners. Although officials refused to reconvene the court without its records,[62] the free miners apparently continued to meet to deliberate mining matters, and in 1807 a group of 48 of them, a reference to the jury of 48 which had been the court's highest authority, called at the Speech House for the court's revival to implement new rules for the mining industry. That group, led by William Bradley, a Baptist minister, met regularly until 1809[63] or later but assemblies of free miners at the Speech House had become infrequent by the 1820s.[64]

The lapse of the mine law court left the supervision of mining customs solely to the gaveller. By the later 18th century miners sought, before digging on Crown land, the consent of the gaveller or his deputy, who on receipt of a fee of 5s. marked out and registered the land required for the new mine. Mining rights lapsed if they were not exercised on at least one day in every year and a day. The gaveller also fixed a royalty to be paid for the mine in proportion to the number of men to be employed in it and the payment, deemed a commutation of the Crown's right to put a man in each mine, came to represent a fifth of the output of each pit or level. The gaveller had used the mine law court to enforce payment of the Crown's dues, and the court's discontinuance led to many miners defaulting in their payments. The gaveller took the Crown's mining revenues for his own use and before 1788 farmed them to one of his deputies for £100.[65] That practice continued until c. 1808, when the gavellership became an honorary post vested in the office of Surveyor General of Woods and the Crown's income from mining became part of the general revenues of the Forest.[66] The term 'gale' came to be applied to the grant of a mine and to the land granted for it, as well as to the royalty.[67]

In the 1770s and 1780s the coalfield supplied a large part of the county beyond the Severn, including Gloucester, Stroud, and Berkeley, and Hereford, Monmouth, Chepstow (Mon.), and Bristol remained among its markets,[68] but by the 1790s markets were being lost, because of the high cost of carriage, to pits in Monmouthshire, Shropshire, and Staffordshire. The northern side of the coalfield, which was also affected by the development of the Newent coalfield, depended principally on sales to the Herefordshire

hop yards.[69] The trade in Forest minerals and stone was boosted by the building of tramroads to link the Forest with Bullo Pill, Lydney, Monmouth, and Redbrook in the early 19th century,[70] but some trade to Bristol and other places was lost by the imposition of duty on shipments of coal in the Severn estuary.[71] Mining was also stimulated by the opening of coke-fired blast furnaces in Dean in the late 1790s,[72] and quantities of yellow ochre were dug during the Napoleonic Wars.[73]

In the later 18th century many miners were too impoverished to pay their gale rents[74] and most lacked the money needed for the pumping and winding machines necessary for deeper working.[75] Coal pits remained shallow and once flooded were abandoned in favour of new workings.[76] Coal was hoisted from some pits by bucket or basket using a hand-operated windlass or a horse gin (or whim).[77] By the 1770s two or three crank-driven pumps had been installed in the coalfield.[78] The first mine to use steam power for pumping was a drift near Broadmoor known in 1754 as Water Wheel Engine[79] and later as Oiling Gin. A steam engine was set up there, perhaps as early as 1766, by a group of foreigners, who in 1776 surrendered a major share in the mine to a company of miners.[80] With few exceptions the provision of machines was possible only with the investment of outside capital. Some miners formed partnerships with foreigners and borrowed money from them[81] but only a handful of them benefited in the long term from such co-operation.[82] One was James Teague (d. 1818), who in the 1790s was partnered by several Shropshire industrialists. He acquired coal and ore mines on the west side of the Forest, installed a steam engine at one of them, built the first tramroads in Dean, established ironworks at Whitecliff near Coleford, and employed other free miners.[83] Some miners sold out to foreigners and others continued to work small mines.[84]

Before 1775 foreigners rarely held gales, being forbidden to do so by custom. Following the lapse of the mine law court it became common for them to buy or take leases of gales and for free miners to acquire gales on their behalf.[85] At first foreigners received little return on their capital but by the 1820s they operated nearly all the large mines in the Forest, investing substantial sums in deep mining and tramroads and thereby producing coal competitively with collieries elsewhere.[86] The dominant figure in the coalfield at that time was Edward Protheroe (d. 1856), a West Indies merchant from Bristol and M.P. for the city 1812–20.[87] He acquired several

[62] Ibid. 7; Hart, *Free Miners*, 47–8, 136–8, which includes evidence that the court last met in 1777.
[63] R. Anstis, *Ind. Teagues and Forest of Dean* (1990), 63–5.
[64] Glos. R.O., D 2297.
[65] *3rd Rep. Com. Woods* (1788), 30, 34, 91; Hart, *Free Miners*, 6–7, 249.
[66] Hart, *Free Miners*, 60–1.   [67] *O.E.D.*
[68] *3rd Rep. Com. Woods* (1788), 109; *Glouc. Jnl.* 10 June 1771.
[69] Glos. R.O., D 421/E 48.
[70] Below, tramroads and railways.
[71] Paar, *Severn and Wye Railway*, 14, 145, 147.
[72] Below, ironworks.   [73] Hart, *Ind. Hist. of Dean*, 245.
[74] *3rd Rep. Com. Woods* (1788), 91.
[75] *4th Rep. Dean Forest Com.* 23–4.
[76] Rudder, *Glos.* 36; Rudge, *Hist. of Glos.* ii. 11.

[77] Hart, *Ind. Hist. of Dean*, 259; *4th Rep. Dean Forest Com.* 23.
[78] Rudder, *Glos.* 36.   [79] Hart, *Free Miners*, 136.
[80] *4th Rep. Dean Forest Com.* 7, 12–13, 30, 32–3, 43; in 1839 it was stated that the first steam engine in the coalfield was installed c. 1765 and more powerful engines were introduced from c. 1774: Glos. R.O., D 421/L 19.
[81] *4th Rep. Dean Forest Com.* 23–4; cf, Fisher, *Custom and Capitalism*, 16.
[82] *Award of Dean Forest Mining Com.* (1841), 21–2.
[83] *Glos. Soc. Ind. Arch. Jnl.* (1980), 18–28, 51–60; (1982), 43–5; Anstis, *Ind. Teagues*, 9–75.
[84] *4th Rep. Dean Forest Com.* 23–4.
[85] Ibid. 7, 9; *Award of Dean Forest Mining Com.* (1841), 22.
[86] *4th Rep. Dean Forest Com.* 24–5.
[87] Williams, *Parl. Hist. of Glos.* 135.

TABLE IV: COAL AND IRON ORE RAISED IN DEAN 1841–1965

The figures are tons.

year	coal	iron ore	year	coal	iron ore
1841	145,136	18,872	1894	860,312	27,780
1850	337,948	73,990	1900	1,050,000	*9,769
1860	590,470	192,074	1920	1,206,000	**1,727
1862	474,168	109,056	1930	1,303,000	
1871	837,893	170,611	1940	1,204,200	
1877	638,319	79,646	1950	723,000	
1885	826,167	35,249	1965	46,000	

*fig. for 1901   ** fig. for 1921

Sources: Fisher, *Custom and Capitalism*, 57–8; *Glos. N. & Q.* vi. 140; *Forest of Dean Coalfield* (H.S.M.O. 1946), 17–18; Hart, *Ind. Hist. of Dean*, 235, 290.

collieries at Parkend from his uncle John Protheroe in 1812, purchased Bilson colliery in 1826, and, having gained control of the Forest's principal tramroads, extended deep mining of coal at Parkend and Bilson and opened up ore mines near Milkwall. From the mid 1820s he sent coal to local ironworks and among the collieries which he developed were Crumpmeadow in 1829 and New Fancy in 1831.[88] David Mushet and other iron-masters operating in the Forest were also prominent in the development of mines and tramroads.[89] William Crawshay, owner of the Cyfarthfa ironworks near Merthyr Tydfil (Glam.), collaborated with Moses Teague (d. 1840), a free miner, in sinking deep mines on the east side of the Forest to supply ore and coal to the Cinderford ironworks.[90] Shakemantle and Buckshraft (later Buckshaft) ore mines near Ruspidge were begun in 1829 and 1835,[91] and Lightmoor coal mine further west was deepened in the late 1830s.[92] Also in the late 1830s Sir Josiah John Guest, Bt., sank Westbury Brook (or Edgehills) mine below old workings south of Mitcheldean to supply ore to his Dowlais ironworks near Merthyr Tydfil,[93] and Anthony Hill, a South Wales ironmaster licensed in 1832 to remove cinders from Crown lands, became involved in Dean's mining indus-try.[94] In 1838 G. E. Jackson, a Birmingham ironmaster, sank Old Sling ore mine below old workings at Clearwell Meend.[95] Of 52 collieries in production in Dean in 1841, Strip And At It, one of the deeper mines,[96] was worked from a shaft sunk in the mid 1830s on Serridge green by John Harris, a free miner.[97]

From the 1820s the large coal mines were run on a 'little butty' system. Each stall was devel-oped under contract by a collier and his mate, the buttymen, who employed four or five men or boys on a daily basis. In the 'big butty' system of the Staffordshire coalfield the con-tractors were responsible for a whole seam or even a complete pit. In Dean's large mines perhaps a quarter or third of the workforce were buttymen and the rest day labourers, of whom a few were directly employed by the masters. The larger collieries were thus an important source of casual employment, affording seasonal work after the harvest and attracting men from Wales and elsewhere to the Forest. There were attempts to curb the hiring of workmen other than free miners.[98] Many boys, some as young as six, worked in the larger coal and ore mines in 1841, when of 700 hands employed at Bilson colliery 40 were aged under 13. Female labour was not used at the larger mines[99] but women hoisted coal and loaded it on carts and mules at the free miners' pits.[1]

With the introduction of deep mines and wage labour the customary system of mining in Dean rapidly diminished in economic significance[2] and the industry entered a troubled period. Disputes arose over boundaries, and the principle that mining in any gale was to cease when mattocks clashed, that is when the mine ran up against another, was increasingly ignored by the driving of long narrow headings to secure coal in other gales. The interests of native free miners and

88 *4th Rep. Dean Forest Com.* 22–6; Nicholls, *Forest of Dean*, 107; Hart, *Ind. Hist. of Dean*, 268–9.
89 Cf. Hart, *Ind. Hist. of Dean*, 132–3.
90 *Award of Dean Forest Mining Com.* (1841), 58–60, 63–4, 179–80; Anstis, *Ind. Teagues*, 112–21; for Crawshay, *D.N.B.*
91 Nicholls, *Iron Making*, 61; cf. Sopwith, *Map of Dean Forest* (1835); P.R.O., F 16/63 (nos. 2849, 3102); F 16/70.
92 *Award of Dean Forest Mining Com.* (1841), 58, 63–4, 147; Sopwith, *Map of Dean Forest* (1835); cf. Glos. R.O., Q/RUm 175.
93 *Award of Dean Forest Mining Com.* (1841), 182; Nicholls, *Iron Making*, 62–3; for Guest, *D.N.B.*; cf. Atkinson, *Map of Dean Forest* (1847); O.S. Map 6", Glos. XXXI. NE. (1884 edn.).

94 *10th Rep. Com. Woods*, H.C. 738, p. 28 (1833); *Award of Dean Forest Mining Com.* (1841), 180.
95 *Award of Dean Forest Mining Com.* (1841), 183; Nicholls, *Iron Making*, 63.
96 Glos. R.O., Q/RUm 175.
97 *Award of Dean Forest Mining Com.* (1841), 48, 60–1, 68, 100–3; Atkinson, *Map of Dean Forest* (1847).
98 Fisher, *Custom and Capitalism*, 65–6, 70–2; *4th Rep. Dean Forest Com.* 8–10, 16, 24; cf. *Diary of a Cotswold Parson*, ed. D. Verey (1978), 119–20.
99 Anstis, *Ind. Teagues*, 179–81.
1 Mountjoy, *Dean Collier*, 76.
2 Cf. Fisher, *Custom and Capitalism*, 15–18.

foreign capitalists frequently came into conflict[3] and resentment of foreigners was a potent factor in riots that occurred over commoning rights in 1831.[4] The next year the granting of gales to free miners was halted temporarily and from 1838, following a report by commissioners investigating conditions in the Forest, mining was subject to a statutory framework of regulation.[5] Registered free miners retained the sole right to take gales from the gaveller for mining coal, ore, and ochre within St. Briavels hundred, but, with the confirmation of earlier sales, mortgages, and leases and of the free miners' power to sell or lease, foreigners were able to secure title in law to gales. Mine owners were left free to employ whom they chose. Men born and living in the hundred, aged 21 or more, and having worked a year and a day in a mine in the hundred could register as free miners and 829 had done so by 1841.[6] Their right to take wood for their pits, a custom already withdrawn from those using the Forest's tramroads,[7] was abolished.

Many provisions of the Act passed in 1838 to regulate mining were implemented in 1841 when commissioners set out the boundaries of 104 gales of coal and 20 of iron ore, awarded them to those judged to be entitled to them, fixed the royalty to be paid, and codified the rules for the conduct of mining. Each gale specified the seams to be worked and the royalty was linked to output. The Crown was guaranteed a minimum or dead rent from each gale assessed on an assumed annual tonnage and when output exceeded that figure ('overworkings') the surplus payment could be offset by any previous 'short-workings'. Gales granted after 1841 paid royalties in the same way and the amount from each was revised every 21 years.[8] The office of gaveller remained honorary, being vested in the First Commissioner of Woods, Forests, and Land Revenues in 1838 and assigned to another of the commissioners in 1852. Its duties were performed by the gaveller's deputy and the deputy surveyor.[9]

The reforms of 1838 and 1841 strengthened trends that had been evident in the industry many years earlier. Production expanded and was concentrated in fewer hands as existing pits were enlarged and new deep mines sunk. William Crawshay (d. 1867) and his son Henry (d. 1879)

took a lead in mining coal and ore on the east side of the Forest,[10] primarily to feed the Cinderford furnaces, and their Lightmoor colliery had four shafts open in the mid 1850s.[11] Henry, who took over his father's mining and smelting interests in the Forest and became known as the 'iron king' of the Forest of Dean,[12] employed as many as 250 hands to dig ore in Buckshaft, Shakemantle, and St. Annal's mines in the mid 1860s.[13] He also developed Foxes Bridge colliery, at Crabtree hill next to Crumpmeadow colliery,[14] in partnership in 1858 with Stephen Allaway and Timothy Bennett[15] (d. 1861) and later with Bennett's son-in-law Osman Barrett. In 1861 Bennett, a Mitcheldean maltster and miller with substantial local mining interests,[16] sold Resolution and Safeguard coal pits to Henry Crawshay,[17] and in 1889 the firm of Henry Crawshay & Co. Ltd. was established to run the Crawshays' businesses in the Forest.[18] Of Edward Protheroe's large collieries, Bilson and Crumpmeadow were acquired between 1841 and 1846 by a company headed by Aaron Goold,[19] formerly his agent,[20] and in 1884 by the Lydney & Crumpmeadow Collieries Co.[21] Parkend and New Fancy, which Protheroe retained until his death, later had several owners before their purchase in 1883 by, among others, T. H. Deakin (d. 1935), founder of Parkend Deep Navigation Collieries Ltd.[22] Trafalgar colliery near Cinderford,[23] which was in production in 1860, was developed by the Brain family and was the only large mine in the coalfield run by free miners in the later 19th century. The colliery, which in 1882 became the first in England to have electric pumps,[24] took over the workings of Strip And At It colliery to the north, and a short tramroad through a tunnel connected the pit-heads.[25]

The coalfield's output rose steadily from 145,136 tons in 1841. Production slumped in the early 1860s but it soon recovered and increased to 837,893 tons in 1871.[26] Of the 460,432 tons raised in 1856 Parkend and Lightmoor collieries produced 86,973 and 86,508 respectively and Crumpmeadow colliery 41,507.[27] Many mines had an annual output of less than 5,000 tons. They were drifts and shallow pits in the outcrop worked by free miners supplying surrounding

[3] 4th Rep. Dean Forest Com. 8–10; Hart, Free Miners, 251–3, 317.
[4] R. Anstis, Warren James and Dean Forest Riots (1986), passim.
[5] Dean Forest Mines Act, 1 & 2 Vic. c. 43; 4th Rep. Dean Forest Com., passim.
[6] Award of Dean Forest Mining Com. (1841), 11.
[7] Churchway Engine to Cinderford Bridge Rly. Act, 49 Geo. III, c. 158 (Local and Personal), s. 18; Lydbrook to Lydney Rly. Act, 49 Geo. III, c. 159 (Local and Personal), s. 75.
[8] Award of Dean Forest Mining Com. (1841), 41–208; cf. Glos. R.O., Q/RUm 173/1–2; Dean Forest Mines Act, 1 & 2 Vic. c. 43.
[9] Hart, Free Miners, 61–3.
[10] Glouc. Jnl. 29 Nov. 1879.
[11] Nicholls, Forest of Dean, 241–2; illustration at ibid. reproduced below, Fig. 21.
[12] Glos. N. & Q. iv. 285–6.
[13] Nicholls, Iron Making, 61–2.
[14] Cf. O.S. Map 6", Glos. XXXI. SE. (1883 edn.).
[15] 37th Rep. Com. Woods, H.C. 54, p. 74 (1859 Sess. 2), xi.
[16] Glos. R.O., D 543, deeds 1879–95; Paar, G.W.R. in Dean, 70; for Bennett, Kelly's Dir. Glos. (1856), 326; Slater's

Dir. Glos. (1852–3), 144.
[17] Glos. R.O., D 543, deed 6 Mar. 1861.
[18] Henry Crawshay's Estate Act, 52 & 53 Vic. c. 2 (Private); Glos. R.O., D 6178/2/1.
[19] Plan of Bilson and Crumpmeadow collieries 1841, at Dean Heritage mus., Soudley; 23rd Rep. Com. Woods, H.C. 717, p. 83 (1846), xxiv.
[20] Fisher, Custom and Capitalism, 58.
[21] Fine Forest of Dean Coal (1933), 22: copy in Glos. R.O., D 3921/II/26.
[22] R. Anstis, Story of Parkend (1982), 74–8; Glouc. Jnl. 3 Aug. 1935.
[23] O.S. Map 6", Glos. XXXI. SE. (1883 edn.).
[24] Hart, Ind. Hist. of Dean, 406–7; cf. J. G. Wood, Laws of Dean Forest (1878), 379–80; Fisher, Custom and Capitalism, 58.
[25] Glos. R.O., D 2428/1/28; annotated copies of O.S. Maps 1/2,500, Glos. XXXI. 6, 10 (1902–3 edn.); J. Bellows, Week's Holiday in Forest of Dean (1920), 61; cf. D. E. Bick, Old Ind. of Dean (1980), 36.
[26] Fisher, Custom and Capitalism, 57; above, Table IV.
[27] Nicholls, Forest of Dean, 242.

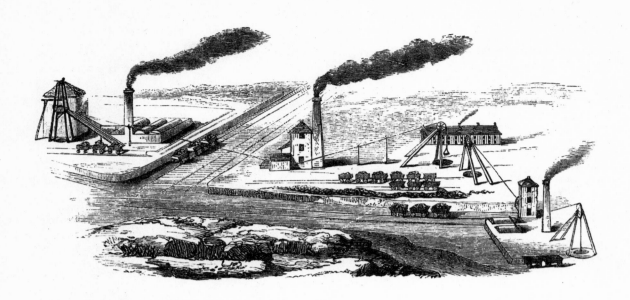

FIG. 21 LIGHTMOOR COLLIERY, *c.* 1850

villages and farmsteads with house coal, and they represented only a fraction of the coalfield's total output. In 1870 nearly half of the 40 working coal mines were in that category while, at the other end of the scale, six collieries (Resolution and Safeguard, Lightmoor, Foxes Bridge, Crumpmeadow, Trafalgar, and New Fancy) each produced more than 50,000 tons and together accounted for almost three quarters of the field's output. Most of the coal was sent to markets outside the Forest but large amounts were used by local industry.[28] The coalfield's output, which fell between 1871 and 1877,[29] did not show any appreciable increase above the 1871 figure until the end of the century,[30] 1,176,712 tons being raised in 1898. At that time most of the principal collieries were near Cinderford or Parkend and worked the upper measures for household and other coal. Elsewhere a few large mines tapped the lower measures, including the Coleford High Delf seam, near the outcrop to produce coal for gasworks and steam engines. On the south side of the coalfield they included Flour Mill colliery in the Oakwood valley near Bream and Park Gutter west of Whitecroft, both worked by the Princess Royal Colliery Co., and on the north side a large colliery at Lydbrook was worked by the tinplaters Richard Thomas & Co.[31]

Exploitation of the lower measures far below the centre of the Forest involved considerable investment in pumping and other machinery and was hampered by the free miners' opposition in the late 19th century to modifications in the system of galing.[32] To expedite the sinking of deep mines the gaveller, using powers acquired in 1904,[33] created seven large holdings by amalgamating many gales and granted them to the free miners. Each united gale, held by several hundred free miners acting through a committee, was leased to a company and the companies paid the galees ½*d.* for each ton of coal raised, the royalty being shared out annually at the Speech House.[34] Within a few years four deep mines operated under that system. Cannop colliery near the bottom of Wimberry Slade[35] began production in 1909,[36] and in the same year H. Crawshay & Co. Ltd. started developing Eastern United colliery, a drift mine at Staple Edge near Ruspidge,[37] and the Lydney & Crumpmeadow Collieries Co. reopened Arthur and Edward (or Waterloo) colliery above Lydbrook.[38] Princess Royal colliery between Whitecroft and Bream's Eaves incorporated the pits of Flour Mill colliery and after 1914 its production centred on a new shaft at Park Gutter.[39] Among the large collieries closed during that period was East Slade near Ruardean Woodside in 1905.[40]

Although output from individual iron-ore

28 Fisher, *Custom and Capitalism*, 58–60; cf. H. R. Insole and C. Z. Bunning, 'Forest of Dean Coalfield', *Jnl. Brit. Soc. Mining Students*, vi (5) (1881–2), 68, 87.
29 Fisher, *Custom and Capitalism*, 57.
30 *Forest of Dean Coalfield* (H.M.S.O. 1946), 17; above, Table IV.
31 *V.C.H. Glos.* ii. 233–4; I. Pope, B. How, and P. Kerau, *Severn & Wye Railway* (3 vols. 1983–8), i. 107–8; iii. 421.
32 *Jnl. Brit. Soc. Mining Students*, vi (5), 67; Fisher, *Custom and Capitalism*, 133–9.

33 Dean Forest (Mines) Act, 4 Edw. VII, c. 156 (Local).
34 Hart, *Free Miners*, 484–7.   35 Above, Plate 21.
36 Pope, How, & Kerau, *Severn & Wye Railway*, ii. 233–9.
37 I. Pope and P. Kerau, *Forest of Dean Branch*, i (1992), 133–5.   38 *Fine Forest of Dean Coal*, 22.
39 Pope, How, & Kerau, *Severn & Wye Railway*, i. 104–11; cf. above, Plate 20.
40 J. Gibbs, 'Development of Educ. in Two Forest of Dean Schs. 1870–1903' (Bristol Univ. Dip. Ed. thesis, 1967), 5.

mines fluctuated, ore production in Dean in the mid 19th century followed the same trend as coal production, rising from 18,872 tons in 1841 to 170,611 tons in 1871.[41] Much of the output was from deep pits but some was from drift mines in the limestone outcropping on the south-western side of the coalfield.[42] Most of the ore, for example almost two thirds of the 1869 output, went to local ironworks.[43] Like the Crawshays, the owners of the Parkend furnaces created deep ore mines, including by the mid 1850s China Engine and others in the Oakwood area and Perseverance and Findall mine in the Cinderford (or Soudley) brook valley below Staple Edge.[44] Beginning in 1854 the Ebbw Vale Co. purchased and worked a number of ore and coal mines near Oakwood, where it had a furnace,[45] and by 1856 the Allaway brothers were developing an ore mine at Wigpool, on the north side of the Forest.[46] Some ore continued to go to South Wales. Henry Crawshay supplied his father through Cardiff in 1858,[47] and the Dowlais Iron Co. employed nearly 200 hands at Westbury Brook mine in the mid 1860s[48] and worked a mine at Mitcheldean Meend on the north side of the Forest.[49] In the mid 1860s Old Sling mine employed nearly 100 hands and Easter, a deep mine at Milkwall, c. 50 men and boys.[50] In the later 19th century several mines, including New Dun at Clearwell Meend, also produced red oxide, that from Buckshaft being sent overseas and becoming known as Crawshay Red.[51] After 1871 the amount of ore raised in Dean declined.[52] Large mines such as Buckshaft, Westbury Brook, Wigpool, Old Sling, and Easter supplied much of the output,[53] but in the deeper workings, particularly on the eastern side of the Forest, water was a constant problem and accessible deposits of ore were mostly exhausted by the early 20th century.[54] Economic depression and competition from Spanish imports reduced ore production to 35,249 tons in 1885 and mines on the south-western side of the Forest, having lost markets in Staffordshire and South Wales, fell idle.[55] Mines elsewhere, including Wigpool, were also abandoned,[56] and the closure of the Cinderford ironworks[57] led to the abandonment of Buckshaft and other ore mines near the town in 1899. With other closures, including Edgehills in 1893,[58] ore output plummeted to 9,769 tons in 1901. In the early 20th century the amount of ore mined continued to

dwindle and more workings were abandoned. A few ore mines were reopened during the First World War and seven were operating in 1917,[59] but by 1921 most, including Easter and Old Sling, had closed.[60] At Wigpool, where the principal mine was abandoned in 1918, an adit driven into a hillside a few years earlier by gold prospectors was used from 1921 to extract ore. Its closure in 1924 marked the end of ore mining on the eastern side of the Forest.[61] By that time ore production on the south-western side of the Forest was restricted mainly to New Dun and in places was incidental to the extraction of oxides and ochres. Much of the mining there was in the hands of the Watkins family and some was undertaken by a company which built colour works at Milkwall in 1926.[62] Ore mining ended with the closure soon after the Second World War of New Dun.[63]

Sedimentary rocks embedded in the Old Red Sandstone underlying, and outcropping around, the Dean coalfield contain traces of gold. In 1906, following a reported discovery near Mitcheldean, the Chaston Syndicate Ltd. was formed to prospect for gold. After test workings at Lea Bailey and Staple Edge, it was concluded that gold and silver could not be extracted economically and the syndicate was wound up in 1908.[64]

The mining population of St. Briavels hundred more than doubled between 1841 and 1871. In those years male employment in the coalfield, which probably did not increase much as a proportion of the total workforce, rose to 3,375 while ore mining saw a fivefold increase in jobs to 1,114. In 1871 over half of the employed men living in the former extraparochial area of the Forest, 3,604 out of 6,782, were miners and 119 were managers and other professionals in the industry.[65]

By the mid 1850s production at larger collieries and other industrial works was occasionally disrupted by strikes.[66] A miners' committee at Cinderford in 1870 had contacts with other coalfields, and following strikes led by buttymen at Trafalgar and Parkend collieries in 1871 an association of Dean miners was formed and affiliated to the Amalgamated Association of Miners. Despite opposition, notably from the Baptist minister and former colliery owner Thomas Nicholson, the union was strongly supported in the coalfield and by the time of its second annual demonstration in 1873 the Dean

41 Fisher, *Custom and Capitalism*, 57–8; above, Table IV.
42 Hart, *Ind. Hist. of Dean*, 228.
43 Fisher, *Custom and Capitalism*, 60.
44 Paar, *Severn and Wye Railway*, 49–50; *36th Rep. Com. Woods*, H.C. 380, pp. 88, 91 (1857–8), xxxi; cf. *Geol. of Dean Coal and Iron-Ore Field* (H.M.S.O. 1942), 68–73.
45 Glos. R.O., EL 172, pp. 12, 18; cf. Paar, *Severn and Wye Railway*, 50; Hart, *Free Miners*, 412.
46 Paar, *G.W.R. in Dean*, 73–4; *36th Rep. Com. Woods* (1857–8), 88.
47 Hart, *Ind. Hist. of Dean*, 230.
48 Nicholls, *Iron Making*, 62–3.
49 Bick, *Old Ind. of Dean*, 40.
50 Nicholls, *Iron Making*, 63–4.
51 Hart, *Ind. Hist. of Dean*, 246–7; O.S. Map 6", Glos. XXXVIII. NE. (1884, 1903 edns.).
52 Above, Table IV; *V.C.H. Glos.* ii. 233.
53 Bick, *Old Ind. of Dean*, 40.
54 Paar, *G.W.R. in Dean*, 68; Glos. R.O., DA 24/100/4, pp. 319–50.

55 *Kelly's Dir. Glos.* (1885), 440; Hart, *Ind. Hist. of Dean*, 233; Paar, *Severn and Wye Railway*, 50; above, Table IV.
56 Paar, *G.W.R. in Dean*, 69, 74; *Glos. Soc. Ind. Arch. Jnl.* (1988), 25.
57 Below, ironworks.
58 *Geol. of Dean Coal and Iron-Ore Field*, 63–74.
59 Hart, *Ind. Hist. of Dean*, 235; above, Table IV.
60 Cf. O.S. Maps 6", Glos. XXXVIII. NE., SE. (1903, 1924 edns.).
61 *Geol. of Dean Coal and Iron-Ore Field*, 63–4; Hart, *Ind. Hist. of Dean*, 318, 321.
62 Hart, *Ind. Hist. of Dean*, 235, 240–1, 246–8; Glos. R.O., D 3921/V/21, newspaper cutting 31 Dec. 1965.
63 Inf. from Mr. Standing.
64 Hart, *Ind. Hist. of Dean*, 316, 318–20; *Glos. Soc. Ind. Arch. Jnl.* (1988), 26; cf. *Glouc. Jnl.* 4 May 1907; 3 Apr. 1982.
65 Fisher, *Custom and Capitalism*, 55–6.
66 *Glouc. Jnl.* 23 Apr. 1853; 12 Apr., 14 June 1856; 23 Aug. 1862; 11 Jan. 1868.

branch had 13 lodges in the Forest. The union, for which Timothy Mountjoy was the local agent, attempted to protect the interests of both buttymen and daymen. Following its defeat in a long strike begun in 1874 membership fell but some lodges continued to meet after the branch organization was disbanded in 1877. An attempt to revive the union in 1882 was repeated successfully in 1886[67] and G. H. Rowlinson, who acted as local agent until 1918, became a respected figure in the Forest.[68] The union organized solid backing for the national coal strikes of 1921 and 1926.[69] Trade unionism also spread among other groups including the Forest's quarrymen; their trade organization attended the miners' 1873 gala.[70] The large collieries employed many hands: in 1922 Princess Royal had 1,138 employees, New Fancy 694, and Cannop 685.[71] In 1930 Cannop became the first in the coalfield to provide pithead baths.[72] The 'butty' system, retained well into the 20th century, was abolished at Eastern United in 1938.[73] There was a number of fatal accidents in the mines in the late 19th century and the early 20th,[74] one of the most serious occurring in 1902 when four men died as a result of flooding in Union pit, in Bixslade.[75]

Coal production, which was boosted during the First World War, was interrupted by the strikes of the 1920s and fell during the economic recession of the early 1930s. In 1936 it rose to 1,439,000 tons and thereafter it declined.[76] During that period several older deep mines closed once they had worked out accessible reserves. Trafalgar, where flooding halted production in 1919,[77] closed in 1925,[78] Crumpmeadow stopped production in 1929, and Foxes Bridge was abandoned in 1930[79] because of flooding from disused mines. The number of jobs in the industry fell from 7,818 in 1920 to 5,276 in 1930 and the closures, besides adding to a high level of unemployment locally, left Lightmoor, with a workforce of 600 in 1934, as the main colliery in the Cinderford area.[80] At that time several mines on the north side of the coalfield were deepened[81] and many miners found work in a deep mine, called Northern United, which H. Crawshay & Co. began sinking north-west of Cinderford by the Mitcheldean–Coleford road in 1933.[82] Mining in the south part of the coalfield was rationalized by the Princess Royal Colliery Co., which from 1937 worked Norchard colliery, adjoining its principal mine, from a new drift entered near Pillowell.[83] Further jobs were lost by the closure of Lightmoor and New Fancy collieries in 1940 and 1944 respectively,[84] but some new ones were created at the remaining large mines[85] and there were many collieries with fewer than 40 employees each. Coal mining remained the principal source of jobs in the Forest, employing 55 per cent of the adult male population, 84.5 per cent in the Cinderford area.[86]

Following nationalization of the coal industry in 1946[87] the National Coal Board operated the principal mines and awarded licences for working smaller ones.[88] Annual production, which including the output of the free miners' workings was 777,000 tons in 1948, continued to decline as rising costs, reflecting particularly drainage problems, led to the closure of most mines. Of the main collieries Eastern United and Arthur and Edward shut in 1959, Cannop in 1960, Princess Royal in 1962, and Norchard Drift and Northern United in 1965, when deep mining ended in Dean.[89] From 1965 some coal was extracted, under licence from the National Coal Board (later British Coal) and the Forestry Commission, by the opencast method. Such mining was piecemeal and short-term, the land afterwards being returned to forestry or used for other industrial purposes. Steam Mills and Yorkley were among places mined by opencast in the later 1960s,[90] and during the late 1970s there was a scheme at Woorgreen, north of the road between Cinderford and the Speech House, where the reclamation of the land created a large pond.[91]

The deputy gaveller, who had worked from an office in Coleford from 1861,[92] continued to deal with matters concerning the free miners, his status and duties being untouched by the vesting of the gavellership in the Forestry Commission in 1924[93] and by the nationalization of royalties from coal mining in 1942.[94] The free miners' rights were not abrogated by the nationalization of the coal industry in 1946,[95] after which a number of small pits and levels were worked privately under grant from the deputy gaveller.[96] Many active free miners, of whom there were 50 in 1975,[97] had full-time jobs elsewhere and the

67 Fisher, *Custom and Capitalism*, 73–81, 91–104; Mountjoy, *Dean Collier*, 35, 56–7, 62; for Nicholson, J. Stratford, *Glos. Biog. Notes* (1887), 228–35.
68 *Trans. B.G.A.S.* c. 242; Glos. Colln. SA 19.18.
69 *Glouc. Jnl.* 9 Apr. 1921; 25 Dec. 1926.
70 Ibid. 2 Aug. 1873. 71 Hart, *Ind. Hist. of Dean*, 289.
72 *Glouc. Jnl.* 27 Dec. 1930.
73 Pope & Kerau, *Forest of Dean Branch*, i. 154–5.
74 Hart, *Ind. Hist. of Dean*, 285–6.
75 Phelps, *Forest in Old Photog.* (1984), 48.
76 *Forest of Dean Coalfield* (H.M.S.O. 1946), 17–19; Hart, *Ind. Hist. of Dean*, 290; above, Table IV.
77 *Glouc. Jnl.* 8 Feb. 1919; Glos. R.O., DA 24/100/8, min. 5 Feb. 1919.
78 Pope, How, & Kerau, *Severn & Wye Railway*, ii. 297–9; according to M. V. Bent, *Highest Point of Dean* (1985), 65, Trafalgar was finally abandoned after flooding during the 1926 strike.
79 Bick, *Old Ind. of Dean*, 14, 16.
80 Glos. R.O., DA 24/100/10, pp. 750–1, 759–61; 11, pp. 278–9; *Forest of Dean Coalfield*, 18.
81 *Geol. of Dean Coal and Iron-Ore Field*, 50–1.
82 M. V. Bent, *Last Deep Mine of Dean* (1988), 20–4.
83 Pope, How, & Kerau, *Severn & Wye Railway*, i. 113; G. J. Field, *Look Back at Norchard* (Cinderford, 1978), 54–7.
84 Hart, *Ind. Hist. of Dean*, 291.
85 Cf. *Dean Forest Mercury*, 30 Mar. 1962.
86 Payne, *Glos. Survey*, 143, 145–6.
87 Coal Industry Nationalization Act, 9 & 10 Geo. VI, c. 59.
88 *Rep. Dean Forest Cttee.* (1958), 36.
89 Hart, *Ind. Hist. of Dean*, 290–1; *Dean Forest Mercury*, 2 Sept. 1960; 30 Mar. 1962; 12 Feb., 31 Dec. 1965; above, Table IV. 90 *Citizen* (Glouc.), 4 Jan. 1968.
91 Glos. R.O., D 6993/1/2.
92 C. E. Hart, *Coleford: The Hist. of a W. Glos. Forest Town* (1983), 372–3.
93 *Lond. Gaz.* 25 Mar. 1924, pp. 2510–13.
94 Hart, *Free Miners*, 64; Coal Act, 1 & 2 Geo. VI, c. 52, s. 43 (1–2).
95 Coal Industry Nationalization Act, 9 & 10 Geo. VI, c. 59, s. 63 (2).
96 *Rep. Dean Forest Cttee.* (1958), 36; cf. above, Plates 25, 44.
97 *Dean Forest Mercury*, 21 Mar. 1975.

number of their workings gradually declined.[98] In 1992, when electricity generating stations were the main customers for their coal, seven mines were operating and the deputy gaveller collected the royalties for British Coal. Of those mines four provided full-time work for c. 11 men and the others part-time jobs for c. 9.[99]

Much of the surface evidence of the mining industry in Dean was removed soon after the closure of the principal workings.[1] The elaborate head-gear of the larger collieries, some of which had three or four shafts, was dismantled and their spoil tips were levelled or planted with trees.[2] By 1992 only a few colliery buildings, including two houses at Trafalgar,[3] survived, and at Lightmoor the coalfield's last remaining engine house was derelict. Some sites were put to other uses. Rank Xerox acquired buildings at Northern United soon after 1965 for warehousing. A small industrial estate was established at Eastern United, and in 1970 a Birmingham college ran a field studies centre in offices at Cannop. From the late 1960s the extensive workings of Old Ham ore mine at Clearwell Meend were developed, under the name Clearwell Caves, as a mining museum and venue for social events.[4]

QUARRYING. Stone has been quarried in the Forest for many centuries, grey, blue, and red sandstones being worked principally for grinding, building, and paving, and limestone being burnt to produce lime.[5] In 1252 lime from Dean was sent by the river Severn to the king's works at Gloucester.[6] Grindstones were produced before the mid 13th century[7] and were quarried at Bixhead on the west side of the Forest in the mid 1430s. At that time several millstone and other quarries in Abenhall, Blakeney, Lea, and Mitcheldean bailiwicks were idle and two active quarries, including one at Hanway south of Ruardean which was worked by John Mason of Mitcheldean, were held for a rent of 3s. 4d. each.[8] Throughout the 16th century grindstones and millstones from the Forest area were shipped to Bridgwater (Som.) for sale,[9] most coming evidently from quarries near the river Wye.[10]

In the early 17th century quarrying and lime burning supported several men living near the Forest.[11] Grindstones were quarried in the south-east, above Blakeney.[12] Much activity centred on Bixhead, where in 1621 Sir Richard Catchmay of Bigsweir, in St. Briavels, attempted to control the digging of grindstones and stone for building windows. Some grindstones were

sent to Bristol for sale. The quarrymen, whose operations were small in scale, claimed the right to dig by ancient custom for an annual payment to the Crown of 3s. 4d. for each quarry.[13] They resisted any interference with that practice and continued to work after 1637, when the Crown granted Edward Terringham a lease for 31 years of all coal mines and grindstone quarries in the Forest. Francis Terringham acquired a new lease of the quarries in 1668, and in 1675 his widow Catherine challenged the quarrymen's rights without success. Under the reafforestation Act of 1668, which safeguarded the Crown's right to grant leases of quarries, quarrying was forbidden in inclosures of timber. In the late 17th century quarrying was concentrated at Bixhead and Ruardean Eaves (later Ruardean Hill and Ruardean Woodside). In 1683 those places had 6 and 4 working quarries respectively and one Bixhead quarry had supplied stone for the Hall family's new mansion at Highmeadow c. 1670.[14]

During the 18th century quarrying evidently continued in small, scattered workings. New limekilns were built at places such as Edge Hills and Vention,[15] the latter on the Forest boundary east of Lydbrook, and in 1758 there was a row of four midway between Blackpool brook and Danby Lodge.[16] In 1787 there were 19 kilns in the Forest and at least 43 quarries, old and new, in Blakeney, Parkend, Ruardean, and Worcester walks.[17] Many of those quarries were on Blakeney hill and Ruardean hill and the industry mainly supplied paving stones.[18] In the years 1746–54 up to 19 quarrymen paid the customary rent of 3s. 4d. to the lessee of the Crown's St. Briavels castle estate.[19] The rent sometimes covered several adjoining quarries or several partners in an enterprise and it was sometimes replaced by a composition from each quarry or from each partner. In the early 1820s one of the deputy gavellers resumed the practice of levying 3s. 4d. for each individual quarry.[20] The quarrymen's rights, though never within the jurisdiction of the mine law court,[21] were assimilated to those of the free miners. The miners claimed an exclusive right to work stone within the Forest under their ancient customs and the gaveller took a fee of 2s., by the end of the 18th century 3s., for galing a quarry. In the 1820s the hereditary woodward of Blakeney claimed control of those in Blakeney bailiwick,[22] a claim that was held to have no legal basis in 1858.[23] In the early 19th century the stone industry benefited from the building of tramroads to Bullo Pill

[98] Citizen, 11 Nov. 1977; The Independent, 23 June 1990.
[99] Inf. from deputy gaveller, Crown Offices, Coleford.
[1] Para. based on Hart, Ind. Hist. of Dean, 242–3, 292–3, 427; Glouc. Jnl. 12 Sept. 1987.
[2] Cf. Citizen, 16 Feb. 1979.
[3] Cf. Dean Forest Mercury, 14 Mar. 1986.
[4] Citizen, 10 Apr. 1974.
[5] Bick, Old Ind. of Dean, 57; Hart, Ind. Hist. of Dean, 297–9.
[6] Cal. Lib. 1251–60, 38.
[7] V.C.H. Glos. ii. 217.
[8] Berkeley Cast. Mun., General Ser. acct. roll 426; P.R.O., E 101/141/1; SC 6/858/14.
[9] Som. R.O., D/B/bw 800, 1432–3, 1537, 1539, 1541, 1561.
[10] New Regard of Forest of Dean, iv. 53–9; vi. 30–7.
[11] Smith, Men and Armour, 36–8.   [12] Ibid. 57.
[13] Glos. R.O., D 2026/L 5; cf. Hart, Free Miners, 175.

[14] Hart, Ind. Hist. of Dean, 298–300; Hart, Free Miners, 187–8, 216–18, 228.
[15] List of Bldgs. of Special Archit. or Hist. Interest (Dept. of the Environment, 1985), s.v. Forest of Dean district, Littledean; Citizen, 20 Feb. 1988.
[16] P.R.O., F 17/2.
[17] Ibid. F 16/31, ff. 16v., 32v.–33, 42v., 50, 63.
[18] W. Marshall, Rural Econ. of Glos. i (1796), 37; Rudge, Hist. of Glos. ii. 20.
[19] Berkeley Cast. Mun., General Ser. T, box 25, accts. for St. Briavels and Newland manors; cf. above, St. Briavels, manors.
[20] 5th Rep. Dean Forest Com. 65–6, 71.
[21] Cf. Hart, Free Miners, 70–1, 228.
[22] 5th Rep. Dean Forest Com. 65–6, 70–4.
[23] Hart, Free Miners, 354–5.

and Lydney.[24] New quarries were opened and foreigners became involved in the industry.[25] In 1816 a Coleford man had 18 quarries in the extraparochial Forest.[26]

Like mining, quarrying in the Forest came under statutory regulation in 1838. Men with the same qualifications as free miners as to birth, residence, and age and having worked a year and a day in a quarry in the Forest were deemed to be free miners but only with the right to quarry stone.[27] Some 175 men meeting those criteria immediately registered.[28] Claims to quarries worked in the period 1833–8 were considered by the mining commissioners, who in 1841 defined the boundaries of 315 quarries or gales, granted leases to the successful claimants, and drew up rules for working all quarries in the Forest. The gaveller or his deputy continued to supervise the industry.[29] New quarries were to be leased by the Commissioners of Woods to free miners, including those with mining privileges.[30] Some leaseholders of quarries sold or assigned their interests to foreigners, a practice acknowledged in 1871 by a relaxation of the rules for granting leases.[31] A minimum rent, paid by quarries up to 20 yards in length, was fixed at the customary sum of 3s. 4d. until 1859 when it was raised to 20s.[32]

Quarrying employed 295 Foresters in 1851 and 340 in 1871.[33] Quarries were worked on all sides of the Forest[34] and most provided blue or grey sandstone for structural and ornamental use.[35] Many of the largest quarries were in the western valleys above the Severn & Wye tramroad (later railway) and some of them supplied stone for Cardiff docks in 1853.[36] Parkend, the meeting-point of several tramroads and railways, became a centre for the industry. E. R. Payne, who had stoneworks there in 1870[37] and worked Point quarry at Fetter Hill,[38] sent stone through Lydney harbour to Birkenhead, Cardiff, and Newport docks in 1872.[39] Although production was often constrained by traditional practices and the industry in general was in decline by the 1880s, some businesses prospered in the later 19th century and works were established alongside the Severn & Wye railway to dress stone for use in building and paving.[40] David & Co., established in 1889, built extensive works at Parkend and in 1892 merged with two other

businesses to form David & Sant, controlling 37 quarries. One of the merged companies, Trotter, Thomas, & Co.,[41] had operated works by the Coleford road in Howler's Slade west of Cannop for many years[42] and had established works by the railway at Cannop more recently.[43] David & Sant invested in new machinery, and in 1898 the firm owned 41 quarries on the west side of the Forest and employed c. 325 men, including 60 at Parkend.[44] Among other quarry owners at that time was the firm of E. Turner & Sons of Cardiff, which in 1901 established works at the bottom of Bixslade south of Cannop ponds.[45] A quarry at Trafalgar colliery provided stone supports for the mine's galleries.[46] On the eastern side of the Forest limestone was quarried extensively and burnt on Wigpool common and Plump hill, above Mitcheldean;[47] at Staple Edge, where several limekilns operated in 1825,[48] a large quarry had been formed near Shakemantle mine by the late 1870s.[49] On the south-western side kilns worked at quarries at Bream Tufts and Clearwell Meend.[50] The production of lime, which during the 19th century was used as flux in local ironworks as well as for farming and building, continued after the First World War in several places, including Shakemantle, Lydbrook, and Milkwall.[51]

Many of the principal quarries were acquired by Forest of Dean Stone Firms Ltd. in 1900 and by United Stone Firms Co. Ltd. in 1910. The latter company, which took over the stoneworks south of Cannop ponds and others at Cannop and Parkend, was in financial difficulties as a result of the contraction in the market for monumental and building stone by 1917. It was reorganized in 1926 and again in 1939, when under the Scott-Russell family its name reverted to Forest of Dean Stone Firms Ltd.[52] The decline of the quarrying industry before the Second World War was felt keenly on the west side of the Forest, where three of the four main stoneworks had shut by 1937.[53] The principal stoneworks at Parkend closed in 1932.[54] Several stoneworks, including one at Fetter Hill, remained in use after the Second World War[55] and the Forest's quarries employed at least 92 men in 1950. Sandstone was supplied for building and limestone for roadworks and other uses.[56] In the 1960s limestone was quarried in several

24 Below, tramroads and railways; cf. *V.C.H. Glos.* iv. 136.
25 *5th Rep. Dean Forest Com.* 70–2.
26 *Glouc. Jnl.* 18 Nov. 1816.
27 Dean Forest Mines Act, 1 & 2 Vic. c. 43.
28 Fisher, *Custom and Capitalism*, 130–1.
29 Glos. R.O., Q/RUm 173/3; *Award as to Quarries by Dean Forest Mining Com.* (1859), *passim*: copy in ibid. D 2511.
30 Dean Forest Mines Act, 1 & 2 Vic. c. 43, s. 83.
31 Wood, *Laws of Dean Forest*, 363.
32 Ibid. 293; Hart, *Ind. Hist. of Dean*, 305.
33 Fisher, *Custom and Capitalism*, 55.
34 Cf. O.S. Maps 6", Glos. XXXI. NE. (1884 edn.); XXXIX. NE., NW., SW. (1883–4 edn.).
35 Nicholls, *Forest of Dean*, 252–3.
36 *Glouc. Jnl.* 12 Feb. 1853.
37 *Kelly's Dir. Glos.* (1870), 617; cf. Pope, How, & Kerau, *Severn & Wye Railway*, i. 150.
38 Bick, *Old Ind. of Dean*, 61.
39 Paar, *Severn and Wye Railway*, 48.
40 Glos. Colln. LR 1.2, pp. 3, 5, 8–11; O.S. Maps 6", Glos. XXXI. SW. (1903 edn.); XXXIX. NW. (1904 edn.);

cf. Glos. R.O., D 3921/II/18.
41 Glos. Colln. LR 1.2, pp. 3, 9.
42 P.R.O., F 16/64 (no. 1087); F 16/71.
43 Pope, How, & Kerau, *Severn & Wye Railway*, ii. 191–2.
44 Glos. Colln. LR 1.2, pp. 3–5, 8–10.
45 Pope, How, & Kerau, *Severn & Wye Railway*, ii. 183–4.
46 Bellows, *Week's Holiday in Dean*, 61
47 P.R.O., F 16/63; F 16/70; O.S. Maps 6", Glos. XXIII. SE. (1883 edn.); XXXI. NE. (1884 edn.).
48 Glos. R.O., Q/RUm 106.
49 O.S. Map 6", Glos. XXXIX. NE. (1884 edn.).
50 P.R.O., F 16/64; F 16/71; O.S. Maps 6", Glos. XXXVIII. NE. (1884 edn.); XXXIX. SW. (1883 edn.).
51 Hart, *Ind. Hist. of Dean*, 121, 313; Mullin, *Forest in Old Photog.* 88; Glos. R.O., DA 24/100/10, p. 687.
52 Hart, *Ind. Hist. of Dean*, 306–8.
53 Glos. R.O., AP/R 1/SP 8/4.
54 Anstis, *Parkend*, 53.
55 Pope, How, & Kerau, *Severn & Wye Railway*, iii. 506–7.
56 Glos. R.O., K 193/10, 28.

places, including Shakemantle,[57] but in 1992 quarrying continued on a large scale only at Bixhead, where 4 men extracted sandstone mostly for restoration and monumental use, and 17 men were employed at the works south of Cannop ponds, where stone from outside the Forest was also dressed.[58]

IRONWORKS. Ore mined in Dean possibly supplied ironmakers there by Roman times.[59] In 1066 the iron was forged at Gloucester, which owed iron goods to the Crown as part of its farm. The Forest sent much iron to the town throughout the Middle Ages[60] and was the chief iron producing district of medieval England at least until the 14th century.[61]

Dean's medieval ironworks included simple forges or bloomeries which were mobile and used charcoal as fuel.[62] In some forges the blast was provided by bellows worked by foot, a feature that survived in some of the more rudimentary ironworks operating in Dean in the mid 1630s.[63] Before smelting the ore was roasted or was crushed by stamping, a practice indicated by personal-name evidence in the mid 13th century. Some improvement in design by the mid 13th century apparently allowed the forges to resmelt cinders or slag left by earlier works.

Under Henry II and his successors some forges active within the Forest's jurisdiction belonged to the Crown and others were in private hands.[64] Private forges were licensed by the Crown often for working in private woodland[65] but some of them operated without permission and many strayed into the royal demesne from nearby settlements. Among the few authorized to enter royal woodland was one at Ardland (St. White's), south-west of Littledean, belonging to Flaxley abbey.[66] The Crown made several attempts to restrict the destruction of woodland by charcoal burning: in 1217 it ordered all forges to be removed, except those belonging to its St. Briavels castle estate and its serjeants-in-fee, four held by hereditary woodwards, and two which Ralph Avenel had by the grant of King John.[67] In 1220 the Crown halted the operation of all private forges and demanded that their owners show warrant for them.[68] In the following months many owners, including 6 woodwards and 10 serjeants-in-fee, were allowed to resume ironmaking[69] and, despite a further attempt to remove all itinerant forges in 1226,[70] ironmaking continued in the

mid 13th century.[71] The forges' impact on the Forest's timber reserves is indicated by Flaxley abbey's right to take two oaks a week for its forge, a right it surrendered in 1258 in return for a grant of Abbots wood in the Forest.[72]

The Crown had 3 forges working within the Forest in 1226[73] and set up 8 forges there in 1237.[74] Those ceased working in 1240.[75] By the later 1240s a great forge belonging to St. Briavels castle was worked in the Crown's woods but, together with several smaller royal forges erected in or shortly before 1255,[76] it was pulled down a few years later to protect timber.[77] A few private forges continued to work within the Crown's woodland. Others, based on outlying settlements and each paying the constable of St. Briavels 7s. a year, may have invaded the royal woodland but in the mid 1240s part of the charcoal consumed by 20 or more forges operating in English Bicknor, Ruardean, Mitcheldean, Littledean, and Lydney came from Wales or other places outside the Forest. The woodwards of Bicknor, Ruardean, Mitcheldean, and Littledean levied a payment from the forges within their bailiwicks.[78] Bristol burgesses visited the area to buy iron,[79] and 43 residents of parishes within the Forest had itinerant forges in 1270[80] and at least 60 people, mostly living on the east or west edge of the area, had them in 1282.[81] One or two years later the number had fallen to 45.[82] Private ironmaking continued in the later Middle Ages, and 49 forges, mostly in St. Briavels, Ruardean, Mitcheldean, and Littledean parishes, were operating in 1317, and 33, mostly in Mitcheldean and Newland, were at work in the mid 1430s.[83] A smiths' court, held presumably to regulate forges throughout the Forest, was then mentioned but no sessions were held during the years 1434–7 and it may have lapsed.[84] Ironworkers were active in the Forest in the mid 16th century[85] and some were sent to operate a royal forge in Glamorganshire c. 1531.[86]

The sites of early ironmaking were later marked by deposits of cinders, which were found, sometimes in large mounds, throughout the Forest. The name Cinderford, recorded in 1258, indicates at least one site near the stream crossed by the Littledean–Coleford road in the eastern part of the Forest.[87] As the forges worked at low temperatures they smelted the ore inefficiently so that the cinders remained rich in iron.[88] Resmelting the cinders may have been practised by the mid 13th century,[89] but most of them were removed in the

57 Hart, Ind. Hist. of Dean, 309.
58 Inf. from general manager, Forest of Dean Stone Firms Ltd.
59 V.C.H. Glos. ii. 216.   60 Ibid. iv. 12, 25–6, 47.
61 H. R. Schubert, Hist. Brit. Iron and Steel Ind. (1957), 98–108; cf. V.C.H. Glos. ii. 216–17.
62 Para. based on Hart, Ind. Hist. of Dean, 2–4; V.C.H. Glos. ii. 218.   63 P.R.O., C 66/2740, no. 18.
64 Nicholls, Iron Making, 12–25.
65 Rot. Litt. Claus. (Rec. Com.), i. 430, 442–3, 449, 452, 464.
66 Flaxley Cart. p. 18.
67 Rot. Litt. Claus. (Rec. Com.), i. 334–5.
68 Ibid. 428.   69 Ibid. 430, 433, 442–3, 449, 464.
70 Ibid. ii. 116, 120.
71 Ibid. 123, 160, 185; P.R.O., E 146/1/25.
72 Flaxley Cart. pp. 109–10.
73 Rot. Litt. Claus. (Rec. Com.), ii. 160; cf. Close R.

1227–31, 138.   74 Close R. 1234–7, 416.
75 Hart, Ind. Hist. of Dean, 4.
76 P.R.O., E 146/1/26; for the great forge, above, St. Briavels, econ. hist. (mills and ironworks).
77 Cal. Fine R. 1337–47, 230.
78 P.R.O., E 146/1/25.   79 V.C.H. Glos. ii. 269.
80 P.R.O., E 32/29, rot. 2.
81 Ibid. E 32/30, rot. 23d.   82 Hart, Royal Forest, 47.
83 Ibid. 65, 69.
84 P.R.O., SC 6/850/20; Berkeley Cast. Mun., General Ser. acct. roll 426.
85 Leland, Itin. ed. Toulmin Smith, ii. 64.
86 Hart, Ind. Hist. of Dean, 7.
87 Cal. Chart. R. 1257-1300, 11.
88 Trans. B.G.A.S. ii. 216–18; Rudge, Hist. of Glos. ii. 12–13; Hart, Ind. Hist. of Dean, 222.
89 Hart, Free Miners, 158.

17th and 18th centuries when they were mixed with the ore to be consumed by more efficient blast furnaces, reliant on water power.[90] Several such furnaces worked near the Forest from the late 16th century and the Crown allowed them to operate within the royal demesne of the Forest from 1612; a lease then gave William Herbert, earl of Pembroke and constable of St. Briavels castle, leave to build ironworks, fell timber, and mine ore and cinders.[91]

Under that lease[92] Edmund Thomas and Thomas Hackett, manager of the Tintern wireworks (Mon.),[93] built and ran four furnaces and three forges, which became known as the king's ironworks. Two furnaces were on Cannop brook at Cannop and Parkend, another was on Greathough (or Lyd, formerly How) brook above Lydbrook, and one was on Cinderford (or Soudley) brook below Staple Edge some distance upstream of Soudley bridge. The forges stood downstream of the Parkend, Lydbrook (or Howbrook), and Soudley furnaces, the Soudley forge being also some way above Soudley bridge.[94] The ironworks consumed large amounts of charcoal, for which the Crown assigned to the lessees an allowance of cordwood from the woodlands,[95] and of ore and cinders, and so posed a serious threat to the woodlands and to the customary rights of the miners. In 1613 the ironworks were shut down, but in 1615 the Parkend and Soudley works were leased to Sir Basil Brooke of Madeley (Salop.) and a partner and the Cannop and Lydbrook works to George Moore and a partner. Illegal felling of timber led the Crown to close them again in 1618. In 1621 it assigned them to Sir Richard Robartes and he handed them over to Philip Harris and Richard Challenor. The Cannop and Soudley works were not in regular use in 1625. From 1628 the ironworks were operated under the earl of Pembroke by Sir Basil Brooke, George Mynne, and Thomas Hackett. The partners, who also ran the Tintern and Whitebrook wireworks (Mon.), built forges on Soudley brook at Bradley and on Cannop brook (or the Newerne stream) at Whitecroft. Hackett later left the partnership and Mynne in 1634 sold his share in it to Sir John Winter. The ironworks, which the Crown closed in 1634, were dilapidated in 1635. Each forge had two or three fineries and a chafery and those at Parkend, Bradley, and Whitecroft two hammers.[96] In 1636 the king's works were leased to the baronets Baynham Throckmorton and Sackville Crowe and the Bristol merchants John Gonning the

younger and John Taylor; the lease restricted the operation of the furnaces and forges and required all unlicensed ironworks to be demolished. The unauthorized works comprised several of the more primitive type[97] and may have included the improved bloomery which John Broughton, deputy surveyor of Dean Forest, worked in 1637.[98] Throckmorton and his partners retained the king's ironworks at Parkend, Whitecroft, Soudley, and Bradley after the grant in 1640 of the bulk of the Forest to Sir John Winter.[99] On the cancellation of Winter's grant in 1642 the Cannop and Lydbrook works were leased to John Browne, the king's gun founder, who assigned them to a partnership headed by William Donning of Purton.[1]

During the Civil War production at the king's ironworks was severely disrupted. The Soudley furnace supplied shot to royalist forces for a time.[2] In 1644 John Brayne of Littledean, who had apparently been ordered by Edward Massey, commander of the garrison at Gloucester, to seize the belongings of Sir John Winter, captured some of the furnaces and forges,[3] and the following year Prince Rupert's troops apparently destroyed some works.[4] Later in 1645, when Brayne was operating the Bradley and Lydbrook forges, the Soudley forge was idle. In the late 1640s John Gifford rebuilt some of the works, including the Parkend furnace, and in 1649 he was running the Lydbrook furnace and forge and several of the other works.[5] Ironmaking ceased in 1650 when parliament ordered the destruction of all works within the Forest. Most of the remains of the early 17th-century king's ironworks were destroyed by later activity on the sites, leaving only traces of building platforms, ponds, and watercourses in the late 20th century. The site of the Soudley furnace, for which two ponds upstream at Cinderford had provided power, was marked by the remains of a building and large deposits of cinders.[6] The Bradley forge may have been at one of two sites, in Newnham, where forges were working in the later 18th century.[7]

In the late 16th century and early 17th iron mills and forges were started at Lydbrook. A hammerman lived there in 1610[8] and a founder in 1612.[9] Ironworks of Robert Devereux, earl of Essex, may have been used shortly before 1597 by Richard Hanbury for trial making of Osmund iron for the Tintern wireworks.[10] From 1600 the earl's works, which retained a connexion with the Tintern works and comprised two forges, were operated with furnaces at Bishopswood by

90 Nicholls, *Iron Making*, 8–9; above, mining to 18th cent.
91 Hart, *Ind. Hist. of Dean*, 8–10; P.R.O., E 112/83/411.
92 Para. based on Hart, *Ind. Hist. of Dean*, 10–43; G. F. Hammersley, 'Hist. of Iron Ind. in Forest of Dean Region, 1562–1660' (London Univ. Ph.D. thesis, 1972), 140–71.
93 Cf. Hart, *Royal Forest*, 89–90.
94 P.R.O., E 178/6917; F 17/2.
95 Below, Forest Admin., exploitation 1603–68.
96 For a description of ironmaking in the charcoal blast furnace period, Schubert, *Hist. Brit. Iron and Steel Ind.* 158–61.
97 P.R.O., C 66/2740, no. 18; cf. *Cal. S.P. Dom.* 1634–5, 487.
98 Hart, *Royal Forest*, 119.
99 Schubert, *Hist. Brit. Iron and Steel Ind.* 187; cf. *Merchants and Merchandise in 17th-Cent. Bristol* (Bristol

Rec. Soc. xix), pp. 110–13.
1 Hart, *Royal Forest*, 129–30; *Cal. S.P. Dom.* 1641–3, 348–9.
2 Hart, *Ind. Hist. of Dean*, 17, 41.
3 P.R.O., LRRO 5/7A, depositions 1645, nos. 7, 13; depositions 1649, no. 5.
4 *Trans. B.G.A.S.* xviii. 104.
5 P.R.O., LRRO 5/7A, depositions 1645, nos. 7, 13; depositions 1649, nos. 47, 60; Glos. R.O., D 2026/X 14, f. 30v.
6 Hart, *Ind. Hist. of Dean*, 18, 40–1, 55, plate facing p. 5; inf. from Mr. Standing.
7 P.R.O., F 17/7; F 17/4; MR 415 (F 16/47); Taylor, *Map of Glos.* (1777); cf. Glos. R.O., Q/RUm 73, 160.
8 Glos. R.O., D 1677/GG 619.
9 P.R.O., E 178/3837.
10 Ibid. E 134/39 Eliz. I Hil./23; *Complete Peerage*, v. 141–2.

George Catchmay.[11] A forge, later called Lower forge, was built *c.* 1600 some way above Lower Lydbrook in place of a grist mill and fulling mill on Greathough brook. Standing on the boundary of a detached part of Ruardean with English Bicknor, it was held in succession by Thomas Hackett, George Moore, Richard Tyler, and John Kyrle. The Crown, which claimed it as an encroachment on the Forest waste,[12] granted the forge to Robert Treswell in 1626[13] but Kyrle, who was made a baronet,[14] remained in possession in 1635.[15] Ownership of the forge descended with the earl's English Bicknor estate,[16] which Benedict Hall purchased in 1634.[17] The lessees of the king's ironworks evidently forced the forge's closure *c.* 1637[18] but it was quickly back in operation with several fineries. Hall remained the owner[19] but in 1648 Baynham Vaughan of Ruardean granted a lease of part of it to Griffantius Phillips.[20] It was apparently rebuilt *c.* 1650.[21]

A short distance upstream a grist mill, within Ruardean parish, had been converted as an iron mill, later known as Middle forge, by 1619. It was then owned by Alexander Baynham and worked, together with the king's Lydbrook forge and furnace some distance above, by George Moore and his partner. In the early 1620s it was worked by the lessees of the king's ironworks. George Vaughan purchased the forge in 1623[22] and held it in 1645, when John Brayne was working it.[23] Benedict Hall was the owner in 1657.[24] Downstream of Lower forge, in a detached part of Newland at Lower Lydbrook, a corn mill was used as a nailer's workshop in 1622. Nearby was apparently a forge worked, possibly from 1611, by Thomas Smart, who in 1622 formed a pond for a battery or plating mill he built there. His assistant Richard Tyler took over the works in 1627 and operated them until *c.* 1637,[25] when the lessees of the king's ironworks evidently suppressed them.[26]

Ironmaking resumed in the royal demesne woodland in 1654 when a new furnace at Parkend was in blast. Built by John Wade, the Forest's chief administrator, to supply the Commonwealth with iron for shot and ordnance, it was a little downstream from the site of the king's furnace. To make use of iron discarded in manufacturing shot Wade built a forge downstream at Whitecroft. In addition to providing shot and fittings for the navy Wade supplied iron to shipbuilders on the river Severn, produced

pig iron and bar iron, and sent chimney backs and baking plates to Bristol.[27] Also in the 1650s several experimental ironworks using local ore were constructed in Dean by a partnership apparently including John Birch and John Wildman, a speculator in royalists' and papists' lands. They employed an Italian glassmaker from Bristol and sought the advice of Dud Dudley, the Worcestershire ironmaster, but their efforts were unsuccessful.[28] At the Restoration supervision of the Parkend and Whitecroft works under the Crown passed to William Carpenter and from 1662 they were operated by Sir John Winter's nominees, Francis Finch of Rushock (Worcs.) and Robert Clayton, a London scrivener, who also worked a furnace at or above Lydbrook.[29] The works possibly remained in use for a while after Winter's connexion with the Forest ended in 1668[30] but, to preserve the woodland, the Crown sold them and a forge at Parkend in 1674 for demolition to Paul Foley, owner of ironworks near the Forest.[31] Cinders sent to Parkend from English Bicknor under an agreement of 1692 were evidently not resmelted there.[32]

After the Restoration Middle and Lower forges at Lydbrook were owned by the Halls of Highmeadow,[33] and in the early 18th century their estate was said also to include a furnace at Lydbrook.[34] In 1671 Paul Foley acquired a lease of both forges and a furnace at Redbrook.[35] He and his partners made Osmund iron for the Tintern and Whitebrook wireworks at Middle (later Upper) forge and, probably until 1694, manufactured anvils at Lydbrook.[36] The Foleys and their partners, including William Rea who was manager of their Gloucestershire, Herefordshire, and Monmouthshire ironworks until 1725, remained lessees of the Lydbrook and Redbrook works in the early 18th century. In the late 1720s they operated three forges at Lydbrook with the Bishopswood furnace.[37] The third forge, which had been a grist mill not long before, was at the bottom of Lower Lydbrook and was part of the Vaughan family's Courtfield estate. It became known as Lower forge[38] and the Foleys retained it after they had relinquished the other forges. In the late 1740s it worked blooms from the Bishopswood forge and pig iron from Lancashire and Scotland.[39]

Upper (formerly Middle) and Middle (formerly Lower) forges at Lydbrook were leased in

[11] P.R.O., E 134/44 Eliz. I Trin./3; *Trans. B.G.A.S.* xxiv. 145.
[12] P.R.O., E 134/4 Chas. I East./40; E 134/4 Chas. I Mich./supplementary 902/2.
[13] Glos. R.O., D 421/E 5.
[14] G. E. C. *Baronetage,* ii. 17.
[15] P.R.O., SP 16/282, f. 253.
[16] Ibid. E 134/4 Chas. I East./40.
[17] Glos. R.O., D 1677/GG 820.
[18] P.R.O., E 134/14 Chas. I Mich./42.
[19] Cf. N.L.W., Courtfield MSS. 107, ct. 11 Apr. 1642.
[20] Heref. R.O., F 8/III/54.
[21] Glos. R.O., D 2026/X 14, f. 3 from end.
[22] Ibid. D 1677/GG 688, 821; Hart, *Ind. Hist. of Dean,* 34, which identifies another forge upstream of Middle Forge and below the king's ironworks; cf. P.R.O., E 178/5304, mm. 3–4.
[23] P.R.O., LRRO 5/7A, depositions 1645, nos. 7, 13.
[24] Hart, *Ind. Hist. of Dean,* 34.
[25] Ibid. 35; Glos. R.O., D 1677/GG 676, 780.
[26] Cf. P.R.O., E 134/14 Chas. I Mich./42.
[27] Hart, *Ind. Hist. of Dean,* 18–19.
[28] Ibid. 256–7; *V.C.H. Glos.* ii. 225; for Birch and Wildman, *D.N.B.*
[29] Hart, *Ind. Hist. of Dean,* 19–23; Glos. R.O., D 421/E 6–7.
[30] Hart, *Free Miners,* 213–14.
[31] Hart, *Ind. Hist. of Dean,* 23.
[32] Glos. R.O., D 33/251.
[33] Ibid. D 1677/GG 950, 1035.
[34] Bodl. MS. Top. Glouc. c. 3, f. 137.
[35] Hart, *Ind. Hist. of Dean,* 34–5, 47.
[36] *Trans. B.G.A.S.* lxxii. 139–40; Glos. R.O., D 1677/GG 1095.
[37] Glos. R.O., D 1677/GG 1557, nos. 1–5; P.R.O., C 108/415; E 134/4 Geo. II East./11; E 134/5 Geo. II Hil./8, 11.
[38] P.R.O., F 14/1; F 14/2A, rot. 1d.; F 17/117(2), p. 22; MR 691 (LRRO 1/240).
[39] *Trans. B.G.A.S.* lxxii. 142–3; N.L.W., Courtfield MSS. 547, 549.

1742 to Rowland Pytt.[40] After his death in 1755[41] they were operated by his son Rowland,[42] and from 1763 Richard Reynolds of Bristol and John Partridge (d. 1791) of Ross-on-Wye (Herefs.) worked them.[43] The partnership was presumably the Bristol company which shortly before 1769 built a forge near Lydbrook,[44] perhaps in place of one of the existing buildings. Partridge's son John[45] worked Upper, Middle, and Lower forges in the late 1780s, when his partners included James Harford of Bristol.[46] About that time an additional finery and a channel to improve the water supply were built.[47] By 1793 Upper and Middle forges and the Redbrook ironworks were worked by David Tanner[48] of Monmouth, who sublet the forges before 1798, when he was declared bankrupt. From 1799 the forges were worked under Viscount Gage, owner of Highmeadow, by his steward James Davies, whose partners included the Gloucester bankers Sir Edwin Jeynes and Robert Morris.[49] Henry Davies held Upper and Middle forges and the Upper Redbrook tinplate works in 1818, when the Crown, which had bought the Highmeadow estate, put them up for sale.[50] Lower forge had been purchased by William Partridge c. 1810.[51]

The first coke-fired furnaces in the extraparochial Forest appeared, almost simultaneously, at Cinderford and Parkend. The Cinderford furnace, built principally at the instigation of Thomas Teague, was probably blown in in 1797.[52] It was situated at a place, then called Daniel ford, on the stream 800 m. north of Cinderford bridge[53] and used coke brought from Broadmoor, to the north, by a short canal.[54] The Parkend furnace dated from 1799 and was possibly operated by Richard Perkins in 1807.[55] Both furnaces fell idle about that time, unable to compete with the iron industry of South Wales and Staffordshire. Their failure reflected in part the poor quality of local coking coal.[56] Problems in the manufacture of iron were addressed by David Mushet of Coleford, whose innovations earned him a high reputation as a metallurgist. In 1818 or 1819 he built a cupola for experimentation at Dark Hill,[57] where a year or two later Moses Teague found a way to make good iron with the coke of local coal. In 1824, to exploit his discovery, Teague formed the Forest of Dean Iron Co. with William Montague of Gloucester, Benjamin Whitehouse of Monmouth and Redbrook, and, later, John James of Lydney. The company reopened the Parkend furnace and later Teague revived smelting operations at Cinderford.[58] Teague's enterprise established Parkend and Cinderford as the main centres, with Lydbrook, of Dean's iron industry, which developed to manufacture tinplate, wire, and metal castings. The industry depended closely on local mines, in which the leading ironmasters invested substantially,[59] and provided many jobs. In 1841 it relied in part on child labour, boys being employed at the blast furnaces and tinplate works and girls at the latter.[60]

The Forest of Dean Iron Co. built a second furnace at the Parkend works and initially derived power from Cannop brook, a large pond being formed in 1825 some way upstream by flooding a quarry at the bottom of Bixslade. In 1827 a large water wheel was installed at the works, which included a bridge or covered way carrying a pipe and rails over the Severn & Wye tramroad. A steam engine was built at the works later in 1827 and a second pond was created at Cannop, upstream of the first, in 1829.[61] The works were closed down in 1841 but were back in use by 1846. Following William Montague's death in 1847 John James (d. 1857) ran the works in partnership with Charles Greenham (d. 1866) and in 1849 a second steam engine was installed.[62] Tinplate works completed north-west of the ironworks by James and Greenham in 1853[63] were worked in 1854 by Nathaniel Daniels, who became insolvent.[64] In 1856 they were sold to Thomas and William Allaway,[65] who enlarged the works and employed 200 men there in 1866. At the ironworks, which had 300 employees at that time, a third blast furnace was built in the late 1860s.[66] Production had begun to decline by 1871 and Henry and Edwin Crawshay, who bought the ironworks and the tinplate works in 1875, closed them in 1877.[67] Charles Morris of Llanelli (Carms.) reopened the tinplate works in 1879 but competition from South Wales was among factors in their closure in 1881.[68] The furnaces at the ironworks were demolished in 1890 and most of the remaining buildings on both sites had been removed by 1900.[69]

Smelting resumed at Cinderford in 1829 at new works provided by Moses Teague, William Montague, and others on the site of the aban-

[40] Glos. R.O., D 421/E 44; cf. ibid. Q/REl 1A, St. Briavels 1776, s.v. Ruardean; P 275/CW 2/2.
[41] V.C.H. Glos. iv. 127.
[42] Hart, Ind. Hist. of Dean, 76.
[43] Glos. R.O., D 1677/GG 1123; for Partridge, Burke, Land. Gent. (1898), ii. 1153.
[44] Hart, Free Miners, 234.
[45] Cf. Glos. R.O., D 1677/GG 1123.
[46] Ibid. Q/REl 1A, St. Briavels 1787, s.v. Ruardean; D 637/III/8; cf. Univ. Brit. Dir. ii (1793), 573.
[47] Glos. R.O., D 1677/GG 1545, nos. 7, 39.
[48] P.R.O., F 17/117(2), pp. 44–5; MR 691.
[49] Glos. R.O., D 1677/GG 1545, nos. 36–50, 81A–104A.
[50] Ibid. D 5844/1.
[51] Ibid. D 637/III/8; Q/REl 1A, St. Briavels, s.v. Ruardean.
[52] Glos. Soc. Ind. Arch. Jnl. (1982), 12–16.
[53] Glos. R.O., D 897, deed 1798; Q/RUm 5, 73.
[54] Nicholls, Forest of Dean, 224.
[55] Ibid. 226–7; Glos. R.O., Q/RUm 5, 10; cf. Anstis, Ind. Teagues, 106.

[56] Nicholls, Forest of Dean, 224–5; Hart, Ind. Hist. of Dean, 119, 121, 127.
[57] F. M. Osborn, Story of the Mushets (1952), 24–8; Glos. Soc. Ind. Arch. Jnl. (1971), 67.
[58] Nicholls, Forest of Dean, 225–6; Anstis, Ind. Teagues, 104–5.
[59] Above, mining from 1770s.
[60] Anstis, Ind. Teagues, 179–83.
[61] Ibid. 108–10; Anstis, Parkend, 35–40.
[62] Nicholls, Forest of Dean, 227; Anstis, Parkend, 42–3; for James, Glos. R.O., P 209/MI 1, p. 75.
[63] Glouc. Jnl. 12 Feb. 1853; cf. O.S. Map 6", Glos. XXXIX. SW. (1883 edn.).
[64] Hart, Ind. Hist. of Dean, 198.
[65] Anstis, Parkend, 50.
[66] Nicholls, Forest of Dean, 228; Nicholls, Iron Making, 58–9.
[67] Jnl. Brit. Soc. Mining Students, vi (5) (1881–2), 88; Glouc. Jnl. 4 Sept. 1875; 29 Nov. 1879.
[68] Anstis, Parkend, 50–2.
[69] Hart, Ind. Hist. of Dean, 129; O.S. Map 6", Glos. XXXIX. SW. (1904 edn.).

doned blast furnace. Activity ceased in 1832, during an economic slump, but was resumed with financial help from the South Wales ironmaster William Crawshay and a second furnace was built. In 1834 or 1835 William Allaway and John Pearce, operators of the Lydbrook tinplate works, joined the partnership running the ironworks[70] and in 1841 there were three furnaces producing 12,000 tons of iron a year[71] and employing 100 men and boys.[72] Crawshay's son Henry, who ran the works from 1847, was given his father's share in the furnaces in 1854 and bought out the only other partner, Stephen Allaway, in 1862.[73] In the mid 1850s the works always had three of its four furnaces in blast[74] but in the later 1870s only two furnaces were in production. Two new furnaces were built in 1880[75] but only one furnace at the works was in blast in 1890 and the works closed in 1894. Demolition of the furnaces was completed by 1901.[76]

Upstream on Bilson green, a forge standing idle in 1856[77] was acquired by James Russell, whose family had wireworks at Lydbrook, and in 1864 it produced wire rods and cable iron using pig iron, chiefly from the Cinderford furnaces.[78] Known as the Forest Vale Ironworks, the works were enlarged in 1867[79] and passed after Russell's death in 1871 to his son A. J. Russell.[80] In 1880 they employed 100 men making wire, some of it from iron smelted by charcoal.[81] The works were demolished in 1892.[82] Further north at Hawkwell new tinplate works were started in 1879 by Jacob Chivers, formerly a tinplate manufacturer at Kidwelly (Carms.). The Hawkwell works, which on Chivers's death in 1883 passed to his brother-in-law A. C. Bright, were shut down in 1895[83] and were converted as brickworks in 1905.[84]

Lydbrook was dominated in the early 19th century by ironworks and mills extending along the stream below Upper Lydbrook almost to the river Wye.[85] Upper and Middle forges were purchased in 1818 by James Russell[86] (d. 1848) and passed to his sons Edward, William, and James.[87] The Russells erected wireworks there before 1848[88] and made telegraphic wire and iron for use by blacksmiths in the mid 1850s.[89] In the mid 1860s,

taking pig iron mostly from Cinderford, they employed 100 hands and also produced fencing wire.[90] Their workforce had been halved by 1880[91] and the works closed by 1896.[92]

Downstream tinplate works and forges were worked by William Allaway and John Pearce in 1834. The tinplate works, a short way below James Russell's mills,[93] were apparently built by Thomas Allaway in 1798 or 1806[94] and were described as extensive in 1807.[95] In 1817 the works, held under William Partridge, comprised three forges, rolling and bar mills, and a tin house,[96] one of the forges being Lower forge, and in the early 1820s, when James Pearce was a partner in the business,[97] they were enlarged.[98] After William Allaway's death in 1849[99] the works, which used iron from Cinderford and dispatched tinplate by boat, were run by his sons.[1] The works were a major source of employment but were virtually idle in 1871 when Richard Thomas became the lessee. Thomas, who later took over the Lydney tinplate works,[2] added many buildings at Lydbrook, where four out of five mills were in use in 1880.[3] Financial difficulties caused by litigation concerning Thomas's mining interests in Dean led to the mills' closure in 1883 and a limited company was formed in 1884 to resume working at Lydbrook and Lydney. The company, headed from 1888 by R. B. Thomas,[4] concentrated production at Lydbrook on the mills at Lower Lydbrook, those higher up being demolished by the early 20th century.[5] The works were closed several times, the men finding temporary employment at local collieries.[6] Tinplate production ceased during the First World War and the works, having reopened in 1919, were closed again in 1925. The buildings were demolished in the 1930s.[7]

In the 19th century several furnaces operated outside the iron industry's main centres of Parkend, Cinderford, and Lydbrook. One established in Ruspidge by 1835[8] was owned by Moses Teague and William Crawshay in 1838. Its building, which also accommodated a foundry,[9] housed workshops and stores in 1849[10] and was unused in 1872.[11] A company formed in 1849 built a furnace at Oakwood, and its prop-

[70] Nicholls, *Forest of Dean*, 226; Anstis, *Ind. Teagues*, 112–14.
[71] Glos. R.O., Q/RUm 175.
[72] Anstis, *Ind. Teagues*, 179.
[73] Ibid. 121–2; Hart, *Ind. Hist. of Dean*, 125.
[74] Nicholls, *Forest of Dean*, 226.
[75] *Jnl. Brit. Soc. Mining Students*, vi (5), 88; cf. above, Plate 31.
[76] Pope & Kerau, *Forest of Dean Branch*, i. 192; O.S. Map 6", Glos. XXXI. SE. (1883, 1903 edns.).
[77] P.R.O., F 16/63 (no. 2437); F 16/70.
[78] Hart, *Ind. Hist. of Dean*, 205.
[79] Nicholls, *Iron Making*, 61; Verey, *Glos.* ii. 160.
[80] Glos. R.O., D 543, Russell fam. papers 1849–98; *Kelly's Dir. Glos.* (1879), 629.
[81] *Jnl. Brit. Soc. Mining Students*, vi (5), 90.
[82] *New Regard of Forest of Dean*, x. 54.
[83] W. H. Morris, *Kidwelly Tinplate Works* (Llanelli, 1987), 13; *Dean Forest Mercury*, 23 Mar. 1990.
[84] Mullin, *Forest in Old Photog.* 72.
[85] G.D.R., T 1/25, 128, 151; cf. above, Fig. 16.
[86] Nicholls, *Iron Making*, 60; *3rd Rep. Com. Woods* (1819), 19.
[87] Glos. R.O., D 543, Russell fam. papers 1849–98.
[88] Hart, *Ind. Hist. of Dean*, 203.
[89] Nicholls, *Forest of Dean*, 228.
[90] Nicholls, *Iron Making*, 60.

[91] *Jnl. Brit. Soc. Mining Students*, vi (5), 90.
[92] Glos. R.O., D 2299/809.
[93] Ibid. D 637/VII/19; D 3921/III/7.
[94] Hart, *Ind. Hist. of Dean*, 172.
[95] Rudge, *Agric. of Glos.* 343.
[96] Nicholls, *Forest of Dean*, 228.
[97] Glos. R.O., Q/REl 1A, St. Briavels, s.v. Ruardean; P 227/OV 1/1.
[98] C. Heath, *Excursion down the Wye* (1826), s.v. Lydbrook.
[99] Glos. R.O., P 138/IN 1/9.
[1] Nicholls, *Forest of Dean*, 228.
[2] D. Wainwright, *Men of Steel* (1986), 12; above, Lydney, econ. hist.
[3] *Jnl. Brit. Soc. Mining Students*, vi (5), 88.
[4] Wainwright, *Men of Steel*, 13–20.
[5] Cf. O.S. Map 1/2,500, Glos. XXXI. 1 (1881 and later edns.).
[6] *Tinplaters of Lydney and Lydbrook*, ed B. Rendell and K. Childs (n.d.), 67: copy in Glos. R.O., PA 209/11.
[7] *The Times*, 20 Dec. 1930; Hart, *Ind. Hist. of Dean*, 177.
[8] Sopwith, *Map of Dean Forest* (1835).
[9] Glos. R.O., Q/RUm 160.
[10] Ibid. 245.
[11] Ibid. Q/RI 52.

erty, including iron-ore and coal mines there, was purchased by the Ebbw Vale Co. in 1854.[12] The furnace was idle in 1859[13] and it had gone out of use by 1870.[14]

At Dark Hill David Mushet built a second furnace before 1845 when he handed the works over to his sons William, David, and Robert. Their partnership ended in 1847.[15] Robert Mushet, who later introduced spiegeleisen to the Bessemer process and also invented a self-hardening tool steel,[16] formed a partnership with T. D. Clare of Birmingham and built small steelworks, known as the Forest Steel Works, some way to the north-west on Gorsty knoll. Mushet, who employed 41 men in 1851, added a cupola and a small Bessemer converter to the works in 1856 and enlarged them again after forming the Titanic Steel and Iron Co. in 1862. Financial difficulties caused the winding up of the company in 1874 and the buildings were used as brickworks in 1928 and fell into ruin later.[17] The Dark Hill ironworks, where the furnace described in 1847 as newly erected was possibly never in blast, were sold before 1874 to the Severn & Wye Railway, which constructed an embankment across the east end of the site to carry the Coleford railway. An archaeological restoration of the site, begun by 1968, was completed in 1987.[18]

In the later 18th century slag from blast furnaces operating in the Forest area was used to mend roads and make green glass. For glassmaking the slag was reduced to powder by large stamping machines, lumps of iron being removed to be worked at the forges with pig iron, and much of the powder was sent to Bristol glass-bottle manufacturers.[19] One stamping machine was installed at Parkend in 1809 by Isaac and Peter Kear. They built a new mill there by Cannop brook c. 1815.[20] It powered twelve stamping blocks in 1841,[21] but was idle in the early 1850s, owing to a cheaper operation at Redbrook. It was restarted by John Morse[22] and apparently continued working until the 1880s.[23] At the end of the century the slag of abandoned ironworks at Cinderford and elsewhere was crushed and sold for ballast or for making concrete.[24]

In the 19th century a number of small foundries were established around the Forest to provide simple castings, mostly for the tramways. The first was built, possibly before 1821, by Samuel Hewlett, who worked a forge at Bradley[25] and in 1851 employed 14 men.[26] The foundry, upstream of the forge between Lower and Upper Soudley,[27] was the principal supplier of tramplates to the Severn & Wye Co.[28] and was run by Thomas Hewlett in 1841.[29] Samuel's son George took over the lease on his father's death in 1852 and the foundry closed after 1862.[30] A foundry in Howler's Slade near Cannop belonged to Trotter, Thomas, & Co. in 1835. Known as the Cannop foundry, it was rebuilt in 1874 and was taken over in the 1890s by Richard Young and Thomas Herbert. Herbert's son Ewart transferred the business to Cinderford in 1957.[31] By the 1840s Cinderford had a number of foundries and small engineering firms supplying the mining industry with machine parts.[32] In the Upper Bilson district a foundry built by Timothy Harris c. 1838 ceased operating before 1852[33] and another foundry, west of High Street and belonging to Timothy Bennett in 1841,[34] was used by the Cowmeadow family as boiler works in 1856 and 1868.[35] Engineering works south of the later Station Street originated as a foundry[36] operated by Joseph Tingle in 1868[37] and were run by his descendants until their closure in 1924.[38] On the west side of the Forest a foundry in the Oakwood valley, dating from 1852, made nails for export.[39] Idle in 1859,[40] it was later worked by the Pearce family and closed c. 1916.[41] Engineering works at Milkwall belonging in 1889 to Tom Morgan continued casting metals after the First World War.[42] Some foundries working in the early 20th century were attached to large collieries such as Lightmoor.[43]

MILLS. In the later Middle Ages there were several mills around the edge of the Forest.[44] The greatest concentration was on the stream at Lydbrook, where at least one was working in 1256.[45] Two mills belonging to English Bicknor manor in 1301, one of them used for fulling,[46]

12   Ibid. EL 172, p. 18; *Glouc. Jnl.* 25 Feb. 1854.
13   P.R.O., F 16/64 (no. 2966); F 16/71.
14   Hart, *Ind. Hist. of Dean*, 150–1; cf. O.S. Map 1/2,500, Glos. XXXIX. 13 (1881 edn.).
15   Hart, *Ind. Hist. of Dean*, 134, 148.
16   Osborn, *Mushets*, 36–47, 60; cf. R. F. Mushet, *The Bessemer-Mushet Process, or Manufacture of Cheap Steel* (Cheltenham, 1883), *passim.*
17   Hart, *Ind. Hist. of Dean*, 168–70; P.R.O., F 16/64 (no. 1507); F 16/71; HO 107/2444, s.v. Newland (Coleford).
18   Hart, *Ind. Hist. of Dean*, 134, 147–9; *New Regard of Forest of Dean*, iii. 85.
19   Hart, *Ind. Hist. of Dean*, 158–60; *Trans. B.G.A.S.* ii. 217; Rudge, *Hist. of Glos.* ii. 12–13.
20   *3rd Rep. Com. Woods* (1819), 80; Nicholls, *Forest of Dean*, 92, 97.
21   Glos. R.O., Q/RUm 175.
22   Anstis, *Parkend*, 47–8; P.R.O., F 16/64 (no. 1965); F 16/71.
23   *Kelly's Dir. Glos.* (1870), 617; (1889), 863.
24   Pope & Kerau, *Forest of Dean Branch*, i. 94–6, 193–4.
25   Glos. R.O., Q/RUm 73; Bryant, *Map of Glos.* (1824).
26   P.R.O., HO 107/1959, s.v. E. Dean (Bradley Ho.).
27   In 1838 the Soudley site was said to be in Ayleford: Glos. R.O., D 3921/III/6.
28   Hart, *Ind. Hist. of Dean*, 161–2.

29   Glos. R.O., Q/RUm 175.
30   Ibid. D 3921/III/6; mon. to S. Hewlett in Awre churchyard.
31   Hart, *Ind. Hist. of Dean*, 164–5; cf. Sopwith, *Map of Dean Forest* (1835); Glos. R.O., Q/RUm 173/3, plan M.
32   P.R.O., HO 107/364, s.v. Littledean walk.
33   Hart, *Ind. Hist. of Dean*, 162–3; for site, *2nd Rep. Dean Forest Com.* 66; Glos. R.O., Q/RGf 1/7.
34   Glos. R.O., Q/RUm 175.
35   P.R.O., F 16/63 (no. 2374); F 17/70; *Slater's Dir. Glos.* (1868), 244; for boiler making, below, other ind. and trade.
36   O.S. Map 1/2,500, Glos. XXXI. 11 (1881 and later edns.).
37   *Slater's Dir. Glos.* (1868), 245.
38   *Morris's Dir. Glos.* (1876), 470; *Kelly's Dir. Glos.* (1879–1923 edns.), s.vv. E. Dean, Cinderford; Hart, *Ind. Hist. of Dean*, 165.
39   Hart, *Ind. Hist. of Dean*, 167; *Glouc. Jnl.* 12 Feb. 1853.
40   P.R.O., F 16/64 (no. 3051); F 16/71.
41   *Kelly's Dir. Glos.* (1885–1919 edns.), s.v. Bream.
42   Ibid. (1889–1923 edns.), s.v. W. Dean.
43   Hart, *Ind. Hist. of Dean*, 166.
44   Cf. above, econ. hist. sections for Abenhall, Mitcheldean, and Ruardean.
45   *Cal. Pat.* 1247–58, 524.
46   *Inq. p.m. Glos.* 1236–1300, 230–1.

were presumably there, as were two to which Richard Talbot had a reversionary right in 1335.[47] Two thirds of another mill at Lydbrook belonged to the Ruardean estate of Alexander of Bicknor in 1306.[48] In 1375 Thomas Hathaway leased his share of a mill at Lydbrook to Alexander Carrant[49] and in 1428 Thomas Carrant granted that mill, together with a manor in Ruardean, to Robert Baynham.[50] Another mill was recorded at Lydbrook in 1437[51] and Flanesford priory (Herefs.) had two mills there in 1535.[52]

At Lower Lydbrook a grist mill called Gabbs Mill, in a detached part of Newland, was probably on the site of a water mill built before 1434.[53] In 1622 it was a nailer's workshop[54] and later it resumed grinding corn.[55] Upstream, on the boundary of a detached part of Ruardean with English Bicknor, a mill was leased in 1501 to Hugh Morse by Alice Baynham,[56] who had a manor in Ruardean.[57] The building later housed both a grist and a fulling mill and was held by John Morse (d. 1596), a Cirencester woollen draper. About 1600 Robert Devereux, earl of Essex, pulled it down to make room for a forge, and Morse's nephew John Morse built a small grist mill on waste land belonging to the earl's Bicknor manor.[58] Two other mills at Lydbrook, owned in 1579 by Christopher Monmouth, were operated by Richard Morse as a corn mill and a fulling mill in 1583.[59] A corn mill held under Bicknor manor in 1577[60] may have been that at Lydbrook held in 1611 by Joseph Baynham, whose son and heir Alexander[61] in 1619 had ironworks there in a building earlier used as a grist mill.[62] Lydbrook's cloth industry was represented by at least three weavers in 1597[63] and presumably by some of the cloth workers recorded under English Bicknor and Ruardean in 1608.[64] One of two corn mills in Lydbrook acquired by Richard Vaughan in 1666[65] and belonging to the Vaughans of Courtfield in the early 18th century was converted for fulling cloth before 1717.[66] Both mills were presumably on the site at the bottom of Lower Lydbrook occupied by a grist mill in 1724 and by a forge

not long afterwards.[67] Corn milling continued elsewhere in Lydbrook in the mid 18th century.[68]

A mill operating at Cinderford in 1275[69] may have been that said in 1282 to have been built by Walter of Huntley.[70] Flaxley abbey had a water mill, known in 1485 as the new mill, elsewhere on the Crown demesne.[71] A mill built c. 1434 on Horwell hill (later Bream's Meend) by Richard Lawrence of Bream[72] was demolished before 1623.[73] It probably stood on a tributary, since disappeared, of Oakwood brook.[74] The latter brook powered Oakwood Mill, a corn mill recorded from 1520 in a detached part of Newland.[75] Another corn mill belonging to Newland was on the stream below Pope's hill at Blackmore's Hale, north-east of Littledean. It was acquired by the Heane family in 1659[76] and was evidently working in 1718.[77] Its building was perhaps that used as a skin house in 1840.[78]

By the mid 19th century the number of corn mills working in the Forest and at Lydbrook had increased. Waterloo Mill, on Greathough brook above Lydbrook,[79] was on or near the site of the king's furnace of the early 17th century.[80] The mill was operated by Thomas Burdock in 1841[81] and steam power had been installed by 1885.[82] Downstream the Cooper family worked a corn mill at Newland bridge in Upper Lydbrook in 1841.[83] A corn mill at the bottom of the valley, on the east side of the main street of Lower Lydbrook, belonged to the Highmeadow estate in 1792.[84] In 1818 or 1819, when it was held by William Partridge, it was sold to James Pearce and in 1856 it was bought by Edward Russell.[85] By the early 1820s it was held with nearby Gabbs Mill, to the south-east,[86] which was worked in 1856 by the Little family.[87]

Whitecroft had two corn mills in the early 19th century. One, on an eastern tributary of Cannop brook (or the Newerne stream),[88] was known as Kidnalls Mill and was possibly in use in 1808.[89] It may have been working in 1841.[90] The other mill, on the west side of Whitecroft, stood at the end of a long race leading from Cannop brook

47 Cal. Pat. 1334–8, 191.
48 Ibid. 1301–7, 446.
49 Heref. R.O., F 8/II/24.
50 Cal. Close, 1422–9, 459; above, Ruardean, manors.
51 Glos. R.O., D 33/355.
52 Valor Eccl. (Rec. Com.), iii. 17.
53 P.R.O., E 101/141/1.
54 Glos. R.O., D 1677/GG 676.
55 Ibid. D 6401/11.
56 P.R.O., E 134/4 Chas. I Mich./supplementary 902/2.
57 Above, Ruardean, manors.
58 P.R.O., E 134/4 Chas. I East./40; N.L.W., Courtfield MSS. 790; G.D.R. wills 1595/90.
59 Glos. R.O., D 33/267–8.
60 Ibid. D 1677/GG 528.
61 Ibid. D 33/271; P.R.O., C 142/335, no. 32.
62 Glos. R.O., D 1677/GG 688.
63 B.L. Harl. MS. 4131, f. 509v.; N.L.W., Courtfield MSS. 116.
64 Smith, Men and Armour, 42–4.
65 P.R.O., CP 25/2/657/18 & 19 Chas. II Hil. no. 10.
66 Glos. R.O., Q/RNc 1, p. 61.
67 P.R.O., F 14/1; F 14/2A, rot. 1d.; F 17/117(2), p. 22; MR 691.
68 G.D.R. wills 1742/148.
69 P.R.O., E 32/30, rot. 6d.

70 Ibid. E 32/31, m. 2.   71 Cal. Pat. 1485–94, 48.
72 P.R.O., SC 6/850/20; MR 879 (F 17/1).
73 Glos. R.O., D 2026/X 19.
74 Inf. from Mr. Standing.
75 Glos. R.O., D 1677/GG 331; G.D.R., T 1/128.
76 Glos. R.O., D 36/T 16; W. C. Heane, Gen. Notes relating to Heane Fam. (1887), 9.
77 P.R.O., CP 25/2/1015/5 Geo. I Mich. no. 6.
78 G.D.R., T 1/128.
79 O.S. Map 6", Glos. XXXI. NW. (1883 edn.).
80 Hart, Ind. Hist. of Dean, 37.
81 P.R.O., HO 107/364, s.v. Worcester walk.
82 Kelly's Dir. Glos. (1885), 519.
83 P.R.O., HO 107/364, s.v. Worcester walk; HO 107/2444, s.v. W. Dean; F 16/64 (no. 242); F 16/71.
84 Ibid. F 17/117(2), p. 7; MR 691.
85 Glos. R.O., D 5844/1; 3rd Rep. Com. Woods (1819), 19.
86 Glos. R.O., P 227/OV 1/1; D 6401/11; G.D.R., T 1/25, 128.
87 Kelly's Dir. Glos. (1856), 322; S. D. Coates and D. G. Tucker, Water Mills of the Middle Wye Valley (Monmouth District Mus. Service, 1983), 22
88 Bryant, Map of Glos. (1824).
89 Glos. R.O., Q/RUm 27.
90 Cf. Paar, Severn and Wye Railway, 44–5.

in Whitemead park.[91] It was worked by the Morse family by 1829[92] and had steam power in 1885.[93] On Cinderford brook Thomas Brace converted a building below Cinderford bridge with an old water wheel, once used for drying coal, as a corn mill in 1818 or 1819.[94] Moses Teague owned it and George Bright operated it in 1839.[95] Downstream below Upper Soudley, at a wood turnery acquired in 1867 by Henry Crawshay, a new building was erected c. 1877 as a flour mill known as Camp Mill[96] and a pond upstream of the site was enlarged.[97] Shortly before 1846 a maltster, Timothy Bennett, built a steam-powered corn mill at a place known later as Steam Mills, north of Cinderford by the road and tramway to Nailbridge.[98] Thomas Wintle worked it in 1856[99] and purchased it later,[1] and in 1890 it passed with his Mitcheldean brewery to his son Francis.[2]

Most of the corn mills were closed in the late 19th century or the early 20th. The mill in the main street of Lower Lydbrook was a paper factory in 1883[3] and for a number of years it made sugar paper for insulating detonator wire.[4] Lydbrook's other corn mills ceased operating later,[5] Waterloo Mill being used before 1912 to pump water to a nearby mine.[6] Camp Mill at Soudley was used for millboard manufacture by 1888 and was sold in 1901 to James Joiner of Dulcote (Som.), who transferred ownership to his Dulcote Leather Board Co.[7] The mill fell idle after the company went into receivership in 1908 and Joiner opened a saw mill there in 1922. That was closed c. 1952[8] and the site later became the premises of the Dean Heritage museum, opened in 1983.[9] Oakwood Mill, which used steam power by 1885, closed c. 1900.[10] Milling stopped at Cinderford bridge when the water supply there was reduced in the early 20th century[11] and at Steam Mills before 1922.[12] The mill in the west part of Whitecroft was abandoned in 1915[13] but by 1919 the Lydney and District Farmers' Co-operative Society had taken it over[14] and it continued to operate it in 1970.[15] The building was disused in 1992.

OTHER INDUSTRY AND TRADE. The timber of the Forest has supported many local industries. Charcoal burning, an essential adjunct of the early iron industry, was widespread by the 13th century and caused much damage in the woodland.[16] Despite a ban on the activity in 1270,[17] many people were making charcoal in the late 1270s,[18] and 2,685 charcoal pits were recorded in the Forest in 1282, most of them in Staunton, Abenhall, and Blakeney bailiwicks.[19] In 1471 the chief forester had the right, by ancient custom, to 20d. from each charcoal pit every 6 weeks.[20] That payment was levied on 47 pits in Abenhall bailiwick in 1478, when the bailiwick's woodward also took some profit from charcoal burning.[21] In 1634 the chief forester, Sir Baynham Throckmorton, Bt., claimed 16d. for each charcoal pit in the Forest.[22] Charcoal continued to be consumed in large quantities by ironworks, particularly the blast furnaces established in or near the Forest from the late 16th century. From the mid 19th century much of the market for Forest of Dean charcoal was supplied by chemical works, but a few families continued traditional charcoal burning and the last charcoal burner was active until after the Second World War.[23]

In 1881 five chemical works produced a range of substances by distilling wood, including charcoal, pyroligneous acid, tar, and naphtha, and employed a total of c. 130 men.[24] The oldest works, near Cannop bridge, were in use in 1835,[25] and George Skipp, who manufactured lead acetate there in 1841,[26] built similar works in the Oakwood valley near Bream in 1844.[27] In 1854 the Oakwood factory belonged to Isaiah Trotter of Coleford.[28] The Cannop factory later produced sulphuric acid and crushed charcoal for making lampblack.[29] At the Upper Lydbrook works, established in 1857,[30] Samuel Russell produced naphtha in 1859[31] and the Broadmoor works, built north of Cinderford by John and Thomas Powell c. 1864, later made lead acetate.[32] In 1870 the firm of Chapman & Morgan operated the chemical works some way south of

91 Glos. R.O., Q/RGf 1/5; O.S. Map 6", Glos. XXXIX. SW. (1883 edn.).
92 G.D.R. wills 1829/173.
93 Kelly's Dir. Glos. (1885), 547.
94 3rd Rep. Com. Woods (1819), 82; 35th Rep. Com. Woods, H.C. 148, p. 93 (1857 Sess. 2), xxiv; cf. Glos. R.O., Q/RUm 73.
95 Glos. R.O., Q/RUm 164.
96 Ibid. D 3921/III/6; Dean Forest Mercury, 12 Feb. 1982.
97 Glos. R.O., Q/RI 52; O.S. Map 6", Glos. XXXIX. NE. (1884 edn.).
98 Glos. R.O., D 543, deed 3 Dec. 1846; abs. title of F. Wintle to Mitcheldean brewery 1923; O.S. Map 6", Glos. XXXI. NE. (1884 edn.).
99 P.R.O., F 16/63 (no. 1821); F 16/70.
1 Glos. R.O., D 543, deed 27 Feb. 1861.
2 Ibid. abs. title to Mitcheldean brewery 1923.
3 Ibid. Russell fam. papers 1849–98.
4 W.I. hist. of Lydbrook (c. 1959, TS. in Glos. Colln.), 2; K. S. Woods, Development of Country Towns in SW. Midlands during the 1960s (Oxf., 1968), 56.
5 O.S. Maps 1/2,500, Glos. XXXI. 1 (1902, 1923 edns.); 5 (1902, 1922 edns.); Kelly's Dir. Glos. (1894 and later edns.).
6 Pope, How, & Kerau, Severn & Wye Railway, iii. 415.
7 P.R.O., F 3/790; Glos. R.O., D 3921/III/6.
8 Hart, Ind. Hist. of Dean, 387–8.
9 Glouc. Jnl. 9 Jan. 1982; Dean Forest Mercury, 29 Apr. 1983.

10 Kelly's Dir. Glos. (1885–1902 edns.), s.v. Bream.
11 Ibid. (1902), 114; (1906), 114; Glos. Soc. Ind. Arch. Newsletter, xiv. 23.
12 O.S. Map 1/2,500, Glos. XXXI. 7 (1922 edn.).
13 G. E. Lawrence, Kindling the Flame (1974), 25: copy in Glos. R.O., D 2598/23/1.
14 Kelly's Dir. Glos. (1919), 265.
15 Hart, Ind. Hist. of Dean, 374.
16 C. E. Hart, 'Charcoal Burning in Royal Forest of Dean', Bull. Hist. Metallurgy Group, ii (1), 33; cf. Close R. 1234–7, 5.
17 P.R.O., E 32/29, rot. 2.
18 Hart, Royal Forest, 44–5.
19 P.R.O., E 32/31, mm. 9–14.
20 Hart, Free Miners, 183 n.
21 Glos. R.O., D 36/M 1, rot. 2d.
22 Hart, Free Miners, 183 and n.
23 Bull. Hist. Metallurgy Group, ii (1), 35–6; above, Plate 24.
24 Jnl. Brit. Soc. Mining Students, vi (5) (1881–2), 89.
25 Sopwith, Map of Dean Forest (1835).
26 Glos. R.O., Q/RUm 175.
27 P.R.O., F 3/230.   28 Ibid. F 3/229.
29 Glos. R.O., D 637/I/60; D 638/6; Hart, Ind. Hist. of Dean, 344–6.
30 Ind. Glos. 1904 (copy in Glos. R.O., IN 11), 58.
31 P.R.O., F 16/64 (no. 204); F 16/71.
32 Hart, Ind. Hist. of Dean, 351; O.S. Map 6", Glos. XXXI. NE. (1884 edn.).

Whitecroft.[33] S. M. Thomas took over the Lydbrook factory in the mid 1870s,[34] acquired the Cannop and Oakwood works c. 1890, and sold them all in 1894 to Thomas Newcomen, who ceased operations at Oakwood and Cannop in 1900 and 1902 respectively.[35] The Whitecroft works, which had closed by 1883,[36] may have been in use again in the late 1880s and early 1890s[37] and the Broadmoor works were abandoned before 1900.[38] The Lydbrook factory, which also made foundry blackings, remained in use until c. 1933.[39] In 1913 the Crown built distillation works at Cannop to turn waste and unsaleable timber to profit. The factory, beside the Severn & Wye railway next to the Mitcheldean–Coleford and Lydbrook–Parkend roads, produced charcoal, tar, alcohol, and acetate of lime. Run by the Ministry of Munitions during the First World War, it was idle from 1919 to 1924 when it was sold to Wood Distillation (England) Ltd. Following a reorganization of the company in the late 1920s the factory was modernized and in 1935 it employed 22 men. From 1960 it produced only charcoal[40] and in 1971 it was closed.[41]

The management of the Forest's timber and its use for naval shipbuilding are discussed elsewhere.[42] Some wood and bark went to craftsmen, tanners, and shipbuilders living in nearby parishes.[43] Within the Forest, where a cardboard maker lived at Moseley Green in 1628,[44] there were possibly a dozen or more saw pits earlier in that century.[45] In the 19th and 20th centuries large saw mills operated on several sites. One at Parkend, run in 1859 by James Hughes, employed 65 men in 1950 but was used as a store for imported hardwoods from 1977.[46] Mining in Dean depended on local wood to shore up workings, and in the late 19th century and the 20th some large collieries ran their own saw mills.[47] The largest saw mill in the Forest in 1992 was that established in 1966 on the site of Lightmoor colliery, near Cinderford, by James Joiner & Sons Ltd.[48] Among trades using local wood were turning and brushmaking. In 1849 Samuel Hewlett had a turning mill next to his foundry at Soudley[49] and for much of the 1860s it was operated by a brush manufacturer,[50] who

created a pond upstream of the building.[51] Upper Bilson had brushworks in 1859.[52] In 1906 a carpenter at Soudley was making carriages and wagons for road use.[53]

Oak bark from the Forest was used in many local tanneries[54] and during the 18th century large quantities were shipped to Ireland, from Newnham and elsewhere.[55] Personal-name evidence suggests that tanning had been introduced to Lydbrook by 1386[56] and two tanners recorded in English Bicknor and Ruardean in 1608[57] presumably lived at Lydbrook. The village had at least three resident tanners in 1638[58] and tanning possibly continued there in 1776.[59] By the later 18th century Lydbrook conducted a thriving river trade in coal and other produce of the Forest[60] carried in barges owned by, among others, the Wheatstone family,[61] and in the early 19th century a few barges and trows were built there.[62] In 1398 John de Montague, earl of Salisbury, took salmon fry at his weir in the Wye at Lydbrook.[63]

In the 19th century the range of activities supporting and supported by the mining industry increased. Several men made and repaired boilers for steam engines. One such business, conducted by James Cowmeadow in 1841,[64] later had works in the Upper Bilson district of Cinderford and apparently in the Drybrook area.[65] In the late 1880s engineering works were started at Steam Mills by M. E. Teague, whose invention of automatic expansion valves for steam engines was adopted widely by the mining industry.[66] The works employed c. 40 men in 1905[67] and specialized in maintaining pumping and winding engines in Dean.[68] Cinderford with its small foundries and engineering workshops[69] remained a centre for metal industries in the early 20th century. They included a business run by the Wheeler family which produced bearings for local collieries and industry.[70] By 1874 electric fuses produced by the Brain family, owners of Trafalgar colliery near Cinderford, were used by the mining and quarrying industries and by civil engineers for blasting. Francis (later Sir Francis) Brain devised improvements in shot-firing mechanisms[71] and by 1900 a fuse factory had been built west of Trafalgar.[72] Insulated wire for the fuses was made at the colliery in the

33 Kelly's Dir. Glos. (1870), 534; O.S. Map 6", Glos. XXXIX. SW. (1883 edn.).   34 Ind. Glos. 1904, 58.
35 Hart, Ind. Hist. of Dean, 346–8.   36 Ibid. 351.
37 Kelly's Dir. Glos. (1889), 863; Harris's Dir. Dean Forest (1891), 51.
38 O.S. Map 6", Glos. XXXI. NE. (1903 edn.).
39 V.C.H. Glos. ii. 211; Kelly's Dir. Glos. (1931), 247; (1935), 247–8.
40 Rep. Forestry Branches 1912–13 [Cd. 7488], pp. 61–3, H.C. (1914), xii; Hart, Ind. Hist. of Dean, 357–67.
41 Dean Forest & Wye Valley (H.M.S.O. 1974), 13.
42 Below, Forest Admin.
43 Above, econ. hist. sections for Lydney, Awre, Littledean, Mitcheldean, and Newland; V.C.H. Glos. x. 72, 96, 113.
44 P.R.O., E 178/5304, m. 11d.
45 Anstis, Parkend, 52.
46 Ibid. 52–3; Glos. R.O., K 193/10.
47 Glos. R.O., DA 24/100/3, pp. 403, 410–11.
48 Citizen, 26 Aug. 1982.
49 Glos. R.O., Q/RUm 245.
50 Ibid. D 3921/III/6; Kelly's Dir. Glos. (1863), 256.
51 45th Rep. Com. Woods, H.C. 410, p. 80 (1867), xix; New Regard of Forest of Dean, vi. 38.
52 P.R.O., F 3/176.   53 Kelly's Dir. Glos. (1906), 114.

54 Hart, Ind. Hist. of Dean, 330–1.
55 Rudder, Glos. 571.
56 Glos. R.O., D 33/420 (abs. of deed in ibid. D 33/55).
57 Smith, Men and Armour, 42–3.
58 P.R.O., E 134/14 Chas. I Mich./42.
59 Glos. R.O., Q/REl 1A, St. Briavels 1776, s.v. Ruardean.
60 Above, mining to 18th cent.; ironworks.
61 G.D.R. wills 1797/6.
62 Farr, Chepstow Ships, 88, 112, 117.
63 Public Works in Med. Law, i. (Selden Soc. xxxii), 157, 166.
64 P.R.O., HO 107/364, s.v. Littledean walk (Mount Pleasant).
65 Ibid. F 16/63 (no. 2374); F 16/70; Slater's Dir. Glos. (1868), 236, 244.
66 Hart, Ind. Hist. of Dean, 165; Kelly's Dir. Glos. (1889), 733; cf. O.S. Map 1/2,500, Glos. XXXI. 7 (1903 edn.).
67 Glos. R.O., DA 24/100/4, p. 119.
68 Bick, Old Ind. of Dean, 69.   69 Above, ironworks.
70 Hart, Ind. Hist. of Dean, 166.
71 Ibid. 406–8; Glouc. Jnl. 12 Dec. 1874; Kelly's Dir. Glos. (1879), 629; (1889), 752; cf. Morris's Dir. Glos. (1876), advertisements, p. 180.
72 O.S. Map 1/2,500, Glos. XXXI. 10 (1903 edn.).

early 20th century[73] and the factory continued to assemble detonators in the First World War.[74] In the mid 1860s a factory was built next to the Severn & Wye railway at Whitecroft to make briquettes from coal dust from a mine at Pillowell. The factory was idle for several periods before its machinery was sold in 1908.[75]

To produce a colouring agent, red oxide may have been burned in Lea bailiwick under licence from the Crown in 1436.[76] Much later, colour and paint works were opened to process ochres and oxides mined locally, and in the mid 19th century red and yellow colouring was used locally in marking sheep and tinting whitewash.[77] In 1831 William Tingle and William Cooper obtained permission to build a machine for grinding ochre on Cinderford (or Soudley) brook in Ruspidge,[78] evidently on the site west of the brook where William Crawshay and Moses Teague owned a paint mill in 1838. The mill was also used as a machine shop,[79] and paint manufacture stopped there before 1856.[80] In 1872 Henry Crawshay had a paint factory downstream near Upper Soudley[81] using pigments, principally red oxide, from his Buckshaft mine.[82] After the First World War colour works were started at Oakwood[83] and Milkwall. The Milkwall factory, built in 1926, employed 7 people in 1965, when in addition to processing oxides mined elsewhere it ground coal for use in the paper and fibreboard industries and in drills.[84] In the 1960s the baths and canteen of the former Eastern United colliery at Ruspidge were taken over by a pigment manufacturer,[85] which in 1992 employed, on two sites, c. 30 people producing material for paint sprays and inks.[86]

Brickmaking had become a Forest industry by the early 19th century[87] and expanded considerably after 1838, when the digging of clay and sand was permitted under licence from the Commissioners of Woods.[88] Brickyards were opened in various places, including Whitecroft,[89] Ellwood,[90] Parkend,[91] and Staple Edge.[92] They usually manufactured fire bricks as well as ordinary bricks and several were attached to local ironworks.[93] David Mushet, who had brickworks next to his ironworks at

Dark Hill in 1832,[94] supplied bricks to South Wales in 1843.[95] Brickworks established by the Coleford–Parkend road at Fetter Hill by 1858 also produced pottery.[96] By the late 1870s, when several brickyards were in production at Steam Mills and Nailbridge,[97] the industry made extensive use of shale from colliery spoil tips. The Brain family used clay from Trafalgar colliery at brickworks at Steam Mills;[98] later the Princess Royal Colliery Co. near Whitecroft manufacured bricks[99] and in 1923 the Lydney & Crumpmeadow Collieries Co. opened brickworks at Broadmoor. Brickworks occupying abandoned steelworks on Gorsty knoll in 1928 were closed in 1937.[1] Brickmaking continued into the later 20th century, particularly in the Cinderford area where the Hawkwell and Broadmoor yards employed 62 people in 1959.[2]

The road haulage industry in the Forest area, which had its origins in the carrying of timber and coal,[3] was well established by the mid 19th century. At that time some haulage businesses were part-time ventures.[4] With the advent of motorized transport the industry expanded and after the First World War a number of bus companies were established, some of them by haulage firms, to handle passenger traffic.[5]

By the 1870s many Forest settlements had small retail shops.[6] A co-operative society formed at Cinderford in 1874 opened shops in the town and elsewhere, and in the early 20th century similar societies were trading in Bream, Pillowell, and Upper Lydbrook. Cinderford became a centre for the retail trade, and the co-operative movement, which had large grocery, furnishing, and hardware stores there in the mid 1960s,[7] built a new supermarket near the town centre c. 1990. In the later 20th century many shops in the Forest closed and from 1991 Lydbrook had only one general store.[8] Livestock sales held at the Speech House from 1857 included an October fair until 1874 or later.[9] Produce markets held in Cinderford town hall from 1869[10] moved to a different site later in the century.[11] In the early 1870s livestock fairs were also held in Cinderford[12] and in 1873 a market

73 Hart, *Ind. Hist. of Dean*, 205–6.
74 P.R.O., F 3/403.
75 Glos. R.O., D 2299/584; *New Regard of Forest of Dean*, ix. 5–7.
76 Berkeley Cast. Mun., General Ser. acct. roll 426.
77 Nicholls, *Forest of Dean*, 247.
78 *9th Rep. Com. Woods*, H.C. 718, p. 56 (1832).
79 Glos. R.O., Q/RUm 160, 164.
80 P.R.O., F 16/63 (no. 2990); F 16/70.
81 Glos. R.O., Q/RI 52.
82 Hart, *Ind. Hist. of Dean*, 247.
83 Ibid. 167.
84 Glos. R.O., D 3921/V/21, newspaper cutting 31 Dec. 1965.
85 Hart, *Ind. Hist. of Dean*, 428.
86 Inf. from works manager, Runnymede Dispersions Ltd., Ruspidge.
87 Cf. Paar, *G.W.R. in Dean*, 21.
88 Dean Forest Mines Act, 1 & 2 Vic. c. 43, s. 84.
89 *Kelly's Dir. Glos.* (1856), 342.
90 O.S. Map 6", Glos. XXXIX. NW. (1883 edn.).
91 Anstis, *Parkend*, 53.
92 Pope & Kerau, *Forest of Dean Branch*, i. 132–3; O.S. Map 6", Glos. XXXIX. NE. (1884 edn.).
93 *Jnl. Brit. Soc. Mining Students*, vi (5) (1881–2), 69;

Hart, *Ind. Hist. of Dean*, 309–12.
94 *Reg. Electors W. Division Glos. 1832–3*, 110; Glos. R.O., Q/RUm 175.
95 Glos. Colln. NQ 15.44.
96 *Slater's Dir. Glos.* (1858–9), 179; P.R.O., F 16/64 (no. 1840); F 16/71; cf. *New Regard of Forest of Dean*, ii. 49–51.
97 O.S. Map 6", Glos. XXXI. NE. (1884 edn.).
98 P.R.O., F 3/402.
99 Lawrence, *Kindling the Flame*, 25.
1 Hart, *Ind. Hist. of Dean*, 170, 311–12.
2 Ibid. 312; Glos. R.O., K 193/48; cf. Mullin, *Forest in Old Photog.* 72–3.
3 Cf. *3rd Rep. Com. Woods* (1788), 83.
4 *Morris's Dir. Glos.* (1876), 467–72, 476–80, 515–16.
5 Hart, *Ind. Hist. of Dean*, 392–3; cf. H. Phelps, *Forest of Dean* (1982), 122.
6 *Morris's Dir. Glos.* (1876), 467–72, 476–80, 515–16.
7 W.I. portrait of Cinderford (1965, copy in Cinderford libr.); Phelps, *Forest of Dean*, 120–2; *Kelly's Dir. Glos.* (1906), 48, 236, 347.
8 *Dean Forest Mercury*, 14 Dec. 1990; 10 May 1991.
9 *Glouc. Jnl.* 24 Oct. 1857; 1 May 1858; 17 Oct. 1874.
10 *Morris's Dir. Glos.* (1876), 466.
11 O.S. Map 1/2,500, Glos. XXXI. 11 (1902, 1922 edns.).
12 *Glouc. Jnl.* 24 Sept., 22 Oct. 1870; 20 June, 17 Oct. 1874.

hall was built at Lydbrook to stimulate trade in cattle and corn from higher up the Wye Valley.[13]

The early 20th century saw the establishment of several enterprises unconnected with the area's traditional industries. The most significant of them was started by the Jarrett family in 1910 to make safety pins at the abandoned briquette factory in Whitecroft.[14] It acquired markets at home and overseas and became the principal employer of female labour in the area. The workforce rose to c. 400, including many outworkers, before the Second World War. During the war the factory also made small components for radio and radar equipment[15] and later the firm, which after its acquisition by an American company in 1964 was known as Whitecroft Scovill Ltd., produced aerosol valves, zip fasteners, and a range of metal haberdashery goods.[16] At Upper Lydbrook a mineral-water factory opened by E. J. Flewelling, a builder, after the First World War[17] ceased production c. 1970.[18]

In 1938, to counteract the large-scale loss of mining and quarrying jobs, a committee representing local government, employers, and trade unions was formed to foster industry in the Forest and its region. The committee, re-formed in 1943 as the Royal Forest of Dean Development Association,[19] was successful from the end of the Second World War in attracting new industries and expanding existing ones. Thereby the area's industrial base diversified and more jobs were provided for local women, many of whom had earlier been in domestic service in Cheltenham. New factories established at Coleford, Lydney, and Mitcheldean employed many Forest residents, who also travelled in increasing numbers to factories and offices in the Gloucester area.[20]

Most projects supported by the development association within the Forest itself centred on Cinderford. To relieve pressure on its Dursley works R. A. Lister & Co. Ltd. established an engine assembly plant in the town in 1944 and built a factory at the bottom of Station Street after the war.[21] The factory manufactured a range of machines, including diesel engines from 1952,[22] and its workforce had risen to 582 by 1969.[23] Rosedale Associated Manufacturers Ltd., a plastics manufacturer, opened a factory in Foundry Road c. 1945 and employed 220

people, mostly women, in 1950.[24] The factory, at which toys and domestic articles were assembled, was destroyed by fire in 1968 and was not rebuilt. By that time some plastic components were made in new works at Steam Mills.[25] On the outskirts of Cinderford brush and biscuit factories were established next to each other in Valley Road, west of the town. In 1959 the brush factory, dating apparently from 1948, employed 43 people and the biscuit factory, built in 1950 for Meredith & Drew Ltd., had 550 employees, mostly women.[26]

The opening of Lister's factory consolidated the importance of the engineering industry in the Forest's economy after the Second World War. Part of the industry was carried on in small, scattered works and foundries, some of them long established. Many were in the Cinderford area,[27] to which the business of the Cannop foundry was transferred in 1957. Occupying the former Bilson gasworks in Valley Road, it produced manhole covers and other castings for road and ornamental use[28] and it was operating in 1992. Among other foundries in the area was that of the engineering works established at Steam Mills in the late 1880s.[29] Those works closed in 1968 and were taken over by a firm of welders.[30] At Lydbrook engineering works were started in 1925 by S. C. Meredith, who made machinery for the cable industry. In 1947 he built a factory at Lower Lydbrook and in 1969 he employed more than 60 people.[31] Fred Watkins, who was dealing in second-hand machinery by 1935, built a factory for repairing boilers at Sling in 1942.[32] The works, later run by his son F. B. Watkins, also made machine tools and employed c. 150 people in the late 1960s.[33] At Whitecroft the engineering firm of Nash & Morgan was building motor coaches in 1954[34] and the J. Allen (later the London) Rubber Co. of Lydney acquired a new factory for warehousing in 1964.[35] In 1983 the factory was purchased by a firm which made insulation material for the building trade and employed 20 people in 1992.[36] Other new businesses included a small oil refinery occupying the buildings of the former Flour Mill colliery near Bream from 1940. It produced lubricants and in 1976 employed c. 20 people.[37] In 1949 Remploy established a factory at Parkend to employ disabled people, including former miners.[38] The factory made various

[13] *Forest of Dean Examiner*, 20 Sept. 1873.
[14] Hart, *Ind. Hist. of Dean*, 406; Glos. R.O., D 3921/II/30.
[15] *Dean Forest Mercury*, 29 June 1945; Glos. R.O., K 193/10.
[16] Hart, *Ind. Hist. of Dean*, 430–1.
[17] W.I. hist. of Lydbrook (c. 1959, TS. in Glos. Colln.), p. 7A; *Kelly's Dir. Glos.* (1931), 247.
[18] Inf. from manager, Lydbrook Valley Springs.
[19] Glos. R.O., AP/R 1/SM10; cf. ibid. AP/R 1/SP 8/3–4; in 1994 the association's min. bks. were at Dean Heritage mus.
[20] Payne, *Glos. Survey*, 145–7; Hart, *Ind. Hist. of Dean*, 422–4; Phelps, *Forest of Dean*, 123.
[21] D. E. Evans, *Lister's: The First Hundred Years* (Glouc. 1979), 184–5.
[22] *Royal Forest of Dean Ind. Handbook* (copy in Glos. R.O., D 3921/V/21), p. 32.
[23] *Dean Forest Mercury*, 13 Dec. 1985.
[24] Glos. R.O., D 3168/3/1; K 193/10, 28, 48.

[25] *Dean Forest Mercury*, 23 Aug. 1968.
[26] Hart, *Ind. Hist. of Dean*, 334, 423–4; Glos. R.O., K 193/10, 48.
[27] Above, ironworks.
[28] Hart, *Ind. Hist. of Dean*, 165; *Citizen*, 11 Nov. 1980.
[29] Cf. W.I. portrait of Cinderford.
[30] *Citizen*, 6 July 1968; Hart, *Ind. Hist. of Dean*, 428.
[31] W.I. hist. of Lydbrook, p. 7A; Glos. R.O., D 3921/III/7; *Forest of Dean Ind. Handbook*, pp. 33–4.
[32] *Kelly's Dir. Glos.* (1935), 144; Pope, How, & Kerau, *Severn & Wye Railway*, iii. 529–30.
[33] Inf. from Dr. C. E. Hart, of Coleford; Glos. R.O., D 3921/V/21, newspaper cutting 31 Dec. 1965.
[34] Glos. R.O., DA 25/132/15; cf. Lawrence, *Kindling the Flame*, 25.
[35] Glos. R.O., DA 25/100/32, pp. 3297–8, 3305–6; Hart, *Ind. Hist. of Dean*, 431; above, Lydney, econ. hist.
[36] Inf. from admin. off., Vensil Resil, Whitecroft.
[37] *Glos. Soc. Ind. Arch. Jnl.* (1976), 62.
[38] Anstis, *Parkend*, 84.

goods, including brushes and protective clothing, and packed spare parts for Rank Xerox Ltd. of Mitcheldean and in 1992, when it was producing small items such as photograph frames, purses, wallets, oven gloves, and washbags, its workforce numbered 60.[39]

Further loss of mining jobs from the late 1950s and the closure of cable works near Lydbrook in 1965[40] prompted renewed initiatives to increase industrial employment in the Forest. Many miners found work in established concerns such as Lister's factory in Cinderford and Rank Xerox's factory in Mitcheldean, both of which were enlarged at that time. With the successful creation of new jobs, the development association lapsed in the late 1960s.[41] Among businesses brought to Cinderford was that of Engelhard Industries Ltd., which purchased the biscuit factory in Valley Road in 1962 to refine precious metals and produce industrial chemicals, catalysts, inks, and paints; it employed 430 people in 1984.[42] An industrial estate was created at Whimsey, northwest of the town. Its first factory, built in 1965 for constructing and galvanizing transmission pylons,[43] had been acquired by 1970 by Rank Xerox Ltd.[44] In 1985 it became the home of Temco Ltd., a specialist wire manufacturer, which moved from a factory near Lydbrook[45] and in 1992 employed 95 people.[46] Beginning in 1975 the district council laid out the Forest Vale industrial estate, covering 104 a. (40 ha.) on the west side of Cinderford; 40 businesses had premises there by 1985 and more factory space was provided in 1986.[47] A smaller industrial estate was laid out south of the town on part of the abandoned Eastern United colliery site at Ruspidge.[48]

With economic recession in the early 1980s many jobs in the Forest disappeared, notably at Lister's Cinderford factory which closed in 1985.[49] Later the workforce at Engelhard's factory fell as its operations were gradually transferred elsewhere and in 1992 it numbered 67, including those engaged in refining and in providing sales and technical services.[50] In the early 1990s other established businesses, including Whitecroft Schaeffer (formerly Whitecroft Scovill), shed jobs[51] and, although the Forest retained many small employers in traditional and newer industries, its inhabitants increasingly looked to centres such as Gloucester, Lydney, Hereford, and Ross-on-Wye for work.

TRAMROADS AND RAILWAYS. Before the late 18th century coal and iron ore from the Forest were moved by packhorse.[52] Given the lack of roads, carts and wagons were of limited use, and the blast furnace commissioned at Cinderford in 1797 received coke brought by a private canal and ore brought by mules.[53] Coal and ore for more distant markets were taken to wharves on the rivers Severn and Wye[54] and the capitalization of the mining industry from the late 18th century was accompanied by the provision of tramroads to carry coal and stone to the rivers. Schemes for building tramroads were supported by the wealthier mine owners, other local industrialists, and merchants in the coalfield's traditional markets and opposed by the Crown, which viewed tramroads as a threat to its woodland, and free miners anxious to protect their claim to a monopoly of carrying.[55]

The first tramroad was a short line built in 1795 by James Teague from his mine called Engine pit, in Perch Inclosure, to the Coleford–Mitcheldean road. Teague and his partners began a second line between the same pit and road the following year and had extended it to the Wye at Lydbrook by 1803. That line enabled Teague to sell coal more cheaply in Hereford, whose citizens had for some years been in favour of such a venture. It was in use in 1808 but the track was lifted in 1815.[56]

By that time Crown opposition to mineral lines had been withdrawn and three tramroads linked the Forest with the Severn and Wye. Those lines, the Bullo Pill, the Severn & Wye, and the Monmouth, were to form the basis of the Forest's tramroad network. Construction of the tramroad to the Severn at Bullo Pill was begun in 1807 by Roynon Jones in collaboration with Margaret Roberts and the Gloucester bankers William Fendall and James Jelf. It ran alongside Soudley brook from Cinderford bridge, on the east side of the Forest, through Abbots wood and Jones's estate in Newnham, and before its completion in 1810 it was extended northwards from Cinderford bridge over Crown land to the summit above Churchway Engine colliery. The proprietors set up a company to make use of the line. Instead of rent for the section through Abbots wood the Crawley-Boeveys received a tonnage, which they retained in 1836 when they sold the estate.[57] The tramroad linking the Severn at Lydney with the Wye at Lydbrook was built by a partnership including John Protheroe, other local industrialists, and several Herefordshire gentlemen and known from 1810 as the Severn & Wye Railway & Canal Co. The line, which was completed in 1812 or 1813, followed the course of Cannop brook in the west part of the Forest and included a tunnel at Mirystock. The steep descent to the Wye at Lydbrook was an inclined plane controlled by

39 Inf. from manager, Remploy Ltd., Parkend.
40 Cf. above, Eng. Bicknor, econ. hist.
41 Hart, *Ind. Hist. of Dean*, 424–5, 431; *Dean Forest Mercury*, 13 Dec. 1985.
42 *Lydney Observer*, 16 Dec. 1983; inf. from general manager, Engelhard Ltd.
43 *Dean Forest Mercury*, 30 Apr. 1965; W.I. portrait of Cinderford.
44 Hart, *Ind. Hist. of Dean*, 429.
45 *Citizen*, 3 Oct. 1985; cf. above, Eng. Bicknor, econ. hist.
46 Inf. from senior secretary, Temco. Ltd.
47 *Dean Forest Mercury*, 1 Feb. 1985; 14 Nov. 1986.
48 *Guide to Ind. Estates in Glos.* (co. planning dept. 1984), 27.

49 *Dean Forest Mercury*, 7 Jan. 1983; 1 Feb., 13 Dec. 1985.
50 *Citizen*, 19 June 1991; inf. from general manager, Engelhard Ltd.   51 *Citizen*, 21 May 1991.
52 Hart, *Free Miners*, 79–80, 87; G.D.R., V 5/254T 3.
53 Nicholls, *Forest of Dean*, 224–5.
54 Above, mining to 18th cent.
55 Glos. R.O., D 421/E 48–9; Fisher, *Custom and Capitalism*, 22–4.
56 Anstis, *Ind. Teagues*, 22–45; Paar, *G.W.R. in Dean*, 13–17; *Glos. Soc. Ind. Arch. Jnl.* (1980), 51–60; (1986), 18.
57 Paar, *G.W.R. in Dean*, 19–22, 24, 27, 34–5; Churchway Engine to Cinderford Bridge Rly. Act, 49 Geo. III, c. 158 (Local and Personal).

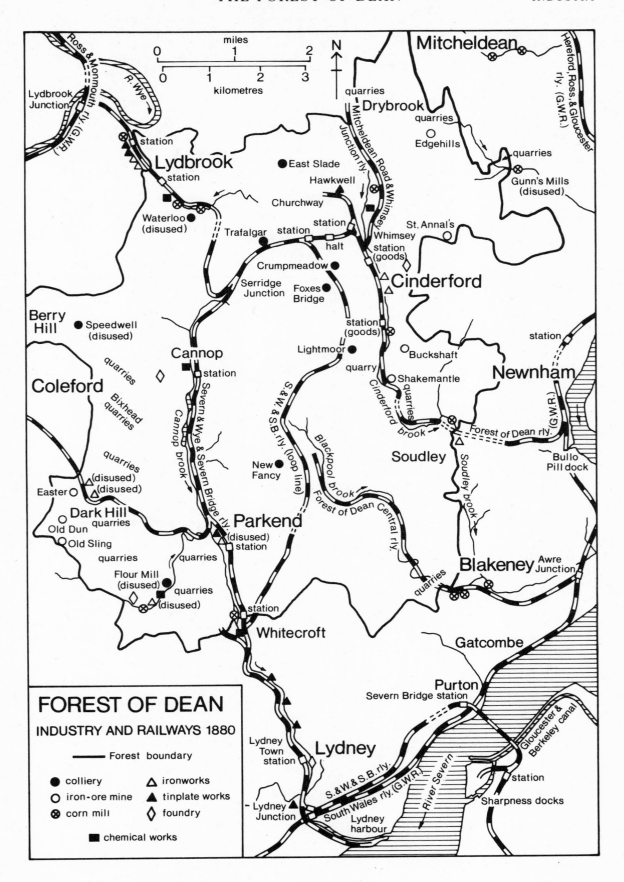

miles
0   1   2

0   1   2   3
kilometres

N

Mitcheldean

Ross & Monmouth rly. (G.W.R.)

R. Wye

Hereford, Ross, & Gloucester rly. (G.W.R.)

Lydbrook
Junction

station

Lydbrook

station

Waterloo
(disused)

East Slade

Hawkwell

Churchway

Trafalgar   station

halt

Whimsey

station
(goods)

St. Annal's

quarries

Drybrook

quarries

Edgehills

quarries

Gunn's Mills
(disused)

Mitcheldean Road & Whimsey

Junction rly.

station

Crumpmeadow

Serridge
Junction

Foxes
Bridge

Cinderford

station
(goods)

**Berry
Hill**

Speedwell
(disused)

Cannop

station

Lightmoor

quarry

Buckshaft

Shakemantle

station

Newnham

Coleford

quarries

Bixhead
quarries

quarries

Severn & Wye & Severn Bridge rly.

Cannop brook

S. & W. & S.B. rly. (loop line)

New
Fancy

Blackpool brook

Forest of Dean Central rly.

Cinderford brook

quarries

Soudley

Soudley brook

Forest of Dean rly. (G.W.R.)

Bullo
Pill dock

quarries

(disused)

(disused)

Easter

Dark Hill
quarries

Old Dun

Old Sling

quarries

Flour Mill
(disused)

quarries

quarries

(disused)

Parkend

(disused)
station

station

Whitecroft

Blakeney

Awre
Junction

quarries

Gatcombe

Purton
Severn Bridge station

Lydney
Town
station

Lydney

Gloucester & Berkeley canal

station

Sharpness docks

S. & W. & S.B. rly.

South Wales rly. (G.W.R.)

River Severn

Lydney
Junction

Lydney
harbour

FOREST OF DEAN

INDUSTRY AND RAILWAYS 1880

——— Forest boundary

● colliery   △ ironworks

○ iron-ore mine   ▲ tinplate works

⊗ corn mill   ◇ foundry

■ chemical works

FIG. 22

ropes.[58] The Monmouth tramroad, opened in 1812, served the western edge of the Forest and ran through Coleford to the Wye at Redbrook and Monmouth.[59]

The Bullo Pill and the Severn & Wye tramroads in particular provided outlets for numerous branch lines supplying local ironworks with coal and iron ore and transporting coal, ore, and stone out of the Forest.[60] Several early branches were constructed by the tramroad companies but most were laid down by mine and quarry owners. Some included rope-operated inclines. The pattern of subsidiary lines was frequently varied and extended. In 1812 the Severn & Wye Co. built a branch from Mirystock to Churchway, where a permanent junction with the Bullo Pill tramroad, involving a change of gauge, was formed in 1823. The company also provided early branch lines to serve mines and quarries in the slades west of Cannop brook and built a line from the top of the Lydbrook incline down to the Wye at Bishopswood.[61] Parkend, on the company's main line, became the junction for four tramroads, of which the Dark Hill branch, built by the company before 1814 and extended to Milkwall later, possibly had a short-lived connexion with a branch of the Monmouth tramroad. The Bullo Pill tramroad, which included a branch to Whimsey constructed in 1822, was in 1826 sold to Edward Protheroe, already the principal shareholder in the Severn & Wye Co., and vested in a new company, the Forest of Dean Railway.[62] The principal collieries on the east side of the Forest were linked to the Bullo Pill tramroad by private tramroads, long lines from Lightmoor and Crumpmeadow having been constructed by the late 1830s.[63] Whimsey became the terminus for several lines from mines further north and north-east; one was built by Sir J. J. Guest, Bt., in 1841 to enable ore from Westbury Brook mine to be shipped from Bullo Pill to his ironworks in South Wales. In the early 1820s there were also short private tramroads, unconnected to the main lines, serving a mine at Moorwood and quarries at Lea Bailey.[64]

The tramroad companies delayed the use of steam traction in the Forest for many years. By clinging to old working methods, neglecting investment in new lines, and charging high tolls they retarded the development of the mining industry. Criticism of them from the Crown, other railway companies, mine owners, and industrialists mounted as the tramroad network proved increasingly inadequate.

The Forest of Dean or Bullo Pill line was replaced by a broad-gauge steam railway after it had been purchased by the South Wales Railway in 1849. The new railway, which opened in 1854, ran from Churchway and Whimsey to the main Gloucester–South Wales line in Newnham. It overlaid the tramroad in places and it included tunnels south of Ruspidge and under Bradley hill. Goods stations were provided at Bilson and Cinderford bridge in the early 1860s and at Whimsey in 1884.[65] Of the branch tramroads some were retained and some replaced by railways often following different courses. The Severn & Wye Co. constructed a short loop line at Mirystock in 1847 to give access from the south to its Churchway branch, but required financial help from the South Wales Railway before it made other improvements in the mid 1850s. Little traffic used the northern end of its tramroad and the incline at Lydbrook had been abandoned by 1856. The company's dilatory attitude encouraged support for other ventures such as the Forest of Dean Central railway. Schemes for a steam railway from collieries in the centre of the Forest to the Severn were first mooted in 1826, and Charles Mathias of Lamphey (Pemb.) started to build one to Purton Pill but failed to complete it.[66] Under powers obtained in 1856 a railway was built to link the central collieries with the South Wales line in Awre. Construction of the railway, which entered the Forest along the valley of Blackpool brook, was slowed by lack of funds and the Great Western Railway opened the line to just beyond Brandrick's green in 1868.[67] A branch line to New Fancy colliery, which provided most of the traffic, was completed the following year.

In 1864 the Severn & Wye introduced steam locomotives on its tramroads and in 1865 it opened up the tunnel at Mirystock and constructed a new spur to the Churchway branch line. In the following decade the company established a railway network in a change of policy prompted by rivalry with the G.W.R., owner from 1863 of the Forest of Dean railway, and by the demand from South Wales industry for iron ore and timber. In 1869 a broad-gauge railway was opened alongside the tramroad between Lydney and the bottom of Wimberry Slade, and in 1872 a standard-gauge loop line was completed leaving the railway at the Tufts, south of Whitecroft, and rejoining it below Wimberry Slade. The loop, which included a tunnel at Moseley Green, ran near several large collieries, and a short branch making a junction with the Forest of Dean railway at Bilson in 1873 aided the movement of minerals between the eastern and western sides of the Forest. Beginning in 1872 the Severn & Wye constructed a standard-gauge railway from Lydney to Bilson and Lydbrook. That line, which replaced the main tramroad, followed the existing railway track to Wimberry Junction and incorporated the section of the loop line to the north-east. The Lydbrook branch, which left the loop line at Serridge green and joined the Ross–Monmouth railway at Stowfield, in English Bicknor, included a tunnel

[58] Paar, *Severn and Wye Railway*, 19–24, 29, 57; Lydbrook to Lydney Rly. Act, 49 Geo. III, c. 159 (Local and Personal).　　[59] Paar, *G.W.R. in Dean*, 85–90.

[60] Cf. Sopwith, *Map of Dean Forest* (1835). The rest of this section is based on Paar, *Severn and Wye Railway* and *G.W.R. in Dean*.

[61] Cf. above, Ruardean, econ. hist. (other ind. and trade).

[62] Cf. Dean Forest Rly. Act, 7 Geo. IV, c. 47 (Local and Personal).

[63] Cf. Nicholls, *Forest of Dean*, 107.

[64] Bryant, *Map of Glos.* (1824); cf. above, Ruardean, econ. hist. (other ind. and trade); Paar, *G.W.R. in Dean*, 143; Glos. R.O., Q/RUm 173/3.

[65] Pope & Kerau, *Forest of Dean Branch*, i. 3, 6, 176.

[66] Anstis, *Ind. Teagues*, 123–48; cf. above, Awre, intro.

[67] O.S. Map 6", Glos. XXXIX. NW. (1883 edn.).

at Mirystock and a viaduct on piers *c.* 90 ft. high at Lower Lydbrook.[68] After that work was completed in 1874 surviving sections of the tramroad and some of its branches were abandoned.[69] In 1875 the company, ahead of the G.W.R., opened a railway to Coleford. It left the main line at Parkend and in places shadowed the Milkwall branch tramroad. The Monmouth tramroad carried little traffic by that time and its track east of Coleford was lifted in the late 1870s. The Severn & Wye amalgamated with the Severn Bridge Railway in 1879, when the opening of the Severn bridge gave Forest mines direct access to Sharpness docks; the combined company was purchased jointly by the Midland Railway and the G.W.R. in 1894. The traffic carried by the branch line between Coleford and Parkend increased in 1916, on the closure of the G.W.R.'s own Coleford line west of Whitecliff.

The enterprise of the Severn & Wye Railway in the early 1870s ultimately destroyed two rival ventures. The Forest of Dean Central railway, which the G.W.R. worked at a loss, lost much of its traffic to the loop line and was idle for a few years from 1875, when mines in the central area were temporarily shut. The section above Howbeach colliery was abandoned at that time and regular traffic ended above Blakeney when the colliery closed in 1921. The G.W.R., which officially took over the Central company in 1923, continued to run some trains above Blakeney until 1932. The completion of the Lydbrook railway in 1874 severely curtailed the potential of a new railway linking the Forest of Dean line at Whimsey with the Gloucester–Hereford line in Lea. The new line was intended to carry South Wales traffic and stimulate iron-ore mining around Drybrook, and it had the support of the Crawshays and Alfred Goold, owner of the Lower Soudley ironworks.[70] Construction began in 1874 and was completed by the G.W.R. after it took over the project in 1880, but the line, which included tunnels at Drybrook and Euroclydon, was never worked throughout. The section northwards from Whimsey was opened to Nailbridge for mineral traffic in 1885 and to Drybrook for passengers in 1907. The track north of Drybrook was taken up in 1917[71] but was reinstated as far as the Drybrook quarries in 1928.

Following the conversion of the Forest of Dean railway to steam traction in 1854 mine owners and industrialists in the eastern part of the Forest, led by the Crawshays, built mineral lines and sidings to bring their works into the railway network. Several lines converged on Bilson green, where wagons were marshalled in sidings belonging to the G.W.R.[72] Among the first collieries to have railway links were Lightmoor and Crumpmeadow, and the Crawshays ran their own locomotives on the Lightmoor line, which had a branch to the Cinderford ironworks. Horse tramroads and rope-controlled inclines

served many mines and quarries in the later 19th century where steep gradients made the use of steam railways impracticable.[73] Among the longer tramroads was one built by the Allaways to Wigpool and extended northwards to meet the Gloucester–Hereford line in Lea.[74] A tramroad from two collieries near Ruardean Woodside to the Forest of Dean railway's Churchway terminus was replaced *c.* 1863 by a long rope-controlled incline connecting East Slade mine with screens for sorting coal in the railway sidings by the Mitcheldean–Coleford road. Foxes Bridge colliery sent coal down to Bilson by a long inclined plane built *c.* 1868. With the proliferation of differing gauges 'wharves' were built at many places in the Forest for the exchange of goods.

From the 1870s mines in many parts of the Forest were served by the Severn & Wye's lines. New Fancy, Lightmoor, Crumpmeadow, and Foxes Bridge collieries were all soon joined to that network, the loop line of 1872 having many advantages over the Bilson sidings for them.[75] Trafalgar colliery, which had been linked to the tramroad network in 1860, was served by a narrow-gauge railway, built by Cornelius Brain *c.* 1862 and leading to the Bilson sidings. A branch line, begun by Brain and completed in the mid 1870s, ran northwards by way of Steam Mills and Nailbridge to iron-ore workings near Drybrook. In 1890 the Severn & Wye provided Trafalgar with a line to Bilson but the narrow-gauge railway continued to carry coal to Steam Mills and Nailbridge.[76] The needs of the mining and quarrying industries shaped the pattern of railways in the Forest well into the 20th century.[77] Among its more striking features in 1913 was a long rope-worked tramway running from the Arthur and Edward pithead, above Lydbrook, and over the Mirystock and Mitcheldean roads to screens at Mirystock.[78]

Passenger services were introduced on the Severn & Wye railway in 1875. Stations or halts were provided at Whitecroft, Parkend, Cannop (Speech House Road), and Drybrook Road (for Cinderford) on the main line from Lydney, at Upper and Lower Lydbrook on the Lydbrook branch, and at Milkwall on the Coleford branch. In 1876 a halt was built nearer Cinderford at Bilson, east of Drybrook Road, and in 1878 a station was opened on a spur to the north-east, even nearer the town. That station was abandoned in 1900 when the company extended its track to a new station on the east side of Bilson green. In the early 1890s a halt at the junction of the Coleford line north of Parkend served a nearby stoneworks. The station at Lower Lydbrook closed in 1903. Passenger services from Gloucester and Newnham were started on the Forest of Dean railway in 1907. Stations or halts were provided at Upper Soudley, Staple Edge, Cinderford bridge (Ruspidge), Bilson, Whimsey, Steam Mills, Nailbridge, and Drybrook. Bilson

[68]   Above, Plate 30.
[69]   Cf. E. T. MacDermot, *Hist. G.W.R.* revised C. R. Clinker (1972), ii. 344.
[70]   For Goold, Paar, *G.W.R. in Dean*, 65–6.
[71]   Pope & Kerau, *Forest of Dean Branch*, i. 19.
[72]   O.S. Map 6", Glos. XXXI. SE. (1883 edn.).
[73]   Cf. above, Plate 28.

[74]   Cf. O. S. Map 6", Glos. XXIII. SE. (1883, 1891, 1903 edns.).
[75]   Cf. ibid. Glos. XXXI. SE.; XXXIX. NW. (1883 edn.).
[76]   Paar, *G.W.R. in Dean*, 145–8; Glos. R.O., D 262/T 1.
[77]   Cf. *New Regard of Forest of Dean*, ii. 52–5.
[78]   A. O. Cooke, *Forest of Dean* (1913), 108–9; Pope, How, & Kerau, *Severn & Wye Railway*, iii. 384–95.

halt closed in 1908, when the completion of a new loop line enabled trains to run into the Severn & Wye Co.'s station at Cinderford. To continue to Drybrook trains had to reverse to Bilson, where the halt was later used by miners going to and from work.[79]

Passenger traffic was always of secondary importance to the Forest's railways. Most services were withdrawn in 1929 and 1930, leaving only that from Gloucester to Cinderford, which continued until 1958. The decline of mineral traffic as a result of the closure of the larger collieries from the later 1920s led to the abandonment of branch lines, tramroads, and inclined planes and, after the Second World War, to the virtual disappearance of the railways. Closure of the main lines was piecemeal, the line between Serridge Junction and Cinderford being closed in 1949, that

between Mirystock and Stowfield in 1956, and that between Speech House Road and Mirystock in 1960. The Lydbrook viaduct was demolished in 1965.[80] On the loop line track was lifted north of Pillowell in 1951 and the northern end was abandoned in 1953. The southern end carried coal until 1957. The Coleford–Parkend railway, which was used by traffic from Whitecliff quarry in Coleford, was abandoned in 1967.[81] The Forest of Dean railway, on which the extension from Whimsey to the Drybrook quarries closed in 1953, was abandoned in 1966 when Cinderford station was closed to freight.[82] The last working section of railway in the Forest, that from Parkend to Lydney, carried stone ballast until 1976 and was purchased in 1983 by the Dean Forest Railway Preservation Society (later the Dean Forest Railway Co.).[83]

FOREST ADMINISTRATION

EARLY HISTORY. In the earliest reference to the Forest of Dean as an administrative unit, Domesday Book records that Edward the Confessor had exempted from tax the manor called Dean, comprising land in the area of Mitcheldean, in return for the service of custody of the Forest. The lord of the manor, William son of Norman,[84] was the first of a family which was later surnamed Forester and kept forests under the Crown until the early 13th century.[85] The Forest was thus in the late 11th century administered from an estate based on the valleys at its eastern edge, and a significant role was perhaps played by a Norman castle at Littledean, called the old castle of Dean c. 1150 and well placed to command the main approach from Gloucester.[86] The later administrative centre, St. Briavels by the Wye on the western edge, was not a royal manor at Domesday and there was no mention of its castle or the liberty later centred on it. William I, who probably hunted in Dean when his court was at Gloucester,[87] enlarged the royal hunting grounds before 1086 by adding two manors near the Wye; some decayed manors in the same area were left as part of the Forest waste, probably by deliberate policy.[88]

A grant by Henry I of the tithes of venison from his forests of Dean and the Severn area c. 1105, addressed to his foresters, huntsmen, and bowmen of the region,[89] reveals little of the administrative arrangements then in place. Hugh, the son of William son of Norman, retained custody of the Forest in 1130, paying a farm of £13 for it and forests in Herefordshire,

so it is likely that it was still administered from the manor of Dean. St. Briavels castle had been built by then but was in the custody of the hereditary sheriff of Gloucestershire, Miles of Gloucester,[90] and may have then been of military significance only. In 1139 when Miles became one of the principal supporters of the Empress Maud she granted him St. Briavels castle and the Forest of Dean in fee.[91] Miles, who was created earl of Hereford in 1141 and died in 1143, and his son Roger, earl of Hereford, held the Forest during the wars of Stephen's reign. A grant made by Miles was addressed to all his officers and foresters of Dean and one by Roger was addressed to his sheriffs and all his foresters of Dean. Both grants concerned forges,[92] a reminder that its ironworking industry gave the Forest an additional value in wartime. Roger used part of the Forest woodland and waste to found and endow Flaxley abbey, reputedly sited on the spot where his father met his death in a hunting accident,[93] and the earls also held former royal demesne manors at Newnham, Awre, Rodley, Minsterworth, and probably elsewhere in the region. In 1154 or 1155 Earl Roger released his rights in the Forest and St. Briavels castle to Henry II.[94]

At Henry II's accession the area under forest law probably comprised the royal demesne woodland and the manors of St. Briavels hundred. Before 1228, however, the Forest was enlarged to include all the Gloucestershire and Herefordshire manors in an area bounded by the rivers Severn and Wye and extending as far north as Newent. As elsewhere in England, the main motive for the enlargement was financial.

79 Pope & Kerau, *Forest of Dean Branch*, i. 201.
80 *Dean Forest Mercury*, 30 July 1965.
81 Anstis, *Parkend*, 68.
82 *Dean Forest Mercury*, 17 Dec. 1965.
83 Inf. from publicity director, Dean Forest Railway.
84 *Dom. Bk.* (Rec. Com.), i. 167v. For a full account of the early medieval admin., M. L. Bazeley, 'Forest of Dean and its relations with the Crown during the 12th and 13th centuries', *Trans. B.G.A.S.* xxxiii. 153–286. For location of sources, the later sections of this article have drawn heavily on the comprehensive account of the Forest's admin. in C. E. Hart, *Royal Forest* (1966), though the original sources have been re-examined.

85 *Trans B.G.A.S.* cvi. 90; *Pipe R.* 1172 (P.R.S. xviii), 120; 1173 (P.R.S. xix), 40; 1199 (P.R.S. N.S. x), 215: 1206 (P.R.S. N.S. xx) 65–6.
86 *Trans. B.G.A.S.* lxxvii. 57–9.
87 Cf. *V.C.H. Glos.* iv. 18.
88 Above, Bounds.
89 *Hist. & Cart. Mon. Glouc.* (Rolls Ser.), ii. 177, 301; *Reg. Regum Anglo-Norm.* ii, no. 594.
90 *Pipe R.* 1130 (H.M.S.O. facsimile), 76–7.
91 B.L. Lansd. MS. 229, f. 123v.; cf. *Trans. B.G.A.S.* lxxvii. 73.   92 *Camd. Misc.* xxii. 5, 15, 28.
93 Above, Flaxley, manor.
94 *Rot. Chart.* (Rec. Com.), 53.

The wider bounds included substantial private woodlands but in several, notably those in Tidenham and Woolaston belonging to the Marcher lordship of Striguil (Chepstow), private chases were sanctioned,[95] while others, such as Birdwood, in Churcham, and Kilcot, in Newent, were too far distant from the main block of woodland to add much to the preservation of game. The hunting rights in Dean, though often used by huntsmen with orders to supply the royal household with venison or wild boar, were apparently not often enjoyed by the monarchs in person. Henry II hunted there on one or more occasions.[96] King John, who was recorded at St. Briavels castle on five occasions and for whom the castle's royal apartments were probably constructed, appears to have been the most frequent royal visitor. Henry III stayed at the castle on five occasions, only one of them probably more than a brief break in his journeyings, and Edward II went there in 1321 for reasons connected with threatening levies of men in the Marches rather than for the hunting.[97] Edward III, who stayed several times at Flaxley abbey before 1353,[98] was possibly the last monarch to enter the royal demesne woodlands of Dean until the 20th century.

Between 1155 and 1166 the Forest was administered by royal appointees, paying an annual farm of £10. No later record of its administrators appears to survive until 1194; from then until 1206, William Marshal, earl of Pembroke, lord of Striguil, and sheriff of Gloucestershire, held it at the same farm.[99] St. Briavels castle, which was recorded in possession of the Forest's custodians in 1160 and in 1198,[1] appears to have been the administrative centre of the Forest throughout the period. It certainly was so by 1207 when the custodian, or warden, was termed constable of St. Briavels.[2]

FOREST OFFICERS AND COURTS. By the early 13th century, when its main elements become clear, the administration of the Forest was firmly centred on St. Briavels. The castle was the headquarters of the chief officer of the Forest, the warden and constable, who ex officio held St. Briavels manor and the adjoining royal manor of Newland and exercised the Crown's rights in the tenanted manors that formed the hundred or liberty of St. Briavels. A number of small estates at St. Briavels were held as serjeanties by foresters, and the manors of the liberty supported the foresters, or woodwards, of 10 bailiwicks in the demesne woodland. The term 'Forest of St. Briavels' was sometimet used during the 13th and 14th centuries, apparently for the demesne woodland alone rather than for the whole area then subject to forest law.[3]

The head of Dean's administration was styled both warden of the Forest of Dean and constable of St. Briavels castle. The two offices were regarded as separate, though it would be difficult to distinguish which duties belonged to which; for convenience the holders are referred to in this account as constables of St. Briavels. During the 13th and 14th centuries, when they usually held during royal pleasure for only a few years, the constables were great magnates or royal administrators with other wide responsibilities.[4] Among those who had local connexions, John of Monmouth, lord of Monmouth[5] and a number of Forest manors, served from 1216 to 1224, and William de Beauchamp, earl of Warwick, who was lord of Lydney manor,[6] served in the early 1270s. William Hathaway, constable 1287–91, who was also chief forester of Dean by tenure of an estate in St. Briavels,[7] was unusual as an appointee from the local gentry.

The constable, whose office was given an enhanced military significance by the Forest's role in supplying weapons and miners as sappers, was inevitably caught up in the struggles between Crown and barons. John Giffard of Brimpsfield, a leading adherent of Simon de Montfort, was appointed in August 1263 and retained the office after his return to the royal cause; he and Gilbert de Clare, earl of Gloucester, took refuge in the Forest with their forces in the spring of 1265 when de Montfort came to Gloucester.[8] The following year Henry III placed St. Briavels castle and the Forest in the charge of his son Edward. During the troubled later years of Edward II's reign there were rapid changes of custody, and local supporters of the dissident barons secured the castle during the fighting of 1321.[9] After Edward's success the following year superior custody over St. Briavels castle and the Forest was given to Hugh le Despenser the younger. In January 1327 castle and Forest passed to Queen Isabella following her successful invasion. Under Edward III the Forest's administration had more stability: Guy Brian, a distinguished soldier,[10] was made constable for life in 1341 and remained in office until his death in 1390.

The status of the holders of the constableship during the 13th and 14th centuries meant that most of the duties were performed by deputies whom they appointed. Some of the deputies were local landowners. In the 1220s the deputy was Hugh of Kinnersley, owner of an estate near Coleford,[11] and Guy Brian's deputies included John Joce and John Greyndour, owners of an important estate in Newland parish.[12] By the mid 16th century the constable was also supported by seven underforesters, one of whom was styled the constable's

95 Above, Bounds.
96 *Giraldi Cambrensis Opera* (Rolls Ser.), iv. 221.
97 Above, St. Briavels, manors; 'Itin. of Hen. III' (1923, TS. at P.R.O.).   98 *Cal. Chart. R.* 1341–1417, 133.
99 Below, Wardens; *Pipe R.* 1156–8 (Rec. Com.), 49; 1194 (P.R.S. N.S. v), 239.
1 *Pipe R.* 1160 (P.R.S. ii), 29; 1198 (P.R.S. N.S. ix), 7.
2 *Rot. Litt. Pat.* (Rec. Com.), 71.
3 e.g. *Pat. R.* 1225–32, 407; *Close R.* 1242–7, 119; *Cal. Close,* 1302–7, 128, 282; *Rot. Hund.* (Rec. Com.), i. 176;

P.R.O., JUST 1/278, rot. 56.
4 For holders of the two offices, below, Wardens.
5 *D.N.B.*   6 Above, Lydney, manors.
7 Above, St. Briavels, manors.
8 *Trans. B.G.A.S.* lxv. 113–17.
9 *Cal. Pat.* 1321–4, 52.   10 *Trans. B.G.A.S.* lxii. 23–4.
11 *Rot. Litt. Claus.* (Rec. Com.), ii. 86; P.R.O., C 115/K 2/6683, f. 86v.; above, Coleford, manors.
12 P.R.O., E 32/33, mm. 3, 6; *Cal. Pat.* 1385–9, 52; above, Newland, manors.

bowbearer.[13] The constable apparently had some of that staff of minor officials from 1350, when Edward III had recently appointed four foresters at wages, to be paid out of the issues farmed by the constable.[14]

The early constables had wide responsibilities, the office combining the roles of forester, manorial steward, military purveyor, justice, and gaveller. A writ *de intendendo* addressed to all foresters and verderers when a new constable took office[15] emphasized that he was the principal forester of Dean with overall charge of its vert and venison. The great majority of the orders addressed to the constable required him to arrange for royal gifts of timber and venison, the former going mainly to religious houses and other local landowners for building purposes,[16] or to provide facilities for huntsmen sent down to take deer or wild boar for the royal household.[17] The constable had also to regulate the exercise of commoning rights in the Forest,[18] and supervise the assarting of land and assess the new rents to be paid.[19] In the administration of the forest law he, or more usually his deputy, presided with the verderers over the attachment court[20] and provided executive support, in particular maintaining a prison in St. Briavels castle.[21] Occasionally the castle was used to house prisoners from outside the region, including some Scots in the reigns of Edward I and Edward II.[22] The constable controlled the Crown's mineral rights in the Forest, collecting the king's share of ore from mines and regulating or attempting to suppress, depending on current policy, itinerant bloomery forges operating in the woodland. In the early 13th century he managed a large royal forge at St. Briavels[23] and throughout that century supervised the manufacture of crossbow bolts, distributing them, and sometimes other products such as horsehoes and pickaxes, to royal armies and castle garrisons throughout England and Wales.[24] He levied men within the Forest for military duty, including those with specialist mining skills.[25] In 1281 or 1282 the king required 100 tree fellers to join the royal army in Wales.[26] Forest men were apparently well thought of as ordinary footmen and archers and large contingents were sometimes levied by the constable: in 1333, when 500 men were to be levied in Gloucestershire, 300 were to come from the Forest area.[27] The constable Guy Brian had Forest men under his

command in France in 1360.[28] Also in the constable's direct management were the manors of St. Briavels and Newland with the castle, demesnes, mills, and fishing weirs. For the tenanted manors of St. Briavels hundred he acted as receiver[29] and escheator.[30] He was also chief judge of the hundred court held at the castle.[31]

The bulk of the profits of Dean were included in the constable's farm in the 13th and 14th centuries, the main exceptions being the fines and forfeitures imposed by the justices and the proceeds of timber sales. The Forest estate was increasing in value in the early 13th century, as a result of rents levied for new assarts and probably also a rise in the profits from mining. In 1210 the farm paid by the constable remained at £10 a year,[32] the same as it had been in the 1150s. By 1230 it had risen to £36 13s. 4d.,[33] by 1255 to £140,[34] and by 1287 to £160.[35] About 1250 the profits collected by the constable were valued at £153 a year: about a third was drawn from the manors of St. Briavels and Newland and the rents paid by the owners of the other manors of the liberty, and about a third from mining and ironworks, including a toll levied on the shipping of sea coal from the Forest, royalties from the iron and coal mines, and rents paid by forge-owners; about a sixth was provided by the herbage and pannage payments of the commoners; and the remaining sixth was supplied by the sale of windfall trees and by other profits of the demesne woodlands. The great forge at St. Briavels castle had formerly contributed another £50 or so but it was declared to be uneconomic and given up at about the time of the valuation.[36] In the year 1279–80 the profits farmed by the constable produced £170 and the following year £143.[37] The profits of the Forest had fallen by 1341 and were valued at just over £117. The alienation from the royal estate of certain assets, such as fishing weirs, was cited as among the causes, but so was the large reduction of the juridical Forest which was finally accepted by the Crown in 1327, suggesting that there were benefits for the constable in the form of fees or other exactions which did not figure in the accounts cited above. On Guy Brian's petition the farm was reduced to £120 in 1341.[38] In 1349, because of losses in the great plague, it was further reduced to £70,[39] and from the following year, to supplement the income that supplied it,

13 Glos. R.O., D 2026/X 3; Badminton Mun. FmE 2/3/1, f. 3.
14 *Cal. Pat.* 1350–4, 5.
15 *Rot. Litt. Pat.* (Rec. Com.), 185; *Cal. Pat.* 1232–47, 48.
16 Hart, *Royal Forest*, 263–6.
17 e.g. *Rot. Litt. Claus.* (Rec. Com.), i. 284, 402, 564; *Cal. Lib.* 1240–5, 3, 8, 23, 57; 1251–60, 213, 235, 314, 389, 408; P.R.O., SC 6/850/18.
18 e.g. *Rot. Litt. Claus.* (Rec. Com.), i. 290, 538; *Close R.* 1231–4, 71, 97; 1247–51, 339.
19 *Pipe R.* 1219 (P.R.S. N.S. xlii), 13; P.R.O., E 146/1/25, 27.
20 P.R.O., E 32/33, m. 1; E 146/1/31.
21 *Close R.* 1234–7, 238; *Ex. e Rot. Fin.* (Rec. Com.), ii. 113; *Cal. Close,* 1341–3, 453.
22 *Cal. Close,* 1288–96, 483; 1307–13, 78, 309.
23 *Rot. Litt. Claus.* (Rec. Com.), i. 334–5, 442–3; P.R.O., E 146/1/26; SC 6/850/19.
24 e.g. *Rot. Litt. Claus.* (Rec. Com.), i. 576; *Close R.* 1227–31, 354, 373, 564; 1254–6, 133, 242, 260; *Cal. Close,*

1313–18, 146–7; 1330–3, 484; cf. above, St. Briavels, econ. hist. (mills and ironworks).
25 Above, Industry, mining to 18th cent.
26 *Cal. Close,* 1313–18, 146–7.
27 *Close R.* 1251–3, 487; *Cal. Pat.* 1313–17, 433; 1321–7, 74, 131; 1330–4, 419; *Cal. Close,* 1313–18, 563.
28 *Cal. Pat.* 1358–61, 384.
29 P.R.O., E 146/1/26; SC 6/850/18–19; *Cal. Close,* 1341–3, 153; above, St. Briavels, manors.
30 *Cal. Fine R.* 1272–1307, 309; *Cal. Inq. Misc.* i, p. 414.
31 Above, St. Briavels hundred.
32 *Pipe R.* 1210 (P.R.S. N.S. xxvi), 142.
33 *Close R.* 1227–31, 378.
34 *Cal. Pat.* 1247–58, 450.
35 *Inq. p.m. Glos.* 1302–58, 289.
36 P.R.O., E 146/1/26.
37 Ibid. SC 6/850/19.
38 *Cal. Close,* 1341–3, 153; *Cal. Fine R.* 1337–47, 230.
39 *Cal. Fine R.* 1347–56, 201; cf. *Cal. Pat.* 1354–8, 4.

Brian was allowed to fell underwood on a regular basis for charcoaling or other purposes.[40]

From the end of the 14th century there was a change in the character of the office of constable. The castle, manors, and general proWts of the Forest once farmed by the holder (which are referred to here as the St. Briavels castle estate) were granted in fee by the Crown, and later, having reverted to the Crown, were granted on long leases.[41] The constableship was evidently subsumed in a grant in fee of the St. Briavels castle estate to John, later duke of Bedford, in 1399, but after his death in 1435 the office was separated from the estate.[42] Constables were appointed at an annual fee paid out of the estate[43] and had the use of parts of St. Briavels castle for keeping the courts and prison.[44] During the next 100 years men from local gentry families often served, including John Ashurst, landowner in English Bicknor, and members of the Baynham and Hyett families. In 1546, however, the earls of Pembroke began a long association with the office, and from the mid 17th century, when the constableship was usually held with the lease of the St. Briavels castle estate, it was the preserve of leading Gloucestershire magnates.[45] The constable continued to appoint a deputy constable, mainly for holding the courts,[46] and his bow-bearer and six under-foresters. The six were later termed rangers or keepers[47] and had the specific task of keeping the deer;[48] they took on an enhanced role at a reorganization of the Forest's administration in the 1670s.[49]

Under the constable's overall control a tier of senior foresters administered ten divisions, called bailiwicks or baileys, in the demesne woodland; they were usually termed foresters-in-fee in the Middle Ages, but to avoid confusion with another group of foresters[50] they are referred to here as woodwards, which was their usual style in the modern period. The woodwards held manors adjoining the demesne woodland by the serjeanty of keeping a bailiwick and paid a chief rent to St. Briavels castle. The bailiwicks and bailiwick manors (listed in clockwise direction around the demesne) were Ruardean, Lea, Mitcheldean, Abenhall, Littledean, Blaize (or Bleyths) which was held with Blythes Court manor in Newnham, Blakeney, Bearse which was held with an estate in Newland and St. Briavels, Staunton, and English Bicknor.[51] About 1245 all the bailiwicks were said to be held by ancient tenure,[52] and some were apparently in existence by the mid 12th century. Before 1155 Roger, earl of Hereford, confirmed to William of Dean an office in the Forest which William had enjoyed under Earl Miles and which owed a rent of 20s. and military service within Gloucestershire, Herefordshire, and Worcestershire. Later William's successors as lords of Mitcheldean manor paid the 20s. rent to the constable, kept Mitcheldean bailiwick with two under-foresters, and owed military service to the Crown, and in 1319 the earl's charter was produced as evidence for the tenure of Mitcheldean manor.[53] The lords of Abenhall held on very similar terms in the late 13th century — 20s. rent, custody of Abenhall bailiwick with two under-foresters, and military service within the bounds of the Forest[54] — and it is likely that their bailiwick, too, was in existence under the earls of Hereford. In 1199 six of the ten bailiwicks, those of Ruardean, Lea, Mitcheldean, Blakeney, Staunton, and Bicknor, were recorded;[55] Abenhall, Blaize, and apparently Bearse, were recorded in the early 1220s,[56] and Littledean, evidently an offshoot of Mitcheldean bailiwick, was possibly a separate bailiwick by 1250[57] and certainly was by 1282.[58]

The woodwards seem to have had a general advisory and supporting role in the constable's administration of the whole Forest. For their individual bailiwicks they presented offenders against the vert at the attachment court[59] and kept rolls of attachments for offences against the vert and venison to present, with other foresters and the verderers, before the justices-in-eyre.[60] At the forest eyre of 1634 each woodward produced a hatchet as the symbol of his office,[61] so their duties probably included marking timber trees that were ordered to be felled in the bailiwick. The direct personal duty of the Staunton woodward, recorded in 1342, of carrying the king's bow when he came to hunt in the bailiwick[62] was presumably common to all, though few holders can ever have performed it. For only Mitcheldean and Abenhall is the obligation of military service recorded. All the woodwards had to maintain under-foresters, two each in the larger bailiwicks like Abenhall and Blakeney and one in the smaller ones like Blaize. Those in Abenhall were bowmen, patrolling on foot, in 1301[63] and that was presumably the case with all. On appointment under-foresters had to make an oath before the attachment court.[64] The woodwards' deputies of the early modern period were evidently their successors.[65]

The woodwards claimed various privileges

40 Cal. Pat. 1350–4, 5.
41 Above, St. Briavels, manors.
42 Below, Wardens.
43 Cal. Close, 1435–41, 293; Cal. Pat. 1441–6, 355; 1485–94, 208; N.L.W., Dunraven MSS. 324.
44 Above, St. Briavels hundred.
45 Below, Wardens.
46 Glos. R.O., D 2026/X 4; Badminton Mun. FmE 2/3/2.
47 Glos. R.O., D 2026/X 3; Badminton Mun. FmE 2/3/1, f. 3; P.R.O., C 99/11, no. 1; in 1565 the earl of Pembroke had a bowbearer and nine other under-foresters.
48 Berkeley Cast. Mun., patents no. 8.
49 Below, reformed admin.
50 Below, this section.
51 For the descents of eight of them, above, parish histories, manors sections; for Blaize, V.C.H. Glos. x. 39–40; for Lea, J. Duncumb, Hist. and Antiquities of Herefs. (edn.

by W. H. Cooke, 1882), ii. 396–9.
52 P.R.O., E 146/1/25.
53 Inq. p.m. Glos. 1302–58, 169–73; Cal. Inq. p.m. i, p. 119; the rent was shared between owners of moieties of the estate: cf. P.R.O., E 146/1/25 (rents ascribed to Wm. of Dean and Ralph of Abenhall).
54 P.R.O., E 32/32, m. 2; Cal. Inq. p.m. iv, p. 13.
55 Pipe R. 1199 (P.R.S. N.S. x), 32.
56 Rot. Litt. Claus. (Rec. Com.), i. 442–3, 553.
57 Cal. Inq. Misc. i, p. 32.
58 P.R.O., E 32/31, m. 14.   59 Ibid. E 32/33.
60 Ibid. E 32/29–30; cf. ibid. E 32/30, rot. 39.
61 Glos. R.O., D 1677/GG 1220.
62 Cal. Inq. p.m. viii, pp. 246–7.
63 P.R.O., E 32/32, mm. 1–2, 7; Cal. Inq. p.m. iv, p. 13.
64 P.R.O., E 32/30, rot. 8.
65 Ibid. E 178/3837, depositions 1622.

within their bailiwicks by right of office. Claims common to all included rights of pannage, herbage, and estovers for themselves and their tenants, and in 1282 all claimed to keep unlawed dogs and some to course for small game.[66] In the early 13th century six or more of the woodwards had the right to operate itinerant forges in the woodland and were exempted from general prohibitions of forges that the Crown attempted to enforce.[67] Claims to take wood probably originated in connexion with their ironmaking operations. In 1223 they had the right to freshly broken wood,[68] presumably the windfallen trees which they all claimed later; in 1565 it was explained that the claim extended only to those trees whose trunk was snapped by the wind, in distinction to those blown over and uprooted, which were the perquisite of the constable.[69] In 1234 a claim made by the woodward of Staunton established that all had the right to the loppings of oaks granted as gifts by the Crown,[70] and c. 1282 several claimed an oak trunk at Christmas. Other claims advanced by various woodwards c. 1282 and evidently not uniform throughout the bailiwicks included eyries of hawks and falcons, honey, and nuts, and the woodwards of Blakeney and Abenhall made the more ambitious claim, possibly never secured in full, to iron ore and sea coal in their bailiwicks.[71] In 1634 when the woodwards entered their claims of privileges before the forest eyre there was still considerable diversity: windfalls were claimed by almost all, but only three claimed the trunk at Christmas, five claimed the bark from trees felled as gifts, and four claimed eyries. Only Blakeney then claimed ore and coal.[72]

The differing privileges and terms of tenure suggest that the pattern of bailiwicks was not devised as a coherent scheme at one date, and the boundaries of the bailiwicks as described in a Forest regard of 1282[73] (in so far as the landmarks are now identifiable) suggest that they were always of disparate size. By 1282, however, the pattern had already been much obscured by assarting. Staunton bailiwick was by then divided from its parent manor by the south part of Coleford tithing in Newland, but that part seems formerly to have been within the bailiwick to judge from rights in it later claimed and chief rents from it received by the lords of Staunton.[74] Blaize had lost a large part of its area by the Crown's grant in 1258 of what was later called Abbots wood to Flaxley abbey.[75] Much of Bearse had been lost to Newland and St. Briavels parishes and by further depletions in the earlier 14th century it was left as scattered parcels.[76]

In 1250 for various misdemeanours by the

woodwards six of the bailiwicks were forfeited to the Crown.[77] Lea[78] and Staunton were returned to the owners of the manors later in the century, but Mitcheldean and Littledean remained divorced from their parent manors in 1319, as did Ruardean in 1385 and Blakeney until the early 16th century.[79] By the mid 16th century all ten bailiwicks were once more held with their manors and they remained with them for as long as the office of woodward continued to be officially recorded. In the early modern period there were usually no more than seven woodwards in all, as some of the bailiwick manors were in joint ownerships, and in the 18th century Littledean bailiwick, which had become known as Badcocks Bailey, ceased to be separately distinguished.[80] Their duties having become nominal, the woodwards figured in the late records of the administration of Dean mainly in connexion with claims to perquisites.

Another group of foresters were usually called serjeants-in-fee in the Middle Ages but later foresters-in-fee. Unlike the woodwards, they performed the duty of protecting the venison and vert and attaching offenders throughout the Forest woodlands.[81] They were headed by a chief serjeant, also called the chief forester, who held a small manor in St. Briavels by his service and enjoyed valuable privileges, including an allowance of venison. He performed his duties on horseback, whereas the other serjeants went on foot, and he appointed an under-forester, known as the bowbearer. There were as many as 11 other serjeants-in-fee during the 13th century, and five or more of them held small estates in St. Briavels by the service.[82] They presented hunting-horns as their symbols of office at the forest eyre of 1634,[83] and a horn and a short sword are among the accoutrements shown on the effigy of the serjeant John Wyrall (d. 1457) at Newland church.[84] By the early modern period the office of the ordinary serjeants-in-fee appears to have become purely hereditary, with only the chief forestership, held for many centuries by the owners of the Clearwell estate, still served in right of its St. Briavels estate.[85] The chief forester and eight serjeants continued to be listed on the swanimote rolls until the late 18th century,[86] but the office was probably purely nominal by the mid 17th.

An officer called the riding forester or rider was recorded from 1282 and two rangers from 1390. The three officers were salaried and were directly appointed by the Crown.[87] All three officers apparently had the power of making attachments throughout the Forest, but in 1565

66 Ibid. E 32/31, mm. 17–18.
67 Rot. Litt. Claus. (Rec. Com.), i. 334–5, 442–3.
68 Ibid. 533.
69 Badminton Mun. FmE 2/3/1, f. 9v.
70 Close R. 1231–4, 528; 1234–7, 468–9.
71 P.R.O., E 32/32.
72 Ibid. C 99/10, nos. 2, 4–9, 107; C 99/11, no. 3.
73 Ibid. E 32/31, mm. 9–14.
74 Above, Coleford, manors.
75 P.R.O., E 32/31, m. 12; Cal. Chart. R. 1257–1300, 11.
76 Above, Newland, intro.; St. Briavels, intro.; cf. Hart, Royal Forest, 281.
77 P.R.O., C 60/47, m. 13.
78 Cal. Pat. 1258–66, 525.

79 Above, parish histories, manors sections.
80 For lists of the holders, Glos. R.O., D 2026/X 3; D 4431, swanimote roll 1637; D 36/Q 2; 3rd Rep. Com. Woods (1788), 76.
81 P.R.O., E 32/30, rot. 22; Glos. R.O., D 2026/X 3.
82 Above, St. Briavels, manors.
83 Glos. R.O., D 1677/GG 1220.
84 Above, Newland, churches.
85 Glos. R.O., D 2026/X 3; cf. above, St. Briavels, manors.
86 Glos. R.O., D 4431, swanimote roll 1637; D 36/Q 2; 3rd Rep. Com. Woods (1788), 76.
87 P.R.O., E 32/30, rot. 6d.; Cal. Pat. 1374–7, 429; 1388–92, 236; Cal. Close, 1461–8, 286, 291.

the rangers were said to have particular responsibility for policing the 'lands', the Forest glades.[88] In 1634 the rangers were required to appear at the eyre with bags of hogrings, presumably symbolic of an ancient duty of regulating pannage.[89] By the early 16th century the rangerships were held with posts in the royal household and had presumably become sinecures.[90] The offices of rider and rangers have not been found mentioned after 1673.[91] Two minor offices in existence by the mid 16th century were a bailiff at large and a beadle.[92]

Dean's verderers were recorded from the early 13th century. During the Middle Ages there appear to have been four or five of them,[93] but three was the usual complement in the 16th and 17th centuries,[94] and there were consistently four from the early 18th.[95] As in other forests the office was an appointment for life, made by royal writ, under the authority of the county sheriff.[96] In the 13th century the verderers acted as coroners for St. Briavels hundred,[97] and they were also distinguished from the other foresters by their duty of presiding over the attachment court;[98] otherwise they shared in the foresters' functions of supervising assarts,[99] selecting timber for royal gifts,[1] and presenting offenders at the eyre.[2] Their perquisites, as claimed in 1634, were the taking annually of two does and one oak and one beech.[3] Dean had the usual body of 12 regarders, appointed before the eyre and responsible for enquiring into and reporting at the eyre encroachments and other invasions of royal rights under a series of heads, such as forges, assarts, and waste of private woods.[4]

The forest eyre, usually referred to in the early modern period as the justice seat, was held in Dean at regular intervals in the late 12th century and the 13th.[5] Records of the proceedings survive for 1258, 1270, and 1282,[6] and for the last eyre there is also the roll of the regard, drawn up by the regarders for the coming of the justices.[7] The session of 1282 was possibly the last time until 1634 that the full apparatus of the forest eyre, including not only the determination of vert and venison offences but also the enrolment and punishment of offences brought to light by the regard and a general inquiry into the privileges and conduct of the forest officers, was invoked in Dean.[8] In the early 15th century,

however, justices of the forest occasionally visited Dean to punish offenders.[9]

As in other royal forests, an attachment court, in Dean in the early modern period usually called the 'speech court',[10] was held for taking cognizance of offences against the vert.[11] Records of its proceedings survive for 1335–41,[12] 1566, and 1568,[13] and estreats for most years in the period 1601–25.[14] It met about every six weeks — the customary interval was 40 days — and was presided over by the deputy constable and the verderers. By the 1330s some sessions at least were held in a courthouse on or near the site of the later Speech House at Kensley, in the centre of the royal demesne woodland. Most attachments recorded at the period had been made by the woodwards within their respective bailiwicks; occasionally they had been made by the serjeants-in-fee or other foresters. Most of the offenders were taken to St. Briavels castle, presumably there to be bailed against the coming of the justices, but in some cases the woodwards who had attached them were charged with producing them. No fines are mentioned as levied by the court, and all offences were presumably then reserved for punishment by the justices. The court at that period aimed to account for all timber taken from the forest for whatever reason: apart from trees stolen, it recorded those delivered by custom to the miners for shoring their workings, those taken for building work or other needs of the Crown, and those granted to neighbouring religious houses or other landowners.[15]

By the 1430s the attachment court was apparently imposing small fines for at least some offences, for profits of the court amounting to c. £9–13 a year were then recorded among the profits of the Forest received by the duke of Bedford and his successors.[16] By the 1560s, when Forest eyres and presumably also visits of justices had long since lapsed, the attachment court had begun to impose a fixed scale of fines for offences, the standard items being 6d. for hewing timber with a bill, 12d. for felling with an axe, 6d. for being caught with a packhorse load of timber, and 2s. for being caught with a wagon load.[17] Later, with growing concern about illegal destruction of the woodland, higher fines were imposed. In 1601 and 1602 felling an oak or even destroying underwood could incur 5s. and cart-

88 Glos. R.O., D 2026/X 3.
89 Ibid. D 1677/GG 1220.
90 L. & P. Hen. VIII, i (1), p. 365; iii, p. 121; viii, p. 122; Glos. R.O., D 326/X 5; D 1677/GG 1552.
91 Glos. R.O., D 36/Q 2.   92 Ibid. D 2026/X 3.
93 Pleas of the Crown for Glos. ed. Maitland, p. 47; Cal. Close, 1288–96, 165; P.R.O., C 143/125, no. 11; C 143/239, no. 20; E 101/140/19.
94 Glos. R.O., D 2026/X 3; D 36/Q 2; P.R.O., E 146/1/32, 34.
95 N.L.W., Dunraven MSS. 330, order for holding swanimote 1713.
96 Cal. Close, 1288–96, 165, 178; 1327–30, 323, 468, 497; 1354–60, 468, 483; 1468–76, p. 148.
97 Pleas of the Crown for Glos. ed. Maitland, p. 47; P.R.O., JUST 1/274, rot. 11d.
98 Below, this section.
99 Close R. 1227–31, 563; P.R.O., C 143/157, no. 9.
1 Rot. Litt. Claus. (Rec. Com.), i. 490, 533; Close R. 1237–42, 224.
2 P.R.O., E 32/28–30.   3 Ibid. C 99/10, nos. 13, 111.

4 Ibid. E 32/30, rot. 18; E 32/31; cf. Select Pleas of the Forest (Selden Soc. xiii), pp. lxxv–xciii.
5 Trans. B.G.A.S. xxxiii. 214–15.
6 P.R.O., E 32/28–30.   7 Ibid. E 32/31.
8 Below, exploitation 1603–68.
9 P.R.O., E 101/141/1; cf. Berkeley Cast. Mun., General Ser. acct. roll 426.
10 Badminton Mun. FmE 2/3/1, f. 4; P.R.O., E 178/3837, certificate 1617; depositions 1622.
11 Cf. Select Pleas of Forest, pp. xxx–xxxvi.
12 P.R.O., E 32/33.   13 Ibid. E 146/1/31–2.
14 Ibid. E 137/13/4; E 146/1/32, 34.
15 Ibid. E 32/33, where the miners' timber is that described as delivered 'pro orbold': cf. Hart, Royal Forest, 56.
16 P.R.O., SC 6/850/20; SC 6/858/15; Berkeley Cast. Mun., General Ser. acct. roll 426, where the item 'pleas of the Forest' in the beadle's acct. was evidently for the attachment court and the court included in the hayward's acct. was evidently the St. Briavels hundred court.
17 P.R.O., E 146/1/30–1; cf. Badminton Mun. FmE 2/3/1, f. 4.

ing timber away 20s.[18] By the 1620s there was a scale based on the size of a stolen tree in terms of 'loads' of timber: for example an oak measured at three loads might incur a fine of 30s.[19] In the first decade of the 17th century the total of the fines levied by the court, by then paid directly to the royal Exchequer, averaged c. £20 a year.[20]

The term 'swanimote', which in forests in general originally denoted seasonal gatherings for regulating pannage and other commoning rights,[21] was sometimes used in Dean as a term for the attachment court. At the forest eyre of 1282 an under-forester of one of the bailiwicks was said to have made his oath of office before the deputy constable and verderers in the 'swanimote', an event which in 1622 was said to happen at the speech (i.e. attachment) court by ancient custom, and the justices also complained in 1282 that the pleas of vert had been insufficiently presented in the 'swanimote'.[22] In 1565 there was an unequivocal reference to the 'speech court alias the swanimote'.[23] In the 17th century, however, the term swanimote was used for gatherings which were distinct from the attachment court and had a wider range of responsibility. In 1634 and 1656 swanimotes were held to record presentments under the articles of the regard in preparation for the forest eyres of those years,[24] and a swanimote held before the verderers at Littledean in 1637 was attended by all the forest officers, including regarders, and four men and a reeve from each township in the Forest bounds.[25] In the late 1670s and 1680s the swanimote was held once or twice a year before the verderers and attended by the officers and the township representatives, to record presentments concerning the vert, venison, and encroachment,[26] but it may have only recently been given an enhanced role in support of the new government policy of managing the Forest as a nursery of timber. The use earlier of the term swanimote for the attachment court, taken with the character of the 17th-century swanimotes, may indicate that there were in the Middle Ages one or two special sessions each year of the attachment court, attended by all the Forest officers and the township representatives and dealing with a wider range of matters than the vert.

Courts held in the Forest for purposes other than the administration of the forest law — the hundred court and leet for St. Briavels hundred[27] and the mine law court — are described elsewhere.[28]

COMMONING TO THE EARLY 17TH CENTURY. A central strand in the Forest's

history and often a cause of dispute and violent confrontation was the exercise of commoning rights in the demesne woodland and waste. Up to the early 17th century, with beeches equal in number to oaks among the great trees of the Forest, it was the feeding of pigs on the mast in autumn which was of most importance. The pannage in Dean yielded £3 6s. 1d. for the Crown in the year 1184–5[29] and £24 for the four years ending in 1194.[30] About 1250 the receipts from pannage averaged £20 a year compared to £5 from the herbage of cattle.[31] Rights of estovers enjoyed in the woodlands by the local inhabitants were recorded from 1223.[32]

Dues for the exercise of the rights were paid to the constable and later to the St. Briavels castle estate. By the early 15th century they took the form of fixed collective payments of a few shillings a year by each parish or tithing. In 1435 the total owed was £5 8s. 1d.,[33] in 1591 it was c. £7,[34] and in 1746 £5 11s. 9d.[35] In the early 17th century, with pigs presumably still preponderating, the levy was termed swine silver,[36] but later it was called herbage money. Some places were exempt from the payment, including the royal manor of St. Briavels and, perhaps as a result of being granted to religious houses in the Middle Ages, Flaxley and Hewelsfield.[37] The regulation of commoning, which included keeping a pound and driving the Forest to check on those pasturing illegally and at prohibited seasons, passed from the constable to the lessee of the St. Briavels castle estate, and in the 16th century and early 17th the court leet for St. Briavels hundred, from which the lessee received the profits, heard presentments of and levied fines for commoning offences.[38] The eyre of 1634, which in its meticulous observance of procedure attempted to account for all the customary offices of a royal forest, decided that Sir Richard Catchmay, who was then under-tenant of part of the estate including the herbage money, was in effect agister for Dean.[39] In the mid 17th century Whitemead park, long held by the constable and lessees, was claimed to have originated as the pound for the Forest,[40] and in 1835 the gaoler of the castle prison was said to be responsible for impounding stray animals in St. Briavels park, another part of the lessees' estate.[41] After the 1670s the responsibility for driving and impounding was assumed by the keepers of the six walks then established, but the herbage money continued to be paid to the lessee of the castle estate.[42]

In the 13th century all freeholders within the wider bounds of the Forest then in force enjoyed

18 P.R.O., E 146/1/32.
19 Ibid. E 146/1/34.   20 Ibid. E 137/13/4.
21 Select Pleas of Forest, pp. xxvii–xxx.
22 P.R.O., E 32/30, rott. 8, 39; cf. E 178/3837, depositions 1622.   23 Glos. R.O., D 2026/X 3.
24 Ibid. D 1677/GG 1220; D 2026/X 14.
25 Ibid. D 4431.
26 Ibid. D 36/Q 2; below, reformed admin.
27 Above, St. Briavels hundred.
28 Above, Industry, mining to 18th cent.
29 Pipe R. 1185 (P.R.S. xxxiv), 28.
30 Ibid. 1194 (P.R.S. N.S. v), 239.
31 P.R.O., E 146/1/26.

32 Rot. Litt. Claus. (Rec. Com.), i. 538.
33 P.R.O., E 101/141/1; C 139/84, no. 76.
34 Ibid. E 112/16, no. 120.
35 Berkeley Cast. Mun., General Ser. 16.
36 P.R.O., E 112/82, no. 300; Glos. R.O., D 2026/X 19.
37 For lists of places paying, Glos. R.O., D 2026/X 19; N.L.W., Mynde Park MS. 1629; Berkeley Cast Mun., General Ser. 16; P.R.O., F 14/13.
38 P.R.O., E 134/34 Eliz. I Hil./23; Glos. R.O., D 2026/L 4, L 8.   39 Glos. R.O., D 1677/GG 1220.
40 Cal. S.P. Dom. 1653–4, pp. 326, 405.
41 P.R.O., F 3/587, surv. 1835.
42 Below, commoning and management 1820–1914.

the common rights;[43] later, exercise of the rights became restricted to places immediately adjoining the demesne woodlands, though still including some places which were removed from the Forest by the perambulation of 1300. From the mid 16th century the general body of commoners, with the backing of the lessee of the St. Briavels castle estate, objected to tenants of the duchy of Lancaster manors of Minsterworth, Tibberton, and Bulley exercising rights; their animals were impounded by officers of the lessee and fines were imposed in the hundred leet. The men of Bulley were excluded in the 1540s, but those of Minsterworth and Tibberton clung obstinately to their claim and later made armed incursions into the Forest to enforce it. On one occasion they established themselves and their pigs in a fenced encampment in the woods and were attacked by a large mob from the other parishes. A suit in 1592 secured a decree provisonally excluding the men of the two parishes, but leaving it open to them to prove their title.[44] Minsterworth resumed the claim on the grounds that the parish lay within the Forest bounds but its opponents countered with some blatantly manipulated evidence as to the Forest perambulation of 1300. The premise was faulty, for if the Forest bounds were to be the criterion many of Minsterworth's opponents, such as those from Lydney, Blaisdon, and Longhope, would also be excluded. In 1597, however, Minsterworth was judged to lie outside the Forest and its exclusion from commoning confirmed.[45] In 1612 the places claiming rights were all the villages and hamlets in the 14 parishes of St. Briavels and Bledisloe hundreds, together with Blaisdon, Longhope, Ruddle and other parts of Newnham, Rodley in Westbury, and, in Herefordshire, Hope Mansell, Weston-under-Penyard, and Huntsham.[46] Rodley's right, though it had been confirmed by the Crown in 1256,[47] was annulled in 1667.[48]

One of the earliest statements of the nature of the rights was incorporated in a decree of 1628 following a full inquiry. The rights were stated as herbage for cattle, with the restrictions usual in royal forests of a 'winter haining' (11 November to 23 April) and a 'fence month' when the deer were fawning (four weeks at Midsummer), pannage of pigs at the time of mast, pasture for sheep in the non-wooded parts of the Forest, and estovers, comprising firebote of dead wood and housebote to be taken on application to the attachment court and under supervision of the officers; ploughbote and cartbote were also accepted by the Crown as de facto rights. Also enunciated was the rule that the rights belonged only to ancient messuages in the parishes and could not be claimed for new-built ones. No mention was made of a stint[49] and none was

apparently ever enforced. At the justice seat of 1634 claims made by individual tenants were similar, though vitally they did not specify sheep, only cattle (under the vague term *averia*) and pigs.[50] The claims of 1634 proved more significant than the decree of 1628, for rights that could be shown to be enjoyed in 1634 were guaranteed under an Act of 1668, which also precluded the acquisition later of a prescriptive right.[51] That evidence was cited by the authorities in the modern period, when large numbers of sheep were run in the Forest, often by people who did not hold ancient messuages in the parochial lands.[52]

ADMINISTRATION AND WOODLAND MANAGEMENT TO 1603. The early medieval administration of Dean, as of other large royal forests, was cumbersome, inefficient, and tardy. The large body of foresters, often with overlapping duties, was difficult to supervise because of the size and nature of the terrain. There was much scope for corruption and embezzlement, which could sometimes be carried on under the cloak of the officers' customary and ill-defined privileges. Even the territory in which the forest law was to be enforced was never clear: the wide area of the 13th-century Forest had privileged enclaves, such as Tidenham chase, whose status was not clearly understood.[53] Special privileges granted to Gloucester abbey and to the bishop of Hereford in repect of woods within the perambulation[54] were probably a further cause of confusion. The evidence for Dean in the 13th century supports the general picture of the royal forest system as one of the least satisfactory and least successful parts of the medieval administration of England. Underlying the whole forest system were serious inconsistencies of policy, while the complex apparatus of petty restrictions brought only a modest financial profit at the same time as causing tension between the Crown and many of its subjects.[55]

Fines levied in 1199 by King John on most of the woodwards of bailiwicks may merely exemplify the policy of arbitrary exactions of that reign,[56] but a major purge of officers under Henry III in 1250, when five woodwards and eight serjeants-in-fee forfeited their offices,[57] suggests a deep-seated malaise. Ralph of Abenhall, one of the manorial lords still in charge of his Forest bailiwick, was accused of a catalogue of offences in 1282, and the eyre of that year also noted the serjeants' practice of taking bribes for ignoring illegal charcoal pits.[58] Successive deputy constables, left in charge of the Forest by their superiors, were reported in 1270 to have permitted numerous abuses; Robert le Waleys, who was in office c. 1260, was said to have taken

43 *Rot. Litt. Claus.* (Rec. Com.), i. 538; P.R.O., E 146/1/25.
44 P.R.O., E 134/34 Eliz. I Hil./23; E 123/19, ff. 151–152v.
45 Ibid. E 134/36 Eliz. I Hil./21; Glos. R.O., D 2026/X 5; cf. above, Bounds.
46 P.R.O., E 112/82, no. 300.
47 *Cal. Inq. Misc.* i, pp. 73–4; *Close R.* 1254–6, 355.
48 P.R.O., E 126/9, ff. 188v.–191.
49 Ibid. E 125/4, ff. 269–74.

50 Ibid. C 99/10.
51 Dean Forest Act, 19 & 20 Chas. II, c. 8.
52 Below, commoning and management 1820–1914.
53 Above, Bounds.
54 *Hist. & Cart. Mon. Glouc.* (Rolls Ser.), ii. 187–8; *Close R.* 1237–42, 226.
55 Cf. M. F. Bazeley, in *Trans. B.G.A.S.* xxxiii. 275–82.
56 *Pipe R.* 1199 (P.R.S. N.S. x), 32.
57 P.R.O., C 60/47, m. 13.
58 Ibid. E 32/30, rot. 22.

bribes for appointing corrupt officials and ignoring waste of private woodlands.[59] The verderers, who were expected to be less open to corruption than the officers by tenure, had abused their position, removing from their rolls of offenders the names of the living and substituting the names of the dead.[60]

The eyre of 1282[61] revealed the geographical difficulties of checking depredations in the Forest: the two navigable rivers which provided much of its boundary aided the speedy carriage of venison and stolen timber away and into other jurisdictions. Venison had found its way to many aristocratic and monastic households beyond the two rivers, and much was taken to Bristol, whose citizens had secured in their charter of 1252 the franchise that none of them could be indicted on account of venison found within the city walls.[62] Owners of river craft, based at landing places on the Severn in Lydney, Aylburton, and Awre, carried on a regular traffic in stolen timber, mainly to Bristol. Lydney and Aylburton men also figured in notable numbers among offenders in general, reflecting the fact that those places contained one of the largest areas of private woodland outside the Forest demesne. The total number of offences showed a considerable increase through the three eyres for which records survive, the venison offences rising from 43 in 1258 to 59 in 1270 and 120 in 1282. Modest fines, averaging under 2s., were imposed for the much more numerous vert offences, while venison offences commonly incurred as much as 40s.[63]

The potential for mineral extraction and ironworking in Dean was the chief cause of inconsistency in the Crown's policy. Long-term preservation of the woodland constantly gave way before the lure of short-term profit from industry. Measures in the early 13th century to restrict ironworking to a few licensed forges were probably not successful, but preservation was still ostensibly the priority in the 1250s when the king's own 'great forge' at St. Briavels was given up, on the ground that it consumed wood of a greater value than the profit it produced.[64] By 1282, however, when as many as 60 itinerant forges were working in the Forest, efforts to restrict ironworking were apparently little more than for form's sake and the fines levied in effect a licensing system. At the same date as many as 2,685 charcoal pits were enumerated in the demesne woodland.[65]

The few records of the Forest and the working of its administration between the mid 14th century and the mid 16th include mention of two disturbances among inhabitants of the area. In 1356 members of the Gainer family of St. Briavels and Aylburton, having refused service as mounted archers in the North of England, led an armed band in the Forest, committing depredations against the vert and venison and attacking and intimidating officers.[66] In 1375 the arrest was ordered of another group of men, some of whom were known by pseudonyms.[67] Whether those disturbances arose from discontent with the irksome forest laws and with the local administration or had more transitory origins is not apparent. Certainly a strain of lawlessness was evident among inhabitants of parishes of the Forest area centuries before it was noted as characteristic of those of them who settled as squatters on the demesne itself. It manifested itself in a complaint of 1429 that shipping on the Severn was being raided when passing the Forest[68] and in the violence associated with commoning disputes from the 16th century onwards. As regards the forest law, much potential for trouble had been removed and the task of administering the Forest simplified by the new perambulation made in 1300 and finally accepted by the Crown in 1327. The exclusion of the private chases from the Forest was confirmed and most of the other large private woodlands, in Lydney, Newent, Churcham, Longhope, and elsewhere, were taken out. Also in the early 14th century the Crown authorized substantial sales of outlying areas of the demesne woodland,[69] leaving the demesne more compact and easier to police; pressure on its bounds by illegal encroachment was presumably also much reduced by the general slump in arable farming of the period and by the great plague of 1349.

The administration of Dean begins to emerge clearly again in the mid 16th century, when the Crown was seeking to profit more systematically from its woodland and imposing by statute a national policy for the preservation of woodland.[70] By the beginning of Elizabeth I's reign eight coppices on the fringes of the demesne woodland were cut and inclosed on a regular cycle and the underwood and thinnings from them were sold to local ironworkers for making charcoal. The largest coppice was the Chestnuts, near Littledean, and the others were in the Bradley hill area west of Soudley brook and at Kidnalls above Lydney.[71] There were also more regular sales of timber trees for building and other purposes, but no consistent policy had apparently been evolved for Dean, and it has been estimated that the sales of timber and coppice wood from the Forest never produced more than c. £100 a year during the 16th century. There is no evidence that any timber was taken by the government for naval shipbuilding at that period.[72] The whole demesne woodland came within the terms of an Act of 1559 which prohibited felling of timber trees for ironworking within 14 miles of the Severn or Wye[73] and its future potential for naval use was no doubt recognized. A story that the Spanish Armada had orders to burn the Forest, as a lethal

59 Ibid. E 32/29, rot. 1d.
60 Ibid. E 32/30, rot. 2d.
61 Ibid. E 32/30 records its proceedings.
62 Ibid. rot. 36; *Bristol Charters, 1155–1373* (Bristol Rec. Soc. i), 26.
63 *Trans. B.G.A.S.* xxxiii. 254, 260, 263.
64 Above, Industry, ironworks; P.R.O., E 146/1/26.
65 P.R.O., E 32/30, rot. 23d.; E 32/31, mm. 9–14.
66 *Cal. Pat.* 1354–8, 399.

67 Ibid. 1374–7, 220–1.
68 *Rot. Parl.* iv. 345–6.
69 Above, Bounds.
70 Hart, *Royal Forest*, 73; G. Hammersley, 'Crown Woods and their Exploitation in 16th and 17th Centuries', *Bull. Inst. Hist. Res.* xxx. 136–61.
71 Glos. R.O., D 2026/X 3.
72 *Bull. Inst. Hist. Res.* xxx. 140, 143, 151–2.
73 Timber Preservation Act, 1 Eliz. I c. 15.

blow to English sea-power, appears, however, to be an invention of the mid 17th century.[74]

In 1565 when Roger Taverner, deputy surveyor general of woods south of the Trent, visited Dean as part of a survey of the royal forests[75] he found much to criticize in the way it was managed under the local officers. Most of the great oaks and beeches, which were the staple of the Forest, were 'shred' of their branches to supply the iron industry. Taverner's exasperation led to exaggerated claims: he said that on the borders of the woods there was as much oak timber cut and stacked as there was standing and no branch was to be seen on oak or beech as thick as the arm of a two-year old child. He concluded that the spoil was encouraged partly by a system of fees paid by charcoal burners: from each charcoal pit worked for up to six weeks, the lessee of the St. Briavels castle estate took 5s., the constable 20d., the woodward of the local bailiwick 18d., and the chief forester and rider 10d. each. The protection of the vert under forest law was undermined also by the officers' practice of making private agreements with offenders to release them from attachment at fines of as little as 1d. or 2d., whereas the scale of fines imposed by the attachment court ranged from 6d. to 2s.[76] Rolls of the attachment court for the late 1560s which survived in the Exchequer were perhaps sent there so that government officials could check on the court's effectiveness.[77]

Taverner's criticisms were levelled in particular at the lessee of the St. Briavels estate, William Guise of Elmore, who, apparently by virtue of his lease, was in charge of the sales of the coppice wood to ironworkers. Guise had failed to enforce a statutory requirement of 1543 to leave in coppices 12 timber trees to the acre, and had not ensured that the coppices were inclosed, after cutting, to protect new growth from the commoners' animals.[78] In an attempt to remedy the situation Taverner obtained a lease of the estate for himself in 1571 but he failed to oust Guise, who at his death in 1574 was succeeded by his son John.[79] Taverner did, however, cause a massive fine of £1,300 to be imposed on Guise, who had paid off a small part by the time of his death.[80] The lessee's role in woodland management was probably ended in 1583 when a renewal of the lease, though still granting 'the whole Forest of Dean', contained a clause reserving all great trees and underwood.[81]

As further evidence of central government's concern, in 1600 the chief justice of the forests south of Trent, prompted by reports of the building of new ironworks and water mills, ordered an inquiry into encroachments. The voracious blast furnaces, including some built right at the borders of the demesne woodland at Lydbrook and Lydney, were beginning to have an impact on the Forest.[82]

EXPLOITATION OF THE FOREST 1603-68. Under the first two Stuart kings the Forest of Dean was managed for short-term monetary benefit with little care for preserving the future value of its woodlands. The Crown's main opportunity for raising revenue was provided by the needs of the ironmasters. The wood required to make charcoal for the blast furnaces, comprising coppice wood or the lops and tops of felled timber trees, was estimated for and supplied in standard stacks called cords, 8 ft. 4 in. in length and 4 ft. 3 in. in both width and height;[83] in 1611 it was calculated that 1 a. of coppice produced 80 cords.[84]

Licensed exploitation of the demesne woods began in 1611 when Sir Edward Winter, owner of ironworks at Lydney, was given a five-year lease of the 331 a. of the old coppices in the Bradley hill area; for the sum of £800, he was given a free hand to work them, the statutory obligations to reinclose and preserve timber trees being waived.[85] In 1612 a policy began of leasing the right to ironworks on the royal demesne, usually known as the king's ironworks, together with an allowance of cordwood. William Herbert, earl of Pembroke, who was both constable and lessee of the St. Briavels castle estate, was empowered to build ironworks and take 12,000 cords a year at a price of 4s. a cord.[86] In that case the statutes for preserving timber were to be enforced, and commissioners were appointed to supervise the cutting and delivery of the cordwood and the inclosure of the areas cut. Irregularities in the commissioners' execution of their task soon became evident, however: in 1614 they were found to have failed to prevent, or connived at, the felling of large timber trees, the embezzlement of wood by the making up of irregularly-sized cords, the sale of wood to coopers, trencher makers, and carpenters, and the invasion of the woodlands by squatters. Abuses in the exercise of the cordwood concessions continued under successive lessees of the king's ironworks[87] during the next 30 years. The lessees' allowance was usually restricted to 12–14,000 cords a year,[88] but in the 1620s and 1630s other rights were granted, including in 1627 wood to the value of £1,500 a year to a cooper for barrel staves,[89] and there were additional sales of cordwood to Sir John Winter of Lydney and other private ironmasters.[90] The Crown also profited from the regular sales of oak bark to tanners of neighbouring parishes[91] and to bark merchants exporting to Ireland and

74 Hart, *Royal Forest*, 83.
75 P.R.O., E 315/429, f. 126; E 407/168.
76 Badminton Mun. FmE 2/3/1, ff. 4–5.
77 P.R.O., E 146/1/30–1.
78 Badminton Mun. FmE 2/3/1, ff. 5–7; Glos. R.O., D 2026/X 3; cf. Preservation of Woods Act, 35 Hen. VIII, c. 17.
79 P.R.O., E 112/15, no. 58; cf. above, St. Briavels, manors.
80 P.R.O., E 407/168.
81 Ibid. C 60/401, m. 43.
82 Glos. R.O., D 2026/X 7.

83 P.R.O., LRRO 5/7A, inq. Sept. 1649; C 99/34.
84 Ibid. E 178/3837, depositions 1611.
85 Ibid. C 99/33; B.L. Lansd. MS. 166, ff. 350, 352 and v., 356.
86 P.R.O., C 99/34.
87 Ibid. E 178/3837; E 178/5304.
88 *Cal. S.P. Dom.* 1627–8, 457; 1628–9, 408; Glos. R.O., D 421/E 5; P.R.O., SP 16/257, no. 94.
89 *Cal. S.P. Dom.* 1627–8, 314.
90 Ibid. 96; Glos. R.O., D 421/E 2.
91 e.g. P.R.O., E 178/3837, acct. Jan. 1618.

elsewhere. In 1630 John Duncombe had a grant of all the bark from the oak cut under the current cordwood concession.[92]

The first evidence found of the use of Dean's oak for the royal navy was in 1617,[93] and throughout the period all timber suitable for shipbuilding was, in theory, safeguarded and reserved in the grants to ironmasters and others. In 1628 the woodland of Lea Bailey in the north-east of the Forest was ordered to be excluded from the operation of all grants.[94] In the 1630s the government became more purposeful in its attempts to preserve timber for the navy's use: in 1633 a deputy surveyor for Dean, directly responsible to the surveyor of Crown woods, was appointed,[95] and the new officer, John Broughton, made a detailed survey of the surviving timber, finding the 1,000 a. of Lea Bailey at least relatively unscathed and stocked with excellent oak for shipbuilding.[96] In practice, however, the safeguarding of navy timber was imperfectly achieved during the period, for many people — the ironmasters with their woodcutters and charcoal burners, the cordwood commissioners, and the patentees, besides the commoners and free miners — then had access to the demesne woodlands and could do damage.

In the 1620s Charles I made grants of parts of the demesne woodland, totalling almost 3,000 a., to raise funds and reward courtiers. The Chestnuts was leased for 21 years in 1624, Kidnalls and an adjoining wood called the Snead for three lives in 1626, and the Bradley hill coppices for 41 years from 1629. Outlying pieces of waste at Staunton were sold in 1629.[97] More significantly, the large Mailscot wood adjoining English Bicknor was given at a nominal fee-farm rent to Sir Edward Villiers in 1625[98] and another large freehold was created in the centre of the demesne at Cannop. A lease of 1,070 a. at Cannop made c. 1628 to John Gibbons, secretary to the Lord Treasurer, was sold by him to Sir Robert Banastre, who secured a grant in fee and left it to his grandson Banastre Maynard.[99]

The activities of the ironmasters and patentees under their grants inevitably brought them into conflict with the many local inhabitants who claimed common pasture and estovers and the right, as free miners, to open mines throughout the demesne woodlands and take timber for shoring them. The earl of Pembroke's grant in 1612 and his heavy-handed exercise of it, which included securing an injunction against the miners to enforce an unrestricted right to minerals from the royal demesne,[1] provoked both legal action by representatives of the commoners[2] and riots and the firing of the woods.[3] In the 1620s, when in aid of the inclosure of coppices for cordwood the Forest officers attempted a stricter regulation of commoning, opposition was led by two local landowners, Sir John Winter and Benedict Hall of Highmeadow. With such influential support the commoners secured an authoritative statement of their rights and the concession that due notice would be given before the Forest was driven to check on illegal pasturing. They were, however, forced to agree that the estates of the patentees were closed to their animals,[4] and a few years later the most serious outbreak of rioting in the period was directed against one of those estates when Barbara, Lady Villiers, widow of the grantee of 1625, began the inclosure of Mailscot wood. On Lady Day 1631 about 500 men, armed and with drums and colours, destroyed the new mounds and ditches and attacked the house of one of Lady Villiers's agents, and shortly afterwards there was an even larger riotous assembly. Later in the year 86 rioters were indicted. The dissidents were from the parishes in the north and west of the Forest and some gentry and clergy were accused of involvement, but the outbreak was given a more than local significance by the leadership of John Williams, alias 'Skimmington', who had been involved in anti-inclosure riots in two other royal forests, Gillingham (Dors.) and Braydon (Wilts.). Williams was arrested early in 1632, and two men who had helped to capture him were attacked by a mob at Newland church later in the year.[5]

The first two Stuart kings also re-interpreted and exploited the Crown's ancient rights. Early in his reign James I declared much of what was presumed to be established freehold in the Forest's parishes to be illegal assarts, the holders being treated as untitled occupants until they had compounded with the Crown at substantial sums. Some owners paid for their lands in 1609 and others settled with patentees who received grants from the Crown of large tracts of the land in 1618 and 1619. Altogether £5,492 was levied for a total of 10,758 a., much of it in the parishes of Newland, St. Briavels, and English Bicknor, where among other landlords the Halls compounded for c. 800 a. and the Wyralls for c. 550 a.[6]

In 1634 Charles I, when reviving the ancient prerogatives of the Crown, convened a forest eyre (or justice seat) for Dean, which in its rigorous examination of rights and detailed cataloguing of offences set the pattern for a series of such eyres for the royal forests. On patently flimsy evidence Sir John Finch, the Crown's chief counsel at the eyre, succeeded in returning to the forest law the many parishes which had been excluded by the perambulation of 1300, confirmed in 1327, but it was decided not to proceed against offenders in those parishes. In the reduced bounds, however, a total of c. £130,000 in fines was imposed for encroachments, waste of woods, and other offences against the vert and venison. Many

92 Cal. S.P. Dom. 1629–31, 277.
93 Bull. Inst. Hist. Res. xxx. 151–2.
94 P.R.O., E 125/4, ff. 273v.–274.
95 Cal. S.P. Dom. 1633–4, 20, 191, 333, 484.
96 Hart, Royal Forest, 274–7.
97 Glos. R.O., D 421/E 5, grant to Sir J. Winter 1640; P.R.O., C 99/26.   98 P.R.O., C 99/28.
99 Cal. S.P. Dom. 1656–7, 316–17; 1660–1, 588.
1 P.R.O., C 99/34; Hart, Free Miners, 166–8.

2 P.R.O., E 112/82, no. 300.
3 Cal. S.P. Dom. 1611–18, 144.
4 P.R.O., E 125/4, ff. 269–74.
5 D. G. C. Allan, 'Rising in the West, 1628–31', Econ. H.R. 2nd ser. v. 76–85; Acts of P.C. 1630–1, 284–5, 289–90, 357, 390–1; Cal. S.P. Dom. 1631–3, 4, 62–3, 87–8, 90–1, 178, 182, 192, 312.
6 Glos. R.O., D 33/188A–G, 272–3; D 34/1/1; D 421/E 3; D 1677/GG 656–7; D 2026/E 21; D 3921/I/48.

offenders incurred only small fines but some of the ironmasters and grantees of lands were made liable for massive sums: Sir Basil Brooke and George Mynne, the lessees of the king's ironworks, were fined £59,040 for irregularities in their exercise of the cordwood concession, Sir John Winter £20,230, mainly for illegal cutting and charcoaling in the demesne woods by him and his father for their Lydney works, and John Gibbons £8,600 for supposed offences in connexion with his Cannop estate. In the event the principal offenders had their fines considerably reduced, and it is thought that no more than about one fifth of the total originally imposed was collected.[7] In the following years, however, the Crown profited by the willingness of landowners in the revived bounds to pay to disafforest their lands: Winter paid £1,000 to free his large and well-wooded Lydney estate, and other sums came from estates in Tidenham chase,[8] which had been effectively free of the forest law even before 1300.

By 1638 Charles I's government had decided that the best means of capitalizing on the Forest was to disafforest and sell the bulk of the royal demesne. It was argued, unrealistically in the light of previous experience, that a private owner would more efficiently and more economically manage the coppices, administer the cordwood concession, and preserve the navy timber. Sir John Winter, who had cleared himself of the fines levied by the justice seat and had become secretary to the queen, was probably the main advocate of the scheme. In March 1640, in return for £106,000 to be paid over six years and an annual fee-farm of £1,951, he was granted c. 18,000 a. of the demesne with the minerals, underwood, and game. He was to provide the lessees of the king's ironworks with 13,550 cords each year and allow them to carry on the works for six years and was required to preserve for the Crown 15,000 tons of ship timber. By an agreement made with representatives of the commoners 4,000 a. of the demesne were to remain open to the rights of common and estovers. Lea Bailey woods were once more wholly reserved to the Crown.[9]

Winter began inclosing and felling under his grant but met with much opposition from the commoners, many of whom claimed they had not been parties to the agreement. His position became untenable after the opening of the Long Parliament, which after ordering an inquiry and collecting evidence of misappropriation of the ship timber and other abuses[10] deprived him of his grant in 1642.[11] Winter's inclosures were demolished by the commoners, who then en-

joyed a virtually unrestricted right until inclosure was again attempted in the mid 1650s.[12]

For most of the Civil War the administration of the Forest was disrupted as royalists under Sir John Winter contested control with the parliamentary garrison of Gloucester. Parliament's victory deprived the area of the influence and leadership of most of its leading gentry and holders of forest offices: Winter,[13] his cousin, the marquess of Worcester, who had estates in Tidenham and Woolaston and in neighbouring Monmouthshire, his brother-in-law Benedict Hall of Highmeadow,[14] the Throckmortons of Clearwell,[15] the Vaughans of Ruardean,[16] and the Colchesters of Westbury-on-Severn[17] were all dispossessed or heavily fined. In that situation the Forest was dominated between 1645 and 1649 by a group of former parliamentary army officers, John Giffard, Robert Kyrle, Griffantius Phillips, John Brayne of Littledean, and Thomas Pury the younger of Gloucester. They secured control of the ironworks on the royal demesne and on the surrounding estates and carried on their operations with little interference: the remaining woodwards, the minor foresters, and a surveyor and four preservators appointed by parliament to supervise the supply of cordwood were intimidated by or colluded with them. Great damage was inflicted: much navy timber was felled and used for cordwood, and abuses, such as fraudulent cords and the misappropriation of cordwood, once again went unchecked. It was estimated that over 35,000 oaks and beeches were felled in the demesne woods during the 1640s, over half of them marked earlier for use as ship timber. The woods were also invaded by several hundred cabiners, often supporting themselves by making barrel staves and trenchers from stolen wood and by keeping goats. There was also destruction in the woodlands of the royalist gentry, particularly in Lydney, Tidenham, and part of the Highmeadow estate at Hadnock (Mon.).[18] Parliament issued an ordinance against any further felling of timber in 1648[19] and a wide-ranging inquiry was carried out the following year, but there was apparently little improvement in the management of the Forest until 1653 when the government appointed Major John Wade to run the ironworks.[20]

Under Wade, who was reappointed with general powers to administer the woodlands in 1656,[21] the ironworks, the felling and delivery of the cordwood, and sales of wood to makers of barrel staves and trenchers were retained under a centralized control and the worst abuses checked; also the bulk of the cabiners were

7 G. Hammersley, 'Revival of Forest Laws under Chas. I', *History*, xlv. 85–102; for the proceedings, Glos. R.O., D 1677/GG 1220; for the Winters' offences, ibid. D 421/E 4.

8 P.R.O., E 401/1924, entries for 29 July, 5 Dec. 1637; 24 Jan., 22 Feb. 1637/8; E 401/1925, entry for 12 June 1638.

9 Glos. R.O., D 421/E 5; P.R.O., E 126/9, ff. 188v.–189.

10 Glos. R.O., D 421/E 5, petition to parl. *c.* 1660; P.R.O., LRRO 5/7A, coms. of inquiry 1641, 1642.

11 P.R.O., E 178/6080, bk. of parl. ordinances, ff. 20–21v.; *Cal. S.P. Dom.* 1641–3, 285, 348–9.

12 P.R.O., E 126/9, f. 189.

13 Above, Lydney, manors.

14 *V.C.H. Glos.* x. 63, 106; above, Staunton, manor; cf. Bigland, *Glos.* ii. 263.

15 Above, Newland, manors.

16 Above, Ruardean, manors.

17 *V.C.H. Glos.* x. 87.

18 P.R.O., LRRO 5/7A, com. of inquiry and depositions 1649; for the surveyor and preservators, ibid. E 178/6080, bk. of parl. ordinances, ff. 13–15v.

19 *Acts & Ords. of Interr.* ed. Firth & Rait, i. 1125–6.

20 *Cal. S.P. Dom.* 1656–7, 155.

21 Ibid. 155–6.

expelled from the demesne woods.[22] With most of the ancient offices by tenure in abeyance, Wade ran the Forest through a staff of the salaried, minor foresters, namely a bowbearer, the six keepers (two of whom also acted as clerks), and the two rangers. Wade himself served as verderer, together with two others from the well-disposed local gentry, William Cooke of Highnam and Richard Machen of Eastbach, in Bicknor, and 12 new regarders were appointed.[23] In 1656 a justice seat was convened at Mitcheldean in the Protector's name and presided over by Maj.-Gen. John Desborough,[24] who had been appointed constable of St. Briavels in 1654.[25] Under a navy purveyor appointed in 1655 the Commonwealth government ensured a regular supply of ship timber. Much was shipped out to the dockyards, mainly through Lydney,[26] where a shipbuilding yard was also established to build frigates.[27]

Under an Act of 1657 which authorized the inclosure of up to one third of the demesne,[28] Wade inclosed a large tract in the south-west part; rather than relying solely on natural regeneration, he sowed acorns and beech mast and planted out saplings.[29] His inclosure produced the usual response from some of the commoners, who broke the fences and fired parts of the woods.[30] The government's failure to take effective action against the rioters made Wade disillusioned with the task of governing Dean: shortly before leaving his post at the Restoration, he described the Forest as a 'forlorn, disowned piece of ground, so much talked of and so little cared for in reality'.[31]

At the Restoration the government ordered a commission of inquiry, which, reporting in 1662, advised it to resume as much as possible of the alienated lands and follow a determined policy of inclosing the Forest as a nursery for ship timber.[32] Initially, however, Sir John Winter and other patentees reasserted their rights, and the ironworks on the demesne continued. In 1662 Winter surrendered his rights under his grant of 1640 in return for a payment of £30,000 but had a new grant of all the timber trees surviving on almost the whole demesne and the use of the ironworks; the Crown reserved Lea Bailey and another 11,335 tons of timber for the navy, to be supplied by Winter.[33] In 1663 he was said to have 500 woodcutters at work in the Forest.[34] In 1665 or 1666 under a new agreement he was given 8,000 a. of his former land in return for managing the other 10,000 a. as a nursery for ship timber,[35] but in 1668, after more opposition

and irregularities in his delivery of the navy's timber, he surrendered all his rights and was discharged of the obligation to supply the timber.[36] The same year an Act was passed to return the whole demesne to government control and establish it as a permanent source of ship timber.

THE REFORMED ADMINISTRATION. The Dean Forest Reafforestation Act of 1668[37] remained for many years the governing instrument of the Forest, which subsequently comprised in practice only the 23–24,000 a. of the royal demesne. The operation of the forest law was confirmed in the demesne, while the manorial lands were freed from its restrictions, confirming a measure of the Commonwealth government in 1657;[38] officially, however, they remained part of the Forest until the 1830s.[39] The main provision of the Act was that 11,000 a. of the demesne should be inclosed, to be progressively laid open and replaced by other inclosures as the new growth of timber reached sufficient size to be safe from browsing animals. Rights to common of pasture, defined as those lawfully used in 1634, and mining rights were to continue in the uninclosed land, but the commoners agreed to give up estovers in response to the Crown's offer to lift the forest law from the manorial lands and end ironworking on the demesne.[40] The deer, if the Crown decided to continue to maintain them in the Forest, were to be limited to 800 beasts. Of the alienated lands of the demesne, the Cannop estate was bought back from its owner Banastre Maynard in 1670,[41] in which year the lease of the coppices at Bradley hill also fell in. The sale of Mailscot was, however, confirmed, and it soon afterwards became part of the Highmeadow estate, while Kidnalls and the Snead were left in the possession of the owners of the Lydney estate, who had obtained the reversion in fee.[42] The Act brought in the local justices of the peace to aid the implementation of the new policy: they were to be represented among the commissioners carrying out the inclosure, they were to supervise the felling of any timber, and they were to mark timber to be preserved for future growth. To pay for the inclosure and buy out Maynard £3,000 was raised by the sale of coppice wood and decayed timber, most of it to the ironmaster Paul Foley and his partners.[43]

By 1671, when Samuel Pepys and colleagues from the Navy Office visited the Forest, c. 8,500 a. had already been inclosed.[44] Five separate

22 Hart, *Royal Forest*, 289.
23 P.R.O., SP 18/130, accts. of John Wade, pp. 689, 697; E 178/6080, ff. 41, 42.
24 Glos. R.O., D 2026/X 14.
25 Below, Wardens.
26 e.g. *Cal. S.P. Dom.* 1653–4, 575; 1655, 403, 435, 469, 515, 552; 1655–6, 449, 493, 529; 1656–7, 562, 568; 1657–8, 390, 516, 547; 1658–9, 552; 1659–60, 544.
27 Above, Lydney, econ. hist. (other ind. and trade).
28 *Acts & Ords. of Interr.* ii. 1114–15.
29 P.R.O., E 178/6080, ff. 32v.–33.
30 *Cal. S.P. Dom.* 1658–9, 328, 361.
31 Ibid. 1659–60, 413, 421.
32 Hart, *Royal Forest*, 286–90.
33 Glos. R.O., D 421/E 7; *Cal. S.P. Dom.* 1661–2, 430.
34 *3rd Rep. Com. Woods* (1788), 14.

35 *Cal. S.P. Dom.* 1665–6, 222; *Cal. Treas. Bks.* 1667–8, 131, 168, 174.
36 *Cal. S.P. Dom.* 1667–8, 466.
37 Dean Forest Act, 19 & 20 Chas. II, c. 8.
38 *Acts & Ords. of Interr.* ii. 1114.
39 Above, Bounds.
40 Hart, *Royal Forest*, 155–7; N.L.W., Mynde Park MS. 2700.
41 The Maynards had been bought out by the government in 1657 but, claiming to have received less than the value of the est., were reinstated at the Restoration: *Cal. S.P. Dom.* 1656–7, 316–17; 1660–1, 588; P.R.O., E 178/6080, f. 33.
42 Above, exploitation 1603–68; Eng. Bicknor, manor; Lydney, intro.
43 *Cal. Treas. Bks.* 1669–72, 78, 90, 112–13.
44 Hart, *Royal Forest*, 296–7.

inclosures were formed, the largest covering the whole of the west side of the demesne and another comprising Lea Bailey and Linings wood (later Lower Lea Bailey) in the north-east part. The intention was mainly to encourage natural regeneration of oak and beech and preserve what healthy trees survived,[45] though some acorns were sown.[46]

To enforce its new policy the government relied principally on its main supporter in the county, Henry Somerset, Lord Herbert, who succeeded his father as marquess of Worcester in 1667 and was created duke of Beaufort in 1682.[47] He had been made constable of St. Briavels and warden of the Forest for life in 1660 and he acquired the lease of the St. Briavels castle estate then or soon afterwards.[48] Among the royalist gentry, Sir Baynham Throckmorton of Clearwell and Sir Duncombe Colchester of Westbury were active in support, as was William Cooke of Highnam, who had successfully accommodated himself to the restoration of the monarchy. Cooke retained his office of verderer, serving in the 1670s with his brother Edward and Colchester.[49] The determination to pursue a policy of preservation was shown by the dismantling of the ironworks in 1674, by the expulsion of the remaining cabiners later that decade,[50] and by important modifications to the Forest's administration.

In preserving the new inclosures little was expected of the principal tier of Forest officers, the woodwards of the bailiwicks. One adviser to the government cited the proven ineffectiveness of the deputies appointed by the woodwards, the impossibility of disciplining the woodwards without holding regular eyres, which he predicted, correctly, would be unlikely in the future, and the debilitating effect on their zeal of their right to common.[51] Instead the administration relied mainly on salaried and easily replaceable officers. In the mid 1670s the demesne was divided into six walks, each provided with a lodge and placed in charge of a keeper.[52] The keepers were, in an enhanced role, the six under-foresters traditionally appointed by the constable, and he continued to appoint them after the 1670s to hold office at his pleasure, besides directing some aspects of their work. Initially, the man who kept King's walk was styled bowbearer, continuing the old title of the constable's chief under-forester, but that usage soon lapsed.[53] Each keeper was assigned a small farm of cleared land adjoining his lodge and an annual salary, paid by the Treasury;[54] after an augmentation out of the proceeds of the St.

Briavels castle estate, the salary was £18 6s. 8d. in 1686.[55] It was £22 in 1787 and by then each keeper received a large income in the form of fees.[56] In addition, a new office was created in 1674, that of the conservator, or supervisor, with the specific role of supervising the new inclosures. It was a direct appointment of the Treasury and carried a salary of £100.[57]

The six new walks, which superseded the ten ancient bailiwicks as the main administrative units of the demesne woodland, were named respectively the King's (or Charles II's) walk, York walk (after the king's brother), Danby walk (after the earl of Danby, the Lord Treasurer), Latimer walk (after another of the earl's titles), Worcester walk (after the constable, the marquess of Worcester), and Herbert walk (after another of the marquess's titles).[58] By the later 18th century the King's was usually called Speech House walk, after the building that served as its keeper's lodge, and York, Danby, Latimer, and Herbert had become known, from geographical location, as respectively Parkend, Blakeney, Littledean, and Ruardean walks. Worcester walk, which was on the west side of the demesne, adjoining Coleford, retained it old title.[59] The new Speech House, built on the site of the old courthouse at Kensley, served as both courthouse and lodge.[60]

The intended role of the six keepers is revealed by instructions drawn up by the marquess of Worcester shortly after 1675. They were to make regular perambulations of their walks, checking for cattle in the inclosures and for encroachments and the building of cabins. They were to take over the regulation of commoning and impound animals found in the Forest in the prohibited seasons (the fence month and winter haining), those turned in by people without rights, and uncommonable beasts, which the instructions declared to include sheep. A new Forest pound for the use of the keepers was built at Parkend, though by the mid 18th century there was one adjoining each keeper's lodge. A particular responsibility of the keepers was the preservation of the deer: they were to search houses for venison and for guns or nets, checking on dressers of skins and gunsmiths in the locality, and keeping records of all deer killed in their walks.[61]

The new office of conservator was given in 1674 to Sir Baynham Throckmorton,[62] and it was usually filled later by a local landowner. For more than 100 years from 1714, except for a brief tenure in the 1730s by members of the Bond family of Redbrook, the office was held by successive generations of the Jones family of Nass.[63] The conservator was intended to be a

45   Glos. R.O., D 1677/GG 1223.
46   Hart, *Royal Forest*, 298.
47   *Complete Peerage*, ii. 52.
48   Below, Wardens; above, St. Briavels, manors.
49   Glos. R.O., D 36/Q 2; Badminton Mun. FmF 1/8/32; cf. *Visit. Glos. 1682–3*, 47.
50   Above, Industry, ironworks; Settlement, intro.
51   Glos. Colln. LX 10.3 (3).
52   *Cal. Treas. Bks.* 1672–5, 228–9; Glos. R.O., D 1677/GG 1223.
53   Badminton Mun. FmS/G 2/4/3–4; Berkeley Cast. Mun., patents nos. 8, 14, 29; *3rd Rep. Com. Woods* (1788), 77.
54   *Cal. Treas. Bks.* 1672–5, 307, 317; 1676–9, 250; 1685–9, 1059.
55   Berkeley Cast. Mun., patents no. 8; cf. *Cal. Treas. Bks.*

1685–9, 1059; Oct. 1700–Dec. 1701, 170.
56   *3rd Rep. Com. Woods* (1788), 84–7.
57   *Cal. Treas. Bks.* 1672–5, 228–9, 319, 508.
58   Glos. R.O., D 1677/GG 1223.
59   *3rd Rep. Com. Woods* (1788), 111–12; P.R.O., F 17/17.
60   Above, Settlement, forest lodges.
61   Badminton Mun. FmS/G 2/4/4; for the pounds, Berkeley Cast. Mun., General Ser. T, box 25, papers about keepers' misdemeanours 1742; *Glouc. Jnl.* 22 July 1735.
62   *Cal. Treas. Bks.* 1672–5, 508.
63   For holders of the office, ibid. 1681–5, 279; 1685–9, 1265; Oct. 1697–Aug. 1698, 216; 1712, 456; 1714–15, 150; *Cal. Treas. Bks. & Papers*, 1731–4, 358, 535; 1735–8, 187, 231; 1739–41, 68, 207; *Cal. H.O. Papers*, 1760–5, p. 94; *3rd Rep. Com. Woods* (1788), 80; P.R.O., LR 4/27.

figure of authority, having supervisory powers over the other officers, including those by tenure and heredity,[64] but failure to achieve a continuing programme of inclosure reduced his role. It was the deputy surveyor, responsible, under the surveyor general of Crown woods, for the general management of the timber, who emerged as the key figure in the Forest administration in the 18th century.[65]

The Forest's courts were continued, apparently with enhanced powers, to aid the policy of preservation. In the years 1673–84, for which records survive, the swanimote was convened before the verderers once a year at traditional venues for Forest business, St. Briavels castle, the Speech House, or the market town of Mitcheldean. In some ways it was a purely formal gathering of the old administration, all the Forest officers and the reeve and four men from each of the parishes within the bounds being summoned to attend; but some forest offences, including poaching, damage to the vert, and encroachments, were presented by the foresters and a jury and fined by the court. Occasionally offenders were bound over to await the justices-in-eyre,[66] and in 1680 an eyre was planned to meet at Coleford,[67] but it was never held.

The attachment court, with its regular six-weekly sessions before the verderers at the Speech House, was also intended as an instrument for disciplining those damaging the plantations, and it was envisaged that it would have responsibility for more than just the vert, as formerly. Worcester's instructions to the keepers imply a role in regulating commoning and preserving the venison: animals impounded for a third offence of straying into the inclosures were to be presented to the verderers in the court and sold by them, the keepers were to report to the court all the fines that they levied as a result of driving the Forest at the prohibited seasons, and were also to present there any deer found dead. The court continued to control the supply of wood to the miners, who had to make a request to the court, which then allowed delivery under the supervision of the keeper of the relevant walk.[68] In 1677 the supply to the miners was being tightly controlled, no oak or beech being allotted but only underwood, such as birch and holly.[69] The main business of the attachment court presumably remained the punishment of vert offences, but how it functioned in practice during the late 17th and the 18th centuries is not known, as no court records have been found.

Opposition to the inclosures from the commoners took its usual form, with incidents of fence-breaking and arson reported in the late 1670s, but the reformed administration remained in control of the situation. In 1677 it was

reported that the timber trees in the inclosures were doing well and three years later some inclosures were said to be ready to be laid open.[70] By 1688 most had been opened and plans were put in hand to make new ones.[71] At the close of the year, however, the programme received a serious setback. The Revolution was a signal for riots, and the new plantations were damaged, the Speech House attacked, and two other lodges badly damaged.[72] In the new reign Sir John Guise, who was in favour with William III, tried to obtain a grant to manage the inclosures, but a commission of inquiry, reporting in 1692, decided in favour of continuing public control.[73]

The position of the Tory duke of Beaufort (formerly marquess of Worcester), the mainstay of government policy towards the Forest, was severely weakened by the Revolution. The riots took a personal direction by the breaking of the fences of Whitemead park, which he held as part of his lease of the St. Briavels castle estate. Tacit support for the rioters came from some local gentry, who revived a claim made under the Commonwealth that Whitemead was not legally imparked, and incidents of fence-breaking continued there for the next 10 years.[74] In 1697 Beaufort, having failed to sign the Association in support of William III, forfeited his offices and was replaced by Lord Dursley, later earl of Berkeley, whose son some years later acquired the lease of the St. Briavels castle estate. Together with the lord lieutenancy of the county, the constableship remained with the Berkeleys for all but a few years of the 18th century; during the minority of the 5th earl in mid century their political allies, the lords Ducie and Chedworth, held it but were followed briefly by Norborne Berkeley, who was of the rival Beaufort interest.[75] The office of deputy constable was multiplied in the 18th century, the constables deputing up to six of their friends from among the local gentry.[76]

The constableship, through the power of appointing the keepers and directing part of their work, remained a more than purely formal post. It had been intended that the other chief foresters would also continue to have a role in the reformed administration: Worcester's instructions of c. 1680 assigned the woodwards and the serjeants-in-fee to act in support of the keepers.[77] By the early 18th century, however, those offices had only a nominal function. The office of woodward retained significance in the 18th century only through the ancient privileges still claimed by some holders, particularly the Gage family. The Gage's Highmeadow estate,[78] besides incorporating the offices of woodwards of Staunton and Bicknor, also had ironworks, so that rights in the demesne woods had a value in terms of cordwood. In 1743 Thomas Gage, 1st

[64] *Cal. Treas. Bks.* 1672–5, 508.
[65] Cf. *3rd Rep. Com. Woods* (1788), 25, 27.
[66] Glos. R.O., D 36/Q 2.
[67] *Cal. Treas. Bks.* 1679–80, 641.
[68] Badminton Mun. FmS/G 2/4/4.
[69] Glos. R.O., D 1677/GG 1223.
[70] Ibid.; Hart, *Royal Forest*, 298–9.
[71] *Cal. Treas. Bks.* 1685–9, 2001.
[72] Ibid. 1689–92, 586–7.

[73] Ibid. 901, 1047, 1156–7, 1495–7; for Guise, cf. ibid. 1693–6, 117, 381.
[74] Badminton Mun. FmH 2/1/1; N.L.W., Mynde Park MS. 1666; for the earlier claim, *Cal. S.P. Dom.* 1653–4, 326, 405.
[75] Below, Wardens; cf. Badminton Mun. FmS/G 2/4/5; Glos. R.O., D 340A/C 26.
[76] Badminton Mun. FmS/G 2/3/3, f. 6.
[77] Ibid. FmS/G 2/4/4.
[78] For the est., above, Staunton, manor.

Viscount Gage, laid claim to all windfall trees and the bark of all trees felled by Treasury warrant in his bailiwicks, and his son was still pursuing those claims in 1782 and seems to have established the right to windfalls. A claim by the 1st Viscount to the right of soil in part of the demesne woodland at Hangerberry adjoining his English Bicknor manor was resolved in the Crown's favour in 1753, but another of his claims, to the manorial waste of part of Coleford against the earl of Berkeley, lessee of the royal manor of Newland, was a source of dispute for the rest of the century. In the disputes, particularly the last mentioned, political rivalry played an important part; the large number of freeholders in the Forest parishes gave a particular value to influence enjoyed there by county magnates.[79]

Other officers of the old administration, the verderers, had a continuing role as presidents of the courts of attachment and swanimote and they sometimes acted in a more general representative role, for example memorializing the government about abuses by other Forest officers.[80] During the period the four posts remained firmly in the control of the local gentry, the Colchesters of Westbury, Pyrkes of Littledean, Joneses of Nass, and Crawley-Boeveys of Flaxley serving for several generations in succession.[81]

The reorganized administration maintained a firm hold on the Forest into the early 18th century. The inclosure policy was continued c. 1706 when a new 353-acre inclosure called Buckholt was fenced off,[82] and at about the same time the thinning of beech and other species from around the oaks in the older plantations was instituted on a rolling programme.[83] It would be many years before the oaks matured for use as ship timber, but the Forest produced a regular income by the sale of cordwood to ironmasters. Until c. 1712 most was taken by the Foleys and their partners for their local ironworks.[84]

NEGLECT AND ABUSES 1720-1808. From c. 1720 the Treasury and its officals ceased their close attention to the affairs of the Forest, allowing the salaried local officers to become lax. The pressure from commoners, miners, and potential wood-stealers and encroachers, kept in check during the late 17th century by energetic management backed by regular commissions of inquiry, was no longer contained. In 1722 the faltering inclosure programme was commented on.[85] In 1736 the conservator Christopher Bond reported that the plantations were being raided by wood-stealers, the commoners' animals were being allowed in at the prohibited seasons, encroachment and the building of cabins had

begun again, and officers were conniving at the offences.[86] In 1742 the keepers, on whom much depended, were accused of poaching and of corruption in executing royal warrants for venison, and one was said to have taken wood for his own cooperage business.[87] In 1746 the Forest courts were said to be greatly neglected;[88] the attachment court later lapsed, and by 1788 the annual swanimote was said to be held largely as a matter of form.[89]

Throughout the mid 18th century wood stealing flourished, encroachments made a steady advance, and commoning escaped regulation. Two attempts to revive the inclosure programme in the period both failed. In 1758 John Pitt, the Crown's surveyor general of woods, was authorized to make an inclosure of 2,000 a. in the centre of the Forest south of the Cinderford to Speech House road, but it was soon broken open. In another scheme in 1770 Pitt made six dispersed inclosures, which he thought would be easier to police than a single large block,[90] but in them also the walls were broken down, the fencing carried off for fuel or for sale, and the young trees destroyed. Only one of the six contained a worthwhile quantity of young timber in 1788.[91] Much of the stolen wood was sold to coopers for barrel staves, for which cider production on Severnside and in south Herefordshire created a constant demand, or to wheelwrights. As in the 13th century, Bristol was one of the main markets for the trade in stolen wood, which c. 1780 was said to be brazenly carried on through Gatcombe. Much of the wood ostensibly supplied to miners was sold by the recipients, because no inquiry was made into how much was needed or its eventual destination; in 1787 the deputy surveyor of the Forest, Thomas Blunt, himself offered the opinion that less than half of that supplied went into the mines.[92]

The failure to check encroachment on the edges of the royal demesne allowed the beginnings of its fringe of hamlets. By 1752 there were already 134 cottages on the demesne, and by 1787 there were 585 and 1,359 a. of land had been encroached.[93] The number of commoners increased during the period, with the new squatters on the demesne and some men from parishes which had no customary right putting in animals. With the failure of the inclosure programme, the animals ranged through most of the demesne woodland and waste. Such measures as were taken by the keepers were mainly for their own pecuniary benefit rather than in the interests of strict enforcement. The prohibition on sheep had lapsed again by the 1780s.[94]

The burgeoning illegalities were backed by

79   Glos. R.O., D 1677/GG 1180–1228, 1259–94, 1299; Berkeley Cast. Mun., General Ser. T, box 25.
80   Berkeley Cast. Mun., General Ser. T, box 25, papers about keepers' misdemeanours 1742; petition about roads 1736/7; 3rd Rep. Com. Woods (1788), 77–8.
81   Hart, Verderers, 117–21, 135.
82   3rd Rep. Com. Woods (1788), 113; cf. Glos. R.O., D 2026/X 28.   83   Cal. Treas. Bks. 1705–6, 547.
84   Ibid. 1703, 313; 1705–6, 43, 62, 477; Cal. Treas. Papers, 1702–7, pp. 408, 412–13; 1708–14, pp. 305, 353.
85   Cal. Treas. Papers, 1720–8, p. 121.

86   3rd Rep. Com. Woods (1788), 22–3.
87   Berkeley Cast. Mun., General Ser. T, box 25, papers about keepers' misdemeanours.
88   Glos. R.O., D 1677/GG 1235.
89   3rd Rep. Com. Woods (1788), 38.
90   P.R.O., E 178/6917; Glos. R.O., D 1677/GG 1270.
91   3rd Rep. Com. Woods (1788), 108, 113.
92   Ibid. 29, 82–3, 88–9, 105–6, 109.
93   Above, Settlement, intro. (Table II).
94   Below, this section; 3rd Rep. Com. Woods (1788), 28, 85, 109–10.

violence or the threat of it. In 1735 a gang, thought to come from the Clearwell area, attacked several of the keepers' lodges and pulled down the adjoining pounds; later it returned, armed, in an attempt to rescue one of its number who had been arrested by a magistrate.[95] In 1742 two of the keepers claimed that they lived in fear of their lives, beleaguered by assaults on their lodges and threatened by anonymous letters.[96] In an incident at Yorkley in 1780 some of the keepers were wounded while attempting to prevent a gang of men in disguise from felling trees.[97]

The abuses were encouraged by a system of fees and benefits that the officers received in the course of their various duties. It was to their financial advantage that wood should be stolen, timber felled unnecessarily, and animals illegally commoned. Thomas Blunt, who was appointed deputy surveyor of the Forest in 1780 at a salary of £50, received in addition between £300 and £500 a year from other perquisites, for which he was not required to make any account. He received a small cash fee for each cord of wood made from timber trees felled by Treasury warrant for the navy and for each tree felled for the miners, and he took the tops of all trees felled for the navy but rejected by the navy purveyors, a share of the offal wood from the miners' timber, and parts of any trees stolen and then recovered. The perquisites of the six keepers included fees for providing the miners' timber, taking deer for the Crown, and releasing impounded cattle. The last encouraged them to make regular drifts of their walks during the fence month and winter haining but not to prevent cattle being put back in those periods or to limit the numbers by keeping a check on who was running them. In the case of stolen trees that were recovered, they took the wood if, when found, it was already cut into pieces for coopers or wheelwrights, an incentive to delay action. In the early 1780s the keepers' salaries of £22 each were supplemented to over £100 a year by the fees and perquisites, and the keeper of Speech House walk, whose beat supplied most of the miners' timber, received more than £200. There were accusations that bribes in cash were taken by the keepers to overlook encroachments and by the deputy surveyor for awarding cordwood contracts, but the system made it possible for the officers to profit without the more blatant, and verifiable, forms of corruption.[98]

Local controls on the officers had mostly lapsed. The execution of all warrants for felling should, under the Act of 1668, have been supervised by two J.P.s, but in 1787 one local J.P., Charles Edwin of Clearwell, said that he had given up attending when he found his advice ignored. The lapse of the attachment court removed a means of monitoring regularly the supply of wood to the mines; in the 1780s the keepers made a return only once a year, to the swanimote.[99]

Commissioners reporting on the Crown woodlands in 1788 summed up the situation in Dean as one in which the different fees, perquisites, and emoluments 'are so many premiums for the encouragement of waste in the felling, measurement, and sale of the timber, of extravagance in the expenditure of the produce, and of profusion in the delivery of the timber to the miners, while they tend to the destruction of the inclosures, and the prevention of the growth of wood in succession'. They could find no documentary record of how 'a system of management so absurd and ruinous' had evolved, and concluded that it had been introduced gradually in the years since government control lapsed.[1]

In spite of all the problems, supplies of good ship timber were provided by the Forest in the later 18th century. The work of the administrators of Charles II's reign began to bear fruit in the 1760s as the oaks in their inclosures came to maturity. In the 26 years from 1761 to 1786 the naval dockyards at Plymouth, Deptford, and Woolwich received a total of 16,573 loads of oak; a load was 50 cubic feet, providing on average a ton of shipping. Dean supplied only a very small proportion of navy's total annual requirement, but much of the estimated 2,000 loads a year from the royal forests as a whole came from Dean and in quality it was regarded as second to none. The timber supplied to the navy in those 26 years was valued at £31,723; timber rejected for navy use and sold to local shipbuilders at Chepstow, Newnham, Gatcombe, and elsewhere produced £16,226; and of the side products of fellings and thinnings, cordwood sold to ironmasters produced £17,178 and oak bark, which went to local tanners and for export from Severnside to Ireland, produced £3,914. During the 26 years administrative costs totalled £41,657, including over £11,000 spent on roads, which served purposes besides timber production, and other sums on Crown projects unconnected with the Forest. It could be shown, therefore, that for all the waste and abuse, the woods were being run at a profit.[2]

Lord Gage, pursuing his claims in 1782, believed that because of the strength of the commoners' opposition and the dispiriting effect of the failure of the inclosures of 1758 and 1770 the Forest would never be replanted.[3] By that time, however, its demonstrable value to the navy, highlighted by the onset of another naval war, had encouraged a further attempt to halt the decline. John Pitt, who since 1771 had made a number of representations to the Treasury for firmer measures, was authorized to try a limited new scheme; 323 a. were inclosed c. 1783 and the old Buckholt inclosure was repaired. Thanks to tighter policing, including the appointment of a watchman, the new inclosures remained intact in 1788,[4] though still under threat; early the following year the fence at Buckholt was deliberately set on fire.[5] Also introduced was a system of financial rewards to informers, which led to regular convictions of timber-stealers before the

95 *Glouc. Jnl.* 22 July 1735.
96 Berkeley Cast. Mun., General Ser. T, box 25, papers about keepers' misdemeanours.   97 *Glouc. Jnl.* 1 Jan. 1781.
98 *3rd Rep. Com. Woods* (1788), 27–39, 81, 84–7, 109–10.
99 Ibid. 32, 79, 81.   1 Ibid. 38–9.

2 Ibid. 56, 99–101; for the load, Hart, *Royal Forest*, 323 and n.
3 Glos. R.O., D 1677/GG 1290.
4 *3rd Rep. Com. Woods* (1788), 24, 30, 92, 113.
5 *Glouc. Jnl.* 19 Jan. 1789.

magistrates in the 1780s. As it swelled the emoluments of the officers, who were usually the claimants to the rewards, it was not in other ways conducive to good management.[6]

In 1788, the first time for many years that Dean received close attention from the government, the commission of inquiry into Crown woods and land revenues made a detailed critique of the Forest's administration and suggested remedies and future policy. It recommended inclosure up to the statutory 11,000 a., appeasement of the commoners by allowing grazing in the open land all the year round, negotiation with the miners to give legal status to their rights in return for the surrender of their free timber, tough action against encroachers other than those holding anciently established plots, stricter procedure for felling timber, destruction of the deer as a cause of damage to new inclosures and an incentive to lawlessness, and introduction of turnpikes.[7]

Little was done, however, during the next 20 years, and most of the commission's proposals were not implemented until the 1830s. The recent small inclosures and Buckholt, a total of c. 680 a., remained the only land managed for future timber needs, and abuses continued. No steps were taken to check the encroachers, who took a further 725 a. of the demesne and built almost 300 new cottages between 1787 and 1812.[8] The earlier encroachments were not disturbed, so that those made before 1787 had eventually to be accepted as freeholds. Claims to rights in Staunton and Bicknor bailiwicks continued to disturb the Forest administration in 1801, though at that time the woodward by tenure, the 3rd Viscount Gage, was prompted and eventually embarrassed by his local agent, James Davies of Eastbach; Davies had a personal interest through his share in an ironmaking firm that enjoyed the Highmeadow cordwood concession and he had also developed an antipathy to certain Forest officials.[9]

The only recommendation of the commissioners carried out before the close of the century was the turnpiking of the roads under an Act of 1796. The motive was partly to aid the removal of the navy's timber, for the road leading to the main shipping points at Gatcombe and Purton was included.[10] Supplies to the dockyards continued in increased volume during the French wars, with 18,839 loads sent in the six years 1803–8.[11] It required c. 500,000 loads[12] to maintain the navy on its wartime footing over those six years, so the Forest's contribution was a small one, but Dean, together with the New Forest, came to loom large in government plans to meet future needs. The authority of Admiral Nelson was given to those plans in a report written in 1803 after he visited the area the previous year.[13]

REPLANTING AND REORGANIZATION.

A replanting programme for the Forest, equal in scale to that of the 1660s, was carried out under an Act of parliament of 1808. The Act confirmed the provision in the Act of 1668 for the inclosure of 11,000 a., empowered the making of new inclosures up to that amount, and imposed heavy penalties to protect inclosures.[14] The programme was planned and partly executed under the direction of Sylvester Douglas, Lord Glenbervie, surveyor general of woods 1803–6 and 1807–14 and chief commissioner from 1810 in the new body set up to manage the Crown estates, the Commissioners of Woods, Forests, and Land Revenues. James Davies of Eastbach was appointed deputy surveyor for Dean in 1806 with his son Edward as his assistant, and in 1808 Edward (called Edward Machen from 1816) succeeded to his father's post.[15]

Work on the new inclosures began by 1806, before the passing of the new Act,[16] and by 1818 over 25 had been planted and surrounded by stone walls or earth banks topped with gorse. They were planted almost entirely with oak, though other species, including conifers, were planted to shelter the young oaks.[17] The new plantations included most of Whitemead park, which was surrendered by the earl of Berkeley, lessee of the St. Briavels castle estate, in 1807, and farmland at Ellwood, in Newland, which the Commissioners of Woods bought in 1817. A farmhouse at Whitemead was improved to become the official residence of the deputy surveyor.[18] In 1817 the Commissioners bought Lord Gage's Highmeadow estate, which included c. 2,350 a. of woodland, mainly at Mailscot and Hadnock (Mon.), and in the late 1820s they planted large areas of the estate's farmland in Staunton and English Bicknor parishes and Coleford tithing. Highmeadow woods were subsequently administered with the Forest though accounted for as a separate Crown estate; in 1849 they covered 3,438 a. and in terms of net income occupied third place among the Crown woodlands in England, after the New Forest and Dean and before the various small royal forests.[19]

Under Glenbervie and Edward Machen, the administration was strengthened and improved, partly by installing woodmen, housed in a series of small lodges and each paid a salary of £39 a year, to police and maintain the inclosures.[20] Timber sales were more closely supervised, with

[6] 3rd Rep. Com. Woods (1788), 35; Glouc. Jnl. 15, 22 Dec. 1788; 19 Jan. 1789.
[7] 3rd Rep. Com. Woods (1789), 41–8.
[8] Above, Settlement, intro. (Table II).
[9] Glos. R.O., D 1677/GG 1545, nos. 64–80; cf. N.L.W., Dunraven MSS. 273, letter 6 Mar. 1790.
[10] Above, Settlement, intro.
[11] Hart, Royal Forest, 206–7.
[12] 1st Rep. Com. Woods, H.C. 357, p. 19 (1812), xii.
[13] Hart, Royal Forest, 312–14.
[14] Dean and New Forest Act, 48 Geo. III, c. 72.
[15] D.N.B. s.v. Douglas, Sylvester; P.R.O., LR 4/20/1–9; LR

4/21–4; for the Davieses, Trans. B.G.A.S. lxiv. 96–7, 105.
[16] Barnhill Inclosure was dated 1806 on its woodman's lodge: inscr. on stone at Dean Heritage mus., Soudley (1994); and the first of the new lodges, at Lea Bailey, were built in 1806 or 1807: P.R.O., LR 4/20/6.
[17] Nicholls, Forest of Dean, 91–103, 107; for the inclosures, ibid. map at end; Atkinson, Map of Dean Forest (1847).
[18] Above, Newland, intro.; manors.
[19] Above, Staunton, manor; Select Cttee. on Woods (1849), 145, 482.
[20] P.R.O., LR 4/26; Select Cttee. on Woods (1849), 163; above, Settlement, forest lodges.

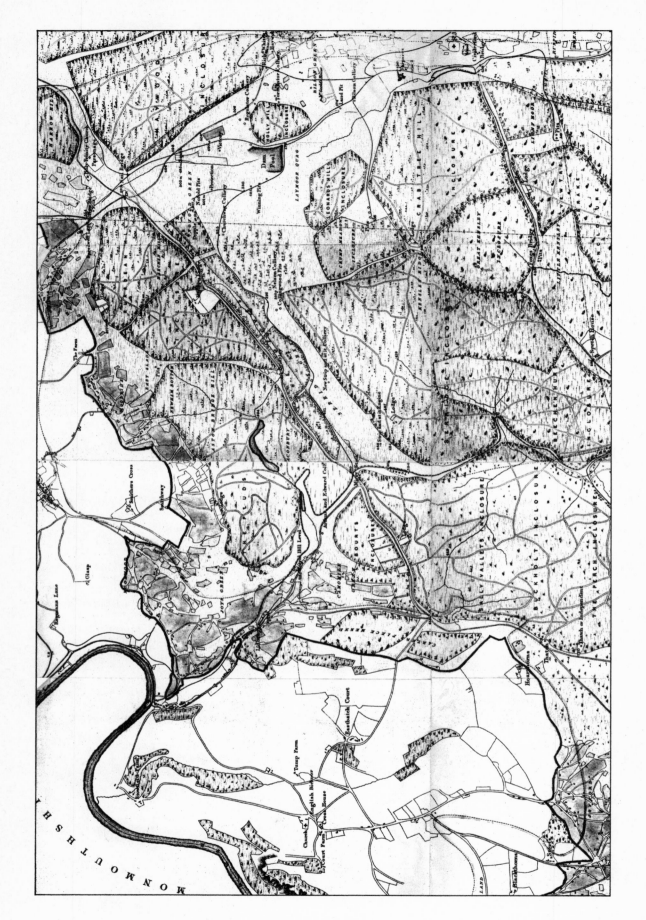

FIG. 23. INCLOSURES IN THE NORTH OF THE FOREST AND COTTAGES AND OLD ENCROACHMENTS AT JOY'S GREEN, RUARDEAN WOODSIDE, AND RUARDEAN HILL, 1847

J.P.s, the verderers, and the keepers all required to sign the deputy surveyor's accounts.[21] The amount of timber supplied to the miners was much restricted after 1809 when an Act for building the Severn and Wye tramroad, which became the main means of carrying out coal, ruled that no miner in receipt of free timber could make use of the tramroad.[22] The right to timber was abolished altogether by an Act regulating the mines in 1838.[23]

To help preserve the inclosures and prevent further reduction of the royal demesne, the attachment court of the verderers was revived. In 1829 verderers in royal forests were empowered to summon and convict those damaging inclosures or making encroachments,[24] and in 1838 an Act regularizing the tenure of the encroachments in Dean confirmed that new role of its verderers and required them to make annual returns of informations and convictions.[25] From c. 1830 the attachment court was held again at the Speech House before the verderers with a local solicitor as steward. The steward, who had the style of steward of the courts of attachment and swanimote, though only the former was revived, received the fines in payment; a small salary was added in 1870. Informations were presented to the court by the keepers of the walks,[26] who were instructed to patrol the whole of their walks twice a week, watching for encroachment, illegal digging of turf or soil, and offences against the vert and venison. The encroachments presented were usually minor, such as garden walls and outbuildings of cottages intruding a short way over the boundaries, and were fined at small sums of 5s. or of 10s. Timber stealing and poaching offences were rarely presented, most being dealt with before the magistrates, and poaching cases ended altogether with the removal of the deer from the Forest in the early 1850s.[27] In the early 1840s the court was held eight times a year, roughly the ancient 40-day interval, but the volume of business did not warrant that number of sessions and by the early 1860s the number was reduced by adjournments to only two a year.[28] In the period 1863–73 the court made c. 10 convictions a year and imposed a total of £60 in fines.[29] By the end of the century the court was often adjourned through many months because of lack of business,[30] and after 1903, apart from a token exercise in 1924, it dealt with no offences.[31]

The established landowning families of the area, the Crawley-Boeveys, Bathursts, Colchesters (later Colchester-Wemysses), Pyrkes, Probyns, and Joneses, continued to dominate the office of verderer in the 19th century. Vacancies were usually filled without a contested election, son often replacing father.[32] In 1863 when some

of the coalowners threatened a contest it was seen as a challenge to a long-established tacit understanding, besides raising fears of expensive and divisive contests, all freeholders of the county being entitled to vote.[33] A contest at the next vacancy was, however, the last until 1930.[34]

Otherwise, the ancient Forest administration ended in the early 19th century. In 1836, following the death of the duke of Beaufort, constable of St. Briavels and warden of the Forest, the two offices were vested in the Commissioners of Woods.[35] The St. Briavels castle estate, by then with only few assets, was taken in hand by the Crown in 1858.[36] Two of the woodwardships, those of Staunton and English Bicknor bailiwicks, passed to the Commissioners by the purchase of the Highmeadow estate, and no mention of the woodwardships has been found after the 1830s when the holder of Blakeney revived a claim to grant gales of quarries.[37]

WOODLAND MANAGEMENT AND COMMONING 1820-1914.

The new inclosures and the tighter administration brought to prominence again the question of commoning rights in the Forest. Increasingly during the 19th century the rights were exercised by inhabitants of the Forest hamlets rather than by those of the surrounding parishes. Forest commoners, mostly working or retired miners with small flocks of sheep, were putting in the greater number of animals by 1839,[38] though in 1860 people from 15 parishes still put in animals, the largest numbers from Newland and Ruardean. The payment of herbage money to the lessee of St. Briavels lapsed c. 1835, probably because the majority of places had paid it out of the old parish poor rate.[39] The commoners from the parishes were more open to schemes for extinguishing or regulating the rights, while the Foresters defended their claims with the traditional belligerence.

By the start of the 19th century regular drifts of the Forest in the prohibited seasons had been largely abandoned, the owners of animals paying fees to the keepers to leave them in. The commoners petitioned to end those fees in 1820 and 1823, but in 1823 the Commissioners of Woods ordered that clearance in the prohibited seasons be resumed.[40] Reinclosure of much of the Forest had at first been accepted without trouble, but resentment grew later and became combined with the Foresters' grievances about the invasion of their mining rights by outsider capitalists. Over several days in June 1831, under the leadership of Warren James, a Bream miner, groups of commoners assembled and, after giving notice of their intention to the authorities, destroyed about half of the estimated 120 miles

[21] *Select Cttee. on Woods* (1849), 131.
[22] Lydney and Lydbrook Rly. Act, 49 Geo. III, c. 159 (Local and Personal), s. 75.
[23] Dean Forest Mines Act, 1 & 2 Vic. c. 43, s. 30.
[24] Crown Forests Act, 10 Geo. IV, c. 50, ss. 100–5.
[25] Dean Forest Encroachments Act, 1 & 2 Vic. c. 42.
[26] P.R.O., F 3/145–6.
[27] Ibid. F 16/20–1.
[28] Ibid. F 3/145.
[29] *Dean Forest Select Cttee.* (1874), 34.
[30] P.R.O., F 16/22.
[31] Glos. R.O., D 6993/1/1.
[32] Ibid. list at front; Hart, *Verderers*, 135–49.
[33] P.R.O., F 3/145.
[34] Glos. R.O., D 6993/1/1, press cutting 3 Nov. 1930.
[35] Below, Wardens.
[36] Above, St. Briavels, manors.
[37] *5th Rep. Dean Forest Com.* 66, 71.
[38] *Select Cttee. on Woods* (1849), 134–5.
[39] P.R.O., F 3/128, letters 29 Nov. 1860; 1 Jan., 4 Feb. 1861.
[40] Badminton Mun. FmM 2/5/3.

of the walls and banks around the inclosures. The riot Act was read several times but no person was attacked by the rioters and order was easily restored when troops were brought in. The rioters were treated fairly leniently: James was sentenced to death but his sentence commuted to transportation, a few others were imprisoned or bound over, and some escaped prosecution by agreeing to help repair the inclosures.[41] The main result was to highlight local grievances, prompting a commission of inquiry into the Forest in 1832, which laid the groundwork for regularizing mining and the tenure of the encroachments. Commoning rights, however, remained a seemingly intractable problem. A meeting called to discuss plans for extinguishing the rights in 1836 broke up when intimidated by a mob of Foresters.[42] Tension eased for a few years after that, however, when to aid the negotiations to settle the regulation of mining there was a tacit agreement to end the regular drifts.[43]

In 1849 the Forest administration comprised the deputy surveyor Edward Machen, two assistant deputy surveyors, four keepers, whose numbers had been reduced from six before 1841, in the old lodges, and 24 woodmen occupying the new lodges in the inclosures. The office of conservator of the Forest, still held by a member of the Jones family in the early 1820s, had apparently lapsed by the middle of the century. About 70 woodcutters were permanently employed in 1849 and another 100 or so labourers might be taken on when new inclosures were made or old ones opened.[44] After c. 13 or 14 years' growth, thinning of the plantations began and after c. 30 years the inclosures were opened. The first was opened in 1841, and c. 2,040 a. more land were inclosed during the 1840s.[45] In the new inclosures much greater use was made of conifers (usually larch) as 'nurses' to protect the young oaks.

The surviving ancient plantations continued to supply the navy until 1833 when there was failure to agree a price; no more was then sent until 1852 and 1853, when great 'falls' of timber produced 7,800 loads for the dockyards. Timber rejected by the navy continued to be sold to local merchants and shipbuilders, but in the 1840s the operation of a 'ring' restricted profits: Thomas Swift, a Monmouth shipbuilder and timber merchant, took the bulk of the timber from the Forest and Highmeadow woods, leaving other local buyers to tender for the private woodlands of the area. In the early 1850s, however, there were several Monmouth, Chepstow, and Bristol buyers, besides one or two railway builders from Birmingham and Newcastle. In the old woodlands, which had been estimated to contain 22,880 loads in 1808, only 4,500 loads remained by 1854. The thinnings from the new planta-

tions, mainly offered to the coalowners at monthly sales, provided a steadily increasing income, £611 in 1828, £2,927 in 1838, and, after the final abolition of the free allocation to miners, £4,711 in 1848.[46] Over all, however, the woodlands were a potential rather than immediate asset, particularly in the years when no timber was supplied to the navy: in the eight years ending at Easter 1852, the income from sales of timber, thinnings, and oak bark averaged £10,033 a year while management costs averaged £11,220, though the addition of the income from the Crown's mineral rights, averaging £4,420 a year, brought the whole Forest estate into modest profit.[47]

The bulk of the oak planted in the years 1808–18 was expected to mature for naval shipbuilding in the first or second decade of the 20th century.[48] Even while warships were still being built with wooden hulls there were doubts about the concentration on that long-term investment and suggestions that some unplanted areas should be used for cultivation.[49] Machen, the deputy surveyor, remained wedded to the original policy and unsympathetic to schemes that deviated in favour of more immediate profit. In the early 1850s, when he had been in the post more than 40 years, T. F. Kennedy, one of the Commissioners of Woods, criticized his administration as overmanned and hidebound, lacking energy in finding markets for the remaining old timber and inefficient in some of its forestry practices. Against Machen's wishes Kennedy had a sawmill set up to produce plank in the hope of attracting more buyers from further afield; local buyers took the trees away uncut.[50] Machen offered his resignation in 1853 but he was supported by the Treasury, and he retired the following year, to be replaced by Sir James Campbell, Bt.[51]

With the introduction of ironclad warships in the 1860s discussion about the future of the Forest became more urgent. Supplies to the navy ceased c. 1865, the dockyards having a good stock in hand and later finding it easier to meet their limited needs from private contractors.[52] In 1869 a meeting called at the Speech House showed strong support among the wealthier local inhabitants for inclosing and selling the Forest, reserving a portion for public recreation grounds and cottage gardens. The scheme was not pursued: negotiations with the miners, at that time over wages, once more made the opening of the commoning question unwise. The scheme was revived in 1874 when a Select Committee inquired into Dean,[53] but a Bill introduced in parliament in 1875 was allowed to lapse after evidence of continuing strong opposition.[54]

During the late 19th century the Crown's profits from the woodland of the Forest were modest, as

41 For a detailed account, R. Anstis, *Warren James and Dean Forest Riots* (1986).
42 *Select Cttee. on Woods* (1849), 135.
43 Fisher, *Custom and Capitalism*, 148.
44 *Select Cttee. on Woods* (1849), 128, 137–8, 163; for the conservator, P.R.O., LR 4/27, 31.
45 *Select Cttee. on Woods* (1849) 132, 164; P.R.O., E 178/6917.
46 *Select Cttee. on Woods* (1849), 129–32, 146, 160, 163–4; *Select Cttee. on Crown Forests* (1854), 10–17.

47 *Select Cttee. on Crown Forests* (1854), 161.
48 *Select Cttee. on Woods* (1849), 133; *Select Cttee. on Crown Forests* (1854), 14.
49 *Select Cttee. on Woods* (1849), 184 sqq.
50 *Select Cttee. on Crown Forests* (1854), 13–14, 17–18, 34–5, 43–8. 51 Ibid. 53; Nicholls, *Forest of Dean*, 137–8.
52 *Dean Forest Select Cttee.* (1874), 127, 136.
53 Ibid. 124–7, 144, 152.
54 Fisher, *Custom and Capitalism*, 161–2; Glos. R.O., D 3921/I/66.

distinct from those from the mineral rights, where the new deep coal mines yielded substantial sums in royalties. The net annual profit from the woods in the ten years 1865–75 averaged £2,992, and in the years 1875–85 £2,878.[55] The mines, as they got deeper, were an increasingly important market for timber and were taking 6–7,000 tons a year by 1874, but the mineowners kept the price low by refusing to bid against each other in public auctions.[56] In the 1880s the price fell because of competition from imported timber.[57]

In 1897, when only 4,665 a. of the Forest remained inclosed, the permanent staff had been reduced to the deputy surveyor and 4 chief administrative officers, 3 keepers, and 14 woodmen. Only 229 a. of older oak, from the planting in the late 17th century and the 1780s, then remained; 10,833 a. of early 19th-century oak dominated the Forest, and there were another 3,002 a. of plantations of the 1840s and later.[58] The drastic thinning out of the plantations had produced stunted trees with long, low branches, suitable for shipbuilding timber but not for other purposes. Past management policies were criticized by two forestry experts, who maintained that the planting of pure oak had damaged the fertility of the soil, which in the past had been preserved by the mixture of beech and oak.[59] New inclosures made from 1897 onwards under Philip Baylis, who succeeded Campbell as deputy surveyor in 1893, were planted with a mixture of oak, beech, larch, and chestnut; only where the ground was suitable was oak alone planted. By 1911 the inclosed woods had reached again the statutory 11,000 a.[60] The Forest began to be used to train foresters when a forestry school was opened in 1904.[61] In 1913 to provide another use for loppings and thinnings of the hardwood trees a wood distillery plant was established at Cannop.[62]

Both Campbell and Baylis challenged the claims of the commoners, testing the legality of the exercise of rights by holders of the former encroachments and of the commoning of sheep. Sheep, which were harder than cattle to exclude from the inclosures, had become the dominant animal commoned. A drift ordered by Campbell at the start of the winter haining of 1864 found 5,868 sheep, 233 horned cattle, 218 horses and colts, 246 donkeys, 86 pigs, and 1 goat. The drift was repeated in 1865, causing some unrest and forcible rescues of impounded animals, but the Commissioners of Woods, worried at the possibility of a serious outbreak of violence, persuaded Campbell to follow a more cautious policy.[63] In 1889, while still maintaining that the majority of commoners had no legal right, he was not restricting or interfering with any who

put animals in.[64] Baylis, before embarking on his new inclosures, sought counsel's opinion in 1896. A barrister concluded that the Act of 1668, while confirming the rights of the parishioners as claimed in 1634, ruled out the acquisition of any right by prescription, and that such rights could not in any case be attached to encroachments. He was less certain whether the claims of 1634 could be interpreted as excluding sheep. The Crown law officers, to whom the question was twice referred, agreed that there was no prima facie case for commoning sheep.[65] The numbers of sheep in the Forest continued to grow, a census of 1898 finding 10,851. The 236 different owners were then almost all Foresters, the great majority having flocks of under 50.[66] By 1905, when the impounding of animals found in the new inclosures and on a new road built between Whitecroft and Mirystock reawakened the issue, the commoners had organized themselves in a protection society, and a new Commoners' Association was formed in 1919.[67]

THE FOREST IN THE 20TH CENTURY. In the First World War the need for timber for military purposes gave a new value to Dean's oak plantations, which were then reaching maturity. Established management practices were subordinated to the immediate demand: some areas were clear felled and any replanting was usually wholly with conifers. The early 19th-century plantations had been reduced to c. 5,000 a. by the end of the war. The wood distillation operation was also much enlarged to supply the munitions industry.[68] In 1919, with the policy of providing a strategic timber reserve dominating forestry, a plan to progressively change the composition of Dean's woods to three quarters conifer was devised. In the 1920s, however, when the Forestry Commission had been established and had acquired much land elsewhere suitable for conifers, it was decided to plant hardwood, mainly oak, wherever Dean's soil was suitable.[69] The Forest, together with Highmeadow woods and some smaller Crown woods in the area, was transferred from the Commissioners of Woods to the Forestry Commission in 1924.[70] In the Second World War production was again massively increased, both in the form of hardwood from the 19th-century oaks and softwood from the more recently planted conifers. The forestry company of the Royal Engineers worked in the woodlands and by 1942 had 11 sawmills at work; 4,864 a. were clear felled. The cover of the trees was also used to store large quantities of ammunition and other equipment.[71]

55 Select Cttee. on Woods (1889), 302–3.
56 Dean Forest Select Cttee. (1874), 138–9.
57 Select Cttee. on Woods (1889), 32.
58 Hart, Royal Forest, 227; P.R.O., F 3/319.
59 Hart, Royal Forest, 226–8; Rep. Dean Forest Cttee. (1958), 6.
60 Glos. R.O., D 6993/1/1, mins. of incl. com. 1911; Hart, Royal Forest, 229–30.
61 Below, Educ., technical schs. and colleges.
62 Above, Industry, other ind. and trade.
63 Fisher, Custom and Capitalism, 148–58.

64 Select Cttee. on Woods (1889), 30.
65 Rep. Dean Forest Cttee. (1958), 21–4.
66 Fisher, Custom and Capitalism, 148.
67 P.R.O., F 3/265; Glos. R.O., D 3921/II/8.
68 Hart, Royal Forest, 234–5; National Forest Park Guide to Dean Forest (Forestry Com. 1947), 40.
69 P.R.O., F 3/1286; Rep. Dean Forest Cttee. (1958), 13.
70 Lond. Gaz. 25 Mar. 1924, pp. 2510–13; 5th Rep. Forestry Com. H.C. 107, pp. 13–14 (1924–5), xii.
71 Hart, Royal Forest, 337–8; National Forest Park Guide (1947), 41.

In the post-war replanting programme, which was completed by 1952, the predominance of broad-leaved trees over conifers was maintained:[72] in 1958 in the Forest, Highmeadow woods, and a number of smaller local woods acquired by the Forestry Commission 12,530 a. were under oak and other broadleaved trees, 5,886 a. under conifer, and 1,430 a. were mixed woodland.[73] During the earlier 20th century the usual peacetime markets for the larger timber produced were local sawmills at Parkend, Soudley, Monmouth, and elswhere and the Forest's mines continued to take large quantites for pit props. Much cordwood went to the Cannop distillation factory, which made charcoal until 1971, and a variety of uses for smaller produce included brush handles and agricultural tools, made at Longhope, and fences and hurdles, made at Huntley.[74]

In 1958 the surviving royal demesne of the Forest was calculated at 19,120 a., c. 16,400 a. of it woodland and the remainder waste (adjoining the Forest hamlets), roads, or the sites of mines and quarries. The Forestry Commission's Dean surveyorship then also administered another c. 8,000 a. in adjoining areas, including Highmeadow woods, the Tidenham Chase woods (1,865 a.) of the former Sedbury Park estate, acquired in the 1920s, and more recently acquired estate woodlands at Flaxley, Lydney, Clanna in Alvington, and Chase and Penyard in Herefordshire. The administration, still headed by a deputy surveyor with a small administrative staff at Whitemead Park, then employed 18 foresters and c. 180 forestry workers.[75] Following a reorganization in 1968, Whitemead Park was sold and a new local office opened at Coleford. Most of the woodman's and keeper's lodges, many of which had long been tenanted, were also sold.[76] In 1994, after further reorganization of the Forestry Commission, Dean and the outlying woods of the area formed an administrative district of the South and West Region of Forest Enterprise, the branch of the Commission concerned with state woodlands; the district's 11,113 ha. (27,460 a.) of woodland included 7,880 ha. (19,471 a.) in the Forest, where much former industrial land and waste had been planted. Under the deputy surveyor, based at Coleford, the employees were 8 administrative staff, 12 technical and supervisory staff, and 30 forestry workers; there were usually also 30 or 40 workers employed in the woods by contractors felling for buyers of timber.[77]

From 1960, as the national policy for a strategic timber reserve was modified, management plans for the Forest laid more stress on commercial enterprise and the planting of the most profitable species. Planting in the 1960s was mainly of conifer, so that broadleaved trees covered only 42 per cent by 1971 when, after public protests, the Minister of Agriculture

directed that the proportion should decrease no further. New broadleaf plantations were made later, and the policy being followed in 1994 was intended to achieve and maintain equal areas of conifer and broadleaf.[78] In 1991 oak remained the principal broadleaved species, forming 28 per cent of all the trees in the Forest and the outlying woods of the district, with 11 per cent beech and smaller amounts of ash, birch, and chestnut; the principal conifers were Douglas fir (16 per cent), Norway spruce (11 per cent), and larch and Corsican pine (each 7 per cent).[79] Large areas of the broadleaf woodland of the district, 1,708 ha. out of 5,290 ha. in 1992, were classed as conservation woods and managed as a public amenity with only limited commercial exploitation. They included the surviving early 19th-century oaks, which were mostly concentrated in the Cannop valley and around the Speech House, and the district's Wye Valley woodland. Also to be preserved as an amenity were 86 ha. of 'community woods', which bordered villages and hamlets, and some older stands conifers.[80] In the early 1990s the commercial enterprise in the district produced c. 50,000 cubic metres of timber a year, mostly in softwood. About 55 per cent of the output was in the form of saw logs, c. 20 per cent in chipwood for furniture and other uses, c. 15 per cent in pulpwood for paper and board, and the rest in firewood and fencing material; all timber was then sold standing. Coppicing was then employed only in parts of the conservation woodland, as a means of encouraging the growth of wild flowers.[81]

The running of sheep in the Forest, though a matter of less bitterness between the commoners and the authorities, had become of more general concern by the mid 20th century. Many traffic accidents were caused by sheep straying on the Forest's roads, there were complaints from the growing residential population about damage to gardens, and the Ministry of Agriculture was concerned at the possible spread of diseases by the unregulated grazing. In 1958, in the months before the autumn sheep sales, it was estimated that c. 6,000 sheep and 4,000 lambs were being grazed by c. 250 owners, still mostly part-time or retired miners. By then no horned cattle were pastured in the open Forest, but considerable numbers of pigs were turned into areas adjoining the villages and hamlets, and some geese and poultry. A parliamentary committee, appointed in 1955 and reporting in 1958, was largely concerned with that aspect of the Forest administration. Besides registration, branding, and the introduction of a stint, it suggested that parts of the Forest be set aside as fenced sheep reservations.[82] The Forestry Commission experimented inconclusively with a sheep inclosure, but other recommendations of the committee were not implemented.[83] In the 1970s, however, negotiations between the Commission

---

72 P.R.O., F 3/1286; Glos. R.O., D 6993/1/1, min. 5 Sept. 1952.
73 Hart, *Royal Forest*, 342; *Rep. Dean Forest Cttee.* (1958), 13.
74 P.R.O., F 3/1286, annual receipts 1925–30; *National Forest Park Guide* (1947), 43; cf. *Kelly's Dir. Glos.* (1931), 23, 245.   75 *Rep. Dean Forest Cttee.* (1958), 9, 11.
76 Glos. R.O., D 6993/1/1, mins. 26 Nov. 1967; 30 Aug. 1968; 20 Aug. 1969.
77 Inf. from Mr. J. E. Everard, deputy surveyor, Forest Enterprise, Coleford.

78 *Management of Broadleaf Woodland in Forest of Dean* (Forest Enterprise, 1992), 7; inf. from Mr. Everard.
79 *Forest Facts: Forest of Dean* (Forest Enterprise, c. 1992), 7.
80 *Management of Broadleaf Woodland*, 15–19, App. D.
81 Inf. from Mr. Everard.
82 *Rep. Dean Forest Cttee.* (1958), 18–20, 26–34; cf. *Country Life*, 31 Mar. 1960, 688–9.
83 Glos. R.O., D 6993/1/1, mins. 4 Sept. 1961; 6 Oct. 1962; 21 Dec. 1964; 26 Nov. 1967.

and the Commoners' Association led to an agreement in 1981, under which a limit of 5,000 ewes was introduced, 4,500 to be grazed by Association members and 500 by owners approved by the Commission.[84] That agreement remained in operation in 1994 when grazing was supervised by a shepherd appointed by the Commission and a pound was maintained at Yorkley. Some of the problems caused by the freely wandering sheep remained. A plan to surround Cinderford, the main centre of population in the commonable area, with cattle grids had not been implemented, though some new housing estates were protected by grids. Over 30 sheep a year were killed in road accidents. A few pigs were still pastured, restricted to a pannage season of 25 September to 22 November.[85]

The verderers' court survived in the 20th century as an advisory body to the Forest authorities and a means of representing the views of local inhabitants. An Act of 1927 provided that the verderers be consulted on all bylaws made by the Forestry Commission. The deputy surveyor had attended the court since the 1860s or earlier,[86] and from the mid 20th century other Commission officers also came to discuss matters such as the provision of amenities, opencast mining schemes, and commoning rights.[87] From the early 19th century the verderers had usually been appointed to commissions for new inclosures,[88] and their consent was necessary for exchanges of small parcels of commonable waste for other parcels of Crown freehold which were permitted under an Act of 1906.[89] The old landowning families were represented as verderers into the later 20th century by Sir Launcelot Crawley-Boevey (d. 1968) and by Charles Bathurst, later Viscount Bledisloe, who served from 1907 to his death in 1958 when his son, the 2nd Viscount (d. 1979), succeeded. A local coalowner, Sir Francis Brain, served from 1912 to 1921, and later verderers included John Watts (d. 1972), a Lydney industrialist, Reginald Sanzen-Baker (d. 1991), a former deputy surveyor of the Forest, and Dr. Cyril Hart, a forestry consultant and historian of Dean, who was senior verderer in 1994. From the mid 1970s the symbolic 40-day adjournments of the court were no longer recorded and the court was convened quarterly under the style of the special court of

attachment. Those meetings continued in 1994 at the Speech House hotel.[90] Elections of new verderers continued to be made at county courts, convened by the high sheriff at the Shire Hall in Gloucester.[91] The role of the verderers, the last vestige of the medieval administration, was confirmed by an Act of 1971 which ended the forest law and the Crown's game rights in Dean and other Crown forests and repealed much of the old legislation, including the Act of 1668.[92]

The Forest had long attracted visitors, partly because of its proximity to the more widely known Wye Valley region, and its use for public recreation had become part of Forestry Commission policy by 1938 when, with other surrounding woodlands, it was made into a National Forest Park under a committee. A camping ground was opened at Christchurch, Berry Hill, in 1939.[93] The main development of the area for recreation was from the 1960s when the last deep mines and railways closed, to be followed by new planting and landscaping to remove the scars of the industrial past. The Commission's role included the signposting of footpaths, introduced in 1965, the opening of bicycle paths on some of the old railway tracks, and the provision of sites for camping, picnicking, and car parking. By 1994 it had established 10 picnic sites, of which the most frequented were at Symonds Yat rock, above the Wye Valley, and at Beechenhurst, in the Cannop valley near the Speech House, and four main camp sites, besides others for the use of youth groups.[94] Nature reserves were formed in association with amenity bodies, and several areas of woodland, a total of 600 ha. by 1992, were protected as Sites of Special Scientific Interest.[95] The sale of leaflet footpath guides and fees from the camp sites and car parks provided additonal income for the Commission, though in 1994 80 per cent of its income from the Dean district still came from the timber enterprise. The Dean National Forest Park, though the designation was still used, had no separate administrative body in 1994, but the Commission had recently instituted a general advisory panel on recreational use of the Forest, composed equally of representatives of local government bodies and of clubs and societies.[96]

LOCAL GOVERNMENT AND PUBLIC SERVICES

Since the Forest was extraparochial, provisions for poor relief and other functions of parish government were unusual. In the 1670s and the following decades a few people, mostly women, received financial help from the county stock,

which also occasionally paid apprenticeship and funeral expenses.[97] Seven women, one of them a foster mother, received regular help in 1726[98] and a child abandoned at St. White's was reared at the county's expense from 1768.[99] Because

---

[84] Ibid. D 6993/1/2, mins. 16 Mar. 1977; 9 Oct. 1978; 25 Apr. 1980; 8 May 1981; 30 July 1982.
[85] Inf. from Mr. Everard.   [86] P.R.O., F 3/146; F 16/22.
[87] Glos. R.O., D 6993/1/1–5 (verderers' mins. 1892–1991); Rep. Dean Forest Cttee. (1958), 15.
[88] Nicholls, Forest of Dean, 89; P.R.O., E 178/6917.
[89] Dean Forest Act, 1906, 6 Edw. VII, c. 119 (Local).
[90] Glos. R.O., D 6993/1/1; inf. from Dr. Hart.
[91] For the procedure, Hart, Verderers, 157–66.
[92] Wild Creatures and Forest Laws Act, 1971, c. 47.

[93] National Forest Park Guide (1947), 3–4.
[94] Glos. R.O., D 6993/1/1, mins. 21 Dec. 1964; 20 Aug. 1969; 'Out and About: Forest of Dean' (Forest Enterprise leaflet, 1994); inf. from Mr. Everard.
[95] Management of Broadleaf Woodland, 11–12, 16.
[96] Inf. from Mr. Everard.
[97] Glos. R.O., Q/SO 1, ff. 34v., 157v., 183v., 190v., 211, 214v.; 2, f. 150v.; 3, ff. 10, 17, 64v., 92, 143v., 150v.; 4, pp. 76, 216, 349.   [98] Ibid. Q/FAc 1, ff. 4v.–10v., 20.
[99] Ibid. Q/SO 9, ff. 64v., 92, 114.

paternity orders could not be obtained for ille-gitimate children born on extraparochial land it became increasingly common in the late 18th century for unmarried women from neighbour-ing parishes to enter the Forest for childbirth.[1] Poverty was the general condition of miners in the 1740s[2] and it remained widespread in the Forest in the late 18th century. Although most Foresters had legal settlement in adjoining par-ishes they often relied on the charity of their neighbours and of others and at times of greatest distress, when the parishes were unwilling or unable to provide help, many faced starvation. In 1801, at a time of exceptionally high grain prices, local magistrates used £1,000 given by the Crown for the Foresters' relief to sell them rice, fish, potatoes, and other food at reduced prices, the sales being conducted by the keepers of the Forest walks.[3] The general poverty per-sisted in the early 19th century but the Foresters, of whom a quarter had legal settlement in New-land parish in 1834, sought help from their parishes only as a last resort and continued to depend on voluntary gifts and subscriptions raised by local farmers and other people. In 1834, when 102 of the Forest's 1,530 families were receiving parish relief, many inhabitants belonged to provident societies and some em-ployers retained a surgeon for their workmen.[4] A committee organizing relief for Foresters in 1842[5] apparently employed them in building a road between Hawthorns and Stenders, above Mitcheldean.[6]

In 1835 a majority of commissioners consider-ing a proposal to create civil parishes for the Forest rejected it, citing among their reasons difficulties in levying and collecting rates.[7] In 1842, however, the main part of the extrapar-ochial area was divided for poor-law purposes into two townships, that of East Dean being included in the Westbury-on-Severn union and that of West Dean in the Monmouth union.[8] At Cinderford, where new building was mostly on land in East Dean township, Flaxley parish, and Lea Bailey tithing, three small extraparochial places on Littledean hill remained outside the poor-law system until 1869 when they were constituted the parish of Hinder's Lane and Dockham within the Westbury union.[9] That parish disappeared in 1884 when East Dean's boundaries were extended to include most of the town.[10] Lea Bailey tithing, where Newland par-ish officers had administered relief only intermittently and had never levied poor rates, relieved its own poor from the late 17th cen-tury.[11] It came to be regarded as a separate parish

and in 1836 became part of the new Hereford-shire poor-law union of Ross.[12] In the 1880s Lea Bailey was dismembered and its constituent parts added to various adjoining parishes.[13] Lydbrook, which grew up on land in both East and West Dean as well as the ancient parishes of English Bicknor, Ruardean, and Newland,[14] became in 1935 a new civil parish including Stowfield, Worrall Hill, and Joy's Green.[15] East Dean was divided in 1953 into the new civil parishes of Cinderford, Drybrook, and Rus-pidge.[16] In 1895 West Dean had become part of West Dean rural district and East Dean part of East Dean and United Parishes rural district,[17] which in 1935 was reorganized as East Dean rural district, Lydbrook parish being assigned to West Dean district.[18] In 1974 Cinderford, Drybrook, Ruspidge, Lydbrook, and West Dean parishes all became part of the new Forest of Dean district.

In the later 19th century periods of economic depression, particularly in the coal industry, were marked by widespread unemployment and some emigration. Plans to lower wages often precipitated strikes.[19] Voluntary relief remained of considerable importance and a committee set up in 1877, during a particularly severe slump, employed men in repairing roads. One member of the committee, Thomas Nicholson, Baptist minister of Yorkley, organized other forms of help, including the distribution of cash, food, seed potatoes, and clothing, and helped families to emigrate and young people to find jobs else-where.[20] In 1897 another Baptist minister, A. W. Latham, organized relief during a strike of tin-platers at Lydbrook.[21] In the early 20th century widespread poverty led to strikes in the coal industry,[22] notably the national strike of 1926 when many hundreds of Foresters received emergency relief and there were hunger marches to the Westbury-on-Severn workhouse.[23] Road building figured among schemes to alleviate unemployment in the 1920s and 1930s.[24]

In the 1670s responsibility for maintaining roads and bridges within the Forest fell on the inhabitants of St. Briavels hundred. The roads included those converging on Coleford from Mitcheldean, Littledean, and Purton passage on the river Severn and the Dean road linking Mitcheldean with Newnham and Blakeney, and the bridges included those at Cinderford, Can-nop, Parkend, and Whitecroft and those carrying the Dean road over Soudley and Blackpool brooks.[25] Although there was a levy on the hundred as late as 1719 to pay for repairs,[26] by that time roads and bridges were repaired by the surveyor general of woods and his local deputy

1 Ibid. D 421/X 5/3.
2 Ibid. D 1677/GG 1205.
3 Ibid. D 421/X 5/1–5.
4 3rd Rep. Dean Forest Com. 6–7, 9, 12–16.
5 Glouc. Jnl. 20 Aug. 1842.
6 Nicholls, Forest of Dean, 197.
7 3rd Rep. Dean Forest Com. 3.
8 Dean Forest Poor-Relief Act, 5 & 6 Vic. c. 48.
9 Glos. R.O., G/WE 8A/8, pp. 334, 358, 412; 9C/2, f. 57; above, Fig. 15.   10 Census, 1891.
11 Glos. R.O., D 2026/R 6; above, Newland, local govt.
12 Poor Law Com. 2nd Rep. p. 526.
13 Above, Newland, intro. (Table I).
14 O.S. Map 6", Glos. XXXI. NW. (1883 edn.).
15 Census, 1931 (pt. ii); O.S. Maps 1/25,000, SO 51 (1958

edn.); SO 61 (1957 edn.).   16 Census, 1961.
17 Glos. R.O., DA 24/100/1; DA 25/100/1.
18 Census, 1931 (pt. ii).
19 Glouc. Jnl. 12 Apr., 14 June 1856; 23 Aug. 1862; 8 July, 16 Sept., 4 Nov. 1871; Mountjoy, Dean Collier, 63.
20 Glouc. Jnl. 16 Feb. 1878; Glos. Colln. LR 10.1; J. Stratford, Glos. Biog. Notes (1887), 233.
21 Glouc. Jnl. 30 Oct. 1897.
22 Ibid. 30 Mar. 1912; 9 Apr. 1921.
23 Ibid. 22 May, 3 July, 21, 28 Aug. 1926; Glos. R.O., G/WE 8A/30, pp. 176–8, 232, 245–58.
24 Glos. R.O., DA 24/100/8, min. 18 Oct. 1921; 10, pp. 593–4; 11, p. 122.
25 Ibid. Q/SO 1, ff. 71 and v., 182v.; D 2026/X 23.
26 Ibid. Q/SO 4, p. 258.

on instruction from the Treasury and the costs were met by sales of timber. In 1721 the Forest's roads were described as impassable[27] and in 1737 Parkend bridge, which carried the Purton road, was in danger of being swept away.[28] Later a contractor made a causeway, presumably as part of the Purton road, to take timber out of the Forest[29] and in the period 1761–86 the Crown spent over £11,500 on repairing roads and bridges.[30] From 1796 the main roads crossing Crown land, including a road to Lydbrook branching from the Mitcheldean–Coleford road at Mirystock and the section of the Dean road between Mitcheldean and Littledean, were administered by a turnpike trust. The Crown, which was to be relieved of its responsibility for those roads on payment of £10,645 by way of a loan to the trustees,[31] incurred some expenditure on the Parkend–Coleford road in 1813.[32] The turnpike trustees, who also looked after roads in adjoining parishes, became responsible for more roads in 1827[33] and built several new roads within the Forest. They levied tolls at gates on the Forest boundary and elsewhere, and of the 16 gates operating in 1856 the most profitable were those at Lydbrook and Drybrook, followed by those west of Parkend and at the foot of Plump hill.[34]

In the mid 19th century roads on the Abbots wood estate were maintained by its owner, Henry Crawshay. Several of them were declared public rights of way in 1870[35] but throughout the whole Forest no highway rates were levied and many roads, including sections of some turnpikes, remained unmetalled in the early 1870s. Sometimes road users raised a subscription to repair a particular route and on one occasion the Crown contributed to the cost of work on the Yorkley–Whitecroft road.[36] Roads in detached parts of Newland at Lower Lydbrook and Pope's Hill were maintained from 1871 by the Coleford board of health.[37] The Westbury poor-law guardians were designated the highway authority in East Dean in 1876 and the Monmouth guardians were given similar powers in West Dean in 1883. Both authorities maintained roads built with their consent by the Crown.[38] After the Forest turnpike trust was abolished in 1888[39] the county council took over the main roads.[40]

For much of the 19th century settlement in the

Forest grew with an almost total lack of services. Squalid conditions developed in Cinderford, where in the late 1860s sewage flowed down the hillside in open drains from house to house, water was obtained from a few wells, and overcrowding, particularly in terraces near Cinderford bridge, caused outbreaks of disease.[41] In 1867 a local board of health was formed to improve sanitary conditions in the East Dean part of Cinderford but its schemes were thwarted by the Crown's refusal and ratepayers' reluctance to contribute towards their cost and in 1870 it was dissolved.[42] Following a resolution of the Flaxley parish vestry in 1869 a drainage authority was appointed for the Flaxley Meend district of Cinderford but the task of laying sewers was delayed by the absence of an outfall system in East Dean.[43] Conditions in Cinderford improved after 1875 when the sanitary authority, at that time the Westbury guardians, acquired greater powers there.[44] The Flaxley Meend drainage authority, despite the wish of the Flaxley vestry to have it dissolved,[45] remained in existence until 1884.[46] An underground drainage and sewerage system built for Cinderford and Ruspidge between 1876 and 1878 emptied into Soudley brook at treatment works above Soudley.[47] The system was extended later and the sewage works were enlarged several times before 1936 when they were rebuilt in a scheme, completed in 1938, serving part of Drybrook.[48] By 1973 there were also sewage works west of the town beyond Bilson green.[49]

In 1877 the Westbury guardians began constructing what became known as the Cinderford works to supply Cinderford, Ruspidge, and parts of Ruardean Hill, Harrow Hill, and Drybrook with water pumped from an ore mine near Green Bottom.[50] The system, which included a small circular reservoir on Littledean hill, was gradually extended and 841 houses had mains water by 1885. The reservoir was enlarged and covered over in 1896 and, to increase supplies, a well was sunk at the pumping station in 1907.[51] From 1923, when a reservoir was completed on Ruardean hill, the system reached as far as Upper Lydbrook and in 1924 mains were laid to Plump Hill and down the Soudley valley to Blakeney Hill.[52] At Blakeney Hill the supply superseded an earlier scheme, which from 1891 had pumped water from a well beside Blackpool

27 *Cal. Treas. Papers*, 1720–8, 81, 330; *Cal. Treas. Bks. & Papers*, 1731–4, 238, 302; 1735–8, 298, 363.
28 Berkeley Cast. Mun., General Ser. T, box 25, petition to Treasury about road repairs 1736/7.
29 P.R.O., F 16/31, f. 66.
30 *3rd Rep. Com. Woods* (1788), 100–1.
31 Dean Forest Roads Act, 36 Geo. III, c. 131.
32 P.R.O., LR 4/20/23.
33 Dean Forest Roads Acts, 36 Geo. III, c. 131; 7 & 8 Geo. IV, c. 12 (Local and Personal).
34 Nicholls, *Forest of Dean*, 197; O.S. Maps 6", Glos. XXXIX. SW. (1883 edn.); XXXI. NE. (1884 edn.).
35 Glos. R.O., Q/RI 52.
36 *Dean Forest Select Cttee.* (1874), 19, 23.
37 T. Bright, 'Hist. Coleford Bd. of Health' (1956, TS. in Glos. R.O., PA 93/1), 12.
38 E. and W. Dean (Highways) Act, 47 & 48 Vic. c. 87 (Local); cf. Glos. R.O., DA 40/100/2, pp. 166–7; 3, pp. 115–16.
39 Dean Forest Turnpike Trust Abolition Act, 51 & 52

Vic. c. 193.
40 Glos. R.O., DA 40/100/3, p. 148.
41 *Dean Forest Select Cttee.* (1874), 172–8.
42 Ibid. 15, 19–20; Glos. R.O., DA 6/100; *Glouc. Jnl.* 14 May 1870.
43 Glos. R.O., P 145/OV 2/1, mins. 21 Sept. 1869; 3 Aug. 1871.
44 *Lond. Gaz.* 5 Jan. 1875, p. 37.
45 Glos. R.O., DA 24/100/1, pp. 80–1, 92, 97, 104.
46 L.G.B. Prov. Orders Conf. (No. 4) Act, 1884, 47 & 48 Vic. c. 210 (Local).
47 Glos. R.O., DA 40/100/1, pp. 98–100, 160–3; O.S. Map 6", Glos. XXXIX. NE. (1884 edn.).
48 Glos. R.O., DA 40/100/3, p. 18; DA 24/100/5, p. 9; DA 24/100/12, pp. 132, 275; DA 24/124/4.
49 O.S. Map 1/2,500, SO 6413 (1974 edn.).
50 Glos. R.O., DA 40/100/1, pp. 106, 108, 133, 142.
51 Ibid. 2, p. 60; Pearce, 'Water Supply in Dean', 18–28; *Proc. C.N.F.C.* xxi. 223–7.
52 Pearce, 'Water Supply in Dean', 30–4.

brook up to a reservoir.[53] Other small systems replaced by the main supply included one in Horsepool bottom, built from a spring by 1897, and one at Joy's Green, built from a mine in 1921.[54] In the late 1920s houses at Lower Lydbrook still relied on a standpipe supplied from a spring.[55] To improve the main supply a second well was completed at Green Bottom in 1937 and a new reservoir was commissioned on Littledean hill in 1939. After the Second World War the supply, which also served neighbouring parishes such as Mitcheldean, was augmented from springs at Blakeney Hill and Lydbrook. The Blakeney Hill scheme, which included a pumping station and a reservoir, also served Awre and Viney Hill and was completed in 1952. The Lydbrook scheme, a joint venture of East and West Dean rural district councils involving a reservoir at the Pludds, was finished in 1954.[56] In the western part of the Forest piped water was supplied from Upper Redbrook from 1931 in a scheme incorporating a reservoir at Sling and a tower at Yorkley.[57]

In 1965 the undertakings of East and West Dean rural districts were acquired by the North West Gloucestershire water board, which in 1974 was superseded by the new Severn-Trent water authority. In 1969 supplies in the Cinderford area, which had been augmented from the Newent works, were increased by the completion of a pumping station at Buckshaft, in Ruspidge, to extract water from flooded ore mines. From 1973 a water shortage in the Bream and Yorkley areas was relieved from a new pumping station near Redbrook. From 1976 much of the Forest region and some other parts of the county were supplied with water from the river Wye through treatment works at Wigpool, above Mitcheldean, and in the following years new reservoirs were built on Ruardean and Littledean hills and at Sling.[58]

In 1859 local businessmen headed by Aaron Goold formed a limited company to provide gas in the Cinderford area for industrial and domestic use. The company, which built its works on Bilson green and started production the following year, was known as the Bilson Gas Light & Coke Co. until 1907[59] when it was re-formed as the Cinderford Gas Co.[60] By 1885 gas lamps provided by a local tradesmen's association lit parts of Cinderford's streets.[61] Oil lamps were also provided but the town's street lighting remained inadequate in 1905 when East Dean parish council assumed responsibilty for it. The gas company erected new lamps for the council,

which from 1913 also provided street lighting in Ruspidge.[62] There were 113 public lamps in Cinderford and Ruspidge in 1925 when electricity, newly introduced to the town by the West Gloucestershire Power Co. from its Norchard works, at Lydney, was first used for street lighting.[63] Abbotswood and several other houses in Ruspidge received electricity from Eastern United colliery from 1919 and until the colliery joined the electricity company's supply in 1924.[64] The Bilson gasworks, which were modernized after nationalization in 1948, closed in 1955 and Cinderford's gas supply, along with that of much of west Gloucestershire, was piped from Bristol by way of the Severn railway bridge.[65] After the bridge was partially destroyed in 1960 the supply was rerouted to a crossing higher up the river.[66]

The Forest of Dean Recreative and Medical Aid Association, formed before 1889 and based in Cinderford,[67] provided an ambulance, and M. W. Colchester-Wemyss, one of the association's founders,[68] gave East Dean parish council a horse-drawn vehicle for an ambulance in 1903.[69] An ambulance kept at Cannop for taking injured miners to hospitals in Gloucester or Monmouth was perhaps that recorded in 1917.[70] In 1923 a hospital built in memory of Sir Charles Dilke, a former M.P. for the Forest, opened on the road between Cinderford and the Speech House. Paid for by grants and voluntary contributions, many of them from miners, it was a single-storeyed building with 16 beds and its running costs were met by subscriptions. The subscribers received free treatment. A three-storeyed block was added in 1926 and a maternity ward in 1940. The Dilke Memorial hospital became part of the National Health Service in 1948 and a geriatric wing was opened in 1968. The maternity ward closed in 1988.[71] In 1993 the hospital was run by the Gloucester district health authority.

In 1893 the Westbury guardians had a small isolation hospital at Soudley.[72] It closed in 1896 when East Dean and United Parishes rural district council, acting as a sanitary authority, took over an iron hospital near Green Bottom put up by the guardians earlier that year during a smallpox epidemic in Gloucester.[73] In 1908 that hospital was moved a short distance[74] and from 1911 it was run by a joint board representing also the urban districts of Awre, Newnham, and Westbury.[75] It closed in 1921 but the building was retained as a smallpox hospital for west Gloucestershire and additional wards were erected in 1923. The hospital was

53 Ibid. 22.
54 Ibid. 32; Glos. R.O., DA 24/100/1, p. 256.
55 Richardson, *Wells and Springs of Glos.* 92.
56 Pearce, 'Water Supply in Dean', 36–7, 42–4; *Citizen* (Glouc.), 28 Sept. 1951.
57 Pearce, 'Water Supply in Dean', 51–4.
58 Ibid. 99–118; *Dean Forest Mercury*, 30 May 1969.
59 Glos. R.O., D 2516/6/1; P.R.O., F 3/176.
60 Glos. R.O., D 4853/3.
61 *New Regard of Forest of Dean*, x. 53.
62 Glos. R.O., DA 24/950/1, pp. 160, 165–6; 2, p. 33; 8, min. 23 Feb. 1906.
63 Ibid. 3, p. 14; D 2516/6/2, undated newspaper cutting.
64 I. Pope and P. Kerau, *Forest of Dean Branch*, i (1992), 143–4.
65 W.I. portrait of Cinderford (1965, copy in Cinderford

libr.); *New Regard of Forest of Dean*, x. 60.
66 R. M. Huxley, *Rise and Fall of Severn Bridge Railway* (1984), 121.
67 *Kelly's Dir. Glos.* (1889), 733.
68 G.D.R., V 6/29.
69 Glos. R.O., DA 24/950/1, pp. 137, 156.
70 Ibid. 2, p. 97; *Dean Forest Mercury*, 10 June 1988.
71 *Glouc. Jnl.* 1 June 1922; 30 June 1923; 17 Oct. 1925; 4 Sept. 1926; for hist. of hosp., *Dean Forest Mercury*, 10 June–29 July 1988.
72 Glos. R.O., DA 24/124/1, p. 1.
73 Ibid. DA 24/100/1, pp. 201, 205; G/WE 8A/15, pp. 102, 114; P.R.O., F 3/496.
74 Glos. R.O., DA 24/100/5, pp. 114–15, 230, 252–3; O.S. Maps 6", Glos. XXXI. NE., SE. (1903, 1924 edns.).
75 Glos. R.O., DA 24/100/6, pp. 156, 234.

dismantled after the Second World War.[76] A tuberculosis dispensary opened in Cinderford by 1925[77] had moved from Belle Vue Road to Station Street by 1935.[78] A mental hospital for elderly people was opened in the town in 1988.[79] To meet a shortage of burial places within the Forest the East Dean rural district council opened a cemetery on the road from Cinderford to the Speech House in 1956[80] and the West Dean district council a cemetery at Mile End for an area covering Milkwall, Berry Hill, and Lydbrook in 1967.[81]

The county police authority opened stations in several places in the Forest in the mid 19th century. The first, recorded from 1848, was at Upper Lydbrook.[82] In Lower Lydbrook some policing was undertaken by constables appointed by the English Bicknor parish vestry in the early 1860s.[83] A police station at Littledean Hill in 1869[84] moved to a new building in Cinderford town centre in 1877.[85] Parkend had a police station in 1876[86] and among other places with a police presence later were Drybrook by 1897[87] and Yorkley by 1920.[88]

Cinderford had no fire service in 1869 when a blaze at the town hall, then under construction, was attended by the Coleford fire brigade.[89] East Dean and United Parishes rural district council provided fire-fighting equipment for the town and for Ruspidge and Drybrook in 1895[90] but there was no regular fire brigade in Cinderford until after 1923.[91] A fire station in Belle Vue Road, built by the county fire service in the mid 1960s, was replaced by a new station in Valley Road in 1987.[92]

SOCIAL LIFE

In the 18th century the remote scattered settlements of the extraparochial Forest of Dean, beyond the usual controls of local government, fostered individualism and disdain for authority.[93] An introspective society evolved with its own pronounced dialect and with customs and attitudes shaped by the Foresters' claims as free miners and commoners. Denied easy access to religious worship and education, Foresters were regarded as uncouth and ignorant, and their propensity to violence and riotous gatherings intimidated the inhabitants of surrounding districts. Despite certain improvements,[94] the Foresters continued in the early 19th century to display many of those traits which had informed an earlier description of the region's residents as 'a sort of robustic wild people'.[95] Excitable and pugnacious in character, they remained proud of their independence, suspicious of outsiders, and fierce in the defence of their customs. Their tendency to lawlessness was readily expressed in collective action, such as the bread riots of 1795 and 1801 and the inclosure riots of 1831, and their disregard of authority later manifested itself in a reluctance to pay local taxes.[96] Poaching and the violent incidents associated with it led the Crown to clear the Forest of deer in the early 1850s.[97]

Preachers began to evangelize the Foresters in the later 18th century and the first missionaries were nonconformists, some of them local men.[98]

From the early 19th century a handful of Anglican clergy from neighbouring parishes also undertook missionary work. They built churches and schools[99] and one of them likened his work to that of a missionary in New Zealand.[1] Missionary work effected some improvement in Foresters' behaviour and moral character and increased Sunday observance, but in the mid 19th century superstitious belief, notably in the efficacy of charms and spells, remained widespread[2] and as late as 1865, twenty years after the first marriages were celebrated in the Forest's churches,[3] some couples lived together under fixed-term agreements drawn up like legal contracts.[4] Despite the achievements of Anglican clergy the Forest became a stronghold of religious nonconformity and chapels were important as meeting places and bastions of the temperance movement. In the later 19th century some congregations, notably the Baptists at Cinderford, numbered several hundreds.[5]

Beer had replaced cider as the Foresters' favoured beverage by 1841[6] when, excluding the Speech House, there were 4 inns and 49 beerhouses in the main part of the extraparochial area.[7] In the 1850s and 1860s the illegal sale of beer, cider, and perry was widespread and even the smallest hamlets such as Shapridge, Fetter Hill, Palmer's Flat near Coleford, and Moseley Green had or were near one or more beerhouses.[8] Although some beerhouses were short

76   Ibid. DA 24/880; DA 24/980; DA 24/984/2.
77   Ibid. CE/M 2/17, pp. 307–8.
78   *Kelly's Dir. Glos.* (1927), 126; (1935), 118.
79   *Dean Forest Mercury*, 4 Dec. 1987.
80   Glos. R.O., DA 24/100/23, p. 585; 24, p. 144.
81   Ibid. DA 25/111/2, p. 970; DA 25/209/2.
82   Ibid. Q/CL 1/13; P.R.O., F 16/64 (no. 219); F 16/71.
83   Glos. R.O., P 138/VE 2/1.
84   *Glouc. Jnl.* 12 June 1869.
85   Date on police station, in Station Street.
86   *Morris's Dir. Glos.* (1876), 478.
87   *Kelly's Dir. Glos.* (1897), 134.
88   O.S. Map 1/2,500, Glos. XXXIX. 11 (1922 edn.).
89   *Glouc. Jnl.* 23 Jan. 1869.
90   Glos. R.O., DA 24/100/1, pp. 81–2, 99–100.
91   Ibid. FD 60.
92   W.I. portrait of Cinderford; *Citizen*, 19 June 1987.
93   Para. based on Nicholls, *Forest of Dean*, 83–6, 110–12,

145, 150–2; Nicholls, *Personalities of Dean*, 175–6, 180–2, 187, 190; *Diary of a Cotswold Parson*, ed. D. Verey (1978), 119; *Glouc. Jnl.* 30 July 1864; Glos. R.O., D 421/X 5/1, 3–4.
94   Rudder, *Glos.* 37.
95   Bodl. MS. Rawl. B. 323, f. 99v.
96   *Glouc. Jnl.* 5 Mar., 9 Apr. 1870.
97   Hart, *Verderers*, 180–3.
98   Below, Prot. Nonconf.
99   Below, Churches; Educ., elementary schs.
1   *3rd Rep. Dean Forest Com.* 31.
2   *Wesleyan Meth. Mag.* xlvii. 409; Nicholls, *Forest of Dean*, 149–50.
3   *B. & G. Par. Rec.* 96, 122, 218.
4   Fisher, *Custom and Capitalism*, 32.
5   Below, Prot. Nonconf.   6   Nicholls, *Forest of Dean*, 151.
7   Glos. R.O., Q/FR 4/1.
8   *Glouc. Jnl.* 23 Apr., 4 June 1853; 20 Feb., 4 Sept. 1858; 30 July 1864; 5 Sept. 1868.

lived, the number of licensed houses grew in the mid 19th century and East and West Dean contained 31 alehouses, 53 beerhouses, and 47 other licensed premises in 1891. Many adopted names reflecting the region's forestry, its mining and other industries, or its inhabitants' character[9] and many were meeting places for local societies, clubs, and lodges.[10] The practice of paying miners at them drew criticism from local temperance organizations in the 1860s.[11] The number of inns and beerhouses declined throughout the 20th century.[12]

The Speech House, the principal courthouse for the Forest[13] in the centre of the woodland beside the Littledean–Coleford road, had become an inn by 1841.[14] It had long been used for banquets on occasions such as the election of verderers,[15] and by 1851 and until the First World War the principal mine owners dined there after the biannual gale audit, when mining rents were paid to the Crown.[16] The Speech House also played an important role in the life of the wider Forest region. Sales of timber and bark, livestock markets and fairs, sporting events, and rallies were held in its grounds or nearby.[17] Large gatherings, notably a demonstration in 1850 to support the proposed Great Exhibition, took on the character of pleasure fairs[18] and the local miners' annual gala was held there from 1872 until the late 1930s.[19] The building, which was enlarged c. 1882,[20] was the scene of royal visits by Prince Albert in 1861 and Elizabeth II in 1957[21] and remained open as a hotel in 1993.

Friendly societies, some of which originated as lodges of free miners,[22] abounded in the Forest in the mid 19th century and several co-operative societies were formed in the later 19th century. The deputy surveyor, some clergy and neighbouring landowners, and a few industrialists sponsored religious, educational, and recreational projects.[23] After the First World War the Miners' Welfare Fund assisted the building of village halls and institutes, often as memorials to the war dead, and the provision of playing fields, often created with voluntary labour on the sites of abandoned colliery tips.[24] In the later 20th century several new halls, social clubs, and recreation grounds were provided, and from the

1970s the county and district councils collaborated to build sports and arts facilities at Cinderford and Five Acres for school and public use.[25] Although the Forest had become a less isolated society by the mid 19th century,[26] it retained its distinct character until after the Second World War,[27] when mining and other traditional industries virtually disappeared and wider social changes affected the area. As in other coalfields in the 19th century, working-class culture flowered with the formation of brass bands, choral societies, and football clubs,[28] some of which survived in 1993. In the mid 19th century club anniversaries and school treats were often marked by parades and religious services.[29] Until the mid 1850s those events were usually attended by musicians from neighbouring places such as Blakeney, Littledean, Mitcheldean, and Ross-on-Wye (Herefs.).[30] Marching bands later proliferated within the Forest[31] and local band contests became important events.[32] In 1864 a commentator noted that, like miners elsewhere, Foresters had excellent voices and enjoyed music.[33] The later burgeoning of chapel choirs and of local choral competitions led to the formation of choral societies and male voice choirs.[34] One annual competition, the Forest of Dean eisteddfod started in 1897, was usually held at Double View school in Cinderford.[35]

In the late 18th century Foresters regularly entertained themselves with open-air revels and sport.[36] In the mid 19th century several places were remembered as venues for country dancing.[37] Horse races were held in the region before 1734 when animals used for carrying coal and ore competed for a trophy at Crump meadow near the centre of the Forest.[38] In the mid 1870s horse races were held at the Speech House and on a meadow at Courtfield, across the river Wye from Lydbrook,[39] and in the early 20th century pony racing continued in a long ride running north from Cinderford to Merring Meend.[40] Cricket, and possibly rounders, were popular in the late 18th century[41] but early cricket clubs, one of which played in a field by the Speech House from 1858, had few Foresters among their members.[42] An archery club established before

9 *Licensed Houses in Glos. 1891*, 56–61, 144–53; for alehouses at Bream and Lower Lydbrook, ibid. 54–5, 156–7.
10 Below, this chapter.
11 *Glouc. Jnl.* 10 May 1856; 20 Aug., 3 Dec. 1864; 15 Apr., 20 May 1865.
12 e.g. W. A. Camm, *Bream through the Ages* (1979), 29, 45.
13 Above, Settlement, forest lodges.
14 P.R.O., HO 107/364, s.v. Speech Ho. walk; Hart, *Verderers*, 147.
15 *Glouc. Jnl.* 4 Oct. 1834.
16 Ibid. 23 Aug. 1851; 16 Feb. 1856; 24 Feb. 1912.
17 Ibid. 6 Apr. 1848; 17 Apr. 1852; 2 June 1855; 13 June, 24 Oct. 1857; 1 May 1858; 15 June 1861; 24 Sept. 1870; 17 Oct. 1874.
18 Ibid. 15 June 1850; Nicholls, *Forest of Dean*, 135–6.
19 *Glouc. Jnl.* 3 Aug. 1872; 2 Aug. 1873; 17 July 1897; H. Phelps, *Forest of Dean* (1982), 64.
20 Above, Settlement, forest lodges.
21 Hart, *Royal Forest*, plates at pp. 168–9, 184–5.
22 *Glouc. Jnl.* 1 Aug. 1846; 6 Aug. 1864.
23 Below, this chapter; Churches; Prot. Nonconf.; Educ., elementary schs.
24 Glos. R.O., D 3168/3/4; P.R.O., F 3/1442; *Glouc. Jnl.* 25 Jan. 1930; M. V. Bent, *Highest Point of Dean* (1985), 77–

8; Phelps, *Forest of Dean*, 136.
25 *Dean Forest Mercury*, 3 Apr. 1987; 25 Oct. 1991.
26 Nicholls, *Forest of Dean*, 150.
27 D. Potter, *Changing Forest* (1962), 49–51.
28 *Glouc. Jnl.* 30 July 1864; below, this chapter.
29 *Glouc. Jnl.* 24 Sept. 1853; 29 Aug. 1863; 5 Aug. 1865; 29 June 1870.
30 Ibid. 8 July 1848; 9 June 1849; 5 July 1851; 7 Aug. 1852; 21 May, 25 June, 30 July 1853.
31 Below, this chapter.
32 *Glouc. Jnl.* 24 Apr., 10 July 1897; *Citizen* (Glouc.), 25 Jan. 1988.
33 *Glouc. Jnl.* 30 July 1864.
34 Below, this chapter.
35 *Glouc. Jnl.* 12 June 1897; Glos. R.O., SB 15/4, p. 408; 5, p. 66.
36 P. M. Procter, *Origin of Established Ch. and Nat. Day Sch. in Forest of Dean* (1819), 3, 42.
37 Nicholls, *Forest of Dean*, 152.
38 *Glouc. Jnl.* 16 July 1734.
39 *Forest of Dean Examiner*, 9 June 1876; 10 Aug. 1877.
40 Phelps, *Forest of Dean*, 124.
41 Procter, *Origin of Ch. in Dean*, 42; *Glos. Chron.* 6 Aug. 1864.
42 *Glouc. Jnl.* 21 May 1842; 5, 19 June 1858.

1857 and patronized by members of fashionable society outside the Forest held summer meetings at the Speech House until 1867.[43] Football had become the Foresters' favourite sport by the 1850s[44] and nearly every village and large hamlet had a football club at the end of the century.[45] The Forest's sporting tradition owed much to the successes of its leading rugby union clubs before the First World War[46] and many players went on to join the Gloucester club.[47] Some ponds created for industrial purposes were used for recreation. One in the Oakwood valley near Bream had a boathouse in 1859[48] and was used as a swimming pool later.[49] In 1993 several ponds, notably those at Cannop and Soudley, provided sport for anglers.[50] A local caving club was formed in 1964 to explore abandoned mines in the Forest area.[51] Sheep dog trials were held in several places in the later 20th century.[52]

In the early 19th century Dean's miners, many of whom were paid under the truck system, were often destitute[53] and when there was large-scale unemployment, as at the time of the 1831 inclosure riots, radical ideas were discussed widely.[54] In 1839 Foresters lent the Chartist rebels at Newport (Mon.) little support[55] but in the summer of 1842, after 300 colliers had demonstrated at Mitcheldean for the distribution of relief, a Chartist orator addressed large crowds at Cinderford Tump and Bilson.[56] Dean's miners first formed a trade union in 1871.[57] In the later 19th century the Liberal party had widespread support in the Forest. On polling day in 1874 antipathy to the Conservative party culminated at Cinderford in a riot during which the party's headquarters were ransacked and several houses were damaged.[58] Following that election a Liberal association was formed at Cinderford.[59] From 1885 the miners' vote was of crucial importance in the new Forest of Dean parliamentary division, which also embraced many outlying parishes, and it influenced the selection of Thomas Blake of Ross-on-Wye, a radical Liberal, as candidate, and his election as member, for the seat. Blake's successor as M.P., a man not as sympathetic to the Labour movement, stepped down in 1892 in favour of Sir Charles Dilke, Bt., the former Liberal cabinet minister.[60] Dilke, whom the Dean miners had

long regarded as their champion,[61] served as the Forest's M.P. until his death in 1911. His successor Henry Webb, a colliery owner raised to a baronetcy in 1916, did not enjoy wholehearted backing from local Labour organizations and in 1918 their candidate took the seat from him.[62]

In the mid 19th century several publications called the *Forester*, the first of which appeared at the time of the 1831 riots, were produced for the mining communities of west Gloucestershire. The miners' union introduced the weekly *Forest of Dean Examiner*, part of a syndicated Labour press, published between 1873 and 1877.[63] Of newspapers published at Cinderford[64] the most successful was the Liberal *Dean Forest Mercury* started in 1881 by the printer John Cooksey with help from Samuel Charley, a Blakeney shopkeeper and newspaper reporter.[65] The *Mercury*, a weekly publication, abandoned its political affiliation after the First World War[66] and under the title of the *Forester* was amalgamated with weekly newspapers for Coleford and Lydney in 1991.[67]

Vernacular literature of the Forest region included in the 1830s the poetry of Catherine Drew of Littledean Woodside, which reflected on the impact of industrial and social change in the Forest,[68] and the more naïve writings of Richard Morse of Yorkley.[69] Among later writers the poet F. W. Harvey (1888–1957) spent his last years at Pillowell and Yorkley.[70] Recollections of Brierley in the 1920s appeared in *A Child in the Forest*, the reminiscences of Winifred Foley,[71] and the writer and dramatist Dennis Potter (1935–94), a native of Berry Hill, often drew on his Forest background for his plays.[72] In 1983 a museum illustrating the Forest's industrial heritage opened at Soudley.[73]

At CINDERFORD in 1841 there were two inns and at least ten beerhouses within that part of the extraparochial Forest extending to Upper Bilson, St. White's, and Ruspidge.[74] The White Hart inn, on the Littledean–Coleford road above Cinderford bridge, was recorded from 1834[75] and was among the town's first meeting places.[76] The other inn, near the Cinderford ironworks, was built after 1834[77] and was known as the

43 Ibid. 13 June 1857; 5 June 1858; 4 Aug. 1860; 22 June 1867; 20 June 1868.
44 Nicholls, *Forest of Dean*, 152.
45 *Glouc. Jnl.* 4 Sept. 1897.
46 Glos. R.O., SP 32, pp. 9–10.
47 Phelps, *Forest of Dean*, 26.
48 P.R.O., F 16/64 (no. 2912); F 16/71.
49 Camm, *Bream through the Ages*, 15; at O.S. Nat. Grid 603066.
50 For the Soudley ponds, *New Regard of Forest of Dean*, vi. 38–44.
51 *Royal Forest of Dean Caving Club Newsletter*, cxiv. 14.
52 *Dean Forest Mercury*, 16 Jan. 1987; Bent, *Highest Point of Dean*, 68; Phelps, *Forest of Dean*, 94.
53 *3rd Rep. Dean Forest Com.* 13–14.
54 Fisher, *Custom and Capitalism*, 37–43.
55 C. Drew, *Collection of Poems on Forest of Dean and Neighbourhood* (Coleford, 1841), 34–6.
56 *Glouc. Jnl.* 20 Aug., 3, 10 Sept. 1842; Fisher, *Custom and Capitalism*, 52–3.
57 Above, Industry, mining from 1770s.
58 *Glouc. Jnl.* 14 Feb. 1874.
59 *Forest of Dean Examiner*, 27 Feb. 1874.
60 Fisher, *Custom and Capitalism*, 140–1; *Trans.*

B.G.A.S. c. 241–8.
61 *Glouc. Jnl.* 2 Aug. 1873.
62 *Trans. B.G.A.S.* li. 326–9; Glos. Colln., newspaper cuttings, xxiii. 94–5.
63 Nicholls, *Forest of Dean*, 112; Fisher, *Custom and Capitalism*, 43–4, 74, 80–1; Glos. Colln. has microfilm copies of *Forest of Dean Examiner*.
64 Cf. B.L. index of newspapers at Colindale.
65 *Glouc. Jnl.* 18 Sept. 1915; for Charley, *Kelly's Dir. Glos.* (1879), 571.
66 C. E. Hart, *Coleford* (1983), 401; Phelps, *Forest of Dean*, 22, 102.
67 *Forester*, 1 Oct. 1991.
68 C. Drew, *Collection of Poems on Forest of Dean and Neighbourhood* (Coleford, 1841).
69 Nicholls, *Forest of Dean*, 149–50; for Morse's writings, Glos. Colln. 10958 (2–4).
70 Phelps, *Forest of Dean*, 30, 95; *Citizen*, 26 Mar. 1988.
71 W. Foley, *Child in the Forest* (1974); *Citizen*, 9 Apr. 1974.
72 *The Times*, 8 June 1994; Potter, *Changing Forest*, 11–12.
73 *Dean Forest Mercury*, 29 Apr. 1983.
74 Glos. R.O., Q/FR 4/1, ff. 78–86, 136; Q/RGf 1/7.
75 *Glouc. Jnl.* 6 Sept. 1834.
76 Ibid. 25 Aug. 1855; Glos. R.O., D 2593/1/9/1; DA 6/100.
77 Glos. R.O., Q/FR 4/1, f. 81; Q/RGf 1/7.

Victoria hotel in 1851.[78] It had closed by 1901.[79] Of the beerhouses, one at the ironworks was known in 1832 as the Forge Hammer[80] and one on Bilson green later as the Barley Corn.[81] Outside the Forest there were two inns, the Royal Forester and the Royal Oak, on Littledean hill in 1838.[82] In the later 19th century Cinderford's principal inns were in High Street. The Royal Union, at the top of the street, was built in 1854,[83] and by the late 1860s several more inns, notably the Swan, the Lion (formerly the Dolphin), and the Fleece, had opened nearby and the Globe and the Seven Stars had opened lower down the street.[84] The Royal Union, closed by 1955, and the Fleece were demolished during remodelling of the town centre c. 1960.[85] In Ruspidge the New Inn and the Rising Sun, two of four inns at the bottom of Ruspidge Road in 1872,[86] remained open in 1993.

In the 1850s and 1860s many friendly societies, including several Odd Fellows' lodges, were based on inns in Cinderford and Ruspidge.[87] Of those meeting at the White Hart one, formed in the mid 1830s, had nearly 300 members and another was the Prince of Wales lodge of free miners.[88] In 1838 the Royal Forester and the Royal Oak each accommodated a friendly society[89] and in 1855 the former was used by a women's society.[90] Some societies, including at least two formed by miners at large pits, met at chapels, and several, notably the East Dean Economic Benefit Society formed at the Baptist chapel in 1854 by Timothy Mountjoy, promoted temperance.[91] In 1877 the opening of a temperance hotel and hall in the town was disturbed by the playing of a band employed by a local publican.[92] The town had several coffee houses in the late 1880s.[93] A co-operative society started by miners at Cinderford bridge in 1874[94] came to dominate the town's retail trade.[95] The society's penny bank for children had 700 subscribers in 1897 and its anniversary celebration was a major event in the town's calendar until after the First World War.[96] The society, which also opened shops elsewhere in the Forest and in neighbouring towns and villages, took over several other societies and had c. 9,000 members in 1965.[97] It was later incorporated in the Gloucester & Severnside co-operative society,[98] which had several shops in the town in 1993.

The colliery owners Edward Protheroe (d. 1856) and Aaron Goold (d. 1862) influenced the development of Cinderford,[99] and the ironmaster Edwin Crawshay took an interest in the town while he lived at Abbotswood, in Ruspidge, in the 1860s and 1870s.[1] In the later 19th century the Crawley-Boeveys of Flaxley Abbey, whose estate included the town's Flaxley Meend district, assisted the building of a school and church there.[2] From 1869 the main public meeting place was the new town hall in High Street. Built by a company[3] and acquired before 1894 by the Cinderford co-operative society,[4] it was demolished c. 1960.[5] An iron hall built in Commercial Street in 1897 for public meetings and entertainments[6] became known as the Empire theatre. It closed after a fire in 1919.[7] A cinema was built in Belle Vue Road c. 1909. Rebuilt in 1919 after a fire and known from 1923 as the Palace theatre, it closed in 1966 and the building was adapted for a club.[8] The Miners' Welfare hall in Wesley Road opened in 1930 and had basement rooms for an institute.[9] It was the town's main public meeting place in the later 20th century. Mechanics' institutes started in the Cinderford area by Aaron Goold and others in the mid 19th century failed to attract members.[10] The Forest of Dean Recreative and Medical Aid Association formed before 1889 by F. L. Lucas of Newnham, a barrister, M. W. Colchester-Wemyss, a local landowner, and others established institutes for Cinderford and Ruspidge and provided books for their libraries. While the Cinderford institute, in High Street, was short lived the Ruspidge institute, housed in the former schoolroom next to St. John's church, had some success. In 1919 its use of the room was threatened by a dispute with St. John's parish[11] and later it moved to Ruspidge Road,[12] where a memorial hall was built in 1923.[13] In 1907 Cinderford's Baptists opened an interdenominational institute at St. Annals in Belle Vue Road,[14] which was used as offices by the rural district council from 1929. A branch of the county library opened there in 1933[15] moved to new premises next to the house in 1961.[16] The

78 P.R.O., HO 107/1959, s.v. E. Dean.
79 O.S. Map 6″, Glos. XXXI. SE. (1903 edn.).
80 Ibid. (1883 edn.); *Reg. Electors W. Division Glos. 1832–3*, 112.
81 *Licensed Houses in Glos. 1891*, 146.
82 Glos. R.O., Q/RZ 1; O.S. Map 6″, Glos. XXXI. SE. (1883 edn.).
83 Glos. R.O., DC/H 59; *Glouc. Jnl.* 7 July 1855.
84 *Glouc. Jnl.* 3 Mar. 1866; 5 Sept., 5 Dec. 1868; 5 June 1869; 2 July 1870; Mountjoy, *Dean Collier*, 26; O.S. Map 1/2,500, Glos. XXXI. 11 (1881 edn.).
85 Glos. R.O., DA 24/132/75.
86 Ibid. Q/RI 52.
87 P.R.O., FS 2/3; *Glouc. Jnl.* 7 July 1855; 9 June 1860; 6 Aug. 1864.
88 *Glouc. Jnl.* 7 Aug. 1852; 25 June, 30 July, 27 Aug. 1853; 1 Aug., 26 Sept. 1857.
89 Glos. R.O., Q/RZ 1.   90 *Glouc. Jnl.* 28 July 1855.
91 P.R.O., FS 2/3; Mountjoy, *Dean Collier*, 38; Fisher, *Custom and Capitalism*, 92.
92 *Forest of Dean Examiner*, 3 Aug. 1877.
93 *Kelly's Dir. Glos.* (1889), 733.
94 *Morris's Dir. Glos.* (1876), 468; W.I. portrait of Cinderford (1965, copy in Cinderford libr.).
95 Potter, *Changing Forest*, 22; Phelps, *Forest of Dean*, 120.
96 *Glouc. Jnl.* 21 Aug. 1897; 29 June 1912; Phelps, *Forest of Dean*, 122.
97 W.I. portrait of Cinderford; below, this chapter.
98 Personal observation.
99 Above, Settlement; Industry; below, Prot. Nonconf., Wesleyan Methodists; Educ., elementary schs.
1 *Glouc. Jnl.* 12 Aug. 1865; 10 Aug. 1867; Glos. R.O., DA 6/100.
2 Above, Flaxley, manor; below, Churches (St. Stephen); Educ., elementary schs.
3 *Glouc. Jnl.* 15 May 1869; Glos. R.O., D 2593/1/9/1.
4 *Kelly's Dir. Glos.* (1894), 109.
5 Glos. R.O., DA 24/132/75.
6 *Kelly's Dir. Glos.* (1897), 110.
7 *Glouc. Jnl.* 12 July 1919.
8 Glos. R.O., FD 60; O.S. Map 1/2,500, SO 6513 (1960, 1974 edns.).
9 *Glouc. Jnl.* 25 Jan. 1930.   10 Ibid. 5 Mar. 1870.
11 G.D.R., V 6/29; *Kelly's Dir. Glos.* (1889), 733; (1894), 110–11, 248.
12 *Kelly's Dir. Glos.* (1931), 117.
13 Date on bldg.
14 *Glouc. Jnl.* 27 July 1907; P.R.O., F 3/1272.
15 Glos. R.O., DA 24/100/10, pp. 677–9; 11, pp. 165, 178.
16 W.I. portrait of Cinderford.

Y.M.C.A. was active in the town for several years before 1917 when it bought a chapel in lower High Street.[17] Among social clubs in the town in 1993 was one in Commercial Street started just after the First World War for former soldiers and sailors.[18] In the later 19th century pleasure fairs accompanied livestock fairs in Cinderford.[19]

A recreation ground formed on land granted for public use in or before 1887[20] was presumably that on Bilson green acquired as a site for the town's railway station, opened in 1900.[21] A recreation ground recorded nearby in 1911[22] belonged to the miners' welfare association in 1925.[23] In the late 1880s land at Littledean Hill next to the Royal Oak was also used for recreation and by 1894 there was a recreation gound in Dockham Road.[24] A park or pleasure ground laid out by East Dean parish council in the Church Road area in 1902 was abandoned during the First World War.[25] In the mid 20th century playing fields were opened elsewhere in Cinderford and Ruspidge[26] and a field next to St. John's vicarage in St. White's Road, which was used for sports,[27] came under the management of Cinderford parish council.[28] In 1991 a sports centre opened next to the Heywood school in Causeway Road. Intended for school and public use, it had been built in stages, the first being a swimming pool in the 1970s, and it included a theatre in a converted gymnasium.[29]

A cricket club formed by members of St. John's church in 1880 played on waste ground before moving to Abbotswood in Ruspidge, where a cricket ground had been laid out by 1856 on Henry Crawshay's land. In 1899 the club built a pavilion there.[30] In 1910 Cinderford also had the Red Rose cricket club.[31] The Abbotswood ground was ploughed up in 1940, and after the Second World War St. John's club played in several places before moving in 1970 to a new ground at Whimsey.[32] Although not the first rugby football club in the town, Cinderford Football club, formed in 1886 and playing on the Dockham Road recreation ground from 1894, was one of the most successful in the county before the First World War. During that

period the town had at least five other rugby clubs, including one called the White Rose. An annual competition between local colliery teams, established in 1926 by A. J. Morgan of Abbotswood to raise funds for Cinderford Football club, was short lived. The revival of rugby in Cinderford after the Second World War rested on the White Rose club. It played on a ground at Cinderford bridge and in 1955 it was reformed as Cinderford R.F.C. In 1963 the club moved to the Dockham Road ground, where a new clubhouse was opened in 1972.[33] The town's most successful association football club, Cinderford A.F.C. formed by 1935,[34] purchased its ground in Causeway Road before 1956.[35] A golf club had links at St. White's in 1926.[36] It disbanded after 1956.[37]

Prominent among Cinderford's brass bands in the mid 1850s was one called the Robin Hood band.[38] Temperance advocates started a fife and drum band at Ruspidge in 1864 and employees of the Forest Vale ironworks formed a band before 1869.[39] The Excelsior brass band, founded before 1897,[40] met at the Methodist chapel in Church Road and lapsed in the mid 20th century. The Town brass band originated in 1896 as a military recruiting band and in the 1980s had its headquarters at the Globe inn.[41] Cinderford had a new choral society in 1898 and a male voice choir in 1912, and Ruspidge a choral society in 1892.[42]

The earliest inns in LYDBROOK, including one recorded in 1686,[43] were at Lower Lydbrook. There the New Inn, opened by 1806,[44] was known as the Old New Inn in 1845[45] and had been renamed the Courtfield Arms by 1897.[46] Higher up the village the Bell and the Anchor had opened by 1792 and 1807 respectively.[47] In the mid 19th century there were numerous inns and beerhouses in the village; names included the Royal Forester, the Sawyers' Arms, the Puddlers' Arms, and the Yew Tree.[48] Lower Lydbrook had the Recruiting Sergeant in 1846[49] and the Forge Hammer in 1870[50] and Upper Lydbrook, where there were three beerhouses in 1841,[51] the Jovial Colliers in 1854[52] and the Crown and Sceptre in 1859.[53] In 1885 the owners of tinplate works in the village, headed by

[17] Ibid.; below, Prot. Nonconf., Bible Christians.
[18] *Kelly's Dir. Glos.* (1923), 122.
[19] *Glouc. Jnl.* 23 June 1866; 24 Sept. 1870; 20 June 1874.
[20] P.R.O., F 3/473.
[21] I. Pope, B. How, and P. Kerau, *Severn & Wye Railway*, ii. 323–5.
[22] P.R.O., F 3/177.
[23] Glos. R.O., SM 109/2/M 2, p. 123.
[24] Ibid. SP 32, pp. 17–27, 168.
[25] Ibid. DA 24/950/1, pp. 113–14, 158; 2, pp. 79, 87.
[26] O.S. Maps 1/2,500, SO 6411 (1983 edn.); SO 6415 (1961 edn.); SO 6512–14 (1960 edn.).
[27] *St. White's Sch. 1887–1987* (copy in Glos. Colln. R 78.10), 13.
[28] O.S. Map 1/2,500, SO 6512 (1960 edn.); W.I. portrait of Cinderford.
[29] *Dean Forest Mercury*, 25 Oct. 1991.
[30] Ibid. 12 Apr. 1985; P.R.O., F 16/63 (no. 2852); F 16/70.
[31] Phelps, *Forest in Old Photog.* (1984), 131.
[32] *Dean Forest Mercury*, 12 Apr. 1985.
[33] *Kelly's Dir. Glos.* (1894), 110; Glos. R.O., SP 32 (a hist. of Cinderford R.F.C.), *passim*.
[34] *Kelly's Dir. Glos.* (1935), 117.

[35] *Dean Forest Mercury*, 27 Apr. 1956; O.S. Map 1/2,500, SO 6614 (1960 edn.).
[36] Glos. R.O., SM 109/2/M 2, p. 148; *Kelly's Dir. Glos.* (1935), 117.
[37] *Dean Forest & Wye Valley* (H.M.S.O. 1956), 6.
[38] *Glouc. Jnl.* 30 July, 27 Aug. 1853; 28 July, 25 Aug. 1855; 16 Aug. 1856.
[39] Ibid. 20 Aug. 1864; 5 June 1869.
[40] Ibid. 24 Apr. 1897.
[41] Phelps, *Forest of Dean*, 122; *Dean Forest Mercury*, 15 Oct. 1971.
[42] Glos. R.O., SB 15/4, pp. 74, 391; *Glouc. Jnl.* 7 Sept. 1912.
[43] P.R.O., E 134/2 Jas. II Mich./18.
[44] *Glouc. Jnl.* 7 Apr. 1806.
[45] Glos. R.O., Q/RZ 1.
[46] *Glouc. Jnl.* 31 July 1897.
[47] P.R.O., MR 691 (LRRO 1/240); *Glouc. Jnl.* 30 Nov. 1807.
[48] *Glouc. Jnl.* 6 Nov. 1852; 9 Sept. 1854; 30 June, 22 Dec. 1855.
[49] Glos. R.O., Q/RZ 1.
[50] *Glouc. Jnl.* 15 Jan. 1870.
[51] Glos. R.O., Q/FR 4/1, ff. 19, 21, 31; Q/RGf 1/4.
[52] *Glouc. Jnl.* 1 July 1854.
[53] P.R.O., FS 2/3.

temperance advocate R. B. Thomas, planned to open a coffee house.[54] Four inns, the Courtfield Arms, the Anchor, the Forge Hammer, and the Jovial Colliers, were open in 1993. A friendly society met at the Bell in 1808[55] and there were many societies, including branches of the Odd Fellows and the Ancient Order of Foresters, based on Lydbrook's inns in the mid 19th century.[56] One of the largest, the Royal William Benefit Society formed in 1834, had 170 members in 1853.[57] A friendly society for women was started in 1853.[58] A co-operative society formed at Upper Lydbrook in 1880[59] was wound up during the 1926 miners' strike and the Cinderford society bought its store in 1933.[60] Another co-operative society traded at Lower Lydbrook in the late 19th century.[61]

In the later 19th century and the early 20th the Vaughans of Courtfield played an important role in the life of Lydbrook. Their meadow across the river Wye from the village was used for sports and such events as an annual horticultural show founded in the mid 1890s.[62] In 1868 a public reading room was opened in a former chapel at Lower Lydbrook under the patronage of local landowners and industrialists,[63] and from 1873 the village's principal meeting place was a new wooden market hall provided next to the Anchor inn by the ironmaster William Russell.[64] The hall, used as a cinema just after the First World War,[65] was demolished before 1974.[66] At Upper Lydbrook, where an institute was formed, probably by the Forest of Dean Recreative and Medical Aid Association, in 1892,[67] a memorial hall opened in 1926 became a centre of social and educational activities.[68] It was also used as a cinema until the 1960s and an adjoining building, housing a library in 1959,[69] was replaced by a health centre, opened in 1976.[70] A British Legion club had new premises in the village in 1980.[71] The Trafalgar brass band, the most notable colliery band in the Forest, was formed before 1866 and was one of several bands in the village in the early 20th century. It later became the Lydbrook silver band.[72] Lydbrook had at least one rugby club in 1892[73] and one of two rugby clubs there in the early 20th century played on the meadow at Courtfield. Rugby

ceased to be the village's main sport in the late 1920s when an association football club, formed in 1919 by local Baptists, took over the Courtfield ground. That club, which became one of the more successful clubs in the region, later played on a recreation ground at Upper Lydbrook.[74] The ground, near the memorial hall, was created in 1934 and 1935 by removing a massive colliery tip from the site.[75]

Leading figures in the early life of PARKEND included the Revd. Henry Poole (d. 1857), who built St. Paul's church, and Edward Machen, who as deputy surveyor of the Forest until 1854 lived at Whitemead Park.[76] In 1841 the village had the Fountain inn[77] and a beerhouse at its ironworks.[78] Among Parkend's other inns the British Lion opened as a beerhouse in 1849[79] and closed in the 1920s.[80] The Fountain and the Woodman, the latter known in the late 1870s as the New Inn,[81] were open in 1993. Several friendly societies met at the Fountain in the mid 1850s[82] and a branch of the Ancient Order of Foresters dined at another inn in 1863.[83] A co-operative society had a store in the village in 1870[84] but did not long survive. By 1901 a reading room and institute had opened with the help of Philip Baylis, the deputy surveyor, in a pavilion brought from the Speech House[85] and in 1909, under Baylis's successor V. F. Leese, the institute moved together with a forestry school to a building which had been part of the Parkend ironworks. The school used the whole of that building from 1914[86] and the institute's funds were assigned to a new memorial hall in the village in 1920.[87] A working men's club had its own premises in 1960.[88] Parkend had a brass band in 1863.[89] A silver band was formed in 1893 from the pipe and fife band of New Fancy colliery.[90] There was a cricket club in the village in 1892[91] and an association football club in 1923.[92] A field in the centre of Parkend was used as a sports ground by the late 1950s.[93]

Among the settlements east of Lydbrook, the changing character of Forest society in the later 20th century was clearly illustrated at the Pludds, where the village beerhouse, shops, choral society, cricket club, and the chapel at nearby Knights Hill had closed or been disbanded by the late 1980s.[94]

54   *Tinplaters of Lydney and Lydbrook*, ed. B. Rendell and K. Childs (n.d.), 31–2: copy in Glos. R.O., PA 209/11.
55   Glos. R.O., Q/RSf 2.
56   Ibid. Q/RZ 1; P.R.O., FS 2/3; *Glouc. Jnl.* 6 July 1844; 9 June 1849; 12 July 1851; 6 Nov. 1852; 10 June, 1, 8 July 1854.
57   P.R.O., FS 2/3; *Glouc. Jnl.* 21 May 1853.
58   *Glouc. Jnl.* 1 July 1854.
59   Glos. R.O., D 2754/8/3, p. 688.
60   *New Regard of Forest of Dean*, ix. 17.
61   *Kelly's Dir. Glos.* (1889), 834; (1897), 231.
62   *Glouc. Jnl.* 12 June, 31 July 1897; 1 June, 10 Aug. 1912.
63   *Glos. Chron.* 18 Apr. 1868.
64   *Forest of Dean Examiner*, 20 Sept. 1873.
65   W.I. hist. of Lydbrook (c. 1959, TS. in Glos. Colln.), 15.
66   O.S. Map 1/2,500, SO 5916 (1976 edn.).
67   W.I. hist. of Lydbrook, 15; for the association, above, this chapter.
68   W.I. hist. of Lydbrook, 17–18.
69   O.S. Map 1/2,500, SO 6015 (1961 edn.).
70   *Dean Forest Mercury*, 26 Mar. 1976.
71   *Citizen*, 1 Nov. 1980.
72   *Glouc. Jnl.* 15 Sept. 1866; W.I. hist. of Lydbrook, 23A.
73   Glos. R.O., SP 32, p. 25.
74   W.I. hist. of Lydbrook, 16–17; *Tinplaters of Lydney*

and Lydbrook, 67.
75   *Glos. Countryside*, Jan. 1935, 16, 27–8; Glos. R.O., D 3168/3/16.
76   Nicholls, *Personalities of Dean*, 88–92, 152–60; below, Churches; Educ., elementary schs.
77   Glos. R.O., Q/FR 4/1, f. 55.
78   Ibid. Q/RUm 175, p. 6.
79   Ibid. D 1443, W. Dean deeds 1842–58; *Glouc. Jnl.* 11 Sept. 1852.
80   R. Anstis, *Story of Parkend* (1982), 33.
81   O.S. Map 6", Glos. XXXIX. SW. (1883 edn.).
82   *Glouc. Jnl.* 21 May, 23 July 1853; 10 June, 22 July 1854; 2 June, 14 July 1855.
83   Ibid. 29 Aug. 1863.
84   *Kelly's Dir. Glos.* (1870), 617.   85   P.R.O., F 3/856.
86   Ibid. F 3/1120; F 3/1162; for Leese, Hart, *Royal Forest*, 232.
87   P.R.O., F 3/856; F 3/1484; the hall is dated 1919.
88   O.S. Map 1/2,500, SO 6108 (1960 edn.).
89   *Glouc. Jnl.* 29 Aug. 1863.
90   Phelps, *Forest of Dean*, 92.
91   *Harris's Dir. Dean Forest* (1892), 43.
92   Phelps, *Forest in Old Photog.* (1984), 130.
93   O.S. Map 1/2,500, SO 6108 (1960 edn.).
94   *Citizen*, 19 June 1989.

The wooden village hall, built in 1975,[95] was in use in 1993. At Ruardean Woodside there was a beerhouse on the Forest boundary in 1841[96] and another nearby in 1862;[97] the Roebuck, the survivor of the two, closed in the early 1990s. A memorial hall was built there in 1922.[98] In 1841 RUARDEAN HILL and Nailbridge each had two beerhouses[99] and by 1853 there was a beerhouse called the China Court on Morse Road.[1] In the early 20th century Ruardean Hill had cricket and rugby and association football clubs, some based on public houses in the adjoining part of Ruardean parish, and in 1927 a recreation ground was opened on the hill.[2] The Baptist chapel, an early centre of social life on the hill, had a fife and drum band in the late 1890s and was the home of a choral society formed in 1914. That society incorporated an older choir formed by members of the Cinderford male voice choir.[3]

DRYBROOK'S principal inn, the Hearts of Oak, was built as a beerhouse in 1838[4] and was known for a long time as the New Inn. A friendly society for miners was meeting there in 1849.[5] Later inns in the village centre, including the Royal Oak recorded in 1852,[6] had been closed by 1993. Drybrook also had a coffee house in 1889.[7] From the mid 19th century members of the Brain family of industrialists lived in or near Drybrook and attended its Congregational chapel.[8] A women's choir attached to the chapel continued to meet after the Second World War[9] and a male voice choir had its own hall in the village by 1990. A memorial hall and institute, built shortly after the First World War,[10] housed a library in 1947[11] and was used for social functions in 1993. In 1921 Drybrook also had a cinema and a recreation ground.[12] Of the village's early rugby clubs[13] one, formed in 1892 and later called Drybrook R.F.C., acquired a ground by the Mitcheldean road in the mid 20th century and fielded nine teams in the early 1990s.[14] The Drybrook band, re-formed in 1924, became a silver band in 1926[15] and built its own hall in 1984.[16]

On the east side of the Forest there was a beerhouse called the Odd Fellows' Arms at Stenders, above Mitcheldean, in 1841.[17] At Plump Hill the Miners' Arms, in 1857 the meeting place of a friendly society with 130 members, was the principal beerhouse.[18] Known later as the Point inn,[19] it closed after 1960.[20] Of the two beerhouses at Pope's Hill in 1841[21] that known later as the Greyhound[22] was open in 1993. Pope's Hill had its own association football club in 1924.[23]

In the SOUDLEY area there were two beerhouses on Bradley hill in 1841[24] and a friendly society met in 1857 in the one called the White Horse.[25] In 1993 there was a public house on the hill and Soudley village had the White Horse inn. A memorial hall built in the village c. 1924[26] was later demolished. A new hall built in the mid 1970s on a different site next to a recreation ground[27] was used for village activities and by Soudley A.F.C. in 1993. The recreation ground was laid out on land given to the people of Soudley and Blakeney Hill c. 1904[28] and an open-air service on it in 1906 was attended by a band from Two Bridges.[29] Two Bridges also had an association football club in the mid 1930s.[30]

The villages and hamlets on the southern edge of the Forest, from Blakeney Hill in the east to Whitecroft in the west, benefited from the benevolence of Charles Bathurst (d. 1863) and his successors as owners of the Lydney Park estate to the south.[31] In 1841 the YORKLEY area contained seven beerhouses on Crown land, one each at Old Furnace bottom, Viney Hill, Yorkley, and Pillowell, and three at Whitecroft.[32] In Old Furnace bottom there were three inns near the new Blakeney–Parkend road in 1851; they included the Tump House[33] which remained open until 1969.[34] At Viney Hill the Albion inn, where a burial club met and a Blakeney friendly society held its anniversary in 1855,[35] closed after 1957[36] and the New Inn, recorded from 1876,[37] was open in 1993. The Nag's Head, the oldest inn in Yorkley, had opened by 1788.[38] Later inns there, including the Stag opened by 1870,[39] have closed, apart from the Bailey (formerly the Royal Oak) inn.[40] At Pillowell a beerhouse known in

95 *Dean Forest Mercury*, 12 Sept. 1975.
96 Above, Ruardean, intro.
97 Above, Settlement; O.S. Map 6", Glos. XXXI. NW. (1883 edn.).
98 Date on bldg.
99 Glos. R.O., Q/FR 4/1, ff. 110, 113, 115, 133; Q/RGf 1/8.
1 *Glouc. Jnl.* 24 Dec. 1853; O.S. Map 6", Glos. XXXI. NE. (1884 edn.).
2 Bent, *Highest Point of Dean*, 57, 66, 77–8, 95–8.
3 Ibid. 34–42.
4 Date on bldg.; Glos. R.O., FR 4/1, f. 115; Q/RGf 1/8.
5 P.R.O., FS 2/3; O.S. Map 6", Glos. XXXI. NE. (1884 edn.).
6 *Glouc. Jnl.* 18 Dec. 1852; Glos. R.O., D 2428/1/28; annotated copy of O.S. Map 1/2,500, Glos. XXXI. 3 (1903 edn.).
7 *Kelly's Dir. Glos.* (1889), 753.
8 G.D.R., T 1/151; *Kelly's Dir. Glos.* (1870), 532; *Kelly's Dir. Herefs.* (1870), 334; below, Industry, mining from 1770s; other ind. and trade; tramroads and railways; Prot. Nonconf.
9 Phelps, *Forest in Old Photog.* (1984), 122.
10 O.S. Map 1/2,500, Glos. XXXI. 3 (1923 edn.).
11 Glos. R.O., CE/M 2/30, f. 161.
12 O.S. Map 1/2,500, Glos. XXXI. 3 (1923 edn.).
13 Cf. Glos. R.O., SP 32, p. 9.
14 *Forester*, 4 Sept. 1992; O.S. Map 1/2,500, SO 6517 (1974 edn.).
15 *Glouc. Jnl.* 4 Apr. 1981.

16 Date on bldg.
17 P.R.O., HO 107/364, s.v. Herbert walk; Glos. R.O., Q/FR 4/1, f. 120.
18 *Glouc. Jnl.* 18 July 1857.   19 Ibid. 13 July 1867.
20 O.S. Map 1/2,500, SO 6617 (1960 edn.).
21 Glos. R.O., Q/FR 4/1, ff. 90–1; Q/RGf 1/7.
22 O.S. Map 1/2,500, Glos. XXXII. 9 (1881 edn.).
23 Phelps, *Forest in Old Photog.* (1983), 81.
24 Glos. R.O., Q/FR 4/1, f. 58; Q/RGf 1/6.
25 P.R.O., FS 2/3.
26 Glos. R.O., P 85/IN 3/5.
27 O.S. Map 1/2,500, SO 6510 (1978 edn.); Phelps, *Forest of Dean*, 55.
28 P.R.O., F 3/473.
29 *Glouc. Jnl.* 6 Oct. 1906.
30 Photogs. at Dean Heritage mus., Soudley.
31 Below, Churches; Educ., elementary schs.; for Bathurst and his successors, above, Lydney, manors.
32 Glos. R.O., Q/FR 4/1, ff. 34, 36, 38, 64, 71; Q/RGf 1/5–6.
33 P.R.O., HO 107/1959, s.v. E. Dean.
34 Phelps, *Forest of Dean*, 51.
35 G.D.R. wills 1857/126; *Glouc. Jnl.* 21 July 1855.
36 O.S. Map 1/2,500, SO 6506 (1958, 1976 edns.).
37 *Forest of Dean Examiner*, 7 July 1876.
38 P.R.O., F 17/6.
39 *Kelly's Dir. Glos.* (1870), 534.
40 Glos. R.O., D 2428/1/23/2; annotated copy of O.S. Map 1/2,500, Glos. XXXIX. 11 (1903 edn.).

1901 as the Royal Foresters' Arms closed after 1958[41] but at Phipps Bottom the Swan, so called in 1891,[42] was open in 1993. In 1993 Whitecroft had the Miners' Arms, one of the beerhouses there in 1841.[43] Among friendly societies meeting at the Nag's Head was a branch of the Odd Fellows established in 1834 and, in 1853, a women's benefit society.[44] The Yorkley and Pillowell co-operative society, formed by 1892,[45] traded at Pillowell.[46] In 1955 it merged with the Gloucester society.[47] Yorkley had a working men's institute in 1892.[48] A new institute was built on Bailey hill c. 1910 and a recreation ground was laid out next to it in the early 1920s as the district's war memorial.[49] The area's earliest recreation ground was between Yorkley and Oldcroft on waste land given for public use c. 1893 and was used by a cricket club in 1914.[50] Further east towards Viney Hill a football ground laid out opposite All Saints' school before 1957[51] included the new building of a sports and social club in 1993. At Pillowell the earliest recreation ground was on land at the edge of Kidnalls wood, to the south, donated by Lord Bledisloe c. 1919.[52] Among brass bands in the area was one at Yorkley in 1853[53] and one founded at Pillowell in 1889. Yorkley Onward band started in 1903 as an offshoot of the Pillowell band and its hall, built in 1913, has been used for village activities.[54] In 1897 there was a mutual improvement and choral society in Pillowell.[55] In 1993 Whitecroft had a memorial hall dating from 1924.[56] A later building next to it has been used as an institute and by local societies and clubs.[57] The village had a successful rugby club before the First World War[58] and a male voice choir in the mid 20th century.[59] At Brockhollands a small hall was built by the miners' welfare committee in the early 1930s.[60]

In the BREAM area the Rising Sun, on the edge of the Forest north of the old part of Bream village, was the meeting place of a friendly society in 1787.[61] Later licensed houses in the area included a beerhouse at Bream's Eaves in 1841,[62] the Two Swans in High Street south-west of the Rising Sun in 1869, and the King's Head at Bream Woodside, the Miners' Rest at Bream's Meend, and the Miners' Arms on the

Coleford road at Bream Tufts in the late 1870s.[63] They had all closed by 1993, when Bream retained the Rising Sun, renamed the Village Inn, and the Cross Keys, which had moved from the old village centre to a building on the Parkend road c. 1960.[64] A co-operative society trading at Bream in 1897 was absorbed by the Cinderford society before 1935.[65] J. F. Gosling, vicar of Bream 1869–82,[66] started a coffee and reading room at the village school.[67] Sun green, to the south-west, was given to the people of Bream for their recreation c. 1887 and a village institute started in the early 20th century moved in 1908 to a new temporary building next to the ground.[68] That building was replaced after 1970 by a new social club on the same site.[69] From 1927 the village's main meeting place was a new Miners' Welfare hall in High Street. Later the hall was a cinema and in the 1960s it was rebuilt as the headquarters of the Bream rugby club. That club traced its origins to 1878.[70] Several other halls and huts in the area have been used for meetings and entertainments. One was a cinema until it was dismantled during the First World War.[71] A branch of the county library service occupied an iron building on the Whitecroft road in 1959[72] and moved to a building vacated by the village school in the mid 1970s.[73] Among local societies was a male voice choir started in the late 1940s.[74]

In the hamlets north-west of Bream a beerhouse, known locally as the Dog and Muffler, had opened in the mill house at Oakwood by 1856.[75] It closed after 1960.[76] A beerhouse on Clements End green in 1878[77] was known as the Montague inn in 1993. On Clearwell Meend a beerhouse in the Sling area was called the Miners' Arms in 1841.[78] Another building nearby had adopted that name by the late 1870s[79] and remained an inn in 1993. A memorial hall built at Sling c. 1921 was superseded by a new Miners' Welfare institute in 1931.[80] It was a social club in 1993. Further north on Clearwell Meend a bandstand erected in the early 20th century near the Coleford road[81] was replaced c. 1980 by a stand on a different site.[82] At Milkwall a beerhouse opened by the late 1870s[83] was known as the Tufthorn inn in 1993. A wooden village hall

41 O.S. Maps 1/2,500, Glos. XXXIX. 14 (1903 edn.); SO 6206 (1959 edn.).
42 *Licensed Houses in Glos. 1891*, 58.
43 Glos. R.O., Q/FR 4/1, f. 38; Q/RGf 1/5.
44 *Glouc. Jnl.* 19 June 1852; 25 June, 23 July 1853.
45 G. E. Lawrence, *Kindling the Flame*, 50: copy in Glos. R.O., D 2598/23/1.
46 *Kelly's Dir. Glos.* (1894), 335.
47 Glos. R.O., D 2754/9/2, p. 5.
48 *Harris's Dir. Dean Forest* (1892), 52.
49 P.R.O., F 3/1190; F 3/1442.
50 Ibid. F 3/473.
51 O.S. Map 1/2,500, SO 6506 (1958 edn.).
52 P.R.O., F 3/1484.
53 *Glouc. Jnl.* 25 June 1853.
54 Phelps, *Forest of Dean*, 95; *Citizen*, 17 Aug. 1978.
55 Glos. R.O., SB 15/4, p. 327.
56 Date on bldg.
57 O.S. Map 1/2,500, SO 6106 (1960 edn.).
58 Glos. R.O., SP 32, pp. 10, 107–8.
59 Phelps, *Forest in Old Photog.* (1984), 123.
60 Glos. R.O., DA 25/711/7.
61 Ibid. Q/RSf 2.
62 Ibid. Q/FR 4/1, f. 41; Q/RGf 1/5.
63 *Glouc. Jnl.* 13 Nov. 1869; O.S. Map 6", Glos. XXXIX.

SW. (1883 edn.).
64 Camm, *Bream through the Ages* (1979), 44.
65 *Kelly's Dir. Glos.* (1897), 48; (1935), 53.
66 Glos. R.O., P 57/IN 1/17.
67 *Harris's Dir. Dean Forest* (1887), 21.
68 P.R.O., F 3/473; F 3/1039.
69 O.S. Map 1/2,500, SO 6005 (1971 edn.).
70 Camm, *Bream through the Ages*, 25, 39; O.S. Map 1/2,500, SO 6005 (1960, 1971 edns.).
71 Camm, *Bream through the Ages*, 23, 26.
72 O.S. Map 1/2,500, SO 6006 (1960 edn.); personal observation.
73 W. A. Camm, *Bream through the Ages* (1980), 14; below, Educ., elementary schs.
74 Phelps, *Forest of Dean*, 94.
75 Ibid.; *Glouc. Jnl.* 10 May 1856.
76 Camm, *Bream through the Ages* (1979), 29.
77 O.S. Map 1/2,500, Glos. XXXVIII. 12 (1881 edn.).
78 Glos. R.O., Q/FR 4/1, f. 45; Q/RGf 1/5; *Reg. Electors W. Division Glos. 1841–2*, 143.
79 O.S. Map 6", Glos. XXXVIII. SE. (1883 edn.).
80 *Glouc. Jnl.* 30 May 1931.
81 O.S. Map 6", Glos. XXXVIII. NE. (1903, 1924 edns.).
82 Phelps, *Forest of Dean*, 104.
83 O.S. Map 6", Glos. XXXVIII. NE. (1884 edn.).

was built after the First World War and a recreation ground was laid out in the mid 1930s.[84] An association football club had its own ground by the later 1950s. A social club built at Milkwall by 1959 was later enlarged.[85]

There were four beerhouses on extraparochial land in the Lane End district in 1841, one at COALWAY and three at BROADWELL.[86] Of Coalway's three public houses in the late 1870s[87] the Crown remained open in 1993 together with a later inn called the Britannia. A recreation ground was laid out at Coalway in the later 1930s and a village hall was built on it in 1988.[88] At Broadwell the Bird in Hand, one of the beerhouses there in 1841,[89] remained open in 1993, but other inns, including the Rising Sun recorded in the late 1870s,[90] had closed. In 1886 a fife and drum band was based on Broadwell.[91] Broadwell's memorial hall, built in 1921,[92] housed a library in 1955.[93] A social club next to the hall was enlarged after 1959.[94] Broadwell also had a football ground by 1959.[95] At Mile End the Royal Forester inn had opened by the mid 1870s.[96]

Of the beerhouses and inns opened in the BERRY HILL area in the mid 19th century the King's Head at Berry Hill, the Rising Sun at Five Acres, and the Dog and Muffler (in 1838 the New Inn and later the Britannia) at Joyford[97] remained open in 1993. Short Standing, where there was a beerhouse in 1841[98] and two public houses in the later 19th century,[99] was without a public house from c. 1990. An inn between Berry Hill and Five Acres, in the late 1870s the Globe beerhouse,[1] reopened in 1993 after a few

years' closure. In 1919 there was a recreation ground at Five Acres and in the early 1920s a Y.M.C.A. hut was erected next to it as an institute and war memorial for the Berry Hill area.[2] A recreation ground created nearby in 1926 became the home of Berry Hill Rugby Football club. The club, one of the most successful in the Forest, had its origins in the early 1890s and its senior team was the county's champion side several times in the 1980s.[3] In 1987 a leisure centre opened on the school campus at Five Acres, then occupied by Lakers school and the Royal Forest of Dean College. The centre, which took over 10 years to build, included a swimming pool and, together with the college theatre, was for public as well as school use.[4] A social club was built in Berry Hill before 1960.[5] In the early 1880s there were two brass bands in the area, one made up of members of a temperance organization and the other of employees of Speedwell colliery.[6] A silver band based on Salem chapel in the 1930s[7] practised in an iron hut behind the chapel in 1993. Worrall Hill had a recreation ground in the mid 1950s.[8]

In the hamlets towards the centre of the Forest a beerhouse recorded at Brierley in 1841 became known as the Quarryman's Arms[9] and was the meeting place of a friendly society in 1853;[10] the hamlet had the Swan inn in 1993. Brierley also had an institute in 1921[11] and an association football club in 1936,[12] and a recreation ground had been laid out there by the late 1950s.[13] In the small hamlet of Moseley Green a public house called the Rising Sun in 1879[14] remained open in 1993.

CHURCHES

BEFORE the 19th century the royal demesne land of the Forest of Dean was extraparochial and had no churches. Newland church, the rector of which was entitled under grants of 1283 and 1305 to the tithes of Whitemead and of new closes and assarts within the Forest,[15] was regarded as the Foresters' parish church[16] and in the early 16th century one of its chantry priests was required to preach the gospel twice a week at forges and mines within the parish.[17] By the late 18th century Foresters and inhabitants of

detached parts of Newland lying intermingled with the Forest attended several churches near the extraparochial area.[18] A society formed at Coleford under the auspices of Henry Ryder, the new bishop of Gloucester, in 1815 to sell bibles cheaply in the Forest region was supported by local clergy, both Anglican and nonconformist,[19] and a similar society was started at Lydbrook in 1830.[20] The Forest's first consecrated churches or chapels, Christ Church (1816) at Berry Hill, Holy Trinity (1817) near Drybrook, and St. Paul

84 Glos. R.O., D 3168/3/4, 6.
85 *Coleford Social Guide* (1955), 13; O.S. Map 1/2,500, SO 5809 (1960, 1978 edns.).
86 Glos. R.O., Q/FR 4/1, ff. 2, 53; Q/RGf 1/4-5.
87 O.S. Maps 6", Glos. XXXVIII. NE. (1884 edn.); XXXIX. NW. (1883 edn.).
88 Glos. R.O., D 3168/3/4; *Dean Forest Mercury*, 8 July 1988.
89 Glos. R.O., Q/FR 4/1, f. 2; Q/RGf 1/4.
90 O.S. Map 6", Glos. XXXVIII. NE. (1884 edn.).
91 Glos. R.O., P 93/MI 1/1.
92 Date on bldg.   93 *Coleford Social Guide*, 41.
94 O.S. Map 1/2,500, SO 5811 (1960, 1974 edns.).
95 Ibid. SO 5810 (1960 edn.).
96 *Morris's Dir. Glos.* (1876), 476.
97 Above, Settlement; for the Dog and Muffler's earlier names, *Reg. Electors W. Division Glos. 1838–9*, 135; O.S. Map 6", Glos. XXX. SE. (1884 edn.).
98 Glos. R.O., Q/FR 4/1, f. 16; Q/RGf 1/4.
99 O.S. Map 6", Glos. XXX. SE. (1884 edn.).
1 Ibid.
2 P.R.O., F 3/1484; postcard postmarked 1924 at Dean

Heritage mus.; *Kelly's Dir. Glos.* (1927), 123.
3 J. Belcher, *Breathe on 'um Berry* (Coleford, 1992), *passim*.   4 *Dean Forest Mercury*, 3 Apr. 1987.
5 O.S. Map 1/2,500, SO 5712 (1960 edn.).
6 Glos. R.O., P 93/MI 1/1.
7 Potter, *Changing Forest*, 11–12.
8 *Coleford Social Guide*, 13.
9 Glos. R.O., Q/FR 4/1, f. 109; Q/RGf 1/8; *Kelly's Dir. Glos.* (1856), 278.   10 P.R.O., FS 2/3.
11 O.S. Map 1/2,500, Glos. XXXI. 6 (1922 edn.).
12 Glos. R.O., D 3168/3/10.
13 O.S. Map 1/2,500, SO 6215 (1961 edn.).
14 Ibid. 6", Glos. XXXIX. NE. (1884 edn.).
15 *Cal. Close, 1279–88*, 219; *Cal. Pat. 1301–7*, 319.
16 P. M. Procter, *Origin of Established Ch. and Nat. Day Sch. in Forest of Dean* (1819), 2.
17 Hockaday Abs. ccxcv, 1548.
18 Glos. R.O., P 30/IN 1/1; P 209/IN 1/2; *3rd Rep. Dean Forest Com.* 32.
19 Glos. R.O., D 2722/28; *Handbook of Brit. Chronology* (1961), 228.
20 Glos. R.O., D 2297.

(1822) at Parkend, were built with some assistance from the Crown, acting mostly through the Commissioners of Woods, Forests, and Land Revenues, for missions conducted by neighbouring clergymen, one of whom also provided a Sunday schoolroom at Lydbrook. The cost of the chapels, which had congregations of poor people drawn from surrounding settlements, was largely borne by their clergy, and in 1830 the Commissioners of Woods established a trust fund to keep the three buildings in repair. The chapels remained without parishes and some parts of the Forest continued under the clergy of adjoining parishes[21] until the mid 1840s when, under an Act of 1842, the Forest was divided into four ecclesiastical districts, one being for a new church at Cinderford,[22] dedicated to St. John the Evangelist in 1844. More churches and school-chapels were built in the later 19th century, including the churches at Lydbrook and Viney Hill, and missions were opened in lesser hamlets before the First World War, some of them organized by Bream, Clearwell, and Coleford churches,[23] which in the later 19th century were given charge over parts of the Forest.[24]

The church of *ALL SAINTS*, Viney Hill, begun in 1865 and consecrated in 1867, was built as a memorial to Charles Bathurst (d. 1863) of Lydney Park by his wife Mary and his brother and heir, the Revd. W. H. Bathurst.[25] In the mid 1830s the Viney Hill area was visited by the curate of Blakeney and the vicar of Awre.[26] Later Henry Poole organized missions from St. Paul's church, Parkend, and in the early 1850s he built school-chapels between Viney Hill and Oldcroft and at Blakeney Woodside with the help of Charles Bathurst and Edward Machen, deputy surveyor of the Forest.[27] That between Viney Hill and Oldcroft, which became known as St. Swithin,[28] was replaced for services by All Saints' church, further east. All Saints was in 1866 assigned a parish taken from that of St. Paul's church and including Blakeney Hill and Yorkley Slade.[29] The benefice, described as a perpetual curacy (later a vicarage), was given a stipend of £150, of which £100 was secured by an endowment from Mary and W. H. Bathurst,[30] and a new house north of the church.[31] The patronage was vested in W. H. Bathurst[32] and

descended with the Lydney Park estate[33] until 1936 when Viscount Bledisloe gave it to University College, Oxford.[34]

All Saints' church, built of local red sandstone with grey sandstone dressings, was designed by Ewan Christian[35] in a late 13th-century style with an apsidal chancel flanked by quadrant chapels and a nave with north transept and south aisle and porch. The north chapel was used as a vestry and the south chapel was converted in the early 20th century as a choir vestry. Of the fittings the organ, in the transept, was bought between 1900 and 1904 to replace another instrument.[36] The two bells hanging in a bellcot over the chancel were cast in 1867 by Mears & Stainbank.[37] The plate includes an almsdish donated in 1901 by Charles Bathurst (later Viscount Bledisloe)[38] and a chalice and paten given in memory of C. R. Williams, vicar 1922–50.[39] The mission to Blakeney Woodside continued under All Saints' church until its abandonment before 1950.[40] In 1875 A. D. Pringle, vicar of Blakeney, began holding Sunday services in a former Baptist meeting house at Blakeney Hill.[41] The building was presumably that used as a mission hall until at least 1901.[42]

CHRIST CHURCH, Berry Hill, was consecrated in 1816[43] but dates from 1812 when P. M. Procter, vicar of Newland, built a school-chapel for his mission to the Forest. The site was acquired from Thomas Morgan, a coal miner in whose cottage, to the north, Procter had started preaching in 1804,[44] and grants and subscriptions towards the school-chapel came from, among others, the duke of Beaufort, the bishop, and the National Society.[45] The building was opened in 1813 and after a year or so was used solely as a free chapel[46] by people from the settlements around Berry Hill and sometimes from as far afield as Lydbrook, Worrall Hill, Hillersland, and the Lane End district.[47] To endow the chapel Procter obtained a grant of 5 a. in the Forest from the Commissioners of the Treasury in 1813 and, having raised funds by a public appeal, purchased 26 a. in Coleford in 1815 and Morgan's cottage. The endowment, which he vested with the chapel and its patronage in trustees,[48] was augmented by Queen Anne's Bounty in 1817 with a grant of £2,000[49] and included *c.* 92 a. of glebe in Coleford in

[21] *3rd Rep. Dean Forest Com.* 18; *8th Rep. Com. Woods,* H.C. 179, p. 10 (1831).
[22] Dean Forest Eccl. Districts Act, 5 & 6 Vic. c. 65.
[23] Above, Coleford, churches; Newland, churches.
[24] *Lond. Gaz.* 16 June 1854, p. 1863; 18 Apr. 1856, pp. 1464–5; 8 July 1890, pp. 3775–7.
[25] *Glouc. Jnl.* 25 Nov. 1865; 27 Apr. 1867.
[26] *3rd Rep. Dean Forest Com.* 32.
[27] Nicholls, *Forest of Dean,* 170; Nicholls, *Personalities of Dean,* 88, 159; cf. Hockaday Abs. clxxvi, St. Paul; for sites of school-chapels, P.R.O., F 16/63 (nos. 3542, 3773); F 16/70.
[28] *Glouc. Jnl.* 27 Apr. 1867; 26 Dec. 1874; in ibid. 30 July 1853, it was called the Sweden chapel of ease.
[29] *Lond. Gaz.* 18 Sept. 1866, pp. 5081–2; cf. Glos. R.O., P 348/CW 3/1.
[30] G.D.R. vol. 385, p. 81; *Lond. Gaz.* 18 Sept. 1866, pp. 5081–2; 5 Apr. 1867, pp. 2126–7.
[31] Glos. R.O., P 348/MI 3.
[32] *Lond. Gaz.* 18 Sept. 1866, pp. 5081–2.
[33] G.D.R., D 5/1/46; Burke, *Peerage* (1963), 257–8;

above, Lydney, manors.
[34] Glos. R.O., P 348/MI 3.
[35] *Glouc. Jnl.* 27 Apr. 1867; in ibid. 25 Nov. 1865, the architect was said to be Mr. Colston.
[36] Glos. R.O., D 3921/II/5.
[37] *Glos. Ch. Bells,* 632.
[38] *Glos. Ch. Plate,* 86–7; Burke, *Peerage* (1963), 258.
[39] Glos. Colln. R 102.1.
[40] Glos. R.O., D 3921/II/5.
[41] *Glouc. Jnl.* 29 May 1875; *Morris's Dir. Glos.* (1876), 436.
[42] O.S. Map 1/2,500, Glos. XXXIX. 11 (1878 edn.); Glos. R.O., DA 24/100/3, pp. 277–8.
[43] *Glouc. Jnl.* 22 July 1816.
[44] Procter, *Origin of Ch. in Dean,* 2–22; cf. G.D.R. vol. 334B, p. 189. [45] Nicholls, *Forest of Dean,* 98.
[46] Procter, *Origin of Ch. in Dean,* 21–2, 26–7, 30; cf. *3rd Rep. Dean Forest Com.* 19.
[47] Procter, *Origin of Ch. in Dean,* vol. cxxxix; Glos. R.O., P 82/IN 1/1.
[48] G.D.R. vol. 334B, pp. 155–91; Procter, *Origin of Ch. in Dean,* 25–6, 31.
[49] Hodgson, *Queen Anne's Bounty* (1845), p. cclxxxiv.

1840.[50] It provided an income of £140 in 1832[51] and £118 10s. 6d. in 1842.[52] Procter, who paid part of his debt arising from the chapel's foundation with £500 in grants obtained in 1818 with the help of Nicholas Vansittart, Chancellor of the Exchequer,[53] was minister until his death in 1822. His successors, sometimes described as perpetual curates, included from 1824 T. R. Garnsey (d. 1847), who held weekday meetings in the Lane End district, Joyford, and elsewhere.[54]

In 1844 Christ Church was assigned a district or parish extending to Mirystock, Cannop, and Broadwell Lane End.[55] It lost Broadwell in 1890 to the ecclesiastical parish of Coleford.[56] Under the Act of 1842 the patronage of Christ Church was transferred to the Crown and the chapel became a perpetual curacy with an income increased to £150 by an endowment from the Commissioners of Woods.[57] The benefice, later styled a vicarage,[58] was united with English Bicknor in 1972. The patronage of the new benefice was shared by the Crown and the Society for the Maintenance of the Faith, the latter having the right to fill the second of every four vacancies.[59] Christ Church vicarage house in what had been Thomas Morgan's cottage, enlarged c. 1840[60] with later additions, was retained for the benefice in 1972.[61] By 1989 it was used for retreats and conferences,[62] the incumbent living in a new bungalow south of the church.

The original church, on the road between Coleford and English Bicknor, was the school-chapel of 1812, a simple building with a west bellcot.[63] The chapel became a north aisle in 1815 when a new nave was added to double its size and a west gallery was erected. A west tower, designed by the Revd. Henry Poole, was added a few years after 1819[64] and a chancel with octagonal apse and north organ chamber, designed by the firm of Waller, Son, and Wood for the vicar, Christopher Barnes, in 1884 and 1885.[65] The church was restored in 1913, when a south-west vestry was added, the gallery removed, the nave repewed, and a chancel screen erected; the screen was removed before 1966.[66] The church has one bell[67] and its font is similar

to that provided for the church which Henry Poole built at Parkend in the early 1820s.[68]

The church of *HOLY JESUS*, Lydbrook, was begun in 1850 and consecrated in 1851.[69] It was built in Upper Lydbrook in the grounds of a Sunday schoolroom[70] which Henry Berkin, minister of Holy Trinity church, Harrow Hill, had erected in 1821. Services were held in the room from 1822, the mission to Lydbrook being conducted by Berkin's curate.[71] Some Lydbrook people attended church at Welsh Bicknor (Herefs., formerly Mon.), on the opposite side of the river Wye.[72] Impetus for building Lydbrook church came from John Burdon, rector of English Bicknor,[73] and £2,000 for the project was given by Edward Machen and his relatives. The remaining cost was met by grants and voluntary contributions, including £250 from local tinplate manufacturers Allaway & Partridge.[74] The church served an area centred on Lydbrook and created a consolidated chapelry in 1852 out of parts of the parishes of Holy Trinity, English Bicknor, Newland, and Ruardean. The living was styled a perpetual curacy[75] (later a vicarage)[76] and its initial endowments included a stipend of £90 from the Commissioners of Woods and, by the grant of John Burdon, £30 from the English Bicknor tithe rent charge.[77] The Crown and the patrons of English Bicknor had alternate rights of presentation. The bishop, to whom the right for English Bicknor was transferred in 1884,[78] became sole patron after 1939.[79] The endowments were augmented in 1854 when Queen Anne's Bounty gave £200 to meet gifts totalling £800.[80] Soon afterwards a parsonage was built some way south-east of the church on land given by the Commissioners of Woods.[81] The house was sold after the Second World War and the incumbent was provided with a new house at Mirystock, to the south-east.[82] The Sunday schoolroom, which housed a day school from 1849 to 1909 and served as a church hall after that,[83] was pulled down in 1975 and a new vicarage house was built on its site.[84]

The church, built of local gritstone with Bath stone dressings, was designed by Henry Woodyer in a 14th-century style, having a chan-

50 G.D.R., T 1/128.
51 *3rd Rep. Dean Forest Com.* 6.
52 Dean Forest Eccl. Districts Act, 5 & 6 Vic. c. 65.
53 Procter, *Origin of Ch. in Dean*, 32–4; Nicholls, *Forest of Dean*, 166–7; Hodgson, *Queen Anne's Bounty*, pp. cxcv, cclxxxiv; for Vansittart, *D.N.B.*
54 Hockaday Abs. clxxvi; Nicholls, *Personalities of Dean*, 148–51, 171.
55 G.D.R. vol. 361, ff. 101v.–103v.; cf. ibid. V 6/138; *Kelly's Dir. Glos.* (1870), 533.
56 *Lond. Gaz.* 8 July 1890, pp. 3775–7.
57 Dean Forest Eccl. Districts Act, 5 & 6 Vic. c. 65; G.D.R. vol. 384, f. 76.
58 *Kelly's Dir. Glos.* (1870), 533.
59 Glos. R.O., P 227/IN 3/5.
60 Nicholls, *Forest of Dean*, 166; cf. *3rd Rep. Dean Forest Com.* 19; P.R.O., HO 129/577/1/5/18.
61 Glos. R.O., P 227/IN 3/5.
62 *Dioc. of Glouc. Dir.* (1989), 115.
63 *Gent. Mag.* lxxxiv (1), plate facing p. 545, reproduced above, Plate 37.
64 Procter, *Origin of Ch. in Dean*, 26–7, 35 n.; Nicholls, *Forest of Dean*, 165–6; Nicholls, *Personalities of Dean*, 157.
65 Glos. R.O., D 1381/XJ.

66 *Glouc. Jnl.* 15 Feb. 1913; cf. Glos. R.O., P 278/VE 3/3.
67 *Kelly's Dir. Glos.* (1870), 533; *Glos. Ch. Bells*, 211–12.
68 Below, this chapter (St. Paul).
69 Nicholls, *Forest of Dean*, 174.
70 G.D.R. vol. 361, ff. 252v.–253v.
71 Glos. R.O., D 2297; Nicholls, *Personalities of Dean*, 140; Glos. Colln. L 9.4; cf. P.R.O., F 17/17; HO129/577/1/5/19.
72 P.R.O., HO 129/577/2/1/1.
73 G.D.R., F 3/2, pp. 55–6, 58–9.
74 Nicholls, *Forest of Dean*, 172–3.
75 *Lond. Gaz.* 20 Apr. 1852, pp. 1118–19.
76 *Kelly's Dir. Glos.* (1870), 592.
77 G.D.R., F 3/2, pp. 55–6; Nicholls, *Forest of Dean*, 174.
78 *Lond. Gaz.* 20 Apr. 1852, pp. 1118–19; 11 July 1884, pp. 3161–2.
79 Cf. *Kelly's Dir. Glos.* (1939), 253; *Dioc. of Glouc. Dir.* (1989), 57.
80 Hodgson, *Queen Anne's Bounty* (suppl. 1864), pp. xxxi, lxv.
81 Nicholls, *Forest of Dean*, 137; Glos. R.O., D 1381/6K.
82 O.S. Map 1/2,500, SO 6114 (1974 edn.).
83 Below, Educ., elementary schs.; Nat. Soc. files, Lydbrook.   84 Inf. from vicar (1990).

FIG. 24. HOLY TRINITY CHURCH AND SCHOOL, HARROW HILL, BUILT IN 1817.

cel with north sacristy, a clerestoried and aisled nave with south porch, and a west tower with saddle-back roof.[85] In 1912 an organ chamber was built between the sacristy and the north aisle and a choir vestry was added at the north-west corner of the church. A few windows have been filled with memorial glass, that in the east window of the chancel being provided in 1908 by Richard Thomas, formerly owner of the Lydbrook tinplate works.[86] The church has a bell cast in 1850 by John Warner and Sons of London[87] and a set of plate made in the same year by John Keith.[88]

HOLY TRINITY at Harrow Hill, near Drybrook, known locally as the Forest church,[89] was opened in 1817 and consecrated later the same year. It was built as a free chapel by its first minister, Henry Berkin,[90] then curate of Weston under Penyard (Herefs.), who began holding services in the Forest in 1812 while at Mitcheldean.[91] In 1816 the Commissioners of the Treasury acting for the Crown granted 5 a. for the church to trustees. The land lay in two

pieces, the smaller on Quarry hill where Berkin built the church and a schoolroom and the larger to the south-east where he built a parsonage.[92] The costs were met partly by grants, including £500 from the Treasury, and by a public subscription to which the duke of Beaufort, constable of St. Briavels, contributed.[93] In 1817 Queen Anne's Bounty endowed the church with £2,200, which produced an income of £88, and in 1825 the endowment was augmented with grants totalling £500. The income from the endowments fell in 1829 from £108 to £91 13s.[94] and in 1832 Berkin's income was £97 16s.[95] Berkin, under whom the church was attended by people from as far away as Lea Bailey, Pope's Hill, Blaize Bailey, Cinderford, and Lydbrook,[96] was sometimes styled a perpetual curate.[97] From 1821, when he also had the cure of Hope Mansell (Herefs.) adjoining the Forest, he was assisted by a curate,[98] whose stipend was paid by a benefactor. Berkin entrusted the curate with a mission to Lydbrook, for which he built a Sunday schoolroom.[99] Isaac Bridgman, the first

85 *Ecclesiologist*, N.S. xlv. 258–9.
86 Glos. R.O., P 208/CW 3/1–2; ibid. IN 4/1; ibid. MI 3; *Kelly's Dir. Glos.* (1910), 241; (1931), 246.
87 *Glos. Ch. Bells*, 421–2.
88 *Glos. Ch. Plate*, 140.
89 Cf. Nicholls, *Personalities of Dean*, 144.
90 *Glouc. Jnl.* 10 Feb., 30 June 1817.
91 Procter, *Origin of Ch. in Dean*, 23 and n.; cf. Nicholls, *Forest of Dean*, 157–61; Nicholls, *Personalities of Dean*, 130–8.
92 Hockaday Abs. clxxvi; Glos. R.O., Q/RGf 1/8; cf.

P.R.O., F 16/63 (nos. 576–7, 857); F 16/70.
93 Nicholls, *Personalities of Dean*, 138–9; Nicholls, *Forest of Dean*, 98.
94 Hodgson, *Queen Anne's Bounty* (1845), pp. cciii, cclxxxiv; Nicholls, *Personalities of Dean*, 138–9.
95 *3rd Rep. Dean Forest Com.* 6.
96 Ibid. 11; Glos. R.O., P 109/IN 1/1.
97 G.D.R. vol. 383, no. cxl.
98 Glos. Colln. L 9.3; Hockaday Abs. clxxvi.
99 *3rd Rep. Dean Forest Com.* 11–12; Nicholls, *Personalities of Dean*, 140; above, this chapter (Holy Jesus).

curate, also preached at Littledean Hill, Cinderford, and Gunn's Mills but his affinities with nonconformist preachers led to his estrangement from Berkin[1] and in 1822 to the revoking of his licence and to an interdict against his officiating in any church in the diocese.[2]

In 1844 Holy Trinity was assigned a district or parish comprising the northern part of the Forest and extending from Pope's Hill in the east to Lydbrook in the west. The parish was created under the 1842 Act,[3] by which the patronage of Holy Trinity, vested in 1816 in its trustees,[4] was transferred to the Crown and the church became a perpetual curacy with an income of £150 secured by a further endowment from the Commissioners of Woods.[5] The living was later styled a vicarage.[6] Berkin, who conducted cottage lectures as part of his mission to the Forest, remained at Holy Trinity until his death in 1847.[7] His successor H. G. Nicholls, author of a history of the Forest,[8] also organized missions to outlying parts of the parish, where services were held on Sunday evenings in a factory, called the Mill, from 1849 and in school-chapels opened at Ruardean Woodside, Hawthorns, and Littledean Hill in the early 1850s.[9] Under William Barker, minister 1866–97, services were held for a time at Ruardean Woodside and at the new Drybrook school.[10] Berkin's successors lived in his parsonage until the 1970s when it was sold.[11] A new vicarage house was built north of the church. Holy Trinity parish was reduced in size in 1852 and 1880 when parts were transferred to new parishes at Lydbrook and Cinderford respectively[12] and between 1909 and 1912 when outlying areas in the north and east passed to ancient parishes adjoining the Forest.[13]

The church, of roughly coursed stone with ashlar dressings, was built under Henry Berkin's personal supervision[14] to a plan comprising a small chancel with north vestry, a broad nave with north and south porches, and a west tower.[15] It had galleries running along three sides of the nave[16] until 1853 when those on the north and south sides were taken down and other fittings were rearranged. In 1902 the church was reseated, a new pulpit installed, and the organ moved from the west gallery.[17] The font presum-

ably provided by Berkin was kept in the church in 1992 when another font, given in 1904, was in use. The east window contains a stained-glass memorial to James Lawton, vicar 1897–1922. The church has two bells, one for the sanctus, cast by John Rudhall in 1817 and a set of eight tubular bells installed as part of a memorial to the dead of the First World War.[18]

The church of *ST. JOHN THE EVANGELIST*, Cinderford, was begun in 1843 and consecrated in 1844.[19] The site on Cinderford Tump, the hill north-east of Cinderford bridge, was given by the Crown, which in 1855 also provided a few acres of land to the north-east for the minister's glebe and parsonage.[20] The cost of the church was borne principally by Charles Bathurst together with the Crown, the philanthropist the Revd. S. W. Warneford, and the solicitor Thomas Graham, formerly clerk to the Dean Forest commissioners.[21] During its construction T. G. Smythies, who was to become the first minister, held services in Edward Protheroe's new school to the south.[22] Under the 1842 Act the church was a perpetual curacy in the gift of the Crown and its fabric was maintained by the Commissioners of Woods from a trust fund.[23] In 1845 the church was given a district or parish comprising the eastern part of the Forest from Blaize Bailey in the east to Cannop in the west and including Ruspidge and Soudley in the south.[24] The benefice, which under the Act had an income of £150 secured by an endowment from the Commissioners of Woods,[25] was later styled a vicarage.[26] Its parsonage, built to designs by Francis Niblett in 1855,[27] was sold in the later 20th century and a house provided elsewhere. Missions were sent from the church to the northern part of Cinderford, which became a separate parish in 1880,[28] and to Soudley, where a permanent church was built.[29]

St. John's church, built of sandstone rubble with ashlar dressings, was designed by Edward Blore[30] in an early 13th-century style with an apsidal sanctuary with north vestry and an aisled nave with short transepts, south porch, and small south-west tower and spire.[31] Galleries in the transepts and at the west end were taken down during restoration work in 1874 when the

[1] Glos. Colln. L 9.3–4.   [2] Hockaday Abs. clxxvi.
[3] G.D.R. vol. 361, ff. 101v.–103v.; cf. ibid. V 6/138.
[4] Hockaday Abs. clxxvi.
[5] Dean Forest Eccl. Districts Act, 5 & 6 Vic. c. 65; G.D.R. vol. 384, f. 77.
[6] *Kelly's Dir. Glos.* (1870), 531.
[7] Nicholls, *Personalities of Dean*, 144–7.
[8] I. Gray, *Antiquaries of Glos. and Bristol* (B.G.A.S. 1981), 117–18.
[9] Nicholls, *Forest of Dean*, 163; Hockaday Abs. clxxvi; Glos. R.O., P 109/CW 2/1; for the Mill, also P.R.O., HO 129/332/1/3/9; cf. below, Educ., elementary schs.
[10] Glos. R.O., P 109/CW 2/1; PA 109/1.
[11] Cf. *Citizen* (Glouc.), 18 July 1978.
[12] *Lond. Gaz.* 20 Apr. 1852, pp. 1118–19; 13 Aug. 1880, pp. 4451–3.
[13] Glos. R.O., P 1/IN 3/2; P 354/VE 3/4.
[14] Nicholls, *Personalities of Dean*, 137.
[15] Nicholls, *Forest of Dean*, illustration at p. 162, reproduced above, Fig. 24.
[16] *3rd Rep. Dean Forest Com.* 10.
[17] Glos. R.O., P 109/VE 2/1; *Glouc. Jnl.* 29 Nov. 1902.
[18] Glos. R.O., PA 109/1; *Glos. Ch. Bells*, 269.

[19] Sheila Smith, *Hist. of St. John the Evang. Ch., Cinderford* (1984), 7; Glos. R.O., P 85/IN 1/1; Nicholls, *Forest of Dean*, 172, gives the dedication as St. John the Apostle.
[20] Glos. R.O., P 85/CW 3/1; *34th Rep. Com. Woods*, H.C. 330, p. 127 (1856), xxxvii; cf. G.D.R., F 3/1, pp. 21–4, 85.
[21] *21st Rep. Com. Woods*, H.C. 590, p. 12 (1844), xxxi; Smith, *St. John's Ch.* 9; cf. Nicholls, *Forest of Dean*, 175.
[22] Hockaday Abs. clxxvi; Nicholls, *Forest of Dean*, 171; cf. G.D.R., F 3/1, pp. 78, 82.
[23] Dean Forest Eccl. Districts Act, 5 & 6 Vic. c. 65; G.D.R. vol. 384, f. 76; *26th Rep. Com. Woods*, H.C. 611, pp. 124–5 (1849), xxvii.
[24] G.D.R. vol. 361, ff. 115v.–116v.; cf. ibid. V 6/138.
[25] Dean Forest Eccl. Districts Act, 5 & 6 Vic. c. 65; G.D.R. vol. 384, f. 76.
[26] *Kelly's Dir. Glos.* (1870), 531–2; *Dioc. of Glouc. Dir.* (1989), 55.
[27] Glos. R.O., D 4335/258; P 85/IN 3/1.
[28] Below, this chapter (St. Stephen).
[29] Below, this chapter (mission churches).
[30] Colvin, *Biog. Dict. Brit. Architects* (1978), 120.
[31] Glos. R.O., P 85/CW 3/1; Nicholls, *Forest of Dean*, illustration at p. 171, reproduced below, Fig. 25.

internal walls of the nave were lined with brick and the west gallery was rebuilt. In 1905 a new organ was put in the north transept and in 1912 a chancel was formed by raising the floor at the eastern end and erecting a low stone screen between it and the rest of the church. A wooden screen was added to the partition in 1913 and a wooden reredos was erected in 1923.[32] A bell cast by Thomas Mears in 1844 was replaced in 1927 by a chime of eight bells given by A. J. Morgan of Abbotswood, Ruspidge.[33]

The church of *ST. PAUL*, Parkend, was consecrated in 1822.[34] It was built by Henry Poole, minister of Bream and Coleford chapels, who in 1819 appealed publicly for funds for a church and school at Parkend. The Crown gave 5 a. for the project and contributed towards the cost of the church, which was paid for primarily by voluntary contributions. Edward Machen of Whitemead Park and Edward Protheroe were among the principal benefactors. The patronage was vested in the bishop,[35] and in 1822 Queen Anne's Bounty endowed the church with £2,200. The benefice, augmented in 1826 and 1827 by two grants of £300 from Queen Anne's Bounty and gifts totalling £400,[36] was worth c. £74 in 1832.[37] Poole, who as the first minister was sometimes called a perpetual curate,[38] in 1828 took up residence in the parsonage built north the church and in a similar style.[39]

The church, which contained free benches for most of its congregation and pews for Forest officials and colliery masters and agents,[40] served Yorkley, Pillowell, Whitecroft, and Ellwood[41] and was assigned a district or parish covering the southern part of the Forest in 1844. The parish, extending from Blakeney Hill in the east to Clearwell Meend in the west and reaching Cannop and the Speech House in the north, was created under the 1842 Act,[42] by which the church became a perpetual curacy with an income of £150 secured by a further endowment from the Commissioners of Woods.[43] The benefice was later called a vicarage[44] and in 1920, because of its poverty, it was assigned part of the endowment of Bream vicarage.[45] Poole, who remained incumbent until his death in 1857, started missions to Yorkley[46] and to the settlements around Viney Hill and Blakeney Hill.[47] The parish has been much altered. Parts in the west were lost to the churches at Bream and Clearwell in 1854 and 1856 respectively, the eastern part, including Viney Hill and Blakeney Hill, became a separate parish in 1866, and the north-western part at Coalway Lane End was transferred to Coleford church in 1890.[48] In 1909 St. Paul's parish gained two detached parts of Newland at Yorkley, to the south.[49]

St. Paul's church, built of ashlar, was designed by Henry Poole in a Gothick style. The plan is octagonal and cruciform, the arms formed by the sanctuary, north and south transepts, and the west end of the church. There is also an east vestry, north and south porches, and a west tower.[50] The transepts and west end contained galleries and in the late 1890s, when much of the church was repewed, a screen under the west gallery was removed and the space below the south gallery adapted as a choir vestry. That vestry and platforms introduced at the same time to raise the altar were removed as part of alterations begun in 1957.[51] Among the original fittings retained in 1992 were the wooden gallery fronts, reredos, and pulpit and the font. The organ, in the west gallery, incorporates part of an instrument built for Salisbury cathedral in the early 18th century and brought to Parkend from Ross-on-Wye (Herefs.) church by 1858.[52] Edward Machen gave a bell, cast in 1831 by Thomas Mears, and a clock. A set of eight tubular bells was installed apparently as a memorial to the dead of the First World War.[53]

The church of *ST. STEPHEN*, Cinderford, begun in 1888 and consecrated in 1890,[54] was built for a new ecclesiastical parish called Woodside at the northern end of Cinderford. Several missions had been sent to the area, including one by William Barker, minister of Holy Trinity, Harrow Hill, from 1866.[55] Woodside parish, formed in 1880 out of parts of the parishes of Flaxley, Newland, St. John, and Holy Trinity with the extraparochial place known as Hinder's Lane and Dockham,[56] had its origins in a scheme launched in 1870 by Thomas Wetherell, vicar of Flaxley, for a school-chapel in Flaxley Meend.[57] St. John's church, Cinderford, held services in a room at Flaxley Meend and in Dockham chapel, a new building on Littledean hill, from 1872[58] and also in Cinderford town hall in 1873.[59] In that year Woodside was made a conventional district with its own curate[60] and from 1875 a new school at the corner of Abbey Street and Forest Road, next to the Flaxley Meend mission room, served as a temporary church.[61] In 1992

---

32   Smith, *St. John's Ch.* 9–14, 22; cf. Glos. R.O., P 85/CW 3/4–5.
33   *Glos. Ch. Bells*, 218–19; Glos. R.O., P 85/CW 3/7.
34   *Glouc. Jnl.* 29 Apr. 1822.
35   Nicholls, *Forest of Dean*, 168–70; Nicholls, *Personalities of Dean*, 155–7; P.R.O., HO 129/577/1/5/17.
36   Hodgson, *Queen Anne's Bounty*, pp. ccvi, ccviii, cclxxxv.   37 *3rd Rep. Dean Forest Com.* 6, 16.
38   Hockaday Abs. clxxvi.
39   *3rd Rep. Dean Forest Com.* 21; Nicholls, *Personalities of Dean*, 159.   40 *3rd Rep. Dean Forest Com.* 21.
41   G.D.R. vol. 383, no. cxli.
42   Ibid. 361, ff. 101v.–103v.; cf. ibid. V 6/138.
43   Dean Forest Eccl. Districts Act, 5 & 6 Vic. c. 65; G.D.R. vol. 384, f. 77.
44   *Kelly's Dir. Glos.* (1870), 617; *Dioc. of Glouc. Dir.* (1989), 56.
45   *Lond. Gaz.* 10 Feb. 1920, pp. 1679–81; G.D.R., V 6/14.
46   Below, this chapter (mission churches).
47   Nicholls, *Personalities of Dean*, 160; above, this chapter (All Saints).

48   *Lond. Gaz.* 16 June 1854, p. 1863; 18 Apr. 1856, pp. 1464–5; 18 Sept. 1866, pp. 5081–2; 8 July 1890, pp. 3775–7; cf. Glos. R.O., P 93/IN 3/3; P 348/CW 3/1.
49   *Lond. Gaz.* 13 Apr. 1909, p. 2899.
50   *Glouc. Jnl.* 29 Apr. 1822; Nicholls, *Forest of Dean*, 169; above, Plate 36; for Poole's archit., Nicholls, *Personalities of Dean*, 155–9; Colvin, *Biog. Dict. Brit. Architects*, 650–1.
51   Glos. R.O., D 3921/II/6; D 1381/9B; D 3867/III/35.
52   Nicholls, *Forest of Dean*, 169; *Trans. B.G.A.S.* xciii. 175.
53   Nicholls, *Forest of Dean*, 169; *Glos. Ch. Bells*, 495.
54   *Glouc. Jnl.* 3 Nov. 1888; 31 May 1890.
55   G. A. Allan, *Church Work in Forest of Dean* (copy in Glos. Colln. L 9.6), 19.
56   *Lond. Gaz.* 13 Aug. 1880, pp. 4451–3; cf. G.D.R., V 6/126.   57 Allan, *Church Work in Dean*, 20.
58   Glos. R.O., P 85/2/IN 3/1; D 543, Littledean Hill chap. deeds 1867–1904; cf. G.D.R. vol. 377, f. 55.
59   Glos. R.O., P 85/2/MI 4.
60   Allan, *Church Work in Dean*, 21.
61   *Glouc. Jnl.* 29 May 1875; 31 May 1890; cf. Glos. R.O., D 2186/41.

the building was St. Stephen's church hall. The establishment of Woodside parish was funded privately and in 1880 the scheme's promoters, chief among whom was Sir Thomas Crawley-Boevey, Bt., of Flaxley Abbey, endowed the benefice, styled a perpetual curacy, with £2,500 stock and assigned the patronage to the Church Patronage Society.[62] Part of the endowment may have derived from a gift by James Parsons (d. 1847), incumbent of Newnham and Littledean.[63] The benefice, later called a vicarage,[64] was united in 1984 with Littledean, which had the same patrons,[65] and the vicarage house built next to St. Stephen's church c. 1912[66] was retained by the united benefice in 1992. Within the parish missions were sent to Upper Bilson and Littledean Hill. In the latter place Dockham chapel, which the Primitive Methodists had acquired in 1879, was used by the Anglicans again in 1901[67] and was closed after 1936.[68]

St. Stephen's church, designed by E. H. L. Barker in an early 14th-century style, has a chancel with north vestry and organ chamber and a clerestoried and aisled nave. It was paid for mainly by voluntary contributions, including a gift of £700 from a Mrs. Rogers of Weston under Penyard (Herefs.), and was built of grey sandstone with Bath stone dressings. The nave, which has a west gallery, was completed in 1890, the chancel was built in 1892 and 1893, the cost being met by Sir Thomas Crawley-Boevey's wife Frances for a memorial to her parents, and the vestry and organ chamber were added in 1896.[69] Elizabeth Crawley-Boevey, widow of Sir Martin, gave a set of communion plate in 1890.[70] The single bell had been taken down and stored in the building by 1981.[71]

In the 19th and 20th centuries several mission churches or chapels were established by some churches within or near the Forest. At Ellwood, where the assistant curate of Coleford held cottage lectures c. 1830,[72] a chapel opened for a mission from Clearwell by 1876.[73] It stood west of Marsh Lane and was closed not long afterwards.[74] Christ Church, Berry Hill, also organized early missions to the west side of the Forest, the Revd. T. R. Garnsey (d. 1847) holding weekday

services in the Lane End district[75] and Sunday services being conducted in the National school built at Broadwell Lane End in 1863.[76] Between 1883 and 1888 a mission from Coleford held services in a former Baptist chapel at Mitcheldean Lane End[77] and in 1890 the Lane End district, parts of which had been included in the ecclesiastical parishes of St. Paul, Parkend, and of Clearwell, was transferred to the ecclesiastical parish of Coleford[78] and services resumed in Broadwell school. An iron mission church, dedicated to the Good Shepherd and paid for by voluntary contributions, was erected next to the school in 1891.[79] It was replaced by a permanent church designed by William Leah and built to the north-west in 1938.[80] The iron building was retained as a church hall.[81] Coleford church also organized a mission to Milkwall from 1895. A wooden hall erected for it in 1909[82] was brought from Moseley Green by Thomas Morgan[83] and was replaced in 1935 by a small brick church designed by William Leah and dedicated to St. Luke. The new church, much of the cost of which was met by a gift of £500, had fittings taken from St. Luke's church in Gloucester.[84] The single bell was cast in 1840 by Thomas Mears.[85]

On the east side of the Forest a mission to Soudley was begun from St. John's church, Cinderford, in 1869.[86] The mission, which conducted services in an iron schoolroom in Upper Soudley from 1875,[87] was abandoned temporarily in 1905.[88] In 1909 and 1910 a stone church was built west of the room. Dedicated to St. Michael, it was designed by W. Whitehouse of Cinderford in an early 13th-century style and has a sanctuary, a nave, and a west porch.[89] By 1885 services were held in a room at Upper Bilson within Woodside parish.[90] The mission, which was later served from St. Stephen's church, Cinderford, occupied an iron building in what became Upper Bilson Road[91] and was run by a Mr. Underhill in the early 20th century.[92] It continued in 1992[93] and its church had a bell cast probably in 1887.[94]

At Yorkley the Revd. Henry Poole of Parkend conducted cottage services in the late 1820s.[95] In 1867 the perpetual curate of Bream was licensed to hold services in a schoolroom at Yorkley

62 Glos. R.O., P 85/2/IN 3/1; *Lond. Gaz.* 13 Aug. 1880, pp. 4451–3; cf. *Kelly's Dir. Glos.* (1885), 420.
63 Allan, *Church Work in Dean*, 21; cf. *V.C.H. Glos.* x. 47–8; above, Littledean, church.
64 *Kelly's Dir. Glos.* (1910), 115.
65 Glos. R.O., P 110/MI 1/1; *Dioc. of Glouc. Dir.* (1989), 56; cf. G.D.R., D 5/1/31.
66 Glos. R.O., P 85/2/IN 3/9; cf. *Kelly's Dir. Glos.* (1910), 115; (1914), 118.
67 Glos. R.O., P 85/2/VE 2/2; D 543, Littledean Hill chap. deeds.
68 Ibid. P 85/2/VE 2/5.
69 Ibid. CW 3/1–4; ibid. VE 2/2; Glos. Colln. R 78.3; cf. Burke, *Peerage* (1963), 269.
70 Glos. R.O., P 85/2/VE 2/2; *Glos. Ch. Plate*, 86; cf. Burke, *Peerage* (1963), 269.
71 *Glos. Ch. Bells*, 219–20.
72 Glos. R.O., D 2297.
73 *Morris's Dir. Glos.* (1876), 475; cf. *Lond. Gaz.* 18 Apr. 1856, pp. 1464–5.
74 O.S. Map 6″, Glos. XXXVIII. SE. (1884, 1903 edns.).
75 Nicholls, *Personalities of Dean*, 150–1.
76 *Morris's Dir. Glos.* (1876), 475; P.R.O., ED 7/35/350.
77 Glos. R.O., P 93/IN 4/3/4–5.
78 *Lond. Gaz.* 8 July 1890, pp. 3775–7; cf. G.D.R., V

6/138.
79 Glos. R.O., P 93/IN 3/3; ibid. IN 4/3/6; *Glouc. Jnl.* 28 Nov. 1891.
80 Glos. R.O., D 3921/II/6; Glos. Colln. RQ 102.1.
81 Glos. R.O., P 93/IN 3/3.
82 Ibid. IN 4/3/6–9.
83 Ibid. D 3921/II/5.
84 Ibid. P 93/IN 3/5; *Glouc. Jnl.* 30 Nov. 1935; Glos. Colln. RQ 102.1.
85 *Glos. Ch. Bells*, 431; cf. *Glos. N. & Q.* ix. 189.
86 Glos. R.O., P 85/MI 2, which mentions an earlier mission of Isaac Bridgman.
87 G.D.R. vol. 377, f. 76; cf. O.S. Map 6″, Glos. XXXIX. NE. (1884 edn.); below, Educ., elementary schs.
88 Allan, *Church Work in Dean*, 23–4; *Glouc. Jnl.* 6 Oct. 1906.
89 *Glouc. Jnl.* 18 Sept. 1909; 14 May 1910.
90 Glos. R.O., P 85/2/CW 2/15.
91 *Kelly's Dir. Glos.* (1894), 109.
92 Glos. R.O., P 85/2/IN 4/1; ibid. VE 2/3, min. 30 Apr. 1919.
93 *Dioc. of Glouc. Dir.* (1989), 56.
94 *Glos. Ch. Bells*, 146.
95 Glos. R.O., D 2297.

Wood.[96] The mission continued in the 1870s[97] and the schoolroom, formerly a workshop, was remodelled as a church in 1884.[98] St. Paul's church, Parkend, ran the mission from 1909[99] and Caroline Gosling (d. 1917) gave £500 stock for a charity to keep the mission chuch in repair.[1] In 1968 the mission church, which was known

as St. Luke's, was closed[2] and the fittings, including a bell cast in 1882, were moved to a house on Captain's green, lower down in Yorkley, the ground floor of which was adapted for the mission.[3] The abandoned church was later converted as a house and the mission was ended in 1991.[4]

ROMAN CATHOLICISM

IN the early 19th century priests from the Monmouth mission visited parts of the Forest of Dean[5] and a few people in the Lydbrook area were members of a Roman Catholic congregation at Courtfield, across the Wye in Welsh Bicknor (Mon., later Herefs.).[6] Later Catholics from the Forest also heard mass at Gloucester, Chepstow (Mon.), Monmouth, Ross-on-Wye (Herefs.), or Hereford, and most priests active in the Forest had parishes to the west. J. B. Chard, priest at Gloucester from 1894, was an occasional visitor. In 1915 a chapel dedicated to SS. Mary and Claudia was opened at Lydbrook. Used for occasional masses, said by a priest from Courtfield, in the early 1930s, it had closed by 1938.[7] Lydbrook Catholics continued to attend the Courtfield chapel after the Second World War.[8]

From 1930, when a Roman Catholic mission covering the Forest was established at Coleford, mass was said in a hotel in Cinderford. The mission to Cinderford was served by priests from Ross-on-Wye in 1935[9] and by priests from

Blaisdon Hall in 1938.[10] Later in 1938 Cinderford became a separate mission and a room of a house was converted as an oratory, and in 1939 a church was built in Flaxley Street. Designed by the Liverpool firm of Badger and Hutton, it was dedicated to Our Lady of Victories[11] and was given a parish including Lydney and Mitcheldean. In 1992 it had an average congregation of 90, drawn from Cinderford, Newnham, Ruardean, and other places in the north of the parish.[12] The presbytery west of the church was built after 1959.[13]

In 1939 the Sisters of Hope, who belonged to the Sisters of the Holy Family, purchased Abbotswood in Ruspidge for a convent and a nursing home. The nuns apparently gave up their nursing work in 1956 and the convent had closed by 1959.[14] In 1960 the Franciscan Sisters of the Immaculate Conception established a convent and a school in a house in Cinderford next to the church of Our Lady of Victories. Their educational work in Cinderford continued in 1992.[15]

PROTESTANT NONCONFORMITY

EVIDENCE for the religious affiliations of early Foresters is fragmentary. The Baptist church in the Forest area in 1653 was evidently in Weston under Penyard (Herefs.)[16] and the Quaker meeting attended by George Fox in 1668[17] was presumably at Aylburton.[18] Baptist and possibly Methodist preachers made occasional forays into the Forest before the late 18th century, when more sustained missionary work began. Itinerant Baptist and Independent preachers attracted congregations and some Foresters belonged to a Methodist society in Coleford.[19]

The growth of industrial settlement and the absence until the early 19th century of the established church favoured the spread of religious nonconformity and fundamentalism in the Forest. Early progress was slow but

chapels were eventually opened in almost every community. Most belonged to one or other of the Methodist churches, principally the more fundamentalist Bible Christian and Primitive Methodist sects which began work in the Forest in 1823. In 1822 the evangelical minister Rowland Hill visited the area and Isaac Bridgman, the curate of Holy Trinity church, was suspended by the ecclesiastical authorities after receiving him. Bridgman continued to preach in the area and his missionary effort came to be directed from a dissenting chapel just outside the Forest at Brain's Green, in Awre parish.[20] His congregations included the ironmaster James Russell at Lydbrook and the carpenter and foundry owner Samuel Hewlett at Bradley.[21] In the later 19th century the most successful

96 G.D.R. vol. 377, f. 13; Yorkley Wood was in a detached part of Newland: above, Newland, intro.; cf. *Lond Gaz.* 16 June 1854, p. 1863.
97 Nat. Soc. files, Bream St. John; *Morris's Dir. Glos.* (1876), 536.
98 *Kelly's Dir. Glos.* (1885), 372; cf. O.S. Map 6", Glos. XXXIX. SW. (1883, 1904 edns.).
99 *Lond. Gaz.* 13 Apr. 1909, p. 2899; cf. *Kelly's Dir. Glos.* (1931), 281.
1 Glos. R.O., D 3469/5/112.
2 *Dean Forest Guardian,* 15 Mar. 1991.
3 *Christian Herald,* 8 June 1974; *Glos. Ch. Bells,* 677.
4 *Dean Forest Guardian,* 15 Mar. 1991.
5 *Misc.* vii (Cath. Rec. Soc. ix), 153 and n. This chapter is based principally on Glos. R.O., D 5467/6/1.
6 *Misc.* iv (Cath. Rec. Soc. iv), 416.
7 Cf. *Cath. Dir.* (1931 and later edns.).
8 W.I. hist. of Lydbrook (c. 1959, TS. in Glos. Colln.),

12–13.
9 *Kelly's Dir. Glos.* (1935), 116.
10 *Cath. Dir.* (1938), 176; for Blaisdon Hall, *V.C.H. Glos.* x. 8.
11 *Glouc. Jnl.* 6 May, 24 June, 8 July 1939.
12 Inf. from par. priest.
13 O.S. Map 1/2,500, SO 6513 (1960, 1974 edns.).
14 Cf. *Cath. Dir.* (1959), 158.
15 Cf. ibid. (1960), 165; (1962), 169; below, Educ., elementary schs.
16 J. Stratford, *Good and Great Men of Glos.* (1867), 406; *Calamy Revised,* ed. A. G. Matthews, 444.
17 *Jnl. of Geo. Fox,* ed. J. L. Nickalls (Camb. 1952), 522.
18 Cf. above, Lydney, prot. nonconf.
19 Glos. R.O., D 1050.
20 Bright, *Nonconf. in Dean,* 17–18; Glos. Colln. L 9.3–4; cf. above, Churches (Holy Trin.); Awre, nonconf.
21 G.D.R. vol. 344, ff. 65v., 111v.–112; for Russell and Hewlett, above, Industry, ironworks; other ind. and trade.

denominations were the Baptists and Primitive Methodists and there were some thriving congregations of Wesleyan Methodists and Independents or Congregationalists. Cinderford had several particularly large meetings. The power of the chapels was revealed in 1875 in the first elections to the Forest school board in which nonconformist candidates received two thirds of the votes cast and two Anglican clergymen failed to win seats.[22] In the later 19th century and the early 20th some other denominations, mostly newer fundamentalist sects, gained adherents in the Forest.

Nonconformist chapels remained at the centre of Foresters' religious, social, political, and intellectual life until well into the 20th century. The Methodist Church, created by the union of Primitive, United, and Wesleyan Methodists in 1932,[23] began with 29 chapels in Dean. Membership of many meetings was falling by the 1950s, when an acceleration in social change allied to the gradual disappearance of traditional Forest industries led to a rapid decline in the chapels' importance within their communities.[24] Many were closed and others reduced to a handful of members. At the end of 1992 the Methodist Church retained 12 chapels and the Baptists and the United Reformed Church, which the Congregational meetings had joined, 6 and 3 chapels respectively.

BAPTISTS. Baptist teachings were introduced to the Forest of Dean by preachers visiting the Coleford church in the 18th century. One conducted baptisms in Cannop brook in 1722 and another entered the Forest c. 1780 to evangelize coal miners. William Bradley, a miner who was to become minister of the Coleford Baptists, preached throughout the Forest[25] and in 1797 had a congregation at Littledean Hill in the east.[26] In the mid 1790s a Coleford Baptist preached many times in a public house in Yorkley.[27] The Coleford Baptists, whose church was behind the registration in 1818 and 1820 of houses at Five Acres and in the Lane End district for services,[28] established mission stations at Mitcheldean Lane End, Milkwall, and Little Drybrook. In 1851 those missions attracted small congregations and the Mitcheldean Lane End chapel, which 40 persons attended, also served as a schoolroom.[29] It was used in the 1880s by an Anglican mission from Coleford.[30]

The Baptist presence in Lydbrook probably began with a mission from the Ryeford church

in Weston under Penyard (Herefs.), for which a house in English Bicknor was licensed in 1823.[31] The same year Thomas Wright, a minister, built a small Baptist chapel at Lower Lydbrook[32] with help from Edward Goff's charity, founded to provide free schools in Herefordshire and adjoining counties and used to establish Baptist missions. Wright remained in charge of the chapel and its Sunday school in the 1830s[33] and there were morning and evening congregations of 30 and 100 at services in 1851.[34] Following the loss of support from Goff's charity the chapel was dependent on the Baptist church at Leys Hill in Walford (Herefs.) until 1857 when it became a separate church with 12 members. The Lydbrook church had its own minister from 1863 and moved to a new chapel further up the valley in 1864.[35] The old chapel was sold and fitted as a public reading room, opened in 1868.[36] In 1875 galleries were erected in the new chapel, and a schoolroom next to it, under construction from 1872, was in use.[37] The church's fortunes in the late 19th century mirrored those of the nearby Lydbrook tinplate works and its membership in 1881 was 102. A. W. Latham held open-air services outside the village at the start of a pastorate lasting from 1883 to 1899.[38] By the mid 1980s the chapel shared a minister with the Ross-on-Wye Baptist church (Herefs.), and in 1992, when it was without a minister, it had average attendances of 25 and 15 on Sunday mornings and evenings respectively.[39]

Baptist missions to Cinderford were attempted before 1842[40] when, with help from Gloucester, services were held in the house of W. F. Rhodes, a grocer and a member of the Coleford church. The following year the Cinderford meeting became a separate church with 10 members and it built a chapel in the later Commercial Street. The church, which had its own minister from 1845, became by far the largest Baptist meeting in the Forest and supported missionary work in several places. The chapel, in which a gallery was erected in 1847,[41] attracted morning and evening congregations of 170 and 280 and taught 170 children in its Sunday school in 1851.[42] It was pulled down following its replacement in 1860 by a larger building immediately to the south. The new chapel had a pedimented street front and an end gallery, and its sloping site afforded accommodation for a schoolroom under it.[43] In 1862 a Strict or Particular Baptist church also met in Cinderford and its minister Richard Snaith[44] conducted baptisms in St. Anthony's well near Gunn's Mills in 1864.[45] The meeting

[22] *Glouc. Jnl.* 27 Mar. 1875.

[23] G. E. Lawrence, *Kindling the Flame* (1974), 50–1: copy in Glos. R.O., D 2598/23/1.

[24] Cf. D. Potter, *Changing Forest* (1962), 11–12, 32–3, 49–51, 54–67.

[25] Bright, *Nonconf. in Dean*, 23–6; above, Coleford, prot. nonconf.; for Bradley, R. Anstis, *Industrial Teagues and Forest of Dean* (1990), 15, 63, 65.

[26] *Glouc. Jnl.* 20 Nov. 1797; Glos. R.O., D 2297.

[27] Glos. R.O., D 2297; cf. Hockaday Abs. ccxcvii, 1786.

[28] Hockaday Abs. ccxcvii; clxv, Coleford; Glos. R.O., D 2722/13.

[29] P.R.O., HO 129/577/1/4/11–12; HO 129/577/1/5/21; O.S. Map 6", Glos. XXX. SE. (1884 edn.).

[30] Glos. R.O., P 93/IN 4/3/4–5.

[31] G.D.R. vol. 344, f. 114v.

[32] Ibid. f. 117v.; T 1/151 (no. 22).

[33] Glos. R.O., D 2297; cf. *32nd Rep. Com. Char. Pt. 2*

[140], pp. 297–8, H.C. (1837–8), xxvi.

[34] P.R.O., HO 129/347/2/7/14, which states that the chap. was erected by subscription by Mr. Boyce and was licensed in 1812.

[35] *Centenary of Bapt. Witness in Lydbrook 1857–1957* (photocopy in Glos. R.O., NC 43), 4–6.

[36] *Glos. Chron.* 18 Apr. 1868.

[37] *Forest of Dean Examiner*, 1 Oct. 1875; *Glouc. Jnl.* 1 Feb. 1873.   [38] *Bapt. Witness in Lydbrook*, 8–9.

[39] *Bapt. Union Dir.* (1988–9), 76; inf. from Mr. J. E. Powell, of Lydbrook.

[40] Bright, *Nonconf. in Dean*, 47.

[41] *Hist. Cinderford Bapt. Ch.* (1910) (photocopy in Glos. R.O., NC 40), 1–6; Hockaday Abs. clxxvi, St. John, 1842.

[42] P.R.O., HO 129/334/1/3/17.

[43] *Cinderford Bapt. Ch.* 9–10; cf. P.R.O., F 16/63 (no. 2560); F 16/70; O.S. Map 1/2,500, Glos. XXXI. 11 (1881 edn.).

[44] Glos. R.O., D 4714/4/1, p. 2.   [45] *Glouc. Jnl.* 13 Aug. 1864.

had a chapel in Flaxley Meend and has not been traced after 1879.[46] Under Cornelius Griffiths, minister 1873–81, the Commercial Street church saw its membership double to nearly 400 and it sent missions to places nearby and to Newnham. Its chapel had side galleries from 1875 and new rooms, opened in 1887 and 1903, were added at the rear for the Sunday school, which in 1901 taught 1,208 children and young adults.[47] The church, which in 1907 opened an institute in Belle Vue Road[48] and at the end of the First World War held open-air services at Mousell barn just outside Cinderford, was in decline by the later 1920s. It had 46 members in 1992.[49]

The extension of Baptist preaching to other parts of the Forest in the later 19th century led to the building of six or seven more chapels. The first, opened in 1854, was at Ruardean Hill, where Joseph Mountjoy, a Cinderford butcher, had started a mission in 1852. The meeting, with Mountjoy as pastor until his death in 1879, separated from the Cinderford church in 1855[50] and had 40 members in 1868.[51] In 1898 two cottages were converted as a manse, which was sold when a new manse was built in the mid 1920s. The chapel fittings including a gallery and an organ installed in 1907 were rearranged several times in the 20th century, and its choir became a focal point in church life.[52] By 1992 the church had ceased to have its own minister and the average congregation numbered 33.[53]

At Viney Hill, where a Baptist minister active in Blakeney and Lydney lived in 1841,[54] a Primitive Methodist chapel was used for a Baptist school anniversary in 1856.[55] A Baptist meeting house at Blakeney Hill had been sold by 1875 to the vicar of Blakeney.[56] In 1860 Richard Snaith, a Baptist living at Whitecroft, began holding open-air and cottage services at Pillowell and Yorkley Wood and started a Sunday school. In 1862, after Snaith's departure for Cinderford, a room at Pillowell was acquired for services and classes and the meeting, which in 1863 joined the Baptist church at Parkend, continued to organize open-air services in neighbouring communities. In 1864 the meeting moved to a larger room at Yorkley, where a chapel was built for it in 1868.[57] Ties with the mother church were severed in 1881 when the Parkend meeting ended the ministry of Thomas Nicholson and joined the Coleford church. The Yorkley church, which Nicholson served until 1883,[58] had 23 members and a Sunday school with 132

children in 1884. In 1887 it engaged as minister S. J. Elsom,[59] the leader of the free miners,[60] and through his ministry resumed a connexion with Parkend in 1891.[61] Following Elsom's death in 1919 the Yorkley church continued to have a shared ministry, usually with the Parkend meeting, and from 1937 it was without a minister.[62] The chapel closed in 1980[63] and was converted as a house.

Parkend Baptist church was established with help from Coleford and Cinderford. Built on land acquired in 1860, it opened in 1862 and incorporated materials from the recently demolished chapel at Cinderford. It was enlarged in 1865, schoolrooms being among the additions.[64] The church, which in 1868 had 46 members, including those attending its daughter meeting at Yorkley,[65] was often without a pastor. For a time it employed Thomas Nicholson, a former colliery owner at Parkend who became a champion of the Foresters' customary rights,[66] but in 1881 it dispensed with his services and joined the Coleford church. That union had ended by 1886 and Parkend later shared a minister with one or other of the Baptist churches at Yorkley, Lydney, and Blakeney. From 1958 the pastorate was unfilled and in 1992 the chapel had 7 members.[67]

Small chapels in use at Green Bottom and Steam Mills in 1992 were built for missions of the Cinderford Baptist church begun in the mid 1870s. Beulah at Green Bottom opened in 1877 and Bethel at Steam Mills in 1880. In the 1890s Bethel was enlarged and schoolrooms were added to both chapels.[68] In the mid or late 1870s a small Baptist cause at Edge End affiliated to the Lydbrook church.[69] It has not been traced later and a congregation meeting at Drybrook under the minister of the Ruardean Hill church in 1885 disbanded a few years later.[70] In 1886 Baptists built a small chapel at Joyford. Known as Bethel,[71] it joined the Coleford church in 1902.[72] It closed c. 1960 and was converted as a house a few years later.[73]

BIBLE CHRISTIANS AND UNITED METHODISTS.

The Bible Christian movement apparently reached the Forest at Drybrook from Monmouth in 1823 and was introduced to many communities by a mission established in 1826. The mission, conducted by two preachers holding open-air and cottage services, gained early converts in and around Drybrook and also

46 *Morris's Dir. Glos.* (1876), 496; *Kelly's Dir. Glos.* (1879), 647; cf. O.S. Map 1/2,500, Glos. XXXI. 11 (1881 edn.).
47 *Cinderford Bapt. Ch.* 12–22; *Glouc. Jnl.* 18 Sept. 1875; 12 Mar. 1881; 16 May 1885; 26 Mar. 1887; 28 Mar. 1903.
48 Above, Social Life.
49 *Cent. of Witness. Cinderford Bapt. Ch. 1860–1960* (copy in Glos. R.O., NC 41), 6; *Bapt. Union Dir.* (1992–3), 78.
50 *Ruardean Hill Bapt. Ch. 1854–1954* (copy in Glos. R.O., NC 75), 1–2. 51 Glos. Colln. J 11.61 (1).
52 *Ruardean Hill Bapt. Ch.* 2, 6, 8–15; M. V. Bent, *Highest Point of Dean* (1985), 34, 39–50.
53 Inf. from Mrs. D. E. Brain, of Drybrook.
54 P.R.O., HO 107/364, s.v. Danby walk; Bright, *Nonconf. in Dean*, 27, 29. 55 Glos. R.O., D 2598/4/6.
56 *Glouc. Jnl.* 29 May 1875; cf. above, Churches (All Saints).
57 Glos. R.O., D 4714/1/1, pp. 2–5.
58 *Parkend Bapt. Ch. 1862–1962* (copy in Glos. R.O.,

NC 44), 3; J. Stratford, *Glos. Biog. Notes* (1887), 231–4.
59 Glos. R.O., D 4714/1/1, pp. 5–6, 10.
60 Fisher, *Custom and Capitalism*, 142.
61 *Parkend Bapt. Ch.* 4.
62 Glos. R.O., D 4714/4/1, pp. 4–6.   63 Ibid. 1/1.
64 *Parkend Bapt. Ch.* 2–3.
65 Glos. Colln. J 11.61 (1).
66 Stratford, *Glos. Biog. Notes*, 320–1; Fisher, *Custom and Capitalism*, 124.
67 *Parkend Bapt. Ch.* 3–8; *Bapt Union Dir.* (1992–3), 79.
68 *Cinderford Bapt. Ch.* 14–15, 20.
69 *Bapt. Witness in Lydbrook*, 7–8.
70 *Kelly's Dir. Glos.* (1885), 439; (1889), 752; cf. *Ruardean Hill Bapt. Ch.* 3–4.
71 Date and name on bldg.; for site, O.S. Map 6", Glos. XXX. SE. (1903 edn.).
72 Glos. R.O., D 2722/2, pp. 32–4.
73 Ibid. 17.

spread beyond the Forest. Its first chapel within the Forest was Bethel, built at Drybrook in 1836 and opened in 1837.[74] Later that year Bible Christian societies at Drybrook, Edge Hills, Soudley, and High Beech had memberships of 17, 15, 6, and 3 respectively. The High Beech meeting lapsed soon afterwards but that at Soudley grew[75] and in 1846 it built a small chapel on Bradley hill near Upper Soudley. The chapel, a square stone building, was called Zion.[76] The Edge Hills society dwindled in the later 1840s and lapsed before 1856.[77] It was represented in 1851 by a congregation of c. 14 attending morning services on Quarry hill near Drybrook.[78] At that time Bethel had afternoon and evening congregations of up to c. 110 and Zion morning and evening congregations of c. 60 and their respective Sunday schools taught more than 50 and 30 children.[79]

By 1850 the mission had visited many places on the eastern and southern sides of the Forest and had established small societies at Bream, Lea Bailey, and Yorkley Slade. Services were held at Bream from 1841[80] and the society, led by Henry Jones, built a chapel on the Parkend road at Bream's Eaves in 1851.[81] At Ruspidge, where the mission resumed its work in 1856,[82] a small chapel was built in 1857.[83] Such successes enabled the mission to become a separate circuit in 1858.[84] The following year the Bream's Eaves chapel was rebuilt to include a schoolroom,[85] the new building being retained as a schoolroom in 1906 when another chapel was built alongside it.[86] Also in 1859 the Drybrook society built a larger chapel on a site some way south-east of Bethel. Called Providence, it opened in 1860[87] and housed a schoolroom on its lower floor. New schoolrooms were built next to it in 1899.[88] Bethel was converted as a house.[89]

In the later 19th century Bible Christians opened chapels in five more places within the Forest. At Yorkley Slade, where the cause was revived by Henry Jones in 1858, a chapel was built in 1862.[90] It became part of the Methodist Church in 1932 and a large schoolroom was added to it in 1955.[91] It closed in 1992. At Lea Bailey, which the mission reached in 1847,[92] open-air meetings were held at the Dancing green. Later, services at Red House, just within Weston under Penyard (Herefs.), drew a congregation from the north of the Forest and adjoining parts of Herefordshire and continued intermittently for some time after 1869, when a

chapel called Bethel was built to the south-east at Bailey Lane End.[93] The chapel was rebuilt in 1930[94] and became part of the Methodist Church in 1932. In 1869 also a small chapel was built on the south-western side of the Forest at Clements End,[95] where preaching had begun in 1856.[96] Apart from their chapels the Bible Christians had several preaching stations in the Forest in the 1860s but only one, at Ruardean Woodside, in 1875. In that year the total membership of their eight chapels, including one newly opened at Cinderford, was 166, with Drybrook (44) and Bream's Eaves (43) attracting the largest numbers.[97] The Cinderford chapel, at Flaxley Meend,[98] closed in 1879 but the society was revived in 1884. It held services and a Sunday school at Zion, the Wesleyan Methodists' chapel in lower High Street, which it purchased the following year. The Bible Christians had little success in Cinderford and in 1917 their successors, the United Methodists, sold Zion to the Y.M.C.A.[99] The Bible Christian cause at Ruardean Woodside was renewed several times before 1881, when a handful of people built a chapel at Knights Hill, to the west. The chapel, called Zion, became part of the Methodist Church in 1932 but closed in 1973[1] and was a house in 1992.

The fortunes of the Forest's Bible Christians fluctuated considerably and several missions were organized to reverse a decline in congregations. Most chapels continued to attract small congregations and underwent little change but the larger societies increased their accommodation.[2] In one advance after 1907 when the Bible Christians joined with other denominations to form the United Methodist Church,[3] a small iron chapel was built at Plump Hill in 1913.[4] It became part of the Methodist Church in 1932 but closed in 1972[5] and was used as a store in 1992. Of the Forest's eight Bible Christian chapels which passed to the Methodist Church formed in 1932,[6] that on Bradley hill, to which a brick schoolroom had been added in 1914,[7] closed c. 1988[8] and became part of the Dean Heritage museum in the early 1990s. After the closure of the Ruspidge chapel in 1992 only the chapels at Bailey Lane End, Bream's Eaves (Parkend Road), Clements End, and Drybrook were in use.[9]

CONGREGATIONALISTS AND INDEPENDENTS. In 1783 the preacher Richard Stiff,

74 G. E. Lawrence, *Bible Christians of Forest of Dean*, ed. H. R. Jarrett (1985), 23–5, 38–9; for site, P.R.O., F 16/63 (no. 436); F 16/70; for later hist., below, this section.
75 Glos. R.O., D 2598/5/8.
76 Date and name on bldg.; above, Plate 17; for later hist., below, this section.
77 Glos. R.O., D 2598/5/1.
78 P.R.O., HO 129/334/1/3/14.
79 Ibid. HO 129/334/1/3/12; HO 129/334/1/2/8.
80 Glos. R.O., D 2598/5/1, 8.
81 Inscr. on bldg.; Lawrence, *Bible Christians*, 58; for later hist., below, this para.
82 Glos. R.O., D 2598/5/1.   83 Inscr. on bldg.
84 Glos. R.O., D 2598/5/1.
85 Inscr. on bldg.; Lawrence, *Bible Christians*, 43, 58.
86 Glos. R.O., D 2598/6/1; D 4337/3/1.
87 Lawrence, *Kindling the Flame*, 42.
88 Lawrence, *Bible Christians*, 39.
89 *Dean Forest Mercury*, 7 Sept. 1984.

90 Glos. R.O., D 2598/5/1; Lawrence, *Bible Christians*, 58–9.
91 Glos. R.O., D 2598/28/25–6.   92 Ibid. 5/8.
93 Lawrence, *Bible Christians*, 40–1; Glos. R.O., D 2598/5/2; G.R.O. Worship Reg. nos. 19356, 19591.
94 Lawrence, *Kindling the Flame*, 48.
95 Inscr. on bldg.
96 Glos. R.O., D 2598/5/1.   97 Ibid. 2.
98 O.S. Map 1/2,500, Glos. XXXI. 11 (1881 edn.).
99 Glos. R.O., D 2598/5/2; 7/6.
1 Ibid. 5/1–2, 8; Lawrence, *Kindling the Flame*, 36.
2 Glos. R.O., D 2598/5/2.
3 Lawrence, *Kindling the Flame*, 48.
4 Glos. R.O., D 2598/21/1.   5 Ibid. 2.
6 Cf. Lawrence, *Kindling the Flame*, 50–1.
7 *Glouc. Jnl.* 3 Oct. 1914.
8 Glos. R.O., D 2598/1/54.
9 Inf. from Mr. P. Hyne, of Ruspidge, Forest of Dean circuit archivist.

an Independent, moved from Dursley to Blakeney and began to hold open-air Sunday services in the Forest.[10] Among his congregations may have been the Independents who in 1787 registered a house at Whitecroft for worship.[11] Stiff's work was bolstered by a missionary society formed c. 1795 by Gloucestershire ministers[12] such as Robert McCall of the Countess of Huntingdon's chapel in Gloucester,[13] and in 1797 and 1802 houses at Littledean Hill and Yorkley were licensed for use by Stiff's followers.[14] The Littledean Hill meeting, established after a mission to Newnham had encountered hostility, moved in 1805 to Littledean,[15] from where it supported missionary work in the Forest. Its members registered houses at Cinderford in 1819, Soudley in 1821[16] and 1822, and Pope's Hill in 1822,[17] and David Prain, its minister from 1826, preached in the surrounding area.[18] In 1833 an Independent Sunday school, started in 1827 possibly at Cinderford, taught 35 children and another in the Drybrook or Ruardean Hill area had c. 70 pupils.[19] The longest mission from Littledean was to Pope's Hill, where a chapel built in 1844 had a congregation of 70 and a Sunday school in 1851.[20] It was enlarged c. 1870 and it remained a mission station of the Littledean church[21] until falling attendances forced its closure in 1970.[22] The building had been converted as a house by 1990.

A mission to the Drybrook area supervised from Littledean by the Revd. Benjamin Jenkyn held cottage services at Hawthorns in the mid 1840s[23] and at Harrow Hill in 1851.[24] A chapel east of the Nailbridge road, begun by Jenkyn in the early 1850s, was opened in 1857[25] and enlarged in 1858 with the help of the mine owner Cornelius Brain.[26] The meeting, which established itself as a separate Independent church with 9 members in 1859 and became the largest Congregational church in the Forest, employed its own minister from 1870. In the early 1870s the chapel, known as Rehoboth, was freed from debt by Cornelius Brain's executors[27] and was given a gabled street front with pilasters and round-headed windows as part of alterations completed by his sons in 1872.[28] A schoolroom was added to the building in 1874 and a block of schoolrooms was built to the north in 1888. From 1893 a manse was provided for the minister. In 1908 the church had 205 members,

including those attending two daughter meetings,[29] and in 1924 it had 109 members.[30] From 1932 the chapel shared a minister with the Littledean church and later, as membership continued to decline, the pastorate was shared with other Congregational churches. The manse was sold in 1964 and the schoolrooms were abandoned in the mid 1980s. In 1992 the chapel, which had joined the United Reformed Church, had a congregation of 20, swelled on special occasions to c. 65.[31]

In its heyday the Drybrook church undertook missions to Brierley and Cinderford. At Brierley, where services began in the early 1880s,[32] a small chapel was built in 1884.[33] It later became a separate church[34] and, having joined the United Reformed Church, was used by a small congregation in 1992. Independents had organized meetings in Cinderford before 1830[35] and the Drybrook church began a mission there in, or just before, 1904. A house at the corner of Forest Road and Woodside Street was converted as a mission church.[36] It was sold c. 1958[37] and was later used by Jehovah's Witnesses.[38]

Independents led by a Gloucester minister held cottage services at Viney Hill in 1849.[39] Coleford's Independents also sent missionaries into the Forest. In 1860 they were holding services at Berry Hill and Coalway Lane End[40] and in 1865 they had a small congregation at Moseley Green.[41] That congregation, worshipping in a room at an abandoned colliery, included Mary Young, keeper of the Yorkley turnpike gate, with whose assistance Samuel Ford of Blakeney built a chapel at Moseley Green.[42] The chapel, opened in 1866,[43] was called Bethlehem[44] and was sold to the Primitive Methodists in 1894.[45] Longer lasting was a Congregational church at Worrall Hill established with help from the Coleford meeting. Services were held in cottages and a schoolroom before 1884 when a small chapel was built. The chapel was enlarged in 1888 and had 18 members in 1908.[46] In 1992 it was used by a small congregation of the United Reformed Church.

PRIMITIVE METHODISTS. The spread of Primitive Methodism in the Forest, where it gained a foothold in the mid 1820s, was slow and unspectacular. Despite frequent setbacks many

10 Glos. R.O., D 2297.
11 Ibid. Q/SO 10, f. 265.   12 Ibid. D 2297.
13 Cf. V.C.H. Glos. iv. 325.
14 Hockaday Abs. cclx, Littledean, 1797; ccxcvii, 1802.
15 Glos. R.O., D 2297; above, Littledean, nonconf.
16 Hockaday Abs. clxxvi, St. John.
17 G.D.R. vol. 344, ff. 21v.–22.
18 Glos. R.O., D 2297; cf. Mountjoy, Dean Collier, 7.
19 Educ. Enq. Abstract, 312; cf. Glos. R.O., D 2297.
20 P.R.O., HO 129/334/1/3/16.
21 Glos. R.O., D 2052, Littledean.
22 Dean Forest Mercury, 16 Oct. 1970.
23 Para. based on a hist. in Drybrook United Reformed Ch. min. bk. 1881–91: in possession of ch. sec. (1992); for Jenkyn, Glos. R.O., D 2052, Littledean.
24 P.R.O., HO 129/334/1/3/15.
25 Poster in Drybrook United Reformed Ch. min. bk. 1914–36.
26 Drybrook United Reformed Ch. min. bk. 1937–88, which includes mins. for 1858 and acct. for 1858–9.
27 Cf. Glos. R.O., reg. wills 1870, f. 211.
28 Inscr. on bldg.

29 Glos. Colln. J 11.48 (16).
30 Inf. from Mr. K. Hale, of Drybook, based on ch. min. bks.
31 Inf. from Mr. Hale.
32 Hist. in Drybrook United Reformed Ch. min. bk. 1881–91.   33 Date on bldg.
34 Cf. Cong. Year Bk. (1972), 94.
35 Above, this section; below, Wesleyan Methodists.
36 Drybrook United Reformed Ch. acct. bk. 1897–1933; O.S. Map 1/2,500, Glos. XXXI. 11 (1902, 1922 edns.); Kelly's Dir. Glos. (1910), says the church was built in 1902.
37 Drybrook United Reformed Ch. min. bk. 1937–88.
38 W.I. portrait of Cinderford (1965, copy in Cinderford libr.).
39 Glos. R.O., Q/RZ 1; cf. V.C.H. Glos. iv. 324.
40 Glos. R.O., D 2052, Coleford.
41 Ibid. D 5533/1/1.
42 M. Young, Life of Faith (1900, copy in Dean Heritage museum), 12–14; for Ford, Kelly's Dir. Glos. (1870), 468.
43 Glouc. Jnl. 12 May 1866.
44 O.S. Map 6", Glos. XXXIX. NW. (1883 edn.).
45 Glos. R.O., D 2598/4/5–6.
46 Dean Forest Mercury, 25 May 1984; Glos. Colln. J 11.48 (4, 6, 16).

chapels were built and, with over a dozen, often small, meeting places scattered throughout the Forest in the late 1860s, Primitive Methodism became the most prevalent sect there. It sustained that position until after the First World War.

Primitive Methodism was probably brought to Lydbrook by a Gloucester man in 1823.[47] The following year James Roles, a preacher from the Oakengates circuit in Shropshire, arrived in Pillowell to evangelize the mining communities of west Gloucestershire. Cottage services were held in several places, including Lydbrook and Yorkley, and the mission became a separate circuit in 1826 or soon after.[48] The first circuit chapel was built at Upper Lydbrook in 1828[49] and the mission gradually extended far beyond the Forest. The resident minister moved to Monmouth in the mid 1830s and circuits based on Hereford, Monmouth and Lydbrook, and Lydney were carved out of the Pillowell circuit in 1850, 1868, and 1879 respectively.[50]

Within the Forest the Primitive Methodists built a chapel between Pillowell and Yorkley in 1835[51] and another at Ellwood in 1841[52] and registered a house at the Lonk near Joyford for worship in 1846.[53] In 1850 they had small societies with less than ten members each at Joyford and in the Lane End district in the north-west, at Viney Hill and Oldcroft in the south-east, and at Littledean Hill in the north-east. Their three chapels attracted larger numbers of people[54] and in 1851 congregations at Pillowell and Ellwood averaged well over 100 and 60 respectively and included many children attending their Sunday schools.[55] The Lydbrook chapel, which at that time had an average attendance of c. 57,[56] was rebuilt in 1852[57] and took the name Ebenezer.[58] Later a gallery was erected in it and a schoolroom was added, and in 1868 the chapel became the joint head of a circuit including Monmouth.[59] It was replaced in 1912 by a larger building with a schoolroom on its lower floor.[60] That chapel, which became part of the Methodist Church in 1932, closed in 1991. The Pillowell chapel was altered in 1856[61] and a new meeting house incorporating a schoolroom under the chapel was built on another site to the south-west in 1885.[62] The original building, known as Jubilee chapel,[63] was sold in 1892 to the Pillowell and Yorkley co-operative society[64] and was used

in 1990 as dwellings. The Ellwood chapel was retained as a schoolroom in 1876 when a new chapel was opened to the west. Services in the new building, known as Providence, were attended by 230 people in 1879.[65]

Of the smaller meetings in 1850 two built their own chapels. Zion at Five Acres, erected by the Joyford society in 1851, was enlarged in 1869.[66] It became part of the Methodist Church in 1932 and was closed in 1991. Mount Pleasant at Viney Hill dated from 1856 and had a schoolroom added to it in 1887.[67] It became part of the Methodist Church in 1932 but was closed in 1969 and was a house in 1992.[68] A society formed at Bream's Eaves in 1851 built a chapel there in 1858. Known as Mount Sion,[69] it attracted people from Whitecroft village, where Primitive Methodists had held cottage meetings,[70] and had a congregation of 150 in 1879.[71] A new schoolroom was added during alterations in 1903.[72] The chapel, which was part of the Methodist Church from 1932, closed in 1991. After several attempts the Primitive Methodists revived their mission to the Lane End district in 1857 and built a chapel called Pisgah at Coalway in 1861.[73] The following year they established a meeting at Reddings, near Lydbrook, and built a small chapel called Mount Tabor there.[74] A schoolroom was erected alongside it probably in the late 1880s.[75] The chapel became part of the Methodist Church in 1932 but after services ended in 1961[76] it was used as a builder's store.[77] From the mid 1850s preachers also visited the Drybrook and Cinderford areas and in 1861 a small chapel was built north-west of Nailbridge on Morse Road, below Ruardean hill.[78] The chapel, part of the Methodist Church from 1932, closed in 1989.[79] Cinderford's Primitive Methodists met in a rented room in 1859 and built a chapel in 1864 in what was to become Church Road. Soon afterwards they opened a Sunday school in rooms under the chapel[80] and in 1908 they built more schoolrooms behind it.[81] The Primitives also continued to evangelize Littledean Hill near Cinderford[82] and in 1877 they had a mission to the Cinderford ironworks which regularly drew attendances of 45.[83] Their membership at Littledean Hill, where they bought Dockham chapel in 1879, remained small and, having failed to clear its debt, turned the

47 G.D.R. vol. 344, f. 119v.; cf. P.R.O., HO 129/577/1/5/26.
48 Lawrence, *Kindling the Flame*, 11, 50; cf. *V.C.H. Salop.* ii. 14.
49 P.R.O., HO 129/577/1/5/26; Hockaday Abs. cclxiv, 1829; for later hist., below, this section.
50 Glos. R.O., D 2598/4/4–6, 9; Bright, *Nonconf. in Dean*, 36.
51 P.R.O., HO 129/577/1/5/22; cf. O.S. Map 6", Glos. XXXIX. SW. (1883 edn.).
52 P.R.O., HO 129/577/1/5/24; date on bldg.
53 Hockaday Abs. clxxvi, Christ Church.
54 Glos. R.O., D 2598/4/9.
55 P.R.O., HO 129/577/1/5/22; HO 129/577/1/5/24.
56 Ibid. HO 129/577/1/5/26.
57 *Kelly's Dir. Glos.* (1889), 834.
58 G.R.O. Worship Reg. no. 1038.
59 Glos. R.O., D 2598/4/6.
60 *Glouc. Jnl.* 10 Aug., 21 Sept. 1912; O.S. Map 1/2,500, Glos. XXXI. 5 (1902, 1922 edns.).
61 Lawrence, *Kindling the Flame*, 50.
62 Inscr. on bldg.

63 O.S. Map 6", Glos. XXXIX. SW. (1883 edn.).
64 Lawrence, *Kindling the Flame*, 50.
65 Glos. R.O., D 2598/4/4–5; inscr. on new chap.
66 Glos. R.O., D 2598/4/6; inscr. on bldg.
67 Glos. R.O., D 2598/4/5; O.S. Map 1/2,500, Glos. XXXIX. 15 (1881 edn.).
68 Lawrence, *Kindling the Flame*, 56.
69 Glos. R.O., D 2598/4/6, 9; inscr. on bldg.
70 Lawrence, *Kindling the Flame*, 26.
71 Glos. R.O., D 2598/4/4.
72 *Glouc. Jnl.* 21 Nov. 1903; inscr. on bldg.
73 Glos. R.O., D 2598/4/6, 9; G.R.O. Worship Reg. no. 14611.
74 Inscr. on bldg.; Glos. R.O., D 2598/4/6, which says the chap. was built in 1863.
75 Cf. *66th Rep. Com. Woods*, H.C. 251, p. 15 (1888), xxxiv. 76 Glos. R.O., D 2598/1/28, 37.
77 Local inf. (1990). 78 Glos. R.O., D 2598/4/6, 9.
79 Ibid. 1/54. 80 Ibid. 4/5–6; inscr. on bldg.
81 *Glouc. Jnl.* 19 Sept. 1908; cf. Mullin, *Forest in Old Photog.* 78.
82 Glos. R.O., D 2598/4/6, 9. 83 Ibid. 5.

chapel over to the Anglicans in or just before 1901.[84]

In the centre of the Forest Primitive Methodist services held at Moseley Green from 1859 were discontinued in 1864 for want of a congregation. They were resumed in 1867[85] and a chapel called Providence, standing north-east of the Barracks, was registered in 1879.[86] In 1894 the meeting moved to the Independent chapel some way south but in 1898 it returned to its former home. The return led to a drop in support and in 1907 a new chapel was built on the Blakeney–Parkend road to the south.[87] That chapel, which was abandoned in the mid 1950s,[88] fell into ruin[89] but in the late 1980s it was rebuilt as part of a new house. In 1868 the Primitive Methodists had 13 meetings and 339 members in the Forest. Most of the chapels were well supported, particularly those at Coalway Lane End (42), Pillowell (38), Ellwood (36), Viney Hill (33), and Bream's Eaves (32).[90] The Primitive Methodists failed to win many adherents at Parkend, where they soon disbanded a society formed in 1870,[91] but in the mid 1870s they provided two more small chapels in the south-east of the Forest. Fairview near the top of Blakeney Hill, where a society met from 1861, was built in 1874.[92] The chapel, which became part of the Methodist Church in 1932, closed in 1990. Bethesda at Oldcroft, where the Primitives revived their cause in 1873,[93] opened in 1876[94] and closed, following storm damage, in 1929.[95] Members of the congregation later reopened it as an independent church,[96] which closed in the early 1960s, and from 1975 until 1991 the building was an electrical engineer's workshop.[97]

The Primitives erected two more chapels in the north-west of the Forest, an area visited by their missionaries in the 1850s.[98] Edge End's iron chapel was built in 1892[99] and Mount Hermon at Mile End in 1904.[1] From that time there were 15 Primitive Methodist chapels in the Forest. Those at Cinderford, Pillowell, Bream's Eaves, Lydbrook, and Five Acres had the largest congregations and each retained over 40 members in 1932. At that time the Mile End chapel, with over 30 members, was also well attended and the cause was weakest at Viney Hill and at Oldcroft,[2] where the chapel had been closed. Of the fourteen chapels that became part of the

Methodist Church in 1932,[3] only those at Cinderford (Church Road), Coalway Lane End, Edge End, Ellwood, Mile End, and Pillowell were in use in 1992.[4]

WESLEYAN METHODISTS. Methodism had gained at least one Lydbrook family as converts by 1751[5] but was not properly introduced to the Forest until 1808 or 1809, when two ministers of the Monmouth Wesleyan circuit holding open-air services were attacked and driven off.[6] Later their reception was more peaceable and William Woodall, one of the first to visit the area regularly, registered a chapel at Lower Lydbrook and a room at Clay Lane, near Clearwell Meend, in 1813[7] and established a meeting at Ellwood,[8] where a house was licensed for worship in 1821. Wesleyan meetings were also begun at Pillowell and Viney Hill, where houses were registered in 1816 and 1817 respectively,[9] and at Joyford, where preaching began in 1820[10] and cottages were registered in 1822 and 1824.[11]

Several small chapels were built as Wesleyan Methodism made progress on the fringes of the Forest. A mission to the colliers of Littledean Hill undertaken by George Robinson in 1821 proved successful and within three months a society was formed there. Robert Meredith's house was registered for the mission but a barn was used for services attended by several hundred people. Following Robinson's departure the Ledbury circuit supplied occasional preachers until the Wesleyan Conference, in response to Meredith's petition on the society's behalf, sent a missionary to the area.[12] Soon afterwards, in 1824, a chapel was built at Littledean Hill;[13] it had a gallery under which a Sunday school was held.[14] In the following months the missionary, Isaac Denison, also preached at Cinderford, Drybrook, Lydbrook, and Parkend and outside the Forest. He also took his mission to Lea Bailey[15] and a chapel was built there in 1836.[16] In 1824 a small square chapel, the first to be built by the Wesleyans in the Forest proper, was opened on a hillside between Whitecroft and Pillowell. Its congregation included members who earlier had attended services at Redbrook[17] and in 1834 its minister was the collier Edward

84 Ibid. 6; D 543, Littledean Hill chap. deeds; P 85/2/VE 2/2.
85 Ibid. D 2598/4/6, 9.
86 G.R.O. Worship Reg. no. 24840; O.S. Map 6", Glos. XXXIX. NW. (1904 edn.).
87 Glos. R.O., D 2598/4/5–6.
88 Ibid. 12/1.
89 Citizen (Glouc.), 17 Mar. 1972; 31 Oct. 1986.
90 Glos. R.O., D 2598/4/9.
91 Ibid. 5, 9.
92 Ibid. 6, 9; inscr. on bldg.
93 Glos. R.O., D 2598/4/9.
94 Inscr. on bldg.
95 Glos. R.O., D 2598/4/6.
96 Lawrence, Kindling the Flame, 56; O.S. Map 1/2,500, SO 6406 (1958 edn.).
97 Inf. from Mrs. Averil Kear, of Oldcroft.
98 Glos. R.O., D 2598/4/6, 9.
99 Ibid. 1/3; Glos. Colln. RR 86.10 (1), p. 17.
1 Inscr. on bldg.
2 Glos. R.O., D 2598/2/9; 4/9, 13.
3 Cf. Lawrence, Kindling the Flame, 50–1.

4 Inf. from Mr. Hyne.
5 Hart, Ind. Hist. of Dean, 114.
6 Nicholls, Forest of Dean, 160; Bright, Nonconf. in Dean, 36.
7 Hockaday Abs. cclxiv, ccxcvii; for later hist. of Lydbrook meeting, below, this section.
8 Glos. R.O., D 2297.
9 Hockaday Abs. ccxcvii; cix, 1817.
10 Glos. R.O., D 2297.
11 G.D.R. vol. 344, f. 36v.; Hockaday Abs. ccxcvii.
12 Wesleyan Meth. Mag. xlvii. 409; Glos. R.O., D 2297; G.D.R. vol. 344, f. 21.
13 Glos. R.O., D 2297; date on bldg.; for site, Glos. R.O., Q/RUm 107; for later hist., below, this section.
14 Mountjoy, Dean Collier, 2.
15 Wesleyan Meth. Mag. xlviii. 407–8; Hockaday Abs. clxxvi, St. John.
16 Glos. R.O., D 2297; for site, O.S. Map 6", Glos. XXIII. SE. (1883 edn.); for later hist., below, this section.
17 Whitecroft Wesleyan Chap. Centenary and Jubilee Souvenir (copy in Glos. R.O., NC 80), 9.

Kear, known locally as 'Clergy Ned'.[18] A chapel built at Joyford in 1825[19] was attended by Thomas James, a Coleford solicitor,[20] and had *c.* 14 members in the early 1830s. At that time the Ellwood society had *c.* 11 members and the Wesleyan cause at Lydbrook was very low.[21] By 1833 Wesleyans were holding cottage services at Bream's Eaves.[22]

The course of Wesleyan Methodism in the Forest owed much to Aaron Goold, a colliery agent and later a colliery owner.[23] Goold, with whose assistance the Littledean Hill and White-croft chapels were built,[24] was particularly influential in Cinderford, where a mission room for use by Baptists, Independents, and Method-ists was opened with his help in 1829.[25] In 1841, when they had a meeting house at Cinderford bridge,[26] the Wesleyans built a chapel at the Cinderford ironworks,[27] and in 1850 their circuit plan for Ledbury and the Forest also included Wesley,[28] a large chapel in Belle Vue Road built by Goold in a 14th-century style. Opened in 1850, Wesley replaced the Littledean Hill chapel,[29] but with Goold's active espousal of the reform movement within the Wesleyan Meth-odist Church those loyal to the Wesleyan Conference reopened the older chapel and late in 1850 moved to a cottage in the Mousell Lane area.[30] Goold appointed Wesleyan Reformers to supply the pulpit at Wesley[31] and in 1851 his minister claimed congregations of up to 500. The ironworks' chapel, which also sided with the Reformers, had congregations of up to 150.[32] The Reformers, who also used the Littledean Hill chapel, were part of the United Methodist Free Churches in 1860.[33] Services continued at Wesley after Goold's death in 1862 and the chapel, which the United Methodist Free Churches retained together with a meeting place at Soudley in 1867, was closed in 1873.[34] The Littledean Hill chapel was converted as a house before 1895.[35]

The Wesleyan loyalists, who following the schism of 1850 numbered *c.* 20,[36] had several meeting places in Cinderford before 1860 when they opened a new chapel called Zion in lower High Street.[37] In 1875 the chapel became the head of a new circuit taken out of the Ross circuit and covering Coleford and Lydney besides much of the Forest.[38] Zion's congregation, which included colliery owners and managers, outgrew the accommodation and in 1880, with the help of the industrialist Jacob Chivers, it took over Wesley chapel. Zion, which it finally left in 1881,[39] was later used by the Bible Christians.[40] At Wesley the Wesleyans, who increased their membership to well over 100 by the end of the century,[41] built a block of classrooms behind the chapel in 1893 and a hall in 1905.[42]

Among the Forest's other Wesleyan societies the reform controversy of 1849 and 1850 had most impact at Whitecroft. There half of the 102 mem-bers left the chapel and, with the support of Aaron Goold, held services nearby in 1859.[43] The chapel's congregation, which averaged *c.* 50 in 1851,[44] was later boosted by the return of many of the seceders and in 1874 a larger chapel was built. The original chapel, which it adjoined, was re-tained as a schoolroom. Other additions to the building included, in 1905, a block containing a schoolroom and a meeting room on separate floors.[45]

In the later 19th century the Wesleyans were not successful in all parts of the Forest and many of their attempts to secure footholds failed. The cause at Lea Bailey, where the congregation in 1851 rarely surpassed 50,[46] was probably always small and the chapel, which was derelict in 1990, was converted as a house soon afterwards. At Lydbrook a similarly sized congregation[47] moved to a new chapel at Lower Lydbrook in 1864,[48] but the cause was overshadowed by other non-conformist churches. The chapel, which became part of the Methodist Church in 1932, closed in 1956[49] and, after being used as a store,[50] was demolished. The Joyford chapel, for which an average attendance of 120 was claimed in 1851,[51] closed in the 1860s or 1870s.[52] The Wesleyan congregation at Bream's Eaves averaged 100 in 1851[53] and moved to a new chapel at Bream Woodside in 1860. Later a rear block was added to the building.[54] The chapel, which became part of the Methodist Church in 1932, closed in 1959[55] and was used by a pentecostalist church in 1992.[56] A Wesleyan meeting at Parkend, established by 1862,[57] was disbanded in 1876.[58]

[18] *2nd Rep. Dean Forest Com.* 51; Stratford, *Good and Great Men*, 416; for later hist. of meeting, below, this section.
[19] P.R.O., HO 129/577/1/5/25; for site, *2nd Rep. Dean Forest Com.* 42; Glos. R.O., Q/RGf 1/4.
[20] Hockaday Abs. clxxvi, Christ Church, 1829; Bright, *Nonconf. in Dean*, 33 n.
[21] Glos. R.O., D 2297.
[22] Hockaday Abs. cxxxii, Bream.
[23] For Goold, above, Industry, mining from 1770s.
[24] Lawrence, *Kindling the Flame*, 17.
[25] Glos. R.O., D 2297; Hockaday Abs. clxxvi, St. John.
[26] Glos. R.O., Q/FR 4/1, f. 136; for site, ibid. Q/RUm 245.
[27] P.R.O., HO 129/334/1/7/19; for site, ibid. F 16/63 (no. 2482); F 16/70.
[28] Glos. R.O., D 2598/2/17.
[29] *Glouc. Jnl.* 28 July 1849; 6 July 1850.
[30] Ibid. 26 Oct., 16 Nov. 1850; Glos. R.O., Q/RZ 1.
[31] F. Balch, *Story of Wesley Church* (1927), 7.
[32] P.R.O., HO 129/334/1/8/23; HO 129/334/1/7/19.
[33] G.R.O. Worship Reg. nos. 11016–19.
[34] Balch, *Wesley Ch.* 7–8; Stratford, *Good and Great Men*, 417–18; cf. *Glouc. Jnl.* 29 June 1872.
[35] *Meth. Recorder*, xxxvi. 57.
[36] P.R.O., HO 129/334/1/8/22.
[37] Balch, *Wesley Ch.* 8; O.S. Map 1/2,500, Glos. XXXI.

[38] Glos. R.O., D 2598/2/6, 10.
[39] Ibid. 7/7–8; *Glouc. Jnl.* 13 Nov. 1880; Balch, *Wesley Ch.* 8–12. [40] Above, Bible Christians.
[41] Glos. R.O., D 2598/2/6–7.
[42] Balch, *Wesley Ch.* 12–13.
[43] *Whitecroft Chap. Souvenir*, 11; P.R.O., F 16/64 (nos. 2598, 2601); F 16/71.
[44] P.R.O., HO 129/577/1/5/23.
[45] *Whitecroft Chap. Souvenir*, 11–17; *Glouc. Jnl.* 30 May 1891; 16 Sept. 1905.
[46] P.R.O., HO 129/334/1/3/13.
[47] Cf. ibid. HO 129/577/1/5/20.
[48] *Morris's Dir. Glos.* (1876), 515.
[49] Glos. R.O., D 2598/1/26.
[50] W.I. hist. of Lydbrook (*c.* 1959, TS. in Glos. Colln.), 11–12.
[51] P.R.O., HO 129/577/1/5/25.
[52] Ibid. F 16/64 (no. 519); F 16/71; O.S. Map 6", Glos. XXX. SE. (1884 edn.).
[53] P.R.O., HO 129/577/1/1/2.
[54] Inscr. on bldg.; cf. O.S. Map 1/2,500, Glos. XXXIX. 13 (1881 edn.).
[55] Glos. R.O., D 2598/1/28, 37.
[56] Below, other churches.
[57] Glos. R.O., D 2598/2/14. [58] Ibid. 10.

At Cinderford bridge, where they resumed preaching in 1864,[59] Wesleyans built a large chapel with a schoolroom under it in 1869.[60] They also founded a church at Ruardean Woodside, where they began services in a workshop at East Slade colliery in 1878 and built a chapel called Ebenezer in 1885.[61] A schoolroom added to the chapel in 1901 was enlarged in 1926.[62] The chapel became part of the Methodist Church in 1932 but closed c. 1981[63] and was a house in 1992. The last attempt by Wesleyans to break new ground in the Forest, at Cannop where they furnished a room at a disused factory for services in 1915, was abandoned in 1916.[64] In 1932, when they helped to form the Methodist Church,[65] the Wesleyans had six chapels in the Forest and Lydbrook with 327 members, and Cinderford and Whitecroft remained their principal meetings.[66] The chapels at Lower Lydbrook and Bream Woodside, in villages where the Methodists inherited several meeting places, were closed in the 1950s[67] and that at Cinderford bridge in 1992. The chapels at Cinderford (Wesley) and Whitecroft remained open.[68]

OTHER CHURCHES AND MISSIONS.

A chapel at Ruardean Hill in 1856 was possibly opened by John Herbert, a dissenting minister.[69] No later record of the meeting has been found. Christadelphians, who apparently had a short lived meeting in Cinderford in 1870, met at the Pludds, near Ruardean, from 1890 until 1914. They held services elsewhere in the Forest, including Ellwood where they formed a congregation in 1916. That group worshipped at Fetter Hill from 1919 and moved in 1928 to a new iron and stone hall at Ellwood,[70] which was in use in 1992. Plymouth Brethren met in Cinderford, in a small chapel at Flaxley Meend, by 1879. The chapel, in Abbey Street,[71] was used by a pentecostal church in the mid 1960s[72] and had closed by the early 1990s. Also in Cinderford a mission hall in the later Station Street, an iron building which became known as the Ark, was registered in 1886 by a group called the Blue Ribbon Gospel Army.[73] The mission, which the 'Forward Movement' of the South Wales

Presbyterian Church revived in 1901, was undenominational and under A. H. Hirst, its pastor for much of its life before 1938, it had over 30 members.[74] In 1973, the mission having been abandoned, the Ark was sold to Cinderford Town band for musical activities[75] and later it was pulled down. Another mission hall in Station Street, occupied from 1921 by a group of Brethren,[76] remained in use in 1992. The Brethren, who gained adherents outside Cinderford in the 1890s, opened other meeting places.[77] One at Yorkley Slade, in use in 1920,[78] was sold in 1957 to the parish of All Saints, Viney Hill, for use as a church hall[79] and another at Plump Hill was abandoned after 1965.[80] Lydbrook had a free mission hall in 1881,[81] and at Lower Lydbrook a mission hall built alongside an abandoned tramroad in 1889[82] was disused in 1990. A mission room at Blind Meend near Clements End was recorded only in 1900.[83] Salem at Berry Hill, a small stone chapel built for a free church in 1900,[84] remained open in 1992.

The Salvation Army held meetings in Cinderford town hall in 1886[85] and had its own place of worship nearby in Woodside Street c. 1930.[86] Jehovah's Witnesses, who were active in the town in the early 1920s, registered Kingdom Hall, formerly a Congregational chapel at the corner of Forest Road and Woodside Street, in 1964[87] and remained there in 1992. Jehovah's Witnesses registered a meeting place at Brockhollands in 1971[88] and their Lydney congregation built a church at Parkend in the early 1990s.[89] Friends or Quakers had a wooden meeting house in Station Street, Cinderford, in 1931.[90] It was dismantled in the early 1970s.[91] A Quaker meeting house at Ruardean Hill, built in 1934, closed in 1960.[92] A Christian Spiritualist church meeting at Lydbrook by 1934 was disbanded before 1964.[93] Pentecostalists meeting in Bream[94] registered the former Methodist chapel at Bream Woodside in 1964[95] and held services there in 1992. In 1958 a congregation of the Assemblies of God had a chapel at Oldcroft, demolished by 1975.[96] In 1976 Latter Day Saints registered a new church in the Lane End district at Wynols Hill, just within Coleford between Coalway and Broadwell.[97]

59 *Glouc. Jnl.* 19 Nov. 1864.
60 Inscr. on bldg.
61 Lawrence, *Kindling the Flame*, 35; Glos. R.O., D 2598/2/14.
62 Glos. R.O., D 2598/14/1-2.
63 Ibid. D 5410/4/2.   64 Ibid. D 2598/2/14.
65 Cf. Lawrence, *Kindling the Flame*, 50-1.
66 Glos. R.O., D 2598/2/9: figures do not include Lea Bailey chapel.
67 Above, this section.   68 Inf. from Mr. Hyne.
69 P.R.O., F 16/63 (no. 969B); F 16/70; *2nd Rep. Dean Forest Com.* 75; Glos. R.O., Q/RGf 1/8; cf. Glos. R.O., reg. wills 1873, ff. 460v.–461.
70 *Dean Forest Mercury*, 16 Aug. 1968.
71 *Kelly's Dir. Glos.* (1879), 647; (1885), 420; Glos. R.O., D 2299/1518.
72 W.I. portrait of Cinderford; Glos. R.O., PA 85/1.
73 G.R.O. Worship Reg. no. 29176; for site, O.S. Map 6", Glos. XXXI. SE. (1903 edn.).
74 Glos. R.O., D 2908/1-2; W.I. portrait of Cinderford.
75 *Citizen*, 18 July 1973.
76 W.I. portrait of Cinderford; G.R.O. Worship Reg. no. 52623.
77 Glos. R.O., D 2598/4/6; cf. C. E. Hart, *Coleford* (1983), 457.

78 O.S. Map 1/2,500, Glos. XXXIX. 11 (1922 edn.).
79 Glos. R.O., P 348/VE 2/2; D 3921/II/5.
80 'Memories of Mitcheldean' (Bristol Univ. dept. of extra-mural studies, 1965), 14: copy in Glos. Colln. RR 203.4.
81 *Bapt. Witness in Lydbrook*, 8.
82 Inscr. on bldg.; O.S. Map 1/2,500, Glos. XXXI. 1 (1923 edn.).
83 O.S. Map 1/2,500, Glos. XXXVIII. 12 (1902 edn.).
84 Inscr. on bldg.; O.S. Map 6", Glos. XXX. SE. (1903 edn.).
85 G.R.O. Worship Reg. no. 29188.
86 *Kelly's Dir. Glos.* (1927), 125; (1931), 118.
87 W.I. portrait of Cinderford; G.R.O. Worship Reg. no. 69374.
88 G.R.O. Worship Reg. no. 72431.
89 Notice outside Kingdom Hall, Parkend.
90 *Kelly's Dir. Glos.* (1931), 118; W.I. portrait of Cinderford.
91 Cf. O.S. Map 1/2,500, SO 6514 (1960, 1974 edns.).
92 Bent, *Highest Point of Dean*, 54.
93 Glos. R.O., DA 24/100/11, p. 304; G.R.O. Worship Reg. no. 55390.
94 Cf. W. A. Camm, *Bream through the Ages* (1980), 13.
95 G.R.O. Worship Reg. no. 69699.
96 O.S. Map 1/2,500, SO 6406 (1958, 1977 edns.).
97 G.R.O. Worship Reg. no. 74476.

EDUCATION

ELEMENTARY SCHOOLS. The educational system of the Forest of Dean has its roots principally in the missionary work of Anglican ministers in the early 19th century. P. M. Procter led the way in 1813 by opening a day school in his new chapel at Berry Hill and was followed by Henry Berkin, who established a similar school at Holy Trinity church near Drybrook in 1819, and by Henry Poole, who provided schools for Parkend and Bream in 1824 and 1830 respectively. Those schools were on the National plan and, deriving only a small part of their income from pence and other parental contributions, depended for survival on financial assistance from the Crown, acting through the Commissioners of Woods, Forests, and Land Revenues, and a few wealthy patrons. In the 1820s and 1830s several smaller, presumably dame, schools funded solely by parental payments were opened mostly in or near Cinderford.[98] The Forest's chief colliery owner built a large school in Cinderford in 1840 but in general mine owners and ironmasters paid education little attention at that time.[99] Apart from a British school started by a colliery owner in 1851, nonconformist endeavours in education were, until the advent of a school board, confined mostly to the running of Sunday schools and bible classes.[1] Two of the four Sunday schools recorded in 1833 were supported by Independent congregations[2] and many chapels, particularly those built after 1850, had their own schoolrooms.[3] In the mid 19th century six more National or church schools supported by the Crown were established, largely through the efforts of local clergy such as Henry Poole and H. G. Nicholls in the face of opposition from the chapels,[4] and Cinderford's principal school came under church control.

Following the Education Act of 1870 there was an acute shortage of school places within the Forest. The voluntary system supported ten church schools and there was an unknown number of private schools. In 1874 the Education Department, in giving notice that a school board would be formed for the Forest if enough places were not supplied, identified ten districts in want of schools or increased accommodation.[5] A board was formed in 1875; its area included the detached parts of Newland belonging to Lea Bailey, the parish of Hinder's Lane and Dockham,[6] and, from 1883, the Flaxley Meend district of Cinderford.[7] It was dominated by

nonconformist members[8] and became the focus of disputes between church and chapel over education.[9] The board had built five schools by 1878 and the voluntary system attempted to start two new schools, but in 1879, when the board schools and nine voluntary schools provided 3,433 places and 221 children attended schools outside the Forest, another 1,150 places were needed.[10] The board, its programme slowed by an increasing burden of debt,[11] reopened two schools which had closed and built three new ones in the 1880s and enlarged many of its buildings and provided a school in Cinderford for older children in the mid 1890s. From 1903 the Forest's board schools were managed, under the county education committee, by a local committee using the board's office in Cinderford.[12] To them were added four new council schools built before the First World War to relieve overcrowding in existing buildings. In those predominantly nonconformist communities served by a church school antagonism between church and chapel continued.[13] The county later took over most of the Forest's remaining voluntary schools and after the Second World War it provided several new schools to replace some older buildings. Management of the county council's schools passed to smaller local committees in 1969 and the Cinderford education office closed in 1978.[14] In 1992 the education authority ran 17 elementary schools for the Forest and there was an independent Roman Catholic school, started in 1960, in Cinderford.

The earliest day schools in CINDERFORD were evidently small private schools such as the seven recorded in that part of the Forest in 1833. They taught between 7 and 30 children and five had been started after 1822.[15] In 1840 the colliery owner Edward Protheroe built a school at Cinderford Tump for the benefit of families in his employ[16] and funded it by fees and a levy on his workforce.[17] After 1843, when he handed it over to the Crown in part payment of debts, Protheroe was in dispute with the minister of the neighbouring church of St. John the Evangelist about the school's management and in 1847 the Commissioners of Woods acting for the Crown placed it under the sole care of the deputy surveyor of the Forest.[18] During that period attendances, by children and adults up to the age of 22, sometimes exceeded 280,[19] and income included a grant from the Great Western

98 *Educ. Enq. Abstract*, 312.
99 *34th Rep. Com. Woods*, H.C. 330, p. 91 (1856), xxxvii.
1 Cf. G.D.R., F 3/1, p. 57.
2 *Educ. Enq. Abstract*, 312.   3 Above, Prot. Nonconf.
4 Nat. Soc. files, Dean West Christ Church; Dean West Coleford Lane End; Flaxley Meend.
5 Glos. R.O., SB 15/1, pp. 4–5, 20.
6 *Lond. Gaz.* 26 Feb. 1875, p. 810.
7 Glos. R.O., SB 15/2, pp. 36–7.
8 *Glouc. Jnl.* 27 Mar. 1875; 6 Apr. 1878; cf. J. Gibbs, 'Development of Educ. in Two Forest of Dean Schs. 1870–1903' (Bristol Univ. Dip. Ed. thesis, 1967), 33–4.
9 Nat. Soc. files, Dean West Christ Church; Dean West

Coleford Lane End; Dean West Parkend; Flaxley Meend.
10 Glos. R.O., SB 15/1, pp. 261–2.
11 Gibbs, 'Educ. in Two Forest of Dean Schs.' 35–8.
12 Glos. R.O., SM 85/1/M 1–6.
13 Nat. Soc. files, Dean East Holy Trin.
14 E. Olivey, *There's nothing like Education* (1978), 33: a hist. of Bilson sch., copy in Glos. Colln. RQ 78.5.
15 *Educ. Enq. Abstract*, 312.
16 Nicholls, *Forest of Dean*, 171 including illustration, reproduced below, Fig. 25.
17 *St. White's Sch. 1887–1987* (copy in Glos. Colln. R 78.10), 2.   18 *34th Rep. Com. Woods* (1856), 92–3.
19 Nicholls, *Forest of Dean*, 171–2.

FIG. 25. ST JOHN'S CHURCH, CINDERFORD, BUILT IN 1844, AND THE SCHOOL OF 1840

Railway Co. besides the Crown's contribution and school pence.[20] In 1855, following a reduction in funds, control of the school was transferred to St. John's parish.[21] As St. John's school it reopened in 1857 with boys' and girls' departments and soon had an average attendance of 112.[22] A National school, it received regular financial support from the Crawshay family and the Crown.[23] In 1883 it passed to the school board, which ran it with junior mixed and infants' departments until 1887, when it was replaced by St. White's school.[24] The building was a church hall in 1992.

In 1851 the colliery owner Aaron Goold opened a British school at Cinderford in connexion with Wesley, his chapel in Belle Vue Road. The school, which from 1853 occupied a new building north-east of St. John's church, in the later Church Road, had boys' and girls' departments and was intended by Goold for his employees' children. Its income came from subscriptions paid by the workmen. Goold's sons ran the school after his death in 1862 and it had an average attendance of 170 in 1863.[25] Although from 1871 it apparently received a Treasury grant in addition to a parliamentary grant[26] it had closed by 1874.[27] Children from the north part of Cinderford attended short lived National

schools at Littledean Hill and Flaxley Meend. The Littledean Hill school was opened in 1852 by H. G. Nicholls, minister of Holy Trinity church, Harrow Hill.[28] The schoolroom, which was also used as a chapel, closed in 1857.[29] Flaxley Meend National or C. of E. school, opened in 1875,[30] was built at the instigation of G. A. Allan, minister of St. John's church, on land at the corner of Abbey Street and Forest Road given by Sir Thomas Crawley-Boevey, Bt., and was also used as a chapel.[31] The school had junior mixed and infants' departments and an average attendance of 137 in 1876, when its income, from pence, did not meet its expenditure.[32] Following the opening of a board school at Bilson in 1877 attendances at Cinderford's older schools declined.[33] Flaxley Meend school, which was kept open principally by a local surgeon William Heane from 1878, became an infants' school and closed in 1881.[34] A school board formed for Flaxley Meend later that year[35] lapsed in 1883 when the area became part of East Dean township.[36]

Bilson school, one of the first to be provided by the Forest board, had new buildings in the later Station Street with 433 places in boys', girls', and infants' departments and a detached pair of schoolhouses.[37] The school was enlarged

20 Nat. Soc. *Inquiry, 1846–7*, Glos. 9.
21 *34th Rep. Com. Woods* (1856), 93, 127.
22 P.R.O., ED 7/37, Cinderford St. John's sch.; Glos. R.O., D 2186/40.
23 *Kelly's Dir. Glos.* (1870), 532; (1879), 629; Glos. R.O., P 85/SC 1/1.
24 Glos. R.O., SB 15/2, pp. 28–35; P.R.O., ED 7/34/124; below, this section.
25 P.R.O., ED 7/37, Cinderford Brit. sch.; *Glouc. Jnl.* 24 Sept. 1853; 25 Feb. 1860; J. Stratford, *Good and Great Men of Glos.* (1867), 418; for site, P.R.O., F 16/63 (no. 2740); F 16/70.
26 *Select Cttee. on Woods* (1889), 172.

27 *Dean Forest Select Cttee.* (1874), 136.
28 Glos. R.O., P 109/CW 2/1; site not known.
29 *Glouc. Jnl.* 5 Sept., 17 Oct. 1857.
30 Ibid. 29 May 1875; for site, O.S. Map 6", Glos. XXXI. SE. (1883 edn.).
31 Nat. Soc. files, Flaxley Meend; above, Churches (St. Stephen).
32 P.R.O., ED 7/37, Flaxley Meend C. of E. sch.
33 Olivey, *There's nothing like Education*, 4.
34 Nat. Soc. files, Flaxley Meend; Glos. R.O., P 85/2/SC 1–3.
35 *Lond. Gaz.* 16 Sept. 1881, p. 4726.
36 Glos. R.O., SB 15/2, pp. 36–7.
37 *Glouc. Jnl.* 8 Dec. 1877; P.R.O., ED 7/34/118.

in 1879 and 1886[38] and the average attendance was 670 in 1889[39] and, after the older children had been moved to Double View school in 1896, 542 in 1910.[40] Remodelled in 1914, it had junior mixed and infants' departments from 1932[41] and an average attendance of 429 in 1938.[42] From 1974 it took only infants, the juniors being transferred to new buildings in Latimer Road,[43] and in 1992, as Bilson County Infants' school, it had 190 pupils and Latimer school 251.[44] In 1887 the school board opened St. White's school in Ruspidge to replace St. John's school.[45] St. White's school, in new buildings on the Littledean–Coleford road, had junior mixed and infants' departments and the average attendance in 1889 was 440.[46] Double View school took the older children from 1896,[47] and attendances fell to 323 in 1910 and 289 in 1938.[48] In 1964 its two departments were amalgamated[49] and in 1992, as St. White's Primary school, it had 364 children on its roll.[50]

Cinderford retained one or two private schools in the late 19th century and the early 20th. They included a boarding and day school for girls at St. White's in 1876[51] and a school recorded in 1902 and 1931. There was also a preparatory school in the town in the 1930s.[52] In 1960 a Roman Catholic school was established in a house in Belle Vue Road next to the Catholic church in Flaxley Street. Called St. Anthony's, it was attached to a convent and as it grew new buildings were provided and the house to the north was taken over. In 1992 it remained independent, teaching c. 110 children up to the age of 11 and including a nursery school.[53]

In LYDBROOK, where a schoolmaster was living in 1837,[54] a day school was established in the C. of E. schoolroom at Upper Lydbrook in 1849.[55] At the end of 1851 the building housed separate boys' and girls' schools or departments with a combined average attendance of 92.[56] They were funded by an annual grant from the Crown, voluntary contributions, and pence and were managed by the minister of Holy Jesus church, which had been built next to them. In 1873 new rooms were added for the girls to leave the original building for the boys,[57] and by 1875 an infants' class had been started. At that time there

were many dame schools in the area, including Worrall Hill,[58] and a few years later a board school was provided at Joy's Green to meet a continuing shortage of places.[59] The church school, which was reorganized with junior mixed and infants' departments, had average attendances of 193 in 1889[60] and 185 in 1904,[61] by which time the county council had decided to replace it. Disputes over the choice of site for the new school delayed its construction, which became more necessary with overcrowding at the church school, and in 1908 the older boys were transferred to a temporary school established in the Baptist schoolroom at Lower Lydbrook. The council school opened at Upper Lydbrook in 1909[62] in brick buildings with places for 246 children. Average attendance was 210 in 1910 and, after enlargement, 251 in 1938,[63] just before the junior and infants' departments were amalgamated.[64] As Lydbrook County Primary school it had 108 children on its roll in 1992.[65] The church school was abandoned in 1909 and its building reverted to use as a church hall and Sunday school. It fell into disrepair[66] and was pulled down in 1975.[67]

Joy's Green board school, built for the Lydbrook district, opened in 1883 in new buildings including a detached schoolhouse.[68] The school had junior mixed and infants' departments with places for 227 children and in 1889 the average attendance was 200.[69] The building was enlarged in 1894[70] and the average attendance was 287 in 1910, falling to 110 in 1938.[71] As Joy's Green County Primary school it had 58 children on the roll in 1992.[72]

PARKEND school, opened in 1824, was founded by Henry Poole on the National plan with the sexes taught separately. It occupied a new building on the Yorkley road north of St. Paul's church and Poole, who bore most of the expense, also built a schoolhouse to the east.[73] Although some way from any settlement, the school in 1825 claimed attendances of 150 on weekdays and 190 on Sundays[74] and in 1833 had a daily attendance of 140.[75] In 1842 the building was closed as unsafe through mining subsidence and a year or two later the school was rebuilt on a site further east.[76] Despite an annual grant from

38 Glos. R.O., SB 15/1, p. 261; 3, p. 111.
39 Kelly's Dir. Glos. (1889), 732.
40 Glos. R.O., SB 15/4, pp. 264–5; below, secondary schs.; Bd. of Educ., List 21, 1911 (H.M.S.O.), 161.
41 Dean Forest Mercury, 25 Oct. 1974; Olivey, There's nothing like Education, 19, 23.
42 Bd. of Educ., List 21, 1938, 126.
43 Olivey, There's nothing like Education, 33; Dean Forest Mercury, 25 Oct. 1974.
44 Schools and Establishments Dir. 1992–3 (co. educ. dept.), 8, 22.   45 St. White's Sch. 2.
46 Kelly's Dir. Glos. (1889), 732.
47 Glos. R.O., SB 15/4, pp. 264–5; below, secondary schs.
48 Bd. of Educ., List 21, 1911, 161; 1938, 127.
49 St. White's Sch. 21.
50 Schools and Establishments Dir. 1992–3, 32.
51 Morris's Dir. Glos. (1876), 469.
52 Kelly's Dir. Glos. (1902 and later edns.).
53 Notice outside sch.; inf. from Rom. Cath. par. priest of Cinderford.
54 Glos. R.O., P 93/IN 1/5.
55 P.R.O., ED 7/37, Lydbrook C. of E. sch.; for site, O.S. Map 6″, Glos. XXXI. NW. (1883 edn.).
56 Glos. R.O., D 33/442.

57 P.R.O., ED 7/37, Lydbrook C. of E. sch.; Lydbrook C. of E. Girls' sch.; above, Churches (Holy Jesus).
58 Glos. R.O., SB 15/1, pp. 8–10; Dean Forest Mercury, 25 May 1984.
59 Glos. R.O., SB 15/1, p. 249.
60 Kelly's Dir. Glos. (1889), 834.
61 Public Elem. Schs. 1906, 191.
62 Glos. R.O., CE/M 2/1, p. 115; 2, pp. 52–3; 5, pp. 250–1, 295–6; Glouc. Jnl. 4 Sept. 1909.
63 Bd. of Educ., List 21, 1911, 168; 1938, 128.
64 Glos. R.O., CE/M 2/24, p. 90.
65 Schools and Establishments Dir. 1992–3, 23.
66 Nat. Soc. files, Lydbrook; Glos. R.O., P 208/MI 3.
67 Inf. from vicar of Lydbrook (1990).
68 Glos. R.O., SB 15/1, p. 240; 2, p. 10; P.R.O., ED 7/34/121.   69 Kelly's Dir. Glos. (1889), 834.
70 Glos. R.O., SB 15/4, p. 164.
71 Bd. of Educ., List 21, 1911, 161; 1938, 128.
72 Schools and Establishments Dir. 1992–3, 20.
73 Nat. Soc. files, Dean West Parkend; for site of sch., 2nd Rep. Dean Forest Com. 57; Glos. R.O., Q/RGf 1/5.
74 G.D.R. vol. 383, no. cxli.
75 Educ. Enq. Abstract, 312.
76 Nat. Soc. files, Dean West Parkend.

the Crown[77] Poole relied on financial help from Edward Machen and Alice Davies of Whitemead Park to keep the school open,[78] and on at least one occasion he closed it for lack of funds.[79] As minister of St. Paul's church from 1858 J. J. Ebsworth managed the school,[80] which had a mixed department and, by the later 1870s, an infants' class,[81] and he closed it in 1879 following the loss of children to board schools at Pillowell and Ellwood and the closure of local ironworks.[82] The school board reopened the school in 1885[83] and it had an average attendance of 104 in 1889.[84] It was enlarged in the mid 1890s, when temporary use was made of the Baptist schoolroom at Parkend,[85] and had an average attendance of 150 in 1910. In 1938 it usually taught 89 children[86] and in 1992, as Parkend County Primary school, it had 52 children on its roll.[87]

RUARDEAN WOODSIDE and RUARDEAN HILL had a few dame schools in 1850 when H. G. Nicholls, assisted by the National Society, built a schoolroom for infants at Ruardean Woodside. The room, to which a schoolhouse was added,[88] also served as a chapel. The school was supported by the Crown[89] and had an average attendance of 30 in 1873.[90] It closed a year or so after a board school opened at Ruardean Woodside in 1878 but one or more dame schools remained in the area until the mid 1880s.[91] The board school, known officially as Ruardean Hill school[92] and locally as the Slad from a neighbouring colliery,[93] occupied a new building with places for 191 children in boys', girls', and infants' departments[94] and served the hamlets of Ruardean Hill, the Pludds, and Brierley.[95] It was remodelled in 1883, when the junior departments were amalgamated,[96] and had an average attendance of 178 in 1889[97] and, after the building was enlarged in 1893 and 1902,[98] of 311 in 1910 and 231 in 1938.[99] The school, in which the junior and infants' departments had been merged in 1926,[1] was later renamed Woodside Primary school and in 1992 it had 115 children on the roll.[2]

The first day school for the DRYBROOK district was opened by Henry Berkin in 1819 in the schoolroom next to Holy Trinity church at Harrow Hill. The school, on the National plan,

was closed in 1824 for lack of pupils and funds.[3] In 1833 ten children from that part of the Forest attended a day school funded with bequests producing £5 5s. a year.[4] In 1835 Berkin revived his school.[5] Known later as Holy Trinity C. of E. school, it received an annual grant from the Crown[6] and was affiliated to the National Society, and in 1847 it taught 57 boys and 93 girls in separate departments. Many more children attended on Sundays.[7] H. G. Nicholls, Berkin's successor at Holy Trinity in 1847,[8] started National schools in several mining communities in his parish[9] and in 1862 he moved Holy Trinity school to a new building to the north.[10] The new school, which had places for 175 children in junior mixed and infants' departments and an adjacent schoolhouse, became overcrowded and another classroom was added in 1870.[11] The infants' department formed a separate school from 1874.[12] In 1870 members of Drybrook Independent chapel began building a school at Harrow Hill[13] but if it ever opened it was short lived. Drybrook had a private school in the mid 1870s.[14] The Holy Trinity schools, supported financially by M. W. Colchester-Wemyss, Sir James Campbell, and the Crown,[15] had a total average attendance of 240 in 1889.[16] The building was enlarged further in 1891 and 1904 to relieve overcrowding[17] and the average attendance in 1910 was 268.[18] Most of the children were from poor mining and nonconformist families. In 1926, in the absence of funds to maintain them,[19] the schools were handed over to the county education authority,[20] which merged them. In 1938 the school had an average attendance of 164[21] and in 1992, as Drybrook County Primary school, it had 119 children on the roll.[22]

A school at Hawthorns, north of Drybrook, was started by H. G. Nicholls, who built a room for an infants' school and church services in 1851.[23] The school, despite an annual grant from the Crown, lapsed soon after 1857.[24] To supply extra places for the Drybrook, Ruardean Hill, and Bilson areas the school board built a school at STEAM MILLS, north of Cinderford. The school, which opened in 1883, had boys', girls', and infants' departments.[25] It had 416 places and

77 Cf. *Educ. Enq. Abstract*, 312; Nicholls, *Forest of Dean*, 175.
78 Nicholls, *Personalities of Dean*, 158.
79 R. Anstis, *Story of Parkend* (1982), 31.
80 G.D.R. vol. 384, f. 77.
81 *Kelly's Dir. Glos.* (1870), 617; (1879), 722.
82 Nat. Soc. files, Dean West Parkend.
83 Glos. R.O., SB 15/2, pp. 241–2; P.R.O., ED 7/35/353.
84 *Kelly's Dir. Glos.* (1889), 863.
85 Glos. R.O., SB 15/4, pp. 164, 169–70, 250.
86 *Bd. of Educ., List 21, 1911*, 168; *1938*, 131.
87 *Schools and Establishments Dir. 1992–3*, 27.
88 Nat. Soc. files, Blakeney Woodside; for site, O.S. Map 6", Glos. XXXI. NW. (1883 edn.).
89 Nicholls, *Forest of Dean*, 163, 175.
90 P.R.O., ED 7/37, Ruardean Woodside sch.
91 Ibid. F 3/29; Glos. R.O., S 109/2/3/1, pp. 1, 15, 20–1, 24–5, 38, 130, 158.   92 P.R.O., ED 7/34/123.
93 M. V. Bent, *Highest Point of Dean* (1985), 82.
94 Glos. R.O., SB 15/1, p. 261; P.R.O., ED 7/34/123.
95 Glos. Colln. RF 254.2, pp. 13, 19, 25.
96 Glos. R.O., S 109/2/2/1, p. 64; 3/1, pp. 130, 135.
97 *Kelly's Dir. Glos.* (1889), 752.
98 Glos. R.O., S 109/2/1/2, pp. 9, 250; 3/2, pp. 308, 310, 313.
99 *Bd. of Educ., List 21, 1911*, 161; *1938*, 126.
1 Glos. R.O., CE/M 2/18, p. 165.
2 *Schools and Establishments Dir. 1992–3*, 39.

3 Nicholls, *Personalities of Dean*, 138; *3rd Rep. Dean Forest Com.* 10.
4 *Educ. Enq. Abstract*, 312.
5 Nicholls, *Personalities of Dean*, 140.
6 P.R.O., ED 7/34/127.
7 Nat. Soc. *Inquiry, 1846–7*, Glos. 8–9.
8 Hockaday Abs. clxxvi.
9 Above and below, this section.
10 Glos. R.O., P 109/VE 2/1.
11 Nat. Soc. files, Dean East Holy Trin.
12 Glos. R.O., S 109/1/1/1; 2/1.
13 *Glouc. Jnl.* 3 Dec. 1870.
14 *Morris's Dir. Glos.* (1876), 471.
15 Glos. R.O., P 109/SC 4.
16 *Kelly's Dir. Glos.* (1889), 752.
17 Ibid. (1910), 140.
18 *Bd. of Educ., List 21, 1911*, 161.
19 Nat. Soc. files, Dean East Holy Trin.
20 Glos. R.O., CE/M 2/18, p. 221.
21 *Bd. of Educ., List 21, 1938*, 126.
22 *Schools and Establishments Dir. 1992–3*, 14.
23 Nat. Soc. files, Hawthorns; Nicholls, *Forest of Dean*, 163; for site, P.R.O., F 16/63 (no. 359); F 16/70.
24 Cf. Nicholls, *Forest of Dean*, 175.
25 Glos. R.O., SB 15/1, p. 290; 2, p. 10; P.R.O., ED 7/34/126.

the average attendance in 1889 was 241.[26] The school was reorganized with junior mixed and infants' departments in 1906[27] and had an attendance averaging 211 in 1910 and 198 in 1938.[28] The departments were merged in 1943.[29] Part of its premises was used as a teachers' centre in 1990[30] and the school, as Steam Mills County Primary school, had 51 children on its roll in 1992.[31]

PLUMP HILL school was opened by the school board in 1878 in a new building incorporating a schoolhouse. The school had 151 places in junior mixed and infants' departments,[32] which were merged in 1883,[33] and an average attendance in 1889 of 147.[34] More classrooms were added in 1890[35] and the average attendance was 137 in 1910, falling to 85 in 1938.[36] The school was closed in 1984, the children being transferred to schools in Mitcheldean, Littledean, and Westbury-on-Severn,[37] and the building became an annexe of the county's field studies centre at the Wilderness near Mitcheldean.

A church school for SOUDLEY was opened in 1875 by G. A. Allan, vicar of St. John's, Cinderford. It was a single mixed department in an iron room at Upper Soudley provided by Henry Crawshay and used also for Anglican worship. The school soon closed for lack of pupils, many children continuing to attend a school outside Soudley,[38] but in 1880 it was successfully revived as a board school.[39] In 1885 a brick building was erected north of the iron room[40] and in 1889 the school included an infants' department and had an average attendance of 136. It was enlarged in 1893[41] and the average attendance was 167 in 1910, falling to 87 in 1938.[42] As Soudley County Primary school it taught 54 children in 1992.[43] The iron schoolroom, which the school board vacated in 1886,[44] was removed before 1920.[45]

Henry Poole founded two National infants' schools for the hamlets around VINEY HILL and BLAKENEY HILL in the south-eastern part of the Forest. One, between Oldcroft and Viney Hill, dated from 1850 and the other, at Blakeney Woodside on the west side of Blakeney Hill, from 1851. Both occupied new buildings pro-

vided with help from Edward Machen and Charles Bathurst of Lydney Park and were cruciform for use also as chapels. Next to each stood a new schoolhouse.[46] The schools, particularly that at Blakeney Woodside, had little income apart from annual grants from the Crown and Poole spent money to keep them open.[47] After 1866 they were managed by the minister of All Saints' church, Viney Hill, who received some financial help from the Bathurst family and others.[48] The Oldcroft and Viney Hill school, which became known as St. Swithin[49] and later as All Saints' school, was apparently a junior mixed school in 1856 and it also taught infants in 1871.[50] In 1889 it had an average attendance of 106.[51] The building was enlarged several times, the first in 1893,[52] and attendances averaged 191 in 1910, when it was overcrowded, and 111 in 1938.[53] It became a controlled school in 1948[54] and closed in 1965.[55] The building was later converted as three dwellings. Blakeney Woodside school, which was also reorganized to take juniors as well as infants,[56] had an average attendance of only 48 in 1889.[57] In 1894 the Revd. E. S. Smith closed it for want of funds to make improvements required by the Department of Education, but efforts by local people to raise money won the school a reprieve until 1908 when it finally closed.[58] In 1904 the average attendance had been 90.[59] The schoolroom, which remained in use for services and a Sunday school, was demolished in the 1950s.[60]

A church school at Yorkley Wood, established as part of a mission from Bream church in 1867,[61] taught mostly infants in 1871.[62] Other settlements along the southern edge of the Forest between Yorkley and Whitecroft were without an official day school until 1877 when PILLOWELL school, one of the first board schools in the Forest, opened between Pillowell and Whitecroft. It had places for 400 children in detached blocks for boys', girls', and infants' departments and a pair of schoolhouses.[63] The average attendance was 281 in 1889[64] and, after enlargement,[65] 505 in 1904.[66] To relieve overcrowding the county opened a temporary school at Whitecroft

26   Kelly's Dir. Glos. (1889), 732.
27   Glos. R.O., CE/M 2/3, p. 394.
28   Bd. of Educ., List 21, 1911, 161; 1938, 127.
29   Glos. R.O., CE/M 2/27, f. 160.
30   Personal observation.
31   Schools and Establishments Dir. 1992–3, 34.
32   Glos. R.O., SB 15/1, pp. 151, 261; P.R.O., ED 7/34/122; for site, O.S. Map 6", Glos. XXXI. NE. (1884 edn.).
33   Glos. R.O., S 220/2/1.
34   Kelly's Dir. Glos. (1889), 752.
35   Glos. R.O., S 220/2/1.
36   Bd. of Educ., List 21, 1911, 161; 1938, 126.
37   Glos. R.O., SM 220/2/M 2; local inf.
38   P.R.O., ED 7/37, Soudley C. of E. sch.; Glos. R.O., SB 15/1, pp. 11, 20, 48.
39   P.R.O., ED 7/34/125; Glos. R.O., SB 15/1, pp. 309, 315.
40   Glos. R.O., SB 15/3, p. 1; O.S. Map 6", Glos. XXXIX. NE. (1903 edn.).
41   Kelly's Dir. Glos. (1889), 732; (1910), 116.
42   Bd. of Educ., List 21, 1911, 161; 1938, 127.
43   Schools and Establishments Dir. 1992–3, 33.
44   Glos. R.O., SB 15/3, pp. 111, 116.
45   O. S. Map 6", Glos. XXXIX. NE. (1924 edn.).
46   Nicholls, Forest of Dean, 170; Nicholls, Personalities of Dean, 157–9; cf. Glos. R.O., A 111/1/2; for sites of schs., O.S. Map 6", Glos. XXXIX. SE. (1884 edn.).

47   Nicholls, Forest of Dean, 175; P.R.O., ED 7/37, Oldcroft and Viney C. of E. sch.; Blakeney Valley C. of E. Infants' sch.
48   Glos. R.O., P 348/IN 4/1.
49   Glouc. Jnl. 27 Apr. 1867; 26 Dec. 1874.
50   P.R.O., ED 7/34/128; ED 7/37, Oldcroft and Viney C. of E. sch.
51   Kelly's Dir. Glos. (1889), 930.
52   Ibid. (1910), 351; C. R. Johnson, 'Hist. Viney Hill Sch.' (1960, TS. in Glos. Colln. RR 102.2), 4–5.
53   Bd. of Educ., List 21, 1911, 161; 1938, 127.
54   Glos. R.O., CE/M 2/31, f. 229.
55   Ibid. S 348/8.
56   P.R.O., ED 7/37, Blakeney Valley C. of E. Infants' sch.; Blakeney Woodside Mixed Nat. sch.
57   Kelly's Dir. Glos. (1889), 930.
58   Nat. Soc. files, Blakeney Woodside.
59   Public Elem. Schs. 1906, 184.
60   Glos. R.O., D 3921/II/5; Johnson, 'Viney Hill Sch.' 7.
61   G.D.R. vol. 377, f. 13; for the mission, above, Churches.
62   Nat. Soc. files, Bream St. John.
63   Glouc. Jnl. 8 Dec. 1877; cf. above, Plate 38.
64   Kelly's Dir. Glos. (1889), 863.
65   Glos. R.O., K 874/12.
66   Public Elem. Schs. 1906, 191.

Wesleyan Methodist chapel in 1907 and built a council school on the Lydney road at YORKLEY in 1909.[67] Attendance at Pillowell fell to 459 in 1910 and to 150 in 1938.[68] The school's departments were merged in 1938 and 1939[69] and, as Pillowell County Primary school, it had 61 children on its roll in 1992.[70] Yorkley Council school, which took children also from All Saints' school, Viney Hill, had junior mixed and infants' departments[71] and average attendances of 259 in 1910 and 181 in 1938.[72] In 1992, as Yorkley County Primary school, it had 155 children on its roll.[73]

Henry Poole established a day school for the children of BREAM, where he was minister, and the adjoining part of the Forest in 1830.[74] It occupied a new building north of the Coleford road at Bream Tufts,[75] erected by subscription and incorporating a schoolhouse, and was run on the National plan with boys' and girls' departments.[76] It taught 80 children in 1847.[77] Poole supplied the deficiency in its funds, which, despite support from the Crown and Mary Gough's educational charity for Bream, were insufficient because of the poverty of local residents. Poole's successors at Bream kept the school open[78] and in 1862 the Revd. Cornelius Witherby moved it to a more central position at Bream's Eaves, where the Bible Christians had started a short lived day school at their chapel the previous year.[79] The new National school and schoolhouse, provided with financial help from Alice Davies,[80] stood east of the Parkend road with separate accommodation for the junior boys and for the junior girls and infants.[81] From 1865 the departments were run as separate schools and in 1874, following some additions to the building, an infants' department was formed. In 1888 the junior schools were merged[82] and in 1889 the school had an average attendance of 176. The building was enlarged in 1893 and 1900[83] but was overcrowded in 1904 when the attendance was 382. To provide more places the county established a temporary infants' school in the Primitive Methodists' nearby schoolroom in 1905[84] and opened a new infants' school opposite the C. of E. (formerly National) school in 1907.[85] In 1910 the new building, called Bream Council school, had an average attendance of 153, including some juniors, and the C.

of E. school remained overcrowded with an attendance of 311.[86] The council school was enlarged in 1912[87] and again in 1927, when it was reorganized to take junior girls and infants[88] and the C. of E. school was left with junior boys. In 1938, when their average attendances totalled 367, both schools had many spare places[89] and in 1951 the C. of E. school, which had accepted controlled status in 1948, became a junior mixed school and the girls' department at the council school a secondary modern school.[90] Following the secondary school's closure in 1973[91] the C. of E. school moved into the buildings west of the Parkend road[92] and in 1992, as Bream C. of E. (Voluntary Controlled) Primary school, it had 222 children, both infants and juniors, on its roll.[93] The building which it had vacated became a youth centre and library.

ELLWOOD had a dame school in the mid 1870s[94] when it was chosen as the place for one of the Forest's first board schools. That school opened in stages in 1877 and 1878 in a new building incorporating a schoolhouse, and had places for 278 children in boys', girls', and infants' departments.[95] It was reorganized several times and in 1889 had an average attendance of 174 in junior mixed and infants' departments.[96] It was enlarged in 1894 but had many spare places in the early 20th century.[97] The average attendance was 279 in 1910 and almost the same in 1922.[98] The building was remodelled in the later 1920s to provide more accommodation[99] but the average attendance fell to 177 in 1938.[1] A special school used part of the building between 1959 and 1964[2] and the elementary school, known as Ellwood County Primary school, had 88 pupils in 1992.[3]

To mark the Golden Jubilee of P. M. Procter's school and chapel at Berry Hill[4] W. H. Taylor, minister of Christ Church,[5] built a National school for the Lane End district, east of Coleford. The district had a day school in a Baptist chapel at Mitcheldean Lane End in 1851[6] and one or two small dame schools in 1862. Known as the Forest Church Jubilee school, the National school with its adjacent schoolhouse was at BROADWELL LANE END and was paid for by subscriptions and grants. It opened in 1864 with 70 pupils, including infants, and was enlarged by Taylor several times.[7] In 1889 it had 270

67 Glos. R.O., CE/M 2/4, pp. 170, 282; 7, p. 137.
68 Bd. of Educ., List 21, 1911, 169; 1938, 131.
69 Glos. R.O., CE/M 2/23 (2), pp. 254–5; 24, p. 90.
70 Schools and Establishments Dir. 1992–3 (co. educ. dept.), 27.
71 P.R.O., ED 7/35/354A; Glouc. Jnl. 11 Sept. 1909.
72 Bd. of Educ., List 21, 1911, 168; 1938, 131.
73 Schools and Establishments Dir. 1992–3, 39.
74 Nicholls, Personalities of Dean, 156–8; cf. Glos. R.O., P 57/CH 1/1, min. 20 Jan. 1831.
75 2nd Rep. Dean Forest Com. 52; Glos. R.O., Q/RGf 1/5.
76 P.R.O., ED 7/35/348; cf. Glos. R.O., D 2186/94.
77 Nat. Soc. Inquiry, 1846–7, Glos. 12.
78 P.R.O., ED 7/35/348; Nicholls, Forest of Dean, 175; cf. G.D.R. wills 1699/29; 19th Rep. Com. Char. 104.
79 Nat. Soc. files, Bream; G. E. Lawrence, Bible Christians of Forest of Dean, ed. H. R. Jarrett (1985), 21.
80 Nicholls, Personalities of Dean, 158.
81 Glos. R.O., K 511; D 2186/94.
82 Ibid. S 57/1/1–2; 2/1; Nat. Soc. files, Bream.
83 Kelly's Dir. Glos. (1889), 681; (1910), 52.
84 Public Elem. Schs. 1906, 190 and n.; Glos. R.O., CE/M 2/2, pp. 302–3, 518.
85 Glouc. Jnl. 2 Nov. 1907; P.R.O., ED 7/35/347A.

86 Bd. of Educ., List 21, 1911, 168.
87 Glos. R.O., CE/M 2/10, pp. 13–14; K 874/3.
88 Ibid. CE/M 2/19, p. 77.
89 Bd. of Educ., List 21, 1932, 119; 1938, 130.
90 Glos. R.O., CE/M 2/31, ff. 20, 231; 33, pp. 254–5, 341.
91 Cf. Lydney Grammar Sch. 1903–73 (copy in Glos. R.O., SC 32), 4.
92 Glos. R.O., CE/O 31.
93 Schools and Establishments Dir. 1992–3, 9.
94 Morris's Dir. Glos. (1876), 478.
95 P.R.O., ED 7/35/351; Glos. R.O., SB 15/1, p. 261.
96 Kelly's Dir. Glos. (1885), 440; (1889), 754.
97 Ibid. (1910), 142; Public Elem. Schs. 1906, 190.
98 Bd. of Educ., List 21, 1911, 168; 1922, 108.
99 Glos. R.O., CE/M 2/18, pp. 148, 202.
1 Bd. of Educ., List 21, 1932, 119; 1938, 130.
2 Dean Forest Mercury, 26 June 1964.
3 Schools and Establishments Dir. 1992–3, 15.
4 Below, this section; above, Churches (Christ Church).
5 Kelly's Dir. Glos. (1865), 271.
6 P.R.O., HO 129/577/1/4/11; above, Prot. Nonconf.
7 Nat. Soc. files, Dean West Coleford Lane End; P.R.O., ED 7/35/350; name on bldg.; for site, O.S. Map 6", Glos. XXXIX. NW. (1883 edn.).

places and an average attendance of 230 in junior mixed and infants' departments or schools,[8] which in 1890, when the Lane End district became part of Coleford for ecclesiastical purposes, were renamed Coleford Lane End National schools.[9] The building was enlarged further in 1893 and 1904[10] but was overcrowded in 1910, when the schools' average attendance was 340.[11] In 1914 the older children were transferred to a new school at Five Acres.[12] Coleford Lane End schools, which the local education authority took over in 1926,[13] had a total average attendance of 261 in 1938.[14] Renamed Broadwell Lane End schools in 1954,[15] they later moved to new buildings at Coalway Lane End, just within Coleford, the infants being transferred in 1966[16] and the juniors in 1977,[17] to become Coalway Infants' and Coalway Junior schools. In 1992 they had 148 and 218 children on their respective rolls.[18]

In 1813 P. M. Procter opened a day school on the National plan at BERRY HILL. For a year or so it used his school-chapel,[19] for the building of which the Treasury and the National Society made grants, and then it moved to a new room to the north, the original building being enlarged to form the chapel consecrated under the name of Christ Church in 1816. The new school had boys' and girls' departments. It received an annual grant from the Crown and depended principally on voluntary contributions.[20] The school, under the control of successive ministers of Christ Church,[21] taught 115 children in 1847.[22] It admitted infants by 1852 when, known as Christ Church C. of E. Mixed school, it received little financial support locally. Over half of its income came from a grant of the Commissioners of Woods, acting for the Crown, and the rest from pence, a few subscriptions, and the minister's share of a trust fund intended for repairing his church.[23] W. H. Taylor, perpetual curate 1852–83,[24] made several additions to the school and in 1856 built a schoolhouse some way to the south-west.[25] There was a separate infants' school at Berry Hill in 1870.[26] In 1889 the National school had 260 places and an average attendance of 195 in junior mixed and infants' departments.[27] To meet the requirements of the Board of Education the Revd. Christopher Barnes in 1897 added more rooms and converted some outbuildings of his adjacent parsonage for

school use.[28] The school was overcrowded in 1910 when the average attendance was 303,[29] and in 1914 the older children were transferred to a new school at Five Acres.[30] Christ Church school, which became so neglected that the local education authority condemned its buildings, was handed over to the authority in 1936[31] and had an average attendance of 195 in 1938.[32] In 1954 it moved to a new building in Nine Wells Road and was renamed Berry Hill County Primary school.[33] In 1992 it had 261 children on its roll[34] and the original schoolrooms north of Christ Church were used for church purposes and a nursery school.

SPECIAL SCHOOLS. Dean Hall (formerly Old Dean Hall) school for educationally subnormal children was opened by the county council in 1958 in a building south of the Speech House originally intended for a school of forestry. Children of secondary age were accommodated in part of Ellwood school from 1959 until 1964 when new buildings at Dean Hall school came into use.[35] In 1992 there were 93 children aged from 5 to 16 on the roll.[36] Oakdene school, so called from 1970, was built by the county council in Dockham Road, Cinderford, in 1962 as a training establishment for educationally subnormal adults and children. From 1967 it admitted persons under the age of 20[37] and in 1992 it taught 25 children aged from 3 to 19.[38]

SECONDARY SCHOOLS. In the mid 19th century a number of night schools continued the education of older children in the Forest. Classes for young colliers were held in the Methodist chapel at Littledean Hill and elsewhere[39] and Henry Poole ran classes in his schools at Bream Tufts and between Oldcroft and Viney Hill. The Bream Tufts night school, which taught 30 children in 1847, had been suspended by 1854 apparently for irregularities by its teachers.[40] Cinderford's principal school, which older children attended in the daytime, was apparently used for a winter evening school funded largely by the South Wales Railway Co. and teaching as many as 90 adults in the mid 1850s.[41] More winter night schools for older children were opened after the school board's decision in 1879

8 Kelly's Dir. Glos. (1889), 672.
9 Glos. R.O., P 93/SC 3/1.
10 Nat. Soc. files, Dean West Coleford Lane End.
11 Bd. of Educ., List 21, 1911, 168.
12 Below, secondary schs.
13 Glos. R.O., CE/M 2/18, p. 221.
14 Bd. of Educ., List 21, 1938, 130.
15 Glos. R.O., K 392/1/2, p. 284.
16 Ibid. SM 111/1/M 1.
17 Ibid. 2/M 1.
18 Schools and Establishments Dir. 1992–3, 13.
19 For the school-chapel, above, Plate 37.
20 P. M. Procter, Origin of Established Ch. and Nat. Day Sch. in Forest of Dean (1819), 21–2, 25–6, 30–1, 38 n.; Nat. Soc. files, Dean West Christ Church; for site, O.S. Map 6", Glos. XXX. SE. (1884 edn.).
21 Nicholls, Forest of Dean, 167; Glos. R.O., D 33/442.
22 Nat. Soc. Inquiry, 1846–7, Glos. 8.
23 P.R.O., ED 7/35/349; cf. Dean Forest Eccl. Districts Act, 5 & 6 Vic. c. 65.
24 Kelly's Dir. Glos. (1894), 107.
25 Nat. Soc. files, Dean West Christ Church; inscr. on ho.

26 Kelly's Dir. Glos. (1870), 533.
27 Ibid. (1889), 672.
28 Ibid. (1910), 113; Glos. R.O., D 33/442.
29 Bd. of Educ., List 21, 1911 (H.M.S.O.), 168.
30 Below, secondary schs.
31 Nat. Soc. files, Dean West Christ Church; Glos. R.O., CE/M 2/23, pp. 349–50.
32 Bd. of Educ., List 21, 1938, 130.
33 Glos. R.O., SM 93/1/M 1.
34 Schools and Establishments Dir. 1992–3, 7.
35 Dean Forest Mercury, 26 June 1964; Glos. R.O., SM 93/4/M 1; for forestry sch., below, technical schs. and colleges.
36 Schools and Establishments Dir. 1992–3, 46.
37 Glos. R.O., SM 85/5/M 1; Citizen (Glouc.), 23 Nov. 1962.
38 Schools and Establishments Dir. 1992–3, 46.
39 Mountjoy, Dean Collier, 42–3; D. E. Bick, Old Ind. of Dean (1980), 55.
40 Nat. Soc. Inquiry, 1846–7, Glos. 12; P.R.O., ED 7/35/348; ED 7/37, Oldcroft and Viney C. of E. sch.
41 Nicholls, Forest of Dean, 171–2.

to make its buildings available. They were run at first privately and later by the board, and most were discontinued just after the First World War.[42] From the early 1890s education of a more vocational nature was provided throughout the Forest by science and art classes organized from Lydney and by mining and domestic science classes financed by the county council. The classes were usually held in elementary school buildings in the evenings and most were conducted at Cinderford.[43] Although it had a senior elementary school from 1896, Cinderford did not replace Lydney as the centre of secondary and technical education for the Forest until 1910, when the county council opened a secondary school there. A few years later the county opened a senior elementary school on the west side of the Forest at Five Acres. Some Foresters attended secondary schools in Monmouth before the First World War[44] and some a secondary school near Mitcheldean after 1930.[45] In the 1930s the county ran technical classes in several Forest schools,[46] and following the Education Act of 1944 it had secondary grammar, modern, and technical schools in Cinderford and secondary modern schools at Five Acres and Bream. All of those schools were affected by later reorganizations of secondary education in the Forest area.

Double View school, Cinderford, was opened by the school board in 1896 to take older children from local elementary schools. It had new buildings in Woodville Road[47] and in 1904 an average attendance of 413.[48] The curriculum had been broadened to include industrial and technical subjects by the First World War.[49] The school, which had an average attendance of 287 in 1938,[50] became a secondary modern school under the 1944 Act.[51] Between 1968 and 1978 it moved in stages to new buildings in Causeway Road[52] and in 1980 it had 748 pupils on its roll.[53] In 1985 it became a comprehensive school, called the Heywood school after the neighbouring plantation, for children up to 16 years.[54] There were 1,064 pupils on the roll in 1992.[55]

East Dean Grammar school originated as Cinderford Higher Elementary school, which the county council opened in 1910 as a secondary school and centre for training elementary school teachers. Occupying new buildings south of Station Street, the school took children from 12 years and its curriculum included industrial and commercial subjects appropriate for local employment. It charged a tuition fee of £1 a pupil a year and awarded some free places to children selected from elementary schools in and around the Forest.[56] Known as Cinderford Secondary school from 1919 and East Dean Grammar school from 1927, it had 367 pupils in 1932[57] and remained a grammar school following the 1944 Act.[58] Among buildings added to the Station Street site were those of a mining school,[59] which ran secondary technical classes in many places in the Forest area and in 1945 established the *Forest of Dean Secondary Technical* school on the Station Street site.[60] The technical school admitted many boys from Ross-on-Wye (Herefs.). In 1959 it merged with the grammar school,[61] which had more than 500 pupils in 1968 when it was replaced by a new school at Five Acres.[62]

Berry Hill Secondary school was originally Five Acres Council school, opened in 1914 to take older children from local elementary schools. It had new buildings at Five Acres with places for 260 pupils[63] and average attendances of 215 in 1922 and 146 in 1938.[64] It became a secondary modern school under the 1944 Act[65] and, having been renamed in 1946,[66] its catchment area was widened in 1966 on the closure of Coleford secondary modern school.[67] The group of school buildings was enlarged by the construction, on the east side of the site, of the *Royal Forest of Dean Grammar* school, opened in 1968 to replace grammar schools at Cinderford and Coleford.[68] In 1980 the secondary modern school had 933 pupils on its roll and the grammar school, which admitted children from the secondary modern school and from Double View school to its sixth form, had 770.[69] The secondary modern and grammar schools at Five Acres were amalgamated in 1985 to form a comprehensive school for children up to 16 years[70] and older children subsequently attended the Royal Forest of Dean College.[71] The comprehensive school, named Lakers school, had 794 pupils on its roll in 1992.[72]

Bream Secondary school, opened in 1951, was a secondary modern school housed in part of the county council's school west of the Parkend road at Bream's Eaves. It had over 200 pupils[73] and its catchment area included Parkend and Yorkley. It closed in 1973 as part of a reorganization of secondary education in the Lydney area and the pupils were transferred to schools at Lydney and Five Acres.[74]

42 Glos. R.O., SB 15/1, p. 260; A. Platts and G. H. Hainton, *Educ. in Glos.: A Short Hist.* (1954), 79–80, 102.
43 Glos. R.O., SB 15/3, pp. 372, 439; 4, pp. 7–8, 64, 84, 88, 105; D 4880/4–5; Platts and Hainton, *Educ. in Glos.* 80, 90.
44 Glos. Colln. RF 254.2, p. 8.
45 Glos. R.O., CE/M 2/22, p. 265; above, Abenhall, educ.
46 *Dean Forest Mercury*, 31 Oct. 1975.
47 Glos. R.O., SB 15/4, pp. 264–5; P.R.O., ED 7/34/120.
48 *Public Elem. Schs. 1906*, 184.
49 Glos. R.O., CE/M 2/11, p. 154.
50 *Bd. of Educ., List 21, 1938*, 126.
51 Glos. R.O., CE/M 2/28, f. 138.
52 Ibid. SM 85/4/M 2, p. 144; M 3, pp. 35, 55, 60.
53 Inf. from Glos. R.O., modern rec. section.
54 *Citizen*, 20 Sept. 1985; *Forest of Dean and Wye Valley Review*, 6 Sept. 1985; O.S. Map 1/25,000, SO 61/71 (1983 edn.), where the traditional spelling of Haywood was used for the plantation; cf. O.S. Map 6", Glos. XXXI. SE. (1883 edn.).
55 *Schools and Establishments Dir. 1992–3*, 42.
56 Glos. R.O., CE/M 2/8, p. 97; *Glouc. Jnl.* 4 June 1910.
57 Glos. R.O., SM 109/2/M 1, pp. 62–5; M 3, pp. 1–3, 78.
58 Ibid. CE/M 2/28, f. 138.
59 Below, technical schs. and colleges.
60 Glos. R.O., SM 85/6/M 1; Glos. Colln. R 78.1.
61 Glos. R.O., SM 85/6/M 2, pp. 2–3, 27.
62 W.I. portrait of Cinderford (1965, copy in Cinderford libr.); E. Dean Grammar sch. mag. July 1968: copy in Glos. Colln. RQ 100.3.
63 *Glouc. Jnl.* 4 Apr. 1914.
64 *Bd. of Educ., List 21, 1922*, 108; *1938*, 131.
65 Glos. R.O., CE/M 2/28, f. 138.
66 Ibid. 29, f. 84.
67 Ibid. SM 93/3/M 2.
68 C. E. Hart, *Coleford* (1983), 431.
69 Inf. from Glos. R.O., modern rec. session
70 *Citizen*, 20 Sept. 1985; *Forest of Dean and Wye Valley Review*, 6 Sept. 1985.
71 Below, technical schs. and colleges.
72 *Schools and Establishments Dir. 1992–3*, 42.
73 Glos. R.O., CE/M 2/33, pp. 144, 254–5, 341, 420, 574.
74 Ibid. SM 57/3/M 1–3.

TECHNICAL SCHOOLS AND COLL-
EGES. Advanced technical instruction in the
Forest developed principally from mining
classes started by the county council in the early
1890s.[75] Classes, including some at a less advanced level,[76] were held in school buildings
in many places, including Bream's Eaves, Cinderford, Coleford, Lydbrook, and Yorkley.[77]
Under the supervision of Francis Brain and
later J. J. Joynes they attracted c. 100 students
and from 1900 operated a scholarship
scheme.[78] Later the classes were run from the
Forest of Dean Mining School,[79] which the
county education committee opened in Cinderford in 1925. Occupying a new building
next to the secondary school in Station Street,
the mining school was built and equipped
using grants from the Miners' Welfare Fund.[80]
More buildings were provided later, and by
1935, when the school had 126 students, the
curriculum had been broadened to embrace
engineering, commerce, languages, and construction.[81] That year the education authority
entrusted the school to governors representing
all sides of the mining industry.[82] As the
industry declined locally the school, which in
1937 became known as the Forest of Dean
Mining and Technical school (college from
1953),[83] introduced new subjects, including
forestry and domestic science, and dropped
mining from its curriculum.[84] In 1966 it amalgamated with an art college in Lydney to form
the *West Gloucestershire College of Further
Education*, which was based on the Station
Street campus[85] where it took over buildings
vacated by East Dean Grammar school in
1968. The college, which took students from

the age of 16, kept its art department at Lydney
until 1970 and used buildings in Woodville
Road, Cinderford, given up by Double View
school.[86] Following the reorganization of secondary education in the Forest area in 1985 the
college was replaced by the *Royal Forest of Dean
College*, which offered full-time and part-time
courses to students from 16 to 18 years and to
adults. It was provided with new buildings on
the campus at Five Acres, where all the full-
time courses were held from 1989. In that year
it admitted students from the Lydney area and
in 1992, when it used some of the Station
Street buildings for technical and employment
training schemes and ran courses in schools and
community centres throughout west Gloucestershire, it had c. 5,000 enrolled students.[87]
Working foresters visited the Forest of Dean
for practical instruction long before 1904[88] when
the Commissioners of Woods established a
school for them there.[89] Known as the *School
of Forestry for Working Foresters*,[90] it moved
from the deputy gaveller's office in Coleford to
Parkend in 1905 and occupied part of the former
ironworks there from 1909.[91] Between 1915 and
1917 a new building was put up near the Speech
House for the school,[92] which, however, remained at Parkend. It provided a course for boys
learning forestry from 1952[93] and had 40 students in the mid 1960s.[94] On the closure of the
school in 1971 the Forestry Commission sold
the premises to Bristol city corporation for a
field studies centre for secondary pupils from
the city. The centre, opened in 1972, was
run by Avon county council from 1974 and its
use was extended to include adventure activities.[95]

WARDENS OF THE FOREST OF DEAN AND
CONSTABLES OF ST. BRIAVELS

By 1207 the keepers or wardens (*custodes*) of the
Forest under the Crown also had the style of
constable of St. Briavels castle, the castle having
probably remained with the custody of the Forest
since 1139. During the 13th and 14th centuries the
constable-wardens held at farm the castle, St.
Briavels manor, Newland manor, and most of the
profits of the Forest, but after the duke of Bedford's death in 1435 that estate was leased
separately under the Crown, while the constable-
wardens received an annual fee paid out of the
estate; between 1611 and 1810, however, the
holders of the offices usually had (though by a
separate patent) the lease of the estate.[96] Between

1660 and 1835, except for two short intervals,
the holders were the lord lieutenants of the
county.
It should be noted that deputies appointed by
the holders to perform the offices in the Middle
Ages were often styled, confusingly, 'constable'
rather than, as later, 'deputy constable'.
From the 16th century the style 'keeper of the
deer and woods' was used in the patents rather
than 'warden', and the later holders sometimes
affected the style of 'lord warden'.
In the following list appointments were during
royal pleasure unless otherwise stated. When the
year of appointment or departure from office is

75 Ibid. SB 15/3, p. 439; 4, pp. 7–8.
76 Above, secondary schs.
77 Glos. R.O., CE/M 2/7, p. 164; 8, p. 171; 10, p. 81; D 4880/4; ED 13; Glos. Colln. RQ 78.1.
78 *Glouc. Jnl.* 7 Nov. 1925; Platts and Hainton, *Educ. in Glos.* 90.
79 Glos. R.O., SM 85/6/M 1.
80 *Glouc. Jnl.* 7 Nov. 1925.
81 Glos. Colln. RQ 78.1.
82 Platts and Hainton, *Educ. in Glos.* 90.
83 Glos. R.O., SM 85/6/M 1.
84 Glos. Colln. R 78.1; W.I. portrait of Cinderford.
85 Glos. R.O., K 521/6.
86 Ibid. SM 209/2/M 5; Glos. Colln. R 78.7; *Dean Forest Mercury*, 31 Oct. 1975.

87 *Forest of Dean and Wye Valley Review*, 6 Sept. 1985; inf. from principal, Royal Forest of Dean College.
88 Hart, *Royal Forest*, 232 n.
89 *82nd Rep. Com. Woods*, H.C. 237, p. 4 (1904), xvii.
90 *Kelly's Dir. Glos.* (1923), 279.
91 *Rep. Forestry Branches 1912–13* [Cd. 7488], p. 58, H.C. (1914), xii; Hart, *Coleford*, 373.
92 *93rd Rep. Com. Woods*, H.C. 285, p. 37 (1914–16), xxxvii; *95th Rep. Com. Woods*, H.C. 104, p. 19 (1917–18), xviii; cf. O.S. Map 1/2,500, Glos. XXXI. 14 (1922 edn.).
93 *Rep. Dean Forest Cttee.* (1958), 12.
94 *Dean Forest Mercury*, 25 Mar. 1966.
95 Inf. from warden, Dean Field Studies Centre, Parkend.
96 Above, St. Briavels, manors.

not known the years of occurrence in office are given in brackets. Some holders of the offices are, of course, unrecorded before 1200, as possibly are some afterwards.

(1086)	William son of Norman (held 'Dean' manor by custody of the Forest)[97]
(1130)	Hugh, son of William son of Norman[98]
1139–43	Miles of Gloucester, earl of Hereford (held castle and Forest in fee)[99]
1143–54/5	Roger of Gloucester, earl of Hereford (as preceding)[1]
(1156)–7	Niel son of Arthur[2]
1157–64	Roger of Powis[3]
1164–(6)	William de Neville[4]
(1194–1206)	William Marshal, earl of Pembroke and lord of Striguil[5]
1207–16	Hugh de Neville[6]
1216–24	John of Monmouth, lord of Monmouth[7]
1224	Walter Asmeins[8]
1224–(30)	Roger de Clifford[9]
1231–2	Gilbert Basset[10]
1232–(3)	Peter des Rivaux[11]
1234–(7)	Emery de St. Amand[12]
1241–	Emery de Cancellis[13]
(1246)–7	Richard de Clifford[14]
1248–55	Peter Chaceporc[15]
1255	James Fresel[16]
1255–63	Robert Walrond (two grants for terms of years)[17]
1263	Roger de Mortimer[18]
1263–6	John Giffard[19]
1266	castle and Forest granted to Edward, the king's son[20]
(late 1260s)	Thomas de Clare[21]
1272–5	William de Beauchamp, earl of Warwick[22]
1275–81	Ralph of Sandwich[23]
1281–7	Grimbald Pauncefoot (grant for years)[24]
1287–91	William Hathaway[25]
1291–1308	John Botetourt[26]
1308–(9)	John de Handlo[27]
1310–18	John of Wyesham (grant for life 1311)[28]
1318–(20)	Roger Damory[29]
1321	William de Beauchamp[30]
1322	Simon de Dryby[31]
1322	James de Broughton[32]
1322–5	Robert de Sapy (Hugh le Despenser the younger given superior custody 1322)[33]
1325–6	John de Mynors[34]
1326	John de Hardredshull[35]
1327	castle and Forest granted to Queen Isabella[36]
1330–5	Robert de Sapy[37]
1335–90	Guy Brian (grant for life 1341)[38]
1390–7	Thomas, duke of Gloucester (assumed to have held in right of grant of castle and Forest)[39]
1397–9	Thomas le Despenser, earl of Gloucester (as preceding)[40]
1399	Hugh Waterton[41]
1399–1435	John, duke of Bedford (in right of grant in fee of castle and Forest)[42]
1435–(6)	Robert Greyndour[43]
1436–(45)	John Mone (grant for life 1438)[44]
1449–	John Ashurst (grant for life)[45]
1461–(76)	James Hyett (grant for life)[46]
1475–	Roger Hyett (grant with father Jas. in survivorship)[47]
1478–?1483	Anthony Woodville, Earl Rivers
1478–(83)	Thomas Baynham
1481–	Robert Poyntz
1483–	Richard Williams (grants in survivorship made to Rivers and Baynham in 1478, to them and Poyntz in 1481, and during pleasure to Baynham and Williams in 1483)[48]

97 *Dom. Bk.* (Rec. Com.), i. 167v.
98 *Pipe R.* 1130 (H.M.S.O. facsimile), 77.
99 B.L. Lansdowne MS. 229, f. 123v.
1 *Camd. Misc.* xxii. 28–9; *Rot. Chart.* (Rec. Com.), 53, 61. 2 *Pipe R.* 1156–8 (Rec. Com.), 49, 100.
3 Ibid. 169; *Pipe R.* 1160 (P.R.S. ii), 29; 1161 (P.R.S. iv), 22; 1162 (P.R.S. v), 60; 1163 (P.R.S. vi), 9; 1164 (P.R.S. vii), 18.
4 Ibid. 1166 (P.R.S. ix), 78.
5 Ibid. 1194 (P.R.S. N.S. v), 239; 1198 (P.R.S. N.S. ix), 7; 1199 (P.R.S. N.S. x), 26; 1200 (P.R.S. N.S. xii), 121; 1203 (P.R.S. N.S. xvi), 60; 1204 (P.R.S. N.S. xviii), 147; 1205 (P.R.S. N.S. xix), 96; 1206 (P.R.S. N.S. xx), 10.
6 *Rot. Litt. Pat.* (Rec. Com.), i. 71.
7 Ibid. i. 185.
8 *Pat. R.* 1216–25, 419–20.
9 *Rot. Litt. Claus.* (Rec. Com.), i. 586, 623; *Close R.* 1227–31, 378.
10 *Pat. R.* 1225–32, 452, 477.
11 *Cal Chart. R.* 1226–57, 169; *Close R.* 1231–4, 198.
12 *Cal. Pat.* 1232–47, 48, 55, 160, 175.
13 Ibid. 252.
14 *Close R.* 1242–7, 414, 526; *Cal. Lib.* 1245–51, 122.
15 *Cal. Pat.* 1247–58, 13; *Inq. p.m. Glos.* 1302–58, 287. 16 *Cal. Pat.* 1247–58, 394.
17 Ibid. 450; 1258–66, 87; *Cal. Lib.* 1260–7, 218.
18 P.R.O., E 32/29, rot. 1d.
19 *Cal. Pat.* 1258–66, 273, 472–3, 548.
20 Ibid. 548; *Cat. Anct. D.* i, A 910.
21 P.R.O., E 32/29, rot. 1d.

22 Ibid. E 32/30, rot. 36.
23 Ibid.; *Hist. & Cart. Mon. Glouc.* (Rolls Ser.), ii. 183–5.
24 P.R.O., E 32/30, rot. 36; *Trans. B.G.A.S.* lxxi. 125–7. 25 *Cal. Close,* 1279–88, 461.
26 *Cal. Pat.* 1281–92, 412; *Cal. Fine R.* 1307–19, 2.
27 *Cal. Fine R.* 1307–19, 18; *Cal. Close,* 1307–13, 170.
28 *Cal. Fine R.* 1307–19, 76; *Cal. Pat.* 1307–13, 355.
29 *Cal. Fine R.* 1307–19, 363; *Cal. Close,* 1318–23, 199.
30 *Cal. Fine R.* 1319–27, 51.
31 Ibid. 96. 32 Ibid. 175.
33 Ibid. 182; *Cal. Pat.* 1321–4, 214.
34 *Cal. Fine R.* 1319–27, 331; *Cal. Mem. R.* 1326–7, p. 3.
35 *Cal. Fine R.* 1319–27, 424.
36 *Cal. Pat.* 1327–30, 69; *Cal. Mem. R.* 1326–7, p. 10.
37 *Cal. Fine R.* 1327–31, 211.
38 Ibid. 461; 1337–47, 243.
39 *Cal. Pat.* 1388–92, 297, 360.
40 Ibid. 1396–9, 224.
41 *Cal. Fine R.* 1399–1405, 14.
42 *Cal. Pat.* 1399–1401, 159; cf. P.R.O., E 101/141/1, where a reference to the appointment of a (deputy) constable by the duke confirms that he was regarded as constable-warden. 43 *Cal. Pat.* 1429–36, 492.
44 Ibid. 513; 1436–41, 153. Ric. Roos had a grant in reversion in 1445 and may have succeeded Mone: ibid. 1441–6, 355.
45 Ibid. 1446–52, 225; Glos. R.O., D 33/107.
46 *Cal. Pat.* 1461–7, 117; Glos. R.O., D 33/120.
47 *Cal. Pat.* 1467–77, 484.
48 Ibid. 1476–85, 261, 405.

1484–	Giles Bridges (grant for life)[49]		1660–97	Henry Somerset, Lord Herbert, later marquess of Worcester and duke of Beaufort (grant for life, forfeited)[58]
1485–(90)	Robert Poyntz			
1485–(95)	Alexander Baynham (grant to them in survivorship)[50]		1697–1710	Charles Berkeley, Vct. Dursley, later earl of Berkeley[59]
1522–	Thomas ap Gwilliam		1711–36	James Berkeley, earl of Berkeley; constable only 1712–14[60]
1522–?1540	Sir William Kingston			
1528–?1546	George Baynham (later Sir George) (during pleasure to ap Gwilliam and Kingston 1522, and in survivorship to Kingston and Baynham 1528)[51]		1712–14	Thomas Thynne, Vct. Weymouth, warden only[61]
			1737–55	Augustus Berkeley, earl of Berkeley[62]
			1755–8	Matthew Ducie Moreton, Lord Ducie[63]
1546–	Richard Bream			
1546–70	Sir William Herbert, later earl of Pembroke		1758–62	John Thynne Howe, Lord Chedworth[64]
1549–1601	Henry Herbert, later earl of Pembroke (grant in survivorship to Bream and Sir William 1546, and to Sir William and son Henry 1549)[52]		1762–6	Norborne Berkeley, later Lord Botetourt[65]
			1766–1810	Frederick Augustus Berkeley, earl of Berkeley[66]
			1810–12	offices vacant[67]
1601–8	Sir Edward Winter (grant for life, surrendered)[53]		1812–35	Henry Charles Somerset, duke of Beaufort[68]
1608–30	William Herbert, earl of Pembroke[54]			
1631–?1650	Philip Herbert, earl of Pembroke[55]			
1650–4	? offices vacant[56]			
1654–(9)	Maj.-Gen. John Desborough, later Lord Desborough[57]			

In 1836 the office of constable was vested in the First Commissioner of H.M. Woods, Forests, and Land Revenues and the office of warden in the Commissioners in general.[69]

49 Ibid. 384.
50 Ibid. 1485–94, 97, a grant made in Mar. 1486, as from Mich. 1485; Glos. R.O., D 33/124.
51 L. & P. Hen. VIII, iii (2), p. 942; iv (2), p. 1773.
52 Ibid. xxi (2), pp. 85–6; Cal. Pat. 1575–8, p. 531. Sir Wm. Winter had a grant for life in reversion in 1577 but died before Pembroke; his son was the next constable.
53 Glos. R.O., D 421/E 3.
54 Cal. S.P. Dom. 1603–10, 395.
55 P.R.O., C 99/11, no. 1; Glos. R.O., D 33/310.
56 Cf. Glos. R.O., D 2026/X 17, an undated petition to parl. by local inhabitants, asking that Cromwell should be appointed.
57 Badminton Mun. FmE 2/3/2; Berkeley Cast. Mun., General Ser. T, box 25, appointment of recorder and deputy warden 1659.

58 Berkeley Cast. Mun., patents no. 8; the duke surrendered his public offices in 1697.
59 Ibid. no. 8. In 1704, because it was thought that the office of constable could not be held separately from St. Briavels castle, the earl was reappointed as warden only with the power to hold the courts attached to the constableship: ibid. no. 10; General Ser. T, box 25, petition of earl of Berkeley to Queen Anne, and legal opinion.
60 Ibid. patents nos. 14–15, 22.   61 Ibid. no. 15.
62 Ibid. no. 29.   63 Glos. R.O., D 340A/C 26, X 8.
64 Ibid. C 26; cf. Glos. Colln. 15931, cts. 1759, 1762.
65 Badminton Mun. FmS/G 2/4/1.
66 Berkeley Cast. Mun., General Ser. T, box 25, patent 1766.
67 1st Rep. Dean Forest Com. 12.
68 Badminton Mun. FmM 2/5/1.
69 Constable of St. Briavels Act, 6 Wm. IV, c. 3.

INDEX

NOTE. Page numbers in bold-face type are those of the principal reference. A page number followed by *n* is a reference only to the footnotes on that page.